The Whole Hiker's Handbook

THE WHOLE HIKER'S HANDBOOK

edited by
William Kemsley, Jr.

William Morrow and Company, Inc.
New York 1979

This book is dedicated to my favorite hiking companions—Marcella, Diane, Molly, Katie, Will, Andrew and Maggie.

TABLE OF CONTENTS

INTRODUCTION

Seldom do I find a book on any subject that lives up to its title entirely. And that bothers me. Hence, I was reluctant to use so ambitious a title as **The Whole Hiker's Handbook** when it was suggested by Julie Houston, our William Morrow editor. Now that the book is in print, though, I agree wholeheartedly that it does in fact live up to the title's promise. I say this with no embarrassment, since the book is a compilation of contributions from over ninety different authors, many of whom are authorities in their fields.

Many pieces that are in this book were originally published in the pages of **Backpacker** magazine. But those articles were meant for magazine publication, not for a book. When we assembled them for **The Whole Hiker's Handbook,** there appeared to be some very striking gaps in the completeness implied by the title. So where there were gaps we commissioned new pieces, and this has rounded out the book. This book is now like none other I've seen in terms of its depth of material of interest to hikers, all in one piece. The information is good. It is presented in an interesting and entertaining manner.

There are many people who helped to bring this book to reality; some of them deserve special mention. Ms. Ellen Ramirez-Quisa, no doubt, deserves the most. She painstakingly tracked down authors, articles, just the right photos and illustrations. She patiently husbanded the thousands of details that made the book what it is. Then there were a whole complement of other people who contributed importantly to the assemblage. There were too many to name each individually, but they include John O'Toole, Jeff O'Connor, Jane Lewis, Arlene Schleifer Goldberg, and Maureen Sugden. I am deeply indebted to them for the care and concern they had in bringing this book to fruition.

Chapter One

GETTING BACK TO NATURE

Getting back to nature is important to us today, as important as getting away from nature was to our forebears. Many of us are finding that we need to take time on a regular basis to get away from the man-made world we live in and let ourselves get back into sync with the rhythms of nature.

When we step off along a trail with our hiking gear, we leave behind all the stresses and hang-ups of our urban lives. All is different. Instead of chairs, tables, typewriters, cash registers, and curtains, we confront trees, rocks, leaves, sun, wind, rain—the elements. They shock us awake to a world we had forgotten was there. It puts us into an entirely different frame of mind that has a spiritually uplifting effect upon us. We find peace of mind and beauty.

But there is also another aspect of it, which I believe to be of equal importance to us. Nature is uncritical of us. It does not matter how we are dressed, whether our hair is combed, what we say, how we act. Nature could care less. It is a freedom we seldom find in our urban, workaday world. And this too has a therapeutic effect, soothing our sensibilities as few other things can.

Going backpacking is like going to Walden Pond. And we are modern-day Thoreaus. On the trail, we cannot help but think sometimes, What would it be like if we just never went back to our city lives?

Norman Clyde is someone who actually tried it—and succeeded. He lived the life of a mountaineer without a care. How did he make out? Winfred Blevins tells Clyde's story in the article that follows.

W.K.

A MOUNTAINEER'S MOUNTAINEER

by WINFRED BLEVINS

When Norman Clyde went "home" in 1928, the course of his remaining life ran over 40 years, stretched across the peaks of the Sierras, and was always unequivocally his own.

IMAGINE for a moment that you have backpacked into Thousand Island Lake, below the Minarets in the Sierra Nevada. As you ease across the last couple of hundred yards to the water where you will camp, your eyes draw south toward the Minarets, a rugged massif topped by a sawtooth ridge of peaks and moated by a steep glacier. Peak-gazing, you nearly step on the gear of a small, stocky old geezer, about seventy years old, camped alone by the lake. He is sitting in the sun and reading the New Testament in Portuguese. He greets you with a Victorian courtesy that does not quite disguise cantankerousness and impatience at your blundering right in on him. Spread about his camp is an awesome array of equipment: heavy iron frying pans, cameras, a rope and ice axe, three or four pistols, a fishing rod, an assortment of cups and dishes, cans on cans of food, and several more books—a volume of novellas in French, Catullus in Latin, Goethe in German and Dante in Italian.

The next morning you see him load all this equipment into a battered wooden-frame pack, shoulder what looks like 100 pounds, and head cross-country to the Minarets before you have started breakfast. At midmorning you see him angling up the glacier, now unburdened of the pack. After noon he is climbing, solo, up the sheer cliffs of the Minarets.

As you do your own climbing over the next week, you find his name in the register just ahead of yours. The difference is that he has been averaging two of these 12 and 13,000-foot peaks a day. He has chosen routes possible only for roped parties and has done them alone. You begin to wonder whether the old guy might be a Hobbit, or whether you are suffering from hallucinations.

Norman Clyde was the man who went to Walden and never came back. Quoting Emerson over his shoulder—"Goodbye, proud world, I'm going home"—he went into the mountains in 1928 and stayed forty years.

He became *the* legendary American mountaineer of the first half of this century, climbing alone in the Sierra and widely in all the other ranges of the West; he wrote innumerable articles about the mountains, and published two books. When he died late in 1972, California lost the man who knew most about its backcountry.

That first peak you saw him climb, for instance, was Clyde Minaret (12,281 feet). He made the first ascent alone on a fine June day forty-six years ago. He walked up from Thousand Island Lake to Garnet Lake, Shadow Lake and Iceberg Lake. Then he cut steeply up to that glacier-moat, chopped steps across it with his ice axe, and paused to consider his circumstances. It was four o'clock already. If he tried to climb the peak,

the glacier would be frozen when he came down. Cutting steps across a steep glacier in the dark was, he knew, a difficult and dangerous task. He went anyway.

The climb itself is still precarious, but his description in *Norman Clyde of the Sierra Nevada* slurs over the difficulties. He almost took a bad, perhaps fatal fall on the descent. After cutting his way across the glacier, he bivouacked for the night. The next day, though he was hungry, he decided to return to camp at Thousand Island Lake over the top of Mount Ritter (13,157 feet) and around Mount Banner. His idea of a nice excursion.

His adventures were full of awesome episodes. He wrote of them with such casualness, and such a strange scholarliness combined with modesty, that reading them can put an experienced climber-backpacker into hysterical laughter. Often enough he talked of having climbed three peaks in a day, in a grand circle or a long traverse—three peaks that most of us could take on one at a time, at best.

Clyde lived for forty years in the High Sierra—not near the Sierra but literally in them—and his home was where he happened to make camp. Every day when the weather permitted (except during the snowbound winters), he was climbing some peak. When he started the Sierra was relatively untouched. No one knows how many first ascents he made. One book lists 130 first ascents of mountains in the Sierra; if first ascents of particular routes were added, the number would surely exceed 1,000. Climbers still, from time to time, find a small cairn at the top of a peak that indicates that they have just completed a first ascent, except for Norman Clyde who was there two or three decades earlier.

Clyde was born in 1885, to a Presbyterian minister who was old-fashioned enough to believe that boys should be raised on the classics. Clyde read Latin and Greek even as a small child, and later was graduated from Geneva College in Pennsylvania with a degree in classics. In 1911 he enrolled at the University of California to get an M.A. in English; but two years later he left without the degree, short a course in Anglo-Saxon because he took Catullus instead. Six decades later he was still annoyed enough to cuss quietly at the professors and their "damn fool ideas."

Then began his unparalleled mountaineering career. He taught school all over California for nine months a year and spent his summers in the mountains. His passion for the mountains grew: In 1925 he made at least 48 climbs, 42 of them alone and 24 of them first ascents. In 1926 the figure rose to 60. In the fall of 1927 he was forced to resign as principal of the high school at Independence, near Mount Williamson, "because of the fluke idea of some damned old women," he said. The biographical sketch in his *Close Ups of the High Sierra* says he left because the townspeople thought they should have a principal who was a proper member of the community, not some crazed mountaineer who could never be found on weekends.

Suddenly free from employment and all ties, Clyde headed for the mountains and said good-bye to civilization for forty years.

When I met him in 1972, on a gorgeously clear February afternoon, he was living at the County Sanitorium at Big Pine. Though he had known almost no sickness in his life, he could no longer go to the mountains. He could see from the sanitorium the great eastern escarpment of the

mountains where he spent his life, rising 10,000 feet above his head. He was reading, typically, a volume called *Nouvelles Francaises*.

Most of the mountaineers I know are well-educated men; many of them have doctorates. Clyde was one of the most cultured. Studying in six foreign languages, he read French about as well as English. He took some civilization into the mountains with him, in the form of a substantial library in a number of languages. Greek served him well at times because he was rusty at it and reading was slower. His friend Smoke Blanchard reports finding him at Big Pine "churning through Goethe in German . . . [plus] a New Testament in Portuguese which he bought for Spanish but was reading anyway. On his nightstand was a *Life of Napoleon* in French, which he has already read three times."

He listed some of his favorites: Goethe, Schiller, Heine and Emerson. "Thoreau's spotty," he said. "Damned old quack—took a canoe trip [described in Thoreau's *A Week on the Concord and Merrimack Rivers*] and spent most of his time thinking about transcendentalism. Besides, *Walden* is inconsistent. Why did he move back to town?"

Clyde was no boaster. His essays on his climbs speak much more about the flora and the scenic beauty than about what he did. On that particular day he spoke of his skills as "just common sense," with perhaps a mere hint that no one in the mountains had any common sense but himself and maybe a dozen others. He was impatient with people who treated him like a hero.

But sparks could still fly. For example, we spoke of his lone, mid-winter ascent of Mount Whitney

Norman Clyde about 1930.
PHOTO: COURTESY OF THE SIERRA CLUB

(14,495 feet)—a dangerous excursion because a blizzard would surely be fatal for a man alone. He had snowshoed up one day in January and reached the summit late in the afternoon. The weather was mild, he noted—12 degrees below zero. A snowstorm struck. Thinking quickly, he started down a gully, chopping steps in the high-angle, frozen snow for 1,000 feet in the dark. Then he snowshoed back to camp, arriving at 1:20 A.M. My photographer-friend indicated that he knew the route Clyde had taken, and Clyde misunderstood him to be suggesting that the feat was not awe-inspiring. Clyde fixed him hard with a look, and said, "Well, many mountaineers wouldn't have made it, I can tell you that."

We walked outside to look up at the snow conditions in the mountains. The photographer and I were thinking, for the purposes of this article, of repeating Clyde's climb (the first ascent, of course) of the east face of Mount Whitney, this time doing it in winter. He peered up. "You might make it, boys," he judged, "but that snow is unstable." It had been a winter of little snow in the Sierra, meaning that the snow was not well enough packed to make travel safe. We had had a mountaineering lesson all winter long: Since Christmas, we had been trying to get the Whitney climb going. Several weekends we were snowed out. On two others we couldn't get climbing partners. Both of us were aware, standing there gazing at the awesome Sierra crest, that Clyde had climbed for forty years with no companions; and if the weather was bad, he stayed home—home in the mountains.

Climbing stories lead to climbing stories. We recollected a painfully tiring time on a climb when we were pushing our way up through mushy snow with fifty- or sixty-pound packs. "Weight never bothered me," Clyde mumbled. He never went in for modern, lightweight equipment. He carried instead a duffle bag lashed to a wooden frame. He carried in it four pairs of boots and shoes, five cameras (including one "to throw in the lake"), six large kettles, cups and spoons, dishes and bowls, condiments, servers, graters, a special stickmop for wash-

ing dishes, and a variety of canned goods. Not to mention his books, a fishing rod and several pistols. "If I want to carry a rock in my pack," Smoke Blanchard quotes him as saying, "to keep me steady down the trail, that's my business."

Blanchard weighed one of Clyde's packs once at 92 pounds, and it wasn't carrying more than emergency food. When he came back six weeks later, the pack weighed 106 pounds. The extra weight was in pots and pans he had picked up, some food, and a string of fish. Clyde himself weighed only about 140, and he was 65 years old at the time.

"Many people might find his way of travel in the mountains quite strange, especially with today's gear, but, you see," comments Blanchard, "Norman was not just visiting the mountains or passing through the peaks. He lived there."

Yes, he lived there. He spent twenty winters at Glacier Lodge on Big Pine Creek, snowbound at 8,000 feet and utterly alone for months at a time. To those who wonder what he did up there alone all that time, he presented a characteristic answer in his essay "Snowbound in the Sierra Nevada": "I am well aware that for many people who know of no better way to employ their time than to play solitaire, this would indeed be a problem. For someone, however, who has more hobbies than he can keep abreast of, the problem is not so much having too much free time, but rather not having enough. With reading and writing, taking pictures, occasional practice with rifle and pistol, and during the months of deep snow, rather frequent ski trips to timberline and beyond, I have more than ample use for all the spare time at my disposal."

He also spent nearly twenty winters at Baker Creek ranch, less isolated from civilization. That sojourn came to an end in 1971 when some "adolescent and adult hoodlums" ransacked his cabin, destroying and stealing his property senselessly. The vandals took what were the necessities of life for Clyde—his cooking utensils, kerosene reading lanterns and so on—and left his mountain photographs, notes and manuscripts in incredible disarray. Clyde estimated that he would need

$150 to fix the cabin up again, and that was money he did not have. Thus he was delegated to the sanitorium a mile away for the last year of his life.

The Baker Creek cabin, though, suited him. He had an outdoor living room—made from three sofas he resurrected from the town dump—where he could entertain visitors or relax and read. He had a wickiup for sleeping out. And he had three rooms for storing all the gear he collected, with the instincts of a pack rat, over the decades. He lived there during the winter, free of charge, in return for a certain amount of maintenance work. (He had the same deal at Glacier Lodge, where he was winter watchman.) He supported himself by his nature writing, regularly published in WESTWAYS and in its predecessor *Touring Topics*, and in *Motorland, National Motorist, American Alpine Journal* and *Sierra Club Bulletin*.

When spring came, he would have to leave the cabin to make way for the fishermen who rented it during the season. The cabin was always running over with gear—Blanchard called it "the largest one-man Seattle Co-op mountain equipment store I've ever seen"—and Clyde had to stash it somewhere while his mailing address was on the trail. He hid most of it in a cluster of rocks. But his collections of snowshoes, three kinds of skis, traps, classics, shovels and ice axes, boots, hatchets, saws, twenty toolboxes of handguns, and cartons of writings and photographs would have to go to town for safekeeping.

Then he would go into the wilderness. He had his creature comforts there too. Aside from what he carried, he had hundreds of hotels. These were campsites discovered and used by Clyde alone, chosen for their scenic beauty. He had one in every corner of the Sierra. His favorite was one that overlooked the Palisades; he called it the Palace Hotel, and claimed that the view alone was worth fifty dollars.

He also had his own hospital. It was a sunny little clearing by a stream, completely private and free of cost. Clyde was sure that three weeks of lounging there on a bed of leaves could cure almost anything.

Perhaps Clyde should be seen as a

kind of Thoreau, who took Thoreau's principle of "economy," for instance, and lived on it fully (as Thoreau did not, quite). He organized his life so that he spent virtually no time merely providing himself with necessities; he gave all his life to doing precisely what he wanted to do. He minimized his burdensome possessions and creature comforts in favor of pursuing his passion; yet clearly, in his own eyes, he had far more of the good things of life.

But he did not give us a *Walden*. Clyde's writings are intriguing, but they are limited by the man. He was not interested in telling us about himself. As a result he told us what he saw and what happened in objective terms. We get only cryptic hints of what he felt. He gave us his physical journeys but not his spiritual journey. Since he was something of a Victorian gentleman, he may have found interior disclosures embarrassing. Yet I yearn for a fuller scrutiny of his spiritual life—an understanding of the interplay of his mind and feelings with the great and dramatic world he lived in. He was capable of communicating that, but seems to have regarded it as a private matter.

His adherence to the principle of economy directed his life away from some of what we usually admire in men. Reducing and expanding his life simultaneously, he moved unswervingly toward what he wanted, toward what mattered personally to him. He did not dramatize his life to gain the awe or affection of others.

These choices led him away from participating in the community, helping others, working toward a common betterment. The standards of people who devote their lives to public service, or to large, publicly visible accomplishments, were foreign to Clyde. He thought of his life in terms of John Stuart Mill's metaphor of the tree—a thing whose purpose is to grow fully into what is contained in the seed. He may, in his way, have achieved an adamantly private stature —not by the standards of this century, but of the nineteenth century.

When Prentice Hall tried to get him to write an autobiography, he replied that he knew of no subject he was less interested in writing about than himself.

He predicted some years ago what the end would be for him: He would just keep climbing in the Sierra until one day he forgot to come back. If life were art, it would have happened that way. Three years ago, after much delay, his second book was published. In it was a tribute from his long-time climbing friend, Jules Eichorn, of which even so modest a man as Clyde must have been proud. In *Norman Clyde of the Sierra Nevada*, Eichorn wrote: "For me there can never be another human being so completely in tune with his environment—the mountains—as Norman Clyde."

MORE THAN A DAY'S WALK

A Story in 20 Stanzas

by COLIN FLETCHER

What do you do when you try to capture a glowing moment and not let it pass? Many of us take photos of the occasion. I fall into that category. Other folks write about it. Colin Fletcher falls into that category. And the following piece encapsulates a rare moment from a trip he took to Alaska.

W. K.

At my shoulder loom the mountains. If I looked I'd see new clouds hiding old peaks. But I could not go back. Not now, after yesterday's snow.

And at last I am walking toward the gap. A week ago, through this gap in a line of low hills that furrow the plain, I saw the tips of dark spruce trees. It seemed only a small stand of trees, but the tips pointed and promised. Although I had already reached the foothills of the mountains when I saw the trees, I knew that to stand among them I would have to make more than a day's journey.

No trees stand in the mountains. You live between rock and cloud. But I was born into the mountains. And once, when I was young, before the rock eroded, I believed in them.

No trees stand in their foothills either, or on this tundra before the gap. And in the foothills, among the caribou, rifles thump. I languished many days among the rifles, while rain fell on soft moss. Peering through my tent door across the sodden tundra, I told myself each day that the Promised Land always lies on the other side of a wilderness.

But now at last the gap lies just ahead. I think it's the right gap, the one through which I glimpsed the tips of those dark spruce trees. I wish I were sure, though. Yet perhaps I do not really wish I were sure, or without fear.

The trees looked very dark, I remember. But although I saw only their tips I knew how they stood. They stood conical and elegant, standing as trees should, reaching for the sky. Should trees have standing?

Knowing it was more than a day's walk, I left the foothills late yesterday afternoon as soon as the rain stopped and the clouds lifted to show new snow on the mountains. I walked westward across the tundra, eagerly, toward the distant gap. I had no map. For me, for all of us, this is uncharted country.

I camped last night beside a sullen, windswept tarn. No moon rose. But this morning, early, a herd of caribou drifted past, cropping lichen. Through glasses, I could see veins and arteries standing out on their brown faces.

The caribou drifted eastward, unknowing, toward the rifles. I walked on westward, knowing, toward the gap. Above me soared seven ravens. I walked on across the treeless tundra, alone yet accompanied, toward the trees that would stand as trees should stand.

Should trees have standing? I see a stone's inscription. I read the inscription yesterday, warm in my tent while rain fell on the soft moss and new snow fell on the mountain's rock. The words of the inscription stood clear.

And now it is afternoon again, and late, and still I stride across the tundra. Ahead, sunlight slants; but here the wind slides cold off the mountains. It is no longer summer now, as it was when I came to this place such a little time ago. Perhaps it is later than we think.

I walk on. The cold, clean air quickens my lungs. Perhaps the knowing is the difference: I think, therefore I have a brain. And the stone's inscription ended: "Perhaps we are the brain of the living planet."

This cold, clean air cannot think—this envelope that is our planet's lung. Not, at least, the way I do, you do. No more than my lungs think the way my brain does, yours does. Yet if the lungs falter, our brains die.

I stride on, climbing now. Over my shoulder, back in the foothills, a rifle thumps; and now another. And beyond the rifles, inside the closing "Arco" Circle, they are slashing an artery across the tundra—are slashing

more than one artery. Yes, perhaps it is later than we think.

But many have read the stone's inscription, and a few have spoken. The old man leaned closer and whispered: "A tree. A rock. A cloud. . . . The weather was like this . . . ," he said, "at the time my science was begun."

The tundra steepens. Beneath my feet, small leaves are almost red, berries almost blue: each organ heeds our planet's pulse. Only a hundred yards to go. But no trees yet.

Behind, another rifle thumps. And far beyond the Arco Circle lie cities shrouded, rivers damned and atolls immolated. Fifty yards, now. But can the brain slash arteries, defile the lungs, maim vital organs—and survive?

I take the last few steps and gain my gap. The trees stand thick and dark, conical and elegant, softening the valley, reaching for the sky, standing as trees should. A river feeds this rich new land. The clouds part: sunlight streams.

So far, no shape has fanned my creature fears. No straight line mars. Beside the trees, a herd of caribou stands brown and calm. Here, all have standing.

I move beyond my gap, into the new land. Old mountains finally dissolve: a brain that cherishes its body can mature—and may transcend. I pass the quiet caribou. And now I stand among the trees. 🥾

PHOTO: COLIN FLETCHER

CAN BACKPACKING BE A MYSTICAL TRIP?

by WILLIAM KEMSLEY, JR.

A growing number of truckers of varying religious persuasions say "yes."

Among the many research studies that I have seen that have tried to construct a profile of what a backpacker is like and why he goes backpacking, there seems to be almost unanimity that the backpacker goes into the backcountry primarily for a type of experience which some call esthetic, and others call spiritual. It would be my guess that the same type of experience is being described in different language. It would seem to me that if religious language is comfortable for a person, he uses it to describe the experience. On the other hand, if the person finds that scientific nomenclature comes more easily, he describes the experience with those words.

But, beyond the esthetic/spiritual aspect of backpacking, there are those who actually use the wilderness to try to kindle religious experience and training. I became intrigued with a group of very fine, strong, handsome young people out in southern California, and wrote the following piece about them.

W. K.

Scattered groups of religious young people believe backpacking can be a sacred experience that is outright mystical, that not only brings solace to the soul but spiritual development to the whole person.

One of the most fully developed of these groups is called Summit Expedition, which recruits its students from a small San Dimas office before taking them out into the wilds of the Sierra Nevadas.

Summit is the brainchild of Tim Hansel—a tough, muscular, backpacking sonofabitch. Tim is 38 years old and spends most of his time in the wilderness. Although he is tough, he is not mean. He is as handsome as he is tough. When you meet him, you wonder if he isn't a movie star. He also speaks beautifully, with confidence and authority. Furthermore, Tim unabashedly admits that he is all of these things—tough, handsome, articulate, and persuasive. For Tim believes that he cannot really claim credit for anything that he is or does. He says God has merely loaned him these earthly attributes for the short time he will be on planet Earth. And he believes that it is his duty to use them as God has directed. For the time being, his duty is to rekindle the Christian spirit within the hearts of young people by taking them into the mountain wilderness.

Tim takes his recruits on 3- to 21-day backpacking trips into the High Sierras. Those who go with him claim they have never had so much fun. But, more important to Tim, they come back baptized into a new life. They are changed people.

Tim uses places like Jackass Lake below Madera Peak instead of the River Jordan. He eats gorp and orange-blossom honey instead of locusts and wild honey. He dresses in coarse army surplus instead of camel's hair garments and leather girdle. But if Cecil B. DeMille were casting for a John the Baptist, he would likely make Tim a fat offer. Tim does believe that he is acting out a role. But for him it is in the drama of real life, and the casting director as well as the scenarist is not DeMille but God.

Tim has a staff of 37 instructors, including his wife, Pam. Over an eight-year period they have taken 2,400 high school and college students on these trips.

Summit has attracted its instructors from Outward Bound and other similar wilderness schools. They are highly qualified mountaineers, some of whom could boast of rather extraordinary climbing feats. Tom Miller, for example, has scaled some of

Yosemite's big walls with climbers like Royal Robbins, Tom Frost, and Yvon Chouinard.

Summit conducts three 21-day trips every summer. There are usually 60 students per trip, with a ratio of one instructor to each four students, traveling in small groups of 8 to 10.

The trips are similar to Outward Bound programs except for a deeper emphasis on the spiritual. There is a 150-mile backpack, some rock climbing, and ice and snow work. But to its trips Summit adds a psycho-spiritual aspect, a strong mix of Bible homilies, Tao-te Ching, Zen koans, Transcendental Meditation, Knute Rockne, and Dale Carnegie.

In the first week the students are given basic camp-craft instruction with emphasis upon no-trace camping, first aid, mountain safety, map and compass, ecology and conservation, and instruction in rock-climbing techniques—rope handling, knot tying, bouldering, and belaying. In the second week they do some rock climbing, rappelling, and stream crossings on rope bridges. They learn basic survival techniques.

During the final week, they go on a night hike. They make a bivouac at high altitude, learn ice and snow techniques—roping, prusiking, self-arrest, belaying, chopping steps. And they build up to their "three-day solo," on which they must survive with six matches, a knife, no food, no tent, no axe, no shelter—all alone in the wilderness for three days. When this is over, on their final three days, they make an expedition. And on their last day they run a 15-mile marathon. On the physical level, Summit follows closely the Outward Bound format with its emphasis upon Stress Education.

Because Tim taught psychology before he started Summit, he understands the importance of stress for teaching. He says, "Psychologists believe that controlled stress is an optimum condition for learning. At Summit we use stress situations to enhance the learning possibilities of our kids. But, the situations are *controlled* for safety factors.

"Apathy is one of the big things to deal with for today's kids. So we put them into stress situations. We get them on a three-pitch rock climb. They concentrate entirely upon what they are doing, bringing their awareness up to a peak. There's no room for apathy. It's scary for them. But we have lots of outs if it gets too rough for them. Each experience is designed to be a little more difficult than the one before it—so that the kids get the excitement of accomplishing a difficult task.

"This gives them the groundwork for solving a problem quickly and efficiently. That's the way you act when you are under fire. And by learning to face the stress situations the students gain confidence.

"The students also learn that the body doesn't quit until the mind does. The mind is the controlling factor. And the spirit controls the mind." Emphasizing this last point may be the pivotal departure of Tim's Summit Expedition from Outward Bound. He says, "Our program gets the students into research in the *other realm* of their being."

At the beginning of each Summit trip, students are given packs and shown how to load them. They are divided into groups of eight with two instructors to a group. They gather at the trailhead ready to get going. Tim gives them a pep talk. Many of the kids have never been on a backpacking trip before. It is all new. In the religious area, they are seeking a newer and deeper interpretation of Christ.

Tim tells them what they can expect on the trip. He tells them they will probably get tired and have to push themselves. "Your bodies will be willing but your minds will have to give direction." To help him illustrate the point, Tim holds up a little jug which he bought in a magician's supply house. He turns the jug over, empties all the water out of it and then rights it. He says, "Just when you think you're empty and you can't go on you can call upon another supply of energy." Then he turns the jug upside down again and more water pours out. "The body doesn't stop until the mind does. There is always more energy. If you have a purpose in life you can draw on this energy almost without limit. Summit offers time and challenge to a strong purpose that can give life deeper meaning. The man or woman who has discovered why to live can and will endure almost anything."

He tells them, "I think the Bible is one of the finest books on survival ever written. It's also a great psychology text. It's one of the most radical books ever written as well. It says that every person—you, me—can have a personal relationship with God.

"First, we've got to find out who we are. We've got to become more aware. We begin to find out through silence. Listening. And we are going to do a lot of that on this trip. You are going to get a little bit at a time, and then if you can do it—and you will be able to—you will get a lot more of it on your three-day *solo*. [Groans from the students.] And once you have learned about the power of silence you will move on to meditation, to prayer, and to true solitude.

"We are all coming to this trip from different points of view. But I am not *selling* Christ or Zen or Yoga. Nothing turns me off more than religious arrogance. No one has all the answers. I personally believe that Christ has all the answers that I am seeking for myself. But that doesn't mean that I have all the answers.

"The reason I've chosen Jesus is that he stands out more than any other personality in history for me. Some people have made such a milquetoast character out of Jesus. And yet, according to the evidence, that's impossible. Jesus had to be tough. He couldn't have endured what he did if he weren't.

"And yet, forgiveness is really what Christ is all about. It is really practical stuff. The feeling of guilt is the predominant source of mental illness in our world today. Christ came to set us free

Students hike 150 miles in groups of 8 to 10 with two leaders. The program follows the structure of Outward Bound in most aspects.
PHOTO: JIM BAKER

from this."

Before the groups depart on their hike, Tim gets everyone working on a Zen koan to get their minds *focused,* to interrupt the undisciplined stream of consciousness that is constantly running through our minds. "We are going to do a lot of things to get your mind centered on just one thing, and keep it from wandering. Try it."

He hands out a little book that contains a number of Biblical quotations that also are meant to be used for centering the mind.

Once the groups depart, there are a variety of mind-bending techniques used to get the students more aware of themselves.

One technique may be a trivial thing like having everyone pick an adjective to go with his own name, such as *Daffy* Diane, *Tough* Tina, *Jovial* John, *Beautiful* Bob, *Dreamy* Deborah. This seems to do at least two things: It makes it easier for everyone to get to know everyone else's name quickly, but also, because they have to pick an adjective quickly, they come up with a word that at some level is their own impression of who they are. Or, a technique as trite as having students write the name of their favorite animal or plant on a piece of white tape and stick it to the back of their packs. Thus, one becomes *Fox;* others *Coyote, Mole, Mouse,* and *Aardvark.*

This, too, reveals a little more about a person's character—not much, but one more bit in the mosaic that is pieced together of the whole person during the trip.

These character revelations build as the trip progresses. Beginning one night early in the trip, everyone is required to take initiative tests. One of these is to try to climb over a rope that is strung overhead between two trees, eight feet above the ground. It is obvious that no one can get over it by himself. It becomes apparent that a method will have to be developed to get over it. That enlists the cooperation of all the others in the group. The instructors make the point over and over again that we can do a lot with the help of others that we can't do by ourselves.

Another night the students are asked to write their biggest fear on a piece of paper; the papers are put into a hat. Then, one at a time, students draw a paper from the hat and act out the fear in the light of the campfire. It becomes obvious in a very intimate way that any one person's fear is not much different from the fears everyone else has.

After each of these experiences, the students hold hands in a circle to get the feeling of togetherness. They draw closer together as the trip progresses. Tim says mountaineering courses afford many

natural opportunities to build trusting relationships—each person coming to depend upon the others more as the stresses build up in their rock climbing, rappelling, ice and snow climbing. And as they get to know themselves better through the group activities, and see others getting to know themselves better, they discover that they are quite like their companions, having the same fears, the same hopes and desires and inner concerns.

Then in the evenings there are long rap sessions around the campfire which sometimes extend into the wee hours of the morning.

In the morning there are meditations and prayers. Occasionally, students are asked to read aloud something they find inspirational.

On the last evening on the trail, all of the groups gather together again at a predesignated spot. Fresh food is brought in from the outside—a great treat after living on freeze-dried fare for 20 days. They turn in their equipment and then have an Agape Feast. This consists of some singing and a dinner of the fresh food, after which they wash each other's feet. Mind you, they've been hiking for 20 days without a bath. The feet are grundgy, and thus the point of the Last Supper rite described in the New Testament becomes very vivid.

This is an emotional high point of the trip because the students also know that the next day it is all over and that they will not be seeing each other—perhaps never again. The intensity of emotions at the feet-washing rite is overpowering. It is rare for a student not to blink back tears.

The final day is the marathon. They are supposed to run 15 miles, and this at an altitude of 8,000 feet. All of them try. They have to run at least eight miles; most make it the whole distance. They call it "running toward life." And they think of their parting as the beginning of life and a new relationship with the world and with themselves and each other.

One of the students I talked to right after a trip said, "Well, it is not as *religious* as I had assumed, but much more powerful. I got a lot deeper into it than I thought I would, and into the people around me and how they actually affected me. With all honesty I can say I really grew from this experience."

Another said, "The nearest thing I saw to mysticism on the trip was eating when you're really hungry and drinking when you're really thirsty. Maybe that's what it is all about."

Perhaps it is. Or maybe it is one's attitude about it. In Zen, for instance, there are many "centering" exercises that focus on the mere physical acts of eating and drinking. Lakshmanjoo's is typical: "When eating or drinking, become the taste of the food or drink, and be filled."

Is Summit merely transporting religion to an outdoors setting? Or is there something actually spiritual in the backcountry experience itself?

Vincent Bolduc, a sociologist at the University of Connecticut, tried to find out. He interviewed 850 hikers during the summer of 1973, and asked each of them this question: "What special appeal does hiking have for you?" Almost 83 percent said that hiking had a spiritual, emotional, or esthetic appeal. And of those a full 18 percent specifically mentioned that spiritual experiences were their prime reasons for hiking. Bolduc said, "For a large number of the persons in this category, backpacking seems to be a substitute for formal religious activity and church affiliation."

Albert Saijo, in his delightful little book, *The Backpacker,* gives us a clue as to how backpackers do get into a spiritual trip while trucking. In a short section called "Your Head" he says:

"Don't let yourself get bogged down in a negative space. When you're doing a tough stretch, you need to boost your body with a certain psychic drive. Do your mantra, if you have a mantra. Take a rosary and say it as you walk. If you have a koan, work on it.

"Say you're climbing a pass and find it rough going. You're thinking of how far you've come and of the thousand feet you still have to go. Take it a step at a time. As a psychic booster, you might think of each step as bringing you one step closer to the time and place of your death. Not in a morbid sense, but in the sense that your life is a journey from one place to another place, and that this wilderness trip is a short segment of that journey, a thing you have to do, a place you have to come to in order to reach the next place. You can't hold back. You've got to go on. If you weren't supposed to be in wilderness, you wouldn't be there. It is a step-by-step revelation of your fate. Let each step be whole, conscious and clear. Keep your head wide open."

Saijo brings to mind a book I read back in the early 1960s by a British admiral who described a course in spiritual instruction he had taken in a Buddhist monastery in Rangoon, Burma. The monks gave the admiral only two simple spiritual exercises which he was instructed to practice over and over continually, filling all of his days during the entire four weeks of his stay at the monastery. Half of the time each day he had to sit cross-legged in a lotus position; the rest of the time he merely walked back and forth 50 paces in each direction. Of course, the key to both exercises was what was going on inside his mind while he was doing them.

"The attention was to be kept on the movement of each foot as it was lifted, swung forward, and put down; and each of these separate actions of walking was to be accompanied by saying mentally 'up,' 'forward,' 'down,' or 'lift,' 'swing,' 'down,' or whatever other words were preferred. During each successive step the attention must not be allowed to wander from the activity of the feet ... Each time the mind strayed or its attention was attracted by something outside, a mental note must be made of the fact and the mind gently but firmly brought back to the subject of contemplation. In this there was to be no furrowing of the brows, no mental clenching of the teeth, no anger or impatience. Tireless persistence in noting, checking, and pressing on was all that was required."

I have tried this exercise while trudging up long, hard slogs. It has an amazing effect. First, it takes all the pain out of the climb; second, it seems to give me endless energy. Was this a spiritual experience?

I suspect it was the same thing that one of the hikers sociologist Bolduc interviewed meant when he said: "I find hiking a substitute for religion. To me there is a kind of mystic communion, even a ritual to walking up a mountain."

Tim Hansel seems to put all of this together with still another dimension: human relations.

One Summit student said: "I found people I care for and who care for me. I found friendship, comradeship, and the ability to live with other people. I found that I can take much both physically and mentally. But most important, I found a kind of satisfaction and peace in my search for God."

And to be a little inexpressible about it, one of the instructors says: "Most of our education in the wilderness is derived from within ourselves and is therefore very unique—hardly anything teachable in the traditional sense."

THE DEEPER THE STREAM THE LOUDER IT SOUNDS

by BOB NERO

Is it possible to see with one's whole body?

You could set me down blindfolded in almost any part of the country, and then again in the Catskill Mountains, not telling me which is which. And within an hour I could tell you which was the Catskills. You would not even have to remove the blindfold.

I think the sounds, scents, and touch of a place are important clues that for most of us are "felt" subliminally. But, if we focus our attention on these clues, we can tell much about our surroundings. One time on a backpacking trip alone in the Catskills I made a game of trying to guess what caused the differ-ent sounds I heard. It was a snap. I could tell a bird rustling through the dry leaves, compared to chipmunk running across the leaves. I could tell the sound of a breeze blowing in the trees from the sound of a light drizzle coming down through the leaves. I could discern the sound of a leaf falling on the ground. I don't think I could do so well with my sense of scent. But I am sensitive to the sounds.

I've often wondered just how much of nature we do experience with our whole bodies. Bob Nero explores this idea as he reports on a memorable hike with blind youngsters.

W.K.

Some of the kids are eating piñon nuts, cracking them with their teeth and then spitting out the thin shells onto the ground. The earth is still damp from last night's rain and the youngsters seem to feel the presence of the storm clouds gathering around us at 10,000 feet.

Les Beaman speaks to his girl friend, Nancy Mollica, "All last night I kept wondering if the mud was going to come in the tube tent."

Although it is no longer raining, the late morning air is still wet and heavy. One of the kids is marveling at the smells following the rain, how different the air tastes.

We get moving and in a short while pass a thicket of poison oak. Bob Oehlman warns the kids to watch out for poison oak. He tells them the native California Indians seemed to be little affected by the poison. "They ate the fresh leaves in the spring and used the plant in everything," he explains, "from dyes for basket-making to cures for warts and snakebite."

Coming up a rock-strewn western slope, we move slowly through a sizable stand of Douglas fir. The youngsters reach out to touch the big trees and are told how the wood was used in a number of ways by the Indians and is now the most important lumber source of North America.

Thick moss grows on the north side of the trees and nearby rocks. The kids take in the smell and feel of the lichens. One of the guides starts talking. "If you're lost in the wilderness, just find where the moss is on the rocks or trees and then you'll know where north is, and you can take it from there."

We have travelled ten miles in four days; this is the third high mountain lake we have come across. I watch to see if any of the kids can sense that they are near water. But it is crystal and absolutely quiet.

"There's no sound from a lake," says young Rob Jenkins, "unless someone throws a rock in it."

Some youngsters strip down to their shorts and test the water gingerly. "There are boulders in here, of course, so you've got to be a little wary of getting cut up," says Jenkins, venturing in only up to his waist. "It's *freezing!*"

After recovering from the initial icy impact, 12-year-old Peggy Martinez goes swimming. She emerges shivering and enthusiastic.

A staff guide is talking to Jess Tyree, who is pumping a Primus stove. "Just give me a knife and a bag of salt, and I can survive in game country. That's what the old timers say." The kids are

The kids take in the smell and feel of the lichens.
PHOTO: BOB OEHIMAN, BRAILLE INSTITUTE OF AMERICA

PHOTO: BOB OEHIMAN, BRAILLE INSTITUTE OF AMERICA

teamed up in fours (two blind and two sighted) to share their daily cooking and packing chores. When cooking they listen to the hum of the flame to tell them when the Primus stove is ready. Hands held at a discreet distance above the flame, they slowly center the frying pan.

Bob, who is a staff member of the Los Angeles Braille Institute, is cooking tonight. He is preparing tumbleweed, dandelion greens cooked with bacon and fiddlehead ferns, all served with tasty mesquite beans. Ironically, he has packed in all of his wild food.

He passes around raw crinkle root, which is eaten with salt like a radish, but the teenagers find it a little on the sharp side. Afterward Bob steeps some green *ephedra* stems in boiling water to make "squaw tea." Many of the youngsters don't care for the flavor, but when Bob tells them the Panamint Indians on the other side of the Sierras used this tea for ailing kidneys and to purify the blood, a few try to empty their cups. The squaw tea is no match for cans of Coca-Cola.

It starts to rain and hailstones the size of dimes fall for a few minutes. The youngsters seem to sense the thick clouds sliding down the rock faces overlooking Chicken Foot Lake and gradually enveloping our campsite.

The night is heavy with rain and thunder and hail. Although obscured by cloud cover, the lightning feels very near. It is not defined in sharp jagged lines, but instead the entire sky turns a dirty white and then returns to blackness. I wonder if the kids can perceive this bright drama.

The next morning the blind are busy helping the girl scouts with the dehydrated Dry-Lite breakfasts. One of the boys who has been "volunteered" to do the dishes is telling about a dream he had last night in which a bear with gleaming white claws came up and spoke to him. "'Don't be afraid,'" the bear said. "'I won't hurt you.'"

"And then what happened?" somebody asks. "That was all. Then I woke up."

* * *

Kathy Martinez has been down by Chicken Foot Lake. She heard a lotus blossom open before breakfast. A forest ranger visiting camp verifies Kathy's perspicacity. The ranger maintains that a person with an exceptionally sensitive ear might be able to hear such a sound.

Most of Kathy's sightless friends, including her sister Peggy, aren't sure, and they, along with a few girl scouts, go down to the lake to listen for other lotuses opening.

* * *

Today we are packing to a new campsite. The kids are having a difficult time shoving their down bags into the small nylon stuff bags. They roll up their Ensolite sleeping pads, strap on their 35-lb packs and we're off.

Each blind backpacker uses a different orientation method while hiking.

"The sound of a stream carries a long way," Rob Jenkins says, "and it'll echo against the mountainside. I use it, but it's terribly confusing until you become oriented and get the basic idea of where the stream is. But a stream is bubbling and churning all the time. The deeper it is, the louder the sound gets."

Lea Beaman uses another method: he listens for the conversation and sounds of his fellow backpackers to judge how far he can wander from the group to explore territory by himself and still be able to find his way back.

"I listen to the footsteps of the person in front of me," Kathy Martinez says, "to see how narrow or rough the trail is. If the footsteps in front of me are uneven, I can tell the rocks are going to be jagged." To protect herself from dangling limbs and branches, Kathy extends her arm diagonally across her chest and face.

We pass alongside a thicket of manzanita bushes, and the kids pull off some fresh berries and eat them. As they run their hands over the smooth leaves, Bob tells them that the early white settlers of California used to mix them with Indian tobacco.

A mile or so later, after a lunch of cheese, nuts and cookies, we come upon some blooming mariposa lilies. A few of the youngsters take off their packs and kneel down on the side of the steep slope to take in the small yellow sweetness of the delicate flowers, rubbing the velvet petals sensually between their fingers. Their hands seem to be able to sense the presence of the tiny red bloodspots on the petals.

Because these blind children cannot see in the way most people understand seeing, they seem smaller than most. They must feel their way through the wilderness: feel the water in the lake, feel the language of a million years printed in a rock, feel the sky at sunset,

feel with two outstretched fingers the evolution etched in an animal track.

* * *

Leaving our packs at camp, we hike up to Morgan Pass to do some rock climbing. We stop by a stream. To Peggy Martinez the sparkling water has a definite smell. "When I get back home," she says, "the water will taste so bad I won't be able to drink it!"

With ropes securely around their waists, the blind are the first to inch their way up the 30-foot rock wall. Their hands search the rock face for cracks and crevices as they are belayed up the cliff. Because they cannot see the precariousness of their position, they do not hesitate. For Kathy Martinez the climb is "lots of fun" but "spooky." Others find it simply too strenuous.

A Braille Institute staff member blindfolds himself and begins working his way up the ledge. A Sufi proverb comes to mind: "Please do not start to teach the blind until you have practiced living with closed eyes."

* * *

As we sit around the campfire this last night, one small blonde girl says, "Our teacher in school told us once about the Havasupais who live down in the bottom of the Grand Canyon. He said they have a saying that goes: 'White man build a big fire, stand way back. Havasupai build a small fire, get real close.'" We laugh and continue to "watch" the medium-sized blaze. If it is true that we can see with our whole bodies and not just with our eyes, perceive with our hearts and not just with our heads, then perhaps these youngsters do see the fire.

One of the girl scouts is reading aloud from the poems of Gary Snyder:

"In ten thousand years the Sierras
Will be dry and dead, home of
    the scorpion.
Ice-scratched slabs and bent trees."

* * *

"A clear, attentive mind
Has no meaning but that
Which sees is truly seen."

Some of the backpackers sit around playing mumbly peg, others soak their feet or munch on strawberry shortcake biscuits. The wind rustles the treetops causing heads to turn.

"What was that?" one of the scouts asks.

"Bats, probably," a blind girl answers.

"Oh," the first girl says. ➥

ROY KERSWILL:

The Backpacker as Artist

by EDITH JOHNSON and WILLIAM KEMSLEY, JR.

The intensity of your perception makes a great deal of difference in what you see. If you race by a forest on a highway, there is no doubt that you miss it all and are not likely to hear a cricket sing nor see a leaf fall. If you backpack into the forest and spend time there you will no doubt hear and see things you had not known were there. And if you do this without the distraction of others along with you, you will see and hear and feel and smell and taste things more intensely.

Now, if you add one more dimension to your perceptual armory, if you train yourself to ob-serve the smallest details in the natural world around you with photographic accuracy so that you can reconstruct them in paintings, your perception is even keener. Does this keen perception enable you to see even beyond what the normal senses see?

Let Roy Kerswill tell you his views. I met Roy Kerswill in the Teton mountains of Wyoming, went on a hike with him on the glaciers at 10,000 feet up in the mountains while he told me about his work. He is a very strong back-packer, snowshoer, and technical mountain climber. And he is a painter of nature subjects.

W.K.

The knickered, bearded, barrel-chested man said, "I find it difficult to believe I am being paid to do this. I got to be the happiest guy on earth." What he was doing was backpacking through the Snowy Range in Wyoming. What he gets paid for is painting pictures. To him, these two activities are inseparable. Artist Roy Kerswill is America's foremost painter of mountain men of the Old West.

Backpacking is a working tool, for Kerswill, like his brush and pallet. It provides him with just as vital research material for his paintings as his library of books and historic documents and his collection of old guns, powder pouches, buckskin clothing, hatchets and other Old West artifacts.

Each summer Kerswill spends upwards of 30 days hiking in the Teton, Wind River and Gros Ventre mountains near his large sprawling home on the side of Rendezvous Mountain beneath the aerial tramway in Jackson, Wyoming. With camera and sketch pad, he picks up details of mountain wildlife and land-scapes for later use in his paintings.

"With his discipline and training, Kerswill is able to see things that most of the rest of us do not see."

"Details are important in historical painting," Kerswill says. "Collectors look for accuracy—the carvings on the gun stock, the shape of a whiskey jug and its markings, the kind of clothes people are wearing, the harness on a horse, the hinge on a box, the way a knife was made, even the knots in a cord tying together a bale of beaver pelts.

"Collectors are very choosy. They pay a lot of money for this type of painting. I have to be accurate."

Some of the people who have bought Kerswill's paintings are Laurance Rockefeller, actor Dick Van Dyke, Senator Barry Goldwater, the Scott Libbys and at least 15 governors of western states. There is even a Kerswill historical painting, "Colter's Hell," hanging in the office of the secretary of the interior. John Colter, the mountain man from the Lewis and Clark Expedition, was the first white person to discover Yellowstone country. Kerswill's painting was presented to Interior Secretary Rogers C. B. Morton in commemoration of the centennial celebration of the National Park System, which had its beginnings in 1872 with the establishment of Yellowstone as the world's first national park.

Kerswill is a prolific painter. Yet, despite painting 16 to 18 hours a day, with time off only for research and other business-related chores, he cannot keep pace with the demand.

Painting makes him a different kind of backpacker—rather an eighteenth-century type. He carries very little of the new-generation nylon and aluminum equipment. Actually, there is very little of anything in his pack. For a typical five-day hike, his load totals only 16½ pounds, including camera, extra lens, film, sketch pad and brushes. He takes no tent, mattress pad or ground cloth. Nor does he carry a sleeping bag, as such. Instead he beds down in an "elephant foot," which is short, like the bottom half of a sleeping bag, and weighs a mere 22 ounces. It reaches only to the waist, but together with a 36-ounce jacket which he carries anyway, Kerswill sleeps quite comfortably in most kinds of weather.

He carries no cooking equipment because he eats "cold" and only one meal a day. His food for a five-day hike consists of 2½ pounds of mixed dry fruit, so he doesn't need to carry dishes or a spoon. He carries neither water nor cup. But he does take one small plastic bowl for his watercolor sketching.

Kerswill usually makes his camp beneath a tree or under a rock. He makes no fire. He says, "When I leave my camp I have hardly disturbed the place at all. I've just lived there a little bit, like a bear. No more than that."

Traveling light and spending so little time making camp and preparing meals, Kerswill hikes an average of 27 miles a day and still has time enough for photography and sketching.

While he usually isn't looking on his trips for any specific detail for any particular painting, he does go to places which may figure in several paintings he has in mind. For instance, a hike to Graves Lake, made while he was thinking about picturing the Wind River Range, has had a conscious influence on some nine paintings he has done since then.

He photographs a variety of things usually too fleeting to sketch—a squirrel sitting on a branch, a tiny corner of a creek pool, a sunrise, an intricate shadow formation sweeping across a grassy meadow.

He carries a 200mm lens as well as a lens extender, which doubles the power to 400mm so he can pull details off the tops of mountains or out of distant valleys.

The photos go into Kerswill's reference files to supply himself with details for future paintings.

In Kerswill's painting "Night Watch," a coyote lurks in the night outside a pioneers' covered-wagon circle encampment. Kerswill saw this coyote sniffing the breeze while he was on a hike in the Superstition Mountain area of Arizona in the winter of 1965. He got several good shots of the animal with his 400mm lens set-up. These photos, along with the others from the hike, were filed away. It wasn't until five years later, when he was working on the "Night Watch" painting, that he needed the coyote. He fetched the photo from his files and painted it into the wagon camp.

Kerswill has trained himself to become a keen observer. And his backpacking trips help him to develop a greater perspicacity. He notices fleeting shapes and changing colors. Sagebrush and buffalo grass and willow trees are all green, for example. But their shades of green vary greatly from one another, as their shapes do. And none of them looks the same at different seasons of the year, on different days, or even at different times in the same day. It is important to Kerswill to be able to convey the way willows move in the wind in the gray light of dawn. Or the way sagebrush looks under a sudden darkening storm cloud, or the image of buffalo grass in the blaze of a hot August midday sun.

Kerswill sketches mostly for his own discipline. He first studies the scene he is about to sketch, making mental note

He hikes to places that may figure in several paintings. For a five-day hike, Kerswill carries only 16½ pounds, including camera.

of all the details he can absorb. After several minutes, he turns his back on it and then sketches it as best he can from memory, a practice somewhat like the game Rudyard Kipling's Kim played to sharpen *his* memory. Kerswill claims that the details he can recall are the only ones important for his paintings. More than that is too much or the wrong ones.

Kerswill is a very disciplined artist in several other respects. He believes that only through strict self-discipline is it possible to achieve the heights to which he strives. To make himself a better painter of mountain men, he has tried to understand exactly what it was like to be a mountain man during the nineteenth century. He reads all the books he can find, including original diaries. He studies historic maps and documents. He has backpacked over thousands of miles of country where the mountain men lived. He has handled their very guns, knives, hatchets, powder kegs, whiskey kegs, fur pelts and other relics. He puts on buckskins, camps where they camped, the *way* they camped, trying to imagine what it was like.

Having trained himself so well, Roy Kerswill is able to see things that most of the rest of us do not see. Furthermore, he has developed his skills to a level touching upon the uncanny. When he holds an object in his hand, for instance, he gets "vibrations" from it which tell him the history of the object and its owners. This faculty of divining image-pictures is called psychometry.

Kerswill is fond of pointing out that everyone does such visualizing. He says, "Think of a cat. A black cat. Can you see him? Now tie a red ribbon around his neck. Can you see him now? Or think of a car. What kind of a car is it? What color? How many doors does it have? What color upholstery? These pictures you see are similar to the pictures I get when I hold an object in my hand.

"I hold this old flintlock rifle. You know what I get? A fox. A little animal...The gun came from Kentucky, or what is now Kentucky. I get a long, lean guy, kinda boney fellow. He doesn't have a hat on. He's got a big shock of hair—that he keeps flipping back—hanging down over his eyes. Doesn't have any fat on him at all. Not much muscle for that matter. He's just wiry. Big red hands. His name seems to be C. Long. There is a date...1838. I see the open woods..."

In much the same way, Kerswill uses his power of mental imagery to get a mind's view of every picture before he starts painting it. He says he imagines it vividly, every single detail.

Kerswill's mental imagery reaches another level quite beyond the average person's capability of understanding: it carries him outside the realm of his current lifetime.

Kerswill claims that his interest in mountain men and the Old West derives from another life he once lived. In that former life he was born in 1808 in Mintley, Pennsylvania. His name was Jacob Plummer. At 18 he married Sarah Bradley. They had two children named John and Vanity. In 1834 they took to the Oregon Trail. At a camp near Independence Rock, Wyoming, his son, aged seven, was kicked in the head by a horse and died. This was a great loss to them. They went on to Sacramento, California, instead of Oregon. And they stayed there for the rest of their lives, where Jacob worked as a blacksmith.

He was born again in 1925 as Roy Kerswill in Bigbury-on-Sea, England. Following military service in World War II, Roy Kerswill headed for New Zealand where he intended to live. But his plan was interrupted when he took a 7,000-mile, two-year canoe trip through the western United States. While paddling down the Snake River in the Teton valley of Wyoming, he developed an unaccountable yearning to stay there. The region is near the spot where Jacob Plummer's son John is buried.

In time, Roy Kerswill did return to live in Wyoming instead of New Zealand and to paint pictures of the period when the Plummer family had passed through.

Any other explanation that would establish an Englishman in Jackson Hole to devote the rest of his life to the study and painting of mountain men has got to be at least as mysterious as this version, no matter how "scientific." Why didn't Kerswill stay put in the upper reaches of the Columbia River, where he started his canoe trip? Why not in New Orleans, where he ended it? Why not in Scottsbluff, Nebraska, where he met his wife-to-be and returned to marry her and lived for awhile?

Whatever the explanation for Roy Kerswill's zeal in painting mountain men, he pursues his interest with enviable enthusiasm and joy. All his friends and acquaintances have something to do with his backpacking or his painting — which really are inseparable. He has

climbed many times with friend Bill Briggs, head of the Exum Climbing School. Another friend, the manager of sedate old Jenny Lake Lodge, boasts of his sole mountain climb—up Symmetry Spire, a good class-5 climb—with Roy Kerswill leading.

Scattered across the valley are countless other Kerswill backpacking buddies. Kerswill frequently is off on hiking trips with anyone who promises him remote and romantic spots. He climbs with ranchers to hidden lakes in the Wind River Mountains, and with whiskey-soaked prospectors to remote historic spots in the Gros Ventre Mountains.

He has climbed almost all of the peaks in the Teton Range. He knows them so well that he can paint a picture of almost any side of any mountain from memory. He did so once when *Ford Times* asked him to illustrate a story titled "The Other Side of the Tetons." They needed the painting in the middle of the winter when it would have been impossible to get into the other side of the Tetons.

Kerswill goes backpacking, also, because he feels it is essential to his art for him to be always in top physical condition. It keeps his mind alert. Every evening, furthermore, he hikes briskly about a mile and a half up some mountain for an ascent of 1,500 feet and then runs back down. In Jackson he gets this exercise on Rendezvous Mountain behind his house. In Phoenix, Arizona, where he spends the winter months, he works out on Squaw Peak.

Kerswill is like a boxer who is perpetually in training. He does not drink strong beverages. He does not smoke. He is almost a vegetarian. His one aim is to keep his body and mind fit for painting.

As Kerswill sees it, the discipline is vital to his art. And his art is vital to his life. "I paint with the same need as I eat," he says. "I paint because it is an adventure into something strange and beautiful. I paint because it is pleasurable, like smelling the rain, touching a little child, loving a woman, listening to the hushed roar of the mountain glaciers....

"As I strive to reach and understand this thing that I but barely sense, I become imbued with something very beautiful, and it is this exciting sensation which drives me on. I suppose I am addicted to painting, to this inner urge, this selfish need to create." ☙

Chapter Two

BEST FOOT FORWARD: NEW IDEAS FOR PACKING FOOD AND EQUIPMENT

Ask two backpackers what they would carry along in the way of food and necessary equipment and chances are their response will be as different as day and night.

Today, the range of equipment available for backpackers is staggering. Some hikers make it a pleasurable hobby to collect, test, and replace as much of it as they can manage, hiking over the course of a year. Others just can't be bothered and stick with the same gear until it wears out. Today, it's all up to the individual. And yet, equipment—or the lack of it—should not impede the backpacker's enthusiasm for getting out onto the trail. Rank ama-

teurs can take a lesson in reading about Grandma Gatewood in the piece that follows, whose "raincoat and a bag of nuts" served her very well. What counts is what's right for you. Every hiker will agree that a comfortable pair of boots is the first order of business. Add to that a light, rainproof shelter, a pack that suits your body frame, and food that suits your stomach and that's about all there is to serious hiking.

In this chapter, there are lots of ideas for developing one's own personal approach to both food and equipment, from some of the more maverick and outspoken of today's hikers.

GRANDMA GATEWOOD (1887–1973)

by LOUISE B. MARSHALL

Most people quit distance hiking at 65; Grandma Gatewood decided to start. She was an instant celebrity wherever she went and word of her progress on the trail often preceded her. She was tough, determined, and a real Elder of the Tribe. Individualism as a hiker is perhaps understood best by reading about what she took along with her, in the article that follows.

GRANDMA GATEWOOD RAISED eleven children. Most people would consider that enough of an accomplishment to justify sitting back and taking it easy, but not Grandma Gatewood. Instead of retiring to a rocking chair, she took up hiking—*distance* hiking.

She traveled the entire Appalachian National Scenic Trail from Georgia to Maine when she was 67, becoming the first woman to walk the 2,000 miles consecutively in one season.

And she did it alone.

Two years later she hiked the famous trail from one end to the other again. Still alone.

And over a period of five years she walked long stretches of the trail, which equaled a third traverse—still by herself.

Surely after hiking the AT three times Grandma Gatewood would hang up her hiking shoes and retire. Not a chance—unaccompanied and in her seventies, she walked across most of the United States, along the route of the pioneers' Oregon Trail.

Born on October 25, 1887, to farming parents in Raccoon Creek, Ohio, Emma Rowena Caldwell grew up in a log house as the middle child in a family of 15. She attended a one-room school, where instruction went through the eighth grade, until the age of 18, repeating the final grade several times to assuage an obvious thirst for education.

She married 26-year-old Perry Clayton Gatewood after finishing her schooling, and their offspring began to arrive at roughly two-year intervals. Her life revolved around cooking, gardening, doing the laundry and taking care of her ever-growing family. It was a hard life, and not always a happy one: Perry and Emma Gatewood, after rearing a family of 11 children, were divorced.

Emma Gatewood was practical, conservative, patriotic and highly ethical. She insisted that those around her behave in accordance with her moral concepts, perhaps to the point of being dogmatic. One person who knew her says, "She was not always one to mind her own business when she came across something she disapproved of."

Mrs. Gatewood was active in community affairs, particularly the Grange and the Ladies Aid Society. She was a hard worker but a very warm and friendly person who always had time to help people in need and to visit the elderly and the infirm.

She became a skilled practical nurse, and in her later years found occasional employment nursing and housekeeping for families incapacitated by illness, which bolstered a small social security income.

She made a duffel bag of denim, which she slung over one shoulder

---

AFTER A DAY'S work in the house and fields Grandma Gatewood enjoyed tending her garden; her flower beds and rock gardens were lovely. She also liked to get out and explore the woods. Hiking and backpacking, however, were not among her

---

"Her gait was her gait. It was steady but slow. She didn't want anybody passing her, ever. She let them know she didn't like that."

---

recreations. Oh, she walked, but not as sport or relaxation. One of her children recalls, "If she wanted to see her sister, Diane, who lived 25 miles away, she would simply walk. None of us questioned why she was walking, for we knew she was frugal and didn't have much income."

Emma Gatewood was a hard-working, dutiful wife and mother. "My mother seemed to accept that there were certain things which were a woman's responsibility, which were part of a woman's role," explains Lucy, one of Emma's daughters. "She seemed to feel that a woman should not let anything interfere with fulfilling that part of her destiny." But Emma Gatewood believed also that once the obligations were discharged, a woman was entitled to follow her inclinations to adventure.

It was not until she read about the Appalachian Trail in a magazine article that Grandma Gatewood got hooked on distance hiking. She learned that no woman had ever hiked the entire trail in one season; she resolved to try it. By July of 1954 she figured she was ready for it.

To carry her belongings, she made a duffel bag of denim, which she slung over one shoulder. She was an inexperienced trail hiker, and her sack contained the minimum of gear—no tent, no stove, no maps, no compass and not much food or clothing. She carried a plain wooden staff and wore tennis shoes.

For her first attempt she traveled to Mount Katahdin, in Maine, the northern terminus of the AT. She climbed to the top of the mountain and back down again in one day, a good start. But on day two she encountered a hazard well known to experienced hikers: a poorly marked trail junction. She guessed wrong, and by afternoon she was lost.

She went down to a stream to bathe, took off her glasses and promptly stepped on them. Crack! A broken lens. Without her glasses, Grandma was at a distinct disadvantage, and for another day wandered around the woods, totally lost, until she chanced upon a forest warden's cabin at Rainbow Lake. She realized that in many ways she was not prepared as yet for a 2,000-mile hike, and she returned to her home.

She didn't tell her family about the episode. Her children and their families knew nothing of the incident until after she completed the AT the following year. And they found out then that she was

---

GRANDMA'S STYLE: A RAINCOAT & A BAG OF NUTS

Grandma Gatewood's hiking equipment and techniques were as unique as she was. In contrast with today's emphasis on equipment, her methods looked foolishly simple, but they worked for her. And that's what counts.

Says a fellow hiker who saw her often on club hikes in Ohio, "Her technique for day hikes was to wear a raincoat and carry in the pockets some raisins and some nuts and maybe a little bag of dried oatmeal. She'd chew on that. She didn't cook *anything*. She did carry water in a little plastic bottle.

"She had some foibles, all right. Her gait was *her* gait. It was steady, but it was slow. But she didn't want anybody passing her, ever. She let them know she didn't like that."

Even for backpacking, Grandma shunned fancy, expensive paraphernalia. She carried simple foodstuffs—cheese, dried meat, bouillon cubes, powdered milk, raisins, nuts or crackers.

She had a sweater, a jacket, a scarf, an army blanket to sleep in and a plastic curtain for shelter. Her raincoat was used as a ground cloth. She also carried a flashlight, a Swiss Army knife, a spoon, a small pot, first-aid supplies, safety pins, needle and thread, soap and towel. Her pack never weighed more than 20 pounds.

But she always took along a change of "dress-up" clothes in that denim bag. She would carry a dress and a beret and a pair of lightweight roll-up shoes. She could leave the trail, go to stay with someone, clean up and then return to the trail, looking quite fresh.

At night she slept in trailside lean-tos, under a tree, in a barn or in a home near the trail. She often paid for her bed or for food, but most people wouldn't accept money. If they did, when they found out who she was they would insist she take it back.

She often supplemented her supplies along the trail. If she found wasted food that was clean, she wouldn't let it go to waste. One time in Virginia—Grandma said she was rather embarrassed about this—she ran out of food and was short of funds, too. She passed through a park full of picnickers. She thought, "I'll bet they're going to leave all kinds of food." So after they left she went over to the trash can, and there were an unopened loaf of bread, apples, oranges and enough to keep her going for another couple of days.

Grandma seldom did such things, but she did eat wild foods along the way, berries or young sassafras leaves. And if she needed food or if her tennis shoes wore out, she would catch a ride into town, buy what she needed, accept a ride back to where she had left the trail and continue on.

She wasn't a fast hiker; on the AT she made about 12 miles a day. There were times, however, when she traveled just a few miles, particularly on the later hikes when she knew so many people. But she didn't stop for any length of time. Grandma Gatewood had hiking in her blood, and she made sure she was walking on that trail some distance—every day.

Grandma eschewed conventional hiking gear and chose instead sneakers and a denim sack, which contained her trailside essentials—a sweater, jacket, needle and thread, cheese, dried meat, a Swiss Army knife, and other oddments. Her pack never weighed more than 20 pounds.
PHOTO: TIMOTHY SULLIVAN, COURTESY OF THE APPALACHIAN TRAIL CONFERENCE

hiking the trail only when they read about her exploits in a newspaper.

REMEMBERING THE EPISODE, youngest daughter Lucy comments, "We kids didn't worry about her. We were all self-reliant and took care of ourselves, just as my mother did. We felt that if she was going to hike the Appalachian Trail, it was with enough planning that she had the pitfalls considered."

After that disastrous first attempt at Mount Katahdin, Grandma deemed it wiser to start at the southern end and go north, and in 1955 that's just what she did, completing the journey on September 25 after 146 days of hiking.

Again in 1957 Grandma Gatewood tackled a stretch of the AT. She was well known by this time to many residents along the route and rapidly becoming a legend among hikers. Everyone knew her and spoke of her as "Grandma."

She hiked long sections of the trail in 1958, 1960 and 1963. Then, in a jaded moment, she announced to her kinfolk that she had had enough and was going to hang up her sneakers. Nevertheless, the next summer she laced them back on and walked a segment of the trail from Shelburne Pass in Vermont to Rainbow Lake in Maine, completing a third traverse of the AT. And she continued to hike other famous eastern trails, such as the Long Trail in Vermont, the Chesapeake and Ohio Canal Towpath Trail in Maryland, and the Horse Show Trail and Baker Trail in Pennsylvania.

IN 1959 OREGON CELEBRATED its centennial. The festivities included a reenactment of the first settlers' traverse of the Oregon Trail: a wagon train would leave Independence and follow the migration route. Grandma decided it would be fun to go along, so she headed for Independence. But the wagon train had left two weeks before she arrived.

So Grandma made the trek alone. As on many of her other long walks, word of her progress preceded her, and she was sought out by newspaper, radio and television interviewers. Grandma arrived in Portland, Oregon, a week *ahead* of the wagon train; and was greeted at the city limits by Governor Mark O. Hatfield.

While she visited in Oregon, Grandma climbed Mount Hood and hiked on nearby trails. She wanted to attempt the Pacific Crest Trail, but at 71 she just wasn't up to the demands of such remote hiking—her feet and knees frequently gave out, and she had to rest often. She never added the PCT to her list of conquests.

Back home in Gallia County in southern Ohio, Grandma Gatewood joined the National Campers and Hikers Association. When they called a meeting anywhere in Ohio, Grandma would *walk* to it.

During the meetings Grandma met people interested in establishing a trail system for the state. Eventually, eight or ten of these individuals formed the Buckeye Trail Association. Grandma was one of the charter members and became a vigorous worker for the association's goal.

In typical Grandma Gatewood fashion, she decided what she thought was right and set about doing it. Without anyone's authorization, she planned a segment of the Buckeye Trail from one corner of Gallia County to the other—some 35 miles. She secured permissions from landowners, cleared brush and developed a pretty good path.

BUT THE BUCKEYE Trail Association determined that the charter group's original plan—to have the state trail run east from Cincinnati parallel to the Ohio River, passing through Gallia County, then north to Lake Erie at the town of Conneaut—just wasn't feasible. The trail would cross too much private land.

Instead, the official route would pass through Hocking County over publicly owned lands, bypassing Grandma's Gallia County section. She was heartbroken.

A lesser individual might have dropped out of the association, but Grandma kept her membership and hoped to the end that somehow her trail would be included in the Ohio trail system. Perhaps someday it will.

For many years the Ohio Department of Natural Resources and the Buckeye Trail Association sponsored a get-together every January for hikers from across the state. Grandma always attended, to visit with friends and lead one of several short hikes that emanated from the meeting place. As a leader, it was Grandma's job to set the pace, but she was getting old—she had trouble negotiating the trail and often had to be carried over the rougher spots. Grandma could no longer hike.

The organizers of the 1973 Winter Hike were in a quandary: Grandma had been invited, but they knew she would not be able to lead a group. How could she take part in the meeting and still feel that she had a role to play? Finally, someone suggested that she serve as hostess, officially greeting her many friends from all over the state of Ohio.

The organizers went one step further: they held the entire Winter Hike in her honor. Grandma was the queen, the honored guest, the one to whom all others paid homage that day. She was installed in a place of honor at the hikers' home base. There she received her friends and companions from the trail and took part in the gathering without drawing attention to her failing health. That Winter Hike was a fitting finale to Grandma's hiking career.

In the spring she went on a bus tour of all the contiguous states, a trip she found exhausting. In June she returned to her long-time home on one acre of land in Thurman, Ohio. Following her custom, she planted her garden, but one day while working in it Grandma became very tired and went into the house to rest. Later the members of her family were notified that she was ill and was in the hospital.

DAUGHTER LUCY RECALLS: "I rested easy for I thought my mother would pull through; it couldn't be quite this sudden. The next day I went down to the hospital to see her with two of my brothers—the youngest boy and the oldest boy—and their wives. She died while we were visiting her."

On June 5, 1973, Grandma Gatewood quietly set out on that last long journey. She was 85 years of age.

JOHN MUIR (1838–1914)

by ALBERT SAIJO

Backpacking in the nineteenth century was makeshift at best, though, by necessity, there was probably more of it than there is today. People walking, or going by horse, from one remote location to another often had to make camp beside the trail for lack of any other facilities. And if you wanted to explore much of the backcountry, you made camp where you were.

To me the most amazing backpacker of old was John Muir. He spent much of his time living in the Sierra, once he discovered this mountain range. And he virtually carried his entire backpacking gear in the pockets of an old wool overcoat. No doubt he lived somewhat like the animals who inhabit the mountains. His story follows, to remind us of the ultimate simplicity in backpacking gear.

W.K.

In 1867, as John Muir started his 1,000-mile walk from Kentucky to Florida, he wrote on the flyleaf of his notebook: "John Muir, Earth-Planet, Universe." He could not have characterized himself more precisely. It was exactly where he was. This 1,000-mile walk was not his first excursion; he had already rambled through parts of midwestern and Canadian wilderness. But it was with this walk that he properly commenced the wanderings that eventually took him over much of earth-planet and made him, by the end of his life, the archetypal figure of earth-planet wilderness consciousness. He is still that for us.

He was entirely unique. His eyes were uncommonly blue with a deep, open gaze, and his features were regular and handsome. His hair was auburn, his complexion clear, and he wore a full beard. Some people thought he looked like Jesus Christ. Lithe, strong and athletic, he could say after climbing Whitney direct from the east side, "Give me a summer and a bunch of matches and a sack of meal and I will climb every mountain in the region." His feet were extra big. He walked flatfooted with a long, loping stride. He stood a lean five-foot nine-inches tall. By all accounts he had a beautiful male presence.

Muir had an alert, questing mind that could focus in on the tiny flower of Cassiope or space out to contemplate broad glacial history. In wilderness he was a combination of desert father and Taoist mountain sage, with the asceticism and God-hunger of the one and the deep philosophical comprehension of the other. His body knowledge of wilderness calls to mind the Yaqui Indian Don Juan, renowned in the books of Carlos Castaneda. It was this that made him a great mountaineer. At the same time, Muir's botanico-geologic interest kept his observation of wilderness accurate and vivid. Nature he understood both as mechanism and as a form of wisdom. In the following passage he describes his method of study during the years he spent in the Sierra Nevada investigating glacial action:

I drifted from rock to rock, from stream to stream, from grove to grove. Where night found me, there I camped. When I discovered a new plant, I sat down beside it for a minute or a day to make its acquaintance and hear what it had to tell. When I came to moraines, or ice-scratches upon the rocks, I traced them back, learning what I could of the glacier that made them. I asked the boulders I met, whence they came and whither they were going. I followed to their fountains the traces of the various soils upon which forests and meadows are planted; and when I discovered a mountain or rock or marked form and structure, I climbed about it, comparing it with its neighbors, marking its relations to living or dead glaciers, streams of water, avalanches of snow, etc., in seeking to account for its existence and character. It is astonishing how high and far we can climb in mountains that we love.

Muir wrote a prose as strong as any in the English language. He is generally considered a transcendentalist in the tradition of Emerson and Thoreau, but he exceeds any category. A master of descriptive narrative, he had a limber, energetic line, and his periods were beautifully paced. Accuracy was the heart of his style. He had a power of exact observation that was at the same time scientific and aesthetic, and when these two elements meshed perfectly, it would put him in a state of ecstatic contemplation. His book describing his initiation into the mountains, *My First Summer in the Sierra,* is surely a classic. He was also a great letter writer, and these contain some of his finest prose.

"Give me a summer and a bunch of matches and a sack of wheat and I will climb every mountain in the region."

His drawings show the same observant eye as his writings. He had a strong, expressive hand. There is a subtle natural humor in his art, like the humor of saguaro cactus. Linnie Marsh Wolfe's biography of Muir, *Son of Wilderness,* has a copy of a holograph letter he wrote from Yosemite, beginning, "I have been down bathing in the Ganges ...." At the head of the letter is a drawing of a grasshopper, and all around the border of the page runs a lacy design that turns out to be the track of a grasshopper walking. The effect is wholly charming. The drawing sets off his calligraphy just right.

We cannot understand John Muir without understanding his relationship to his father. Daniel Muir is usually written off as a religious fanatic and tyrannical parent. But everything his famous son achieved stemmed from his upbringing, harsh as it was. In no way could he have accomplished the things he did without the upbringing his father gave him.

John Muir was born April 21, 1838, in Dunbar, Scotland, to Daniel and Ann Gilrye Muir. He was the eldest son and the third of eight children. Of his mother Muir once wrote, "She was a representative Scotch woman, quiet, conservative, of pious, affectionate character, fond of painting and poetry." She gave him loving support and encouragement throughout her life. Muir's father was another story.

Daniel Muir's character was greatly determined by a religious conversion he had experienced as an adolescent, when what he called "the ecstasy of

the Apostles" flooded his soul. He became a religious zealot. The Bible — especially the Old Testament and Revelations — was the only book. Life on earth was an endless struggle between God and Satan, and the only salvation was a perpetual state of emotional excitement called "worshiping the Lord."

Here is how Daniel Muir brought up his son John. Although he himself had no formal schooling, he put John in school at age three. He thrashed him every day whether or not John did anything wrong, explaining, "I dinna ken any wrong ye have done this day but I'll thrash ye the same for I hae no doot ye deserve it." Muir once described the whippings his father dealt him as being "outrageously severe, and utterly without fun." He was thrashed not only at home but also at school. Yet young Muir learned. At age 11, he had committed to memory the whole of the French, Latin and English grammars, three-fourths of the Old Testament, and all of the New Testament. Spelling, history, arithmetic and geography had also been beaten into him.

John was an eager, curious, savage kid. He was by his own account a "little fighting, biting, climbing pagan." A friend once said of him, "He grew up savagely strong." He loved escapades, and no amount of thrashing could quench his vigor and joy. This capacity for enjoyment — and a great love of nature — John also learned from his father. Daniel Muir was an excellent fiddler; he loved to play and sing ballads and hymns, and he taught all his family to sing. His love of plants and flowers was transmitted to John, together with a knack for whittling and carving.

Meanwhile, the elder Muir had wandered through denomination after denomination seeking a church with a zeal equal to his own. He finally found what he was looking for in a group called the Disciples of Christ, which was then urging its members to emigrate to America, where they had already established colonies. Muir's father had always had America in the back of his mind, and now in a rush he decided to sell his prospering food and grain business and move his family to Wisconsin. They found land in the wilderness near Portage. This was in 1849, and John was 11.

In his book, *The Story of My Boyhood and Youth,* Muir described the impact

of his first wilderness experience: "This sudden plash into pure wilderness — baptism in Nature's warm heart — how utterly happy it made us! Nature streaming into us, wooingly teaching her wonderful glowing lessons, so unlike the dismal grammar ashes and cinders so long thrashed into us. Here without knowing it we still were at school; every wild lesson a love lesson, not whipped but charmed into us. Oh, that glorious Wisconsin wilderness!"

But this idyllic phase was to last only a short while before the beginning of the sustained labor of transforming the wilderness into a farm. The father's relentless drive bore down hard on John. From age 12, John was out in the field from dawn to dark doing a man's work. The whippings continued. But worse than the whippings was the endless grind of work. "We were all made slaves through the vice of over-industry....We were called during summertime in the morning at four o'clock and seldom got to bed before nine, making a broiling, seething day seventeen hours long loaded with heavy work, while I was only a small stunted boy...." Muir always believed that his growth had been stunted by the severe labor of his youth. And while John sweated, his father gave more and more time to Bible study and preaching and less to working in the field.

There was no school for the children. But snatching time here and there Muir taught himself higher arithmetic, algebra, geometry and trigonometry. At age 15 he got fired on poetry. He speaks of "a great and sudden discovery of the Bible, Shakespeare, and Milton, sources of inspiring, exhilarating, uplifting pleasure...." Although his father censored his reading, John sneak-read novels, and the works of the explorer-naturalists Humboldt and Mungo Park.

It was during this time, too, that Muir got into his inventions. He started getting up at one o'clock in the morning to work on them, devising clocks, thermometers, pyrometers, hygrometers and barometers. These were made out of scrap metal and parts patiently whittled out of wood. His thermometer was so sensitive that in cold weather the dial hand would move at the approach of a person. He made a small self-setting sawmill with a double rotary saw and ran it with the water power of a dammed-up creek. Most ingenious of all was his "early-rising machine." This gadget, a clock connected to a bed, could strike, register hours and dates, light fires and a lamp at set times and, by means of levers and cogwheels, tip the bed up to throw the sleeper onto his feet at any set hour. He began to think of mechanical inventions as a possible means of making his way in the world.

After eight years of hard labor the farm was complete, all the land fenced and brought under the plow, with outbuildings and a roomy frame house overlooking a lake. Muir tells us in his memoirs that in spite of the unending work, he and his brothers and sisters did have some recreation. They had Sundays off. The father, again showing his light side, bought them a horse to ride and gave them wood to build a boat in which they floated over the lake.

But now, just when this farm had become a comfort, Daniel Muir decided to sell it and buy another section of virgin land to start another farm from scratch. The father's motivation seems to have been to make more money for the Disciples of Christ.

The backbreaking work of clearing land started over again. Because his father no longer worked in the field, most of the responsibility for this work fell on John. He was 19 years old and prided himself on his physical hardiness and his ability to endure whatever was required of him.

Now his father gave him what might be thought of as his final test of strength. He ordered John to dig a well. After digging ten feet down John struck fine-grained sandstone. A neighbor advised blasting with dynamite, but it didn't work, so his father decided to have John do the work with hammer and chisel. The bore of the well was three feet in diameter. He sat in that cramped space and chipped away from early morning until dark, day after day, for weeks and months. In the morning he was lowered in a wooden bucket by a windlass, then hoisted out for lunch, then lowered again to work till dark. About 80 feet down he almost lost his life to deadly choke-damp. Carbonic acid gas had settled to the bottom one night and he had been lowered into it. When they didn't hear the sound of his chisel, his father and his brother David

were alarmed; after some confusion, they hoisted him out unconscious. After a couple of days' rest he went down again. Finally at 90 feet he struck a "hearty gush of water." Muir ends his account of this episode with the laconic comment: "Father never spent an hour in that well. He trusted me to sink it straight and plumb, and I did...."

As Muir came of age he began thinking about leaving home. "My brothers left the farm when they came of age, but I stayed a year longer, loath to leave home. Mother hoped I might be a minister some day; my sisters that I would be a great inventor. I often thought I should like to be a physician, but I saw no way of making money and getting the necessary education, excepting as an inventor. So, as a beginning, I decided to try to get into a big shop or factory and live awhile among machines."

His apprenticeship to his father was over. When John told him that he was about to leave home and asked if a little money could be sent him, if ever he needed it, his father answered, "No; depend entirely on yourself." The year was 1860. Muir was 22 years old. He had $15.

This was the time when industry was just beginning to supplant agriculture as the economic force in the North. Industrial cities like Buffalo, Detroit, Indianapolis and Chicago had become centers for great foundries and machine shops. Opportunities were limitless for young men with an inventive gift. A friend suggested that John take some of his inventions to the State Fair in Madison, that he had only to exhibit them and every machine shop thereabouts would be open to him. As it happened, his inventions were a great success at the fair. But the hoped-for job in a machine shop did not materialize. Instead, he applied to the University of Wisconsin, which accepted him even though he had had no meaningful formal schooling since Scotland. Supporting himself with odd jobs, he stayed at the university two and a half years and studied chemistry, mathematics, physics, Greek, Latin, botany and geology. He did not work toward a degree but the knowledge he gained there, especially in the last two subjects, was the foundation for his later scientific work.

Outside school the world was in

turmoil. The Civil War had started, and war frenzy gripped the country. When Lincoln called for 75,000 volunteers, excitement swept through the campus. Students rushed off to the war. Muir could not see the sense of it. He wrote home that he could hear the noise and commotion from his room, "but the thrushes in that fine grove don't seem to care . . . I always keep my window open so I can hear them fine." But he worried about being drafted.

During the long summer vacations he worked at home. His father even agreed to pay him a wage. The old man had begun to mellow and was even sending money from time to time to help John out at school.

At this time John thought of going to the University of Michigan to study medicine. He was restless. The war was like a blight over everything. The draft hung over him, and he was going through heavy soul changes. "I was tormented with soul hunger. I began to doubt whether I was fully born . . . I was on the world. But was I in it? . . ."

It was now that he took his first real excursion into wilderness. Accompanied by friends along part of the way, he walked down the Wisconsin River doing botany and geology. Coming to the Mississippi, he crossed over into Iowa and walked south along the bluffs of the mighty river.

Perhaps the main lesson of this trip was the great destructive power of the lumber industry. He saw the forests of Wisconsin and Minnesota bound in rafts and strings floating downstream to the sawmills below. He returned the way he came. Overall he had walked 300 or 400 miles.

This first long exposure to wilderness made a tremendous impression on him. For one thing, it gave him a way to measure civilization, which he found generally wanting. To go into wilderness "not as a mere sport or plaything excursion, but to find the plan that governs the relations subsisting between human beings and Nature" seemed the most worthwhile thing he could do.

It was at Wisconsin that he first studied the subject of glaciers through the writings of Agassiz. He read Agassiz in the original French—the French that had been thrashed into him as a child. (The Latin he had acquired in the same way had become very useful in his botanical inquiries.) His study of Agassiz' methods for measuring the movement of glaciers was the basis for his investigation of the glacial origins of Yosemite.

The social life of the university had broadened him. His friendship with Jeanne and Ezra Carr proved invaluable. Dr. Ezra Carr, his chemistry and geology professor, opened Muir to the very latest scientific studies; his wife, Jeanne, herself a talented botanist, artist and musician, taught him humanities. To Muir their home was "a revelation of gracious living"—so different from the austerities of the home he grew up in. The lifelong correspondence between Mrs. Carr and Muir forms a small biography of the mature John Muir. It was through the Carrs that Muir met Emerson in Yosemite Valley.

But finally, with the war nearly over, he had to trade "Wisconsin University for the University of the Wilderness." In the spring of 1864, at age 26, he started north through Wisconsin and upper Michigan to Lake Superior, and then into Canada. "I quietly wandered away....I traveled free as a bird, independent alike of roads and people. I entered at once into harmonious relations with Nature....Faculties were set in motion, fed and filled. The vague unrest and longing...vanished.... I felt a plain, simple relationship to the Cosmos."

He went east along the north shore of Lake Huron, then south across lower Ontario to Niagara Falls. It was a walk of well over 500 miles. Along the way he did chores and day labor for food. It was on this trip that he established the simple diet that he never really varied on all his subsequent wilderness excursions: bread and tea. "Oftentimes I had to sleep without blankets, and sometimes without supper, but usually I had no great difficulty in finding a loaf of bread here and there."

He got very much into the plant life of the bogs and swamps of Manitoulin Island and Georgian Bay, and he spent days sloshing happily through them.

At Niagara Falls, by prearrangement, he met his younger brother Dan. Winter was coming on, and they needed work and a place to stay. They found work

in a sawmill attached to a factory that turned out rake, broom and fork handles. It was in beautiful forested country on the south shore of Georgian Bay.

Before long Muir found himself inventing machinery for the factory. In 1865 he says, "I was haunted with inventions that tortured me sleeping or waking until I worked them into visible forms." Most of his inventions were devices to automate production. His employer, William Trout, said of him: "He was a real live inventive, designing mechanic, systematic, practical; and it was a delight to see those machines at work." Muir doubled the production of the factory.

He contracted to produce 30,000 broom handles and 12,000 rakes, for which he was to receive half the profits. This would provide money for travel. He had been reading the South American travels of Humboldt, the naturalist-explorer. South America became his next goal: he would push southward along the Orinoco to its headwaters, cross over the divide to a tributary of the Amazon, and float down on a raft or skiff the whole length of this greatest of rivers. But one blizzardy night, with just a little more to go to finish the contract, the factory caught fire and burned to the ground. It was a total loss; there was no insurance. Muir took it as a sign to leave, though Trout offered him a partnership if he would stay and help rebuild the factory. Instead, he resumed his wanderings.

Canada had given him a breather. He had been content "to work and study and dream in this retirement, happy in being so comfortably separated from the world's noisy dust."

⸻

He headed south. "Looking over the map I saw that Indianapolis was an important railroad center, and probably had many factories of different sorts in which I could find employment, with the advantage of being in the heart of one of the very richest forests of deciduous hardwood trees on the continent." His intention was to make a few hundred dollars, then move on farther.

He found work with a manufacturer of hubs, spokes, rims and other carriage wheel parts. The business was one of the largest of its kind in the country. Muir advanced rapidly and was soon inventing machinery again. He invented a machine that completely automated the making of wooden

wheels. Of this job he said: "I liked the inventive work and the earnest rush and roar and whirl of the factory." But his botanical and geological studies were being interrupted. Then he suffered the accident that changed his life.

While he was unlacing a machine belt to make it tighter, the sharp-ended file he was using slipped and flew upward, piercing his right eye at the edge of the cornea. He put his hand to the eye and could feel the aqueous humor dripping out onto his fingers. His sight in that eye failed completely, and—worse still—his other eye went sympathetically blind. The darkness was total.

The first days after the accident he lay in bed, utterly shattered. "My days were terrible beyond what I can tell, and my nights were if possible more terrible. Frightful dreams exhausted and terrified me." The first doctor to see the damaged eye said it was gone. But a specialist was called in; after a careful examination, he told Muir that sight would return in both eyes. When this diagnosis proved true, Muir felt resurrected. While recuperating in his darkened room, he made up his mind to leave the factory and mechanical inventing forever. He would devote the rest of his life "to the study of the inventions of God."

During his convalescence, someone had given him an illustrated booklet on Yosemite Valley. He must see it and the Amazon. He quit his job at the factory, even though, as in Canada, he was offered a partnership to stay. He wanted wild nature. "Now I propose to go south and see something of the vegetation of the warm end of the country, and if possible wander far enough into South America to see tropical vegetation in all its palmy glory."

But first he went back to Wisconsin to visit his family. He found his father sitting in the shade of a tree, copying a quarto edition of Foxe's *Book of Martyrs*. The visit wasn't a happy one. The rest of the family was overjoyed to see him, but his father carped at him. The old man believed that botany and geology were blasphemous and that John's wanderings were in the "paths of the Deevil." According to a well-authenticated story, as John was saying good-bye to his mother and sisters, the father broke in and said:

"My son, hae ye na forgotten something?"

"What have I forgotten, Father?"

"Hae ye na forgotten to pay for your board and lodging?"

John handed him a gold piece and said, "Father, you asked me to come home for a visit. I thought I was welcome. You may be sure it will be a long time before I come again."

They did not meet again until 18 years later, at the old man's death bed. During those 18 years Muir made the famous journeys that would enable him to know this continent as few others have known it before or since. These were not just walks but revelations, a nature lover's Pilgrim's Progress. Perhaps his greatest gift to us is his restatement of the American Indian idea of wilderness as a place to go in search of a vision.

First came the famous 1,000-mile walk, almost allegorical in its unfolding. It was September, and John was 29. In a small rubberized bag he carried a comb, brush, towel, soap, a change of underclothing, a copy of Burns' poems, Milton's *Paradise Lost* and a small New Testament. In addition he had his plant press. He would pick up food along the way. Beg it or buy it. As on all his trips he often went hungry.

⸻

The ground, plant life and winds of Kentucky and Tennessee were similar to the country he knew up north. But the people were different and wary. The countryside in its civilized parts was devastated by war. He kept mostly to the wild. In Tennessee he saw the first mountains of his life, the Cumberlands and Alleghenies. Crossing over, he came to the sandy, pine-covered piedmont of Georgia. Then things began to change. The plant life was new. The sky was different. He heard strange sounds in the wind. It was hot and sultry. "Now I began to feel myself 'a stranger in a strange land.'" As he passed through pine barrens and swamps he began to feel slightly feverish. He reached the port of Savannah, where his brother was to have sent him money. It hadn't come. Wandering around the city weary and hungry, he spent most of his time resting and sleeping in a cemetery outside the city. Finally the money arrived.

From Savannah he went by boat to the north coast of Florida and walked across the base of the peninsula to the town of Cedar Keys. The tropical vegetation turned him on completely. "These palms and winds severed the last strands of the cord that united me with home. Now I was a stranger indeed.

I was delighted, astonished, confounded, and gazed in wonderment blank and overwhelming as if I had fallen on another star." He ate bread, when he had it, and drank the brown water of the swamps.

He was planning to go from Florida to South America. But at Cedar Keys he fell ill with malarial fever. For days he was unconscious and close to death. Only the care of a family he met on first coming to Cedar Keys pulled him through. It took him three months to get back on his feet.

During his convalescence he pondered the relation between man and nature. Muir was antianthropocentric. He saw that the human enterprise must be rescaled to a more realistic and aware relationship with the rest of nature. Civilized man was "as purely a manufactured article as any puppet of a half-penny theater," yet he believed himself to be the lord of creation. "A numerous class of men are painfully astonished whenever they find anything, living or dead, in all God's universe, which they cannot eat or render in some way...useful to themselves." But, Muir asks, "Why should man value himself as more than a small part of the one great unit of creation?...The universe would be incomplete without man; but it would also be incomplete without the smallest transmicroscopic creature that dwells beyond our conceitful eye and knowledge. From the dust of the earth...the Creator has made Homo Sapiens...from the same material he has made every other creature ...they are earthborn companions and our fellow mortals." Of the green and mineral worlds he wrote, "Plants are credited with but dim and uncertain sensation, and minerals with positively none at all. But why may not even a mineral arrangement of matter be endowed with sensation of a kind that we in our blind exclusive perfection can have no manner of communication with?"

From Florida, weak and feverish, he crossed over a stormy sea to Cuba, still intent on reaching South America. He was a month in Cuba. "I made free with fine oranges and bananas and many other fruits. Pineapple I had never seen before. Wandered about the narrow streets, stunned with the babel of strange sounds and sights...." He wanted "to climb the central mountain range of the island and trace it through all its forests and valleys and over its sum-

mit peaks, a distance of seven or eight hundred miles." But in his weakened state he thought better of it.

Unable to find a ship to South America, he decided to go to California. However, California-bound ships didn't touch Cuba. He would go instead to New York, find a boat to the Isthmus of Panama, cross over to the Pacific and catch another boat to San Francisco. He found passage on a fast-sailing schooner loaded with oranges for New York. It was a beautiful voyage, and as he drew north his fever abated. The city was under snow. He said of New York, "[Often] I thought I would like to explore the city if, like a lot of hills and valleys, it was clear of inhabitants."

While shipping out of this port in steerage, he wrote, "Never before had I seen such a barbarous mob, especially at meals." Crossing over the isthmus, he discovered that its tropical flora exceeded both Florida's and Cuba's. It was a fast trip north to San Francisco. He found the quickest way out of San Francisco and made a leisurely walk toward the thin, cool air and radiant light of the Sierra Nevada. Yosemite. It was now April 1868, eight months since he had started from Kentucky.

⸻

Muir's Yosemite experience is well known. From 1869 to 1874 he was in the mountains almost continually. By 1874 he knew the Sierra Nevada from Tuolumne south to Whitney as well as anyone, and he knew Yosemite Valley

and its watershed better than anyone.

There could not have been a happier meeting of a man and a place. He gave himself up completely to the mountains, and the mountains told him whatever he wanted to know. He was at the height of his powers. His mind was open and clear, his body strong and immediately responsive to the alpine setting. It was a case of absolute engagement—almost a religion. The Chinese had an ideal of this type of man. The backcountry rustic scholar, artist, eccentric—a man on the outs with civilization who turns to mountains and waters to draw out expressions of a free and fluid existence. Thoreau also approached this ideal, but he wasn't wild enough. Such men are not common among us.

Muir saw Yosemite Valley as an invention of God and for that reason wanted to figure out the mechanics of its formation. From the beginning he perceived glacial action as a major determinant in forming Yosemite-type valleys. Thus, he became deeply engrossed in a study of the glacial history of the Sierra Nevada and Yosemite Valley in particular. "I soon had a key to every Yosemite rock and perpendicular and sloping wall. The grandeur of these forces and their glorious results overpower me, and inhabit my whole being. Waking and sleeping I have no rest. In dreams I read blurred sheets of glacial writing or follow lines of cleavage or struggle with the difficulties of some extraordinary rock form."

During five years of intense study he unraveled the mystery to his own satisfaction. Muir began to publish his findings in 1871. By 1874 he had written seven essays on the glaciology of the Sierra Nevada. Together these are titled *Studies in the Sierra*.

But beyond his scientific work was the ecstatic contemplation he developed in the mountains. He became "like a flake of glass through which light passes." And when he looked around he saw that "all terrestrial things are essentially celestial." These Sierra writings, the letters and journals as well as the formal accounts, comprise the most accurate description on record of a beautifully intelligent mind made ecstatic by an exploration of alpine wilderness. There is nothing else like it in world literature.

He could not have accomplished what he did in the Sierra Nevada with-

out his extremely simple backcountry outlook. From his earliest excursions he had seen lightness as the primary virtue of a mobile wilderness style. In the California mountains he traveled lighter than ever. Food was generally white bread broken up into small pieces, or some kind of grain meal, sugar and tea. On occasion he would supplement this with items like dried meat or dried plums. Mostly he ate plain bread. He liked it hard-crusted, and would sun-dry it thoroughly to keep off mold. His food was carried in a bag tied to his belt. Underlying his food style was the knowledge that he could go without food for up to eight or ten days provided he had water. Experienced in fasting, he would expend himself to the limit on his trips and then come down and eat, rest and recover.

⸻

His equipment sometimes included a couple of blankets. But he knew if he was caught by nightfall in freezing weather without blankets or fire he could find a level spot and dance on it till morning to keep warm. He was not afraid of wet and cold. His backcountry "outfit" was his agile and very durable mind-body and not much else. Which is about as light as you can get.

After his spiritual achievement at Yosemite, his subsequent scholarly and political accomplishments—powerful as they were—may seem like an anticlimax. He was in and out of the Sierra Nevada through most of the 1870's. From the summit of Half Dome in 1875 he saw the rare optical phenomenon called the specter of Brocken. His shadow spread out a half-mile on a cloud beneath him. During this time he also studied Mount Shasta to the north and went into the wilderness of Nevada and Utah. And he was hard at his writing, beginning the steady stream of articles that within 20 years would make him the pre-eminent voice of wilderness conservation in America. It was now too that his life took a social turn. He became a part of the very interesting intellectual life of San Francisco-Berkeley. However, despite his reputation for gregariousness among close friends, he could not stand society for any length of time. The wilderness tugged at him, and he always scampered back to it.

In 1879 he made the first of five trips to Alaska. Alaska made an overwhelming impression on him, for here were the kinds of glaciers whose effects he

had studied in the Sierra Nevada. On his first trip he made a long voyage of 800 miles by canoe from Fort Wrangell to Glacier Bay and back again through straits, sounds, inlets and bays, investigating glaciers. He traveled with a small party that included two Indian chiefs. Muir is credited with being the first westerner to see Glacier Bay and the numerous glaciers that empty into it. He visited one of the largest of these glaciers (named after him) on his third trip to Alaska, in 1890. He describes this ten-day solo excursion to the upper reaches of Muir Glacier—one of his greatest adventures—in *Travels in Alaska*, which contains some of his finest writing. When he went back to Alaska for the last time in 1899, he visited his glacier again and knelt to the ice and kissed it. The Indians called him the Great Ice Chief.

In 1880, at age 42, Muir married Louise Wanda Strentzel, whose family had a large fruit ranch in Martinez up the bay from San Francisco. He took over the management of the ranch and devoted a large part of the next ten years to its expansion and development. With his usual thoroughness he made a complete success of the ranch and retired from active management of it around 1890 after making a substantial amount of money. Two daughters were born during this time, and Muir wrote little.

It had been understood from the first that Muir would have from July to October of each year for his excursions. He often started earlier and stayed later. Just three months after his wedding he was in Alaska. Less than two months after the birth of his first child he left for a six-month cruise of the Arctic Ocean. On the face of it, his behavior seems unfeeling to us now, though Muir himself claimed that his health always suffered in the lowlands from "coughs, grippe and business" and that only wilderness could revive him.

Muir's cruise aboard the revenue cutter *Thomas Corwin* in 1881 took him into the Arctic Ocean and along the northeastern coast of Siberia. The mission was to search for a polar expedition that had vanished off Wrangel Island. *Cruise of the Corwin* is Muir's story of this trip.

In 1885, Muir went to his dying father. The old man had left home and family ten years earlier and had gone to Canada to preach in the streets and minister to the sick and dying. Once he wrote home saying; "I am renewing my youth as the eagles....I have had truly an apostolic experience, and I cannot be pleased with anything else." Now he was dying in Kansas City at the home of a daughter. Muir writes that when he went to him, "He drew me down with a low moaning sound to kiss him and held my hand for a long time and would not let me go." Later he added, "Few lives I know were more restless and eventful as his—few more toilsome and full of enthusiastic endeavor onward towards light and truth and eternal love...." In many ways, the son relived his father's life in his own.

With the founding of the Sierra Club in 1892, Muir stepped fully into the politics of conservation. By the 1890's it was clear that the unchecked exploitation of wilderness by corporate monopolies, carried on with increasing vigor since the Civil War, had to stop. Land, mining, and timber speculators, together with cattle and sheep interests, were running riot over wilderness. To the freewheeling laissez-faire capitalism of the day, the idea that government could withdraw public wilderness from private exploitation was novel and disturbing, and the added idea that wilderness should be preserved solely for beauty seemed outrageous. The battle lines were drawn.

Muir became the master publicist of the conservation movement and a lobbyist for conservation at the highest levels of government. His articles and public proposals and his book *Mountains of California* were instrumental in creating the sentiment for conservation in America at the turn of the century.

Muir's work greatly influenced Presidents Harrison, Cleveland and Roosevelt to establish close to 200 million acres of forest reserves. He had a hand in the creation of the U.S. Forest Service and also helped establish many national parks and monuments.

As a result of this work, Muir found himself a famous and influential man. He counted among his acquaintances some of the most powerful men of his time. But what he called the "Political Quag" took a lot out of him. He traveled as much as he could.

During the 1890's Muir traveled more extensively than ever: to Alaska three times; to Europe, where he visited his old Scottish home, then on to Switzerland for a ramble through the Alps; to the great forests of the western United States and the Canadian Rockies. Everywhere he saw reckless exploitation. He wrote home, "Wherever the white man goes, the groves vanish." In 1898, down with grippe and a cough, he revived with a tour of the eastern seaboard from Florida to Canada, revisiting some parts of the trail he had taken on his 1,000-mile walk.

In 1903 he took a year-long tour of the world. He went through Europe visiting parks, gardens and art galleries. Then he traveled to Russia. From St. Petersburg (Leningrad) he made a short trip to Finland to view its forests, then proceeded to Moscow and south through the Ukraine to the Black Sea and the Caucasus. Returning north to Moscow, he then crossed the Volga basin to the Urals and over into Siberia. He found tundra, vast forests of birch, and north-flowing rivers. At Vladivostok he became desperately ill with ptomaine poisoning, shriveling to 90 pounds. A journal note states, "Still alive. Morphine to stupify pain and brandy to hold on to life." But he pushed on, down the coast of Korea to Shanghai and from there to India for the deodar forests and the Himalayas. He saw the Himalayas from Darjeeling and Simla. Then he journeyed to Egypt for the desert, the pyramids and the Nile. After that he struck out east again to Ceylon, Australia, and New Zealand. From there he headed north through the Malay Archipelago to Manila, then across to Canton, Japan, Hawaii, and finally home. It was a grand tour, and he sketched and botanized on the way.

Muir was growing old, and so were those around him. In 1905 his wife died; his mother had died nine years earlier. Nevertheless, he worked harder than ever on his writing. Out of these years came almost all the books he published in his lifetime. Then, in 1911, at the age of 73, he decided to go to the Amazon alone. His friends tried to dissuade him. But nothing could hold him back. "Have I forgotten the Amazon, Earth's greatest river? Never, never, never."

He must have known it would be his last adventure. From New York he sailed to the mouth of the Amazon, then went upriver by steamboat to Manaus. Sketching and botanizing, he gloried in the beauty of the tropical rain forest. Returning to the mouth of the Amazon, he sailed down to Rio de Janeiro and then to Santos, from where he struck inland to see the primeval forests of *Araucaria braziliana*. He proceeded to Buenos Aires and across the central plateau of Argentina and over the Andes to Santiago, Chile. On the western slopes of the Andes near snow line he found the rare tree *Araucaria imbricata*. Returning to Montevideo, he now wanted to see the baobab tree in its native habitat—Africa!

To fulfill his wish he sailed a roundabout course north to the Canary Islands, then back south to Cape Town. From there he went directly to the baobab forests around Victoria Falls, then north to Lake Victoria to see the headwaters of the Nile and finally home to California, by way of Suez, Naples and New York.

He returned to the final rounds of perhaps his greatest conservation fight: the battle to save Hetch Hetchy Valley in Yosemite National Park from being dammed and flooded by the city of San Francisco. The political issue was the inviolability of a national park, but the larger issue was saving a spot of earth-planet beauty. He lost this battle, and the loss was bitter. He had no choice but to return to work on his *Travels in Alaska* ("A fine change from faithless politics to crystal ice and snow").

Alone now in Martinez in a big house on the knoll overlooking his orchards, he used only his study and a small sleeping porch. "I'm in my old library den," he wrote, "the house desolate, nobody living in it save a hungry mouse or two...." He worked on his book from seven in the morning to ten at night. For some odd reason, in the summer of 1914 he had the old house completely redone, even installing electricity.

That December he went south to visit his daughter Helen, who was farming alfalfa with her family on the edge of the Mojave Desert. He intended to finish *Travels in Alaska* there. But soon after arriving he caught cold, and it turned into pneumonia. He was rushed to a hospital in Los Angeles. There, alone in his room on Christmas Eve, 1914, he died, the Alaska manuscript beside him.

BACKPACKING EQUIPMENT ESSENTIALS

by WILLIAM KEMSLEY, JR.

It is a shame to invest your money in backpacking equipment. To get started, you might invest in a pair of lightweight boots. But it is much better to rent or borrow most other equipment for your first few trips. You can't possibly know exactly what you'll want until after you have tried various items a few times.

Having qualified thusly, here are some basics:

BOOTS

This is your most important piece of gear. And most important about buying boots is seeing that they fit you properly.

Take the socks you'll wear on the trail with you when you shop for boots. Try on the boots with these socks on. Many back-

The most common hiking boot worn by backpackers today is a sturdy though lightweight model, such as these. They have lug soles, but are thin enough to flex when you walk. Comfort is the most important consideration when you buy boots.

packers like to wear two pairs of socks, a light pair with a heavier pair of wool socks over them. If this is what you'll be wearing, then put on both pairs when trying on boots.

Try on both boots. Most people's left and right feet are different. And it is important that both of your feet be comfortable.

There are ways to tell if your boots fit properly. A good salesclerk can help you determine proper fit.

Buy boots that are not too heavy. They'll wear you out and blister your feet quicker than lighterweight trail boots. If you need all the "support" that heavy boots supposedly provide for your feet, you probably ought to be exercising your ankles before taking up backpacking.

And break in your boots before you go on your first hike with them. Wear them around town to get your feet used to them.

PACKS

First of all, a pack ought to fit you comfortably. Second, it ought to be big enough to carry the gear you'll need on your trip—but not so big your gear will be flopping around in it, making a racket when you walk.

There are several hundred packs to choose from. That complicates matters. But if you use common sense and buy one for your commonest needs—which would be weekend trips—and not for that two-week trek to the Al-

About four out of five packs that are used on the trails are external frame packs like this one, with a pack bag divided into two main compartments and a wraparound hip belt. This particular pack also has the commonest cluster of side pockets.

askan Brooks Range which you *may* take someday—you'll do all right.

The pack for this purpose is about 2,500- to 4,000-cubic-inch capacity, and has a hip belt and some side pockets.

SLEEPING BAGS

Here is where many people overbuy. Buy a sleeping bag for the average nighttime temperatures you'll be using it in, *not for the lowest temperatures* you may use it in.

If you do have an exceptionally cold night, you can put on a few layers of clothing before getting into your sleeping bag.

If you make the mistake of buying a bag good for the lowest temperatures you might encounter, you'll be too warm on your average night out. My brother Mike, who lives in Vermont and camps out many nights each winter, has a great sleeping bag which is good for 60° below zero—which he's never been able to use, and is willing to sell cheap.

For backpacking, the most popular choice of sleeping bags is the mummy shape of the one illustrated here. The mummy shape is best for conserving body warmth inside the bag, and because it does not have wasted material in unused square corners, it is lighter and uses less insulation material to give the same amount of warmth as a square-cut bag. Although down is the lightest insulation material used in backpacking sleeping bags, the new synthetic polyester insulation materials like PolarGuard and Hollofil II are less expensive and not that much heavier, and hence very popular.

Many synthetic fillers are now on the market, as well as the goose and duck downs, and a great variety of designs. You'll need to do some studying before leaping in this area. If it gets too complicated, you can always take up racquetball instead of backpacking.

The most commonly used backpacking tent is made of "breathable" nylon fabric which is not itself waterproof. This is because waterproof material would cause body vapor to condense on the inside of the tent and produce excessive moisture. To keep the rain out of the tent, a waterproof fly is needed to pitch over the top of the tent, as in the photo here.

In recent years there has been a spate of domelike tent designs for backpackers. This has been made possible because of new fiberglass materials that are light, flexible, and strong enough to use as tent poles. The advantage of the dome shape is that it gives more headroom inside the tent. This is a three-person model.

TENTS

If you think packs, boots, and sleeping bags are complicated, tents will surely be your undoing.

The sturdiest tent construction over the years has been the A-frame model such as the one here. The sturdiest of the A-frame models are those whose tent poles also form an "A" at each end. They are guyed out front and back. And the canopy of the tent top has a built-in sag along the ridgeline, known as a "catenary cut," which keeps the fabric of the tent walls from developing wrinkles that flap in the breeze.

For a beginning tent I'd stay away from complicated designs. I'd be sure it had good insect-net doors, windows, and vents and plenty of openings for cross ventilation. It should be waterproof yet breathable, so that your own body moisture does not condense on the inside of the tent and get you wet.

And from this point on you're going to have to make trade-offs. The more features you want your tent to have, the costlier it will be. If you want it really lightweight you're going to be cramped in small space. And so on.

You'll have to do some studying and some shopping around to find out what features are important to you.

STOVES

Today, in most national parks and many wilderness areas, open campfires are not permitted. This means you'll have to carry one of the small backpacking cookstoves. That's not so bad. There are some pluses to this. Stoves don't get soot on the outside of your pots, they cook your meals quicker and better, and you don't have to gather firewood.

In buying a stove there are a

A lightweight backpacking stove is an essential today. In most national parks and wilderness areas, campfires are taboo. This particular camp stove will bring a pot of water to a boil in less than six minutes and will leave pots soot-free. Its temperatures are so easy to regulate that cooking is almost as convenient as on a kitchen range.

number of choices. The basic choice is between cannister stoves, fueled by propane or butane cartridges, and liquid-fuel stoves. There are advantages to each type. You can light cannisters more easily and regulate them better than the liquid fuel stoves. But there are some inconveniences as well, such as running out of fuel in the middle of cooking a meal, and not getting a strong enough heat for some foods.

Again, you're better off if you can wait to buy a stove until after you've gotten more experience in actual trail use with some of the models available.

HOW TO PACK YOUR PACK

What you'll carry in your pack will depend largely upon the length of your trip and the season of the year. Also, regardless of books you read and advice of friends, there'll be some personal items which you'll always take along because you are you. One person I know brings along pa-

Weekend backpack (hot summer weekend)

Qty.	Item	Weight
1	pack	28 oz.
1	tent	62 oz.
1	ground cloth	10 oz.
1	sleeping bag	68 oz.
1	sleeping pad	16 oz.
1	stove	16 oz.
2	cooking pots	12 oz.
1	can opener	½ oz.
1	pot lifter	¾ oz.
1	Sigg pt. bottle w/ fuel	21 oz.
1	funnel	¼ oz.
1	pocketknife	2 oz.
1	plastic plate or bowl	2 oz.
1	plastic cup	1 oz.
1	spoon	¼ oz.
1	salt and pepper shaker	1 oz.
2	books matches in watertight plastic bag	¼ oz.
1	small roll toilet paper	2 oz.
1	toothbrush and tube toothpaste	1 oz.
1	comb	¼ oz.
1	first-aid kit	12 oz.
1	package mole-skins (for blisters)	1 oz.
1	insect repellent	1 ½ oz.
1	snakebite kit	1 oz.
1	compass/maps	4 oz.
1	canteen	2 oz.
1	rain cover for pack	6 oz.
1	camera	39 oz.
1	film	2 oz.
1	garbage bag	1 oz.
	food	32 oz.

Clothing

Qty.	Item	Weight
1	pair hiking boots	59 oz.
1	extra pair socks	2 oz.
1	bandanna	1 oz.
1	hat	3 oz.
1	pair long pants	28 oz.
1	pair shorts	14 oz.
1	belt	5 oz.
1	long-sleeve shirt	6 oz.
1	short-sleeve shirt	4 oz.
1	wool or down sweater	22 oz.
1	rain jacket	12 oz.
1 pr.	camp mocassins	16 oz.
2 pr.	nylon boot laces	1 oz.
1	repair kit	2 oz.
1 pr.	binoculars	4½ oz.
1	flashlight	8 oz.

TOTAL WT. FOR WEEKEND 33⅓ LBS.

Week-long trip (in hot summer weather)

Duplicate the above and add the following items:

1	pair extra underwear	7 oz.
1	pair rain pants	8 oz.
1	pair gloves	1 oz.
1	wool hat	4 oz.
2	spare flash-light batteries and bulb	6 oz.
1	candle lantern	6 oz
2	candles	8 oz.
1	towel	4 oz.
	food	112 oz.

Total additional 9⅔ lbs.
TOTAL WT. FOR WEEK 43 LBS.

Winter Weekend Trip

Add to weekend trip list (leave off the shorts, boots, camp moccasins, and short-sleeve shirt):

1 pr.	skis or snow-shoes	72 oz.
1	ice ax or ski poles	38 oz.
1 pr.	crampons	33 oz.
1 pr.	gaiters	4 oz.
1 pr.	wool pants	25 oz.
1	down parka	44 oz.
1	wind parka (60/40 type)	38 oz.
1 pr.	long johns	12 oz.
1 pr.	down booties	12 oz.
2 prs.	wool mittens	10 oz.
1 pr.	nylon mitten shells	4 oz.
1	wool balaclava	4 oz.
1 pr.	winter boots	96 oz.

Total additional winter
18 lbs. 8 oz.
TOTAL FOR WINTER WEEKEND
51 LBS. 14 OZ.

jamas. He can't sleep without them. Another friend always brings along camp moccasins to change into at the end of a day's hiking. Someone else I know brings a book to read. Another brings binoculars. And so on.

Here are suggested equipment lists for different types of trips. I've listed all items I carry, and their weights. Some of these items, of course, are worn, while the rest goes in your pack. Nevertheless, it gives you an idea of the amount of gear you will be carrying for each type of trip.

This is a check list of gear for one person. If a second goes along, that pack will weigh considerably less, because you won't need to duplicate some of the heavier items—tent, stove, fuel, cook pots, first aid kit. These community items weigh about 8⅓ pounds. And hence, a second person's pack should weigh in at about 25 pounds.

Of course, you can vary this list considerably. I have gone on trips with as little as 12 pounds and as much as 52 pounds in my pack for a weekend trip in summer.

Here is a lightweight folding candle lantern, which makes camps bright and cheery in the evening.

In the past few years, miniaturization of binoculars has made it quite practical now for a backpacker to tuck a pair like these into his shirt pocket. It is one of the thrills of backpacking to be able to sight and watch wildlife.

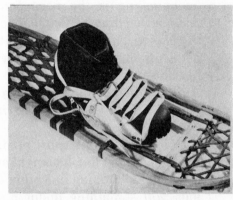

Although snowshoes are still made of wood and rawhide, there has been a lot of innovation in showshoe bindings, making it possible to get them on and off with a good deal more ease than ever before.

Today's backpacking equipment enables you to take the whole family along. There is a wide range of children's packs available, as well as kiddy carriers to tote infants on your back.

BACKPACKING EQUIPMENT:

A Personal View

by LIONEL ATWILL

Backpackers are individualists to begin with. One of the underlying needs that is satisfied by backpacking is the need for self-sufficiency. Anyone needing self-sufficiency badly enough to take to backpacking is obviously an independent cuss. Ergo, an individualist. People like this don't generally like to follow fashions. And no better place can you see a backpacker's individuality than in his choice of equipment.

Unlike his counterpart on the ski slopes or the golf links, the backpacker usually has a revulsion to looking like other backpackers. He tells you something about his personality by the individuated collection of gear he takes on a trip, by the way he carries his gear, and by how he customizes his gear once he owns it.

There are go-light backpackers, who make an art of trimming excess weight from their pack load. There is the lunatic fringe of this group, who take film cartridges from their cardboard boxes before putting them in their packs, cut off the handle of their toothbrush and the tags off their tea bags—in the name of lightness.

The other extreme has those who carry bulging packs with 100 pounds of lightweight gear. Because all the latest gadgets are so lightweight, they tend to toss them all into their packs, not realizing what a load they're shouldering.

There are tent campers and tarp campers; Dutch-oven gourmet cuisine nuts and cold, uncooked-oatmeal ascetics; poncho stalwarts versus the order of the cagoules; thick-soled mountaineering boot freaks versus running-shoe zealots. Its like watching Coxey's army when you see a group of really experienced hikers marching out on the trail together. But that's a contradiction, too. The chances are a group of really experienced hikers won't be marching along together very long. They'll scatter out along the trail—each at his own individual pace.

The following piece was written by a highly experienced backpacker, who admits to being as opinionated as he is experienced. Tony Atwill grew up hiking in the mountains of the Northeast. His outdoors experience was further broadened (and his opinions more hardened) in the U.S. Army Rangers, where he learned how to catch and eat animals, fish, and reptiles, which he is wont to tell about around an evening campfire just as you are about to enjoy your chicken fricassee. Guaranteed to ruin your appetite. Here is Tony's slant on equipment.

W. K.

On August 4, 1913, Joe Knowles, an unknown portrait painter with a romantic bent, sauntered into the Maine woods wearing a breechcloth and carrying only the conviction that man could still survive in the wilderness alone and unaided. Two months later he emerged tan and fit and the next year repeated his performance in the Siskiyou Mountains of Washington, proving that man need not live by equipment alone . . . but it helps.

Modern backpacking equipment—superbly engineered, meticulously manufactured—is especially helpful. It makes life in the backcountry not only possible but eminently palatable and, more importantly, has opened the wilderness to the masses. Armed with Gore-Tex, Cordura, ripstop nylon, mosquito netting, ensolite, aluminium, magnesium, down, and wool, the average backpacker can tackle any climate or terrain within reason (unfortunately, not all backpackers are reasonable, and every year fools disregard their instincts for survival and bet their lives on the mystical properties of bird feathers and nylon. They inevitably lose).

Besides preparing the backpacker for the elements, the proliferation of today's backpacking equipment permits the wilderness traveler to fine-tune his load to match his taste and style. Don't think for a moment that backpacking equipment is not an extension of the packer's personality; there are schools of backpacking equipage: the go-lighters, the old-woodsman wanderers, the army-surplus olive-drab outfitters, and the portable handwarmer hedonists, to name a few. They all subscribe to styles of dress and equipment that often have little to do with weather and terrain. For example, as a member of the old-woodsman school, I would no more go into the woods without my rancid poplin hat and ripped fishing shirt than I would wearing only Joe Knowles's attire. I can spout pragmatic reasons for my costume—and I will—but my outfit really boils down to style and taste. My hat and shirt look good and feel good. To hell with your hat and shirt.

Granted, there is almost too much equipment around. Packs, tents, sleeping bags, clothes, boots, and sundries ranging from collapsible lanterns to portable showers have been designed, refined, and combined to a point where the weight of decision of what to take is often heavier than one's final pack. But there is a benefit to all the planning and fretting that must go into such a decision, too: the thrill of backpacking is extended. Only ptarmigan and fools go out in winter, as far as I am concerned, but I don't stop backpacking come November. I sit by a warm fire with my library of catalogs from L. L. Bean, EMS, Ski Hut, REI, Snow Lion, Kelty, and Stephenson's (who can resist all that flash) and backpack my way through specification charts and fine print.

There are three salient points about equipment that all backpackers should memorize, although few do: Everything is a compromise, and no one piece of equipment will fill all needs; no matter what backpacking item you lust for—be it a high-altitude tent or a pocket barometer—you probably don't need it (remember Joe Knowles); and whatever advice anyone gives you, he or she is grossly prejudiced.

That is the best advice I can give you, and I should stop here, but no one who relishes the smell of damp woods, the comforting, settled weight of a pack, and the gentle thud of boot on trail can pause with such a mouthful of generalities. Backpackers spend too much time fine-tuning their loads not to proselytize whenever possible. I am no exception. I shall, however, preface my ranting and raving with two qualifications: I am an eastern backpacker and as such am more concerned with warmth in wet weather and less concerned with weight than my western counterpart (I eschew down in favor of wool, which will keep you warm in wet weather rather than turning into a ball of soggy feathers). I also speak to the three-season hiker. Winter hiking and the equipment for it are highly specialized, and since on two occasions I have pulled the bodies of inexperienced winter backpackers from the snow, I prefer to skip any discussion of the merits of wool over down and give this simple advice: do not go backpacking in winter. If you insist on ignoring me, make sure you read everything available on winter camping, attend a class (with a field trip) on winter technique, and go out only with experienced winter backpackers. With those warnings in mind, read on, if you must, while I bare my soul and hide.

COVERING FOR THE HIDE

Joe Knowles wore a breechcloth. Such attire may still suffice for some, but most of us need more clothing for protection, warmth, and modesty. I will start with Joe's outfit and add on.

I haven't worn underpants in the woods for years. I find them constricting and unnecessary. They chafe, get dirty, and look foolish hanging from the ridge of a tent after a washing. I recommend doing without—for both men and women—but if you are a slave to convention, wear cotton, the baggier the better. Tight nylon panties for women restrict circulation, do not absorb sweat, and constantly ride up, necessitating frequent undignified tugs. For men, I don't advise wearing them in or out of the woods.

In hot weather I dispense with undershirts, too, preferring to walk bare-chested. In moderate to cool weather, however, I wear a cotton T-shirt or a fishnet T-shirt, which wicks away moisture quite well but also traps air efficiently when worn under a buttoned-up, long-sleeved shirt. That air sandwiched between the strings of the fishnet and the shirt keeps me surprisingly warm. There is one drawback to fishnet: pack straps will impress the netting into the shoulders, leaving a waffle pattern in the skin that is uncomfortable and ugly. Buy a fishnet with solid cotton shoulders if you don't like your flesh quilted.

There are only two sensible types of pants to take on the trail, shorts and tightly woven long wool trousers. My favorite shorts are a cotton-and-synthetic blend with a touch of Spandex, which allows the pants to expand over my ever-increasing gut and to

33

stretch with the movement of my legs. They are covered with pockets—handy receptacles for litter collected along the trail—and have served me well for four years. I wear them all day in almost all weather down to 40°. And I wear them on the trail and off. My legs are scarred from losing battles with blackberry bushes and wait-a-minute vines, but such wounds are certainly no more foolish than Heidelberg dueling scars.

When rain falls and temperatures drop I switch to long wool pants, which keep me warm no matter how wet the weather. And nothing is more luxurious than climbing out of my shorts and slipping into my woollies at the end of the day.

If you are so proud of your unscarred gams that you demand long pants for warm-weather wear, get a pair of baggy cotton trousers from an army-surplus store or backpacking shop. Don't consider blue jeans; they are much too constricting, and when wet they take an interminable length of time to dry. If you insist on wearing jeans, wear cowboy boots, too. Then people will think you are a wayward bronco buster instead of a misinformed backpacker.

For chest protection I favor a 100-percent cotton shirt from Orvis, which specializes in fishing gear. It is held together with pockets (it is designed for fly-fishing, and fly-fishermen carry more gear than backpackers), has baggy long sleeves which roll up easily and will dry out on a hot rock within 15 minutes if I should decide to rinse it out after 10 or 15 days of wear. In the rain or cold, I wear my fishing shirt over an army-surplus jungle sweater—100 percent wool with a shawl collar—and if the wind is blowing I add a light nylon wind shirt that I bought at a downhill ski shop that was going out of business. If temperatures fall below freezing, I add a down sweater.

In a drizzle I dispense with conventional rain gear and jump into my wool. In a downpour I pitch my tent or set up a tarp and sit it out. To hell with walking in the rain. I do carry a poncho for around-camp wear in the rain, but I try not to walk in it—the condensation inside is far more annoying to me than fresh rainwater. I have tried cagoules and anoraks but find them much too confining—they remind me of shrouds for burial at sea. Gore-Tex and Bukflex vapor-penetrable rainwear is relatively new, and I have not tried either brand. And I probably never will, for I am terribly suspicious of people who walk in the rain.

What separates the experienced backpacker from the novice is his choice of accessories. Listen up, here, if you want to dress as if you know what you are doing.

Throw out your three-inch-thick leather belt with its two-pound brass buckle. It will inevitably go to war with the waist belt of your pack—and lose. Instead, wear suspenders or a soft, flexible belt. A length of solid nylon webbing, the sort used by rock climbers, will hold up your pants quite well if you sew two brass rings onto one end.

Bandannas are a must for the trail. They can serve as towels, sweat bands, pot holders, place mats for formal dining, and they will plug that gap around your neck when the blackflies are out in force. They look good, too.

Some people carry swimsuits; I find them as useless as underpants. If I were hiking around a Holiday Inn, I would probably carry a pair, but in the wilderness, who needs them? And if I embarrass someone with a flash of my nudity, then let him or her leave. I'm not going to.

Hats are imperative, and I say hats because I always take two. A floppy, high-crowned cotton model to keep the rain out of my glasses, cool my crown in the sun, and keep the bugs off my brow when saturated with insect repellent. My other hat is a wool tam-o'-shanter, which I wear in the evenings and on retiring. I am slightly claustrophobic in a sleeping bag that envelops my head, but on a cool night I freeze unless something keeps the heat from escaping from my noggin. So I wear my tam to bed, pulled right down over my ears. It is dashing as hell, too.

Backpacking clothing is dictated by the weather. If you hike in the rain in the East, you will need wool. If you hike in the desert, you will need cotton that will absorb sweat and dry out quickly. Just make sure you take sufficient clothing to cope with the worst weather you might encounter; that means if you hike in the White Mountains or the Adirondacks in August, you will need clothing to protect you from the snow. However, don't think you must spend a fortune to be sartorially splendid on the trail. Almost all the clothing you need for a summer hike is already in your closet; or it was there, and you can now buy it back from Goodwill.

FOOT POWER

A crusty, professional woodsman friend who has spent at least 50 years in the backcountry performs this ritual every day on the trail: precisely at noon he finds a moss-covered log, preferably by a stream, sits down, removes his boots and socks, contemplates his toes for 10 minutes, dusts them liberally with foot powder, puts on new socks, massages his feet for another five minutes, eats lunch, replaces his boots, and finally hits the trail. Remember, he is no tenderfoot, literally or figuratively.

I once asked him why he spent so much time on his feet. He looked at me quizzically, shook his head in disbelief, and muttered, "When my damn feet give out, you don't think I'm gonna call a cab out here, now do you?"

Ever since that condescending reply, I've observed the same ritual, and I have not had a blister in years. My feet are ugly, but I like them. And I take care of them, beginning with the socks and boots I slip them into.

There is only one type of sock for the backpacker, as far as I am concerned: 100-percent, fluffy, scratchy, moisture-absorbing wool.

I always wear two pairs, a thin inner sock, usually a well-worn white athletic sock left over from my competitive days, and a Ragg wool outer sock. I like two socks not so much for the conventional reason that friction in the boot will occur between the two socks rather than between one sock and my foot, but because of the extra cushioning two socks afford. My boots fit and my feet are ugly and tough, so I don't worry about blisters, but after a long walk on a hot day, my feet expand to the size of flippers, and I need the extra resilience I get with two socks.

I swear by wool because it keeps my feet warm even when wet, wicks off sweat better than any other fabric, provides that excellent cushion, and feels almost comfortable when wet (I don't bother to remove my boots or socks when crossing a stream; I just plod through the water, and on my next break wring out my socks and put them back on). I have found only one drawback to Ragg socks: after one washing—either by hand or machine—they look as if they should be hanging from someone's rearview mirror. Shrinkproof Ragg wool socks with a touch of elastic eliminate that problem.

Backpackers habitually overbuy on boots. The average hiker doesn't need seven-pound, inflexible, lug-soled stompers to walk along a level trail, but time and again that is what you will see on the majority of "fashionable" hikers. Do not wear more boot than you need.

If you limit your hiking to the occasional overnight jaunt, stick with sneakers. Grandma Gatewood walked the Appalachian Trail in a pair; you should be able to negotiate your local park. If you take three- or four-day trips, consider a pair of sturdy, rubber-soled work boots or moccasin-toe hunting boots. Both are flexible, light, and inexpensive.

Since no one will heed that advice, sound as it is, I'm forced to say something about backpacking boots. Buy boots that are light and boots that fit.

Backpacking boots come in all sizes, weights, shapes, and colors. They are sold in backpacking stores and in J.C. Penney's. They can be the most comfortable or the most excruciatingly painful piece of equipment you can buy.

Any boot that weighs more than five pounds a pair, doesn't bend across the instep when you walk in it, or costs more than $65 should automatically be eliminated. Such a boot is designed for heavy-duty mountain work, usually with crampons, and has no place on the average backpacker's foot. Try on every other boot in the store. (Yes, in the store; you cannot buy boots by mail—at least you shouldn't unless you live in the heart of nowhere and cannot find a well-equipped backpacking store. I advocate backpacking stores, too. Your corner shoestore may carry boots, but chances are good that your corner shoe salesman hasn't the slightest idea about proper fit.)

Make sure you put on the same socks you plan to wear on the trail. Lace the boots up snugly and walk around the store for 10 minutes. If you feel anything rubbing, chuck those boots like the plague and try another pair. You may go through every boot in the store before you find something that fits, but your efforts will pay off on the trail.

Once you have selected a pair that feel relatively comfortable, try them out on a slanted fitting board, an inclined ramp designed to simulate uphill or downhill walking. If the store doesn't have such a board, leave, or at least go to the wall and kick the hell out of the molding. On either the slant board or the kick test, your toe should jam forward in the boot, and you should be able to get one finger down the back of the boot just aft of your heel. Two fingers and the boots are too large; no fingers and they are too small. Try again.

When you find a pair that fit, buy them with the provision that you can wear them at home for a few days and bring them back if a blister develops. Remember, if they don't fit when you buy them, they never will. You can soak your feet in water, soak your boots in water, stretch the leather, or cut off a toe, but you will still have problems.

Do not eliminate a boot because it does not have a lug sole. Such soles work well on snow and on certain types of rock, but on all other terrain a smooth rubber sole will do the job just as effectively and will not prepare the ground for erosion at the first rain. If you have a pair of boots with lug soles, look behind you the next time you go on a walk. You will see hundreds of small waffles following you, and as soon as a rain hits, those tiny mounds of earth will wash away. Lug soles are slowly wearing away many of our trails, and even Vibram, the largest manufacturer of lug soles, is introducing a shallower lug sole for the average backpacker.

Three other pieces of equipment are important for your feet: foot powder, the merits of which I have already discussed; moleskin, which will protect the blisters that are formed by those overweight, stiff mountain boots you insisted on buying; and a soft, cuddly pair of moccasins or tennis shoes to slip into at the end of the day. Don't leave home without them.

HOUSE ON YOUR BACK

The modern frame pack has taken the backache out of backpacking. It has replaced the Trapper Nelson, the Adirondack packbasket, the Duluth sack, and a myriad of other torture devices, and anyone who still adheres to those old carriers deserves the slipped discs and contorted vertebrae that accompany them.

Next to tents, more design goes into packs than into any other piece of backpacking equipment. There are packs with internal frames, external frames, flexible frames, rigid frames, padded belts, padded backs, pockets, straps, and every other gewgaw conceivable. What has made the modern pack so revolutionary, however, are not all these trappings but a hip belt, which distributes the weight of the pack across the pelvic girdle rather than concentrating it on the shoulders, and a curve to the pack's frame that follows the curve of the spine and places the center of gravity of the load over the center of gravity of the average person.

One should therefore look for a frame that fits (so the center of gravity will be correctly positioned) and for a sturdy, padded waist belt. Beyond those two considerations, the most important criteria are workmanship, for a pack will take a terrible beating over the years, and design features that fit your needs. Check a top-of-the-line pack, say a Kelty, to get an idea of proper workmanship; you'll find that the more money you spend, the better workmanship you'll find.

There is an old adage in backpacking that no matter how long you will be out—a day or a month—no matter what the weather, and no matter how long you have been backpacking, you will fill up your pack—to the top. Succinctly stated, "Backpacking gear expands to fill the volume of its container." Now there are some packs on the market that can haul over 100 pounds and still have room to tuck in a few mastodon bones which you might happen to pick up along the way. You don't need such a pack. Granted, it is tempting with all its extra patches and pockets, but remember that you will fill it up.

My favorite pack for more than a two-day trip is a Kelty Tioga, a sturdy, simple pack which holds more than I need but not more than I take. My system for packing it is hardly unique, but it has served me well, and I have stuck to it for several years so that now I know immediately where my first-aid kit is without having to rummage around for 20 minutes while a hiking companion writhes in agony from a blister demanding treatment.

The items I use most frequently on the trail—first-aid kit, toilet paper, flashlight, canteen, poncho, pack rain cover, and something to nibble—all go in the small outside pockets. Clothing, wrapped in a plastic bag, resides in the lower main compartment. Sleeping bag and pad are strapped onto the bottom of the frame. Everything else—and at times that can be an impressive amount of equipment—is jammed into the top compartment. I do subdivide food from stoves and pots by using small nylon stuff sacks, but I have never been successful at organizing that top compartment. You can find tidy diagrams of perfectly organized packs, and if you can get everything into your pack according to a schematic, more power to you; I have had an aversion to overorganization since my Army days and find that the cram-and-jam method serves me well.

Carrying a pack is a fine art. I start a trip with my waist cinched in to Victorian proportions—my hips are more conditioned to carrying weight at the start than my shoulders—but after a few miles I loosen my hip belt, tighten my shoulder straps, and the load is effectively shifted without stopping for a break. I repeat this transfer every mile or so, and occasionally I will rig a tumpline from the frame so I can carry my load from a third point, my forehead. All this adjusting keeps me busy but saves overtaxing any one set of flabby muscles.

Hip belts have made packing pleasurable, but they also can be dangerous. When crossing water—a trickling stream or the Colorado—take off your hip belt. If you fell off a slippery rock and landed face down with your hip belt cinched tight, you might have a difficult time getting out of your pack. Glug!

BEDDING DOWN

If I get a good night's sleep, I can put up with all sorts of discomforts and injustices during the day, so I consider a sleeping bag and, equally important, a mattress or pad the two most important items in a backpacker's kit.

A trail bed serves two functions: it insulates you from the ground (the filling in almost any sleeping bag will compress under your weight, drastically diminishing its insulating powers), and it makes the ground softer. Nothing wrong with comfort—in moderation.

The old woodsman traditionally cut boughs, preferably balsam, and arranged them meticulously on the ground to build up a mattress 8 or 10 inches high. Sleeping on a bough bed was a glorious experience, but today such a luxury is irresponsible and incomprehensible—forests cannot stand such heavyhanded treatment.

The air mattress and foam pad have replaced the bough bed. Air mattresses no longer need be of the army-surplus or imported-from-Taiwan varieties that weighed four pounds apiece and inevitably went flat at 3:45 A.M. My favorite air mattress consists of a light nylon shell enclosing nine individual vinyl tubes, each of which will inflate with a single breath. By overinflating the outer tubes and underinflating the tubes in the middle, I can create a delightful sleeping platform that gently cradles me like a small waterbed. And the whole package weighs around a pound.

Air mattresses are most comfortable, but they have two drawbacks: they must be inflated and deflated every day (I always hyperventilated blowing up my old surplus model, and on several occasions I passed out at the feet of my hiking companions, who immediately went into their first-aid acts, tying tourniquets around my neck and practicing mouth-to-mouth in my ear); also, air mattresses are terrible insulators. All that air moving around inside conducts heat away from your body and carries the cold from the ground right up to your back.

One can circumvent these drawbacks by using a foam pad, either open-cell or closed-cell, neither of which requires inflation and both of which are fine insulators. There is a flood of foam on the market with frightening names, Ensolite E, Volarafoam, Duralite, and on and on. To simplify all that, it is best to look at foam in two families, closed-cell and open-cell.

Closed-cell foam, as its name implies, is a foam with encapsulated bubbles, each isolated from its neighbor. Open-cell foam, on the other hand, resembles Swiss cheese under magnification—the foam is tunneled with interconnecting cells. Both have unique characteristics.

Open-cell foam is more compressible and therefore softer than closed-cell. It is more comfortable but is subject to wear and must be encased in a cover. Also, open-cell will absorb water, which will destroy its insulating ability, and because all of those interconnecting cells permit air to circulate within the foam, a much thicker piece of open-cell foam is needed to deliver the same insulation as a piece of closed-cell.

Closed-cell foam is the best insulator, is relatively easy to roll up and pack, but offers little more comfort than a bed of roots. I solve the comfort/insulation problem by slipping a piece of closed-cell into the nylon cover of my open-cell pad. The resulting mattress is on the bulky side, but I sleep warmly and comfortably and rarely feel the rocks that inevitably find their way under my bed.

Sleeping bags will see you through the night, and I wouldn't go out without a good one. Two factors determine their efficiency: what they are filled with and how they are cut.

Traditionally, better bags have been filled with fluffy down—usually plucked from an accommodating goose. Down has the unique properties of being extremely light, compressible and of providing a high loft for its weight and volume, all of which equals great warmth. Unfortunately, down has a serious flaw: when it gets wet, it is useless (have you ever seen a bird sitting on a telephone line in a rainstorm? He isn't comfortable and he is using down.) Wet down, unlike wet wool, takes ages to dry out and fluff up.

Some of the newer synthetics, notably PolarGuard and Hollofil II, have overcome down's weakness without adding too much weight and bulk. These synthetics, when wet, can be wrung out, and their insulating properties quickly restored. For any given amount of insulation, they are heavier and bulkier than down, but many backpackers are willing to make those small sacrifices for the comfort of knowing that they still can get a good night's sleep if their bag gets wet.

A good sleeping bag is cut snugly to fit your body and should not have any stitching passing from the inside to the outside of the bag. Baffles should be sewn in the bag to keep the filler from lumping up at the bottom, and a good zipper should extend from head to foot so that one may control the temperature inside the bag by opening it up at head and foot. Some people cannot stand a close-cut mummy bag—they feel as if they are being laid out for their final rest—and they should certainly consider a semi-rectangular bag and perhaps an extra-long bag. Everyone, however, should stay away from those cute square bags with the flap at the head which can be propped up with sticks to form a mini-tent. They look great and work well in the living room, but I have never been able to figure out what that overhead tent is really for; it certainly would offer no protection from rain or snow. Perhaps one could tape a mirror to it and watch television while lying down.

There is one other item available to the backpacker that can make sleeping out more enjoyable—a pillow. Not long ago a friend who claims he spends a minimum of 150 nights per year sleeping out under the stars amazed me and our hiking companions by reaching into his cavernous pack and pulling out a small airline pillow. Like a 16-year-old forced to wear shorts to the junior prom, he was subjected to no less than an hour of ridicule, but when all the tormenting died down and we all settled into our wilderness beds, he was snoring before the rest of us had zipped up. I don't carry a pillow yet—instead I fill the stuff bag for my sleeping bag with clothes and boots—but the next time I am on a plane, I will be tempted to make off with one.

KITCHEN IN A SACK

Not long ago cooking on the trail could be complex. One needed to know how to start a fire in rain and snow. A frying pan was a must, as were pots, pancake flippers, can openers, steak grills, Dutch ovens, reflector ovens, soup ladles, and assorted condiments. All that to heat up some beans, fry an occasional trout, or drown a piece of Spam in grease.

Today, the backpacker's kitchen can be outrageously simple. Fires are as archaic as bough beds and just as damaging to the wilderness. Small stoves solve the heating problem. Foods are freeze-dried or dehydrated and rarely need more than hot water to make them palatable—and believe me, they are much better tasting than the slop we put up with a few years ago.

Building a fire used to be the ultimate test of a woodsman, but it was also the ultimate inconvenience. A stove solves that and should be considered mandatory. There are all sorts of stoves available fueled by butane, white gas, kerosene, Sterno, and even buffalo chips. Most are light and efficient, although some do certain jobs better than others.

Butane stoves, employing a small cylinder of gas attached to a burner, are clean and easy, but they do not operate well in cold weather, and one must always pack along an extra cylinder of fuel—it is impossible to determine accurately how much gas is left in the cylinder attached to the burner. White gas and kerosene stoves come in a variety of sizes, are hot-burning, and work well in the cold, but they can be a curse to start. My Svea 123, a popular, compact gas stove, demands a ritual before it will fire up. I kneel before it, perform a short incantation, shield the stove from wind, prime the burner, light a match, pray that the fuel will vaporize as it is supposed to, discover that the nozzle is plugged, repeat all of the above, and eventually light a match, which ignites a spurt of gas, singeing my eyebrows. The entire ritual is similar to meditation but with physical pain and frustration thrown in.

Sterno, an old standby, should not be overlooked. The flame is not particularly hot, but it is easy to start and does a fine job of heating up just enough water for a quick cup of soup at lunch. It is also a good backup stove.

I've seen backpackers prepare sumptuous meals in coffee cans, but backpacking pots that fit together and have lids that serve as frying pans are more compact and versatile. Since most backpacking meals need little more than a shot of hot water and a stir, I never take more than two pots; if I do, I use all of them, and that means more after dinner cleanup. Remember to carry a bandanna, which makes a fine potholder, or a pot gripper, a pair of pliers with the gripping head set at a right angle to the handle. Until you have etched a burn across the tips of your fingers with the hot bail of a pot, you will not appreciate these two accessories.

Difficult-to-pack foods like jam and honey may be carried in special squeeze tubes which open from the bottom. It is impossible to force jam through the small hole of a conventional plastic bottle, but it is quite easy to spoon it into the bottom of a backpacking squeeze tube and then secure the tube by folding over the end and clipping it shut. Backpacking stores sell other types of plastic bottles for coffee, powdered milk, sugar, and the like, but I prefer baby bottles from the grocery store. They work just as well and are cheaper.

Water is a must for the kitchen, and a canteen is the answer. Many packers use a large-mouthed plastic bottle, which is easy to drink from and which simplifies the addition of lemonade or Tang—nice additives to mask the taste of purified water. I prefer a plastic army canteen, which fits neatly into a matching canteen cup. The cup is

my plate, too, and has several advantages over the popular Sierra cup, a shallow metal container with a wire rim extending into a handle which keeps the lip of the cup cool.

When I am backpacking with a group and dinner is a community affair, I can hold three times as much food in my canteen cup as my companions can spoon into their Sierra cups—and no one is the wiser. Also, I can heat up just enough water for a lunchtime cup of soup, carry enough water for a head-to-toe sponge bath, and when camping in winter when cold winds may confine me to a tent for several days, my half-quart-capacity canteen cup eliminates the need to go outside when nature calls. Try that with a Sierra cup!

The last part of my cooking kit is a spoon, once part of a slip-together knife-fork-spoon combination. On its handle are two small knobs that used to hold the set together. Now they serve as efficient pot lifters. I slip the handle of the spoon under the wire bail of the pot, catch the wire on the knob, and lift. I rarely spill my soup more than once a day.

TENTS: HOME AWAY FROM HOME

The backpacking tent is an engineering masterpiece, providing shelter from wind, rain, snow, and bugs and a psychological barrier to things that go bump in the night. A good backpacking tent can be as cozy as a two-story chalet; that's why I rarely take one. As a firm believer that a little misery afield is good for you, I gave up tents several years ago for most summer trips in favor of a tarp. I would only be caught dead in the winter without a tent, but summer backpacking can be most enjoyable without one. A friend of mine becomes psychotic if she has to sleep under the stars, but I find the experience one of the most rewarding parts of backpacking. Occasionally I suffer from bugs—especially in the Adirondacks in early summer—and occasionally I am caught

with my tarp down at 3 A.M. when a rainstorm breaks, but I am willing to put up with such inconveniences to enjoy sleeping out.

I switch among several tarps as fancy moves me. One is a three-mil-thick sheet of clear plastic, available in 25-foot rolls at any hardware store. I can string it up in a variety of configurations using parachute cord tied around small pebbles gathered in the corners of the plastic. I have also used just the fly of my tent, which is waterproof, light, sturdy, and ringed with tie-down points.

When the bugs are too much or I expect three or four days of bad weather, I'll break down and take one of two tents I have for summer packing. The first is a large A-frame with coated walls—no fly is necessary, and since the tent is well ventilated, condensation, the biggest bugaboo in coated tents, is kept to a minimum. The tent is light, but more importantly it is large, and with two inside there is still room for gear and the occasional card game. My wife, who is slightly claustrophobic, refuses to go out in anything smaller. I can't blame her, for I find my other tent, a two-man mountain model, quite confining. I use it only when I am camping by myself, and then I grow tired of my company after three days; however, it does have a number of features that my coated monster lacks.

Most importantly, the tent is not waterproof. The moisture generated by my sweltering body inside easily passes through the fabric without condensing. When rains arrive, I can erect a waterproof fly over the tent within a minute, forming a waterproof covering for the tent but still maintaining air circulation, which will sweep away vapor. The waterproof fabric on the bottom of the tent extends some seven inches up the wall, so runoff and ground moisture don't come in. The mosquito netting at the entrance and at the back window is quite effective—for stopping mosquitoes; no-see-ums pass right through, but then they let you know you are camping out and not basking at some Ramada Inn. The poles are shock-cord loaded, and the material is cut well enough so the ridge doesn't flap in a breeze—a most satisfactory tent.

Like boots and packs, tents are often oversold, and I am always distressed when I see some poor backpacker camping below timberline on a warm summer evening in a high-altitude mountain tent loaded with unnecessary features: snow tunnels and flaps, frost liners and enough structural support to keep the tent upright in a hurricane. Such a sight makes me go back to my tarp. Reverse snobbery, I suppose.

There are some interesting new designs out today: geodesic domes, external frames, and even a tent that can be erected by just throwing it up in the air. Someday I shall buy that tent if only for a conversation piece. If it keeps the rain and the bugs out, all the better.

ESSENTIALS AND NONESSENTIALS

Everything else that goes into pockets and pack can be divided into two groups: essentials and nonessentials. Unfortunately, no two backpackers can agree on what belongs where. Since I am neither bent on re-creating the feats of Joe Knowles nor am I a member of the go-light school, I list more items under the essential category than most packers. In fact, I do not discriminate between the groups and am often tempted to leave out an essential to make room for a nonessential. Here is my breakdown:

ESSENTIALS

Map and compass. I won't get out of my car at a drive-in without a map and compass. Never rely on simplistic trail maps with dotted lines to follow. Always take a topographical map, and if there is a remote chance you might stray from your proposed route, take all the adjoining map sheets. Waterproof your map by covering it with clear contact paper. Your compass should be a good one. Stay away from the cheap models where the needle never stops spinning. It is also handy if you know how to read a compass—and yes, Virginia, declination does make a difference.

Knife. Indispensible. I always take two, a Swiss Army knife for splinter removal, fingernail paring and cutting out paper dolls on rainy days, and a folding single-blade knife for general cutting of onions and for whittling. Make certain your knife is sharp—sharp enough to shave your thumbnail.

Flashlight. No matter how carefully I plan, the sun always goes down before I have done my dishes, so I use a flashlight a great deal. I prefer a small, cylindrical penlight that takes two AA batteries. It fits nicely into my mouth so my hands are free to wash dishes. I also carry an extra set of heavy-duty batteries and two spare bulbs. Strange quirk, but the only time I had to replace a bulb, my spare didn't work. Now I am covered.

First-aid kit. Start with a pre-packaged kit, available from most outfitters, and add to it, depending on your needs. I have never met two doctors who agree on what should go into a first-aid kit. Some suggest sutures and a generator for nighttime surgery; others subscribe to the Boy Scout school, which advocates only a knife and a bullet to bite on. I change the contents of my first-aid kit regularly, depending on the advice I have most recently received, but I always include something for diarrhea and some morphine. The first can be purchased over the counter, but you will need a prescription for the morphine—and many doctors will not give it to you. There are other pain-killers, of course, but if I break a leg in the woods, I don't want some idiot trying to overdose me with aspirin. I want a heavy-hitter pain-killer, and morphine fills the bill.

Toilet paper. Self-explanatory.

Insect repellent. Army-surplus jungle juice is best. Cutter is a strong second and for sheer perfume, try Old Woodsman. It smells like a new telephone pole and is effective on blackflies and amorous companions.

Fire starter. If someone becomes hypothermic, you will need to start a fire. Some backpackers spend hours cutting down kitchen matches, dipping their heads in wax, and packaging them in 35mm film cans. I carry two Bik Cliks. Why fight progress?

Whistle. Three blasts means you are in trouble. Yelling will only give you a sore throat.

NONESSENTIALS

Candle and lantern. A small candle is an efficient fire starter, and a candle and lantern make a superb fireplace substitute if you yearn for the romance of a flickering flame.

Sunglasses. If you are backpacking in snow or on the desert, sunglasses are a must. Otherwise, you can probably get along without them, although if you bushwhack, you should wear something for eye protection. Take polarized glasses if you are a fisherman.

Plastic bags. Very handy for keeping clothes dry and for packaging food. Remember to pack them out.

Condiments. I carry two 35mm film cans filled with assorted spices and salt. Does wonders for freeze-dried foods.

Thermometer, barometer. There are only three weather conditions I wish to record: cold, hot, and comfortable. I never take a thermometer. A barometer can be of help in the mountains to warn you of approaching bad weather and can be used as a navigational aid, although I would feel like an airline pilot if I had to watch a barometer as well as a compass to tell me where I was.

Hammock. I always take one, a

light nylon model. People laugh—until they try it.

Fishing rod. Trout are my nemeses, and I pursue them relentlessly. My fishing rod, a three-piece, 6½-foot graphite rod by Orvis, is the most expensive piece of backpacking gear I own ($155). It breaks down to less than 28 inches, throws a tight loop and lays out a straight line. It comes with a tubular aluminium case, which I tape to the frame of my pack. We all have our weaknesses; fly fishing and trout eating are mine.

Cameras and binoculars. Great to have if you use them.

There are a few things that no one needs: soap, toothbrush (use the end of a twig and salt), comb, mirror, razor blade, and guns, although I have thought of filling a water pistol with insect repellent and shooting deerflies out of the air.

That's it. That's all you need to go backpacking, and if you think back to Joe Knowles you will realize that everything I have suggested is an extra. One final word

on equipment from John M. Gould, the author of a comprehensive book on camping entitled *How to Camp Out,* published in 1877:

> Do not be in a hurry to spend money on new inventions. Every year there is put upon the market some patent knapsack, folding stove, cooking-utensil, or camp trunk and cot combination; and there are always for sale patent knives, forks, and spoons all in one, drinking cups, folding portfolios, and marvels of tools.

Not bad for 100-year-old advice.

GO-LIGHT BACKPACKING

by ALBERT SAIJO

Illustration by Gompers Saijo

Albert Saijo is undisputably one of the most colorful individuals on the trail today. In his piece, he reports on the newest trend in backpacking—to carry as little as possible. It cuts back on the load, and it cuts back on the damage to the wilderness. It also leads to a radically different head-trip.

W.K.

It's early summer and you're in the mountains. You walked up a long canyon that started as a deep gorge and ends here at its upper reach as an alpine meadow between parallel ridges. Ahead is a series of high basins with lakes nestled among snowy peaks. The meadow is covered with thick grass, and down the middle of it runs a stream with a slight meander. Though it's summer at home, at this elevation it's just spring with flowers all around. Scattered over the meadow are pearly-gray granite boulders and exposed mounds and low swells of the same rock. Conifers border the meadow and grow up the ridges to thin out at treeline. The ridges have a rounded, smooth look in their lower parts but are fractured and jagged along their crests.

Late afternoon. The light is oblique and soft under a pale blue dome of perfectly cloudless sky. The air is still, the day's upwind has stopped, the night's downwind not yet begun. You're sitting on a polished granite swell in a bend of the stream. The stream is running over its banks from snowmelt above.

It slows around the bend with a strong flat current. Winged insects make busy toward the end of day. Violet-green swallows catch them on the wing. Trout rise to them. It occurs to you that insects have a lineage more ancient than the granite you're sitting on, insects being Devonian, the granite of these mountains Cretaceous. As a living form, they're more ancient than conifers and the grass of the meadow. Being among these skillful ancients in this alpine set-

ting makes you feel primeval. Natural wonder lays you back.

Then, like a visitation, you see, for a moment, the Indians that used to summer here. You hear voices in a soft language. It is a family encamped by the stream right where you are, doing their life. You realize you must be on a camping spot that's centuries old. You think of the vision of life the Indians had that enabled them to spend all their summers here. You see that it was the clear purpose and precision of their very light techniques that allowed them their lives in the open. This and their idea of what constituted living a human life. A kind of sophistication we no longer understand, it was elegant in the way scientists speak of an elegant solution: when it gets too hot for comfort in the valley below, go up into the cool mountains; when it gets too cold in the mountains, go down to the warm valley. In either place the Indians had all they needed, and they knew how to do all the things that needed to be done. They were onto the same superintelligent level as the insect. They were in concert with plants, minerals and animals and they survived by using what was before them, requiring nothing more.

But now, as if out of nowhere, a white gull goes floating by, seated high on the water. It brings you back to where you are. Seagulls in the mountains? Then you remember: they summer here too.

The light is beginning to fade. You must find your place for the night. You're not making elaborate camp. All you need is a level spot big enough to lie down on. You don't need fire. You aren't cooking. You'll drink water and eat raw out of your store. Toward the upper end of the meadow you see the rise of a glacial step with the stream cascading down it. To one side is a multijointed, smooth granite eminence with conifers growing in its fractures and on its terraces. On one of these terraces you will find a small bed of white sand. It will have a view to the peaks ahead and the meadow below.

You have everything you need, you can go where you want. You've come in spare for ease of travel. You have leaned toward not enough rather than more than enough, because you know that you can make do with not enough. You are going light.

It comes about this way. You find you always return home from a wilderness trip with leftover food and stuff you took in and didn't use. You look at the excess and you remember you carried it all the way for nothing, and how hard it was to carry. After you've done this a number of times, it occurs to you, as an ideal, to go as light as possible next time.

But why do we take more than we need? In a strange way, we generally calculate the amount of stuff we're going to take not on how much we need but on how much we can bear. The packs that are offered to us by designers of outdoor equipment seem to encourage this tendency to overload. When we see the more-than-generous space they give us, we feel obliged to fill it. Chock-full of stuff, our packs end up weighing just over what we can bear comfortably. We assuage our doubt about the weight with the thought that the pack will lighten each succeeding

day, but it never seems to. Are we in wilderness to prove how much we can carry? Is backpacking a form of punishment? Are we beasts of burden? There is a vicious cycle involved here. The more stuff we take, the more exertion necessary to bear it; the more exertion, the more food we feel we need to keep up our strength, and so on. The only way to break this cycle is to begin thinking in terms of an ultralight wilderness style. And relief from our present burdensome style is not the only consideration—ultralight comes to mean not only cutting back on the load, but also treading very light on wilderness, thus helping to preserve it.

As more people go into wilderness, it becomes necessary to rethink the wilderness experience in terms of right now. How not to despoil wilderness has become the primary issue. Without some clear thinking on this matter, a whole bunch of backpackers are going to repeat the depredations of sheep, cattle and lumberers. We've got to learn to go light.

LIGHT ON THE MUSTARD!

My meals were easily made, for they were all alike and simple, only a cupful of tea and bread. JOHN MUIR.

In America we have a strange attitude toward food and eating. It's a part of our abundant supply of food, and the way it's dealt to us commercially and highly advertised. We're led to believe we must eat more food than is necessary or good for us. We end up believing that unless we have three square meals a day, every day, we'll starve or immediately become sick. Something called "dietary deficiency" is presented to us as a constant threat to our health and wellbeing. You wonder how our species managed to survive to this point without knowing the minimum daily requirements.

And because the food that's purveyed to us is highly processed and generally thin of nutrition, great amounts of it must be eaten to feel nourished. So we eat and eat, and we do it on schedule. We end up eating not so much because we're hungry as because it's time.

It's compulsive behavior. We eat to fill a maw of insecurity. Every sign seems to say: Eat. So we eat, and grow fat and partially secure. If we take this food style into wilderness, we're bound to take more than we need.

The psychology of abundance and the impact of advertising are reflected in the variety of specially prepared

camping foods offered the backpacker. Check the catalog of any store that carries a complete line of dehydrated and freeze-dried dishes. It reads like the fantasy of a starving man: Tuna à la Neptune, Chili Con Carne Ranchero, Beef Almondine, Turkey Tetrazzini, Chicken Chop Suey . . . . Packaged menus for breakfast, lunch, dinner and snacks read the same way. The whole American food trip has been freeze-dried.

It seems something better could be thought up, something more in keeping with the spirit of wilderness. How long can we go on using a gift of such beauty as fire to cook up freeze-dried Turkey Supreme? Even white flour biscuits, bacon grease and coffee have more the feeling of proper outdoor grub.

Freeze-drieds do have the great advantage of light weight, but at what price? They have a deadness that no amount of culinary skill can liven. It's hard to see how a food could be submitted to the extreme temperatures required by freeze-drying without destroying its vitality. Your freeze-dried dish is twice cooked, first before packaging and again when you prepare to eat it. It's a pretty limp food that finally enters your mouth. There's also a large consensus that these foods don't digest well. And the cooking they require means carrying kitchen paraphernalia, which means finding a campsite with wood if you aren't carrying a stove and fuel. You will also need a good supply of water for cooking and washing up after. All of these are limiting factors if you have a mind to go light and free.

What are the alternatives? Here, as in all things having to do with living in the wild, we can turn to the Indians for instruction. They mastered the way to live on foot on this continent. When they traveled they carried such foods as pemmican, jerky, parched corn, pinole and buccan. They understood how to lighten and preserve food by drying out the water. As we mechanically dehydrate and freeze-dry, they dried out their stuff with sun and wind and over slow smoky fire, a gentler method that left more food value intact.

Pemmican was made with jerky and rendered fat. Jerky is lean meat cut in strips and dried in the sun and wind or over a small smoky fire of nonresinous wood; the fire must not cook the meat. The jerky was shredded by pounding, then mixed with hot rendered fat in a proportion of half to half, then packed

ILLUSTRATION BY GOMPERS SAIJO

ing happen? Then eat raw out of your store while still in your bag. Then emerge from bag nice and warm and start the day just as direct sunlight hits you. In the evening, when the chill begins to make you shake, get into your bag and eat foods of high caloric content such as fats and carbohydrates.

The comfort of being warmed by your own body heat under down cover is a form of pure luxury. And this method requires no hunting of wood, no fireplace building, no cooking, no kitchen cleanup. No muss, fuss or bother.

Still, cooking is ancient to us. And fire is possibly the oldest distinctly human acquisition. Cooking by fire must be the vestige of an old sacrificial ritual. There is a beauty in sitting by a fire in wilderness, at twilight, with a pot of slumgullion at a bubbling simmer before you. But there's also great beauty in the simplicity of hiking to the end of your day, then finding that level spot just big enough to lie down on and eating raw out of your store while you watch night fall. As John Muir put it: "One may take a little simple clean bread and have nothing to do on these fine excursions but enjoy oneself."

Now that we've worked our way somewhat out of the cooking imperative, we can go back to thinking of kinds of flavorsome staple foods that can be eaten every day and don't require cooking in the field. We return to the idea of a pemmican.

The Indian pemmican was mainly protein and fat. The early American outdoorsman made a pemmican of jerky, fat, raisins, and sugar (which added some carbohydrates, minerals and plain sugar). If we could make a pemmican of high caloric content that contained protein, fat, carbohydrates, minerals and vitamins, we might have something more like a fully nutritious food. Here, let's broaden the definition of pemmican to mean any compact, nutritious, tasty, uncooked or precooked foodstuff that carries well and keeps for a long time — for at least a month, say, without spoiling or getting rancid. It may or may not contain meat and animal fat. Most important, it must serve as a staple food: it must take the place of the traditional collection of separate and various foods that require cooking.

A light, relatively nonfatty, nonmeat, uncooked pemmican might include the following:

Seeds: Sunflower, pumpkin, chia. High caloric content, both saturated

in hide bags. It was a kind of sausage. Parched corn is corn roast-dried. Pinole is a meal made from parched corn flour mixed with the sweet flower of mesquite beans or with sugar and spices. Buccan is smoked meat, buccan being the wood frame on which the meat was placed over the smoky fire. Then, of course, the Indians knew all the wild edible plants along the way.

If we could come up with a modern equivalent of these Indian foods we might have something better than freeze-drieds. The idea would be to find a few staple foods that are compact, digestible and nutritious, that would taste good to us at all times of day, day after day. They should not require cooking.

The notion that we must cook outback is really an encumbering one. Must we carry a kitchen everyplace we go? Why should we want to eat in the wild as we

do at home? Aside from the taste of cooked food, we eat cooked food for its warmth. Putting something hot into the stomach is a fast way to bring heat to the vitals and make us feel warm. Outdoors it's in the chill of morning and evening that we want a fire and hot food. But it's good to remember here that a simple cup of hot water will do as well as a hot meal to warm your innards and is much easier to prepare. And eating hot food and hugging a fire are not the only ways to get warm. In fact, outdoors, fire isn't that great a method for getting warm since it heats just one side of you at a time.

A more efficient and expeditious way to be warm is to take advantage of the down sleeping bag. If you wake into a chill morning, instead of running around cold, building a fire and cooking, why not stay in your bag and watch morn-

42

and unsaturated fats, rich in both protein and minerals, some vitamins. Best raw.

Nuts: Pinole, almond. Much like seeds nutritionally. Best raw.

Dried fruits: Pitted dates. apricots. raisins or currants. Good for calories, minerals, some protein. Dates are an excellent carbohydrate source, better in fact. than most grains. Dates are a fine all-around food. In addition to carbohydrates, they have high caloric content, some protein, and are rich in minerals — a natural sweet bread. There are many varieties: the Empress is excellent. Dried apricots are extremely high in vitamin A. Dried fruits are best sun-dried.

To these basic ingredients might be added raw wheat germ, wheat-germ oil, a little salt, some vitamin C powder — just enough to give the pemmican a slightly tart, clean aftertaste. (If you can find powdered-fruit vitamin C, all the better.) Also, some kind of high-protein powder, bittersweet chocolate chips, etc. You can either mix all these ingredients as they are or put the whole thing through a hand grinder set at "coarse." When you compress the stuff to pack it, the stickiness of the dried fruit will bind it nicely. About three-quarters of a pound a day should do you well.

This pemmican can also be made into a biscuit. Simply add flour, milk and egg to the pemmican mixture in quantity sufficient to make a biscuit batter, mix well, roll it out and cut it into flat, rectangular biscuits for efficient packing. Then bake them on a cookie tin at 300° for 20 to 30 minutes on each side until you have a dry biscuit. Check often to test. Here again, you may use the ingredients as they are, or coarse-grind some or all of them. Carob powder, powdered chocolate, or something like Ovaltine will make a sweeter biscuit.

A meat pemmican can be made by adding shredded jerky, crumbled-up bacon bar, or ground-up dry salami to the seeds, nuts, dried fruits, etc. Salami ground up becomes more perishable, so use it accordingly. Lecithin might be added to this mixture to help the body assimilate the animal fat.

In this discussion of pemmican no specific recipe has been given. You must instruct yourself in this matter. Everyone must figure out his own pemmican. It will take some experimenting. The important thing is to find the combination of ingredients that suits your taste.

Now the question is, will it work? Can you eat pemmican day after day as your staple food outdoors? It would seem to be mostly a question of attitude. If you have no expectation but pemmican, and you're relaxed and not overtired when you eat, and you chew well and attend to flavors, and you're in a beautiful setting, and you remember Muir with his bread and tea, and you have an interesting pemmican, there's no reason why it shouldn't work.

You may want to take both kinds of pemmican to appreciate the contrast between the saltier meat pemmican and the sweeter pemmican biscuit. In addition to your pemmican, you might carry a few items like powdered fruit drink, powdered milk, some fresh, good-keeping fruits and vegetables like orange, apple, cucumber, carrot and sweet onion tucked away in your pack.

If the idea of pemmican puts you off entirely, instead of mixing up the different ingredients, carry them separately. All the ingredients for pemmican are good by themselves. Other foods that don't require cooking include cheese, granola-type cereals, roasted soybeans, fig paste, nut butters, dry breads and crackers, or dense pumpernickel that comes in a well-sealed package.

You might also consider the foods just lately brought to public attention, such as bee pollen and the royal jelly of bees. Bee pollen, which is pollen as it's brought to the hive by the worker bee, is an extremely nutritious food containing protein, minerals, vitamins (especially B complex), free amino acids and enzymes. It has a flavor unlike any other food, like very concentrated natural, bittersweet, tart bread candy. You must taste it to believe it. It is said to be good for cardiac action and intestinal function. Its purported ability to increase the hemoglobin count would make it an excellent high-altitude food. Buy it in its natural pellet form. Royal jelly is a glandular substance produced by the worker bee and fed to bee larvae together with honey and pollen. It is rich in nucleic acids. The Chinese make a kind of tonic based on royal jelly. It is called Peking Royal Jelly and comes in a 10 cc. glass vial. Taste it on an empty stomach to see what it does for you. A vial of this is a fine way to start an extra-hard wilderness day. If your health food connection can't get it for you, try a Chinese pharmacy.

Someday a dedicated backpacker will go through the whole Chinese pharmacopoeia in search of herbs and medicaments helpful to the outdoor life. Modern research, for instance, has shown the legendary ginseng to be an excellent central nervous system tonic and regulator of blood pressure. If you are in the mountains, which is a yin condition, the yang of ginseng will provide a nice balance.

So if pemmican doesn't appeal to you, there are many alternatives. You could go far and high on a store of raw almonds, a jar of raw honey (or a brick of maple sugar), a bag of bee pollen, a small chunk of ginseng, some vials of Peking Royal Jelly, a bag of dates, a bag of dried apricots and some fresh stuff perhaps, together with whatever supplements you might need or want.

The ideal is to take the minimum to get you by without a feeling of terrible deprivation or hardship. There's no need for fanaticism. On the other hand, say that you've taken the bare minimum, stayed longer than planned, and run out of food a day or two away from your car. Well, what's wrong with an honest fast, if it comes to that? Our body has great reserves available to it at all times. The capacity to fast is an interesting and valuable thing to know. How far can you go without food? To know this could be considered an outdoor skill.

Muir's bread and tea diet is probably impossible for us to keep over any length of time. It's simply too austere, and we're too conscious of nutritional factors to accept it. Then again, even Muir varied his diet on occasion. Somewhere in his writings he speaks of a breakfast of crystal clear water and nectar sucked out of flowers. His example continues to be inspiring and provides a rock-bottom model of what's possible.

GEAR & STUFF

The bundle I carried on my thin, bony shoulders was the cause of my first discomfort on this journey. I had intended to set off just as I was; however, a kamiko (kimono made of white paper, prepared with persimmon juice, and crumpled soft) to protect me from the cold at night, a yukata (thin cotton kimono), a waterproof, and writing materials and so on — all these things I had received from my friends as parting gifts, and I could hardly leave them behind, but they were necessarily a cause of discomfort and vexation all the way. BASHO.

Gear is everything besides food. We all know where we can cut back and simplify on gear: it's the doing that's hard. We have a thing about things. Things make us feel secure. We have a need to be surrounded by our personal things. They provide comforts we're loath to give up. So when we leave home for wilderness, by some intricate mathematic we scale down our belongings to make up a mobile environment that matches the home environment almost point for point, only smaller and more compact. We have a light that can be turned on with a switch. A stove that can be lit with a match and the turn of a knob. A water supply right at hand in canteens. A kitchen with pots, pans, dishes and utensils. A waterproof shelter. A complete ensemble of clothes for every possible wilderness occasion. A medicine cabinet. A pantry full of food. And so forth. Someone will soon invent a collapsible portable chemical toilet that can be flushed into a sack—which may not be a bad idea, considering how thoughtless some people are with their toilet in wilderness. Then, of course, there must be hearth and fire. We want to be in wilderness but safely shielded from it at the same time.

The overload psychology of too much food and gear, and the heavy, home-outdoors style of camp ultimately rest on the early American urbanite pioneer's idea of wilderness as a foe to be fought·and subdued—a domain of unfriendly forces to be penetrated at great risk to life and limb. Following this psychology, we often try to provision ourselves absolutely fail-safe.

Looking for an exemplar of a new wilderness style, we inevitably return to John Muir. He saw wilderness as a nonhuman realm of sacred nature with its own set of moves, and he learned these moves so that he could go with them. He never set foot in wilderness except with curiosity, wonder and reverence. There was no need to fight or trample it.

Gear was little burden: no one traveled lighter. In the Sierra, at his most elaborate, he would carry two blankets, bread and tea, a notebook, perhaps an aerometer and small stuff he could carry in his trouser pockets. If he wanted to bear less he dispensed with the blankets.

For us, gear is a problem, and we must find the smallest amount of the very lightest gear to do wilderness right. The ideal, at this point, would seem to be a collection of gear that would make us self-contained units capable of passing through wilderness without in any way despoiling it. Uplift and water would be all that we'd take. In other words, we need gear to help keep our weight off wilderness as much as possible.

Basic gear for a temperate-zone summer trip might include something like the following: a down sleeping bag, a lightweight sleeping pad to enable you to bed down anywhere, the long over-pack poncho, perhaps a space blanket, or a small (say five-by-seven) waterproofed nylon tarp (which could either be used as a ground cloth or, in combination with the poncho, be pitched as a tent when it rains) and the most versatile and spare ensemble of clothes possible. There's really not too much else you need.

But is the kind of gear we need for ultralight traveling available? For instance, is the present sack-type pack the best solution for our need as packs go? Couldn't there be a pack of some other design? Perhaps a pack that spreads out open, so that gear and food can be wrapped into a bundle in it and tightly lashed by some arrangement of belts? It would be like wrapping stuff in a blanket and lashing the bundle to a frame. The advantage of this design would be that you could make the shape and disposition of the load suit you exactly. And the pack would always be just the size that holds what you have. It could attach to the frame with clevis pins. Ingeniously designed, it could be as convenient as the sack-type pack.

How about a boot as light as high-top canvas shoes that would still give the support and protection of a medium-weight four-pound hiking boot? In the same way, we could go through every item of gear and redesign it ultralight yet capable of doing its function in the best way. The ultralight gear will follow as soon as we get our heads ultralight.

It's a provident and saving backcountry style we want. A lean style, appreciative of the wild as a refuge. And because we know wild earth to be a kind of flesh, we go in a way not to wound it. We go light. As though being stalked, we don't leave a trace. ◣

GOING LIGHT WITH SAIJO

by MELVA ENGERS

When the article "Go-Light Backpacking," by Albert Saijo, appeared in BACKPACKER magazine, it elicited a good deal of response. Putting Saijo's ideas to the test, Melva and Joe Engers report on their own firsthand experiences.

W.K.

On Friday, August 2, at 4:04 A.M., I broached the subject in a very sneaky way to my spouse. Counting on the power of subliminal persuasion, I talked to him while he was still asleep: "Let's try to go ultra light on our backpack trip next week."

Later in the morning he showed signs of my success: "You know," he said, "I had the funniest dream last night. We were backpacking, and you left all our food at home. It was crazy."

I was ready. My next gambit was to hand him BACKPACKER-3, opened to Albert Saijo's article, "Go Light Backpacking." After 29 years of marriage Joe knows when I'm serious. So he read the article.

Secretly, I too wondered if old-timers like us could break 13 years of California trail habits. Joe has always enjoyed fashioning freeze-dried foods into gastronomical delights. The pemmican route would be a whole new experience.

After 15 minutes I began to fidget. Finally, Joe declared, "This guy might have something. Now, if we could just get an interesting gorp."

I don't really know whether he was sold on going light or whether he wanted an excuse to visit Hadleys Fruit Orchard 30 miles east of River-side, which has a marvelous selection of plump dates, wrinkled figs, prunes, banana crisps and buckets of granola mixes. Anyway, we went to Hadleys and bought the following: two pounds of sunflower seeds, one pound of pumpkin seeds, two pounds of almonds, one pound of shredded coconut, two pounds of date nuggets, one pound of dried apples, two pounds of dried apricots and one pound of dried currants. The total cost was $14.87.

That night we ground and mixed the ingredients of our pemmican. We seasoned it with Tang and Wheat Germ. It tasted good. Then we divided it into thirds and added jerky to one-third of the mix and bacon bar to one-third, keeping one-third plain.

By then, Joe was fascinated by the possibilities of unusual combinations. He discovered Denise Van Lear's recipe for gorp in BACKPACKER-6, and he couldn't resist. He substituted currants for the raisins and granola for the oatmeal in Ms. Van Lear's recipe. Addition of chocolate chips and butterscotch chips to the Van Lear recipe gave us dessert bars.

Packing was a breeze. We left at home stove, extra fuel, skillet, pots, bottles, freeze-dried dinners, breakfast and trail lunches. Instead we each packed 4½ pounds of pemmican. Joe's pack weighed 40 pounds instead of 50; mine weighed 31 pounds instead of 38.

We planned to hike continuously, covering the Big Pine Lakes near Bishop. We would fish when we wanted, eat when we wanted, camp

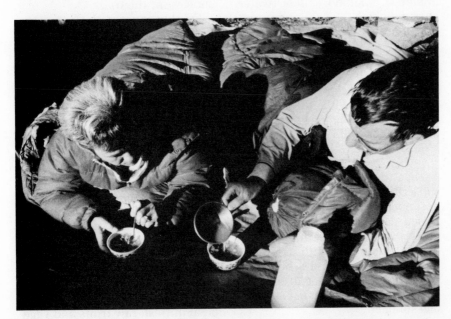

While still in their sleeping bags, Melva and Joe Engers breakfast on pemmican in a cup of Tang.

where we wanted.

Lunches would consist of a half-cup of jerky pemmican and a half-bar of dessert pemmican. We packed them into one-cup margarine containers, which we tucked into side pockets of our packs. These containers would be replenished each day from our bulk food store, packed in milk cartons. We secured fishing poles to the sides of the packs. The bait—earthworms, salmon eggs and flies—was packed very carefully because there was a possibility that fishing might become our lifeline if the pemmican didn't pan out.

After leaving the car at 10 A.M., we followed the stream up Big Pine Canyon, a hike of seven miles, and ate our first lunch. Not bad.

Camp that night at Third Lake was different from any of our previous experiences. Where had all the camp duties gone? We fished at the inlet and cooked the trout we caught on a wire grill over the hot coals of a fire. But we both agreed the pemmican would have been adequate.

In the morning we stayed in our sleeping bags while we ate breakfast—a half-cup of plain pemmican in a cup of Tang.

When we reached Sixth Lake that afternoon, we set up the tent on a knoll above the lake. Work was done. The rest of the day was duty free. Below us, the canyon stretched like a canvas. Despite ample fishing time, we had no luck. Then we faced the real test: sitting on a log, we feasted incredulously on a half-cup of pemmican each. Believe it or not, it was fun differentiating among the crunchies. The dessert pemmican was too much for us to finish.

On the third day we still liked the pemmican. The fourth, fifth and sixth days were equally satisfying. We did have trout the fourth night. Yet the fifth night we gave the fish we'd caught to a young boy camping nearby, for the pemmican was satisfying enough.

On the sixth day we ate pemmican for breakfast and lunch, then capped off our week's adventure with a steak dinner at a restaurant on the drive home.

Our adventure proved the thesis: pemmican is practical and even enjoyable for old-timers. ◣

FOOD FOR THE TRAIL
by WILLIAM KEMSLEY, JR.

Food is probably the thing that reveals more about a backpacker than anything else. There are no two packers that I know who are in agreement about what kind and what amounts of food to carry on a trip of any length. And I have heard—or been a party to—more squabbles about food among backpacking companions than about any other subject.

There are backpackers—and I tend to fall into this category—who are lazy as hell about their trail food and will only take the simplest foods to prepare. They tend to want to get meals over with quickly. At the other extreme are the trailside gourmets. They'll take along the most complex ingredients and cooking gear and spend hours preparing gourmet meals that they'd never think of preparing at home. I recently witnessed a group of seven hikers in the White Mountains filleting a luxurious steak into thin strips and chopping a cornucopia of vegetables—broccoli, cauliflower, green peppers, scallions, tomatoes, bamboo shoots, water chestnuts, whole pea pods, and such—into a huge iron skillet with a variety of Chinese oils, sauces, and spices. It smelled delicious. It looked mouth-watering. I would gladly have accepted an invitation to dine with these folks, though they didn't ask me. But never, ever would I prepare such a meal—on the trail or at home.

Then there is BACKPACKER subscriber William Schaefer, who describes a meal he prepared of tossed salad, char-broiled fillets, green peas and pearl onions, and French apple pie with whipped cream for dessert and a bottle of Cabernet Sauvignon at 10,600 feet altitude in the Sierra snows early one summer.

But each packer has his own food tastes. That is what makes horse races. And I'm always curious—as I think most people are—to hear about someone else's food choices for the trail.

Frankly, one of the joys I get from backpacking with others is learning about their trailside culinary considerations.

One couple I go backpacking with from time to time take along delicious whole-grain dishes which take entirely too long to prepare both at home and on the trail so far as I'm concerned. But delicious! And I don't mind sharing the meals—like couscous with salmon, bulghur and chicken, brown rice with onions and carrots—provided my friends do both the prehike preparation as well as the cooking on the trail.

Another backpacker whom I've been out with numerous times brings along an amazing assortment of fresh raw fruits and vegetables. They're not difficult to cook, I know. But the weight in the pack is more excessive than I care to carry.

A number of other packers I know are big on steaks. I've eaten one of the most tasty aged steaks I've ever had at a campsite beside a mountain lake at 9,000-foot elevation in western Montana. Most recently I shared a very enjoyable broiled steak, boiled fresh summer squash, and fried potatoes at a camp deep in a Florida swamp, with good trail companions.

There are no hard-and-fast rules regarding backpacking foods. Generally speaking, you can take just about anything you care to carry on short two- and three-day trips. Your pack is pretty lightweight on trips of this length. So, why not enjoy just about any imaginable food you care to carry and cook. You can even find small utensils that work on the top of your stove, such as a backpacker's oven. So even baking is possible on short hikes. I've even known a packer who takes along a Chinese wok for Chinese cooking. (For me, as I've indicated before, a can of Chun King chop suey and a can of Chinese noodles is as exotic as I'll go when I'm doing the cooking.)

For breakfast take eggs and toast or biscuits, cold cereal or hot cereal, doughnuts, coffee cake, or Pop Tarts. Add coffee, tea, hot chocolate, milk, whatever you like. Incidentally, coffee is one thing I like to take time to do right. I find it takes no more room and is no more trouble to make real coffee than it is to make instant coffee. But the taste is so much better. My recipe is simple: Add a tablespoon of coffee to the pot for each cup of water. Bring water to boil and let boil for one minute. Remove from heat, flick a few drops of cold water onto the top of the water, cover and let sit for two minutes. Then, carefully pour the coffee into your cups so that you don't get the grounds in the cup as well. Tastes terrific!

For lunch some people cook up soup or tea and a light meal. Not me. I go for sandwiches of canned corned beef and hard-crust rolls, or canned boneless chicken, potted meat, deviled ham, sardines, or kippered snacks. I also love cheeses—Gouda, Edam, Cheddar, Swiss—with Rye Krisps, crackers, or bread. Lunch is the least problem. There are so many possibilities.

Dinners can be steaks, chops, fish, stew, or a wide variety of one-pot dishes. I like soup first. Almost any flavor of the Cup-a-Soup variety does just fine. As for the main course, as I say, it can be just about anything—hamburgers, steak, hot dogs, pork and beans, macaroni and cheese (I have eaten my way through several cases of Kraft Macaroni and Cheese over the past twenty years). And dessert can be whatever you can carry without crushing it. Cookies, candies, cakes, what have you. Something that I find especially good are candied dried fruits, such

One of the greatest thrills of backpacking is sleeping under the stars and waking up as the sun begins to rise above the horizon. It is a special time of day, and the birds let you know it. Author Bill Kemsley with his brother Brian at dawn in the Grand Canyon.
PHOTO: MICHAEL KEMSLEY

as pineapple slices, candied pears or apricots, figs or dates. And I almost always drink tea with dinner.

I think it is ludicrous to see someone carry freeze-dried food on an overnight hike. But on a long trek, you have to deal with food in an entirely different way. All of the meals have to be carried on your back. And the food has to keep much longer without spoiling. I have recently carried food for 18 days without resupplying. When you do that you have to be very careful about weight. And I have developed several rules of thumb for the long trek.

I try to keep the food weight down to a pound per person per day. It can be done. Though the portions are not as generous, they are perfectly adequate. Here, of course, is where the real benefits of freeze-dried food come in.

I also repackage all the food, taking it out of the boxes, jars and cans that it comes in from the store. I repackage all items in plastic bags—all the food for each meal in a separate bag—and label them "Breakfast—Day 1," "Lunch—Day 1," "Dinner—Day 1," "Breakfast—Day 2," etc. On a really long trip it makes sense to pack the meal packets on the bottom of the pack starting with the last day first, working up so that the first day's food is on the top. It is a good idea to apportion the food packets among the hikers in your group so that one person carries the first day's food, the second carries the next day's, the third the following day's food.

In shopping for a long trip I buy about a third of the food at a backpacking equipment store, about a third in the supermarket, and a third in a gourmet shop. Though I never skimp, I have never spent more than $3.00 per person per day for food. I doubt you can eat that well at home for the money. No matter what else you buy, there are a few staples that most backpackers take:

GRANOLA

There are so many excellent granolas on the market today, at reasonable-enough prices, that I rarely make it myself anymore, except for extended trips. When I do make it, here is my recipe. It is Sun Cloud Granola, a concoction first introduced to me by my brother, Brian, who got it from his wife, Sarah. She named it in honor of their first son, Isaac Sun Cloud.

Dry ingredients: 3 cups rolled oats, 1 cup rolled wheat, 2 cups coconut, ½ cup wheat germ, ½ cup sunflower seeds, ½ cup sesame seeds, ½ cup soy grits, ½ cup bran, ½ cup pumpkin seeds, 1 cup cashews, 1 cup walnuts

Liquid ingredients: ⅔ cup oil (I use safflower), 1 cup honey, 3 tsp. vanilla

Dried fruit: 1 cup chopped dates, 2 cups raisins (or any other chopped dried fruit)

Add liquid ingredients to dry ingredients. Mix well. Bake in shallow baking pans in 250° oven till golden brown. Stir often. Remove from oven and add dried fruit. Let cool. Eat and enjoy.

GORP

A good friend of mine has said that anyone who uses a recipe for gorp is too fastidious to be a true backpacker.

Perhaps.

At the risk of my trail reputation, I'll say a few words about gorp. First of all, the name. What does it mean? The question has been debated for a very long time, and there are numerous etymological attributions. I prefer this one: *Good Old Raisins and Peanuts.*

Gorp is basically a mixture of fruit and nuts. And some people add candies.

Some of the general rules of gorp making that I follow are: 1) Make it with about the same quantity of fruits, whatever ones you use, as of nuts, whichever nuts you use. 2) If you use fine nuts or seeds, like sesame seeds or chopped nuts, try rolling chopped dates in the seeds first before tossing everything together into the mixture. The dates pick up the seeds and keep them from sticking together in the gorp. 3) Understand that gorp is about as concentrated a shot of calories as you can find. It beats candy bars, ice cream, and strawberry shortcake for putting on weight. And it is difficult to stop nibbling at it. If you are like me, you will come back from hikes weighing more than when you started out, even though you may burn up 5,000 calories a day on a strenuous trip!

Since I like two different gorps so well, herewith are the recipes for both.

SUNSHINE GORP

10 oz. pitted dates
3 oz. dried papaya
3 oz. currants
3 oz. seedless raisins
3 oz. white raisins
3 oz. shelled sunflower seeds
3 oz. shelled pumpkin seeds
3 oz. shelled pecans
3 oz. shelled hazelnuts
3 oz. shelled walnuts
3 oz. shelled almonds

Spread sesame seeds on a cookie tin and place in an oven at 200°. Stirring the seeds often, to keep from burning, bake them until they are just slightly browned. Be careful not to overbake.

Cut dates in quarters lengthwise. Then, roll in sesame seeds until they are no longer recognizable. Chop nuts into pea-size chunks.

Toss the entire mixture together into a bowl, mix, and then fill individual Baggies with sufficient portions. Store on your shelf, and keep handy for your next hike.

Then there is Kaibab Gorp, which was first shared with me by Tommy Davison, a ranger in Grand Canyon National Park. Tommy claims to go out for week-long treks with nothing to eat except Kaibab Gorp—breakfast, lunch, and dinner. I don't advise that. But, it is good and certainly can be a meal in itself.

KAIBAB GORP

1 lb. commercial granola
12 oz. dry-roasted almonds
6 oz. dehydrated apples
6 oz. shelled sunflower seeds
1 lb. M&Ms

Mix all ingredients together.

Portion out into Baggies. Watch the calories!

BREAD

Then there is bread—or the delicious *cakes* which we call bread. Try my favorite, Mt. Logan Bread. One time while climbing in the Cascade Mountains I lived on Mt. Logan Bread bought from Recreation Equipment, Inc. (REI), spread with strawberry preserves every day for lunch for three weeks. That was twenty years ago—and I can still taste it! Here's one recipe for Mt. Logan Bread from my good friend Laura Waterman.

MT. LOGAN BREAD

3 cups flour (2 cups rye, 1 cup whole wheat)
¾ cup wheat germ
¼ cup brown sugar
½ cup powdered milk
2 tbsp. peanut oil
½ cup honey
¼ cup molasses
¼ cup sorghum syrup or maple syrup
½ cup shelled walnuts or pecans
½ cup raisins
½ cup chopped dried peaches, apricots, or dates
6 eggs

Mix flour, wheat germ, milk, sugar, nuts, raisins, and dried fruit. Stir in peanut oil, honey, molasses, and eggs. Mixture should be heavier than bread dough. Makes two loaves. Press into oiled pans (about one inch deep).

Bake at 275° for two hours or until done. The bread burns easily. It can be baked successfully with the oven turned on as low as possible for two hours. The bread should be like fruitcake in appearance.

JERKY

Jerky is very popular, though I hardly ever take it. If I do, it is not the commercially prepared type. I like the homemade variety. Here's a recipe for it.

BEEF JERKY

1½ lbs. beef (flank or round)
1 tsp. seasoned salt
1 tsp. onion powder
½ tsp. garlic powder
¼ tsp. pepper
½ cup Worcestershire sauce
½ cup soy sauce.

Remove all fat from meat. Cut into ¼" slices along grain. It is easier to slice if partially frozen.

Combine dry and liquid ingredients to make marinade. Marinate meat overnight in refrigerator. Drain. Lay meat strips on oven rack and place foil on bottom rack to catch drippings. Leave door ajar. Set oven at 150°. Dry meat for 6 hours. Turn oven off and leave meat in oven for another 6 hours.

Store Jerky in covered container with holes punched in lid. Makes one pound.

FOOD ON THE TRAIL

by FRED POWLEDGE

The following article by my good friend, Fred Powledge, the author of The Backpacker's Budget Food Book, exemplifies so well the individuality of backpackers when it comes to food. There is a current of truth to all that he says, though he would admit to his own particular prejudices. Read it. It has good advice. And it will stand you in good stead until you can become your own man and be just as opinionated as Fred. If you want a good deal of fun, read his book. It is more than a recipe book. It is a lot of fun to read.

W.K.

For the backpacker, food might be considered something of a mixed blessing. It is essential to the trailwalker's life, of course, just as it is to those who sport about on snowmobiles or sit on front porches and rock. It produces satisfaction in piney forests and on mountainsides, just as it does in expensive restaurants and fast-food hamburger joints. For the backpacker, food takes on even greater importance: It can make the rigorous climb to the top of a mountain actually possible; it can make a cold, wet night in a cold, wet sleeping bag actually bearable. The proper kinds of food can prevent the cramps that invade the muscles of back-packers who spend too much of their time sitting at desks in the sedentary world. And food—even a few bits of chocolate, eaten during a snowy night—can help stave off hypothermia, the potentially fatal disease of lowered body temperature.

But food also can be a pain in the neck—or, more appropriately, in the back. For food and the tools needed to prepare it, like everything else used by the backpacker, must be carried into the woods, and if you're a backpacker that means carried on your back. The more food you carry, the heavier your burden will be until you eat it, and, presumably, the more uncomfortable you will become and the less enjoyment you'll get out of backpacking.

Similarly, food that contains a great deal of water or that must be packed in metal, such as cans of stewed tomatoes or the old woods tramp's standby, pork and beans, will be heavy. Food that requires elaborate utensils for preparation (and in the woods, "elaborate" means pretty much anything that can't be eaten raw, boiled, or cooked quickly above an open flame) will weight down your pack unconscionably. Foods that might be low in water content but that require long cooking times, such as dried legumes or grains, will cause trouble if you use a mechanical backpacker's stove, because you'll have to carry along extra fuel.

So what's the solution? It's not an easy one. Obviously, you want food that is lightweight, low in water content, nutritious, tasty, and satisfying—seeming contradictions in terms. That last requirement, satisfaction, is in some ways the most important one. Even the most experienced backpackers have days and nights in the woods when the goal of backpacking seems to have become completely lost behind the horizon; they feel as much "as one with nature" as a strip miner, they are cold and wet, and their feet hurt. That's the time one badly needs a meal that is *satisfying*— that meets all those childish requirements that used to be fulfilled with a bowl of hot soup and a delicious peanut butter sandwich and a hug around the neck. It's the sort of meal that quite literally gets us through the night.

How does one put all that into a tiny package that weighs nothing, cooks quickly, and takes up virtually no room inside an already bulging backpack? A lot of backpackers solve the problem by purchasing, from the same places they get their boots and ponchos, freeze-dried foods made especially for trailwalkers. Most of these foods come in plastic or foil pouches, require a minimum of cooking (some ask only that you pour a certain amount of boiling water into them and wait a decent interval before eating), and promise you, in return for a rather heavy outlay of cash, the delights of foods you might never have at home—beef Stroganoff, beef almondine, turkey Tetrazzini.

That's fine. There are times when the prepared backpackers' foods are the logical choice—indeed, when they are the only proper choice. Their light weight and compact nature make them ideal for extended trips into the woods where many days' provisions must be carried. They're excellent, too, for winter camping when the packbag becomes crammed fuller than usual with clothing and heavier sleeping equipment.

But they're expensive. And, I and many others feel, they are disappointing. They frequently fail to deliver that all-important element of satisfaction. They represent, at least for me, an unwelcome intrusion into the world of backpacking by those qualities that I'm trying to get away from— exaggeration, hype, undelivered promises, claims of instancy and quality that don't work out; feelings that best can be summed up in the word *plastic*.

We have allowed ourselves to fall for the notion in recent years that a society that can send people to the moon really *can* achieve anything else it wants to. We can miniaturize anything, dehydrate anything, cook anything in less time with no fuss, no muss, no more ring around the collar. What some of us overlook (and, more sadly, what some of our latter-born may never know since they have no means of comparison) is that invariably these "advances" are achieved only in conjunction with big losses of quality. We have watches now, for instance, that tell us with great insistency, in lighted digits so that there can be no mistake, precisely what time it is. The unfortunate trade-off is that these watches don't last very long, and when they go haywire nobody can, or will, fix them.

We're similarly fooling ourselves, I believe, if we allow ourselves to think that we can open up a tiny foil package on some cold and windy mountainside, pour a small amount of hot water into it, and be rewarded with a delicious meal of shrimp Creole. What I'm trying to say is that maybe backpackers should keep their sights and expectations low in the food department. Maybe it's wise to stick with what you know is filling, nutritious, and moderately tasty. You're out in the woods or on the side of a mountain or at the bottom of a canyon or on the berm of an uninhabited beach for the experience of being there, not for some epicurean debauch.

Once you get into *that* frame of mind, the experience can be more delightful and the food may even become satisfying. Dishes that you hardly ever thought twice about at home, because of their blandness or ordinariness, may take on new values. I was backpacking not long ago in Shining Rock Wilderness in the North Carolina mountains and received one morning an invitation from a couple down the way, who were more or less on their honeymoon, to drop by for breakfast biscuits. The groom mixed up some dry batter with water, shaped it with his hands into biscuit shapes, put them into a simple aluminum frying pan, covered them with another pan to create a simulated oven, and very carefully cooked them over the lowest possible flame of a tiny butane stove.

I am something of a biscuit fancier, and I have never eaten better ones than that morning. The surroundings, and the shattering of the belief that I had up until then had that baking was just too much trouble for the backpacking chef, elevated the common biscuit to a status at least as high as that of the French *croissant*. Now I make biscuits almost every time I go packing.

One of the things that backpacking is, is an escape from the world of *things*. Computers, electricity, money, internal-combustion engines—you leave all these behind when you head down the trail. And yet backpacking itself requires a certain amount of equipment in order to be safe and enjoyable. (Or at least we think it does. John Muir, the quintessential backpacker, did pretty well on a blanket and a cup of tea. And Emma Gatewood, a grandmother, hiked the Appalachian Trail three times, shod in sneakers.)

It might seem at first glance that one piece of cooking equipment easily left behind would be the stove. A small cooking fire does the same job, weighs nothing in your pack, and has the added value of stirring ancient feelings of pleasure that go all the way back to our caveperson ancestors. John Muir used fires a lot. All this is true, but it runs head-on into something that has evolved in recent years, that a lot of people know about, but that still not enough of them practice: the new backpacking ethic.

It's not at all complicated. It merely holds that things aren't the way they used to be back when a woodswalker could in good conscience tear a few boughs off a fir tree to line his bed; when it was de rigueur to excavate a little drainage ditch around your tent; and when a campfire, suitably roaring, was the only proper way to cook your meal and end your day and, probably, keep you warm through at least the early part of the night.

Those days are over because we know more now about the impact that human beings make on nature when they go walking in the wilderness. A single footprint made with a heavily lugged sole, we now know, can have a quite lasting and bad effect on some parts of the environment. The drainage ditch becomes a source of erosion, and modern tents don't need it anyway. And the fire ring that is left when the fire is dead and the camp is broken remains behind a long time—years, in some cases—and the scorch marks may not fade until the next ice age. In addition, a lot more people head into the woods now than ever did before, and if each of them requires some timber for a campfire some serious damage will result.

So backpackers who subscribe to the new ethic (and those who don't shouldn't be called backpackers) never make bough beds and they never dig drainage ditches. And very few of them use anything but a mechanical stove to cook their meals in the woods.

Which brings us directly to the question of cookery equipment. The major element is going to have to be the stove.

It comes, as far as most backpackers are concerned, in two basic forms: stoves that burn compressed gas, usually butane, and those that run on white gasoline-type fuel, often referred to as Coleman fuel. Some less popular forms of stoves include those that operate on propane (which require heavy cannisters best suited to car-campers), liquid petroleum gas, alcohol, kerosene, and jellied fuel such as Sterno.

There is a large variety of stoves available in both butane and white gasoline, and the beginning backpacker who's trying to make a choice is in danger of becoming confused to the point of frustration. There's no substitute for actually getting your hands on one and using it and seeing whether it likes you and vice versa, but in the absence of that a choice might well be based on some of the following factors:

Do you want simplicity and ease of operation, or do you want predictably high heat? As in most everything else, there are tradeoffs involved in choosing between butane and gasoline. In general, the butane stoves are simplicity themselves to operate: Make sure that a fuel cannister is attached; turn the valve; apply a match flame to the burner head; and you have a flame that's ready for cooking. If you need to relight the stove later, the process is identical. A gasoline stove has more working parts, is more complicated to light, and is very likely to be more temperamental. Most of those that are small enough to use in single-handed backpacking require that you introduce a small quantity of fuel from the regular tank into a little cup beneath the burner head (I use an eyedropper for this); light it; encourage it to heat the stove's generator so that enough pressure is created within the tank to vaporize the fuel; then open the valve at the right moment to create a roaring and adequately hot pressurized flame.

There are advantages and drawbacks to both sorts of stove. Butane has lower heat output than gasoline, which means it takes longer to boil water, and it loses efficiency in cold weather. The cannisters are just dead weight and space in your pack once they are exhausted, and some of them can't be removed from the stoves until they're completely empty, leaving you with a pathetic little flame and seriously reduced heat as pressure drops toward zero. Gasoline stoves are more finicky, take longer to light, and can be frustrating to relight. The fuel is dangerous when spilled, and the stoves are likely to be heavier than their butane-driven counterparts. But their ability to turn cold water into boiling water is much more advanced than is butane's. Coleman-type fuel is widely available in the United States, while many butane cannisters are not interchangeable and may not be available close to some trailheads.

So it may, as we say in these matters, boil down to a question of how willing you are to go through the ritual of filling, priming, and lighting a white-gasoline stove. If you *are* willing—and the routine takes no more than a couple of minutes, once you learn it—then gasoline stoves are probably for you and you can start comparing prices. Which can be quite a shock, since those prices have been rising rapidly in recent years, as more people become interested in the out-of-doors. The Optimus 99 white-gasoline stove, my favorite among the light-weights, was running in late 1978 at $30 to $35, or about double its price of five years before. The relatively new Coleman Peak 1, which uses a little pump to generate its initial pressure, is by far the sturdiest, hottest, and heaviest of the gasoline stoves suitable for single-person use and the only one I know of that can throttle down to a real simmer. It costs around $28. By contrast, butane stoves cost from around $12 to $20.

Obviously you need to do some homework and comparison shopping before sinking a fairly large sum of money into a piece of backpacking machinery that may or may not satisfactorily boil water for your morning coffee and that you're going to be very dependent on for meals in the woods. Comparisons are not all that easy to make, since backpacking supply stores tend to carry a few brands each, but not anywhere near all.

It's a great help to be able to study weights, prices, capacities, and model numbers before you go into the store, and this can be done in several ways. Both Recreational Equipment, Inc., the West Coast-based cooperative (P.O. Box C-88125, Seattle, Washington 98188), and Eastern Mountain Sports (Vose Farm Road, Peterborough, New Hampshire 03458) are mail-order backpacking supply houses whose catalogues contain a wealth of information on stoves. And the best source of unimpassioned, factual, comparative information is *Backpacking Equipment Buyer's Guide*, by William Kemsley, Jr., and the editors of BACKPACKER magazine (New York: Collier Books, $8.95).

By comparison with stoves, the selection of the remainder of your kitchen equipment is quite simple. You'll more than likely need the following:

A *pot* to cook in. Bear in mind that much of your food will be stew-type in form and texture, and that you might be best off with a simple spun-aluminum pot, with bail handle and cover, that will serve essentially as a device for boiling water. The pot's size (usually given as 1, 1½, or 3 quarts) will depend on the number of people who ordinarily will be using it. Ninety-five per cent of your cooking and eating can be done in and from this pot. If you go in for occasional pancakes or freeze-dried scrambled eggs, or have a tendency to catch trout, you'll need some sort of frying pan. The pot lid may well serve, although somewhat inadequately, this purpose.

A *pot grabber*, a lightweight pliers-looking gizmo, that takes the place of a pot handle and keeps your fingers from getting roasted. A cheap pair of cotton *work gloves* will help in this regard, too, and double as hand protection on nights when it gets unexpectedly cold.

A *cup*, which can be either metal or plastic, that can serve both as drinking cup and measuring device. If it's metal, water can be boiled directly in it—an advantage when the cooking pot is filled with stew and you want another cup of coffee in a hurry.

A *spoon*, large and metal, of the sort that's found in camping utensil kits. Set the accompanying knife and fork aside and forget about them; a spoon is perfectly adequate for almost all trailside eating, and it is an excellent utensil to use in preparing the food as well. A folding, pocket-type *knife*, kept respectably and respectfully sharp, will handle any real cutting jobs. Mount your eight-inch killer-macho hunting knife on a plaque and leave it at home as a reminder of the way things were back before we discovered that going out into nature didn't have to be an *assault*.

Containers: You'll need several different kinds, to hold your condiments, spices, soap, and foodstuffs, and there's a great variety to choose from. There are tiny plastic Austrian bottles (the ones with nubby green tops; try to get those with gaskets), and Gerry tubes (they look like toothpaste tubes except the other end is open; you fill with peanut butter or whatever and then seal it with a clip); large plastic bottles to carry your water supply; and an assortment of plastic bags. These can include good old Baggies and Ziplocs, and (for something sturdier) heavy-duty bags bought from aquariums, where they are used to transport goldfish; and heat-sealable bags, which are not only very strong but also tolerate boiling water (you can, for instance, load dry cereal, powdered milk, and sugar into one at home, pour hot or boiling water into it in the woods, and have a warm breakfast that doesn't mess up any pots). And one of your most important containers will be a plastic garbage bag or two, for carrying your trash out of the woods. It's amazing how many people who call themselves "backpackers" forget about that garbage bag.

Other is a category that will get heavy if you aren't careful. It can include matches or lighter; a small rectangle of closed-cell foam (similar to that used beneath sleeping bags) to steady and insulate your stove when you're snow-camping; sturdy fuel tanks if you're using a gasoline stove and extra cannisters if you're using butane; and sanitation materials. This includes some kitchen detergent in a tightly sealing plastic squirt-bottle from the dime store, tablets for water purification (and a notation as to their expiration date), a small towel and washcloth, a scrubbing pad, and the smallest can opener you can find. And, if you're properly pessimistic about mechanical objects in the woods, spare parts for your precious stove.

Once you've got the equipment put away (and it's amazing how much of it you can cajole inside a 1½-quart pot), you can start worrying about food. If you've decided to live off the prepackaged, freeze-dried foods you buy at backpacking stores, your job will be limited to picking out the dishes that appeal to you. If you're more of a do-it-yourself-type person, you'll need to get down to the pleasant task of establishing a modest system of backpacking cookery.

System, here, doesn't mean anything complicated. It means only a set of recipes, and components of recipes, that work out for you and that can be easily interchanged. What follows here is an abbreviated version of the system that works best for me. Most of the foodstuffs that go into it can be obtained at any large, garish, modern supermarket:

Breakfast: I keep this very simple, largely because scrubbing pots can really slow you down if you're moving from place to place every day. I boil a quantity of water, use most of it for tea or coffee, and pour the rest into a small boilable bag in which I have packed a hot cereal, usually oatmeal because of its well-known tendency to stick to your ribs. Or, in hot weather, cold water gets poured into a mixture of cereal such as Grape-Nuts and nonfat dry milk. In either case I stir the mixture with my spoon, eat it, and am left with only a flattened plastic bag with wet insides. Not scrubbing burned-on oatmeal off the bottom of a thin aluminum pot is an excellent way to start the day in the woods.

A dry fruit-flavored drink, such as Tang, is mixed with water for breakfast. I have found that I am not alone in being someone who would not dare drink Tang at home—I guess it's just my silly aversion to a "natural-tasting" drink that's made from sugar, calcium phosphates, gum arabic, cellulose gum, hydrogenated coconut oil, and other chemicals—but who doesn't mind it at all in the woods. Same way with Vienna sausage and a number of other backpacking staples.

Lunch is similarly uninspiring. Most backpackers I know advocate a very simple midday meal—some cheese, nuts, fruit if they can carry it, and peanut butter. The last-mentioned is one of the finest foods ever devised for the walking person, and for humanity in general: It's portable, fairly cheap, doesn't require refrigeration, tastes swell, and is full of protein and the calories one needs to get on down (or more often, I have found, up) the trail. The same foods listed above, by the way, serve as excellent snacks that may be eaten during midmorning or -afternoon breaks on the trail.

If it's cold at lunchtime, it takes but a little longer to prepare a hot meal. Instant soup is good—particularly pea soup—and it can easily be augmented with the contents of a small can of Vienna sausages, or slices of the hard sausage that needs no refrigeration until it's cut open. Even homemade croutons would be welcome here. They weigh practically nothing.

Dinner is the big meal, the one you have when the day's walking is done and the inside of the sleeping bag looks more and more inviting. Indeed, you sometimes will end up doing your cooking from inside the bag when the evening chill sets in.

Because you're a backpacker, you're going to want this meal to be comforting, filling, nutritious, and our old friend *satisfying,* and you're going to want to create all that in one relatively small pot over one relatively small flame. The obvious form such a meal should take is some sort of a stew. Stews are a respectable and time-honored means of fighting off starvation, and if it is true that they are rarely served in the high-stakes restaurants, who cares? If you backpack alone, nobody's going to know that you ate a stew with a big spoon and actually enjoyed it.

The elements of backpacking stews are quite interchangeable, providing you with a vast repertoire of foods that may be bland, but that at least are *varied* bland. I usually build my stews on three major components: a starch base, a source of protein, and a source of vegetable and liquid.

The starch can be pasta (some brands and shapes of macaroni cook in as little as four minutes), or quick-cooking rice, or instant mashed potatoes. The protein comes from small (or larger, if more people are involved) cans of tuna fish, chicken, turkey, shrimp, or the infamous Vienna sausage. It can come, too, from hard sausage, homemade jerky and dehydrated beef, or from one of several meats that can be purchased in freeze-dried form at backpacking supply stores: meat and pork bars, which come in little foil-wrapped loaves and need no refrigeration until they're opened, and foil pouches of freeze-dried chicken and ham. And peanuts and cashews are excellent sources of protein and require virtually no packaging at all.

The liquid-vegetable component is usually nothing more than a packet or two of instant or otherwise dehydrated soup, reconstituted with water at the campsite. The sort of soup is limited only by availability, your imagination, and your taste buds; those that I seem to use most are tomato, vegetable, and especially, cream of mushroom. The last imparts a creamy texture to dishes that is reminiscent (in the woods, at least) of the flour-butter sauce used in a great deal of cooking.

The components could typically be combined into a meal such as this one, adapted from my book, *The Backpacker's Budget Food Book* (New York: David McKay Company, $3.95):

CREAMED TUNA, MACARONI AND CHEESE

dash of salt
2 cups water
1 cup macaroni
2 envelopes instant cream-of-mushroom soup mix
1 small can tuna fish, any kind
4 tbsps. dried American cheese food
1 tbsps. instant dry milk

At home, package the cheese food and dry milk together in plastic film and put the packet inside a bag that contains the loose macaroni, the envelopes of soup mix, and the can of tuna.

In the field, drain the tuna in its can but leave it moist. Bring salted water to a boil. Add the macaroni and cook until almost done. Drain, leaving about 1¼ cup of the liquid. Add soup mix and tuna and stir vigorously. Sprinkle the cheese-milk mixture over the whole works and simmer a few minutes, stirring frequently.

Experiment with the various elements, and you'll come up with other combinations, such as creamed tuna on rice, shrimp Creole, spaghetti with meat sauce—enough different meals to provide anyone with the variety that's needed on a backpacking trip.

I *did* warn you about blandness. These meals are not, shall we say, exciting. But they can be pepped up quite a bit by the addition of other ingredients that are cheap, easy to use, and so lightweight that they practically fly out of your pack. There are, of course, herbs and spices that can be added to ordinary dishes to give them more interesting tastes. And—most importantly as far as the backpacker's kitchen is concerned—they can fool the taste buds into thinking that this pathetic freeze-dried stew you're eating is actually a work of some culinary merit.

A greater degree of merit could

be achieved, of course, if you executed the dish at home and with more nearly proper ingredients, but I have found that a lot can be accomplished by blending a tablespoon or two of curry powder into, say, a tuna and rice dish, along with a handful of raisins. Chili powder goes into an otherwise tasteless beef stew. Commercial poultry seasoning helps with dishes containing chicken and turkey. I have a home-blended Italian spice mixture for the trail that includes basil, oregano, bay leaf, and whatever else I have handy. A similar mixture for Creole-type dishes includes dried cayenne pepper, bay leaf, basil, rosemary, thyme, filé, marjoram, savory, mace, brown sugar, garlic, onions, green pepper, and celery. And folks who grow things at home in window boxes may want to take dill, chives, and mint.

The point is that the food on a backpacking excursion doesn't have to be bland beyond belief. It should not become so important that the real purpose of walking is obscured, but that doesn't mean you have to eat tasteless little ampuls of boring goop like an astronaut. With a little preparation and planning (which any backpacker can tell you are important and gratifying parts of the trip), and a trip to the supermarket and the spice rack, you can come up with meals that do what meals should do—leave you nutritionally and emotionally satisfied, and ready for another day of walking tomorrow.

CULPRIT COOKERY

by JACK HOPE

We had a good deal of fun publishing this piece in BACKPACKER. It may be a spoof on cooking, but there are quite a few messages between the lines as well.

W.K.

The recipes below, tried and tested in actual wilderness settings, will delight the most discriminating of backcountry gourmets. They are tasty, filling, and nutritious. Yet their basic ingredients can be found easily—fresh, and in great abundance—in most wilderness environments. They do not require that the backcountry chef resort to bland, freeze-dried preparations, or that he burden his pack with unnecessary weight.

Most important, these meals strive for what may be described as an "esthetic and ecological balance" in the American outdoors. As the modern hiker knows, today's backcountry experience is often marred by a variety of disrupting forces, forces that shatter the serenity of the wilderness and impair natural esthetics and ecology. In response to this, each of the following recipes is intended to remove certain of these forces, thereby improving the backcountry setting and insuring its natural character for the enjoyment of future generations of Americans.

At first, the reader may be reluctant to attempt these new dishes. This is understandable. But persist, and you will be rewarded: not only with the ultimate in dining pleasure, but also with the knowledge that your efforts will aid—in some small way—in rendering the American wilderness a truly lovely place to visit.

SCOUT-KABOB

Ingredients
2 lbs. sliced bacon
4 lbs. fresh vegetables
1 hatchet-wielding
  Scout (either sex), 60-80 lbs.

Utensils
1 hardwood skewer, 2-inch
  diameter, 6 feet long
  (peel bark before using)
large pile firewood
2 matches

History and comment. A dish designed to modify the aggressive outdoor behavior of large youth groups. While an authentic "Scout" need not be used (the gourmet should not be bound to mere labels), care should be taken to maintain the proper ratio of meat to vegetables.

Preparation. Secure one Scout. Not just any Scout, but one who persists in using his hatchet on live and standing trees around camp. After said Scout has felled a sapling of the dimensions approximate to those of the needed skewer, use hatchet to chop Scout into 6-oz. pieces. Sharpen one end of skewer and insert it through pieces, alternating fresh vegetables with chunks of Scout. Wrap pieces with strips of bacon. Place skewer over wood fire and turn slowly for half hour. Remove from flame and serve to remaining Scouts—impressing upon them the inevitably negative consequences of excessive use of the hatchet. Season to taste. Pack out uniform, hatchet, merit badges.

TRAILBIKE TARTARE

Ingredients
1 trailbike
1 trailbike rider
½ dozen fresh eggs (or 4 oz. dehydrated)
2 loaves whole wheat bread
salt and pepper

Utensils
large mixing bowl
meat grinder
hacksaw

History and comment. This is a
relatively new dish, developed in
1965 to counter the rapid proliferation of noise-making, resource-
consuming, trail-eroding machinery
in the American wilderness. A summer recipe, its winter equivalent is
known as "Snowmobile Supreme."
Preparation. Any trailbiker encountered in the backcountry may
be used in this recipe, other than
park or forest rangers, who may be
using their machinery in the line of
duty. Divide trailbike and trailbiker into tiny particles, using
hacksaw and meat grinder, respec-
tively. Remove gas tank, tires, and
fuel line from trailbike. (If these
are left in, they impart a disagree-
able "industrial" taste to the meal.)
In a large bowl, mix eggs, spices,
trailbike, trailbike rider. Spread
mixture on slices of bread. Serve
cold. Excellent for quick camp
meals where firewood is scarce.
Rich in iron.

PITON à FOIE GRAS

Ingredients
1 strand (3) mountain climbers
1 quart cognac
2 lbs. pork fat
2 cups heavy cream
1 clove garlic

Utensils
large, hotel-size saucepan
sharp carving knife

History and comment. Originated
by Nepalese sherpas who early fore-
saw the need to dispose of western
climbers who littered Himalayan
mountainsides with discarded oxygen
tanks, food tins and disposable
butane containers in recent years, this
has become a popular favorite in the
continental United States, where it is
used to discourage those technical
climbers who have cracked, chiseled
and splintered natural rock surfaces
with their pitons and other climbing
weapons. Appropriate preparation requires the utmost coordination between the chef and his assistant.
Thus, it should be attempted only by
the most accomplished of backcountry gourmets.

Preparation. Locate a group of
above-described rock climbers. Half-
fill saucepan with fresh water and
place on wood fire at base of cliff,
below climbers. Chef attends to fire
while his assistant ascends to top of
cliff, using hiker's route. As water
comes to roiling boil, chef signals
assistant who then removes the up-
permost piton. Or, if piton is firmly
imbedded, assistant uses carving
knife to sever belaying rope. Chef
must then be prepared to move saucepan in order to catch entire string of
climbers as they fall from cliff. (This
fall may be facilitated by greasing
climbing rope with pork fat before
climb. However, it is an imprecise
technique, since climbers may fall
before water comes to full boil.) With
climbers in saucepan, cook gently for
one hour—stirring continually—blending in cream, cognac, garlic. Remove
saucepan from flame. As the mixture
cools and solidifies, it may be ladled
from pan and pressed into molds.
(Climbers' boots, which should be
removed before mixture reaches second boil, make ideal molds.) Any
excess mixture should be used to fill
in eroded rock crevices that climbers
have created with their pitons. May
be eaten as hors d'oeuvre or entree.
An ideal on-the-trail snack.

BAKED ALASKA

Ingredients
1 barrel crude oil
1 bushel snow
1 Interior Secretary, Atlantic Rich-
field executive or other individual
responsible for the construction of
Alaska pipeline.

Utensils
1 oil drill

History and comment. This recipe
came to me from a northern backpacker who had hurriedly designed
the dish as a last attempt to thwart
the then-proposed 800-mile petroleum pipeline that would destroy several hundred thousand acres of
Alaskan wilderness. The ingredients
and utensils for this recipe—in its
pure form—dictate that it be prepared
only in northern Alaska, where several American firms are now conducting oil explorations. With a little
imagination, however, I suspect that
the recipe could be adapted to other
situations in other regions of the
country.
Preparation. If proper equipment is
available, this preparation is simplicity itself. Insert Interior Secretary
or oil executive into the shaft of a
freshly-dug oil well. Lower drill into
shaft and run at high speed for two
minutes, whipping the chosen individual into a smooth, pudding-like
consistency. Remove this "pudding"
from the shaft. (It will now be essentially "baked," I am told, due to the
heat generated by the whipping process.) Blend together the snow and
crude oil and use as topping. Serve in
50-gallon oil drums.
The reader should feel free to experiment with these dishes, substitut-
ing ingredients to suit his own tastes,
or altering the recipe in subtle ways
to meet the needs of a particular
back-country environment. Select
your ingredients with care and
discrimination. Do not be inhibited
by tradition nor intimidated by the
skepticism of an occasional onlooker.
We who share an interest in fine food,
and in the future of the American
outdoors, look forward to exchanging
culinary techniques with our readers.
For it is only in this manner that new
and better dishes can be developed,
and that perfection can ultimately be
achieved. *Bon appétit!*

Chapter Three
PHYSICAL FITNESS

No backpacker, beginner or expert, can ignore the matter of physical fitness. The body must be prepared for exertion in any physical activity, and hiking is no exception. If you are a beginner, it is foolhardy to set out on even a day's walk in the woods without some kind of preliminary warm-up exercise. If you run or jog, you are pretty well on your way to optimum fitness for hiking. If not, some of the ideas and pointers in this chapter should get you moving in this area. Staying in shape for backpacking is not easy. The single best method of doing so is to backpack a lot. The hardiest hikers I know are those who spend a great deal of their time hiking, backpacking, climbing, canoeing, and kayaking.

Take the old-time outdoorsman. There is not much in the old outdoors literature about exercises to get into shape for outdoor trips. Instead, the outdoors was regarded by old-timers as a place to get into good physical condition. In this chapter, we start out with a fitting account of one of our "Elders of the Tribe"— Theodore Roosevelt. If ever there was an inspiring story of a man's overcoming his hard battle with poor health to go on to become one of our country's most rugged outdoorsmen, this is it.

TEDDY YOU'RE A BEAR:

Theodore Roosevelt (1858–1919)

by KENT DANNEN

It seems almost a cliché for the image of Teddy Roosevelt to come to mind when thinking of a physically fit outdoorsman. He seems the epitome of the tough old breed.

Though the popular image of him is mainly as an outdoorsman, Teddy Roosevelt, of course, was much more than that—president, statesman, conservationist. In the following article there is emphasis upon another aspect of Roosevelt's life, and an underlying reason why he was in such good physical condition all his life. He was an insatiable naturalist. This little-known fact about Roosevelt explains why he was so enthusiastic an outdoorsman. And, of course, being outdoors a lot is the best way of staying in shape for outdoors activities, especially for backpacking.

W.K.

Americans tend to think of Theodore Roosevelt as the high-spirited Rough Rider, grinning widely as he led a charge up San Juan Hill. Or they remember the political cartoons of T. R. menacingly swinging a big stick over the world.

But I believe these were public images manufactured by Roosevelt for political purposes. Basically, Roosevelt was a naturalist who loved hiking and camping. And as a politician he knew how to encourage, organize, and mold the burgeoning conservation sentiment of the nation into a strong movement.

Roosevelt's enthusiasm for conservation began when he was seven or eight. "We children," he wrote, "loved the country beyond anything. We disliked the city." As he learned to read, animal books were his favorites, although he also enjoyed some heavier tomes such as David Livingstone's *Missionary Travels and Researches in Africa.*

He came from a family of outdoors enthusiasts. His lawyer uncle wrote books about outdoor subjects and campaigned for the protection of wildlife. The Roosevelt family was active in the New York State Game Protective Association's fight to protect Adirondack deer and improve sport-hunting ethics. His father, Theodore Roosevelt, Sr., was a major contributor to societies for the prevention of cruelty to animals and helped found the American Museum of Natural History in New York City.

It is not surprising, then, that T.R., Jr., also founded his own museum. When he was nine years old, he established the Roosevelt Museum of Natural History in his bedroom. But when the family maid complained about the seal's skull, shells, insects, birds' eggs and nests, the museum was moved to a case in the upstairs hall.

His parents traveled widely, seeking climates that would help young T.R.'s asthma. These trips gave Roosevelt opportunity to gather specimens in wild areas of Europe, Egypt, and Palestine.

At first he collected everything he could find, but later he began to specialize in birds. Using a double-barreled shotgun given him by his father, T.R. collected hundreds of bird skins, each carefully tagged with the bird's location, habits, diet, body structure, and scientific name.

At age 11, Roosevelt began to study taxidermy under John G. Bell, who had been an associate of the famous bird painter John James Audubon. Four specimens that T.R. collected and mounted are on display in the American Museum of Natural History.

In 1876 Roosevelt enrolled at Harvard University with the intention of becoming a naturalist. The following year he made his first published contribution to the body of zoological knowledge, *The Summer Birds of the Adirondacks in Franklin County, N.Y.*, a list of 97 species.

But by his senior year he had decided to give up his original ambition and to devote his life to politics. Perhaps his political science professors influenced him, or maybe it was his fiancée Alice Lee, whose family was prominent in politics. Roosevelt himself claimed that he switched fields because Harvard couldn't train an outdoor naturalist. T.R. had aspired to be a field man, to get outside and observe what was going on firsthand; the straight-laced biology faculty at Harvard, however, emulated the German universities and their obsession

President Theodore Roosevelt at Yellowstone National Park, April 1903.

U.S. DEPARTMENT OF THE INTERIOR PHOTO

with microscopes, insisting that the work of a biologist was to dissect, embalm, and magnify tissues and embryos.

Whatever the cause of his shift from natural science to political science, Roosevelt was destined to be a great public leader, although it would have been bad politics for him to admit any special advantage. In an age that admired Horatio Alger heroes, poor-boy-made-good was the best political image. Since he could not claim to have risen from poverty, T.R. emphasized his poor health as a child, against which he had waged and won a hard fight. During that time, and indeed all his life, Roosevelt threw his formidable energies into all manner of rugged outdoor exercise.

"I was fond of walking and climbing," he wrote in his later years. "As a lad I used to go to the north woods in Maine, both in fall and winter. . . I canoed [and] tramped through the woods. . . visiting the winter logging camps on snowshoes." Snowshoeing is not an activity for the sickly!

Three years after his graduation from Harvard, it was New York State Assemblyman Roosevelt who boarded a train for the Badlands of the Dakota Territory. Arriving in the West while it was still fairly wild, he hired a guide and set out to hunt bison. After two weeks of camping in the rain, Roosevelt had experienced cold, hunger, and being thrown by his horse but had seen no live bison, thanks to hide hunters who had butchered them by the thousands. He wrote, "No sight is more common on the plains than that of a bleached buffalo skull; and their countless numbers attest the abundance of the animal at a time not so very long past." He had come to love the West and to see what ignorant or unscrupulous men could do to destroy its wild resources.

He bought a ranch and began dividing his time between East and West. Roosevelt became a devoted expert on the wildlife of the plains around his property and used the ranch as a base for long camping trips into the mountains. During the course of these trips he became more familiar with the life histories of large western animals than any other naturalist of his time.

Of course, Roosevelt's western expeditions were hunting trips. There always has been a split within the conservation movement between sport hunters and nonhunters. Like most backpackers, I belong to the latter group and have difficulty understanding the hunter's point of view. Some of the greatest American conservationists, however, have been hunters. So great is my respect for these men, including Roosevelt, that I do not yet have the nerve to say that hunting is wrong. I can only remain puzzled by the motives.

Inevitably, Roosevelt's hunting got him into plenty of trouble with nonhunting conservationists, but much of this resulted from hostile or sensational journalism. For example, when he went on a winter trip to Colorado between his term as governor of New York and his inauguration as vice president, Roosevelt was accompanied by some reporters. Unable or unwilling to follow T.R. into the cold wilds, the newsmen sat around a cozy stove and made up stories that were far more "newsworthy" than "No luck today." So the United States read how the vice president-elect killed vicious lions, escaped miraculously from a huge grizzly (in winter, remember), was treed for hours by a pack of 100 wolves, and shot nearly all the predators in Colorado.

Actually, Roosevelt was researching mountain lions. He collected 14 specimens and sent them to the U.S. Biological Survey. Killing this many lions today, with far more sophisticated techniques of field research available, would be excessive. But in T.R.'s time, government-planned and financed predator extermination had not yet had serious effect on the lion population, and Roosevelt's collecting did not reduce significantly the number of big cats in the area.

Fourteen lions collected for the U.S. Biological Survey is a far cry from the hundreds of "varmints" that the press had him kill. Small wonder Roosevelt was condemned by conservationists for "ruthlessly taking the lives of innocent and unoffending animals without provocation and with the sole aim of gratifying a desire for killing."

Repeated reports like this made Roosevelt hostile toward the press. On one occasion, however, newspaper enterprise enhanced Roosevelt's conservationist reputation. Late in 1902 he was on a bear hunt in Mississippi. Other members of his party caught a small cub, stunned it with a blow over the head, and tied it to a tree for the president to shoot. Roosevelt was outraged and ordered the bear's release. A political cartoonist for the *Washington Post* picked up the story and produced a cartoon that showed Roosevelt refusing to shoot a wide-eyed little bear. Soon the whole country was talking about the cartoon as it was reprinted again and again. An enterprising toy maker then produced the teddy bear, and soon no nursery or Republican meeting would be without one. The popularity of these toys was a significant sign of how sentiment for wildlife was growing in America.

Roosevelt did all he could to encourage respect for wildlife among Americans. In 1888 he served as the first president of the Boone and Crockett Club, and made this group of big-game hunters into a powerful conservation lobby. It was largely because of club pressure that Yellowstone National Park was saved by the Park Protection Act of 1894: it had been created by law in 1872, but there was no provision for the enforcement of that law. People did as they pleased and the park suffered greatly until the Park Protection Act literally sent the cavalry to the rescue.

Roosevelt also threw the club's weight behind the passage of the Forest Reserve Act of 1891. This legislation gave the President authority to preserve federal forest lands from private exploitation. Roosevelt's predecessors had set aside nearly 50 million acres; when he became president, T.R. increased the acreage by 148 million, changed forest reserves to national forests, and put them under the supervision of trained foresters. He was determined to change the pioneer mentality by which "the American had but one thought about a tree, and that was to cut it down."

The president influenced Congress to create five national parks. But this was not enough for T.R. He allied himself with the chairman of the House Public Lands Committee to pass the National Monuments Act in

1906, which enabled the President to create national monuments without congressional approval. He then established 16 national monuments.

Roosevelt had been a dedicated bird lover since childhood, and early in his term as governor of New York had banned the use of bird skins in

---

Theodore Roosevelt's Conservation Accomplishments

• Set aside over 148 million acres as national forests.

• Set aside 86 million acres as national mineral reserves.

• Approved five national parks.

• Signed National Monuments Act of 1906, then used it to create 16 national monuments.

• Created 55 national wildlife refuges.

• Wrote 16 books and pamphlets and numerous magazine articles on natural history.

• Brought about game laws for Alaska.

• Wrote 17 unpublished manuscripts on natural history.

• Collected many specimens of North American mammals for U.S. Biological Survey.

• Collected North American bird specimens for the American Museum of Natural History.

• Led wildlife collecting expedition to Africa for the Smithsonian Institution, discovering many new species and subspecies.

---

the manufacture of clothing. Then in 1903 ornithologists came to the White House complaining that plume hunters were exterminating the egrets and other gaily plumed birds on four acres of federal land in Florida's Indian River. T.R. responded by proclaiming Pelican Island the first national wildlife refuge. He liked the idea so much that he went ahead and created 50 more refuges all over the country, including Alaska, Hawaii, and Puerto Rico. His decisive actions gave such momentum to the refuge movement that today there are more than 300 federal refuges. At the same time, states, municipalities and even individuals responded to the federal effort and established refuges of their own.

Roosevelt was quick to note that besides the direct presidential power he could wield for conservation, he

could also use the prestige of his office as clout. He utilized this indirect power to great advantage by encouraging, praising, and assisting other naturalists and conservationists. Never before had naturalists found themselves the center of so much important attention. One after another was called to the White House to advise the president of the United States, which gave them incentive to continue and to improve their work.

Roosevelt also sought the company of naturalists when he traveled. In 1903 when Roosevelt was on a camping trip in Yosemite National Park, John Muir convinced him that California should cede control of Yosemite Valley to the federal government for inclusion in the adjacent national park. Strings were pulled and this was accomplished in 1906. Two years later, Muir again influenced Roosevelt to preserve Grand Canyon as a national park. T.R. was unable to get it through Congress, though, so he made the canyon a national monument instead.

In 1908 Roosevelt made his last big conservation effort as president by calling a conference of governors. Not only governors but congressmen, Supreme Court justices, and naturalists attended; the states were urged to undertake vital conservation actions that the federal government could not manage. The results were dramatic and far-reaching. Thirty-six states created conservation commissions to establish policy and solve conservation problems. Various scientific organizations set up conservation committees, and the National Conservation Association was organized. The conference of governors gave the conservation movement the momentum it needed to survive reversals suffered later under different political situations.

Even before he left the White House, Roosevelt began to organize a collecting expedition to Africa for the Smithsonian Institution. He supervised every detail of how a 200-man expedition would survive in the wilderness for the better part of a year. What kind of food and tents? How much mosquito netting? What books to take? How many portable bathtubs? How should specimens be preserved and sent back to Washington? How many pairs of easily broken glasses should he take? (He finally took nine.) With T.R. looking after each detail, the expedition was a huge success. The Smithsonian gained a valuable collection of new species of African fauna, and much information was added to the sum of knowledge about African wildlife. For Roosevelt it was the highlight of his life and provided some of his fondest memories.

Very different was an expedition in 1913 to the Amazon River basin for the American Museum of Natural History. It began as a collecting trip but ended as an exploration of the uncharted River of Doubt, tributary to the Amazon. For some reason, T.R. as a private citizen left the preparation to others, and the result was death and disaster on a 47-day ordeal down the unknown river now called Rio Roosevelt. Although the important new data gathered went a long way to enhance the geographic and biological knowledge of the Amazon basin, T.R. never recovered physically.

After T.R. left office he sustained his love of "the silent places . . . the wild waste places of the earth, unworn of man, and changed only by the slow change of the ages through time everlasting." He already had written several widely praised books on natural history. He managed to carry on his naturalist activities and wrote more natural history books as well as magazine articles and reviews of other books on biology. He organ-ized a bird club and urged homeowners to create backyard habitat for wildlife.

On the evening of January 5, 1919, T.R. wrote an enthusiastic letter to the author of a book on pheasants that he planned to review. He died in his sleep early the following morning. He had written around 150,000 letters in his life. The first was about birds; the last was about birds. In between, of course, were letters on a multitude of subjects, but wildlife and conservation always held first place among his interests. He dedicated a lifetime, creatively mixing politics and conservation, to structure a wilderness heritage for Americans that still bears his definitive hallmark. ⚘

PHYSICAL FITNESS AND THE BACKPACKER

by DON HARDIN AND BRIAN KELLY

An account of tests that were done to determine the weight a backpacker can manage, here's a piece that will help you gauge the load an individual can safely manage.

While backpacking is itself an activity which is very good at building physical fitness, how much backpacking can you do if you aren't in pretty good physical condition? Two scientists conducted an experiment recently to determine how important age, overweight, and physical fitness were to the amount of weight a backpacker should carry. Their conclusions are quite interesting. And draw some good broad-gauge guidelines for setting goals for the beginning backpacker.

W.K.

In the summer of 1974, at the University of Texas at El Paso, we completed a research project to help identify some of the factors that determine how much weight can be effectively carried in a backpack and to what extent the backpacker's performance is affected by his age, lack of fitness or being overweight.

The 15 men who volunteered as subjects ranged in age from 21 to 45 years. In order to find their levels of physical fitness, they were given an exhaustive test. A prediction was made for each volunteer's maximum ability to utilize oxygen during hard exercise. The ability to utilize oxygen is considered to be the best indication of cardiovascular efficiency or fitness because it indicates how well the body can respond to hard physical work. The greater the ability to utilize oxygen, the higher the level of physical fitness.

For each person, there is theoretically an ideal body weight. By taking measurements of how much fat a person has at such places as the abdomen and back of the upper arm, and measuring the width of the knee, it is possible to come up with a predicted ideal body weight for people of varying heights and ages. The difference between each man's predicted weight and actual weight was used to determine how far overweight he was. It is frequently claimed that excess body weight has the same effect as the addition of that amount of weight to his pack.

Consideration of age as a factor in backpacking is important because there are many people past the first flush of youth who feel they are too old to backpack.

Our research team used a motor-driven treadmill running at three miles per hour at a 12 percent grade. The subjects carried pack loads of 20, 25 and 30 percent of their own body weights until their heart rates reached predetermined levels indicating they were becoming inefficient at handling the load. The level in most cases was approximately 160 beats per minute. The scores for each subject were calculated by how many minutes and seconds it took his heart to reach 160 beats while carrying the differing loads. All data were then treated to determine the relationships between levels of fitness, age, degree of overweight, and performance with packs of different weights.

The walking pace chosen, three mph at 12 percent grade, was considerably more than a hiker would undertake under normal circumstances. Most hikers average two to 2.5 miles per hour on a level trail if they are carrying loads like those we used. But we wanted to develop a stressful situation in a relatively short while to yield data relevant to actual packing.

After we analyzed the data, it became apparent that physical fitness was the factor most influential in backpacking performance.

As could be expected, the subjects as a group performed better with 20 per cent of their body weight as pack loads than they did with the heavier

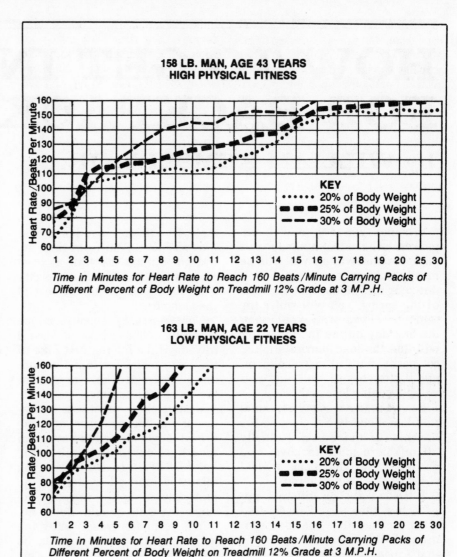

158 LB. MAN, AGE 43 YEARS HIGH PHYSICAL FITNESS

KEY
• • • • 20% of Body Weight
▬ ▬ 25% of Body Weight
– – – 30% of Body Weight

Time in Minutes for Heart Rate to Reach 160 Beats/Minute Carrying Packs of Different Percent of Body Weight on Treadmill 12% Grade at 3 M.P.H.

163 LB. MAN, AGE 22 YEARS LOW PHYSICAL FITNESS

KEY
• • • • 20% of Body Weight
▬ ▬ 25% of Body Weight
– – – 30% of Body Weight

Time in Minutes for Heart Rate to Reach 160 Beats/Minute Carrying Packs of Different Percent of Body Weight on Treadmill 12% Grade at 3 M.P.H.

loads. It appears, furthermore, that individuals who carry light loads well also carry heavy loads better than other people do. In other words, they demonstrated the highest levels of physical fitness. Some of the best performers were overweight men in their forties, while some of the worst performances were turned in by men in their twenties who were not overweight.

The results of our study are summarized as follows:

Physical Fitness
Physical fitness appears to be more closely related to pack-carrying performance than to either age or weight. Therefore we concluded that packers should be physically fit before attempting difficult hikes.

Pack Loads
Lighter loads are desirable. Never-

theless, up to 30 per cent of body weight can be easily handled by fit packers in fairly difficult situations.
Overweight
Excess body weight will affect performance to some degree, but it decreases as a factor with higher levels of physical fitness.

Age
Physically fit older people should not find backpacking too strenuous.

A prospective backpacker should be in at least average physical condition before attempting a trip of more than one day's duration. If not, he may be a burden to the rest of his party. Guidelines that may be used to judge adequate levels of fitness are the ability to run, jog or walk 1¼ miles in 12 minutes or the ability to walk without a pack two miles on a good surface in 28 minutes. ◣

HOW TO GET IN SHAPE FOR BACKPACKING

by WILLIAM KEMSLEY, JR.

Whether you're a new backpacker, or have just hung up your pack for the winter and will be mostly sedentary until you take it down again for the first big hike of the spring, you will suffer the same problems with your pack the first day out on the trail. You will find the load uncomfortable, get easily winded, especially on uphill stretches of trail, and you will get aching legs and feet.

For years this was my perennial problem. Eagerly anticipating the first hike of the season, I usually bit off more miles to cover and carried a heavier pack than I should have. And suffered.

I tried a lot of different approaches. One year I discovered what I called the "four-day syndrome." What I mean by this is that I discovered that on the first day of a long backpack I suffered all the pains of being out of shape. And fell asleep early the first night, exhausted. The second day was probably the worst, because I started out with all the sore muscles. So I did not even have the break of starting out fresh the first few hundred yards of trail. I suffered the entire day. At the end of the second day I could care less whether or not I even ate dinner before going to sleep. The third day was somewhat miraculous. While I was sore from the first step out on the trail, I found that I had more strength than I had on either of the first two days. This was always encouraging, and it spurred me on with my hike. Then, the glorious transformation of the fourth day. Almost always on the fourth day of my hike I would not be sore, but would have an enormous store of

strength. All of a sudden, I was a super-hiker! And from then on, if I got out on the trail at least once a month, I was in pretty good hiking shape for the rest of the summer.

This knowledge encouraged me to do two things: plan at least a four-day hike for the first hike of the season, and see that I got out on at least one hike a month for the rest of the summer.

Despite these practices, I wonder if anyone else has had the same thoughts I used to have each time I got out on the trail on the first hike of the season after being relatively inert all winter? In the first mile of uphill slogging the same thoughts would flood my mind, year after year: "Why the hell am I doing this? I could be back home at a good movie. This isn't even fun. This is all pain. This is the last backpacking trip I'll *ever* take. I'm hanging it up for good when I get back home. So help me, I am."

Those were not just occasional, whimsical thoughts. I was dead serious.

Of course, if you are an experienced backpacker you already know that once you have reached your first good viewpoint on the trail, stopped, taken off your pack, and sat awhile, you have completely changed your mind. That was the way it was with me. And after the fourth day, when I was turned into a super-hiker again, I sheepishly reversed my thinking of the first day's agony and was ready for the next hike.

I had tried calisthenics of all sorts to keep in shape. At one time, prior to an extended summer of mountain climbing and

backpacking, I had worked out strenuously all winter on the track at the YMCA, as well as with weights. That had gotten me into pretty good shape for that summer's activity. But, in the years since then, I have found calisthenics to be the most boring way to spend time that I could imagine. Nothing worse. I hated it. And despite occasional resolve to work out during the winter months to stay in shape for backpacking, my workouts usually faded out by late January. And so I would again be out of shape when it came time for the first hike of the spring.

Something else, too. It takes a great deal of working out to keep in shape at all for backpacking. Just your run-of-the-mill Royal Canadian Air Force sort of thing doesn't do too much for you, when you sling on a 50-pound pack and start up Agony Grind Trail.

A simple thought occurred to me. So simple, I wondered why I hadn't thought of it before. Why not continue hiking through the winter months? I could at least hike all winter, if not backpack. And from my mountaineering experience of having camped at high altitudes on glaciers, I knew how to camp out in cold weather. So why not do it all winter long? That would keep me in good shape for the summer backpacks.

That was the answer I needed. I resolved to get in a hike a month, all winter long. And I found I really enjoyed cold-weather hiking. I bought some snowshoes and a good winter tent, and I went out backpacking in January, then in February and March. Then it was already time for my first backpack of the year in April. That did it. Ever since then I have not suffered the spring agonies of being completely out of shape again.

Now, however, I have found a new way of augmenting the year-round hiking system of staying in shape. I have started a new system of running. I have found a way of making running fun for myself. And that has made a lot of difference in my backpacking.

On and off over the past twenty years, I have taken up running. Usually I get about four to six months of regular running workouts, and then gradually taper off. At first my running had mainly been on indoor tracks at YMCAs. And that was my problem. What is more boring than trying to keep count of whether you have gone around the track 36 times, or was it 37? Admittedly, it was somewhat easier running with a group. And the longest stints of running I ever did over the years was when I belonged to a cardiac-prevention program, comprised mainly of middle-aged executives in midtown Manhattan. It became a social thing, meeting with them three or four times a week for our runs.

But now my running life is different. I enjoy it. There is nothing boring about it. I actually look forward to going on my runs, and I am running farther than I ever ran before.

There are two key differences in the way I run today. One is that I am running on roads instead of tracks. The second is that I have given myself an edict, that the run must be fun. So I do not try to set any distance or time records for myself. I don't even use a stopwatch. Ever. So I can't tell you how fast or slow I am running. Two things are important for me: distance and regularity. I try to run every day. Obviously, that is an impossible goal. But, it does guarantee my attaining a good level of running without really trying. I find that I run about three to five days a week, all year round. On the days that I don't feel like running, I force myself to put on my running shoes and get

outside anyway. That's the only forced part of my program—get on the shoes and get outside. Then, even if I run only a quarter of a mile, I have had a victory. And in the beginning of this running regimen, there were days, in fact, on which I ran only a quarter of a mile. The important thing for me was that I develop a pleasant habit.

Now, of course, I don't have

any trouble getting my shoes on, and getting out for a four-mile run. Usually my runs are a minimum of two miles, and average about three. I have a wide variety of routes. When I set out for my run I take the route that seems best suited to how I feel. There are some routes that are just two miles long, with no hills. There are others 2¼, 2½, 3, 3½, 4, 5, and 7 miles in length. Some of them

Runners' early-morning yoga practice in a remote part of the Grand Canyon.
PHOTO: WILLIAM KEMSLEY, JR.

have more hills than others. The variety makes the running more fun.

As a result of my running, my backpacking is easier than it ever was. I can carry more weight, hike faster, climb hills with less huffing and puffing. This does not necessarily mean I go on longer hikes or hike faster, or carry more weight. At my age, I am not out to set records. I have found a lot of things that I enjoy doing on backpack trips, but seldom is setting records one of them.

However, I have noticed that I have been able to keep up to hikers half my age if they aren't trying to race with me. More important, I have found that at higher altitudes, I am in better shape to handle the thin air.

Many avid backpackers I know are avid runners, too. They feel that running is the next-best thing to backpacking itself for keeping in shape for backpacking. Some of my friends are actual running nuts.

For instance, on a 15-day trek in the Grand Canyon last year, four of my friends were competitive runners from Montana. Our backpacking trip was not all that strenuous—other than the fact that we had to carry extra water on some parts of the trip, which meant packs weighing close to 80 pounds at those times. The run-

ners made a practice of getting up early in the morning and running short distances back and forth and around camp before we started our day's hike. To underline their fanaticism, let me also tell you they got into catatonic contorted poses for a half hour before both breakfast and dinner each day. They called it runners yoga!

Still another of my friends runs a weird kind of race each year, and it is his only race a year—from Fairplay, Colorado, to Leadville, a distance of 25 miles. Two aspects of this race point up its fanaticism. First, the altitude. The run is from 9,964 feet altitude at Fairplay up to 10,190 feet at Leadville. Secondly, the competitors are chasing burros along the racecourse. It is a reenactment of a race that the old prospectors used to run back in the days of gold fever on the Colorado frontier. My friend has won second place in this race for the past few years.

He is a heck of a good backpacker. Carries enormous amounts of weight, and covers long distances quickly. Actually, he has reversed the fitness process. He uses backpacking to keep in shape for his annual jackass race!

From my experience then, I would recommend the following program for getting into physical fitness for backpacking:

1. Go hiking without a pack as often as you can, preferably once a month, year round.

2. Get into showshoeing or ski touring or both. Get out at least once a month during the season. Get good workouts on the times you get out. Work up a sweat.

3. If you cannot keep active between backpack trips, then plan your next trip to be of four days' duration. Plan to cover a modest distance the first day, gradually increasing the distance each of the following days. (Depending upon the terrain, about four or five miles is a reasonable distance to hike the first day out, regardless of whether or not you are in shape.)

4. Get into a good program of regular running. Keep it up year round. Make it pleasant for yourself. Use the principle of LSD, i.e., Long Slow Distance. It is the miles you run, not how fast you run them, that count. Another point to keep in mind is that you get 90 per cent of the physical-fitness value from running in the first mile you run, three days a week. All the rest of the physical-fitness benefits you get from running more miles, more often, is mere frosting on the cake.

Chapter Four

FINDING THE WAY

In this chapter, you will find some of the basic on-land "navigation" techniques—skills every hiker can well afford to learn. We are often too dependent on the trails themselves for giving us a sense of direction, and yet being prepared to "read the land" can in its extreme truly mark the difference between survival and death if one is lost.

HOW TO USE A MAP AND COMPASS

by LESTER H. LOBLE II

Knowing how to use a map and compass is, in my opinion, the single most important knowledge you need to go hiking into any backcountry. Without this basic knowledge I think you ought not to venture very far off the highway.

There is so much interest in "survival kits" today. And so little need for them. But the same people who are interested in survival kits really ought to get to know how to use a map and compass—and be sure they have an adequate one of each before going for a hike.

What happens is that most new hikers follow trails and use detailed trail-description guides. This is all well and good. But what if they get off the trail, turned around, disoriented—and lost? Then what? What chance do they have with their survival kits, if they do not have a map and compass and know how to use them?

The following article tells you how to use a map and compass.

These are basics. And the real way to know how to use them is to use them; practice taking compass bearings. Don't assume you know it all. I've known seasoned foresters who tell tales of having gotten lost, panicked, and then forgotten how to use their compass.

What I do is to carry the basic instructions that came with my compass when I bought it, right in the plastic wrap with my compass. In case I do get lost, and panic, which would be an entirely human reaction, then I'd feel confident in knowing that I could read my compass bearings without fail.

The following article was written by Lester Loble II for Montana magazine. Les is a partner in High Country Adventures, an outfitter that takes people on trips to the Montana wilderness areas.

W.K.

Act I: The Publisher of this handbook and the Author of this article are on the move. They have only the vaguest idea of where they are. Other than a brief glance at the map at the start of the trip, they have not looked at it again or at a compass at all. Why? Well, the Publisher has remembered the time they traveled 4½ miles in 1¼ hours in the Bob Marshall Wilderness. He is determined to better that time. Even if the Publisher and Author had time to stop and use the map and compass, their vision would have been blurred by fatigue and by the sweat running into their eyes.

Act II: Less fanatic and more thoughtful hikers have spent time examining their map and the route of the proposed trip. From time to time they have stopped and—using the compass—have oriented the map with the lay of the land. Using both a compass and altimeter they have kept a continuous check on their progress. They know where they are throughout the hike. They miss no opportunities for shortcuts over passes nor miss small lakes for side trips and they know the names of the nearby mountains.

Act I is known as a "bad act" (as in, "Boy, that was a bad act"). Act II is obviously preferable to Act I. Furthermore, it is easy and more fun. This article presents a simplified approach to the use of map, compass, and altimeter which will keep the hiker knowledgeable of his whereabouts and the whereabouts of his objectives.

Orienteering with map and compass should not be an end in itself. It is a tool to get the hiker from point A to point B. In my belief, any tool which is inordinately complicated to use will not be used. Many methods proposed for the use of a compass are very complicated. It has been my experience, though, that the method described in this article, using the compass to orient the map with the lay of the land, is at once simple and will see a hiker through with little or no chance of getting lost.

Your first need is for a good map. The best maps available for showing the topographic features are the maps published by the United States Geological Survey. An index map for the state of

Montana can be obtained free by writing to the USGS at the following address: Distribution Section, Geological Survey, Denver Federal Center, Denver, Colorado 80225. A postcard will reward you with a map of Montana with a grid overlay, each square of the grid bearing a name for the map that it represents. The best maps for hiking purposes are the 7½-minute and 15-minute maps. The 7½-minute maps are gradually replacing the 15-minute maps. The 7½-minute maps are of larger scale and show more detail than the 15-minute maps. The 7½-minute maps are on a scale of 1:24,-000, about 2½ inches to the mile, and the 15-minute maps are on a scale of 1:62,500, about one inch to the mile. Maps of smaller scale, showing more area, are generally not helpful, because the detail is lost. Special maps for the national parks showing all trails are also available. The order form sent with the index map will specify the price of the maps ($1.75-$2.25 each).

A word about trails: Although the USGS topographical quadrangle maps (referred to as "topos" or "quads") are excellent in their pictorial description of topographic features, they do only a fair job of showing the trails. The maps which most completely show the trails are those available from the U.S. Forest Service. These can generally be obtained free by writing the U.S. Forest Service office which has jurisdiction over the area in which you wish to hike. Unfortunately, the U.S. Forest Service maps are otherwise inadequate. They show only the barest suggestion of topographical features. A combination of the two maps is best, if you have the inclination. Otherwise, stick with the USGS topos.

The margin on a USGS topo contains the following information: The name of the quadrangle in the upper and lower right-hand corners: This is taken from a major topographical feature on the map or a major town, (for example, the Helena quadrangle shows Helena, Montana, and surrounding area); the scale, shown in miles, feet, and kilometers; the

contour interval: the distance in altitude between the contour lines which show the hills and valleys on the map; magnetic declination or variation (a graphic drawing showing true and magnetic north); the name of the quadrangles adjacent to the subject quadrangle (these are shown in parentheses on the edges of the map and on the corners); the latitude and longitude in degrees; the date of drawing of the first map and the date of any revision.

This is all very important information. The date of the drawing of the map and any revision will often explain why your trail is not shown on the map. It may have been built after the map was either drawn or revised. The scale is important so that you know the distances that you are traveling. The magnetic declination is important so that you correctly orient the map with the lay of the land. The differences between the contours are important so that you know the height of the ridges and mountains you will be crossing. The names of adjacent quadrangles tell you which quad to use next when the trail leaves the quad you are using. It seems to be a corollary of Murphy's Law that

hikes always require more than one quad.

Roads and other man-made features are shown in black, (dotted, dashed lines, squares); water features are shown in blue (a solid blue line is a perennially running stream, a dotted blue line is an intermittent stream); vegetation features in green; elevation features in brown (thin squiggly lines).

With your index map of Montana, you will receive a booklet published by the USGS entitled "Topographic Maps." This small booklet explains how maps are made, the various sizes of maps available, and contains a complete set of map symbols. These symbols are generally not found in a legend at the bottom of the map. This booklet is well worth reading.

STEPS OF USING A MAP AND COMPASS

First, study your map and the proposed route. This is a matter of 10 to 20 minutes. Do it at home the night before the trip. It is helpful to mark the trail on the map by using either a yellow Hi-

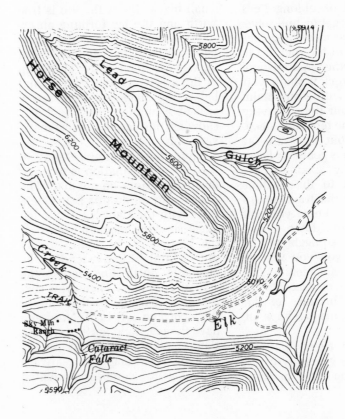

Liter so the map will not be obscured, or using a pencil or pen, being careful not to obscure important features. Then you have no trouble on the hike locating your trail on the map. Next, try to envision what the terrain is going to look like. The map shows forested areas in green shades and clear areas in white. Does your trail go by a stream? Does it cross open spaces? Or is it predominantly in the timber? This knowledge will help you recognize the trail when you hike it. It will help you decide which trail to take. Do you want open vistas? Or do you want a quiet walk in the forest? With your map you can decide in your living room.

Examine the contour lines. These squiggly lines connect places of equal altitude above sea level. If you want to see a graphic representation of contour lines and how they work, get a rock about 4 inches by 6 inches. This will represent a mountain. Looking at the rock from the side, use a felt-tipped pen or a piece of chalk to draw a series of lines around the rock, each line being level and parallel to the others. After you have drawn several of these lines place the rock on a table and look at it from the top. You'll see a series of round or oblong lines like a warped target or bull's-eye. The lines will be closer together where the pitch of the rock is the steepest and farther apart where the pitch of the rock is shallow. It works the same with a mountain. Where the contour lines are very close together, the terrain is steep. Where the contour lines are far apart, the terrain is gentle or level.

Now, carefully examine the trail in relation to the contour lines. Whenever the trail crosses contour lines, you know you will be going up or down. Look closely: a slight squiggle of the trail may show you you will be climbing 100 or 200 feet in altitude. Long climbs or descents are usually obvious because of the switchback or hairpin shape of the trail.

If the contour lines of a particular mountain are generally circular and about the same distance apart on all sides, then you know the mountain will be shaped like a cone or rounded hump. If at the center of the contour lines there are two small series of circles, then you know the mountain has twin peaks. If the contour lines at one end of the mountain are far apart and close together at the other, then the mountain has one gentle slope to the top and a sheer or steep slope down the other side. Obviously, if your goal is to reach the top of the mountain, you will take the gentle slope where the contour lines are farther apart.

Now that you have planned your trip, the second step occurs at the trailhead. Lay your map on the ground and roughly orient it with the features that you can see around you compared to the same features shown on the map. The third step is to orient the map using the compass. This requires understanding what magnetic declination or magnetic deviation is.

Magnetic north is not true north. In most places in the state of Montana the variation from magnetic north is 18° to 20° to the east. At the bottom of your map you will find a triangle with two legs: the vertical leg with the small black star at the top is true north and the leg forming an arrow pointing to the right is magnetic north. The magnetic north leg will also have "MN" at the top of the arrow. To the right of and below the magnetic north arrow will be a number, such as "19°," showing the degrees of magnetic variation.

I find that the simplest way to correct for declination is to draw declination lines on my map. The easiest way to do this is to line a ruler with the right leg of the triangle showing magnetic north at the bottom of the map. Simply draw a straight line extending the magnetic north line across the face of your map. Then draw several lines parallel to that line to the right and left of it. Now you have the magnetic north shown in slanted parallel lines across the face of your map. You always leave your compass oriented

toward true north and simply use the magnetic north lines drawn on your map as if they were true north. This will automatically orient your map in the right direction.

If you are using a Silva compass, then this means that you will almost always use the compass so that magnetic north (represented by "N") is lined up with the arrow showing "DIRECTION OF TRAVEL" on the compass card or base plate. The Silva compasses are the most widely distributed and reasonably priced compasses. They have generally been found to offer the most value for their price in product testing by such organizations as BACK-PACKER magazine.

Now to orient the map: place the straight edge of the base plate of the compass along one of the parallel magnetic-north lines that you have drawn on your map or make sure that your compass needle is parallel to one of the magnetic-north lines. To do this, you will have to orient the map itself. In other words, you have to turn it until the compass, resting on the map, and its needle both point in the magnetic-north direction. You then place the map on the ground, weighting it with stones on the corners if it is windy. You should now have the map and its pictorial description of the topographic features around you in the same position as the features themselves are. The top of the map is pointed true north, the right is east, the left side is west. Now you can tell where you are and where you want to go.

If, for example, you have come to a branch in the stream or a fork in the trail, and if you orient the map so that the pictorial description of the topographic features is in the same position as the features themselves, then it is a simple matter to decide whether you should go right or left on the branch of the stream or fork of the trail. Also, by looking at the direction your trail is going and finding that portion of the trail going in the same direction on your map, you can usually determine where you are. You can then check that determination by seeing where that part of the trail on the map is with relation to the features shown on the map. You then look at the real features around you to confirm your estimate of where you are.

If you have failed (despite my good advice) to mark your map with lines showing magnetic north, then you must compensate for magnetic declination before putting the compass on the map and orienting the map. There are two ways: the first is to align the compass along the right leg of the triangle at the bottom of the map (the one that is an arrow with "MN" at the top). This is the same as lining the compass up with the magnetic-north lines I suggested that you draw on the map. The compass needle will be parallel with the right leg of the triangle. The second method is to subtract the variation shown from 360° (true north) and set the compass accordingly. Example: assuming declination is 19° to the east, set your compass so that the arrow showing "direction of travel" intersects the compass ring at 341° marked on the ring (360° −19° =341°). Or, to state it another way, assume that 341° is true north, orient the map (with the compass on it) so that 341° points to the top of the map and the compass needle points to 360°.

A third dimension which you can add to your orienteering is an altimeter. Altimeters range in price from $13 to over $100. The $13 altimeters are, of course, much less accurate and are not temperature-corrected. However, they seem to be accurate enough for the use I have in mind. You have to remember when using an altimeter to set it every day because the altimeter is the same as a barometer and reacts to changes in pressure caused by the movement of weather systems. This means you must set the altimeter to a known altitude at the beginning of the trip and, having established where you are from time to time on the trip, set it to the altitude shown by the contour lines on your map. The beauty of an altimeter is that by checking your altitude of the various parts of the trail (shown by the contour lines), you can almost always pinpoint precisely where you are on the trail. You now have a number of factors helping you pinpoint your position: the direction of the trail as shown by a properly oriented map, the major topographical features and their relationship to the trail, the positions of streams which cross the trail, and, finally, your altimeter, which helps you select the contour lines crossing the trail. All of these are usually quite sufficient for giving you a clear idea where you are.

I believe that using the compass to carefully orient the map in the same relationship as the topographical features around you will produce the necessary degree of accuracy for happy and carefree hiking. The addition of the altimeter, if you choose to purchase one, should give you more certainty than most hikers would need.

The best way to become skilled in the use of a map and compass following this suggested procedure is to spend a few minutes every hour or so looking at your map, orienting with your compass, as you move up the trail. Try to imagine what the topographic features look like by first examining the map and then see if you can find them. Pretty soon you will be able to have a fair idea by looking at contours the way mountains are shaped and how they look in visual three dimensions. It is particularly helpful to do in an area with which you are quite familiar, so you know where you are and are sure that the contour lines that you pick out on the map do show Sugarloaf Mountain, or whatever. If you have drawn declination lines across the map, then you can keep the map folded to a handy size showing the general area. You can check your heading and location as you walk. Using this method, you will be able to navigate in the summertime or in the wintertime, as shown in the accompanying photo.

Remember the four easy steps to orienteering: (1) Study your map and your proposed route before the hike; (2) at the beginning of the hike orient your map visually with the surrounding topography so that the pictorial description on the map matches the existing natural and manmade features around you; (3) use your compass to orient the map exactly; (4) repeat steps (2) and (3) from time to time as you hike to verify where you are on the trail and to choose which alternative route to take as the alternatives present themselves. Finally, an added tool, giving you a third dimension for locating yourself, is an inexpensive altimeter. Happy hiking!

TRY AN ALTIMETER

by W. S. KALS

My first altimeter was purchased pretty much as a novelty—expensive, but fun to fool with.

Then, one October day, I got completely disoriented bushwhacking through a fir thicket on the shoulder of Table Mountain in the Catskills. It took us eight hours to thrash our way through roughly two miles of this thicket. And it was almost sundown by the time we got out of it. We heard water running down in the valley below us and made our way down to the stream to make camp for the night.

You can imagine my companion's comments when I said, "Hey, that stream is going the wrong way. If we are where I thought we were, it should be flowing the opposite direction." Well, ha ha ha for our navigator. We're lost. We'll figure it out in the morning. In the meantime, let's eat and go to sleep.

Now, this time I had both map and compass with me. But in clawing our way through the fir thicket with its blowdown we could only see at most three feet ahead of ourselves for about eight hours that day. Hence, frequent compass readings could only tell us where the compass directions were—and were useless in telling us where on the map we were at any one time.

In the morning when we tried to locate ourselves on the map, all we could get was one compass bearing. We had a pretty good idea which valley we were in, and we had a fair idea what the mountain peak was that we could see at the end of the valley. But whereabouts in the valley were we? The bright idea occurred to me to get an altimeter reading and to find the contour mark on the map that corresponded to that reading, and where that intersected the stream would be our location. Eureka.

Simple. But all of a sudden I realized that with an altimeter and a compass you could triangulate your position on a contour map, just as you do with two compass bearings. The only difference is that you are using orienting lines on two different planes, a vertical as well as a horizontal plane with your altimeter/compass triangulation, instead of the two orienting lines on a horizontal plane when you use two compass bearings for triangulating.

If this sounds at all confusing, read W. S. Kals's article on using altimeters for finding your way. He's developed it into a science.

W.K.

To some backpackers, an altimeter is a fascinating toy, like Colin Fletcher's thermometer. And, at several times the price, an altimeter is several times more beguiling than a thermometer.

Other backpackers use their altimeters for measuring their progress, for scheduling rest stops and for estimating the amount of time it will take to travel a certain route.

Still other backpackers use their altimeters as navigational aids to locate their position. They set the instrument to the correct elevation at the trailhead and trust the altimeter to show the correct elevation later on. When they come to a point identifiable on a topographic map—a peak, pass or creek crossing—they take the elevation reading on the map as the correct one and

reset their altimeter to that elevation. Most users accept the fact that the altimeter reading almost always differs from the elevation on the map.

But with a thermometer and a little patience, an altimeter can become an accurate navigation tool, especially useful for cross-country travel and route finding in areas where getting a compass bearing is difficult.

SIMPLE USES OF ALTIMETERS

All pocket altimeters are cousins of the aneroid barometers used to forecast weather. Both types of instruments measure changes in air pressure, usually expressed as "inches of mercury." And because air pressure decreases

with altitude, an altimeter's scale can be calibrated in feet or meters to reflect changes in elevation. Like their cousins, the barometers, altimeters need a light tap or two to make the needle read correctly.

Measuring progress. If, when you start your climb, you set the height scale of your altimeter to zero, any later reading will indicate the approximate gain in elevation. When the needle, after a tap or two, is on 1000, you have climbed about 1000 feet. If you know from your map that you must climb 1500 feet altogether and you still can't see the summit, your altimeter lets you know that you have come more than halfway.

Scheduling rest stops. You may want to reward yourself with rests measured by altitude rather than by time. You may decide to break a 3000-foot climb, for instance, into three stretches of about equal gains in elevation. You then rest when the height scale on the altimeter reads 1000 feet, 2000 feet, and when you reach the top.

For going down a mountain or ridge, set the scale so that 10,000 appears under the needle. Then a reading of 9000 would mean you have come down about 1000 feet, and so on.

Estimating time of travel. Everyone has his or her own personal equation for estimating time of travel. It depends on one's style, fitness, load and other factors. Here are calculations suggested by two experts.

Robert S. Wood, in *Pleasure Packing*, figures on covering two miles per hour on flat or mildly descending trails with a moderate load (less than 30 pounds). For each 1000-foot rise, he allows an extra hour. For steeply descending trail sections, he adds one-half hour per 1000 feet.

James R. Wolf, whose climb and descent data for the entire length of the Appalachian Trail appear in volume II of *Hiking the Appalachian Trail*, gives this basic formula: 2.3 miles per hour plus one additional hour for each 700-foot rise. He then allows a maximum correction of 15 percent, plus or minus, for the condition of the trail.

Those are starting points for developing your own equation for travel time. Take into consideration time spent sniffing flowers, taking pictures and other trailside activities.

You won't be far wrong if you reason like this: "Today, with this load, it has taken me 1½ hours to gain the first 1000 feet of elevation. The spacing of the contours on the topo map is about the same for the next 2000 vertical feet. It should take me approximately three more hours to get there."

For such simple uses, the less expensive altimeters are all you need. Most of their scales are marked for 200-foot intervals.

BASIC NAVIGATION WITH ALTIMETERS

For navigation in the mountains, cheap altimeters are unsatisfactory. The trouble is not in their coarse graduations. It is this: these altimeters do not compensate for temperature.

The heart of the instrument, the barometric cell, is supposed to expand in the lower air pressure at higher elevations and contract in the higher pressure at lower elevations. That's the principle of all pocket altimeters. But unfortunately the cell of an inexpensive altimeter also expands when the instrument gets warmer, thus indicating too much altitude. If the instru-

ment gets colder, it indicates too little altitude. (The error may be reversed, however, by the expansion or contraction of other parts of the altimeter.)

The better—and, of course, more expensive—altimeters are made to compensate for temperature changes. Theoretically, that means the needle does not move when you warm or cool the instrument. But to completely compensate for all temperature changes, from summer heat at the bottom of Grand Canyon to blizzard conditions on Mount McKinley, would put the price out of reach. So the better altimeters actually are only fairly well compensated.

If You Want to Know More about Altimeters . . .

The Sportsman's Altimeter/Barometer: A Where, When and Weather Guide by William J. Peet II
This booklet explains in detail how altimeters work, how to use them. Has an entire chapter on using an altimeter to forecast the weather. Available for $2.00 from Peet Bros. Co. Inc., P.O. Box 2007, Ocean, N.J. 07712.

You can increase your altimeter's accuracy by not setting it *inside* a heated hut and then expecting it to show the correct elevation outside. On a cold day the economy models will indicate that you've descended several hundred feet when you've merely stepped out onto the porch.

With a temperature-compensated altimeter, it pays to set the starting elevation as precisely as possible. Some trail guides supply the elevation at the trailhead. If not, you can read it from the topo map.

The intervals between contour lines on topo maps vary with their scale and the steepness of the terrain. Typically, on 7½-minute sheets the contours are 40 feet apart. The interval is printed at the bottom of each map.

If you have cut off the margins of your map to save weight or if you carry only a portion of the map, you still can puzzle out the interval. Look for two numbered and heavily inked contour lines, say the 3200-and 3400-foot lines. If the area between them is divided into five zones—by four lines in lighter ink—the interval is 40 feet. The first line above 3200 indicates 3240, the second 3280, and the last line before 3400 indicates 3360 feet above sea level.

Suppose you have set the altimeter to the correct elevation at the trailhead. You have tapped it and perhaps readjusted it to allow for the jump after you snapped the case closed. The altimeter from now on should show about the

same elevations above sea level as does your map.

Using an altimeter, you need only one point on your topographical map—a creek, trail or single compass bearing—to fix your position.

Example. You have set your altimeter at the confluence of two branches of a creek before the road crosses them at the point marked "1" on the map. A bench mark here reads 3120 feet. (On the original map, which showed contours every 40 feet, you could also have determined the elevation from the contour lines. In this illustration, to keep things simple, contour lines are drawn only at 200-foot intervals.)

You hike along the northern branch of the creek; your altimeter reads 3800. You must be at or near point "2," where the 3800-foot contour crosses the creek.

Example. You are on the trail that enters near the southwest corner of the map. Your altimeter indicates 3600 feet. You must be at or near point "3," where the trail crosses the 3600-foot contour.

Most people know that two accurate compass bearings, with proper allowance for local declination, fix their position. You don't need an altimeter for that. On forest trails, however, you'll seldom have two identifiable landmarks at suitable angles in sight at the same time. You'll be lucky if from time to time you get a glimpse of even one. But you can use that single bearing and your altitude, read from the altimeter, to fix your position.

Example. You are bushwhacking and get a glimpse of a fire tower on the next mountain; it bears 80° True (that is, when corrected for declination); your altimeter now reads 3800 feet. You must be at or near point "4," where the 3800-foot contour crosses the line drawn toward the fire tower.

You get the idea. In each of the above examples, you were at the intersection of two position lines. One position line in each example was the contour line corresponding to your altimeter reading. The other was a line on your topo map—creek, trail or bearing line (drawn or simulated by the edge of your compass).

But remember, *you get the most reliable position when the two lines cross at right angles.* Avoid using lines that cross at small angles; here a small error in calculation mislocates the intersec-

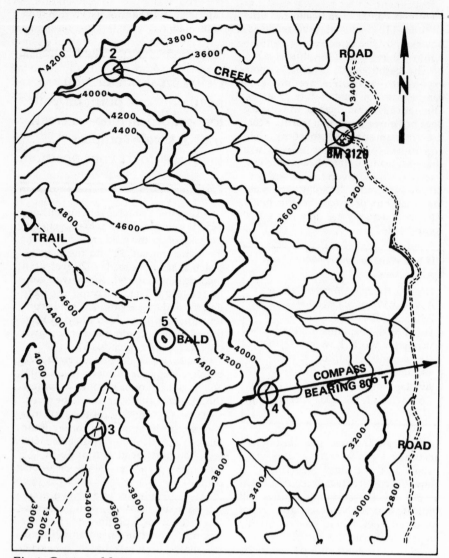

Fig 1. Contour Map

altimeter to that height.

You could have used a peak, a saddle, a fork in the trail or a creek crossing to get the elevation from the topo map. You could also have gotten it from a reliable trail guide or from a sign at a lookout, trail shelter or cross trail.

The more often you reset your altimeter during a hike, the more accurate your readings will be. The process takes only a few moments. It can be done without breaking stride, or it can be combined with a rest stop.

Here is a trick for almost eliminating the effect on your altimeter of changes in barometric pressure or temperature while you are *not* moving. As soon as you arrive at your campsite, read your altimeter and write down your elevation. Stay a few hours, a night or several days. Then, when you are ready to move on, set the altimeter to the elevation indicated on arrival. It will be more accurate than the present reading, which may be off as much as a few hundred feet after just one night.

MORE ACCURATE NAVIGATION WITH ALTIMETERS

Even if you set your altimeter at the start of a hike and several more times a day, you'll notice that at almost every resetting point the instrument is somewhat off. That means that the readings between setting points probably are somewhat off, too. The inaccuracy is unimportant when hiking well-defined trails. But in cross-country travel—especially in places where landmarks are hard to come by—your altimeter is such a useful navigational tool that you want your readings to be as accurate as possible. At the very least, you may want to know what causes even the best altimeter to be off. The answer: mainly the temperature of the air through which you have moved.

Although a temperature-compensated altimeter ignores most changes in temperature, the air through which you are traveling does not. As air gets colder, it gets heavier and registers more pressure on your

Weather and humidity, as well as altitude, can change an altimeter's reading. With a thermometer and a little calculation, you can minimize the error.

tion by a considerable distance. (This rule is not new to you if you have used it whenever you crossed two compass bearings to find your position.)

You may wonder why I said "at or near point so-and-so" in each of the examples. The reason is that no pocket altimeter is absolutely accurate; in every one there is likely to be an error resulting from incomplete temperature compensation or the inevitable margin of error in plotting compass bearings.

That error is likely to be small. Much more important is that this method of measuring heights assumes—among other things—that the barometric pressure in your area will remain the same after you set your altimeter. And everybody knows that the barometric pressure changes with the weather. In one hour the change in air pressure probably will be small. But the longer the time elapsed between setting the altimeter to a known elevation and taking a reading, the greater the possibility of error.

Surveyors leave a barometer at a base station and later correct their elevations to account for changes in barometric pressure. (You may have read in BP-10 that Mount Le Conte in the Great Smoky Mountains was named after the man who supplied readings of a barometer in a valley while another scientist, Samuel Buckley, climbed to the mountain's summit.)

How can a backpacker solve the problem of change in barometric pressure? It's simple. Keep the elapsed time between settings of your altimeter as short as possible. Whenever you come to a point where the elevation is clearly discernible—a stream crossing, mountaintop or trail junction—reset your altimeter.

Example. While hiking on the trail shown on the map, you see the open area marked point "5." You climb to it for the view. You notice that on the map it's the only isolated spot roundabout that rises to 4600 feet. You reset your

Getting to Know Your Altimeter

A good way to get acquainted or reacquainted with your altimeter is to take it for an automobile ride through mountains with someone else doing the driving.

If comfort permits, use neither heater nor air conditioner, keep a window open, and don't let the sun shine on the altimeter. Set the instrument at your starting point. Then watch for places along the road where the elevation is posted. Mountain passes are good reference points. In many states an elevation appears on the sign announcing town or city limits. (Since this elevation is not that of the exact spot where the sign is posted but probably of the post office or city hall when the town was first surveyed, disregard signs for localities that slope.)

When you find a posted elevation, write it down along with the reading from your altimeter. Even the best altimeter will show some differences. The main reason for the differences is that the temperature where you are traveling is likely to differ from the one assumed in the calibration of all altimeters, that of the "standard atmosphere." Here is what you must expect:

When the temperature of the air you passed through was *colder* than the standard atmosphere, whether you were going up or down, the altitude difference shown by your altimeter between reference points will be *too great*. When the temperature of the air you passed through was *warmer* than the standard atmosphere, whether you were going up or down, the altitude difference shown by your altimeter between reference points will be *too small*.

You can measure air temperature by holding a thermometer out the window—on the shady side—while the car is moving. For comparison, here are temperatures in the standard atmosphere used to calibrate altimeters:

Sea level	59°F	Sea level	15°C
2000 feet	52	1000 meters	8.5
4000 feet	45	2000 meters	2
6000 feet	38	3000 meters	−4.5
8000 feet	31	4000 meters	−11
10,000 feet	23		
12,000 feet	16		

As in walking, you can minimize the effect of change in atmospheric pressure resulting from changing weather by resetting the altimeter approximately every hour. But by traveling in an automobile you can be moving rapidly toward higher (or lower) pressure systems, an effect that is negligible when you walk.

instrument; as air gets warmer, it gets lighter and registers less pressure.

"Cold" and "warm" are relative terms. So all altimeters are calibrated for a standard temperature at sea level—59°F (15°C)—and a standard drop in temperature with elevation gain.

On any given day it is most unlikely that the temperature where you are is exactly what the standard calibration assumes it to be. Whether the air is warmer or colder after you have climbed exactly 1000 feet from where you last set your altimeter, your instrument will indicate an altitude reading that differs from the map.

If the air through which you climbed averaged 20°F warmer than the standard, the altimeter will indicate a 960-foot gain instead of a 1000-foot gain. If the air was 20° colder than the standard, it will indicate a 1040-foot gain. (In metric units: If you climbed exactly 1000 meters and the air was 10° warmer than the standard, your altimeter will indicate only 965 meters. If the air was 10° colder than the standard, it will indicate 1035 meters.)

A 40-foot error in a 1000-foot climb may not make much difference to you. It merely puts you on the next contour line on a 7½-minute topo map. But the higher you go after setting the altimeter, the greater the error. In 3000 feet, you'd be three contours off.

It is possible to calculate the correction to apply to the reading of an altimeter to determine true elevation above sea level. A surveyor, for instance, would measure the temperature and amount of water vapor at the setting point and at the reading point. (Altimeters are calibrated for zero moisture content of the air.) Later, in the office, the correction would be figured out on a calculator.

Does this mean that for accurate use of your altimeter you need to pack, besides a thermometer, a humidity-measuring instrument and a pocket calculator as well? The answer is no, and you don't even have to do much arithmetic. For BACKPACKER readers I have worked out a graphic method that eliminates most calculations. You'll do only one multiplication (never more than a two-place figure times a two-place figure); it will provide a single correction for nonstandard temperature which includes an allowance for average humidity.

Before making the calculation, take the temperature at the point where you set the altimeter to a known height—the set point—and again at the point where you read the altimeter—the read point. A thermometer will add one ounce to your load and costs about $5.00.

You want the *air* temperature, so don't lay the thermometer on a hot rock or cool moss, and don't let the sun heat it. The best procedure is to make a loop from a piece of string to fit your hand, attach the other end of the string to the eye at the end of the thermometer, and whirl the thermometer in front of you for a minute.

Once you have the four measurements—two temperature readings and two altimeter readings—you can make the calculation.

Example. At the set point the elevation was 4000 feet, the air temperature 70°F. Make a mark at 4000 on the left, or height, scale of the graph. Make another mark at 70 on the middle, or temperature, scale.

At the read point the elevation is 6000 feet on your altimeter, the air temperature 64°F on the thermometer. Mark 6000 on the height scale and 64 on the temperature scale.

Now mark a point halfway between the two heights and another halfway between the two temperatures. Draw a line through these points, or lay your thermometer case or another straight edge across them; the point where the line meets the scale on the right is the proper correction for 1000 feet—in this case, +59 feet.

Because you have climbed from 4000 to 6000 feet, or 2000 feet, you must double the correction: 2 × +59 = 118. The plus sign indicates that this correction should be added to the altimeter reading. Your corrected altimeter reading, therefore, is 6118 feet.

(When the figures are not so conveniently round, you can get the altitude gain by counting the marks on the altimeter dial between the set point and read point. If you arrive at a count of 1800 feet, multiply +59 by 1.8. The margin of the topo map is a handy place to multiply.)

The plus and minus signs on the correction scale are for climbing, that is, for situations when the read point is higher than the set point. When you are descending and the read point is lower than the set point, reverse the signs. Read minus for the plus sign, and plus for the minus sign.

Example. You are going down a ridge. You started at 6000 feet (set point) and now read 4000 feet on your altimeter. The temperature was 64°; it now is 70°. The graph shows that the correction per 1000 feet is −59 feet. The final correction (for a 2000-foot loss) is *minus* 118 feet. The corrected altimeter reading: 4000 − 118 = 3882 feet. Of course, it's silly to talk about two feet when the finest calibrations on your altimeter are 20 feet and there are small errors still present. So round off the figure and call your elevation 3880 feet.

ALTIMETER CORRECTION CHARTS

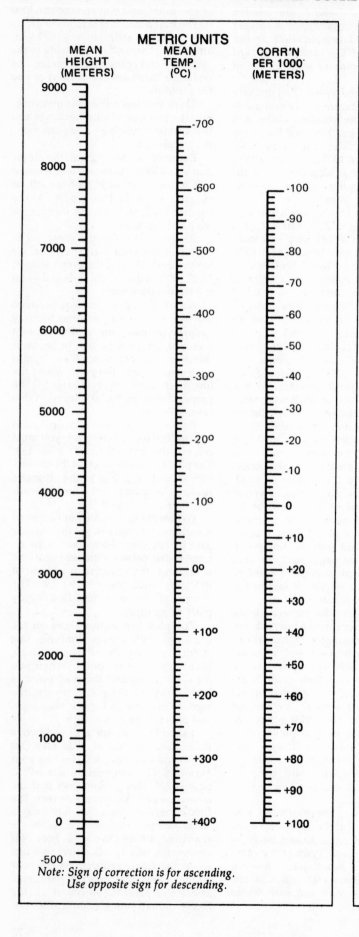

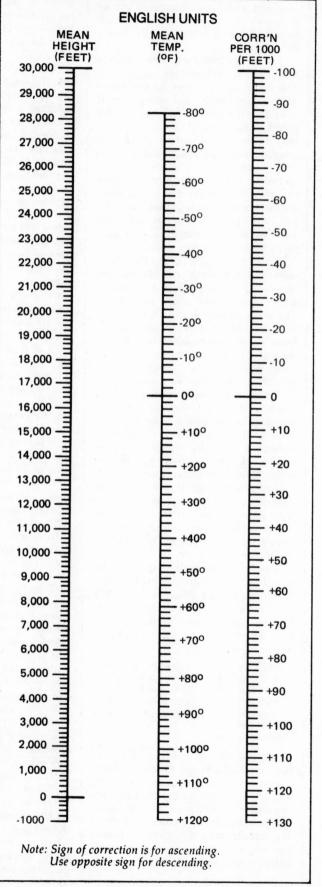

Note: Sign of correction is for ascending.
Use opposite sign for descending.

Note: Sign of correction is for ascending.
Use opposite sign for descending.

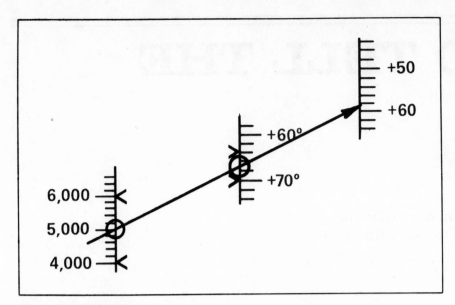

Fig 2. Small Scale

Mathematically inclined readers may prefer a slightly different method. Instead of marking the heights and temperatures at set and read points and halving the distance between them, you can write down the data and find the means.

Example: Set point: 10,000 feet, 53°F; read point: 13,000 feet, 43°F. Mean height: $10,000 + 13,000 = 23,000 \div 2 = 11,500$ feet. Mean temperature is $53 + 43 = 96 \div 2 = 48°$.

As in the graphic method, connect 11,500 on the *Mean Height* scale with 48 on the *Mean Temperature* scale. A connecting line will point to +66 feet on the *Correction per 1000 feet* scale. The elevation gain was 3000 feet, so multiply the correction by 3: $3 \times 66 = 198$ feet. Round it off to +200 feet. The corrected altimeter reading is 200 plus 13,000—13,200 feet.

Example. You started out at 13,000 feet and descended to an altimeter reading of 10,000 feet. The temperature was 43°; it now is 53°. The +200 foot correction becomes −200, and your corrected elevation is 10,000 less 200—9800 feet.

When you use an altimeter with its altitude scale in the metric system, use a thermometer calibrated in degrees Celsius and find the correction on the metric graph. The method is exactly the same as for English units.

You can find out just how much more accurate my method is, compared to using uncorrected altimeter readings, by using the graphs to doublecheck well-known elevations.

Using a graph and making a simple calculation is well worth the trouble when you need as accurate an elevation reading as possible. The process could mean the difference between arriving at an impassable ravine or finding the trail home. ☙

HOW TO TELL THE STARS

by W. S. KALS

A new, simple method for identifying
stars, telling time by them, and finding
directions at night

*Stars were the traditional navigation aids of
sailors until just a few years ago. Though they
have also been used by travelers on land, this
has never been so common as for sailors.*

*Still, if you are really lost, say for several
days, and do not have a compass, you can get
your rough orientation by identifying some celestial bodies. The North Star, of course, is the
obvious one. W. S. Kals, in the following article, has a simplified method which would be of
help under these circumstances.*

W.K.

If you find "How to Tell the
Stars" intriguing, you can find a
much more complete presentation
in the author's book, *How To
Read The Night Sky* (New York:
Doubleday, 1974). It will add 13
ounces to your pack and lighten
your wallet by $6.

A KNOWLEDGE OF THE STARS and
planets will enrich your backpacking
experiences, just as will knowing
about plants and birds. An understanding of the orderly motion of the
sky can even be useful for telling time
and determining direction.

For thousands of years star lore
concentrated on constellations, the
patterns of stars. There are a lot of
them—88 by official count. Many are
hard to remember. Few resemble the
beasts, things or people for which
they are named. They often are difficult to find, especially when they lie
on their sides as they rise or set in
the sky. Result: Few people can identify more than three constellations.

I have a different approach for

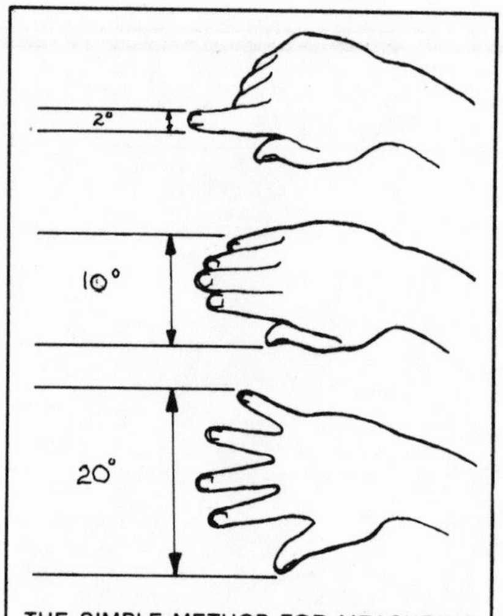

THE SIMPLE METHOD FOR MEASURING
DEGREES OF LATITUDE.

learning to identify the stars. Instead
of concentrating on *patterns* of
stars—sometimes quite dim stars—
the system is based on the *brightest*
stars. There aren't many of them.
Only 15 first-magnitude stars can be
seen everywhere in the northern
hemisphere between the tropics and
the arctic circle. Six more become
visible at times in the southernmost
part of the area.

These are all "fixed" stars. That is,
they do not move in relation to their
neighbors. Additionally, you may see
up to five planets that look like bright
stars. The planets change position
among the fixed stars.

The 15 first-magnitude stars are
identified—the brightest the most
prominently—on the star chart on
page 45. The horizontal line at zero
is the celestial equator. Scales, in degrees, appear at the right and left
sides. (What would be north or south
latitude on a map is called declination by astronomers.)

You can measure degrees in the
sky to locate the stars without any
special equipment.

Here is the way you do it: At arm's
length the width of your hand, with
the fingers and thumb together,
covers 10 degrees in the sky. At the
same distance, each of your fingers
covers two degrees. And the span of
your spread hand—between the tip of
the thumb and the little finger—
covers 20 degrees. Using this system,
you can take the measurements from
the left or right margin of the star
chart and transfer them to the sky by
using your hands.

For example, Deneb is about 30

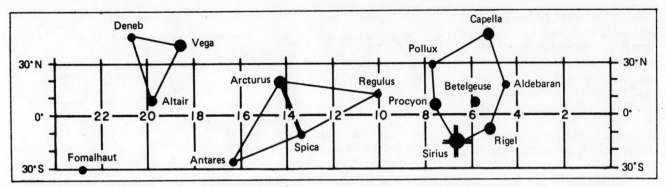

These are the 15 brightest stars visible in the northern temperate zone. Fourteen of them have been arranged in three superconstellations. The degree scales on the left and right margins of the chart will enable you to measure the angle between any two stars. The degrees can be measured off in the sky with your hand. The horizontal line in the chart's center is the celestial equator; the numbers along it label the vertical hour lines. Both are used to align the chart with the sky.

THE PLANETS

The five planets you can see with the naked eye look like bright stars. Star charts don't show them. If they did, the charts would soon be out of date because the planets keep moving among the fixed stars.

Mercury is seldom seen. It is visible for only a few days or weeks, always low on the horizon, either in the east just before sunrise or in the west shortly after sunset. Sailors who know Mercury's period of visibility sometimes wait years before spotting it. Clouds near the horizon regularly interfere.

Venus is easy to see and to identify. It is by far the brightest starlike object in the sky. As a morning star, it appears in an easterly direction up to three hours before sunrise; as an evening star, it can be seen in a westerly direction up to three hours after sunset. Venus must get tired of being the last star to disappear in the morning and the first to appear in the evening, for it takes regular vacations that sometimes last for several months. Here is Venus' schedule from 1976 to 1980:

1976   P.M. after beginning of August
1977   P.M. to end of March
      A.M. mid-April to end of November
1978   P.M. April to October
      A.M. after mid-November

1979   A.M. to mid-July
      P.M. after mid-October
1980   P.M. to beginning of June
      A.M. after end of June

Saturn moves so slowly among the stars that it's easy to find even when you haven't seen the sky for months. Between 1976 and 1979 it will move only from the vicinity of Pollux to that of Regulus.

Jupiter seems to try to catch up with Saturn but never quite makes it. Until 1980 it always will be west (right) of Saturn. Jupiter is the brighter of the two planets, at least as bright as the brightest fixed star.

Some people claim they can always recognize Mars from its reddish color. But Antares is almost as red, and every two years or so it and Mars appear together. Additionally, Mars is sometimes brighter than Jupiter; at other

times it's no brighter than Polaris. At any rate, it always will be near the curve on the star chart.

Mars returns to the same place among the stars in a little less than two years (22.6 months). Like Jupiter and Saturn it moves most of the time eastward—left, in the Northern hemisphere—against the background of the fixed stars. But near its period of greatest brightness, when it is about south of you at midnight, it stalls, moves westward for a while and stalls again before resuming its normal eastward motion.

Mars is dimmest when it appears nearest the sun in the sky. That is, low in the west just after sunset, or low in the east just before sunrise. Between its last appearance in the western sky and its reappearance in the eastern, it is hidden by the glare of the sun for a few months.

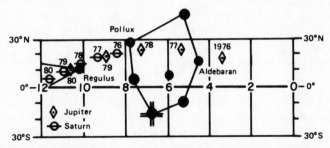

The planets Jupiter and Saturn look like bright stars. Unlike stars, however, they change their position. The chart shows their position at midyear for the next four years. In the first half of each year they will be a little west (right) of the marked location; in the second half, east (left).

degrees from Vega. In the sky you will find these stars three hands apart. Or you first can measure the stars in the sky with your hands and then check the measurements on the star chart.

The labels along the equator of the star chart, which on a map would be in degrees of longitude, are in hours. These correspond to the meridians in the sky which astronomers call "hour circles."

To make the brightest stars easier to remember—the ones visible everywhere in the area—I have arranged 14 of them into three superconstellations.

On the right near the six o'clock line is Betelgeuse, pronounced BED-uhl-jooz. (Its reddish tint may be the reason that sailors dubbed it "beetle juice.") Around Betelgeuse is a rough hexagon of stars measuring two or three hands on a side.

To help remember them, I think of a fastidious ship's captain. The first mate reports to him, "Captain, all de rigging seems properly polished." That gives me, clockwise from the right: Capella (kuh-PELL-uh), Aldebaran (AL-de-buh-ruhn), Rigel (RYE-jel), Sirius (SEE-ree-uhs), Procyon (PHRO-see-uhn) and Pollux (POL-luhks).

Between 10^h and 16^h I have drawn a double triangle (each half measuring three hands by five hands) formed by four stars. To remember their names, I think of broccoli being served to the impossible captain. Its ingredients: Regular spices and arsenic. That reminds me of Regulus (REG-gyou-luhs), Spica (SPY-kuh), Antares (an-TARE-eez) and Arcturus

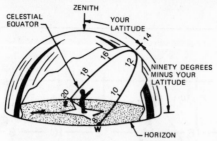
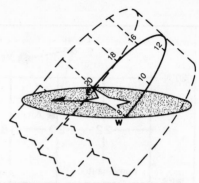

To fit the star chart to the sky, you must first locate the celestial equator in the sky. To do this, face due south. Then, using your hand, measure down from the zenith the number of degrees in your latitude (or subtract your latitude from 90 degrees and measure up from the southern horizon). Point to the spot just found in the sky and swing your arm from right to left to the horizon. The arc traced in the sky by your hand will be the celestial equator.

(ark-TOO-ruhs).

Near 20^h I have drawn a nearly equilateral triangle measuring three hands on a side. I remember the stars in the triangle by the newspaper headline following the arrest of the cook: "Vegetable Alteration Denied." That gives me Vega (VEE-gah), Altair (al-TARE) and Deneb (DEN-eb).

Only one of the 15 stars, Fomalhaut (FOH-muhl-hot), is left out of the three superconstellations.

FITTING THE STAR CHART TO THE SKY

Once you become familiar with the superconstellations, they are simple to remember and find. In the meantime, the star chart will allow you to

Imagine the star chart curved so that its celestial equator lies over the line you have traced in the sky. Only half of the chart will be above your horizon showing the stars visible now. What astronomers call "local star time" determines which hour line on the chart should be due south of you. In the diagram, the chart is aligned for a local star time of 14^h.

find them anywhere in the area and for any date and time of night.

To do this, you need to know south, your latitude and what astronomers call "local star time." (Local star time indicates how much time has elapsed since a reference point in the sky—the vernal equinox—has passed due south of you.) A simple way to find all three uses Polaris (PO-lah-ruhs) and stars that appear nearby.

You probably know how to find Polaris—the Pole Star or North Star. You look for the best-known of all star patterns, the Big Dipper. A line through the two stars farthest from the handle of the dipper leads to Polaris. Its distance from the nearer

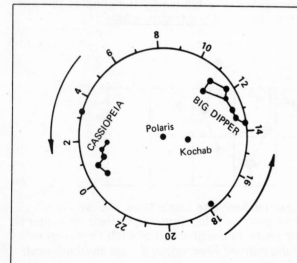

HOW TO TELL TIME FROM THE STARS

Here's a simple method of telling time from the stars: Imagine Polaris as the center of an ordinary clock. Kochab (KOH-kab), the star 1½ hands from Polaris and of approximately the same brightness, makes the tip of the hour hand. Like other stars, it turns counterclockwise around Polaris once every 24 hours. That's half the speed of an ordinary clock hand. To get elapsed time, you merely double the hours Kochab seems to have moved backward around the clock face. For instance, suppose you turn in at 9 P.M. and see Kochab to the right of Polaris in the three o'clock position. During the night you see Kochab directly above Polaris in the twelve o'clock spot. The difference is three hours; doubling that provides the elapsed time—six hours. And six hours past 9 P.M. means that the time is three o'clock in the morning.

How To Find Local Star Time: Alternative Method

To fit the star chart to the sky, you need to know your local star time, i.e. how much time has elapsed since the vernal equinox has passed due south of you. (It passes due south of you every 23 hours and 56 minutes.)

There are two methods for telling local star time. The simplest uses the North Star and the constellations that appear nearby (see the text on page 80). But it works only when you can see the northern sky.

The second method will work anywhere. Here's how: Use the table (right) to determine the approximate local star time for midnight. On March 20, for example, the local star time at midnight is about 12^h. (The table applies to any standard time zone.)

If you want local star time for any time other than midnight, simply add hours after midnight or subtract hours before midnight. On the same date at 5 A.M., five hours after midnight, star time is $12 + 5 = 17^h$; at 7 P.M., five hours before midnight, the star time is $12 - 5 = 7^h$. Sometimes a morning calculation may provide a nonsense figure. For instance, at 5 A.M. on September 6 the addition $23 + 5 = 28^h$, and there's no such star time. But remembering that 24^h and 0^h are the same thing, you deduct 24^h. Therefore, the correct answer is that local star time is $28 - 24 = 4^h$. At other times subtraction will seem impossible. At 7 P.M. on November 20, five hours before midnight, you'd get $4 - 5^h$. To avoid that, borrow 24^h and add it to the star time before you subtract: $4 + 24 = 28^h$. Then the local star time will be $28 - 5 = 23^h$.

When daylight time is in effect, you must subtract one hour to get standard time. You can subtract it from the time your watch shows or from the star time. For example, at midnight on June 21 local star time will be 17^h, not 18^h. Or, on the same date, 4 A.M. daylight saving time is only 3 A.M. standard time, so star time then is about 21^h. These calculations become quite automatic after you've done them a few times.

The times in all these calculations are approximate, for the same midnight star time is used for about a week. Also, for a precise calculation, local time should be used instead of standard time. To keep an entire state, province or country on the same standard time, that half-hour limit is exceeded in some areas. But even in such areas the star time calculated from the table will be accurate enough for aligning the star chart to spot the superconstellations and identify the brightest stars.

Day of month	1-7	8-15	16-23	24-end
Jan.	7	7½	8	8½
Feb.	9	9½	10	10½
Mar.	11	11½	12	12½
Apr.	13	13½	14	14½
May	15	15½	16	16½
June	17	17½	18	18½
July	19	19½	20	20½
Aug.	21	21½	22	22½
Sep.	23	23½	0	½
Oct.	1	1½	2	2½
Nov.	3	3½	4	4½
Dec.	5	5½	6	6½

Local star time for approximately midnight (standard time) for any date

You can get approximate local star time at midnight on any date of the year from this table. (It is based on standard time and can be used in any time zone. For daylight saving time, subtract one hour.) For any other time of night, add hours after midnight to the star time; subtract hours before midnight. For example: On November 20 at midnight, local star time is about 4^h. At 2 A.M., two hours later, it is 6^h; at 10 P.M., two hours earlier, local star time is 2^h.

pointer is three hands. Polaris, a second-magnitude star, is about as bright as the pointers and is the only such star in the vicinity. Because Polaris is always due north, the opposite direction is, of course, south.

You can find your latitude by measuring the distance between Polaris and your horizon. For example: At latitude 40 degrees north, Polaris will be two hand spans above the north horizon. Since there are 90 degrees between the zenith—the point directly above you—and the horizon, you also can measure from the zenith down to Polaris and subtract that from 90 degrees to find your latitude when the north horizon is obstructed.

Polaris appears to stand still, but the stars near it seem to turn around it because of the Earth's rotation. That allows you to get local star time from Polaris. To do this, turn the star chart on page 47 until the Big Dipper and Cassiopeia (kass-i-UH-pee-uh) match their position in the sky. The chart shows a local star time of 8^h. If you had to turn the page 90 degrees to the left (the handle of the Dipper would be above Polaris), local star time would be 14^h.

Finally, to fit the star chart to the sky, you need to find the celestial equator. Here's how: 1) Face south. 2) Measure your latitude down from the zenith or subtract your latitude from 90 degrees and measure up from the horizon. Mark that spot mentally by some star or the space between two stars. 3) With outstretched arm, point to the spot just found. 4) Swing your arm from the horizon at the right (west) up through the measured high spot (south) and down to the horizon at the left (east). The arc of your hand was the celestial equator.

Now align that arc with the celestial equator on the star chart.

Next, find the hour line on the chart which corresponds to the local star time you found (14^h in the example). Finally, move the chart right or left until that hour line is due south of you. In the example, the 14^h line would be straight up and down in the sky and running through the celestial equator to the zenith. The point on the chart marked 8^h—exactly six hours to the right on the equator—would be due west on your horizon.

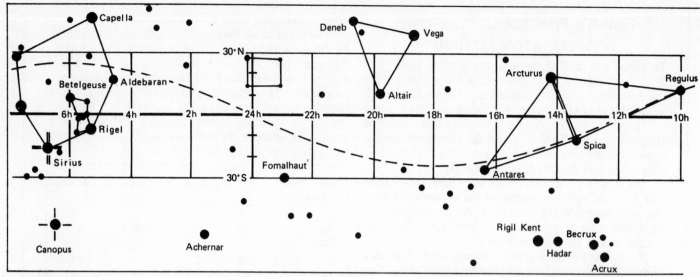

This star chart shows all the stars you are likely to see on a full-moon night except these on the Polaris and local star time chart. The larger the dot, the brighter the star. The dotted curve is the path Mars, Jupiter,

And the point marked 20ʰ—six hours to the left—would be due east on the horizon.

The Polaris method for finding south, your latitude and local star time works only when you can see the northern sky. If you're camped on a south slope, determine south from your compass, allowing in the usual way for declination if it is more than a few degrees. Next, find your latitude on the right or left margin of your hiking map. Only the degrees are needed. (The same figure will do for several nights even if you have covered a lot of ground; it changes only by one degree for every 69 miles [111 km] you walk north or south.) Then, determine the approximate local star time by using the alternate method described on page 79.

After doing this a few times, you won't need to find local star time but will be able to align the chart by looking at the stars themselves.

MORE STARS

The star chart below shows more stars than the 15 brightest ones. In the hexagon there is Castor (KAS-tor), the twin of Pollux. It's two fingers west (right) of Pollux and barely misses qualifying for first-magnitude status.

In addition to the stars that make up the superconstellations in the northern temperate zone, this star chart shows the six first-magnitude (brightest) stars that become visible south of latitude 35 degrees north. Also shown are several second-magnitude stars: Castor, the twin of Pollux, and the stars that make up the Square of Pegasus and the constellation Orion. The three central stars of Orion are directly on the chart's celestial equator. Whenever Orion is visible, the line you trace in the sky with your arm should go right through them.

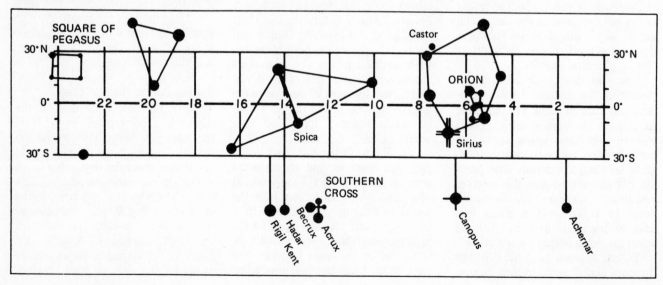

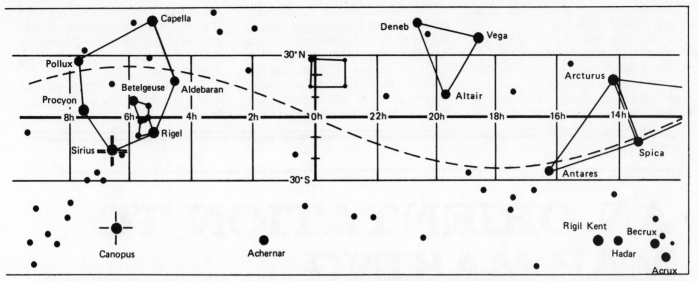

and Saturn follow as they wander among the stars. All stars and hour lines appear twice on the chart. To align the chart with the sky, use the hour line nearest the fold.

In the same area I have added the outline of Orion, one of the best-known constellations. The three stars between Betelgeuse and Rigel—the "belt" of Orion—are virtually on the celestial equator. That fact lets you check on your positioning of the star chart whenever Orion is visible: The celestial equator should go right through the belt. Another helpful fact is that whenever you see Orion set on the horizon, the three stars accurately will indicate true west. And if you recognize Orion when it rises, you'll have an accurate east. This holds true anywhere from the Arctic to the Antarctic.

Near the left margin of the star chart I have placed a rough square formed by four dimmer stars, the Square of Pegasus (PEG-uh-suhs). Its western (right) edge is on the same hour line as Fomalhaut, the first-magnitude star that fails to fit into a superconstellation. That means that Fomalhaut will be south of you whenever the right edge of the Square is due south. At all other times it will be roughly in the direction of that edge, a little more than two spans below it.

I have also added the six first-magnitude stars that become visible only after you travel south of about 35 degrees north. The only one that ever will appear brightly is Canopus (kuh-NOH-puhs). Theoretically it should shine briefly on the southern horizon at about latitude 37 degrees

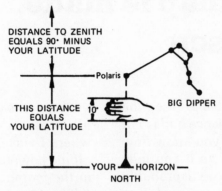

Distances in the sky can be measured by using your hand. At arm's length the width of your hand, with the fingers together, covers 10 degrees in the sky. Each finger covers 2 degrees, and the span of your spread hand covers 20 degrees. Using your hand, you can find your latitude by measuring the distance between Polaris and your horizon. At latitude 40 degrees north, for example, Polaris will always be four hands (or two spans) above the north horizon. If the northern horizon is obstructed, you can measure from the zenith down to Polaris and subtract that from 90 degrees to find your latitude (50 degrees in the example). Since Polaris is always due north of you, south is in exactly the opposite direction.

north. But near the horizon all stars appear dimmer than they do higher in the sky. The same effect makes the rising and setting sun less bright—and redder—than at other times. Canopus is the second brightest fixed star (Sirius is the brightest). To see Canopus as a first-magnitude star, you must be no farther north than latitude 33 degrees north. There it will appear barely above the southern horizon when Sirius bears south. As you travel farther south, Canopus will get a finger or so higher for every additional two degrees of latitude. In latitude 25 degrees north, it will be one hand above the horizon when Sirius bears south.

At latitude 25 degrees north, four more first-magnitude stars will appear one or two fingers above the southern horizon when Spica bears south (local star time, about 13½ʰ). But they will look like second-magnitude stars. To raise them higher above the horizon and make them appear brighter, you have to travel farther south. The four stars: Rigil Kent (RYE-jel KENT)—also known as Alpha Centauri—Hadar (HA-dar) or Beta Centauri, Becrux (BAY-kruhks) and Acrux (AK-ruhks). Becrux and Acrux help form the constellation Crux, the Southern Cross.

Achernar (AK-uhr-nar), the last of the six first-magnitude stars, doesn't look that bright even at latitude 25 degrees north. There it will be less than four fingers above your southern horizon, bearing south when local star time is about 1½ʰ.

To summarize the use of the star chart: 1) Find approximate south, opposite Polaris or by compass. 2) Find your approximate latitude from Polaris (in spans, hands and fingers) or from the right or left margin of a map.

3) Determine approximate local star time from the constellations around Polaris or from the alternate method described on page 79. 4) Trace the equator in the sky. 5) Imagine the star chart bowed over the sky so that its equator falls on the line you just traced. 6) Mentally slide the star chart

left or right until your local star time is south. 7) If you recognize a bright star bearing south, slide the chart to match it without bothering about local star time.

It all sounds a lot more difficult than it is. With a little practice you'll be surprised at your proficiency. ☛

AN ORIENTATION TO MAP MAKING

To know how to use a map, you should know how a map is made.

by GARY BRAASCH

There is no substitute to being able to "read the land." This takes years of experience and is not fail-safe in all situations. But if you know how to do it, and you do get lost—even if you misread the land a time or two, you'll probably ultimately read it right and get reoriented.

There was a time in Snowdonia National Park in Wales that I recall getting lost. I had no map or compass with me. Nor did I have sufficient food for more than a day. However, I could read the land and when I took stock of my situation I could see that I could no doubt survive without food if I had to for several days. I had a plentiful supply of water in the mountain streams and, while I was not sufficiently clad for comfort, I knew my clothes could keep me warm enough to survive a night or even more. I did misread the land the first couple of times and I estimate I walked about ten miles out of my way by following the wrong ridge. But before dark I had made my way to the top of a third ridge and suddenly knew where I was; from that point it was just a matter of putting one foot in front of the other.

There was a real thrill in my getting lost and all of a sudden realizing that I did not know where I was. I had been busy taking photos of alpine flowers and had apparently taken a fork in the footpath that had not been on the maps I'd used to plan my hike that day. Hence, when I'd expected to come down off Lliwedd Mountain and to my inn, I discovered there was not the slightest landmark that was at all familiar. I told myself that I was going to allow myself the full advantage of being lost. And I was going to take in this experience to its fullest. I did enjoy it, though I was very tired that night and I was too late for dinner when I did get to the inn.

While, as I say, the only way you can get skilled at reading the land is by hiking a great deal and trying to find your route with map and compass (and not a guide book!), a knowledge of how maps are made can also be a help.

Gary Braasch's article is very informative.

W.K.

Org, the pithecanthrope, didn't have a map when he first ventured from his cave. Nor did Caesar as he led his legions into far Gaul. Cabot, Columbus, Burton, Amundsen, Lewis and Clark, all wandered with the sketchiest of charts to guide them.

Today, the average backpacker would sooner leave his boots at home than forget the map.

The age of discovery has passed. It may be true that much land remains to be viewed intimately for the first time, but even Armstrong, Aldrin, and Collins were preceded by Ranger and Surveyor cameras. Modern Man wandering over territory new to him has the benefit (some would say crutch) of excellent relief maps based on aerial photography that leaves little of the lay of the land in mystery. There are a few exceptions, especially in northern North America and even in some of the Lower Forty-eight states. But generally the number and variety of maps available is overwhelming.

Twenty-two federal agencies publish about 40 different types of charts. They range from the familiar topographic maps of the U.S. Geological Survey and weather charts of the National Weather Service to more obscure layouts of ground conductivity, buried treasure and minor governmental divisions, to name only a few. The biggest names in government mapping are the Library of Congress and National Archives collections (historic maps), the Defense Mapping Agency (which now handles the army's superb world and foreign-nation charts), and the Geological Survey (U.S.G.S.), an agency of the Interior Department.

The U.S.G.S. is the prime producer of maps on which so much of the nation's scientific, informational and recreational data is affixed. In addition to nearly 40,000 different topo maps, the U.S.G.S. issues state base, shaded relief, water and mineral resource, geologic and river survey maps. It prints maps from many other agencies. Recently, it has issued special publications on the Moon and Antarctica, and even an Atlas of Volcanic Phenomena. Because hikers make large use of Geological Survey charts, this agency will be emphasized in this article.

A major tributary of the modern map stream issues from local and private cartographers. Every state and most cities issue information in map form on highways, recreation areas and re-

sources. At least 27 major firms in this country and Great Britain produce and distribute maps of interest to the public: political maps, wall maps, school maps, Bible maps, ski maps, vacation maps— a staggering production.

Several firms produce plastic relief maps, including quadrangles and inch-to-four-mile jobs that can make planning a backpacking trip a visual experience beyond all reasonable need. Hundreds of mapping companies do topographic work under contract.

Foreign countries have their own government cartographic agencies, the most important being those of Britain, France, Switzerland, the USSR and Japan. In Canada, surveyors and draftsmen work for the Department of Energy, Mines and Resources. In Mexico, mapping is done by the Dirección General de Geografía y Meteorología.

All this because, in the million years or so between Org and the "one small step" onto the Moon, Man has never lost his desire to know "where the heck I *am*" and to let everyone in on it once he finds out. The Romans followed itinerary-type maps as they traveled the *via*; so hikers use trail guidebooks Aristagoras's brass plate map convinced the Spartans it was too far to march to Persia; backpackers think twice about attempting a climb over stacks of contour lines.

In the United States, modern mapping is generally believed to have begun with the Lewis and Clark Expedition. After that, military survey crews were out nearly every season. The Coast Survey (forerunner of the Coast and Geodetic Survey, now the National Ocean Survey) was established in 1807. The U.S. Army Corps of Topographical Engineers (which also went through name changes on its way to becoming a part of the Defense Mapping Agency) began operations six years later. Many states had their own geological surveys begun in 1867 with the Fortieth Parallel Survey from Colorado to California. Three other major western surveys followed.

In 1879 the Geological Survey was established for the purpose of itemizing the mineral wealth of the public lands and producing a national geologic map. There was no mention of topographic mapping in the U.S.G.S. charter, but leaders felt a standard series of relief maps was needed in order to make the geologic chart. So accurate was this topo work that it soon assumed an importance of its own. In 1888 Congress

appropriated the first money solely for relief maps. A year later, the U.S.G.S. got permission to sell them to the public —and the Survey's most widely renowned public service was under way.

Early maps were at 1:250,000 scale with 200-foot contours, painstakingly hand drawn by surveyors and artists in the field who clambered up to high vantage points to view as much land as possible at once. As more people wanted maps, the scale steadily got

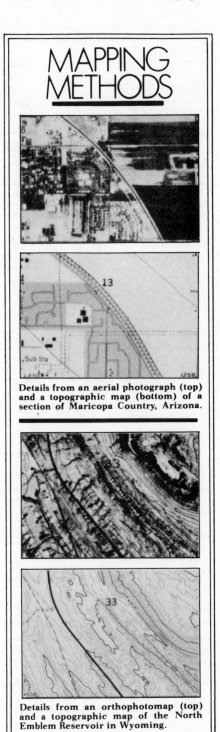

MAPPING METHODS

Details from an aerial photograph (top) and a topographic map (bottom) of a section of Maricopa Country, Arizona.

Details from an orthophotomap (top) and a topographic map of the North Emblem Reservoir in Wyoming.

SCALE

These maps of the town of Victorville, California, show the three most common scales used by the U.S.G.S. The map above is considered a large scale map, i.e., one unit on the map is equivalent to 24,000 units of actual terrain. Thus, one mapped inch represents 24,000 inches, or about 2,000 feet of actual distance.

One inch on this medium scale map represents 62,500 actual inches, or approximately one mile. This medium scale therefore represents a larger area than the large scale map but describes it in less detail.

On this small scale map, one mapped inch represents 250,000 inches, or about four miles, of actual terrain. The shaded areas further illustrate how the large, medium and small scale maps compare in depicting the town of Victorville.

Representative U.S.G.S. Map Scales

series	scale	1 inch equals	coordinate size of quadrangle	area covered (square miles)	scale classification
7½-minute	1:24,000	2,000 feet	7½ X 7½ min	49 to 70	large
15-minute	1:62,500	about 1 mile	15 X 15 min	197 to 282	medium
Alaska Quad	1:63,360	1 mile	15 X 20-36 min	207 to 281	medium
US 1:250,000	1:250,000	about 4 miles	1 X 2 degrees	4580 to 8669	small
State Base	1: million	about 16 miles	4 X 6 degrees	73,734 to 102,759	small

larger. In 1941 modern accuracy standards were adopted. By the fifties it was clear the contiguous 48 states should be mapped on 7½-minute quadrangles. Today 14 states, mostly in the East, are either completed or nearly completed at 1:24,000 scale. Nine others are covered by a combination of 1:24,000 and 1:62,500 scale charts. In the other states work goes on to bring areas into the 7½-minute series or to revise existing maps (except in Alaska, which continues to be charted on 15-minute quads).

It's a giant job, producing 60,000 detailed relief maps to illustrate this nation's diverse topography. Here's how the U.S.G.S. does it.

Modern mapping is best understood as three steps: (1) geodesy—the determination of exact locations and elevations of certain points on the Earth, and the relationships and sizes of land masses; (2) photogrammetry—making surveys and maps by detecting elevations and surface features in stereo photographs of the Earth; (3) cartography—production of maps, including projections, compilation of details, design and reproduction.

First, someone makes the decision to map an area. This is the responsibility of the plans and programs office, where money is alloted to unmapped areas based on government needs, geologic interest and state requirements. Technical planners at four regional mapping centers schedule overlapping aerial photography by private contractors. The best photos are taken during periods of no snow, no leaves, and no floods—which made 1973 a poor year for mapping in much of the United States. Flights are made at altitudes of 5,000 to 14,000 feet, depending on the terrain, and produce from three to hundreds of photos per quadrangle. All of them overlap about 50 percent with the next shot so that a stereo view is possible with optical equipment.

Technicians in the aerotriangulation section get the first look. They choose easily identifiable landmarks to be *control points* that will provide the basic latitude, longitude and elevation framework. If these points are plotted incorrectly, the entire map will be inaccurate.

Then a field party of surveyors, aerial photos in hand, enters the area to find the control points and measure their exact positions and/or elevations. The surveyors are aided by an existing grid of more than 400,000 marked geodetic bench marks, and by modern equipment such as helicopters and microwave distance-measuring gear which is accurate down to two-tenths of a foot.

Armed with this control information, the technician at the mapping center views the stereo image (the *model*) and through a complex optical-mechanical linkup transfers data to a computer. The computer does the figuring necessary to transform the three-dimensional map. The data is used to operate a rectangular coordinate plotter or *coordinatograph*, which marks out the map grid, control points, elevations and correct longitude and latitude on a yellow-plastic-coated sheet of mylar that is the exact size of the eventual map. This becomes the *base sheet* for all subsequent mapping actions.

Now the base sheets and stereo photos go to the compilation section. Again, a stereo viewer comes into play. It projects the three-dimensional model

Reading a Map at a Glance

SCALE. Scale expresses the size relationship between the map and the terrain it represents. It is usually shown as ratio of map distance to distance on the ground, such as 1:24,000 or 1/24,000 for any convenient units. In general, scales are classified as large or small. *Large-scale* maps show a *small* area in great detail, and have a *small* number as denominator of the ratio. *Small-scale* maps show a *great* deal of territory and have a very *large* number in the denominator.

MAP SERIES. These are families of maps conforming to the same general specifications or having a unifying feature, usually scale. The U.S.G.S. publishes 10 major series of topographic maps. The relationship of scale to size is shown on the chart on page 33.

PROJECTION. A systematic construction of lines drawn on a plane surface, representing the meridians and parallels of the curved surface of the Earth. The problems involved can easily be seen by trying to flatten out an orange peel, or cover a ball smoothly with a piece of paper. No single projection is good for all map scales and uses, so several families of projections have evolved and are commonly used for topo maps:

Mercator: Based on a cylinder of paper circling the globe touching only one line. This line can be the equator or any other chosen line. Weakness: away from this line distortion increases rapidly.

Conic: Picture the Earth wearing a dunce cap. Again, a standard center line is chosen. Polyconic projections combine cones of varying angles to provide several touching points and thereby reduce distortion.

Equal-area formulas: Derived from Mercator, conic and other basic projections but processed through complex mathematical procedures to hold shape, distance or direction constant at the expense of other factors. Lambert Conformal Conic and Albers Equal Area often appear on small-scale U.S.G.S. maps.

A TOPO MAP SPEAKS. Down at the bottom of Geological Survey maps, you'll find a full run-down on the factors that went into its production. If you're concerned with accuracy and timeliness of detail, you may want to check it out.

Lower Left: Tells what agency made it, by what method (photogrammetry and multiplex-stereo photomapping, photo interpretation for features, ground-based surveys or a combination), when the aerial photos and surveys were taken, when and how it was revised, what projection was used, what the margin ticks mean (usually they are grids for interlocking the quad into national and world geodetic systems). Some of the older maps even supply the names of the cartographer and surveyor who collaborated on drawing the map in the days before aerial photography.

Center: Shows the scale of the map in both ratio and distance, and the contour interval of the elevation overprint. A quick glance just below will tell if the map conforms to national standards. If it does, you know that horizontal points are mapped within ⅕₀th of an inch on the chart and that vertical elevations can be interpolated to within one-half the contour interval. If it doesn't, accuracy can vary over wide limits, since photogrammetric stereo mapping was probably not used.

Right: In tiny print just under the map edge is the name of the printing agency and date of the press run, which reveals how long it took to complete the map after the final survey—the official date of the map.

CONTOURS. The brown contour lines on U.S.G.S. topo maps connect points of equal elevation. Learning how to "read" their bends and twists gives a picture of the terrain. A few tips: The closer the lines are together, the steeper the ground. A circle or a loop indicates the summit of a mountain. A pattern of V's pointing upstream indicates a valley. A downhill-pointing V indicates a ridge.

SYMBOLOGY. Cartographers have to make certain compromises between dead accuracy and legibility of map symbols and lines. Thus, the following cautions are in order when reading Geological Survey relief maps:

Water: Single lines represent streams and canals less than 40 feet wide on 7½-minute quads (80 feet on 15s). Larger streams or rivers are shown to scale. The blue line marking coastal waters equals Mean High Water — which is always higher than contour reference level, which is Mean Sea Level.

Buildings: Structures smaller than the average dwelling are not shown. Heavily built-up areas are depicted by a red tint with most individual structures omitted. The tint usually does not coincide with municipal boundaries.

Property and fence lines: These lines are not intended to show conclusive evidence of land ownership or boundary locations.

Small features: Symbols for wells, springs, mines, fences, landmarks and control stations nearly always cover relatively more area on the map than their real-life counterparts do on the ground.

Trails: Trails that lead to mapped features (mines, lakes, etc.) usually are shown only if they do *not* parallel a road. Those in recreational areas, however, will be mapped regardless of roads. Public trails in remote areas are mapped, but those intended for private use usually aren't. Major trails are labeled, but many connecting paths are omitted entirely. It is important to remember that trail routes in some areas change rapidly, putting maps out of date. In other words, *caveat backpacker.* Don't expect the Geological Survey to lead you by the hand.

onto a small moveable tracing table, and it has an optical system that detects small elevation differences on the model. The operator moves the tracing table to follow ground features or imaginary contour levels, sensing terrain changes by watching a tiny spot of light on the table. He moves the table to keep that dot from seeming to either float above or sink below the image of the ground. As he adjusts the table for changing elevations, a pantograph attached to the table traces out a two-dimensional representation of the model on a plastic base sheet.

Later, the compiler uses sharp *scribers* to hand engrave the base sheet along the feature and contour lines so formed. He makes three sheets: one with drainage, man-made features and the control diagram; a second with contours; and a third showing woodland areas. This process of compilation can take as long as three months, with a sole operator—who must have an artist's feeling for natural curves and shapes—scribing an entire quad.

Next, cartographers take over to interpret the map in names, symbols and color. They make basic decisions as to how much information is needed on the map, which spellings to use and which symbols are needed where. In other words, they decide how the chart will communicate. They rely on field checks to clarify boundaries, ascertain local names, determine building uses and double-check elevations and locations. For very flat terrain that is difficult to map from stereo photos, they often perform freehand plane-table sketching, just as mappers did in the early days.

As many as seven plastic sheets emerge from this interpretation process. Each sheet provides for a different subject in a different color: man-made features and control (black), road fill (red), contour lines (brown), water (blue), large water areas (blue screen), forest and vegetation (green) and urban areas (red screen). After being checked, the images are transferred to high speed offset lithographic press plates for printing.

Total time from initial flight planning to distribution of the map to sales offices: about three years. Cost: an average of $17,000 per 7½-minute quadrangle.

Three years to produce a map? Some maps are already out of date the minute the photo planes land. Obviously, many others are old by the time they're published. To minimize this problem and to

THE MAP INFORMATION OFFICE

If you can't figure out what those map symbols mean; if you can't find the maps you need locally; or if you're having trouble locating Blue Lake where the camping was so good last year, then the U.S. Geological Survey (U.S.G.S.) has the answers for you.

The Map Information Office in Washington, D.C. is set up just to provide information about the U.S.G.S., its products and the land they illustrate. This office annually fields thousands of questions about elevations, legal boundaries, highest and lowest points, availability of maps, map reading, location of features and man-made objects, and foreign and state map sources. In its files are answers to the puzzles most often posed by scientists, almanac publishers, boy scouts, treasure hunters, gamblers—and, of course, backpackers.

But before you drop your questions into the mailbag bound for Washington, here's some advice from the man who set up most of the Information Office files—Kenwood Markussen, chief of the Special Research Unit. He suggests you try local sources first.

Much map information can be had at libraries that maintain files of topographic maps and U.S.G.S. brochures.

(You can probably copy what you need at the cost of a few dimes.) Next, try local map dealers, outdoor stores, and state information centers. Visit, if you can, one of the Geological Survey Public Inquiries offices in Salt Lake City, Denver, Dallas, Los Angeles, San Francisco, Spokane, Anchorage, Fairbanks, Menlo Park, California, Rolla, Missouri, or Arlington, Virginia. If you still come up short, Markussen and his co-workers will be happy to deal with your problem at the Map Information Office, U.S. Geological Survey, Washington, D.C. 20242.

He cautions you to be very clear about what you need, and where: "We get requests to locate Mud Pond...but which Mud Pond...and in which state?" Further, he warns, "Don't expect us to tell you where to hike or fish." But the Map Information Office can very quickly describe which topos to buy for a hike on the Pacific Crest Trail, help locate ghost towns in Colorado, or provide addresses for obtaining recreational information in Maine.

Markussen understands your problems—he enjoys camping, and his sons hike the Appalachian Trail—but after 30 years in the Survey he'd really rather handle only the tough questions.

get maps updated as quickly as possible, the U.S.G.S. uses three revision methods. Complete revision amounts to a new map. The standard revision uses field-checked photos to change parts of an existing map: the new map bears the dates of the original and second field surveys. Since 1967, a third technique has been employed: *photorevision*. New aerial photo information is overprinted in purple on the quad without field checking, thus lopping about a year off the normal revision process. During a recent month, the U.S.G.S. issued 146 revised maps, of which all but 14 were photorevisions.

The U.S.G.S. prints about 6,000 different topographic maps each year. Two-thirds are new ones, and most are at 1:24,000 scale.

Sales are enormous. In fiscal 1972,

the Geological Survey sold just short of 9.5 million relief maps. Figures on sales to other government offices (the biggest customers) are obscured by budget paperwork. But fiscal 1972 public sales amounted to $2.5 million.

At an average cost of $17,000 per quad, does the U.S.G.S. break even? Yes, according to Joe O'Neill, the Survey's assistant chief of distribution. He says, "We are required to recover costs on maps. And the public is getting a bargain at 75 cents a quad."

Every hiker who's squinted from map to terrain and back again trying to figure out exactly where he is has wondered what kind of bargain he *did* get how accurate the information is. Today's answer: accurate to within a few feet. The 1941 U.S.G.S. guidelines call for horizontal accuracy of 90 percent on a

1:24,000 scale map, or 40 feet on the ground. Vertical accuracy standards require at least 90 percent of the elevations interpolated from contour lines to be correct to within one-half the contour interval, which could be as little as 2½ feet. Obviously, the greater the area a map covers, the greater the chance for inaccuracy.

The key to getting the required accuracy is the control between the map and those ground points selected in aerotriangulation.

According to Lawrence Corn, assistant chief of the Survey's Eastern Mapping Center in Arlington, Virginia, "The better your ground control is, the better your map's going to be. Modern photogrammetric equipment can provide positions so accurate that they can't be plotted due to reproduction limitations, human error and even atmospheric changes in equipment and paper."

Even when photos are scaled to 1 inch equals 100 feet, measurements on corresponding U.S.G.S. quads at 1 inch to 2,000 feet often hold up well in comparison. The occasional errors usually have resulted from difficulties that photogrammetric methods face in correctly adjusting to rapid, extreme changes in elevation.

Of the many places where error can occur, the hand scribing of terrain features by the compiler is the most obvious. Errors and adjustments sometimes creep into the cartographic process too, since symbols may be larger than scale in order to be legible and printing plates may be slightly out of register.

Of all the users of U.S.G.S. maps, the ones most aware of their shortcomings are private map makers. These aerial photo and charting firms use quads to plan their flights, then check their photos against the maps.

"We find discrepancies all the time on the early maps done with plane table," says one official of an Oregon-based mapping service. "Apparently there was a lot of imagination used in those days. However, the accuracy of the new 7½-minute maps is amazing."

Marin Bacheller, vice-president and editor-in-chief of Hammond, Inc., in Maplewood, New Jersey, says much the same thing: "You have to consider the date the survey map was published. If it's an old map—especially of an urban area with streets and houses, then of course we'll have to supplement it. But in general there's nothing better in terms of accuracy. Survey maps are the best."

If you're not happy with U.S.G.S. maps, as people living in poorly mapped areas might not be, is there any place to turn? Not really.

Although there are many map suppliers and their products are diverse, the government is the only source of inexpensive, high quality, large-scale topographic charts. Most private firms use the government maps to compile their own, which usually are at small scales. City maps, of course, are sometimes at very large scales, and the National Geographic Society's cartographers produce beautiful large-scale maps to illustrate magazine and book articles.

For the wealthy backpacker whose favorite backwoods haunt is not mapped to his satisfaction, there is one out, nevertheless. Some small companies specialize in making photogrammetric maps on contract. They are capable of producing incredibly large-scale maps that are virtually error free. But if you want one, you'd better have thousands of dollars ready to pour into the project.

Sometimes American mappers need the aid of foreign government cartographic agencies. The Swiss Federal Mapping Bureau, which is world renowned for its depiction of rocks and glacial formations, collaborated with Bradford Washburn of the Boston Museum of Science to produce an awe-inspiring topographic chart of Mount McKinley. The National Geographic Society called Swiss cartographer Paul Ulmer to the United States in 1967 to learn his airbrush relief technique. The Society and many other large mapping concerns use foreign government maps to produce atlas sheets. The only drawback is the usual one, modern mapping methods have yet to be applied to all parts of the world.

There are recent developments in mapping which should increase the accuracy and usefulness of charts manyfold in the future. One new technique that the U.S.G.S. is using more frequently is *orthophotomapping*—direct application of an aerial photographic image as a map. Stereo photos are projected through an orthophotoscope, which corrects distortion and like a very complicated darkroom enlarger prints the image onto a quad-sized sheet of film. The Survey has issued more than 125 orthophoto sheets for areas in Alaska, Florida, Georgia, North Carolina, Texas, Utah and Arizona. Minnesota is next.

Some of these black-and-white maps are mosaics of many photos. But the beginning of each project was orthophotomaps, printed from single photos and enhanced by colors to bring out terrain features. These maps show vividly rock formations, vegetation zones, homes and buildings, farm fields and even ocean shallows.

Work continues toward discovering the best color system and methods of speeding production. Reduced need for human scribing of terrain symbols will make orthophotomaps faster and cheaper to produce than normal topos. They'll also be different for map users because cartographers will no longer have to interpret contour and terrain. You'll see the land more clearly—*provided* you first understand more about it.

Because of this proviso, some Survey officials believe the photomaps will have limited application. "I don't think they're too good in mountainous terrain," says Lawrence Corn of the Eastern Mapping Center, "and not too good in cities. Their use is for identification of terrain, not interpretation of relief."

Orthophotomapping now is being concentrated on wetlands and deserts. Yet, one experimental photomap of Dallas is quite beautiful, with terrain types highly enhanced by vivid colors. Striking, when compared to the "perfect view" of an ordinary topo map, are the visible cars on the roads, aircraft on runways, houses, gardens and even details of large roofs.

Will all parts of the country eventually get orthophotomap coverage? Corn doesn't think so. Nodding toward the Status of Mapping chart on his office wall, he says, "Our primary target is to get that map all pink"—indicating 7½-minute coverage. "Mapping is a costly process, so we're not looking for maps to do over. We use the technique where it's appropriate."

There are other new techniques. In 1971, the U.S.G.S. issued an experimental map of Phoenix at 1:250,000 scale, developed from two space photos taken by Apollo astronauts. It combines imagery with the color brown and several parts of a conventional line map to provide an incredible view of desert, irrigated fields and urban sprawl. Some private firms are beginning to use the thousands of photos available from NASA to update their old maps and produce new ones. The photos are fascinating and full of information, but combined with conventional map symbology they become nearly perfect representations of the Earth.

Another new way of seeing the world that is beginning to find an application in cartography is the use of laser beam distance-measuring equipment. Using this technique, Dr. Washburn of Boston is on the way to doing for the central portion of the Grand Canyon what he's already accomplished for Mount McKinley. Starting with all-new aerial photographs in 1970, his teams selected 42 control points on both rims and inside the canyon, and began triangulation and distance measuring from the bench mark on Yaki Point.

Coherent beams of helium-neon light are shot out to other control locations, where grids of quartz prism reflectors bounce it back. Sensors detect the time lag to give the most precise measurements ever of the great gulf—microseconds that help bridge billions of years of earth history. With all 42 control points measured, the project will produce manuscript charts at a scale of one foot to a mile, and a topographic map at three inches to a mile for use by canyon visitors. It will be a boon to backpacking canyon-crawlers. The project is supported by the Boston Museum of Science, the National Geographic Society and the National Park Service.

In another use of modern tools, U.S.G.S. topographers and NASA engineers are working to combine the environments of space and Antarctica. Photoimagery mosaics from the new Earth Resources Technology Satellite (ERTS-1) are revealing previously unknown mountains and unsuspected changes in glaciers and ice shelves. This will help revise the Geological Survey Antarctica maps series up to a scale of 1:250,000. It also will enable the Survey to build an historical record of geologic changes of Antarctica.

Thousands of pictures produced by 1973's Skylab project provide the same kind of eye-opening glimpse of the terrain of the United States. They have the advantage of being produced by thinking human beings applying knowledge during photo sessions—changing subjects, lenses, cameras and film as required.

Other new developments: radar altimeters and continuous-flight profile recorders enabling geodetic data to be gained in one pass from aloft. Side-looking radar cutting through atmosphere and vegetation to show oblique views of bare terrain. Infrared sensors clearly depicting changes in vegetation and soils. Satellite geodesy measuring long distances with unheard of accuracy.

Scientists in the United States, Canada and Britain are developing techniques for totally computer-driven map making. In one system, optical scanning of the photo-model feeds basic terrain information into memory banks. Later, an operator at a console draws out the facts he desires and combines them with symbology, scale contour interval and control points to produce a map on an automatic plotter. Recently, Canadian government mappers produced a computer-compiled and -drafted quadrangle map in only 40 hours.

Clearly, automated cartography will soon "eliminate much of today's time-consuming drudgery, without loss of either the precision or of the elegance of maps," as one British researcher puts it.

If Org could only be here. And Ptolemy, Caesar, Columbus and Amundsen. They would agree that although Man is still not sure where he's going, he now knows a lot more about where he is. ◣

Chapter Five

HAZARDS AND SAFETY

Survival is often a state of mind. And the proper state of mind, calm and collected, can help when you suddenly face danger. As any seasoned hiker knows, however, it pays to know the hazards that backpackers can encounter and be ready to avoid them—both by prevention and by as full a knowledge of trail safety as possible.

STRANDED!

by DAVID HEILLER

After waist-deep snows were dumped onto the trails by an early blizzard, barring the way out, it was too late to wish he'd let Yosemite Park rangers know his itinerary or wish he'd brought a map.

Here is a story that tells a lot about what not to do as well as what to do in a backcountry emergency. The author is gracious enough to share his entire story with us, his wisdom as well as his folly. And not only does it have good information in it, but it also is highly interesting reading.

W.K.

Only fifty yards to go; I was almost there.

I blinked as the wind swirled down the trail, powdering everything with snow. Looming above me was 10,485-foot Tuolumne Peak. It appeared ghostly; gray-white against white. So close. So deceptively close.

"The most crucial 150 feet of my life," I thought as I stood shivering in the snow. For the past six hours of that fateful November 10, 1973 day, I had waded through drifts up steep switchbacks below the peak. Now, standing on a small bare patch of soil protected by a dozen large pines, I scanned the outline of the snow-choked trail as it rose steeply over a crest.

Beyond the crest was Yosemite Valley, 20 *downhill* miles to the south. For seven days I had backpacked over mountainous trails, many like this one, always managing

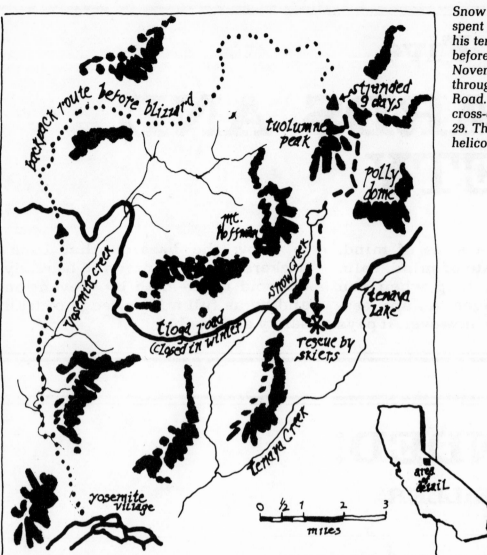

Snow came November 10. He spent nine days snowbound in his tent below Tuolumne Peak before the weather stabilized. On November 19 he struck off through the snow toward Tioga Road. There, he chanced upon a cross-country skier on November 29. The next morning a helicopter flew Heiller to safety.

to stay one step ahead of the deep snow. But now?

This was the most crucial distance. The final 50 yards. The chilling wind, my snow-soaked clothes and numbed hands were forgotten. With all my remaining strength, I began wading up the drifted trail. Twenty steps brought knee-deep snow; each successive step was worse. Leaning forward, hands pawing uselessly, I crawled through the snow as it drifted around my waist. But it was no use. I could go no farther.

The long day's bout with snow and wind had taken its toll. Defeated, I waded back to the shelter of the pine grove. With hands that had no sensation, I clumsily tied my nylon pup tent between two trees, staked down the sides, threw my sleeping bag, food bag, mess kit, matches and notebooks into the tent, and myself with

them. My body was deeply chilled; I shook uncontrollably from head to foot as I slowly stripped off wet jeans and long-johns. My mind was numb. There were no thoughts of the magnitude of my predicament, or of home or death; only of the freezing cold and my savior—my down sleeping bag. But as I reached in the stuff sack, my

heart sank: the bag was soaked! The night before, a steady drizzle had infiltrated my tent and seeped into the bottom of the bag. My spare clothes also were soaked. I hadn't taken the time to dry anything. Now, lying cold and nude in the half-wet bag, with darkness falling and the wind beginning to howl from the mountaintops,

"It became a ritual for me to sing Christmas carols or play my harmonica to take my mind off the pain."

I started to cry. My fight to survive the snow and cold and find civilization in the Sierra Nevada had begun.

FROM SATURDAY NIGHT to Monday's dawn, as a blizzard raged, I reflected on the past month. I had taken a fall vacation from my University of Minnesota studies to try backpacking and see some of the country. The week I'd spent in Yosemite National Park had been my first extensive backpacking. Now, beginning my second week, totally unprepared for snow and freezing temperature, I chided myself for being such a greenhorn.

By Monday morning three feet of fresh snow, blown by roaring winds, had piled up against the tent, pressing in upon me like an icy iron maiden. Initially I had tapped the inside of the tent to knock off the snow, but my fist soon met with a heavy thud. Now the tent was almost buried.

I put on my wet clothes again, crawled out into the tempest and waded a trench around the tent. The dim morning light made the scene eerie and unreal. The blue tent sagged like a squeezed marshmallow under the snow's weight. The bare ground of two days before was covered with swirling, flowing mounds of silvery snow. And there was no sound, save for the wind as it sifted over snow and through pine boughs.

A few hours later on that morning of November 12, I began writing a diary in one of my notebooks. "The wind howls and blows snow over my tent as I write this. I can only hope and pray (I've done a lot of both in the last 48 hours) that the storm will soon blow itself out, and I can make it back to civilization on my own two feet, not on a stretcher or over a horse. With the help of God, I'll do all within my power to get out of this hellhole. I don't want to die."

When the wind quieted down an hour later, I put on my wet clothes and stepped out into the white stillness. Common sense told me to stay where I was: to wait for rescue, build a fire, get warm. Common sense warned of the futility and danger of retracing the 30 miles I had come, especially in three feet of fresh snow. But fear overpowered common sense. I stuffed everything into my pack and started wading.

It was nearly my last living mistake. I was much weaker than on Saturday. During the last two days I'd eaten only a raw trout left over from Friday and a bowl of granola. My stomach muscles ached.

I went 50 yards before hitting a drift up to my waist. I tried pulling myself out, but the snow held me fast.

In the deathly silence a tiring but peaceful calm settled over me. "It would be so easy," I thought, "just to lie here and sleep."

Flashes of death crossed my mind, first with vivid scenes of my mother's heartbroken sorrow; scenes of grief, tears, the funeral. Then with a face-to-face confrontation with death. I realized that the past 20 years were all in vain. Only the unknown lay ahead. It was the most frightening, awesome vision I have ever had, enough to give me the strength to roll out of the drift and wade back to my campsite among the pines. There I determinedly secured the tent to four trees and began another phase of my ordeal—waiting for rescue.

I HAD NO REASON to be optimistic about search planes ever finding me. Because of my inexperience I had not checked in with Yosemite Park headquarters, had not obtained a wilderness permit and had not told any ranger about my trip. No one except my mother knew where I was.

Nevertheless, I hoped for rescue. "Let me say what I hope and pray happens, and what is really my only chance for rescue," I wrote in my journal. "Mom gets worried after she doesn't hear from me by Thanksgiving (two weeks away). She calls up park headquarters and asks whether they have any information. Perhaps they'll have found the food and clothes that I left in storage locker 41, and she'll verify that they're mine, which will indicate that I'm still in Yosemite somewhere. Maybe they'll check the past weather records and recall the big storm of November 10, and they'll assume that I'm either dead or snowbound. Either way they'll send out search parties, most likely by small plane, and scour the area. With a signal fire or an SOS in the snow, they should find me. So I've got to hang on for a long month."

Underneath this, I added a postscript: "Of course, I doubt things will go exactly like that. The rangers might not discover the locker, in which case they won't even be sure I'm in the park and might not search at all."

I did my best during the next week to prepare for search planes. After a pair of denims and a shirt had dried on Tuesday, I broke off all the dry dead wood I could reach from the trees and put it in my backpack on a rise 20 yards away, along with some white gas fuel. Beside this I piled some large dead boughs wrapped in my tarp. If any search planes did come, I'd be ready with a quick signal fire. I also kept a small mirror handy to signal planes.

Monday and Tuesday were both sunny with a slight breeze. By Tuesday evening, after two days on a makeshift clothesline, all my clothes and, more importantly, the sleeping bag, had dried. And I made the crucially important discovery of a creek, about 75 yards away. I had crossed the foot-wide stream flowing off Tuolumne Peak on Saturday. On Tuesday I waded back through thigh-deep drifts to look for it. There was hardly a trace in the deep smooth snow, merely a single hole about three feet across, but I could hear the beautiful sound of gurgling water. After three days of eating snow, the

David Heiller in Lewis Memorial Hospital after being snowbound for 18 days in Yosemite National Park. Though he had lost 40 pounds, his only injuries were blisters on his heels.
PHOTO: RALPH V. THRONEBERY, STAFF PHOTOGRAPHER *Fresno Bee*

How to Avoid a Cold Weather Emergency

Some people get into trouble in the wilderness because they are not prepared for adverse weather. Here's what you should do to minimize the risks:

✔ Plan your hike before you leave. Consult trail books and maps. Draw up an itinerary.

✔ Be prepared for the worst. Pack adequate clothing and food. *Always* carry a map and compass, knife, flashlight, matches and first-aid kit.

✔ Let the rangers know where you will be in the backcountry and when you expect to return.

✔ Do not hike alone.

✔ Know your limits. Avoid places beyond your capabilities. If you become tired, stop.

✔ Don't be afraid to turn back. Reaching your objective is not worth risking weather changes.

✔ Stay on the trail. Cutting cross-country increases the danger of becoming lost.

✔ Let the rangers know when you return. Call, or drop them a postcard.

Here's what to do if you get into trouble

✔ Stay calm. Panic will only increase the dangers.

✔ Get out of the weather. Improvise the quickest adequate shelter for terrain and conditions.

✔ Get warm. Add clothing, using rainproof garments to reduce heat loss. Shelter the head and neck from wind and cold. Use your stove or build a fire.

✔ Keep warm. Sit and stand on thick insulation. Wiggle toes and fingers. Prewarm inhaled air by breathing through a wool sock.

✔ Drink hot liquids and nibble on food to resupply energy.

✔ If food is not available, remain quiet to conserve energy.

✔ Stay put until conditions improve. Traveling in a storm will use up precious energy and expose you to wet and cold.

✔ Don't walk aimlessly. Consult your map and compass. If you need to orient yourself, find a vantage point.

✔ Avoid getting wet. Wet clothing loses body heat 240 times faster than dry clothing.

✔ Avoid excessive perspiration. It indicates energy loss and wets clothing from the inside.

✔ Guard against frostbite and hypothermia.

✔ If you become lost, find shelter and stay put.

✔ Be prepared to signal for help.

sweet, icy liquid couldn't have tasted better. From then on I had a full canteen.

Knowing any rescue would probably be at least a month away, I began rationing my two-week food supply. The inventory, as I recorded it in my journal, consisted of: one-half bag (pint size) brown sugar, one-half bag Malt-O'Meal, one-half bag instant rice, one-half bag instant potatoes, one-third bag granola, 12 servings pancake mix, one serving instant eggs, one quart instant milk, two instant breakfasts, three one-cup cocoa mixes, three packets Lipton Instant Soup, four packets Lipton Cup-a-Soup, three packets chili seasoning mix, one-half packet Spanish rice seasoning mix, three ounces cooking oil, one packet freeze-dried chicken and rice, one-half Gerry tube of peanut butter and jelly and seven tea bags.

I began limiting myself to one two-course meal daily. For the main course, I had half a bowl of mixed granola, rice, instant cereal, instant potatoes pancake batter, cooking oil and dried soup mixed with water. Along with this paste I ate "snow salad"—brown sugar and snow. I was constantly, ravenously hungry, but the prospect of running out of food before getting rescued reinforced my will power.

The worst hardship I encountered the first week, though, was loneliness. I reread Thoreau's *Walden*, then finished Mark Twain's *Huckleberry Finn* in two days. *Walden's* reverence for nature and simplicity seemed to befit my predicament. I wrote daily accounts of my thoughts and plight in my journal; I played my harmonica; I sang Christmas carols. But most of all, I reflected on my past. I began to realize the value of life and how much I had taken for granted. A Wednesday, November 15, entry in my journal reads: "All I really want is to get back home, back to school, to see my friends and loved ones again, to live out my life. If I could only see everyone again; I'd be more aware and loving, more appreciative."

For the first time ever, I began believing in Christ. Maybe it was only "pocket Providence," pulled out under the stress of silence and thoughts of death. But at the time it was sincere. It grew into a faith that kept me going when I thought I lacked the physical strength to continue.

As my mind cleared during the week, my hopes for rescue grew dimmer. By Thursday evening I was in a mental dilemma. I wouldn't admit that my chance of rescue was almost nonexistent, for I needed that hope to keep my spirits up. It had spurred me through the first four days, sustaining my will to live. But on Thursday evening it received a deathblow. As I lay looking at a park brochure and map, I read, "This is Yosemite National Park, a 1189-square-mile scenic wonderland of sculptured peaks and domes. . ." With that much territory to cover and not knowing where to begin looking, the National Park Service would never find me, even with a signal fire.

I PINPOINTED MY location on the sketchy map, just north of Tuolumne Peak, and then it occurred to me that I might be able to walk out on my own. To the east and stretching north–south was a large valley with a creek. Even though the creek flowed north into the Grand Canyon of the Tuolumne River, I figured it had to cut a natural pass through the mountains to the south and might even intercept May Lake and Tioga Road, which were seven miles due south of Tuolumne Peak and my campsite.

I had seen the valley every day, a wide one with a dense pine forest and small mountains sprinkled throughout. No longer content with waiting, and with the snow more compact, I planned my escape for the first weather-permitting day.

Friday and Saturday brought another storm, though nothing like the blizzard a week earlier. Sunday held hurricanelike winds. When Monday dawned clear, windless and warm, I packed my gear and started toward the valley. I was exchanging security for the unknown. Although frightened, I felt strength and pride for assuming the burden of my rescue. It was no longer up to my family or the rangers; it was up to me and the grace of God to make it back alive.

During the week from Monday, November 19, to Sunday, November 25, I hiked south, using a compass and common sense as guides. My hypothesis that the valley creek would cut a natural pass through the mountains to the south proved to be correct. Except for two days when I rested, I followed the creek south, passing through dense conifer forest. The hiking was slow and treacherous. Not only did my progressing weakness force me to take four or five breaths with each step, but I had to avoid streams, rocks and trees obscured beneath the snow. At first the streams were nearly impossible to spot ahead of time; I'd suddenly sink up to my crotch and feel my boots fill with icy water. After this had happened twice, I began to recognize warning signs—a barely perceptible crease in the snow, a soft swish of flowing water. I also improved at detecting boulders and young pines by the slight mounds they made in the snow. Sometimes, however, they were unavoidable. I'd step gingerly on a half-inch mound only to go crashing down on a buried tree that had formed an air pocket under the snow.

I learned a few other important tactics by experience, such as erecting my tent in a position for the morning sun to warm it quickly and thaw out my boots early enough for me to get in a full day's hiking. I learned to wear wool socks on both hands and feet while hiking; only wool kept them warm, even when wet, and saved them from frostbite. I learned to wrap my two-quart aluminum canteen in spare clothes at night, preventing it from becoming a two-quart ice cube by morning. And I learned how to withstand intense pain. Both heels developed blisters the size of a

quarter from the unnatural motion of walking in deep snow. At night when I was drying and thawing my cold, clammy feet, my heels would ache for 15 minutes, badly enough to bring tears. It became a ritual to sing Christmas carols or play my harmonica at this time to take my mind off the stabbing pain.

I HAD MY SHARE of frightening and frustrating experiences. On the first day, just 150 yards below my campsite, I came to a sheer 15-foot drop-off. The only way off the ridge was down the smooth, almost 90-degree face of a huge boulder. I sat down and gingerly pushed myself feet-first toward the snow below. Not reckoning the influence my pack would have, I belly-flopped, miring myself up to the waist. My glasses were gone, but no bones were broken. I quickly scanned the snow, sighing in relief when I spotted my wire-rimmed glasses lying a few feet away. With my 20-200 vision, lost glasses would have been disastrous.

Weighed down by the pack, I discovered I could not walk through the deep snow at the foot of the slope. So I slipped off the pack, unrolled my Ensolite sleeping pad, cut four holes in it and lashed my pack onto it. The makeshift sled pulled with ease, enabling me to wade through a half-mile of snow before the drifts lessened and I could resume hiking normally.

The most frustrating experience occurred late Friday afternoon. After spending all day hiking up a steep incline paralleling the creek, I was able to look to the south and east, in the direction of Yosemite Valley. The sight was discouraging—a solid wave of Sierra mountain range lay across the horizon as far as I could see. As I stood on the ridge, weary and depressed, a low droning sound gradually drifted nearer. I looked up eagerly and spotted a speck in the distance. A small plane was heading directly for me, flying low. I pulled out my mirror and frantically tried to flash to the plane in the dimming light. I waved my arms and yelled, "Hey I'm here, I'm here! Stop, please stop!" But the plane kept going.

By Sunday the creek had dwindled to almost nothing, an important sign that I was nearing the summit of the gradual rise I'd been climbing for three days. After one last knoll, I found myself on an expansive, open ridge which offered a good view to both the southeast and southwest. Jagged peaks were everywhere. To the southwest, however, a pine forest sliced between the mountains. If there was any way through the mountains to Tioga Road and May Lake, it was via that forest. But three days of steady drift-wading on my starvation diet had drained me physically. I pitched camp and rested the remainder of Sunday and all day Monday, trying to decide what to do.

"NOW IS THE BIG debate, and my life hinges on my decision," I wrote in the journal. "Do I push south and hope I hit Tioga Road and not another mountain range; or do I pitch camp here, where it is open, and pray I'm rescued before I starve? I'm tempted to push on, but I'm getting weaker. I might last for two weeks if I stay put, keep warm and eat a bare essential every day. If I push on into the valley, I might become even more lost and exhausted, and they'd never spot me in that forest. I don't know what's beyond it. Maybe May Lake and Tioga Road. Maybe not."

Tuesday, acting on the impulse of clear, snow-melting weather; I decided to push on. It was the toughest hiking I'd encountered in eight days. Dense pines dropped clumps of melting snow on me; dead logs, boulders and my arch-enemies, hidden streams, were constant obstacles. Yet despite them, I was in good spirits. I repeated the Lord's Prayer, saying one word with each step. I'd had uncanny good fortune, both physically and with the weather. There had been no severe storms for 17 days, and now the temperature was above freezing. But I hardly expected the beautiful sight I beheld in a clearing that afternoon. Jutting from the snow were two rusty punch-letter trail signs. I knelt in silent thanks as I read, "May Lake—3.7 miles, Yosemite Valley—14.5 miles." It seemed as if God had heard my prayers, and answered them.

I followed trail markers blazed on trees for two hours, then set up camp as dusk approached. It was the happiest night in 17 days. Before I had been only hopeful; now I began to gain a wary confidence. I had enough food for 10 more days; still, the 13

miles to Yosemite Valley would take a long time to walk with the progress I had been making. Yet I knew that once I found May Lake I would find Snow Creek, which would eventually take me to Yosemite Valley. "If this good weather holds out, I'll be in the valley in three to four days," I wrote in my journal Wednesday morning. "Thank God. I kept faith when there didn't seem to be much hope. I've got a lot of promises to keep to the Lord now, and I plan on doing it."

Some of my promises were concise, like not smoking, stealing, lying or eating meat. Others were closer to convictions than promises. I vowed never to take anyone or anything for granted again. During the previous two weeks I had thought much about people I knew and loved, almost to the point of being unrealistic, as we do when dear friends have died. We tend to overpraise their good traits, forget the bad and wish to God we had another chance to meet again, just to say, "I love you." It seemed I would be getting that second chance.

Although I lost the trail 10 minutes after I started out Wednesday morning, I wasn't worried or upset. The descending valley had to pass May Lake, and I'd be sure to see it. Skirting the forest's edge, I happily discovered a hard crust on the snow along the perimeter of the valley. I stayed on it most of the day, making what I thought was good time and expecting to see May Lake around every corner. I even made up a song entitled "Just Around the Corner," which I sang while I walked and marveled at the pristine, snow-covered valley and mountains.

But as the sun dipped behind the mountains, I still hadn't come to May Lake. I was positive I couldn't have missed it; it had to lie close ahead. I pitched camp, confident that I would find it early the next day.

Ominous gray clouds were filling the sky when I packed up and started hiking Thursday morning. A storm was heading my way. Half an hour later, my song came true. As I rounded one last corner, the most beautiful and anticipated object of 10 days of sweat, tumbles, blisters and tears—May Lake—stretched away to the south, a quarter-mile of ice and open water. From my high vantage point, I could see several drainage

streams merging at the end of the lake into a wide pine forest that converged on Snow Creek. The creek wound southward to Yosemite Valley. There lay my final haul. Ten more miles.

Feeling more drained than usual, with stops every 10 steps, I found Snow Creek and alongside it a wide alpine meadow. Slowly, methodically, I trudged through the meadow's knee-deep snow, eyes downcast. Gray clouds were moving swiftly toward me from the south. "They're hurrying to make life a little harder," I thought. "Ten miles, another blizzard and a week of food. Who's going to win?"

A movement ahead snapped me out of my reflections. For one or two seconds, nothing registered. Then, for the first time in 26 days, I recognized a human being, gliding along a hundred yards ahead.

I didn't scream crazily at the cross-country skier. I yelled loudly yet calmly, and at my same pace slowly made it to where the man stood watching me. A "Speed Limit, 40" sign just to his left told me I had finally found the closed Tioga Road.

"I've been stuck in the mountains for three weeks," I said. "I need some help."

"You've been out there, like that," he asked, scrutinizing my snow-shoeless feet and sock-covered hands, "for three weeks?" He couldn't believe his eyes. Nor could I. In an instant all had changed, and I was in touch with humanity and civilization again. Chuck Cochran handed me a fresh orange, and I realized my ordeal was ending.

A summer Search and Rescue employee of Yosemite, Chuck was skiing to Tuolumne Meadows to visit two young ranger friends. With the aid of Tom and Carolyn, two more friends who were skiing an hour behind him, we made it to a bathroom at the east end of Tanaya Lake by mid-afternoon. While Chuck and Tom went on to the ranger station to radio park headquarters in Yosemite Valley, Carolyn heated freeze-dried food and hot jello for me on their white-gas stove. Later that afternoon Tom and one ranger returned and checked my hands and feet for frostbite, thinking I might be an emergency case.

The ranger whistled when he saw the blisters on my heels. I couldn't feel anything in my feet, but the blisters, black and the size of half-dollars, were ugly enough to make me wince. Yet no sign of frostbite showed on my toes, and there was only a touch of black on the tips of four fingers.

The next morning a helicopter flew in to pick me up, and I waved goodbye to my rescuers. Ten minutes later I stepped onto a grassy field in Yosemite Valley. What a contrast! Twenty days of deep snow, then 10 minutes later, bare ground all around!

A gruff, gray-haired ranger drove me to Lewis Memorial Hospital.

Looking angry, he said nothing until we arrived there. Then, as nurses started fussing over my blisters and skinny body, he told me what I already knew, that I was a very lucky young man.

"Every spring we haul three or four people just like you out of the mountains." He didn't have to go much further. He could see I'd learned the lesson the hard way.

My body temperature had dropped two degrees; and at 145 pounds, my six-foot frame was 40

pounds lighter than a month before. Amazingly, there were no lasting injuries. I was all right except for the painful blisters.

Nearly everybody—nurses, family, reporters—marveled at my story and my strength. But I take credit for only part of the survival: keeping a clear, level head that enabled me to make the right decisions. For the rest, I credit some other Force, one which some call Fortune and others call God. ❧

JOHN WESLEY POWELL (1834–1902)

by ANNE KOLB

Getting lost is probably the least dangerous of the perils that can befall you in the wilderness. Far worse, for instance, would be to fall and drown in a swollen mountain stream, to get mauled by a bear, to get wet and cold without the gear that could warm you up, to break your leg a long way back in the wilds.

Should you get lost, the worst thing to do is to panic. If you have sufficient food, water, and

shelter you could no doubt survive long enough either to find your way back out or to be found by searchers.

Consider the plight of John Wesley Powell in his explorations—especially the exploration of the Colorado River. Survival clearly meant staying alive long enough to find the way out— which on some of his journeys took a number of months.

W.K.

Exhausted, starving and with one boat and most of their supplies already destroyed by the raging rapids, Major John Wesley Powell and his eight-man exploration team had entered the Grand Canyon in a cold torrential rain. For 82 days the expedition had battled the treacherous Green and Colorado rivers, passing through wild, largely unexplored and savagely beautiful canyon country. And now, as they prepared to break camp on the banks of the Little Colorado and proceed through the great uncharted canyon, Major Powell said nothing to his men about the danger he sensed ahead. But in his journal on the morning of August 13, 1869, he confided:

"We are three quarters of a mile in the depths of the earth, and the great river shrinks into insignificance as it dashes its angry waves against the walls and cliffs that rise to the world above; the waves are but puny ripples, and we but pigmies running up and down the sands or lost among the boulders.

"We have an unknown distance yet to run, an unknown river to explore. What falls there are, we know not; what rocks beset the channel, we know not; what walls rise over the river, we know not. Ah, well! we may conjecture many things. The men talk as cheerfully as ever; jests are bandied about freely this morning; but to me the cheer is somber

and the jests are ghastly."

Before the day was over the foreboding prophecy was fulfilled. The river grew narrower and wilder, and the canyons soared higher and steeper into ominous granite walls. For the next 16 days death ruthlessly stalked Powell and his men down the mad, boiling river. They ran almost continuous rapids, made numerous back-breaking portages, slept perched on ledges in driving rain and were down to their last sack of flour when early on the morning of August 27 they encountered black perpendicular walls of granite and the worst of all rapids.

That evening one of the men informed

VINCENT PUCCIARELLI

Powell that he and two others felt it was madness to continue. They wanted to abandon the river and take their chances climbing out of the canyon. At nightfall the worried major, using his sextant, estimated they were about 80 to 100 miles from the Rio Virgen and Mormon settlements, or three or four days from the end of their journey. Quickly, the major awakened the spokesman of the disheartened men to tell him about his calculations. But it was to no avail. At daybreak the men reiterated their desire to leave, and the major ordered that the departing trio be given two rifles, a shotgun, half the biscuits and a record of the expedition, which had been kept in duplicate. Then both parties left the fateful spot which has since been called Separation Rapids. Those who climbed out were never seen again, killed by Indians. Powell and his five remaining

crewmen survived the rapids and arrived at the Mormon settlements on the Rio Virgen three days later.

News of the successful expedition soon spread. The major emerged from the Grand Canyon a national folk hero as well as a scientist of distinction. He was the first man to lead an expedition some 1,000 miles down the Green and Colorado rivers, to map this hostile land, to chart its wild rivers, to sample its archaeological ruins, to unlock its geologic mysteries, and to lecture and write on the wonders of the Grand Canyon.

In looking over the long, productive life of John Wesley Powell; it is clear that this first Colorado River expedition was the high point of Powell's multifaceted career as a college professor, linguist, naturalist, geologist, ethnologist, conservationist and philosopher. Following a second Colorado River expedi-

tion, he made many contributions to knowledge and the nation. He organized the Bureau of Ethnology, turned the U.S. Geological Survey into a world-renowned scientific bureau, originated many scientific theories which are still valid and fought against enormous political odds for a land conservation program. All these were monumental achievements. Yet, it was the drama of the Colorado River explorations and Powell's fame as a scientist-explorer that set the stage for his later contributions.

As if preordained, Powell's youth and early manhood amply prepared him for his western wilderness adventures. Born March 24, 1834, in Mount Morris, New York, he spent his childhood at his mother's knee, learning his letters and committing the Bible to memory. His father, Joseph Powell, was a part-time farmer, tailor and circuit preacher who strictly disciplined his eight children and believed the most noble calling was the ministry. He deliberately chose the name John Wesley for his second son in hopes that the appellation would inspire him to become a man of the cloth. This paternal desire delayed Powell's scientific training and caused endless conflicts between him and his father.

Although young Powell refused to join the ministry, he did subscribe to many of his father's liberal beliefs. Perhaps the most important was the reverend's staunch stand against slavery, a highly controversial issue in the town of Jackson, Ohio, where the Powells lived. Like his father, the boy spoke out against the evils of slavery, which prompted some of his classmates to taunt and stone him. This so upset Mrs. Powell that she withdrew the boy from school and asked George Crookham, a learned family friend and abolitionist, to take her son into his home and give him lessons there. Crookham had an extensive library and sizable collections of plants and animals. He taught the boy by reading him the classics and taking him on field trips. On these nature walks Powell was first exposed to the elements of geology, archaeology and natural history.

By the time Wes was 12, the family had moved to a 160-acre farm in South Grove, Wisconsin. He was put in charge of the family spread while his father preached in neighboring communities. For four years all formal schooling ended for him. But when he turned 16, he left the farm to resume his education at a one-room schoolhouse in Janesville, some 20 miles from home. To support himself during this period, he worked as a hired hand.

A year later Reverend Powell asked his son to leave his studies to help the family move to a larger farm in Bonus Prairie, Wisconsin. If Wes would set up the new farm operation, the father promised to send him to Oberlin College where he could train as a minister. Wes dutifully helped his family but again flatly refused to become a preacher.

In 1852 at the age of 18 Powell, striking out on his own, secured a teaching position for $14 a week in a spartan one-room schoolhouse. He hoped to save $100 to attend a college of his own choosing. His classes were a big success. An innovator, he set geography lessons to music. The singing geography classes were popular with the children, and adults flocked to his evening lectures on geology and geography.

Finally, at the age of 21 Powell entered Illinois College. During the same year he made his first long collecting trip, to study mollusks of the upper Mississippi River. Though information about this trip is sketchy, we do know Powell walked across Wisconsin to Mackinaw collecting specimens as he went.

In succeeding years he alternately taught school, attended college and traveled the entire Mississippi basin by skiff and on foot, taking with him nothing but a little food, pocket change and the tools of his profession—pencils, notebooks and collecting bags. By 1861 when he was elected curator of conchology by the Illinois State Natural History Society, he had amassed an impressive collection of plants, animals, fossils and mollusks. His reputation as a naturalist was firmly established.

That same year his life took another direction. On May 3, 1861, President Abraham Lincoln called for 42,000 volunteers to save the Union. John Wesley Powell, a slender bearded man of 27, responded by enlisting in the army. During the war two significant events occurred in his life. In November, 1861, General Ulysses S. Grant gave him a week's furlough to marry his first cousin and childhood sweetheart, Emma Dean. Six months later Powell's right arm was

shattered by a Minié ball in the battle of Shiloh. Doctors amputated the infected arm. Within two months Powell returned to active duty and participated in the Battles of Vicksburg and Nashville. Throughout these engagements, his interest in science continued. Fossil seashells uncovered in trenches were sent home for his collection; during lulls in the fighting around Vicksburg he studied the hydrology of the Mississippi River.

When the war ended, Major Powell was a gaunt shadow of his former self. Though he had always been thin, he now weighed barely 100 pounds. It was many months before he was well enough to become a professor of geology at Illinois Wesleyan University. While there and later at Normal University he frequently took his classes on walking trips to deal with the natural sciences firsthand. Additionally, he turned into a persuasive lecturer and organizer, and succeeded in having the Illinois State Legislature appropriate $2,500 for the Illinois Natural History Museum. When he was named curator of that museum, he asked that $500 of the appropriation be spent on the exploration of the Rocky Mountains. A new chapter in his life had begun.

If any man was prepared to deal with the wild American West, it was John Wesley Powell. He had labored on a farm, struggled for an education, navigated the Mississippi alone, trekked across Wisconsin and Illinois on foot, and successfully commanded a battery of soldiers in two of the hardest fought battles of the Civil War. He was a leader, and he was fearless.

On his first trip to the Rockies the major was accompanied by 12 men with scientific backgrounds, and his wife. The expedition had two missions: to broaden the collections of the natural history museum and to climb Pikes Peak. The collecting mission was enormously successful. So was the climb, although there was one slight mishap. Because Powell was a novice at mountain climbing, when the party reached the summit on the afternoon of July 27, 1867, they were so enthralled with the view that they stayed too long. Night overtook them on the descent; they had to inch their way down the precipices in the dark. It should be noted that Mrs. Powell was the first woman to climb Pikes Peak and that she made the historic hike in high-top shoes, a long dress and a profusion of petticoats.

No sooner was his first expedition over than Powell was out raising funds for another. The first had cost $2,100; Powell had paid for half of it from his meager salary as a university professor. He did the same for the second trip. Once again a railroad provided free

travel, the Smithsonian Institution lent scientific instruments, the federal government furnished rations and educational institutions contributed less than $1,500.

The goal of the 1868 expedition was the same as the previous year's except the group elected to scale Longs Peak, 14,256 feet high and never previously climbed. On the morning of August 20, Powell and a party of six began the ascent on horseback. On August 22 they abandoned the horses and spent the entire day searching on foot for a route to the summit. Late that night one of the climbers announced he had discovered one. Early the next morning the group reached the summit. L. W. Keplinger, the man who had found the safe route, was the first over the top, followed by Powell. The party celebrated by implanting an American flag, toasting their success and listening to the major make a short speech of appreciation. They also wrote their names on scraps of paper which they placed in a tin can and buried in a hastily built monument of rocks.

Two other important events occurred on the second Rocky Mountain expedition. The major made contact with the chief of the Ute Indians and began a systematic study of the tribe; it resulted in a life-long interest in ethnology. And he mapped out his plans for the first expedition down the Colorado River the following year.

Many amazing feats characterized the Colorado River exploration. Not the least was Powell's success in recruiting eight men for a trip down an unknown river rumored to flow underground, one with terrifying rapids and waterfalls higher than Niagara. What's more, he offered his recruits no pay . . . only wooden oar-powered boats stocked with scientific instruments, a few tools, blankets and rations (beans, flour, salt bacon, coffee, dried apples, tea, rice, sugar).

The men Powell selected were rugged outdoorsmen who knew how to cope with the wilderness. They served him well. He later wrote, "Their bronzed, hardy, brave faces come before me as they appeared in the vigor of life; their lithe but powerful forms seem to move around me; and the memory of the men and their heroic deeds, their generous acts, overwhelms me with a joy that seems almost a grief, for it starts a fountain of tears. I was a maimed man; my right arm was gone; and these brave men, these good men never forgot it. In every danger my safety was their first care, and in every waking hour some kind service was rendered me, and they transfigured my miscomfort into a boon."

Powell's scientific training also was an important factor in the trip's success. He had done his homework on the canyon country and correctly predicted on the basis of available data that the journey could be made in boats, provided they were designed to withstand whitewater. His crippled arm proved an asset: Unable to help with the portages, his strength was saved for climbing the canyon walls at night to take scientific sightings and for keeping a journal which has been acclaimed a literary masterpiece.

Two years later Powell persuaded Congress to give him $10,000 and organized a second Colorado River expedition which became known as the "Geographical and Topographical Survey of the Colorado River of the West." It was not only better equipped than the first but included four trained scientists as well as an artist and a professional photographer. Although Powell regarded this expedition as purely scientific, it was touched by high adventure.

For the first month the river behaved itself, and the major whiled away the time reading Sir Walter Scott's *Lady of the Lake* while perched in his captain's chair lashed to the boat deck. But by June the rapids grew fiercer because the water was low; at one stretch the crew made 100 portages where the previous expedition had made only 3. During the winter and spring of 1872 Powell halted the river survey in order to survey the Kanab and Kaibab plateaus. In late summer when the river exploration did get under way again, the Colorado was flooding at dangerous levels. The party encountered continuous whirlpools, vicious rapids, and once the river rose 15 feet overnight. Finally, on September 9 at Kanab Creek, mid-way through the Grand Canyon, Powell told his men at breakfast, "Well, boys, our voyage is done." The scientific mission had been completed, and the major believed that continuing further would endanger lives.

The following year the Powell party continued survey work in the canyon while the major devoted most of his time to studying and helping the Indians of Nevada and Utah He always traveled unarmed among these tribes and was so trusted by them that he was the first white man to be able to record their languages and life style. His writings on their linguistics are considered classics. The artifacts the Indians gave him are housed in the Smithsonian.

For the next 15 years Powell's life was studded with stunning accomplishments. He founded the Bureau of American Ethnology at the Smithsonian at a time when not a single American university offered regular courses in ethnology or anthropology. He set this fledgling science on its feet through brilliant research, writing and organization. Meanwhile he worked for the establishment of the U.S. Geological Survey and became its director in 1881.

Both of these bureaus flourished under Powell's direction. He respected his men and gave them a great deal of freedom to pursue their wide-ranging interests. To Powell, geology meant the earth and virtually everything upon it, so by 1885 the Survey was studying metallurgy, geography, paleontology, mineral resources, soils, ground waters, rivers, runoff, flood control, irrigation, topographic surveying and geology. He persuaded Congress to approve the drafting of a topographical atlas of the United States, a task so enormous that it is still unfinished. He correctly believed this map would be essential to any intelligent land classification and land-use policy. Long concerned about the misuse of land in the arid West, he thought it was time to challenge government policies that served vested interests at the expense of the public domain. He recognized the West's water limitations and argued for limited development and conservation practices there. In short, he advocated protecting natural resources for "future generations."

Powell did not confine his ideas to scientific papers. He spoke out, and in his usual fearless fashion, crossed swords with powerful private interests and some western congressmen who thought the sole purpose of the public domain was to build private fortunes. Powell's outspokenness, logic, and irrefutable facts incensed his critics.

Meanwhile, the major's accomplishments as a scientist, administrator and explorer were being recognized by leading educational institutions around the world. He received numerous honorary degrees, sat on the boards of many prestigious professional organizations and was a leader in Washington's intellectual society.

For some of his less able colleagues, all this was too much to swallow. They believed Powell wielded too much power. They began nit-picking and criticizing the Survey, backstabbing its director and cozying up to his congressional enemies. For five years a handful of scientists and self-motivated congressmen circled like buzzards over the Survey and its director, watching for any sign of weakness that might discredit the Survey and topple Powell.

Although the Survey's reputation survived untarnished, the critics did manage to undermine its programs by cutting appropriations. Their attack came at a time when Powell was nearing 60, in failing health and wearying of political dog fights. Staying only long enough to groom a successor, in June 30, 1884, he resigned, citing his "failing health." The man who had survived the western wilderness and its mightiest river met defeat at the hands of a pack of politicians with questionable motives.

Despite this blow, Powell remained one of the nation's leading scientists, working and writing from his office in the Smithsonian where he continued to direct the Bureau of Ethnology. But his health steadily declined. On a January morning in 1902, an aide was called to help him make his daily walk from his home to his office. While en route, the major, now feeble and gravely ill, told his young helper, "I used to climb mountains." Eight months later at a summer cottage in Maine, John Wesley Powell slipped into a coma and died.

Only a few friends gathered at the Arlington grave to mourn this remarkable pioneer. It took other generations to fully recognize his genius and to see his land conservation programs enacted. Nor have his great explorations been forgotten. Every year the thousands who hike into the depths of the Colorado canyons and venture out on the raging river marvel anew at the courage of the one-armed major who was able to preserve so much of the character of the American West. ☙

THE PERILS OF PAID TREKS

by CHARLES F. BRUSH

He needed the sleeping bag that was supposed to be there in the hut. Violent shivering—the first stage of hypothermia. Now he knew—

When you go into the wilderness you are taking risks. You should know what these risks are.

Just paying a guide to take you into a wilderness area or up a mountain does not remove all the risk. Yes, it may lessen some of the risk that would result from inexperience. But it won't make your trip fail-safe.

Charles Brush tells of the kind of trouble you can encounter—even on commercial trips. Brush was 50 years old when he climbed his first mountain. Over the next five years he got himself in shape to be able to climb Aconcagua, highest peak outside the Himalayas. And now he is a runner, having just this past year completed the New York Marathon.

W.K.

THREE OF US almost died on a mountain in Argentina we paid to climb. On another commercial climb in Mexico, our guide quit before we reached the summit. On Chimborazo, in Ecuador, we had to carry our leader off the mountain. And on Kilimanjaro in Africa, scheming guides tried to cheat us out of the summit. Nonetheless, I hope the commercial outfitters won't get too angry at me for writing this article. I still want to climb more mountains with them.

Four years ago the only climbing I had ever done was out of pits I dug myself. I am an archeologist, not a mountaineer. In fact, climbing always seemed dumb—all that effort to end up where you started. But when I was on digs in Mexico, I had been curious about the three big volcanoes. I had looked up at them many times and wondered what it would be like to look down. So when I got an advertisement from Mountain Travel in Albany, California, promising to guide me to the Mexican summits and

teach me all the techniques I needed to know, I signed up.

The problems began when I met the group in Mexico City. I had no ice axe. Mountain Travel's equipment list had not mentioned an ice axe, though it did list crampons. The salesman in the mountaineering shop picked up on that. "If you need crampons, you also need an ice axe," he argued. Who did he think I was, some country bumpkin? I was too sophisticated for that game. But he was right, as I would have known had I read any simple book on mountaineering. Fortunately, I was able to rent an axe in Mexico City.

TOM ERWIN WAS OUR LEADER, and 17,887-foot Popocatepetl was our first volcano. Just before snow line Tom's girlfriend quit; her feet were cold. Just after snow line another member turned back; no one had told him that crampons would not work with the flexible boots he was wearing. The rest of us continued upward

toward the crater. Eventually we stood on the rim, a narrow plateau that separated the volcano's outer slope from the precipice that plunged into the crater. More than 400 years earlier Cortez's men had struggled up to that spot. I wondered how those conquistadors had felt.

Music drifted through the thin air. A singsong commercial interrupted the music; it was a radio. It belonged to a couple who were throwing orange peels about. Suddenly our accomplishment did not seem such a big deal. "Congratulations," said Tom. He pumped my down-mitted hand, turned and started down.

"But the top is up there," I said, and pointed to the summit, a half-mile away. I set out, and Tom followed, protesting. Fifty yards from the top he sat down. "To hell with it," he said. "You can have the honor of going up alone."

On the summit I met a Mexican and a German climber. We embraced and took each other's pictures. By the

Brush on the 22,834-foot summit of the Aconcagua, highest peak outside the Himalayas. During the climb his guide had become sick and descended. It was the third time a guide on a paid trek had failed to accompany Brush all the way to a mountain's summit.
PHOTO: DOUG MAYNARD

time we started back down, Tom had long since hurried off and left me.

In some spots the rim narrows and steepens, but climbing up I had not noticed that. If I skidded to the right, I would go over the precipice into the crater. To the left, clouds pressed against the mountain a long way below. I crept downward, digging in my crampons.

"It is your first mountain," said my new friends. "Would you feel more comfortable with a rope?" I said yes.

WHEN WE REACHED a level spot, they untied me and asked whether I knew "self-arrest." I said I didn't. So they taught me how to use my ice axe to break a fall and made me practice several times before we continued.

"Someone should have shown you," they said. I agreed. Mountain Travel's advertisement had stated I would be taught all the techniques I needed. I hadn't been, but maybe I should have known to ask.

A few other details also bothered me. Such as not being warned that when you're high in the mountains the pressure differential in a jar of freeze-dried coffee can propel the powder like shrapnel when you break the paper seal. Hilarious? I guess so, but coffee in my eyes was not. And then there was Cheyne-Stokes respiration. As soon as I dropped off to sleep, I stopped breathing and awoke gasping for air. It felt as if a feather pillow were pressed against my face. Cheyne-Stokes is common among mountaineers, and virtually everyone will experience it if he goes high enough. Yet it scared the hell out of me until I questioned the trip doctor. No one had told us about Cheyne-Stokes, either. But in climbing mountains you can't really expect anyone to hold your hand or wipe your nose.

Our next volcano was Ixtaccihuatl, 500 feet lower than Popo. While waiting to start for the summit, I peered at the mountain with dreadful fascination. I was so preoccupied that I did not notice the argument between our leader and Leo Le Bon, one of the owners of Mountain Travel, until, right there in the middle of the mountain at 4 A.M., Tom quit. Leo was with us to learn about the volcanoes so he could lead the next tour. He said not to worry, now he would lead. Leo had demonstrated a love of good food, good wine and good times. Some of the members, however, questioned his ability to lead and remained behind. As it turned out, Leo had more leadership and patience than Tom, and the climb became an exhilarating adventure.

A few months later I was in Africa and took my second mountain tour, a five-day luxury trip up 19,321-foot Kilimanjaro. It was run by the Marangu Hotel in Marangu, Tanzania. A porter carried my gear on his head, unrolled my sleeping bag at night and in the morning brought me tea in bed. But there were problems. On Kilimanjaro the guides try to exhaust their clients by rushing them up to the crater. If they are successful and the clients poop out, the guides are spared the four-mile round trip to the summit. In my group of 10 only four of us persevered to the summit.

THE FOLLOWING SUMMER I saw an advertisement that said a professional alpine guide was leading a trip up 20,702-foot Chimborazo, in Ecuador. I queried organizer-leader Frank Ashley about the amount of climbing experience needed. He wrote back that Chimborazo was the easiest 20,000-footer to climb. Later, I learned he had never climbed it.

Only two other people, Stan Stephan and Bob Nelson, both from Colorado and both experienced mountaineers, showed up for the tour. From the first they were disenchanted with the leader, Frank. "You can tell a mountaineer by the way he keeps his ropes," they muttered, and Frank's ropes always seemed a tangled mess. I reserved judgment until Frank collapsed at 16,000 feet. He could not go on, and we had to help him off the mountain.

Bob was so disgusted that he went home. Stan and I still wanted to climb, so we went back and scaled the mountain together.

A YEAR LATER I paid $965 plus round-trip travel expenses to Argentina to take a climbing tour up the Aconcagua, whose 22,834-foot summit is the highest outside central Asia.

The tour was run by Mountain Travel, and Leo Le Bon was our leader. He had three assistants: John Fischer, an instructor at a West Coast climbing school; Miguel Alfonso, a solidly built Argentinian who had scaled the Aconcagua several times; and Raphael, who was to assist Miguel. Engineers Herb Packard and Doug Maynard were from the East, as I was. Physicians Don Brown, Reinhold Ullrich and Peter Stevens, vocational coordinator Gene Markley and nuclear engineer Jeff Baier came from California. The youngest member of the group, 25-year-old Glenn Porzak, was an attorney from Colorado. Although most of us met for the first time on this trip, there were no personality problems; in fact one of the pluses of commercial tours is that I have never experienced any personality conflicts on one.

To climb the Aconcagua it is necessary to get permits from both the police and the army. Sometimes the Aconcagua can be easy to climb; in 1934 an Italian party even led two dogs up it. Yet altitude, intense cold and blizzards have made it the most deadly of the major mountains. Sixty-eight people have died trying to conquer it, and the mountain broods over its own private cemetery for mountaineers killed on its slopes.

The Aconcagua tour the year before had stalled at 18,000 feet while the guides went to the aid of an expedition from Oregon. Two members of that expedition died. By the time the others were safe, the Mountain Travel guides were too exhausted to continue, so the tour went back down. Leo said all his organization could guarantee this year was adventure.

THE FORMALITIES STARTED in a dimly lit room in a police station. We were photographed, fingerprinted and our pictures drawn. Then a police doctor listened to our hearts, took our blood pressure and told us to come back later because the electrocardiogram machine was unavailable. We had heard of climbers without local friends who had been delayed for weeks trying to get the necessary climbing approvals. But Miguel was able to get the cardiograms waived because there were three doctors in our party. Our police permissions had been obtained in a single day—something of a record.

Suddenly, word came that we must be ready to leave in two hours, a day early. The mountain road was being repaired, and blasting would close it for the next four days. We waited. Darkness came. The chartered bus had broken down. By 11 P.M. another bus had been located. We squeezed ourselves and our luggage inside and rushed off into the night. Three A.M. We turned off the paved road, bounced a few miles and stopped.

Our equipment was unceremoniously dumped; the driver had to be back past the blasting point before dawn. We had driven a hundred miles and climbed to 9500 feet. The stars were bright with a crisp winter look. Everyone shivered while poking through baggage for sleeping bags.

The next morning we packed and hiked four miles to the army post, 1500 feet below our camp. If disaster came, the army would be obligated to attempt a rescue. Therefore they wanted to make sure our equipment was adequate.

A soldier poked silently through the pile of clothing in front of me. He picked up my parka, shook it till the down expanded to full thickness, looked at the hood, peered down a sleeve. "Nice," he said in English.

Then came another physical examination. Two clerks pounded furiously at typewriters as the doctor's cold stethoscope traveled slowly over my chest.

"Stop!" The doctor waved his hand curtly at the clerks. The typing ceased, and the icy stethoscope started probing again. When I am

On Kilimanjaro, the guides try to exhaust their clients by rushing them up the mountain to save themselves the extra work of climbing all the way to the summit.

nervous, my heart sometimes skips a beat. I was nervous now. The doctor's face was absolutely blank as he listened. Then he barked out 64, 120/80 in Spanish and started listening to the next man's chest. When he finished, we had the last of the needed permissions. We could try to climb the Aconcagua.

O N OUR SECOND DAY we climbed the 13,000-foot Cerro Banderita. To do it we had to hike down to the army camp again and through Puenta del Inca, a former hot spring resort. We walked past the ruins of a hotel and the resort's old sulfur baths to the base of Cerro Banderita. It is an enormous slag heap, and its summit was almost a mile above us.

The going in the loose scree was rough, and my knees creaked in rebellion. Although I had climbed a hundred flights of stairs a day for a month before leaving home, it had not been enough, and I was exhausted at the end of the practice climb. Aching and discouraged, I stripped and slid with the others into one of the old resort's steaming sulfur pools.

Half an hour in the hot sulfur water worked miracles. Afterward, the four-mile trek up to camp seemed a breeze.

The following morning a pack of mules arrived. They would transport our gear while we carried only daytime necessities: water, lunch and sweaters.

For two days we hiked up austere, boulder-strewn valleys to become acclimated and to get a better view of the Aconcagua's south face. It loomed increasingly large, then towered above us, a 10,000-foot cliff of snow and ice, one of the world's most imposing precipices.

Next morning we headed for the *ruta normal,* which ascends the northwest side of the mountain, up the Horcones Valley. To reach it we had to cross a murky torrent of water. "Too deep," the mule skinners said, "but we can cross in the morning."

Next morning we hurled our possessions across a narrow gorge through which the river cascaded around automobile-sized boulders. The mules were led to a wider, calmer place a hundred yards downstream. The rushing water rose to their bellies; it was too swift and too deep for

us to ford there. The literature Mountain Travel had supplied prior to the tour strongly advised use of a rope for such crossings. I do not know whether we ever had a rope, or whether it had been lost. As it was, we had to jump across the narrow gorge. There was no time to think "What if?" The man in front of me jumped; someone behind me was waiting. I took a mighty leap and was safely across.

Raphael, one of Leo's three assistants, was not as lucky. During the crossing, a rock smashed his foot. Our doctors decided a bone had been chipped. He could not continue and had to return with one of the mules.

The valley before us was without vegetation. At first its stony floor was crisscrossed by a number of rivulets, easily stepped across. But as the day grew hotter and the mountain snows melted, the streams coalesced and grew in size.

Then the valley narrowed and a trail became visible, winding along the rubble-heaped side of the canyon toward the first mountain shelter, Lower Plaza de Mulas.

W E SHARED THE HOSTELRY that night with some Mexicans and Germans. During our sojourn we met climbers from six countries and as far away as South Africa. Some had reached the summit, some had not. Successful or not, the climbers coming down looked beat.

The following day we walked up to the second shelter, Upper Plaza de Mulas, a thousand feet above. This was the mules' last stop; they would return for us in a week.

The summit was 9,000 feet up, a three-day climb. But the supplies were too heavy to permit going straight to the top. We would have to haul some of the gear to 18,000 feet, cache it, climb back down, and then start for the summit with more gear. That afternoon we divided food and fuel, some tents and two of the three oxygen cylinders into piles of 50 pounds each. The oxygen was for medical emergency. One cylinder was to be left at the Upper Plaza de Mulas, the second at 18,000 feet and the third at the Berlin huts, our last night's stop before the summit.

We left early the next morning. Soon we encountered the only topo-

graphic obstacle the mountain offered, the Nieves Penitentes, a field of ice pinnacles caused by differential melting of the glacier. These fields expand and contract, and in some years may be completely absent. With our bulky frame packs, it took us an hour to maneuver between the six- to 10-foot spires.

Slowly, rhythmically, trudging one step after another, we climbed on. In six hours we reached the Antarctica hut, an aluminum shed six feet square. Snow had started to fall. We hurriedly piled the gear outside the hut, covered it with lightweight tarpaulins, anchored them with rocks against the developing gale and hurried back down the mountain.

The next day we rested and puttered with our equipment. The energy required to carry each additional pound to the summit would be equal to loading 500 bags of cement onto a truck. We combed our pockets and packs for items to eliminate and hid them among the boulders. There was talk of taking only a few cameras, of sharing films and pictures, but we reached no agreement, so we each lugged our own camera.

The second trip up was enjoyable; the added acclimatization time and lighter loads made the difference.

W E CAMPED A FEW hundred yards from the Antarctica shelter on Portachuelo Pass, 5,000 feet below the summit. A series of 18,000- to 20,-000-foot peaks extended on three sides. Behind us the Aconcagua loomed upward into dark clouds.

That night the condition of Jean, who had been suffering from diarrhea for several days, grew worse. In the morning he descended alone and we continued upward through alternating periods of snow and sun. The ascent to Berlin, two small A-frame shelters and a boxlike hut perched at 20,500 feet, was short and easy. But the wind had increased, and the temperature dropped precipitously. I crawled into one of the A-frames. The slanting sides seemed to press down on me and restrict my breathing. I rushed out, panting from the sudden exertion. My tent-mate, John, was a smoker, but anything was better than the hut, and the swirling snowstorm made sleeping without a tent impossible. After creeping into my sleeping bag, I pulled in my boots and water bottle to keep them from freezing. They crowded me uncomfortably, but no one slept much that night anyway.

Then: 4:30 A.M. I switched on the flashlight and looked at my thermometer: 18 below zero. I pulled on my boots and put on all my clothing. Outside, we stood about, stamping our feet, trying to keep warm. We wanted breakfast, hot tea, anything. But there was nothing. The night was clear; the first fringes of light were just appearing. High altitude kills the appetite, and there were problems over breakfast. To hell with it. Reinhold, Glenn, John and I started out.

In the gloom the trail was difficult to follow. Once we lost it and wasted 20 minutes. Glenn raced ahead. This day the route was steeper, and I made no attempt to catch him. Reinhold joined me. The sun rose, and we worked slowly upward. John, the professional mountain guide, had disappeared. Later we learned that he had become sick and turned back. Ahead of us was another A-frame hut. The door was missing, and a ragged hole gaped in the roof; inside there was nothing but snow. This was the Independencia shelter, 21,300 feet above the sea, the highest shelter in the world.

From there the trail rose in a series of switchbacks to a ridge, became level as it skirted the side of the mountain, then ended abruptly in the Canaleta, a great field of jumbled rocks. They ranged from pebbles to Volkswagen-sized boulders tilted at a 45-degree angle to the summit, only 200 yards higher. A thin coating of snow covered the smaller rocks; everything underfoot rolled and slid. It was no place to climb one behind another, so Reinhold and I separated. Each would find his way to the summit alone.

I lurch up the steep incline, panting. Ahead is one of the auto-sized rocks. Can I make it in 10 steps? I count them. One. Two. My breath is coming faster, but my whole being is tied to completing those 10 steps. At last, I place my foot on a flat rock. It tips toward me. I stagger and almost fall. I move one foot forward and bring the other up to it. Ten steps completed. The "Volkswagen" is still ahead. I luxuriate, conscious of breathing. Ten breaths, 10 steps, I must move on. I pull one heavy,

booted foot up and set it down, then lift the other. I am immersed in a nightmare; I am running in a sea of molasses from some unspeakable monster.

But this is not a bad dream; the monster is a part of me. I plod mindlessly on, making all of 50 yards per hour. Is this how it is with salmon struggling upstream? I look back. Some members of the group are closer now. They will tell me I have to turn back, that we must be off the mountain before dark. I try to hurry. A rock rolls from under my feet, I fall and a cloud of feathers wafts away from a rip in my down overpants. I creak upward, propping myself on ski poles. Self-indulgent, I take an extra five breaths. Why not pave the Canaleta? The thought seeps into my anoxic mind. I laugh out loud. The sound of my own voice snaps me from the reverie. I am horrified: I do not want to hallucinate. The year before, some members of the Oregon expedition swore they had seen road-building machinery on the Canaleta; two of those people died.

Time passes; I am almost there. Doug, who is on the summit, waves a ski pole at me. The last 20 feet are almost vertical. I stop to breathe. To the left a yellow-clad figure is sprawled on its stomach, black hair tousled among the stones. It is a Japanese climber who died a year ago.

The last few feet are excruciating. Then, suddenly, I am on a small, upward-tilting triangular plateau strewn with stones. At one end stands a low cross made of iron pipe. I lift my ski poles above my head, and Doug takes my picture. We shake hands, and he starts down.

I was alone atop the southern and western hemispheres. Inexplicably, I cried. Then came intense aliveness, a quiet exhilaration. Crowded peaks extended in every direction below me. I had won something. But what? The pleasures of climbing are very private, a secret from even the mountaineer himself.

Reinhold arrived. We took more pictures. Half an hour later we left and picked our separate ways down.

THE NEED TO BALANCE, to twist, to make all those minute muscular adjustments that prevent falling remain when descending. But the energy requirements are less, the body does not sob for air, and fatigue is more in the consciousness.

At the base of the Canaleta, Peter, Herb and Miguel, who had reached the summit just after Reinhold, joined us. We would travel back to the Berlin shelters together. Single file, we set out.

"Stop, Jeff's sick." It was Herb's voice. But Jeff? None of us had seen him all day. Yet there he was, lurching against me as Herb led him forward. I learned he had climbed with Leo and Don until they separated for the struggle up the Canaleta. Both Don and Leo had abandoned the climb and descended. Jeff, feeling ill, had sat down to rest, dozed and, fortunately for him, had awakened as we passed. Now he was desperately ill with cerebral edema, a potentially fatal affliction of high altitude. Peter and Miguel left to hurry down and seek help.

The route just before the Canaleta crosses a great, uptilting scree field, but the path is only slightly pitched and walking was easier. Nevertheless, Jeff was like a drunkard. Staggering, he kept slipping away from whoever was supporting him. Then he would roll a short distance down the mountain and have to be led back.

Our progress was slow. We decided that I should go ahead to the Independencia shelter, try to clear away some of the accumulated snow and make it as habitable as possible. As I started down the switchbacks, Herb passed me. Jeff's condition had deteriorated; Herb was returning to Berlin to urge haste. Help was imperative. But what help?

One of the problems of high altitude is that the oxygen-deprived brain does not think clearly. Because all 11 members of our tour had attempted the summit, the only ones who might be at Berlin to help were John and Glenn—John, who had turned back because of sickness and Glenn, who had reached the top hours ahead of everyone else. Nobody knew when Leo and Don turned back, but as their climb had not been successful, it was doubtful whether they could ascend again.

There is danger in the Aconcagua's technical ease, which permits unroped, solitary travel. Two members of the Oregon expedition had wandered away from the party and died. Now, our group had fragmented into small segments. Possibly tour owner–leader Leo should have waited to shepherd us down, like the captain of a ship being the last to leave. But at altitude an almost mystical drive to climb is requisite; money alone cannot compensate for physical travail. Thus on commercial tours the potential for lack of commitment can make leadership problematical.

I peered inside the Independencia shelter. Wind had compacted the snow in the back half as high as the roof. The front half was covered with two inches of powder. I crawled in. An advertising brochure from Mountain Travel promised sleeping bags would be in the hut "in case a bivouac is needed." But they were not there.

In a corner was a little stove, its gas cylinder in place, ready to light. A pot for melting snow made me aware of my thirst. I needed a match, and there weren't any. Suddenly I was angry and much thirstier and colder.

"Pave the Canaleta!" I thought. It would make the most esoteric of bumper stickers; I would get some made when I returned home. I cleared the snow from the front of the hut with an iron bar and prodded the drift in the back. Too hard. I would never get it cleared away. I crawled outside.

THE WIND WAS STARTING to blow. It was mercilessly cold. I fumbled with the zipper of my down parka. It had never worked easily, and I had to take my gloves off. No use. The zipper would not close. I put the mitts back on and started to make a rock wall where the door should have been. The work exhausted me. It got darker and colder. I crawled back into the hut.

The wind was pushing through the empty door and rushing from the gaping hole in the roof. I crouched in one side, the wind swirling everywhere. I squirmed to become as small as possible and cowered, shivering, in the farthest corner. I crept outside and crouched behind the hut. There had to be a lee someplace, but I couldn't find it. I shouted and for some reason

it helped. "Hello! This way! Pave the Canaleta!" I crawled back in, hid in a corner and clutched the parka around me. Violent shaking . . . the start of hypothermia. I was dying on that damn mountain. A boulder for a marker, and the epitaph: "He couldn't get his zipper zipped."

Outside again. "Goddamn it, pave the Canaleta!" Inside again. An embracing lassitude scared the hell out of me and drove me outside again.

John and Glenn came at 2 A.M., pushing sleeping bags through the hole in the roof. "Where are the others?" they asked. Somewhere higher on the mountain. But the rescuers were too exhausted to push on. We wedged tightly together in the hut—the snow bank on one side, the empty doorway on the other, stars shining through the ragged hole overhead. Within my sleeping bag warmth slowly returned.

The stars faded . . . dawn . . . daylight. There seemed little hope for anyone being alive higher on the mountain, little urgency to push up toward Reinhold and Jeff. So we continued to lie there, huddled together.

"Hello, Charlie. Are you there?" A ghost, a voice that could not be. But there was Reinhold, supporting Jeff. Elation!

"The wind, Reinhold. How did you survive the wind?" I asked.

"Why, we didn't have much wind. We just bundled up and lay down on the scree. It wasn't too bad." They had been on the other side of the ridge, in the lee of the mountain. Even so, their survival seemed a miracle.

John and Glenn helped Jeff back to the Berlin huts, and Reinhold and I followed. After resting a few hours, we descended all the way to Upper Plaza de Mulas. We waited a day for the mules, then walked 26 miles back to the roadhead. That night the mule skinners barbecued great chunks of kid, which we consumed with quantities of beer and rich red wine. The bus came for us next morning.

Jeff has since completely recovered. For a few weeks my fingertips felt wooden. Then the dead, frozen

skin sloughed off, the fingers returned to normal, and I started thinking about my next tour, to the summit of 18,465-foot Mount Elbrus, the highest peak in Europe.

Another commercial tour? Why not? The tourist organizations provide a lot of services. In Mexico I did not know how to find out about climbing the volcanoes; in Argentina local contacts saved days, perhaps weeks, in completing the formalities. Elbrus is in the Soviet Caucasus—it would have been a hassle without professional travel know-how. That trip was led by Jim Henriot, a Tacoma attorney, chairman of The American Alpine Club Expeditions Committee and a prominent climber. Jim's able leadership coupled with Mountain Travel's know-how produced a magnificent trip and proved that trauma need not be a part of mountain tours.

I HAVE SENSED A condescension among some mountaineers toward people who take climbing tours, as if the idea of financial profits sullies the mountains.

Not true. How else could an overage, East Coast archeologist gain the experience necessary to participate in a private climb? If you live far from the mountains and want to try climbing, paid tours might be just the ticket for you. Just be sure to check the organization and leadership.

Elbrus was my last commercial tour. Since then I have been on two private mountaineering expeditions, one to the Canadian Arctic and one to the Hindu Kush, in Afghanistan. For both, the necessary logistics consumed several months' time. This summer I will climb Mount McKinley with Glenn Porzak, who led the Hindu Kush expedition. After Afghanistan, organizing an Alaskan climb should be child's play for him.

But time is valuable, and when a competent commercial organization such as Ray Genet's is available to attend to details, why not use it? That is what we are doing. So do not denigrate commercial tours. Despite their failings, they fill a need. ◢

BACKPACKING IN GRIZZLY COUNTRY

by ORVILLE E. BACH, JR.

There is only one really big fear that I have in the wilderness—and that is bears. I know that grizzlies are supposed to be the only bears that would attack you unprovoked. But I'm not sure that I can always live so carefully in the wilds that I don't inadvertently do something to provoke a brown or black bear.

While my fear doesn't keep me out of bear country, it does make me very cautious. The grizzly is unequivocally the most powerful and ferocious wild animal in the United States. It is aggressive, fast enough to run down a race horse and unpredictable. Every year a few people are mauled or killed by this great beast. What should you do if you are backpacking in grizzly country?

The following pieces on grizzlies, the first by Orville Bach and the second by Bill Schneider, have some good advice about hiking and camping in any bear country.

W.K.

Last summer Barrie Gilbert, a biologist studying grizzly bears in Yellowstone National Park, got too close to a grizzly sow. The bear charged and severely mauled Gilbert's head. Extensive reconstructive surgery was required to treat the wounds. Fawn Pass, the area in which the mauling took place, was immediately closed while park rangers investigated the incident. Gilbert believed the mauling to be his fault for trying to get too near the bear. The rangers, therefore, did not attempt to relocate or destroy it. But park officials did urge all hikers applying for permits to hike in that area to have at least four persons in their parties because larger groups are less likely to be attacked by bears.

This mauling was the only injury definitely caused by a grizzly last year in Yellowstone and Glacier National Park. Other grizzly incidents did occur in Canada and Alaska, though. In Waterton Lakes National Park, the Canadian counterpart of Glacier National Park, a grizzly killed a girl, and in Mount McKinley National Park in Alaska, a woman lost both arms from a mauling. Each year there is an increase in backpacker use of areas that are grizzly habitats. Park officials, despite their efforts to keep humans and grizzlies apart, are more and more concerned.

HOW TO BEARPROOF YOUR CAMP

How to bearproof your camp in grizzly country. *Pitch your tent at least 150 feet* <u>*upwind*</u> *from your cooking area and your food and garbage. Try to place its door near climbable trees. Suspend food and garbage in sealed plastic bags at least 12 feet above the ground, five to ten feet from the tree trunk, and five feet below the limb on which they hang. A clean campsite without tempting or strange odors will best insure a night's sleep untroubled by bear visits.*

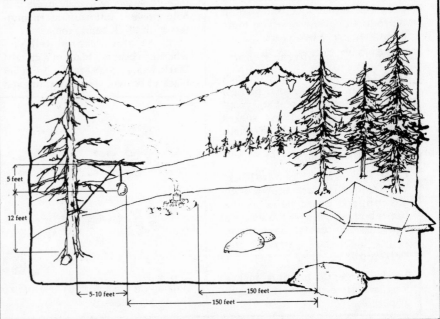

Hikers going into grizzly country can do much to reduce the risk of encountering bears. Although grizzlies are the most ferocious mammals in North America, they are usually anxious to avoid humans. They don't like to be surprised, however, and they will fight to defend their food or their cubs. In hundreds of days of hiking in grizzly country, I have had only one close call—and that because I wasn't as careful as I should have been.

Coincidentally, my encounter was near Yellowstone's Fawn Pass, where the biologist was attacked last summer. A friend and I were approaching a spruce thicket. Our scent couldn't precede us because of a strong headwind, nor could we see very far ahead on the trail. What noise we made was obliterated by wind in the trees. Just as we entered the woods, the trail made a sharp left turn. And there on the trail was a grizzly cub. It let out a wail and scooted away into the trees.

Rod threw off his pack and zoomed up a tree. I tried to do the same, but in my panic I forgot to unfasten my waist belt. On my knees, I frantically tore at the buckle. I glanced over my shoulder and saw a big grizzly mamma about 15 yards away and closing fast.

Finally free of the pack, I bolted for a tree. This reaction was a mistake because you can't outrun a grizzly. I was in luck. For some reason, the grizzly stopped chasing me. I was 20 feet up the tree when she nonchalantly loped away into the forest with her cub.

We had made many mistakes and got away unharmed. We were lucky.

Before entering grizzly country—for even a few hours—you should take some basic precautions and be mentally prepared for the slight chance you may encounter a grizzly. By understanding the animal and using proper hiking and camping procedures, you can further reduce that risk.

▶ *Know the bear.* While planning your trip, read one of the many books on the grizzly to help understand its characteristics, capabilities, and behavior. Your pre-trip research should include learning to distinguish between black bears and grizzly bears. If possible, ask a park or forest ranger for

Bear Facts

THE GRIZZLY BEAR

Scientific Name: Ursus horribilis.

Present Range: Yellowstone National Park and the surrounding national forests in Idaho, Montana, and Wyoming; northwestern Montana; north-central Washington; much of Alaska and western Canada.

Size: South of Canada, 350 to 800 pounds, with a few old-timers reaching 1,000 pounds. Slightly larger in Alaska and northern Canada. Females usually smaller than males.

Number of Young: One to four, but usually two. Born in a den in January or February. Females retain their cubs well into their second year, so reproduction cannot occur more often than every two years.

Life Span: Twenty-five to 35 years.

Diet: Omnivorous. Heavy on such vegetable matter as roots, berries, and succulent forbs. Eats small animals like gophers and snakes and a few large mammals. In certain places such as Alaskan salmon streams, fish are important.

Color: Ranges from blond to black, but frequently dark brown with silver-tipped guard hairs on the upper body which give the animal a "grizzled" or "frosty" appearance. Hence the names "grizzly" and "silvertip."

Track: Large, 10 or more inches long, with five claw marks usually apparent.

Grizzly bear   *Black bear*

HOW TO TELL A GRIZZLY FROM A BLACK BEAR

Grizzlies are more fearsome, yet black bears also require respect and great caution. Black bears, better able to cope with human encroachment upon wild lands, are more numerous and, in Yellowstone and Glacier national parks, have caused more human injuries and property damage than grizzlies. Precautions taken because of grizzly bears will help prevent unfortunate encounters with black bears, too.

Color alone cannot tell you whether a bear is a black or a grizzly. Black bears' coats range from jet black to brown, cinnamon, or even blond. Better criteria are shape of face, size, and body profile.

Grizzlies have a concave or dished face, similar to that of a dog; black bears' muzzles are fairly straight, and the head is small in proportion to the body. An erect adult grizzly stands six to eight feet high; a black bear only five to six. Grizzlies' claws are alarmingly long; black bears' are not as noticeable. But the best way to distinguish the two is provided by the prominent hump on the back of the grizzly bear. The black bear has no such hump.

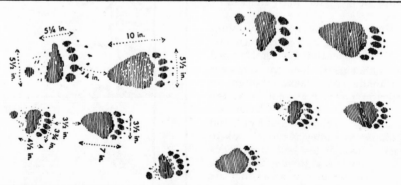

Walking gaits of a grizzly (top) and a black bear. Notice the longer claw marks in the grizzly tracks.

literature before hiking in grizzly country. This is especially important for day hikers, since overnight campers often are given this information along with their backcountry use permits.

▶ *Be alert.* While hiking, carefully watch the trail ahead and on both sides. Avoid areas obviously used by bears.

▶ *Make your presence known.* A wild grizzly usually will avoid hikers—*if* it knows where they are. So make noise constantly. Surprising a grizzly—particularly a female with cubs—may be the worst thing a hiker can do. If possible, hike with the wind at your back. Wearing a "bear bell" on your pack probably is better than trying to keep up steady conversation on long trips. It's easy to forget to announce your approach at every blind spot in the trail, and human voices tend to be muffled by the trees.

▶ *Never hike alone in grizzly country.* Not to hike alone is good advice for any backpacking trip. But it goes double for hikes in grizzly country because bear attacks occur less often on large parties than on small groups or solitary hikers.

▶ *Stay away from carrion.* Carefully detour around any carrion, which grizzlies relish. It can attract bears from miles away.

▶ *Pick a good campsite.* Set up your camp with the possibility of bear trouble in mind. Keep it clean and odor-free. Pitch your tent at least 50 yards upwind from the cooking area. Try to camp near climbable trees. Avoid campsites near such signs of bear activity as scratchings and scat.

▶ *Be careful with food and garbage.* Next to startling a grizzly, careless handling of food and garbage is most likely to bring bear trouble. Smelly foods are taboo; carry dried or freeze-dried foods instead. Eat in one spot and wipe up any food that spills. When fires are permitted, burn leftover scraps, fish entrails, and empty food containers to erase lingering odors. (Remember to dig the remains from the ashes and pack them out with the rest of your garbage.) If fires are forbidden, seal garbage tightly in a plastic bag and store it at least 50 yards downwind from your sleeping area, preferably suspended 12 or more feet off the ground. Do not sleep in the same clothes in which you cook and eat—especially if you habitually wipe your hands on your pants. Before retiring, wash the odors of food and insect repellent off your hands and face.

▶ *Special precautions for women.* The National Park Service recommends that women stay out of grizzly country during their menstrual periods, since bears have attacked women in this condition.

▶ *Avoid all cosmetics.* Don't use or carry perfume, hair spray, or other cosmetics because their smells can attract and infuriate bears. Additionally, there are indications that the odors of human sexual intercourse may incite bear attacks, especially during bear mating season in June and early July.

▶ *Leave pets home.* Pets are usually banned in national park backcountry but may not be in national forests. Nonetheless, don't take your pet along. There is evidence that pets, especially dogs, attract bears to campsites and hiking parties.

▶ *Give any bear plenty of room.* If you see a bear at a distance, make a wide detour around it, keeping upwind so it will get your scent. If you can't detour, hold your ground until it moves out of the area, but stay as far from it as possible. If you can't get around the bear, abandon your trip.

▶ *Stay cool in a confrontation.* If all precautionary measures fail and you come face-to-face with a grizzly, try to react calmly and correctly. The typical reaction of an unprepared backpacker —to panic, scream, and flee—generally is the worst possible response. You cannot outrun a grizzly that wants to catch you, and by trying you might excite it into pursuit. So keep calm.

If the bear is not aggressive, you should cautiously and slowly retreat. Unfasten your waist belt and look for a tree. If the animal moves toward you, walk slowly to the tree and climb as high as possible. Adult grizzlies cannot climb trees, but they may be able to "walk" up stout lower branches.

If the bear advances rapidly, your response should depend on the distance to the tree. This decision—to run or not to run for the tree—is vital.

Don't overestimate your ability or underestimate the bear's. Before running, drop your pack or some other object to distract or delay the animal. Run downhill if possible; since bears have short forelegs and long hindlegs, they run downhill more clumsily than uphill.

If you cannot make the tree, play dead. In the summer of 1976, two hikers in Yellowstone Park who surprised a female grizzly with cubs were charged. They played dead. The bear sniffed at them, rolled them around, and then departed, leaving them scared but uninjured. What could have been a fatal encounter was averted by their quick thinking. Other hikers have likewise avoided serious injury by playing possum.

When playing possum, you should protect your most vulnerable parts— belly, neck, and the insides of arms and legs—by clasping your hands tightly behind your neck and lying face down with your legs pressed together. If the bear rolls you around, try to stay curled in the fetal position to guard your neck and abdomen. Don't struggle, cry out, or resist.

These rules will not assure a trip without bear trouble. But if all hikers strictly adhered to them, the number of bear encounters would decrease. ▰

WHO NEEDS GRIZZLY BEARS?

by BILL SCHNEIDER

WHEN GRIZZLY BEAR AND MAN happen onto the same spot at the same time, the results are never dull. Packs, tents, even entire camps get demolished. Wilderness vacations, long-planned and eagerly awaited, come to untimely and occasionally tragic conclusions. Some hikers are frightened out of the woods into a lifetime of martini drinking. A few others—about a dozen each year—are mauled, sometimes fatally.

Most grizzlies live in national forests and parks heavily used for backcountry recreation. Aren't these public lands intended for people as well as for animals? So who needs grizzly bears?

A mere 175 years ago the grizzly ranged from the Mississippi River to the Pacific Ocean and from central Mexico to the Arctic Circle. Over this vast habitat it reigned supreme among the native fauna, fearing nothing.

In 1804 and 1805, Lewis and Clark led the "Corps of Discovery" from St. Louis to the West Coast and back. One of their more notable discoveries was the grizzly, which they called the white bear. The explorers had many colorful confrontations with the awesome creature and killed at least 43 of them during the two-year expedition.

Mountain men next invaded the high country, and after many bloody battles named the grizzly Old Ephraim. These early adventurers seemed obsessed with the challenge the grizzly presented. Perhaps they were contesting to see who was king of the mountains.

The extermination of many local bear populations came when the livestock industry spread like a tidal wave over the oceans of grass. The only good grizzly was a dead one—a theory cowmen and woolgrowers went to great lengths to prove. The grizzly couldn't endure against repeating rifles, leghold traps too strong to be set by hand, poison, trained hunting dogs and, when all else failed, guns set so

grizzlies (and other animals) could trip over wires and shoot themselves. In short order, mountain range after mountain range became bearless. Before long entire states were without their magnificent menace.

A grizzly population of 100,000 or more south of Canada shrank to fewer than 1,000. And the infinite wilderness so vital to the animal was whittled down to a few slivers of security in Idaho, Montana, Washington, and Wyoming. Here, *Ursus horribilis* now is making its last stand in the continental United States. It is, perhaps, a losing battle. *Progress* keeps coming to grizzly country, and the beleaguered bear doesn't fit into the scheme of modern America.

BUT THIS IS HARDLY NEWS. All backpackers worth their freeze-dried ice cream know that wilderness is in trouble. Some backpackers, though, fail to realize the link between the grizzly and

wilderness. "Permanent grizzly ranges and permanent wilderness areas are of course two names for one problem," Aldo Leopold noted in his conservation classic *A Sand County Almanac*.

"As surely as the sun rises every morning," agrees Andy Russell in his book *Grizzly Country*, "grizzly country is wilderness country, and we cannot live without it."

In September, 1975, the U.S. Department of the Interior (using the authority of the Endangered Species Act of 1973) designated the grizzly a threatened species south of Canada. This action started a bitter debate over whether publicly owned grizzly habitat (particularly national forests) should be kept livable for the big bear or should continue to be developed by commercial interests.

The controversy came to a head this year when the Interior Department revealed its draft recommendations to declare about 13 million acres of the

**Grizzly Country
1800**

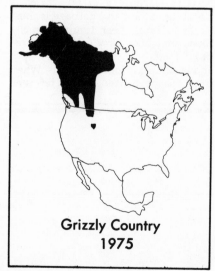

**Grizzly Country
1975**

Although grizzlies still thrive in Alaska and western Canada, in the lower 48 states their population has shrunk from over 100,000 in 1800 to less than 1,000 today.

northern Rockies as critical grizzly habitat—a protective status specifically required by the Endangered Species Act. When finalized, the plan will make it a crime to develop critical habitat to the bear's detriment.

Even a casual evaluation leads a reader to conclude that the plan can help keep national forests free of extensive development without placing roadless land in the Wilderness Preservation System authorized by the Wilderness Act of 1964. There is, of course, nothing wrong with protecting areas by including them in the Wilderness Preservation System, but critical habitat status might be easier to obtain because under it more latitude would be allowed for commercial uses.

When parts of national forests are declared critical habitat, many commercial and recreational uses will continue, but there will be a *limit*. Development will *stop* when it jeopardizes the grizzly population. Significantly, the land will remain open to some commercial uses such as limited logging, but it will remain desirable terrain for both grizzly bears and backpackers—which means it will remain wild.

Unfortunately, many westerners loathe this plan just as they do most government plans. Of their reaction, Montana conservation leader Don Al-drich observed: "They say it's dangerous to get caught between a female grizzly and her cubs. But it's much more dangerous to be caught between *Homo sapiens* and his nickel."

Opposition was omnipresent and violent. A few spoke bravely for the plan, but amid the criticism of stockmen, miners, outfitters, resort developers, loggers, off-road vehicle clubs, realtors, western politicians, game departments, and chambers of commerce, their voices were lost.

The plan to give long-needed protection to the grizzly's last domain is therefore floundering. It isn't dead, but its future resembles that of the bear itself—uncertain.

AS BACKPACKERS, should we care? What does the grizzly do for us besides rip up our camps and chew on our flanks while we frantically climb the closest tree, which wasn't close enough?

So far, certain backpackers have recognized the umbilical cord-like connection between grizzly bears, wild country, and quality hiking. But as a group, the presence of backpackers has not been felt. At this time no backpacking lobby is strong enough to save the grizzly. It is clear that backpackers won't work long hours for critical habitat designation, wilderness pres-ervation, or any other plan to help the big bear unless they wish its salvation. But why should they want forests to be inhabited with these beasts? Exactly how dangerous is the grizzly?

After extensive study, Dr. Stephen Herrero of the University of Calgary concluded that the probability of getting mauled by a grizzly was a mere seven-thousandths of one percent. That sounds awfully safe compared with the chances of getting killed in an auto accident or murdered on the streets of Detroit. Despite such statistics, however, someone will sooner or later be hurt or killed by a bear.

Since Montana's Glacier National Park started keeping records in 1913, 138 people have died there from causes *other than bear maulings*—drownings, falls, vehicle accidents, hypothermia, avalanches, etc. During the same period, only three individuals have been killed by grizzlies—three of 29 million visitors. Other national parks in the United States and Canada have similar statistics.

I view the remote chance of a bear mauling as part of the backpacking deal, along with hazards such as wildfires, avalanches, sudden illness, falling trees, and unexpected storms. Wilderness camping cannot be totally safe. Do we even want it to be?

I've researched and written about

THE CATCH-22 OF BEAR MANAGEMENT

The conflict between grizzly bears and hikers in national parks isn't going away. And whatever park officials do to reduce the number of confrontations, it seems somebody always thinks it's wrong, too late, or doesn't go far enough.

The conflict came to a head in August, 1967, when two young women camping in Montana's Glacier National Park were fatally mauled. These were the first lethal bear incidents in the park's history. Since then, interest in bear maulings has been extremely high. As one park administrator put it, "We could have a multiple-death car accident and it wouldn't even make the local paper. But if somebody gets scratched by a grizzly, it's on every front page in America."

Since 1967 park officials have worked hard to prevent confrontations. Park visitors get warnings about hiking in grizzly country when they enter the park, and warning signs are posted at every trailhead.

Such education, however, has failed to stop maulings. In the early 1970s bloody meetings between bears and people increased dramatically in Yellowstone National Park after the National Park Service started closing garbage dumps where the bears habitually fed. The closures went against the recommendations of two noted wildlife scientists, Drs. Frank and John Craighead, and initiated a bitter debate between the Craigheads and park wildlife managers.

In 1972, after a young man was fatally mauled in Yellowstone Park, his parents sued the National Park Service. They claimed that the Park Service had created an overly dangerous situation by abruptly closing the dumps. They won the case and were awarded $87,000 in damages. The Federal Government, however, appealed to a higher court, which overturned the decision.

This case brought up another issue, liability. Park administrators reacted accordingly. Researchers began looking for ways to route people more safely through grizzly habitats. At the first hint of bear trouble, trails, campgrounds, and, at times, even entire drainages were closed to public use. Education programs were intensified for an ever-increasing number of tourists. But the problem still persisted. In 1976 grizzlies killed three persons in Canadian and U.S. national parks. Another Canadian park visitor died in 1977. And there were a few nonfatal incidents.

Many park administrators and hikers are beginning to think this may be a "no win" situation. Certainly, more efforts by both groups will reduce the number of incidents. But there's no sure solution. As long as grizzly bears and backpackers frequent the same places, they will occasionally meet.

—Bill Schneider

the grizzly extensively, and one problem continues to gnaw at me. At a typical 500 pounds, the grizzly is unequivocally the most powerful wild animal in the continental United States. In addition, it has a bad temper and enough speed to run down a race horse. It stalks and kills elk and moose. It is a supreme example of strength and unpredictability. Meanwhile, thousands of day and overnight hikers tramp into every corner of its domain every summer. We should be easy prey for such a great omnivore. Why, then are there so few maulings? To me it seems a miracle that so *few* backpackers are attacked.

WHEN I HEAD FOR THE HILLS, I'm looking for a wilderness experience—a serene intimacy where living systems work as naturally as possible, where only nature's sounds are heard in a place without man's "improvements." I could experience wild country without worrying about rubbing noses with a 500-pound ursine. I could go to eastern wilderness areas or to one of many western wildernesses where the grizzly has been exterminated. But after hiking hundreds of days, I find that I get the richest rewards in grizzly country. The remote possibility of seeing the great bear adds an extra dimension to the trip. It makes for a real wilderness trip rather than just a walk in the woods.

I consider the grizzly the wilderness king, not only because it is still the dominant species in wild places but because it embodies the spirit of roadless country. Seeing its massive, 10-inch tracks pressed into mud or snow thrills me as no other spoor can. When I recall my best trips, I invariably recount the hikes when I was afforded a rare glance at a grizzly, or when I spot-

ted its tracks along a crescendoing mountain stream.

In the summer of 1968 Robert Hahn was severely mauled by a female grizzly while trying to take a picture. Upon recovery, he had a surprising view of the confrontation.

"The thing that makes me very unhappy," Hahn remarked, "is my fear that this will only add fuel to the fire for those people who advocate destruction of the grizzly to make the national parks safe. There is no reason, in the name of civilized progress, to kill an animal for doing what is natural . . . I feel no malice toward the bear."

"The only thing that will prevent me from hiking in the wilderness again is the eventual destruction of the wilderness itself," he added. "And when anyone advocates the destruction of grizzlies, he is in essence advocating the destruction of true wilderness."

WILD ANIMALS HAVE BECOME indicators of environmental quality, and there is no better example than the grizzly. Where the grizzly walks, the land has retained most of its natural integrity. There, we find invisible air, drinkable streams, incredible vistas—including entire horizons without pollution plumes, native trout, climax forests, large drainages without any works of man. Stately pines, untainted breezes, wild creatures, and quiet sounds blend together into a wilderness song as old and proud as the mountain summits and as rich as life itself. Through this high country, along the perilous peaks of the Great Divide, marches the majestic grizzly, truly the wilderness king.

Miners used to take canaries underground with them; when their birds died, they scrambled to the surface because they knew that the air was

going bad and that they would die next. Today we must watch *our* canaries, the wild creatures around us. When they start to die, though, we may have no safe surface to scramble to.

One of our canaries, the mighty grizzly bear, may be dying. We can't afford to lose it. The sky won't fall if the grizzly disappears, but it will be a sure sign that the future won't be worth living.

Who needs grizzly bears?
We all do. ●

ADDITIONAL READING
• *Where the Grizzly Walks* by Bill Schneider. Mountain Press Publishing, Missoula, Montana, 1977.
• "The Great Grizzly Controversy" by Bil Gilbert in *Audubon*, January 1976.
• *The Night of the Grizzlies* by Jack Olsen. Putnam, 1969.
• *Grizzly Country* by Andy Russell. Alfred A. Knopf, 1968.
• *The World of the Grizzly Bear* by Walter Schoonmaker. Lippincott, 1968.
• *The Beast That Walks like a Man* by Harold McCracken. Hanover House, 1965.
• *The Grizzly Bear* by Bessie and Edgar Haynes. University of Oklahoma Press, 1953.
• *A Sand County Almanac* by Aldo Leopold. Oxford University Press, 1949.
• *The Grizzly: Our Greatest Wild Animal* by Enos A. Mills. Houghton Mifflin, 1919.
• *The Grizzly Bear* by William Wright. Charles Scribner's Sons, 1909.

SNAKES, SNAKEBITES, FIRST AID, AND TREATMENT

by LOU PEREZ, M.D., AND DAVID SUMNER

Blind snakes, water snakes, racers, king snakes, boas, garter snakes, rattlesnakes, more. To the average backpacker who sees only half a dozen snakes along the trail in a year, the diversity of species is astonishing. There are more than 2,000 species worldwide—nearly 200 of them in the United States—and many additional subspecies. Snakes are found on every continent except Antarctica. In North America they are virtually ubiquitous. Red-sided garter snakes have been reported north of Fort Smith in Canada's Northwest Territories, while king snakes, garters, and several species of rattler have been noted at elevations above 10,000 feet in the mountains of New Mexico, southern Utah, Arizona, and southern California.

Except in Australia, poisonous snakes are the minority. Of the species native to the United States, only about 10 percent are venomous: 19 different species and 42 subspecies. In popular terminology, they include rattlesnakes, copperheads, cottonmouths, and the beautifully colored coral snakes. But the actual dividing line between dangerous venomous snakes and harmless snakes is shadowy. The lyre snakes of California and the Southwest have poison but lack the technology to injure humans: their fangs are at the rear of the jaw and can reach only very small prey such as lizards.

About 45,000 snakebites, by all species, occur annually in the United States. Of these, between 15 and 20 percent (something between 6,000 and 9,000) are made by harmful poisonous snakes. Precise figures are hard to come by because many bites are not reported.

More than half of all recorded cases occur in only six states: North Carolina, Texas, Georgia, Florida, Louisiana, and Arkansas. North Carolina is the national leader with almost 19 bites per 100,000 people. Maine, Alaska, and Hawaii bring up the rear; few, if any, poisonous snakes live in these states.

There is a great difference, however, between raw statistics and a backpacker actually being bitten by a poisonous snake. Furthermore, not all bites are serious. Much of the popular literature about snakebite and its treatment sensationalizes the danger with grisly artwork, low-angle photos that enlarge the snake's size, and exaggerated horror stories. There's no question that a poisonous snakebite is serious, but there's no sense in living in constant fear either. Consider these facts:

• A major percentage of bites are incurred by people who are, so to speak, asking for trouble. They include amateur and professional snake handlers, herpetologists who handle snakes regularly in laboratories or zoos, devotees who use snakes in religious ceremonies, hobbyists, exotic dancers, etc. Persons who hunt or attempt to kill poisonous snakes also fall in this category. A 1976 report in *Patient Care*, a medical magazine, states that 30 percent of all snakebites seen in the United States are made by captive snakes.

• Clinical records show that most

cases occur close to home. Examples include children playing in woodpiles, farmers working fields, people stepping off their porches at night, and cotton and berry pickers—largely in rural settings. Of the ample cases cited in medical literature on poisonous bites, a substantial number reached hospitals within 30 minutes, and the overwhelming majority within 2½ hours. The inference is clear: instances of bites deep in the wilds, many hours from the nearest hospital, are comparatively rare.

• As a group, backpackers favor mountains. Though many exceptions exist, America's poisonous snakes tend to inhabit lowlands. In the East, of course, this tendency is blurred by the mountains being low. Timber rattlesnakes have been identified atop Wayah Bald (5,316 feet) in North Carolina and just below the summit of Indau Knob (5,941 feet) in Tennessee. A more typical statement comes from a Forest Service employee in Andrews, North Carolina: "About the highest elevations we have in this region are 6,000 feet," he says. "We find rattlers right to the highest tops. However, they are never as plentiful as on some of the lower slopes." In the West, despite a number of high altitude exceptions, rattlesnakes are rare in or above the montane life zone. In Colorado, where the prairie rattlesnake is the major species of concern, few hikers worry about bite danger above 8,000 feet. The snakes stay lower.

• Medical authorities agree that 25 to 30 percent of all poisonous snakebites result in *no envenomation (injection of poison) at all.* Less unanimously, they say that up to 50 percent of all cases require no treatment for poisoning.

• Nearly 60 percent of those bitten are under the age of 21. A major portion are children who lack the caution that comes from knowledge and are wont to poke hands in holes under rocks, veer off the trail, and play around logs and

Central American Rattlesnake in striking position. Reprinted from the book Rattlesnakes *by Laurence Klauber,* University of California Press.

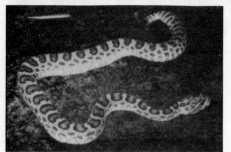

PRAIRIE RATTLESNAKE
Crotalus v. viridus

COTTON MOUTH
Agkistrodon piscivorus

WESTERN DIAMONDBACK RATTLESNAKE
Crotalus atrox

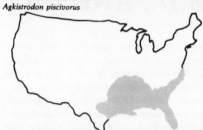

MASSASAUGA RATTLESNAKE
Sistrurus c. catenatus

COPPER HEAD
Agkistrodon contortrix

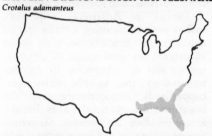

EASTERN DIAMONDBACK RATTLESNAKE
Crotalus adamanteus

PACIFIC RATTLESNAKE
Crotalus u. oreganus

TIMBER RATTLESNAKE
Crotalus horridus

CORAL SNAKE
Micrurus f. fulvius

other snake habitats. Dr. Nathan Strickland of the University of Arkansas notes "a decreasing incidence of snakebites with increasing age."

There is little question, then, that the incidence of harmful bites is overrated. In six years at Everglades National Park, Chief Ranger Jerry Hammond recalls three cases. Two were pygmy rattlesnake bites received by park personnel who were working daily in the bush. "The occurrence of snakebites is more a myth than anything else," he says. "Our snakes will do anything they can to get away from a human. We have antivenin kits placed around the park. Most have never been used."

Dr. Nicholas C. Johns, director of the medical clinic at Grand Canyon National Park, echoes Hammond's sentiments to the word: "The idea that there's a high risk of encountering poisonous snakes is basically a great myth." Johns has spent three summers at the clinic and normally sees 30 to 50 people daily—most for ailments such as heatstroke and sunburn. During that period five snakebite cases have come into the clinic. Grand Canyon's Chief Ranger Dave Ochsner recalls a research team from Southern Illinois University that was expressly looking for rattlers, which are presumed to be common in the park. The scientists couldn't find any.

So, for the backpacker, the chance of dangerous snakebite is very low. For those sticking to established trails, it is even less likely than for those given to bushwhacking or rockwhacking. No one has ever worked up any kind of figures for the ratio of poisonous snake encounters to bites, but statements like this are common: "I've been backpacking intensively for eight years in the Rockies and the Southwest. In that time I've seen six rattlers. Four buzzed [rattled] courteously, and I gave them a wide berth; the other two were heading for cover when I saw them."

Despite the rarity, however, backpackers can and do get bitten by poisonous snakes. Although the odds are a million to one against, somebody loses. Because the possibility exists, snakebite is something to know about, and the first rule is: *Take bites seriously.*

If you are bitten by a rattler, copperhead, cottonmouth, or coral snake, the consequences of going without treatment range *between none and death.* Since 1960, the estimated annual deaths in the United States have numbered between 12 and 20—approximately 0.035 percent of all bites. Although incidence of bites is rising because more people are outdoors, the fatality rate is dropping because of greater public knowledge and improved medical care. The eastern and western diamondback rattlesnakes account for about 95 percent of all deaths. Both species are large and aggressive; they inject the greatest amounts of venom, and it is highly potent. The venoms of the coral snake and the Mojave rattlesnake are equally lethal, but

---

How to Avoid Snakebites

The first American flag pictured a rattlesnake with 13 rattles representing the colonies and bore the words, "Don't Tread on Me." No creature likes to be walked on by any other. This is a basic territorial fact. The best way to avoid snakebite is to avoid snakes. But that's not always easy. All poisonous snakes except the coral are naturally camouflaged. When a human approaches, they usually freeze. Those two characteristics make sighting difficult. Be attentive and watchful in snake country.

• Don't step where you can't see or, when climbing, reach up where you can't see. Many bites occur when someone reaches over a ledge or steps blindly over a log.

• Don't put your hands inside holes, in logs, trees, or rocks.

• Don't wander around camp in the dark without a flashlight. Many poisonous snakes are nocturnal creatures for much of the year.

• If you hear a rattler buzz, stop! Find out where it is, then make a careful retreat. Normally, rattlers will strike only at a moving object.

• When camping in snake country, choose a clear area away from rock piles, brush, and other suitable snake cover. If you're using a tent, zip the mosquito netting closed. While the old stories about snakes in your bedroll are probably not true, there is always the possibility of rolling over on a snake while you are sleeping or accidentally hitting one with your hand.

Combining these basic precautions with a knowledge of snakes in your area and their habitats will go a long way toward protecting you from harmful bites.

Two volumes in the Peterson Field Guide Series will give you a good start on identifying poisonous snakes:

• *A Field Guide to Reptiles and Amphibians of Eastern and Central North America* by Roger Conant, Houghton Mifflin, Boston, 1975.

• *A Field Guide to Western Reptiles and Amphibians* by Robert C. Stebbins, Houghton Mifflin, Boston, 1966.

---

these species are retiring and must usually be provoked to bite.

If death from snakebite is rare, injuries—painful, ugly, and crippling—are not. Almost all result from wounds inflicted by members of the pit viper fami-

ly (Viperidae: rattlesnakes, copperheads, and cottonmouths). Pit viper wounds constitute 98 percent of all incidents in the United States, and the various poisons act similarly, causing both local and systemic (i.e., affecting the entire body) harm. The remaining two percent of bites are made by the coral snake, a very different species belonging to the Elapidae family, which also includes the Old World cobras, kraits, and mambas. The poison of the coral snake generally produces little local damage; it works systemically on the nervous, respiratory, and heart functions. Its treatment is a special case not covered here.

Almost all (96 percent) pit viper bites occur on the extremities, most often the ankle or the top of the foot. Next most frequently bitten are fingers and thumbs.

Pit viper venoms vary, but all are extraordinarily complex substances. Says Dr. Strickland: "They contain five to 15 enzymes, three to 12 nonenzymatic proteins, and at least half a dozen other substances known and unknown." For the snake, their function is simple: they poison a prey to death, then help digest it. When applied to humans, the venoms quickly begin to destroy red and other blood cells, lymphatic vessels, capillaries, and muscle tissue. Blood may lose its ability to coagulate. There is pain, swelling, discoloration, and often blistering. In effect your foot—or leg or hand—is being readied for digestion by the snake.

Not to treat such an injury is to ask for much pain over a long period of time. To ignore a pit viper bite is to toy with losing a limb or use of the limb, if not from the venom itself, then from secondary infection or gangrene. To ignore any sort of poisonous snakebite is to chance heart and nerve damage and assorted breakdowns of other systems. In short, it's stupid.

Not surprisingly, snakebite remedies and treatment date back to antiquity both in Europe and North America. Aristotle had a cure for asp bites; Nicander (150 B.C.) listed many herbal remedies, and Pliny the Elder (60 A.D.) recommended chemical caustics, agents derived from snakes, a split chicken, goat's or cow's milk, and 196 different plant preparations. Not all at once, but in various situations. Among North American Indians, almost every tribe had its own prescriptions, often accompanied by ceremonies and medicine priests trained or designated to cure bites. Plants were the most common remedy—pulped in a poultice, boiled as a tea, or both. Ethnobotanists have identified more than 75 plants used as poisonous snakebite remedies, including goldenrod, plantain, white ash bark, tobacco, and peyote. Indians of the American Southwest often used yucca leaves, jabbing the area of the wound with the needlelike spines in a manner that combined acupuncture and blood-letting.

American settlers and immigrants picked up many of the Indian cures. Were one to do a dissertation entitled "Poisonous Snakebite Treatment in the United States from Colonial Times to the Present," he would produce a grand brew of folklore, humbug, hucksterism, and groping, trial-and-error medical progress. Fads in treatment came and went. And the dividing line between worthless antidotes and true treatment was shadowy and blurred. Cutting and sucking, today's most frequently recommended field treatment, dates back to antiquity in the Old and New Worlds; it is commonly recommended in North American medical treatises of the 1700s.

Colonists and pioneers used tourniquets in conjunction with cutting and sucking. Cooling as a method of treatment goes back to 1906, antivenin research to 1887.

Some old-time methods, once highly recommended, have slipped into seemingly permanent disrepute. A few are worth noting because of former popularity.

• <u>Ammonia</u>. Snake venom was thought to be an acid which could be neutralized by alkaline ammonia. The notion appeared first in the United States in a 1738 treatise. It was tested and found worthless in 1765. In the early 1800s, it was touted as a new miracle cure. Then it fell to disrepute once again, only to be revived in the 1890s as, you guessed it, a new and sure remedy. Today's verdict: useless.

• <u>Cauterization</u>. Earliest mention was in 1648. John James Audubon rec-

ommended using a hot iron in 1827, and Wyoming cowboys of the 1870s substituted the handier branding iron. Black gunpowder was an acceptable substitute: just sprinkle a portion on the wound and ignite. The best that can be said for this method is that it distracted the victim's attention from the bite.

• <u>The Split Chicken</u>. Mice, swallows, pigeons, kids, lambs, toads, frogs, rabbits, and cows all have been used, but the common chicken eventually won out. The Rx: Slit a chicken and apply as a poultice to the wound area. When the chicken's flesh turns green or its comb blue, the poison has been removed. This method, a fowl litmus test, is bogus.

• <u>Exertion</u>. One O.F. Potter, in an article in the *Buffalo Medical and Surgical Journal* of 1870, cited a case in which a rattlesnake bite victim was forced to run beside a buggy as it carried his rescuers to the nearest doctor.

Striking Coil

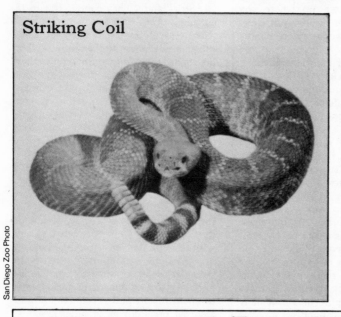

San Diego Zoo Photo

Sleeping Coil

Twelve *Snake* Facts

1. Rattlesnakes have two coiling postures, one for resting and one from which to strike. In the former the coil is flat like a pancake; in the latter the body rises in a vertical spiral, with a large, open loop on the ground for support. Many snakes alleged to be "coiled and ready to strike" actually are asleep.

2. The strike is astonishingly quick, usually faster than the human eye can register, but not, as has been said, "the fastest thing in nature." A striking human fist is faster.

3. A rattlesnake can strike a distance of one-half to two-thirds its length. Nevertheless, that is not to be taken as an indication of safe range, for it's very difficult to estimate a coiled snake's length.

4. Rattlesnakes can bite from any position; the coil-and-strike position is

merely the most efficient.

5. Snakes do not jump through the air like flying bed springs. Rattlesnakes do not throw venom any more than porcupines throw quills.

6. Why the rattle? Various suggestions have included a poisonous device, a repository of lethal dust, a mating noise or a means of calling nearby snakes for help, of charming prey with sweet sounds, or of paralyzing prey with a deadly sound. It's now agreed that the purpose of the rattle is to warn off creatures that might harm the snake.

7. Rattlesnakes do not always rattle before they strike. Chances are that one will rattle if it has time to get itself into a defensive coil.

8. Rattlesnakes do not, like certain

wasps, die after striking. They can and will strike repeatedly.

9. The venom of juvenile pit vipers, age six to 12 months, tends to be more toxic than that of adults. The size of a snake has little bearing on the strength of its poison.

10. Rattlers are not out and around only when it is hot. When temperatures are high, they're more apt to be hidden in the shade, becoming more active when temperatures moderate.

11. Rattlesnakes can climb trees and bushes, and they can swim.

12. This year in the United States, more people will die of bee stings than of poisonous snakebite. Perhaps the biggest snake myth of all is the one of constant, lurking danger—under every green tree and on every high hill—of a dangerous viper.

Results of this treatment were not disclosed. Today it's generally agreed that exercise speeds circulation of the blood, spreading venom through the body. Now, flogging, pinching, and massaging also are rejected along with exercise.

• Liquor. J. Frank Dobie, the Texas historian and folklorist, notes the common use of "pure old bald-face, white mule, red eye, prickly pear juice, forty-rod liquor" in his book, *Rattlesnakes* (Boston: Little, Brown, 1965). He is talking about whiskey which, he adds, "is as good for rattlesnake bites as it is for colds." To Dobie's list, one might add cancer, poison ivy, measles, and loneliness. At best, the effect of alcohol on snakebite is indirect and psychological only; it can calm a hysterical victim who demands that "something" be done at once. Medically, alcohol increases the circulation of blood and speeds the spread of venom.

• Snakeweed. Various plants are called master weed, snakeroot, snakeweed, or *hierba de vibora* because of a belief that where the Almighty has placed a danger, He has also provided a cure. In Arkansas the medicinal plant is reputed to be a certain wild hyacinth; in Oklahoma, the purple coneflower; in Texas, a milkweed; elsewhere, plantain, horehound, and garlic. The only thing any of these plants has ever supplied is false confidence to travelers and dwellers in poisonous snake country.

The list of folk cures goes on: tobacco, indigo, vinegar, turpentine, kerosene, iodine, adrenalin, mud. What each attests to is a deep fear of poisonous snakebite, an equally deep desire to counter that fear, and the intricate working of evolution which has created venoms so complex that the finest medical, pharmacological, and biochemical research of the 1970s has failed to discover the still-dreamed-of sure

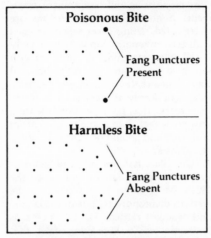

cure. Today there are many proposed methods of care for snakebite, and tomorrow there will be more. Most will come and go while the dream lingers on.

Predictably, present-day medicine exhibits substantial differences about how to treat poisonous snakebite—both in regard to first aid in the field and treatment in the hospital. When a pit viper strikes, what do you do? Use a tourniquet? Where? How tight? Do you cut and suck? Cut where and how deeply? Suck with what? Do you apply ice? Use antivenin? Use the scalpel? Administer corticoids? Give aspirin? These are but a few of the questions.

BACKPACKER's review of medical journal articles authored or coauthored by 24 authorities in the United States, plus work by another 13 who have dealt with venomous wounds in Nigeria, Rhodesia, and South Africa (specifically the Johannesburg area), revealed no consensus. Instead, a contrary state of affairs prevails for both specific and general procedures.

Making the basic distinction between *field* first aid and *hospital* treatment, here are some of the differences, and a few of the agreements.

First Aid

All authorities concur that anyone bitten by a pit viper should get to a hospital as soon as possible; they recommend calming the victim and immobilizing the injured limb. From then on, controversy rages.

Tourniquet. Most authorities say yes and right away; some say only if moderate-to-severe symptoms appear. Dr. Robert E. Arnold of Louisville, Kentucky, says only if you're half a day or more from a hospital; his theory is that otherwise the tourniquet reduces circulation and increases the chance of loss of tissue. Some say to place a tourniquet above the wound; some say both above and below. Some say the tourniquet should impede lymphatic and venous flow; some say lymphatic flow only. There is general agreement, however,

How Bad is the Bite?

Grade	Signs and Symptoms				
	Fang marks	**Local pain**	**Local swelling**	**Discoloration**	**Systemic symptoms can include**
MINIMAL	Yes	Slight	Slight	None	None
MILD	Yes	Sharp and burning; throbbing	Moderate	Yes	None
MODERATE	Yes and oozing blood	Severe and burning; throbbing; tingling and numbness	Moderate to severe	Yes	Shortness of breath Quickened or lowered pulse Weakness Dimmed vision Giddiness Nausea and vomiting
SEVERE	Yes and oozing blood	Agonizing; numbness	Rapid and severe	Rapid and spreading	Same as for moderate bite, plus: Enlarged and aching lymph nodes Tingling around mouth, face, scalp Pinpoint pupils Slurred speech Shock and unconsciousness

that arterial flow should not be blocked—you should be able to feel a pulse below the tourniquet.

An April 1978 American Red Cross paper on poisonous snakebite says to apply a tourniquet if any symptoms appear. It says the tourniquet should be "from ¾ to 1½ inches wide, not thin like a rubber band." But Dr. Alan Dimick of the University of Alabama recommends use of a string tourniquet to ensure the blockage of just lymphatic flow. One of these is included in the widely marketed Cutter's snakebite kit.

People who recommend a tourniquet say it slows movement of the poison to other parts of the body. Dr. Arnold, however, says that dilution of the venom through the bloodstream can cut down on damage to tissue at the bite site.

Cut and Suck. The purpose is to remove venom from the bite area. Most authorities say yes, cut longitudinally (along the axis of the limb) at the fang marks, not in an "X" and not from one mark to the other. Proponents say cutting and sucking can withdraw up to 50 percent of the poison. Others agree with Dr. Robert H. Dreisbach, of the University of Washington and Stanford University School of Medicine, who says that incision is too hazardous to underlying structures and at best removes only 20 percent of the venom. Still others argue that it's not worth recommending because the victim is likely to be butchered. Dr. Arnold recommends using the rubber suction cup from a snakebite kit on the bite but is strongly opposed to any cutting by nondoctors.

Some say cutting must start within three minutes to be truly effective; others, including the Red Cross, say wait until symptoms appear; others that it's okay if begun within 45 minutes. Most agree that sucking accomplishes little after 30 minutes.

Some say it's all right to suck with the mouth. Others denounce that as unsafe for the person who's sucking (if he has a mouth sore, *he* may be poisoned too) and for the victim (because the human mouth is a sewer of pathogenic bacteria).

Cooling. Prolonged immersion in ice water (cryotherapy) is generally discouraged. Some say use no ice at all, anywhere, ever. Others, such as Dr. Thomas G. Glass, Jr., of San Antonio, Texas, say ice packs (or a synthetic substitute) applied around the bite, en route to the hospital and until formal treatment begins, help reduce pain and the spread of venom.

Treatment

Most disagreement about treatment in the hospital appears to originate from authorities' personal philosophies about medicine and their relative confidence in medication as opposed to surgery.

Antivenin. The aggressive approach to medication urges that antivenin be administered promptly and intravenously, even if serum sickness (a common complication) is likely. The more conservative approach encourages close monitoring and symptomatic treatment. It notes that many victims are overtreated, citing cases when patients with zero envenomation were needlessly dosed with antivenin and burdened with serum sickness and a costly hospital stay. Doctors favoring more vigorous treatment imply it's better to be safe than sorry, that pit viper poisons are a greater danger than complications from antivenin and should be guarded against at all costs.

Dr. Glass has treated some 200 rattlesnake bites in San Antonio since the 1950s. Most of the bites were from the western diamondback, one of the largest and deadliest rattlers. Dr. Glass regards antivenin as "a life-saving *drug* that should be reserved for the most serious bites."

Surgery. Dr. Glass's approach to snakebite treatment, which has gained considerable support and attention nationwide, is surgical.

Dr. Glass discourages cutting and sucking in the field. He recommends application of a tourniquet above and below the wound, plus ice or similar cooling because it "definitely decreases the activity of the venom." He also recommends taking the offending snake to the hospital, "preferably dead." Once a case is before him, he evaluates it and, when serious, proceeds to surgically remove the tissue affected by the poison. Dr. Glass's critics regard him as overzealous with the knife; Dr. Glass, however, regards most antivenin adherents as overzealous with a drug.

So the controversy goes on. In the end, it testifies most clearly to the complexity of the pit vipers' poison and the great variability among cases. What kind of snake caused the bite? What is the nature of its venom? What is the general health of the victim? Is the victim a child or an adult? How serious is the bite? How long ago did the bite occur? How advanced is the poisoning? What is the victim's psychological state—terrified, calm, somewhere between? What complications are likely in this case? What's available in the hospital? What are the attending physician's best knowledge and skills?

Today, answers to these and similar questions, carefully and quickly thought out, are among the prerequisites for curing a pit viper bite.

THE BACKPACKER MAGAZINE

Recommended Method for Snakebite First Aid

The controversy over snakebite first aid and treatment in the United States stems from many causes. Pit viper venoms are complex substances: they vary in strength and properties. Victims vary too. Each case is different, and what works smoothly for some won't do the job for others. Additionally, all treatments are involved and multiple—reflecting the nature and effects of the injury. Were one to manage a wound from the instant of the bite until the victim was pronounced well, he would make and remake hundreds of decisions—assessing evidence, drawing on medical background, checking test results, etc. With such a complex procedure, differences are inevitable.

BACKPACKER's recommendation for what to do in cases of pit viper poisoning in the United States follows. It is not intended for the bites of coral snakes, which present a very different toxicology. This is a first-aid prescription *for the field* that presumes medication (i.e., antivenin) will be the primary treatment *in the hospital*—if warranted. So far, antivenin remains the mainstay of treatment in all but a few regions of the country. It is only logical that first aid in the field dovetail with what happens in the emergency room.

1. **Get the victim to a hospital.** Any suspected case of poisonous snakebite should reach a hospital as quickly as possible. *En route*, the victim should be kept still and calm; he should lie down if possible. The bitten limb should be immobilized; it should be kept at or below heart level. But first, *be sure it's a poisonous snakebite.* A few species have harmless look-alikes. When in doubt, assume the snake was poisonous until symptoms become clear. With youngsters, if no adult is around at the time of the bite, you should also assume the snake was poisonous until proved otherwise. If there's any doubt at all, get to a hospital.

Evacuation. What do you do when you're deep in the wilds, at least eight or ten hours from the nearest hospital? The answer is to know what the emergency evacuation possibilities are when you assess the severity of the bite—and then mesh the two accordingly. A bad bite by a western diamondback rattler far from help in Texas's Big Bend National Park probably means sending someone for a helicopter. A light bite in the arm in South Dakota's Badlands can come only from a prairie rattler, a species with moderately dangerous venom. A slow, watchful walk to the nearest road may do the job. If you're hiking with a strong group and can improvise a litter, that's an option. Balance the variables and choose the most appropriate course.

2. **Assess the wound.** Pit viper venom generally acts fast. Most reactions begin within five minutes; onset very rarely begins after four hours. If nothing happens within an hour, the victim probably is one of the fortunate 30 percent who get bitten but not envenomated.

As with burns, medical authorities have devised a scale of grading the severity of poisonous snakebite. A layman's version follows:

Minimal. Fang marks, but only slight local pain and just a trace of swelling. No symptoms elsewhere in the body. Often no envenomation.

Mild. Fang marks, sharp burning pain with swelling, discoloration (blueness like a bruise), and sometimes throbbing immediately around the bite. Only local symptoms.

Moderate. Fang marks, severe burning pain, and substantial, progressive swelling, throbbing, and discoloration. Bloody substance oozing from fang marks. Possibly a tingling and slight numbness. Systemic signs and symptoms (i.e., those occurring elsewhere in the body) may include quickened or lowered pulse, shortness of breath, weakness, dimmed vision, giddiness, vomiting, nausea.

Severe. Fang marks, rapid swelling and blue discoloration spreading quickly, pronounced numbness, agonizing pain. Early systemic signs may include enlarging and hurting lymph nodes and tingling around the mouth, face, and scalp. The same systemic signs as with a moderate bite are likely; others may be pinpoint pupils, slurred speech, and progression toward shock or even unconsciousness.

Fear is a primitive, natural, and immediate response to snakebites. It can cause weakness, dizziness, clammy skin, and fainting—symptoms often impossible to distinguish from systemic effects of venom. Therefore, *it's very important to reassure the victim from the moment of the bite.*

3. **Tourniquet.** Tourniquets both above and below the wound are good first steps and should be put in place quickly. Minimally, they assure the victim you are doing something. They will also help contain any venom that may have been injected. Place them from two to four inches on each side of the bite. If the bite is on a toe or finger, apply a tourniquet just above the ankle or wrist. The bands should be between three-fourths inch and two inches wide. String tourniquets may not adequately block lymphatic flow. That's *all* you should do. Do *NOT* block arterial flow to the wounded limb. Be sure you can slip a finger beneath the tourniquet. If swelling increases, loosen the tourniquet accordingly. Constantly monitor the swelling. The most severe problem with tourniquets is making them too tight.

4. **Cut and suck.** If you are within four to five hours of a hospital and if the symptoms are not severe, *do not* cut and suck. The cut-and-suck method, especially as done by an amateur, has hazards which are best avoided if possible. Much opposition to cutting and sucking is due to its frequent mishandling rather than its intrinsic merits.

But if it will take you more than five hours to get to a doctor and if severe symptoms occur, you should be prepared to use this measure, observing the cautions stated below.

The purpose of the cutting is to open the wound enough to draw out some of the venom. Incisions 1/8 inch deep in fleshy places, less on wrists, ankles, and around the eyes, will do the job. Go no deeper and make only two cuts measuring 1/8 to 1/4 inch long. The slits should be parallel. They should begin at the fang marks and extend along the path of the fang, at right angles to an imaginary line connecting the two punctures.

If you can, make the cuts along the skin's lines of stretch—the way the skin folds. Never make "X" cuts. If the bite is on a finger or toe or over a vein or superficial artery, don't cut at all; the risk of damage is too great. The wound should be swabbed with disinfectant before cutting; likewise, the razor or small knife (lancet) from the snakebite kit.

Sucking should be done only with the cup or pump from the kit. Do not use your mouth, for that would endanger you (poison could enter a sore) and the victim (your mouth has more pathogens than do the mouths of most dogs). If you cannot cut, sucking at the fang marks is still advised. A recent study using radioactive tagged venom showed that 50 percent of the poison can be withdrawn if sucking is begun within three minutes after the bite. After 30 minutes, little is accomplished. When you are finished sucking, swab the cut or wound once again, apply a light dressing to keep out dirt, and go to the hospital!

5. **Other considerations.** Good emergency medicine is the rule. If the victim lapses into shock, treat accordingly. If breathing stops, use mouth-to-mouth resuscitation. If both breathing and pulse stop, use cardiopulmonary resuscitation (CPR). For pain, give Tylenol. Do not use aspirin, alcohol, or sedatives. For anxiety, give reassurance. Be sure to stay calm yourself.

6. **Some don'ts.** Pit viper antivenin is manufactured solely by the Wyeth Laboratories of Philadelphia. It requires intravenous administration. It is a hospital treatment only. It can cause severe reactions which must be countered by sophisticated life-support measures. *Antivenin is not for use in the field.*

Ice as a first-aid measure is still controversial. It may do no more than lessen pain. Application of ice or chemical cold packs does slow the activity of the venom for the first three or four hours. Possible adverse side effects, including inhibition of the working of antivenin and reactivation of the venom when the ice is removed, are under hot debate. Until there is further clinical validation, the use of ice is not recommended here.

Some authorities say that the offending snake should be killed and taken to the hospital, with the victim, for positive identification. This is an unsound practice. It wastes time and can be dangerous. Laurence M. Klauber, the world's foremost authority on rattlesnake behavior, once decapitated 13 snakes and found their jaws active for as long as an hour thereafter. For up to 40 minutes the severed heads would open mouths, erect fangs, and bite sticks. The bodies did not coil as for a strike but did writhe. The evidence speaks for itself. Leave the snake behind; learn instead to identify the poisonous snakes in your area by sight. ▲

DEATH ON THE MOUNTAIN

by ED HALE

The Lake Placid News

When most people think of the dangers that lurk in the wilderness they usually have in mind two things, in this order: snakes and bears.

Now, while both of these dangers do exist in some backpacking areas, by far the biggest cause of death in the outdoors is a sneaky killer known as hypothermia.

When I was a kid you used to hear of people dying of "exposure." The new term is now hypothermia. The following article is true. It is a classic case and it is worth studying before hiking in cold weather.

W.K.

The following account of a tragic Thanksgiving weekend death in the nearby High Peak area of the Adirondacks has been pieced together from extensive interviews with those closely involved. It is presented in a straightforward chronological fashion using the participants' own words whenever possible. In effect, it is a case history of a mountaineering accident written to prevent and learn of the dangers inherent in hypothermia—"killer of the unprepared." With increasing numbers of novices finding their winter recreational opportunities in the mountains each year, knowledge of nature's rules is imperative. Readers will find related stories on hypothermia also included in today's paper. The time in developing these stories will be well worth the effort if even one potential accident is averted.—Editor.

Steven L. Collier—fit, lean and 23 with red hair and beard—arrived in the Upper Works parking lot in the Town of Newcomb at dusk Thanksgiving Day.

A hint of snow was in the air.

While Patrick J. Eagan, 27, organized his equipment in his Kelty pack from the jumble in the back of his 1974 Toyota station wagon, Steven contemplated his first backpacking trip.

For him, the trip would be the beginning of the end. About 29 hours and 15 minutes later, he would be dead.

The companions were college friends who met while attending Northeast Louisiana State University in Monroe, where they had worked in a pizza restaurant together in 1969.

Steven now worked in the supply room of the Eureka Tent Company in Binghamton. Patrick is a school teacher in Falls, Pennsylvania. His parents live in Binghamton.

Finally, they were organized.

Steven—5-feet 9-inches tall, weighing 165 pounds—was dressed in waffle-type cotton long johns, blue jeans, a cotton flannel shirt, Ragg wool socks, and summer hiking boots.

Patrick was dressed similarly except he wore cotton corduroy knickers.

About 5 P.M., they started the

1.75 miles to Henderson lean-to, following the yellow trail markers. At six o'clock they arrived to find five others occupying the shelter.

"We didn't feel like going on to Wallface [an additional mile]," Patrick remembers, "so we stayed there with them. They shoved over for us."

On the six-hour drive from Binghamton, they had bought only doughnuts to eat. So they were hungry.

They broke out their Teakettle brand freeze-dried casseroles and Lipton Cup-a-Soup, heating up the lightweight foods on Patrick's Primus gas stove.

AWAKE AT 8:30 A.M.

"Everybody else crawled in about 7:30," Patrick said, "and I think we waited until about 8."

Patrick had his thermometer along. The temperature was 19° F.

They snuggled down in their sleeping bags as about an inch of snow began to fall.

Steven's equipment was new—a Camp Trails pack, a Gerry sleeping bag, a foam pad, and a down

118

jacket. All good equipment.

The companions awoke about 8:30 Friday morning, had a breakfast of tea and oatmeal, and were on the trail by 9:30.

The pair did not carry any liquids with them except for Patrick's flask of brandy.

The party of five with whom they had shared the lean-to was on the trail, too. That group was made up of four hikers from Rochester—three of them apparently photography majors at the Rochester Institute of Technology—and the fifth from Ballston Spa.

Three hours later, at 12:30 P.M., after following red trail markers, the friends reached Summit Rock at Indian Pass, a distance of 2.67 miles from Henderson lean-to during which they had gained about 800 feet of elevation.

They ate a light lunch of rolls, cheese, deviled ham, and a mouthful of brandy each.

"My flask was leaking," Patrick said, "so we had hardly any left."

The pair had expected to bring candy bars to use as trail snacks, but Patrick said they had forgotten to buy them.

The day was bright—about 20 percent cloud cover, Patrick remembers—but the temperature was in the low 20s. They were on their way within 30 minutes.

"I would say," Patrick recalls, "that we left within half an hour. It was kind of cold."

So they started through Indian Pass toward the Cold Brook trail junction about 1.1 miles away, which leads between Mt. Clinton and Iroquois Peak of the MacIntyre range to Lake Colden.

TROUBLES BEGIN

"That's where it first started. We left the trail junction at 2:15. I got the time from the other party. They were sort of still with us at the time—we passed them; they passed us.

"But we were doing a bit better than they were because there were more of them and they traveled slower.

"But at the junction, we stopped for about 10 minutes and I asked the time. One fellow said it was about 2:15 and we should be there (Lake Colden) about 4:15. I remember 2:15 stuck in my mind."

At this point, Patrick felt Steven was "absolutely normal."

With 3.3 miles to go, they hiked up the trail to the height of land between Clinton and Iroquois as a light snow began to fall. Patrick was breaking trail. The climbing was strenuous.

Although Patrick is not clear about the length of time it took to reach the top of the pass, he said:

"I didn't have a watch with me. Neither did Steve. All I can say is that at the top of the pass it was getting sufficiently dark to be difficult to see the trail. The moon hadn't come out yet; it was still cloudy."

Steven began to slow down. Here's how Patrick remembers the situation:

"He was slowing down before we got to the top—as I was, too. I didn't want to stop until I got to the high point.

"When I did, I took my pack off and waited. The first person around was from the other party. He said: 'Your friend is back there a ways; he's not doing too good.'

"These are almost his exact words: 'He's got that I-don't-care-if-I-make-it attitude. And that's not a good attitude to have up here.'

"And all five of them just tromped right on past. They were making pretty good time. So I went back down the trail—maybe 100 yards—before I finally found him. He was coming kind of slow. He was tired."

STEVEN FALLS CONSTANTLY

Steven told his companion he was tired.

"I kind of walked him up to where I'd left my pack and gave him a piece of cheese," Patrick continued. "He ate it and I said to him let's take a breather for a minute."

Now Patrick was becoming concerned about the oncoming darkness and the cold. Steven said:

"Can I take my pack off and rest?"

His companion replied:

"The longer we wait here, the longer it's going to take to get down to Charlie Nolan's cabin."

Charles Nolan is the year-round caretaker who lives in the Ranger Station at Lake Colden.

They started off again. The snow was 12-18 inches deep, but the going was easier for Patrick since the party of five was now breaking trail.

But the situation was becoming more and more difficult for Steven.

"The thing that struck me," Patrick said, "was that he couldn't walk more than ten paces without falling.

"I had assumed that maybe his pack was throwing him off balance. I told him to stop trying to run and take it easy—heels first and just kind of shuffle along. We weren't floundering in the dark or anything because the light on the snow was good enough to see the trail.

"But he just could not keep his balance. He said once or twice: 'Why am I the only one who seems to be falling?'

"I said, 'You're trying to hurry too much—just take it easy.'"

Nevertheless, they proceeded. Patrick recalls Steven wanting to stop.

"Look," Patrick said, "that's not getting us there. The best thing for us is to get down and get warm."

Patrick was aware of the tent and warm clothing in their packs. He even thought of bivouacking.

"But I didn't think we were that far from Charlie's cabin," Patrick added.

ICE ON BROOK BREAKS

Shortly before the point where Steven became unable to walk, he had broken through the ice covering a shallow brook—wetting his legs primarily. Moreover, he had a good deal of snow melting into his clothing from his stumbling and falls in the snow.

"He was walking across a shallow brook and the ice broke," Patrick said. "He fell in the water twice because he could not keep his balance at that point. He got his pants wet; I couldn't see that he got his body wet."

Down the trail a bit, Patrick decided he needed help. He estimated that they were one-quarter mile from the ranger station at Colden, when the distance was, in fact, about a half mile.

"Looking down," Patrick said, "I could see the lake. I thought the best thing for me to do was to get down there quick and get back instead of taking time to get him in some kind of bag."

Patrick put his Eddie Bauer down jacket on Steven.

"He could hardly get his arms into it," Patrick recalls.

He remembers Steven sitting on the trail "on sort of a humpy thing."

When he left Steven, he said he appeared exhausted. Both had lost their hats by this time. Patrick said he was not familiar with hypothermia.

"Exhaustion," he said, "was what I thought he had really."

Would Patrick have done anything differently now?

"I realize, now," he said, "I should have put him in a sleeping bag or should have set the tent up. But then time was of the essence for me. And it was steep—not a good area for tents."

Patrick also assesses Steven's attitude as "very positive" about the trip in general.

"He was very positive," Patrick said, "about the whole thing up to maybe an hour before he couldn't walk. He enjoyed it. I told him it was one of the most beautiful trips I've ever had because of the snow. And he said how could it be more beautiful. He was really impressed by the scenery. I even asked him on the way up the yellow trail if it was worth driving six hours to get up here and he said it was worth it."

ALONE FOR MORE THAN TWO HOURS

As Patrick dashed down the steep mountainside, Steven sat alone with his new pack beside him—with its down jacket, sleeping bag, pad, and empty water bottle. He was to remain there alone for about two hours. Patrick said:

"I assumed I was closer and thought I could do it quickly. I thought it would be better to get him into the warm cabin—I know Charlie always has hot soup on—instead of trying to get the tent set up because it was extremely difficult terrain to try to get situated."

As the snow and darkness widened between the two friends, another phase of the tragedy began—the rescue.

At Lake Colden, the party of five, with whom Steven and Patrick had shared a lean-to the previous night, had arrived. They established themselves in a lean-to just across the dam and facing the Opalescent.

Arthur H. Reidel, 24, a computer programmer from Medford, Mass., was up at Lake Colden for what he termed a "lazy weekend—poking around on day trips and taking a few pictures." He had visited Charlie earlier for tea and conversation.

On returning to his lean-to, he was a bit annoyed to find five others occupying it.

"They were sprawled out all over the place—all over my things," he said. "They didn't even cook themselves supper or anything hot to drink. They just got in their sleeping bags and were going to zonk out."

At the ranger station, shortly after 7 P.M., Charlie Nolan remembers Patrick coming to his cabin. He said:

"Pat got here a little after seven. I told him there's an M.I.T. graduate here who has had a lot of experience in the mountains—a chap I've known for some time."

So Charlie sent Patrick across to get Arthur Reidel, just beginning his supper, as the party of five were going to sleep. Patrick went across the lake wearing only his flannel shirt and two T-shirts. Arthur Reidel said:

"I was cooking my supper when Pat came over looking for me. So I asked these people if any of them felt up to coming with me. They were photography majors or something from R.I.T. with 10-15 pounds of camera gear. Their sensitive camera gear was covered with snow and ice. That didn't impress me."

DIFFICULTY MET IN GETTING RESCUE PARTY

"When I asked them if anyone wanted to come along, they didn't rush to volunteer. I didn't push them because I didn't know how good they were going to be anyhow."

He observed that they seemed cold, wet and tired—thus, unable to be helpful on a rescue. Arthur Reidel continued:

"Then I ran to the next lean-to up the brook. There were a couple of people in there. I shouted at the top of my lungs. And nobody answered. It couldn't have been 8 P.M. yet. They couldn't be asleep.

"I knew there were people up on Cedar Point and Beaver Point, so I went that way. At Cedar Point, it was the same story. Nobody answered.

"Fortunately, at Beaver Point there were decent people. There were five of them. I stuck my head in and explained the situation. Right away two said they felt pretty good and would be glad to come along. So I just hoofed from there up to Charlie's while they put their boots on."

The two who took part in the rescue were:

Dexter Dimarco of Willow Grove, Pa., and George Herman of Glenside, Pa.

The four rescuers—Reidel, Dimarco, Herman, and Patrick Eagan—gathered at the ranger station. They took a hot Thermos of tea Charlie had prepared, a Coleman lantern, and the snow boat—a six-foot fiberglass rescue sled.

Charlie estimates the rescue party's departure time from the ranger station at about 8:30 P.M. Arthur Reidel agrees. Steven Collier had been alone for about an hour and a half. The temperature was 16° with a 5-10-mile-an-hour wind, Arthur said. He continued:

"We started right up the trail

dragging the snow boat. He was about a half mile up. It was very hard because it's very steep in a few places and there isn't quite enough snow so there is a lot of exposed rock. It's very narrow and twisting and the brook is open in a lot of places.

"We got up there and got to him—and geez, when we got to him he was pretty far gone."

Arthur estimates the time at about 9:15. Patrick believes it took them less time to get there than 45 minutes.

LAST STAGES OF HYPOTHERMIA

"I can't see that it took us 45 minutes to get there," Patrick said, "but it took us an awful long time to get down."

Arthur continued:

"Anyhow, we got up there and I took a look at him. He was pretty far gone already. He seemed to be in the last stages of hypothermia. I couldn't estimate what his core temperature was, but it was pretty darn low.

"I took his pulse and am pretty sure he was in shock already. I didn't time his pulse but it was pretty shallow. He was just barely conscious then.

"He couldn't talk and he was moaning a lot but he seemed to moan in response to his name. He had a little muscle control and we managed to sit him up and he could sort of cooperate a little bit.

"First, we tried to feed him some tea. He swallowed just a couple of sips and then wouldn't swallow any more. So we gave up on that.

"There were only two possibilities—one was to attempt to warm him up there, which would have been real tough. And I'm not sure how much we could have done for him. So the other alternative—since we couldn't have done an adequate job up there—was to get him down, to the cabin as fast as possible."

The party wrapped him in his sleeping bag, that they took from his new pack, and put him in the snow boat.

"We put him in his down bag," Patrick said. "It got wet, but it wasn't wet at the time. It got very wet at the end because a lot of snow was pulled in on it."

Arthur Reidel explained:

"The thought was that the best thing for him was to get him down as fast as possible. We weren't sure what shape he was in. When I went up, I thought we'd be able to dump some tea down him, stand him up, and march him down. But it didn't turn out that way . . .

"He was just barely conscious at this point. We put him in the snow boat and started down. It was really hell getting him down. It was really steep and in places the brook was open."

PULSE STOPS

"About 15 minutes from the cabin, we noticed that he had stopped breathing. I tried for his pulse again and he didn't have one that I could discern.

"But there wasn't going to be any good stopping then so we went as fast as we could for the cabin. When we got him to the cabin, he had no heartbeat at all. I put my ear right to his chest. Nothing.

"I wasn't sure just how far up the trail his heart had stopped so we quickly got him out of his clothes and I started cardiac massage and got somebody else to start mouth-to-mouth resuscitation. But he was dead. There were just no two ways about it . . .

"We gave him a fairly rough ride on the way down. There was no alternative to that. I'm sure we didn't do him any good, but he wasn't doing any good sitting up where he was.

"One of the worst things about it—and there were several—is that he was dressed in cotton from head to toe. I'm sure if he were dressed in wool from the skin out he would have lived.

"And the other thing, evidently his pal, Pat, although he had a fair amount of experience, he didn't know about hypothermia . . .

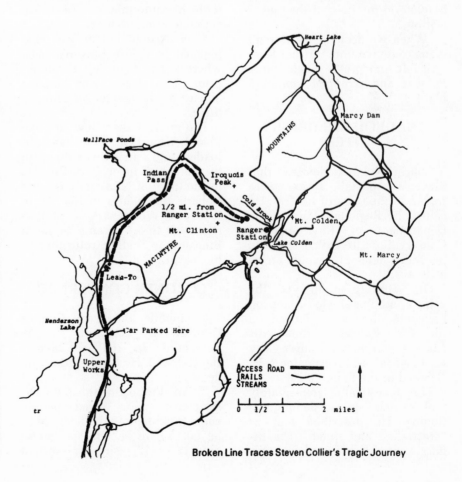

Broken Line Traces Steven Collier's Tragic Journey

"The cotton clothing was a disaster. Then, the last thing that really did him in was ... that he was sitting there in his blue jeans in the snow when we found him. If we'd gotten to him a half hour earlier, we might have pulled him out ... It was a real combination of tragedies—one of which, if it hadn't happened would have pulled him through. He died just 15 minutes outside the cabin."

Arthur Reidel said he'd been involved with mountaineering for the past six years, but had no formal training for first-aid certification.

"I have an awful lot of training," he said, "but none of it is with official certification. I've studied a lot with people who have and I've read books. And, unfortunately, I've been involved in a fair number of situations—rock climbing, ice climbing, and winter mountaineering—for six years now."

After the attempt to revive Steven with cardiac massage and mouth-to-mouth resuscitation in the cabin, they wrapped him in a blanket on the floor of the ranger station.

"When we decided we weren't going to revive him," Arthur said, "we left him pretty much where he was and wrapped him in a blanket."

INADEQUATE DRESS CITED

Charlie Nolan remembers that Steven's soaked socks were frozen to the soles of his feet. He called the Regional Office of the Department of Environmental Conservation. It called back to tell him a helicopter would arrive at 10 A.M.

On Saturday at 10 A.M., the yellow and blue single-turbo-prop helicopter arrived. It landed on the Old Ranger Station site. Aboard were Forest Ranger Gary K. Hodgson and Investigator R. H. Garrand of the State Police.

The investigator immediately took Patrick Eagan aside for questioning. He described him as "crestfallen and quiet." The officer wanted to get Patrick's story while it was fresh in his mind.

Gary Hodgson, who has taken part in many Adirondack rescues, said:

"Of course, hindsight's perfect. But my feeling is that his best chance was his partner, Pat, understanding what was happening."

He pointed to the inadequate dress and the fact that his socks were frozen to the soles of his feet. The ranger added:

"This is the first death I've been involved with that is definitely hypothermia. It's like reading it in a textbook—the sequence of fatigue, confusion and dehydration. It falls into a pattern."

He cited an earlier brush with hypothermia, saying:

"Maybe three years ago, we brought two young boys in from Indian Pass by snowmobile ...

"We made two trips to Adirondack Loj with the snowmobile, but I guess the boys forgot about it pretty quick. Fortunately, the leader recognized it early so we could get them out right away."

That was another encounter with hypothermia where quick action averted tragedy.

After Arthur Reidel was dispatched to obtain Steven's pack where it had been left the night prior, the body was loaded aboard the helicopter on a stokes litter.

The aircraft then flew to Lake Placid Airport, the body was unloaded, and Patrick was flown to the yard of Ranger Gary Roberts in the town of Newcomb. Ranger Roberts drove him to his car in the Upper Works parking lot. Patrick went to his parents' home in Binghamton, before returning to his teaching job.

CORONER CONCERNED

Meanwhile, the Essex County Coroner, Dr. Herbert V. W. Bergamini, was at Placid Memorial Hospital. He had heard of the death.

"While I'm sorting this out," Dr. Bergamini said, "other people come trickling into the hospital to be taken care of. One's a young boy—11 or 12 years old—with a broken arm.

"Well, how did you get this? The boy said he fell and broke it. He's there with his uncle, who has a bad back so he stayed at Adirondack Loj and was delegated to bring the boy in because the family was out hiking.

"I said, 'What did you do yesterday?' 'Well,' the boy said, 'I was going with my mother and grandmother and somebody up one of the trailless peaks (Tabletop), but we couldn't really find the trail to get there and came back.' "

Dr. Bergamini ascertained that the boy had done some summer hiking and projected a hypothetical case of the boy's grandmother breaking her hip.

"They had no idea," he said, "what to do if one of their party became injured."

Dr. Bergamini said this is the first case of death due to hypothermia he can recall during the 17 or 18 years he has lived here.

"The outstanding thing about this," he said, "is you had a healthy young man on Thursday and a corpse on Friday night."

The body was transported to Moses Ludington Hospital in Ticonderoga for autopsy. It revealed he had died from hypothermia. The medical words and physical characteristics of the cold injury attributed death to cerebral edema, and anoxia associated with hypothermia.

The examination showed hypoglycemia, or a low blood sugar level, and an empty stomach. In addition, the death certificate noted subpleural hemorrhages due to poor respiration.

Moreover, Steven had recently had a physical examination which verified his good health.

Patrick Egan also reported that Steven felt he was in good physical condition as a result of the lifting involved in his supply-room job at Eureka Tent.

Steven's body was taken to Monroe, La., where his parents, Mr. and Mrs. Walter A. Collier, Jr., live at 1009 Florida St. His brother, Gary, returned home from Houston, Tex. He is also survived by a sister, Karen.

Preventing Hypothermia

What is hypothermia?

Dr. Theodore G. Lathrop has termed it "Killer of the Unprepared."

In fact, it is a cold injury resulting from exposure and exhaustion that causes the core temperature of the body to drop.

Usually associated with the outdoorsman, mountaineer, canoeist, and hunter, it can also occur in more urban settings. Hypothermia can attack:

—the elderly poor who suffer from malnutrition and lack of heat;

—the alcoholic lying listlessly in a skid-row doorway;

—the drug addict oblivious to weather; and

—infants wrapped in clammy clothing in a cold room.

Hypothermia is a sort of system breakdown, which can occur at temperatures well above freezing, where the body's core temperature drops. Death can result within two hours.

SYMPTOMS LISTED

As the core temperature drops, the symptoms change. You should be alert for the following:

99-96°— Intense shivering.

95-91°— Violent shivering, speech difficulty, thinking sluggish, amnesia starts.

90-86°— Shivering decreases or stops; replaced by muscular rigidity; skin may be blue or puffy; muscle coordination affected with erratic and jerky movements; thinking less clear. Victim can usually retain posture and some contact with environment.

85-81°— Stupor, irrationality, pulse and respiration slow, and muscle rigidity continues.

80-78°— Unconsciousness, erratic heartbeat, and reflexes cease.

Below 78°— The heart fibrillates, edema and hemorrhage in lungs, death.

If you follow the case study of Steven Collier, you can almost follow the physical deterioration as his core temperature drops as he starts up the Cold Brook trail.

How do you treat a suspected victim of hypothermia? Three actions are necessary:

REWARM QUICKLY

—Prevent heat loss;

—Rewarm as quickly and safely as possible; and

—Avoid complications.

Specifically, if you judged someone to have hypothermia with a core temperature of 81-95°, you should stop immediately and seek shelter, replace any wet clothing, insulate the victim from cold, and add heat. Heat can be added through a large volume of hot, sweet liquids, the use of a warm canteen in a sleeping bag or by using your own body to warm the victim.

Total immersion in a bath of 105-110° is a remote possibility that is rarely practical in the out-of-doors. A hydraulic sarong has been developed that pumps hot water through plastic tubes in a blanket—but again such devices are rarely available.

The susceptibility of a victim to hypothermia can be greater if he does not eat properly, sleep properly, and control his muscular activity to avoid sweating.

Alcohol and tobacco also hinder the body's ability to adjust to cold. Alcohol causes the blood vessels to dilate in the extremities, while tobacco causes a constriction which can drop skin temperature 10° in toes and fingers.

WAYS OF LOSING HEAT

The forces that work against you in the cold environment are lack of physical conditioning, wind, temperature, and wetness caused by rain, snow, or sweat. You can lose heat through:

Radiation— The radiation of the body's own heat outward. For example, an uncovered head can loose up to 50 percent of body heat production at 40° F. and up to 74 percent at 5°.

Conduction— Touching cold objects, sitting on the snow, handling hardware or stoves. Use silk gloves and watch out for gasoline in filling stoves because it can supercool, causing instant frostbite.

Convection— Air movement carries away body heat. Windchill temperatures are dramatically lower than regular temperatures. Clothing forms the barrier to retain heat around the body.

Evaporation— Sweating. Adjust your muscular activity and ventilate properly to avoid wetness.

Respiration— Heat is lost when inhaled air is raised to body temperature.

BODY GENERATES HEAT

Remember the body is a heat-generating machine. The outdoorsman must concern himself with heat production, heat conservation, and heat loss. You can get heat from external sources such as the sun, fire, hot food and drink. Or from internal sources such as your body's metabolism in burning of food or through muscular activity. Shivering, for instance, increases your body's heat production.

The News's science columnist Bob Emerson explains:

"Under normal conditions there is a balance between heat production and heat loss. If the heat loss is greater than heat production, the balance is upset and eventual hypothermia results."

This means you should dress properly—ventilate, insulate, and protect from wind and wet—eat properly, and adjust your muscular activity to the situation.

The above explanation was

RADIATION
Losses to Distant
Cold Areas

EVAPORATION
Losses in Breath
and Perspiration

CONVECTION
Losses to Moving
Air

CONDUCTION
Direct Contact Losses

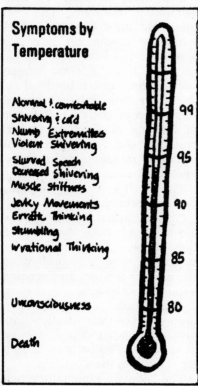

Symptoms by Temperature

Normal & comfortable
Shivering & cold
Numb Extremities
Violent Shivering — 99

Slurred Speech
Decreased Shivering
Muscle stiffness — 95

Jerky Movements
Erratic Thinking
Stumbling
Irrational Thinking — 90

— 85

Unconsciousness — 80

Death

weather, it can be fun to cook more complex meals. In the winter, the simpler the better.

Three types of food should be kept in mind:

Carbohydrates— A quick source of energy. More readily digested than fats and proteins. If you're cold at night eat a candy bar.

Fats— High-energy, low-bulk food. For a given unit of weight they yield over twice the amount of calories afforded from carbohydrates and proteins. Fats help digest carbohydrates and proteins.

Proteins— These are most important for the maintenance and repair of body tissue. Eat them last thing at night and first thing in the morning.

Weight is of great importance when backpacking. There is a large variety of freeze-dried and dehydrated foods available at mountaineering shops. They are expensive. Many substitutes can be found in the supermarket. Example: Buy Lipton's beef Stroganoff at the supermarket and freeze-dried peas to cook with it at a mountain store. One-pot meals are easiest.

Breakfasts:— Granola or small packages of instant oatmeal are the easiest. Hot Russian tea (tea, Tang, sugar, and spices) is a good winter starter. Eggs, meat, pancakes, etc., are all great if it's not winter and you have time.

Lunches:— A standby is crackers, cheese, and meat. Small party rye bread, peanut butter, jam, sardines, tiny tins of ham; corned beef, and other meat spreads. Oranges, raisins, candy bars, cookies.

Dinners:— Try one-pot dinners. Rice-a-Roni with the addition of canned boned chicken and freeze-dried vegetables. Study your grocery shelves.

Snacks:— Candy bars, hard candy, cookies, nuts, jerky, gorp, fruit (dried).

written from lecture notes developed for National Ski Patrol courses. The sources are varied. However, excellent articles have been written and published on the subject, particularly Dr. Theodore G. Lathrop's piece, "Hypothermia: Killer of the Unprepared," in the *NSPS* manuals, *Off Belay* (February 1974), *Wilderness Camping, Outdoor Living*, published by the Tacoma Unit of the Mountain Rescue Council and others. Such publications can be purchased in mountaineering stores; Eastern Mountain Sports here has an extensive catalogue of publications.

FOOD IMPORTANT

All right, what do you eat and wear? Here are some ideas:

What you plan depends on the time of the year. In warm

CLOTHING NEEDS NOTED

And what about clothing?

Keep in mind that the name of the game is not to sweat. Dress in layers. When climbing you may only need an undershirt and shirt. When you stop you may need a down jacket and windproof garment over that.

Warmth in clothing comes from dead air trapped in small spaces or cells. Two light layers trap more air than one heavy, tight-woven layer. Regulate the required amount of warmth by adding or subtracting layers. Wool is the only thing that will keep you warm, even if wet. If you are in need of winter underwear, buy wool instead of cotton. At 40° F. the body can lose 50 percent of its heat through the head, which can result in chilling of the feet and the entire body. It is wise to stop and adjust clothing, rather than sweat, which results in loss of heat. When you stop, immediately put on more clothing. Don't wait to overcool. It takes much less energy to maintain heat than to have to regenerate it.

RIVER CROSSINGS

How do you do it?

by BILL MARCH

Next to hypothermia, stream crossings take more lives of backpackers than any other cause. Yet I believe few backpackers know anything about the safety of stream crossings.

I think the biggest danger in stream crossings is a simple failure to unbuckle your hip belt on your pack when stepping off from a stream bank—onto a log or rock. If you fall into a stream with your belt fastened, your pack will float and force your face down below the surface of the water. And thus, the stream doesn't even have to be fast in order to drown you. It is a good safety precaution to unbuckle your hip belt at every stream crossing. Make it automatic and you won't forget to do it when it's essential.

The following article is excellent in its description of other safety considerations in stream crossings.

W.K.

River and stream crossings can be the most dangerous part of backpacking. They cause far more backpacking deaths than do snakebites. Yet backpackers are more likely to be aware of snakebite precautions than of the dangers of river crossings.

One of the first problems is to recognize the point at which a stream becomes a river and therefore dangerous to cross. It frequently happens that a hiker crosses a gentle stream on the way in and on the hike back out finds the stream swollen to dangerous proportions. A sudden hot spell can melt snow and cause floodwaters in the small stream. A rainstorm of an inch or more can similarly swell a stream. In canyon and desert country, a rainstorm can occur 100 miles upstream, go unnoticed by you, and cause a flash flood in a mild stream. When a stream becomes a river, it is dangerous.

River crossings should be regarded as emergency procedures to be used only when you have reconnoitered the river and found a suitable ford and when the alternatives to crossing are more hazardous than the crossing itself.

There are many sorts of rivers and streams. They can be broadly summarized into three types:

Rivers with large boulders and with the current varying greatly from place to place due to turbulence and obstacles. These are young, immature rivers found high in mountain areas and present serious problems when they are flooding.

Rivers where the banks and bottom are coarse gravel and the water does not flow so fast. These are more mature streams and are found lower down in larger valleys or where rivers flow into lakes.

Rivers where the water is deep and flows slowly. These are mature rivers found in lower valleys where the gradients are gentle.

Each kind of river requires a different approach, but the selection of a satisfactory ford is always of critical importance. A river may be impossible to cross at one place and yet be quite possible to ford a short distance away. In addition, a ford can easily change from safe to dangerous or impossible with a rise in water level.

The decision to cross or not to cross depends upon an assessment of the total situation. The color of the water, the nature of the bottom, the width of the river, the speed and volume of the water all are factors to consider. It is inadvisable to attempt to cross a river in which boulders can be heard rolling and trees or logs are being swept along. If no satisfactory ford can be found, it may be better to make a detour upstream and find a route there. If the river is obviously in flood and you have time, it may be best to mark the water level and then wait, especially if the weather is fine and there is little prospect of rain. The level may fall quite rapidly, exposing a suitable ford. In headwater areas with extensive snowpack or glaciers, streams are lowest in the morning after a cold night and highest in the afternoon, with snow and ice melted by the day's heat.

When a river has to be forded, spend some time finding the easiest and safest place. If possible, examine the river from a high vantage point, where it is easier to ascertain width, speed, turbulence, obstructions, and in clear water, the nature of the bottom. The form, slope, and material of the riverbank may give a clue to the nature of the riverbed. The best crossing is on a firm bed of gravel. Large rocks, smooth slabs, sand, mud, and high banks should be avoided. A ford should be free of obstructions, submerged or otherwise, which can snag your rope, and the outflow below the ford should be reasonable. Care should be taken when crossing silt or sand at the edge of a glacial stream or glacial terminal lake, as it may be quicksand. If the river is clouded with glacial flour (pulverized rock), look out for submerged boulders and rocks. Sometimes it is possible to cross the headwaters of these rocky mountain streams by boulder hopping or by utilizing stable logjams. But great care should be taken to avoid long jumps with heavy packs, as a slip could prove dangerous. Care should also be taken if it is very cold, as the rocks may be glazed with ice. Even under warmer conditions, logs and boulders can be slippery and slimy.

The force of moving water, even if it isn't white water, is considerable, and its speed should be determined by throwing a small stick into it and noting the rate of movement. Never underestimate the velocity of shallow water.

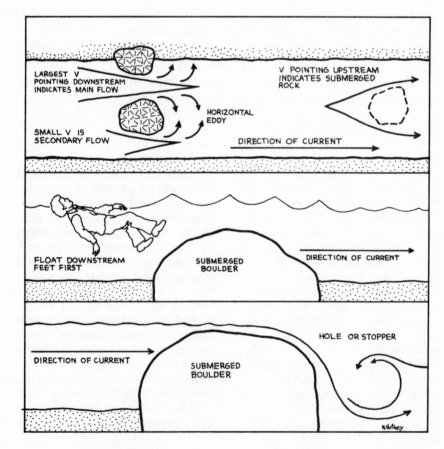

Reading Moving Water
A. Horizontal Eddies (top view)
B. Standing Waves (side view)
C. Stopper Vertical Eddy (side view)

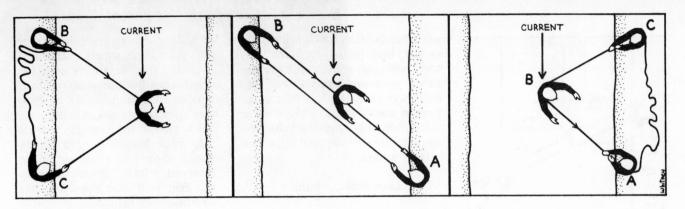

Continuous Loop System
(i) First Person (ii) Second Person (iii) Last Person Carabiner and sit sling

When reading river water and attempting to find a crossing point, a knowledge of water hydraulics and river behavior is extremely useful.

When a river widens, the water is more likely to be shallow and slow-flowing.

When a mature river increases its gradient, there is often a gravel bar running diagonally across the river above the change in grade.

When a river's gradient decreases, the river often widens and runs in braided channels which can be easier to cross than the mainstream.

Bends of rivers are poor places to cross as the water is usually deeper and flowing more strongly and the outside bank is often steep and undercut. Water between the bends is likely to be shallower and less powerful.

When a river is deep but flowing slowly in pools, a crossing can be made by swimming.

The main flow is where the biggest V of water points downstream. This is the most powerful section of the current and the most difficult to cross. Ripple formations pointing upstream indicate a submerged obstacle at the apex of the V.

Obstructions, or rock projections above the water level should be avoided, since it is possible to be pinned against them by a force of water on the upstream side. On the downstream side of obstruc-

tions, there is always an eddy current running upstream, and this is often a good place to rest.

When an obstacle is deeply submerged, the water surface will be broken by large standing waves gradually diminishing in size on the downstream side. The largest wave upstream marks the position of the obstruction. These "haystacks" are indications of fast, deep water and an irregular riverbed. Although spectacular, they are not particularly dangerous.

When an obstacle is large and just below the surface, a small waterfall may form and a strong vertical eddy flow upstream on the downhill side of the obstacle. This is called a stopper, or hole, and is capable of trapping and drowning a person who has been swept into it, especially if the obstruction extends across the entire width of the river. Such holes and falls are to be avoided at all costs because of the great difficulty in escaping from them. To rescue someone trapped in a hole, throw a rope with a bowline loop tied in the end and pull the person out downstream. If there is no rope available, the trapped person may take a deep breath and dive to the river bottom, where he should theoretically be swept downstream by the current.

CROSSING WITH A ROPE

The best way to cross a river is with a rope as a safeguard. An exception to this rule is when

there is a danger of the rope snagging on a rock. If the rope snags, the person crossing may be held underwater and rescue may be impossible. There are several types of roped crossings.

Continuous Loop System

The leader, A, ties on in a loop passed high under his armpits and sets off across the river, supporting himself on the upstream rope held by B. B is not tied into the rope but may be protected by a sling tied to a tree. Downstream a third person, C—also not attached to the rope—passes the rope through his hands as A crosses. In the event of A's losing his footing and being swept away, B pays out rope and C pulls in A while always remaining downstream of him. If you try to pull a man onto the bank while upstream, he will be dragged under. When A reaches the far bank, he slips out of the loop and pays the rope through until the loop is passed to C on the other side. C then steps into the loop and crosses diagonally while belayed by B and A. If C slips, B pays out rope and A pulls in, downstream. The last man, B, crosses supported upstream by C and, if he falls, is pulled in by A.

Fixed Rope, Sling, and Carabiner

An alternative method of crossing, when high banks or trees permit a rope to be stretched across the water, is by using a fixed rope, a sling, and a carabiner. The leader crosses as in

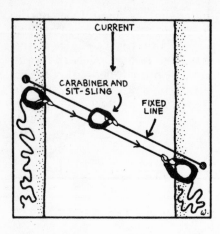

the continuous loop system. One rope is rigged across the river as a fixed line, and the next person crossing uses a sit sling, and clips into the fixed line with a carabiner. A second rope is used to pull him across. The last man dismantles the fixed line and crosses in the same manner as the first. Separate carabiners and slings are required for everyone except the first and last persons crossing.

Before any method of roped-river crossing is attempted, a clear system of calls and hand signals should be agreed upon. The noise of a river makes conversation difficult between those on opposite banks.

CROSSING WITHOUT A ROPE

If a rope is not available, then other methods must be used, but with the greatest care. In such circumstances, the following methods have been used successfully:

Triangle of Support Method

Three people face inward with

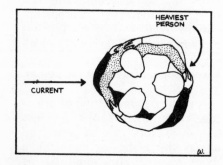

Triangle of support

arms firmly linked, heads close together, and feet apart. One person, who is also the heaviest, faces upstream, the other two sideways to the current. Only one person moves through the river at a time. In this way the two who are stationary support the one who is moving.

Line Astern Method

Three or more people stand one behind the other, facing into the current, and give each other support by holding onto each other's belts. The front person moves

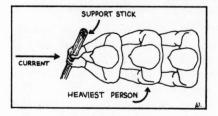

Line astern

first, then number two, who should also be the heaviest, and finally the third, until the party is in one line again. In very heavy water, each member of the group moves at the same time.

Line Abreast Using a Pole

Three or more persons stand in line abreast, side to the current,

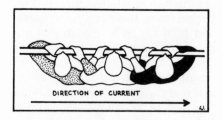

Line abreast using pole

with arms interlocked and holding onto a long tree branch. Everyone moves together, giving each other support.

No matter which method of crossing is used, there are certain rules and precautions that should be observed.

• Keep your boots on. They

protect feet from injury and provide a more secure placement, reducing the possibility of a slip or stumble. Socks can be removed and carried in the pack to keep them dry, and wearing gaiters will keep gravel from being worked into your boot tops. On no account should a crossing be attempted without boots, because the feet will numb quickly and can be easily bruised.

• Baggy trousers offer resistance to water flow and should be removed. If the water is very cold, woolen long johns can provide some protection for the lower body without offering resistance to water flow.

• Your pack should be kept on but with the waist belt undone so it can be removed easily if you lose your footing. The extra weight of the pack increases stability in fast, shallow water. In slow, deep water, the pack will be a source of flotation if saucepans are inverted and clothes and sleeping bags are packed in sealed polyethylene bags. If the pack has a bivouac extension, it should be securely fastened to trap air and increase buoyancy. When you are swimming a slow, deep river, the pack should be floated in front of you and used for additional buoyancy.

• When crossing, never face downstream. The force of the current would push against the back of your knees and cause your legs to buckle. It is better to stand sideways to the current with hips angled diagonally toward the opposite bank so the current exerts a force in that direction. This "ferryglide" effect assists in conserving energy and makes crossing easier.

• Move one foot only when the other is firmly placed, and shuffle rather than take big steps. Do not cross your legs—keep them apart in a stable, braced position. A stout stick is useful as a third leg and allows two-point contact when moving. That is, move stick, then left leg, right leg, repeat. The stick should be used as a support on the upstream side.

If you lose your footing and are swept away, keep calm, jettison your pack, and float feet first downstream. Keep your feet up to fend off rocks and swim across, not against, the current to try to reach an eddy or slower water. On no account allow yourself to be swept up against logjams or fallen trees, as you might be trapped and drowned by the force of the water pushing you under.

A river crossing may chill those involved, especially if it is a glacial-melt stream, and it is advisable to change into dry clothes and have some hot food and drink before proceeding.

Remember that crossing rivers is hazardous and should not be undertaken without full consideration of all the factors involved and a thorough knowledge of the area. Far better to change your route or retreat than risk a life in a dangerous crossing. And always give serious consideration to possible river crossings when planning your intinerary.

HIGH-ALTITUDE SICKNESS

by CHARLES S. HOUSTON

One of the saddest mountain stories I have ever heard is the one about the death of Nanda Devi Unsoeld.

She was the daughter of mountain climber Willy Unsoeld, who was one of the first Americans to climb Mount Everest. When his daughter was born, Willy wanted her named Nanda Devi, after the Himalayan mountain of that name. The mountain is a beauty. And Willy dreamed of climbing it, perhaps even with his daughter when she grew up.

Then, when Nanda Devi Unsoeld was 22 years old, his dream was about to be fulfilled. His lovely daughter had become an accomplished mountain climber, quite capable of joining her father on an expedition to climb Nanda Devi.

The party had climbed for 57 days. One group of the party had already made the summit. Nanda Devi Unsoeld was in the second group that was to go for it. They waited out the weather for four days at Camp IV at 24,000 feet. She had complained of diarrhea for the entire trip. But since she had been able to carry heavy loads they had not given it much concern. Then on the morning of September 7, 1976, she suddenly was stricken by cerebral edema. She had time only to say, "I'm going to die." In 15 minutes she was dead despite mouth-to-mouth resuscitation and CPR. Her father and companions were turned back down the mountain in their grief, and they laid Nanda Devi Unsoeld out to rest on a shoulder of the namesake mountain.

Altitude sickness is a mystery illness that comes in a variety of forms. It is a mystery because it is not predictable. You can be in top physical condition, and it can bring you down. You can have climbed to high altitude many times before, and it can bring you down on your next climb. It can nail you at elevations as low as 8,500 feet. It is no respecter of age— can cut down a youngster just as quickly as an oldster. But few who climb in mountains of this elevation or higher know much about it, or what to do if they are stricken.

The following article was written by the world's foremost authority on altitude sickness, Dr. Charles Houston.

W.K.

BILL DEMAREST had been skiing and climbing for 13 years when he started into the Wind River Range. It did not occur to him or his companions that he might meet disaster at an altitude well below what he had attained many times before. Having been a physical education major in college, he believed in keeping fit and at 38 was in better shape than most of his contemporaries. He and four friends prepared for their

12-day ski trip with great care, and all were in good shape when they reached Jackson, Wyoming (6,200 feet) on March 18, 1973.

In Jackson, the group spent two days sorting their gear before driving to Pinedale (8,400 feet). After lunch on March 20 they set off in a light snowfall and easily made six miles. Their camp that night was at 9,800 feet. They were tired and slept well. The next day Bill broke trail in deep new snow, but after a few hours developed a bad headache and moved to the rear of the small group. It snowed hard throughout the day, and the party took six hours to cover three miles and climb 400 feet. All were exhausted and had headaches that night.

On March 22 more fresh snow made the going even tougher, and they camped that night at 10,100 feet, a hundred feet lower than the night before. Bill had a "roaring headache" and did not help to set up camp. In contrast to his usual high spirits and energy, he was quiet and withdrawn and ate almost nothing. In the morning, after a poor night's sleep, he was sluggish and slow. Despite the deep snow, the party covered six more miles, mostly on the level, and since the sun broke through from time to time, their spirits rose and everyone felt better. Except Bill. That evening he crawled right into his sleeping bag, refusing to eat or to drink anything but a few sips of tea. He seemed to be really sick, and for the first time his friends were alarmed.

THEY HAD REASON to be. Bill was developing the most serious form of altitude illness, even though the party had climbed quite slowly to a moderate elevation. His friends had no way of being certain he did not have some type of infection, but the evidence pointed to altitude as the cause.

Altitude sickness has been recognized for centuries by travelers and climbers. The most celebrated description comes from José de Acosta, a sixteenth-century Spanish missionary to Peru, who wrote in 1590: "I was suddenly surprised with so mortall and strange a pang that I was ready to fall from the top to the ground . . . I was surprised with such pangs of straining and casting as I thought to cast my hearte out too . . ." Acosta offered an explanation: "I therefore perswade myself that the element of air is there so subtile and delicate, as is not proportionable with the breathing of man . . ."

Acosta was describing a common form of altitude illness, what we today call acute mountain sickness, which typically causes vomiting, weakness,

dizziness, and headache. He correctly suspected the "thinne air" as the cause, but it would take hundreds of years for science to have the instruments and basic knowledge to show that (1) the weight of the air above the Earth (barometric pressure) decreases as altitude increases, (2) the composition of air everywhere is constant at 21 percent oxygen and 79 percent nitrogen, and as a result (3) the pressure or weight of oxygen in air decreases as altitude increases, though it still occupies 21 percent of the air in volume. Today all this is common knowledge but rests upon the invention of the barometer (1643), demonstration of the composition of air (1655–80), and a century later the isolation of oxygen and proof that it was essential to life.

Through the seventeenth and eighteenth centuries scientists all over Europe were studying the passage of air in and out of the lungs, speculating about the circulation of blood and the nature of metabolism. Meanwhile, travelers were crossing mountain ranges for trade between Europe and Asia, and others were climbing high into the mountains searching for gold or gems or for sulfur to make gunpowder. Many reported headache, weakness, vomiting, and collapse but attributed their symptoms to poisonous vapors from plants or to emanations from minerals containing antimony or lead. Toward the end of the eighteenth century, balloons were first used, but not until the mid-1800s could they carry men high enough to become ill; then, in the intense competition to set altitude records, a number of people died.

These developments set the stage for the research of Paul Bert, a French physician and politician and the true father of altitude science. In 1878 Bert published an immense collection of travelers' tales and accounts of hundreds of experiments in decompression chambers and balloons. Bert was inquisitive, conscientious, and thorough. He concluded that at higher altitudes there was a shortage of oxygen which caused experimental animals and humans to become ill and even die. He realized that breathing extra oxygen would protect against this mortal illness and began to study hemoglobin, the red pigment in blood which carries oxygen to the tissues. At about

the same time, Angelo Mosso, under the patronage of the queen of Italy, was studying altitude illness on the summit of Monte Rosa (14,300 feet). He published his own account in 1898. Mosso was not as certain as Bert of the exact nature of altitude sickness.

The first complete and accurate medical description of the various types of altitude illness—for there are three distinct groups of symptoms—was made by Dr. T. H. Ravenhill, a physician to a mining company in Peru. In 1913 Ravenhill described "common puna" (today known as *acute mountain sickness*), "cardiac puna" (*high altitude pulmonary edema*), and "nervous puna," which is due to excess water in the brain, or *cerebral edema*. Ravenhill used one of the local names for the conditions: "puna" means "high barren deserts." Another name, "soroche," means lead or antimony in Spanish; Argentinians speak of "Locura Blanca," snow madness. Today these conditions often are considered separately, but each is part of a continuous spectrum of illness with a common cause—lack of oxygen.

No medication, no treatment—not even oxygen—can substitute for getting down to the richer oxygen supply at lower altitudes. Waiting to see what weather or medication will bring can be fatal.

ANOTHER NIGHT'S SLEEP was no help to Bill Demarest. On the morning of March 24 he was weak and groggy. Though he had trouble standing and his lungs felt congested, he insisted that he could ski back to Pinedale and resisted a decision to send for help. Indeed, he seemed to improve a little during the day but still moved very slowly and fell asleep instantly whenever the party stopped. By that afternoon they had covered only a few miles and gotten down a hundred feet, but Bill could go no farther. His face was puffy, he could scarcely stand, and the few times he spoke, he was incoherent. After drinking thirstily he fell into deep yet restless sleep.

It was a dreadful night for the whole party. Bill mumbled and tossed and snuffled, coughing weakly and ineffectively. He could not sit without help and was unaware of his condition and surroundings. He was desperately ill. At first light, two of his friends set off to get help from a ranger station 30 miles away. Bill was almost unconscious. His eyes were vacant and unfocused, and he remained most of the day in a rigid position—legs out straight, arms folded, head and shoulders bent forward. He was close to death when a helicopter arrived at 5:30 the next morning. It was the sixth day after leaving Pinedale, and the elevation was 10,100 feet.

THE MOST OBVIOUS and serious of Bill's problems was what Ravenhill called "nervous puna," which we recognize as being caused by excessive accumulation of water in the brain—cerebral edema (CE). CE is not as common as water accumulating in the lungs—high altitude pulmonary edema—but it is more dangerous. CE can cause permanent brain damage—if the victim survives. Its manifestations depend on the location of the fluid, and this varies among individuals. As pressure increases within the rigid case of the skull, CE causes an intense throbbing headache as if the head might burst. Staggering walk, difficulty using fingers or hands, or double vision occurs if the parts of the brain controlling those functions become waterlogged. Hallucinations are common. Frank Smythe, alone on Mount Everest in 1933, was so certain he was accompanied that he actually offered to share his candy with an illusory companion. The survivors of a party stricken near the top of Aconcagua in the Andes were convinced that they saw bulldozers and palm trees on the summit and that tourists were stealing their supplies.

The exact mechanism for the accumulation of fluid in the brain is not fully understood. It is believed to be the result of a temporary breakdown of the "sodium pump," the term used to describe the delicate "machinery" with which each cell maintains its balance of sodium, potassium, and water. Normally, bioelectric changes in the cell membrane are constantly shifting sodium ions and water out of and potassium ions into each cell. This mechanism is invisible, of course, and still hypothetical. When insufficient oxygen is being supplied, the process reverses—so we believe—and water tends to follow sodium ions into the cell, causing it to swell.

Although lack of oxygen is the ultimate cause of CE, it seems to be such responses to oxygen lack that produce the symptoms. This impression is supported by the fact that a victim may develop no problems until many hours after arrival, depending on the altitude—even though oxygen cannot be stored in the body and must be replaced as rapidly as it is used. (Similar signs, symptoms, and pathology are seen in victims of carbon monoxide poisoning, where oxygen is displaced by carbon monoxide in combination with hemoglobin, as well as in victims of acute lack of oxygen at sea level from other causes.)

BILL DEMAREST arrived at the Jackson hospital at 7:30 A.M., motionless, rigid, nonresponsive, and breathing with great difficulty. Dr. John Walker, recognizing the desperate condition of his patient, immediately started high-flow oxygen and an intravenous line for medication and drew arterial blood for gas analyses. His examination confirmed the presence of neurological pathology: all of Bill's reflexes were hyperactive, and an abnormal Babinski reflex, which made his toes turn upward when the soles of his feet were stroked, was another ominous indication of brain damage. Examination of the retina of each eye showed that the optic nerves were slightly swollen where they enter the eyeball from the brain—additional evidence that the brain was swollen.

Dr. Walker next discovered signs of an abundance of fluid within Bill's lungs, a finding—confirmed by X-rays—characteristic of high altitude pulmonary edema (HAPE). The results of the gas tests of the blood, reported later that morning, showed moderate lack of oxygen in the blood and a slight decrease in carbon dioxide due to overbreathing, which also slightly increased the blood's alkalinity. There was no evidence of pneumonia or any other disease. Bill was critically ill from lack of oxygen manifested as both HAPE and CE, and it seemed unlikely that he would recover without permanent damage. Dr. Walker increased the flow of oxygen and gave him a strong kidney stimulant in an effort to remove excess water from brain and lungs. Then he waited.

HAPE IS LESS COMMON than acute mountain sickness (AMS) but more common than and as serious as CE. Pulmonary edema as a complication of other problems such as heart disease, anemia, shock, and brain damage is not uncommon. It occurs when blood serum seeps from the lung's capillaries into the tiny air sacs, or alveoli, which they surround. As fluid accumulates in the air sacs, the transfer of oxygen and carbon dioxide between lungs and blood is disrupted. Lack of oxygen develops rapidly, further aggravating the problem. The victim literally drowns in his own juices unless drastic measures are taken.

A trained observer with a stethoscope can detect the seepage before it actually starts to fill the alveoli, and at this point the condition is easily reversible. By the time fluid accumulates in the air sacs, it can be heard even without a stethoscope. Anyone so afflicted is in grave danger, and getting down, eliminating the fluid, and receiving more oxygen will be his only hope of survival.

Just why fluid seeps through the capillary walls is not understood. One likely contributor is an increase in blood pressure in the pulmonary artery. But the exact mechanism of pulmonary edema is very complicated.

Although Mosso's book described two probable cases of HAPE and Ravenhill's case descriptions were unmistakable, not until the last 20 years has HAPE become widely recognized as a dangerous result of too rapid ascent. In the 1930s several South American physicians published case reports, but in Spanish only, and they received limited attention.

In 1959, I happened to be in my office when a call came to rescue a young skier taken ill while crossing a 12,000-foot pass in the Colorado Rockies. He had been barely able to get down to 9,000 feet because of weakness, cough, and shortness of breath. When he was brought to the hospital, he showed classical signs of pulmonary edema. He recovered rapidly, but the cause of his illness was unclear.

Several months later I had the privilege of discussing the case with cardiologist Paul Dudley White. White believed this edema might be the product of oxygen lack combined with cold and exertion, and he urged me to publish a paper on the subject. With the addition of several suggestive though anecdotal accounts of similar illness among climbers, my paper appeared in the *New England Journal of Medicine* in 1961. It was the first account of such phenomena in English after Ravenhill's, and it stimulated interest around the world.

Since then hundreds of cases of HAPE have been identified and reported. Excellent medical articles by Drs. Herbert Hultgren and Robert

Grover, among others, have pointed out various features of this "physiological disease." Doctors Peter Hackett and Drummond Rennie have reported many cases in trekkers taken too rapidly on tours toward Everest Base Camp. Dr. John Dickinson in Kathmandu has seen several fatalities from HAPE and from CE.

One outbreak of altitude illness is particularly significant. Along the spine of the Himalaya, the troubled frontier between Chinese-occupied Tibet and India has been the scene of small sporadic skirmishes for decades. In the fall of 1962 the Chinese suddenly attacked in force. Large numbers of Indian troops were hastily flown to the mountains from the low plains of India and sent into combat, often at altitudes above 14,000 feet, only a few days after leaving sea level. Several thousand became ill with various forms of altitude sickness, while the Chinese, adapted to the altitude by months or years of residing on the high Tibetan plateau, were unaffected. From this experience Indian military physicians learned much about the causes and effects of altitude illness and shared their knowledge through many good articles for the scientific community.

Perhaps more important in the long run, the Indian experience alerted the armed forces of other countries, including the United States, Canada, and the Soviet Union, to the hazards of combat at high altitude. Government interest in altitude research, keen during the early years of World War II when aircraft were flying too high for conventional oxygen-breathing equipment, had declined following the perfection of pressurized airplane cabins. But now much research into many aspects of oxygen lack, not only at altitude but due to illness or injury at sea level, is in progress again.

DURING THE 16 HOURS after being admitted to the hospital, Bill Demarest urinated four quarts more water than he had received by vein because of the powerful kidney stimulant, and the moisture in his lungs decreased. A day after admission, however, he was still comatose, although the abnormal reflexes had disappeared. Dr. Walker gave him an intravenous steroid to decrease the swelling in the brain. Twelve hours later Bill became lucid and coordinated, but he responded only slowly and with difficulty. He was much taken by the persisting hallucination that Jane Fonda was on the wall of his hospital room, live and in color. He was definitely on the mend. On March 30, 4½ days after entering the hospital nearly dead, Bill Demarest, evidently completely normal, walked out of the hospital and flew home.

Not everyone is so fortunate. Of 12 cases of severe CE reported by John Dickinson and me, two patients died, two had prolonged convalescence, and two more showed evidence of permanent brain damage. Moreover, some persons who have had unusually severe headache at high altitude feel that they took many weeks or months to regain full mental function, even though they had not required hospital care.

Experiences like Bill's are becoming increasingly common. Because of helicopters, small aircraft, and jeeps, thousands of people are now able to reach dangerous altitudes rapidly and easily. As a result, many otherwise healthy and fit trekkers and climbers are being hit by altitude illness. As Drummond Rennie, mountaineer and physician, put it: "Because these are the people who go into the mountains, altitude illness kills the young, the fit, the enthusiastic, and audacious and hard-working, and it is killing them in ever increasing numbers." The incidence may begin to fall when more persons become aware of the risks and learn to take time for their travel.

NOVICES ARE NOT the only victims. HAPE and CE show no respect for seniority or experience, and some of the finest climbers in the world have been made critically ill or have died from altitude. In the fall of 1977, Sir Edmund Hillary, hurrying up Narayan Parbat in Nepal, had to be evacuated by helicopter at 17,000 feet. An experienced Japanese climber on a hurried reconnaissance preliminary to an attempt on Mount Everest died of CE and HAPE within 48 hours of passing 14,000 feet. A great Italian guide had to be evacuated from Mount McKinley because of HAPE. Most serious cases are combinations of HAPE and CE, with features of AMS as well. One condition or another may dominate.

Although firm figures are impossible to obtain, it seems likely that several million persons each year go from low to high altitudes to ski or climb or trek. Based on the crude figures we do have, perhaps more than 100,000 people have severe symptoms and 20,000 may require evacuation or have to descend. As many as 200 may die annually from these preventable dysfunctions. Nor are the problems limited to very high mountains, as Bill Demarest's experience shows. Several deaths and near-deaths have occurred in resort areas as low as 9,500 feet when both summer and winter visitors have tried to do too much too soon after arrival. In fact, both CE and HAPE seem to be more common between 10,000

ACUTE MOUNTAIN SICKNESS (AMS)	HIGH ALTITUDE PULMONARY EDEMA (HAPE)	CEREBRAL EDEMA (CE)
Common above 7,000 or 8,000 feet. Headache, nausea, perhaps vomiting, shortness of breath. Usually some improvement after a day or two.	Rare below 10,000 feet. Weakness, shortness of breath, increasing cough begin 12 to 48 hours after too rapid ascent and progress to coma and death.	Rare. Severe headache, hallucinations, weakness, staggering gait, and coma develop 24 to 60 hours after too rapid ascent or strenuous work, usually above 12,000 feet.
Fluids, aspirin, and limited activity are best treatment. Descent usually unnecessary.	Descent is best treatment; Lasix by mouth or vein and oxygen may help.	Descent is mandatory; intravenous steroids helpful. There is a chance of permanent damage if the victim survives.

and 17,000 feet than above 17,000 feet, probably because so few people are able to go much higher without adjusting to the altitude.

Strenuous exertion increases the risk of altitude illness. Young children are more vulnerable than adults; perhaps because they are more active. Men and women are equally susceptible, and women have a special risk during the water-retaining week before menstruation. Physical fitness confers no protection, although by enabling the climber to be more efficient in using muscles, a fit person requires less oxygen for a given task. Persons who have had one attack may be more likely to have another, but this has not been proved.

Several authorities believe that a person adapted to altitude who descends and then returns within a few days or weeks is more likely to develop HAPE than a new arrival. Increasing evidence supports this impression, and it seems prudent to counsel reentrants to take more time and to be extra alert to symptoms. Finally, a small group of HAPE victims at unusually low altitudes have been found to have abnormal lung circulation. I counsel such people to undergo some rather sophisticated studies of lung function to be sure there is no built-in hazard before they return to the same altitudes.

RETINAL HEMORRHAGE is a special problem whose exact place in the spectrum of altitude illness is unclear. I first observed these tiny bleeding spots in the back of the eyes of two persons going to 17,500 feet in 1968; since then the Arctic Institute of North America's Mount Logan high altitude research group and other scientists have confirmed that more than a third of all persons going above 17,000 feet will have such hemorrhages, though very few are aware of them. They disappear in a few weeks and are believed to leave no permanent scar. Two severe cases have been reported, however, in which persistent visual defects remained after the hemorrhages healed.

The cause of the hemorrhaging is not yet known, nor can we be sure that similar bleeding spots don't occur in other, less visible, parts of the body. Since the Indian physicians saw only a few hemorrhages in the soldiers rushed to 14,000 feet, and they were in a different part of the eye, what little evidence exists suggests that retinal hemorrhage is most common above 17,000 feet. (A fascinating aspect of this problem is that a third of all newborn infants also have rapidly healing retinal hemorrhages.) Since retinal hemorrhages can be seen only with special instruments, they are usually not observed, and much more study is needed to learn their importance. At present we do not believe retinal hemorrhage is cause for descent. We know no treatment, but taking time for the climb seems to minimize the occurrence of retinal hemorrhage and the condition appears to be exaggerated by strenuous exertion.

CURRENTLY, THE BEST and only way to prevent high altitude illness is to take time for the climb. There's no substitute for time; no training, no experience, no medication works as well. Climbing a maximum of 1,000 feet a day will protect most people from serious problems, though as Bill Demarest's experience shows, some will still be affected. Bob Gerhard, a ranger in Mount McKinley National Park, described an experienced climber with severe HAPE who had to be taken down from 16,300 feet, even though the party had climbed well within the recommended limit of 1,000 feet per day. The individual had suffered before from HAPE at 14,500 feet and at 21,000 feet in the Himalaya and thus was at greater risk.

In 1976 several parties taking ample time to reach 17,000 feet on Mount McKinley were nevertheless seriously affected by HAPE or CE. Some 30 persons had to be evacuated from the peak that year, mostly because of problems caused by altitude. Gerhard has instituted an effective educational program consisting of pamphlets and discussion of the risks of altitude with climbers. Phil Snyder, a ranger on Mount Kenya, where there has been a high incidence of serious problems among the 5,000 persons who try that climb each year, has started a similar program, as has Dr. Peter Hackett near Mount Everest.

Advice might therefore be amended to read: "Allow at least one day to climb each 1,000 feet above 8,000 feet, but go even more slowly if warning signs appear." In Bill Demarest's case the warnings began on the second day; for others the warnings lie in previous episodes of altitude illness.

Various medications have been recommended to help prevent high altitude illness. Among them are ammonium chloride (to acidify urine, thus expediting loss of bicarbonate), cytochrome C or methylene blue (to increase cell efficiency in using oxygen), and acetazolamide or Diamox (to permit overbreathing with less risk of changing the pH of the blood). Only the latter has been proven to minimize AMS, and it has little or no effect in preventing HAPE or CE. It must be taken for several days before and during the rapid ascent, and it is no substitute for time.

Recently, an antacid has been proposed as treatment on the tenuous

BOOKS

Additional reading about the effects of altitude

• *Man at High Altitude*
by Donald Heath and David Williams, Churchill Livingstone, London and New York, 1977. An excellent book intended primarily for doctors and scientists but rich in technical information understandable by any intelligent reader. More basic science than warning or applied medical advice.

• *Mountain Medicine*
by Michael Ward, William Clowes, London, 1975. An encyclopedic reference book on all aspects of mountain medicine. The style is curt, chopped, and authoritative, and there are many references. Altitude is given only brief attention, however.

• *Medicine for Mountaineering*
edited by James Wilkerson, The Mountaineers, Seattle, 1975. Probably the best of the handbooks for nondoctors. The section on altitude is complete and understandable.

• "See Nuptse and Die"
by Drummond Rennie, in *Lancet*, November 27, 1976, pp. 1177–79. A concise summary of recent medical articles on altitude illness, with special reference to a paper in the same issue of the publication devoted to observations by Peter Hackett at Pheriche near Mount Everest Base Camp.

• "High Altitude Illness: Disease with Protean Manifestations"
by Charles Houston, in *Journal of the American Medical Association*, November 8, 1976, pp. 2193–95. A short summary of current knowledge and theory about cause and management of various types of altitude illness, with special reference to climbers.

• "Altitude Illness—1976 Version"
by Charles Houston, in *American Alpine Journal*, June 1976. Written primarily for nondoctors, this is a summary of cause, prevention, and management of the various forms of altitude illness as of 1976.

A more complete bibliography of 40 annotated titles is available, for $2.50 postpaid, from Dr. Charles S. Houston, 77 Ledge Road, Burlington, Vermont 05401.

theory that by decreasing stomach acidity, the antacid will also decrease the acidity which may rarely develop in the blood. Both theory and evidence are weak. Taking iron or blood stimulants—or even transfusions—has been proposed because an increase in red blood cells and hemoglobin is one of the beneficial changes occurring during adaptation. None is thought to be much help. Europeans have tried a variety of respiratory, circulatory, and brain stimulants; all seem about as beneficial as a placebo.

One medication which has been in use for a long time would seem to be a logical preventive for all forms of altitude illness. Diphenylhydantoin, also known as Dilantin, is so valuable in controlling epilepsy that it has been regarded as good for that disease alone. But Dilantin is a stabilizer of cell membranes, which means that it restores to normal the shifts of sodium, potassium, and other ions in and out of the cell when they have been disturbed. It is reasonable to think that Dilantin would reverse or prevent the disruption of the "sodium pump" believed to be the fundamental cause of altitude illness. Animal studies confirm this protective action, but the drug has rarely been used to protect humans from lack of oxygen.

Taking time is still the best, the most natural way to avoid altitude illness. Given time, the body's many systems will adjust to a lower oxygen supply, so adapted climbers can, for a few weeks or days, do prodigious feats far past 20,000 feet. Above this altitude, deterioration due to chronic lack of oxygen or inadequate food, water, or rest—or a combination of these—seems to proceed faster than acclimatization. Most climbers believe you can't adapt to such altitudes for more than a few weeks.

BUT UNDER THE BEST of circumstances, some cases of altitude illness are likely to happen. How should they be treated? AMS usually improves within a day or two if the individual takes plenty of liquids and aspirin for headache, and stays mildly active. Tempting though bed and self-pity may be, it is better to be up and around. Those who "can't keep anything down" may need to descend or be given intravenous fluids. Taking oxygen helps but only while it is being breathed. Low-flow oxygen during sleep has been of great benefit on high Himalayan peaks but should not be needed at lower elevations.

HAPE and CE, on the other hand, are always serious. Once either is suspected, the victim should start down without delay. In the early stages of HAPE and CE even a short descent works wonders, but if the party delays ("Perhaps he'll be better tomorrow"), the risks increase greatly. Extra oxygen helps, but only in the early stages, and it is no substitute for descent. The possible benefits of morphine are probably outweighed by its bad effects. Digitalis, tourniquets to the extremities, and other methods of handling heart failure are useless because the heart is not failing and refuses to be spurred to greater effort. Some other respiratory and circulatory stimulants are still experimental.

Because HAPE kills by drowning the victim in an excess of water in the lungs, there is a rationale for giving a kidney stimulant to "squeeze" fluid from the lungs and other boggy tissues. Furosemide (Lasix) is most often used and can be quite valuable, though no controlled study of its benefits has been made. Lasix is most helpful if given by mouth early in the disease. It can also be administered intravenously, but caution should be taken because of the risk of further depleting blood volume and causing shock. Lasix does not help CE. Intravenous cortisone derivatives, most often dexamethasone, do improve this condition. (Carbon monoxide poisoning is also helped by dexamethasone. Hypertonic solutions, which draw blood out of tissues, are administered for other forms of brain edema occurring most often at sea level. We have little experience with them in treatment of CE.)

If special treatments like intravenous injections or morphine are needed, a doctor is certainly helpful—perhaps essential. But not all climbing parties include doctors. I usually advise groups going on extended trips to high mountains to get some medical instruction. I provide lists and procedural outlines and have even taught a few people how to give injections as a last resort. Some doctors object, and I acknowledge that a risk is involved. But I feel a well-informed lay person is better than nobody in an urgent or desperate situation.

No medication, no treatment—not even oxygen—can substitute for getting down to the richer oxygen supply of lower altitude. A mild case will improve rapidly, possibly fast enough for the person to go back a few weeks later and finish the climb. Waiting to see what weather or medication will bring may be fatal.

HOW DOES ONE DECIDE when altitude illness is becoming serious? Obviously, not everyone with headache or cough or shortness of breath will need evacuation. The speed with which symptoms appear and worsen is a valuable guide—and when things are changing fast, descent is imperative. If a cough produces pink or bloody sputum, or if one hears rattles or wheezes when the victim breathes, then it is time to move down. Hallucinations, however mild and even if recognized as such by the individual, are ominous. A staggering walk is only an advance warning. If one person is clearly slower, more short of breath, and obviously sicker than others, the pace must be slowed or halted. Perhaps the best guide is simple common sense and caution.

Can HAPE or CE be differentiated from such infections as pneumonia or meningitis? Experts find it difficult without good laboratory or hospital facilities. But infections usually cause high fever and chills, which are uncommon in altitude illness. Infection gives a person a feverish flush, what doctors call a "toxic" look, and the pulse is usually faster. Still, none of these signs is certain, so the best course of action is to descend. Infections are more dangerous at altitude, anyway. If in doubt, get down.

If Bill Demarest's rescue had been delayed even half a day, he probably would have died. But if the party had turned back a day sooner, he would not have become so desperately ill. Just a year later and fully recovered, Bill made a similar eight-day ski trip from 8,500 to 11,500 feet. The group set a pace to suit his comfort and, except for a mild headache the first day or two, he had no trouble. "We were, of course, very conscious of my condition," he wrote afterward. Bill will go on climbing and skiing.

Altitude does not respect age or experience nor does it differentiate between the fit and the feeble. Various forms of altitude illness can disable anyone who goes too high too fast, but there may be a special danger to some persons at any pace and to others only under certain conditions. Though lack of oxygen is the ultimate cause, it is the inappropriate or failed responses of the body to oxygen lack which create signs and symptoms. They appear at a speed and severity dictated primarily by rate of ascent and by altitude reached. Though some medications may be helpful, getting down is the best and only sure cure. Taking time to climb, to enjoy the rewards that mountains have for their devotees, is the best and surest preventive. ♣

LIGHTNING ALMOST ALWAYS STRIKES TWICE

Once is enough to frazzle you. But lightning follows certain rules. Understanding them keeps you ahead of the law of averages.

by GEOFFREY CHILDS

While the National Park Service has told me that there are very few deaths that have occurred to backpackers struck by lightning, there are nonetheless some very real dangers to people in the mountains during electrical storms. Knowing what to do to avoid being struck makes it possible to avoid danger with almost complete certainty.

Geoffrey Childs's article gives sound advice.
W.K.

The friend with whom I do most of my hiking is into survival. Given a sheath knife, a match, and a yard of string, he can serve up a three-course supper (with or without a meat dish), throw together a sleeping shelter, and build a fire in about the same amount of time it takes me to do it using all the modern amenities of camping. He claims he could do as well in the desert or stranded on an island in the middle of the ocean, and no doubt he probably could, assuming that the law of averages would protect him from being killed by lightning.

As it stands, the law of averages is *all* that is protecting a lot of people like my friend. They have adopted a kind of fatalism where lightning is concerned, the kind of thing men are apt to do when trying somehow to confront the unconfrontable. Yet despite its longstanding reputation for unpredictable behavior, lightning is actually one of Nature's most consistent performers. Unfortunately, one of its most consistent statistics happens to be the number of people it kills each year, the vast majority of whom spend enough time outdoors to be fully aware of the potential dangers.

Considering the amount of time that backpackers, mountaineers, survivalists, and rock-climbers spend above treeline and in other areas particularly vulnerable to lightning, their general ignorance about protecting themselves from it is lamentable.

For example, in late August, 1957, two middle-aged couples were approaching the Chasm Lake area on a hike up Colorado's Longs Peak, when they noticed a thunderstorm moving rapidly in their direction. The decision was to head back down immediately. The storm overtook them as they were passing through the open near Mill's Morraine. A sudden bolt of lightning struck and killed one of the women, knocked the other three people off

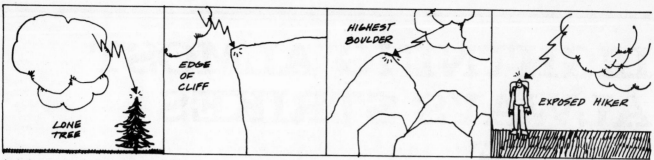

LONE TREE · EDGE OF CLIFF · HIGHEST BOULDER · EXPOSED HIKER

their feet, and sent the second woman into deep shock. This incident probably best typifies the real danger climbers expose themselves to when caught on open terrain during a thunderstorm. Whereas the city or suburban athlete has only to step indoors to be reasonably safe, the hiker's situation is considerably more complex. Dramatic as it may sound, his initial response is absolutely critical and potentially the difference between life and death.

According to a leading authority, Professor Martin A. Uman, lightning is no more than a "very long spark which discharges regions of excess electrical charge developed in thunderclouds"—much the same as the spark that leaps between your finger and a light switch after you have dragged your feet across a nylon rug. That is: when two dissimilar surfaces rub together, frictional charging is produced. Thus, lightning seeks to ground itself by discharging a spark "of enormous voltage" (once the air resistance between source and ground is overcome). It can be very dangerous if you happen to be the ground it is seeking to connect itself to.

There are three varieties of lightning. The first occurs within a cloud, from cloud to cloud, or from charged air down to a cloud. Although this phenomenon may be of interest to us, it represents no threat. The second and most frequent variety—called *down stroke* because it travels from the cloud down to earth — usually strikes the highest object on a flat surface. Although the *down stroke* may actually hit some-

one directly, more often than not it causes a voltage-robbing "breakdown" in the air around the body, in which case the individual usually has to sustain only a few thousand volts of what is known as *arc-voltage* for no more than a small fraction of one microsecond. Quite frequently, that can be enough to cause death — but in over 70 percent of the cases, the victim recovers entirely.

Much the opposite is true with the third variety — *upward stroke* lightning — which is almost always lethal. It is called *upward stroke* because the lightning actually begins on the ground and shoots upward to the cloud. As this kind of stroke is limited to the tops of mountains, it was very probably the cause of the woman's death in the previously mentioned incident.

A person struck by upward stroke lightning may draw as many as 100 to 300 amperes for several hundredths of a second, at a temperature of up to 50,000°F. This internal heating, combined with the electrical shock to the cardiac system, almost always results in death. Typically, burns are found on the body and clothing; metallic items such as zippers, bobby pins, and buttons may be welded together.

Most lightning-caused casualties, however, do not result from direct hits. More often, they are the result of a radial diffusion of the lightning's voltage through the ground, in what is called *step voltage*. In other words, when lightning strikes, it sends out its charge in an expanding and slowly dissipating circle around the point of impact. The

shock you receive depends on how close you are to the strike, and how good a conductor the ground you are standing on happens to be. A few years ago, two teenage boys were camping on the summit of Mt. Lafayette, New Hampshire, when a lightning bolt struck and shattered a boulder 35 feet away. Because the rock on which they had pitched their tent was such a good conductor, both were charged severely; one suffering burns and lacerations, the other falling into shock.

With an estimated 2,000 thunderstorms going on at any given moment, with about 100 bolts of lightning striking the earth each second, the same law of averages most of us depend on to save us from lightning also dictates that if you spend much time outdoors, you are probably going to encounter it one way or the other.

Contrary to popular myth, lightning almost always strikes twice. It is drawn to the tallest object of the topography and will consistently strike it time and time again, year after year. From this it follows that you should neither allow yourself to become the tallest object, nor try to shelter beneath the tallest object. That sounds like common sense, yet 15 percent of the people killed by lightning are found lying under trees. Though there are no statistics available on it, probably at least as many are killed standing out in the middle of a meadow. Experts like Professor Uman suggest the wiser course is to wait out the storm in a stand of smaller trees or conceal yourself in a depression twice as deep

UNSAFE POSITIONS

UNSAFE RECESS · EXPOSED POSITION · RAPPELLING · CLIMBING

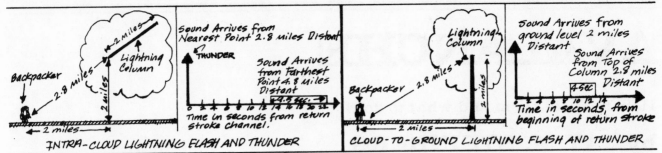

INTRA-CLOUD LIGHTNING FLASH AND THUNDER

CLOUD-TO-GROUND LIGHTNING FLASH AND THUNDER

as the tallest nearby object.

It is also wise to avoid grouping with either animals or other people, ten meters of separation being the advisable minimum. Though step voltage goes out in all directions, it obviously will follow the line of least resistance, dispersing along natural leads like splits or cracks in mountains, small streams, vegetation or debris at the base of a cliff. Consequently, it is wise to avoid these, particularly a depression with a small stream flowing through it.

Because thunderstorms usually travel at a speed of well over 25 mph, trying to outrun one seems futile. It is more advisable to use your time trying to find a safe and dry place to wait it out. You can judge pretty accurately how much time you have by counting the seconds between a flash of lightning and its thunder. For every five-second interval, it is one mile away. Using this system you can pretty well predict whether the storm is coming or going and how fast it is moving—though once you've decided it is coming towards you, your time can probably be better spent looking for a place to hide.

If you're caught out in the open, the ideal position is away from all steel objects, crouching low on the knees or haunches with the feet close together. If possible, you should try to put at least ten centimeters of insulation between you and the ground. Coiled rope or sleeping pads function better than most things in this capacity. Lying down, as the two boys were doing in the preceding example, is obviously a very bad position

to be caught in. If you are in a tent during a storm and it does not seem to offer itself as a particularly good target, you may as well stay inside—crouching on your sleeping pad, not lying down.

The predicament of a rock-climber is both the most critical and the most complex. Obviously, if there is enough time, he should try and get down off the face, but frequently there is not enough time, and rappelling during a storm is only asking to be struck. Shallow caves or recesses are equally unsafe because a bolt of lightning "can arch across the entrance and bring disaster," as the Sierra Club's *Basic Mountaineering Manual* puts it. "A safe position may be regarded as 50-80 feet from the face of a cliff or between and below the top of two flat boulders."

Jettisoning all steel technical climbing aids is also of great importance. If you are too slow in doing so, you may notice a buzzing of pitons and carabiners or other metal objects in contact with each other, and the head of an ice-ax may begin to glow. This effect is known as *St. Elmo's Fire,* and demands separating yourself from the objects immediately. Occasionally, it is possible to notice the same effects climbing into a cloud, with the addition that you may notice a tingling sensation through your legs. When electrical potentials differ at various ends of the same cloud, static energy is created and poses the threat of discharging itself within the cloud as lightning. In any case, the sensible course is to retreat immediately.

Still, no matter how conscious one

is of the danger and the steps to take to avoid it, lightning is erratic and always capable of creating an emergency situation. However, it should be emphasized that as many as 70 percent of all lightning victims make full recoveries; thus, artificial respiration in the form of heart massage and mouth-to-mouth breathing should always be attempted. Often a person's heart and breathing will cease immediately upon being struck; the heart will usually begin again on its own, but breathing will not. Not breathing for a prolonged period will cause brain damage, though cases have been reported where victims went for as long as thirteen to 22 minutes without respiring and still made full recoveries.

Injuries from diffusion are considerably more varied, ranging from burns, lacerations, and contusions to amnesia, paralysis, and internal injuries. Broken bones and head injuries often result from falls taken after being struck.

In the final analysis, the best way to avoid running the danger of being struck by lightning is to listen to the weather forecasts and stay out of the mountains or other areas where you are likely to encounter lightning. If that's impossible, then remember that Nature is not without a heart. Lightning provides you with an early warning system: thunder. There is no lightning without thunder; the sound should be warning enough to set about finding some kind of shelter or, if there is time, to retreat until the storm blows over. Even if it were true that lightning never strikes twice, once would be sufficient.

RECOMMENDED POSITIONS

BETWEEN FLAT ROCKS

CROUCHED LOW ON INSULATION

50-80 FEET FROM FACE OF CLIFF

SPACIOUS DRY CAVE

AVALANCHE

How to avoid them and what to do if . . .

by JAY M. STEINBERG

In mountain snows avalanche is one of the greatest perils to the skier or snowshoer. Knowing how to avoid avalanche is not difficult—generally speaking. But knowing how to survive one if you're caught in one is, at best, an uncertain art.

You should definitely not travel in the mountains in the winter without knowing the basics about avalanche. The following article could save your life.

W.K.

In the falling snow the line of searchers standing almost toe-to-toe moved forward scarcely a foot. Avalanche probes were thrust into the snow, and withdrawn. A team leader, alert for some evidence of a buried victim, examined the bottom of a probe that had hit a spongy object. Nothing. The rescuers kept on probing as snow continued to fall. What had begun in the morning as a pleasant snowshoe outing had ended in an avalanche disaster.

That Sunday morning in January, members of two Seattle families and several friends had put on snowshoes at the Snoqualmie Pass parking lot, 50 miles east of home, for a day hike to Source Lake. The ski area around the pass was avalanche controlled and patrolled, but a large U.S. Forest Service sign straddling the trailhead warned that the area around Source Lake was hazardous because of avalanches. Still, the father of one family had gone snow hiking at Source Lake for years without incident, so the group set out up the trail. The route ran through a forested valley divided by a stream tumbling down from the lake, two miles away.

Arriving at the lake, which is small and bounded by the steep slopes of a natural bowl, most of the group started to build snow shelters on a bench above the lake, opposite 6,000-foot Chair Peak. But two young girls, one from each family, decided to hike around the lake. It was cold, and they thought that snowshoeing would be warmer than making snow houses.

There was soft new powder snow on Chair Peak. The mountain was overburdened. Some of the snow had sloughed off, fanning out in white chunks. Suddenly, several layers high on the mountain peeled off in a giant slab. There was a brief, ominous roar of warning, but it wasn't enough for the little girls at the base of the peak. They started to run across the frozen lake on their snowshoes, were overtaken by churning snow and ice, and disappeared. The massive flow stopped at the feet of the horrified fathers.

Frantic, they and the other members of the group dug and clawed into the debris now piled in the basin. It was 20 to 30 feet deep. Their minds were dizzy from seeing a mountainside fall, and they were stricken with grief, yet they managed to mark the spot where they last saw the girls. Finding nothing, they sent for help from the ski area at Snoqualmie Pass, where there were people trained in avalanche-rescue technique. Under the threat of the rumblings of smaller avalanches, the rescuers probed systematically and frantically, and dug empty holes. The continuous avalanching, bad weather and darkness

finally brought the search to a halt. Since chances of survival after one hour of burial by avalanche are only 50 percent, time—the enemy—was winning.

Early the following morning, a rescue team from the county and a small army of volunteers gathered at the ski resort. They came from all over the Pacific Northwest: students, teachers, engineers, scouts, army reservists. But it was a gray dawn, and foreboding snow showers shrouded the mountains. A U.S. Army helicopter that was supposed to drop avalanche-control explosives on the steep slopes above Source Lake was grounded because the basin was souped in. The rescue leaders vetoed any search efforts but did send a select team to survey the area. The team reported that resuming the search would be too dangerous because of the probability of more avalanches. Snow was still falling. The fathers of the lost girls braved interviews with members of the press and television. Everybody knew that hope was fading. In a rare case, a man in Switzerland had once survived being buried for 24 hours.

Days passed. The search for the living changed into a search for the dead. Handling cold metal probe poles became part of life for the grieved family and their friends. Memorial services were held for the missing girls. Snow piled deeper. Even the efforts of a small bulldozer hired by the families yielded nothing. Spring came, and went. Summer arrived. Finally, with the big thaw in August, the search ended. Scuba divers recorded the final chapter of the disaster.

The two girls are now at rest. The story of their deaths, however, and of the torment of their families and friends, lives on.

This tragedy is only one of many that have created mounting concern among members of the U.S. Forest Service, National Park Service and National Ski Patrol. These groups are worried about the increasing number of winter backcountry travelers who are exposing themselves to the danger of avalanches. Officials dealing with recreation are being pressed with the responsibility of informing the public about the hazards of mountainous backcountry travel during the winter. "You simply can't patrol the backcountry then," says one experienced snow ranger. "Established ski trails can be checked and avalanche-control work accomplished, but not in the thousands of square miles of wilderness under deep snows."

Evidently, most backpackers exercise reasonable care while fording wild mountain streams and crossing the thin ice of snow-covered lakes. But when it comes to winter backcountry travel in the mountains, most of them are not knowledgeable. They do not know that even the most experienced mountaineers fear avalanches. Tons of snow moving down a mountain at speeds no one can outrun have no respect for age or experience.

The common assumption that all snow is alike invites catastrophe. In the mountains snow builds up in slablike layers. It freezes, thaws, becomes water-saturated from melt and rain, and is snowed on again. One layer fractures or buckles and has a tendency to slide off another layer. All that is needed is a trigger. A skier, snowshoer, additional snow falling from the sky or higher up the slope, or simply the tremendous weight of the snow itself on an incline may become the trigger of a massive avalanche.

In a most discouraging statistic, the National Ski Patrol points out that only 19 percent of the people who are completely buried in an avalanche survive. Obviously, avalanche safety must consist of more than knowing how to camp in winter, being sure to carry a shovel and probe pole, and dragging an avalanche cord along behind.

"If you are looking for a cookbook solution to staying alive in avalanche country," says Leo Hoeffer, a Squaw Valley ski patrolman and mountaineering instructor, "there just isn't any." Pete Martinelli, a Fort Collins, Colorado, project leader for U.S. Forest Service alpine snow avalanche research, believes that the only safe way to avoid avalanche hazards is to avoid the open, steep slopes and chutes and valleys in which avalanches habitually run. "There is no avalanche hazard until man invades the natural environment. Most avalanches fall unobserved far from man and his facilities."

The authorities are not trying to scare everyone away. (If they did, they would be out of work.) They are merely trying to get people to use their heads rather than take off on winter trips with little or no preparation.

What is involved in planning and carrying out a winter trip?

First of all, if you are not an experienced winter sports enthusiast, you have no business going into the mountains without experienced leadership. In the summer beginning hikers can go for a three- to five-mile backpack on an established trail without a leader, but that same hike during the winter could spell disas-

---

Condensed primer on avalanches

✔Most avalanches occur on slopes of 30 to 45 degrees, but large ones can occur on slopes of as little as 25 degrees.

✔Snow is most unstable after and during snowfalls or prolonged heating by the sun, especially on steep inclines.

✔Sunballs and cartwheels on the surface during a warming period could indicate instability in deeper layers.

✔The most dangerous avalanches usually occur on convex slopes.

✔Avalanches can take place on short slopes as well as long ones.

✔Leeward slopes are dangerous because wind-blown snow adds depth, creating hard, hollow-sounding wind slabs.

✔South-facing slopes are most dangerous in the spring.

✔Smooth grassy slopes are the most dangerous spots, but avalanches can start among trees under conditions of stress.

✔Avalanche danger can vary within a slope.

✔Following an old track does not necessarily mean a slope is safe.

✔Down-slanting trees and brush indicate previous avalanches.

✔Sun crusts on old snow can cause new snow to slide off.

✔Rough surfaces generally favor stability of new snow cover.

✔Loose, underlying snow layers are more dangerous than compacted ones.

✔Recent avalanches indicate dangerous conditions.

✔Snow falling at the rate of an inch or more per hour increases avalanche danger.

✔Snow crystals in the shape of needles and pellets result in more unstable snow conditions than the typical star-shaped snowflakes.

✔Snow saturated with water can avalanche, especially on south slopes and beneath exposed rock.

✔Rapid changes in wind, temperature and snowfall cause changes in the snowpack and may affect stability.

✔If the snow cracks and the crack runs as you step, the danger of slab avalanche, the most serious type of winter hazard, is high.

✔Gullies are many times more hazardous than open slopes because they act as natural avalanche chutes.

There is no expert who can accurately determine avalanche risk!

ter. An experienced leader will be aware of many possibilities for trouble.

The key to the safest winter travel in the mountains is taking the proper route. All cross-country trips should be planned well in advance using the most recent topographic map available. Details of the route and of alternative and emergency evacuation routes should be checked with appropriate authorities, such as the U.S. Forest Service, National Park Service, National Ski Patrol or state department of forests.

Let's suppose you have naively decided to make a snowshoe trip to a favorite lake via the same narrow valley you hiked through last summer. In August you could clearly see that it was ribbed with avalanche chutes. Debris from past avalanches, large boulders lying about and an absence of trees were further indications of avalanche danger.

But in winter a passive white winter coat covers those scars; everything looks smooth, inviting and lovely. You probably cannot see the massive cornice hanging over the ridge above. And you certainly cannot see the slick frozen snow several layers beneath you, gradually becoming a potential runway for the layers on top. You know that a nice switchback trail on the steep unforested mountainside lies buried just ahead. You can't see the trail, but you want to go up, so you start to zigzag. Then you notice that the snow is cracking with every step. Fracture lines begin running out for several yards. Well, my friend, you are about to become a statistic or have one helluva scare, depending on when, where and how the snow decides to follow Newton's old idea and take off downhill.

This little scenario is totally unnecessary, for in winter you can still hike to that favorite lake with relative safety by using a winter route. It usually means going a longer way around. You might have to keep to a well-forested area and work your way to the top of a ridge, the safest place to travel, by avoiding all cornices and steep, barren slopes. Heavily forested pockets and large rock outcroppings are natural avalanche barriers that tend to hold snow in place, so take advantage of them. The topo map and a consultation with the local authorities should make the winter route

plain before you start out.

The timing of a winter trip can be crucial. Now, not many summer hikers would start out in the teeth of a storm; they wait until the storm lets up. In winter the same procedure should be followed except that a longer interval should be allowed because snow conditions are most unstable after a snowfall. If bad weather is forecast, it is best to cancel a trip altogether. During storms even rescue efforts are shelved so that no additional lives will be endangered. Safe travel requires good weather! Everyone who has anything to do

with winter recreation emphasizes the importance of "weather wisdom." The rule from the experts is to simply stay out of the mountains when weather conditions threaten blizzards, fog, avalanches or other extremes.

The National Weather Service now provides avalanche-warning advice on its radio broadcasts in most mountainous regions of the United States. Additionally, the National Ski Patrol and local government officials are usually aware of weather conditions and can provide informed advice when they are consulted.

Rescuers keep probing as the snow continues to fall. What had begun in the morning as a pleasant snowshoe outing had ended in an avalanche disaster.

Well, you have planned your trip, done some informative reading, acquired adequate equipment and clothing, consulted the weather forecasters, and you are on your way.

Despite all your careful preparations, problems can occur. Your group may happen to be high on a mountain when a storm threatens, and want out. You will need all your thought processes, a knowledge of winter hazards and a good dose of common sense. The experts advise using the early hours of a storm to get away if visibility permits. But if you can't make it, try to find a safe place to bivouac or camp to wait out the storm. Use the survival techniques you learned ahead of time. Unfortunately, there is no "cookbook" answer for when to move on; every situation is different. You have to watch for sloughing snow and fractures and listen to nature at work. At least, you will know how much new snow has accumulated and the condition of the layer below it.

Even without storms, there is danger. You should not cross open treeless slopes or travel at the base of such slopes. Detour around them. But if you have no choice—if you find your group in a situation when it becomes necessary to traverse these places—plan your actions carefully. Before proceeding, test the snow on small steep slopes oriented like the slope you wish to cross. Or, if you are anchored, try to release an avalanche by stamping. Then climb across the slope in short zigzag patterns below any protective barriers. Use these barriers as resting places. If long traverses become unavoidable, make them either high on the slope above possible fracture zones or well beyond the point where snow will pile up at the bottom. Space your people apart, each following the tracks of the person in front. The greater the danger, the greater the distance should be between individuals. If extreme danger develops, that is, if it becomes obvious you will cause or be caught in an avalanche, abandon your equipment and climb directly up or down the slope.

If you know ahead of time that an unavoidable slope is extremely dangerous, you should follow the procedures recommended by the National Avalanche School:

Establish an avalanche guard and select a backup leader. Distribute the rescue equipment (probes and snow shovels) in the middle and at the end of the column. Tie red avalanche cords at least 35 feet long to each person's body, not to his clothing, where it might rip off. Be ready to quickly cover your mouth and nose with a scarf, parka or sweater. If you are using ski poles, remove the wrist loops. Be able to quickly jettison your pack and any other gear. Space the members of the party so that only one person at a time is in the danger area. All others should keep their eyes on his exact position.

If the worst happens and an avalanche occurs, the experts say that you should try to get out of its path or to the side by hooking onto any tree trunks or shrubs. If you are caught, try to get rid of your equipment. Use a skulling or backstroke swimming action to try to remain on the surface. It is best to be in a half-sitting position on your back facing downhill, with your legs together and knees bent. Then fight the avalanche all the way down, keeping your mouth shut to prevent snow from entering your lungs. As the avalanche stops, make breathing room for your chest and face. Try not to panic. Frantic attempts to free yourself will only use up valuable oxygen. In soft snow, you may be able to dig yourself out. Be sure to dig in the proper direction—up, not down.

If you should happen to witness an avalanche in which someone gets buried, you can do several things to effect a live recovery. Remember, time is of the essence, and you will need to keep a cool head. Mark the place where the victim was caught in the avalanche and the place where he was last seen. These two reference points will give a good indication of the victim's line of travel. Place someone on guard to warn rescuers in case of new avalanche threats, and select a direction of escape for the rescuers.

Experts recommend first visually exploring the surface of the avalanche deposition zone down the fall line from the spot where the victim was last seen. Most victims who live are rescued in this operation. You might find an article of clothing, avalanche cord or some clue as to where the victim is fully or partially buried. The experts also suggest using a dog if one is available because its natural curiosity and sensitivity will often lead it to the victim.

The next step is to systematically coarse probe the deposition zone, probing the most likely spots first. If there are no probe poles, use ski poles, skis or even tree branches. Coarse probing calls for a probe line that is established by lining people up elbow to elbow in a hands-on-hips position. Each person makes one probe insertion between his feet, and then the line advances two feet. Each area probed should be marked.

If rescue is not immediate, someone should go for help—or preferably, two people if the party can spare them or if the accident has occurred in the backcountry. The rest of the group should continue to search vigorously, coarse probing all likely areas several times for two hours.

After two hours of coarse probing, fine probing should begin in the most likely places, which are the toe of the avalanche (the place of the greatest deposition) and any terrain features that catch or hold snow (because they can also catch a human being). The line is arranged in the same manner as the coarse probe, with 20 inches between each prober's feet and 10 inches between him and the next person. But instead of making one probe, each participant probes between his feet and at the toe of both feet. The line then advances only one foot at a time. It is a desperate business, but it must be done carefully.

Once the victim is located, you should uncover his face and immediately treat him for suffocation by clearing snow from his mouth and giving mouth-to-mouth artificial respiration. Then dig him all the way out of the snow, apply first aid to any injuries, and do what you can to warm him before transporting him away. During the evacuation, you should watch his breathing carefully for any relapse or cessation.

The cry of "Avalanche!" is enough to chill the spine of the most experienced mountaineers. If winter recreationists would make adequate trip preparations and exercise more caution, this cry would be heard less, and more people would survive to enjoy another winter. ♣

A SIMPLE, SAFE METHOD OF WATER PURIFICATION FOR BACKPACKERS

by FREDRICK H. KAHN and BARBARA R. VISSCHER

That clear, cold mountain stream is not as pure as you think. And that halazone you've been carrying in your pack probably won't work. Do you have to risk giardiasis, dysentery, or some other disease? Not necessarily.

For forty years I've done little about purifying the water I've drunk in the backcountry. I've not gotten sick from it, so far as I know. I've been lucky.

From what we know recently, even the purest mountain streams can carry giardiasis. And if you get infected with it you may not know it for six weeks later, and hence you may not relate it to the crystal-clear mountain springwater you drank on your last hike.

Certainly when hiking in areas where you drink from streams with less certain origins, you ought to treat the water before drinking it.

At BACKPACKER we have tried to determine the effectiveness of the various techniques advocated for purifying water—boiling, halazone, chlorine, iodine treatment, filtration. It gets complicated. We believe, though, that the method prescribed in the following article is both simple to use and effective.

W.K.

IT HAS ALWAYS BEEN ASSUMED that mountain streams were pure. With improved surveillance it is now known that most streams of the United States are polluted. Reliable data on the incidence of waterborne disease among hikers and backpackers are unavailable, yet potentially waterborne diseases including Salmonella infections, amoebic dysentery, giardiasis and infectious hepatitis are commonly observed among travelers returning from abroad and from remote areas of the United States.

The authors' interest in water disinfection was sharpened when they acquired giardiasis after drinking from a partly frozen stream on the Long Valley trail to Mount San Jacinto in California, in early May, 1971. Human habitation was sparse, and snow covered the ground. Cold weather, however, is no protection from intestinal parasitism and may actually present a problem in water purification, as will be explained below.

A water disinfectant must be able to kill the hardiest organisms, especially amoebic cysts and enteroviruses, the most resistant to disinfection of the pathogenic microorganisms. At the same time, the toxicity of the chemical must be very low. A water disinfectant for the traveler presents special requirements which are of less importance to a sanitary engineer. These include simplicity, effectiveness in the presence of nitrogenous pollutants, rapidity of antimicrobial action over a wide pH range, and immediate palatability. The backpacker will, of course, also demand light weight.

DURING WORLD WAR II, Halazone (p-dichlorosulfamoyl benzoic acid) was issued for individual use when other forms of water treatment were not available. Though Halazone

142

1 The water purification kit consists of a one-ounce clear glass bottle with a hard plastic cap and 4 to 8 grams of USP-grade resublimed iodine—iodine crystals. Since iodine in large quantities is a poison, you may need a doctor's prescription to get it at your pharmacy. Eight grams costs about $2.00.

2 When water needs to be treated, fill the bottle with water, cap it, and shake it vigorously for 30 to 60 seconds. Shaking will cause some iodine from the crystals to be dissolved in the water. The amount of iodine that will be dissolved depends on the temperature of the water (see table).

3 What is used to disinfect the drinking water is this saturated iodine solution, not the crystals themselves. So hold the bottle upright for a few moments until the iodine crystals fall to the bottom. The one-ounce bottle holds 30 cc's altogether, and you can use the cap to measure the right amount.

4 Carefully pour the correct amount of iodine solution into a liter (a little more than a quart) of water. Then let the treated water sit until the iodine disinfects it. If you can wait, adding less iodine and letting the treated water stand longer will produce the same effect, and the water will taste better.

water germicide, yet Halazone continues to be widely used and is often the only commercially available agent.

CHLORINATION BY HALAZONE in the recommended dose depends on the slow release of 2.8 parts per million (ppm) of free chlorine for immediate antimicrobial action. Chlorine under ideal conditions, namely a pH of 7 or lower (neutral or acidic water) and the absence of nitrogenous compounds, hydrolyzes to hypochlorous acid (HClO), an excellent germicide. But HClO is highly reactive and in the presence of such nitrogen-containing compounds as amino and ammonia ions, it is quickly converted to relatively inactive monochloramine. Moreover, above pH 7 (alkaline water) HClO hydrolyzes to the less active hypochlorite.

These two problems are solved in water purification plants by the practice of breakpoint chlorination, the application of sufficient chlorine to bind with the organic materials in the water while leaving a biocidal residual of free chlorine. But this technique requires continual testing and is impractical for rapid treatment of small quantities of water. The individual traveler must resort to simple chlorination, the practice of adding a fixed dose of chlorine compound to water of uncertain quality. Simple chlorination is unpredictable and may be useless against bacteria and enteroviruses when water is contaminated with organic material.

Additional disadvantages of Halazone are slow solubility and a short shelf life of five months when stored at 32°C. (89.6°F.). Potency is reduced 50 percent when stored at 40° to 50°C. (104° to 122°F.), the temperature range one might expect in an automobile glove compartment on a summer day. Halazone also loses 75 percent of its activity when exposed to air for two days.

produced potable water in the absence of heavy contamination, its efficacy in treating cold, heavily polluted water containing resistant forms such as viruses and amoebic cysts was seriously questioned. In 1942, at the request of the armed forces, investigators at Harvard University initiated a search for a more dependable technique of water sterilization. Their study recommended the use of iodine for treatment of small quantities of water. A technique for iodination was developed and adapted by the armed forces. Subsequent investigations confirm the superiority of iodination as a personal

How Much Saturated Iodine Solution You Add Depends on the Temperature.

The amount of iodine that will go into solution in your one-ounce bottle depends on the temperature of the water. The following quantities of nearly saturated iodine solution will yield an iodine concentration of four parts per million when added to one liter of water.

Temperature	Volume	Concentration	Capfuls*
3°C (37°F)	20.0 cc	200 ppm.	8
20°C (68°F)	13.0 cc	300 ppm.	5+
25°C (77°F)	12.5 cc	320 ppm.	5
40°C (104°F)	10.0 cc	400 ppm.	4

*Assuming a capful of standard 1 ounce glass bottle is 2½ cc.

IODINATION, IN CONTRAST, with a weak aqueous solution of 3 to 5 ppm of elemental iodine (I_2) will destroy amoebae and their cysts, bacteria and their spores, algae, and enteroviruses at 25°C. (77°F.) in 15 minutes or less (see chart). At near freezing (3°C., 37.4°F.) disinfection will require 20 to 30 minutes at the same concentration of iodine, since germicidal potency is roughly proportional to temperature. Elemental iodine does not react readily with ammonia and amino ions and therefore will remain an effective disinfectant in water polluted with nitrogenous wastes. Iodine is effective over a wide pH range, hydrolyzing at pH above 6 to hydroiodous acid, which is a faster virucide than I_2.

Iodination can be accomplished in three ways. One method is the addition of eight drops of two percent tincture of iodine to a quart of water, but this results in water of less than acceptable palatability. A second is the addition of a tablet of Globaline (tetraglycine hydroperiodide) to a quart of water, releasing active iodine in a concentration of 8 ppm. The disadvantages of Globaline Tablets include a fixed, high concentration of iodine and a 33 percent loss of their initial activity when exposed to air for four days. The third method is the use of crystals of elemental iodine.

THE ONLY EQUIPMENT needed for iodination with crystalline iodine is a one-ounce clear glass bottle, with a leak-proof bakelite cap, containing 4 to 8 grams (or any small quantity) of USP grade resublimed iodine (I_2). The bottle is filled with water and capped, shaken vigorously for 30 to 60 seconds, then held upright for a few moments to permit the heavy iodine crystals (specific gravity 4.6) to fall to the bottom. *The iodine crystals are not to be used directly.* What is used is the *water* in the bottle, now a nearly saturated iodine solution. Disinfection is accomplished at 25°C. (77°F.) by the addition of 12½ cubic centimeters (cc) of this nearly saturated solution to one liter of water (1.06 quarts) to achieve a final concentration of 4 ppm iodine. Since the concentration of the saturated iodine solution varies with its temperature (see table), only 10 cc of iodine solution would be needed if the bottle were kept at body temperature. At near freezing, 20 cc of iodine solution would be used per liter. (The cap of the iodine bottle may serve as a measuring device.) After a contact time of 15 minutes, the water is disinfected. When more disinfected water is desired, the above steps can be repeated almost 1,000 times without replenishing the iodine crystals. The shelf life of crystalline iodine is unlimited.

Under usual circumstances, a 2 ppm iodine solution with a contact time of 40 minutes offers improved palatability and effective disinfection. If increased germicidal potency is necessary because the water is turbid, cold, or heavily contaminated, the concentration of the iodine solution could be increased to 8 ppm, with a contact time of 20 minutes. However, in the interest of palatability, one may prefer not to increase the concentration, but instead increase the contact time (see chart).

A clear glass bottle is recommended to permit observation of the iodine crystals. Plastic bottles of all types take on an opaque brown stain after long exposure to the working solution. Furthermore, plastic bottles tend to leak as one travels to high elevations and distort and crack on descent to low elevations.

THE TOXICITY OF IODINE is remarkably low in the concentrations used for water disinfection. Only persons with a specific sensitivity to iodine, and perhaps those who have been treated for hyperthyroidism, risk any ill effects. The only danger of the iodination procedure is the inadvertent ingestion of iodine crystals, although an ounce of nearly saturated iodine solution would be harmless. No fatality from ingestion of less than 15 grams of iodine has been reported.

Chlorine, except when breakpoint chlorination is practiced, is an unreliable disinfectant. Iodination, on the other hand, rapidly inactivates the known human pathogens, including the enteroviruses which are the most resistant to disinfection. Iodination is effective over a wide pH range and in the presence of nitrogenous pollutants. There is a need among travelers and hikers for an effective, palatable water disinfectant with rapid action and long shelf life. The iodine disinfection method described above meets these requirements. ♣

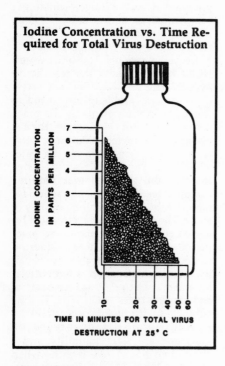

Iodine Concentration vs. Time Required for Total Virus Destruction

IODINE CONCENTRATION IN PARTS PER MILLION

7 6 5 4 3 2

TIME IN MINUTES FOR TOTAL VIRUS DESTRUCTION AT 25° C

Because the concentration of iodine is inversely proportional to the time required for disinfection, a lower concentration of iodine left in water for a longer period of time will have the same disinfection effect and make the treated water taste better. The virus that produced these figures is one of the hardiest, comparable to the infectious hepatitis virus.

Chapter Six

GOING IT ALONE

One of the most talked-about aspects of the wilderness education courses such as Outward Bound and National Outdoor Leadership School (NOLS) is the three-day solo. This is a dramatic experience for those who undertake it. Usually it comes after three weeks of training in outdoors skills. The student is left by himself in the wilderness with no food or shelter or matches. And is expected to survive by what he has learned from the course.

What is so dramatic about this experience, though, is not so much the survival skills employed as it is the psychological experience of finding yourself alone in a world you have not known before. What kind of beasts lurk out there in the darkness? What if I roll over in the night on a rattlesnake? Other, far more bizarre, thoughts prey on your mind. You listen through the night to sounds you are not familiar with. It is difficult.

Completely by yourself for three days, you also listen to yourself—and come to realize that you never ever got acquainted with yourself before. It is a frightening experience for most people, but having lived through the three-day solo, you gain confidence that you can endure lots of less frightening things in your daily life.

The first time I found myself completely alone in the wilderness was in 1958 in the Bugaboo Mountains in British Columbia. I was going climbing with friends of mine from New York. I arrived two days late at the approach, and they had already gone in ahead of me to the boulder camp, high on the edge of the glacier. It took two days to get into the high camp, which meant I had to camp out a night by myself, and to backpack in on my own.

At that time the area was rarely visited, and there were no trails. I had to find my way by topographical map and hope that I would be able to find my friends' camp.

For the first time in my life I felt really alone. A lot of different kinds of thoughts ran through my mind. What if I fell and broke a leg? How long would it be before someone would find me? If ever? What if I missed finding my friends' camp? What if they had changed their minds and decided to camp somewhere else instead of where we had agreed upon back in New York? What if . . . ? That was the frightening part.

But there was another part that was equally compelling. That was a new sense of the aesthetics of the mountains. By myself everything seemed to be so much more sharply in focus. The air seemed tangier, the sun more sparkling, the pine scent more powerful, the taste of the mountain stream water sweeter and cooler. All more intense. I had never enjoyed the wilderness more.

Still another aspect of this trip stands out very prominently in my memory, after twenty years. The feeling of independence that I got on that hike into boulder camp was exhilarating. I went at my own pace without a care for anyone else. It did not even matter if I didn't get up to boulder camp by night. My friends did not know when I would be arriving, and it didn't matter to them.

So when I stopped to drink, I dawdled as long as I liked. When I was hiking along a river, I can recall that I raced along for a mile or more. I can still feel how my legs were like matchsticks under the enormous weight of my pack—but how good it felt to trot along the riverside, jumping from boulder to boulder. That, of course, is when I got the frightening thoughts about what if . . . I should break a leg.

There was one time I stopped for a long time—took a dip in the stream and lay out nude on a warm, flat rock, letting the sun dry my body. Absolutely no cares. After all those years, that moment is still so rare that it stands out in my mind as perfect peace.

Another aspect of hiking alone on that memorable trip is with me still as a lesson. I came to realize that a lot of the silly worries that I had been ruminating about before starting my hike into the Bugaboos gradually diminished in their intensity and their effect upon my feelings until, in that apex experience of peace on that flat rock, they were gone altogether, and I was completely joyous in my heart.

In this chapter, several contributors share their very personal experiences with hiking alone.

THE PLEASURES OF GOING ALONE ON BAFFIN ISLAND

by JAMES KERN

Most of us live in a man-made environment. Take a look around you as you read this sentence. Where are you? Most likely you are in a room with walls made by humans, filled with furniture made by people, holding a book printed and written and sold to you by human beings. Very likely the room is lit by lights manufactured by humans and electricity supplied by human efforts. And if there is anything of nature in your room it is probably a potted plant, a caged bird, a fish in an aquarium. So, what is your relationship with nature? I mean right now, as you read this book?

Chances are that you do not know whether the stars were out last night, or what time the sun went down and the time the moon came up, and what phase the moon is in. Don't fret. Neither do I. The point I am making is that most of our lives we live secluded from nature. Hence, when we go out into the wilderness it is like a foreign place for us.

In a way, that is good. Perhaps it makes us appreciate it more. The author of the following piece, Jim Kern, thinks so. He spends much time by himself in the wilderness. And he tells what significance it has for him in this article.

W.K.

I was trying to explain to my Eskimo guide when he should come back down the ice to get me. We had finished offloading my camera equipment and hiking gear. The sealskin tarps that had protected them were again lashed to the empty sled. The Eskimo was ready to start his Ski-doo and return the 20 miles to the town of Frobischer Bay, on Baffin Island at the edge of the Arctic Circle. I would be left alone to hike the surrounding hills and search for nesting shore birds to photograph.

Did he understand I wanted him to come back in five days? We were dependent on English, and his wasn't too good. I wrote the return date on the palm of his hand with my ball-point pen. When he saw the numbers, he nodded, and I felt better.

In a few minutes his Ski-doo and sled were specks on the ice, heading west. The engine became a distant drone. Quiet settled in. I looked around. My gear was piled on a narrow, steeply sloping beach of coarse brown sand. A rivulet ran across the tundra nearby and then across the sand. By walking up the slope a few yards, I could see a narrow lake that wound away for several hundred feet. I thought I saw two geese at the end of the lake.

The idea of having this place entirely to myself was exhilarating. It was the first week of June. The ice would break up on Frobischer Bay in another couple of weeks. Most of the snow was off the tundra, and the birds had arrived. I found Canada geese, common eider, sanderlings, and semipalmated plover nesting close by. Each day I hiked farther from camp.

They were five glorious days of exploring, hiking, making wildlife pictures, and not much sleep, since it didn't get dark at night. I found glaucous gulls wheeling against the rock face of a miniature fjord, identified and photographed dozens of tundra wildflowers, took long mid-day naps, read L. David Mech's book *The Wolf,* even took sunbaths by facing the front of my tent to the sun, the back to the wind, and stretching out inside.

Author James Kern.
PHOTO: RICHARD KERN

Hiking alone, for me, produces a curious mix of emotions. Walking in the outdoors with little or no evidence of humans heightens my sense of peace and freedom. The amount of each varies with the time and place: peace at early morning in the Big Cypress Swamp in Florida; freedom in the blustery, salty whip of the wind on an Oregon dune.

But there is the excitement, too, of deliberately exposing myself to the vicissitudes of nature. Satisfaction in handling what comes. And contentment once I've made myself secure. Discovering in the dark that after the downpour quits I am still warm and dry in my sleeping bag is sweet pleasure. Drifting back to sleep is heaven. Doing it alone is more exciting and adventurous than when I have friends within reach.

Long before I read Thoreau or Muir, I was required to read for an English class an essay about going on walks alone. I never forgot the ideas in that essay, though more than once I had wished I could remember the author and title.

At my twenty-fifth school reunion I sat opposite a member of the class literati and told him about the essay. "Try Hazlitt," he suggested. An hour later, in the

library stacks, I rediscovered British essayist William Hazlitt, who wrote from 1805 to 1830. "On Going a Journey" was written for people like me:

One of the pleasantest things in the world is going a journey; but I like to go by myself. I can enjoy society in a room; but out of doors, nature is company enough for me. I am then never less alone than when alone. . . .

I cannot see the wit of walking and talking at the same time. When I am in the country, I wish to vegetate like the country. I am not for criticizing hedge-rows and black cattle. I go out of town in order to forget the town and all that is in it. There are those who for this purpose go to watering-places, and carry the metropolis with them. I like more elbow-room, and fewer encumbrances. I like solitude, when I give myself up to it, for the sake of solitude. . . .

The soul of a journey is liberty; perfect liberty, to think, feel, do, just as one pleases. We go a journey chiefly to be free of all impediments and of all inconveniences; to leave ourselves behind, much more to get rid of others.

I have some additional simple reasons for going alone. To begin with, I can leave my watch at home or at the bottom of my pack. I don't end up rushing because I told someone I would meet him at a certain hour, perhaps at some halfway spot where he will be kept waiting if I don't arrive on time.

One of my first backpacking trips started in this way. It was an overnight hike through Ocala National Forest in Florida with three other people whom I had never met, a survey trip to locate the Florida Trail. I was late. The others, now good friends, have long since forgotten it, but I still remember keeping them waiting.

So at the outset, when going alone, I can nullify one of the great impositions of modern society—the sense of urgency. Just yesterday my life went like this: Mowed the lawn at daylight (teenage son out of town). A meeting at 9:00 A.M. to try to sell a business ran to 10:30, later than I thought it would. A hiker calls from California, needing help and equipment; there are other calls I don't have time to return. Can my secretary speak to me about vacations before the 11 o'clock appointment? Can it wait until after lunch? 11:05. I help a client select mats and frames for photographs. Noon. A lunch downtown to discuss the sale of the business with another prospect. Eye appointment at 2:45; make business calls from doctor's office. Inspect house I am building; many decisions with the builder. 6:00 P.M. Haven't flown lately and decide to do touch and go's at the airport before dark. Call home: feed the kids, I'll make it by eight o'clock. Most people have similar stories of being too busy. On hikes I try to make time unimportant. Alone, it is much easier.

Next, I like to indulge myself in the route selection. What haven't I seen? Where do I want to loll, getting back on the trail only when the spirit moves me? One summer at a family reunion in the Smokies, I decided to take an overnight hike on a moment's notice. No one cared to join me, but my wife, sister, and her husband were willing to drive me to a trailhead. En route, park map in hand, I decided on the trail I would take and asked to be met at Newfound Gap in the late afternoon of the following day. I had no pack. Instead, I wrapped some food in a blanket and, after tying the ends of the blanket, slung it over my shoulder and across my chest like a bandolier. I also took a knife and some twine.

That night I slept alone in a lean-to. In the morning at a table in front of the lean-to, the cool, still air was warmed by patches of sunlight. There I lingered and got back on the trail who knew when. It didn't matter.

When I go by myself, I can start with a route in mind and change all of it before I reach the first fork in the road without a comment. If I am meticulous or fickle as a planner, no one knows. If I pick a destination and then decide not to make it, I need make no elaborate explanation. I just stop and set up camp.

The pleasure of these whims applies to canoe travel as well. Once, in the 10,000 Islands of Everglades National Park, I started out alone for Indian Key. I never got there. While studying the map along the way, I decided to paddle for Rabbit Key, found it unoccupied by boating campers, brought in my canoe, and had the place to myself. That evening by moonlight I watched a family of raccoons for more than a hour as they worked the marl flats at low tide, looking for a late-night meal. There were no sounds except the lap of receding water and the whistle of black-bellied plovers. It was a night I won't forget.

Once I step off alone, the pace I set is my own, a reflection of my current mood, ambition, and physical shape. Few hikers know this simple pleasure. I walk until I wish to stop. With a group, rest stops normally come at regular intervals, an accommodation to the average need. But each body varies from the average, of course. Occasionally I want to keep moving when the rest break arrives. Usually, though, I get tired before the group leader decides to stop. What a pleasure it is to rest from labor just when you feel like doing so. Rare among fellow workers. Difficult in your own home with a hundred things to do. Usually awkward with hiking companions. Deciding to goof off at such times is tainted with guilt. No accounting is necessary when I hike alone.

One way to try hiking alone is to plan for an extra day on a hike with companions. On that day everyone goes his own way. The Florida Trail Association sponsored a six-day hike in Vanoise National Park in France. Six of us went. I spent half the extra day stretched out amid mountain grasses and wildflowers, watching ibex, my nose sucking up the earth's good odors, belly half-chilled, back comfortably warmed by a brilliant sun in a cloudless sky.

Burdens on my mind instead of my back? I can't lay them down while talking to others on the trail the way I can when going alone. Talk gravitates to relationships, expectations, problems, hopes, discomforts, fears, worries, dreams. I defy anyone to keep his mind on such things under the massaging rhythm of his own footfalls. Even when I hit the trail with the most intense workday pressures riling me up, half a day of walking alone is all I need.

During the Florida real estate collapse of 1974-76, I was trying to hold on to a large parcel of land and was under enormous financial pressure. Several times during the winter months of those years, solo walks into the Big Cypress along the Florida Trail calmed me down.

If I want to shout for joy, I shout. If I want to skip, I skip. If I want to sing, it doesn't matter that I "can't" sing. I sing. Once, a view from an unnamed ridge in northeastern Nevada so overwhelmed me that tears rolled down my cheeks. Just the view. No need to feel self-conscious; no one else was around. To feel emotions as they come without having to assess how others will respond, in unlimited space, amidst wild things, adds to my sense of freedom.

Usually in early morning, once I have broken camp and am on the trail, my spirits are high.

That's when I am most likely to let random emotions tumble out. Sometimes irrepressibly I let out ungodly whoops of joy. Because no one hears me, it saves explanations.

At first light one cold morning in Rocky Mountain National Park, I left my family in their sleeping bags and drove to a pass for a chance at hearing elk bugle. High up on the slopes a fellow was dancing alone in the first rays of the morning sunlight, whirling like a dervish. Some kind of nut? Perhaps. But I envied him.

The delights nature serves up to me create some real problems if I'm hiking with companions. I may want to stop for only a minute to watch a skink rustle its tail in the dry leaves, but the moment I stop, I fall behind. And any time I spend on my knees is matched by an urgency to be on my way, to catch up. It may be a crab spider hiding in a daisy or a brightly bibbed yellow-throated warbler working the branches of a slash pine. If I suggest we all stop, together we will not enjoy the sight as much as I would have alone.

Part of the reason is the problem of verbalizing impressions for the benefit of companions, and they for you. Of course we want to share such things. But words fail us, and we know it. Nature is so marvelous that whatever we say proves inadequate. Hazlitt said it best, first:

In my opinion, this continual comparing of notes interferes with the involuntary impression of things upon the mind, and hurts the sentiment. If you only hint what you feel in a kind of dumb show, it is insipid: if you have to explain it, it is making a toil of pleasure. You cannot read the book of nature, without being perpetually put to the trouble of translating it for the benefit of others. I am for the synthetical method on a journey, in preference to the analytical. I am content to lay in a stock of ideas then, and to examine and anatomize them afterward. I want to see my vague notions float like the down of the thistle before the breeze, and not to have them entangled in the briars and thorns of controversy. For once, I like to have it all my own way; and this is impossible, unless you are alone, or in such company as I do not covet.

Walking alone sets a person free; resting alone unites him with nature. Hiking is a penetration; sitting quietly, attentively, is a revelation.

One spring at Seven Mile Camp in Florida's Big Cypress, I was lying in my sleeping bag at dawn, cozy and secure, my eyes not yet ready to focus. I heard a catlike screech that was too short for my ears to make a good connection with my brain. I would guess a bobcat. What did it want? What had it done? Now I was alert. Waiting. But I waited in vain. Moments later the unmistakable, quivering, melodic gobble of a tom turkey summoned the hens of his harem. Not long after came the mewing call of a red-cockaded woodpecker. An endangered species! What a way to start a day. These experiences in wild sound were heightened because I was in the midst of them by myself. Others might have been talking or rustling in their beds, mixing society and wilderness in a dubious colloid and scarring these moments for me.

While my rule is to leave society at home when I enter the woods, I make an exception: a good book. Preferably one that fits the setting. Something by John Burroughs or John Muir would be a first choice. *Walden* or *A Sand County Almanac* to reread. But other books of similar spirit are just as good: McPhee's *The Survival of the Bark Canoe,* Schumacher's *Small is Beautiful,* even Rawling's *Cross Creek.* With such a book, I am a walk-read-walk hiker. I walk until I am tired, read until I start to get stiff, then walk again. The two activities activate alternately the mind and the body.

Two years ago I started into the Big Cypress Swamp in April, bushwhacking much of the way. At that time of year, the "swamp" is very hot and dry. No creeks, no ponds. Wells along the Florida Trail provided the only water for miles around. I tired easily and rested often, but that suited my plan, for I had Roderick Nash's *Wilderness and the American Mind* in my pack, and could hardly wait to get into it. I would lean against the shady side of a giant slash pine and read until the perspiration dried, be off until my T-shirt was soaked, then sink down again into the shade.

An earlier walking-reading-walking experience profoundly affected my life. During college I had a summer job as a pipe walker with the U.S. Smelting, Mining & Refining Company in Fairbanks, Alaska. We needed a small river of water for our gold-mining operation. The water was brought part of the way through old pipes 24 inches in diameter and sealed at the joints with burlap. Leaks occurred frequently. My job was to walk back and forth along four miles of pipe, checking for leaks. I kept a paperback of Emerson's essays in my back pocket. Out came the essays on Nature, Self Reliance, and Character at every rest break. And they paid me for doing that job!

Talking about solo hiking with friends has turned up a lot of agreement I did not realize was there. Margaret Scruggs, executive secretary of the Florida Trail Association, calls going alone her "high." David Wells, section leader for the Big Cypress Section of the Florida Trail, was continually organizing and leading trail maintenance hikes. He eventually set out over the same terrain on a day hike by himself and got so carried away with the pleasure of it, he walked 32 miles before dark.

On another level, the experience of going alone is one way back to individuality in a society in which we eliminate risk, remove uniqueness, and join the herd.

I'm not saying a life of solitude—hermithood—is the best kind of life. Solitude is an alternative form of pleasure. And in the same way remembrance of quiet solitary moments in the outdoors enhances my enjoyment of life within human society, knowledge of our culture gives me a deeper appreciation of nature. Handel and Beethoven quicken my sense to bird song. Newton has helped me wonder at the spider's orb. The psalmist David speaks more eloquently than I can of God's creation.

Sigurd Olson noticed that the Cree Indians in the Athabasca wilderness, living their entire lives in the wilds, did not appreciate their world as much as Olson, whose culture prepared him to appreciate it. We hikers often tend to be romantics, imagining ourselves laden with pack and heading into the sunset. A more realistic and meaningful course is a balance of both worlds, a coming and going from the world of man to the world of nature.

This alternation between wilderness and civilization was seen as the solution for living by John P. Milton, author of *Nameless Valleys:* "A life spent contrasting and living alternately in both worlds ... seems best to me." Frank Dobie, an essayist on the Southwest, wrote: "The greatest happiness possible to a man ... is to become civilized, to know the pageant of the past, to love the beautiful, to have just ideas of values and proportions, and then retaining his animal spirits and appetites, to live in a wilderness."

"I am never less alone than when alone," said Hazlitt. With our culture cut off and left behind, we are free to draw deep breaths of clean air, to receive a thousand sensations altogether new since our last visit. To explore the bark of a tree with your fingernail, to feel the velvet undersurface of a mushroom, to wait for the end of a vireo's song, to look at stars in a black night and struggle alone with what infinity means, to be startled by an exploding snipe, to drink runoff from a snowfield with cupped hands, to be frightened by a bear print, to think about those we love from our temporary otherworld—these are the kinds of deep pleasures that await us.

WHAT ARE THE RISKS OF GOING ALONE?

A physical adventure involves physical risk. Going alone involves the risk you will get hurt and that there will be no one to help you. I'll take the risk. Try to eliminate it, and you will suck out of your trip much excitement and exhilaration. There isn't much actual risk, but it doesn't take much to make the adventure real. Driving downtown to work each day is much more perilous, and is also devoid of adventure.

Tell someone where you are going and when to start a search if you're not back. Don't forget to report in. If you break a leg, you won't die. Sit down in your sleeping bag and wait a few days for help. Having a red or orange tent fly, easily seen from the air, is wise when hiking alone.

Perhaps exposure—hypothermia—is the greatest risk. There is a lot of room for foolish mistakes: getting wet when it is cold, running out of water when there is none on the trail, exhausting yourself in a climb as the temperature drops. These mistakes could cost you your life in an extreme situation. But you are more likely to walk off a curb without looking and come out worse.

People who speak Spanish will tell you that Spanish is easy to learn. Pilots say it is easy to fly a plane. As one who is completely at home alone in the woods—who longs, in fact, for the experience of solitude—I say it is easy to prepare yourself for the adventure of going alone, and it is joyful to do it. I leave the details to you.

ALONE IN THE BLACK FOREST OF PENNSYLVANIA

When you backpack alone, you can feel selfish without feeling the least bit guilty.

by CHARLES FERGUS

One of the most important reasons for backpacking instead of just day hiking, in my opinion, is that it enables you to be out in the backcountry later at night and earlier in the morning, to savor more of the cycle and rhythms of nature. Charles Fergus is acutely aware of this aspect of solo backpacking in his article about Pennsylvania's Black Forest.

Since all of your perceptions seem so much more intense when you backpack alone—sunshine is more joyous, birdsongs louder and more distinct, ferns softer—so, too, are the more unpleasant aspects. What about when it rains? The backcountry can be its loneliest at those times, lonelier still if you are alone. Hear what Charles Fergus has to say about this.

W.K.

I WAS HALF A MILE from the trailhead, and already sweat was running down my forehead and soaking my shirt. I climbed through a cluster of mountain laurel topped with blossoms like heavy, pink-tinged snow. The grade leveled off, and the trail swung past a gap in the trees. I stopped to rest and take in the view of forested Pennsylvania mountains all the way to the horizon. The wind felt good, but I felt even better because I was back in the Alleghenies—my mountains, rough, rock-spined, bunched up like a green rug kicked into a corner.

I stood a long time, just looking, listening, and smelling the breeze. Ahead lay 40 miles of trail. I was looking forward to the birds and animals, the stream-crossings and switchbacks, and even the rain, if it came—and to being alone. Overhead a pair of ravens and a band of vultures kited in the wind, and on the opposite mountain the maple leaves flashed their pale undersides. I snugged up my hip belt and started off.

I was on the Black Forest Trail, a hiking loop constructed and maintained by the Pennsylvania Bureau of Forestry. Why "Black Forest"? Because the region once was covered with stands of virgin pine and hemlock so dark and forbidding they reminded German settlers of the forests of their native land. Much of north-central Pennsylvania was that way until the late 1800s, when logging began. By the time the saws stopped and the mills closed, the big trees were gone. Today two forest types predominate: an oak-white birch-pitch pine mixture; and northern hardwoods—beech, birch, maple, ash, and cherry.

This was my first trip on the Black Forest Trail. Opened in 1970, it is laid out with cross-trails so hikers can vary their routes and trek as far as they like. I'd picked mid-June for my trip, since flies and gnats aren't as plentiful then as they can be later, and the mountain laurel is in bloom. I planned to do the main loop of the trail, which begins and ends near Slate Run, a sleepy little collection of hunting camps, old houses, and a few stores.

THE TRAIL WOUND THROUGH a burn grown up in huckleberry, and then sent me over a field of loose, fist-sized rocks. I was getting into the walking rhythm—feeling the tug of the pack, extending and flexing my legs.

Again the trail swung out to a vista, and I welcomed a chance to have a drink and sit on one of the sandstone boulders that stuck out of the mountain. Below, four streams fed Slate Run; the sound of merging water was barely audible over the wind in the trees. A sharp-shinned hawk swooped past carrying a limp snake in its talons.

As I rested I pondered the advantages of backpacking alone. Probably the greatest is that you come and go as you please. There's no need to dovetail a trip into others' vacations or schedules. You set your own pace, decide when and where to spend the night, sleep late or rise at dawn. In short, you are selfish without feeling the least bit guilty.

I sat a long time on that rock. The sun beat on the back of my neck, and the wind developed an edge. I finally put on my pack again and went on.

I kept up a good pace for the next hour. The trail left the mountain and made a steep descent of Red Run. In north-central Pennsylvania, the mountains are so diverse and jumbled that many remain unnamed. More often places are identified by their proximity to streams, which are referred to as drafts, forks, and branches but are usually called runs: Whiskey Run, Slate Run, and Lushbaugh Run; the Wild Boy Run, Bear Trap Draft, Sinnemahoning Creek. The names tumble off the tongue with the fluid grace of water pitching over moss-covered rocks.

Red Run was full of sandstone boulders that had broken off the mountain cap and had, over the centuries, slid downhill. At one point the water had cut a narrow gorge; it pooled dark green beneath the hemlocks, and trout dimpled the surface. Phoebes flew through the gloom, catching the same insects for which the trout were rising.

I HAD PLANNED TO CAMP along the run, but tent after tent covered the good sites. I met a big pork barrel of a man puffing along the trail, no pack and a .44 revolver strapped to his thigh. He was followed by a woman wearing a leather coat and carrying a styrofoam cooler. A forestry road passed within a half-mile of the run, providing easy access for those too soft or unwilling to walk far for solitude.

I filled my water bottle and started up the next mountain.

I climbed slowly. The most obvious disadvantage to backpacking alone is that you have to carry everything yourself. But you soon learn tricks to keep your pack as light as possible. A poncho doubles as a sleeping fly, I take only half a bottle of gas for the stove, and I stick to dehydrated food as much as possible. Despite my planning, though, and my hard-hearted rejection of bird guide, soft moccasins, extra candy bars—the pack weighed almost 40 pounds. By the time I topped the mountain, I was in the lowest hiking gear.

The sun was almost down when I slipped out of my pack and felt that day's-end, unfettered feeling. There was no mini-city of tents. To my chagrin, the spring, which the trail guide described as unreliable, was a sluggish trickle—unappetizing at best and possibly unpotable. It would be a dry camp. All the water I had was the quart from Red Run.

I made a mental note to add "second water bottle" to my equipment list when I got home. In the waning light I cooked supper, listening to thrush calls percolating up from the hollows.

In the night I had visitors. Apparently I'd camped near a game trail, for I heard deer and saw their shapes in the starlight. They approached my poncho, stopped, pawed the ground, and snorted loudly. This went on, it seemed, at least five minutes per deer, until the animal detoured around the camp or pounded off through the woods. I slept like an animal myself, waking and listening, going back to sleep, waking again.

I rose early and was breaking camp as the sun's first rays slanted through the trees. The canopy of beech and birch under which I'd slept was pale green, separated by gray columnar trunks from shimmering, pale green ferns. Vireos and peewees sang from the treetops. I cinched my pack shut, slid into the straps, and made an evaluation: back, stiff from sleeping on a thin foam pad; shoulders, sore; toes, tender; hips, chafed by the pressure of the hip belt; spirits, high, ready for the day, readjusting to being alone.

THE SUN HELPED. I'LL be the first to admit that backpacking solo in rain can be lonely as hell. At dusk you lie under a tarp, shivering in a damp sleeping bag, wondering what craziness has driven you to leave friends, warm houses, and hot showers. You're miserable, the days stretch ahead, the miles are struggled over and not fully enjoyed or understood.

The kinks worked out as I walked. I passed a heavy stand of white birch and stopped for the view across Big Dam Hollow. Thin clouds began to cover the sun, taking some of its light and most of its warmth. The weather in these mountains is, to say the least, changeable.

I found a spring near a cluster of closed-up hunting camps, then reached the trail junction with Sentiero Di Shay, an alternate route which can be used during high water or, in winter, for cross-country skiing. Sentiero Di Shay is Italian for "pathway of the Shay." A Shay was a steam-powered logging locomotive geared to climb mountain grades. The grades were cut by Italian laborers, who used picks, shovels, and black powder to knock out the big stuff; it was backbreaking

On his way down to Callahan Run, Fergus finds a pool to soak his tired feet.
PHOTO: CHARLES FERGUS

SIDEPOCKET

Maps

The area traversed by the Black Forest Trail is covered by three 7.5 minute USGS quadrangles: Lee Fire Tower, Cedar Run, and Slate Run. They are available for $1.25 each from the U.S. Geological Survey, 1200 South Eads Street, Arlington, Virginia 22202. Allow three weeks for delivery.

An excellent map entitled "Black Forest Trail" is available from the Tiadaghton Firefighters Association, 423 East Central Avenue, South Williamsport, Pennsylvania 17701. This map is also a booklet giving trail distances in miles and kilometers, and information on campsites, springs, geology, forest types, history, cross-country skiing, and high water routes. It is well worth its $1.25 price.

Books

• *Forbidden Land: Strange Events in the Black Forest*, compiled by Robert R. Lyman, Sr., available for $2.65 from the Potter Enterprise, Coudersport, Pennsylvania.
• *Sunset along Susquehanna Waters*, volume 4, by Thomas T. Taber III in a 13-volume set on logging in Pennsylvania. A 99-page book detailing timber operations in the area traversed by the Black Forest Trail. Available for $3.00 at the Pennsylvania Lumber Museum.

The Pennsylvania Lumber Museum

This excellent indoor/outdoor museum depicts the early wood industry in the state. Indoors are pictures, exhibits, models, tools, and slide presentations. Outside are a reconstructed logging camp including bunk house, mess hall, laundry, and blacksmith shop; a Shay logging locomotive; and a lumber mill.

The museum is located on U.S. Route 6 ten miles east of Coudersport and ten miles west of Galeton, approximately 35 miles from Slate Run (trailhead and end of the Black Forest Trail). It is open daily.

Cross-Country Skiing

Two well-marked and maintained trails, the Sentiero Di Shay and the George B. Will Trail, are laid out primarily for cross-country skiing. Both are high elevation or mountaintop trails passing through diverse forest types, open meadows, and tree plantations, and offering excellent views of the surrounding mountains. Both are near Pennsylvania Route 44. (The "Black Forest Trail" map booklet shows these trails.)

If you see a deer in winter, *never chase it*—simply ski away as unobtrusively as you can. This region has harsh winters, and to avoid starvation wildlife must conserve every bit of energy. Deer could use precious energy trying to get away from you, then weaken and die.

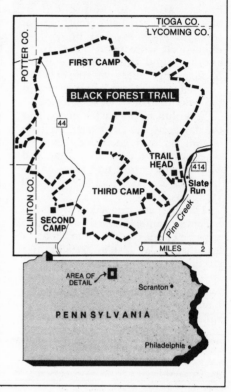

work, but the grades are straight and steady, and you can feel depressions where the ties used to lie.

I made my way unnoticed past fishermen and met groups of backpackers walking the loop in the opposite direction. A balding man as lean and brown as boot leather spoke of seeing a rattlesnake ("Yellow-phase, he was") and a sow black bear with two cubs. Then the trail led me out of the hollow and switchbacked up the mountain. It was the first hard walking I'd done that day.

Topping the slope, I hiked through an aspen meadow. Another descent, a second climb, and I found myself on an open, barren plateau with a view of endless mountains. A light drizzle began to fall.

A NOTHER REMINDER of the primal forest jutted from the slope: charred pine stumps. More than three feet across, they bore the axe notches which had determined the direction of their fall. There was a saying in the lumber country that even though a man could cut down a pine, he would die long before its stump rotted to dust.

From the stumps' bases, roots thicker than my leg crawled over the ground where two feet of soil had been burned and washed away. I sat on a gray, weathered root and looked around. Pines this big were cut early—perhaps in the 1850s, 30 years before the railroads—and, if they were straight enough, rafted to Chesapeake Bay to be made into masts for clipper ships.

The drizzle stepped up, and I left the open plateau for the shelter of the trees. It wasn't raining quite hard enough for me to put on the poncho; I prefer a little exterior dampness to the immediate sweat caused by my raingear.

My steps wet and quiet, I walked within 50 feet of a browsing buck. He was piebald—a rare partial albino, his red-brown coat spotted white around the middle and pure white from flanks to tail. He shifted one ear forward, then the other; he sensed something was out of kilter. Finally he eased off through the woods, tail half-raised and head down.

That night, as I heated water to make supper, I realized I hadn't seen another person since leaving County Line Run about noon. Most of the roads were behind me and it was late Sunday, so perhaps all the weekenders had left. It suited me fine. Somewhere in the darkening forest a ruffled grouse drummed. The hollow pops of beating wings sounded like a far-off lawnmower engine starting, accelerating to a rapid whir, and fading away. Dinner was a nasty surprise: the freeze-dried food tasted like chemicals. I boiled more water and tried a second package. Same thing. Disgruntled, I sat on a log and tried to fill the hole in my belly with bread and cheese.

I T RAINED IN THE NIGHT, and the woods sparkled the next morning. Warblers played among the leaves as I broke camp. I'd seen many before—black-and-whites, parulas, magnolias, black-throated blues. Now several Blackburnian warblers flitted from tree to tree, orange throats jewel-bright against the green backdrop.

The sun rose higher, heating the air and making leaves steam. Steep sections of trail were slippery, forcing me to jam my walking stick into the dirt at each step. After a few miles I surprised a hen grouse with eight chicks. She flew at me, crying; she stopped only a few feet away and tried to lure me from her young by hobbling along with tail fanned and a wing dragging. I sat down against a tree and waited, motionless. A half-hour later the hen came back, called her young out of hiding—one had been crouching not ten feet from my left boot—and trooped off with brood intact. That's another good thing about solitary backpacking: unless you sing or talk to yourself, you have a better chance to see wildlife than when with a group.

After lunch, the air felt heavy, and the day grew steadily hazier. Sections of trail led over good, wild country, where even with the wind dead and birds silent, I heard no traffic—an increasingly rare situation in the state of Pennsylvania.

I doubt if any true wilderness is left in Pennsylvania. Plunked down almost anywhere, one could hike to a road in less than a day just by walking in a straight line. But there's something special about the way nature reclaims what man has used. In the woods I have found trees twisted around old rails; grass knee-deep on railroad grades; and logging camps grown up in cherry and hornbeam, where the only signs of human occupation were a flat spot and a broken-down, frost-ravaged apple tree looking so completely out of place that I knew it came from an apple core some logger had tossed away.

AS I DESCENDED to Callahan Run, I came upon a stand of virgin hemlocks that somehow had escaped the logging 70 years earlier. The thick trunks rose free of branches for 50 feet. The crowns, feathery and black, towered above the oaks and maples like the fletchings of huge arrows shot into the earth; it would have been a black forest indeed when these giants covered the mountains. Underneath, the ground was cushioned with needles, and a chipmunk foraged a few yards away, heedless of my presence.

That night I camped by Naval Run in a hollow so deep that only a small strip of sky showed between the mountains on either side of the stream. A barred owl sounded its plaintive call and was answered by another from the opposite slope. I pulled on a wool shirt and brewed a cup of hot chocolate; nights are always cool in the mountains, and the hollows fill with the chilliest air. Fireflies bobbed like lanterns up and down the stream. I listened, and heard only the owls and the constant rush of water.

It had been a good day. I had seen no one, and I thought back to the last time that had happened, in a homesteader's cabin in the Wyoming high country. Then, as now, the chaff had blown away, and only truths remained—simple, often-ignored truths, the truest things about life and death.

I knew I would hike out the next day, doing the final 12 miles in a rush, coming out to the car sweated and drained and dirty on the outside and absolutely clean on the inside. Under my belt would be four days into which I'd crammed two weeks of good living.

The hollow darkened, and I thought about going to bed. But I turned up the collar of my shirt and listened a while longer to the flow of the run. The truths were still there, sharpened by weariness and hunger. The scent of the nighttime fern was almost unbearably sweet. I savored all these things, and finally went to bed ▲

ACROSS THE ADIRONDACKS

by ANNE LABASTILLE

The psychology of a woman alone in the woods is different from a man's. There are special fears that girls have instilled in them at early ages. It is no doubt wise to have such fears ingrained early. But they do present special problems for a woman backpacking alone, as Anne Labastille admits in her article about hiking the 132-mile-long Northville-Placid Trail in New York's Adirondacks. Her candor is to be admired. How many women would face these fears by backpacking alone, and then admit to their fears in a public statement that can be read by everyone?

W.K.

For fifteen years I've been hiking and camping around the Adirondacks, gradually getting to know this rugged, scenic mountain mass, which is my home in northern New York State. Just five years ago I was granted a guide's license by the state's Department of Environmental Conservation, making me one of about 250 individuals registered to take people into the woods and the only active female guide. Yet in all this time and with all the required training, I had never tackled the Northville-Placid Trail, the major backpacking trail in our mountains. Built in 1922-23 by the Adirondack Mountain Club, this 132-mile footpath is a miniature version of the Appalachian Trail. It cuts north-south across six-million-acre Adirondack Park and bisects four of its true wilderness areas.

Suddenly the ideal reason to travel the NP Trail presented itself. I was commissioned by *National Geographic* magazine as a free-lance writer–photographer to do an article on the Adirondacks. What better way to become more thoroughly acquainted with the region and increase my expertise as a guide than to backpack the length of the 9,000-square-mile area?

But there were two problems: I had done little backpacking over long periods, and I would have to go alone.

All my outdoor friends were away on summer vacations or entertaining guests. None of my indoor friends could stand such a trip. Moreover, I sensed that the *right* way to feel and photograph the Adirondacks was to travel quietly on my own. By setting my own pace, I would pause to sniff, touch, look, swim, taste, drink and deepen my awareness.

So in June, 1973, I started outfitting for the challenging trip. From the Adirondack Mountain Club, I purchased their *Guide to Adirondack Trails—High Peak Region and Northville–Placid Trail,* eighth edition. In the local hardware store, I thumbed through stacks of U.S. Geological survey maps, pulling out fresh green sheets for the places crossed by the trail (Lake Pleasant, Piseco Lake, West Canada Lakes, Indian Lake, Blue Mountain, Long Lake, Santanoni, Saranac Lake and Lake Placid). Mail orders went out for freeze-dried foods. I bought a new aluminum frame pack and measured my big German shepherd, Pitzi, for a stout nylon and leather dog pack.

It was easy to assemble the basic necessities: a lightweight tent and rain fly, sleeping bag and short pad, rain gear and extra clothing, medical kit and cooking set, rope, knife, matches and compass. But when it came to packing the essential cameras, film, lenses, notebook and waterproof pens, I was stumped. Every inch of my pack was stuffed, and I didn't trust such delicate equipment to my dog, knowing his inclination to chase squirrels and rabbits through swamps and thickets.

Finally I attached rawhide straps to each camera body and hung them from the pack posts. The bodies and lenses were wrapped in double plastic bags with rubber bands. The bags would cushion and silence the cameras swinging under my arms, keep them dry and could be removed as easily as leather cases, yet weighed far less. Next, I packed 20 rolls of 36-exposure film, a telephoto lens, small tripod, and a pair of pliers in a waterproof fanny pack. This I planned to wear backward across my belly with the zipper facing up for easy access.

I was feeling confident about these arrangements until I weighed all my gear. More than 50 pounds! I knew it was too much for me for a sustained, two-week trip. After a scrupulous sorting (and a surreptitious juggling of tripod and pliers into Pitzi's pack), my things weighed in at 43 pounds. Without the cameras, the pack would have been 35 pounds, an ideal weight. But there was no alternative; I would have to manage 43 and Pitzi 12.

I planned to start in mid-July when the worst of the black fly season would be over, days warm and lots of hikers on the trail. Pitzi and I would leave from Upper Benson at the south end and work into shape for the higher ranges to the north. On the first lap, we would carry food for seven days. I planned to come out for fresh supplies on the dirt road near Wakely Dam in the Moose River Primitive Area. Actually there were two other access points where I could walk out to stores, but I wanted to cover half the distance, 58 miles. Stopping to take photos and carrying that heavy pack would slow me down, but I figured on covering at least eight miles a day.

As the jump-off date approached, I grew more and more nervous. I wondered whether any other woman had ever hiked the NP Trail alone. Was I in shape for such a challenge, physically and psychically? What would I do if I met a couple of tough men way back in the woods? Even worse, what if I broke a leg or slipped a disc in my back? One misstep and I might lie alone in pain for hours or days until help came. How well-traveled was the trail?

With such spectral thoughts rushing through my head, I called a good friend, a policeman, for reassurance. "Take a handful of morphine tablets," he commanded. "And if you meet any funny customers, tell them your husband's just down the trail a ways. That'll give you time to hide."

The morning of July 14 I parked my pickup beside the farmhouse of a cordial, leathery-faced lady who offered to keep the keys. Two of my friends would pick them up later and drive my pickup to the checkpoint at Wakely Dam. "Sure I'll watch your car," she said pleasantly, "but

if the barn and it burn up, I won't be responsible."

The woods seemed very green, dim and close as I shouldered my pack and strapped Pitzi into his saddlebags. I hung the cameras from the pack posts, belted the fanny pack around my middle and donned my red felt guide's hat. Lastly, I grabbed my old hiking stick. Feeling very much like an overloaded, teetering mule, I took my first steps along the NP Trail.

Adrenalin started pumping at dusk eight miles later as I neared the first state lean-to at Silver Lake. Who might be there? To my relief, the three-sided log structure was empty and the fireplace cold. I decided to sleep in it this first night to save time and energy. Pitzi and I were very tired. Strange-looking salmon and purple clouds piled up over the dark hills. A distant loon called eerily across the lake. Somehow the shelter beckoned.

The next morning it was raining. Just before I left, two teen-age boys staggered into the lean-to and collapsed on the floor. "You leaving, lady?" one asked hopefully. I nodded yes.

"We're staying *here* then," sighed the chubby one, exhausted. "We've got 25 days' food in our packs, and I ain't walking no farther!"

Shaking my head in disbelief, I stepped off on the trail again. Those youngsters had just begun, and already they were quitting. My shoulders ached unmercifully, and my arches pained as never before, but there was no turning back now. Pitzi and I passed Mud Lake (well named), ate a trail lunch and stopped for a welcome swim close to the foot suspension bridge over the west branch of the Sacandaga River. Suddenly I saw a man leaning over the railing. Stiffening in my wet bathing suit, I called out warily, "Good evening." He answered in a mutter, barely looking my way. Then I saw him jerk a fishing rod and begin to play a spirited 12-inch brook trout. Fishing was the only thing on *his* mind.

I set up camp at Whitehouse in a beautiful meadow where old houses once stood. A single cobblestone chimney still towered above the flower fields, bushy young pines and a small farm pond. As the embers burned low and bullfrogs began their "chunk-chunk-chunking," I crawled into the tent and fell asleep.

It was a short morning's walk to Route 8 near Piseco Village, then almost a mile on paved road to the next section of the trail. Now the path entered one of the wildest regions of the Adirondacks. The next road, store or hotel lay 38 miles north. These woods had been logged years before, yet the remaining trees were tall and formed a dense canopy. It was dark as a church, so I pitched camp early that night near a bubbling brook out of sight of passing hikers.

Not a sound broke the stillness until midnight when a snowshoe hare thumped past, followed moments later by the dainty drumming of fox feet. Pitzi gave one sharp bark. Thoroughly awakened, I lay awake thinking about predators and prey. Pitzi and I were truly the top predators on the most intricate of food chains. We had selected the lightest, tastiest, highest calorie-producing foods available to carry. They came from distant places—granola and dried beef from western prairies, coffee and chocolate from Latin America, peanuts, raisins and dates from Georgia, California and Africa, pemmican from Canada. It all had ended up on our backs, giving us an extraordinary independence from the land. Yet we were irrevocably linked to those far-away plants, fibers and animals—and to the trucks, trains and planes that had carried them. Such ironical musings soon sent me to sleep again.

We were due to reach Spruce Lake, highest of all bodies of water on the NP Trail (2,378 feet) by the next afternoon. It was a perfect summer day, with the temperature above 80 degrees Fahrenheit. At lunchtime I stripped and splashed into the ice cold water of Jessup River. Then I stretched out in the sun on a log to dry. Deep male voices suddenly sent me scut-

tling behind a bush to don my clothes. Two fishermen had also stopped there for lunch. I said hello and quickly pushed off for Spruce Lake.

The lake was so lovely that I decided to stay and photograph at the closest lean-to, but when I reached up to the shoreline, I discovered two teen-age boys emptying their packs on the floor. From their self-conscious manner, it was plain to see they felt odd with a woman around. They kept staring at me disapprovingly and then turning red-faced.

Even though state law deems that lean-tos are open to anyone, most back-packers like their privacy, so I decided to walk up the lakeshore to the next shelter. On the way a pack of 14 boy scouts approached from the north. Pitzi confronted them boldly. The troop stopped abruptly and looked scared. I assured the leaders that he wouldn't bite, and we visited awhile. They told me that another larger scout group was coming from behind and was due to pass them at Spruce Lake. "They'll stay here tonight," said one leader, "cause they've come nonstop from Piseco."

It occurred to me that if I wanted to secure a shelter along the heavily forested lakeshore, I had better hustle. I needed a

lean-to where I could take pictures of the lake and sunset, write up my notes, swim and rest in privacy. The map showed three lean-tos at Spruce Lake. The first was taken. That meant one for me and the dog, and another for the scouts. Behind me I now heard the high-pitched wrangling of youngsters. Pitzi and I tried to speed up, but we were both exhausted. We reached the second lean-to minutes before the troop. It was perfect. A tiny sand beach was artistically framed by huge spruce. Inspiration struck. I scrawled out a note: "OCCUPIED—JULY 17," and hung it on a branch at the junction of the main trail and the lean-to path. Pitzi stayed on guard. The pack passed like so many noisy beagles, and 15 minutes later I saw them descend on lean-to number 3 across a bay, yelling and shouting. Maybe it was a dirty trick to pull, but I was left in peace. I just couldn't sleep with 20 noisy boy scouts.

South and West Canada lakes were the highlight ahead. I had heard of them for years. They are two of the highest, wildest lakes in our mountains—the former home of the famed hermit French Louie and presently the site of a rustic state ranger headquarters. The first glimpse of South Lake was enchanting: a yellow sand beach edged with paper birches looking out on a two-mile sweep of blue water. A marsh

---

SIDEPOCKET

Recommended reading, tips and trivia to add to your understanding and enjoyment of the Adirondacks.

Books

Woodswoman by Anne Labastille, E. P. Dutton, $10.95.
The Adirondacks by Clyde H. Smith, Viking Press, $15.95.
The Ancient Adirondacks, Time-Life Books, $6.95.
Adirondack Country by William Chapman White, Alfred Knopf, $10.00.
Forever Wild: The Adirondacks by Eliot Porter, The Adirondack Museum and Harper & Row, $25.00.
Guide to Adirondack Trails by the Adirondack Mountain Club, Glens Falls, New York, $6.00.
Noah John Rondeau, Adirondack Hermit, by Maitland DeSormo, Adirondack Yesteryears, Saranac Lake, New York, $9.00.

Maps

The following USGS quadrangles cover almost all the Northville–Placid Trail: Lake Pleasant, Piseco, West Canada Lakes, Indian Lake, Blue Mountain Lake, Long Lake and Santanoni.

The trail does dip for a few miles into the Northville and Jackson quads at the southern end and through the Lake Placid and Saranac Lake quads up north but a road map will suffice at both of these points.

USGS maps may be purchased locally or by mail from: Geological Survey, 1200 South Eads Street, Arlington, Virginia 22202. Orders take approximately three weeks to be filled. The cost is $1.25 per map.

Additional information on the NP Trail and on feeder trails may be obtained from: The Adirondack Mountain Club, R.D.1, Ridge Road, Glens Falls, New York 12801.

Adirondack Lean-Tos

The lean-to is part of the history and tradition of the Adirondacks. A three-sided open shelter, it was originally designed as temporary quarters for hunters and fishermen in the 1800s but soon evolved into a more permanent structure, often used as a base camp by turn-of-the-century vacationers. There are now some 250 lean-

tos in the Adirondacks, all built and maintained by New York's Department of Environmental Conservation.

Older lean-tos were constructed from logs cut on the site, but recently the DEC has been flying in precut logs. Lean-tos measure approximately 8 x 12 feet inside and have a sloping roof covered with either asphalt or cedar shingles. The floors are dirt or planked. Five 16-foot logs, usually white pine, go into the back wall, with 12-foot logs forming the side walls. A 14-foot log at least 17 inches in diameter across the front of the lean-to serves as a deacon's seat.

A fairly comprehensive list of all the lean-tos in the Adirondacks is included in the Adirondack Mountain Club's *Trail Guide.*

The Adirondack Museum

The Adirondack Museum is located in Blue Mountain Lake, New York, smack dab in the center of the Adirondacks. It is regarded as one of the finest regional museums in the country, and hikers of the NP Trail should certainly allow at least a day for exploring its many exhibits. Open from June 15 through October 15.

Heading into the High Peaks of the Adirondacks, author Anne Labastille pauses to admire the flush of fall color spreading across the mountains. Vermont and Lake Champlain are visible to the extreme right.
PHOTO: ANNE LABASTILLE

filled with waterlilies and fringed with black spruce ran toward Mud Lake and West Lake. On the small bridge crossing it, I met Earl Overacres, the interior caretaker, and his wife, Thelma. It felt warm and friendly to talk to people after four days alone—people who weren't preoccupied with fishing, exhaustion or the embarrassment of finding a woman in the woods. The Overacres invited me into their stout log station house. Thelma graciously offered me ice-cold root beer and sandwiches. Never had any food tasted so good. Earl showed me the register kept for the Department of Environmental Conservation. Nine hundred thirty-five hikers had come through in 1972, a few less in 1973. He remembered seeing only two or three girls traveling on their own during the previous few summers.

I could see a citizen's band radio and telephone on his desk. "Do you actually have a phone line way back here?" I asked incredulously.

"Yes," smiled Earl. "It's for accidents, lost people and firefighting. We maintain one line through the woods along part of the trail so we can call a seaplane or state helicopter in case of an emergency."

I felt better knowing that a backpacker with a broken bone could be reported and rescued. Before I left, Thelma took me out front to a field that sloped down toward the rocky, rectangular shore of West Canada.

"Here's where French Louie lived for years," she said, pointing proudly to the remains of a stone fireplace. I could envision the gnarled, blue-eyed French Canadian who some described as "hard as Laurentian granite and as tough as Adirondack spruce" crouched over his hearth, stirring venison stew or grilling a trout. He had hunted, fished and trapped the West Canada area for years and knew it as few others ever have.

I was anxious to put more miles under my feet that day, so I reluctantly said goodbye to Earl and Thelma. The day was clouding up, so I hoped to stay at one of the three state shelters at Cedar Lakes. The muggy, hot weather had brought out black flies, mosquitoes and deer flies. Several followed me obstinately, buzzing over and under my hat. As I walked, I kept alternating repellents—6-12, Off, and Old Woodsman—to see which worked best.

Judging from the bites on my arms and legs, none of them did.

Midafternoon, I approached the second Cedar Lakes lean-to from behind. It seemed deserted. No sounds. On rounding the corner, however, I saw lace curtains hanging across the opening! Gingerly I parted them and peered in. A young couple sat inside on foam pads reading a Chinese philosophy book and brewing green tea on Sterno. The interior was as cool, neat and quiet as a monastery.

"Welcome," they said in unison. "Come join us."

Pitzi and I slipped through the filmy barrier. The pretty girl with long braids offered me a cup of tea. I drank thirstily, eyeing them and their belongings. "Where did you come from?" I asked, noting a fine guitar and case in the corner.

"Oh, we started in Lake Placid three weeks ago," her lanky companion said, stroking his beard. "We walk three miles a day. Stop where we want. Our home is where our packs are."

"How can you carry enough food?" I marveled.

"Easy," replied the girl. "We just eat granola (she pointed to a huge plastic jar), oatmeal, powdered milk, tea and a little cheese. We're vegetarians."

I glanced at Pitzi, sprawled out on his side, and wondered if the two of us could manage on such a diet. It didn't seem possible, even sensible, as hard as we were working. Even so I felt a bit embarrassed as I opened a can of Alpo and prepared my freeze-dried beef stew for supper. While Pitzi and I gobbled our food, the man said, "You-all can sleep right in here with us. The skeeters can't get you with these curtains up." It seemed much easier than finding a flat spot and setting up my tent, so I thanked him and laid out my bag and pad beside theirs.

By dark, the mosquitoes found us, penetrating the lace. They began a relentless whining and biting. Then the 'coons, mice and bears began to rummage around the site. Pitzi kept charging through the curtains into the night in a paroxysm of barking. By midnight it looked as if several cannonballs had been shot through. Finally I set up my tent *inside* the lean-to to have some mosquito-netting protection and keep him quiet. My poor bedfellows, however, were kept awake. Around 2 A.M. they began a long story about the year they spent sailing a 40-foot ketch around the Caribbean. They had been wrecked in a storm off Turks Island, rescued by a Norwegian freighter, dropped off in Florida and had hitchhiked their way to the Adirondacks!

Having lost everything, they truly did carry their home on their backs. "Funny thing, though," yawned the man about 5 A.M., "I find backpackers and sailors have a similar mentality. They both *have* to get there."

It was an entertaining night, climaxed by the couple's frolicking into the water at dawn and cooking up oatmeal and tea in the nude.

I left these natural children in mid-morning and headed toward the Cedar Lakes ranger station. The lack of sleep was bothering me, and I resolved to avoid lean-tos and their associated two- and four-legged wildlife from then on unless the weather was bad. My little tent set up on a lakeshore or deep in the woods would be quieter, cleaner and free of insects.

I met John Remius, the interior caretaker, at his handsome log station house, and shared a cup of camp coffee while we chatted. He told me about some emergency problems he dealt with—bears stealing packs, sprained ankles, a rare heart attack, dogs getting jabbed by porcupine quills. I was glad I'd brought pliers and a strong rope in case I had to tie up Pitzi and yank out any quills. Refreshed, I left Cedar Lakes and pushed on for Cedar River Flow where I'd pass my last night before reaching the road, my truck and fresh supplies.

We were down to one freeze-dried meal, odd candy bars, a cup of dry dog ration and two Gainesburgers. We *had* to make those next ten miles by noon next day, or go hungry.

And our packs had not lightened much. All along the trail and in lean-tos, I'd found campers' bounty: three bars of soap, a can of tuna fish, a lens cap for my camera, a pair of maroon jeans, which fit perfectly, a new denim jacket with a hole burned in one elbow, and an exquisitely tied trout fly. Being a pack rat at heart, I'd filled up all the new space in my pack created by eating food.

We spent a peaceful night at the Flow on a sand beach overlooking a marsh where grebes, ducks, beaver, muskrats, loons and bass swam by. It was the most idyllic spot on the trail. At dawn a great blue heron flapped lazily over my tent in silhouette as a giant red sun rose behind smoky-blue hills. It promised to be another hot summer day.

At the truck I found a note. It read: "Go home immediately. Do not continue on trail. Murderer on loose." It was signed by my policeman friend. Astounded and dismayed, I opened the cab and switched on the radio. In a few moments, the noon news was broadcast. I learned that Robert Garrow, a psychotic killer, was loose in the Adirondacks. He had killed two campers during the past few days, and a massive man-hunt was under way. Reportedly, he might be heading for the Northville–Placid Trail. He was believed armed and extremely dangerous.

From the news reports that continued all day, I figured that Garrow might have been only 15 to 20 miles from where I'd slept the night before. I was horrified, imagining what Pitzi and I might have done if we'd met the murderer on the trail. We'd either both be dead or taken hostage.

The manhunt held the Adirondacks in terror for almost two weeks. Nothing like it had ever happened before. In the seven days I'd been backpacking, I'd met 43 people and two boy scout troops. All had been courteous and harmless. It was not until they caught the killer near Lake Champlain that I relaxed. I didn't give up the rest of my trek because I calculated that the chances of such an event happening again were one in a million. Nevertheless, I did postpone resuming the trip until after Labor Day. Days would be cooler, autumn colors approaching, insects gone and there would be fewer people on the trail.

In the middle of September, Pitzi and I started again with another seven days' supply of food, a down jacket and a foam pad for the dog to sleep on. I knew we could expect frost and heavy rain anytime.

The nip in the air made me fairly skip over the seven miles of dirt road from

Wakely Dam to where the trail headed off to Stephens Pond. I sidetracked into Blue Mountain Lake village where I planned to visit the famed Adirondack Museum. This is one of the finest regional historical museums in the United States. It occupies a commanding view over chains of lakes and the somber slopes of Blue Mountain (3,759 ft).

Leaving my pack in the admissions lobby and Pitzi tied under a tree outside, I spent half a day in the fascinating exhibits. On a wall in the main hall I read Article 14, that amazing bit of legislation written in 1894, which has fortuitously kept almost half the Adirondack Park wild and undeveloped. Because of it, my backpacking route wound through the wildest and largest state park in the United States, almost as vast as the combined acreage of Yellowstone, Great Smoky Mountains, Grand Canyon, Yosemite, Olympic and Glacier national parks. The article reads:

> The lands of the State, now owned or hereafter acquired, constituting the forest preserve as now fixed by law, shall not be sold, exchanged, or be taken by any corporation public or private, nor shall the timber thereon be removed or destroyed.

Pitzi and I hitchhiked back Route 28 three miles to pick up the trail again and made a fast walk to the south end of Tirrell Pond. Under a lowering sky, I started a fire and put the sleeping pad on the floor of the lean-to; then a deluge burst over the forest. As darkness fell, three soaked hikers and their collie piled into the lean-to. I was glad to have a roaring fire ready to dry and warm them, but soon wished for a mop, as the collie dripped all over the wooden floor.

At 7 A.M. a stiff north wind with autumn cold front was blowing over Tirrell Pond, twisting streamers of mist and fog into grotesque shapes. The temperature was just above freezing. I shivered into my boots, ignored the drenched fire, packed up and quickly started down the trail to warm up. The front had left the sky faultlessly blue. The air was as invigorating as chilled cider. The sheer rock face above the lake glistened in the bright September sun. Gradually the day warmed. Barely sweating or pausing for breath, Pitzi and I toiled up the side of Burnt Mountain, the steepest climb yet, and down the other side toward Long Lake. We made it out to Route 28N by midafternoon.

On impulse I decided to break the trip and chance a short run into Long Lake village for more tent pegs and boot dubbing. A friendly native took me the 1½ miles to the general store. There I succumbed to the sight of fresh produce, tinned meats and home-baked pies. How tasty a cooked dinner would be! I walked into the Adirondack Hotel and ordered a roast beef dinner, blueberry pie and plenty of bones for Pitzi. Almost too full to walk, I accepted a ride back to the trailhead 1½ miles up Jennings Park Road. It was dark as Pitzi and I groaned into our packs again. But there would be a full moon that night which promised light in the woods. Meanwhile I walked by the glow of a pen-light. The path was wide and hard-packed. It was only two miles to the Catlin Bay lean-tos. As I picked my way through the night, it occurred to me that I must be the luckiest girl in the world to go on such an exciting adventure.

Continuing up the picturesque east shore of Long Lake the next day, I glimpsed the Seward and Santanoni ranges ahead. I was eager to reach the High Peaks region, which is so different from the rest of the Adirondacks. We camped near Plumley's Point and pressed on past Shattuck Clearing and another ranger outpost station next morning. Now the trail edged the Cold River. Pitzi and I spent a drizzly night on the dirt floor of the old Seward lean-to, with the temperature about 40 degrees Fahrenheit. The dog shivered so hard I finally unzipped my sleeping bag and drew him against my tummy to warm him. When breakfast time came round, I was very grateful to the anonymous camper who had left extra firewood inside the shelter.

By this time, having passed so many lean-tos, I had amassed a large collection of graffiti from the walls. Some was humorous, some sad, some informative. I read that a girl named Helen had walked the trail alone in May, 1963. There were hundreds of other names, among them Big Foot, The Turnip King and Minnie-Ha-Ha. There was: "Here to enjoy a delicious meal of beaver steaks and suffer the cold night. Four feet of snow on the ground yet." And, "Jack cut the wrong kind of meat. Sat. 11 A.M. had to go to Dr.'s in Saranac Lake for emergency surgery. Nine stitches. Came back in with flashlite Sat. nite." Also, "Rain, rain, go away. Come again some other—and we ran out of wine—day. Muscatel Kid."

As I was jotting down more quotes at the Ouluska Pass lean-to, hopefully waiting for the rain to stop, two men trudged in from the opposite direction. They joined me and before long had offered cheese sandwiches and a jug of what looked like grape juice. I took a big swallow and almost choked. It was 86-proof dark rum! We spent a cheerful interlude warming ourselves that damp afternoon.

The rain continued to pour next day as I passed Noah Rondeau's old hermit camp set on a high point above the Cold River. The dreary weather made it seem more dilapidated and mournful than it deserved. Actually Noah lived happily there for 33 years in his tiny town hall and hall of records buildings. He had easy access to hunting, trapping and fishing grounds and good visibility for approaching game wardens. The famous hermit finally passed away practically a pauper.

I was drawing near the end of the trail. Only one night remained in the woods. I decided to stay at an inky black pond called Duck Hole, long having heard of it as "the beauty spot of the Adirondacks." The bad weather was lifting, although the ground was soaking wet and big drops still hung from the balsams and pines. A pearly pink wreath surrounded the tops of MacNaughton and other peaks which backdropped the pond.

Only a few other people were camped there that Friday night—unlike the more than 200 on a usual July weekend. I joined a group of Adirondack "46-ers" (hikers who've climbed the 46 peaks over 4,000 feet). We sipped tea and watched dusk fall over the High Peaks.

Next noon Pitzi and I were standing by the large sign at the crossroads of the Averyville Road and Old Military Road which marks the official end of the North-ville–Placid Trail. For the last time I set up my tripod and snapped a few self-timed pictures. For the last time I signed Pitzi's and my name in a register. For the last time I eased out of my pack and un-snapped the dog's saddlebags. I felt extraordinarily proud as I stood on the black-topped road leading to Lake Placid village, five miles away. Soon a good friend would meet me and shuttle me back to my truck. My muscles were sound, and my every sense seemed vibrant and acutely aware of surrounding stimuli. I felt strong, fearless and free. Then a whiff of car exhaust hit me, and the honk of a horn made me jump. I'd forgotten how noisy and smelly the civilized world really was. Suddenly I wished I could go on for several days more. Pitzi must have felt the same, for he snuggled against my leg and looked back toward the silent forest.

Then I smiled. How different my attitude now. All those niggling fears had vanished. I felt capable of going anywhere and meeting anyone on the trail. Tomorrow I'd send for the Adirondack Mountain Club badge issued to people who have traveled the entire trail. Soon, I'd have hundreds of photos developed and start on the proposed *National Geographic* article [published May, 1975, Ed.]. But best of all, my Adirondack adventure had deepened my attachment for these mountains. ▰

Chapter Seven

ALL TOGETHER NOW: FAMILIES ON THE TRAIL

A few years ago, after we had our first child, my wife and I were forced to make a hard choice: give up either sailing or hiking. Married life, and children, did not allow enough time for us to both maintain a sailboat and invest the time in planning our hikes as well.

Our sailboat consumed evenings and weekends in scraping, painting, and fixing. That's part of the fun we had in sailing.

Our hiking, especially the backpacking trips with our children, required evenings planning routes, cooking and packaging foods, sorting out and packing gear, and of course weekends of shakedown hikes before the big trips.

We chose hiking. And we sold our sailboat. Our decision was not easy, for we passionately enjoyed both. The deciding factor was that we could more likely keep our family together over the most number of years with hiking. We had known sailing families whose children found sailing boring after they reached toddling age, and few sailing families could count on their teenagers' participation in their sport.

With hiking it was different. I'd never known a youngster who really didn't like the woods—especially if he'd been introduced to the outdoors at an early enough age. Further, it has always seemed to us that teenagers love the woods. Perhaps we saw it so much that way because both Marcella and I had loved the outdoors when we were teenagers. And then, it always seemed to us that you are never too old to hike. There have been people in their late 80s who've hiked the entire Appalachian Trail. So it seemed to us that we'd be able to enjoy hiking with our children when they were very young, enjoy their company on the trail as teenagers, and it was our deep hope that they'd enjoy our company on hikes after they had grown up and had their own families and we had grown old. So far it has worked out as we had hoped.

You are lucky if you were a hiker before you got married. It is easier, I think, to get your family into hiking as you acquire the family—first just you and your spouse, then you and your first infant, then the child as a toddler, and another infant as your family increases. Your family hiking evolves. It is far easier to develop your techniques as you evolve rather than have to hatch them for immediate use for a full-blown family that's never hiked before. If you're starting from that point of view you'll have to go about it a little differently. But you'll still have to introduce your family to it gradually—or you'll lose them as hiking partners.

TURNING CHILDREN INTO BACKPACKERS

by MARLYN S. DOAN

Turning children into backpackers requires considerable resolve on the part of the parents. You have to approach hiking in an entirely different way. But, being the father of six youngsters who've become backpackers, I can attest that it makes very interesting backpacking. As a matter of fact, I believe that even my backpacking without children has greatly improved since we started introducing our children to hiking.

For one thing, you simply must throttle down—way down—almost to a crawl—if you expect your children to become backpackers and expect to enjoy it with them. But suddenly you'll find out all you missed by hiking so fast before that.

For another, they'll see things you never even noticed before. And if you can only have the patience to forbear their unrelenting questions, you will enjoy seeing things with the freshness of a child's eye. It's really exciting.

You've got a lot in store for yourself if you do manage to turn your children into backpackers.

Marlyn Doan tells the basics of how to do it better than anyone I've ever known. Except for some of the details, Marcella and I have done with our children exactly as Marlyn and her husband have done with theirs.

W.K.

YOUNG CHILDREN do not love backpacking automatically. It hurts—going up the trail hurts; so can coming down. If backpacking parents introduce their children to the outdoors in the right way, however, even a four- or five-year-old child can be transformed into a serious, enthusiastic backpacker.

But be warned: a crying, wailing, I-can't-go-any-farther child can make the most dedicated parent wonder why hiking with kids ever sounded like fun. Yet, don't despair. Remember that a youngster at home can be equally difficult and cantankerous, and if you persist, the rewards of being a bona fide backpacking family will more than make up for bad moments.

The conversion of a child into a backpacker takes time. Parents must work at it with patience and determination. In our family we begin by introducing car–tent camping and day hiking, and carrying our children, still babies, in child carriers. A variety of comfortable carriers are available, but we prefer models in which the child faces the parent's back, since sleeping is easier. Perhaps the baby only breathes in the atmosphere, the relaxed pace of the walk, the serene quiet of the woods, but these are important seeds to plant early.

Then, still day hiking, our two-year-olds alternate riding and walking. At three each one is expected to change into a hiker—not a backpacker, mind you, we wait a year for that, but a real trail walker. We consider these day trips training sessions. When the child graduates into backpacking overnight, we are adding just a small twist to a familiar experience.

WITH CHILDREN ALONG one of the most important considerations is the length and difficulty of the hike. Any early trip has to be short: the lower limit may be a half-mile to a mile each way for a walking three-year-old; the upper limit probably averages four miles round trip for day hikes, or five miles each way on an overnight. Young children often can do much more, but if you push too hard, they will not want to come back.

The terrain chosen also is significant. A slight gradient in a trail is better than a steep pitch. Some of our most successful early day hikes have been along level lakeshore. For a four-year-old's first backpack trip, ocean beach hiking is ideal—it provides an easy, flat walk. Wherever you go, allow plenty of time. An early family backpack trip over a fairly level five miles took from nine in the morning until four in the afternoon. Slow and broken travel is the rule.

To please hiking youngsters, the destination of each trip must be carefully chosen. An adult may seek alpine meadows with breeze-fluttered flowers or a view-laden ridge where jagged peaks erupt on the horizon, but a child may be unimpressed. When you plan your hikes, think like a child. What do all children enjoy? Water, mud, animals, games and food. Any combination thereof may make the day, but in our experience arriving at water, preferably a lake but sometimes just a stream, is the ultimate pleasure.

When the cry "I'm too tired . . . I want to go back" arises, countering it with "We're almost there" means nothing. To a tired child, "almost" isn't anywhere. But paint a picture of something definite and appealing ahead, and miracles happen:

"There's a big lake. You can wade along the edge, maybe even swim. You might find some nice salamanders, or a frog or two." Each child immediately finds a second wind. Beach hikes, whether lake or ocean, are ideal since the fascination of water is at hand throughout the walk.

If in that water your child discovers some wriggling tadpoles, a frog or a garumphing toad, you will instantly have a happy small hiker. Our children still are talking about breeding ponds we once

found, with black tadpoles squirming bank-to-bank. On other trips newts and salamanders have appeared and erased memories of sore muscles in short legs.

IN OUR YEARS OF HIKING with children, only a manned ranger lookout ever competed with the appeal of water. With a little checking, you can find out where rangers are on duty. A trip to a fire tower took us an extra, very steep mile. The children were exhausted, but the friendly ranger made up for their struggle. He showed them about lightning chairs and sighting forest fires, and pointed out where he slept and how he kept mice out of his food supply. Everyone was entranced, and exhaustion was forgotten. "Say, when can we come here again?" the five-year-old wanted to know on the way down, and the four-year-old girl declared she was going to be a ranger when she grew up. We had a good memory to take home, and such memories are vital—they get children back on the trail and make possible harder and longer hikes.

Being a photographer, I underscore the good times by collecting pictures of trip highlights. Enlargements of animals we have seen, from chipmunks and marmots to frogs and deer, line the walls of the children's rooms and provide daily reminders of the exciting things discovered while hiking and backpacking.

Although getting away is often hard for parents with young children, the best way to discover appropriate places for family overnight trips is by scouting locations alone. We have found innumerable possibilities on our own longer trips, and we catalogue the finds so we have a wealth of information on safe, interesting places. Thus, we can avoid taking the children into areas they could not handle. We once scouted two alpine lakes where we had planned a family trip, only to discover dangerous cliffs and drop-offs into frigid, deep water. We quickly scratched that place from our list of possible hikes.

To make backpacking palatable to children one must convert the drudgery of hiking into fun. One of the best ways is to use games they naturally love; our family's favorite is hide-and-seek. Other hikers may think that seeing a grown man hunched behind a bush or log is a little strange, but no matter. The children quiver with excitement as they plow up the trail to find Dad. Fatigue is forgotten, and suddenly you have reached your destination, painlessly.

Another workable, on-trail diversion is a who-can-gather-the-most-litter contest, with extra treats for all participants at the end of the hike. By helping to clean up after the careless, children begin to learn basic conservation which will last them a lifetime. The game is painless except that

Proper equipment is important; without sturdy foot gear, for example, the Doan children would not be able to safely negotiate this rough footing near Hurricane Ridge in Olympic National Park.
PHOTO: MARLYN S. DOAN

The seashore is the perfect setting for introducing children to backpacking: the terrain is easy and there are plenty of diversions—flotsam and jetsam to collect, tidal pools to explore, and sandcastles to be built whenever a rest stop is called, which should be often.
PHOTO: MARLYN S. DOAN

youngsters are like pack rats: they love to find shiny treasures. So don't be surprised if all the bottle caps go home with you for a collection.

ONCE CHILDREN HAVE HIKED awhile, a naming-nature contest is fun. Everyone moves along more quickly in search of known natural objects. Although the game is another ploy to get you there, it doubles also as a good way to learn more about the out-of-doors.

Besides using games to encourage a positive attitude toward hiking, we carry plenty of food, drinks and treats, and we make innumerable refueling stops. A good procedure is to stop and eat and rest before a child is overtired, which may help you avoid a real energy crisis later. A favorite treat for our youngsters is trail snacks we put together and affectionately call squirrel bags. Suit your fancy and your child's tastes: you can combine granola, chocolate chips, raisins, coconut, nuts—you name it. Everyone, even the little guy, gets a bag to carry in a pocket or a pack, and children love to munch as they walk.

There is great motivation in hiking with other families who have children. A variety of ages is fine—younger children imitate the older ones, and no older child wants a half-pint showing him up. Our three-year-old took her first five-mile hike

with a friend's older child along. Determined to stay with her friend, she accomplished what would ordinarily have been close to impossible.

The trade-a-parent plan helps, too. You walk with your friends' kids while they take responsibility for your children. Somehow, saying "I give up" is harder when the adult with you is not a parent.

Arousing a child's enthusiasm for hiking is vital, yet without the proper gear the trail experience can be negative, despite parents' efforts to make backpacking fun. A backpack must be comfortable, but when you look for a child's first real pack, problems arise. A youngster's slender body is not built for most packs. Shoulder straps can bury into bones and leave welts, even if scant weight is carried, and the hip belt can dangle uselessly.

One of the best first packs for youngsters is a harness designed to hold a small sleeping bag. Some child-sized packs on lightweight frames are manufactured.† Although none we have tried works perfectly, a real pack has certain psychological advantages: every child wants to be like Mom and Dad, and having a miniature adult pack means a youngster has "arrived." In addition, children can carry more in a pack, and as they get stronger, there is room to increase the load.

Probably the single most important

piece of gear for hiking children is a lug-soled hiking boot. At first we hedged and tried sturdy oxfords, play boots with smooth soles and finally rough-soled boots with flimsy tops, but slipping and falling on trails was a major problem. When our first three-year-old hiked, we took a short trail to a waterfall. He was a walking accident, slipping and stumbling on every small pebble.

BY THE NEXT TRIP, I had located children's hiking boots. They were too big, but cotton in the toes fixed that, and he suddenly became a sure-footed mountain goat. To cushion that initial expense, we save boots and pass them down to the younger children, and we trade with other hiking families.

We decided also that with children along, a tent is a necessity. As adults we often manage pleasantly with a tarp, but with a good tent we can survive almost anything, and our children are assured of relative comfort.

Initially we used a two-man mountain tent that weighed only 4½ pounds. With two small children it was enough for four of us—though we didn't dare to exhale at the same time. Because of the tight fit we carried a light tarp to use as cooking shelter, for children need to stretch their legs on a rainy day.

We know a number of families who find adequate room in three-man tents, but now that our children are larger and a third youngster is hiking, we have graduated into an 8½-pound four-man model, which proved its value on a recent trip when we were deluged by a record-breaking rain. By morning a puddle had created a two-inch-deep waterbed, but we were dry and warm. Instead of a disaster, we experienced an adventure the kids loved.

Every child needs a good sleeping bag. Unless he or she has an allergy and must use synthetic fill, down bags give the most warmth for the least weight, and small sizes are available. If you are going into mountains or along beaches where nights are cold, beware of lightweight summertime bags. You can always cool a warm bag, but compensating for an inadequate sleeping bag is difficult. And don't forget a sleeping pad; for little added weight, warmth is guaranteed.

Particular attention should be given to keeping children warm and dry during the day. Once we camped in a meadow at the foot of a high mountain and faced rain, snow, sleet, sun and a wind storm, all in a 36-hour period. At such moments children have to be protected, and their gear must work. If a raincoat is new, don't hesitate to stand a child under the backyard sprinkler to test the coat's ability to shed water. Better to find out at home that the seams leak than to have a wet, miserable youngster in the wilderness.

For warmth, light layers, preferably wool, are ideal. Avoid sweatshirts, which act like sponges when wet (and children manage to get wet even when the sun shines). We insist on long pants; they protect against cold, nettles, insects and sometimes the sun.

Rain gear, which we always carry, serves both as rain protection as well as a windbreaker. Slickers with hoods usually are available in children's sizes and do the job, although they are a bit heavy. We have found, too, that rain pants are as important as tops. They shed not only water but mud and dirt. They are not, however, easy to find in small sizes, but with a simple pattern I have made children's sizes from coated nylon material.

Our standard "keep-kids-dry" gear includes plenty of extra socks. Boots can be thoroughly waterproofed, but a child inevitably will step in mud or water at least knee-deep. With a change of socks, comfort returns, even when shoes are damp. If the weather turns cold, wool socks can do double duty as mittens.

The best rule when packing is to know your child's needs. If your youngster is easily chilled, a down jacket will have to be standard equipment. Our middle child is a bug attractor and swells when bitten. We know now to double or triple our bug repellent supply and to carry antihistamine. Another child sweats a lot and needs his own juice bottle to keep going.

From the beginning of your family hiking you should be testing all of *your* gear and skills. Don't discover when the kids are along that you do not know how to read a compass or use a map. Check your flashlight and routinely carry extra batteries and a spare bulb. The first-aid kit may have to be revamped to meet your children's needs. Certainly you should double your band-aid supply.

While you are convincing your children that backpacking is pleasurable, you must also teach each one about safety on the trail. Rules are absolute and must be enforced. The cardinal rule: Never get ahead or out of sight of an adult.

Some families hang a whistle around each child's neck in case of emergency. A good idea, but we have seen bewhistled youngsters as much as a quarter-mile from their parents. That separation creates a danger no whistle can eliminate. And there are difficult places where children should walk hand in hand with adults.

With proper motivation, plenty of day hikes and car camping initially, the right gear and a special regard for safety, you can begin to become a backpacking family. But do not think your troubles will end when your children get older and stronger. You may discover, as I did, that the challenges increase as the youngsters grow.

This irony was underlined on a recent trip with our seven- and eight-year-olds when we climbed a steep six miles to a chain of alpine lakes. The children made good time, and their packs bulged with more than token loads. At our destination I collapsed, muscles tingling and back sore, but not the kids. The hike hadn't phased them.

"Let's fish."

"No, I want to collect rocks."

"Hey, look, a frog, over in that pond."

"Mom, come here and take a picture of this gorgeous flower."

Enthusiasm for everything sparked through the air. We had succeeded, all right; we had converted our reluctant toddlers into backpacking fanatics.

"Say, Mom, let's walk over to that next ridge. The view must be super." My daughter was at my elbow prying me off my comfortable perch.

I groaned, then thought, "Well, we asked for it." Now the trick will be keeping up with our backpacking children. ☙

END-TO-END ON THE APPALACHIAN TRAIL

by SHIRLEY PEARSON

Another family, Bob and Shirley Pearson and their children, Kris and Robin, put it all together and hiked end-to-end on the Appalachian Trail—2,050 miles. They did it all mostly on weekend hikes, with a style of hiking that any family can adapt.

W.K.

"BETTER NOT go that way," warned my husband as I felt the warm, murky water of the spruce bog slowly gurgle into my boots and ooze up the side of my legs.

"Mommy's sinking," the two children calmly informed their father. They watched from a slightly submerged log they had managed to reach safely and dryly.

Somehow mommy had missed the log in the churned-up, muddy water and had stepped off into a seemingly bottomless pit, wearing a 35-pound pack as a sinker.

Clutching at the nearest limb, I managed to haul myself up onto the invisible bridge and teeter my way to drier territory. We continued to squish our way across the moist state of Maine after an early summer flood.

We were on the longest continuous hike of our 2½-year project of walking the Appalachian Trail end-to-end on weekends. Except for five nine-day trips and this one of three weeks' duration, we had walked the rest of the 2,000 miles on weekends only, driving from our home in Ohio to various points on the trail. Then, after 85 trips and 91,000 miles, we finally climbed Mount Katahdin and achieved our goal on August 16, 1973.

The family involved in this adventure consisted of Bob, my 51-year-old carpenter husband; Kris, our 11-year-old son; Robin, our nine-year-old daughter; and me, a 44-year-old elementary-school teacher. Kevin, our 14-year-old, accompanied us on 600 miles of the trail but was not really interested in outdoor life and much preferred other activities. Our three oldest sons were grown up, married, and had other interests.

Robin and Kris were just young enough not to be mixed up in weekend sports or social activities, but I think that they would have protested if we had continued much longer with our regular weekly trips. Now they seem quite content to stay home and be free to do other things, though they still like to hike and love the outdoors. For over two years, however, "The Trail" was really a way of life for us.

OUR WEEKEND schedule became a regular routine. As soon as Bob arrived home from work on Friday, he took a quick shower and dressed in hiking clothes. By 5:30 P.M. we were usually on the nearby interstate highway. Our van had been packed the night before, and supper was eaten picnic-style as we rode along. Since we spent Friday night and most of Sunday in our "Green Monster," Bob had made it as comfortable as possible with two double bunk beds, a cupboard for snacks, toys, books, and tools, and a portable toilet to eliminate extra stops. He and I took two-hour turns at the wheel while the one not driving relaxed or slept. The children did homework, played, and went to bed at their usual bedtime. They were quite accustomed to their home on the road and slept well with only an occasional inquiry like, "What state are we in, Daddy?"

We drove steadily from midnight to dawn until we reached the point on the trail where we planned to stop hiking on Sunday. At daylight Bob would find a good hiding place nearby and chain his motorcycle to a solid object there. Then we would drive to our starting point. By the time we arrived, we had eaten breakfast and were dressed in the proper attire, ready to "hit the trail." In zero winter weather it was no simple task to route sleepy children from warm sleeping bags and into the awkward array of cold-weather hiking gear.

We generally kept the Saturday hike to between eight and 15 miles, except near the end when we did manage 20 miles a day a few times. We tried to make camp in the early afternoon, allowing plenty of time for the children to do their usual chores and still have time to explore and get their feet wet in the nearest stream. We used trail shelters when they were available in the winter or early spring but usually camped in our homemade nylon tent.

Sunday we hiked another eight to 10 miles until we reached the hidden motorcycle. Bob would ride it on the highway back to the van, fasten the cycle to the rear-end carrier, and return for his family. This was often a long, cold, and rainy ride for him, and it was always a great relief when we were all safely together again and headed home to Ohio.

We often did consecutive sections for a few weekends and then for variety would skip to an entirely different area. One week we might hike in Tennessee, and the next would find us in Vermont. I carefully checked off each section as we completed it, and marked it on a large map, filling nine albums with daily logs and color prints. We planned longer weekends and vacations months in advance, using them to cover parts of the trail that were more difficult or that involved longer mileage. Our hiking continued through every season including winter; unfavorable weather reports might affect only the direction in which we headed.

HAVING YOUNG CHILDREN along can sometimes cause slight catastrophes and anxieties. One evening after a long day's hike south of the Smokies, Bob was preparing supper while Robin and Kris rested in the bunks at Cable Cap Shelter. Our skillet was balanced precariously on our little stove, and the whole apparatus was resting on a board that lay across the front of the lean-to. Just as Bob had the beef stroganoff bubbling deliciously, Kris decided to alight from the top bunk by doing a trampoline act off the springy board that held the meal. The skillet did a perfect flip, dinner landed in the dirt, and the Pearsons had soup for supper!

Occasionally we spent a few anxious moments when an adventurous child got too far ahead or behind and became lost. Bisecting trails or logging roads sometimes led them astray when they were watching something other than white paint blazes. They were taught not to go far without a marker in sight, so after a time they always returned.

But this strategy didn't work one day in Maryland's Washington Monument State Park when we were waiting for Bob to return for us at the end of a Sunday hike. After climbing the monument we planned to meet at the campground near the park entrance. Robin and I started down the road, and Kris was going to race us via the trail. He took the A.T., all right—but north, instead of south to the campground. When he didn't show up after a reasonable length of time, I went back to where I had left him and realized what had happened. Kris was headed for Pennsylvania on our following week's section! The next road crossing was three miles beyond the park, so when Bob came for us he started out on the trail while I drove around to the crossing. No

"Victory" kiss on summit of Maine's Mount Baxter, the end of the trail.
PHOTO: SHIRLEY PEARSON

Kris there, so I returned and finally met the two of them just coming off the trail in the park. Kris had gone the whole three miles and back before his father met him. He had asked other hikers which way to the park and had gotten confusing answers because there was a park in each direction.

The children bore up well under the usual hardships suffered by backpackers. They endured black flies, mosquitoes, deer flies, and bees without too much complaining. While hiking in Virginia's George Washington National Forest, we were plagued with yellowjacket stings. Each day on the trail someone got stung at least once until only I had escaped. As we drove along the Blue Ridge Parkway toward home after our last trip to that area, I felt a burning sensation on my thigh. The Virginia bees had accomplished their mission—they had got us all.

Knee-deep mud and a week with wet feet and clothes made things a little unpleasant during the three weeks in Maine. After wincing under the initial shock of pulling cold, wet shorts on bodies warm from a down sleeping bag, Robin and Kris would bravely attack the task of wiggling into wrung-out, clammy socks. It rained so long that it was impossible

to dry anything for a week. Few children have learned to appreciate the ultimate in comfort: putting on clean, dry shoes and socks.

One thing we found hard to understand was the "mystery of the shoes." Shoes usually disintegrated very gradually, giving us plenty of time to replace them before it was too late, except for Kris's footwear. For some reason, his always came to a dramatic end with flapping soles and gaping holes at the most inconvenient times—usually on long hikes. On our seven-day hike of the area south of the Smokies, his soles came off. So for the next three days the nylon straps that held the sleeping bags on the packs had to do double duty. At night the straps held the broken wire bunks together, and during the day they were wrapped around Kris's feet. They worked fine on the descents but had to be replaced constantly when climbing *up* mountains.

BOTH CHILDREN usually cleaned up the small trash around lean-tos; Kris collected dry firewood to leave for the next occupants and offered to help other hikers with their chores. At No Business Knob Lean-to, where the spring was 400 yards down the mountain, he offered to fetch drinks for tired people just arriving. One boy

promised to give him a dime for filling all his canteens and water bottles. Kris sped eagerly down to the spring, but came back up a little slower, loaded with several pounds of water. He soon returned to our tent looking disheartened: his "employer" said he had been too slow and wouldn't give him the dime. Bob replied, "Boy, I would have dumped the water *out* after that!" Kris disappeared, and a few minutes later we heard a loud protest followed by the sound of water splashing on the shelter floor.

Most of the people we met on the trail were exceptionally kind, however, and we value the many friendships we made. Robin still writes to Steve, a hut boy in New Hampshire whom we met first in Georgia and again at Pinkham Notch. An Adventure Bound leader named Perry carved her a wooden spoon in Maine, and another twice-met hiker named Barney was encouraged to finish his trip to Mount Katahdin after seeing her determination during the rainy week. Kris remembers Jeff, from Wisconsin, who befriended him on our Easter trip in the Cherokee National Forest, and many other older hikers who treated him as a worthy fellow-backpacker.

We were especially fortunate to have few injuries occur during the

2,000 miles. Robin accidentally walked into Kris's fishing line and pulled the hook through the skin on her thigh one day near a Vermont lean-to. Several rugged hikers looked a little pale as Bob operated and cut out the hook with a sterilized razor blade. That was really Robin's bad day because soon after we resumed the remaining eight miles to our destination, she stumbled and fell flat on her face. This was an unusual accident for her since it happened on a rough, rocky trail—she usually did all her spectacular falls on smooth, level "tourist's" trails.

Kris, too, had his share of skinned knees, twisted ankles, and stomach aches. We suffered no broken bones, however, nor serious illnesses. Growing legs and feet sometimes developed muscle cramps in the middle of the night, and many a shelter mouse stopped gnawing to hear a little hiker's sniffles. But this happened less frequently as our children grew and our hikes became very regular.

NIGHTTIME bathroom trips were not frequent after our week-long hike in Georgia. I was awakened suddenly one night by the frightened cry, *"A bear!"* and a body hurtled headfirst into the bag beside me. Kris had made a hurried return from the latrine after hearing something crashing through the bushes.

More real than the Georgia bear was the cow moose that came galloping down the trail toward Kris on White Cap Mountain. It was frightened and trapped between Bob and Kris ahead and Robin and me behind. After half a dozen frantic trips back and forth, it finally leaped into the scrub spruce and vanished down the slope, leaving a breathless family with a moose story to take home.

Other wildlife also kept our walks interesting. A litter-conscious skunk in Georgia politely picked up and ate all the popcorn that we had spilled on the dirt of the floor shelter. But as we were sleeping on top of the popcorn, the skunk nudged its nose under our feet to paw out the goodies. We were careful not to complain too loudly.

The resident shelter mice usually performed their nightly gymnastics just before bedtime. We would watch them peek out from the cracks and then daringly run the rafters or, if they were really talented, climb up and down the walls. Bob always left an offering of popcorn or peanuts to fill their tummies before they reached our packs.

We had a few meetings with poisonous snakes. Once when we stopped for a break, I almost set Robin's pack on a beautiful brown and pink copperhead. It was in no position to complain, luckily, as it was devouring a salamander that hung part way out of its mouth. We all watched quietly from a distance until the meal was almost out of sight, and then went farther down the trail for *our* snack.

Another snake incident occurred in Shenandoah National Park on a cold and rainy October day. Kris was leading and turned to ask his dad a question. Instead of answering, Bob yanked him back just in time to keep him from stepping on a timber rattler stretched completely across the trail. The snake was so cold it could hardly move. We gingerly walked around it while Bob took its picture, getting as close as possible. When our film was developed we were surprised to see nothing in the print but brown autumn leaves. The snake blended so well that it was entirely invisible.

We have tried to teach our children to respect all wildlife and appreciate the wilderness they see. They are all properly horrified when they notice anyone throwing trash around or breaking green boughs from trees.

Many interests evolved from our trips. Robin became expert at identifying wildflowers from field guides, and Kris developed an interest in geology. There seems no end to the chain of learning attached to the trail.

With so much history along the way, we tried to expose the children to as much as possible. We never passed museums without a visit, and we followed several blue trails to other interesting places. We took the alternative route through Harpers Ferry in order to spend a Sunday afternoon exploring the historical park. Twice we ended hikes at Bear Mountain Park so we could see the zoo and all the museums and go home via New York City, only 30 miles south.

AS OUR MILEAGE grew every weekend, so did our children. We often looked at them striding ahead of us with their 20-pound packs and remembered how little they had seemed when we first started out many months before. As we hurried to finish the trail and climb Mount Katahdin before school started in the fall, they were both able to carry their well-filled packs as much as 20 miles a day. On the first real hike Robin was only seven, and it took two of her steps to match one of her dad's. Her pack weighed in at a staggering three pounds, but we were happy just to have her cover the miles on her own feet. As time went on, however, we noticed that complaining boy scouts we encountered would grow strangely quiet as they watched Robin trudge along under a pack almost as big as she was.

Now that we are back to civilization, Robin and Kris both insist on hard beds and open bedroom windows at all times. I tip-toed into Robin's room one stormy night recently and found sleet and rain blowing in her face. As I started to close the window, she startled me by saying, "Don't shut that! I'm smelling the rain!" Each winter Kris spends a few nights in a cave he builds into a natural snowdrift on our patio. So far his sleeping arrangement has been tested in temperatures as low as five degrees, and he has been comfortable.

We would advise anyone doing winter backpacking to be sure children are dressed warmly, as ours always seemed to get chilled long before my husband and I did, and we were always on the watch for hypothermia. Robin's cheeks were easily frostbitten in the strong winds, although she never noticed it herself. As soon as we reached our campsite, everyone had to remove sweat-dampened socks and boots to put on down bootees. A hot bedtime snack in our down bags usually made us all comfortable and ready for sleep.

Now that we have attained our goal, we are left with a lost feeling that is hard to describe. To fill the void, we are hoping to learn cross-country skiing and do more winter camping. Additionally, there are many places we would like to return to. We always seemed to pass the nicest lean-tos and campsites at noon or too early to stop for the night. ◗

A FAMILY BACKPACK IN THE GRAND CANYON

by WILLIAM KEMSLEY, JR.

Once mastered, backpacking with your family can become addictive. You can take on even a week-long trek in the Grand Canyon, as we tell about in the following article.

W.K.

It was snowing again on the morning that we were to begin our hike down into the Grand Canyon. We had already waited three days at the South Rim. If we were to keep the schedule called for on our camping permit, we had to get moving. As we adjusted our heavy packs and started down the Kaibab Trail at Yaki Point, the snow stopped briefly, just long enough to give us a clear view of the wonderland below.

Do you know that thrill you get when you realize that you are finally on your way? For me, there is hardly anything else like it. It's a soaring feeling. My family and I began to sing as we headed down the first switchback. The trail is wide as it winds back and forth down the side of the canyon, but we were carefully watching our footing. We were the first people to go down the steep, slippery trail since the last snow fell, and we had no ice creepers on our boots.

Soon the snow-covered piñon and juniper anchored in the trailside rock gave way to an occasional bare blackbrush as the snowy trail became a muddy path. Still, it was a relief. With the mud came warmer temperatures. At our first rest stop in a clearing on top of O'Neill Butte, I pulled out a sack of pistachio nuts which no one knew I had packed.

We had been building up to this trip for nine long months and here we were enjoying our first rest stop on the trail with a special treat to boot. As we gazed out across the mile-deep canyon and down onto the tops of the mountains within it, my wife, Marcella, and I had a sense of triumph that our commitment to family backpacking had survived all the preparations for this, our most ambitious trek.

Because Marcella and I had backpacked most of our lives, we had to find ways to continue when our first child arrived. And as the children kept coming, we had to devise ever more ingenious ways of coping with youngsters on the trails. We were living in White Plains, a suburb of New York City, when we decided the time had come for the whole family to explore the Grand Canyon. To allow time for the children's slower pace, we set aside a two-week vacation for it. At that time Molly was 11; Katie, 6; Will, 5; Andrew, 3; and Maggie, 9 months.

With children of these ages, we knew we would have to have some other experienced backpackers along in case of an emergency. It made good sense to invite our nephew, Kenn Petsch, 21, a camera salesman in Arizona and one of the most experienced desert hikers we know. Next, we asked Gary Page, my charge from the Big Brother program in Queens. At 16, Gary was a veteran backpacker, having been my most frequent hiking companion in the past eight years.

With Kenn and Gary, we felt we could cope with any problem on the trail. Since Kenn and I had backpacked in Grand Canyon before, we felt we had had enough experience to get the park rangers' permission for our party to spend several days in a wilderness part of the canyon. Later we added one more competent and enthusiastic trekker, a 15-year-old neighborhood girl, Jana Bergins, who offered an enticing bonus: she would baby-sit for us on the trip.

We had planned our great adventure for mid-March, at the time of the children's spring vacation. We also chose this time of year partly because the temperatures in the canyon would be perfect for hiking. But more important, mid-March is still too early in the season for snakes and scorpions. With young children, one of the most serious considerations is the possibility of their reaching behind rocks or into bushes and surprising a rattler or scorpion. This danger is considerably reduced by avoiding the hot summer season.

Because we wanted everything

about the trip to go right, we began our planning the preceding July. First we ordered topographical maps of the canyon. By Labor Day we had decided upon a route, requested camping reservations from the Park Service, and started to list the gear we would take.

Right after Christmas I began shopping for the special items we would need to add to our backpacking equipment. Soon we were all involved in the excitement of searching catalogs and discussing choices. Two items looked particularly useful for the trip. One was a varmint-proof container for storing our food supplies in the wilderness. (The plan was for our strongest backpackers to precede the family on our proposed route and set up food caches.) We ordered six of the five gallon metal cans from an outfitter in San Francisco who sells them for use on packhorse trips in the Sierras.

We also needed a water container that was collapsible enough to be carried conveniently in our packs when not in use. At one of our wilderness campsites we would be waterless for three days, so we would need enough of these containers to carry 10 gallons at a time. We chose large, army-surplus, leakproof polyvinyl bottles from a supply house in Buena Vista, Colorado.

With our equipment problems solved, we turned to that part of the trip preparations that always gets our whole family involved: the food. Early in January I made out a week's menus. Then the fun began. First, the shopping. For large trips we usually find about a third of the goods we need in a supermarket, about a third in a backpacking supply store, and about a third in a gourmet food shop.

By mid-February we were cooking for a trip that was still one month away. I made three kinds of the trail snack known to all backpackers as gorp, while Marcella made a date-nut-molasses loaf, and granola from our own recipe. The granola requires long, slow baking and sends an aroma through the house that gets

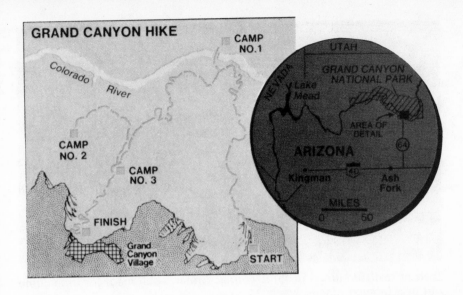

GRAND CANYON HIKE

everyone's taste buds clamoring for a sample. Of course we had some, warm right out of the oven, in bowls with fresh milk. I portioned out the rest into plastic bags, one for each day it appeared on the breakfast menu. To save weight, we repackaged all the store-bought goods into plastic bags, in single-meal quantities. The gorp was divided into 63 individual bags, so each person (except Maggie) could carry his daily supply in a pocket. Altogether, the bottles and cans we emptied for this Canyon trip weighed 8½ pounds.

The shopping, cooking, and packing made us feel as if the countdown had started. We pitched the tents in the backyard to make sure that everything was still there—poles, stakes, tie downs—and that no repairs were needed. Will, Katie, and Andrew played inside them and got underfoot, but I really enjoyed their excitement. Everyone tried on his pack and boots to be sure they still fit. Katie and Molly had outgrown their boots, so Marcella took them shopping for new ones, and the girls broke them in by wearing them to school day after day. One of the last jobs was to pack our sleeping bags in small nylon stuff sacks so the down would not get too compacted.

The children told everyone at school about their coming trip to the Grand Canyon. Katie's first-

Molly and Will Kemsley, ages 11 and 5, pause on a muddy switchback of the Kaibab Trail to survey the awesome dimensions of the family adventure unfolding before them—a 40-mile hike in the Grand Canyon.
PHOTO: THOMAS DAVISON

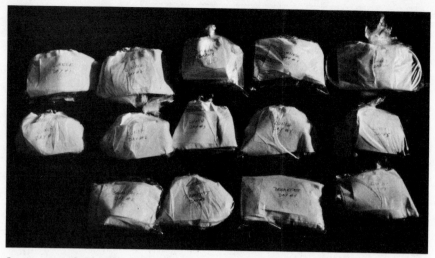

Instant trailside lunch or three-course dinner, each meal for nine came out of a labeled plastic bag.
PHOTO: WILLIAM KEMSLEY, JR.

grade teacher got her to write a story about the trip. Molly's teacher asked her to read a book about Navajo and Havasupai Indians because the canyon country is their homeland. Jana called several times to ask about cacti, an essay subject she had chosen for her science course. Gary wanted to know about the controversy over deer and burros in the Grand Canyon because he had made a bet with his study-hall adviser. I began to read about John Hance, Seth Tanner, Ben Beamer, and other nineteenth-century prospectors who explored the canyon.

Suddenly departure day was here—March 12. Jana's father drove us to the airport. There was barely breathing room with all of us and our gear in his station wagon. When we landed at Grand Canyon Village, we found six inches of snow on the ground and more falling. We stayed at Moqui Lodge while completing our plans and spent our first day sightseeing and meeting with the backcountry rangers. They wanted to know how much canyon backpacking experience we had had, what gear we were taking, names and addresses of all members of our party, and a list of places we would be staying each night. Satisfied that we met all requirements, they confirmed our permit.

Then a freak accident threatened to undo our months of plan-

ning. I broke my thumb and had to go to a hospital in Flagstaff to have it set. Suddenly, I was something of a liability to our party instead of a strength, and I felt it would not be wise for us to travel so deeply into the more remote wilderness parts of the canyon as we had planned. The rangers adjusted our permit and we resigned ourselves to spending part of our time in what is known as the "heavy-use corridor" in the canyon. It is the route of daily mule trains to Phantom Ranch, the tourist hotel at the bottom of the canyon next to highly developed, ranger-attended campgrounds.

We had to wait yet another day while Kenn and Gary set up our food cache. We kept hoping that it would stop snowing long enough for us to hike safely down through the snow zone. We knew that each 1,000 feet we descended would be like traveling 300 miles south and that we would pass through several biotic life zones, ending up in the Lower Sonoran Zone which is pretty much like a tropical desert. Though it was still snowing at the Rim, we expected it to end about 1,500 2,000 feet down and evaporate altogether before it hit the bottom. As I kept telling everyone, "It never rains on the bottom of Grand Canyon." So I thought.

By the time we stopped for lunch that first morning, the snow

had stopped. We were enjoying our Gouda cheese and pilot biscuits when it suddenly began to hail and then to rain. We pushed on anyway, and the children had already begun to ask, "When will we be there, Dad?" when we dropped down over the edge of the Tonto Plateau into the Inner Gorge. There the clouds opened up—thunder, lightning, and a torrential downpour. Soon everyone was soaked to the skin. The thunderstorm set first Katie, then Will and Andrew off in a constant wail. We had already hiked about seven miles. For the first time in my life I wondered if I could be something of a sadist to inflict this kind of abusive treatment upon our children.

What to do? Hike on. We simply kept right on hiking. What was the point in stopping? There was no place to get out of the pelting rain.

Well, the children survived. When we arrived at the bottom of the canyon, it stopped raining. I left the family by the side of the trail while I went to inquire about our campsite. When I returned, I jokingly said, "It's only another mile."

Little Will stamped his foot. "Damn it, Daddy, I don't want to hike anymore." He so well expressed the feelings of everyone that we all broke up laughing. I didn't have the heart to reprimand him for his language.

My family was amazed to discover how dry the air is at the bottom of the canyon. Our clothes dried completely right on our backs by the time we had finished cooking dinner and unrolled our sleeping bags.

The next morning was sunny and clear. It was as if we had hiked down through a fairy maelstrom, weathered the storm, and were now in the garden of paradise. Springtime was in full bloom at the bottom of the canyon. The cottonwoods and arrow weed were clothed in their light green leaves. Beavertail cactus, turpentine broom, and globemallow were in full blossom.

We dawdled about camp until midmorning, then took a day hike down to the sandy north bank of the Colorado where it is joined by Bright Angel Creek, so named by John Wesley Powell in 1869 when his party stopped there for a few days' rest. One of the vital secrets we have learned about successful family backpacking trips is to allow for frequent rest days, and this was the first one for this trip. Gary, Kenn, and Jana tried to throw stones across the Colorado. In the midst of a hearty game of Capture the Flag, we were all amazed to find a brown pelican among the cottonwoods. We learned later that the bottom of the canyon is a minor flyway for such varied species as juncos, Canada geese, and other migrating birds that sometimes follow the Colorado River into the canyon and winter there.

After lunch the little children occupied themselves by building a fort in the sand while Maggie napped. The roar of the river rapids washed away all sound of voices around us as Marcella and I basked, reveling in the remoteness wrought by the canyon's vertical walls. Recalling our seven-hour journey of yesterday, down through the layers of gray-white limestone and pale brown sandstone at the distant Rim, past the blues, greens, and purples of the Tonto Platform and the red rock of the Inner Gorge, we tried to fathom the Colorado River's journey down through five million years of rock formation.

Time itself acquires a different meaning in this place of vast heights, depths, and distances. The children felt it in the shortness of the day. The sun never came over the Rim until midmorning and passed the other Rim by midafternoon. As soon as the shadows fell, the temperature cooled rapidly from around 75° to the low 40s, summoning us back to camp. Along the way Molly was the first to notice several bats swooping about in the twilight.

Our third day required our longest hike, 10¼ miles and an ascent of 1,700 feet. It would take us up to Horn Creek, the most primitive campsite of our trek and the place where our food was cached.

Food accounted for more of the weight in our packs than it normally does because Maggie is allergic to milk and her special soybean formula had to be carried in cans.

The next day Gary and Kenn went on ahead of us to set camp. Then they hiked back three miles from the new camp and met us for lunch at Indian Gardens, excited over some mule deer they had seen. Since the new camp had no water supply, we filled our army-surplus bottles at Indian Gardens with enough water to last us through the first night and morning there. Then, because we decided to stay at our new wilderness campsite for three nights, some of us would hike back the six miles' round trip for more water.

On our way to Horn Creek, it was very revealing to us to be hiking the "heavy-use corridor," where we met other hikers and long mule trains carrying either passengers or supplies. We had never intentionally hiked such a crowded trail before. It took us through Indian Gardens which, like our Phantom Ranch campground of the two previous nights, was one of the most heavily used backcountry campsites in Grand Canyon National Park. Here were some 75 people jammed side by side into campsites with picnic tables, plumbing, electric lights, and pumped water. Yet only a very easy three-mile hike away was Horn Creek—completely undeveloped, no sad scars of man, quiet, and almost completely unoccupied except for us. We saw one camper there the first night, a Flagstaff minister, William H. Denlinger, and only two other hikers the rest of the time we were there. I have a hunch that most backpackers do not really want solitude, but rather want to do their social thing in a nature setting.

Mr. Denlinger told us he had seen a desert bighorn sheep the day before, so we spent our first day at Horn Creek exploring the side canyons to the west of our camp in the vicinity of Mr. Denlinger's bighorn sighting. We did

not find the bighorn, but we did find deer tracks and a pair of burros. Skunks visited our campsite at night, forcing us to rig our hiking staffs into a derrick to suspend some foods out of their reach. Fortunately they didn't vent their frustration on us.

When our time at Horn Creek was up, there was a sadness among us. While the trip was not yet over, we knew we were now on the last leg. We had only 7½ miles to hike back out. Still, we had allowed two whole days to do it, because it included 4,000 feet of vertical ascent. By midmorning we were back at Indian Gardens, in good time to set up camp and take off on a day hike to some Anasazi ruins. Surprisingly, these Indian ruins, located within sight of the most heavily used trail in the park, the Bright Angel Trail, are remarkably unscathed.

That night we reorganized our gear and prepared for an early morning departure back up to the Rim. Of the 308 pounds of supplies we had carried into the canyon, we had 45 pounds of trash to carry out in our now empty metal cans. The 45 pounds included an excessive amount of trash from

Only Maggie ate in her usual style.
PHOTO: KENN PETSCH

the baby—empty food jars and cans, and disposable diapers—but our theory is that if you change very little in the way the baby is accustomed to being treated at home, you'll have a more contented baby and, ergo, a more enjoyable trip.

We began the long climb out of the canyon about eight o'clock that last morning. We let three-year-old Andrew lead the procession because it would be particularly difficult for him. Kenn and Gary were far ahead of us on the premise that they could get to the Rim, leave their packs, and come back to help us, if need be. Since the rangers do not allow any camping along this stretch of trail, we had to go all the way to the top. We were confident the children could do it, after their week of trailhardening.

What we could not have imagined, though, was how easily it would go. We made it all the way out—four miles—in 4½ hours, not counting stops. I doubt Andrew could have, or would have been willing to try to make this record during the first days of the trip. But because the whole adventure had been so much fun, he was willing to put forth the effort. We've found that youngsters have far more hiking stamina than we think they do. The trick is to make it interesting enough for them. The ever-changing rocks, plants, and animals beside Bright Angel Trail were a big help, as was the trail itself, twisting its way upward through one ecosystem after another. Back on the South Rim we turned for a last look into the canyon. Already it was hard to believe we had really been part of it. We found we had no way to express the sense of vastness and the mystery of time that it had given us. So, just as Andrew and Will and Katie had mastered it one little step at a time, it was the little things we talked about—the lizards and the burros, the bats, the prickly pear cactus, and the Indian ruins—and how much we all wanted to come back to see them again sometime.

SIDEPOCKET

More information for planning a trip to the Grand Canyon . . .

Reservations for backcountry camping permits should be made well in advance with the Backcountry Ranger, Grand Canyon National Park Office, Canyon Village, Arizona 86023, telephone (602) 638-2411.

Maps

USGS Bright Angel quadrangle can be purchased from the U.S. Geological Survey, Denver, Colorado 80225, for $1.25. A geological cross section map is published by the Zion Natural History Association, Springvale, Utah 84767, and costs $1.00.

Trail Guides

• *Grand Canyon Treks: A Guide to Inner Canyon Routes* by Harvey Butchart, *La Siesta Press, Glendale, California, 1976, $2.50.*

• *Grand Canyon Treks II: A Guide to Extended Canyon Routes* by Harvey Butchart, *La Siesta Press, 1975, $1.50.*

• *Inner Canyon Hiking*, Grand Canyon Natural History Association, 1977, $1.25.

Books

• *Geology of the Grand Canyon*, William Breed, ed., Museum of Northern Arizona, *1974, $5.00.*

• *The Man Who Walked Through Time* by Colin Fletcher, *Random House, 1972, $2.45.*

• *Grand Canyon Place Names* by Byrd H. Granger, *University of Arizona Press, 1960, $1.00.*

• *Grand Canyon: Today and All Its Yesterdays* by Joseph Wood Krutch, *William Morrow, 1958, $3.50.*

• *Grand Canyon Wildflowers* by W.B. McDougal, Museum of Northern Arizona, *1964, $3.50.*

• *Grand Canyon Venture: Sightseeing and Hiking Tips for One of the World's Greatest Experiences* by Carl A. Munson, *Signpost Books, Lynnwood, Washington, 1977, $2.00.*

• *Exploration of the Colorado River and Its Canyons* by John Wesley Powell, *Dover reprint, 1895, $3.50.*

• *The Grand Colorado: The Story of a River and Its Canyons* by T.H. Watkins, et al., *Crown Publishing, 1969, $15.00.*

Pamphlets

Numerous pamphlets and brochures are available from the Visitor Center, Grand Canyon National Park, Grand Canyon, Arizona 86023. Among them are "Grand Canyon Rim Trail," "The Grand Canyon: A Slice of Time," "Hiking the Bright Angel and Kaibab Trails," "Life Zones and Ecosystems," and "South Rim Grand Canyon: Your Step by Step Guide."

ONCE BEFORE I DIE

by EDITH FREUND

Bill had heard the admonition: the Bridger Wilderness is only for the most experienced backpackers. Nonetheless he was going to hike it with his wife and three children.

It is important to view a family trip as you would a mountaineering expedition. It takes all the planning, preparation, logistics and leadership that a mountaineering expedition requires. The only difference is that it is not as strenuous, nor as dangerous.

The piece that follows, describing Bill Krampert's family backpacking trip in the Wind River Mountains of Wyoming, accentuates some of the precautions that families ought to take, if they are to venture onto wilderness trails with youngsters. The Krampert family made several mistakes, which under adverse conditions could have been disastrous. They have been willing to relate them in this narrative in order to help others who would undertake such a venture.

But there is a more positive side to this piece. It proves again that families can take on some quite adventurous backpacking trips and experience the tremendous joy of the wilderness. The Kramperts had an experience of a lifetime. And one that is a very special way of bonding the family together.

W.K.

BILL KRAMPERT has visited the Wyoming wilderness areas often during the past 20 years.

Now he, his wife, Jane, and three of their four children were camped at Lake Ethel inside the Boulder Lake entrance of the Bridger Wilderness. On several vacations they had nibbled away at the Bridger, camping a few miles inside one entrance, then another, not daring to venture too far into the wilds with their young children. The family was watching a sunset when Bill said, "Someday I'd like to hike the length of it. Someday before I die." Jane is the kind of individual who says, "Why not?"

Bill described his dream of backpacking the 90-mile length of the rugged Bridger in terms of a family expedition. He wanted to show his wife and children the backbone of the continent, to return to the backcountry of the Wind River Range for two weeks with only the provisions they could carry on their backs.

Bill nurtured his dream back home in Illinois, where the winter days track one after another like the obedient cars of the suburban train on which he commutes to his job as a business consultant in Chicago. He is 50 years old, but he has the innate stubbornness of his German ancestors. When he thought of the Bridger, the image of Square Top Mountain came to mind; it began to symbolize the trip, to be his Mecca.

On a map, the Bridger nestles like a bumpy sausage against the western shore of the Wind River, forming 120 miles of the continental divide. The northern portion of the Bridger is still in the ice age; seven of the largest glaciers in the Rockies are located there. The area is subject to more storms than any other Wyoming mountains. Before the middle of July, melting snow makes hiking impractical. Soon after Labor Day, possibly before, there is a chance of new snow. The season for backpacking in the Bridger is short.

Five spur trails intersect the length of the Bridger. They run horizontally on the map, from west to east, to meet the parallel north–south trails, the High Line and Fremont. Backpackers are encouraged to travel near the entrances of the five spurs, either going in or coming out on the parallel north–south trails. Even then, it can be a 70-mile hike eastward into the craggy mountains or west to civilization.

The Bridger has been described by its veterans as a place for only the fit and skilled, people who know mountain ways. In fact, one school of thought recommends that family groups camp no farther than three miles from the car and leave the wilderness to more rugged parties. Bill had undertaken a difficult task for someone accustomed to desk work most of the year. But the Kram-

The Kramperts—Diana, Jane, Peter, Bill, and Patty.
It was their first extensive backpacking trip
together.
PHOTO: FRED C. LOGAN

perts are strong and capable.

As for the Krampert children, Patty, 20, a student
at the University of Denver, was eager to join the trip.
Eighteen-year-old Jenny, who likes soft beds and comfort,
declined. Eleven-year-old Diana and Peter, 14, joined immediately. Now the family began planning in earnest.
They wrote letters for maps and information, read books
and spent weekends near home hiking with full packs.

WHEN THE BIG day came, the jumping off place was
Big Sandy entrance at the south end of the wilderness. There Bill checked in at the ranger's station to leave
their itinerary and note how long they would be
gone.

"I planned to start at the south because the north end
is at a lower elevation and I felt we would be tired on
the last half of the trip," Bill says. "My original idea was
to hike two days and take the third day off. Too many
of the accounts we have read became a grim chronicle—
'We hiked, we carried, we set up camp, we slept and we
carried again.' I wanted a different kind of experience for
my family."

Bill learned from the ranger that sheep had just used
Fremont Trail. This was the trail they had intended to
hike because it parallels the continental divide a mile
closer than the High Line Trail. Stock has the right of
way in the mountains and leaves unpleasant evidence
behind. On the advice of the ranger, they chose the High
Line instead. The switch was not a success.

Late in the day, after the Kramperts had hiked seven
miles on the steadily rising High Line to Poston Meadows,
they discovered a shepherd guiding his rolling woolen
sea of animals across a meadow. It was too late to continue
on, so they pitched camp under the pine trees and upwind
of the sheep, and fixed dinner. Bill touched the glacial
waters of the East Fork River with a dry fly and immediately landed trout to go with their freeze-dried hashed-
brown potatoes, instant soup and cocoa.

That night they shared the dark mountain with the
sheep, who passed the hours muttering, as flocks do, on
the hillside. It wasn't a restful night, and both Bill and
Patty woke the next morning with headaches, symptoms
of their lack of acclimatization to the altitude.

Because of their bad night, the family was able to travel
only 3½ miles the second day, and Bill soon realized he
would have to revise his plan for two days on and one
day off the trail. Despite his desire for a leisurely pace,
they were subject to time limits—the food supply, the
weather and the day they had told the ranger they would
return. They didn't want to be the object of an unnecessary
search.

From Poston Meadows the Kramperts followed a sin-
uous trail that wove in and out of high lodgepole pine,
across crests of rubble-strewn hills, then down again into
surprising mountain meadows, soft as green feather beds
and cut through by ice-cold creeks. Each meadow lay at
a higher elevation than the previous one as the family
moved upward toward the continental divide. Soon they
had increased their elevation another 1000 to 1500
feet.

"We didn't talk much on the trail," Jane recalls.
"Especially when we were tired and pressing to make the
top of a rise. But then we'd come over the top of a difficult
climb and see one of those valleys. When I saw the size
and scope of everything, I felt a strange all-pervading
sense of order; it was a definite religious feeling. I began
to understand why Bill had brought us there."

Long hours passed. The mountains lay before them
as they traveled, authoritative, listening without ears to
the approach of their feet. The only sound of the twentieth
century was the distant whine of mammoth jets flying
high above the dangerous peaks.

The children were straining their bodies to the
utmost. At times they were bone-tired. They fought
with each other. The girls complained Peter was
lazy. Diana and Peter grumbled that Patty took up
too much room in their three-man tent. And Patty
would forge too far ahead on the trail to be reached
by the sound of her parent's voices. By the third day
the irritations had begun to accumulate. But they
were somewhat offset by a minor crisis that was
developing, a crisis which kept them all laughing.

Jane had tried to keep the weight and bulk of the
children's packs at less than one fifth their body
weight. Unfortunately, she had seriously underestimated one vital need: she had failed to pack enough
toilet paper. On the morning of the fourth day the
family came upon the only man-made building on
the trip—a ranger's shack, complete with outhouse.
Diana, who made the discovery, immediately rushed
toward it. By the time the rest of the group caught
up, she was hopping like a happy frog from stone to
stone across a creek, waving a toilet-paper flag. They
were saved from civilized disaster.

On into the Bridger. Crowned by imperial mountains, the wilderness has remained as it began, a
place of passage. No man makes his home there;
Indians found it hospitable only for hunting and
fishing. The westward-rolling wagons penetrated

Union Pass and South Pass, but they were mere notches in a bitter wall. The notorious Wind River storms are replete with erratic wind and wild electricity, and visitors often find they have come for nothing but a demonstration of immensity and power. The land gives up little but beauty. Mineral deposits are rare, timber is scarce and the growing season is short.

As they moved upward through the rubble and scree above tree line, the Kramperts felt successful, if a bit tired. They had reached the first spur trail to the west where they could make an escape to civilization, and they bypassed it, waving to a party on horseback in from North Fork for a short day's ride. The Kramperts felt like seasoned backpackers with no need for horses or guides.

On the sixth day the family took the wrong trail. Before

Back in Illinois the family had accepted Bill's dream without knowing its reality.

---

they realized their mistake, they had crossed Hat Pass on the divide. Bill decided they should not go forward but should retrace their steps until they could find an identifiable spot that matched something on their maps.

THEY LOST SEVERAL hours and began to quarrel softly among themselves. Bill was disturbed by the tension, yet said nothing as they descended from the pass. It was not a happy silence.

In their attempt to retrace their steps, the Kramperts again took a wrong turn. They were on a trail, but not the one they had followed to reach the pass. Still, it was frighteningly familiar. Everything had begun to look alike.

During the planning stages for the trip, the Kramperts had written for USGS topographical maps. On the eve of their departure the maps arrived. Unfortunately, they were the wrong ones; they covered peripheral areas not on their itinerary. It was too late to write for the others, so they had started the trip with the only ones they had.

Now Bill realized that this had been a serious error. They should not have left home or entered the wilderness without the correct topographical maps. On the other hand, Bill is an engineer and a graduate of Massachusetts Institute of Technology, and he was a navigator in World War II. He was confident he could find his way in the wilderness.

"We had lost a particular trail," he says, "but we weren't lost. I never had any doubt about being able to bring the family out of there. Still, for that extra margin of safety, nothing should have forced us to enter the wilderness without the proper maps."

In his frustration and anger at himself, Bill turned on Jane and accused her of misreading the maps. He knew they looked falsely easy to follow; nevertheless, he refused to concede and had worked up a good German head of steam by the time they realized they were on the wrong

trail for the second time and were not retracing their steps. Finally they found Horseshoe Lake. But Bill would take no chances; he insisted on a signpost to match the identification on the map. They found one. "See," Jane snapped. *"Horseshoe Lake,* in big letters."

The family sat down beside the sign and held a council. They were tired, and the frustration of being lost had made them irascible. More than that, they had lost confidence in themselves; they were no longer sure they should go on. They took a vote, and the vote was clear: three to two in favor of aborting the trip and finding a spur trail that would carry them west to civilization, where they could phone for their car.

The vote had gone against Jane and Diana, who wanted to continue as planned. Bill knew Jane could finish the original itinerary, as could Patty and Peter, but he was concerned about Diana. She was pale, partly from fatigue and partly from the tensions she felt within the family. Diana looked at her father with urgency. "We want to see the rest of it," she pleaded.

UNDERNEATH HIS concern, Bill felt admiration for her determination and spunk. He knew she really *wanted* to continue. "Okay," he relented, "we'll continue. But," he added over Diana's whoop, "no more voting, no more democracy. Until we get out of here, I'm captain."

Back in Illinois the family had accepted Bill's dream without knowing its reality, and plans for the trip had been laid with idealistic fervor. Only Bill had understood that the party would need a leader and that, regardless of votes or of individual preferences, the final decision of what was best for the group would be his. Now the others accepted this, too. They went on.

On August 23 the Kramperts stood on 11,580-foot Lester Pass and looked back at the 60 miles they had climbed in 10 days. It seemed an impossible distance to have come on foot. Four days and 30 miles lay ahead to civilization, but the sight reinforced their confidence.

From Lester Pass the Kramperts went down to Island Lake, where they camped on a peninsula at water's edge. There they left their packs and tents and took lunch for a hike toward Titcomb Basin at 10,000 feet, where Bill had been told elusive golden trout lie in the glacial waters. The lightened load and the lightened mood were increased by the success of his fishing.

"Come see this; come see it! I don't know if I can land it," shouted Bill. He had a golden trout on the line, 19 inches, approximately 3½ pounds and scarred from other fishing battles in previous years. Bill took two trout from Titcomb Lakes.

On to Shannon Pass, guardian of Peak Lake, which is a sharp turquoise blue and filled with the heavy water called glacier milk, a product of the grinding action of glacier against mountain. Clutching Diana as they edged over the high places, watching Peter for signs of weariness and ever mindful of Patty's tendency to march ahead too fast, Bill and Jane headed down toward civilization and the final leg of their journey.

Their britches were worn through from sitting on rocks, their bodies were tired and the trail wound back and forth, frustratingly interlaced with the Green River and Clear Creek but overshadowed at last by Square Top

Mountain. Bill had succeeded in bringing his family to his Mecca.

Bill remembers a party of horseback riders from Green River Camp who looked over the ragged family as they neared the end of the trail. Patty was far ahead as usual, marching up the path with her hat flopping and a walking stick marking off her energetic stride. Bill and Pete were together, father and son, somewhere behind her. Jane and Diana, the two mavericks, brought up the rear, satisfied that they had held the rest to their original goal.

"I wanted to shout at those riders," Bill says. "I wanted to tell them where we'd been. The last day as we approached Square Top, I had an intense feeling of kinship with the old pioneers, the ones who finally made it across South Pass. They passed the Bridger by. They needed tillable land, and they couldn't see anything useful in the place. They left it intact, and now it's the last frontier."

SLICK ROCK CANYON

by WILLIAM KEMSLEY, JR.

Adjusting your pace to that of others can give you pleasures you would not have believed possible. Don't make it just a wait-until-they-catch-their-breath kind of adjustment. That will never work. That makes the slower ones feel that the pressure is still on even at rest stops. No. You've got to sincerely get into going at a slower pace, stopping often—and enjoying it. Or else forget about going with families.

If you're willing to adjust the pace, however, you can take older people along backpacking, too—even those who've gotten ruefully out of shape. And the joys are exceptional. Let me be more specific about those joys. Here's a piece about a trip that I went on with my 66-year-old dad and my two brothers. It was the best time we ever had all together.

W.K.

We planned to hike only 50 miles in eight days. We wanted to set no records, only to be sure we had enough time to enjoy our trek.

Our ages spanned several generations: my father is 66, I 46, my brothers, Brian and Michael, 30 and 23. Could a backpack trek keep all of us interested? Could we tolerate each other's close company for that length of time? We had not been all together for more than 15 minutes in over 17 years. We had such different lifestyles. Brian is a silversmith eking out a subsistence on a homestead in the foothills of Oregon's coastal range. Michael is a student at the University of Vermont. Dad is a retired trade union leader. I am a New York editor. We approached the hike with as much anticipation for the adventure of our personal relationships as for the wilderness itself.

We decided to hike down a long side canyon of the Colorado River. It is one of the great network of canyons

that weaves in and out of several states through national parks, national forests and other categories of land supervised by a variety of federal and state governmental agencies. Ours was a slick rock canyon.

On March 14 we embraced each other warmly in the Phoenix airport, then drove north on Route 89 toward the Utah border. Since it would require a full day to set up the logistics of the hike, we could become acquainted with the country and reacquainted with one another in a relaxed, leisurely manner.

We picked up a few last-minute items, checked the five-day weather report and registered with the Bureau of Land Management rangers. As we planned to hike through the canyon, our car had to be driven to the point where we would emerge. The $60 to arrange this seemed high, but the drivers had to travel 300 miles to set it up for us. This was the only big expense other than our airfare. Food,

for instance, came to only $3.18 per day for each of us.

Finally, at 6:00 P.M. on March 15, we were on our way. We hiked a short distance along the river before making camp at the last safe spot before entering the narrows, the most dangerous spot in the canyon. (Of the fourfold dangers of the canyon—flash floods, quick sand, rattle snakes and scorpions—the only serious danger is flooding.) Beyond our first camp we would enter a narrow section of canyon, seven miles long, where there would be no escape should a flash flood be caused by a rain storm several hundred miles up stream. The walls of the canyon here rise 800 feet in sheer sandstone cliffs on both sides of the river.

Our first full day of hiking, therefore, took us deep into what, for all intent and purposes, was really a cave. The walls at the river's narrowest point were 12 feet apart with wall-to-wall river between them.

They rose in serpentine configurations above us; the sun peeped through only at midday, and then as if through the mouth of the cave. At first it was exciting and breathtaking; we rubber-necked the entire morning. By late afternoon, however, we confessed we were glad to have left behind the narrowest part of the canyon and be where the walls were a little farther apart.

That first day was an adventure in other ways, too. For one thing, we ran out of water. At the start of our hike, we carried only enough water for one day's dinner, breakfast and lunch. We were counting on replenishing at the water sources indicated on the maps. But the maps are not accurate, and the water sources were all dry.

We had been warned by the rangers that the muddy river water was not safe to drink. That night we had no choice. We filled our pans, let the water settle for an hour, then skimmed off the clearest water from the top and boiled it for 20 minutes. This probably did kill any germs, but the water was also full of alkalines that boiling could not remove. Everything we cooked tasted salty and very much like Alka Seltzer. My appetite destroyed, I ate but a few bites of dinner and only a cup of coffee for breakfast.

The next day we stopped often and explored many places, one of which was an ancient stream bed. We spent four hours in this old gully and concluded, not very scientifically but probably not inaccurately either, that the river once had flowed through this ancient ox-bow. And that centuries ago a canyon wall had tumbled down and stopped the river's flow. The river must have built up against this natural dam, we reasoned, and finally carved a new course for itself along its present river banks. Subsequently, the old dry ox-bow had taken on a Zen-garden quality with a special sanctity that held us there. We were in no hurry. We had all the time we cared to take and all the food we could possibly use on the trek, which gave us a wonderfully relaxed feeling. This second day we hiked a total distance of 2¾ miles before making camp next to a fine, flowing freshwater spring.

We had a huge dinner of hot jello, Knorr's Napoli soup, pork chops, green beans, peaches, raisin cookies and hot tea. We had planned this hike so we would be leisurely, comfortable, joyful and well fed.

The sunny weather helped out. Daytime temperatures ranged from 72 to 94 degrees. The temperature dropped to 32 degrees on our first night, the coldest of the entire trip. The evenings were usually warm enough for us to sit and chat late into the night. We slept under the stars on beds of sand so soft that it wasn't necessary to use sleeping pads.

March was still early spring in the canyon, and we saw little wildlife. We did notice tracks and scats of deer, otter and bobcat. The biggest creatures we saw were the numerous small geckos, a few bats, some cliff swallows and a toad. And one evening we were thrilled to hear echoing off the canyon walls, the beautiful, reedy singing of a white-throated sparrow.

Our most exciting encounter with wildlife occurred while we were climbing the canyon wall, searching for evidence of a pipeline built by Mormon farmers in the 1880s. They had attempted to pump water to the desert plateau from the river 1200 feet below! We had climbed the 800-foot scree slope and then began climbing the canyon wall itself. I was following Brian across a narrow ledge when I heard a spine-chilling rattle. In 35 years of hiking I had never heard a rattlesnake, and did not expect it to be so loud. I moved quickly and cautiously away from the crack in the wall from which the sound came. I became aware of the color of my face when Brian asked "Are you all right?"

From a distance we tried to see what was inside the hole. It was not a snake but a long-tailed lizard. Later, a ranger said it was probably a chuckwalla. According to the ranger, chuckwallas are 18 to 24 inches long with loose-hanging skin. They burrow into a hollow in the rock and, when frightened, blow themselves up like a balloon, making an awful rattling sound.

On our fifth day, after only two miles of hiking, we made camp at the entrance to a side canyon. We had heard there were Indian artifacts inside such canyons. We hiked two miles up the side canyon before lunch. There we found a plentiful supply of watercress which we picked to eat with our Tilsit cheese and sourdough bread. It is surprising how good fresh greens taste after only a few days of freeze-dried foods.

In the afternoon we each did our own thing. Dad stayed at camp and stretched out with a book. Brian, Mike and I hiked back up the side canyon. Brian panned for gold in the tiny creek flowing through the canyon. Mike searched for pottery shards. I took pictures—an absorbing activity for me. Each of us, in his own way, came to feel the presence of Indians in the past history of the site. It was a peaceful glen with cottonwood trees, green grass and low bushes—a natural place to camp for Indians, or anyone else, who had to spend extended time in the main canyon.

Mike found several pottery shards. I found petroglyphs on one of the canyon walls. Brian found some flowery gold in the little creek and a piece of turquoise. Late in the afternoon we met again at the farthest end of the side canyon. We followed the creek as far as we could, trying to trace its source through a labyrinth of sandstone crevices, until we could climb no higher. Our search ended part way up a 1400-foot sandstone cliff which boxed in the end of the canyon. As we descended we invented a game of challenge, running up the steep, sloping canyon walls as high as possible, then back down. Even on a steeply angled wall, if we ran fast enough, our feet would cling to the rough sandstone long enough to carry our weight beyond a designated mark on the wall and down to level ground again. First we ran up around one water pocket. Then, as my brothers gained confidence, they ran a figure eight around two water pockets higher up the steep wall. Time passed so quickly that darkness spilled suddenly down from the canyon rim. Since we had no flashlights, we had to make a quick exit. We ran the entire two miles back to the main canyon, yipping and yelling as we ran. It seemed completely natural for us to cavort like this. When we were back in camp that night, we speculated that the Indians also must have been unable to resist running and cavorting in the canyon as we had been doing. For the first time I felt close to what I imagine Indians might have felt in earlier centuries.

Sheer sandstone canyon walls rise 1,000 feet above the river on both sides, giving the feeling at times of being inside a giant cave.
PHOTO: WILLIAM KEMSLEY, JR.

This camp was the high point of our trip. We sat up late talking, feeling very close, perhaps closer than the four of us had ever felt to one another. We felt really tipsy, but, of course, we had no intoxicants. It was simply a spirited high from our activity and the comradeship. In retrospect, I think perhaps another reason for our exhilaration was that each of us had spent the afternoon exactly as he wished, without regard for what the others were doing or thinking. Perhaps we were each, in our own way, tuned to the same vibes as the canyon itself. And, being so in tune with the canyon were better able to

relate to each other.

The next day we hiked eight miles, and our campsite that night was the nicest of the trip: high up on a sand bench, among cottonwood trees close to the rock canyon wall. This day, I noticed I actually lost track of time. Only my diary reminded me what day it was.

That night we had our first and only real altercation. It was over something quite petty. Brian casually mentioned that he'd have coffee instead of tea because he preferred honey with his tea, and he knew we did not have any honey with us. I retorted, "Sugar has the same nutri-

tional value as honey." To which he responded, quite predictably, "No. Honey is a good deal better for you than sugar, which is adulterated." And, again predictably, I responded, "It is proven that honey is no different nutritionally than sugar."

My younger brother, Michael, jumped to the defense of honey. So did my father. I was licked. I had to walk away, come back and apologize for starting the squabble.

On the morning of the eighth day we rose early. We had 15 miles to hike across the hottest part of the desert, where there would be no drinkable water until we reached our car.

Gradually the canyon widened as the canyon floor flared away from both sides of the river bed. Since the beginning of our hike, the river had dropped several hundred feet through the slick rock, penetrating various layers of clays and sands.

Along this stretch of the hike we knew we would find huge rocks profusely illustrated with Indian petroglyphs. When we found them we ate lunch beside them.

We began to encounter other signs of civilization, albeit of much later vintage. First we noticed the remnants of a barbed wire fence, then an old abandoned ranch. High up on one side of the canyon were the obvious remains of a gold-panning sluice. Next was a gauging station. Then, coming toward us up the canyon, a herd of cattle was being driven by a cowboy. Ironically, the cowboy was an Indian and very friendly. This was our first personal contact with the outside world in a week, a very pleasant way of stepping back into civilization.

Next we passed a stock-loading station and a jeep road leading to a ranch house. Finally we reached our car, parked at the end of the gravel road leading in from the highway.

We shook hands and hugged one another and we realized it was over. All too quickly the week was gone. There wasn't much about the hike to discuss except that we would like to do it again. And next time we will stay even longer. We will be sure we have ample time to linger over those precious moments that we had experienced only briefly in our special canyon. They were much too brief, like life itself. ▲

FAMILY HIKING IN BRITAIN

by WILLIAM KEMSLEY, JR.

How one man's family—wife, five children under 12, and mother-in-law—find hiking happiness and adventure on Wales's most cherished crags.

Backpacking is a word of recent coinage. For most of my 43 years of doing it I've heard it referred to mostly just as "hiking" or maybe "overnight hiking" to emphasize the sleeping-out aspect of it. It is only since about 1970 that I've heard the term backpacking used to describe this activity.

While the difference in these two words may seem trivial, it reflects a more fundamental difference in attitude.

When I was a boy we hiked a lot. And we camped a lot. Often we camped near the car and went for hikes, returning at night to our camp. Sometimes we carried all our gear on our bodies in a pack and stayed out in the woods away from the roads. We never made too much of a distinction between the two. Today, though, the emphasis is for some reason on the latter and not on the former. That's too bad. Because for me there's a place for both. And I passionately desire both types of hiking. Sometimes I even prefer the day hiking to the overnighting.

And as it turns out, day hiking is a far better way to get a family, and especially young children, introduced to the woods than it is to plunge them headlong into the more scary part of hiking—sleeping on the ground—and listening to the strange night sounds of the forests. It isn't any less macho to go day hiking. As a matter of fact, I used to have a mountaineering companion, the man who first taught me how to use an ice ax and crampons, who was an excellent and tough technical climber but who never slept out on the trail unless that was the only way possible to climb some mountain. It was not his "thing." But it's always been my thing. I love sleeping out—especially under the stars. But I don't always have to do that to enjoy a hike. In fact, one way to enjoy a good vacation with a family is to stay in inns or motels most nights and hike most days.

In the following article I tell about one of the most enjoyable vacations I have ever taken with my family. On this trip, we introduced my mother-in-law to hiking. It was the first time she'd gone into the woods since she was an adult. She was a city and a night person. She had fallen love with Las Vegas and had spent several of her most recent vacations there—mostly enjoying the floor shows. On this trip we meticulously avoided the large cities, spent most every day on some sort of a hike in the mountains, hills, and beaches of Great Britain. Upon finally arriving in London for the big finale of the trip my mother-in-law said, "I'm disappointed. I'd rather be back in the Welsh mountains." The trip had something for all of us—short day hikes, the ambience of country inns, castles, seashores, Roman ruins, which everyone enjoyed. My wife Marcella, her mother, and the children drove on to Aberystwyth on the Welsh coast, where they traced their family history—while I remained in the mountains a few days longer, backpacking and rock climbing.

W.K.

179

Family snacks on top of little Moel Berfed.
PHOTO: WILLIAM KEMSLEY, JR.

Taking my wife and children to England for a hiking holiday had overtones of a religious pilgrimage for me. I had been building up to this trip for about 20 years. Names of English climbers had come to have a hallowed ring — Mallory, Mummery, Evans, Joe Brown, Hillary — climbers whose names I associated with hallowed places like Snowdon, Idwal Slabs, Wasdale, Borrowdale, Pillar Rock, Communist Convert, Tennis Shoes.

What kind of a climbing vacation could I expect with five children aged 1½ to 12 years old? Well, very interesting question.

It took us a year of planning before we actually departed. We wanted to do it right. I am glad we spent so much time planning, for it made the trip turn out even better than we had hoped. Furthermore, I got another kind of enjoyment from gathering together maps and brochures, studying guidebooks, and writing and talking to people who had been there. The anticipation

of this trip was like savoring the mouthwatering aromas of a fine kitchen for a year before tasting the first morsel of a gourmet meal.

Since our interest was hiking and climbing, we did not plan time for sightseeing. Also, we intended to do as little driving as possible. Each day of driving meant one less day on the trails. Being forewarned about England's weather, we planned to drive on inclement days, saving sunny days for hiking. Despite this, we knew we would be in areas that get upward of 200 inches of rain a year. So we counted on

The children are eager to climb Snowdon to gain admittance into Mr. Briggs' club.

hiking in the rain at times, too. We planned to spend the drizzly days hiking in the valleys, saving the peaks for cloudless days.

We flew to the closest airport to the Lake District, Prestwick in Scotland. Our first day we drove only 150 miles, to Keswick in the northern Lake District. It was a beautiful crisp day — until we approached the mountains. There, the clouds hung low on the mountainsides, shrouding them from view. As we expected, the next few days were rainy, but not rainy enough to prevent us from taking our first walks. We stayed in a small hotel at the upper end of Bassenthwaite Lake. The following morning we got our first view of the mountaintops as the wind wisped away the mist from time to time to give us glimpses of Skiddaw Mountain across the lake. It was a surprise to me that the mountains were almost entirely barren of trees, giving the appearance of being much higher than their 3,000-foot elevation.

It seemed to us that everyone in the Lake District walks. Interests range from casual rambles all the way to full-fledged winter mountaineering and rock climbing. There are those who take short walks along old country roads, rambles that hardly cause them to perspire. We saw English gentlemen with Harris tweed jackets or Welsh wool sweaters, caps, pipes and walking sticks, accompanied by their fashionably attired ladies. Cars, in the Lake District, seem to be a means of getting someplace in order to park and get out and walk. For this type of walking there is a popular series of guidebooks called *Walks for Motorists*. The books describe walks that vary in length from about 1½ to 7½ miles.

At the other extreme, there are sections of the mountains near Wasdale Head and Buttermere where you can hike for some 15 miles without crossing a road. While this does not sound exactly like the Sierra Nevada, if you backpack on these peaks you can experience wilder weather than you will find during summer in the Sierra. The winds frequently rise to 50 miles per hour. Temperatures drop suddenly and dangerously. Rain and snow dampen more than your spirits. I've never been so wet as on some of my hikes in England.

We took advantage of the full spectrum of walks in order to satisfy the varying needs of all members of our family. In addition to my wife and five youngsters, my mother-in-law was with us, and she is not a walker. To persuade her to hike at all we needed the most civilized type of terrain.

Our first walk was the three-mile circle to Lodore Falls and Ashness Bridge overlooking Derwentwater. This is such a famous walk that one of the views of the lake is reputedly the most painted and photographed view in all of Britain. Its likeness is seen on postcards, calendars, greeting cards, tea trays, candy boxes and jigsaw puzzles. It was easy enough for everyone, including two-year-old Andrew who rode in the kiddie carrier part of the way.

I heard that an estimated 25 to 65 percent of the English people consider walking to be one of their major leisure-time activities. In the Lake District it was easy to believe these figures true, if not actually an understatement. It is my opinion that the English are better off for their walking. Not only is it better for their personal health, but also they are even better off as a nation, for they tend to revere their countryside. For instance, there seemed to be less litter than in the United States. There are certainly fewer billboards. And there seems to be far less vandalism.

I believe that if more Americans walked for pleasure, more Americans would treat our countryside with respect. And I also believe something that would encourage more Americans to walk would be a series of guidebooks such as the English *Walks for Motorists.*

One notch above the motorists' walks were the trailless walks we took on the lesser hills in the Lake District. On drizzly or threatening days we would pick one that looked like a nice place for a picnic, hike to its top and remain for the afternoon while the children frolicked in the meadows. A nice feature of hiking in this area is that because the mountains and hills are relatively treeless, you enjoy fine views wherever you are — weather permitting.

For me the most beautiful spot in all of the Lake District is Honister Pass. We crossed it at sundown, and the view dropping down toward Buttermere was as breathtaking as anything I have seen in any mountain range. And right at the top of the pass, with the most commanding view in all of the Lake District, is a youth hostel. It was a surprise for me that was repeated over and over again. So prevalent is hosteling that the Youth Hostel Association has obtained hostels in the choicest locations in Britain; there are 30 hostels in the Lake District alone. In the United States such locations are snatched up by the most commercial enterprises in the resort industry, and the prices are proportionately sky-high. But in Britain the choice sites have gone to the YHA and the prices are low.

At the hostel at Llanberis Pass in Wales, I discussed this with Deputy Warden Trefor Owain. He explained

Our climbing pace was harmonious; our relationship was one of those rare experiences of perfect rapport.

that rates vary from one type of YHA accommodation to another, but that a youth less than 21 years old would pay from $2.56 for dinner, breakfast and bed at the simplest YHA accommodation up to $3.29 at the most deluxe. A hosteler can save even further on these rates by cooking his own meals in the kitchens provided for this purpose. A bed alone costs from 89 cents to $1.61 a night, depending on the hostel. Of course, adults pay more — a big 15 to 40 cents a day more. According to Trefor, the key to why hostels are so inexpensive is that everyone is expected to help with the chores. Thus, the mammoth 140-bed hostel which Trefor operates is run by a permanent staff of only four. (Compare that with the staff of 46 at a Holiday Inn accommodating the same number of guests.)

We drove across Honister Pass and around the mountains to Wasdale Head which is frequented mostly by rock climbers. We spent the next day hiking on the hills near Wastwater, the lake opposite The Screes. At dinnertime that evening I decided to go on my first backpack trek, with a friend, Jim. Our objective was to make camp that night at a higher elevation so that we could get an early start the next morning at climbing the highest mountains in the Lake District, Scafell Pikes and its sister peak, Sca Fell.

We hiked a couple of miles up to Sty Head, arriving at 10:30 P.M. England has so much daylight during the summer that it is not really dark until

Marcella Kemsley goes "fell walking" with daughter, Katie, on crags in Snowdonia National Park in Wales.
PHOTO: WILLIAM KEMSLEY, JR.

almost eleven o'clock. Furthermore, daybreak comes at about 4:30 A.M., which can give you a very long day of walking.

That night the weather changed on us. Winds gusted through the pass at 40 to 45 miles per hour. Toward morning it started raining. By the time we crawled out of our sleeping bags, fog had enshrouded the mountain pass. It was so thick we could not see 25 feet ahead. We did not have time enough to pick our way to the peaks through that weather so we headed back down, walking directly into the wind. It drove the rain through every tiny opening in our waterproofs, especially through the head and sleeve openings. By the time we reached the valley floor we were soaked, despite all of our waterproof clothing.

From the many Englishmen we met afterward we tried to find out how to stay dry. We learned that none of them actually expects to stay dry on days like that one. The most they expect is to keep warm. This explains why the English wear wool clothing rather than down garments when they hike, except in winter. For when down gets wet, it does not keep you warm.

The wet and windy weather partly explains why there is little backpacking in the Lake District. The biggest single group of backpackers is the rock climbers. They often pack in to the foot of some interesting crag and make camp so that they can spend the weekend on the rocks. Most serious hikers camp at large campsites at the base of the mountains, and then take extended day hikes. If they don't camp, they stay in inns, farmhouses or hostels, all of which are very reasonable. We stayed in one farmhouse that cost $2.60 for bed and breakfast for each adult and half that for each child. At the most elegant inn in which we stayed it cost $12.50 for room and all meals for each adult and half that for the children. And because everything worth hiking to can be reached on a day hike, it isn't necessary to carry all of your gear with you.

We did not confine our hikes to the mountains. One particularly bleak and rainy morning, a guest at the hotel suggested we might find some sun if we went to the west coast, which was only an hour's drive from the Lake District. That turned out to be one of our nicest days, at an area near the town of Whitehaven. George Washington's grandmother is buried in Whitehaven, and it has the distinction of being the only place in England that has ever been attacked by the U.S. Navy. That was under John Paul Jones during the Revolutionary War.

The shore was uncrowded and pastoral. Cows grazed in the meadows on top of the hills that roll gently up to the shore and then drop abruptly in cliffs. We walked along a stony beach to St. Bee's Head, which juts up 400 feet from the sea, and incidentally provides interesting rock climbing for English cragsmen.

An important difference between hiking in Britain and the United States came into focus for us that day. In the United States the backcountry gives you a feeling of the pioneering, trailblazing spirit of our forefathers, a feeling that you are treading in virgin wilderness. I think that this is one of the great appeals the backcountry has for us. But in Britain, there is no real wilderness. Instead, you feel wherever you hike that the land has been trodden for thousands of years by many different peoples.

As we climbed St. Bee's Head, this sense of history came over us. St. Bee's had been a busy harbor 2,000 years ago during the Roman occupation. Every school child in the area can tell you that in those days the Romans lit up the entire St. Bee's coastline with torches to guide their ships through the Irish Sea past the Isle of Man to the shore at St. Bee's or further north to Bowness, the western terminus of Hadrian's Wall.

We followed an ancient wall along the edge of the cliffs all the way to the top of St. Bee's Head. The wall was not indicated on any map; it was not a designated historic site; no one locally even seemed to know anything of the wall's origin. We examined it with great curiosity. Obviously, it had been a battlement centuries ago. It had a trench along the inner side where men could move along it, protected from attack by flying objects. We played amateur archeologist and imagined a Roman camp there overlooking the harbor where the ships would have put in. And we probably were right. There are so many Roman remains in Britain.

From the Lake District we drove directly to Snowdonia in North Wales. As we approached Wales, and most especially after we left Betws-y-coed and began climbing into the mountains, an excitement leaped up within me: I felt like a pilgrim approaching Mecca. Back in 1953 I got my first interest in rock climbing from a book called *On Climbing*, whose photos had been taken mostly in Wales. Its author was Dr. Charles Evans. At the very time I was reading the book, Dr. Evans was with Sir Edmund Hillary and Tenzing Norkay on Mount Everest; he was the expedition physician.

I had borrowed the book from the library for a quite practical purpose — to learn how to climb mountains with the aid of ropes. The weekend before I had scrambled up the Huntington Ravine headwall on Mount Washington in New Hampshire and found that it was exhilarating but as steep as I cared to climb without finding out about ropes.

I can vividly remember the book's jacket. It had a photo of a man clinging improbably to the side of a vertical cliff. I couldn't see what it was that he was standing on, or what his fingers clung to. Still, the photo did not prepare me for what was inside. Dr. Evans discussed cavalierly, in my opinion, the most improbable type of cliff climbing. He talked casually of climbing rock cliffs where there were no footholds and handholds at all so you have to use "pressure" or "friction" holds — you jamb your fist or foot into cracks, or make sideways squeezes on smooth vertical rock. This was a great deal more difficult "climbing" than I had had in mind when I checked the book out of the library. I read with complete disbelief and sweaty palms.

Nonetheless, I became fascinated with rock climbing, as well as with Wales. Dr. Evans referred mostly to Welsh crags and cwms as the locale of his climbing. And I came to consider Wales as the most hallowed ground for British rock climbers.

In the years that followed, I became a rock climber myself. I heard many intriguing and romantic tales of the exploits of British rock climbers — especially of a legendary climber named Joe Brown. I heard how the mountains of Wales were craggy and the rock polished smooth, really tough to climb. My yearning to visit Snowdonia, the heart of North Wales climbing, grew over the years. It intensified unbearably as we drove up into Llanberis Pass and stopped in front of what was once the Gorphywysfa Hotel, which I had read about in so many mountaineering books. It was a small inn where climbers had been staying since the 1850s. The hotel had been turned into the youth hostel. Under a museum-type glass case they have the old Gorphywysfa, guest register which contains names like Mummery, Wills, FitzGerald, and Mallory.

We drove through Pen-y-Pass on down to Caernarvon, then around the other side of the Snowdon Range to take a good look. We finally stopped at an inn right below Llanberis Pass, the Pen-y-Gwryd, also an historic stopping place for British climbers. Just the week before we arrived, the twentieth reunion of the Everest team had been celebrated at the Pen-y-Gwryd. Sir John Hunt, Tenzing Norkay, Dr. Evans and many other team members were there.

Before we unpacked our bags, we put on our boots and ran up Moel Berfed, a small mountain next to the inn. It was a beautiful day. From there we got a splendid view of Snowdon and the surrounding peaks. There was a strong, steady, cold wind. We all wanted to climb Snowdon, the highest peak in England and Wales, but we needed to stretch a few times before we could attempt it with the smaller children. William recently had turned three; Katie was only four. Andrew, just under two, would have to stay below. In the next few days we took several short-distance warm-up hikes. On one of these hikes, a three-mile walk on the Miner's Track, my mother-in-law came along for the picnic on the shores of a mountain tarn named Llyn Llydaw. The weather was perfect, the sun brilliant and the temperature warmer than usual, with a slight breeze to keep it comfortable.

The owner of the Pen-y-Gwryd Inn is a great old gentleman named Christopher Briggs, reputed to have been a very powerful climber in his day. Now he thoroughly enjoys playing the host to visiting climbers, nature lovers and conservationists. His dining room is formal, and you feel more comfortable with coat and tie at meal times, but it is by no means the rule. Mr. Briggs has a table in one corner of the room, where he presides, usually with a group of his own personal guests. When he heard that we were going to climb Snowdon with the children, he called them around his table and said he would have a special celebration for them if they made it all the way to the summit and back on their own feet. He told them he had a club whose members were youngsters under the age of 12 who had climbed Snowdon, and that they were given little pins and enrolled on the roster. This spurred the children on. We were all fired up. We decided we would climb Snowdon on the first sunny day.

The next day the sun was brilliant. This was it. We left Andrew at the inn with my mother-in-law, and at 10:15 A.M. we stood beside the PYG track sign and had our picture taken.

We began to climb slowly, too slow for the older children. But just right for the little guys. We stopped often. Took it easy and patiently. When we got married my wife, Marcella, and I decided that our kids would have to enjoy hiking because it is such an important, vital part of our lives. With the children, we have altered our manner of hiking, gearing it down to the smallest walker in our party. We always try to be patient with the littlest one on any hike, try never to scold him, try to make it fun. This hike, our smallest was William. And he was great. He hardly complained until we started up the Zig Zag Trail on the headwall of the cirque between Snowdon and Crib-y-ddysgl mountains. From that point on we had to pamper him. We took turns, first Marcella, then I. We had a pocketful of candies for just such a time. After many hours, we managed to coax him to the top of Snowdon on his own two feet.

At the top there is a snack bar. There is also a cog railway station for the train that comes up the mountain from the other side. We took a long refreshing break, then started down. Going down took a lot longer. William's legs got very rubbery, and each time we stopped to rest he would immediately fall asleep. I began to feel like a criminal for having brought him along on such an extended hike. He and Katie, though, were even amusing in the last stretches. Every few minutes they'd say, "Daddy, I gotta get." I'd say, "Get what?" And they'd reply, "I gotta *get rest*." At 8:45 P.M. we reached the road in the town of Llanberis on the other side of the mountains.

The children were too tired that night for the celebration so it was held the following evening in the Guest's Taproom in the hotel. Then, I knew it had been worth it, for the children were overjoyed with pride in their accomplishment.

We made several other hikes after that. But the highlight for me was the rock climbing. Colin Dickinson, the assistant manager of the Pen-y-Gwryd, volunteered to take me climbing. He is head of the Mountain Rescue team in Llanberis and also a guide.

We climbed a few of the famous routes such as those on Milestone Buttress and the Idwal Slabs. On the latter Colin took me up a classic route known as Tennis Shoes — but with a more severe variation. It was probably the most difficult climb I have ever done, and it made me quite respectful of the "polished" British rock.

On one of these rock climbing days I had the most enjoyable time I have ever spent in the mountains. I had mentioned to Colin one evening in the Pen-y-Gwryd's pub, which is the watering spot for rock climbers in that area, that I was going to climb Mount Trefan, one of the most beautiful mountains in Snowdonia. He offered to plan a rock climbing route up Trefan if I'd wait to go on his day off. How could I pass up a proposition like that?

It turned out to be a perfect day in every respect — sunny and mild and not terribly windy. I had come to enjoy Colin's company a great deal. Our relationship was one of those rare experiences of perfect rapport; our pace of climbing was harmonious. I did not want to climb fast. Rather, I liked to linger with each pitch and embrace the sun-warmed rock. At my age, I greatly enjoy the sensuousness of rock climbing far more than the challenge of difficulty. Nevertheless, I allowed Colin to lead me up the most difficult route on one side of Trefan, and then we traversed across its shoulder to climb the most difficult route on the other side — altogether, about 1,000 feet of difficult rock climbing. Trefan isn't a very high mountain, and the weather was so perfect, there was no reason to hurry. After each pitch we lingered on the belay points, absorbing the beauty.

As we were resting on the summit, eating a piece of chocolate, I had the feeling of actually being high from drinking, though we hadn't had a drop of alcohol. I was giddy. I felt a glow inside, a light-headedness, a perfect peace. It is for moments like that that I go to the mountains. And these moments remain with me long after the climb is over.

That being my final day of climbing, it was a splendid finale. Looking back, I can see that the trip actually grew from the first easy ramble on country lanes in the Lake District, picking up in difficulty, interest, and challenge with each ensuing day of hiking, until I stood on top of the two pillars, Adam and Eve, on the summit of Trefan.

In the course of the trip, I learned a lot of ways to make the most of a family hiking expedition, more ways than I knew beforehand despite 11 years of family hiking.

I learned not to plan to do too much. To plan to travel very short distances and to stay at the same inn or campsite for at least a week. This has several advantages. It gives the children a feeling of security to return to the same bed every night. It is less troublesome and time consuming because it saves hours of packing and unpacking. It gives you an opportunity to wait out the weather so that you are sure to be able to get in the hikes you most want to do. And to take it easy. Going at the slower pace that my children require actually leads to increased enjoyment, for I see a lot more and absorb a lot more than I ever have done before. ✎

TO THE TUNE OF ROLAND'S HORN

by BARBARA PETERS

Family Hiking in the Pyrenees

In Europe there is very little backpacking—but a lot more hiking than there is in the U.S. The best way to go is the way the Europeans do it— enjoying the trails by day and the camaraderie of an inn at night. It's a nice way for a family to hike. And while the Peterses did it with their young children in the Pyrenees, some of the same pleasures are available closer to home, as the articles by Allan Pospisil and Lesley Wright-Barker point up.

W.K.

The sympathetic stranger knew instinctively we were in trouble.

"How much does the rucksack weigh?" he asked, pointing to my husband's pack. "Thirty or thirty-five pounds," I answered, not wanting to make it sound too heavy. As my two young children and I huddled together on the cold bare rock in the gray twilight, the good Samaritan issued orders. "François, take this backpack. Marie-Claude, the little girl's pack. Dominique, the young lad's pack." *"Oui, Monsieur L'Abbé,"* they obediently answered. Then off we went, up the steep incline over the glacier in the dimming light. Part way up, we met my husband, Bruce, returning from an exploratory hike to tell us it would be too difficult a climb. But we were now in safe hands. Our newly found friend turned out to be a Bordeaux abbé on a mountain-climbing holiday with 34 of his young parishioners, aged 14 to 25.

We arrived at the Refuge de la Brèche de Roland in record time. Our efforts were rewarded with a gourmet dinner, the first we had ever had in a high-altitude refuge—rich beef soup, roast lamb with roasted potatoes, buttered fresh carrots and string beans, a pale yellow local mountain cheese, a chewy crunchy fresh-baked loaf of bread—all flown up by heli-

copter from the valley. It was especially appreciated after our meager lunch of leftover bread and ewe's cheese, and a frugal Spanish breakfast which had been hardly enough to sustain us through an eight-hour hike up the mountain from the Spanish town of Bujaruelo, over the pass of Boucharo at the French border, and up to the French refuge.

We felt content and serene that evening as we chatted with the abbé and the young students and teachers. Our children, Andrew, 11, and Claudia, 8, played chess with the younger members of the group. The elusive goal of our trip—the pass called Roland's Breach—was not only in sight but approachable.

The next morning, Bruce and I climbed over the glacier to the Breach, while the children opted for a morning at the refuge. Andrew had learned from the abbé that several members of the youth group did not plan to go rock climbing that morning. Instead they spent the day playing chess, making soup and baking a cake. After having walked more than eight hours each day for almost a week, we could hardly blame Claudia and Andrew for their choice of activities. They are definitely not goal-oriented; they live in the present.

Our family plans our hikes

with a specific objective in mind. On this trip in the Pyrenees, from France into Spain and back to France, we were following the legend of Roland.

I became interested in the story of Roland while I was in college. Our class read the fascinating narrative, *The Song of Roland*, in French and I never forgot it. Written anonymously about 1100, it relates in verse the story of a late eighth century Christian crusade against the Saracens, the infidel invaders from North Africa.

The narrative tells how King Charles of France (crowned Charlemagne in 800) freed all of Spain from the Saracens except the realm of Marsile in Zaragoza in northern Spain. Charles sent Ganelon, the jealous stepfather of Count Roland, the king's nephew, to make a peace pact with Marsile.

Wishing for the death of Roland, the treacherous Ganelon made a deceptive peace plan with Marsile. He told Marsile that Roland was keeping King Charles in Spain. If Roland were dead, the king would no longer trouble Marsile. Ganelon then arranged for Roland to be in charge of the rear guard of the French army. After telling Marsile of the army's strategic plans, he along with King Charles left Spain by way of the pass above Roncevaux.

Roland remained behind as commander of the rear guard. Marsile broke the peace and tried to kill Roland. Despite the wise urgings of his friend Archbishop Turpin, Roland refused to call for aid. But he finally relented and lifted his horn to sound the call of alarm. King Charles heard it but was convinced by Ganelon that it was only a hunter. As Roland lay dying from various wounds and from a broken blood vessel in his temple, caused by forceful blowing on the horn, he vowed that his sword, Durandal, would not be captured. He tried to break it, but in vain.

The legend has a just, if not a happy, ending. Charles arrived as the Saracens were retreating, and God had not forgotten his good deeds in Spain. That evening the sun did not set but lit up the sky, allowing Charles to go in hot pursuit of the Saracens and to vanquish them.

Before our hiking trip, we read the story of Roland and listened to a recorded account of the legend which I had borrowed from the neighborhood library. We ordered several detailed maps of the western and central Pyrenees, but they never arrived. "Let's take a chance. We're bound to find them on the spot in a mountain village," Bruce philosophized. A hometown bookstore had some good small-scale maps. We took off—small-scale maps in hand, just in case.

The Roncevaux Pass crossing began in Saint Jean Pied de Port, a tiny French Basque mountain town with an old walled section dating back to the fourteenth century. Our first attempts at orientation were a complete fizzle. If we had known then that it was to be only number one of a whole flock of fizzles, we probably would have quit before we began.

We knew we shouldn't take small children into the mountains without a large-scale map. Presumably, we would get such a map at a tourist office. But on a Thursday we discovered that the only bus to Val Carlos, where the nearest tourist office was located, ran on Wednesdays. We took a bus instead to the border town of Arneguy and walked to Val Carlos. An erratic rainstorm accompanied us the whole way. The trip was a waste of time: the Tourist Office had an interminable lunch hour which forced us to give up.

Back in Saint Jean, we discov-ered a tiny booklet describing the old Roman road over the Pyrenees which had been used by everyone, from Roman soldiers to a French princess on her way to marry a Spanish noble, until hard-surfaced roads were built less than a hundred years ago. To our delight, the booklet's author, Jean Etchevers, lived in town. The chef-owner of our hotel was a friend of his and arranged a meeting. For a delightful hour we discussed our projected walk over the mountains to Spain, learning details of the route. Our excitement mounted—imagine the thrill of following in the footsteps of Roland and Charlemagne on an ancient Roman road!

The next morning after the children's favorite breakfast—buttery, flaky croissants with strawberry preserves—we hailed a taxi for a quick trip out of town. Finding one's way in the Pyrenees is quite a challenge. There were no signs, cairns or directional indicators, and no other travelers going our way. Even with a compass and the details filled in on our map by Mr. Etchevers, we could not determine which unmapped side path to follow down to the valley. Use one's own best judgment? We tried that and landed in Val Carlos. Fizzle.

Fortunately, a willing taxi driver drove us to Roncevaux on another part of the mountain. We consoled ourselves with the thought that if we had not taken a wrong turn, we would have missed seeing one of the prettiest valleys in the Pyrenees. From high on the mountainside, yellow-blue-green farm patches looked like a beautiful velvety quilt, designed with neat white farm houses and thin-spired churches.

In Burguete, a private home

Following the ancient Roman road over the Pyrenees.
PHOTO: BRUCE PETERS

with a cobblestoned entry way offered us spartan but immaculate accommodations for less than four dollars. Dinner at the inn across the street was very simple but good: six dollars for four including wine and especially good caramel custard.

We spent the next day exploring the monastery of Roncevaux (or Roncesvalles) and the field above—the site of Roland's last stand. Our wanderings took us past the ossuary where his bones are kept. Inside the monastery, we came upon a convocation of priests from far-flung parishes, handsomely dressed in red chasubles, chanting prayers in the candlelit sanctuary. Upstairs, in a tiny, locked treasure room, gold-encrusted vestments and bejeweled church vessels shone from glass cases. Three thorns on display were from Christ's crown, we were told.

Frustrating as the first leg of our trip had been, we were too deeply committed to the history and legend of Roland to quit. We were only 60 miles west of the famous Breach. Torla, a small, centuries-old village near the entrance to the National Park of Ordesa, would be our jumping-off spot.

We were told that to get to Torla we had to take a bus from Sabiñánigo. Two tourist offices and a hotel manager gave us specific itineraries of the buses. Simple. We went to the train station as instructed and found several buses, all going somewhere else. The officials in the train station said buses were not their bailiwick. We finally learned from a knowledgeable bus driver that the bus from Sabiñánigo to Torla had not run for three years. Fizzle No. 3.

Matters would have been even worse had I not been fluent in Spanish. A person not knowing the language would certainly do better renting a car. Transportation facilities in these remote places are few and far between. In larger cities, one meets many English-speaking people, but not in out-of-the-way places. I got a good workout as an interpreter in the villages.

By the time we got into the mountains, the sheer beauty of the clouds of wildflower patches helped us forget about the high cost of getting there. The yellow flowers called *alicones,* our driver told us, are favorites of the grazing sheep; the

pretty yellow blossoms called *mantanillas* are supposedly a very effective headache cure. The lurching of the taxi around hairpin turns and the frequent blaring of the horn made me want to stop to gather blossoms to munch on during the remainder of the 27-mile serpentine drive.

From Torla, a six-hour round-trip hike to the park through the woods served as an orientation. We spent the evening studying detailed maps with seasoned hikers at the Bella Vista Hotel. Rooms were about $1.60 each, and dinner ran from $4 to $5 for all of us.

Claudia and I, the shoppers, made the rounds of bakery and grocery the next morning and bought calories for the hike. Following the advice of our friends at the hotel, we by-passed the woods, saving time by taking yet another taxi to the entrance of the National Park of Ordesa. We were then on our own for the eight-hour hike to Goriz, the refuge high in the mountains.

The national park has a long, narrow canyon similar to Yosemite. The canyon's granite sidewalls are spectacular jagged cliffs which in sunlight take on a rose-golden-silver hue. The valley was formed during the Pleistocene epoch by the slow action of an advancing glacier which caused massive erosion of the sidewalls and floor, resulting in the characteristic U-shape.

On the lower pathways, beside the Arazas River, we joined groups of hikers on a morning's jaunt to see the Horse's Tail, a spectacular cascade named for its shape. A half-dozen cascades indicated that we were definitely going uphill. One particularly high cascade being blown by the wind looked like a crystalline lace wedding veil. Common wildflowers and thistles led the way up the increasingly steep path to a final wide flat section of the valley. It was then time to zigzag up the steep sidewalls. Edelweiss poked its velveteen pointed flowers and razor-sharp leaves out of crevices on the rocky slope.

We found the refuge at Goriz a welcome sight after our exhausting hike. The congenial atmosphere made us overlook the rather uninviting dining area with its cluttered tables, and that black hole of Calcutta which served as a bathroom. Goriz was the

first hotel we came across in northern Spain that wasn't spotless.

We were glad to leave the next morning for the Breach. All went well until we arrived just below the snowfield and the ice cave of Casteret. There we were stymied. We had no ropes, crampons nor ice axes, and we were faced with a steep snowy slope with a path across it only wide enough for one foot. Even if we had found a way around the field, the climb on the other side up to the pass was equally treacherous—steep dirt slopes with abundant piles of loose rock. At the top, just below the pass was a narrow crossway with fixed pitons and rope, attesting to the difficulty of the climb. Turning our backs to the Breach, we headed back toward the refuge and spent a rainy night there. Fizzle No. 4.

The scenery in the canyon during and after the rain was even more beautiful than it had been in the sunlight two days before. The rocks, covered with a lead-gray glaze, shimmered in the haze. At the foot of the zigzagging path we met a shepherd who told us about his sheep, how he trained his dogs to herd and about life in the mountains. We declined to share his lunch of cheese and bread, but gratefully gurgled down some good wine from his goat-skin bag. Andrew was surprised that he too was offered wine. As we said good-by, the shepherd presented me with a full bunch of edelweiss.

Back at the restaurant at the entrance to the park, we gathered energy on a tortilla sandwich (a Spanish western) and a cool beer and tried to figure a way out of the latest dilemma. It would take three hours to walk to Bujaruelo, and we had already walked five.

The next morning we tried a more accessible pass which took us back through France, over a glacier and finally to the impossible 9,210-foot Breach. The forceful rushing Ara River seemed to be in a hurry to make the gorge deeper and steeper.

Hot and exhausted, we rounded a corner of the road leading into the village of Bujaruelo about six-thirty that night. In the distance were only two buildings and an ancient church in ruins. The whitewashed building was clearly the headquarters of the Civil Guard. Could we stay at that other rather dilapidated building? Oh, no. Fizzle Number Five? But this time we were lucky. It turned out to be a centuries-old farmhouse converted into an exceptionally clean hostel. The food was well prepared, spicy and delicious.

We had been assured it was only a three-hour walk to the pass and another hour to the French refuge, so there seemed no sense in having a lunch packed at the hotel. After a small breakfast, we were on our way. Six hours later we realized that some people travel faster than others. At 7:30 P.M. we enjoyed our first substantial meal of the day.

This brings us back to the start of our story when one very good Samaritan found us alone and discouraged, and made all things seem possible to us. After the joy of making the Breach and absorbing the view to satisfaction, we rejoined the children at the refuge and savored a piece of Claudia's cake.

We bade farewell to the abbé and our French friends as they took off after lunch to climb one of the surrounding peaks. We headed downhill to tackle our final project—photographing the dozen waterfalls plummeting 1,500 feet from the Gavarnie Cirque.

The trail down the mountain from the French refuge is called The Staircase. Ropes would not have been out of place. Holding the children's hands over difficult spots or lowering them where steps were farther apart than legs were long slowed us down a bit. But it didn't matter. The clouds were high in the sky. There was still lots of picture-taking time. Suddenly I heard a scratching, then a rumbling of rocks. I looked behind and painfully watched my daughter's rucksack tumble down the mountain. Oh well, what was one more fizzle?

An hour and a half later, after climbing up and down giant boulders that for some crazy reason all looked blue and green plaid, we found the rucksack.

We finally arrived at the base of the falls in time to get a marvelous view—the only one we would have. By the time we backed off enough to get photos of the 12 falls in all their splendor, an ugly cloud sat right on top of them. Fizzle No. . . . I've lost count.

But experience on this trip taught us one thing: fizzles can be fun . . . eventually. This was no exception. We took so long getting down that our friend the abbé and followers caught up with us. An invitation to their chalet led to a superb dinner, folk singing and a peaceful night.

In the morning, the abbé drove us to Lourdes to catch our train. As his car flew in space above the roadway, my only thought was, "We can't possibly die in his hands . . . but, if we do, we shall without a doubt go directly to Heaven."

At the end of our trip, we began to wonder about the wisdom of planning a trip at all. Everyone knows that unplanned events are always more fun. Fizzles, we discovered, are simply a change in plans. The children agreed. "Going from one country to another on foot is o.k.," they concluded, "but what we really like is just walking around." ❧

GRAND MANAN

A Walk with Bed and Board

Article by ALLAN POSPISIL

Tucked into the Bay of Fundy eight miles off the coast of Maine, the New Brunswick island of Grand Manan offers country roads, seashore scenery, and comfortable accommodations to the walker who, like the hiker, disowns mechanized travel—but not civilization.

WE COULD HEAR THE ISLAND before we saw it—a queer electric whistle sounding a high thin echo to the traditional bass blast of the ferry. The ship's horn began blowing about 30 minutes out, and its first powerful note took the boys by surprise—they had been fooling around on the forward deck, just beneath the speaker—and sent them scurrying inside, hands clapped over their ears. They found me sitting with a gnarled and elderly man who tended the fires in one of the smokehouses on the island. Through bites of his cheese sandwich, which he ground between his gums, he told me that the island fishes for herring, smokes herring, and lately has been selling most of its herring to Poland.

"Can't say why," he said, "but they're paying the best now. Been smoking herring all my life; should be retired but I ain't. Some young fellows started a smokehouse a while back, had troubles. So I'm working it now. You going through Grand Harbour?" I said we were, in a day or two. "Well, you stop in, I'll show you around. Talk to anyone on the island," he said, "ask them anything. Everyone's friendly."

THERE WERE 31 CARS on board—the boys had counted—and no room for more. It was Sunday, and there is only one ferry from Black's Harbour, New Brunswick, to Grand Manan, somewhere ahead in the fog. To the island's west lay Grand Manan Channel and the coast of Maine; to the east, the Bay of Fundy and Nova Scotia.

None of the cars on board was ours. The plan—my plan, really, the boys stuck with it—was to walk Grand Manan, some 20 miles long by road and beach and trail, 15 by crow flight. We would be self-propelled but not self-sufficient. I was not above relying on what limited commercial hospitality—inn, hotel, cottage—the island offered. Indeed, I counted on it, and our packs were lighter for the things we didn't have to carry—tents, sleeping bags, food and cooking gear.

The two boys were excited and enthusiastic. But what if the fog condensed into something more liquid, or if they found the walking—four days of it, from one end of the island to the other and back—too dull?

Craig, my son, was 13 and certainly strong enough for the hike, but his eagerness became genuine only when I suggested inviting a friend. Brand Livingstone was 12 and robust, but when he said yes, he didn't ask how far we would walk, he just wanted to know would Craig be along.

WHEN WE WALKED ON BOARD THE FERRY at Black's Harbour the sky was merely overcast. Halfway there, the overcast fell to the sea. I knew of Grand Manan's tendency to shroud itself in fog, had been warned that the island was often dismally blanketed for days, and wanted to experience something of that. The forecast was for clearing weather the following day and maybe the day after.

We walked off the ferry into the village of North Head, Grand Manan's main port. Most of the island's fishing fleet ties up there.

On foot we made for the Marathon Hotel, hardly a half-mile from the landing. It was a several story Victorian affair, built in 1871, and with the fog swirling about I could imagine no cozier accommodation. Dinner was at six, giving us three hours to explore. We broke out raingear and headed for Swallow Tail, a point of land near North Head but practically pinched off from the island. There was a lighthouse there, the source of that strange electric whistle.

Swallow Tail is reached by a narrow wooden bridge high over a gorge that falls away nearly to sea level, the bridge like a stitch clasping the point to the main body of land. From the bridge we could see only as far as a path leading up a grassy slope. As we walked up the path, first a shed, then a residence and at the end of a boardwalk the lighthouse itself came into view. The sea, gray like the fog, lay at the edge of rock cliffs.

We clambered over the cliffs to throw stones into the sea. We followed paths that wound through wet grass leading to more cliffs. Everything was moist green and gray, all blends and no edges. Even the whistle sounded blurred and so did the occasional muted chug of marine diesel engines passing by on the water. They sounded so close we stood and stared into the fog after them, but never saw one.

There was time to walk part of a wooded trail from Swallow Tail to Whale Cove, and we came across the Grand Manan version of a trail blaze—a lobster trap with a splash of red paint.

We stood later on the wharf at North Head. The last of the herring seiners was just leaving. Out every Sunday, back by Friday—that's the rhythm to which the island moves, year-round in almost any kind of weather. It was pleasant to be standing on the wharf in the softness of the fog, watching the last boat disappear into it; better, we thought, than being a fisherman and watching the wharf disappear.

For dinner the Marathon Hotel stuffed us with roast beef, fiddleheads, mashed potatoes, hot apple pie and ice cream. Later we settled in a comfortable living room, and I browsed through the library. What better entertainment on a damp night than the bookshelves of an inn where the collection leans toward local history? On Grand Manan that meant shipwrecks, and I read about the schooner *Lord Ashburton*, which was bound for St. John in a winter gale in 1857 but found the rocks of Grand Manan instead; 21 men died.

A heavy rain began to fall, and the hotelkeeper said that in the previous month, July, there had been 20 consecutive days

After a real breakfast—not granola and powdered milk—the author's son Craig and friend Brand Livingstone continue their trip south along the island's eastern coast and through Seal Cove.
PHOTO: ALLAN POSPISIL

of fog.

Sometime in the night a single crack of thunder shook me awake, and I listened awhile to rain rattling on the roof. The boys slept on. I did not yearn for a sleeping bag and tent.

GRAND MANAN IS ALIGNED on a north–south axis, and although the island is narrow—five miles at the broadest point—it is, geologically speaking, a split personality. Sea level on the eastern shore is a succession of beaches and mud flats, coves and harbors. All of the island's 3,000 residents live along this mostly hospitable coast. By contrast, the island's west side, including the northern and southern headlands, is a forbidding place. Spectacular cliffs with organ-pipe faces rise 200 to 400 feet from the water, capped by thick dark forest. No one lives on this side of the island. There are no roads paralleling this coast.

Our itinerary kept us to the villages along the east shore where we could find accommodations and meals. Each day we walked at least eight miles to our next lodging, and as the days progressed so did we, quickening our pace. On the first day,

from North Head south to Grand Harbour, we started out in a drizzle and wearing rain suits. But the drizzle quit, the clouds thinned and we gradually shed our rain pants and jackets. Since we were walking through civilization we partook of its pleasures, stopping for bottles of Orange Crush pulled chilled and dripping from grocery coolers.

The entire time we were in sight of the sea. The tide was out, exposing long reaches of mud. We walked by homes where women were tending prolific flower gardens. Virtually every yard had some flowers—color to store up against the days of persistent fog.

And we were offered lifts, enough so that we began a count. Number Four was a minister who asked, "Are you still enjoying your walk, or would you like a ride?"

"We'll walk on a bit," I said and he suggested a turnoff just ahead which would take us to the shore. "I often walk there," he said. "You'll like it." The shore route took us into the village of Woodward's Cove by the back door and brought us the first rich odor of herring being smoked.

We reached our lodging, the small Grand Harbour Inn, in midafternoon. The next day, hiking just as far to a cottage a couple of miles past Seal Cove, we flew. Sometimes Craig set the pace, sometimes Brand, but it was fast enough so that by noon we were unlocking our door. That was the halfway point; the next day we would turn around and walk north. Although there was some backtracking to do, there were enough alternate routes so that it would be unnecessary to retrace our paths step for step.

After we checked in at the Grand Harbour Inn, I dropped the boys at a municipal swimming pool close by. The sun was strong now, and I walked on a bit.

My informant on the ferry had spoken of the friendliness of the island people, and as I strolled along proof appeared. A man plowing a fallow field by the side of his house hopped off his tractor when he saw me approach. He stuck out a hand and said, "How do you do? I'm Gordon Foster. It's a beautiful view, isn't it? Least it is when the fog lifts. That's Ross Island, and over there, White Head Island. On a good day you can see Nova Scotia from this hill. It's 40 miles, but you can see it."

Mr. Foster squinted in the sun, looking for Nova Scotia, and pointed out some other landmarks—lighthouses, offshore islands, the distant Gannet Rock and lighthouse.

"I was game warden here for some years," he said, "and maybe just a bit of an outlaw." Smiling, "Takes one to catch one, they figured. Besides, I knew the island better than anyone. There's some deer on the island, ducks, partridge . . . but they're annihilating them. Any time you come by again, stop in for a cup of tea." And he went back to his tractor and his crop of stones.

THERE'S A SMALL MUSEUM in Grand Harbour, and an old log from the Gannet lighthouse lay open to the entry of exactly 100 years earlier—August 18, 1876. The keeper had reported a light west wind at midnight, the air clear after five days of fog; but at 5:00 A.M., fog again, the wind variable.

From our cottage below Seal Cove we made for the very southern tip of the island and its lighthouse. The marked contrast between the two coasts of Grand Manan begins at South Head, and we found ourselves on a high open perch, able to see for the first time the tall cliffs standing away to the north. We walked carefully, for the trail skirts the very edge of the cliffs; waves washed against them 200 feet below.

We faced a long hike of three to four miles back to the cottage, but found some diversion at a small cove where we stopped to watch three seals swimming

SIDEPOCKET

Light information on Grand Manan to tuck into the sidepocket of your pack.

MAPS

Topographical maps on Grand Manan are available from: Canada Map Office, Department of Energy, Mines and Resources, 615 Booth Street, Ottawa, Ontario K1A OH3, Canada.

FERRY INFORMATION

The ferry for Grand Manan leaves from Black's Harbour, New Brunswick. For a schedule, contact: Coastal Transport Limited, P.O. Box 26, St. John, New Brunswick, Canada (506 657-3306).

NOTES, NAMES AND A MUSEUM

The island's name is the French derivative of the Indian word *menane,* meaning "island place," which first appeared on a map drawn by Samuel de Champlain

in 1607. Over the years the island has been claimed by France, Great Britain and the United States. In 1817 claims were settled, and the United States deeded the island to England in exchange for Moose Island, Maine.

John James Audubon probably was Grand Manan's first tourist. In 1833 he went there to study the island's birds, a fine collection of which may be seen at the Grand Manan Museum, operated by the Historical Society, in Grand Harbour.

The birds on display were not picked randomly; only those that actually visit Grand Manan are displayed. The island's life list numbers more than 275 species, so the collection is sizable. Lobstering is important to the island (although in Canada the season is closed during the summer), and the museum has mounted a small replica of a workshop that makes lobster traps. Traps are shown at successive stages of construction. A portion of the museum is devoted to the study of local geology. Since a fault line divides the dissimilar east and west coasts, there's a lot to learn.

The Historical Society's own magazine can be purchased at the museum; on sale, too, is a map of the island pinpointing the dozens of ships that have gone down off Grand Manan.

For more information on Grand Manan, contact: Tourism New Brunswick, P.O. Box 12345, Fredericton, New Brunswick E3B 5H1, Canada (506 453-2377).

close enough to a herring weir to be contemplating supper. Weirs surround Grand Manan; they can be seen from almost any point that overlooks the shore. Birch saplings driven into the muddy bottom in the shape of a lollipop form the frame from which netting is hung. A well-kept weir in a choice spot is a valuable asset, sold like real estate, willed from generation to generation. A 1939 map of Grand Manan, which I found in a New York library, locates and names 86 weirs—including Hardtack, Turnip Patch, Black Prince, King George, Grit, Try Again.

We cooked out that night, grilling hot dogs on the beach, telling ghost stories by the fire. Later I gave instruction in seven-card stud and blackjack.

On our way back through Seal Cove the next morning we paused to visit a herring cannery. Women chopped off heads and tails, packed the plump bodies three to a can, and slid the cans on trays in one swift move; the fish kept coming, the women kept chopping. Next door men were stringing whole "green" herring, slipping them one by one on long sticks, racking the sticks in a smokehouse, packing it nearly to the roof. In two months—kippers.

The boys enjoyed excursions like that, and so did I. Long hikes on the mud flats and scrambling along the rocks at the high-water line rated good marks, too. Along the paved roads, however, with cars flying by, fatigue became a factor, and the boys questioned my contention that the walking was more important than the arriving. By now, more than a dozen motorists had offered us rides. Stubborn, I refused them all. The last two miles back to the Grand Harbour Inn were marched in grim silence.

There, Brand had a choice. His mother and younger brother had arrived on the island—in a car—from their summer home in Calais, Maine, to visit neighbors vacationing on Grand Manan. He could stay with them in a seaside cottage near North Head, or hike on with us. I had in mind our longest day yet—a dash across the island to the west coast and back.

Brand decided: enough walking. Counting side trips and longer shoreline routes, he probably had made 25 miles in three days. Craig might have used Brand's departure as a wedge for his own defection, and I half expected some hints in that direction. But there were none ("I thought about it," he admitted later), so early the next morning he and I started off on a road that led across the island to Dark Harbour, the only real break in the long reach of cliffs.

By a little fancy rationalization I announced we would accept lifts now because we finally had a destination more important than the traveling. And the faster we got there the more we could poke around and look for other routes back across the island and to North Head. We didn't go so far as to extend our thumbs, but we managed two rides. Our second was in a pickup whose driver mentioned a trail, cut the previous winter, that followed the cliff line from Dark Harbour all the way to the Whistle, a lighthouse at the far northern tip of Grand Manan. That was the ticket, I thought. A long way around, but from the Whistle there was a road angling across to North Head.

A natural stone dike encloses Dark Harbour, which isn't a harbor at all. It's fed by a freshwater stream and a tidal flow that washes in and out over a spillway in the dike.

We ate a sandwich lunch and started off for the Whistle. The trail went straight up through a slope of shadowy spruce, but when we reached the top we came out in sunlight. We had an afternoon of unlimited visibility. Perhaps if we had been looking east we could have seen Nova Scotia. As we looked west, the Maine coast stood out clearly across seven miles of water, and far inland I could see the outline of Mount Katahdin. The view at our feet had some interest, too—the drop fell away as much as 400 feet to the water.

EVEN THOUGH WE WERE NEVER more than three miles from the roads and villages of the eastern shore, the places where we were walking could have passed for wilderness. We moved through thick forests, crossed running streams, picked wild raspberries and tramped across high openings where ferns grew waist-high. We skirted a beaver pond and watched an eagle soaring a hundred feet below us along the face of the cliffs.

I had thought two hours would bring us to the Whistle, but I hadn't counted on the trail detouring inland as much as it did to skirt sizable cuts where streams ran to the sea. After three hours Craig began to fade, but when we leaned out from one high lookout and saw the lighthouse a mile ahead, he shouted, "Civilization!" and loped the distance. From there it was still another three miles over an up-and-down road to a room for the night, this time a motel in North Head. It was a wearying walk—even with our two rides I estimated we had tramped ten miles—and we got just a bit silly, the way you do sometimes when the top of one hill reveals yet another hill to climb. But oh, did we finally eat and sleep!

THERE IS ONE CAMPGROUND on Grand Manan, called the Anchorage. Craig, Brand and I passed through on our third day, heading north. A couple of trailers were parked there and a few tents with four-door sedans stood by. Where did we fit, I wondered, in the hierarchy of campers and backpackers? Somewhere below the carry-your-own-food-and-shelter troops, yes; but in truth I didn't think of ourselves as backpackers. We were just out walking, following a path or road from village to village and inn to inn, steering a course that sought rather than avoided encounters with the ports of civilization. There is some historical precedent for that sort of travel (one thinks of English poets), not to mention at day's end those pleasing little touches that civilization can be so good at providing—hot water, soft beds and someone else to make the dinner. ☙

HIKE INN-TO-INN IN VERMONT

by LESLEY WRIGHT-BARKER

Lush eastern forests and fern-filled vales by day, gracious living by night? On 50 miles of the Long Trail, it's possible.

SCOTT SAID we ought to wear tweeds and bring a bottle of cognac. "Will it be that easy?" I asked my husband as our little Datsun truck wound up Vermont Route 17 toward the Appalachian Gap.

James grunted and shifted a finger toward the upper right-hand corner of the windshield. "See for yourself." Above us, in a long line reaching south, the mountains loomed—first General Stark Mountain, then Mount Ellen leaning northward against it, and Mount Lincoln in the distance. Their backsides were etched with three of the biggest ski resorts in Vermont: Mad River, Glen Ellen, and Sugarbush Valley. I wasn't at all sure it would be easy.

Although we were both familiar with backpacking, neither my husband nor myself was in the best of shape. Aside from a rare inspired jog, we'd done nothing in particular to prepare our bodies for this adventure, and it had been at least a year since either of us had done any extended hiking. Living in a small Vermont village and working at full-time jobs, we'd opted for just *looking* at the mountains. Finding a weekend or week to explore them was another matter.

But we were finally doing it—and in style. It was going to be, we had told our friends, a "pastoral experience."

The idea of trekking inn to inn is old and established, but there are only a few opportunities to do it in the United States. Hut systems exist in the Alps, Norway's Jotunheimens, the Himalaya, New Hampshire's White Mountains, and little bed and breakfast places in England.

In my lap lay a small yellow pamphlet titled "Hike Inn to Inn along Vermont's Green Mountain Trails." It listed six inns about 10 miles apart along the Long Trail. Our hike would cover 50 miles of the Long Trail, which follows the main ridge of the Green Mountains for 262 miles between Canada and Massachusetts. We would be walking from north to south. Each morning our truck would be ferried from the trailhead to wherever we planned to be by the end of the day. Our reservations covered dinner, bed, and breakfast, and there would be no 30-pound pack, no struggling to set up a tent, no worrying about damp sleeping bags. It would be a real vacation.

WE ARRIVED at Knoll Farm, our first inn, just before dinner on a Friday. From the road that climbs through the hill town of Fayston, near Waitsfield, we could see only a red barn and a great, sprawling eastern cottonwood tree. The sun was low behind us, and as we approached I felt as though we'd entered another era. A man and a woman were sunning themselves on the porch of the old homestead. To the right a group of children floated in a rowboat in the center of a spring-fed pond, and far off to the left beyond a clump of barns, a garden, and an old horse-drawn carriage, a group of Scottish Highland cattle stood grazing. Pastoral indeed.

Ann Heinzerling, the inn's owner and manager, greeted us, took our luggage, and led us to the backyard. "We're taking advantage of the weather," she said, directing us to a table piled with hamburgers, homemade baked beans, and green-tomato chutney. We sat at picnic tables with 12 other guests—a German couple who'd come here every summer for eight years, and a Swiss family who exclaimed how much like home it was, as they waved at the view of the Mad River and the White Mountains.

That evening we walked with Ann through the fields, where she introduced us to McTavish, the Highland bull, his Jersey girl friend, Nellie, and their shaggy calf. She took us through the century-old barn occupied by goats, carriages, a surrey with a fringe on top, and an old pony pung—a box-shaped sleigh on runners—which they used to get their Christmas tree each winter.

In our room, James and I sat up late, whispering—giddy with ourselves so

SIDEPOCKET

More information for hiking inn-to-inn in Vermont . . .

The six inns—Knoll Farm Country Inn, The Long Run, Chipman House, Churchill House Inn, Tulip Tree Inn, and Mountain Meadows Lodge—are about 10 miles apart along the Long Trail. Hikers can plan their own itineraries, including any combination of inns and any length of stay desired.

Reservations can be made through Mike Shonstrom, Churchill House Inn, RFD 3, Brandon, Vermont 05733. (802) 247-3300.

A typical trip, one night at each of the six nights, costs about $150 per person, double occupancy. That's an average of $25 per night, and it includes lodging, breakfast, dinner, and the transport of one's car from trailhead to trailhead. A deposit of $10 per person per night is required. The balance is payable as you visit each inn.

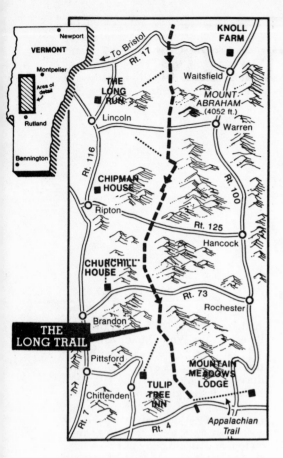

VERMONT — Newport, Montpelier, Area of detail, Rutland, Bennington

To Bristol · Rt. 17 · KNOLL FARM · Waitsfield · THE LONG RUN · MOUNT ABRAHAM (4052 ft.) · Lincoln · Warren · Rt. 116 · Rt. 100 · CHIPMAN HOUSE · Ripton · Rt. 125 · Hancock · CHURCHILL HOUSE · Rt. 73 · Rochester · Brandon · **THE LONG TRAIL** · Pittsford · MOUNTAIN MEADOWS LODGE · Chittenden · TULIP TREE INN · Rt. 7 · Rt. 4 · Appalachian Trail

---

From the summit of Worth Mountain we could see woods in all directions, patched here and there by a circle of houses or a cornfield.

IT HAD BEEN a long time since we'd hiked in deep woods, and we had to stop every few hundred feet to examine such things as a red-pocked mushroom or a spread of lichen. The first mile of trail climbed Stark's Wall, 1,000 feet up, and after that, Mount Ellen, one of the four highest peaks in the entire range.

I hummed to myself, knocked against trees, and revelled in being in dank woods again. I was content until I asked James, the water-bearer, for a drink. "Water?" he replied blankly. Being part camel, he hadn't thought to fill the canteen. "There *should* be streams," he said, "lots of them." There weren't, and I was thirsty. And thirstier. Half-parched, I lagged behind, mumbling that I was going bone-dry and might not make it another inch. Not another half-inch. Then James gave a yelp. And a splash. I found him half-way down a ski slope, knee-deep in a spring, munching on cheese and gorp. Saved. And forgiven—barely.

The Green Mountain Club, which maintains most of the Long Trail, hires caretakers to reside in key shelters along the way. They maintain a stretch of trail and try to educate passing hikers in ecologically sound camping practices. That day we passed three shelters: Stark's Nest, Castlerock, and Battell, and found Wayne Feiden, the caretaker of Castlerock, at home. "We do all kinds of things," he told us. "We build bridges and water bars, encourage people to stay in huts, and ask them not to build fires. Most people know that kind of stuff, but there are other things. The tundra vegetation on Mount Abraham, for instance." He pulled out a Green Mountain Club publication and showed us a list of endangered species, including bog bilberry and toothed cinquefoil.

By this time I was walking barefoot. I'd left the moleskins in the truck, and my heels were hurting in almost new boots. So I stepped gingerly, picking my way with a walking stick across the face of Mount Lincoln and over the fragile tundra of Mount Abe. James's feet, in two-year-old boots, were fine. His legs were buckling slightly, how-

ever, and I had trouble coaxing him down the nearly 2000 feet from the top of Mount Abe to Lincoln Gap.

We stumbled out of the woods at 8 P.M. We recovered quickly in the care of Jim and Genevieve Burke at The Long Run Lodge in Lincoln. They treated us royally, wining and dining us far into the evening. "Often dinner doesn't end until one," Genevieve told us. "We know it's been a good night when the candles are burned down to the nubs." They pulled their chairs up to our table to exchange stories and bits of gossip—oil spills and the price of bread, the Vermont steam train and local history. The lodge itself dated back to 1798. "It used to be a boarding place for loggers," Jim said. "And the old-timers still refer to it as 'The Olde Hotel.'" The walls around us were lined with bits of antique tools Jim had unearthed in the garden and pictures of former boarders who kept coming back. It wasn't hard to see why.

James and I retired at 11:30, full of wine and wondering if there weren't something very special about innkeepers. "They have to be teachers," Ann Heinzerling had said the night before. "They have to like people," Jim and Genevieve had told us tonight.

SUNDAY MORNING we woke at eight, downed a huge breakfast, signed the ledger, and walked with our hosts to their swimming hole in a nearby river. By the time we'd rounded up a tube of first-aid cream and a few sheets of heavy-duty moleskins, and followed the Burkes in our truck to the trailhead, it was noon.

The day's hike would be only seven miles, winding over the peaks of Battell Mountain and Mount Boyce and down a side trail to the third inn— Chipman House in Ripton. The temperature was in the eighties, and our bodies felt slightly more fragile than they had the day before. Nevertheless, we made good time until James, a few paces behind me, hollered that he had "a couple of knobby friends" screaming at him to stop. When I looked back, he had stopped. His knees were remembering all that walking down the backside of Mount Abe.

We lolled for a time. James photographed mushrooms and red berries while I chased toads. Then we hobbled down into the town of Ripton around 5:15.

I had often driven through Ripton

out of context. We knelt in front of the window screen and listened to the peepers, the stir of animals in the barn, McTavish and his family above us in the fields. The room, with its old pine floors and four-poster bed, had once been Ann's daughter's, and she'd named a certain elm on the eastern horizon, visible from this window, the "burst tree." Tomorrow, when it burst with sun, we'd start our trek.

"This summer only one couple's done the whole 13 miles to Lincoln," Ann warned us as we drove to Appalachian Gap Saturday morning. "The others found the trail too muddy or were caught by the dark and came down one of the ski slopes." We gulped. We'd had a long, leisurely breakfast, and it was nearly ten o'clock. The brochure offered sidetrails as an alternative to the long hike between the gaps in the mountains, but we hadn't thought we'd need them the first day. At the trailhead Ann pointed out wildflowers to look for—evening primrose and yarrow. We waved hasty goodbyes.

We woke to find Marion Shonstrom canning tomatoes and her husband Mike pummeling a heap of dough that would become French bread.

192

when I was a child, and the summer before James and I had bicycled in this area. But coming upon it from the mountains, with the sun low in the west and the village stretched along a river, it seemed a different place. It suddenly made sense that it had grown here where the mountains broke, one in a long line of mountain villages—Fayston, Lincoln, Goshen, Ripton. Poet Robert Frost had kept a cabin, still standing, near here, and had founded the Bread Loaf Writers' Conference in this town.

Chipman House spoiled us. Now run by Gina and Buddy Todd, the inn began as a large home back in the 1800s. It houses a restaurant open to the public as well as rooms. At dinner we were told we could choose anything (at no extra cost), so my husband promptly ordered escargots, prime ribs, Yorkshire pudding, and a bottle of Beaujolais. As chasers we each had three big hills of sherbet. It was fine fare for two muddy hikers.

Before going to bed, we strolled down the main street of the village past the one-room schoolhouse and the church. The night was soft and damp, and our bodies, though stiff in places, felt stronger and healthier than they had in a long while.

MONDAY'S HIKE was the nicest to awaken to. We were now physically capable and psychologically prepared to put one foot in front of the other in the sharp climb from Middlebury Gap to the first mountaintop of the day. "It's mind-state that's important," I kept reminding us as we leaned, puffing, against trees. "Mind-state and a staff." James refused to carry a walking stick though I swore it served as an invaluable third leg, pulling me up mountains and balancing me down. I even found sev-eral good used ones at the trailheads.

The trail began by crisscrossing the Snow Bowl ski area, then leading, marked by a series of white blazes, across the tops and hollows of five mountains, the highest 3300 feet. Although the air was still hung with mist, from the summit of Worth Mountain we could see a great spread of woods in all directions, patched here and there by a circle of houses or a cornfield. Someone at Knoll Farm had told us that 85 percent of Vermont is forested. Looking down from the spine of its highest mountain range, we could well believe it. That only 100 years ago 85 percent of the state was cleared and farmed and the remaining woods riddled with loggers seemed scarcely possible.

At Suckerbrook Shelter we ate lunch and drank deeply from a bubbling stream. James sniffed around for deer sign. So far we'd seen nothing bigger than a squirrel, though we often felt "watched," and most of the shelters we passed were pocked with teeth-marks of porcupines.

We met three hikers coming through Romance Gap, and at the top of Romance Mountain, at 3050 feet, we . . . well, it was the nicest stop we had.

The Long Trail guidebook describes this section as once exceeding "any region in Vermont for sheer wilderness." The leader of the six woodsmen who originally carved the trail through the forest crossed this region in 1912, and "all he could say was that he got through."

The trail has become a hiker's joy. It is lined with red spruce, balsam, and yellow birch. In places we found thick roots, long used as stairs, beginning to give under the constant pressure. We tried to step discretely over them, but then there were lichens, mushrooms, and mosses to worry about.

The trail was a continuous climb, up and down, crossing the peaks of White Rocks Mountain and Cape Lookoff. On the cliffs of Mount Horrid, the final peak of the day, we squatted to gaze down on the broad, sunlit sweep of an old beaver pond and Route 73 twisting through the gap. But the height made us queasy, and we scurried back to the trail, rejoicing to find our Datsun waiting at the bottom.

CHURCHILL HOUSE, the fourth inn, was four miles from the trail, toward Brandon. James and I had gone there on the eve of our wedding three months earlier, and it was then we'd first heard about hiking inn to inn. Mike and Marion Shonstrom, the proprietors, bought the century-old farmhouse four years ago and have painstakingly retained the colonial, woodburning elegance of its original owners. The rooms on the third floor had been converted from a ballroom. Mike led us to our room—the "blue room," in a corner of the second floor—and mentioned that we had just missed meeting four other people doing the same hike. "They came last evening," he said. "One couple from the north and one from the south, like ships passing in the night."

After baths and a candlelit dinner of risotto and veal, we sat and talked with two other guests. Tricia and John were from Massachusetts. John worked as a pilgrim on the *Mayflower* in Plymouth and moonlighted as a cockroach exterminator. He upset us with the news that, contrary to school-book history, Squanto the Indian had been a blackguard.

At dinner's end, Mike showed us home movies of another program possible between country inns. Cross-country skiers, poles flailing, bumped across the dining room wall. ("I was

James and Lesley have breakfast with Mike Shonstrom, owner of Churchill House and organizer of the inn-to-inn treks.

PHOTO: JAMES BARKER

skiing when I made this," Mike explained.) Marion slid into view, snowplowed to a stop, and stuck her tongue out at the camera. "Each inn supplies its own guides for a day. We supply a guide for the hiking program, too, but no one's seemed to need one." Indeed, half the joy is in wondering if you're lost.

Again we went to bed late, listening to the rush of the Neshobe River behind the house and the familiar rustle of animals in the neighboring farm. Our walk was more than half over, and now that our limbs had toughened and toned, we wished there were more than two days left.

We woke to find Marion canning tomatoes and Mike pummeling a great heap of dough that would become bars of French bread. Breakfast was lavish—cottage cheese pancakes and sausage—and our pattern of late starts continued. Each morning we were reluctant to leave. So many things were not explored: the knolls in Fayston, the Long Run's swimming hole, the dirt roads of Ripton, and the river behind Churchill House. Were we to do it over, we decided, we'd alternate a day of hiking with a day of poking around. But that would require more time and, of course, more money.

I was convinced, for some reason, that because we were heading south, we were heading downhill. In fact, the trail was getting smoother. On Tuesday we followed the contours of Farr Peak, Bloodroot Mountain, and Mount Carmel without traversing the peaks. The trail meandered through patches of fern and thick woods full of mushroom smells and over streams. We passed two shelters, Sunrise and Carmel Camp, and two more pairs of inn-to-inners trekking north. The trees opened into a view of the foothills running east, and we stopped to look. And munch. Great bunches of wildflowers blooming beside the trail filled the air with honey. We tried to memorize them for later identification.

AFTER SEVEN MILES we left the Long Trail for the New Boston Trail. After two miles of that, we found ourselves walking an additional and unexpected three miles on a dirt road. Our car was not where it ought to have been. Somewhere in those last three miles James and I struck up an argument. My feet began to ache. When we reached the truck I was in a bad humor. By the time we reached the Tulip Tree Inn in Chittenden, I was in a rage.

"Why was our truck parked so far down?" I snapped at Barbara and Gerry Liebert as they greeted us. "What d'ya mean the road's impassable? Because of a little pothole?" I stomped up to our room to soak my feet and mope.

But if an unexpected forced march brings out my temper, it also deprives me of the energy to stay angry. After a slice of Barbara's spinach pie, fresh corn on the cob, cantaloupe, and lemon mousse, my spirits improved. I apologized. By the time we'd gathered in the den, we all were feeling rosy.

James and another guest played chess while the Lieberts told stories of other hikers. "They come in all ages," Barbara said. "In shape and out of shape, some in sneakers, some experienced, and some not. We enjoy them all, and a few of them we worry about." I remembered the Burkes' account of two girls traveling south from Fayston to Lincoln who'd failed to appear. That night they'd gathered together a search party, but it wasn't until the next day that the missing hikers were discovered—in a restaurant in Middlebury, drinking beer. "We were damn concerned," Jim had said. "Anything could have happened to them."

The warmth of the fire, beer, and the ticking of numerous antique clocks all pointing out different times readied us for sleep. On the way upstairs, Gerry explained the inn's name. "We got it from a tulip tree in the garden of our former home. It had grown to symbolize a kind of family welcome. We've planted another one here."

Wednesday morning the Lieberts' son Daniel drove us in his '47 jeep to the Long Trail. This was, alas, our last day. We savored the walk, tredding smoothly over rocks and log bridges, up to our knees in fern. After five miles of easy walking we stopped at the Tucker–Johnson Shelter to chat with another hiker.

Like many people we'd met on the trail, John was there for the age-old therapy of walking without "worrying overmuch" about his destination. "For instance," he said, "there's a junction coming up soon where the Appalachian Trail heads off east to the White Mountains, and the Long Trail just keeps trucking down toward Massachusetts. When I get there, I'll surprise myself. Who knows where I'll be in a week?" The freedom of his plan was enticing. Already his beard was growing in, and the handle of his staff was neatly carved. His pack, however, was heavy. We shifted our light day-packs to our shoulders and, with a wave, headed off toward the junction. We knew exactly where we were going— to Killington. "Mountain Meadows serves dinner at 6:30," Barbara had reminded us that morning. And besides, we had two cats waiting at home.

AFTER TRUDGING A MILE and a half through Willard Gap and around the edge of Deerleap Mountain, we left the Long Trail and followed the blue blazes of the AT east. We'd heard that Mountain Meadows could sleep 90 skiers in the winter, and its location, near the Killington and Pico Peak ski areas, led us to expect a resort atmosphere, colder and more formal than the inns where we'd stayed. In fact, we considered not staying at all, immediately heading home instead.

We approached the lodge by following a series of little scrawled signs around the north end of a pond and over a river. White blazes led us through woods already turning into autumn colors, though it was only August, and we emerged to find the last little red-painted sign: "Bed, Bath, and Breakfast, $4.50."

That sign, we learned later, is legendary along the Appalachian Trail: a promise of home-cooked meals and hot baths to any number of worn and bedraggled "end-to-enders." The special price is for the "serious hiker" only. James and I, on this trip, did not qualify. Instead, for quite a bit more money, we got a private room with a bath.

We spent the evening with some of the finest people we'd met. How do Joanne and Bill Stevens have time to sit and talk for hours with strangers when they have all of Mountain Meadows Lodge, the largest of the six inns, to attend to? Somehow, they did. It was one of the mysteries of the trip. Long after dinner we were still at the hiker's table listening to anecdotes of other hikers who had passed through. Then we visited the Back-Behind Saloon, an old caboose turned tavern, back behind some buildings in West Bridgewater. It was another late night.

At breakfast we compared experiences with Joe and Jane Alper, who had come the same way we had. The peak of Mount Abe and the cliffs of Horrid. The thick foliage of the last two days and the warm welcomes of the innkeepers. The Alpers already were making plans to return.

It was noon when James finally nosed our truck onto the highway. It took us less than two hours to travel the distance we'd hiked in a week. If you ask me which way I'd rather go, the answer is easy. I'd rather walk. ◣

EXPLORING ST. JOHN ISLAND'S HIKE, SWIM AND SNORKEL TRAILS

by WILLIAM KEMSLEY, JR.

Covering two-thirds of the island is the Virgin Islands National Park, which also encompasses 5,650 acres of surrounding water, and offers some of the best diving in the world.

Sometimes the hiking is really incidental to a different kind of vacation. But if you've got to hike, you'll find some trails. It was to have been a typical Caribbean vacation spent in resort hotels and basking on beaches. Then the family discovered the island's hiking trails.

W.K.

I AM NOT MUCH OF A beach person. Broiling in the sun while the sand works its way into my swimming trunks bores me. In fact, my children cheer when they hear I'm going to spend a day with them at the shore, it's so rare. Give me mountains or canyons, anytime.

Occasionally, however, I give in to family pressure, and last winter my wife, Marcella, and I planned a family beach vacation to the Virgin Islands. We never considered the possibilities of backpacking and thought we would enjoy ourselves most from the convenience of a modern resort hotel on St. Thomas. If I were to be bored to death, I would do so in style.

When my children wanted to learn to snorkel at St. Thomas, I readily agreed to learn, too. I fidget after 15 minutes on the sand, so snorkeling seemed a way of passing the time. Besides, snorkeling is *the thing to do* in the Virgin Islands. As the interpretive ranger at the Virgin Islands National Park later said, "This is the second-best snorkeling area in the world. And since the best is on Australia's Great Barrier Reef, you might want to take advantage of the second-best while you're here."

We got masks, snorkels and fins from the dive shop and some instructions on how to use them. All of us, including seven-year-old Katie and six-year-old Will, learned quite fast, and we were soon ready for a dive.

Tourist literature recommended a "marine adventure on an underwater trail" in the Virgin Islands National Park on nearby St. John Island. I could not even imagine what that meant, but we ferried across to St. John, rented a jeep and headed for Trunk Bay.

While driving along the narrow, potholed island road, I began to realize that there was more to St. John than "marine adventures on an underwater trail." I had read about the island and the national park that covered about three fourths of it and knew the statistics: St. John is the smallest of the three most important U.S. Virgin Islands, just 20 square miles, and the least spoiled. Its beaches are beautiful. Its weather is incredibly balmy. Summer temperatures average only six degrees Fahrenheit warmer than winter temperatures, with barely a day going above 90 degrees or below 68 degrees. The island gets only 50 inches of rain a year. When it does rain, it almost never rains all day long. Usually a shower is followed by a lot of sunshine.

But these were clichés, good copy for a retirement brochure, but of no more interest to me when I first read them than the proverbial "marine adventures on an underwater trail." Driving across the island, however, my backpacker senses started to equate this flowery copy to the real St. John: here were intriguing tropical plants, trees and wildlife; historic ruins of Danish sugar plantation days; Arwak Indian relics, and breathtaking landscapes—all surrounded by clear, blue, calm water. I stopped fidgeting from boredom and started twitching from excitement.

WE SOON REACHED TRUNK BAY and donned our diving gear. From the very first trail marker, a bobbing red buoy, the trail was everything promised in the word *ad-*

venture. I went around the circular trail first with my 12-year-old daughter, Molly. At the first trail marker, Molly motioned for me to notice a big fish swimming near her. I watched it for a moment and when I turned my eyes back, was startled to find four of the big devils swimming underneath my stomach, less than a foot away. Hell, each was a good 18 inches long and fat and bold. Later I learned they were bar jacks, a harmless and good-eating species.

From that point on we had the entire fish watchers' course. We saw several varieties of parrotfish, yellowtail snappers, groupers, ferociously frowning trunkfish, beautiful blue and yellow damselfish, and many variously colored, delicate angelfish.

What attracted all these fish was the textbook garden of corals that the trail followed. There was a forest of wide-branching elkhorn coral interspersed with clusters of pillar and brain coral, lacy sea fans, sea whips and sea plums, and, in the deeper water, staghorn coral. And topping all this off was a series of descriptive signs, fastened to the ocean floor, to be read as we snorkeled along.

THE UNDERWATER TRAIL was the turning point of our vacation. You see, there are many beaches on St. John, each quite different from the other, and many of them can only be reached by a hike of some distance. To really enjoy all St. John has to offer, we would have to stay on the island for several days—and do lots of hiking. Thus, we checked out of our St. Thomas resort condominium and found more modest accommodations in the town of Cruz Bay on St. John.

We systematically hiked to and snorkeled at almost every public beach on St. John Island. Since the tropical sun devastated my winter-white flesh, we dove only in the forenoon and late afternoon, which left a large piece of the midday for hiking. That was fortunate, for we became modestly acquainted with tropical plant life and wildlife. Kapok trees, pearly-eyed thrashers, cute little bananaquits, antillean crested hummingbirds and that strange exotic, the mongoose, are a world apart from what we'd been used to seeing in our familiar Catskill Mountains of New York.

Although St. John is little more than five miles wide and nine miles long, it has wide differences in rainfall and, therefore, four distinct types of forest. An interesting feature is that in a two- to three-mile hike over easy terrain you can pass through all four zones—moist forest areas with bay rum, mango and teyer palm trees, dry forest areas with turpentine trees, wild frangipani, calabash and wild tamarinds, cactus woodlands with century plants, barrel cactus, prickly pears and dildo, which looks a lot like a Joshua tree, and shoreline mangrove swamps with sea grapes, red mangroves and button trees.

There is a short trail that pertains to slave life on the sugar plantations of eighteenth-century Danish colonial days, and a longer trail that leads to some unique petroglyphs carved in stone by African slaves, probably during the 1733-34 slave rebellion.

At present the petroglyphs, as well as some other sugar plantation ruins and nearly all the south shore, are accessible only on foot. It would be a tribute to the National Park Service to continue this policy, keeping this section of the park preserved for hikers, and not attempt to build paved roads.

Accommodations on St. John are very limited. There is the elegant Caneel Bay Resort with rooms for two at $155 per day, and there are national park campsites at $3 per day. Otherwise, there are fewer than 150 rentable accommodations for either resorting or camping on the entire island. Of these, some 40 units are cottages renting for $18.50 per day, and 40 units are fully equipped tents at $10.50 at the national park campground at Cinnamon Bay, which leaves some 51 rooms for rent in guest houses, private homes and a few small hotels. The latter are almost all in town at Cruz Bay, the only town of any size on St. John. We stayed in the largest of the hotels, The Serendip, with 10 rooms. It was far too expensive for what we got and far too noisy. There are 24 bars on St. John, one for every 100 men, women and children living on the island. There were bars in front and behind our room, and both had native bands which played late into the night—and very loudly. St. Thomas, for its far greater commercial development, was a good deal quieter.

Since the accommodations on St. John are so limited, you need to plan well ahead. The campgrounds, for instance, can be reserved nine months in advance, and during the busy season—December through March—they are almost always booked solidly no less than eight months ahead of time.

The park rangers told me that this

Will Kemsley totes his snorkel and fins along an island trail to Drunk Bay, an isolated beach at the south end of the island, just a mile from the road.
PHOTO: WILLIAM KEMSLEY, JR.

year a St. Johnian probably will open a new campground on private land inside the park. It'll be called Maho Bay Campsites. From a stateside hitchhiker we picked up on St. John we learned about another possibility: renting rooms in the local native homes. She had obtained a small cottage without plumbing facilities for $50 a week at the quieter end of the island, near Coral Bay. At present there are no facilities for overnight backpacking—only for day hiking. Lameshur Bay already has a resident park ranger. It would be a simple matter to mark off a few dozen primitive campsites with portable outhouse toilets—but not the flush toilets, showers, grocery store, bar and cafeteria of Cinnamon Bay campground—just one very primitive place reserved for overnight campers, where they would have to carry everything in as they do at the Bright Angel campground at the bottom of the Grand Canyon.

Although it might be possible to camp outside the park, the biggest problem would be water. You'd have to get the landowner's permission, as well as find the water, which is very precious because of sparse rainfall. Virtually none is available from pond, stream or spring. Most natives draw their water from cisterns, where rainfall collects, and Cruz Bay has to import an additional supply on tankers from Puerto Rico.

D ESPITE THE LIMITED MILES of trail (181) and the smallness of the island, St. John had sufficient variety to keep us interested for a longer time than we had for our vacations.

By hiking we were able to greatly expand our snorkeling horizons. First we took to the beaches closest to the road. (There are only 35 miles of paved road on St. John.) We tried Cinnamon Bay, Trunk Bay, Hawks Nest Bay, Maho Bay and Leinster Bay. Then we found our favorites, Salt Pond Bay and Drunk Bay, a mile's hike from the road at the far end of the island. There we were almost completely by ourselves. We could snorkel along one reef and then along another.

I discovered *The Fishwatcher's Guide,* the Peterson-like guide to underwater marine life. Incredibly, it was printed on waterproof paper, so we could carry it into the water with us and identify fish while we snorkeled.

In one way, snorkeling at St. John is like hiking in Arizona: you have to be careful where you step and what you touch. Everything seems to be prickly, poisonous or biting. Still, we were assured by park rangers that with sufficient caution we'd be safe. And that turned out to be so, even though we swam in waters only a few yards away from stingrays and barracuda and a few less intimidating species.

St. John has a lot of charm and much of the unspoiled beauty we love so much. Still, its isolation and lack of worldliness can throw you for a loss. If you're used to using credit cards for rooms or meals, you could get caught short, as we did, because virtually no one, not even the Chase Manhattan Bank sub-sub-branch, will honor them. It's strictly cash and carry. And prices for food and other commodities are very high because all supplies are brought over from the mainland via Puerto Rico and St. Thomas. But the inconvenience and making do is part of the experience, part of the charm.

We'll return to St. John for our children plead with us to go there again. To keep them backpacking with me in the mountains, I've had to agree to go with them to the shore once in a while. And wonder of wonders, I've found a shore activity that's as adventurous as mountain backpacking.

UNDERWATER TRAILS DIRECTORY

Hiking seashores and snorkeling are beautiful. Several opportunities now exist for these types of recreation. Here is how to obtain information:

Virgin Islands National Park. Trunk Bay Underwater Trail. Write to: Superintendent, Virgin Islands National Park, Box 806, St. Thomas, Virgin Islands 00801.

The Fishwatcher's Guide. Available in the Virgin Islands, but you may wish to obtain a copy to peruse before your trip (and to practice turning pages underwater). Printed on plastic, the book is waterproof and greaseproof and contains 23 color plates illustrating over 160 species of fish found in the western Atlantic coral reefs. *Fishwatcher's Guide to Western At-* *lantic Coral Reefs,* by Charles C.G. Chaplin, illustrated by Peter Scott, Livingston Publishing Company, Wynnewood, Pennsylvania, $5.95.

Buck Island Reef National Monument. This has a very famous underwater trail. There are no camping facilities nearby. Write to same address as Virgin Islands National Park (above).

John Pennekamp Coral Reef State Park. Underwater trail. Write to: Coral Reef Park Company, P.O. Box M, Key Largo, Florida 33037.

Channel Islands National Monument. An underwater trail is being developed at Cathedral Cove on Anacapa Island. The island has camping facilities and hiking trails. Write to: Superintendent, Channel Islands National Monument, 1699 Anchors Way Drive, Ventura, California 93003.

Grand Cayman Island (British West Indies). Rum Point Underwater Trail. There are also several guided snorkeling trips to sunken ships on the reefs. Write to: Cayman Islands Department of Tourism, P.O. Box 67, Georgetown, Grand Cayman, British West Indies.

Biscayne National Monument. Here there is a self-guiding interpretive boat trip for snorkelers. Four buoys are anchored to various reefs for boats to tie up to. Guidebooks and underwater maps of each reef are available so snorkelers can make undersea excursions from their boats. There is no underwater trail. Write to: Superintendent, Biscayne National Monument, P.O. Box 1369, Homestead, Florida 33030.

Haunauma Bay, Hawaii. This underwater interpretive area for snorkelers is less than 20 miles from downtown Honolulu. A kiosk on the beach provides information on where to go on the offshore reefs to view aquatic life. There is no underwater trail. Write to: Administrator, Division of State Parks, Department of Land and Natural Resources, Box 621, Honolulu, Hawaii 96809.

Okinawa. The Japanese currently are developing several underwater trails. Write to: Marine Parks Center, Toranomon Denki Building, 15 Shiba-Nishikubo-Akefune-Cho, Minato-Ku, Tokyo, Japan.

And there are more opportunities to come. The California Underwater Parks Advisory Board has recommended that four underwater parks be established at Salt Point, north of Point Reyes National Seashore, at Point Lobos (National) Reserve and Julia Pfeiffer Burns State Park, south of Monterey, and at Torrey Pines Beach State Park, north of San Diego. But it will be a while before any of these trails is established. Action has yet to be taken on the recommendations. ❧

SKI CAMPING WITH KIDS

by ANNE RICHARDS

The coup de grace of backpacking is winter backpacking. While Marcella and I have taken our children out many times day hiking in winter, and I've taken most of our children tenting in the backyard in snow and below-zero weather, we've never done what the Richardses have done. We're neither good enough skiers nor competent enough winter campers as a family to try it yet. The Richardses' advice seems very sound. When heading out into the snow with children, you can't afford to make mistakes—any mistakes.

W.K.

When a case of cabin fever attacked our Aspen home two years ago, we decided to mount our first ski camping trip for the entire family. Joining my husband, John, and me were our two daughters, Summer and Brooke—aged seven months and seven years—and our airedale, Chai. Quite frankly, we were not properly prepared, and that experience was a disaster. Educational, but a *disaster.*

We started out with too much equipment, enough to support a minor expedition, including a life-sized toy monkey which dangled from the bottom of the baby carrier. Within a half-mile I realized that skiing with a family load was far more restrictive and unstable than skiing with just my own gear. John discovered that skiing with an animated baby on his back plus 25 pounds of equipment was painful and precarious. He had to dodge low hanging branches to protect the baby's head, and an awkward spill was not comical because of the baby.

Heavy untracked snow, a series of inclines, improperly waxed skis and bulky loads turned the trip to our campsite on the T-Lazy Seven cross-country trail—only a 1½-hour walk from the trailhead in summer—into a four-hour ordeal.

At last John and I set up camp in the fading light. Both children demanded food. Summer was little trouble. I was her sole source of nourishment, and nursing presents few problems for mother or child, even in the snow. But Brooke would not wait patiently while John melted snow, boiled water, shuf-fled pots and rehydrated the freeze-dried dinner. After wolfing down soup and pork chops, we went right to sleep.

At 5:30 in the morning Summer awakened us, crying for breakfast. An hour later Brooke echoed her. We ate a hasty breakfast in the dark. It was still dark when we packed the gear and slipped off toward home.

We skied carefree for an hour, with Summer snoozing in her carrier and Brooke singing and striding out briskly. Then Brooke took a tumble, popped out of her binding and watched her ski disappear forever into an inaccessible ravine. Three hours later we arrived at the car, which a snowplow had surrounded with a two-foot mountain of snow. It was the perfect ending to a less than perfect trip.

Once home, John and I discussed what had gone wrong. Oddly enough, Brooke was willing to try it again. We spent the rest of the winter refining techniques, testing our equipment and devising a plan in family ski camping that works for us.

The blunders we made on the first outing were correctable; they were not the sort that would have endangered our lives or well-being. They taught us, however, that when heading out with small children in winter, one cannot afford to make mistakes—*any* mistakes. Without a thorough knowledge of ski touring, snow camping and winter survival techniques, anyone would be insane to take children along in wintertime.

We also became aware of the tre-mendous physical and emotional demands that a winter family trip places on parents and children. Not all families are suited for it, even if the members are veteran summer backpackers. Know thyself, and thy children.

John, Brooke and I were accustomed to skiing trips that would take us three to five miles from the car. With children along it is best not to go very far. With a baby, we go no more than two miles to a campsite. Flat terrain is preferable to the challenges of the mountains because level, wooded areas are safer and offer diversity. Children find panoramas boring.

So when the winter of 1977 arrived, we were determined to keep our family excursions realistic, short and safe. The winter turned out to be one of the driest seasons on record in Colorado. Despite meager snows, we were able to make eight overnight trips with both children. We chose Difficult Campground in the White River National Forest as our first destination, in early January. It was close to home, in familiar surroundings and only three-quarters of a mile from the parking lot.

A few days before departure we field-tested our gear in the backyard. We filled the packs as if we were headed out onto the trail, then skied around near home. Then we pitched the tent in the backyard, spent the night in it and in every possible way pretended that this was D-Day. The precautions enabled us to calculate our traveling speed and the amount of equipment we could handle comfortably.

The evening before our real trip we stacked our equipment by the front door, ready for an early departure. The morning was gray, with steadily falling snow, and we had to wait for assurance from the weather bureau that the weather would clear. Around 10 A.M., with high spirits and extra diapers, we departed.

Massive supplies of patience and flexibility are prerequisites for camping with children. Both virtues were tested the moment we entered the parking lot. Brooke bolted eagerly from the car, followed by the dog, who knocked down Summer and created general upheaval. While Brooke nagged us to unload her skis and backpack, we tried to soothe the screaming infant.

As I helped Brooke shoulder her pack, I recalled the day we bought it for her and the sense of importance and self-esteem it gave her. At eight, she now can carry up to 15 pounds. What a child can carry depends not only on physical attributes like size, strength and endurance but on personality, experience and mood. Brooke is especially pleased when she gets to tote the "special stuff": candy bars, flashlights, her sleeping gear and red cup, and the dog harness. She carries most of her reserve clothing, too.

After placing Summer in the baby carrier, we skied down the entry road. John, the strongest skier, carried Summer with 25 pounds of gear lashed to and stuffed inside the baby carrier.

We used a frame baby carrier. The sack is water-repellent nylon and allows easy entry to the storage compartments without removing the baby. The upper bars are well padded to prevent a bumped head or wet lips stuck to cold metal. The carrier has a hip strap and flip-open stand which, during rest stops, enables us to set down a sleeping Summer without having to find a tree to prop her against. There is plenty of room to lash a sleeping bag and tent to the bottom of the frame. When Summer was a tiny infant with a floppy neck, she rode in the same carrier with clothing packed around her and a piece of plywood supporting her head.

We hadn't traveled far before the dog tripped John's skis, and he fell. Summer is fearless but quick to sense distress, so we dismissed the accident with a casual "whoops" and continued as if nothing had happened. The act worked. Brooke, who was easily keeping up with us, enjoyed her father's spill immensely.

Brooke uses traditional wooden skis

Brooke Richards and her father skiing to Difficult Campground in the White River National Forest near Aspen, Colorado. Because John Richards is the strongest skier in the family, he carries the baby, Summer, as well as 25 pounds of gear.
PHOTO: ANNE RICHARDS

Do's and Don'ts

PREPARATION: Do not introduce your children to camping with a winter trip.

Take a tour close to home with all your equipment and carefully calculate the travel time under conditions similar to the trip you plan to take. Spend at least one night camped in the backyard to familiarize yourself and your children with the equipment.

ROUTE AND DESTINATION: Select a level route with minimum obstructions. Start early, stop frequently and travel no more than a few miles, especially if you have toddlers perched on your back. Be familiar with the campsite and make sure it is sheltered. Keep the pace slow and limit yourselves to overnight trips.

WEATHER: Do not take children along on trips unless the weather is good and there is a forecast of clear sky and moderate temperature for at least three days. At the first sign of storm, go home.

SKIS, POLES AND BOOTS: Be sure that equipment for children is durable and fits correctly. Cable bindings and high boots are preferable for young children: the bindings will fit any pair of hiking boots, and the boots double as footwear for campside snowball fights. Low-cut boots are a disaster for roughhousing.

BABY CARRIERS: Look for a carrier that protects the child, has room for lashing or packing additional equipment, is comfortable for both passenger and porter and will stand on its own when placed on the ground.

CLOTHING: Synthetic insulators (PolarGuard, Hollofil II) and wool are preferable to down. Children, like adults, should dress in layers for adequate warmth. Make sure that gloves, caps, mittens and other easily lost items are fastened to the child's sweater or jacket with elastic or clips.

DIAPERS: Take only heavy duty, all-night disposable diapers and a good supply of trash bags for disposal (in your pack). Pre-moistened wipes are good for cleanup, but stay away from wipes that are saturated with alcohol. They will literally freeze your child's tail.

EATING: Stop frequently for snacks and have a supply of ready-to-eat munchies to satisfy your child's hunger until dinner is ready. Try cashews, raisins, beef jerky, pepperoni sticks, hard-boiled eggs, butterscotch, Swiss cheese, precooked franks, honey, sardines, tuna, gorp, or dried fruit.

SLEEPING: Consider bivouac bags for small children, and synthetic insulation for possible bed wetters. Washable flannel bag liners keep children from squirming out of their bags, and a waterproof flannel sheet is perfect for protecting the bag of a child not yet toilet trained.

AND ABOVE ALL: Make sure you know what *you* are doing. If you have never camped in winter, don't take kids along on your first trip. Parents should be experienced skiers and winter campers before venturing out with children. On a winter trip the youngsters are totally dependent on you. You must feed them, dress them, put them to bed and look after their welfare just as you do at home. If you are not completely comfortable on a winter trip, don't experiment on children.

---

and bamboo poles. We do the waxing. A few years ago only the elite touring shops carried cross-country skiing equipment for children. Today we can find kids' gear almost anywhere, from inexpensive kits packaged in plastic bags to the newest fiberglass and fish-scale skis. Quality skis and poles are unnecessary for children, but correct length and fit of skis, poles and boots are important. We equipped Brooke with a pair of cable bindings. They give excellent heel support and fast, easy entry, and accommodate hiking boots as well as the cross-country ski boots Brooke uses. We treat every family member's boots with Sno-Seal, and we have equipped all our skis with runaway straps, attaching each binding to the lower laces of the boot.

Proper clothing also is important. Regardless of body size, the secret of staying flexible and warm is the layering of garments. There are, however, a few peculiarities associated with children—at least with our children. Preadolescents have higher rates of metabolism than adults, and our kids require fewer layers than we do under the same conditions. (Of course, when Summer is riding in her carrier, she is not expending the same amount of energy as an active skier, and so she needs more clothing.)

American Indians nested their papooses in dry moss; we use the modern substitute, heavy duty disposable diapers. We combine them with protective, breathable nylon pants, and, just in case, line the seat of Summer's carrier with a flannel-covered, rubberized pad. "Disposable" doesn't mean we junk used diapers in the woods. We tie them tightly in plastic bags and stuff them in corners of our packs. Later, we transfer these small bags to a double-weight garbage bag, which we pack out with us. There is no mess or stink if we carefully secure the packets. Changing is done in a sheltered spot on an Ensolite pad covered with a baby blanket. For cleaning up, pre-moistened wipes saturated with oil or lotion are best. Stay away from towelettes drenched in alcohol—brrr.

Despite the availability of cross-country equipment for children who ski, I have yet to find a camping store that acknowledges infant backpacking needs. The pastel stroller-wear available in department stores is just not warm enough. I have had to make most of Summer's skiing clothes. No one-piece garments; they interfere with changing, and Summer's wardrobe would diminish top and bottom in case of mishap. She wears two-piece wool, footed sleepers; polyester-filled warm-ups, vest and parka; and wool sweaters and long johns in various layers. Additionally, she has a homemade windproof, water-repellent shell parka, a small balaklava which protects the back of her neck, a sun visor hat and a pair of sunglasses. Layers of woolen tube socks that come up over the knees and insulated boots keep her feet warm; woolen mittens and nylon shells, her hands. Except for her parka and snowpants, everything is carried in duplicate or triplicate. And anything that might drop off on the trail, such as mittens, hat or shoes, is securely attached to her clothing with clips or elastic.

Brooke's clothing is basically the same as an adult's. Her vest and parka are insulated with a polyester filling. She uses warmup pants, side-zippered for ventilation and for quick removal while skiing, and knickers. Knee-high nylon gaiters prevent accumulation of snow. She also wears or carries several layers of woolen underclothing—shirts, sweaters and long johns. Her mitts are down-filled and get covered

---

A dress rehearsal of the trip—skiing around the neighborhood with full packs and camping in your backyard—lets both you and the kids know what to expect.

by nylon shells when it is wet.

Eight-year-olds can be stubborn and unmotivated about reaching a destination, and part of John's and my role as parents is to keep the whole party moving. We devise games. For instance, the first person to spot a rabbit track wins a prize; the first person to spot the rabbit itself wins a grand prize. Bionic Indians is another favorite.

At Summer's age, time and distance mean nothing. She has, so far, been a cooperative trail companion. The rhythm, movement and sound of our voices keep her content for hours. Singing delights her, and she often joins in, much to our amusement.

Because frequent breaks for rest and snacks keep our kids happy, we soon stopped by the Roaring Fork River, on our January trip.

Brooke is in charge of purchasing and carrying the trail treats. Occasionally we have had to choke down marshmallow sandwiches and half-squished Ho-Ho's; on this trip we got lucky—Running Bear's Fruit 'n' Nut Pemmican from the natural foods store!

The sky was clearing rapidly, and we decided to ski on. If we spend more than 15 minutes at a rest stop, Brooke becomes engrossed with some find of nature and is less than willing to leave.

We arrived at Difficult Campground in good time, selected a campsite that would be exposed to the early morning sun and set up camp. Brooke's duty was to help her dad pack down the snow and pitch the tent; mine was to keep Summer occupied and happy. I took some pictures and brewed hot drinks for the workers. Later, we went skiing.

Traces of wildlife rarely seen in summer are abundant in winter, and we have become competent at identifying animal tracks. We enjoy guessing

How much a child can carry depends not only on size, strength and endurance but on personality, experience and mood as well.

where the creature was going, how fast, in what mood and why. Brooke once sighted a five-inch-wide set of elk tracks, our prize recording. Playing tracker that afternoon, though, was difficult because of the recent snowfall. We returned to camp with nothing to record in our animal logbook.

Dinner consisted half of foods that required no cooking and half of quickly prepared hot food. While Brooke nibbled ready-to-eat munchies, We did the cooking. This time nobody got the jitters waiting for the snow to melt or the food to cook.

We try to eat meals outside the tent, because grease and oil spilled on sleeping bags or clothing compact down and ruin its efficiency. When we are forced to eat inside the tent, we cover everything—clothing and sleeping bags—with plastic garbage bags.

After dinner, we bunked the kids in the tent. On our first winter outing we used a tent that was too small, and there was a lot of condensation by morning. We switched to a roomier three-person tent for subsequent trips, yet, with the four of us sleeping inside, a fair amount of condensation still collects on tent walls. John and I often leave the tent to the children and sleep outside. We never take the kids ski camping in severely cold weather or when the forecast is for wind or snow, and we pick well-protected tent sites. Thus our tent has never been troubled with snow penetration or buildup.

Both children move around a lot while they sleep, so we provide them with a nearly wall-to-wall ground cover of four Ensolite pads. Brooke sleeps in a down bivouac bag which she has had since she was three. Summer now beds in a child's PolarGuard bag tucked under at the bottom. It is easier to wash than down and better protection if she wets. (When she was seven months old, we wrapped her in sweaters and a sleeping bag stuff sack, and allowed her to bunk with us. This method was convenient for nursing, and the stuff sack prevented wetting of our bag.) Washable flannel bag liners keep the kids from inching out of their cocoons; the one under the baby is waterproof.

I am a light sleeper, and when John and I sleep outside the tent, I awake if one of the children so much as mumbles in her sleep. On this trip all was quiet until around 6 A.M., when Summer cried out. I crawled into the tent and pacified her with a bottle of juice I had kept warm in my sleeping bag. (I share my bag, also, with three pairs of boots, mine and the kids', wrapped in plastic bags. That way our boots are warm when we put them on in the morning.)

John arose around 7:30 and got the stove going. He served us breakfast in bed—hot chocolate, granola, eggs, bacon and pemmican. By 8:30 we were dressed and ready to break camp and go skiing.

Brooke corralled and harnessed Chai. He pulled her on skis a half-mile down the road without mishap.

When we reached home that afternoon, Chai crumpled wearily to the floor. Summer curled up next to him and fell fast asleep. Brooke, John and I sat at the kitchen table, already planning our next weekend trek. ✒

Chapter Eight

THE LONGEST, DARKEST DAYS: HIKING IN WINTER

I got into winter hiking to escape the crowds. It seems all my life I have been seeking ways to do this. Back in the 1940s, it was easy to avoid other hikers, because there simply weren't that many of them in the woods. All I had to do was hike off the road a quarter of a mile or so and I would find solitude. Everyone was so taken with driving that they had forgotten that their feet would get them there, too.

By the 1950s there were more folks discovering camping. But even then I can recall driving across the country from New York to San Francisco and pulling a short way off the road to set up camp without anyone bothering us. And a hike of a mile or so into the woods was still enough to get away from almost everyone. I camped at Cascade Pass in the North Cascades in Washington State for several days in early July back then and didn't see another person the whole time. That same summer I climbed Mt. Rainier without seeing anyone else on the mountain. Today there would be hundreds of people at

these places at any time of the year you'd care to go.

By the late 1950s though, I began to notice that on hot summer days I would bump into people on trails in some of my favorite hiking areas, like in the Catskills or in the Adirondacks. And one of the places I liked so much, Tuckerman's Ravine in the New Hampshire White Mountains, had become so popular that you were sure to find someone there no matter what time of year you hiked in there. I distinctly recall detouring away from Tuckerman around to Huntington Ravine to find more solitude.

In those days when I wanted solitude, all I had to do was go hiking before the Fourth of July or after Labor Day. I would find absolutely no one on the trails then—except, of course, during hunting season.

By the 1960s there were so many people on the trails in the summer that I changed my hiking habits entirely—hiking only in the spring and fall. And I began to seek out places that were less well known than Mount Marcy, Mt. Washington, Grand Teton, Mt. Rainier—places where the crowds were sure to head.

And then I found a new joy. I had been camping later and later into the year, extending my season right up to hunting season. For several years I woke up with snow on my sleeping bag before hanging up my pack for the winter. Since I knew how to camp out in below-zero weather from my mountaineering experiences, why not use the same techniques to backpack on snowshoes in winter? So I got myself a pair of snowshoes and kept on backpacking into January. It was about the biggest turn-on that I've had since I started backpacking as a kid. But, like so many other things in life, I discovered that there had been many people there before me, and I began to find out that there were many techniques for hiking in winter, about which I knew very little. The pieces in this chapter will give you an idea of what I mean. Chapter Five will also provide information about some of the hazards of winter backpacking—hypothermia, for example.

As a matter of fact, it makes me blush to think how many folks, with far less equipment, were traveling across the snow and camping out in severe conditions long before I had been born. Consider the Indians, the trappers, the mountain men—and Snowshoe Thompson, whose winter exploits were for him all in a day's work.

SNOWSHOE THOMPSON (1827–1876)

by CURTIS W. CASEWIT

One of America's first backpackers found his life's work in the grim winter terrain of the Northwest.

Snowshoe Thompson was one of America's first backpackers. He carried heavy mail pouches across the High Sierra, and for many years, from 1856 to 1869, he served as a link between winter-shrouded mining camps. Thompson got through when coaches couldn't—a life line, sometimes a life-saver, a rescuer, a carrier of medicines and food supplies, a package lugger. He was dedicated to nature, nonviolent, nonmaterialistic and altogether selfless. In short, a rare kind of man, hard to find today (even among backpackers and cross-country skiers, who as a group have high standards and resist the march of civilization).

The legendary Snowshoe Thompson was born as Jon Torsteinson Rui on April 30, 1827, in the mountainous Telemark province of Norway. When Jon was old enough to understand, he was told that only health counted; wealth was not important. He learned to use skis, which were then known as "snowshoes." His father brought him to America when he was 10, and his family settled in the Middle West. At the age of 24, Jon headed west, a lean and wiry six-footer burning with a sense of adventure. Before he started on his long journey across the plains, his mother said prophetically, "Perhaps there's something more out there. Something that only *you* can do." He would always remember her words.

The young Scandinavian outdoorsman was not cut out to make money. Most of the people he would deal with—including those in the U.S. government—would exploit him to the hilt. Like John Muir, Thompson was more interested in mountains themselves than in cashing in on them.

Thompson arrived on the western side of the Sierra Nevada in 1851. He met up with some miners who assured him that there was plenty of gold "in them rivers." Thompson, along with most of the immigrants, bought a pan and a rocker and learned to wash gravel. He found little of the precious metal at places like Coon Hollow and Kelsey's Diggings. He did poorly. Maybe a Snowshoe Thompson (or a John Muir) could not be smitten with real gold fever; perhaps competition was too strong and there was not enough gold left in the rivers. Besides, more lucrative mining was soon done in deep tunnels and shafts. Thompson liked the sky and fresh air too much; subterranean mining was not for him. He turned to farming, and he trekked through the High Sierra at all seasons. Late in 1855 he happened to pick up a copy of the *Sacramento Union*. A dramatic headline caught his eye: "People Lost to the World! Uncle Sam Needs Mail Carrier!"

The need was real enough. Each winter, Sierra mining camps were cut off from one another. Because of Indian raids and blizzards, letters from Salt Lake City to the West Coast detoured for hundreds of miles south on mule back or horse; packages often went via Panama or by ship around the length of South America. Four mail carriers had given up on even

relatively short stretches across the Sierra Nevada. Mail from Boston to San Francisco could take a full year.

The postmaster in Placerville, California, was desperate. The winter of 1856 promised to be an especially grim one, with marrow-gnawing temperatures and snows reaching 40-foot depths. Blizzards would sever all

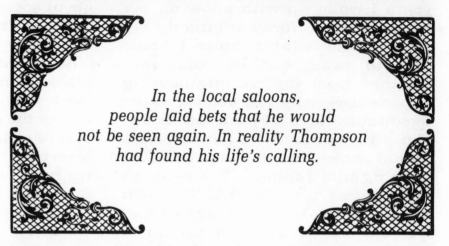

*In the local saloons,
people laid bets that he would
not be seen again. In reality Thompson
had found his life's calling.*

contact with other snowbound settlements. "People Lost to the World!"—unless someone came forward with enough courage and stamina to hurdle the icy spine of the mountains. Someone unafraid of a hundred-mile journey in subzero weather. A person who did not mind solitude.

Thompson was that person. He made a pair of 25-pound skis, tried them out and reported to the Placerville post office. The clerk thought Thompson was a little crazy. Norsky snowshoes? Impossible. Eighty-pound sacks to be carried on a human back for five cold days? Unbelievable.

Still, the clerk fetched Allen M. Thatcher, the postmaster, who was equally doubtful. Wouldn't Thompson get lost in the wintry terrain? According to the written record, Thompson replied: "I can go anywhere in the mountains. Day and night. Storm and shine."

"It's 90 miles to Genoa," the postmaster said.

"A man can find the way. If he has his wits about him."

Thompson started his job in January, 1856. In the local saloons, people laid bets that he would not be seen again. In reality, Thompson had found his life's calling.

All that winter he conquered Ebbetts Pass and Carson Pass. He picked up letters at the Placerville Hotel, at

the Strawberry Station, in Woodfords, at Markleeville, at the tiny Genoa post office and the Genoa stockade, at the St. Charles Hotel in Carson City. The letters were merely folded sheets, sealed with wax. They had stamps on them, just as mail does now. But there were no envelopes in those days.

Merchants who owned stores on either side of the snow-blocked mountains would ask Thompson if he minded carrying boxes with warm socks for the miners. In addition to mail, he supplied camps with tools, writing paper, books, tobacco (he did not smoke himself), pots and pans. Before the spring thaw, he transported seeds of all kinds.

In order to increase his speed, Thompson built lighter skis. To save weight, his own food supply was slim—a few biscuits, a piece of sausage and some jerked beef or other sun-dried meat strips—not much for a constantly moving 180-pound man with a backbreaking load.

Thompson traveled on cool days or during moonlit nights; he stopped rarely. When he had to sleep, he chose caves, using hollow rocks to make fires of dry twigs and cones, and being conscientious about extinguishing fires when he left.

This early conservationist and backpacker soon took on additional duties. Just before Christmas in 1856, the Strawberry Station postmaster drew Thompson aside and told him that three prospectors had failed to return that day from a search for minerals. Would Thompson look for the lost men? He would. The Norwegian followed their boot tracks through drifts for seven uphill miles and found them stuck in snow to their armpits. Local eyewitnesses reported that Thompson brought the weakened men, one by one, back to safety, riding on the back of his skis.

A few days later, Thompson's endurance was put to a much greater test. He was en route from Placerville to Woodfords and Genoa. He saw the blunt 10,000-foot-high Monument Peak, and skiing on, caught sight of Lake Tahoe glinting up through the conifers. He would reach Genoa, his final destination, the next afternoon. Thompson stabbed his man-sized pole into the snow and took the straightest line across the sloping land. If he had veered by a few miles, someone would undoubtedly have died. As it happened, Thompson paused near a small log cabin that night. He heard groaning and sobbing inside. Using the tips of his skis, he shoveled the snow from the door and pushed it inward. The moonlight illuminated a man panting on a thin layer of hay. Trapper John Sisson had been marooned there for 12 days, with only a little raw flour for food. His legs were purple from frostbite.

Thompson skied to Genoa for help, but the gold seekers there seemed to be indifferent, and it took time to gather a small flock of volunteers with webbed snowshoes. Sisson wept at the sight of the rescue party. Thompson, who had traveled throughout the previous night, refused to rest and helped construct a hand sled. Then he led the way on his skis through deep snow, pulling the first-aid vehicle over crests by means of a rope.

It took Thompson until morning (and a second night without sleep) to reach the valley and Genoa, where the local physician—a Dr. Luce—gave the rescuers some bad news. Sisson's legs would have to be amputated, but the old trapper was not strong enough to last through the operation without an anesthetic. Someone had to journey to Sacramento for chloroform. This would mean skiing about 90 miles over the mountains to Placerville, then riding on horseback to the railroad station in Folsom and finally taking a train to the supply house in Sacramento. Apparently, chloroform was unavailable elsewhere. Thompson went. According to an account in the *Territorial Enterprise,* Snowshoe

Thompson, "who did nothing in halves, hurtled the Sierra. The long-delayed operation was performed. So modest was Thompson that what others called great feats, did not appear so to him." Sisson survived the operation. At a time in the history of the West when men shot their best friends, Thompson had risked his own life to save the life of a total stranger.

Like most genuine naturalists, Thompson despised guns. "A gun would slow me down," the Norwegian always said. But what about Indians? his friends wanted to know. What if he encountered a dangerous tribe? Thompson replied that he knew of no Sierra Indians who skied.

One harrowing day in 1857, Thompson came face to face with a pack of six thin, starved-looking timber wolves. He knew that hungry timber wolves could tear a human being to pieces, so he decided to race away down the slope on his skis. And he actually outskied them.

Thompson knew much about the area's fauna, flora and geology. Despite distances—his daily trips averaged 25 miles—he paid attention to his surroundings. For instance, he estimated altitude from rock strata. Brown sandstone told him that he was about 6,000 feet above sea level. A certain red granite could only be found at 10,000 feet. Trees gave him similar clues; between six and eight thousand feet, there were ponderosa pines, with thick trunks and open cones. The bark of the ponderosa pine, he claimed, gave off a scent like vanilla. He carried no compass, he said, because the moss on tree trunks directed him to the north, and on clear nights he used the North Star.

According to the miners, Thompson achieved speeds of 60 miles an hour on skis. He could cover the 90 up-and-down miles between Placerville and Genoa in 15 hours. Dan De Quille, a well-known reporter, wrote, "Thompson, a heavy bag upon his back, has frequently run three miles in five minutes. He glides among the obstructions like a skater on ice; at ever so great a speed he will touch or pass within an inch of any designated object." Thompson also took ski jumps, leaping 50 feet without falling. W. P. Merrill, postmaster of Woodfords, wrote that Thompson

once "made a jump of one hundred and eighty feet without a break."

When Thompson entered races for money, however, he won no purses. Nor did his incredible backpacking feats bring him riches. The *Territorial Enterprise* paid Thompson only 50 cents per pound to transport dismantled presses to a new location and to carry rolls of newsprint to Carson City.

Thompson's marriage in 1866 must have given him some motivation to prod the post offices, which owed him money for his services. But he was in for grave disappointments. All the postmasters slapped him on the back and made promises that he would be remunerated for the 30 to 35 round trips he made each winter with 50 to 80 pounds on his back. Sure, the postal officials told him, he would get $750 per season. But each postmaster passed the buck to the next. By 1859 Thompson had received only $80.22 for his first two winters of mail carrying. Fortunately for him, the merchants and miners would give him a pinch of gold dust or a few coins for his deliveries.

In 1872 the Nevada legislature decided that Thompson should get $6,000 in back wages. A petition was drawn up and duly signed in Carson City by James W. Nye, governor of the Nevada Territory, and other state officials, by the various postmasters and by the residents of Carson Valley—about 1,000 signatures in all. Could Thompson personally take the petition to Washington, D.C.? His appearance would help at the U.S. Senate hearing.

On January 16, 1872, Thompson kissed his wife good-by, strapped a suitcase to his back and boarded a train east for Laramie City (today's Laramie) in Wyoming Territory. Unfortunately, the barren land was hit by a blizzard that stopped the train in its tracks. Thompson waited out one night. After he learned that he would be stranded for days, the Norwegian made up his mind to walk to Laramie City and catch another train from there. One other passenger accepted Thompson's plan. His name was Rufus Turner, and he, too, had an urgent appointment in the East.

Thompson and Turner left the train together in the morning. At once the blizzard hit their bodies, almost

205

toppling them. Thompson strode ahead, breaking trail. On skis it would have been difficult, but afoot, each step through the deep whiteness was agony. The bitter cold clawed at the men's faces, and carrying baggage on their backs made travel even rougher. After about 10 miles, Turner hollered for Thompson to stop. "Suitcase—too heavy," Turner gasped. The Norwegian took his companion's luggage and fought on, following the line of the railroad tracks. Just before darkness Thompson and Turner reached snowbound Laramie City.

After a night's sleep, Thompson was told the trains would not run for days. Still, Cheyenne was 56 miles away. Surely, there had to be transportation east from Cheyenne! The Norwegian then performed an almost incredible feat. He crossed the Medicine Bow Mountains and plodded over the shelterless plains, the first outsider to reach Cheyenne in two weeks. "Mountaineer outruns the Iron Horse!" announced a Cheyenne newspaper headline. It was pure Thompson, pure Jon Torsteinson Rui. His performance was doubly remarkable for a man of 46, which was considered old in those days.

Disheartening news awaited Thompson in Washington. The forty-second Congress of the United States made short shrift of the $6,000 named in the petition. For unknown reasons, the postal officials now claimed that Thompson should be paid only for one season. The figure was to be $750, less the $80.22 which he had already received, leaving him $669.78. Thompson stuck it out in Washington for a few weeks. His back pay never came. What had happened? No one knows for sure, except that the politicians talked much and did little. "I can wait no longer," he wrote to his wife, Agnes, adding in his warmhearted way: "I'm needed at home."

In March, Thompson returned to the High Sierra, only to find that his services were not needed. Trains and stage lines had taken over the postal deliveries. Thompson put his skis

away. Millions of dollars were being made in Carson City, Virginia City, Placerville and other mining towns. Thompson and his wife had settled in the Diamond Valley, 30 miles south of Carson City. They owned some acreage for growing wild hay, alfalfa and wheat.

In May, 1876, Thompson and his nine-year-old son Arthur brought back bags of seed from town. The next morning Thompson got on his horse and sowed seed from the saddle. When he had finished, perspiration ran through his blonde beard, and he was coughing badly. He died in the afternoon of May 15, 1876, a Tuesday.

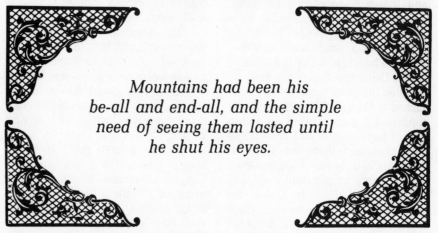

Mountains had been his be-all and end-all, and the simple need of seeing them lasted until he shut his eyes.

From his bed, up to the last minute, he could see the Sierra peaks he loved so much. Mountains had been his be-all and end-all, and the simple need of seeing them lasted until he shut his eyes.

His life's pleasures had been simple enough: the quiet of the peaks, motion for his body, snow for a thirsty tongue, a slice of dried meat to still hunger, a fire for cold hands. Real recognition came only after his death. "Thompson's equal will probably never again be seen," Dan De Quille wrote. "It would be hard to find another man combining his courage, physique, and powers of endurance—a man with such thews and sinews, controlled by such a will. There was no recklessness in anything he did."

Sierra ski races and jumping events were eventually named after

Snowshoe Thompson. Modern cross-country skiers traced his route and reenacted his mail runs. His skis were put on display, first at Sutter's Fort in Sacramento, then at the Plumas Eureka State Park, California. Other relics traveled to the Holmenkollen Ski Museum in Oslo, Norway. For a while, Thompson's log cabin in the Diamond Valley was a shrine for visitors. Even the U.S. Post Office in Washington, D.C., which had treated him so wretchedly, considered issuing a stamp in his memory (although it never paid his wife the back pay). Author Jack Schaefer wrote a study of Thompson, calling him "a good man of the West" and "a hero without glory."

The old backpacker's grave in Genoa, Nevada, is flanked by an apple tree. Over the spot where he sleeps forever stands a white stone monument with a pair of crossed skis chiseled into the granite. The inscription reads, "Native of Norway, departed this life May 15, 1876."

Next year will mark the one-hundredth anniversary of Thompson's death. Groups dedicated to the outdoors have made ambitious plans for the day. A tall bronze statue will be unveiled. Thousands of persons, including Norwegian dignitaries, are expected to attend a memorial ceremony. It will be a fitting tribute to an early backpacker whose gravestone bears a simple but lasting message: "Gone but not forgotten." ▲

HOW TO GET STARTED WINTER BACKPACKING

by JOHN A. DANIELSEN

In recent years winter backpacking has become increasingly popular, yet many people are foolhardy about their approach to it.

Winter camping is a serious business. A small mistake in the summertime can be a mere inconvenience, while the same mistake in winter can cost you your life. A slight change in the weather can become considerably more dangerous in winter than the same degree of change would be in summer.

Winter camping ought to be approached with a great deal of respect. If approached with caution, it can provide immense joy.

John A. Danielsen presents here a simple primer for getting into winter camping.

For further reading, pick up a copy of his famous handbook, Winter Hiking and Camping, second edition, published by the Adirondack Mountain Club in 1977.

W.K.

13 mistakes most beginners make

WINTER BACKPACKING IS a challenging idea for those who have enjoyed the pleasures of extensive summer and fall backpacking. Enjoying the woods and hills in their deep snow mantle and clear freezing air, with fewer people around, and no bugs, has a compelling allure.

It can be an exciting and fascinating experience—but for many the first attempt ends in a cold, unpleasant fiasco. For an unfortunate few, frostbite and hypothermia convert their mistakes, which if made in summertime would be mere inconveniences, into tragic disasters.

It is so tempting to assume that if you have a lot of experience backpacking in summer and fall, even in light November snows, it will be easy to make the transition to winter trips.

But successful winter backpacking is a whole new ball game.

The summer-experienced hiker undertaking a remote backpack on his first winter outing often encounters a new order of problems.

🐾 His canteen freezes up.

🐾 He becomes dehydrated for lack of drinking enough water.

🐾 His clothes get wet, both from perspiration and from snow melting on his parka, his socks or his mittens.

🐾 He does not make nearly the mileage he thought he would and falls short of the spot where he planned on spending the night.

🐾 Darkness seems to come on shortly after lunch because of the shorter days of the winter.

🐾 If he reaches a shelter, it may be filled up—not with people, but with snow.

🐾 His tent is a lot more difficult to set up in deep snow, fading twilight and hand-freezing temperatures.

🐾 The process of melting snow for water is trickier than he expected and requires much more snow than he anticipated.

🐾 He spills his cooking pot at least once, trying to operate in the cramped space inside his tent.

🐾 As his dinner finally cooks, steam clouds fill the tent, and the vapor dampens his down bag, drastically reducing its warmth.

🐾 In the morning, after a cold

207

night, his boots are frozen, and he has a difficult time getting them on.

🔖 Every time he touches the tent wall in the morning, frost showers down on him and his gear, all of which is by now either wet or frozen.

🔖 When he finally blunders out down the trail to his car, the battery is dead.

Before launching on their first winter trip, some people are sensible enough to study up on what to expect, what equipment to take and how to plan a reasonable first-time objective. Many are just plain lucky that the weather treats them gently.

But on far too many occasions, the experiences described above befall the apprentice winter backpacker. Of course, entertaining tales about such trips can be told for many years. But how much safer it would be to do it the right way the first time out.

How should you get started in winter backpacking?

A four-step sequence is advisable.

1. Begin with a solid "experience base" of backpacking in warmer weather. Be thoroughly at home in the backcountry in summer. Know your equipment well, in bad weather as well as good. For example, get to know your cookstove so that you can start it quickly without fuss. Your first winter trip is no time to try to figure out how the thing works. The same goes for boots, pack, headlamp (not flashlight), everything.

Many people buy new equipment for winter and never try it out first in mild weather conditions. For example, they have used a butane stove for summer trekking and have been told that it won't work in winter. So in November they buy a gas-fueled stove, start it once in the cellar and not again until they're camping out at Faroff Lean-to 12 miles from the road in January. The chances of dinner going smoothly that night are pretty slim.

During the summer get to know the area in which you expect to pack. Get acquainted with the mountains, valleys, streams, ponds and trails. Learn to relate hiking areas with topo maps. Learn to see mountains, valleys and other features when you look at those little lines on the topos. Learn to use your compass with more authority. You will come to know which of two trails is longer but easier, and which is the shorter, steeper route. Your sense of time and distance will sharpen. Your judgment will improve. You will get to know how many hours it takes to get from point to point. Later you'll learn how to estimate how much longer winter travel will take.

Know the local roads to the trailhead so that time is not wasted getting started hiking. No problem in summer, but in winter, a valuable hour of daylight may be lost. The delay could be more serious.

2. Learn as much about winter backpacking as you can *before* you ever set boot in snowshoe.

Learn from experienced friends with proven good judgment and leadership ability. It is best if they will take you along with them on one of their trips. There is no better way to learn. And when out there, offer to help with cooking and making camp so that you can get actual experience in these essential tasks.

Reading some good books is useful, too. Until recently there were no basic guides on winter hiking and camping. Today the westerner can consult Bridge's *The Complete Snow Camper's Guide* and the pertinent chapters of *Mountaineering: The Freedom of the Hills.* For the very different problems of eastern winter backpacking, two good sources are the Adirondack Mountain Club's *Winter Hiking and Camping* and Dan H. Allen's *Don't Die on the Mountain.*

You can speed up your learning process by participating in one of the winter camping courses offered by many of the outdoor clubs. These programs usually combine classroom instruction with day hikes and move up to more demanding overnight trips.

3. If you are getting started on your own with the aid of books, get started gradually. Begin with winter day hikes when the ground is bare or has less than a foot of snow. Then try your skis or snowshoes in moderate snow cover. Take short trips at first, with only essentials in a knapsack.

Later, take complete backpacking gear.

This enables you to experience the new problems of winter hiking and camping a few at a time rather than all at once. For instance, take on the problems of learning to snowshoe and of how to adjust snowshoe bindings when you're wearing a day pack and have plenty of time. It's a lot easier and safer than trying to do it with a fully loaded 50-pound backpack and that panicky feeling that if you don't hurry, you'll run out of daylight before you get to a safe place to camp.

You will find it is surprisingly difficult to stay on the trail when several feet of snow blanket the woods. This is specially true when the trail is not broken and sleet or wet snow covers trail markers. In the vicinity of tree line and above, you must be aware that in winter there is virtually no trail. Losing your way on mountaintops is dangerous and a major cause of some parties failing to return.

Day trips will help you judge how slowly you travel in deep snow and, therefore, how far you can expect to travel when you set out for your first overnight trips.

You will learn how short the winter daylight hours are. In Yogi Berra's immortal phrase, this is the time of year when it gets late early.

Practice the endless task of putting on and taking off your clothing—mittens, cap or balaclava, wool shirts and sweaters—so that you don't overheat when going uphill and don't chill down too fast when you stop.

You can learn much on day trips without committing yourself to the dangers of a major "adventure."

4. Learn to operate overnight in some location where a quick retreat to civilization can be made at any time. Your first attempt at winter camping should be close to your car, lodge or home. The first test would best be made early in the winter when the snow cover is thin and temperatures are only moderately cold. Make the next trip in a bit colder weather and later in the winter. Stay below tree line until you feel really at home in the cold and know your equipment well. You will learn a limited number of new things on each trip without risking a too-advanced project.

Do not commit yourself to remote high country until you are thoroughly confident of your equipment, your technique on snowshoes or skis and crampons, your trail-finding ability in deep snow and every facet of daily backcountry living under full winter conditions.

Within this structure for gradually introducing yourself to winter backpacking, here are some additional considerations of winter camping, many of which seem obvious but are frequently underestimated by the novice winter backpacker.

The Cold.
Because we live indoors most of the time, most of us are inclined to be complacent about the cold. This attitude can lead to serious difficulties on the trail. You must make a deliberate effort to adapt mentally to cold. Do not believe that your expensive equipment or physical condition will shield you fully from it. Do not fight it or try to overcome it by brute force. You must do everything to accommodate yourself to low temperatures, including the cooling effects of wind on your body.

Snow and Ice.
Living and moving about on snow and ice present unique problems. Travel takes longer. Visibility is often drastically reduced. Your tracks may disappear quickly behind you beneath new-fallen or blown snow, making it more difficult to retrace your route. Climbing is more strenuous. Icy areas are more hazardous. Erecting your tent and keeping it up are more difficult. A heavy snowfall can quickly cover a camp, collapsing your tent and burying your equipment. Items dropped in the snow get easily lost. And there are special dangers such as avalanches and thin ice on lakes.

Weather.
The longer you stay in the mountains, the more your exposure to vagaries of weather. One day may be mild and damp with sleet or rain that dampens your clothing and sleeping bag. The next can bring a sudden temperature drop that freezes your wet gear.

Your chances of predicting local weather changes are better if you have previous winter experience in the area and—most important—if you use good judgment in deciding whether to continue. Trips have ended in disaster, or nearly so, because a decision was made to go ahead rather than turn back.

Operating.
Understand and anticipate that practically everything you do in the cold will be more difficult and time consuming: moving about, cooking, getting water, erecting your tent, putting on and removing your clothes, putting on and lacing your boots. Functioning while wearing mittens is difficult. If your body is warm enough, you can use your bare hands for a short period to perform tasks with nonmetal equipment. But you'll be able to use your bare hands only as briefly as possible, because rewarming them takes a long time even with mittens back on.

Your winter operating time can be

Trips have ended in disaster because a decision was made to go ahead rather than turn back

significantly reduced, as I said earlier, by practice on introductory trips and by being familiar with all features of your equipment. You can also improve your operating efficiency by "winterizing" your clothing and equipment. Attach rawhide or tape pulls on zipper tabs, secure your mittens with a cord around the neck or to parka sleeves as you do for small children. Use a parka with roomy pockets, a tent that is easy to erect, shock-corded tent poles, a quick-starting easy-to-use stove, simple foods that are quick to prepare, simple-to-use utensils, a larger stuff bag for your sleeping bag, a headlamp instead of a flashlight and tape over metal parts that you are likely to touch with your bare hands.

Keep Warm.
Always keep your clothing as dry as possible. Damp clothing and sleeping bag will not keep you warm because their insulation value is lost. Socks, underwear, mitten liners and down vests will absorb moisture, especially when you are perspiring from vigorous activity. You can minimize moisture absorption by scrupulously brushing snow off your clothes, by ventilating in every possible way and by wearing as little clothing as is necessary to retain your body warmth.

Inadequate food intake can contribute to premature fatigue and lower your body temperature. Your caloric consumption in winter is generally higher. Be sure your body is adequately fueled. You need nutritious meals that include ample beverages. Your pre-trip meals should also be nourishing.

Pack.
Use a roomy pack. Too many hikers get started in winter using packs that are entirely too small. You need extra space in your pack, not just for the extra clothing you must carry but for the clothes you shed as you warm up on the trail. If your pack is too small, it discourages shedding, which is an essential maneuver for keeping your clothes dry. The frame should have lashing studs or D-rings for securing snowshoes, crampons, skis, ice axe. Extra outside pockets are handy for stuffing additional small items you need in winter.

Boots.
Take precautions to avoid getting cold feet and frostbite. You invite trouble if you wear hiking boots that you ordinarily use at other times of year with one pair of socks but which become tight-fitting when you add a second pair of socks. Instead, get larger boots that fit your feet with at least one pair of medium wool socks and another pair of heavy ones and allow sufficient room for wiggling your toes.

Many experienced winter hikers use leather-top, rubber-bottom boots or insulated, all-rubber boots. The former require two pairs of socks and insoles for insulation; the latter need only one pair of socks. Some all-rubber models are designed to be worn at 20 degrees below zero.

Preventing boots from freezing at night is important. The best way is to keep them inside your sleeping bag with you. Be sure to scrape all snow and ice off first. Then put them in your sleeping-bag stuff sack before stowing them at the bottom of the bag. But turn the stuff sack inside out so that any traces of snow from the boots won't dampen your sleeping bag when you stuff *it* into your stuff sack in the morning.

Clothing.
A good ensemble would include wool pants and two wool shirts, a wool sweater, a nylon shell with hood, a pair of wool mittens, outer mitten shells to keep mittens dry, a ski cap or balaclava, and a pair of long johns. All your clothing should be loose fitting with plenty of built-in features for ventilation: full zipper on parka, adjustable closures at sleeves (not knit wristlets), suspenders instead of a belt. For protection around hips and legs, windproof shell pants can be used in deep snow and wind. Prevent snow from entering your boots by wearing gaiters.

When you stop hiking for the day and set up camp, put on additional shirts, sweaters and parka—whatever you have. Maintain your body heat. If temperatures are very cold, get into your sleeping bag as soon as your tent is up; then have your meal.

Stove.
Obviously, a portable cookstove, *not* a campfire, is mandatory in winter. One caution: carbon monoxide is a potential hazard wherever stoves and heaters are used in a confined space and ventilation is limited, such as in a tent. Be sure you keep your tent vents open, even if it is blowing a blizzard outside.

Food.
Nibble-food or "gorp" carried in your pocket is a good idea.

Cold air has an extremely dehydrating effect on the body, so it is important to drink as much liquid as possible. Some people like to carry a hot drink in a thermos bottle. Some people fill their canteens with hot tea or water in the morning before setting out on the trail, and after dinner, and put the warm canteen in their sleeping bag with them. (Be sure it doesn't leak if you do this.) Carry your canteen inside your pack—upside down wrapped inside your extra clothes or inside your parka to prevent its cap from freezing.

Main course meals should be simple and easy to prepare. Many winter campers carry extra margarine or butter to add extra calories and flavor to both their dinner meals and their cereal.

And one final coup de grace for late evening: a piece of candy or other sweet just before going to sleep gives you another extra surge of quick heat. ✒

WEARING THE RIGHT CLOTHES FOR THE MOST WARMTH
from the Editors of BACKPACKER magazine

Probably the most important thing to learn about hiking and backpacking in the winter is how to regulate your body's warmth. I've found that if you follow the simple principle my friend Laura Waterman once told me you'll rarely ever have a problem: "It is a lot easier to stay warm than it is to warm yourself up after you've cooled down."

I find that I am constantly changing clothes on a winter hike—taking off a jacket when the sun comes out, putting it back on or putting on an additional sweater when the sun dodges behind a cloud. Some folks who hike with me think I am a pain in the neck for this. But I have yet to feel the cold on a winter trek. And that makes me feel all the more joyous about being out there.

W.K.

An Exercise in Layering

The morning we began our hike it was still quite cold. The air warmed up some by mid-morning, and as we gained elevation we worked up a sweat. By the time we had gained our first 1,000 feet in altitude, it began to rain. After another 1,000 feet we stopped for lunch. Rain turned to slushy snow, so we pitched a tarp and relaxed beneath it. But we noticed that one of our hikers did not have much appetite. He shivered uncontrollably, his bodily movements were sloppy and uncoordinated, and he had thoroughly lost his strength.

Luckily, we recognized his behavior symptoms as the early stages of hypothermia. The fellow was wearing every item of clothing he had brought with him, and still he could not get warm; his clothes were soaking wet.

He had made a number of errors during the morning's hike which we had not noticed. He had assumed that his 60/40 mountain parka was waterproof; it was not. He did not realize that if his down parka got wet it would not keep him warm. Even worse, he was using a pack designed for rock climbers that was completely unsuitable for the backpacking we were doing. Access to the pack was difficult, so our friend, as he perspired during the morning's hike, did not bother to take off garments and put

them in his pack. The rest of us had been shedding our clothes as the air and our body temperatures warmed up. Our companion was soaked by the rain from the outside and with his own perspiration from the inside.

His errors forced us to abandon our four-day hike after lunch on the first day—a big disappointment to us, but one dictated by our better judgment.

Once down the mountain, our companion bought some better gear at a local shop. The next morning we started out again. Despite the difficulty of getting items in and out of his pack, our friend dutifully took off and put on clothing as conditions required.

At lower elevations we hiked in shirt sleeves. As we ascended higher and circled to the shaded side of the mountain, we put on our mountain parkas. Later we added wool sweaters. Still later, our down sweaters and parkas. That night we slept on snow in a mountain col 2,700 feet above our starting point.

The next morning was cold, damp, and windy, temperatures were in the mid-teens, and our camp was dusted with snow. As we began hiking we each were wearing our cotton chamois shirts, wool sweaters, down sweaters, and mountain parkas. Within fifteen minutes we shed both

our down and wool sweaters. By noon the sun was hot enough for us to hike in shirt sleeves. When we stopped on the summit for lunch, the chilly wind caused us to put on our mountain parkas. After lunch it was shirt sleeves again until our route dropped down to the shaded side of the mountain. We put our parkas back on. In the late afternoon we stopped at a saddle on the shaded side of the mountain. We put wool sweaters under our parkas before we made camp. Finally, as darkness approached we also added our down sweaters.

The next day we began hiking in a snowstorm, which later turned to rain farther down the mountain. This required yet another variation of clothing combinations. But we were warm and dry because, since the aborted first day, we all used the layering principle.

In the interest of lightness of weight, everything in your pack should serve as many purposes as possible. Since clothing and sleeping gear constitute the greatest bulk and probably the most weight, you should choose clothes with a great deal of versatility in mind. Get the maximum use from your various items of clothing and combinations of them.

Liner Bags And Over Bags

The layering principle can be applied to sleeping bags and their accessories, too.

The first sleeping bag for most is a three-season mummy bag. Fine, but what about those occasional chilly weekends in late fall? Or those sultry summer nights? One answer is a liner sleeping bag. A liner bag is a lightweight slim-cut bag that fits inside a standard mummy sleeping bag. Several sleeping bag manufacturers make liners, either with down or polyester fillers. These bags do

not have the finished touches you normally find on conventional down sleeping bags. Draft tubes are missing, seams are sewn through, and the sidewall baffle is omitted. The advantages of the liner sleeping bag are that in hot weather the liner can be used alone; in mild weather you can use your sleeping bag alone; and in colder weather you can use the liner bag inside your sleeping bag.

If you own a slim-cut mummy sleeping bag, however, a liner bag will probably be too snug.

Another solution, is an overbag. It, too, is filled with either polyester or down, is sewn through, and does not have the detailing of standard down bags. The only difference is that it has a wider cut and fits over your regular sleeping bag. It can be used by itself in summer; or over your sleeping bag in cold weather.

And, in dead of winter you can use all three—liner bag, your standard sleeping bag, and your overbag.

Wearing The Right Clothes For The Most Warmth

In the interest of lightness of weight, everything you carry in your pack should serve as many purposes as possible. Clothing and sleeping gear constitute the greatest amount of bulk in your pack and probably the most weight. Thus, you should choose clothes and sleeping gear with a great deal of versatility in mind.

For example, instead of two pairs of long pants, carry one pair of long pants and a pair of shorts. You can wear the shorts alone, or the long pants alone, or both at the same time.

The same with shirts. Instead of one heavy shirt, carry two medium-weight shirts—one with long sleeves, one with short sleeves.

Carry two lightweight wool sweaters instead of a heavy sweater or jacket. Even better, carry a lightweight wool sweater and a wind shell. This gives you three possibilities: sweater alone, shell alone, sweater and shell together.

Additionally you will be warmer in several layers of clothing than in one layer of heavy clothing. The shell, light sweater and two shirts will keep you warmer than one shirt and a heavy sweater or jacket.

This same layering principle applies when you sleep. Better to have a lightweight sleeping bag and wear several layers of clothing than to have a heavy duty low-temperature sleeping bag.

The chart is meant merely to illustrate the incremental warmth gained from layering of clothing and sleeping bag—and the versatility gained thereby. It is not intended to be a guide to any particular sleeping bag or for any particular person, although it was patterned after actual use by one of our editors.

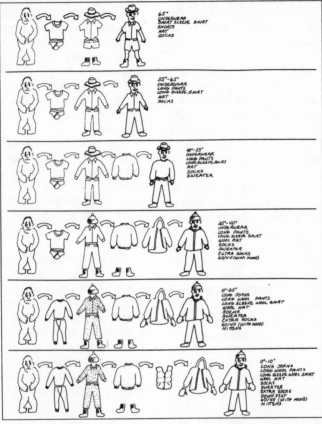

Wear layers of clothing in cold weather or at high altitudes. They will keep you warmer than if you wear thick, bulky garments. Layers also permit you greater flexibility in adding or taking off garments to control your temperature. Layers trap the body warmth and keep it from escaping. Thus, the more layers you wear, the warmer you'll be. Wool garments are warmer than cotton clothes. And wool is better than down in that if it gets wet it will retain its insulating capacity. A parka made of nylon or other windproof material worn over the wool sweaters keeps the wind from whisking away your body heat, trapped in the wool garments. Pullover garments are warmer than those that zip or button up. But zippers and buttons allow you better control over temperature. You can increase or decrease by degrees the amount of ventilation you need as exertion or temperature varies. You can carry your extra garments in your pack until you need them. Best to keep a warm, easily donned sweater or parka on top, so that you can quickly put it on at rest stops. It is easier to keep your body warm than it is to warm it up after it cools down.

Getting The Most Warmth Out Of All Your Gear

Should you find yourself in a freak situation, such as zero temperatures when you started out in weather that should not have dropped below freezing there are a number of things you can do to improve the warmth of your sleep.

1. You can sleep inside a tent, of course. This increases the temperature by 5 to 10 degrees and it cuts the wind chill factor substantially.
2. Make a sheltered camp out of the wind. This cuts down the wind chill factor.
3. Place your sleeping bags close together. This retains the heat for all of you.
4. Camp on the side of a hill instead of on the valley floor, especially on clear nights. Warmer air lifts up off the valley floor on clear nights. There can be as much as 15 degrees difference between the temperature on the valley floor and halfway up a hill.
5. Use stuff sacks, or poly bags to put your feet or hands into on very cold nights, but be aware that when you wrap yourself inside any plastic you will cause moisture to condense inside, and that will cause any clothing you are wearing inside the plastic to get wet.

212

HOW TO KEEP WARM IN WINTER WITHOUT A CAMPFIRE

by LAURA and GUY WATERMAN

There are two theories about fires in winter. Some folks say you ought to know all about campfire techniques in order to survive the worst conditions. Others say no need for fires to survive; it is better if you conserve the energy and stay warmer with the energy you save. There are techniques for both and the following two articles explain them.

W.K.

How high on the list of priorities should fire building be, even as an emergency tool?

Our answer: not very. A fire is a poor way to keep warm, fire-building uses up energy which you may need to perform important life-saving activities and could be harmful to the environment.

Almost everyone now agrees that campfires have lost their place in normal camping routine. If today's millions of backpackers all lit fires, the destruction of trees would be overwhelming.

But what about emergencies? The notion that starting a fire is the proper way to cope with an emergency is a psychological illusion which dies hard.

There *are* circumstances in which an emergency fire could save a life, no question about that. So it's probably desirable for backpackers to know how to build one. But building an emergency fire falls roughly into the same category as treating a snakebite or performing an emergency tracheotomy on the trail. Furthermore, like performing a tracheotomy with a pen knife, it has been done but should be undertaken only as a last resort and *not* be practiced in advance.

The backpacker who aspires to serious winter hiking ought to be taught more generally useful skills than fire building for surviving unexpected cold weather. Some of these skills:

• how to build a snow cave, and what constitutes a minimum effective bivouac cave for surviving one night;

• effective use of compass, both with and without map;

• what emergency gear to pack for each type of trip;

• the uses and limitations of space blankets, bivouac sacks and elephants' feet;

• knowledge of advanced first aid and mountain medicine;

• how to recognize frostbite and hypothermia, and techniques for dealing with them;

• most important of all—how to minimize the risk of having an overnight emergency arise in the first place. This involves everything from prudent trip planning to weather-judging wisdom, avalanche-risk calculation and mountaineering skills learned from other people.

Why is fire building of so little use? There are several reasons:

1. If getting warm is essential, starting a fire will be little help. An outdoor fire is an extremely inefficient source of heat, even for the one side of you that gets any warmth. Great quantities of fuel are required to produce a negligible amount of BTUs.

2. The modern backpacker almost always carries a down sleeping bag, and he's much better off inside it than out. Inside, the considerable heat his own body generates is retained.

3. If the backpacker gets a fire going, he should then get into his bag, anyway. Once inside it, how could he tend a fire effectively?

4. If hot food is the backpacker's greatest need, he should use his cookstove.

5. If above treeline, firebuilding is a useless art because there will be no burnable materials at hand.

6. Most emergencies where fires are alleged to be needed occur in winter situations. If you start a fire on a six-foot snow cover, you'll soon have a pit several feet deep with the fire at the bottom, where it will furnish no heat but plenty of smoke. It's not easy to cook a meal way down there, either.

7. If a backpacker has the energy, tools and daylight to amass many large logs to construct a fire platform in the snow, he should probably use his time and energy instead to do something of more lasting benefit—like walking out.

If you should be caught in an

emergency without tent, sleeping bag or stove, you *might* want to try to get a fire going. But you would probably be better off using the natural protection of deep snow by digging a snow cave, conditions permitting, or by burrowing under a blow-down where natural caves can occur. Minimize the possibility of frostbite or hypothermia by keeping active, if possible; by loosening boots or crampon straps to keep circulation going; and by being rigorously watchful that no snow gets between you and your clothing; where it would melt.

One of the authors was once caught in a somewhat desperate situation at 35 degrees below zero with winds strong enough to knock him over. When camp was finally established, there was a difficult struggle to keep a Svea stove going long enough to melt snow to supply badly needed hot liquids. He recalls that the idea of getting out of his down bag long enough to start a fire would have been patently absurd. ▰

HOW TO BUILD A CAMPFIRE IN DEEP SNOW

by DICK ANDERSON

It is hard to believe that the good old campfire is no longer the key to backwoods success or survival. But most backpackers have adjusted to the idea. Contemporary ecological concerns have forced us to change many backcountry habits.

We're not arguing that you shouldn't try to start a fire if you find yourself in that very exceptional emergency when it seems to be a practical way (or the only way) to obtain heat. Fine, go ahead. But we do say that such situations, like snakebite incisions, are too rare to justify every backpacker's learning to perform the skill under adverse conditions. And just imagine what a tremendous amount of fragile vegetation would be destroyed every year in the process of teaching the art of fire building to everybody.

So why burn down the woods practicing fires that aren't really needed, wouldn't keep you warm, and are out of step with today's environmental concerns? Read up on how to build an emergency fire because you just might need to, just as you might need to perform an emergency tracheotomy. But as for practicing—keep away from our throats with that pen knife and leave the trees alone.

Any outdoorsman worth his down vest can build a crackling campfire. Simple—matches, some tinder, and dry wood. But remember Jack London's tale about the sourdough in *To Build A Fire*, or the fate of the Donner party in the High Sierra?

The combined elements of high mountain country, deep snow, and freezing temperatures can elevate the most rudimentary task to the realm of the near impossible—even in our age of down and nylon. Many of us venture into the winter wilds without sufficient knowledge of how to deal with an unforeseen emergency.

Each winter, groups of ski tourers and backpackers become stranded because of injury or broken equipment, often having to remain immobile for long periods of time. With nighttime temperatures dipping well below zero, the message is clear: build a fire or perish. When the human body is unable to sustain its normal temperature (a condition known as hypothermia), the only salvation is some source of outside heat—a hot drink and a fire.

But the conventionally constructed campfire will not do. It will burn down through the snow until the walls on top of it cave in or melt away clear to the ground. The ill-fated Donner party had fire holes 15 feet deep.

The first step in building a deep-snow fire is selecting a site. Choose a fairly level spot with an accessible supply of firewood. Avoid overhanging snow-covered branches.

Use skis or snowshoes to tramp down the area. Even in deep powder a packed-out platform will set up firmly enough to allow walking without breaking through the crust.

Gather large pieces of wood for a platform to keep the fire above the snow. The platform will sink slowly but will remain close enough to the surface to maintain a satisfactory base. Make it as level as possible, using larger logs on the downhill side if need be. If you must remain in one spot for some time, it is imperative that you use green logs for the platform to prevent their burning through. Only in an emergency should you cut down a living tree.

The best kind of kindling, especially if fresh snow has fallen, is the sheltered undersides of pine or spruce trees. Dried pine needles and dried sap (pitch) will also catch quickly.

Never try to light a fire with a piece of wood larger in diameter than a match. Select sticks at least eight inches long so that plenty of air can reach the fire. Start it at the *bottom* of the kindling and protect it from the wind.

Add wood while the fire is burning well. New wood, particularly in cold temperatures or at high altitudes, will steal enough heat from a dwindling fire to extinguish it completely.

Should you plan to melt snow over the fire for water, don't repeat the mistake often made by the inexperienced winter camper. A surprising thing happens when a full pail of snow is placed over a fire. Only the bottom inch or so will melt and then boil away without melting any more snow. The result is not only no water but also a badly burned pail. Instead, add snow slowly in small amounts.

Even in our age of down and nylon, building a deep-snow fire is an indispensable procedure for the winter backpacker.

THE TECHNIQUE OF SNOWSHOEING

by GENE PRATER

The simplicity of snowshoeing is the greatest advantage over skis in backcountry.

When I first started backpacking in winter, I took to snowshoes. The choice was obvious: I felt that with them I was on firm footing. That was especially important to me because of the heaviness of the pack I needed to carry in the winter. It had never even occurred to me to use skis.

I had never even seen anyone use skis for backpacking loads in the winter. However, I had read a book published by the Sierra Club about ski mountaineering and while the idea fascinated me, the idea of skiing with a pack held no allure.

It was interesting for me to hear of a veteran Seattle-area mountaineer, Gene Prater, who had also taken to snowshoeing rather than skiing in his winter mountaineering. Gene and his family were so much into snowshoeing that he has designed several snowshoe models. And his brother founded the Sherpa Snowshoe Company.

Gene has taught many people over the years how to snowshoe. Here, he tells about the simple techniques that are involved in using snowshoes effectively.

W.K.

Turning and looking back, I could see the smoothly curving line of exclamation points sunk only three inches or so in the four-foot-deep snowpack. A hundred yards behind us, interrupting the continuity of the snowshoe trail, was a man struggling knee-deep through the snow, with only climbing boots on his feet. My wife was ecstatic. She had passed a veteran mountain climber, a member of the 1963 American Mount Everest Expedition, and he was rapidly losing ground.

It must have been the right choice way back in 1950 when I chose snowshoes rather than skis for winter outings in the Cascade Mountains. When a housewife in her mid-thirties, mother of three, can operate snowshoes this well in steep, rugged terrain, their usefulness and feasibility for winter travel becomes readily apparent.

No doubt the simplicity of snowshoeing is the greatest advantage over skis in rugged backcountry. And this same simplicity has made snowshoeing, for me, the most practical means of navigating otherwise unreachable winter terrain.

The basic design of the snowshoe probably ranks second only to the wheel in practicality of form. Its physical composition has undergone occasional alterations, but its general size, shape and structure remain pretty much the same as they've always been.

Because of our rapidly advancing technology, the last few years have seen several new approaches to traditional problems of expense and weight. Plastic and aluminum snowshoes are now available and, within certain limitations, seem to perform well, but the overwhelming majority of people continue to put their trust in the familiar wooden-frame model.

HOW TO PICK A SNOWSHOE

Three snowshoe designs have survived other variations as the most popular: the Yukon (or Trail) with its high toes and an elongated body usually measuring 10 x 56 inches; the Michigan (or Maine), which is teardrop shaped and generally 12 x 48 inches, with a upward turn of the toes; and the Bearpaw, short, flat and rounded and most commonly 12 x 28 inches. Variations of the Bearpaw are only 10 inches wide and three to four feet in length.

Each shape has its own advantages and disadvantages. The Yukon was designed with the deep powder and sparse underbrush of the West in mind, the Bearpaw for the heavy snow and thick vegetation of the Northeast. The Michigan and Maine seem to fall somewhere in between the two. The shoe that works best for you is the right one. It makes good sense to rent, if possible, until you find the model, weight and size snowshoe that best conforms to your needs.

Getting the right size involves a number of factors. Your height and weight are important, but so too are your strength and endurance. And old rule of thumb is that a

Avalanche conditions: Snow may slide on a 25-degree slope, and slides continually on a 60-degree slope. Snow slabs formed by warm winds—crusts up to many inches thick—slide in blocks. Cornices are always dangerous and may, in falling, trigger slides below. Enough new snow on a hard base will slide on any slope. Heavy, wet snow—a springtime danger—will slide if the slope is steep.

pound of weight on the foot is as tiring to carry as five on the back. Thus, a pair of 10-pound Yukon or Michigan shoes will be the equivalent of a 50-pound pack. Unless you are in exceptional condition, a somewhat lighter shoe with a lower "fatigue factor" would be a wise selection.

I usually suggest that a person with a body weight over 200 pounds use a 10 x 56 inch Yukon, or 13 x 48 inch Michigan design. From 175 to 200 pounds, choose a 10 x 46 inch Yukon pattern or 12 x 48 inch Michigan. People weighing between 150 and 175 pounds are best supported by a 10 x 36 inch Bearpaw or 12 x 34 inch Michigan.

For lightweights under 150 pounds there is a wide array of Bearpaws, although the most common size seems to be 12 x 28 inches. Plastic snowshoes are an alternative in this weight-class, but a note of caution: Although they are light, they are also flimsy. The user tends to sink repeatedly deep into the snow — a process which can be especially tedious when carrying a heavy pack.

Recently, aluminum-frame models have been added to the market on an increasing scale. They come in most sizes and at a great reduction in weight. The advantages of a lighter weight snowshoe are fantastic. But they cost up to double the price of wooden-frame webs. Only time will tell if metal and synthetic fiber will replace wood and rawhide.

THE BUSINESS OF WALKING

Your first outing on snowshoes shouldn't be too long. In the beginning they are cumbersome, and special attention is required to keep from stepping on your own snowshoes and tripping yourself. Depending on the terrain, a mile or less should be long enough.

Once you have learned the walk, you are ready for the refinements. In deep, loose snow the feet must be raised unusually high to keep the tips of the snowshoes from catching in the snow.

In wet, heavy snow several pounds of snow seem to adhere to the lead man's snowshoes. Small hazards are myriad, such as stepping into hollows where the snow has covered bent-over spruce trees or even western sagebrush.

Take turns breaking trail. In very heavy snow, three to five minutes is usually long enough in the lead. In a party of five or six this allows for quite a bit of rest between stints. After the first two or three snowshoers have passed, the trail becomes pretty smooth and keeping up is no longer a difficulty. Learn to use the mountaineers' "rest-step," pausing briefly between strides. It may slow your pace slightly, but it will greatly extend your range.

There are a number of techniques that are useful for both mountain country and flat terrain.

Try to walk up a slope until it becomes too steep to be comfortable, then traverse across the slope as on a trail switchback. If the snow is soft, it is possible to edge your snowshoes so that they are level, although the outside shoe will be slightly lower than the uphill foot. The softer the snow, the higher the uphill shoe must be raised to take a step because of the slope rising on that side.

The turn or switchback itself is a little more complicated. A ski pole or an ice axe with a "basket" attached near the bottom of the shaft is a great aid generally and especially in turning. Either one can be driven into the snow in front of you and used for balance during your turn. (A second ski pole can be placed behind you as support, depending on preference and the grade of your maneuver.) In the East where a good deal of snowshoeing is done below treeline, trees can be held or grappled with an ice axe for assisting in turns or just getting up a steep slope.

In making a turn, the feet present the

greatest difficulty. Facing in the direction of movement, the downhill shoe should be planted as firmly as possible so it won't slip. As mentioned above, the ski pole or ice axe is driven into the snow to provide an anchor. The uphill shoe is then reversed so it faces in the new direction and planted firmly so it won't slip as you complete the turn by shifting your weight to it from the downhill shoe.

After you have reached a high viewpoint, your options in descending depend pretty much on slope and snow conditions. Where the slope is very steep or has any avalanche hazard, it is best to return on your ascending trail. With the giant webs on your feet this can be a touchy procedure. Switchbacks are tricky to descend. Where the slope is clear and the bottom visible, glissading or "skiing" on your snowshoes is rapid but strenuous. Before attempting it, you should be proficient in performing an ice-axe self-arrest and be familiar with local avalanche conditions.

Traction devices or crampons affixed to the bottom of your snowshoes are a necessity for hill or mountain travel and are useful for any small ascents or descents in generally flat country. The most common device is a six-inch length of 3/4 x 3/4 inch (or larger) aluminum angle bolted to the bottom of the wooden crosspiece in front of your toe or to the webbing under your foot. A lengthwise piece may be employed to prevent sideslipping, and additional

Snowshoe kick-turn: Begin an uphill turn by firmly stopping on the outside (in this case the left) shoe. For additional stability plant the axe or pole. Then pick up the inside shoe and point it in the new direction. To complete the turn release the outside shoe and walk on.

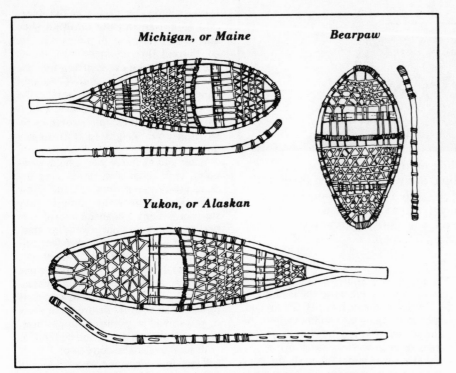

Showshoe types: The bearpaw is for lighter loads and tight turns. Its maneuverability makes it ideal in dense forest and hills where frequent turning is necessary. For flatter trails and fairly open country, the Michigan shoe offers more stability—and a greater bearing surface, making it more suitable for middleweight loads. For open country, very deep snow, and heavy loads, the Yukon design is best, offering still more stability and bearing area than the Michigan.

angles can be bolted on to suit the wearer. Four- and six-point instep crampons also are available and are easily mounted to most makes of snowshoes. Specially built snowshoes with traction mounted under the binding provide the greatest grip.

As a snowshoer gains experience, his bindings will become the focus of increasing importance in adding to his maneuverability and comfort. A loose, sloppy snowshoe binding is as great a drawback to the snowshoer as is a loose ski binding to a skier. For the casual snowshoer, or if the route is level, almost any kind of binding will work. But if there is any up, down, or sidehill climbing, it is vital to have a heavy-duty binding that provides a positive connection between the boot and the snowshoe. For downhill, it is imperative that the binding "trap" the boot and prevent it from slipping forward.

The binding should be of great enough area to spread the pressure over as much of the foot as possible, especially if you wear soft-toe shoe-pacs, the old-stand-by in the East. Mountaineering boots seem to be standard in the mountainous West. The firm toe and sole of the climbing boot provide a

much more solid object to tighten the binding to than does the shoe-pac.

Some bindings are equipped with a metal hinge. These have the advantage of better control of the snowshoe but the drawback of extra weight and expense. Synthetic fabrics are displacing leather for bindings. They are waterproof and so don't become wet or freeze, and they stretch less, as well. The old "H" binding — nicknamed the "Wet Noodle Binding" when it gets soaked and slippery — may be the only variety available in some locations. It leaves a lot to be desired when compared with some of the better-designed newer models.

Finally, footgear should be determined by the amount and type of snowshoeing you actually do. Almost anything warm and comfortable will serve for the once-a-year person. If you intend to do more, you should be a little more concerned with your selection. If you are snowshoeing in mountain country, then you probably will need heavy-duty climbing boots with Vibram soles and laces that won't freeze into a Gordian knot. Gaiters are useful and almost necessary for keeping snow out of the boots and off the laces. Overboots

will add welcome warmth, for climbing boots are not especially warm.

For the general or recreational walker, standard hunting or shoe-pac boots perform well where they are available. When ordering them make sure they are large enough to accommodate heavy socks, are lined, and, of course, are waterproof. If you will be snowshoeing in extremely cold conditions, the Korean War, or "Mickey Mouse," insulated boot is a virtual necessity.

Advanced Procedures

As you improve your technique and expand on your travels, you will find yourself encountering a number of potentially hazardous situations. A little foreknowledge may help you avoid a disaster.

In central Canada, Alaska and some of the western states, frozen streams and lakes are main travel routes; walking on them one always runs the risk of breaking through. The possibility of getting wet feet is even greater in the Northeast and Northwest where snowdrifts form bridges over streams moving too rapidly to freeze. In either case, avoiding a mishap is easier than remedying it.

Obviously, streams and lakes should be by-passed after any prolonged thaw or wherever thin ice is apparent. The ice closest to shore is often soft or thin and should only be crossed with care. The same care should be taken at the point where a lake is fed by springs or streams.

Covered stream locations can be determined by watching for extended depressions or sags on the surface of the snow. You should probe any suspicious spot with ice axe or ski pole before walking on it. Open streams are best crossed by finding a foot log and side-stepping across it, since leaping across streams with snowshoes on your feet is not practical.

In areas of tall luxuriant forest, a constant hazard exists of having branches or entire trees collapse on you under the weight of the snow. Great clumps of snow dropping from fir boughs are rarely fatal but are always a nuisance and are well deserving of the name "Idiot Makers."

Snow avalanches, the most spectacular of winter hazards, are also the most dangerous. It is very fortunate that with a little intelligence they are the most easily avoided. The U.S. Forest Service pamphlet "Snowy Torrents" mentions that a slope as gentle as 20 degrees can avalanche, but the real danger to snowshoers is on steeper terrain. In the East, deaths attributable to avalanches are rare and confined to only a few locations such as Mount Washington's

Huntington Ravine. In the West, the problem is more widespread. The Rockies and Utah's Wasatch Range are famous for high-speed powder snowslides. Both the Cascades and Olympics, with their warmer climates from Pacific storms, are well known for heavy, wet snowslides, equal to any in destructive power.

It is easy to recognize a steep, treeless slope below a rocky mountaintop as a potential snowslide path. So far, however, no one has been able to pinpoint the time when a given slope will avalanche, although certain weather conditions are known to be prime causes of slides. High winds with heavy snowfalls create large accumulations of drifted snow on the lee side of ridges. Such windblown snow adheres poorly to the underlying surface and can become unstable enough for a slide to be triggered by a person snowshoeing across it. At other times this "wind slab," as it is called, is released spontaneously.

In warm weather following a snowfall, snow crystals begin to melt, losing the spikes that make fresh, moist snow pack so well. As the mass loses its cohesion with the surface below it, any small disturbance can cause the entire body to slide.

It is worthwhile to know that sliding snow acts like a fluid and tends to "flow" down gullies and depressions. If snow is falling out of trees and off rocky cliffs onto snow slopes below, if snowballs are spontaneously forming and rolling down past your route of march, the wise decision obviously is to turn back in a hurry. To retreat rather than cross a 200-foot-wide, moderately steep slope with only a foot or so of unstable snow may be an unpopular decision, but research has shown that victims of minor slides are equally as dead as those buried by large-scale avalanches. An all-purpose rule to keep in mind is, "If in doubt — don't!"

Safety and Aesthetics

By its very nature the greatest reward of snowshoeing — experiencing the backcountry in winter — creates the greatest dangers. Whereas fatigue or a minor mishap may mean some inconvenience during the summer, in the dead of winter it can mean tragedy. It is a good policy to always do your snowshoeing as part of a group and to always take along basic first-aid and survival equipment. Because this article concerns snowshoeing and not survival, I will merely say that the fundamental skills of lighting a fire, constructing an emergency shelter and treating injuries may save your life or someone else's. That is reason enough to learn them.

Furthermore, as the leader of a group it will be your responsibility not only to see that the route is followed and the trail-breaker position changed frequently but also that when it becomes foolish to push on, you turn back. Lack of judgment in knowing when to abandon an outing is probably the prime contributing factor to the numerous and needless deaths blamed every year on hypothermia.

I hope that my acquainting you with some of snowshoeing's problems and a few solutions will enable you to avoid such difficulties and to enjoy the spectacular beauty and freedom of the winter landscape that much more.

If you have not yet begun snowshoeing, I envy you the first experience of suddenly finding yourself walking on water — frozen, of course, but no less remarkable.

God has blessed us with a wealth of beautiful mountains and backcountry. Snowshoes can be the vehicle for transporting you from a sedentary urban half-life to a continuing rich and vibrant outdoor experience. 🥾

SNOW CAVES

by DAVID SUMNER

The next best thing to a cabin and fireplace

One of the best survival techniques for staying warm in inhospitable weather is to dig a snow cave. In some of the western national parks, like Rocky Mountain and Rainier, the park service publishes instructions on how to do it.

I know an outfitter, Al McClellan, owner of Rocky Mountain Expeditions, who does a lot of winter camping and uses only snow caves. He never carries a tent.

I suppose if you master the technique this would be okay. Dave Sumner gives instructions on how to get started building caves in his article, which follows.

W.K.

THE PERSON WHO FIRST turned the often-used phrase "blanket of snow" wasn't talking idly; he spoke, perhaps unknowingly, as a pragmatist. In the cold of winter, snow can be a readily available shelter, warm and secure.

Consider the ptarmigan, the plump mountain grouse that molts from mottled brown to snow white and back again with

219

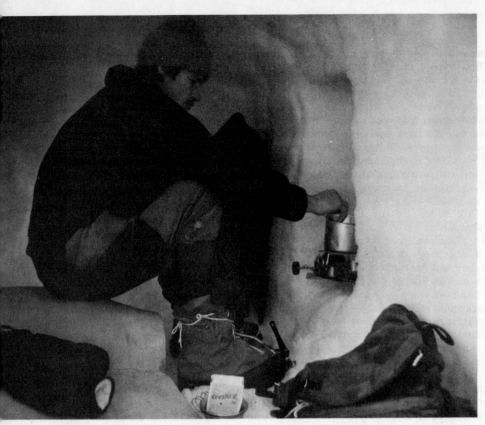

With a bench for sitting and sleeping and a small alcove for the stove, this cave is a cozy home. Note that the snow bench has metamorphosed sufficiently to support the weight of the cave dweller. The ensolite pad on the bench keeps him dry and prevents his body heat from melting the snow.
PHOTO: GARY BRAASCH

caves is notably thin. More often than not, the shelter is treated as a last resort to be used only in emergencies, a grim alternative to spending a night in the open, exposed to wind and storm.

Nevertheless, of all available winter shelters, none is more snug and secure than a snow cave—except a cabin with a fireplace. No shelter is quieter, either. From inside a snow cave, neither a howling blizzard nor a human shout 20 yards away can be heard. Still, most people do not consider snow very hospitable, so the idea of sleeping in a snow cave may require some mental adjustment.

THE INSULATING PROPERTIES of snow are well known. In the Arctic, for example, it's common for areas of deep snow cover to be largely without permafrost; by contrast, areas of light snowfall often have a frost that penetrates deep into the soil year-round.

Scientists at the University of Colorado's Institute of Arctic and Alpine Research describe snow's capacity to insulate by making analogies with feathers and urethane foam. In each, the prime insulating agent is the millions of tiny, trapped, dead air pockets rather than the solid matter. Air itself has an extremely low capacity for conducting heat; as long as substance holds in air and restricts air flow, its success as an insulator is nearly assured. Wet goose down fails as an insulator not because it is soaked but because most of its air pockets have collapsed. A porous material through which air readily passes is equally inefficient at providing warmth.

Snow, however, possesses insulating

the seasons. At night or during a storm, the chunky bird regularly holes up in the lee of a rocky outcrop or protective bush—or occasionally in the open—by scratching out a small, semicircular hole in the snow and snuggling down with its head curled back in the protection of its feathers.

Sometimes, after a wind-driven blizzard, ptarmigans will be all but buried by the insulating snow. In the morning or after the weather breaks (long after the birds are moving about in search of food), one can spot the abandoned remnants of their mini-snow caves: small indentations lined with dung and feathers.

The same lesson can be learned from any of the thickly furred canids of the arctic and alpine regions—wolf, fox, coyote, husky or malamute. In winter, digging into the snow is a practical way to assure both survival and comfort.

Records of snow caves and improvised snow shelters go well back in the nation's history. Indian lore is scattered with references to them, as are accounts of the mountainmen and fur trappers who opened the West in the early 1800s. The diaries of pioneering Arctic and Antarctic explorers and of early Scandinavian ski troops also mention snow caves.

Surprisingly, especially since more and more Americans are exploring the world of winter on touring skis and snowshoes, general knowledge about snow

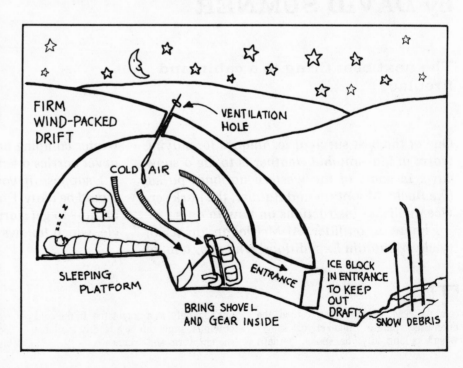

FIRM WIND-PACKED DRIFT

VENTILATION HOLE

COLD AIR

SLEEPING PLATFORM

BRING SHOVEL AND GEAR INSIDE

ENTRANCE

ICE BLOCK IN ENTRANCE TO KEEP OUT DRAFTS

SNOW DEBRIS

qualities in abundance. A fresh layer may hold from 62 to 95 percent air, depending on its structure. (In addition to the classic crystalline hexagon, flakes fall in a variety of other forms: columns, plates, prisms and irregular particles.) Furthermore, the piling and interlocking of the flakes trap air in countless minute pockets.

Once snow has been on the ground for a time, the flakes undergo a process of change known as metamorphism. The rate of change depends on such variables as climatic conditions and the weight and structure of the snowpack, but the general nature of the process is fairly predictable. Sharp points and edges disappear. Under a microscope the snow looks like a mass of tiny kernels or globules. Old snow usually is more dense and contains a lower percentage of air than fresh snow—as little as 40 percent during the melt season. Nevertheless, because firmer bonds tend to develop between these melted flakes, the amount of air, although reduced, may be more effectively trapped, and the insulating qualities of the snow may improve.

Imagine a cave burrowed into such a medium, and the reason why these shelters are warm even in the cruelest of conditions is apparent. The original temperature of snow-trapped air is near the average air temperature during the time the snow fell, but human body heat and heat from candles and cookstoves soon produces a change.

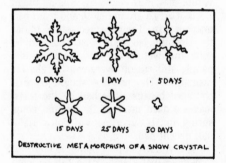

0 DAYS   1 DAY   5 DAYS

15 DAYS   25 DAYS   50 DAYS

DESTRUCTIVE METAMORPHISM OF A SNOW CRYSTAL

Fed by these heat sources, the air temperature in the snow around the interior of the cave rises toward the freezing point, even when it is well below zero outside. Because the heat migrates (or convects) slowly outward into the snowpack, the interior temperature is tolerable.

SOME WINTER CAMPERS have warmed their caves as high as 45 degrees Fahrenheit. The warmth may be welcome, but as a general practice it is not popular, for it may lead to a humid, mushy, drippy cave. Maintaining the temperatures around the freezing point is what most parties shoot for.

(It should be noted that this description does not hold for unusually cold regions. For example, Alaska or Antarctica. Since the temperature within the snow

reflects mean climatic conditions, caves in such zones usually are sufficiently cold to resist all warming. Early in his book, *The Mountain of My Fear,* a classic account of his party's ascent and descent of Mount Huntington in the McKinley range, author David Roberts describes the situation at their cave: interior temperature "a chilly 16 degrees," exterior temperature "an incredible 46 degrees." Nevertheless, the four climbers holed up in the cave were close to comfortable—reading, writing in diaries, cooking, eating, sleeping and playing Monopoly. "Had an avalanche swept over us," writes Roberts, "we would have slept through it, never awakening. Had the Battle of Gettysburg been fought just below us on the Tokositna [Glacier], we might have heard the occasional faint pop of the cannon.")

In short, a snow cave works better than a tent, better than an igloo made of ice blocks and better than almost any other winter shelter. It's all irrelevant to the ptarmigan, but to a skeptic with an inquisitive mind, the knowledge can be reassuring.

For the winter traveler, whether on skis, snowshoes or marooned in a car, three basic ingredients are necessary in planning and building a snow cave: adequate snow, ample time and waterproof clothing.

Of these three, adequate snow is the major stickler because it is not available everywhere. The depth must be sufficient, and the pack should be firm. Digging a cave early in winter before the pack has firmed up or in fresh snow (especially if it happens to be on the wet side) is not impossible, but the risk of a cave-in is there and should not be toyed with.

The ideal spot is a large, wind-packed drift, although a well-covered slope or level terrain will serve the purpose. Anywhere the snow has settled (or metamorphosed) to a stable mass will do. Depth is largely a function of comfort and snow conditions. If you cannot sit up in your cave, you will feel claustrophobic and probably will get wet from rubbing against walls and roof. If the snow is fresh or not firmly packed, however, and you construct too large a cave, you may find it coming down around your ears. The larger the interior, the greater the strain on the roof. As a rule of thumb, construct a cave no larger than necessary for comfortable—not spacious—living. Although western cave builders occasionally get away with a two-inch roof and easterners sometimes need three feet, a roof thickness of at least one foot is recommended.

In the Rockies, the Sierra and the Pacific Northwest, finding a suitable site is seldom a matter of traveling more than a hundred yards. Elsewhere in the United States, a longer search may be necessary. If you're really pressed and absolutely must have a cave, then build your own pile

of snow, allow it to set (depending on temperature and snow conditions, this may take anywhere from five minutes to several hours) and then dig a cave into it. Hardy easterners have built snow caves in two inches of snow!

WHATEVER THE CASE, digging a roomy snow cave does take time, and it's wise to allow at least two hours for the job. Not only is it genuine work but much of the job must be done on your knees, which further slows progress.

Most winter campers believe the time required is the prime disadvantage of building a snow cave. Recently, a number of innovative outdoorsmen have begun experimenting with shortcuts However, these have yet to be proven out on anything more than a regional basis. To dig the standard, time-tested snow cave, a party must plan to stop their travel well before dark and face several hours of strenuous digging.

In cases where a group is moving camp daily, they may prefer to pack tents, which usually can be pitched in five minutes. The trade-off between time and weight is one that must be assessed before the start of any overnight winter trip.

Then there is the matter of staying dry while digging. For the hands, waterproof shells or gloves work well, especially if the temperature is below 20 degrees. In the wet snow of the East, cave builders often use neoprene skin-diving mittens or wear extra-large rubberized work gloves over wool inserts. In dry, cold areas, plastic sacks or even bread wrappers may do. If nothing else is handy, wear woolen mittens, which can be wrung out occasionally to provide some semblance of warmth. For the legs, a pair of rain chaps are unbeatable. If it's on the warm side, slip on a light rain parka but don't zip or snap it—you'd perspire too much.

This preparation may seem excessive, but it's far better than getting wet and then trying to dry out in a humid snow cave. Old adage: He who stays dry stays warm—and alive.

The actual digging is best done with a tough, lightweight aluminum shovel (a small grain scoop works well). Don't trust anything flimsy; a hard snowpack is quite capable of crumpling it. In an emergency, extemporized digging tools are readily available: a spare ski tip, a cooking pot. Then there is the ingenious, Norwegian-made "Tipsaw" manufactured by Weswitco, which folds out into a scoop for just this purpose. (It folds a second way to become a wood saw and a third to become an ice saw.)

Snow caves can also be dug with skis, the point of a snowshoe or a strong stick. Use the implement to break off chunks of snow inside the drift, then scoop them out with your hands. Caves have even been dug with hands alone, but these methods are not recommended.

BASIC SNOW-CAVE DESIGN is the least complex element of the process. A narrow entrance tunnel large enough for one person to crawl through and a dome-shaped room are it. Most people will want enough height so they can kneel comfortably without brushing the roof and knocking the inevitable shower of loose snow down their necks.

Yet, for reasons that probably have more to do with a predilection for order than physical comfort, a snow cave rarely stops with such simplicity. One of the true joys of the shelters is the possibility of infinite, sometimes whimsical variation. Small shelves and alcoves may be carved in the walls to accommodate gear. For larger parties, additional rooms, wings and tiers can be added until the cave becomes almost a catacomb.

The time required for these embellishments is well worth it, especially if the shelter is to serve as a base camp for an extended period. When the National Outdoor Leadership School crew made its pioneering New Year's ascent of Wyoming's Grand Teton in 1970, the man in charge of fashioning the support party's base camp at 11,700 feet was Lawrence Higby. The Byzantine snow cave he created was at the base of a ten-foot vertical shaft and included four rooms, one of them a bridal suite. The cave was affectionately nicknamed "Higby's Hilton."

For the basic snow cave, however, only two additions are truly important. First, there should be a small ventilation hole. It usually is poked in the roof with a ski pole or the handle of a shovel, preferably straight above the cooking area. The possibility of suffocation in an unventilated snow cave is slight, but spending the night in a room with stale, dead air can result in a mean hangover the morning after. If you expect snow during the night or think your air hole might freeze over, thrust a ski pole into the cave from the outside, handle first, and leave the pole in the hole. During the night you can jiggle the pole up and down from the inside, effectively clearing the air passage. A stick left in the hole will work almost as well.

Second, unless the entrance tunnel slants *up* into the cave, it helps to have a raised platform for sleeping. This keeps cold air from flowing down onto you and places you and your sleeping bag closer to the top of the cave where the warmest air collects. In any case, the entrance tunnel should be at least horizontal—never slanting down into the cave—unless there is no choice. Additionally, it is easier to

THE INSTANT CAVE (Can Condominiums Be Far Behind?)

By ERNEST WILKINSON

I have been experimenting with a method of digging a snow cave that is more efficient and involves less stooping and kneeling than standard construction techniques.

I move to the deeper snow of a slope or windblown drift and dig a large entrance hole about three feet wide and four feet high. Utilizing this enlarged entrance rather than the traditional tunnel, I can hollow out a cavern in the snow with a minimum of stooping and kneeling.

After I've removed the bulk of the snow from the cave, I trim the ceiling and walls, shaping them into a dome, and put the loose snow I've removed at the sides of the cave where I pack it into sleeping benches a foot to 18 inches high. Next, I carefully place groundcloths, sleeping pads and fluffed up bags on the benches. I then clean out and smooth a two-foot-wide trench between the benches, sloping the trench downward toward the cave exit (the same way a traditional entrance tunnel slopes down from the sleeping area to the entrance hole).

Outside the cave I gather chunks of snow and, if possible, cut snow blocks which I build into a wall blocking the entrance, making sure the wall comes up under the snow cave roof—not outside it—so as to add support. I chink any cracks with loose snow and wait for the snow to set.

When the snow has hardened, I carve a small entrance hole in the bottom of the wall. My snow cave is completed, my benches have hardened, I'm relatively dry, my sleeping bag has not been dragged through a tight tunnel, and my back is very happy.

dig an upward-slanting tunnel. You can then shovel the snow down and out of the way rather than having to lift it up and out. Advocates of the raised platform point out that it also provides a benchlike arrangement for more comfortable sitting.

A latrine can be added by digging a narrow trench to one side of the entrance below the raised platform. This may not appeal to some people's sense of esthetics, but it does avoid exposure to the elements when nature calls.

For the actual digging process, a couple of guidelines will suffice. Dig at a moderate, measured pace so you don't wear yourself out or perspire excessively. Once the tunnel is complete (strictly a one-man job), two people can dig the remainder of the cave three or four times faster than one person alone. Have one individual inside hollowing out the interior of the cave while another takes up the workhorse post at the entrance, shoveling away the accumulation of snow coming from within. To ward off stiff muscles, switch positions occasionally.

Once you've created a cavity, smooth down the interior walls and roof to create a dome shape. This serves two purposes: the curved surface is stronger than a horizontal roof and vertical walls, and any snow that melts will run along the outside curve to the bottom edge of the cave rather than dripping off the roof and down your neck. If the temperature is warm, you may wish to ditch the edge of the cave to channel this melted snow

away from you and your bag.

From now on it's simply a matter of making a few minor adjustments and of taking some precautions against whatever winter may hurl your way. Among them:

* Carry a ground cloth and foam pad on your trip. They are necessities under the sleeping bag; otherwise you will be cold and wet, or at least damp. Some people still rip off evergreen boughs for insulation. The practice should be discouraged because it is hell on the trees, leaves a dead mess on the ground come spring and is superfluous if you carry a half-decent pad.

* If you're camping in humid country, remember that a snow cave can be even more humid and may decrease the insulating property of down bags. A polyester fiber bag, on the other hand, won't have this problem.

* Take all gear into the cave with you at night except skis, poles and snowshoes. Stand these firmly and straight in the snow outside the entrance. Even a modest storm will bury everything else. Be sure to take in the shovel; for some reason it is easily left outside, where it's no help should you have to dig yourself out in the morning.

* If you're using a cave as a base camp for day trips, be sure it is well marked so you can find it on your return. Snowdrifts and slopes can take on a bewildering sameness, even in a light storm, and you don't want to be groping about.

* If the cave is in a fairly level snow-

field, mark out the area so no one walks or skis across the shelter and pays an unexpected visit through the roof. That can happen more easily than you'd expect.

＊ Inside the cave, keep your bag covered—wrapping the ground cloth around it is the easiest way—while you're cooking and rummaging around. Snow from clothing or the ceiling can fall and melt, producing unwanted wet spots on bags.

＊ To retain heat and avoid drafts at night, or during a daytime storm, prop a block of snow, a pack or a snowshoe and some loose snow in the entrance. The hole in the roof will be all you need for ventilation. If it is snowing, though, you'll want to check periodically during the night to be sure the hole has not become plugged.

＊ A candle or two, plus their reflected light from the interior walls, will illuminate a cave surprisingly well. It is possible to read or write in this light. Indeed, that

can be almost a psychological necessity when you're holed up for any extended spell. Do not, however, let the candles burn through the night; they consume oxygen and may lead to headaches or nausea.

＊ If you're using a cave for more than a day or two, repeated heating and cooling may result in an icy glaze on the interior surface. Scrape it off so the cave will "breathe" better. Even though air moves slowly through snow, having it move at all can make the difference between a pleasant and a stuffy cave.

＊ Make sure you have a place for everything and everything is in its place. Unless you are organized, the cave will mysteriously gobble up cups, spoons, flashlights, candles and almost anything else smaller than a sleeping bag.

＊ After a day or two in a cave, the roof will settle. Shave off one or two inches of snow to preserve your headroom. If the

walls are melting excessively, dripping water all over you and your gear, the roof is probably too thick. Shave off a few inches, and see if life improves. Conversely, if frost forms on the interior, the roof is too thin. Go outside and pile snow on top of the cave.

Some people say caves are the next best thing to returning to the womb; others use them to fulfill long-lost childhood dreams of castle building. Virtually everyone gives ready testimony to their ample warmth, quiet and peace.

Like the ptarmigan and the other animals that turn instinctively to snow for winter shelter, let the cave help you when it can. For an element so commonly regarded as hostile and dangerous, snow is amazingly hospitable. And not unlike a blanket, at that. ◣

WILDERNESS SKIING

Up or Out?

by DAVID SUMNER and WHIT PORTER

One of the most embarrassing moments for me in the wilderness was a time I roped up, ice ax in hand and crampons on feet, plodding up the glaciers on the back side of Mt. Baker in the Cascade Mountains with a couple of climbing friends. We had started our long climb from Kulshan Cabin at about one in the morning. At daybreak another party of two men and two women passed us up, just marched right on by us, clad in stretch pants and ski boots, with skis and poles on their shoulders.

What for us was a mountaineering feat, for them was a slog up a hill, albeit a 10,000-footer. When we arrived on the summit, they had finished their lunch, taken their snapshots, and

were strapping on their skis. Then, whoosh, off they went in one long beautiful schuss back to Kulshan Cabin. I believe they said it would take them just 12 minutes to make the run.

There has been a great deal of interest in wilderness skiing lately—the variety where the skier is off in untracked snow. They go to the wilderness from two directions: the severe downhill skier looking for more challenges like those folks I met on Mt. Baker, and the ski tourer looking to get farther away from the crowds. But I suspect that both of them are seeking to get back to the silence and magic of the winter wilderness.

W.K.

Who is the wilderness skier? Behold him in two of his guises.

• This: setting out on skinny, laminated wood skis; poling with Tonkin bamboo; shod in lightweight,

ankle-high boots; toting a modest day pack loaded with lunch, extra clothes and an assortment of safety gear. He glides through unbroken snow, over rolling terrain, occasionally travers-

ing steeper slopes. The route he follows is chosen for diversity, maximum scenery, and simple, almost casual, pleasure.

• Or this: heading uphill on

stubby plastic/fiberglass skis; poling with variable length, 18mm aircraft aluminum; shod in heavy double mountaineering boots (which he encases in plastic "descent uppers" for firmer support on the downhill run); head sheathed in a crash helmet; toting a substantial frameless assault pack loaded with crampons, ice screws, rope, carabiners, overnight expedition gear but not quite the kitchen sink. He trudges up a 40-degree backcountry slope out of no particular love for climbing. Then he tops the summit of a mountain, ridge, couloir or chute and barrels down, flying over low cliffs and drops, schussing deep powder, carving broad S-turns and trailing a rooster tail of iridescent white, probing something he vaguely senses is "the ultimate."

Attire in both cases is consistent in principle while variable in style. The wilderness skier will dress in layers that can be peeled off or pulled on with the weather to keep his body warm but not overheated. Source of garb may be Abercrombie and Fitch, Eddie Bauer, White Stag, the Salvation Army, Goodwill or Grandma's attic—chic, camp, gross or grundy. But clothing is always functional, always loose enough to allow plenty of freedon of movement.

Motivations are diverse and mixed. Many people get into wilderness skiing because they wish to extend backpacking to a four-season pursuit, to enjoy the freedom of the hills and woods under a blanket of snow. Some people break for the wilds out of disenchantment with 47-minute waits in lift lines, crowded alpine slopes, the show-off mystique of developed areas and $12-per-day lift tickets. Other people head out to push limits and explore the unknown. They want to make a multiday backcountry trek under full pack on narrow, Nordic skis; to do an all-or-nothing ski descent of a 14,000-foot peak using modified alpine gear. Wilderness skiing exists in the 1970s because of this rich blend of yearning and rejection, which has created soul mates and bedfellows of several disparate types.

Distinctions always help, so put it this way: there are two kinds of wilderness skiers—those who go *up and back down* and those who head *out*.

Up high on skinny skis: Colorado's San Juan Range is full of avalanche paths, but this trail up 12,800-foot MacMillan Peak is a safe exception.
PHOTO: DAVID SUMNER

Two examples:

TERRY YOUNG is a 35-year-old "up-and-back-down" wilderness skier. Professionally, he is honcho of an Aspen-based outfit named Company 3 that specializes in equipment suited to his kind of skiing. Personally, he is a dropout from the downhill, ski resort scene, a highly skilled alpine skier who found packed trails and marked runs too confining and itched to explore his own limits. Young and his compadres ski the deep, unbroken powder of steep wilderness mountain slopes. When conditions are less perfect, such challenges as the corn-and-ice crud of a north-facing couloir in May will do just as well. Young will occasionally get into technical mountaineering, and often into cross-country, or Nordic skiing. But both are mainly means to the end of getting him to the height from which he will launch a downhill descent.

"I'm totally willing to die to do this," he says quietly. "I'm willing to risk giving up life to experience that much more of life." He describes the joys of total control and commitment that come from skiing and compares its outer dimensions to the extremes of class-10 kayaking, 5.10 climbing, sky diving and hang gliding.

SVEN WIIK, older and more restrained than Young, is an "out" wilderness skier whose life centers around his very fine lodge and training center on the fringe of the Steamboat ski area in northwestern Colorado. A native Swede, he came to the United States more than two decades ago and soon established himself as one of America's premier cross-country ski racing coaches. At little Western State College in Gunnison, Colorado, he turned out one top runner after another, and in 1960 he was head U.S. Olympic Nordic coach at Squaw Valley. Today his lodge is a haven for the ski touring sport, and Wiik himself is a dedicated guru. Though he still works with racers, he spends most of his time teaching all comers from ages six to 75 how to stride and glide on skinny skis, and he does it extraordinarily well.

Although there is a technique track at Wiik's Lodge and a complex of packed touring trails, Wiik likes to take his charges wilderness skiing. East of Steamboat on Rabbit Ears Pass in the Park Range is some of the loveliest rolling mountain terrain anywhere in Colorado. Here, Wiik and friends head out over the unbroken snow for the afternoon, or the day or overnight, holing up in igloos or snow caves.

Like Young, Wiik is concerned with skiing well, but for him perfection is quieter and less dramatic. It is the rhythmic grace of effortless Nordic technique. "Poetry in motion" he calls it, and Wiik on skis approaches ballet. But unlike Young, who can verge on the mystical, Wiik remains

The Ramer binding for alpine touring, set in the cross-country mode either with downhill ski boots as shown or with climbing boots. The hinged plate locks down with a precision safety release for the descent. It props on a helical spring for climbing.
PHOTO: KENDALL WILLIAMS

eminently practical about his love. He points out that touring exercises the entire body and is an ideal vehicle for fitness. "Arms, lungs, legs and heart," he tells his classes, "all work rhythmically together when you're out there gliding along."

There, basically, are the two breeds of wilderness skiing that are alive and well in the United States today. Young's technique is mostly downhill, and Wiik's Nordic. But both borrow liberally from each other. Wiik, for instance, will sail down a moderately steep powder slope like a dancer, dipping in and out of sweeping telemark turns.

Equipment.

Only three years ago, equipment for the "up-and-back-down" wilderness skier was a hodge-podge of alpine, Nordic and mountaineering gear, much of it ineffective or outdated. Equipment for the "out" skier, however, has changed little in a decade, except for minor refinements and a current revolution in synthetic ski technology.

One of the appealing qualities of the "out" skier's gear is its aura of tradition. Skis are usually handsome, multilaminated wood; poles are often bamboo; cable bindings have changed little in a generation; boots are old-timey, flexible leather. As with most backpacking gear, the goal is maximum strength and support with minimum weight. When there's any doubt, the skier chooses strength and support and puts up with extra weight.

• *Skis.* Prime criteria for a quality wilderness Nordic ski are strength, flex pattern, weight, quality of base and stability.

The need for strength is obvious; a broken ski only 400 yards from the nearest plowed road can be an ugly problem. The flex pattern makes the difference between easy and grueling sliding. A well-designed ski should have a slightly stiff camber so that even when one totes a 50-pound pack, only the tips and tails ride hard on the snow except in mid-stride. Most wood models are bulky compared with the leaner, lighter skis that now dominate the recreational touring market. The new synthetic touring skis (plastic–fiberglass combinations, often with wood, sometimes with aluminum) are stronger per unit of

weight and thus lighter. On the other hand, relatively few manufacturers are making synthetic models wide enough (60mm to 65mm at the tip) for heavy duty wilderness skiing.

Hickory is the only sensible wood bottom; it's tough and holds wax well. The synthetic bottoms, which are usually plastic resins or epoxies, are equally durable, but some lose their wax too quickly. A surprising number of skiers have ducked waxing entirely by turning to skis with fishscale, stepped or mohair-strip bottoms. They're great for beginners because they don't slip, but able technical skiers notice they don't glide as well as properly waxed skis. This deficiency subtly increases fatigue on long overland treks.

The Norwegian-made Bonna 2400 is the premier, all-wood warhorse of wilderness Nordic skiing; a 200cm pair weighs just over 5½ pounds. The new Huski Classic (61mm at the tip, weight about 4½ pounds for a 200cm pair), the Jarvinen Speedglass and the Karhu Titan are solid synthetic

Some Books on Wilderness Skiing

Tejada-Flores, Lito, and Allen Steck, *Wilderness Skiing,* Sierra Club, 1972, $6.95. One of very few books treating wilderness Nordic ("up-and-back-down") skiing in adequate detail. Equipment section is dated. Chapter "The Ski Touring Scene" is a good thumbnail directory of places to ski, with emphasis on the Far West.

Wiik, Sven and David Sumner, *The Regnery Guide to Ski Touring,* Henry Regnery Company, 1974, $4.95. About Nordic ("out") skiing, only. Chapters "The Day Tour," "The Overnight Tour," "The Complete Tour Leader" and "When Winter Turns Mean" bear directly on wilderness skiing.

Williams, Knox, *The Snowy Torrents: Avalanche Accidents in the United States, 1967-1971,* U.S. Forest Service General Technical Report, 1975, $2.50. Precise, lucid and chilling accounts of 76 avalanche incidents in ten western states in which people were trapped; 60 percent involve skiers. Excellent cautionary reading.

models. Trak makes two "Nowax" skis with fish-scale bottoms.

• *Poles.* For years bamboo, especially Tonkin cane, was it—strong, flexible but more apt to break than the aluminum alloys that have now taken over half the market. Nordic poles have forward pointing tips to cut down on jamming in the snow, large baskets up to six inches across and adjustable wrist straps to assure proper grip whether one is wearing thick down mitts or light gloves. Scott USA, Skilom and Liljedahl all make top-of-the-line aluminum alloy poles.

• *Bindings.* Most "out" wilderness skiers touring with medium to heavy packs will want cable bindings similar to those used on downhill skis in the 1940s. These give greater stability and support than the lighter (up to a pound per pair) three-pin "rat-trap" bindings that clamp only toe to ski and leave heel free to lift with the boot's flex. Yet a skilled Nordic stylist will use the lighter binding because his technique gives him all the stability he needs. Jofa's Cortina and the Gresshoppa Cable are among the most dependable heavier bindings.

• *Boots.* A flexible leather touring boot cut just above the ankle is the norm; a pair should weigh as little over two pounds as possible. A lower cut gives less support and less warmth; a higher cut adds unnecessary weight where it's least needed. Fleece-lined boots are of dubious value because once wet, they dry very slowly. Spare socks provide dryness and warmth with more practicality. Gaiters are almost a must in deep snow. Lightweight rubber boot gloves are invaluable on slushy days. Alfa, Fabiano and Norrona are among the more popular Nordic boot brands. Care should be taken to ensure that boots, bindings and skis are well matched to each other.

In contrast to these relatively simple items, the "up-and-back-down" skiers rely on sophisticated high-performance equipment. This is Company 3's thing: manufacturing and marketing the most advanced gear for running the steep and deep. What the firm does not make itself, it finds in the most obscure places in the United States and Europe. For alpine touring equipment, four major challenges stand out: the equipment must perform well under extreme

How to Survive an Avalanche

"I looked uphill and saw the snow hurtling toward me. There was no chance to out-ski the slide; I was knocked down almost immediately. I dropped my poles and began 'swimming' with it in an effort to stay on top of the snow. I finally came to a stop lying on my side, twisted around so my feet were higher than my head. As the snow from above buried me, I managed to move my head around enough to form a small air pocket.

"The avalanche ended as quickly as it had begun. I could hear the muffled crunch above as the snow settled around me. It was solid, like being in a bag of wet cement. I couldn't move at all, but I wasn't uncomfortable. Oddly enough, I felt no sensation of cold, pressure, or even fear . . . just a cozy feeling of being all covered up with a thick, soundproof quilt. Even though I concentrated on breathing slowly to conserve the limited air supply, I soon lapsed into unconsciousness."

So wrote Dick Porter in *Western Skier* of his experience with an avalanche at the Jackson Hole, Wyoming, ski area in a deep gully now known as Dick's Ditch. The date of the accident was January 5, 1967. Rescue action began immediately and, because the slide was small (only 120 feet wide by 80 feet downslope) a line of 20 searchers using avalanche probes were soon able to find Porter.

A total of 65 minutes elapsed between the slide and the time the victim was dug from beneath five feet of snow. He was gray, unconscious and not breathing; mouth-to-mouth resuscitation began at once, then oxygen was given before he started to breathe. He was rushed to shelter where he was stripped and placed in a tub of warm water to counteract hypothermia. Later he was hospitalized and given intra-venous fluids to combat the muscle cramps and blood poisoning that resulted from oxygen starvation.

Porter recovered completely and was skiing again in five days. Obviously, the quick rescue effort at the developed ski area was a major factor in his survival.

But, as Porter notes, "What goes on under the snow is important too. Making that air pocket undoubtedly saved my life. I'm in good shape physically and don't smoke, so my system utilized the available oxygen efficiently. Having skied professionally for almost ten years, I've become acclimated to the high altitude and cold. As a patrolman, I was familiar with avalanches and survival techniques such as making air pockets and breathing slowly. The fact that my head was lower than my feet helped blood circulation to the brain, while lying on my side prevented me from choking."

Porter was lucky. Statistics from 121 U.S. avalanche burials from 1967 to 1974 show that only one avalanche-buried victim in three survived. No one covered by more than six feet of snow lived; neither did anyone buried longer than eight hours. These statistics also show that a victim covered to any depth has only a 50 percent chance of survival after 30 minutes.

The implication is obvious: time is of the essence in avalanche rescues. In the wilderness that means only a victim's companions can save his life, and only by acting swiftly. Skiers should *always* carry an avalanche probe, avalanche cord and a Pieps 1 so that a victim can be located as quickly as possible. Shovels are equally important for prompt digging out, which is not an easy task in hard-packed snow.

Rescuers should never abandon efforts until the victim has been found. Even after six hours, chances of survival are still 2 or 3 percent, and there is one case on record of a 59-year-old man surviving being buried for 25½ hours. He was fortunate enough to have an air space the "size of a washtub" around his head.

stress, it must be reasonably light, it must work together and, although its chief function is the downhill run, it should also follow the Nordic groove. No mean task. Surveying Company 3's array of basic gear, it might appear that Rube Goldberg had gone skiing. Not so. Today's madness is tomorrow's wisdom.

• *Skis.* Company 3's Trucker skis (Mother Trucker, Trucker 2 and plain ole Trucker) are designed to handle the loveliest and lousiest conditions of steep mountain slopes. The Trucker line evolved from the European *Kurzski,* a short backcountry mountain ski used by Swiss, Austrian and German army troops on duty in the Alps. Company 3 has progressively improved its product to the present models made of combined thermo-plastic, fiberglass, rubber, polyethylene and aluminum. Each element has a similar molecular structure so the ski is a very "tight unity." Chattering and vibration are minimal, even at high speeds and banging off bumps.

The Trucker is short: 180cm maximum compared with the 205cm average for thin Nordic skis. And it is wide: 90mm at the tip tapering to 73mm under the boot and back out to 80mm at the tail. Short for tight maneuvering through a stand of trees or down a narrow chute, wide for maximum stability and running surface, and tapered for quick response at all times. Equally important, it is light (7.4 pounds for a 180cm pair) and workable in the Nordic mode. For the flat or traversing uphill, Truckers are waxed like standard cross-country skis. Gone is the old alpine tourer's curse of lugging two pairs of skis—Nordic or ultra-short mountaineering models for the ascent and standard downhillers for the descent.

• *Poles.* The "up-and-back-down" skier used to endure a similar problem with poles: comfortable Nordic length is about eight inches longer than that for downhilling. You either packed two pairs of poles or skied with misfits for half of each outing. But now Company 3's variable length aircraft aluminum poles combine both needs in a single unit. And there's more. When you're climbing a bare, windswept ridge, carrying skis and poles is a drag. Company 3's poles collapse down to

two feet and may be stuffed out of the way in a pack. In the high country, avalanches are always a threat. These same poles may also be extended to maximum length, screwed together, the baskets snapped off and used as avalanche probes measuring almost three meters long. Expedition tents need poles, but there's no reason to carry the extra weight (1½ pounds for a two-man tent) when ski poles will do the job; Company 3 is working on a line of screw-in/snap-on fittings for tent use.

• *Bindings.* For years there has not been an adequate, double-duty alpine/Nordic binding. The Silvretta was long the standard. It was fine for Nordic striding in heavy boots, but its safety release was inadequate for downhill running. The Silvretta has been known as the "bear trap" because of the violence it inflicts on innocent ankles and legs. More recently, Su-Matic and Marker have made alpine touring bindings with excellent safety features, but they allow marginal heel lift for striding.

Now we have the (Paul) Ramer Binding manufactured by Alpine Research, Inc. of Wondervu, Colorado. It is an efficient, two-in-one design— firm and safe in the downhill mode, and easily switched to a very comfortable Nordic mode. In the latter, the heel can be propped as high as four inches on a helical spring (like a child's kangaroo shoe), which makes it possible to walk straight up a 50-degree slope "as easily as you would climb a flight of stairs," says Young. The binding works equally well with conventional downhill and soft-soled climbing boots.

• *Boots.* As yet, there is no mass-marketed boot that switches from Nordic to alpine mode, so most "up-and-back-down" skiers wear heavy or double climbing boots like Galibier's or Lowa's. For added support on the downhill run, they can be stiffened by Galibier's descent upper, a plastic shell that buckles around most climbing boots and up the calf.

Inventive Paul Ramer has developed the first generation of what may become the ultimate omni-boot, a model that triples for hiking and Nordic and alpine skiing. It is made of motorcycle-height plastic, has Vibram soles and features flexible, telescoping lowers and ankle pivots that

can be locked or unlocked according to use. Ramer describes these boots as "radical" and "weird." His major patents went through only last October, and he hopes to make and market 50 pairs this season.

Hazards.

Whether you ski "out" or "up-and-back-down," you must be aware of hazards peculiar to the wilds in winter. A summer backpacker who gets lost can usually hole up for the night and be little the worse for wear; a lost skier, however, is in immediate trouble. A sudden summer shower is unpleasant; a swift blizzard can be a killer.

And there are no avalanches in the summer. Few people ever see these slides, even those who live in the mountain snow belt; common sense normally steers humans and their settlements away from hazardous areas. But this is deluding: out of sight, out of mind. In the last 25 years in the United States, 147 people have been killed in avalanches, all of them except seven in the West. The last slide deaths in the East occurred on April 4, 1964, when two climbers were killed on New Hampshire's Mount Washington. Colorado (48), Washington (22) and Idaho (18) have been the scene of the most avalanche fatalities over this period, and the annual figure throughout the country is rising. The winter of 1974-75 witnessed a total of 17 deaths in seven western states.

Last winter, areas of Colorado were for a while almost under a state of seige by avalanche. Snow information was unusually conducive to the big slides. In one month, January of 1975, and in one range, the San Juan, researchers from the University of Colorado's Institute of Arctic and Alpine Research observed 327 avalanches. Of these, 84 reached a well-traveled U.S. highway. At least 3,000 slides were estimated throughout the range, an average of 100 a day.

During this long winter, seven Colorado wilderness skiers became what are coolly counted as "avalanche victims." Art Evans, veteran of the *Haute Route* in the Alps, and Keith Rush, an experienced Nordic skier, were two of them. Dick Scar of Rocky Mountain Expeditions in Buena Vista recently described the search he led for the pair in Taylor Gulch, a gentle alpine bowl in the Sawatch Range. The skiers were 18 hours overdue at the time, and a U.S. Forest Service helicopter had spotted the aftermath of a slide in the gulch.

"When we got near the gulch," Scar recalled, "it was nothing like I expected. I'd imagined displaced boulders and uprooted trees strewn over a huge area. But it was only a lower portion of a snow slope at the head of the gulch that had sloughed down. From a distance you could hardly tell it had moved. I was relieved at first to see how small the slide was, then a bit disappointed that there wasn't something a little more spectacular. For some reason, the fact that Art and Keith might be dead hadn't made it into my mind. Up close I could see that the slide area was composed of jumbled-up chunks of snow about the size of small boulders. The whole area wasn't much larger than a football field."

Scar and other searchers poked about for a while, found nothing, followed tracks into the next valley and a small cabin, found no one there and returned to Taylor Gulch. It was a glorious, bright, warm morning; the skiers relaxed and several of them even stopped to take pictures before running a probe line.

"Something made me look down," Scar said. "Maybe the color caught my eye. It was a glove and blue jacket sleeve—a hand and forearm—sticking out of the snow. I don't know how we missed it on the way up. I recognized the sleeve as Art's and knew he'd been there since two or three the previous afternoon when the slide was first spotted. I touched the arm with my ski pole; it was almost as though I were afraid to use my bare hand for fear of catching some dread illness. Art's arm was stiff as a board. About that time a numbness settled over me, which lasted several days. All reason dictated that the foreign object in the snow was no

longer a live person, but I started to dig with a ski tip. I couldn't believe how hard and dense that snow was— like concrete. I uncovered Art's pack and could tell he was lying prone under only a foot or two of snow. It seemed incredible that he couldn't have just gotten up and brushed himself off. But there was no air pocket around his face, not even an 'ice mask,' which indicated it happened quickly."

Although they can be classified by types, every avalanche is different, and avalanche knowledge is difficult to come by. Among the best ways to learn is to attend either of a pair of avalanche schools, both in their second year. The American Avalanche Institute of Wilson, Wyoming, offers three different courses. One is for Nordic and alpine wilderness skiers, one is for professionals (ski patrolmen, snow rangers) and one is an advanced field training seminar. The ski tourers' course runs for four days with two sessions each at Jackson Hole and Silverton, Colorado—two of the most avalanche-prone areas in the West. In California the Sierra Avalanche Seminars organized by Norman Wilson are given at Donner Summit four times each winter. These are also for ski tourers and run for four days. Teachers at both schools include several of the country's leading avalanche experts.

Other wilderness skiing hazards are more predictable: blizzards, whiteouts, frostbite, hypothermia, snowblindness, dehydration, sunburn. Ample preparation, due caution, first aid and survival gear will normally take care of them. But no one should ever underestimate the extremes possible during the winter. In the Rockies, for example, the temperature can easily drop 15 degrees in five minutes, and visibility can go from total sunlight to total whiteout. It is wise to carry extra clothing with a 30- to 40-degree temperature margin

beyond what you expect to encounter.

Curiously, however, a surprising number of wilderness skiers who are careful in all other respects incorrectly assume their equipment is infallible. They don't seem to realize that bindings can pop screws, skis break, poles snap and pants rip. The kind of thing that's just a nuisance to the summer backpacker is a genuine danger to the wilderness skier.

Sven Wiik carries a "bag of tricks"—an all-purpose, assemble-it-yourself repair kit that you should carry, too, anytime you venture off the beaten path. Wiik's strong and compact lightweight tools and spare parts can bring off any repair job in no more than five minutes. The idea is to be able to deal with all contingencies by jury rigging. The contents of his bag: screwdriver and screws, extra binding parts, pliers, baling wire, strong tape (tire or gaffer's), small hammer, small drill, safety pins, spare pole strap, spare pole basket, emergency ski tip, simple jackknife. Only the leader of a group tour need carry such a kit; even if only two people are touring, however, one of them has to be the leader.

All these dangers are real, but it's all too easy to sketch a falsely grim picture of the wilds in winter—and to induce fright when no more than caution and respect are in order. The wilderness skier (whatever his guise and gear) need be mindful and aware—but no more. His sport takes place in a season of sharper limits and finer demands than those of the summertime backpacker. He plays and explores within constraints that can be imposed by snow, cold, biting wind and dazzling light. Winter is a realm that tends to subdue the extraneous and drive one toward the essential. Whether he heads *out* or *up and back down,* the seasoned wilderness skier knows and cherishes this well. ➤

SKI TOURING

18 Days Through Yellowstone

by ORVILLE E. BACH, JR.

Here is a ski-touring trip that gives me a twinge of envy. It is one of those trips that I have just got to take one—"one of these days."

Without detracting from the excitement or suspense of the tale, it is worth noting some of the errors the author confessed to me that were made on this trip.

First, the group got lost. They ought to have retraced their tracks until they were sure they knew where they were.

Second, they should not have zigzagged up a steep, snow-covered slope. That is almost sure to cause an avalanche with you in it. They were lucky.

Third, they should never have skied across a frozen lake—especially in an area where there are known thermal currents which could cause thin spots in the ice and a perilous fall into the lake.

Fourth, they continued on their trek in a blizzard, when visibility was zero. This is a very dangerous practice. And again, they were lucky. Not recommended procedure.

W.K.

Every dyed-in-the-wool backpacker has experienced the feeling that pervades the mind and body just prior to embarking on a lengthy trip. The two- and three-day backpacking trips are great, but when you are about to enter the wilderness for two weeks plus, well, it's like being a kid at Christmas. Such were my feelings of excitement as I stood in the doorway of a rustic log cabin at Old Faithful, in Yellowstone National Park, admiring the winter beauty of a cold February morning.

After months of planning meals and eyeballing topo maps (which is at least half the fun), Brian Severin, Steve Veltrie, and I were finally ready for an 18-day ski tour that would take us deep into Yellowstone's winter wilderness. Brian and Steve were adding a few finishing strokes of wax to their skis. In the distance a tremendous cloud of steam began to mushroom above the trees, signaling another eruption of Old Faithful. The minus 14 degree air only magnified the loveliness of the surrounding thermal features in the Upper Geyser Basin, where extreme heat and cold combine to produce unique scenes. The deep blue sky was filled with tiny ice crystals that were the result of geysers erupting throughout the basin; they had the appearance of a million miniature prisms.

Soon our packs were donned and we were gliding toward the trailhead, located only a few hundred yards from the cabin. It appeared that my dream was finally about to come true. Although I had explored Yellowstone's vast backcountry many times during the summer, I had made only a few brief visits to the grand old park during the winter. For several years I had dreamed of making a lengthy cross-country ski tour there, but for lack of time and available companions, the trip had remained only that, a dream. Finally, though, I managed to find the time (20 days) and the companions "crazy" enough to go with me. First, I met Brian Severin, a rugged backpacker and cross-country skier from Great Falls, Montana, who completely shared my enthusiasm for the trip. Two other backpacking friends were eager to go but could not arrange the time: through them, however, I met Steve Veltrie of Spokane, Washington, a rock and ice freak who seemed to spend half the year on the slopes of Mount Rainier. I felt quite satisfied with the experience of our threesome, and trip plans were quickly under way.

Because the Yellowstone country produces some of the nation's coldest winter weather (the record is minus 66 degrees with no chill factor), we had to be ready for anything. Our plans were to make a semicircular tour of the park's backcountry, starting at Old Faithful in the southwest and concluding at Gardiner, Montana, on the northern boundary. The distance to be covered measured about 150 miles, for which we had allotted 18 days. We knew that weather conditions would be the determining factor in the actual distance we would cover, but we did not realize how important the weather would be. According to park records, December and January are mostly stormy with plenty of snowfall; additionally, the days are quite short. The best time for making the trip would be from mid-February to mid-March, when the days are longer and chances for sunshine greater.

Our biggest problem was loading our packs for 18 days. We would cross only one plowed road during the entire trip—the Cooke City road at the northeast entrance. (The other roads are open to over-the-snow vehicles.) We left a cache of steak, potatoes, beans and wine at the Lamar Ranger Station on the Cooke City road. But we would not get there until the fifteenth day. With no other possibilities for caches, we were forced to go 100-percent freeze-dried. Even so, what with food, clothing and camp gear for 15 days, our packs weighed in at 55 pounds. They would certainly be a deterrent to any "hot-dogging."

A bright spot among the plans was being given permission to stay in a few backcountry National Park Service patrol cabins. Several of them date back decades to the early days of the park, and though they are for official use only, permission may occasionally be granted for winter travelers to use them.

Our itinerary would take us past the best the backcountry has to offer. We would visit the geyser basins at Shoshone and Heart Lake, skirt Yellowstone Lake and the Absaroka Mountains, and pass through the Black Canyon of the Yellowstone River, into which many species of animals descend every winter in search of food.

With high spirits, perfect snow conditions and the luxury of a packed trail, we covered the first four miles to Lone Star Geyser (so named because it is the only geyser in the area) with ease. We knew that the geyser performed about every three hours and decided to take a midmorning break in the hope of seeing it in action. But it did not cooperate, and we

witnessed merely a few bursts of water and steam.

There are many hot pools, springs and fumaroles in the vicinity of Lone Star. Although we knew about the danger involved in skiing across these thin-crusted areas, we had no idea how difficult and time-consuming it would be. In many places the underlying heat made just enough snow melt to botch up our skis. Having to stop occasionally to break off chunks of ice and rewax the skis became a necessary chore. It slowed down our progress considerably.

We entered deep, untracked snow as we began the long, slow climb up to Grants Pass, at an elevation of 8800 feet on the Continental Divide. Ski touring was reduced to "ski-shoeing." We did not reach the pass until shortly after darkness had settled into the woods. After stomping out a flat spot with our skis, we pitched the three-man tent, slipped into our sleeping bags and ate a hearty meal of beef and potatoes. Then we were content to soak in the silence and drift off to sleep. It felt great to be back in the wilderness.

The following morning broke clear and cold, with the thermometer reading 8 degrees below zero. Brian started things off right with steaming stewed apricots, granola and hot cocoa. We decided that our evening destination would be Shoshone Lake and Geyser Basin and hoped that there would be enough daylight left to explore the basin.

Almost immediately after breaking camp, we became lost, at least as far as following a trail was concerned. Most of Yellowstone's paths are identified by orange metal markers nailed to trees eight to 10 feet above the ground. At our elevation, however, and in dense lodgepole pines, most of the markers were covered by an accumulation of snow. We set a compass course on the topo map and eventually managed to find the trail and Shoshone Creek, which we knew would lead us directly into the geyser basin. But

we committed a stupid blunder by following the trail along the creek into a steep-walled canyon rather than ascending the ridge above it.

Before we knew it, we were somewhat trapped on a hill that sloped down sharply to become perpendicular a hundred feet above the creek. The snow was beginning to slough around us, and ideal avalanche conditions clearly prevailed. But our avalanche cords would be of no value if we fell here! Behind us, portions of our track were already starting to move, and it was impossible to continue forward because the slope was becoming even steeper. The only choice was to ascend the hill above in a zigzag fashion. As I turned to start up, I heard a shout and turned to see Brian falling backward and sinking into the deep snow. Apparently he had been standing directly on top of a large tree, and his movement had caused the loose snow underneath to give way. To our amazement, he managed to arrest his fall quickly and escape a plunge into the creek. We decided that this one big scare was enough for the entire trip.

Once out of the canyon, we were shocked to hear the abominable sound of snowmobiles on the Old Faithful—Lake road. By 3 P.M. we emerged from heavy timber to see column after column of steam rising ahead. We crossed Shoshone Creek via a precarious snow bridge and entered beautiful Shoshone Geyser Basin. After camp was set, we spent the remaining hours of daylight exploring and admiring our own private thermal area. Brian bet us a beer that he could catch a fish from the creek with the tackle from his survival kit. He failed. We had expected to find some wildlife, attracted by less wintry conditions created by heat below ground, but spotted only a few coyote tracks.

It was very cold the following morning; the thermometer read 14 degrees below zero. The geyser basin was completely enshrouded by a hanging fog, from the thermal activity, which prevented the sun from

Setting up camp on the way across Heart Lake. With little visibility and raging winds, the wind-chill factor plunged the temperature to 12 below zero. Their only cache (steak, potatoes, beans, and wine) would not be reached until the fifteenth day. Until then, all meals were freeze-dried.

PHOTO: ORVILLE E. BACH, JR.

warming things up. I had placed my boots beneath the sleeping bag to prevent them from freezing. To emerge from our warm cocoons and begin breaking camp required some strong words and willpower.

STEVE LED THE WAY out of the basin and soon we were skiing on the ice of Shoshone Lake. We had decided to ski directly across it, Heart Lake and a portion of Yellowstone Lake because the terrain would be flat enough for easy skiing, the snow would be well set from wind packing and we would save several miles. We had fully anticipated, however, the potential danger of skiing across a frozen lake—especially in Yellowstone where thermal features abound. Even a cold spring beneath the ice can cause a "blow hole" or thin spot. In 1960 two rangers died in a tragic mishap while crossing Jackson Lake in Grand Teton National Park after the ice beneath them collapsed, apparently weakened by a nearby hot spring. A similar tragedy involving a snowmobiler occurred on Holter Lake, near Great Falls, Montana.

We attached avalanche cords to our waists as safety precautions and allowed a safe distance between us. If anyone went through, the other two would immediately pull him out, place him in a bag and build a fire. Fortunately, that was never necessary.

Once out on Shoshone Lake, we emerged from the fog of the geyser basin to an intensely blue sky. The seemingly interminable white expanse was awe inspiring. Mount Sheridan (10,308 feet) and the Red Mountains stood out prominently in the distance, while clouds of steam from the Shoshone Geyser Basin rose up behind us.

We found skiing conditions ideal and were making good time. My feet, however, refused to respond to the strenuous activity and became quite numb. The others waited while I took off my boots and attempted to warm them. Several minutes passed, with little success. Then Steve, a true friend indeed, offered to let me place my feet against his bare stomach to restore circulation.

Our most frustrating problem this day was psychological: we had to stare for hours at our destination on the east shore without seeming to get any closer to it. (The lake measures 7.5 miles from the west shore to the east shore.) After lunch, progress was slowed considerably by changing snow conditions. As usually happens in the early afternoon, rising temperatures made the snow rather sloppy, which created a sinking sensation. To avoid this, we had planned to do all our skiing between daybreak and 2 P.M. But we had to pay the penalty for a too lengthy breakfast that foggy morning.

Finally we reached the east shore and managed to locate one of the two cabins we would use during the trip. We dug through five feet of snow to enter the cozy structure and promptly decided to spend a rest day there, washing and drying our clothes and selves, relaxing and day skiing. Late that afternoon a warm front moved in, and a heavy snow began to fall. We did not know, of course, that this snowstorm was to continue, more or less, for 13 days.

Two days later, having left the shelter of the cabin, we skied under miserable conditions through a driving snow. A foot of new snow had fallen during the previous 24 hours, which also slowed us down. After skirting Lewis Lake and crossing the desolate, unpacked south entrance road, we trudged three miles along the Heart Lake Trail to make camp in a protective young grove of lodgepole pines. We had covered only 7.5 miles.

The following morning held some promise: the sky was merely overcast. The snow had finally stopped falling, at least for the time being. Shortly after breaking camp, we encountered a large cow moose standing belly deep in the snow among the dense lodgepoles. It surprised me until I remembered we were nearing Heart Lake Geyser Basin, which extends northwest 1.5 miles from the lake, and that wildlife should be abundant there. Soon we came upon the first of several groups of hot springs. From there we had a beautiful view of the frozen white expanse of Heart Lake, 700 feet below, with Mount Sheridan and Mount Hancock looming up in the darkened sky.

WE DECIDED to leave the trail and descend to the lake instead via the groups of hot springs along Witch Creek. Some of the most exciting scenery of the entire trip rewarded us; group after group of colorful hot pools, springs and brooks marked the way down. Several pools were quite large, deep and colored an intense emerald or milky blue. Steam rising from some pools had completely coated nearby trees with ice, transforming them into the "ghost trees" that are unique to Yellowstone. Additionally, the thermal features had created amazing warmseason sights: the sides of many hot pools and runoff channels were lined with a growth of succulent green plants and a sprinkling of yellow monkey flowers; verdant mats of algae coated the channel beds. The entire basin was almost free of snow, so we attached our skis to our packs and explored the area thoroughly on foot. Brian said he felt like John Colter, the first white man to explore Yellowstone, in 1807. Indeed, we were alone, deep in the wilderness, with Heart Lake and its entire geyser basin all to ourselves. And we were walking in Colter's very footsteps.

Just before reaching the lake, we spotted a group of seven elk, two of them large bulls; coyote tracks were abundant.

We had planned to spend two nights at the Heart Lake patrol cabin so we might explore the geyser basin, and then head east toward Yellowstone Lake. As we neared the cabin, ferocious winds bearing the day's first snowflakes began to sweep across the lake. Our brief spell of decent weather had ended.

WE AWOKE ON March 1, our sixth day out, to a howling blizzard. The thermometer read a balmy 38 degrees Fahrenheit, and the white stuff was really coming down. We were truly disappointed because we had planned to devote the entire day to exploring and photographing the area.

By midafternoon conditions were unchanged. The snow was so wet that it was almost rain—just the type of weather you would expect in Yellowstone in May, but not in March. After feeling very sorry for ourselves, we finally agreed that when in the wilderness, we might as well accept it on its terms and try to enjoy it. So, with winds raging up to 45 mph, visibility perhaps 200 yards and a heavy wet snow dumping down, we skied over to the geyser basin, hoping to catch an eruption of Rustic Geyser.

After half an hour there, Steve decided to appreciate the wilderness back in the cabin. Brian and I stayed on to watch the geyser erupt a few times. The water went 25 feet high and lasted approximately 15 seconds.

A few moments after the second eruption, a tremendous gust of wind swept over the geyser basin at about 55 mph. Bracing myself, I looked up at Mount Sheridan's mighty slopes, which could now be seen through the clouds, and marveled at the raw power of nature. Trees swayed and groaned in the wind and snow flew from their branches. Just then I turned and noticed a very large, dark-colored animal loping into an isolated but thick group of trees along the lake shore, only 100 yards from where I was standing. From its size and gait I guessed it might be a Yellowstone wolf—a species unique to the Yellowstone area and once thought to be extinct. A few recent sightings have raised hopes that the animal is making a comeback.

Excited, I called Brian over and told him what I had just seen and that I thought the animal was well enough "trapped" in the trees so we could get a really fine look when it emerged. We skied down to the shore and confirmed from the fresh tracks that the animal was indeed a wolf. Some of the tracks were imprinted in mud (the result of underlying heat), and the baskets of my ski poles, which measured 4½ inches in diameter, scarcely reached across them. The sly creature

eluded us, however, by slinking behind a small snowbank to return to the heavy timber.

WE SPENT the next 45 minutes tracing the animal's tracks and reconstructing a fascinating predator-prey scene. Apparently, the wolf had crept up on a snowshoe hare beneath a tree, from which it flushed the hare into the open and eventually chased it into the bunch of trees. It was then that I spotted it. Although not certain, we think the wolf became aware of our presence and abandoned its chase. From our vantage point near Rustic Geyser, we could have witnessed the entire chase scene, had we only been looking in the right direction. Still, even that brief glimpse was electrifying, and the afternoon provided the trip's best wilderness vibes.

On March 2 we got up at 5:30 to find the blizzard still howling, and the temperature at 36 degrees. The snow was glop—we would have to wait still another day at Heart Lake before continuing on. Winds during the night, we later learned, had approached 60 mph. At times the cabin had sounded as though it were about to come apart, and several trees in the vicinity had blown down. With visibility almost zero, conditions were intolerable for skiing, so we spent most of the day playing cards. We knew that if we did not move out the following morning, we might be unable to complete the trip as planned. That night the temperature dropped to 18 degrees, giving us new hope.

We awoke on March 3 to find the same blowing snow. But it was still 18 degrees, and the glop was gone. We left before sunrise, with Steve leading the way across Heart Lake. Visibility was absolutely zero, so we had to follow our compass. The wind was raging terribly. If I had not been wearing a 60/40 hooded parka, my face would probably have been frostbitten, for the wind chill factor reduced the temperature to 12 degrees below zero. After sunrise, visibility remained zero because of the blizzard. We were traveling through a whiteout. Everything blended into one; there was no sky, no ground. I felt as though I were superimposed on a white screen. Even Brian and Steve, only a few feet away, continually disappeared from view. I could fully believe the old pioneer stories about men getting lost during a blizzard between the house and the barn. Our avalanche cords kept the three of us together as we groped our way across the lake.

Despite the weather, we managed to make decent time because the wind had packed the snow. By 10 A.M. we had crossed Heart Lake and were only six miles from the south arm of Yellowstone Lake. Disaster, however, struck in the forest in the form of deep, heavy snow. It was so deep and soft that we sank with every stride to the tops of our gaiters and occasionally even to our knees. We lost the trail. Then, to cap it all off, we turned south down the Heart River instead of east up Outlet Creek. We had simply confused the drainages. By the time we discovered our error and returned to Outlet Creek, we had lost two valuable hours, and it was rapidly becoming impossible to make any headway in the snow. So we surrendered to Mother Nature. Because our timetable did not grant us the luxury of waiting out the weather for better conditions, we returned to the Heart Lake cabin to make new plans. The trip back across the lake was more of the same—windy whiteout, with the addition of scares from ice settling. We would be moving along and suddenly sink a couple of inches and hear a sound like a muffled rifle shot beneath our skis.

That night we were all a bit down in spirits. Our original plans were shot, the temperature had returned to a warm 30 degrees, and it was still snowing heavily. The following day it snowed and snowed and snowed. We measured the fall at an astounding three inches per hour.

MARCH 5 started as another snowy, blowing day. Our plans now were to return to the south entrance road, ski north on it to the West Thumb of Yellowstone Lake and west to Old Faithful, catch a park snow coach to Mammoth, drive to the Lamar Ranger Station and there resume our original itinerary. We left the cabin at sunrise and encountered the miserable skiing conditions we had anticipated. I broke a ski pole and toe plate during the first mile. The groups of hot springs bore no resemblance to their appearance five days earlier; we could hardly believe the accumulation of snow. It had fallen too rapidly to be melted by thermal heat. By late afternoon we had trudged seven miles and made camp near the road.

The next morning the snow was falling as heavily as ever. Our exciting trip had been reduced to a slow, agonizing effort. Breaking a trail was extremely tiring; we had to switch lead positions every 15 minutes. We had hoped to find the road packed by a National Park Service snowcat for travel by snowmobiles and snow coaches, but it was untouched, and trudging down it was no different from bucking the trail through the timber. Finally, we reached West Thumb and to our delight found a snowcab operating there. The driver said he was heading for Old Faithful early the next morning and offered us a ride. We were elated to be spared 18 miles of road walking.

The snow finally stopped falling when we arrived at Old Faithful. We learned it had snowed 10 feet in 10 days! Many of the cabins were practically buried. Even snowmobiles and snow coaches had been unable to travel because of the accumulation. That evening we talked with several well-wishers who were surprised we had made it back under such terrible conditions. "Thought we'd find your bones come spring," one laughed. We could laugh, too.

March 8 was spent riding a snow coach to Mammoth, digging out our car and driving to the food cache at the Lamar Ranger Station. We were eager to continue our trip toward the north entrance to visit the Black Canyon of the Yellowstone River, where we would surely see many forms of wildlife. We made camp near the ranger station and enjoyed an evening serenade from a chorus of coyotes.

We awoke March 9 to beautiful clear weather and a temperature of eight degrees. If only we could have had 12 other mornings just like it; it was our first blue sky in 13 days. A small herd of buffalo was spotted grazing only a few hundred yards away from camp. The trip into the Black Canyon was fantastic. The snow was well crusted, and we could really ski for the first time. White mountains stood out against the deep blue sky. We stopped for lunch by a delightful stream, and four bull elk ran up a gully right next to us, apparently unaware of our presence. After lunch, on the segment of trail that descends sharply 1200 feet into the canyon, we entered a completely new world. Rather than bucking snow at 8800 feet, we were approaching 5300 feet, with little snow at all. We attached our skis to our packs and began hiking. The change felt great. We went from the middle of winter almost to the beginning of spring. What a delight to have huge douglas firs towering over us, rather than dense lodgepole pines roundabout.

Our final camp was the most beautiful: we pitched the tent on a ridge overlooking Crevice Lake and the Black Canyon. Just before retiring, I noticed a yellow glow slowly creeping up the cliff above us. I called Brian, and we watched in awe as a huge golden moon began to rise above the head of the canyon, spilling rays upon the shimmering waters of the Yellowstone River. "This is what it's all about," Brian said reverently. He was right. Later, most of the night, we enjoyed the yips and barks of coyotes echoing through the canyon.

ON OUR LAST day we would continue through the Black Canyon and cover eight miles to reach Gardiner. It was an incredible journey. The excitement began as soon as we emerged from the tent and found three coyotes on Crevice Lake. One was very large and required a long look through the field glasses. The recent heavy snows in the high country had crusted, evidently forcing many animals to compete for food in the canyon. There was not enough food to go around; we spotted several winter kills, and the coyotes were making short work of them.

Near Knowles Falls we spotted two bighorn rams, one with a full curl of horns. Shortly thereafter, we confronted 30 elk on the trail. The big bull leading the harem ran right up to us, surveyed the situation and decided to lead his group up a steep, rocky ridge. I felt like a terrible intruder, especially when I noticed that one small cow had a broken leg. Rather than follow the herd, she jumped into the Yellowstone River and barely made it to the opposite shore. She was a pitiful sight, and I knew she would not last the night with coyotes in the immediate area. Within the next few miles we spotted nine more bighorn sheep, a prong-horn antelope and two mule deer. We seemed to be walking through an un-fenced zoo!

We took our lunch break on the banks of the river. With the tempera-ture in the fifties and the constant singing and chirping of birds—a large flock of cedar waxwings had de-scended into the canyon and were really rejoicing—it felt like spring. Everything was so alive and vibrant that it was hard to believe we had been snowbound only a few days ear-lier. An occasional pair of mallards raced along, only inches above the river.

After lunch we soon emerged from the timbered canyon into open country resembling an Arizona desert. In the summer this stretch is very hot, dry and drab, but now it was gorgeous. We spotted a herd of 350 elk on the sage-covered slopes above us, only a quarter-mile away. In the distance the white expanse of Electric Peak was impressive. From our lowly vantage point, it looked Himalayan. Three bald eagles soared over the Yellowstone River. I followed their free flight through my binoculars and truly appreciated John Denver's words in *Rocky Mountain High:* "It's a poorer man who has never seen an eagle fly."

Soon we were approaching Gar-diner. Our 17-day trip was nearing an end, and thoughts about the journey raced through my head. The wildlife show on this day had been simply spectacular. But so had the winter-bound geyser basins, and the wolf . . . and the moon rise. Oddly, the ten feet of snow and the hardships did not seem to occupy much space in my memory.

From the Gardiner Bridge we took a long last look back up the Yellow-stone River to the wilderness from which we had just emerged. "Yel-lowstone," I thought. "Truly a world apart."

EN RAPPEL . . . ON SKIS?

by CONSTANCE STALLINGS

On the summit, ski mountaineer Bill Briggs stepped out of his crampons and onto his skis.

In addition to providing the cleanest and quietest relationship to nature, winter is also, of course, the most severe time to be in the mountains—a time that pits the best you've got against the best nature has to offer in the way of resistance. Hence, a winter climb of a diffi-cult mountain is several notches above a sum-mer ascent of same.

Bill Briggs, of Jackson Hole, Wyoming, wins my admiration for his winter ascents of many difficult peaks. The following account is partly the story of Bill's winter ascent of Grand Teton by a route he thought had never been climbed before. But Bill Briggs earns my triple admira-tion: first for the ascent, next for the most in-credible ski descent it's possible for me to imagine, and finally, he earns my ultimate ad-miration for the strength of will that he has exhibited in dealing with a personal affliction which should have made it impossible to both climb mountains (any mountains) and to ski (on any terrain). But obviously Briggs is not an ordinary man. And perhaps his story will earn as much of your admiration as it has of mine.

W.K.

When you go out to dinner with Bill Briggs, you learn that he can't sit with his right side toward the inside of the steakhouse booth. That may be one of the few things Briggs cannot do.

Ski school director in Jackson, Wyoming, and mountaineering guide in Grand Teton National Park, Briggs's reputation is based upon many ski mountaineering "firsts." They include a 100-mile traverse of the Canadian Rockies, an early descent of Mount Rainier and the first ski descents of the Middle Teton and Mount Moran.

"Excuse me. Bill, I want somebody to meet you. Ed, this is the guy I was telling you about — the one who skied the Grand."

That first was the one that topped everything. On June 16, 1971, Briggs made the first ski descent of the 13,769-foot Grand Teton — a difficult mountain that requires ropes, pitons and carabiners just for the climbing. As surely as he carved himself out a route high on that dizzying peak, he carved himself a niche in skiing history.

Bill Briggs. Native of Maine. Self-taught skier. Dartmouth College.

But not a member of the Dartmouth Ski Team because he was born without a right hip socket. When Briggs was a child, a surgeon drilled a socket in the hip and inserted the leg bone into it. That was satisfactory until he stopped growing. Eventually, the cartilage between the hip and the leg bone ceased to renew itself, so in 1960 doctors fused the hip.

Now, because his hip has no working joint, he can't bend over from there, or crouch down, or raise his right knee and boot in front of him. When dressing or equipping himself for the mountains, he leans his shoulders and upper back against a wall, bends his right foot up behind himself and carries out the routine, foot unseen. And he needs to stretch out his right leg at dinner tables. After you've learned this, his accomplishments seem miraculous.

Briggs doesn't think they are. He believes that accomplishing difficult feats is vitally important for him *because* of his hip. He must stay active in order to keep from stiffening up. Furthermore, he believes that the biggest obstacle to skiing the Grand, as well as other first ski descents, was the popular notion that it was impossible. "Skiing the Grand was a fun thing to do but not a wild thing, from my point of view. It's not far out. It was all things I'd done before, in a new combination, a very nice adventure. I'd like to do it again. I think I will."

He describes himself as being both a ski mountaineer and a downhill skier — that is, he likes the climbing up as well as the skiing down. "I enjoy both. But I used ski boots that day on the Grand."

Four men started on the expedition: Briggs, George Colon, Robbie Garrett and John Bolton. Skis strapped to their backs, they climbed to 11,500 feet and spent the night in a Quonset hut maintained by the local climbing school. At five o'clock the next morning, June 16, they set off for the summit itself, still 2,300 feet above them. They elected a route up through the Stettner Couloir, which involved a difficult 150-foot pitch. Actually, the route had been climbed by another party a year earlier, but Briggs and his companions did not know this at the time. They believed they were making a first ascent.

Upon reaching the most difficult part of the climb, the others in the group had second thoughts about the whole enterprise. "At the one belayed pitch," says Briggs, "George got hit by a rock that came off the roof of a snow cave he was standing in. It sapped his confidence and he didn't want to take any more risks after that. Another fellow hadn't skied that much although he'd done a lot of climbing. The fourth hadn't done much climbing, although he was an experienced skier. When they saw the vertical drop, they said *'No way.'* To me, it was a very straightforward problem — sort of fun to handle."

With no one to belay him, Briggs continued on toward the summit alone. "The hard part was climbing up, because of my fused hip. That was something else. I had those guys along because they were strong — they were supposed to blaze the trail. It was awfully hard going up without them. I had to put the poles in upside down, lean back on them using them as handles, and kick myself forward and up. I could make about three steps, and then I was pooped and had to stop. There were clouds coming over, and I really didn't want to get caught. But the weather didn't change."

Once on the summit, there were new problems.

"Since there was nothing to lean against, to get the crampons off I had to balance on my left foot and bend my right leg up behind me. The straps were frozen so I couldn't get the buckles undone. I had to do it with my gloves off. It took at least five minutes, but on the third attempt, I finally made it.

"Putting on the skis was a pretty good trick because I had to put my right foot into the binding and close the binding with my left foot. It was very icy. I knew I *had* to do it because there was no way to put the crampons back on. Once the right ski was on, the left one was easy."

Briggs's description of his downhill run is epic.

"I had to take it awfully slow and steady; I'm not that good a skier. After the first turn, it was fun. It was narrow and I was turning among rocks on ice — a frozen-snow ice with a hard, hard crust, not like water ice. Below that it was corn snow and really super. I had a wonderful time.

"When I dropped through the crust a foot and took a fall, I didn't have any strength left, though. I rolled over and back up onto my feet, automatically, the way I used to do on Tuckerman's Headwall. I used to be famous for yodeling down the Headwall. Friends joked that I'd spill, the yodel would stop and I'd keep on going. But I wasn't yodeling on this trip.

"It was very touchy on top of the cornice over Ford's Couloir, but the skis were superb, very dependable. I could just cut *so* precisely. It's a very nice feeling to have a piece of equipment you can depend on for the conditions you're in.

"Then the East Snow Field slope got awfully steep, about 45 degrees. People have skied on steeper slopes but not under such conditions. It was pretty rough. When I skied across, it would avalanche off. So I had to cut off an avalanche intentionally, back up and then make my turn. Each turn still set off a great slide of snow that went downhill, bounced off a lip and flew off into the air like a waterfall. My party, down below, could see me again by then, and they literally could not watch. They figured I must be in, if not one avalanche, then the next one. But if you're used to spring snow of this kind and to cutting it off to make it slide, it doesn't present that much of a problem.

"Down where my party was, it became very narrow. I couldn't ski it straight because I'd go way too fast. There was no room to turn, either. And when I was sideways my tips were on one rock face, and my tails on another. So I just slid through on my side. Then it was perfect going into the top of the Stettner Couloir. I could make pure, carved turns. It was just right, all the way down to the rappel. The rappel was lovely — an out-of-sight scene."

And certainly extraordinary: On reaching the edge of the cliff, Briggs secured his climbing rope to a rock. Then, instead of lowering himself backwards over the edge, "I skied right off into the air and never touched the rock. It was *so* delightful. Everyone should do it someday.

"Below the rappel I fell again from sheer carelessness. My friends had gone down first and were below me, and I was afraid I'd fall into them. So as I cartwheeled sideways, I crossed one ski over and pointed it down into the snow. It went in clear up to the foot and anchored me."

The rest of the descent included merely a strenuous climb over a notch, a third fall and outracing an avalanche.

Briggs's first experience with skiing took place in 1938 when his sister put him on too steep a slope. He decided then never to entrust himself to anybody but to teach himself how to ski. It worked. ("By the time I got to college, I was skiing on things

235

very steep.") This beginning undoubtedly accounts for his unorthodox approach to instruction at his ski school.

He does not advocate constant classes. He thinks a learner should take one lesson on a particular slope, work there by himself until he can negotiate it comfortably, move on to a steeper slope where he should take lesson number two, and so on. "Almost all of ski instruction is just a matter of keeping people on the right slope."

His ideas about technique also are unusual and should make every old stemturner happy. "Technique and I have a bit of a problem. It's like dancing. When I was a kid, I had dancing lessons and I hated it — you know, so many steps forward, so many steps backward, so many to the side. Dancing should be natural and spontaneous; so should skiing. These people who come out here aren't looking for precise technique, except for the advanced skiers. They're looking for a way to get down the hill. The fun is in finding a way down; we teach them that. I don't think you can say there's a correct or an incorrect way. If it works, it's correct . . . I teach them the snowplow. I even teach the Telemark, an old-fashioned turn that hardly anybody does anymore. I rediscovered it one day when I was skiing in soft snow, carrying 90 pounds on my back. It was the only turn I could manage; it's super."

The increasing popularity of nonlift skiing pleases Briggs because he himself has done a lot more skiing without the aid of lifts than with. He says that what people like best in the Tetons, far and away, is the off-trail, backwoods kind of skiing. "We take some groups up on Teton Pass at night and ski down in the moonlight, and they enjoy it the *most,*" he says, eyes twinkling. "Sometimes the clouds come over, and it's hard to see. One of my instructors told me one night he put some guy's skis back on twice before he realized he was strapping them to a tree. You can't do super-duper technique there. I challenge anybody to come down from up there at night doing parallel. If you can snowplow, you're okay. These are the people who come back the following year."

The finest skiing of all in Jackson Hole, Briggs thinks, takes place during the month of November when there isn't a single lift operating. Then all levels of skiers arrive, from beginners up to Olympic class. "You have to pack out your own slope; that is the nicest snow to ski in. The turns feel the best; they *are* the best."

During the rest of the season, it is possible for lift skiers everywhere to ski the same slopes so often that they become bored. For these people Briggs recommends two courses of action. One is to use a pair of old skis for a change. "You create a brand-new experience. The value of your hill goes way up. When a sport starts getting boring, you should make it harder." It becomes harder with unfamiliar equipment. The other thing he suggests is skiing behind a small child. "I have a friend who was getting bored, so I told him to follow little Danny, four years old, down the mountain. He did and had the best run of his life." It seems that Danny showed the friend an entirely new way down.

There is a philosophical side to Bill Briggs. His idea about making skiing more difficult is part of a larger pattern of thinking on the subject of land use. He would like to see the National Park Service eliminate maintenance of backcountry hiking trails. That would keep the horses out and reduce erosion. Ultimately, he would like to see maps eliminated from the national parks. Decreasing such services would increase the value of the wilderness experience for the backpacker.

Mountaineers cause some erosion, Briggs knows. He has served as a summer guide for a mountaineering school since 1958, except for the period of his hip operation. He is concerned about the school — "I don't know if it's correct or not" — but firmly believes in the rightness of guiding visitors through Grand Teton National Park. "The person who is guided gets a very good return for his investment. The person who finds his own way without even a guidebook gets a heavy return, too."

Briggs would like to have not only the national park but all of the Jackson Hole country made more difficult to reach so as to increase its value. Accordingly, he is against the pending proposal that Jackson Hole Airport, the only airport located inside a national park, be expanded in order to accommodate Boeing 737s. He explains: "It's not just the airport; it's what will come after. The park has only so many resources. If we let one guy erode them away, the next guy can, too. The question is — do we want to erode the park to that extent? There has to be a decision." *His* decision would be to move the entire airport someplace else.

Bill Briggs: an altogether fascinating man, no less in personality than by accomplishment on the high peaks.

How will Dartmouth ever live it down?

Chapter Nine

THE HIKER AS NATURALIST

For a couple of centuries the rationale for spending any extensive time in the wilderness was to do scientific research. No doubt it was a valid excuse. But an <u>excuse</u> nonetheless. It is my belief that men spend time in the wilderness mainly because nature itself has something spellbinding about it. And that to find the wherewithal to spend the time in the wilds these men found patrons in the financiers of scientific discovery.

Like all summary judgments, no doubt mine is an oversimplification. I'm sure that being a scientific observer in the wilderness is very compatible with the outdoors experience and probably does much to enhance its magic. First of all, being in the wilds on behalf of science requires that you take a closer look at things, that you venture a little farther afield, looking around one more promontory, around one more peninsula, over one more pass to extend your investigation. Thus, it intensifies your involvement with your surroundings.

It also extends your natural curiosity about the things you see in nature, pushes you to be more exacting in finding answers to your questions, deepening your experiences as a result.

Nature observation provides another benefit for the hiker. It gives a sharply focused purpose to your trip. All the planning, preparations, and energies of the trip—no matter how short or long it will be—are focused upon achieving the goals.

Probably by strictest definition, few backpacking trips that purport scientific goals would be recognized by the officialdom of the American Association for the Advancement of Science. They would be too loose in their methodology. However, there is clearly an imaginative side of science which scientists don't seem to like to admit. This is the poking around that one has to do to become familiar with the subject that must precede the development of hypotheses to test. The scientific community would rather keep this aspect of research outside the realm of science and sort of pretend it isn't there. Nonetheless, this creative prelude to any scientific work may actually be the most important in making breakthroughs. It is more likely in this area of scientific work that most observation in the wilderness falls.

During the great push west in the U.S. in the middle of the nineteenth century, most explorations had a scientific justification to them. One famous member of many of these scientific expeditions was not even suggested to be a scientist. He was a landscape painter. His job was to observe and to record on canvas what he saw. To that extent Thomas Moran was a scientist just as John James Audubon was a bird scientist with his bird paintings.

Additionally, many amateurs have enjoyed their own "scientific" pursuits in the activity of hiking, and this is one of the joys we can all share together, as the pieces included in this chapter point out.

THOMAS MORAN (1837–1926)
by ELEANOR STERLING

We can now recognize him as an Elder of the Tribe, but this frail city man went west to paint America's wilderness and to persuade the nation of the need for national parks.

THOMAS MORAN SEEMED poorly equipped for a rough life. Frail, with an almost cadaverous body, he had endured childhood bouts with rheumatic fever and pleurisy. He was a city boy, born early in Queen Victoria's reign in the squalor of Bolton in Lancashire, center of the British cotton industry, a gray milieu of tall chimneys against a smoking sky where there was no ready escape to the countryside. Therefore it was something of a wonder that Moran ever chose a life of travel to the wilderness of the American West. Yet choose it he did, and he became a foremost landscape painter of the nineteenth century.

In Wyoming, as a young man on his first trip into the Yellowstone country with the Hayden Survey Expedition of 1871, Moran tucked his thin frame into a flannel shirt, heavy boots and trousers, and mounted a horse for the first time. His fellow-traveler, photographer William Henry Jackson,

later remembered that Moran "made a picturesque appearance when mounted. The jaunty tilt of his sombrero, long yellowish beard and portfolio under his arm marked him as the artistic type, with something of local color imparted by a rifle hung from the saddle horn." But the hard saddle was a torture on the long ride; only a camp pillow tucked strategically between Moran's spare anatomy and the saddle made the trip possible.

According to his companions, Moran eventually became a seasoned camper. He traveled light. He had the good sense to outfit himself carefully, often journeying with only sketching materials and a small carpetbag stuffed with clothing rather than the big Saratoga trunks popular at that time. In the course of his trips, however, he acquired loads of another kind: he crammed his brain with a teeming accumulation of shapes and colors and ideas. These stored visual impressions later spilled forth from

his studio in the East in more than 1,200 canvases. They profoundly affected American sensibilities and helped to shape the nation's perspective of the American West.

Thomas Moran was a bread-and-butter artist with a family to support. But he rarely had to apply himself to anything except his art—a situation contemporary artists well might envy. He meant his paintings to be shown, not shuttered away against changing tastes and political climates. No honest artwork was above or beneath his talents. In his early years he sketched and painted from other people's descriptions of a place and from photographs, depicting scenes upon his easel which he wouldn't visit until many years afterward. But he felt that working "second hand" handicapped his art, and he later resolved to confine himself to scenes from his own travels and personal observations.

Moran's father, a hand loomer, took his family to America in 1844. Young Thomas began working as an apprentice wood engraver in Philadelphia when he was 16. He was intent upon teaching himself "mastery of the line." Ambition and the fear of becoming just another penniless artist drove him to work a 13-hour day, a schedule he continued for most of his life. Taught to paint by an older brother, Thomas first worked in watercolors, then oils. As he learned his craft, he imagined distant places that were wilder and more exotic than Philadelphia. Then, in August of 1860, in search of actual scenes of majesty, he took his first camping trip to the Pictured Rocks at Lake Superior. There he made many sketches which he stored back East in a studio file; he maintained and added to the file for the rest of his working years. From Lake Superior he wrote to his future wife, Mary:

We have seen the great sight, the Pictured Rocks. They exceeded my expectations ... We left here in a Mackinaw boat with only another man and ourselves on last Sunday morning at 9 o'clock and reached the farthest point about 2 o'clock having rowed the whole distance 12 miles. We then landed and pitched our tent on the sand beach, lit a fire, cooked our dinner of pork fat (it would astonish you to see me bolt the fat out here) took a sail to the great cave and made a sketch. We slept on the beach 3 nights.

Years later, when asked about his trips, Moran explained that he seldom carried an easel or oils. He took merely a good-sized portfolio of sketching paper and some watercolors. He said that the rest of his equipment was the same as any tourist's.

Moran never used many of his sketches. But some, occasionally in combination with others made years apart, inspired many different pictures: oils, watercolors, etchings and wood engravings for books and magazines; and lithographs for prints and calendars. The oils, especially, were strongly influenced by the work of J. M. W. Turner, whose paintings he saw on the first of several European tours. In 1870 much of the nation's energy was directed at taming the vast and little-understood interior of the West. Several government expeditions were in the field, researching and mapping. One was the Washburn–Langford–Doane Expedition to the headwaters of the Yellowstone. Upon its return, Nathaniel P. Lang-

ford submitted to *Scribner's Magazine* a manuscript entitled "The Wonders of the Yellowstone" which described the expedition's discoveries. The manuscript appeared in the magazine as a series of articles illustrated with paintings by Moran. The artist produced the pictures from his imagination, but the assignment so fascinated him that he wangled an invitation to accompany Dr. Ferdinand V. Hayden's survey trip to Yellowstone the following summer. And so, with financing he raised himself, he made his first trip to the Far West in June, 1871. William Henry Jackson was another member of the party.

Moran had a lifelong aversion to greasy foods and almost never ate any, despite his letter describing the Lake Superior camping trip. So, on the Yellowstone expedition, to avoid the torment of flour cake and bacon at every meal, he became an expert trout fisherman and a master of campfire cooking. Once, after some "tall fishing," he promised a better dish than the previous meal. Scraping aside the coals and ashes of the old campfire, he dug a hole and placed the fish in it, cleaned and wrapped in wet brown paper. Then he covered them with earth and hot coals, and left them there to be cooked. Jackson noted, "When the charred paper was removed, we had as dainty a bit of steaming white flesh as the most exacting taste could wish for."

From every point of view, the expedition was a success. Moran proved to be a good explorer and was highly popular with his campmates. His field sketches were superb, and it would be hard to imagine a greater contrast than that between his first, imagined pictures of Yellowstone and the magnificent works that were to result from the Yellowstone trip.

Upon his return, Moran's portfolio of sketches and the images crowding his mind provided months of intensive work in his studio. He painted a watercolor series for financier Jay Gould, who was eager to publicize his Northern Pacific Railroad, and created a series of illustrations to accompany Dr. Hayden's official report to Congress. He made a spectacular group of chromolithographs that were printed in an oversized limited edition, bound in red leather and circulated among congressmen. Graphic artists and printers hailed the collec-

tion as one of the finest examples of chromolithographs ever published in America. Not least, he painted large oils of Yellowstone.

These large landscapes were displayed at the Smithsonian Institution and Library of Congress in Washington during the winter of 1871–72 in connection with congressional hearings for legislation establishing Yellowstone National Park. History was made on March 1, 1872, when the bill establishing the country's first national park was signed into law by President Ulysses S. Grant. There is no doubt that Moran's paintings contributed to the bill's passage. In recognition of this and because Moran later traveled to many other wilderness areas that would receive protection by the National Park Service—the Grand Canyon, the Grand Tetons, the South Dakota Badlands, the Colorado Rockies, Zion and Bryce canyons, the California coast and the Sierra Nevada—Moran soon began to be called "Father of the National Parks." His professional reputation was made.

Moran's success posed a problem for Dr. Hayden: how to retain the brilliant young artist who had been catapulted to fame. Other expeditions also sought his services; Moran was so much in demand that he had to choose from among opportunities that came his way. Never again did he have to finance his travels. Major John Wesley Powell invited him to participate in his exploration of the Grand Canyon in 1872, and the artist had to say no because of previous commitments. But later he did travel in Utah with Powell. And his black felt bowler hat became familiar at encampments of additional Hayden expeditions. He was a popular companion on climbs and difficult treks. He was resourceful and surprisingly tough, and nothing fazed him: no infestation of rattlesnakes, mountain cold or canyon heat.

A typical trip was his descent into the Grand Canyon with W. H. Jackson in 1892. Moran described it in a letter to his wife, who accompanied him only on short sketching trips:

The first descent of about 3000 feet is very steep but we made it rapidly. The views on the way down are very magnificent. All our traps were on pack horses and how they could get down is remark-

The Thomas Moran Legacy

Thomas Moran's name is memorialized in many of the places his paintings popularized. In Grand Teton National Park there is a Mount Moran, a Moran Canyon, a Moran Bay (on Jackson Lake) and a Moran Junction. In Yellowstone National Park there is a Moran Point, a lookout on the Yellowstone Canyon rim named for him by Dr. Ferdinand Hayden, whose report to Congress led to the establishment of the park in 1872. There is another Moran Point in Yosemite National Park, just down-valley from Glacier Point.

Moran was a prolific painter. He produced more than 1200 paintings, illustrated books and made lithographs for calendars. There is hardly a museum or major art collection in the country that does not have one of his works. The largest collection of Morans is in the Gilcrease Institute in Tulsa, Oklahoma, which also has a set of the limited-edition chromolithographs that circulated in Congress in 1871.

Moran's largest Grand Canyon painting, *Chasm of the Colorado,* hangs in the U.S. Department of the Interior Museum in Washington, D.C. It measures seven feet by 12 feet. There are additional Morans of the Grand Canyon in the small museum at the national park visitors center in Grand Canyon Village and in the William Rockhill Nelson Gallery in Kansas City.

Moran painted another panoramic oil with seven-by-12-foot dimensions, *The Grand Canyon of the Yellowstone,* which is featured prominently at the Smithsonian Institution in Washington, D.C. The Yellowstone National Park Museum has more of his paintings of Yellowstone territory.

Other places popularized in Moran paintings include the Colorado Rockies (his large oil, *Mount of the Holy Cross,* is in the Denver Public Library), Zion National Park and Wyoming's Grand Tetons. His *Teton Range* is displayed at the Metropolitan Museum of Art in New York City. The same museum has one of Moran's European oils, *View of Lake Como,* which he painted after a trip to Italy.

The Philbrook Art Center in Tulsa has seven Moran paintings. The Jefferson National Expansion Memorial in St. Louis also has a collection of Moran oils. Other places where the painter's work can be seen are the Heckscher Museum in Huntington, New York, the Fort Worth Art Center and the Dallas Museum of Fine Arts.

---

able as it was the most perpendicular trail I was ever on. They got there all right, however, with the single exception of a fall of one of the horses which did him no damage. Hance went with us as guide and he did his part excellently, being careful and cheerful. About noon we reached his cabin in the canyon and had dinner. After dinner we started for the river. The trail was easy enough until we struck the first waterfall in the lava. Here we let ourselves down with ropes and in the same way of six waterfalls . . . We reached the river about 4 in the afternoon. It was very full and muddy and it seemed to me that the rapids were equal to the Whirlpool rapids at Niagara. Black lava 2000 feet in height was all around us except an occasional glimpse of the higher sandstone peaks in the openings. After photographing an hour, we began the return to where we were going to camp for the night about 2 miles up. We had to mount all the falls again by the ropes we came down on, which we accomplished all right, and just at dark camped under some rocks about 2 miles from Hance's cabin in the canyon. After a good supper we wrapped ourselves in our blankets and laid on the open ground and slept the sleep of the tired.

Next morning we started back, took dinner at Hance's cabin again, rested awhile, and then made the final spurt for the top nearly 5 miles off. We took it easy as possible but mounting the steep trail to the upper edge was hard and slow work, but we got there early in the afternoon having made the journey down and back in 2 days.

As Moran became well known through public exhibitions of his western paintings and the publication of his drawings in magazines, he began to have considerable influence on easterners' impressions of the West. For many people, a Moran painting *was* the West. Eventually, Hayden named a peak after him—Mount Moran, in the Tetons. Yet some art critics criticized his work as being "postcard painting," which annoyed him. Actually, the criticism was unjust, for Moran did not depict nature photographically; he painted his *response* to it, instead. He derived inspiration from the natural scene and then created, not slavish copies, but impressions. He explained his technique in reference to one of his Yellowstone canvases:

> Every form introduced into the picture is within view from a given point, but the relations of the separate parts to one another are not always preserved. For instance, the precipitous rocks on the right were really at my back when I stood at that point, yet in their present position they are strictly true to pictorial nature; and so correct is the whole representation that every member of the expedition with which I was connected declared, when he saw the painting, that he knew the exact spot which had been reproduced. My aim was to bring before

the public the character of that region. The rocks in the foreground are so carefully drawn that a geologist could determine their precise nature.

In fact, before that particular canvas was taken from its easel, Moran asked Hayden to inspect it for the correctness of its geology. Hayden found that Moran had indeed depicted sandstone as sandstone, and volcanic rock as volcanic rock, but also had edited out details whose inclusion would have made a chaotic jumble.

Moran's descriptions of life in the field in his letters and journals are fascinating glimpses of frontier exploration. A journey into Utah with Powell in 1875 resulted in the first pictorial record to reach the public of the land the Mormons called Little Zion and which, a half-century later, became the heart of Zion National Park. On another trip with Powell, he wrote his wife from Fillmore City, Utah:

> The day after I wrote you last we rode to a ranch at the foot of Mt. Nebo and concluded to ascend to the top. Nebo is the highest mountain in Utah or Nevada being 12000 feet. Before sundown we ascended 2000 feet and made our camp for the night, cooked supper, played a game of Euchre, wrapped our blankets

around us and went to sleep. We were up again by 6 o'clock. It was an awful climb but we made the top by 12 o'clock having mounted 6,500 feet. We made coffee from the snow and remained up about 2 hours. It was the most magnificent sight of my life and no person who has not ascended to such an elevation can have the faintest concept of the glorious sight. It seems as if the whole world was laid out before you; and although I do not think I would undergo the labor of another ascent, I would not have missed this for 10 times the fatigue. I stood it first rate, but Powell, Colburn and Pilling were sick and vomited when we got down.

Moran's penchant for climbing led him and Jackson on one of their most famous treks, a trip to locate and sketch the Mount of the Holy Cross in Colorado in 1874. Jackson's excellent photographs of the 14,000-foot mountain and Moran's painting, *Mount of the Holy Cross,* which won a medal at the Centennial Exposition in 1876, made the ordeal worth it. But this is the way Moran described it to his wife:

Thursday we began the ascent of the intervening mountain between us and the Roche Moutonée Valley, and of all the hard climb that I have experienced, this beat it. Almost perpendicular, covered with burnt and fallen timber, lying 3 or 4 deep. It was only by slow and persevering effort that the horses could get through and we had to walk a good part of the way. After we got to the top the view was perfectly magnificent. 2000 feet below us lay the Moutonée Valley with the Holy Cross Creek rushing through it and at the head of the Valley the splendid Peak of the Holy Cross, with the range continuing to the left of us. The descent into the Valley was even steeper than the ascent had been, but was freer from fallen timber. We got down all right and without accident but Horror!!! The way up the Valley was infinitely worse than anything we had yet encountered. A swamp, covered with the worst of fallen logs and projecting through which were the Roche Moutonée or Sheep Rocks, rounded and smooth and slippery, varying from 10 to 40 feet high. We worked our way as best we could, without any serious accident, except one of the horses slipping off a rock about 20 feet and punching a hole in his belly, and a fir bough striking me in the eye which hurt all that day but is all right again. Added to all this it rained on us all the time, making the logs and rocks extremely dangerous and slippery ... The next day, Friday, I and Woods and Jim began the ascent of the mountain, Delano feeling that he was not strong enough to stand the ascent. We started at 8 o'clock, on foot up the Valley over the same kind of ground I have mentioned, for three miles and then commenced the toughest trial of strength that I have ever experienced, with the steepness of ascent added to the usual difficulties. Woods was very weak and came on slowly, but I stood it all right. When we had got up about 2000 feet above the Valley we took lunch of corn bread, sardines and a bottle of excellent German wine that Woods had brought with him for the purpose. After lunch we again started through the timber upward and at 2½ o'clock we were at 12000 feet. Here we were in clear view of the Cross and although still 800 feet below where we intended to reach, we were all so tired that we concluded we had gone far enough.

For all his love of the West, Moran spent most of his life in the East. He lived in places between Philadelphia and eastern Long Island, close to metropolitan New York, where art buyers were numerous and commissions available. In 1916 he moved to Santa Barbara, California, where he continued to paint. He died in 1926 at the age of 90, long after paved roads led millions of tourists in automobiles directly to most of the scenic wonders he had labored to reach on horseback and on foot.

Moran was asked many times to name his favorite spot in the West. He would reply that he had chosen to spend 12 entire winters and long intermittent painting sessions in the Grand Canyon and that the canyon had a special, personal meaning for him. But it was the country of the Yellowstone that had altered his life. Therefore it did not disturb him to be nicknamed "Yellowstone Moran." ▰

I'M IN LOVE WITH TUNDRA

by PATRICIA ARMSTRONG

Tundra is found on arctic icefields and on peaks and plateaus in North and South America and Asia. The small plants that grow there have special biological adaptations which enable them to thrive despite freezing temperatures, harsh winds, and lack of soil.

Pat Armstrong, the author of the following article on tundra, fell in love with mountains the first time she visited them. It changed her entire life. She committed herself to knowing more about them, to climbing them often, and to a career related to them. I came to know about these facts gradually through correspondence with Pat about other articles she was writing for BACKPACKER. And in the end, I asked Pat to write about her love affair. Hence the following article—which itself answers some of the questions I'd always had, such as, How come tree line is at different elevations in different mountain ranges? and, What causes tree line?

W.K.

I HAVE ALWAYS BEEN in love with tundra. It's funny too, because I grew up in the Midwest, farther away from mountains than any other place in the United States. I didn't even see a mountain until I was nearly 25, with a husband and two baby daughters.

We made our first trip to the mountains, accompanied by a babysitter and a rotten old army tent borrowed from friends, at the end of August, 1961. We drove straight through to the Blackfeet Indian Reservation in northwestern Montana. There in the middle of the night we stopped. We were near enough to see the mountains, and we wanted our first view to be at dawn. The five of us contorted around the junk in our beat-up old car and tried to snooze while waiting for the sun. We were awake well before the first fingers of light began to play on the tallest mountains. Ever so gently the peaks began to glow. The rosy luminescence spread slowly from one mountain to another and slid down the ridges to fill the valleys. Every detail stood out against blue shadows. We held our breath.

Too soon, the magic faded and the mountains stood stark and bare, flat and cold, where before they had been so warm and inviting. We crossed into Canada and headed

west from Calgary, directly into the Rockies. We set up our first tent camp in Yoho Valley, British Columbia. We had come 2,113 miles in less than three days. We were tired, yet sleep came hard. It was like Christmas Eve. Takakkaw Falls plunged 1200 feet from the base of the Daly Glacier and the Waputik Icefield, the second tallest waterfall in America. The night wind brought the mist up the valley to settle heavily on our tent. Tomorrow we would walk in the mountains, see them up close, feel them.

Dawn finally came at 5:30. It was cold. All our provisions as well as the camp's water supply were frozen. We left the girls in care of the babysitter and began our first day in the mountains.

When I think of how we slept in newspapers and blankets in that heavy army tent and how we carried our jackets in a bucket and took 30 feet of old clothesline with us, I laugh. We have come a long way since then, but some things have never changed. I will always remember our love-at-first-sight encounter with the alpine world. I have never been the same since.

The subalpine forest of the Canadian Rockies is much

Tundra Areas of the World

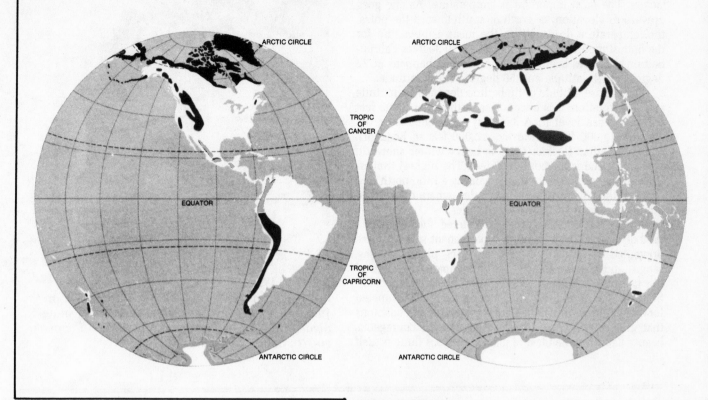

taller and more lush than the boreal forest of our native Michigan. The Engelmann spruce *(Picea engelmannii)* and subalpine fir *(Abies lasiocarpa)* grow tall in the cool, snowy environment. Dense moss carpets and flowers brightened our path as we headed upward. We climbed 1000 feet in the first mile, switchbacking 27 times.

At 6000 feet the trail leveled off in a beautiful mountain meadow. Flowers danced before our eyes: scarlet Indian paintbrushes *(Castilleja miniata)*, pink twinflowers *(Linnaea borealis)*, daisies *(Erigeron peregrinus)*, white valerians *(Valeriana sitchensis)*, grass-of-Parnassus *(Parnassia fimbriata)*, harebells *(Campanula rotundifolia)*, bluebonnets *(Lupinus sericeus)* and golden groundsel *(Senecio triangularis)*. I had never seen so many different colored flowers at one time before. We couldn't even stand without crushing something lovely.

We hiked around Mount Wapta toward Mount Field. The valley fell off on our right. Far below, the greenishwhite Emerald Lake looked like a dish of creamed pea soup. Trees with grizzled bare heads and dense green skirts shrank to our size and even smaller. They clustered behind boulders and in the lea of ridges until, finally, there were none. We had reached timberline, our very first timberline. We seemed to stand taller in relation to the world, to see farther and feel closer to the sky. It was a glorifying yet humbling experience.

At timberline the continuous forest ends. Above it trees appear in clumps and are dwarfed and twisted by

Polar Tundra Regions

The Arctic. North of 72° latitude no trees grow. The arctic is characterized by short, cool summers and long, dark winters. At high altitudes, vegetation is sparse, lichens and bryophytes predominate.

The Antarctic. South of 56° latitude no trees grow. The antarctic is characterized by short, cold summers and long, extremely cold, dark winters. In most of the antarctic, there are no vascular plants. Lichens and bryophytes are restricted to the warmer, moister coastal areas.

High-Latitude Alpine Regions

These areas are contiguous with the arctic and antarctic but have strong seasonal differences between summer and winter. There are definite hot and cold seasons. Summer is short; winter is long. Generally there is much snow and meltwater. Most areas have extensive Krummholz zones and many lichens and bryophytes.

Low-Latitude Alpine Regions

These areas are located in extremely dry latitudes about 30° north and south of the equator where great mountain chains make their own special climate. The Himalayas and Karakorams in Asia, and the Andes in middle South America, are the best examples. There is a long growing season, less snow than in the high-latitude alpine regions and much sublimation. The highest snow lines and vascular plant limits are found here. Vascular plants may grow above 20,000 feet. Krummholz, lichens and bryophytes are scant.

Equatorial Alpine Regions

These areas are located in the tropics near the equator where there are minor temperature variations from summer to winter. Most mountains are isolated volcanoes. Spring and fall are warm and dry; summer and winter are cool and wet. (Clouds in summer keep the temperature down.) Most of the snow sublimates, and there are few Krummholz and lichen–bryophyte zones. Hot- and cold-adapted animals share the same habitats during different times of day. The growing season is almost continuous.

the wind. These elfin trees are called Krummholz. They extend upward to the tree limit above which the only trees are prostrate willows and birches. Above these is tundra.

Timberline and tree limit are determined by several factors. The most important is temperature. As one goes upward in elevation, or north or south toward the poles, the temperature drops. When the mean temperature for the hottest month of the year averages 50 degrees Fahrenheit or less, trees begin to disappear. This happens at 72 degrees north latitude and 56 degrees south latitude.

The precise altitude of timberline depends on latitude and precipitation. It is lower close to the poles (2300 feet in Alaska, sea level in Antarctica) and higher near the equator (13,000 feet in Mexico, 12,000 feet in Ecuador). In the Canadian Rockies there is heavy winter snowfall, and timberline is at about 7000 feet. The highest timberlines in the world are in the Himalayas a little north and south of the equator and in the Andes, where the highest mountains occur in the driest altitudes.

Above the last elfin tree, we entered the enchanted land of tundra. From there until permanent snow and ice prevented the growth of most flowering plants, grasses, sedges and flowers enjoyed the unhampered freedom of the heights. Turflike meadows were ablaze with color. Shrubby heaths and tiny tufts among the rocks competed for our attention. It was the pink star-studded pin cushions that grabbed my fancy. I marveled at such courageous beauty flaunting the blast of glacier winds. I flung myself

Patricia Armstrong explores Snowdrift Peak on the Juneau Icefield to look for red and yellow snow algae. She was the first woman to climb the peak.
PHOTO: CHUCK ARMSTRONG

Vegetation Zones and Boundaries on Mountains

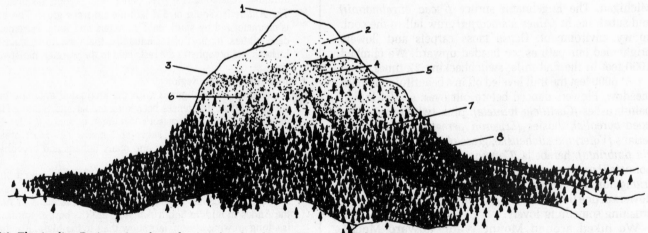

(1) *The Aeolian Region* exists above the vascular plant limit. All life subsists on wind-blown nutrients. Mosses, lichens, algae and liverworts predominate.

(2) *The Vascular Plant Limit,* above which no vascular plant grows, is determined by low temperature. Vascular plants cannot grow where temperatures rarely rise above freezing.

(3) *The Snow Line* occurs where the average temperature for the warmest month of the year is 32 degrees Fahrenheit. Snows accumulate and form permanent snowfields.

(4) *The Alpine Zone* lies below the snow line and above the tree limit. Here many types of vascular plants, bryophytes and lichens flourish.

(5) *The Tree Limit or Scrub Limit.* Woody plants more than a few inches high cease to grow.

(6) *The Krummholz Zone* occurs below the tree limit and above the timberline. Tundra vegetation and subalpine vegetation intermix. This is a zone of transition.

(7) *The Timberline* is the boundary between a continuous forest of trees over six feet high, and dwarf, twisted, isolated trees. The highest mean temperature of the warmest month is no more than 50 degrees Fahrenheit.

(8) *A Subalpine Forest* is a continuous, closed community of trees more than six feet high, usually conifers.

to the ground, eye to eye with moss campion *(Silene acaulis),* my first alpine friend. It is one of the most widespread alpine plants, growing on mountains from Alaska to Mexico and completely around the globe in the arctic. It can be found also in the mountains of New England, and in the Alps, Carpathians, Pyrenees and Apennines of Europe.

Moss campion snuggles its compact cushion among wind-rounded rocks and gravels on the harshest ridges. A long taproot anchors it in granular soil and stores nourishment. It may take 10 years for a cushion to grow big enough to flower, and a 25-year-old plant may be only seven inches in diameter. That day, the plant's flowers smiled among its dense leafy hemisphere only a few

Tundra Conditions: How Plants and People Can Adapt to Them

Condition	Plant Adaptations	Human Adaptations
Increased isolation	Thick, waxy cuticle on leaves; accessory pigments to screen radiation; less chlorophyll; intolerance to shade; vibrant flower colors.	Sunglasses to filter ultraviolet radiation; hat to shade face and head; sun screen such as zinc oxide to protect lips, nose and other exposed skin areas.
Wind—chilling, abrading and drying	Thick, waxy cuticle on leaves; enrolled margins; dense hairs to retard evaporation; cushion shape with little exposed surface; growth behind rocks; succulent leaves; small leaves; water-storing roots; deep taproots; short stems; seeds in wind shaker; seeds with plumes for wind dispersal.	Nylon clothing to cut wind (wind pants, windbreaker, nylon scarf); tent or poncho for shelter; skin surfaces covered to reduce wind chill; lotion for exposed skin to prevent windburn; drinking lots of water.
Cold temperatures and short growing season	Perennial growth, dormant when cold; vegetative reproduction; cushion shape, short and close to ground; dark colors; food-storing roots; low assimilation rates; parabolic flowers track sun to collect heat; buds occur close to ground and are well protected in dense leaves.	Warm clothing: mitts, insulated boots, down booties, hat, heavy sweater, down jacket, down pants, down sleeping bag.
Wetness, rain and soggy ground	Tolerance to saturated soil; preference for peat, and acidic and highly organic soils.	Waterproof boots, heavy wool socks, poncho and rain pants, tent or poncho for shelter.
Snow and ice	Frost resistance; perennial growth; layering under snow.	Mountain boots, gaiters, mitts, ice axe, crampons.
Temperature extremes	Frost resistance; quick start of growth when warm; food storage roots; perennial growth; vegetative reproduction.	Many layers of clothing, added or subtracted as needed; shelter carried along.
Low oxygen at high altitudes	Low assimilation rates (altitude alone has little effect on plants).	Keeping in shape—jogging, swimming, cycling or other daily exercise for heart and lungs. Acclimatizing—four easy days above 7000 feet before going higher, slowly and with light loads at first. Using the step-rest walk. Drinking plenty of liquids; eating simple sugars, starches and vitamins, and less fats.
Unstable substrates (scree slides, avalanches, solifluction)	Deep taproots; adventitious roots, resprouting if buried; stems bending back to vertical.	Good mountain boots; sturdy clothing; hard hat; ice axe; crampons; care in walking; knowledge of hazards of mountain travel and of rescue techniques.
Permafrost and solifluction	Short roots or no roots; adventitious roots; tolerance of soggy substrates; vegetative reproduction; low nutrient requirements.	Travelers should be extremely careful not to disturb plant cover and to dispose of their wastes properly. (Permafrost has little effect on visitors.)
Isolation	Some wind pollination; brilliant colors ensure insects will find and pollinate flowers.	Extra food, shelter and first-aid equipment; carrying map and compass. Protecting plants (which may be rare) by not cutting firewood or tent poles and by staying on established trails to avoid trampling.

inches above the ground, where my cheek felt the warmth of the gravel and the quietness of the wind.

Another plant not far away was the dryad *(Dryas octopetala)*. Its tiny fernlike leaves wove dense mats across the scree and its feathery seed heads were spread like a cockatoo's crest. Back-lit by the sun, they made shimmering islands on the broken stones. A few plumes rode the wind and bumped across rocky places. A butterfly buffeted by the same breeze landed on the moss campion. As the insect sucked its life-giving drink from the flower, I looked up to see an eternity of sky, clouds and rugged peaks. My lifelong love affair with mountains had begun.

THE ALTITUDE, airy views and dazzling clarity of the place struck both of us. Chuck leaped to his feet and jerked me up. We shouted and waved across the valley. Sometimes echoes answered back but mostly there was only the screaming wind. We cavorted on the meadow, dancing hand in hand in wild circles till we fell exhausted to the ground. Then, laughing, we rolled downhill in each other's arms and slid to a stop behind a boulder. We heard the scree go sliding on and on until it vanished and the great silence of the summits shushed us.

Out of the wind, we basked in the warmth of mountain sun. We heard wind-worried sand ping against the rocks and felt the angles and grooves where differential hardness had opposed the eternal etching process. We marveled about the few plants able to smile here despite the hostile winds.

Fellfields, or wind-swept boulder fields, are far better developed in the southern Rockies than in the Canadian Rockies. There, cushions of alpine forget-me-not *(Eritrichium aretioides)*, dwarf clover *(Trifolium nanum)*, Rocky Mountain nailwort *(Paronychia pulvinata)* and alpine phlox *(Phlox condensata* or *P. pulvinata)* mix their bright colors with moss campion. These hardy plants take their shapes from the rocky places where they live. To appreciate their beauty and smell their lovely fragrances, you must lie down and view them at their level.

We resumed climbing, hand in hand, our bucket swinging in the breeze. Plants became scarcer; here and there in the cold shade of craggy places we found snow. We put our jackets on and continued to climb.

The vascular plant limit and the snow line usually occur at the same altitude. It is wherever the average mean for the warmest month of the year is 32 degrees Fahrenheit. There is no time for blooming and setting seed. The soil is almost always frozen and not a source for plant nourishment. The only plants that can survive are those that don't need warm periods to live. Mosses, lichens and algae are well adapted to this harsh environment.

The zone above the vascular plant limit has been called Aeolian, after the Greek god of wind. Since temperatures there rarely go above freezing for long, plants obtain all their nourishment from wind-blown debris and snow melt. In such dry areas as the low-latitude Himalayas and Andes, the snow line is extremely high, and plants grow at 20,000 feet. In northern North America, the snow line is low, and there are extensive Aeolian zones.

Exploring the Aeolian zone of Mount Wapta and Mount Field required technical rock climbing skills. Be-

Botanical Definitions

Bryophyte. A small plant with leaflike structure that lacks vascular tissue. Mosses and liverworts are two types of bryophytes.

Heath. A shrub commonly found on acid soil. Heaths have small leaves and bell-shaped flowers. Many produce edible fruits. Heather, blueberries, cranberries and rhododendrons are common heaths.

Krummholz. A forest of twisted, stunted trees less than six feet high, growing in isolated clumps on a mountain.

Lichen. A plant made up of an alga and a fungus living together for mutual benefit. Lichens are among the heartiest plants on earth and are able to exist on bare rocks, in deserts and in tundras.

Monocot. A grouping of plants based on appearance. Monocots have long linear leaves and produce inconspicuous flowers. Grasses, sedges and rushes are common monocots.

Vascular Plant. A plant containing water pipes in its roots, stems and leaves. All large plants such as trees and shrubs are vascular. Bryophytes, lichens, algae and fungi are nonvascular plants, being small and containing no water pipes.

Woody Plant. A plant containing woody tissue in its stem. These plants may lose their leaves in the winter, but the woody stems and branches remain alive, though dormant, all year. A nonwoody plant, on the other hand, often dies back to the roots in winter.

Geographical Definitions

Fellfield. An area containing rocks, gravel, sand and soil mixed together. Fellfields usually are exposed to wind. They lack snow cover in winter, get direct sunlight and often are located where frost occurs. They are a harsh environment where only hardy tuft or cushion plants can grow.

Glacier. A body of flowing ice.

Insolation. Solar radiation received in a particular area.

Nivation Hollow. A depression in a sheltered location formed by the erosive action of glacial ice. Nivation hollows hold snow late into the summer. Therefore they are a cold, wet environment with a short growing season. Yet certain plants have adapted to this environment.

Nunatak. The Eskimo word for a hill or mountain that has been encircled by a glacier. Most nunataks are Matterhorn-like peaks and are glaciated on all sides.

Permafrost. Perennially frozen subsoil in areas where the temperature is above freezing for only a few months of the year. During the summer only the top few inches or feet of soil thaw out.

Permanent Snowfield. A spot where more snow falls in winter than melts away in summer, usually in a sheltered location. Unlike glaciers, permanent snowfields lack movement and do not contain ice compacted from accumulated snow. But with increased accumulation, they may develop into glaciers.

Solifluction. The gradual slipping of soil downslope caused by the effect of gravity on water-saturated soil. Solifluction often occurs in the tundra: permafrost prevents meltwater from soaking in, so the soil on top becomes saturated and slides downhill.

Sublimation. The process by which snow volatilizes into vapor and then condenses again into a solid, without passing through the liquid state.

fore we had gone far, better judgment got the best of us. We didn't know why mountaineers carried rope or how they used it, but we realized our clothesline wasn't good for much. We stood for a long time looking up at the beckoning skyline and out across the dark green abyss. We dared not go on, yet we were reluctant to leave. Sadly, we finally traced our footsteps down the rocky face, across the scree and cushion plants to the tundra meadow of our rapture, and down to our camp in the fir forest. We kept stopping to look back, to remember how it had been. We knew we would have to return.

IN THE YEARS that followed my husband and I took up climbing. I went back to school to learn about tundra and spent several summers with the University of Colorado in Rocky Mountain National Park, with Michigan State University on the Juneau Icefield in Alaska, and on a 10,000-mile Edlund-Armstrong-Olmsted-Abbott-Corydalis Expedition, of the University of Chicago, to the mountains of the eastern United States. In 1968 I finished my master's research on bryophytes and lichens. Since then the mountains of the Western Hemisphere have become my classroom, and the plants that grow there my instructors and friends.

Nowadays, we carry lightweight mountain tents with snow liners and rain flies. We have good mountain boots, backpacks and down sleeping bags. On the trail I carry a six-by-ten-inch backpacking plant press and some flower books as well as my share of camp gear, climbing and photographic equipment.

Each time I see the forest dwindle into Krummholz—as I pass into the area of "elfinwood"—I feel reborn and free. I still have worldly cares; I must use my judgment to stay alive under conditions often harsh and dangerous. But I am self-sufficient. I have food and shelter on my back and a knowledge of mountains in my head.

I have laughed in the teeth of 100-mile-an-hour winds, slept snuggly in the snow at 30 below, found my way in the darkest night and whitest fog, been soggy wet and mosquito bitten for two weeks straight, and felt the presence of lightning all around and through me. Yet I love it. Like the tundra flowers or the lowly lichens, I have learned to adapt so I can enjoy the worst as well as the best.

There are four basic types of tundra, categorized geographically:

• *Polar Tundra* is characterized by the lowest timberlines; long, cold, dark winters; and short, cool summers. Often the Aeolian zone makes up most of the cover. Spruces and firs are dominant timberline trees.

• *High-Latitude Alpine Tundra* is characterized by low to moderate timberlines, good Krummholz zones and strong summer–winter extremes. All of the United States except for parts of Alaska has this type of tundra. Most summer days have brief afternoon showers or snow, and cool to frosty nights. The amount

ᵃ = Documented specimen.

Comparison of Data from Different Areas

Tundra type	Country area	Mountain	Latitude	Summit elevation	Timberline elevation	Vascular Plant limit elevation	Snow line elevation
Equatorial alpine	Mexico	Orizaba & Citlaltepetl	19°N	18,701	12,000-13,500	16,000–15,200ᵃ	15,000-17,000
Equatorial alpine	Ecuador	Cotopaxi	1°S	19,340	10,700-12,500	17,000	15,600-16,500
Low-latitude alpine	Peru	Huascaran	9½°S	22,205	12,000-14,000	18,000ᵃ	15,000-17,500
Low-latitude alpine	Bolivia	Illimani	16⅔°S	21,200	13,000-14,000	19,000-21,000	16,000-17,000
Low-latitude alpine	Nepal	Everest	30°N	29,028	12,000-13,500	19,000-20,130ᵃ	17,000-20,000
High-latitude alpine	U.S.A. New Hampshire	Washington	44¼°N	6288	4800-5200	above 9000	9900
High-latitude alpine	U.S.A. Colorado	Evans	39½°N	14,264	11,500-12,000	14,500-15,000	14,500
High-latitude alpine	U.S.A. Alaska	Devils Paw	58¾°N	8584	2300-3000	5600-7000 6900ᵃ	3000-6000
Arctic	Canada Ellesmere Is.	Tanquary Fiord	81°N	4950	72°N	83°N	1000
Antarctic	Antarctic MacRobertson Coast	Anniversary Nunataks	68°S	4455	56°S	64°S	sea level

of snow and ice varies with latitude and proximity to moist air masses.

• *Low-Latitude Alpine Tundra* is characterized by the highest timberlines and snow lines. The temperature fluctuates less from season to season than from day to night. There are dry and wet seasons rather than cold and hot seasons. Length of day is constant throughout the year. The world's highest mountains—the Andes and Himalayas—have low-latitude alpine tundra. Here life forms exist at higher altitudes than anywhere else.

• *Equatorial Alpine Tundra* is similar to low-latitude tundra. But climates are warmer, so snow tends to evaporate rather than melt. Wet, cloudy summers keep temperatures down and retard evaporation. As a result, equatorial mountains may have two cool seasons a year. Length of day is constant throughout the year. The timberlines and snow lines are moderately high, but there is less Krummholz and moss–lichen coverage than in other tundra. Most equatorial mountains are isolated volcanoes like those in Ecuador and Mexico.

We started by studying the high-latitude alpine tundra of Colorado and Wyoming. These enchanted gardens make an unbroken, flower-spattered carpet. The soil is thick. Plants come halfway to your knee. Bumblebees buzz busily from pink to blue to yellow to white. Lark-like water pipits trill piercing metallic notes as they skip above bobbing flowers, catching insects. These are the pleasantest of places to lie and dream away summer days. You can count three dozen different plants in one arm's reach and a hundred in the sweep of an eye.

The southern Rockies boast more than 300 species of alpine plants and nearly all the plant communities of tundra. The scrub heath community, however, is absent; to see it I had to head farther north. Twice my family drove the Alaskan Highway to look for scrub heaths and Aeolian zones. In Alaska the high latitude and heavy precipitation force timberlines, vascular plant limits and snow lines downward. The width of tundra is much narrower than in the Lower 48, but the amount of mountain above the vascular plant limit is greater—for instance, 16,000 feet on Mount McKinley. Lichens and mosses are important contributors to the community.

Heathers, the most common scrub heaths, occur occasionally in Wyoming and California but are common in the Cascade Range. These woody shrubs have tightly packed, evergreen-needle leaves and pink to white bell-like flowers. Where snow covers them in winter, they make dense mats. Lichens and mosses grow among them. Other plants sometimes integrate, usually such members of the Ericaceae or heath family as blueberries, Labrador tea, alpine azaleas, laurels, rhododendron and crowberries. Walking in or on scrub heaths is very troublesome. Rocks and holes are hidden by the dense growth. Wet branches scrape waterproofing from boots so your feet get soaked when it isn't even raining.

The two most common heathers are *Cassiope mertensiana*, which has tightly overlapped, waxy leaves that look like a braided cord, and small white flowers; and *Phyllodoce empetriformis*, with leaves like hemlock needles and pink flowers. The names come from Greek mythology. Red stamen clappers chime small bell-like flowers and conjure up visions of the past when gods and goddesses lived among men. The misty places where the heathers grow enhance the mystic mood.

In 1966 I went to Alaska. As one of 3 women among 50 men in the Institute of Glaciological and Arctic Sciences, on the Juneau Icefield, I studied tundra on the arctic mountains and glaciers.

The Aeolian zone was crowded with lichens of black, brown, yellow and white. Most rock surfaces and soil were covered with them, as well as frosted red, brown and gold mosses. In many places a banding occurred: different-colored mosses and lichens grew in zones that depended on the depth of soil, amount of moisture and exposure to the sun. Snow algae dyed the glaciers red and yellow. Daylight lasted most of the night.

It was a different world—stark, forbidding, cold, harsh, sharp, silent, vast, dazzling, infinite. Blinding white icefields undulated as far as I could see, broken here and there by rows of nunatak fangs snapping at the sky. Torn pieces of blue—ice falls and crevasses—lay scattered on the glaciers. I returned two years later to become the first woman instructor on the icefield.

Low-altitude alpine tundra is best displayed in the punas, the high, arid plateaus, of South America. In 1972 I brushed up on my Spanish and took a three-week trip alone to the tundras of Peru, Bolivia and Ecuador.

The puna in Peru was cheerless, mournful, brooding, grim. There, where the massive Andes receive dry Pacific winds across the cold Humboldt Current, glaciers evaporate instead of melt. No spruces and firs point to the peaks. Instead, red paper-barked polylepis trees and orange-flowered buddleias marked the timberline. Snow lines were elevated, and so were plants. The Andes gentian (*Gentiana sedifolia*) grew at 18,000 feet, looking at the blue-blue sky with blue-blue eyes. But when a cloud momentarily passed before the face of the sun, the gentian's petals folded neatly like a circular accordion to hide the flower among the leafy tussock.

After Peru, I spent a five-dollar weekend in Bolivia exploring the highest, driest part of the puna. From the airport, at 13,300 feet, I walked away toward the nearest mountain, hoping I could make it there and back in two days.

I was lucky enough to hitch a ride with two young men: a Bolivian taxi driver, who spoke only Spanish, and his paying passenger, who spoke only French. They, too, were going to the mountain. I had taken along my notebook and collecting bags, but as it turned out, the rock was too frost-shattered for lichens and it was too far above the vascular plant limit for larger plants.

Back in the taxi heading down, the driver asked about my work. He was disappointed I hadn't found any plants on the mountain. "Your trip will be a failure," he said sadly. "Here are some plants. We stop."

"But the Frenchman is paying for this ride, not I," I replied. "I can walk some other place."

"But he is dull. He cannot talk. You speak Spanish pretty good. Besides, you look much better than he does." He stopped the car. "I want your ride with me to be good."

I let them argue about what was happening and made a quick collecting trip beside the road. Five grasses and two herbs were all I found. The Bolivian altiplano was very barren.

In the equatorial alpine tundra of Ecuador, the days and nights pass consistently like the opening and closing of a door—12 hours' light, 12 hours' darkness, no shading twilight, no displays of sunset colors. Winter occurs every night when the temperature falls to freezing; by 10 A.M. it's warm enough for shirt sleeves. Arctic mammals, coldblooded lizards and frogs share the same habitat, alternating their dormant and active periods every 12 hours. The dry season is not as long or severe as it is in low-latitude tundra, so the growing season is almost continuous.

In Ecuador I found shrub meadows at elevations between 10,400 and 14,600 feet, and cushion-mat plants in the fellfields and rocky barrens above. In Mexico I found sedgemeadow turfs (with grasses rather than sedges dominant) from the subalpine pine forests at 11,500 to 13,000 feet on up to 13,500 feet. Higher, only occasional grass tufts and cushion plants grew, in the shelter of rocks where water was more available.

On Cotopaxi, Ecuador, the world's tallest active volcano, I explored the high plateau, the paramo, with special permission and transportation furnished by NASA's rocket and satellite tracking station. When I came upon signs saying "restricted area, absolutely no admittance," I thought they didn't refer to me. I took notes and photographs and collected plants among the radar antennas. When it began to rain and snow, I got out my bright yellow poncho and sat down under the antennas to enjoy the storm.

A pickup truck drove by, and I kept crouched down, keeping my notes and specimens dry beneath the poncho. The truck went by a second time, and a third. Then it stopped and a group of men piled out. The leader gestured frantically in my direction. The men spread out along the road and charged with guns in hand. Before I knew what was happening, I was surrounded, jerked to my feet and hustled off into the truck.

"It's only you!" the director soon said, and apologized. He had neglected to tell the workers about my mission, and I had walked into a restricted zone. When I proved to be only a harmless botanist, the truck driver was embarrassed, but it was a good joke anyway.

My most recent excursion to tundra was a 5½-week family vacation to Mexico to see more equatorial mountains, in December, 1973. Our girls were now 17 and 15 years of age and had a beginning knowledge of Spanish. After six days of hiking above 8000 feet, we were ready to try the big mountains. Roads on Zinantecatl, Ixtaccihuatl and Popocatepetl let us drive to 13,000 feet.

Our excitement grew as we drove through fir and pine forests, straining ever upward with our engine in second gear. The Mexican mountains had little Krummholz. A few small pines were outriggers on the sea of grass. There were no groves of twisted wood or wind-pruned hedges as in the Rockies.

Above the nodding, drooping grass bristled silver-straw *Eryngium protaefolium,* looking like lurking Indians with spears and arrows poised. The wind rasped through barbed leaves, speaking of feathered serpents and Aztec sun gods. Rain and snow hissed and slithered between grassy mounds. Little mustard plants wore woolly underwear and rattled dry seeds in waxed-paper pods. A few yellow flowers smiled bravely in the snow.

Reaching 17,342-foot Ixtaccihuatl, we camped at the end of the mountain road. At midnight a jeep with siren and flashing red lights pulled in beside us. Seventeen young people spilled out and began to unload gear in gay confusion and set up camp. They were preparing a mass climb and practice rescue, complete with walkie-talkies and stretchers. There was no sleeping in that pandemonium, so we got up.

Chuck and I readied ourselves and packs for the climb. At one o'clock in the morning we set out by moonlight to follow the black line of path among the shadows. Rocks and grass hummocks, trees and cliffs appeared as carved shapes in shades of muted ochre and black. The moon was almost full. We walked slowly—step up, straighten knee, rest leg, step up—our breathing keeping pace without a problem. An awe of the night hung heavily over us; we barely spoke. Once or twice we squeezed a signal between clasped hands.

Just before 5 A.M. the moon went down and plunged us into utter darkness. We had to use the flashlight frequently to find the trail. A few minutes later we reached a hut and struggled in to await the dawn.

Chuck had a cold, and it was bothering him. His ears were plugged; he was having trouble breathing deep. At dawn we discussed the situation. I went on alone.

When I reached the summit, clouds were all around me and it was snowing, cold and gray. I was six hours away from the car, miles to the north, several thousand feet higher and in a special world of my own. I turned a cartwheel in the snow, then flung myself down to wave angelwing arms. I hadn't made snow angels since I was a kid in grade school. I guess I did it because I was just so happy to be there. I have suffered all my life from asthma and allergies. Yet on the mountaintop I cavorted like a mountain goat without a single breathless gasp or hurried heartbeat. Conditioning and acclimatization were my secrets.

So the pattern for the mountains of Mexico was

set. Chuck would stay with the girls below, and I would reach the heights alone—gloriously ecstatic, with no one to share my joy.

On Popocatepetl I chopped out a place to sleep on the 45-degree snow at 16,600 feet. On Citlaltepetl I watched Chuck go back to Tlachachuca with the jeep and found myself the only person on Mexico's highest peak. The jeep would return the next day, but what if I weren't there to meet it? This was really isolation.

Within six hours I was poking around the summit crevasses as the sun dipped low and clouds wrapped their shrouds around the mountain. Contrast faded. I could see only one step ahead. The windswept snow was packed hard and somewhat slick. I slipped and did an ice-axe arrest, and lost a mitt. It slid into the mouth of the fog and disappeared.

I could have made the last few feet and claimed the highest summit of my life, but I turned back. Solo climbing was dangerous among the hidden crevasses. The weather was deteriorating fast, and it was late. I was not beaten by the mountain; rather, I decided to call time out. I would return, hopefully with the climbing partner of my life, to share the joy of the magnificent peak.

I glissaded to my abandoned pack, found the lost mitt farther below and found a place out of the snow to spend the night. I went to bed early and lightly clad. My wool knickers and heavy outer socks were so covered with snow that I had to keep them outside my sleeping bag. I weighted them down against the wind and from my snug perch watched the stars through torn fog curtains.

The wind intensified. The fabric of my sleeping bag flapped noisily. My legs and feet got cold. I drew my knees up under my chin, my feet beneath my rear and puppy-cuddled into my down jacket in the sleeping bag.

As the night wore on and Orion chased the Pleiades across the sky, I was unable to sleep. I thought about the push of the wind, the excitement of the climb, the breathless fascination of my aerie, the freedom of the mountains. It was the freedom to chart survival where there is death, to choose a life more abundantly blessed than that on the Earth's plains. I had met the rocks and plants of different mountains and moved well among the frozen steeps. No, not just moved. I had done it with skipping feet and singing heart, with exuberance and exaltation. Now, like a cushion plant tucked in the rocks, I exposed the least amount of surface area and hid my warmth within. I thrived on rarified air and icy winds. I had adapted—I belonged.

Not only I, my whole family. They remind me of certain tundra flowers. My younger daughter, Becky, is a pink mountain heather, *Phyllodoce empetriformis*. Tough, wiry, stormy mornings and sunny afternoons, a snow-bed plant, sleeps late. Somewhat mischievous, slippery footing on the steeps; yet petite and feminine with dainty chiming bells. Imaginative, and talkative.

My older daughter, Jackie, is a dryad, *Dryas octopetala*. A rebel, chumming with her cohorts, taunting the established ways, daring slidey scree. Long shaggy hair back-lit in the sun, radiantly beautiful when happy. Not a part of any community. Aloof, yet clannish with her kind. A hidden potential to heal the world's erosion scars with boundless love.

My best female friend and companion on many tundra treks is an alpine sunflower, *Hymenoxys grandiflora*. A big blonde Swede, she's wholly beautiful. Her sunny countenance and laughing eyes have shared a world of passion and pain with me.

My husband? An elephanthead, *Pedicularis groenlandica*. Unexpected humor, delight of mimicry, cheerful smile despite heavy pack and soaking feet. I take strength and warm comfort from his ever-presence in my mountains.

And me? What flower am I? That's hard for me to say. I might be moss campion, snuggly warm and delicately pretty, until I think of alpine forget-me-nots. My eyes are blue. Then I remember the sky-blue eyes of the Andes gentian in Peru, and I think I'd like to spend forever there at 18,000 feet, watching condors soar over Nevado Cayesh.

When at last I reach the slower, grayer years, I can become an arctic gentian, *Gentiana algida*, pert in blue-black lace and faded scarlet shawl against the eternal snows that must surely come.

ALPENGLOW

by KENT DANNEN

The optimism and joy of a new day dawning cannot be recorded on film.

I love alpenglow, and never gave too much thought about what causes it until Kent Dannen, a curious sort of fellow, asked me one day if I knew the answer. Since I innocently admitted that I didn't, I was set up for Kent's next question: How about an article explaining what alpenglow is and what causes it?

Sure, Kent. So here it is. I found it edifying.

W.K.

The sun is setting; long violet shadows are growing out over the woods from the mountains along the western rim of the park; the Absaroka range is baptized in the divine light of the alpenglow, and its rocks and trees are transfigured. Next to the light of the dawn on high mountain tops, the alpenglow is the most impressive of all the terrestrial manifestations of God."

John Muir, *Our National Parks*

The appearance of either sunrise or sunset colors on mountain summits is called "alpenglow." Usually there are three phases to this optical phenomenon. I shall describe them as they occur in the evening because that is when they are most often observed. Of course, the order is reversed at dawn.

The first phase is the ordinary evening coloration of the peaks when the sun is still a little above the horizon. This takes place when the sun's rays are at an angle of about 88 degrees from the observer, or zenith 88 degrees.

A few minutes after the first color has faded, the second stage appears—the alpenglow proper. The peaks still are in direct sunlight; the sun's zenith angle is a little over 90 degrees. The color, deeper and usually pinker than before, results from the setting sun's rays hitting the atmosphere at a low angle and passing through a greater depth of air. Only those light rays toward the red end of the spectrum are strong enough to penetrate so far.

The pink band of alpenglow proper often begins hundreds of yards below the summit and spreads upward as the sun sets. It gradually blends, and disappears, into the dark segment. The dark segment, a bluish-gray band, indicates the point at which perceptible light rays are not strong enough to pass through the atmosphere. The duration of this dark band increases with the purity of the air but always ends by the time the sun is around zenith 97 degrees. It gradually is extinguished by the third stage of alpenglow: the afterglow.

Crowding the heels of the dark segment, the afterglow begins when the sun is at about zenith 94 degrees. The peaks are no longer in direct sunlight. Their color, ranging from yellow through purple, results from reflected radiation of the purple light that faintly glows in the western sky after sunset. The purple is caused by the reflection of light off a layer of extremely fine dust at an altitude of 6 to 12 miles.

Because its light is reflected, rather than direct, the afterglow is much more diffused than the other two stages, and its boundary is less well defined. It also lasts longer, until the sun is at zenith 99 degrees.

Sometimes there is a second afterglow. It occurs when there is an abnormal second purple light caused by an unusual amount of impurity in the upper air. The impurities can result from both manmade and natural causes, such as volcanic eruptions. Second purple light may last until the sun has reached zenith 101 degrees.

There are a few physical differences between evening and morning alpenglow. The alpenglow seems to be much more common at sunset than at sunrise, and the evening colors—orange and red—are more striking than the morning colors, which run toward pink and purple. The richer colors of sunset result from the evening air's greater humidity and greater turbulence, which enables it to contain more particles of dust than the morning air.

Yet, "Beauty is in the eye of the beholder," and John Muir seemed to prefer the alpenglow at sunrise. The delicate pastels of dawn alpenglow may have seemed more impressive to him because in the morning our eyes are completely rested and therefore more sensitive.

But it seems likely that psychological as well as aesthetic considerations were involved in Muir's judgment. The bright optimism of a new day dawning, the sense of joy and satisfaction at rising early enough to have so much day ahead—these too are factors. Although they do not operate by laws of physics, they definitely affect the viewer's perception and, hence, the beauty that he sees.

The psychological aspects of alpenglow are not easily recorded on film, but the physical qualities can be the subject of spectacular photographs. Even the simplest sort of camera will give excellent results.

Any lens, at one time or another, will be the best one. A short telephoto, however, usually is the most useful for composing the patterns of color and shadow.

251

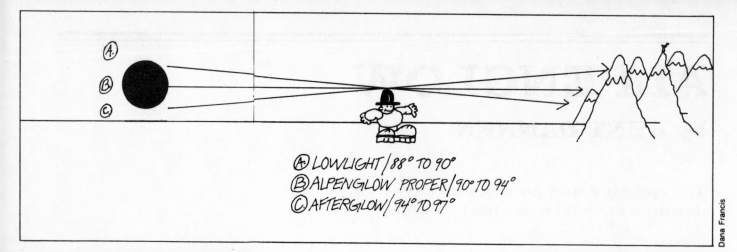

A LOWLIGHT / 88° TO 90°
B ALPENGLOW PROPER / 90° TO 94°
C AFTERGLOW / 94° TO 97°

Dana Francis

Low light. The ordinary coloration of the peaks when the sun is still above the horizon. It is the first phase in the evening; the last in the morning.
PHOTO: KENT AND DONNA DANNEN

Alpenglow proper. The peaks are usually a deeper and pinker color. The sun is at a lower angle and only the red light rays are strong enough to penetrate the atmosphere.
PHOTO: KENT AND DONNA DANNEN

Afterglow. This is the purple phase. The peaks are no longer in direct sunlight. The color results from the reflection of sun rays off a layer of fine atmospheric dust.
PHOTO: KENT AND DONNA DANNEN

When using a normal length lens, there probably will be either a good deal of empty sky or of dark foreground in the picture because you cannot get close enough to the peaks to fill the frame with alpenglow. Usually it is better to include the foreground than the sky. Trees and other foreground objects make a dramatic black frame, give weight to the bottom of the picture and provide contrast to the color of the peaks.

The filters normally used in color photography have no use in alpenglow photography. There is little polarization to the glow. So a polarizing filter may darken the sky, increasing contrast between the peaks and sky. This will create a more dramatic picture without significantly altering the glow's natural color. And because there are few ultraviolet rays, an ultraviolet filter has no effect. A yellow, orange or red filter heightens the natural alpenglow colors but also casts the sky in a decidedly unnatural hue, which is usually not desirable.

To vary alpenglow pictures, you should remember that Muir said, "rocks and trees are transfigured." Small details as well as massive mountains take on new and wonderful colors at this time. The details need not be inanimate ones; people and animals make excellent subjects. To catch the details, the photographer himself must be high enough on the mountain to be caught in the light. Since this is possible only at the extremes of the day, alpenglow photography is especially suited to backpackers.

The causes of the alpenglow are somewhat complex. But remember that Muir spoke of "divine light" as of an earthly manifestation of God. If he was right, then the alpenglow necessarily must be somewhat mysterious. Those who find joy in the outdoors know that beauty need not be completely understood to be appreciated. ▲

252

CHULO

by BIL GILBERT

"Our ostensible objective to find and study a communal, raccoon-like mammal called the coatimundi, was an exotic, quixotic, profoundly necessary one."

The real reasons for studying wild animals in their natural habitat are clearly explained by author Bil Gilbert in the beginning of his article. I found them to make as interesting reading as the actual field study about the raccoon-like animal called coatimundi (or chulo).

Many of us dream of taking an adventure with our families like the one Bil Gilbert has taken here, but few do it.

W.K.

ALL OF US INVOLVED in the move to the mountains along the Arizona-Sonora border, and a good many others who observed it with curiosity, doubts, even alarm, wondered why we would do such a thing. Our ostensible objective, to find and study a communal, raccoon-like mammal called the coatimundi, was an exotic, quixotic, profoundly necessary one. In pursuit of it, we were trading very comfortable circumstances for others which would almost certainly be less comfortable in a measurable way. For example, anyone who in August leaves the cool green Appalachians, a trout stream with a swimming hole, and the shade of big maples, willows, elms, white pines, birch for the blazing pitiless sun, the searing heat, the thorns, and the dust of the Sonora Desert is, at least physically, behaving in a peculiar and impractical way.

The others had various motives for going with me, among the best being that it would have been very difficult for most of them to have done otherwise. However, in the beginning the coati scheme was not the result of group discussion or decision.

For some years, combining certain training and a lifelong interest in natural history with an ability to write,

I have earned a pleasant and easy living as an essayist, a commentator on the affairs of other species. Being moderately successful at an agreeable trade, being forty-three years old, I was consequently restless, feeling now and then that my life was too agreeable, that the soft sheets were getting me, that it would be a good thing to send out the laundry and pick up new challenges, physical, intellectual, emotional. Also I believed or had convinced myself that change would be good for the entire family, that the children would benefit from getting out of their cozy life in the gentle Appalachians, from poking about for a time in the larger world.

Especially I thought a drastic change would be good—was, in fact, necessary—for Ky and Terry, who had been close friends all their lives. Both were in their middle teens and their sap was flowing vigorously. Both were excruciatingly bored with and increasingly hostile toward school, their schoolboy status, the village life style. I thought they had good reason for being bored and hostile. In the interests of an almost worthless education, small-town gentility, their natural exuberance and vitality were being suffocated. Their legitimate ambition for adventure,

real work, freedom was continually thwarted by petty tyrannies and tyrants. It seemed that if I stirred my stumps, got out of the soft sheets, I could release them from the prison to which I had helped commit them, in which they had been left too long.

Such itches, irritations, desires might have been partially soothed by sailing to Australia, packing through Patagonia, moving to Belgrade, or by one of the other ingenious activities designed to alleviate middle-class, middle-aged angst. However, given my tastes, it was inevitable that we should, if not watch coatis, do something similar. For as long as I can remember, I have been a kind of animalcoholic addicted to associating with other beasts.

The range of the coatis made it obvious that if we were to see them in the wild we would have to travel to and live in a new, un-Appalachian-like country. Also, search of mammalian literature confirmed a background impression that very little was known about this creature, virtually nothing about it in the United States. Therefore an obvious objective and attraction was to learn what we could of this mammal, perhaps contribute something to the knowledge of its natural history.

Even in the southern Arizona bush, the coati is an uncommon animal, regarded as something of a curiosity. Prospectors and cowpunchers who see the animals most often, sometimes call them Mexican monkeys. Others believe the coati to be a peculiar kind of arboreal anteater. More generally in this region, coatis are called "chulo bears" or simply "chulos," and will be so referred to hereafter.

The coati *(Nasua narica)* is one of a family of four medium-sized carnivores found in the New World, the Procyonidae. The other members are the kinkajou, the ring-tailed cat, and the more familiar (to North Americans) raccoon. In South and Central America the coati is widely distributed, being relatively common from Argentina to northern Mexico. In the United States, the coati is rare, designated as a peripheral animal by the U.S. Bureau of Fish and Wildlife. It is occasionally reported along the Rio Grande Valley in Texas and New Mexico, but many of these sightings may be of escapees, since imported animals are often stocked in pet shops. The only place where the coati is found regularly and in any abundance in this country is southern Arizona.

ON THE FEBRUARY DAY I first visited Bear Canyon, the temperature was in the seventies, the air dry and clear, the cloudless sky so blue as to be almost black. A year later, we would have seen, lived in so many such winter days as to consider them ordinary, but the first time, fresh from Pennsylvania, the weather seemed remarkable, virtually perfect. I started walking from the gravel road, at 5,000 feet of elevation, at about the eastern limit of the San Rafael Valley, where the short-grass prairie, golden brown in the winter, began to thin out, give way to open thickets of oak and alligator juniper. Within less than a half-mile, I was well into another life zone, a mixed deciduous forest of oak, sycamore, walnut, madròna, mountain mahogany, manzanita, grape, a few maples and piñon and a great many plants, bushes, trees which I did not know. Bear Creek, a clear, musical little stream, spilled down the canyon in a series of gentle steps. Underneath the lip of the ledges there were deep pools fringed with aquatic plants in which there were chub minnows, leopard frogs, turtles. All of which delighted me for no better reason than that it was familiar. The ravine, the brook, the woodland, with a few additions and deletions, could have been Tom's Creek Valley, in which we live in south-central Pennsylvania.

When it comes to natural aesthetics, most of us are strongly conditioned in favor of scenery such as that inside Bear Canyon: a brook, soft grass, shady glades. A principal reason for this preference may be that it is similar to the scene which so appealed to English Romantic poets and landscape artists of the eighteenth century and their cultural descendants, the nineteenth-century New England essayists and naturalists. For better or worse, these critics have largely shaped the notions of many of us as to what is beautiful and what is ugly in nature.

All of which is not to argue that aesthetic standards and prejudices are silly, much less wicked, but only that the mythical boob who says he doesn't know much about art but knows what he likes may not be so silly as critics with a stake in some particular system of aesthetic values have led us to believe. I liked the Appalachian floor at Bear Canyon better than I did the desert country, not because it was formally superior but because of what I am and have been made.

At about 7,000 feet, I climbed out of Pennsylvania into Vermont, or maybe Colorado, a dark forest of tall evergreens: ponderosa, white,

PHOTO: BIL GILBERT

Apache pines; blue and Engelmann spruce; Douglas fir. There were snowbanks under overhanging cliffs, water trickling over moss, and the footing became sloppy, boggy. Stellar jays screamed in the pines and I came across mountain-lion tracks in the snow, scats—droppings—along the trail.

I camped that night at Bear Spring, a big, deep, all-weather outflow which rises in a grove of mature pine and fir. In the woods behind the water there is an old corral, built and used years ago by cowpunchers, prospectors, other trail riders. Beside the spring is a wide ledge, now a foot or so thick with accumulated pine straw. I spread out a poncho and sleeping bag on the needles, arranged in a circle around me everything I could possibly need during the night: two avocados, a piece of cheese, some hard rolls, a can of beer, a chocolate bar, tobacco, a jackknife, a flashlight, and my boots.

The sensual joys of bedding down outside—lungs full of fresh air, with starlight, moonbeams, owl music, wind tunes—have been persistently touted to the point that they have become cliches suitable for cigarette advertisements. These pleasures do exist, but the enjoyment of them rests upon another condition, one which is implied but rarely specified. If you lie down at dusk and plan to be there

**"... I decided that—
come heaven, hell,
or distemper epidemics—
I would return
to these mountains
by fall ..."**

until at least daybreak, you have time and are in a mood for something in addition to the little death of an eight-hour sleep. In such a twelve-hour period, you may wake up half a dozen times and stay awake for five minutes or an hour, not as an insomniac but because there are a lot of pleasant, entertaining things to do: eat an avocado, sip on a beer, chew a little tobacco, listen to a large unidentified animal walk on the mountainside above, look for constella-

tions, and above all let your mind run free. During the night at Bear Spring, in a leisurely way, I wrote a novel, a long essay on the play of dogs, made up spring workout schedules for the members of the girls' track team I coach, catalogued the equipment I would need for the coati project, and visited the Scented Grass Hills, an arctic peninsula in Great Bear Lake. There are always a lot of people around during these dreamy night watches. The people who stop by are the ones you have loved or admired or been interested in, never the fools, rascals, and monsters you have known. A park ranger who had told me about butterflies in the Huachucas, a twelve-year-old quarter miler, a Jamaican botanist, a college roommate, and a girl I had not seen in twenty years were among the group who stopped by Bear Spring.

In the middle of the night, I was awakened by a light snow squall. Directly overhead there were heavy clouds, but elsewhere the moon and stars were visible, reflecting brightly off the rocks below. It was a nice scene and a sort of funny one—traveling across the continent, out of a Pennsylvania winter, to lie on the ground and be snowed on in Arizona. It was the kind of thing that amused my father, who had a lot to do with developing my tastes, and who has been dead thirteen years. So I told him about it, and then we talked for quite a while about other matters of mutual interest.

During the night, it occurred to me that it would be a good thing, as soon as light came, to climb up from the spring to Bear Saddle, on the topmost ridge of the Huachucas, and wait there for the sun. When it got light enough to do this, I had to reconvince myself of the merits of the plan, arguing against the warmth of the sleeping bag. I finally did so by applying the logical crusher—how was I to know if I would ever again have a chance to sit in Bear Saddle at dawn?

The sunrise, from the vantage point of 8,200 feet was—as I had advertised it to myself—well worth seeing. The sun came up behind me, from the direction of Tombstone. The light spilled through the saddle, changing the blues and grays in the canyons below to reds and burnts, then progressed across the San Rafael Valley, up which Coronado, looking for the

golden cities of Kansas, had marched some 155,000 mornings previously. I waited until the sun lit the Canelo Hills, the Patagonia and the Santa Rita mountains, across the valley, to the north of Nogales and the Mexican border.

When I left Bear Canyon that day, I decided that—come heaven, hell, or distemper epidemics—I would return to these mountains by fall, that they were where I wanted to watch coatimundis.

THE HUACHUCAS FELT, looked, and were so different from anything we knew that at first we had the vague notion that there were things which might jump at us; that we were likely to blunder into situations which would require immediate, extemporaneous evasive action. Fear is too sharp, too specific a word to describe this situation. It is rather a kind of generalized wariness which promotes sensitivity, alertness.

We had to learn the properties of the new rocks and ledges on which we were climbing, about the effects of eight and nine thousand feet of altitude, the high ultraviolet content of the unshaded sun beating down through the thin air, the logic and dependability of javelina trails which were often the only paths through the thick scrub. Though we did not like admitting it even to ourselves, we worried at first about rattlesnakes. While we did not have a special interest in herpetology, none of us were phobic about snakes, having collected and carried even venomous species when there was some reason to do so. Nevertheless we could not completely rid ourselves of the notion that we were heading into the heart of poison country. Partly this was because of tall snake stories, which are numerous in southern Arizona, and also partly because it is a fact that the Huachucas are good snake country, as they are good country for so many wild things. (Twelve species of rattlers live in or near these mountains, including several small high-altitude snakes which are found only in the mountain islands. Several venomous oddities—the Arizona coral snake, two rare, mildly poisonous back-fanged creatures—live in the vicinity. For good measure there are a lot of scorpions, and the Gila monster is

255

occasionally found in the high desert at the eastern foot of the Huachucas.)

Once we got settled in the new country, we found that snakewise things were about the same in the Arizona mountains as elsewhere, i.e., we heard a great many more snake stories than we heard or saw snakes. According to our notes, we encountered thirty-two rattlesnakes during the year in which we were constantly poking about in the bush. This does not deny the fact that there are a large variety, perhaps a large number of snakes in the Huachucas; it only confirms the obvious fact that rattlers and men occupy very different niches, meet each other less often than men, at least, fear they will. In Arizona, at the elevations at which we were working, the temperatures began to dip into the forties in November, and at that time snakes of all sorts began to hibernate in dens. They did not emerge until February or later, and thus for a third of the year there were for practical purposes no rattlers abroad. Even during the warmer weather there are phenomena serving to separate our two species. Being cold-blooded, a rattler cannot, for example, survive a ground temperature of over 110 degrees, a mark often recorded on the unshaded slopes and ledges. Therefore we seldom saw these snakes during midday when we and the chulos were most active. The rattlers came out to hunt and travel in the cool of the evening when the chulos had gone to their caves, we to our camp—an arrangement agreeable to all parties.

In point of fact, the American wilderness has always been (what is left of it still is) a benign one, inhabited by remarkably few creatures who could, much less would, dispute the territory with man. Historically the bees and wasps have accounted for more human deaths than any other species, with rattlesnakes in second place and psychotic, tormented, terrified bears a distant third. It is doubtful that in the last seventy-five years all other species combined have done in as many citizens as are scragged on a Labor Day week-end on a moderately busy interstate highway. In fact, the boondocks are now so safe, their inhabitants so timid and docile, that the remaining patches of wilderness currently serve as a kind of sanctuary in which it is possible to temporarily escape the risks and violence of the civilized regions.

While things were still in the early planning stage, I told Ky and Terry that a time I had been anticipating for some years had arrived. In consideration of their age and mine, I was commencing my retirement as a camper. Henceforth they would rustle the wood, fetch the water, try to drive tent pegs into rocks, organize the gear and grub, cook, and clean up while I sat around drinking tea, napping, and bitching about the service. Generally this is how things worked during the year, though after we had settled into our routine I started cooking breakfast. (Being an earlier riser, I found it easier to get started in the morning than to get the boys started.) Otherwise the boys were the domestics. Having been around camps since they were very young, they did not regard their new role as being a promotion or much of an honor. They understood, as many more romantic and less experienced souls do not, that the act of camping is in itself no fun, is simply housework without a house or attendant conveniences. Accepting the fact that camp living always involves—by contemporary standards, at least—some discomfort and inconvenience, the best approach is to do as little camping as possible: eat plainly, wash sparingly, sleep hard, so as to conserve one's energy, enthusiasm, temper for whatever work or pleasure one came to the woods for in the first place. Knowing all this, the boys accepted being the campers stoically, recognized their plight for what it was, another manifestation of the ancient tradition that rank hath its privileges.

So far as practical arrangements were concerned, Terry and Ky decided between themselves that they would rotate the work on a weekly basis; that one would do all the buying, organizing, cooking, cleaning, maintenance for five days, then have the next week free while the other camped. (One reason they warmly welcomed John when he arrived in October was that they could then work a one-on, two-off shift.)

We would leave the campman to his chores and the other three of us would put some water, modeling powder, a snakebite kit, a notebook, a few tortillas, a piece of cheese, an apple, and a can of snuff into a small pack, pick up a pair of binoculars, sometimes also a camera, and after breakfast go off into the mountains and spend the day walking slowly, stopping often to sit, look, and listen. It would be impressive to report that we quickly began to apply logic and woodcraft, developed a high-probability plan for locating chulos, confidently closed in on the animals. However, this would be untrue. As in most natural-history searches, we used our backs more than our brains during the first stages. We continued to walk and look, gradually increased our knowledge of the area, kept hoping to come across some major clue bearing on the question of where chulos might be found, how we could observe them. During the first weeks, there was always a possibility that we might blunder on a chulo, but initially this was not our principal objective. Rather we hoped to find chulo signs, or signs that might have been

"When we approached, he woke up and without great enthusiasm accepted another biscuit from Will's hand."

made by chulos, which would give us better information as to the activities of the animals than would an accidental encounter with one of them.

All terrestrial mammals, except the bat, move across the ground and all of them defecate. Thus the most common mammalian signs are footprints and scats.

The border country is one of the worst possible places to look for tracks. It is rocky and, where not rocky, matted with tough, springy vegetation. It is dry and sun-baked. There are some dusty patches and places, but the steady wind erases marks from the dust almost as soon as they are made.

There were a few mud and sand bars beside certain ponds, streams, and seeps where the wettish earth would take and hold a footprint. We searched these carefully, reasoning that chulos would visit such places.

They did, as it later turned out, but so did everything else that lived in the vicinity, open water being a kind of ecological pivot in such generally dry country. Javelinas, deer, antelope, coyotes, lion, bobcats, bear, skunks, chulos, other small mammals, and particularly cattle regularly come to these water holes. In consequence, there is a rich but usually hopelessly smudged, indecipherable conglomeration of signs on the banks.

Working with guidebooks from isolated impressions over which more often than not cows and wild pigs had walked, we were doubtful for some weeks about being able to distinguish chulo from coon prints. We remained so until we had made dozens of plaster-of-Paris study castings, watched chulos walking about, examined the feet of trapped animals.

Scats are perhaps the best of all signs, since they not only conclusively prove an animal was in a given spot, but tell something about him, specifically what he has recently eaten.

Not until midwinter did we come to recognize the sign which most dependably indicated that an area was being used by a tribe of chulos. We missed it earlier because neither we nor anybody we had talked to knew that such a sign existed. A chulo tribe usually devotes an hour or two a day to resting and socializing (of which more later). Within the tribal territory there may be half a dozen spots favored for this purpose. They are usually located on a broad ledge, on the side of a cliff which is partly covered, protected by scrub. Invariably there is a dead or dying tree growing on or in front of the ledges used by resting chulos. The tribal youngsters swing on and chase each other about the branches of this tree, shred its bark, play tug of war with the shreds. The tree serves the youngsters as a piece of recreational equipment and is useful to the tribal elders in the same way that a swing set or slide is useful to a group of matrons who take their children to a playground. While the young chulos are helling around in the tree, the tribal matriarchs are free to gossip, groom each other, or nap without being mauled by their offspring.

After we had been in the mountains for two months, we found our first chulo tribe in the Cave-Oversight-Ida canyon complex. We found them there the hard way, by walking, watching, going over the ground again and again. Ten months later, when we were making some sentimental farewell walks through the Huachucas, Terry and I came down from the ridge one afternoon through Cave Canyon. There in reasonably plain sight we found, without really looking for them, two chulo resting ledges, the condition of which indicated they had been in use the previous fall. We had hiked this same trail half a dozen times in September and October without seeing these signs—or more accurately, we had probably seen them but did not know what we had seen.

In retrospect, the first chulo was like a drought-breaking rain, or a home run that snaps a slump, for after him we began seeing the animals regularly. Two days later, I drove alone across Montezuma Pass, half-way down the east side of the mountain, to talk to Will Sparks at the State of Texas Mine. Will had grown up around the mine, living with a maiden aunt who owned it. However, after a hitch in the Army he had drifted off to Phoenix, married his wife, Deane, moved to and worked as a mechanic in Los Angeles. Eventually souring on city life, Will and Deane decided to return to Arizona and, in partnership with Deane's sister Dot and her husband Bob, reopen the old mine.

Will and Bob had come to the mountains first, at about the same time we did, and had been working hard all fall to make the abandoned mine compound livable. On the morning I stopped by, they had been struggling since breakfast with an ancient and balky water pump, were glad to take a break, I asked Will about chulos, and he said, "I think they are great animals," insuring during the first five minutes of our acquaintance that we would be what we became, close friends. "In fact, I tell people they are the perfect animal. They take care of themselves, don't bother anybody, and aren't afraid of anything. They are smart and pretty and they are good to each other. Sometimes I think I wouldn't mind being a chulo. You want to see one?" asked Will, a large, handsome man who favors the *Cool Hand Luke* style.

"Sure I want to see one. We've been walking our asses off for six weeks looking for them. Whereabouts?"

"I think right now he is in the sycamore behind the tool shed. He comes down every morning to get Bob's biscuits, which is good, since nobody else can eat them."

"Any time you want, the stove's right in there," Bob offered.

"You better take a look at him now," Will went on, ignoring his brother-in-law. "There's no telling how long he'll last eating Bob's cooking."

As promised, the chulo was sitting on a limb, napping. When we approached, he woke up and without great enthusiasm accepted another biscuit from Will's hand. Though I did not know it at the time, I was meeting a prominent member of the Montezuma Canyon tribe, one with whom we would be much involved. In this case, there was no question later about the identity of the biscuit eater. He stayed around the State of Texas Mine, and Will and Bob kept an eye on him until we moved into the canyon permanently in December, marked and named the animal "the Supervisor," found out that he was the dominant tribal male.

During the next three weeks, we saw ten more chulos—a small band of four, and six singles—and had two good reports of other animals, one from a hiker who had encountered five animals on the top of the ridge, another from a rancher whose dogs had run and lost a solitary animal in Lyle Canyon. In the last week of October, we found our first tribe which in some ways was almost as satisfying as seeing our first chulo. We had to meet tribes if we were to learn anything about chulo society.

The lack of information presented obvious problems as to where and how to begin our study, but there were compensations, principally the rare and exhilarating sense of being explorers, of feeling that we were seeing or knowing things that others had not looked for, or had overlooked. During our eleven months, Terry, Ky, John (who joined us several weeks after we arrived and became the fourth permanent member of the chulo cadre), and I spent 290 days and nights in the Arizona bush, during the course of which we put in some 8,500 "man observation hours," as they are called in the field naturalists' jargon. During these hours, we recorded 5,000 observations of chulos, some being only brief sightings, others representing many consecutive hours, even days, spent with the same animals. Most of our observations were made of two chulo tribes, one in the Baboquivari Mountains, the second in the Huachucas, that we were fortunate to locate, in a sense privileged to associate with intimately. In some ways, we were comparable to students who take themselves off to strange places and become absorbed in the culture of Bushmen or Irishmen. But in a fundamental way ours was a more

foreign trip than any which an anthropologist or a sociologist can take. We and the chulos with whom we lived are, of course, of different bloods.

One evening toward the end of our year, an evening like so many summer ones in these Southwestern mountains, clear, cool, quiet, bugless, we were sitting on the stoop of the cabin which we used in the Huachucas, watching a gang of juvenile chulos, the young of 1970, tribal teen-agers, helling about the premises. Despite the splendor, the satisfactions of the moment, we were all suffering from twinges of depression, thinking that there would be so few

other such evenings, that our days as chulo watchers were very much numbered. In an effort to put a better face on the situation and on us, I said something to the effect that while it might not be much, like being the best snow-shoer in Saudi Arabia, we almost certainly knew more about chulos at that moment, were closer to being adoptive members of a chulo tribe than any other men in the world. I said that whatever else happened to us, I thought we should be able to remember that moment—the whole year—with true pride and satisfaction.

TRACKING THE LANGUR MONKEYS

Article by JOHN MELVILLE BISHOP
Photographs by John and Naomi Bishop

Langurs are found in arid places such as the Rajasthan desert, in congested temples and in cities, and in the tropical rain forests of the Indian Terai. No one had previously studied them in the high temperate forests of the Himalayas.

Studying the langurs required a scientist's patient observation. To determine behavioral patterns, Naomi Bishop spent hours in the field taking notes on the langurs' feeding and grooming habits, their vocalizations, and their sexual encounters. Her observations revealed several variations between the Himalayan langurs and those studied in other areas, the most significant of which was a lower incidence of aggression, a fact that the Bishops theorized was attributable to either the harsher environment or a low population density.

The night duty fell to John Bishop, who would sleep out beneath the towering hemlocks where the langurs took refuge from predatory leopards. The sleeping bag also served as protection from a nighttime peril: whenever one monkey made a nature call, the entire troop followed suit, ensemble.

W.K.

NEEDLES IN HAYSTACKS are not half as elusive as langur monkeys in the Himalayas, or so we felt when we reached Thangbujet after a fruitless week on the trail. It had rained all morning, dampening our spirits. We began preparing lunch in the shelter of a half-constructed house, and the burning wet wood soon filled the room with smoke. As usual when a trekking party stops in a village, a curious crowd gathered; in this instance, 20 people stood in the window frame and scrutinized us. Many were munching popcorn while they whispered comments among themselves; we were a movie and they were the audience. Existence is a tough act to follow, so we packed up all our belongings and moved on.

We were in a black mood: even if we found monkeys, we did not want to live in this village or in any of the others we had visited. What might appear exotic to the casual trekker is often dismaying to someone planning a year's stay, the minimum time we would have to spend with a troop of langurs to understand their adaptation to the temperate mountain environment.

An hour later on the trail, we rounded a bend and were startled by crashing branches and a flurry of activity. There were a dozen langurs in the trees ahead. The effect of seeing in the flesh what we had come halfway around the world to find was overwhelming. The monkeys had the grace and nobility of creatures secure in their forest habitat, and they

Unlike leaf-eating, tree-living langurs elsewhere, those in the Himalayas often came out into the open and ranged up the steep rock faces of the mountains, eating herbs and ground plants, occasionally climbing up to elevations as high as 14,000 feet.
PHOTO: JOHN AND NAOMI BISHOP

Author John Bishop.
PHOTO: NAOMI BISHOP

watched us as intently as we watched them. Langurs are large, and those in the Himalayas somewhat larger than the average langurs: females weigh 35 pounds and males 40 pounds. We watched, unable to take our eyes off them except to note their number, elevation and location. But soon we noticed that there were increasingly fewer animals. A moment later only one large male was visible, which we attempted to follow. Suddenly, in a few long leaps, he too was gone. We found no trace of him or the troop, and realized we had been fooled by the oldest trick in the primate repertoire. He had been a sentinel, and conspicuously maintained eye contact with us while the bulk of the troop melted away into the forest. When they were safe, he also left, and since it is much harder to follow a single animal than a group, we could not relocate them.

Langurs, like all primates, are basically omnivores—they eat a varied diet—but in addition, their stomachs are adapted to extract nutrients from nonnutritious foods such as mature leaves. This characteristic extends their geographic range considerably: they are found in arid places such as the Rajasthan desert, in congested temples and even cities, and, of course, in the tropical rain forests of the Indian Terai. No one had previously studied them in the high temperate forests of the Himalayas, where the combination of northern latitude and high elevation makes them one of the two species of cold-adapted monkeys. We were interested in the Himalayan habitat for what its extremes could tell us about the baseline behavior and ecological adaptations of *Presbytis entellus*; it would be dishonest, however, not to admit that the appeal of living in the Himalayas increased our interest.

It had been very hard to select a study site. Monkeys were essential, of course, but with a limited interface between monkeys and man. We did

not want a population that relied on crop raiding for a major part of its diet. We originally planned to live year-around in a tent, but after the rainy survey trek to Thangbujet, we compromised and decided to look for a house in a village with undisturbed habitat and monkeys nearby.

It took several treks to find a suitable site. Melemchigaon (8500 feet) in the Helambu valley of central Nepal filled the bill. It is surrounded by forests of oak, hemlock and rhododendron that are virtually untouched by man and shelter several troops of langurs. Moreover, the village is only a three- to five-day walk from Katmandu, the nearest source of supplies and medical help, yet is geographically isolated. Although Melemchi is situated between two well-traveled routes, a visit requires a half-day sidetrip and several-thousand-foot climb, so visitors are few.

Not all villages in the Himalayas can support an extra nonproducing household. The inhabitants often have barely enough for themselves and cannot sell food at any price. Melemchi, fortunately, had a surplus and could sell us such items as *tsampa* (toasted barley flour), rice, wheat flour, potatoes and dairy products. Everything else had to be brought from Katmandu. It is sobering how much food a person eats, a fact almost unnoticed when one buys a week in advance. For example, my wife, Naomi, who is an anthropologist, our assistant and I consumed 60 pounds of sugar every three months.

The extra food supplies and the equipment for the monkey project had to be carried up to the village by us and an army of porters because there are no roads in the mountains and pack animals are impractical in all but a few localities. We brought a typewriter, cameras and tape recorders, tents, film and stationery supplies, compasses, thermometers and an altimeter, as well as household supplies for a year's stay. Trekking with an entourage of 16 porters plus a Sherpa guide is somewhat confining, for the ultimate responsibility rests on the employer to keep the group in good spirits and progressing at a decent rate, and the loads undamaged. We three each carried an umbrella, a Himalayan tradition. At first we felt like zany Victorian ladies

carrying parasols through the Alps, but we soon learned there is no more useful hiking implement than the brolly. Not only does it provide protection from sun and rain, but it also allows some privacy for bathroom stops and baths, serves as a walking stick, repels Tibetan mastiff dogs and is excellent for poking off the leeches that crawl over one's boots. Naomi and I have continued the tradition on our backpacking trips in the Sierra, where on sunny days we are frequently met with bemused looks and the question "Is it raining ahead?"

We rented a house in Melemchi village and lived there with Mingma Tenzing, a Khumbu Sherpa born in Thami village a day-and-a-half walk from Everest Base Camp. He was our translator, cook, general assistant and companion. Two village men were hired as mail-runners to take letters to and from Katmandu every few weeks. We stayed in Melemchi for one full year except for three brief trips to Katmandu for supplies.

MELEMCHI SERVED AS base camp for our daily forays after the monkeys. It was ideally situated for this purpose, jutting out on a shelf off the mountain with the forest forming a bowl around it. The monkeys, with their prominent white heads, came to the treetops early each morning for sun, and from our house we could often locate them with binoculars before leaving home. Even with this head start, however, we spent as much time searching through the forest for the monkeys as we did in actual contact with them.

Behavioral observation is a lengthy process based on description. (The description is critical, since one can decide what behavior means only through the accumulation of descriptions of behavior in its surrounding social context. The more times you see something, the more certain you can be about its function.) Data built up slowly. The langurs were not about to go through their entire repertoire in a single day; we had to be there when something noteworthy happened in the normal course of their activity. Mostly, they just sat and ate. We knew this would be the case, but like all children who want animals to *do something,* facing this reality required a period of adjust-

ment. Since we were interested in how they lived naturally, we tried to avoid any interaction with them—we never fed them, caught them or tried to make them behave in any particular way. In addition to following and watching the monkeys, we made botanical collections to determine exactly what they ate and how the forest was made up, and we kept records on the climate, other animals and human activity on the mountain. Though it was slow going at first, our appreciation of the forest shifted from esthetic to knowledgeable, and the monkey troop became familiar as we learned to recognize animals as individuals by differences in their faces, voices or behavior.

After the troop became used to our presence, I began spending nights under their sleeping trees. "Our" troop always slept in hemlocks, the tallest trees in the forest—many well over a hundred feet. In my pack I carried a ground cover, sleeping bag, flashlight, binoculars and notebook. Usually I arrived at the current sleeping grove before the monkeys, which gave me the double advantage of being able to set up my bed without disturbing them and watching them enter the sleeping site.

Progress into the trees was always quick and orderly and took place just as it began to get dark. Some animals were still moving when it was too dark to see more than vague shadows, but by then most had found their spots. They sat singly or in huddles of several animals, on the highest branches. This made them extremely safe from predators because leopards could never climb that high. Mothers kept their infants pressed tightly to their bellies, but did not put their arms around them as langurs often do in other climates. The hands of all the animals were tucked inside their groins against the cold. In the gloaming, as colors faded to darkness, I saw giant flying squirrels swoop through the air and the frenetic fluttering of insectivorous bats, but the langurs took no notice.

During the night an animal might defecate or urinate, which would set off a round of defecating and urinating by the troop. After that quiet would reign for a few more hours. I never heard any vocalizations at night, nor was there moving around in the dark.

As it began to get light, the huddles broke up and some animals moved, but the real activity did not start until the sun shone on the sleeping trees. Then the whole troop moved to the tops of the branches to bask in the sun. (Down on the ground, where I had no respite from the cold, I was not so fortunate.) After as long as a few hours or as little as a few minutes in the sun, the troop moved out to feed.

MOST NIGHTS I SPENT with the monkeys in a grove directly over a trail. While this made access easy, it did cause some embarrassing moments when people came down the trail and found me watching monkeys from my sleeping bag. The villagers considered a penchant for going into the forest a symptom of craziness, so my nocturnal ventures caused some concern.

Sleeping out was regulated by the weather, the location of the monkeys and my disposition. My final night out was in June, shortly before the summer rainy season. Hearing a loud crashing nearby, I put my head in my sleeping bag and played dead. Then a large creature walked over me. I assumed it was a deer and went back to sleep. The next morning, when I had returned to the village, I learned that a leopard had killed a sheep in a pasture less than a quarter-mile from where I had been sleeping. I lost my taste for sleeping alone in the forest.

On days when we could not find the monkeys, there was no dearth of short trips we could make. Our excursions took us up the valley into the increasingly wild forest. Sometimes we would go to the top of a ridge to look at the snow mountains, at other times to high-altitude pastures to see wildflowers and birds. In the early summer Mingma and I went on an expedition to the sacred lakes of Gossainkund and saw the fire-tailed sunbirds courting at 13,500 feet. The females are olive drab, but in this season the males wear elegant nuptual plumage. They have a blue head, red shoulders, yellow breast, a bright red chest patch and, best of all, two long red tail feathers easily twice their body length, which they swish around while whistling at the females. There were dozens of pairs of birds, the males chasing the females and occasionally each other. The males were incredibly vain and always stopping to primp, sometimes stroking the tail feathers with their long curved beaks, stretching a wing or striking a pose before whistling and giving their tails a swish.

Although we followed the monkeys almost daily and knew the direction they took, we could not adequately visualize their range. It is difficult to get a sense of topography from a point halfway up a very steep, sloping mountain. Hiring a helicopter for an aerial survey was out of the question, so Mingma and I undertook a climb up Yangri Gang peak (12,372 feet), on the opposite side of the valley, to make oblique aerial photos.

This expedition involved descending to the Melemchi River at 6500 feet before starting the climb. We got lost almost immediately, still on our side of the river, and had to descend through scrub. We noticed another troop of langurs partway down and stopped to count them and make notes before re-shouldering our packs. At the bottom of the steep valley a herder pointed out the trail up the other side.

At 9700 feet the forest became very beautiful, with large stands of conifers, both fir and hemlock, and everywhere the saturated color of the blooming rhododendrons. The tree rhododendrons are spectacular in bloom, and we walked through groves of the deep-red *barbatum* and the pastel *arboreum*. It is not so much the individual flowers that are attractive, or even the trees. In the dark context of the forest, their bursts of saturated color impart an artificial quality. For sheer surprise, they are one of nature's great works.

TWO THOUSAND FEET BELOW the top of Yangri Gang, the small patches of snow we had seen from Melemchi proved much larger. By late afternoon it became very slow going because the snow was wet and slippery. At 4:30 we reached a saddle at 11,500 feet where there was a stone shelter. We were exhausted, and it seemed foolish to press on. The trail past the saddle was exposed on the north where it got little sun, so every inch of snow that had fallen in the winter lasted on that face when it had burned off everywhere else. As a result, the trail for the remainder of the climb was under five to 10 feet of snow. We decided to spend the night in the shelter.

I wanted to reach the summit and set up my cameras before the sun rose on Melemchi, which necessitated leaving our warm sleeping bags early. In the crisp pre-dawn morning we ate some tea and *tsampa,* and began the final thousand feet. The snow had refrozen during the night, and the first stretch was easy. But unless I was extremely careful, my weight broke through the crust and I sank in past my knees. Mingma was having better luck, partly because he weighed less and also because he had mastered the technique of slowly lowering his weight on the crust so as not to shock it into breaking. It is a Zen discipline, a definite yogic control of mind over matter. No special motor pattern is involved, only one's attitude when taking a step. Under Mingma's tutelage I did much better but still fell often. It seemed a lot longer than 1000 vertical feet.

The summit was a relatively flat area, with several Buddhist monuments made from the ruins of a monastery that had once stood there. I set up for the photographs, and Mingma lit a fire to make tea. The climb had taken two hours, and the sun was well up in Melemchi. The view was superb. The snow mountains to the north were spectacular, and the mountains to the south receded in gentle modulations. Most important, conditions were good for photographing the contours of the land and the langurs' home range.

SENSATIONS EXPERIENCED ON a mountaintop are second to none. There is a moment of communion

261

with the Earth, a sharing of its geological patterns and a glimpse of the forces that mold the planet and the shape that results. I recalled the theory of continental drift, which postulates that the Indian subcontinent broke off from Africa and floated toward Asia at a rate of ten centimeters a year. The impact supposedly caused the uplift of the great Himalayas, a magnificent acknowledgment of that renegade piece of Africa.

I thought of the langurs utilizing the same mountainside generation after generation and considered what we had learned in a year. Unlike many other langur troops, ours had several adult males who were able to coexist peaceably most of the time. Furthermore, there was a low incidence of aggression within the total of 32 animals, and rarely did they meet other troops of langurs. For all the climatic stresses of the temperate environment, they were under remarkably little social stress. Despite reports of early naturalists, we found our langurs used the same range all year round and did not migrate down the mountain to escape winter snows. They did use parts of the range to different degrees during the year, but they always remained within the 8000 to 10,000 foot band, and their movement revolved around food sources rather than weather. (Like langurs in other localities, they showed marked preference for seasonal foods like acorns, mushrooms and berries.) Most of our findings complemented what was known about other langur populations, with whom ours share the same basic behavioral patterns. There are some

variations, of course, because of local traditions, brief geographical isolation and environmental differences, but the adaptable langurs are remarkably similar from Sri Lanka to the top of the Himalayas.

As I stood atop Yangri Gang, my eye lingered on a particular yak pasture to the north. A few weeks before, Naomi, Mingma and I had gone to visit the pasture at a herder's invitation. He claimed there were langurs there, although the pasture, at 12,700 feet, was well above the scrub juniper and rhododendron, which grow only below 12,000 feet. He had reported that the monkey troop sleeps in a cave of overhanging rock, travels up gorges between steep rock faces on the mountain and eats herbs and ground plants—all unusual and unlikely characteristics for leaf-eating, tree-living monkeys.

We had ascended the ridge running along the top of the mountain spur and planned to watch the troop come up the gorge from the sleeping cave. When we reached the top (14,000 feet), the herder had signaled from below that the langurs were indeed climbing up. The fog that had been forming in the valley below started rising, and we knew our visibility would soon be gone. We still could not see the monkeys.

At HIGH ALTITUDES one experiences the unnerving tendency to fall asleep in the most uncomfortable circumstances. As the fog came over us and it began to drizzle, we three sat down to take stock of the situation, and on the wet rocks fell asleep for an hour. The least sound woke us, but these sounds were never monkeys,

and we went back to sleep. As the cloud wisped back and forth there was brief visibility, but still no trace of monkeys. We suspected that the herder was playing a joke on us that would amuse the local people in the coming months. Very disappointed, we finally gave up waiting and started down one of the gorges to the trail 2000 feet below, rather than take the longer, easier ridge route back to camp.

The gorge was very steep, and the going was dangerous over slippery moss-covered rocks and thick wet weeds that provided treacherous footing. For the most part we crawled down on all fours, relying on Mingma's knowledge of the mountains and his yak-herding experience to keep the three of us going in the right direction.

We had descended about 500 feet, which took almost an hour, when Mingma noticed something on the other side of the gorge. Like ships passing in the night, the langurs were moving uphill 30 yards away. The clouds thinned enough to reveal at least 30 animals. They were nervous and barked at us, then continued up the gorge, going quickly over the ridge where we had been napping. Within five minutes they were gone. It had required a three-day backpacking trip and a five-hour morning climb for that brief observation.

The ridge the monkeys had crossed was in excess of 14,000 feet, the highest elevation where any primate has ever been observed. We realized that we must return another year to learn more about these langurs in the clouds. ▰

SNAKES OF THE SOUTHERN APPALACHIANS

by JOHN MACGREGOR

Probably the things most feared by people who go hiking are snakes. Hence, it's difficult for most of us to imagine anyone going backpacking actually looking for them. Yet here is a fellow, John MacGregor, who makes a point of trying to find snakes and their snake pits whenever he goes hiking. Naturally, he finds many of them.

I've been hiking and camping for more than 40 years and I've rarely seen any snakes, never mind poisonous varieties. I've even gone hiking several times in desert country in early spring when rattlers are presumably mating and abundant. But the only rattler I've ever seen is a tiny thing about the length of an earthworm. Like most of us who'd rather not encounter snakes on the trail, I consider myself lucky. To some—especially if you're like John MacGregor and you're looking for them—I may not be considered so lucky. It's all in one's point of view.

In addition to the piece on snakebites in Chapter Five, the article that follows will tell you a lot about how to recognize and avoid poisonous snakes in all parts of the country. Take along a lightweight field guide on snakes if you are heading off the trail. Indentifying a poisonous snake in the eventuality of a snakebite is crucial.

W.K.

You are walking among hemlocks along the Appalachian Trail in North Carolina. A few rays of sunlight filter through the branches and fall upon pink lady's slipper growing beside a hollow log. Stopping to examine the flowers more closely, you hear a sudden rustling. At your feet is the biggest snake you have ever seen, hissing and furiously vibrating its tail. Then it darts toward the log and vanishes.

Were you startled? Or were you pleased at having seen a beautiful snake? Perhaps you were frozen with fear. Or perhaps you knew that it was a pine snake and that it is perfectly harmless to man.

More than 20 types of snakes live in the southern Appalachian Mountains. Only two species are venomous; all of the others are quite harmless.

Despite their abundance in most lowland and certain upland habitats, snakes are seldom seen by even the most observant hikers. They are quick to flee from larger animals, including man. In fact, to find snakes you must know how and where to look. The best places are those that have been unaltered by human beings. Many snakes crawl into the burrows of mice, shrews, or moles. Others tunnel into leaf mold or rotting stumps. Needless to say, these snakes are rarely uncovered except by accident.

Nearly half of the species are small and retiring and don't often venture out of their hiding places beneath stones, logs, or stumps. Most of the large snakes do their hunting and prowling at night and seek shelter during daylight hours. Although it is difficult to see them at night in grass or brush, driving slowly down little-traveled dirt roads on warm summer nights can give you a chance to see one crossing the road.

Additionally, snakes can sometimes be found in places once frequented by man—the ruins of houses, old sawmills and dumps, fallen-down barns, and overgrown fields. These places provide plenty of food and shelter for rodents and are thus good hunting grounds for snakes.

Another reason snakes are so difficult to see is that they have protective coloration. Some snakes are dull and dusty looking; others have color patterns that blend in with their natural surroundings. Anyone who has recognized a copperhead coiled among fallen leaves, a green snake in a honeysuckle vine, or the markings of a large timber rattlesnake can readily understand the life-saving value of protective coloring.

Surprised in the open by a larger animal, a snake will either lie perfectly still and try to remain unnoticed or attempt to escape. Occasionally, when it feels that its escape route is cut off, it chooses to stand its ground. A hiker who comes between a snake and its favorite retreat may be startled as the animal continues to crawl toward him. But by remaining motionless or stepping to one side he can usually avoid further trouble.

The sight of a snake in its native haunts is always a thrilling experience. Some people feel they must have some memento of such an encounter. A snake must usually be captured before it can be photographed. But to attempt to capture or photograph a venomous snake is a foolish undertaking for anyone except an expert.

Hikers who wish to avoid venomous snakes altogether should stay on trails as much as possible, be extremely careful when picking up large branches or logs, watch where they put their feet while walking through brushy places or thickets, and not reach onto ledges or into bushes when they can't see what's there. If, despite these precautions, they come upon a poisonous snake, they should not kill it but leave it alone. Snakes are protected in all our national parks, for they occupy an important position in the food chain of their environment. In addition, many states have passed laws to protect some of their rare or beneficial snakes.

There are actually few snakes to fear in the southern Appalachians. Coral snakes do not inhabit the area. There are, however, some harmless snakes such as scarlet kingsnakes and scarlet snakes that resemble coral snakes and are often mistaken for them. But the red and black bands border one another on these two harmless varieties, while on coral snakes the red bands border the yellow bands. And you aren't likely to see them anyway because they're quite rare.

Northern water snakes, fairly common in the southern Appalachians, are similar in appearance to venomous water moccasins (cottonmouths) and are

Copperhead (Agkistrodon contortrix mokasen). *The chances of a hiker stumbling upon a copperhead during the summer season are practically nil. Both the timber rattlesnake and the copperhead usually migrate to the forests and become completely nocturnal in the summer. The copperhead, known to live nearly as long as the timber rattler, bears its young alive in the early fall.*
PHOTO: JOHN MACGREGOR

Timber rattlesnake (Crotalus horridus). *The timber rattlesnake is one of the only two venomous snakes common to the Southern Appalachian Mountains. It is not uncommon for a timber rattlesnake, which has been known to live as long as 30 years in captivity, to travel several miles during a single season. It is rare to find a rattlesnake near the hiking trails.*
PHOTO: JOHN MACGREGOR

thus frequently slaughtered, although there are no water moccasins in the southern Appalachians.

Young water snakes are slim and brightly colored. Adults of the species develop heavy bodies and take on a dull gray or brown hue. They flatten their bodies and heads when aroused and can sometimes manage to look more menacing than water moccasins. They are found along banks and shorelines of all major streams and lakes throughout the southern Appalachians, where they feed primarily upon fish. Water snakes lack the prominent facial pits and elliptical pupils characteristic of most poisonous snakes native to the United States.

The only two venomous snakes in the southern Appalachians are the timber rattlesnake and the copperhead. During winter they both live on rocky, wooded hillsides where they hibernate in talus slopes and mountain ledges. On warm days in late autumn and early spring they can sometimes be found sunning themselves in such places. During early summer they usually migrate to forests and become almost completely nocturnal. Thus the chances of a summer hiker seeing a venomous snake are practically nil. In mid- to late summer, rattlers and copperheads move down to the grainfields in the valleys in search of rodents. They remain there until the first cool autumn nights send them back toward their winter quarters.

Timber rattlesnakes are wanderers; individual snakes may travel several miles during a single season. Copperheads generally do not wander such distances, although they may do so in search of food.

Both rattlesnakes and copperheads bear their young alive in early fall. A pregnant female usually chooses a large rock or log beneath which to give birth. As soon as the young are born, they are on their own. They remain in the same area for several days before leaving in search of food. Yearling snakes hibernate in small crevices or rodent burrows, and many fail to survive their first winter. At about the age of three they reach adulthood and begin wintering in large dens. They generally trail one another to denning sites. A single den may shelter hundreds of snakes, including copperheads, rattlesnakes, and other species. Not all snakes use dens, though. Many hibernate singly every winter during their entire lifetimes.

Timber rattlesnakes have been known to live as long as 30 years in captivity; wild ones may live even longer. Copperheads probably live nearly as long as this. But the average life-span of either species is generally not more than four to seven years because predators and disease take heavy tolls.

The common notion that you can tell the age of a rattlesnake by the number of rattles on its tail is pure myth. A healthy snake can grow several new rattles in a single year. Additionally, rattles are easily broken off. It is rare to find an adult rattlesnake with a complete set of rattles.

Rattlesnakes as well as nearly all other large snakes—pine snakes, kingsnakes, rat snakes, racers, and copperheads—usually vibrate their tails when angry. Yet rattlesnakes are deaf and cannot even hear the sound of their own rattles.

Snakes exhibit other kinds of behavior when alarmed. Most discharge a foul-smelling musk from their cloacal glands. This accounts for the distinctive "cucumber" scent associated with copperheads, kingsnakes, water snakes, and rat snakes. Tiny red-bellied snakes, which seldom grow longer than 15 inches, flare out their lips, exposing rows of tiny teeth. Some ring-necked snakes curl their tails upward and display bright ventral colors. This behavior serves as a warning to predators, for their flesh is toxic to some animals. Even the innocuous green snakes, which rarely bite under any circumstance, may open their mouths and display the red interior to frighten away enemies.

When molested, the hognose snake, another widely feared creature of the southern mountains, has the most curious behavior of all. It first flattens its head and neck, hissing savagely, and usually strikes in the direction of the intruder. If those tactics do not frighten him away, the snake goes into convulsions—writhing and rolling over onto its back—and "dies." Sometimes it bleeds from the mouth, vomits, and everts its cloaca to add to the realism of the act. The snake is so convincing that it will not react when prodded with a stick or picked up by hand. If it is turned onto its belly, it will quickly flop onto its back again. But once the molester is gone, it speedily comes back to life and crawls away unharmed.

Snakes are essential links in the natural chain of life in wild areas. The small species prey upon slugs, insect larvae, earthworms, salamanders, and lizards. Large species eat mice, rats, frogs, and various other small vertebrates, including smaller snakes. Numerous animals—hawks, owls, shrews, and skunks in particular—eat snakes. Skunks use their keen noses to find clutches of eggs buried in rotting logs or loose soil.

In the southern Appalachians, snakes form a varied and fascinating portion of the local fauna. They have habits that seem unusual to us, but each species has become adapted to a particular mode of living over a long period of time. There are many facets of the natural history of snakes about which man knows remarkably little. No one yet knows, for instance, the origin or the survival value of the death-feigning act of the hognose snake. Likewise, no one is sure how kingsnakes have become immune to the venom of copperheads and rattlesnakes.

Snakes are vital and beautiful creatures. We ought to learn to appreciate them in the same way we do birds, wild flowers, and all other forms of life that share the world with us.

THE HIGHEST CHRISTMAS BIRD COUNT

by KENT DANNEN

For most of us, nature study is an avocation, albeit an intensive one for some. It can be a fine excuse for getting into the outdoors even in the most inclement weather as Kent Dannen relates in the article that follows, on Christmastime bird-watching at 12,000 feet in the Rocky Mountains. Did they see any? Well, he says they did.

W.K.

IN A BLINDING SNOWSTORM driven by 100-mile-per-hour winds, we were climbing a 12,000-foot mountain in search of a white chickenlike bird with feathers on its feet. It was undoubtedly an odd way to celebrate Christmas, but the practice was 76 years old.

During the nineteenth century, so-called sportsmen organized into teams to celebrate Christmas by going into fields and forests to shoot anything that moved (humans excepted, in theory). The winning side had the largest pile of dead wildlife by the end of the day.

Fortunately, in 1900, the concerned editor of *Bird Lore* magazine, Frank Chapman, replaced this gory "side hunt" with a less brutal competition, the Christmas bird count. The new teams competed instead for the number of bird species they could sight within a 15-mile radius during a period of 24 hours. Nowadays, more than 28,000 observers on 1,141 teams trek into the American outdoors at Christmastime to count birds.

Although we admit to watching birds, my wife, Donna, and I used to take small part in the Christmas counts. The harsh climate around our Estes Park, Colorado, home severely limits the number of bird species. Last Christmas, however, we resolved that if we could not be on the highest count in numbers we would be on the highest altitude.

But merely climbing a mountain at Yuletide was not enough. There would have to be at least an outside chance of seeing birds on the heights. For our count we hiked into nearby Rocky Mountain National Park, where a tough grouse species called white-tailed ptarmigan (Tar-muh-gun) lives above treeline all year.

PTARMIGAN TURN white in winter and roost under the snow. They are hard to see during blizzards, when wind-driven snow cuts visibility to a few yards; but on December 27 Donna and I were determined to find them, despite stormy weather.

Starting out with us before dawn were friends Jim and Trish Medlock. They had climbed these mountains often in summer to observe ptarmigan in their mottled-brown breeding plumage, which camouflages them among lichen-covered rocks. The Medlocks, however, wanted to see the grouse in their winter feathers.

Another friend, Becky Lewis, had flown in from San Francisco to join us the day before. Five feet tall and weighing scarcely 100 pounds in her winter clothing, Becky was not about to let a rise of two miles in altitude with no time for acclimatization prevent her from participating in our Christmas bird count.

Leading the group was Dr. Clait Braun, a researcher for the Colorado Division of Wildlife and an expert on white-tailed ptarmigan.

I was confident Clait could show us ptarmigan—until he mentioned the weather was the worst in which he had attempted a Christmas count. During the previous fall, however, he had staked down a small research trailer by Trail Ridge Road, which crosses the ptarmigan habitat. Winter snows blocked the road, yet the trailer would shelter us if we could reach it on foot.

Clait and Becky started the climb on snowshoes; the rest of us opted for cross-country skis. We soon abandoned both, for fierce winds had scoured all snow, except for a few drifts, from the upper part of the road. We walked the remaining six miles to treeline, pushing against gales all the way.

As part of his ptarmigan research Clait often had measured wind velocity with stationary anemometers. At treeline on Tombstone Ridge he estimated we would face 80- to 100-mph gusts. We would have to cross wind gaps, narrow spaces between granite buttresses (the tombstones) on the ridgeline. Into the gaps are funneled volumes of air that rage unhindered across the open tundra. When a volume of air has to pass in the same length of time through a constricted space, the air must move much faster. Other researchers had estimated speeds in excess of 200 mph when their anemometers broke after reaching their 180-mph limit on Tombstone Ridge.

WHEN WE REACHED the ridge, the winds were difficult to fight, and not only snow but pieces of plants and granite pummeled us. Jim pushed stubbornly on into the storm. Clait followed, grabbing Becky before she blew away. I hung back to take pictures and saw that Donna and Trish were having trouble making it across the gaps. They were neither heavy enough nor strong enough and were being forced toward the edge of the ridge.

A particularly strong gust nearly knocked them over and thrust them against a granite buttress. Pinned there by the wind, they were unable to move. I leaned hard into the wind and headed for their rock, making sure one foot was well planted before lifting the other. When we finally linked arms, our combined weights made it easier to fight the gale.

The limber pine around us showed clearly the scars of a centuries-long war with the wind. All were bent and sculpted into forms of weird beauty. On the windward sides, bits of flying granite had sanded off the bark and burnished the surface beneath. Forest fire had added to the trees' distress, killing many and preserving their skeletons in grotesque postures.

Beyond the fire area, the pine gave way, and subalpine fir formed the battleline. These trees, too, were stunted by the wind. Many grew as dense Krummholz behind the shelter of a boulder. Any new growth that dared to venture above the level of the rock soon was killed by the wind.

In other places the trunks of the taller firs (eight feet high at the most) had their own protection for new growth. On the lee of the trunks, green branches streamed out like banners. The windward side, however, was so sandblasted and devoid of branches that new twigs never had a chance.

When Donna, Trish and I finally unlinked arms at the research trailer, Jim and Becky were drying out inside.

Clait had water boiling for hot chocolate and was telling jokes to lift everyone's spirits. Ice formed on my beard by heavy breathing began to melt down my neck.

DURING LUNCH, gales rocked the trailer—a convincing argument against ptarmigan-seeking. Becky was feeling the effects of her sudden rise from sea level and from the high-altitude exertion. Trish was not enthusiastic about being pinned against another rock by the wind, but Jim still wanted to see a white ptarmigan, and Donna and I were eager to begin the Estes Park count. Clait seemed concerned only about the group's safety and comfort.

Becky and Trish decided to keep water boiling on the stove to welcome the rest of us back after we had found our quarry.

Even though Clait knew every bush and rock where the birds might seek shelter, the number of shelters far exceeded the number of grouse. We crisscrossed tundra for more than half an hour before we saw our first white ptarmigan.

It looked like a small chicken. Two small black dots on either side of a larger black triangle marked its eyes and beak. "Isn't it beautiful!" Donna shouted above the wind. It *was* beautiful, both as an unusual bird in rarely seen plumage and as a new mountaineering experience.

Ptarmigan often seem semi-tame because their camouflage hides them even from the eyes of prairie falcons, their chief predators. Their safety usually lies in staying still. But as we tried to move closer, this ptarmigan retreated over deep drifts with its feather-sheathed toes widespread like snowshoes. Clait yelled over the gale that the birds are nervous in roaring wind and become hard to approach.

Having seen one ptarmigan, Donna and I were eager to see more. Clait suggested we try to increase our tally by climbing Sundance Mountain, which rises to 12,466 feet and dominates Trail Ridge. Jim, however, decided he had seen his bird. Drawing the line between stubbornness and fanaticism, he headed back down the road for the trailer's shelter.

Donna, Clait and I spread out in

A white-trailed ptarmigan in winter plumage blends into the snow-covered landscape of Colorado's Rocky Mountain National Park. Beaks and eyes show just a touch of pigmentation in this bird, the only ptarmigan found in the western United States, excluding Alaska.

Participants in annual Christmas Bird Count brace themselves against wind-driven snow while climbing to find white-tailed ptarmigan above tree line on Trail Ridge.
PHOTO: KENT DANNEN

a line to cover as wide an area as possible and trudged up the side of Sundance. Following Clait's instructions, we looked for ptarmigan on the leeward side of rocks and in stunted stands of willow and subalpine fir.

Donna and Clait occasionally faded from my vision in gusts of snow, then rematerialized like characters in an episode from *Lost Horizon*. But still no ptarmigan appeared out of the howling storm.

Then Donna, who was farthest downslope, waved for me to come. I ran toward her after passing the signal on to Clait. When we reached her, two grouse already had flown out on the wind and disappeared with a faint cackling wail into the white void. Nevertheless, our ptarmigan total had jumped to three.

The search continued until we came together again above 12,000 feet. Clait announced that we had passed the limit of ptarmigan country; we now were above winter "birdline," and it was pointless to ascend farther.

AS WE BEGAN TO DESCEND, Clait looked at me sharply, then stepped closer for a better look. "Your cheek is frostbitten," he yelled. He had noticed a dead white spot as big as a quarter where my goggles had slipped away from my tightly drawn down hood.

Donna's only experience with frostbite had been seeing a post-Annapurna photo of Maurice Herzog in BACKPACKER-4. She feared my face was about to fall off, but I only had to turn the injury away from the wind, take off a down glove and press my warm hand against my cheek. The still-gloved hand I placed over the bare one. Soon the frostbitten area warmed back to life.

"In the alpine zone in winter," Clait warned, "we've got to keep an eye on each other to make sure frostbite or exhaustion doesn't catch someone off-guard." Thereafter, we stuck close together and gave up finding ptarmigan. Then, of course, more birds appeared. Donna spotted them near the trailer—four white ptarmigan, easy to approach as the wind stilled momentarily.

I snapped a telephoto lens on my camera. Through the viewfinder I watched one bird grab a willow twig in its beak, shake it until it came loose from the bush and then eat it.

Clait and Donna fell back to avoid disturbing the birds any more than necessary. I shot 10 photos. When the wind rose again, the birds walked nervously away. Then I realized I had left the wind-scoured turf and was up to my waist in snow, crouched behind a half-buried fir.

Inside the trailer, congratulations were brief, for the short day was moving toward darkness, and we had the wind gaps to cross on our descent. On Tombstone Ridge I nearly was blown down. I was tired, and all my muscles ached. Bits of flying granite stung my flesh. But a surge of excitement welled up inside me, and I grinned, for I realized I was having a great time.

Resting in the lee of a boulder below the wind gaps, I asked Donna, "Don't they say that in this kind of weather your mind is the first thing to fail? How could I be having so much fun while we're being battered like this?"

She grinned, too, and looked closely at my face. I could not tell whether she felt the same way or was merely checking for frostbite. ❦

HOW TO TRACK WILDLIFE ON SKIS

by SAM CURTIS

Some of the most productive wildlife sightings come on overnight trips.

Wildlife is different in winter. Tracking and studying it is easier because of the snow. One of the best places to see wildlife in winter is in Yellowstone National Park. Sam Curtis gives a glimpse of what Yellowstone wildlife is like in winter.

W.K.

As we started up the foothills toward Specimen Ridge in Yellowstone National Park, the signs we were looking for became increasingly evident. Elk pits were everywhere. The irregular hollows in the snow, caused by elks' attempts to get at underlying grasses, made progress on touring skis like crossing a frozen sea of three-foot waves.

John muttered, "This kind of skiing is ridiculous," but we kept pushing up through the sparse timber.

After an hour of skiing we approached the first ridge, which promised a good vantage point for surveying the surrounding foothills. I stopped to look back into the valley and to catch my breath while the others continued on. Two owls coasted down through the pines. I checked my watch: only two hours until dusk.

I started to climb the last hundred yards when Chico motioned me to hurry. They'd found elk!

Huffing to a stop beside the others, I could see a herd of 70 animals across the valley. They stood out clearly against the snow. I broke out my camera gear.

Cross-country skiing is a logical extension of hiking. With cross-country skis, the backpacker's realm is expanded to include a world of wildlife seldom seen in milder weather. Wildlife is most visible during the harsh winter months because heavy snow in the high country drives the animals to lower elevations where they can find food. But snow, even at low elevations, hinders their movement and their possibility for escape.

There is a knack to locating and approaching wildlife without frightening them. Most animals rely on a highly developed sense of hearing to warn them of danger. Some species, such as moose, have very poor eyesight, which further increases their dependence on hearing. Skiing is inherently quiet; fallen leaves and branches are blanketed, and skis glide over snow with only the quietest whispers.

These ski whispers should be the only sounds made when approaching animals—no talking, no clacking of ski against ski. To communicate something such as a change in approach route, subtle sign language will suffice. Silence is not only necessary for getting within viewing range of animals but also, and more important, it is consistent with our responsibility not to surprise snow-hampered animals which might be weakened or injured in their attempts to retreat from us.

I will never understand why snowmobilers think they can approach wildlife on their snow machines. The whine is audible for miles; animals can become frightened even though the vehicle is not in sight. Last February, while I was photographing eight mule deer in Bridger Canyon north of Bozeman, Montana, two snow machines screeched along a logging road to within 200 yards of the small herd. As the machines approached, the deer became frightened and retreated through the belly-deep snow. Five minutes later I spotted them straggling up a nearby ridge, the weaker animals struggling to follow the trails broken by the stronger ones. The snowmobilers missed seeing the deer, and I missed getting photos. But the deer suffered most in their winter-weakened condition.

Even the sight and smell of a human can alarm animals. In addition to moving quietly, stay downwind and out of sight. If you suspect that you have been seen, stand perfectly still and watch for

Moose feed on willows along open streams.
PHOTO: SAM CURTIS

the animal's reactions. Often it will turn away, at which point you can quietly move closer. On the other hand, some animals, such as the pronghorn, are very curious creatures and may approach a motionless person. In this case, remain still until the animal has satisfied its curiosity and moved away.

When several people are attempting a quiet approach more precaution is needed. Move very slowly, one at a time, to reach a place of concealment from which the animals can be observed. Don't split up and approach from several directions because you may block their natural avenue of escape. Box canyons and fence corners are no places to push animals since they may be injured or killed in their panic.

The animals themselves will often indicate when they are alarmed. Elk give a little whistle; pronghorn flare their rump hairs; whitetail deer raise their tails. These cues let us know that we shouldn't attempt further approach and should remain silent and motionless until we can depart without causing more alarm.

When to be on the lookout and when to go out looking for animals require an understanding of their behavior. Dawn and dusk are optimum times for wildlife sightings because they usually bed down or take cover during daylight hours.

On clear, calm winter days, animals—particularly deer and elk—often spend a good part of the day in open areas far from roads, pawing through snow cover for grass. Conse-

quently, day trips away from the beaten path can be fruitful.

Chances of sighting wildlife are poor during windy or snowy weather because animals tend to stay in the cover of dense timber or sheltered ravines. After a big storm, however, get out there; they'll be hungry and looking for food.

Optimum sighting locations vary with the species. Deer and elk like the valleys, foothills and open meadows with escape timber nearby. Moose tend to feed along open stream beds where willow browse is available, although I have occasionally seen them on snowy mountain ridges as high as 9,000 feet. Bighorn sheep can often be seen on rock outcroppings in mountain valleys. These beautiful animals are difficult to spot against snow, but they are often visible as they walk in front of exposed rock too steep to hold snow.

A basic awareness of wildlife behavior is certainly helpful in locating certain species. Nevertheless, there are notable exceptions to the rule:

While skiing in the Gallatin Canyon south of Bozeman, I watched four bighorn sheep grazing on exposed grass. This in itself wasn't unusual, but it was high noon, the day was extremely windy and cars could be heard on a nearby road. The sheep ignored all of this and me. They worked their way down the rocks and entered a small grove of pines directly across the river from where I watched.

Later that winter, I saw one bison in the same spot so many times that I nicknamed him Stokely for his Afro hair-do. Stokely evidently lived near

Soda Butte in Montana's Lamar Valley, forsaking the wandering herd. He could always be found within a few hundred yards of a small thermal butte.

Overnight trips afford the opportunity of being where the action is at the time it is most likely to occur. Several friends of mine recently camped on the edge of a large clearing with a view of a herd of 200 elk. They watched them until darkness settled in. The next morning when they poked their heads out of their mountain tent they were amazed to see two huge bulls standing within 25 yards of camp. The rest of the herd pawed at the snow not much farther away. A lot of good photographs came out of that trip.

You shouldn't leave your camera behind for the sake of traveling light, although photographic equipment can get pretty weighty when you take along a high-powered telephoto lens with a tripod. A good telephoto lens—200mm, or better yet, 400mm—allows you to photograph animals from a distance and stand less chance of being detected. I never photograph wildlife with a standard 50mm lens because it necessitates getting too close.

Cold-weather photography requires certain precautions. In subzero temperatures, moving camera parts become sluggish and even freeze. Camera manufacturers can prevent this by cleaning the parts and applying special oil.

Sudden temperature changes can cause your lens to fog. When you travel in the field, don't keep your camera bundled up under your parka because fogging will occur when you bring it out. Keep it out all the time to maintain the same temperature as the surrounding air.

A final must is to keep snow out of your camera. Fine snow is like fine sand: it seems to get into everything. Change film or lenses in a dry place out of the wind.

Don't let these problems influence you to leave your camera at home. With proper preparation and care, the problems are all easily solved. Winter really is the best time to see wildlife, and as long as you take care not to frighten the animals, it offers unexcelled opportunities for photographing and observing them in their natural habitats. ▲

FILMING ENDANGERED SPECIES

by JUDY WARE

Marty and Mark Stouffer consider them
the delicate balance of nature.

There are some who study nature in an advocate's role. Marty and Mark Stouffer play this role. They devote their time lugging heavy movie equipment into the wilderness to make films of endangered species. Their objective is clear: to help save them.

Judith Ware interviewed the Stouffer brothers for BACKPACKER. Her article relates the intensity of the Stouffers' commitment to their cause.

W.K.

The young man stood up and carefully stepped over the empty film spools and piles of paper on the floor to offer me a seat in the crowded office. It was spring in Aspen, Colorado, and I had just walked into the inner sanctum of Stouffer Productions to talk to wildlife photographer Marty Stouffer and his brother, Mark.

The whole office was about the size of a horse's stall. The space along one wall was occupied solely by a huge editing table, thrice-threaded with film, animal background and film narration. All three were synchronized to show what the film would look and sound like in its final form. Against the opposite wall stood another less sophisticated table with the additional asset of a slide-viewing glass. Overhead, neatly lined up on a rack, were large and small tins of film. Large boxes labeled "Surplus Slides" occupied the room's corners. The bulletin board was cluttered with notes, signs, mottos, quotations from Ernest Hemingway and a check list of endangered species. Bob Dylan sang to himself from some inaccessible spot. We seemed a great distance from the subjects of Stouffer Productions.

"You know what just struck me today? The fact that less than one hundred years ago this town did not exist and that only wildlife lived here. Now consider what we have done to this area in that brief time."

Marty is not usually outspoken; he generally allows his work to express his thoughts. He has spent the last six years gathering information and backpacking into remote areas to film endangered or threatened species. The latter animals are threatened with extinction, usually because of low numbers; the former have reached the point where each living creature is critical to the preservation of its species. "Severely endangered" animals are almost extinct.

When asked how he became involved in his exotic life, Marty replied, "It's hard for me to verbalize. It's just that I have always done whatever it was I wanted to do—which seems to be roaming around in the woods and taking pictures."

Having been raised on Walt Disney, National Geographic, and Wild Kingdom films, I was anxious to hear how Marty and Mark make their movies. Marty exploded many myths about the animals in popular commercial programs. For instance, very few scenes are shot in truly natural surroundings. Many of the animals are raised from birth and trained or "socialized" for years before actual film production begins. The "wild" animals seen on screen were probably filmed in a pen from a scaffold. Additionally, some of the cute scenes for which Disney and others are so well known may have cost many animals' lives. In a movie the small animals may escape, but during shooting 2,000 others may have been sacrificed to obtain the proper effect.

Marty and Mark, however, prefer to "capture" their subjects in the real world. They represent a new breed of wildlife photographer, one that reflects a new mentality about our wilderness and its people and animals. With his vast knowledge of wildlife, Marty was quick to point out that a wild animal is different from a socialized one. Any creature is an integral part of its environment; enclosing it with an unnatural wall makes it become unnatural.

The wolf, although characterized in mythology as vicious, appears in Marty's films as an independent animal, a family member, and most important, a shy creature around men. At the same time, the elusive bighorn sheep, usually seen only from a dis-

Peregrine falcon with mourning dove it has just taken in flight. This species is the fastest bird alive, able to reach speeds up to 180 mph in a dive. It is endangered because of poisoning and thinning of eggshells from DDT and other pesticides.
PHOTO: MARK AND MARTY STOUFFER

tance, becomes curiously bold as it befriends the Stouffers while they camp in bighorn territory.

It is true realism Marty patiently seeks as he carries 50 pounds of camera equipment. His activity is engendered by a love of animals and by an obvious talent with the camera. As he put it, "I've never really been that fascinated with the whole photographic process. That was just an expression of my interest in wildlife." Although his movies have won at least six awards, he is modest about his talents.

One of the secrets of good wildlife photography is knowing what one is attempting to capture. In order to produce a good movie Marty does extensive research to learn the best locale and time for filming. There are numerous scientists to be questioned, biologists to be consulted and federal offices to be contacted for permission. Of course, this does not necessarily mean he has the *animal's* permission.

The Stouffer brothers' trip to southwestern Arizona to photograph the endangered Sonoran pronghorn antelope was typical of their work. There are only 75 of these animals left, and, according to the Stouffers, they had never been filmed in the wild—an added challenge. After figuring out the best time to go, Marty and Mark left for Arizona. They camped on the desert 60 miles from the highway running along the Mexican border. Finally, after two weeks, they saw five antelope. They checked the area to find where the animals were feeding and then set up a blind on a lava flow. There they sat from dawn to dusk for eight more days. Eventually, the pronghorns meandered by, and the brothers captured them on film.

This seemingly casual approach to photography makes wildlife filming sound relatively easy. But when pressed for details about what he goes through to reach the chosen areas, Marty admitted that he had had to devise his own backpack to transport his heavy, bulky camera gear. "The ordinary camper takes a day pack and some lunch. He can go anywhere, scampering over rocks and so forth. But with my camera I have to know where I am going and how far. And I always carry more film than I can use in my wildest imagination. I would never go without four to six rolls of 200-foot film."

Shooting in the mountains is comparatively easy, evidently. If Marty keeps his equipment organized, it isn't difficult to keep everything clean and in working order. Shooting in the desert, on the other hand, is not for the fainthearted. There are three basic barriers. First, Marty has to go to the nearest town at least every three days for dry ice to protect the film from excessive heat. Secondly, his camera has batteries that must be electrically charged; that means carrying a small generator. The third problem is the insidious dust that can bring all equipment to a grinding halt. If any of these details has not been taken care of, the two minutes that Marty and Mark saw the Sonoran pronghorns would have been for nothing.

"To catch the pronghorns," Mark said, "we drove as far as we could. Then we worked out of a desert base camp in a radius of five to 10 miles. But we didn't load up all our camera equipment. A lot of the time we were scouting around, and sometimes we used the car. We worked in full cooperation with everybody involved: marine corps, air force, U.S. Fish and Wildlife Service, its regional refuge manager in Yuma, acting refuge manager Jim Creasy of Ajo, Arizona, and REST, the regional endangered species team."

My first reaction to all of this was that it sounded great for the United States government to have so much control—that it is really looking after our animals and wilderness. But

The eastern timber wolf has been widely slaughtered and is now down to about one percent of its original population. The wolf is important in keeping prey species (moose, deer, caribou, elk, etc.) herds healthy. While wolves kill the weak and sickly of the prey herds, human hunters seek out only the healthiest and strongest specimens.

PHOTO: MARK AND MARTY STOUFFER

Marty was watching me closely out of the corner of his eye, and he continued:

"You see, the air force bombs the whole area. They drop bombs all over and shoot up at targets in the air. It didn't affect us because when we arrived we were only supposed to be there for a week. But after a week we decided we didn't want to contact all those people again—letters, telephone calls, telegrams—it was insane, the red tape involved with endangered species. We said 'forget it,' and just stayed in. And you know, we'd see planes coming overhead with machine guns blazing, and heard bombs going off in the distance. The ground would shake and there would be a huge black mushroom cloud rising thousands upon thousands of feet in the air way up the valley maybe 20 or 30 miles away. And there we were, 60 miles from the highway. We did not see another soul. We did see tracks of one Mexican, probably a wetback coming into the country illegally."

I was fascinated and amazed by the government involvement. How can it protect and bomb endangered species at the same time? With that in mind, I asked whether Marty had found non-endangered species in the wilderness areas.

"No," was the quick reply, "because most endangered species are endangered because of disturbance by man. As a result they are found in fairly close proximity to man. An animal like the ptarmigan is doing all right because it lives in almost undisturbed areas; that is, until the snowmobile and helicopters arrive." Then he supplied a list of species and how they have been affected by man:

1) The ivory-billed woodpecker is almost extinct (is severely endangered) because of destruction of mature hard-wood habitat in the southeastern United States.

2) The grizzly bear is threatened because of hunting and destruction of wilderness areas in the western United States.

3) The Indiana bat is endangered because of spelunkers having disturbed its caves because of overcollection by scientists.

4) The Delmarva Peninsula fox squirrel is endangered because of destruction of forests on the East Coast.

5) The Morro Bay kangeroo rat is endangered because of urbanization on the California coast.

6) The salt-marsh harvest mouse is endangered because of rapid development of human population in the San Francisco Bay area, the only place in the world where it is found.

7) The Texas red wolf is endangered by heavy hunting and (Marty believes) by an extensive program of poisoning by the U.S. Fish and Wildlife Service.

8) The San Joaquin kit fox is endangered because of reduction of its habitat for irrigated agriculture.

9) The Utah prairie dog was poisoned because of conflict with agricultural interests.

10) The black-footed ferret became endangered as a result of poisoning of the prairie dog, its chief food, and destruction of grasslands.

11) The Florida panther was killed for sport.

12) The Florida manatee was

Marty Stouffer fording a stream with motion-picture gear.
PHOTO: MARK STOUFFER

killed for sport, for food and by injuries from boat propellers.

13) The Key deer was overhunted but now is killed primarily on highways by automobiles.

14) The Columbian white-tailed deer became endangered because of destruction of its habitat.

15) The Sonoran pronghorn is endangered because of hunting and because vast areas of its desert are overgrazed by cattle.

16) The Mexican duck is endangered because of the draining of marshes, particularly those of central New Mexico, southeastern Arizona and western Texas.

17) The California condor: shooting, specimen collecting and disturbance of nesting habitat.

18) Florida Everglade kite: feeding problems resulting from the lowering of the water table in the Everglades.

19) Southern bald eagle: DDT, shooting, press of human population.

20) Attwater's greater prairie chicken: reduction of prairie.

21) The masked bobwhite became extinct in Arizona because of overgrazing of cattle and droughts in the mid-1800s.

22) The whooping crane, which used to live over all of North America, was shot and interfered with by man until it now is found only in one tiny area in Texas, a wildlife refuge.

23) Yuma Clapper rail: channelization and damming of rivers, which destroyed its marsh habitat.

24) The red-cockaded woodpecker nests only in mature pine trees infected by a disease. Foresters claim it's economically unfeasible to let those pines stand so they cut them down for pulpwood.

25) Kirtland's warbler has suffered from much destruction of its very limited habitat, the jack pines in Michigan.

Marty continued, "So there you see in every single case the danger was man. He either plows up a beach and builds houses or drains the Everglades. He chops down a forest or channelizes a river. He plows the prairie or kills with DDT. He kills directly with his guns or indirectly with his poisons."

It is evident that Marty has done a great deal of research. Why? His answer:

"Before anyone can be interested in anything, he has to know about it first. How can someone care about 75 Sonoran pronghorns if he has never heard of or seen one? How can people care about endangered species if 99 percent of them couldn't name five species that are endangered? The average person could list about four—whooping crane, California condor, bald eagle, timber wolf. He might also mention the grizzly bear and the bighorn sheep because of their size. But he would just leave out the salt-marsh harvest mouse and all the other small species.

"In my latest movie I have dealt with endangered mammals and birds. People can't relate to reptiles, amphibians and fish yet. Maybe in 10 years they'll be ready for them, maybe even endangered plants. Doing a film on just mammals has taken three years and a lot of effort, energy and just money.

"I view my role as increasing public awareness, educating the people. I tell them what endangered means and why species are endangered. I tell them what's going to have to happen before animals are safe. If corrections and human concern do not occur, the animals will become extinct. To get right down to it on a personal level, if the animals go, we're next. If the water can't support fish, it can't support us. If the environment because of pollution by DDT can't support the brown pelican or bald eagle, in another couple of years it's sure as hell not going to be able to support us, either."

In short, human beings are animals too. We have all heard it before, but perhaps in the future when Marty and Mark Stouffer educate us about the delicate balance of nature, we'll really learn the lesson. ▲

PHOTOGRAPHING ALASKAN WILDLIFE

by JOHN WALDVOGEL

Photography is a splendid discipline which has the side benefit of getting us to slow down and take a closer look at the world around us. When taking photos of wildlife, for instance, we must find it and get close enough to get photos. That usually requires studying some- *thing about the habits and behavior of the animals we choose to photograph. Not really scientific, but nature study nonetheless, as John Waldvogel illustrates in his piece on photographing Alaskan wildlife.*

W.K.

I was eager to stand on a sharp windy summit again. Because photographing Dall sheep requires climbing, I decided to make them my first subjects. At Mount McKinley National Park headquarters early in July I was told of an excellent sheep habitat, 70 miles northeast of McKinley's massif.

En route to it I encountered my first Alaskan wildlife: *the mosquito.* I've seen bigger mosquitoes in Vermont and thicker swarms in Florida, but none match the Alaskan variety for viciousness, arrogance and punch.

Upon reaching the area I began immediately to climb 5,000-foot Cathedral Mountain, which is situated between Igloo Creek and the Teklanika River. Its lower slopes were covered by dense alder and willow thickets.

I was carrying about two weeks' worth of food, and my pack felt heavy. Still, I felt great. When I stopped to rest and eat my trail lunch—a chocolate bar and iced tea—through my binoculars I saw a bank of about 80 head of sheep grazing in a meadow high upon a mountain on the other side of the valley. Upon reaching the summit I rested again, drinking in the beauty. To the south were the higher peaks of the Alaska Range. To the southwest Mount McKinley itself, veiled in clouds. Magnificent.

I pitched my tent 50 feet below the summit of Cathedral Mountain. I cooked up some freeze-dried Beef Romanoff for dinner. Then I leisurely studied the closer mountains through my binoculars with a cup of hot chocolate beside me. I spotted another bank of 16 sheep on a ridge two miles away. They appeared to be moving toward me. I watched them throughout the endless Alaskan sunset, and when they finally settled down for the night, I did too.

The next morning the sheep were not in sight. I decided to hike to the spot where I had seen them the night before. Climbing was easiest when I stayed on sheep trails. Scree and talus covered most of the slopes, but the sheep trails were surprisingly stable. Following the trails between towers of rock I began wishing for the safety of a rope. I had to make my way along ledges of very loose rock—like dried mud—with 500-foot drop-offs on both sides of me.

About noon I again located the sheep in my binoculars. They were now below me, on an entirely different mountain, moving in the opposite direction. Since they were too far away to follow and the day was half gone, I headed back to my campsite. While I didn't get any sheep photos, I did luck out with other wildlife. For instance, as I climbed around a large rock outcrop I encountered two rock ptarmigan. One flew up as I approached, but the other stayed long enough to allow me to get some good shots.

The following day I again spotted the sheep, this time on a nearby mountain. But when I climbed across a ridge toward them, they slipped away from me along another ridge to a still more distant mountain. Again, the hour got late, and it would have been useless to continue. So I gave it up once more.

That evening I decided that I would try a new approach. Instead of trying to creep up to the sheep from above, I would approach them from below. In the morning I got an earlier start. After my typical breakfast of Bircher Muesli with powdered milk and a cup of hot chocolate, I ran down the scree until I was below them. Through my binoculars I could see them watching me. But they seemed less concerned this time.

I got to within about 300 yards when the rams and a few ewes suddenly left. I was perplexed. If they were running away from me, why did those remaining seem unperturbed? Then I noticed a flash of red ahead of them. They were chasing a fox. When the lead ram got close, the fox ran up the slope and left them all behind. All I could get was a few long-lens shots of them.

Once the sheep settled down, I began creeping up on them again. As I got closer I could really appreciate their beauty. By moving very, very slowly and speaking softly, as if to small children, I snuck up to within 30 feet of them. And I was rewarded with a good many close-range photos. I had learned the trick.

For the next four days I photographed the sheep from close range without difficulty. Each night I returned to my tent on Cathedral Mountain, a fine "home" for me. And I enjoyed waking up in the brisk air so close to the summit. During my seventh night at this camp, though, a violent storm struck. In the morning the sheep were nowhere to be seen, so I rolled up my tent and packed down the mountain.

As I walked through some willow thickets in the valley in search of a new campsite, I noticed a great deal of moose spoor. I decided to make camp in the valley for a few days to photograph Alaskan moose. I pitched

A sow grizzly and her two cubs finish the kill and feast on a caribou carcass by the Toklat River.
PHOTO: JOHN WALDVOGEL

Solitary hawk owl rests in an aspen tree.
PHOTO: JOHN WALDVOGEL

Above left:
A caribou interrupted while grazing on the tundra. Both sexes of caribou have antlers.
PHOTO: JOHN WALDVOGEL

Dall sheep graze freely on ridges in the Alaska Range. The photograph was taken from Cathedral Mountain, between Igloo Creek and the Teklanika River.
PHOTO: JOHN WALDVOGEL

my tent near the rushing waters of Igloo Creek. That first evening I made friends with a red squirrel.

I searched for moose among the willow thickets, and for the first time I started to worry about meeting a grizzly on the trail. To keep the bears away from my camp I avoided having strong-smelling foods in camp and washed my dishes right after dinner. But on the trails I had been advised to make noise to warn any bears of my presence. My technique had been to sing loudly. But how was I to sneak up on a moose if I were singing? I decided to take the risk and so searched for moose as quietly as I was able—but also with very tense nerves.

That same afternoon I was startled by a snort exploding from the thicket directly ahead of me. All of my dedication to wildlife photography vanished. I got out of the thicket like a shot. Upon regaining my composure, I circled the thicket and climbed a rise to get a better view. I was rewarded by the sound of breaking branches. A huge bull moose emerged. He stood over six feet at the shoulder, and his velvet-covered antlers were the biggest I had ever seen. Next, a cow appeared. She was stripping willow leaves with efficient lips.

I followed them throughout the afternoon, trying to remain unobtrusive, shooting a couple of rolls of film. When they lay down to rest and chew their cuds, I too sat down a safe distance away and ate lunch. This tranquility was shattered by a helicopter swooping down across our area. (I learned later that the helicopter was searching for a lost hiker on the lower Muldrow Glacier.) The bull moose jumped to its feet, ears back, stamped and snorted until the helicopter disappeared. He then lay down again and grunted to himself, no doubt convinced he had frightened away the intruder.

The next day I found another cow moose with two calves. While I was nonchalantly photographing the nursing offspring, the cow charged me. I ran away, expecting any second to be overtaken. Apparently she only wanted to frighten me, for when I looked back she was herding the calves back into the brush.

At the end of two weeks I left the park and headed south toward Anchorage to replenish my supplies. Two days later I returned with several oranges, dehydrated soup, freeze-dried dinners and lots of hot chocolate which I drank at any hour and with any meal. I love it. Also I had a large smoked salmon that I bought from a fisherman along the Nenana River. This latter proved a big mistake. Not that it wasn't perfectly delicious and cheap at one dollar for the whole fish, but that night it attracted a grizzly to my camp.

But how was I to sneak up on a moose if I was singing?

I took the shuttle bus to the Teklanika River where I hiked toward the center of the Alaska Range. The gravel bars of the rivers are the best routes for travel in this backcountry. Five miles up the Teklanika I reached a glacier-fed tributary, Calico Creek. I then followed a route the caribou use in their annual migration across the range.

The next day as I continued south I came upon a light blond grizzly digging roots in the stream bed. I made a wide detour.

I crossed a pass in a snowstorm and descended 1,000 feet on the other side, where I pitched my tent. The next day was beautiful with a clear blue sky, and I could see where I was. To the south was the Refuge Valley, an untouched glacial wilderness nestled between 7,000-foot peaks. Perfect setting. I explored the valley floor during the following days. I photographed bears, foxes and moose among the willows and alders. I found sheep and marmots on the crags.

Throughout the next few weeks I had many interesting experiences exploring other parts of the park. But one experience surpassed all else.

By this time I felt I had obtained photos of a good range of wildlife. But I still had not had the courage to try to get any good grizzly shots. I decided to try my hand at it along the Toklat River. Mother Nature played her cards in my favor.

A pack of wolves had attacked a lone caribou on a gravel bar on the East Fork of the river. While the injured animal had been fighting for its life, a couple of wildlife photographers had tried to capture the scene. When the wolves saw them they ran away. Wolves will not tolerate human presence even if it means losing a good meal. Then, as I arrived on the scene, a sow grizzly and her two cubs also appeared. They finished killing the caribou. I got myself situated in a comfortable spot and set up my camera. Not bothered by my presence, the grizzlies began feasting upon the caribou.

The sow ate until she could eat no more. Then she walked off a short distance, lay down and fell asleep on her belly with her four legs sticking out in opposite directions. The cubs played games around the caribou carcass.

After about an hour's sleep, the sow returned to eat some more. When both she and her cubs had enough, they crossed the river and settled down to sleep again. But when a raven dropped by to nibble on the caribou carcass, the sow charged back across the river and chased it away. From then on, the bears stayed closer to the carcass.

By afternoon of the second day the sow had eaten so much her belly was swollen. She could barely move. Like a drunk, she flopped down in a spot in midstream and fell asleep right in the water.

The following morning was cloudy. It was apparently raining farther to the south, for the East Fork began to rise. Around noon, the carcass began drifting downstream. As the sow realized what was happening, she chased after it and dragged it back ashore. She noticed me for the first time at this point, but she didn't seem to mind my presence. Throughout the rest of that day I managed to get in quite close to photograph the bears feeding, and just in time. That evening the carcass washed away for good. I packed up and left, feeling very satisfied with my photographic take.

I stayed in the park through the rest of the summer and on through fall, leaving it every two weeks to replenish my food supplies.

At the beginning of October, with the Alaskan winter snapping at my heels, I left the park for the last time. The night before I crossed the border into the Yukon Territory, I received my farewell gift from Alaska—a phenomenal display of the Northern Lights. ►

Chapter Ten

THE HIKER AS PHOTOGRAPHER

Carrying a camera while hiking is a very personal matter. Some hikers would never be caught dead with one. Others would not be caught dead without. What complicates matters more is that the same person can experience both extremes of attitude about trailside photography at different times—even at different times on the same hike. Colin Fletcher described this schizoid attitude about his camera on his hike from one end of Grand Canyon to the other. In the first stages of his hike the camera seemed to help him take things in more, got him to take a closer look at the scene around him. But, when he broke his camera about halfway through his hike, he felt relieved not to have to bother with taking pictures. He was able to relax and enjoy the scene more.

Attitudes are further complicated when it comes to someone else's carrying a camera on a hike. Some people won't hike with folks who carry cameras. They don't like to wait while the trip photographer dawdles to take wild flower shots. They hate the constant posing for the trip snapshots. And they begin to feel self-conscious about having their photo taken, which sort of spoils the fun of relaxing out of the sight of others.

I think as both a hiker and a photographer I've felt all these emotions at one time or another. Until 15 years ago I seldom carried a camera on a hike, except to get snapshots to record a memory of a trip. Then I became interested in taking photos of flowers and scenes along the trail. At about the time I started doing this, my hiking companions objected. So I went out alone with my camera. Some of those trips are my most memorable. I became enraptured in my picture taking. And there was no one along to become impatient with me, no one that I had to worry about fidgeting while I got absorbed in some tiny phlox off the side of the trail. I would get mesmerized—and hours would scoot by without my noticing.

The trouble with this kind of photography is that no one ever wanted to look at my slides when I came home from a trip. Sure, they politely viewed them. But, I could tell they were really bored after the third shot of a trillium with a sparkling dewdrop hanging from its petal.

Since, apparently, I'm a showoff by nature, I decided to put people in some of my photos. And since I was alone, that meant getting some device to take my own picture. At first I set the camera on a rock, triggered the self-timer, and ran around to get into the picture. This crude way had some shortcomings. First, a handy place to set the camera with the right camera angle was usually difficult to find. Secondly, once having set the camera, it was so precarious that the mere triggering of the self-timer would knock it off its camera angle. So I soon found a small tripod to solve this problem. Later, I found a neat backpacking device which could be screwed into a tree trunk, clamped onto a tree branch, or set up as a miniature tabletop-type tripod.

That solved a lot of problems. And people became more tolerant of viewing slides of mushrooms and sedges as long as there was an occasional shot of me and my camps tossed into the mix.

Since I had been a professional photographer back in the 1940s when carrying a Speed Graphic, a case of cut film holders, and flashbulbs was something of a backpacking trip itself, I'd tried ever since to keep away from the complicated part of photography. I'd had my fill of interchangeable lenses, filters, film speeds, flash bulbs, shutter speeds, lens stops, and such. It was too damned complicated. I had given it all up in favor of a small pocket folding camera, which served me for many years.

When I started taking pictures of flowers, though, I wanted something that could get me closer to the flowers. I bought a simple 35mm single lens reflex camera with an extension tube. It was all I ever needed, plus the one simple 50mm lens that came standard on the camera body. Oh, also the tripod.

I really got into this macrophotography. But it, too, was a pain in the neck when I wasn't busy taking pictures. I hated having the damned camera hanging from my neck. So I simply developed a schizoid attitude about it. I buried the camera deep in the pack when I was hiking. And when I wanted to take pictures I took it out and hung it around my neck. Simple. Two lives—completely separated by where the camera was. If I saw a great scene and the camera was in the pack—the decision was simple. Leave it there. If, on the other hand, I had the camera out and I felt like lingering over a gently floating beam of sunlight, I did. No sweat. No confusing the two worlds with should-I's or shouldn't-I's.

I believe that sooner or later every backpacker becomes a photographer—if he continues to backpack over a number of years. The two activities seem to go together so naturally. (I read recently that a survey of photographers both amateur and professional revealed that 80 percent considered themselves nature photographers.) The point is simple, that nature is a compelling subject matter for photographing, for everyone, backpacker or not. And since backpackers are already predisposed to an interest in nature, they are more likely to take pictures of nature, if they take pictures.

Many backpackers get into photography as a result of their interest in backpacking. They simply can't stand to see all that beauty in nature without wanting to both capture some of it and save it, and to share it with others later after the trip.

Other nature photographers start off as photographers taking pictures of nature, and get into backpacking as a means of getting closer to nature, of being out in the backcountry later at night and earlier in the morning.

Backpacking and photography have led some to professional careers in photography. But few have been as successful at combining both into a career as enviable as that of Ira Spring. He virtually earns his living backpacking with a camera.

So backpacking photography is a very personal thing. And, in this chapter we will explore more of that in the personal statements by some of the leading photographers in the field, who reveal a good many pointers for the rest of us.

The one subject that most of them do not talk about much is actual techniques for taking photos of backpacking. So before reading further, there are a few tips I can give you that I have developed over a period of many years. They are more the product of my many mistakes than of any deep insights.

The first pointer that I can emphasize is something I have already said, get people into your photos. You can always get people into a photo of even the greatest nature scene. This is important if you want an audience for your photos. There are two reasons for this. First, people always like to see pictures that have people in them, better than they do seeing pictures without. Second, having a person in the picture gives it perspective, a scale to the size of things. Without people in a picture, natural objects such as trees, mountains, caves, rocks, valleys, cliffs, and such cannot be perceived in their true size.

My second piece of advice is to watch the backgrounds of your photos. Try to silhouette your people against a solid-colored background. For instance, a backpacker silhouetted against a sky is far more exciting than one who blends into a mottled background of trees and rocks.

My third bit of advice is to "bracket" your photos. By that I mean a simple procedure that is used by all professional photographers, to be sure that they get good photos. Once you have the correct light-meter reading, take a couple of photos, a half-stop more and a half-stop less than the "correct" light-meter reading. Then take another two shots that are a full stop more and less than the true reading. This is because the light meter reads an "average" light reading of the scene. And outdoors that average can fluctuate from very light to very dark photos. To be sure of getting a good exposure, take the time to "bracket" your shots, taking about five shots for every picture you hope to get. For example, say the proper light reading gives you an exposure indication of 1/250th at f-8. Then take five shots: one at 1/250th at f-8, and others at 1/250th between f-8 and f-5.6, 1/250th at f-5.6, 1/250th between f-8 and f-11, 1/250th at f-11.

Another thing that pays off in the viewing of photos after a trip is to take pictures when you least want to do it, at times when you are setting up camp, cooking meals, eating, when it is raining, at sunrise and sunset, at lunch stops and at rest stops. Get people into your photos doing things besides just standing there looking at the scenery. But, of course, do get good photos of people standing there viewing the scenery. All of this will inevitably make enemies of your hiking friends—but it will give you some really good photos.

Do take photos of scenics without people in them—a few. And take some macro photos. That is a photographically hip way of saying take close-ups of flowers, insects, mushrooms, animals.

But most of all take the photos of people backpacking, silhouetted against that setting sun, against that rosy-red sunrise, against that mirror-surfaced alpine lake.

Another piece of advice that I learned the hard way is to edit your photos before showing them after a trip. I always take 35mm slides, because they can be used so many different ways. They can be projected. And you can make prints of them. And they are best for reproduction purposes.

Before showing your slides, edit out the out-of-focus and off-exposure shots. Then put them into some sort of interesting order, mixing the close-ups in with the scenics and the shots of people doing things. And try to eliminate all shots that are about the same subject in the same sequence. Try to make the photos tell a story. Then edit again, seeing which others you can eliminate. Better to show too few than too many photos. When your friends sit down to view your photographs, you can tell how well you did your job by the response they have to your mini slide show.

H. W. GLEASON (1855–1937)
by ED COOPER

Photography, nature, and conservation go hand in hand, and at a time of life when many people nowadays are beginning to plan for their golden years in retirement communities, a man named Herbert Wendell Gleason embarked on a brand-new career. It eventually took him backpacking with many pounds of photographic gear to the remotest frontiers of the North American continent.

Ironically, it was because of poor health that Gleason in 1899 gave up his career in the ministry at the age of 44. He took his first photograph the same year. There was nothing prophetic about that photo of the "interior of parlor and hall, 1815 Columbus Avenue, Minneapolis. #1, February 2, 1899." But Gleason's photographic interests soon shifted out-of-doors, where he spent much of the next 38 years, until shortly before his death.

Gleason was well ahead of his time. Although most people in the West during the early 1900s were busy subduing the wilderness, Gleason went there solely for the wilderness experience, making some 30 separate trips from the home in Boston where he lived after retiring from the ministry.

He was active in the conservation movement before most people ever heard the word and was instrumental in the preservation and creation of several national parks and monuments.

A good friend of Stephen T. Mather (father of the National Park System, and its first director), Gleason was appointed Interior Department Inspector, a position which presumably helped finance all those trips. His job was photographing the lands of the National Park System and proposed additions to it—a dream assignment. The photographs he took in Yellowstone in 1921 helped save the park from incursions by powerful irrigation interests. Mather used many Gleason pictures when lobbying for the creation of new parklands.

A Christmas card Gleason and his wife sent to friends in 1930 contained some early conservation lobbying, too. It read, "...we beg to make one request:

Altogether he traveled more than 200,000 miles on his trips to Alaska, California, Colorado, the Grand Canyon, Canadian Rockies and Yellowstone.

Will you not, in planning your Christmas decorations, avoid using Mountain Laurel, Ground Pine, American Holly, and (in California) Toyon? Ruthless and commercial gathering has in many places practically exterminated these beautiful evergreens. Other material, in large variety and equally decorative, can be secured, and some of it is surprisingly durable. For instance, a wreath of native spruce kept its shape perfectly in our home for over three months. Yours for the conservation of Natural Beauty."

The most remarkable fact about Gleason, I believe, is the variety of remote locations he managed to photograph at a time when travel was very difficult. All his negatives are numbered in sequence, chronologically, so it is easy to follow his travels. In 1901 he was in Alaska, taking pictures of gold-mining activities. From 1905 to 1907, when he was in his early fifties, he kept up an almost unbelievable pace. Each year he seems to have taken a grand tour two or three months long covering wilderness areas in the western United States and Canada. Many of these spots now are national parks and monuments.

The years 1917-21, when he was in his sixties, were another especially active period. Popular parks we can reach in hours by car took him days by train, horseback and foot. He must have become expert at train travel, which was the only practical way to reach the jumping-off spots for various wilderness enclaves.

The weight and bulk of Gleason's camera equipment must have been considerable. Each 5 x 7 glass plate weighed approximately one pound and took only one black-and-white negative. In addition, there was the weight of his camera, tripod, processing equipment (including chemicals and trays) and light-proof bag or tent for loading film holders. Consequently, when Gleason visited a remote area for a week, he had to be very selective about the number of pictures he could take.

Within the field of nature photography, his interests were varied and not limited to western scenery. Actually, during his lifetime Gleason was better known for his photographs of New England. In 1906 his pictures illustrated a 20-volume edition of Thoreau's works and in 1917, another book, *Through the Year With Thoreau*. In 1916 Gleason wrote:

...[I have] made two trips to Alaska, six to California and the Pacific Coast, three to the Grand Canyon of Arizona, seven to the Canadian Rockies, two to Yellowstone Park, and three to the Rocky Mountains of Colorado. Yet, after every one of these trips, it was a genuine delight to return to the simple beauty of New England.

I think Gleason must have regretted being unable to shoot in color, for he made a subspecialty of photographing wildflowers and formal gardens. Color would have been especially useful for the many illustrated lectures he gave while traveling. One of them was entitled "Personal Memories of Luther Burbank and His Magic Gardens." He didn't do entirely without color, however: Mrs. Gleason became expert at hand coloring the lecture plates.

Fortunately, most of Gleason's original wet-plate negatives have been preserved. More than 6,000 of them now belong to Roland W. Robbins of Lincoln, Massachusetts, who furnished the pictures for this article. In addition, two fine books of Gleason photographs have recently been printed by Barre Publishers in Massachusetts: *Thoreau's Cape Cod*, containing early pictures, and *The Western Wilderness of North America*. A third book, *Gleason's Canada*, will be published in the spring of 1974.

How is Gleason's work rated today? Opinions differ..Some people believe his photographs are a gold mine of superb photography. Others are not enthusiastic about their artistic merit but value them for their historical interest. Ansel

He carried at least 25 pounds of camera equipment on each of his trips. Each wet-plate glass negative alone weighed a full pound.

Adams belongs to the second group. "He made a great contribution in the informative sense," Adams has written, "and revealed many new areas of the wilderness to the public...but his work does not excite me at all."

It is in the field of mountain wilderness photography that I feel the greatest empathy with Gleason. True, he did not always make the best use of the lighting, but this criticism is not entirely fair. An automobile moves me around quickly so I can "strike while the weather is good" in order to arrive at a planned viewpoint during the right weather, with the right lighting. Gleason did not have much choice; he had to take many of his pictures in overcast weather or not at all. Additionally, because many locations were virgin territory, he had no way of knowing when the lighting would be best at a certain location. Until he arrived there, he probably couldn't be sure whether there would be a vantage point from which to shoot or whether he would find any views he wanted at all.

So to Herbert Wendell Gleason, who died the year I was born and in whom I can see a bit of myself, I pay respectful homage. 🐾

ERNEST BRAUN

I first came in contact with Braun's work when we were just beginning to seriously plan to publish a backpacking magazine. At that time, my own life was hectically involved in commercial photography in Manhattan. And I hiked on the Appalachian Trail on weekends to take pictures of nature and mostly to get my head cleared.

When I picked up Ernest Braun's fine book, Living Water, I was fascinated. The more I studied his work, the more I realized that this was the sort of photography I was into myself. I usually went on my backpack trips alone. (I figured I was not fit for anyone else to live with in those days.) I enjoyed being by myself, especially in the mornings, after breakfast, when I wandered about aimlessly with my camera, sometimes wallowing around on my belly for an hour or so, taking pictures of some small corner of a meadow beside the trail.

Thus, when I read the short section in the back of Ernest Braun's book called "About the Pictures," I could really identify with him. Here was a really fine nature photographer who, I discovered, also was involved in commercial photography, who also mindlessly explored nature on his belly in his small patch of wilderness, who also entertained the types of ideas and experiences I was going through.

It seemed natural to me, when we were doping out the philosophy underlying BACK-PACKER's editorial format, that there must be thousands of other people like me, who were happily employed in their professional work during the week, who stole away into their own corners of nearby wilderness with their cameras to get into what I now call my "camera meditation." (Just getting behind my viewfinder, lost to all considerations of time—whether or not I get any worthwhile photos—has a spiritually therapeutic value for me similar to Transcendental Meditation.) Hence, we incorporated the photo interviews as a regular feature in BACKPACKER from the first issue. I seem to have been right. Readers have responded that this is one of the most popular features of the magazine. For our readers at least, a camera appears to be as essential a part of their backpacking gear as their pack and sleeping bag. BACKPACKER readers seem to be sophisticated photographers who already have a substantial understanding of f-stops, shutter speeds, and ASA ratings and who are more interested in a photographer's philosophy than the nitty-gritty of his technique.

When it came time to do a photo interview with Braun, I went back to his book, Living Water, to refresh myself, and I reread the section of the book that had had such an instant appeal for me six years ago. Surprisingly, after having seen so many photographs and having interviewed so many different photographers, I still found Braun's photos and comments as fresh and inspiring to me as they had been before.

It seemed only reasonable for us to share with our readers the original text just as it appeared in Ernest Braun's book, Living Water, which follows.

W.K.

SHARING A DISCOVERY is one of a photographer's joys. Another, for me, is to encourage other people to look closer and to make their own discoveries. As little children we all start out with eyes close to the ground, seeing, feeling, smelling, exploring, and learning. Seeing with a camera is the best way I have found to get close to the earth again.

Imagine that you are wandering with your camera along a wilderness trail, or that you are stretched out in a meadow at dawn, shivering with cold and delight as the rising sun gently prods the frost crystals. This scene will never be repeated. The elements, earth, air, fire, and water, are in a changing balance instant by instant. You see it change and raise your camera. This is a moment of confrontation. You are faced with infinite choices. What will you do? If both the environment and the camera are new to you, a quick snapshot may be enough; but if you have become aware of the endless possibilities for visual discovery, you will work longer and harder, though you will never be completely satisfied.

There is an entrancing subjective quality about nature photography. If you just open yourself to the environment and try to tune in on what is happening, you will begin to see images that almost reach out to be discovered. Pictures will seem to happen to you without any effort. But you will miss all this fun if you cling to rigid preconceived concepts of subject matter or a static way of seeing.

We all need a transition period between home or highway and the reality of the natural world. This is a time for walking, feeling the earth underfoot, visiting with the landscape, watching the light change and the clouds move, or maybe just listening to the many sounds of running water and wind in the trees. One of the best times I can remember was the beginning of a visit to Delaney Creek in Yosemite. I needed three days of solitude to unwind, to forget what day it was, to drop the load of personal problems. I had been up and down the stream, cameras and film in my daypack, walking for hours, sometimes sitting quietly on the rocky banks visually exploring the magic of water, until finally I was content to just be.

ALTHOUGH ALL MY WORKING life has been spent with a camera, I have been photographing in the natural world for a relatively short time—and never too seriously. My purpose has been, more than anything else, to learn and to be refreshed. But as I became better acquainted with nature and nature photography, I realized that the creative work of most con-

temporary photographers was confined to human experience. The rest of the planet was being neglected, and I knew that the visual arts could help by just showing how it is here before the asphalt and concrete take over. We cannot expect people to fight for something they don't even know.

I started camping and backpacking only ten years ago. Before that, I felt I was too busy with photographic assignments, being part of a family, expanding and remodeling an old house on a steep, forested hill. Then I began exploring nature in small ways—wandering on our hill with the children when they were small, exploring beaches and tidepools with them.

My first love was the tideline wilderness. During family vacations at the beach I began to explore its form, color, texture, and motion with a camera. As my work led me up and down the Pacific Coast, I managed a little extra time to explore and photograph other beaches, from San Diego to the Olympic Peninsula. So it was quite natural for me to carry a camera into the mountains.

As my friendship with the high country of the Sierra Nevada grew, my seeing with the camera became more intimate. I discovered that a great unknown exists at ground level. This is where the action is, in living and growing terms. I found, as I had in the tidepools, that when I stayed in one place, close to the ground with eyes and lens alert, my view of the world was transformed, and my op-

portunity for seeing and thinking was expanded. There was enough going on in one place for a whole day's work. Discovery was cut short only when a cloud of mosquitoes or a stiff neck forced me to my feet.

Because of the very limited time I had available and a general dissatisfaction with my random efforts, I decided to concentrate on a visual profile of a small area. By imposing this discipline on myself, I hoped that more intense exploration would be possible and that the feeling of intimacy I hoped to establish would be transferred through the pictures to the viewer. Three years ago, after a lot of looking, I selected a meadow, a stream, and a timberline lake that were easy to get to—the meadow is just four and a half driving hours from home—and planned to return to these places as often as possible through the seasons. It would be better, of course, to spend a whole year in one wilderness place, and I will someday. While I know my meadow and stream better with each visit, the time to complete this project has not been available. (And in honesty I must admit that I have not been disciplined enough to resist knapsack trips through other parts of the high country with my family and with friends.) However, one result of this experience is a growing collection of photographs from which the pictures in this portfolio were selected.

SEEING, THINKING, AND FEELING are the essential acts of photography. The camera is scarcely

Detail of feather in the riverbank jungle, Caswell Memorial Park, on the Stanislaus River west of Modesto. Micro-Nikkor lens, Ektachrome X.
PHOTO: ERNEST BRAUN

more important to a photographer than a typewriter is to a writer; however, photographers have a wider choice of tools than writers do, and there is no denying that the seeing and the tools are related. The traditional large-format view camera and the modern 35mm single-lens reflex camera represent the extremes. A wide range of camera systems lie in between and may be used in all kinds of ways. Each system has its advantages and its limitations. A contact print from an 8x10 negative can represent the ultimate in clarity and perfection. Because of the time, effort, and craftsmanship needed to operate a large view camera, each exposure is an important event that merits careful study and consideration. However, the photographer with his large camera on a tripod tends to be an observer rather than a participant. There is so much heavy equipment between him and his subject that his seeing becomes deliberate and limited. Portability is a problem, especially on long trail trips because pack animals are restricted to altitudes where grazing is available and allowed.

The compact 35mm single-lens camera has many advantages for nature photography. One sees the same image through the lens that is being recorded on film. The mechanical barrier between the photographer and the environment is minimized. Since hardly any effort is needed to operate the camera, more energy is available for seeing. Most important, the camera is light, mobile, and easily used in tight spots. All this freedom must be used wisely. We live in a time of instant everything, and now instant images are here—thirty-six at a time, if one just keeps pushing the little button. The tiny 35mm format demands respect and loving care if the magnificent quality of modern lenses and film is not to be wasted by an unsteady hand or a careless eye.

As part of my preparation for teaching a photography workshop recently, I made a brief historical review of published nature photographs and was again reminded of the incredibly short and successful life of photography as a communication medium. Just one hundred years ago Sullivan and Jackson were recording Yosemite and the West for

the first time. Their work is amazing, considering that there were no highways as we know them and they were using wet glass plates, coated and developed on the site in a tent darkroom carried on muleback. Minimum exposure time was fifteen seconds. About forty years ago Edward Weston was exploring the natural world with his 8x10 view camera. He discovered the texture, form, and symmetry that had always been there but had seldom been seen. In 1938 Kodachrome film became available and in the last ten years the single-lens reflex camera and faster color film arrived on the scene. I can't help wondering what Weston might have done with modern equipment!

WHILE PHOTOGRAPHIC TECHNOLOGY had continued to make picture taking easier, serious photographers of the natural world have tended to be traditional in their seeing and thinking, feeling safer perhaps to work within the limitations of the large format camera. There has been almost a reverence for the needlesharp image, made popular by the ƒ64 group. I think of this as a carryover from the early days of photography when a technically perfect image was a goal in itself. Actually, a totally sharp photograph is an abstraction. Our eyes scan as we look, never projecting a sharp image of the whole scene on the retina, but moving rapidly so that we have an impression of the whole. When we look intently at one point, nothing else is sharp.

My choice for wilderness photography is the 35mm camera. All the photographs in my book, *Living Water,* were made with Nikon or Pentax systems. Most of the pictures could not have been made with any other kind of equipment. I respect and use the view camera and the 2¼x2¼ format for some of my commercial work, but about 70 percent of my editorial, industrial, and advertising assignments are done with the 35mm. I seldom take a picture that gives me personal satisfaction with anything but the 35mm. This format gives me maximum freedom to identify with my subject.

I tend to be impatient with equipment and with myself because the image I see may not exist in another minute—the frost is melting, the bub-

bles under the ice are moving, and so are the clouds and the sun. There is an immediacy about closeup work that is exciting and demanding. You never know if the frog will jump before you are ready—and he usually does.

EXCEPT FOR A FEW telephoto shots and long exposures with neutral density filters, I do not use a tripod. A tripod takes time to set up and is extra weight to carry. Some good pictures are failures because of camera movement, but often there is a rock or a tree handy for extra support. It becomes a question of choosing your limitations.

The micro lenses are great timesavers for closeup work. They focus from infinity up to a point at which the image on the film is the same size as the subject. I also like the different perspective in a closeup image made with a longer focal length lens, such as the 200mm with added extension tubes. I use all the lenses that are available and moderately portable, from the 21mm focal length to the 500mm. If I am traveling very light, as on a long knapsack trip, I take one camera with the 55mm Micro-Nikkor and a 135mm lens. That is a minimum. If my back is up to it, I add a 28mm and the 200mm, plus another camera body.

Dawn and dusk are prime times for any kind of outdoor photography, because the light is soft and warm. Our sun has a tender goodbye caress for the land in the evening, while early morning is a time of cheerful reunion. As the light level diminishes, high speed color film extends the time for working, although I try to use slower fine-grain color film whenever possible. Cloudy or foggy days are ideal for closeups. Storms are a time of celebration for the land and present very special and beautiful conditions for working (it's surprising how wet a camera can get and still keep operating). The harsh light and strong shadows of the midday hours are very difficult, however, and the brightness range of a sunny day may exceed the capabilities of color film. The middle of the day is a good time to move on to the next campsite, to scout locations for work at dusk, or to enjoy a siesta after a dawn picture session. ⚓

THE INTIMATE WORLD OF DAVID CAVAGNARO

David Cavagnaro is truly a Renaissance man. Trained as a scientist, he has worked as an entomologist, museum director, and teacher, and has carried those skills over into his creative endeavors. David now free-lances from his home, photographing, writing, and teaching. He has published more than 700 photographs and articles in books and magazines ranging from Life to Psychic and has co-authored The Amazing Life Games Theater, teaching materials in the sciences for children; Living Water, with Ernest Braun; and Almost Home, a picture book about personal changes. He is the author and illustrator of This Living Earth, which reveals his extraordinary talents as a nature photographer.

BACKPACKER: Your photography makes the viewer feel he is more a participant than an observer of nature.

CAVAGNARO: Photography has been a valuable perceptual tool in my life and has caused me to participate rather than merely observe—to slow down and focus in. When you are out exploring with the camera, you're forced to do it. You are there physically, and you are forced to look—perhaps even to see.

BACKPACKER: Do you think people need a basic knowledge of nature to understand what's going on about them?

CAVAGNARO: Of course. But I believe very strongly that basic learning in the natural world works through a process of personal discovery. The educational system is turned upside down; it's a pyramid reversed. People are crammed full of information first, and allowed to experience only when they've graduated. There are intellectual concepts that anyone can learn from a biology book, but you don't *feel* them from reading the book. You really come to grips with the concepts when you're out in the meadows and mountains, observing what's going on and absorbing the surroundings through every sense of your body.

BACKPACKER: Are there specific techniques you use to heighten the sense that your photos are a part of nature?

CAVAGNARO: There's a very basic one that is often overlooked by photographers. The prerequisite is to change your posture. You really have to crawl, to get down on your belly and look at things closely, because the vast majority of significant events in the natural world are small happenings among small creatures. I've often said adults need to become children, because children have not only an open mind but the smallness of stature that enables them to be intimate. Get down on the ground and look up at the wildflowers. See what a plant looks like from a child's perspective. We're so locked into viewing things from five or six feet off the ground that we forget the world may be perceived in many different ways.

BACKPACKER: It seems to us that your photography requires your repeated exposure to the same area to get a feel for what's going on. But most people prefer to visit new places to take pictures.

CAVAGNARO: Before we began photographing for my book, *This Living Earth,* we had photographed on backpacking trips and other expeditions, always in new places. But *This Living Earth* re-creates a three-year experience that my wife, Maggie, and I shared in grassland areas near our home. We had eight-to-five jobs; in fact, we were working a lot longer than eight to five. So we had to explore the areas early in the morning, on our way home and occasionally on weekends. Many of the pictures were taken in a patch of grass by the side of the road. We discovered that within each small area there is a web of knowledge as well as a web of life. I think people cheat themselves if they don't allow at least some time in their lives for this kind of close exposure. It happens

PHOTO: ERNEST BRAUN

on two levels. Knowledge is gained and, at the same time, there is a spiritual change, because the more one experiences a place, the more familiar one becomes with the moods, the setting and the individual characters at work in it. You come to feel you are a participant, which, of course, you have been all along, even though you didn't know it.

BACKPACKER: Can you transfer the feeling or experience you have gained this way? For instance, when you did the nature walk essays for the Time–Life American Wilderness series and spent only a few days at each location, did you have to develop new techniques?

CAVAGNARO: If I can make an analogy, a person who shops regularly in the local Safeway would be able to walk into any Safeway across the country and very quickly find what he needs. I think it's much the same as going into a new natural area and applying experiences from another one. For the Time–Life essays, I went to 11 widely different wilderness areas in the western United States. In each area I had a very short time—two to four days—to visit several miles of country and to photograph it with intimacy. But knowing something of the significance of natural events, I was able to find my way quickly and locate habitats where I might expect to find something interesting happening. In other words, I had a sense of the significant. In Hawaii or South Dakota or the Sawtooth Mountains, that sense stood me in good stead.

BACKPACKER: What about the mechanical side of photography—equipment and technique?

CAVAGNARO: Very simple. I don't like to be burdened with equipment, and the mechanics of photography are barriers between me and the experience I want to have in the first place. After all it's the experience I'm there for, and the camera is only a tool. So if I had my druthers, I'd carry one camera and maybe two lenses. I use 35mm Nikkormat cameras. I generally use the 55mm Micro-Nikkor lens, a 28mm wide-angle lens and a 105mm telephoto lens. I use extension tubes with the Micro-Nikkor and telephoto lenses. I wear a belt pouch into which I put all my extra accessories and film, so everything is in one little bag and easy to reach. I almost never use a tripod. Again, it's not that I don't believe in it, I just don't want to be burdened with the thing.

BACKPACKER: Part of your style is that some shots are not quite sharp. To us it makes the viewer feel he is getting an insect's view. Did you accidentally discover that effect, or was it a conscious development?

CAVAGNARO: When you're working with tiny close-ups for documentary photography, the best approach is to use electronic flash, primarily for sharpness. But I'm not as interested in documenting the natural world as in relating an experience, documenting a mood or spiritual reaction I am having in communion with the natural world. Therefore, I shun the use of artificial light and extra equipment that would dilute the experience, both for myself and for the final photographic results. When working with natural light close up, the photographer is limited in terms of the motion he can stop, depth of field and other factors. I've tried, at first inadvertently and later with more conscious effort, to develop a technique that makes the best use of limitation, a style that incorporates the inherent lack of depth of field and sharpness into a sort of perceptual frame of reference.

Human attention is always selective, particularly when one is focusing up close. It's the adage about the forest and the trees. To me, working with the camera is like painting with watercolors. When I'm shooting in an out-of-focus realm, backgrounds and foregrounds become splashes of color. They create a mood. They are something subjective, rather than objective.

BACKPACKER: Direct light, especially the sun, seems to be important in your style.

CAVAGNARO: My primary love in photography is light, the sun. I would have been a sun-worshipper in any other culture. I'm drawn to natural sunlight in each of its various moods, and I especially enjoy being out early in the morning and late in the evening when the sun is low. Of course, a biologist would say that the sun is the source of all energy that drives the whole living

"We're so locked into viewing things from five or six feet off the ground that we forget the world may be perceived in many different ways."

fabric. But I think man throughout time has had a spiritual attraction to the sun, and this attraction is expressed in the kinds of things I photograph. I very much like backlighting, too, because of the luster, the radiance, that the sun gives when seen that way.

BACKPACKER: How do you photograph the sun?

CAVAGNARO: When I photograph the sun itself, I use only a part of its light, because otherwise it is too intense. I look for a place

Dew drops adorning a spider web on a seed spike of rye grass.
PHOTO: DAVID CAVAGNARO

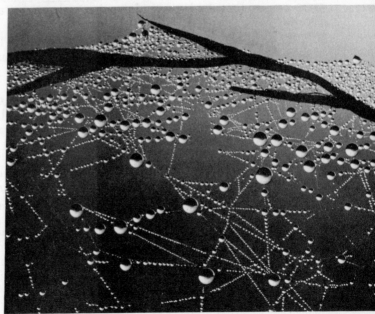

where the sun is partially masked behind a distant tree or shrub, and get down on the ground and prowl around with my camera to find things in that semishaded light. The image of the sun's light in my camera, quite out of focus because I'm doing a close-up, is large and moonlike. But one has to use a wide-open aperture to avoid hexagonal suns, which you would get from the aperture blades if the lens were stopped down.

BACKPACKER: It seems obvious your photographic and scientific philosophies go back many years. They are so well integrated, and you have given them much thought. What were your early influences?

CAVAGNARO: When I was six or seven, I developed an interest in biology, particularly insects. I began taking pictures with a Brownie box camera. But it wasn't until 1964 when I was in the Galápagos Islands on an entomological project that I became seriously involved with photography. One can't go to the Galápagos without being intimately aware of unique animals and plants and interesting biological stories, which all cry out to be recorded.

BACKPACKER: When you returned, did you get involved with Ernest Braun on the book *Living Water?*

CAVAGNARO: Ernie Braun's family and mine had been friends since I was seven years old. When I returned to Marin County, I discovered Ernie's camera work, particularly that of the California coast and the Sierra Nevada. But it was some time later that we collaborated on *Living Water.*

BACKPACKER: Was it Braun who turned you toward intimate nature photography?

CAVAGNARO: In one sense, yes. Ernie and I are drawn to much the same kind of things in the natural world. We did spend quite a bit of time together in the Sierra, photographing, hiking and backpacking. We developed a very strong bond, both personally and visually. I would say his work influenced me in a lot of ways, but my own interest in natural history was actually the stronger influence.

BACKPACKER: It seems you have developed a dual talent—that of the scientist and that of the artist.

CAVAGNARO: I really feel *all* mankind has a dual nature—innate intellectual and spiritual sides. I think our great challenge is to balance the two sides, to use the power for knowledge and to temper it with the particular wisdom that only our spirit can give. For me, photography offers something of this discipline. It enables me to temper a facet of knowledge in the natural world with my own soul and feelings. I believe all people should strive to achieve this balance through one expressive endeavor or another, whether it is writing or photography or another art form. 🥾

MAYNARD SWITZER'S WET-WEATHER PHOTOGRAPHY

A BACKPACKER Interview

BACKPACKER: We understand you grew up in the shadow of the Rockies?

SWITZER: Yes, right there; I lived in Calgary, Alberta, about 70 miles away from Banff which is, you know, right near the mountains.

BACKPACKER: What kind of relationship did you have as a boy with the mountains?

SWITZER: Oh, as long ago as I can remember my parents took me to the Rockies. It used to take quite a while to get up there on the old road. And when I grew up, I went to the mountains with close friends who did a lot of backpacking and hiking, and I got very familiar with the whole area. Often we'd take Friday afternoon off and go up for a long weekend.

BACKPACKER: And you left the mountains when you went to college?

SWITZER: Right, I went to the Art Center, College of Design, in Los Angeles. Ansel Adams taught there. They have a really good photography group.

BACKPACKER: Why did you choose to go into photography?

SWITZER: Well, I was spending so much time at it. I started photographing when I began getting seriously into backpacking. There were so many unique areas that we went to, and none of my friends was interested in photography. It seemed a shame to go on those fantastic hikes and not have anything to bring back. I think I was 12 years old when I was given an old Ricoh camera. It was a straight lens model. I couldn't change the lenses to get close-ups of flowers. So when I was 15 I bought a Nikon so I could change lenses.

BACKPACKER: A Nikon is an expensive camera.

SWITZER: Yes, and I bought it myself, I saved my money for it. And then about six months later I added another lens, and I thought that was incredibly expensive, too. I knew I wanted to be a professional photographer, even then.

BACKPACKER: Why did you pick nature photography?

SWITZER: That's what I thought I was best at—although the Art Center gave me a good background in advertising. When I got out of school I went to work for Richard Avedon, the famous fashion photographer. I worked for him for a year. While I really enjoyed nature photography, I wanted to get a background in advertising photography, too.

BACKPACKER: Did you learn anything during that time that helped you in any way in your nature photography?

SWITZER: They are totally different. Advertising and fashion photography have so much to do with people. But maybe they made me more professional about photography—meeting deadlines and such. It was so specialized; it was fantastic, the people I met. We photographed Charlie Chaplin on his first day back in the United States. We photographed every famous model in the world and many famous personalities, too.

BACKPACKER: When you were working for Avedon, did you take pictures of nature in your spare time?

SWITZER: Yes, I went up to Vermont whenever I could. But it wasn't until after I left Avedon that I took a lot of strictly nature photographs.

BACKPACKER: Do you find a conflict between the two types of photography?

SWITZER: Oh no. I like trying to work in graphics. My fashion theories lead over into nature, and nature leads over into advertising. In my fashion portfolio you can see the lines and symmetry and things like that. I didn't realize it until after I found myself developing a style of shooting. I think anyone can shoot beautiful pictures of nature. I mean, nature puts it all out in front of you. But I think to really take outstanding pictures, you have to study the area and look for the hidden things.

BACKPACKER: Could you explain that a little? What sort of things are you looking for?

SWITZER: Well, I don't run in and shoot and come out. I sometimes take a whole day, just hiking around and making notes of what things interest me and what time I think would be the best to take certain photographs.

BACKPACKER: Does inclement weather give you anything special to work with? Or is it barely possible to take shots at those times?

SWITZER: I like working in inclement weather and overcast days, especially when I'm shooting color. I think the colors become incredibly rich. And I like to use Kodachrome. On an almost monochromatic scene on an overcast day the slightest color will show through. In overcast weather you get a very flat and beautiful light. At those times colors seem to have a brilliance to them, especially when you use Kodachrome.

BACKPACKER: But doesn't inclement weather present problems?

SWITZER: Yes, I shoot most of the time with a tripod when I'm working with Kodachrome because it's very slow. But it's worth the extra effort because I like warm tones when the day is grey and dull. You get a mixture of the warm and the cold on Kodachrome, and the shots usually turn out beautifully. Also, Kodachrome is contrasty, and you need that little bit of sparkle on overcast days.

BACKPACKER: How do you keep your camera from getting wet?

SWITZER: I'm not very worried about that. More important is keeping myself warm. I'm usually wet, and everything else totally soaked. It is a lot more pleasant then if I can keep warm.

BACKPACKER: Do you purposely go out to shoot on inclement days? Or do you just happen to be there?

SWITZER: I go out intentionally. Usually I have checked out an area beforehand, and I know what subjects I'm after.

BACKPACKER: Did you do that for the photos accompanying this interview?

SWITZER: Yes. With the exception of the waterfall they were all shot in Vermont, and all of them were taken on two trips only two weeks apart. And all in the same area. The cobweb, for instance, was shot on the bank of that misty river.

BACKPACKER: When you go backpacking, say for two days, what do you carry in the way of camera equipment?

SWITZER: I carry two Nikon bodies and four different lenses. Usually I have High Speed Ektachrome in one camera and Kodachrome in the other.

BACKPACKER: What else do you take?

SWITZER: A small tripod, a set of extension rings, and filters. I almost always shoot with a polarizing filter.

BACKPACKER: How about backpacking equipment? Clothes and stuff?

SWITZER: I've never worn a great amount of clothing, even in cold weather. The most uncomfortable thing for me is being wet. On the Vermont trips I took along a water-proof nylon shell, a down parka, a sweater, and a turtleneck. The main thing for me is to be comfortable when I'm shooting. I don't think anything is as miserable as trying to shoot when you're cold. You try to rush things, and they simply don't happen that fast. If you're waiting for a sunset or sunrise, you wait for an hour or so, and this is usually the coldest time.

BACKPACKER: You say you don't mind your cameras getting wet.

SWITZER: No, the water really doesn't hurt them. When I'm through shooting for the day I wipe the cameras off, especially around the meter where it attaches to the camera body. The sealing isn't too tight there. I have a little cloth, and I try to daub up as much moisture as possible.

BACKPACKER: You say you use a polarizing filter? On rainy days, too?

SWITZER: No. I use one *almost* all the time. But you're right; in inclement weather the polarizer isn't necessary because there isn't the type of light to polarize.

BACKPACKER: Do you use other kinds of filters?

SWITZER: Yes, I usually check the film to find out what its color balance is before I shoot with it.

BACKPACKER: How do you do that?

SWITZER: I buy film in large quantities; it comes in 20-roll packages. I buy 100 or 200 rolls at a time. Then I shoot one roll of test shots. That's sufficient because all of the rolls in that batch will have the same emulsion. The test shots will give me the filtration factor for the rest of the batch. I find that I have to use filters more often when I use Ektachrome than Kodachrome.

BACKPACKER: You said you work very slowly. How long does it take you to take a picture?

SWITZER: Usually the composing takes a long time. I worked at least an hour to shoot that cobweb, trying to find the right position. I wanted the center of the cobweb to be separated. I decided to align it with the red object in the background, which I threw out of focus, and it gave me the separation I wanted. I guess that's the fashion photographer in me. When you take pictures of clothes you have to show them separating from color values of the background.

BACKPACKER: It took you an hour just to find the right angle?

SWITZER: Yes, it took an hour to compose the picture from the time when

I found the cobweb. It was a very long exposure, taken in the morning, so I had lots of time. I'm sure every photographer has tried to rush through something, and after getting the transparencies back, found he didn't get the results he thought he would get.

BACKPACKER: So your work in fashion made you very conscious of backgrounds in photos. How about this waterfall, as an example?

SWITZER: That's not a good example. Actually, that photo probably took me less time to prepare than all the rest. I was leaning over the stream bank. A friend had to hold me so I wouldn't fall. I couldn't use my tripod. So I wasn't able to pay as much attention to the background as I would have liked. Still, I knew it was a good shot, and the results are good, I believe.

BACKPACKER: What part of the picture-taking process gives you the most kicks?

SWITZER: The preparation. That's about 90 percent of taking the picture. Once it's set up I've done basically all the work; I know my exposure and everything else. The only thing left is pushing the shutter—and I like leading up to that climax.

Incidentally, I usually underexpose my pictures about a quarter to a third of a stop. It gives very rich transparencies.

BACKPACKER: If you could take the ideal photo, just one last shot, what would you take a picture of?

SWITZER: Well, I guess there are two subjects that have excited me the most—snow and sand dunes. I never thought I'd find a place as beautiful as the Rockies, until I saw Death Valley. In its own way it's as beautiful, and I found a great deal there that has opened up new fields for me. But, at this point in my life I still lean a little toward the mountains. ▲

GARRY VALLÉ
The Point-and-Shoot Dude
A BACKPACKER Interview

BACKPACKER: Sounds like you don't plan your photography—or plan trips around it. You just shoot what hits you, relying on serendipity?

VALLE: Yes, normally I don't go into an area with specific images in mind. I'm sure you know what I mean when I say I am like a blank photographic plate: no preconception of what I'm going to see.

BACKPACKER: So just what is it that causes you to stop and make a photograph?

VALLE: Primarily, emotion is what compels me to photograph. As it is difficult to control our emotions in an intensely happy, maddening, or fearful situation, so it is difficult for some people, myself included, *not* to respond to certain situations in a "photographically emotional" manner. There is little doubt when I am confronted by such an image: my feeling is instantaneous and acute. My adrenalin flows, and an agitated feeling persists until I have responded to the situation.

BACKPACKER: In a letter to us you said you wanted other people "to sense something unusual" about your photographs. Is it the unusual that grabs you, mostly?

VALLE: Yes, I think it is some sort of unusual relationship; a stark juxtaposition. But it is hard to say exactly what it is that wells up my emotions.

BACKPACKER: How do *you* feel about your shots when viewing them again?

VALLE: Sometimes I get the adrenalin again—not as strongly as the first time, but there will be a very definite feeling about it. I can see why I took the shot in the first place, and that recognition leads me to feel that such a shot is really representative of what I want to do.

BACKPACKER: Seeing a very striking image is only the first part—and sometimes the easiest. Actually making a photograph that will carry the feeling and presence of what was seen is often difficult. Are you often disappointed by technical difficulties when you get the film back and the instantaneous emotional shot is not successful?

VALLE: I think luck is involved in it, but there is some technical filtering going on. I am just not very aware of it when I'm taking photographs. I use a normal 50mm lens on a 35mm reflex camera. So if I am moved by a scene and am seeing it the same way the camera would see it, there shouldn't be overwhelming technical problems. Of course, lighting could be difficult, but that's not always detrimental to a photograph. All I can say is I haven't been having a lot of technical troubles. Whether it has been luck or some sort of subjective technical correction, it is hard to say.

BACKPACKER: Do you bracket at all?

VALLE: On occasion, if it looks like there may be a lighting problem. In color film, exposure can make a big difference as to whether the picture will be successful or not.

BACKPACKER: Do you have other equipment besides the 50mm lens?

VALLE: I have a doubler that I sometimes use, heaven forbid.

BACKPACKER: Seems like anything you can use to get the image you want is okay.

VALLE: I'm not saying you shouldn't use other equipment. I just feel you

PHOTO: BOB SMITH

Peaks at the headwaters of Mono Creek, Sierra Nevada.
PHOTO: GARY VALLÉ

must use what you have to the best advantage. If I had a 28mm lens, say, I'd use it a lot. But you do learn your primary lens and get a feeling for its particular flavor. You learn to see in a particular perspective, and it is difficult to switch from, say, 18mm one moment to 500mm the next.

BACKPACKER: The perspective one has on his own work also changes. Are you still photographing in the style shown in these shots, which were done several years ago?

VALLE: I still find myself using the same photographic technique; whether the resulting style has changed or not is difficult to evaluate. I don't think you can wish a style upon yourself, saying "I'd like to take pictures like Bruce Davidson or Eliot Porter" or anyone else. And because I feel this way, it irks me when someone says my photographs look like someone else's. Style is too intertwined with the personality of the photographer for simplistic similarities to be important.

BACKPACKER: Your own personality seems to be highly influenced by science. You have a degree in mathematics, right?

VALLE: Yes, but I certainly don't want to characterize myself by that dry connotation. My interests are extensive and varied. They range from astronomy to biology, edible plants to geology. All have in common that they make a would-be naturalist's life a lot more meaningful and interesting. I have been backpacking, mountaineering, ski touring, and rock climbing for several years, primarily in the Sierra. I like to avoid well-worn trails and go cross-country wherever appropriate, many times searching topographic maps for that especially memorable route over "Knapsack Pass" into "Clyde's Crags." I have

climbed many Sierra peaks and outcroppings—some easy, some difficult—all interesting and rewarding. I enjoy ski touring immensely. It is the epitome of the cross-country wilderness experience—no trails, no signs, no people, just the terrain, snow, and you. My most memorable wilderness excursion to date has been a trans-Sierra ski tour a friend and I did during the early spring of 1973. Using light touring equipment, we skied from Bridgeport to Yosemite Valley, our route diagonaling across Yosemite National Park. Much of the tour was through the varied terrain of the Yosemite high country—its glaciated canyons, expansive meadows, and granite topography providing occasional challenges, yet constant and spectacular beauty.

Generally I find great satisfaction in working out the best possible solution to a given problem and its associated restraints. This is true whether the problem is one of discovering a complex mathematical relationship or climbing a difficult route on a Sierra dome. Both are problems of logic and of "routefinding." Perhaps this is why I find hang gliding so enjoyable and own a company that manufactures hang gliders.

BACKPACKER: That doesn't sound like a wilderness pursuit.

VALLE: Hang gliding is perhaps the most misunderstood and misrepresented contemporary recreational pursuit. Mountaineering and technical rock climbing have much in common with hang gliding. The former have great potential for injury; however, through proper instruction, responsible judgment, and use of good equipment, the dangers are minimized. So it is with hang gliding. It is hard to understand why certain individuals and organizations put

down hang gliding. I fly hang gliders from the summit of a mountain for the same reasons—and with the same rationale—that I climb to that summit. The air mass around the mountain is another dynamic wilderness to explore by using an appropriate tool, the hang glider.

BACKPACKER: Do your knowledge and interests interact strongly with photography?

VALLE: It makes my life more meaningful to have a grasp of the things that are going on around me. I feel like I am sharing something instead of looking in from the outside. Undeniably my scientific background must necessarily influence my photography. I believe it does so in the following manner: Science, it would seem, begins with an investigation of a supposed relationship and ends with the satisfaction that the supposed relationship does indeed exist. Likewise, my photography begins with the recognition of a sensed relationship and ends with the satisfaction that the relationship exists—and more—that its essence has been recorded on film. That the relationship is recognizable, recordable, and communicable is proof enough that, in fact, it exists. Interspersed between a recognized beginning and a specific end are always a multitude of newly discovered suppositions and, therefore, a multitude of possible beginnings and endings. Which path I choose is the enchantment of science and of photography.

BACKPACKER: Do you think you can use photography to answer questions about what is going on in nature?

VALLE: No. All it does actually is present another question, perhaps on another level. It is never an answer.

WILLIAM BAKE

A BACKPACKER Interview

BACKPACKER: How do you feel about style? What separates a professional photographer from an amateur?

BAKE: With practice and study, the professional learns to develop a way of approaching a subject that is his alone. Maybe we all go through stages of imitating other people. I think I did. But I've gotten so the main body of my work doesn't look like anybody else's, and it is consistent. Style also depends, of course, on what format you're using. There is a way of photographing with large cameras that is not as appropriate with 35mm, and vice versa. For example, 35mm could be used if you're trying to achieve an impressionistic, interpretive photo. That would be more difficult on 4 x 5 film, where precision and sharpness of focus are critical.

BACKPACKER: Which format do you prefer?

BAKE: 4 x 5. However, 35mm is the best all-around size for most people. I would not recommend that a photographer choose a large camera unless he has a very good reason for doing so. Thirty-five millimeter is less expensive and much more versatile than 2¼ x 2¼ and larger systems. I would use larger cameras, though, if a client seems to need the larger format. The Sierra Club calendar editors, for example, like to see 4 x 5. But a magazine like *National Geographic* doesn't need such a large image; they usually want 35mm. Part of the reason I like 4 x 5 is my personality. When it comes to photography, I'm a perfectionist. I like to be methodical and study what I'm going to shoot. That works best with large cameras. In contrast, I work very rapidly, just like everyone else, when I use 35mm.

BACKPACKER: You prefer a view camera, yet there are times when you use 35mm. Why?

BAKE: I choose the smaller formats—35mm and 2¼ x 2¼—when I must cover the subject in a limited time or when the subject itself is more appropriate to rapid, versatile work. And sometimes I shoot 35mm just for the freedom this format offers. You can't imagine what a joy it is to use a good 35mm until you've made nothing but large format photos for extended periods. In the rain I use only 2¼ or 35mm cameras. There's no way I can keep my 4 x 5 from getting wet.

BACKPACKER: You do a lot of shooting in the rain?

BAKE: Yes. Color is most saturated in wet weather. You get terrific, beautiful colors. Dull scenes are enlivened. So I go out then a lot. Of course, keeping my gear dry is of prime importance. I often use an umbrella. I keep the camera inside my poncho until I want a picture. Then I open the umbrella, take out the camera, wait for any condensation to evaporate and go to work. I suppose it looks rather silly for a backpacker to be carrying a black umbrella—I was once nicknamed Mary Poppins—but it works.

BACKPACKER: Did you take instruction in photography to learn your filtering techniques?

BAKE: My formal education wasn't in photography; it was in education. I've taught junior high, junior college and graduate school. Social sciences, history and audio-visual techniques. It's difficult to say how a person learns to relate to nature, but in my case I think the reason was that I was pretty much on my own during my younger years. I was in a place where I could walk. After school, instead of playing sports, I'd roam the fields. I picked up photography on my own, beginning in college with a camera given me by my grandfather. It was a Leica, model 6. Then I switched to a 2¼ x 2¼, and later I began working with 4 x 5. Now things have merged a bit, and I write, edit and sometimes do photography for the National Park Service Division of Publication. And, of course, I free lance.

BACKPACKER: Do you usually find story and book ideas in the photos you've already taken, or do you develop themes and then shoot for them?

BAKE: It could be done either way. For booklets, I have gone out to get photos after writing the text. But for an actual book, I find years of work are involved to do one the right way. After you see that you've got something unique in your work and you know it's comprehensive, you can start thinking in terms of a book, a really good book. And that's the way the photography evolved for *The Blue Ridge* book that I'm doing for The Viking Press.

BACKPACKER: How did you proceed?

BAKE: I suppose, like other photographers, I feel compelled to take pictures. I happen to live near the Blue Ridge Mountains, and my photos of them began to accumulate over seven or eight years. I realized I had excellent coverage of this range all the way from Georgia to Maryland, and I thought, well, what can I do? The obvious answer was to promote a book. This is not easy. The publisher has to be very certain that the book will make money. I had been communicating with Viking Press for about a year, and the okay finally came through last summer.

BACKPACKER: You began photographing for pleasure, and now you do it for publication. Has your technique changed at all? What are the differences?

BAKE: Some of the considerations are strictly technical. For publication, you generally must use transparency film instead of print film. And the professional must have reliable and versatile equipment that will work under all sorts of adverse weather conditions. When you are out shooting for pleasure, you shoot whatever you want. But for publication you try to cover the subject, either by making photos of the entire assigned area or by representing the high points. You must usually overshoot. I think amateurs would be astounded by the amount of film most professionals use.

Another consideration is how you handle your equipment. You may be able to get by with slightly blurred photos for projection but not for publication. You must know your limits of steadiness and not try to hand hold a camera at slower shutter speeds. You should be able to previsualize and to manipulate both your camera and lenses automatically, just as a carpenter knows his tools and what he can do with them.

BACKPACKER: Each individual learns those things for himself. They are the technical factors, and are relatively easy to learn with practice. What about the more subjective qualities?

BAKE: I'd say that the most important mark of the professional is his attitude. You must approach your work with dedication and a determination to do the very best you can with each photo. Beyond that, I'd say that a successful photographer must become very sensitive to the quality and intensity of light. I've gotten so that if even a cirrus cloud passes between me and the sun, I know it. You also learn to form a mental picture of the way certain kinds of light will look on the film you are using. You must previsualize the effects you want. Editors like photo submissions that show artistic proficiency. And this is the result of constant photography—of being involved in it over months and years. Dedication and commitment are also the marks of a pro. Still, I miss a lot more pictures than I get. Everybody does.

WILLIAM J. WEBER
The Hunter Turned Photographer

BACKPACKER: What do you think makes a good wildlife shot?

WEBER: Rather than just taking portraits of animals, you need to catch them doing things. Any activity that is part of an animal's normal life will make a good picture.

BACKPACKER: Do you get many good shots while merely walking along the trail?

WEBER: Trail walking is very productive for me. I always carry at least two cameras, sometimes three. That way I can take whatever comes up without fumbling to change lenses. Since my camera gear weighs a minimum of 22 pounds, it doesn't leave much room in a pack for sleeping bag and food. I find a good spot for base camp and walk out for day trips. One of the best days I ever had was in the mountains west of Kaycee, Wyoming. I was close enough to photograph 43 deer, including bucks, in one day. I also stalk such large mammals as antelope, bison and moose, the way a hunter does.

BACKPACKER: Aren't good wildlife photos often the result of a lot of drudgery: long waits in a cramped blind or in the rain?

WEBER: Wildlife photography does require lots of time and patience, but it usually isn't drudgery for me. It seems that there are always a lot of things going on.

BACKPACKER: Do you plan trips to photograph a specific subject?

WEBER: No. I pick an area for pictures because something, such as bighorn sheep, is there, but I don't really narrow my field of interest down to one subject. I might never see a sheep, but will get wildflowers, deer, rabbits, lichens, porcupines, aspen leaves and a host of other subjects. Every trip is worthwhile. Learning to see so many picture possibilities requires a degree of practice and concentration.

BACKPACKER: Do you have to use a lot of film to get a really fine photograph depicting an animal's normal life?

WEBER: Yes, I make quite a few exposures because most animals are moving. If I'm shooting scenery, flowers and other things that stay relatively still, most of the shots would be keepers. But if I'm shooting, say, a wild turkey as the sun rises, 10 or 15 good shots out of 36 would be about normal. If five of these were good enough to interest an editor, it would be great. And if I had one outstanding photograph, the roll would be a success for me.

BACKPACKER: You mentioned before that you carry two cameras, sometimes three. How are they fitted out?

WEBER: I carry one Leicaflex S-L with built-in meter and a 400mm lens for wildlife subjects. An identical body has a bellows with a 100mm lens. This setup allows me to focus anywhere from infinity to an area only a few inches away that's the size of a postage stamp. It works well for lichens, flowers, insects and so forth. Then I have a regular 50mm lens which is sometimes on a third camera body. In all of these I used Kodachrome II, though I now use the new 25 speed film.

BACKPACKER: You must have to use a tripod a lot, with such slow film.

WEBER: I don't usually unless I'm in a blind. When I'm walking I carry a walking staff that I use as a unipod. But I frequently rely on resting the camera against a tree or rock, whether using the 400mm or the 50mm lens.

"I remember the day I put my guns away."

Weber quit hunting in 1966 after he downed a four-point buck in Wyoming. As he stared at the dead animal, he could think only of how beautiful it had been moving through the trees and rocks. Now he shoots only with a camera.

Weber carried a Leicaflex S-L with a 400mm lens to capture a baby raccoon in a distant tree. A strobe was used for this photo to fill shadows and increase depth of field.
PHOTO: WILLIAM J. WEBER

the right shots? Like blinds or camouflage?

WEBER: I use blinds a great deal for birds. From songbirds to turkeys to egrets, I find I can get the best pictures that way. I have two blinds set up in rookeries here in Florida which I use during the spring nesting season. I also have a portable, homemade, lightweight blind that I can set up in the woods or on a flat-bottomed boat. For example, to get the pictures of cattle egrets, I went to a blind every day from March 15 to June 4. Sometimes I stayed six hours, and other times only 30 minutes until the light got bad. On several days the temperature in the blind was above 105 degrees, but it was worth the effort.

BACKPACKER: Do you hunt, too? How does that fit in with photography and veterinary work?

WEBER: As a kid I was brought up to hunt. It was a measure of skill and manhood to be able to find rabbits and pheasants and try to get more than your friends. Later I hunted big game, too. But after working seven years to become a veterinarian, my attitude gradually changed without my being aware of it. I think there is a contradiction in being a veterinarian and a hunter. This is apparent to children, even though I can justify my position to adults. But as I got older, I couldn't really justify it to myself. I remember the day I put my guns away. It was on the top of a small forested moun-

> "Wildlife photography has all the elements of the hunt-the stalk, the wait, the challenge of trying to outwit an animal-but the conclusion is more satisfying to me."

tain in Wyoming in 1966. I had just shot a four-point buck and was elated as I ran up to him. But as I looked down on him, all I could think of was how beautiful he had been as he moved around the rocks and through the trees. Now he was just a poor dead blob. I vowed then and there I would never kill another. I guess you can't spend 20 years of your life trying to save animals and then take a weekend off to destroy them. I have no bone to pick with people who hunt. It just isn't for me. Wildlife photography has all the challenge of the hunt with a more satisfying conclusion.

BACKPACKER: Do you ever do the reverse now—healing injured wild animals?

WEBER: Oh, yes. For years my veterinary hospital has been a drop-off point for injured and orphaned wild creatures that people find. We raise

them, heal them when we can and help them to adapt to the wild again. Right now on the back porch we have an owl with a bad wing, a cedar waxwing injured in the spring migration, five baby opossums, three mice, one quail and four flying squirrels. In the backyard are two deer we fixed up for the Florida Game and Fresh Water Fish Commission.

BACKPACKER: Do you take your family on camping and backpacking trips?

WEBER: Sure. Family camping has been a part of our life since my 20-year-old son John could barely walk. It has made us close and provided memories we will all cherish. Our experiences have taught us that all of us who enjoy the out-of-doors should develop a little tolerance toward one another, and judge each person as an individual, not by his equipment. ❧

MARTIN SCHWEITZER

He began taking photographs as an adjunct to backpacking. Before long, he was spending all the time he could on the trail.

BACKPACKER: Do you get as much thrill out of seeing a photograph as you did when you took it?

SCHWEITZER: I find that the photographs I enjoy, that I'm pleased with, do recall the experience of the

trip. I sense the kind of day it was and what happened on the trail. But something else happens. When I'm

backpacking, I may be tired, elated, wet with rain or terribly hot and dry. Then I see something I find quite lovely that I want to photograph, and in that moment everything I have experienced until then falls away. Later on, if the photograph is good, it does more than recall the experience of the trip. Suddenly I can see the scene for itself in a pure sense, isolated from all other sensations.

BACKPACKER: This is a concept of "centering." The act of taking a photo becomes a centering experience.

SCHWEITZER: Very much so. I feel I'm both behind the camera and in front of it. I'm experiencing the nature of what is around me: everything on Earth, all about me, constantly changing, shifting. The light that will never again be the same. The way things are together purely by accident in the wilderness. This to me is very spiritual and exciting. When I photograph, I do indeed center. I concentrate in such a way that everything becomes silent. Suddenly I'm two inches from a brook, photographing, but I don't hear the water. I get very excited when I do that.

BACKPACKER: One would think, looking at your pictures, that you spend a great deal of time finding the right location, setting up and waiting for the right moment to take a picture. Is that true?

SCHWEITZER: No, it's not. Photography is not a thinking process for me at all. It's very spontaneous and joyous. When I'm walking and enjoying something in the wilderness, I don't plan ahead. I see something and just shoot. I hate to use the word "instinctual," but it is a very spontaneous reaction. And I have no patience for technical matters. I don't take notes. I have a 55mm macro lens, a short extension tube and a 105mm lens. That's the extent of my equipment. I like close-ups, the feeling of intimacy, a small segment. Somehow that detail—if it works properly—reveals a sense of the whole. I usually take only one exposure of a scene. I don't bracket. Each image to me is unique, a new experience.

BACKPACKER: What drew you into photography?

SCHWEITZER: I was in graduate school at the University of Chicago, studying the culture and philosophy of India, and had intentions of doing anthropological research in Bengal. In my second graduate year, 13 years ago, I visited California. My friends took me to Yosemite Valley, which I had no concept of. When I entered the valley in late September, it was an unbelievable experience. The famous view seemed to be projected on an invisible screen. It was so mysterious, far beyond my fantasies of wilderness. At the same time it seemed to connect with thoughts and feelings of an earlier time in my life. As a boy growing up in Brooklyn, I read books on nature prior to experiencing true wilderness. I remember a book on the national parks and a longing to be outdoors in nature.

BACKPACKER: Had you been backpacking before that trip to California?

SCHWEITZER: Until then I was not particularly sports minded. The Yosemite trip was my first hike, with or without a pack. The memory of those few days stayed with me during my next graduate year at Chicago, and I knew I would return to California and those mountains. I did return the following September to go backpacking, and a year after that I moved to California. But I didn't expect to leave the academic life for good.

BACKPACKER: Were you taking pictures then?

SCHWEITZER: Before that time I never thought I'd be involved in photography. When I was beginning to backpack, a friend loaned me his Argus C-3, and I started taking pictures without any thought to the future. It was just an adjunct to backpacking. By 1968 it became more than an adjunct; it was a way to fix my experiences—to relive the beauty of the trail, time and time again.

BACKPACKER: When did you buy your own camera?

SCHWEITZER: In 1967. It was a Nikkormat. By 1968 I was backpacking more extensively and photographing more intensively. There was a conflict between the time I had to spend at my job and what I really wanted to do.

BACKPACKER: You moved positively toward photography, rather than negatively away from a job?

SCHWEITZER: Right. It was a move closer to my inner expression. I had to decide it was worth the chance to let my inner flow reveal itself, rather than to never have the opportunity to explore and express.

BACKPACKER: Do you feel your study of Indian culture had anything to do with your outlook today?

SCHWEITZER: Yes. The Indian writings belong to my subconscious. I derived my philosophy by way of the New England transcendentalists, Emerson and Thoreau, and the poetry of Walt Whitman. Later, in college, I came to the source of their thinking in terms of, most particularly, Vedantic thought—concepts postulating that the world is illusion and that beyond the illusion is an ultimate reality. Questions about the root meaning of all we experience. I responded that that which is ultimately real in the microcosm is the same reality in a larger sense.

I'm constantly aware of change. When I feel a calmness and rapport with what I'm photographing, maybe I'm persuading myself that I'm "seeing" a little beyond all the changes. I also reflect on the fact that I'm as much a product of the natural world as the wildflowers on the bank of a Sierra stream. The animate and inanimate blend together. And I find that the camera is definitely an extension of myself.

BACKPACKER: Do your friends get in the way when you are photographing? Or do you get in the way of them?

SCHWEITZER: Sometimes I wonder whether I get in their way when I suddenly slow down, and whether they're just being courteous when they wait for me. But when they've learned my habits, they disappear and we meet farther along the trail. This means that when I photograph I am alone about 90 percent of the time. It's the nature of the process, to pause and

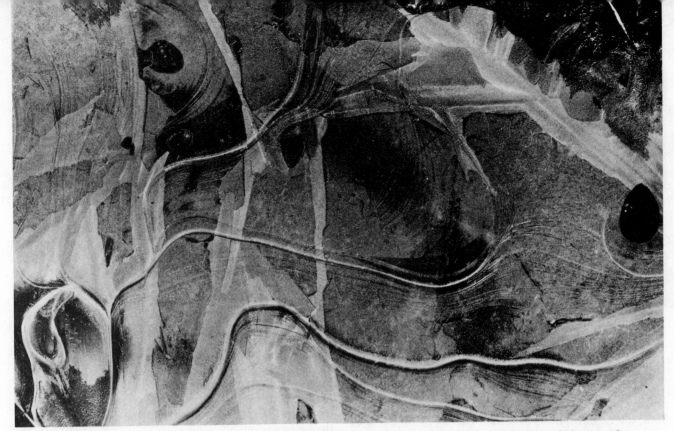

Close-up of ice in a stream taken in Mount Lassen Volcanic Park in Northern California. Taken with Nikkormat 35mm using a macro lens (55mm) and Panatomic-X film, f.8 at 125/sec.
PHOTO: MARTIN SCHWEITZER

experience for myself.

BACKPACKER: That seems to be the nature of your pictures, as well: a very personal, private experience. And a powerful one.

SCHWEITZER: Yes. For me, photography is at once spontaneous and intimate. Much of my work is quite detailed and close up, but the landscape photographs are also a reflection of my way of seeing and experiencing the world. I believe that photography really is as much psychology as art. After returning from the backcountry, the projected image lets me relive what is initially a private experience, tempered by mood and place. Later, through good fortune, some photographs may be published, and the images then are experienced by thousands of people I have never met. To have them share my moments of meditation and joy is a beautiful realization for me. ►

IRA SPRING

America's foremost mountain book
photographer

BACKPACKER: You make your living from the mountains and photography. Have these interests been primary all your life?

SPRING: I grew up in a small logging town, Shelton, Washington. From our window my twin brother Bob and I could look right over into the Olympic Mountains. It was just a morning thing we did when we got up—we went to the window to see if the mountains were up, too. At the same time, 1930, it was Eastman Kodak's fiftieth anniversary, and they gave every 12-year-old kid in the country a Brownie box camera. Right from the start, mountains and hiking and pictures just went together.

BACKPACKER: When you decided to make careers of photography, did you have to take part-time jobs outside the field in order to survive?

SPRING: Oh, yeah. I worked in a pulp mill. Bob worked

297

Ira Spring in the Glacier Peak Wilderness Area.
PHOTO: BOB AND IRA SPRING

at the power company until we saved up enough money. Then we were in the U.S. Army three or four years during the war and actually came out of that a few dollars ahead. Well, the GI Bill sent us to school, and we chose a school of photography in New York. Then we started free-lancing.

BACKPACKER: Starting right in with outdoor shooting?

SPRING: One of the things we began with was mountain climbing and glaciers. We went to New York editors and showed them our work, and it was different enough from what they had that they grabbed it. It got us into . . . well, just about all of the national magazines of that era. *Saturday Evening Post*—we had a lot of climbing stories in that—and *Liberty.* I think we sold to everything but *Life.* We never got in that, but we did get in the backdoor through a lot of ads that used our mountain-climbing pictures. So we got started right off the bat. It didn't make us rich, that's for sure. For the first five years we didn't have to pay income tax. The sixth year we had to pay a little bit. We didn't know whether to be sad or celebrate.

BACKPACKER: Nevertheless, you make it sound easy.

SPRING: Unfortunately, young people have a tendency to think that they can just hop into the business of photography. To start in on photography as a living? I don't recommend it. Selling pictures, that's the pitfall, and the fact is that it may be five years before you can pay your expenses, let alone make enough to eat. Even granola, you know, is pretty darned expensive.

BACKPACKER: The credit lines always say, "Bob and Ira Spring." How has the work evolved between you two?

SPRING: Well, it is an evolution, because during the first few years we actually went out and did stories together. You don't need two photographers to do a story, but we kept our name "Bob and Ira." We do work together on the selling. My interest has always been hiking and climbing. As time went on, Bob's interest proved to be tourism. He's done a lot of photography that's used in travel promotion by airlines.

BACKPACKER: Bob's big interest is Alaska, isn't it? He has several books on that state.

SPRING: That's right. He doesn't hike there, but he's thrilled with the Alaska scenery he sees from some of those out-of-

the-way airplane landings and resorts out in the tules. I don't think he has time to go hiking.

BACKPACKER: But you still hike.

SPRING: Yes, that's me. Bob's the moneymaker. I'd rather go hiking any day.

BACKPACKER: That's very clear from the hiking guides you've illustrated. Are the people in those pictures your family?

SPRING: Quite often. At first we felt we needed a person to show the size. Most of our glacier pictures still have people in them.

BACKPACKER: Do the climbers just happen to be there?

SPRING: No, it takes so much time to get a good picture that you go out there and either find the pictures or find the mountain. You're not going to succeed in both. So I got my own group together for photography. They know they're not going to get to do the greatest climbing of the year.

BACKPACKER: How about on the trail: do you pose them or get ahead and wait for them to come along?

SPRING: Well, this is a problem because it's got to look casual. It can't look stiff and posed. And I'm not that good at posing people. If you're going to have a person in the picture, it's got to be part of the composition, not only part of the picture. I've seen many pictures where a photographer has placed a person in the center without any rhyme or reason.

BACKPACKER: So you tell them where to stand and . . .

SPRING: And they go back and get in the right spot for me and hike along there again, and again. Taking it in color and black and white I've got to do it four or five times to get it casual.

BACKPACKER: Some of your shots ended up in the hiking guide series published by The Mountaineers of Seattle. What's the history of those pictures?

SPRING: They're copies from the hiking books of Europe. The Europeans had had them for years. *100 Hikes in Western Washington* was the first U.S. guide. We felt that maybe we could sell 5,000 of those in a year or two, and do you know, those 5,000 lasted exactly three weeks. The Mountaineers reprinted another 5,000, and by September the doggone thing had to be reprinted again for the Christmas trade—a total of 15,000 books the first year.

BACKPACKER: You sound as if you were very surprised.

SPRING: We were tremendously surprised. And we saw the light: good heavens, 15,000! What was it going to do to those 100 trails? And it did. So we immediately evolved the idea of publishing a more thorough book and covering the trails in all of western Washington.

BACKPACKER: As photographer and trail researcher, what was your technique while preparing the guides?

SPRING: I got a pick-up camper. My family and I would drive to the trailhead and park there overnight; then we'd hit the trail early in the morning. It was not uncommon to walk six or seven miles and find that people who had hiked in the day before were having breakfast or were still in their sacks. We would photograph at our destination for an hour or two, then turn around and go back to the camper, move the camper to its next trailhead and be ready for the next morning. We had two pairs of hiking shoes so that they'd dry out between trips. Some of the trips were backpacks. After all, this is our fun. It gives me a bad feeling to hike to a gorgeous place and be able to spend only an hour or two there.

BACKPACKER: You must have had some problems with the weather not cooperating, especially the Cascades weather. Did you often wait for conditions to change?

SPRING: To do the *100 Hikes* book, I couldn't afford that. If the weather was bad, the photographs were taken anyway. They aren't all good pictures. But if it was really bad, it may have improved the pictures. I tried to get a scenic shot that would display what we were writing about for each hike. But it was only a chance thing when I had to use one with fog.

BACKPACKER: Merely by publishing guidebooks you're encouraging people to use the mountains. This is important, as your co-author Harvey Manning says, because we have to publish information about the wilderness or it will perish. But it's very clear now that because of guidebooks and the great explosion of backpackers a lot of the trails are unbelievably overcrowded. There ought to be a lesson in this.

SPRING: *100 Hikes* just happened to come out as the hiking explosion was gaining momentum. Guidebooks are not responsible for that explosion. Montana and Idaho have never had guidebooks; Wyoming has had one for 20 years. Yet, hiking has been accelerating in all three states at the same rate as in Washington. Guidebooks have played their part, but they also have the best potential to educate and direct hikers. Our recent books are loaded with environmental messages and pleas for the individual to get involved in saving the out-of-doors. I am proud of any part I may have played. At long last the hiker is being heard, and if there are enough voices, we may stop the destruction of our trail country. I estimate there are about 200,000 hikers and backpackers in western Washington. If they would all write one letter a year we would have a tremendous impact.

All right, *100 Hikes* was a mistake because it picked only a few places and hikers congregated there. Before it could be turned off, almost 50,000 books were printed. [*100 Hikes in Western Washington* is permanently out of print. Ed.] Still, I'm not going to apologize for it because the error was unintentional. But even among The Mountaineers' membership there was dissension as to whether it was going to do all that much harm and whether we should keep publishing it.

Now, in *101 Hikes in the North Cascades*, *102 Hikes in the Alpine Lakes, South Cascades, and Olympics*, and *50 Hikes in Mt. Rainier National Park*, we've gone to the extremes of naming every single trail we could find. Two hundred fifty-three trails are described in detail. And in the back of the books there are another 250 listed as "more hikes."

BACKPACKER: Has this attempt to spread knowledge of the lesser-known trails relieved overall congestion?

SPRING: I don't know, but we are hearing criticism from people who used to have their own private trails that there are other people on them now.

BACKPACKER: Do you think that's valid criticism?

SPRING: No. These 200,000 people must go somewhere. Just what would a person recommend doing with 200,000 backpackers—limiting them to so many a weekend? I'm strictly opposed to that because I think backpacking's a way of life that should be encouraged, not destroyed by limiting the number of participants.

BACKPACKER: What about area permits to allow only so many people in each campsite or on each trail?

SPRING: Those would have the same effect. People need somewhere to go. The books attempt to disperse people everywhere on the trails. But solitude, if you want it, is still possible in off-trail ramblings and places without the tremendous attraction of an alpine lake. That's where your crowding is.

BACKPACKER: We've talked about restrictions; we've talked about permits; we've talked about dispersion. Still, the water-side camp areas are overrun. Is there a solution?

SPRING: I, for one, believe that what is spoiling the area is not necessarily the number of people. What is beating it to death is probably camping and horse use. I suspect we could have twice as many people at, say, Image Lake if there weren't any camping allowed there. The Forest Service wouldn't have to eliminate horse riders, just the horses: make the riders park their horses a half-mile, better yet a mile, away in a less fragile spot. The riders ought to be able to stagger that far. Then everyone could hike in to watch the sunset and participate in the scenic spot— twice as many people as now without damaging the terrain. Good old Mother Earth has to come first, but there are ways to accommodate more backpackers without damaging her.

BACKPACKER: That would mean that people would have to lose some of the joy of backpacking—the joy of being able to relax and sleep in camp next to the stream and the view.

SPRING: Well, I'd rather give the people a chance to go— everyone who wants to.

Frankly, I think there should be areas that will accommodate crowds of hikers. If a permit system is used to force people to disperse, there will be fewer people at any one place because the system will push bodies into every nook

Vicky Spring has a visit from the landlord. This inquisitive mountain goat looked over the photographer's camp, which was beside the Blue Glacier on Mt. Olympus. During the night, the goat returned and stumbled over the tent lines.

PHOTO: BOB AND IRA SPRING

and cranny. This has already happened at Mount Rainier. Once it was easy to find solitude in the park, but the camping permit system dispersed people so thoroughly there is no longer any solitude left. If we turn to the permit system for climbers, even the Willis Wall will lose its solitude.

BACKPACKER: A moment ago we were speaking of finding solitude by going off the trail. It's important that the hikers who bushwhack don't leave a personal trail behind them or any sign of their camps.

SPRING: Definitely. One of the joys of going off-trail is finding a place to camp where you believe nobody else has camped before. And you'd better be darn sure that after you've left the next person thinks he's the first one to camp there, too.

BACKPACKER: Since you grew up in timber territory, your conservationist viewpoint might seem unusual to some people.

SPRING: I don't think a conservationist is born; he grows into it. A person just starting out accepts the world as he sees it. He doesn't know what it was like when his parents were young. He doesn't know there were 1,000 more miles of trail the year before. It takes a few years of visiting different areas before he looks back and finds one of his trails has gone. Then suddenly he begins to realize that he's got to speak out.

BACKPACKER: Speaking of growth, there's a growth of style in photography. Other than the mountaineering and guide-book-type shots, what's your personal style now?

SPRING: What turns me on mostly is that great big scene, a gorgeous calendar shot, the photograph that makes you want to go look at the spot yourself. I want to take pictures that I can feel are luring some of the people who see them.

BACKPACKER: Like the ones in your book *North Cascades National Park?*

SPRING: Right. I call them breathtaking. They make you want to stop and stare.

BACKPACKER: What kind of equipment do you use for that kind of shot?

SPRING: The majority of our markets want large film, 4 x 5 or larger. We have one client that has us use an 8 x 20 inch camera.

BACKPACKER: That must weigh . . .

SPRING: About 100 pounds. It's Kodak's Colorama camera. But I also use 2¼ x 3¼ because I need a decent sized telephoto lens with reasonable depth of field for animals, and a close-up lens for flowers. My wife, Pat, uses a 35mm, which once in a while I use, too.

BACKPACKER: Many of the shots in your flower book were taken with that, right?

SPRING: That's right. Close to half of them were taken by Pat with the 35.

BACKPACKER: Do you carry all these cameras with you when you go out shooting?

SPRING: If I'm going on a hike, I take the 4 x 5 because it's so much simpler to print and develop large film. I get better results. If I know I'm going to take close-ups of flowers and other small things, I take the small camera, as well. Or maybe just the small camera because each one weighs about 20 pounds.

BACKPACKER: Your pack must get very heavy. Already it's up to 20 pounds with only one camera.

SPRING: I keep it as light as I can, so long as I have plenty of film. My pack used to be always 50 or 60 pounds, but now anytime I go over 50 pounds I get a sore back, and that takes away all the fun. So I keep cutting down on all the essentials until they become nonessentials. Like food. This is limiting: during the past few years I've been lucky to have a trip when I was out more than three or four nights in a row. I'm not all that much on starving myself.

BACKPACKER: Do you travel to certain places only for specific reasons?

SPRING: Because I have to make a living at photography, I must go where I anticipate a need for pictures. Some places excite me no end; some leave me rather uninspired. We don't have the time to give justice to some of the places. That's my only gripe about my job. Otherwise it's not a job but a perpetual vacation.

BACKPACKER: Yet it's obvious that in order to get some of your very nice scenic shots you've had to wait around and take many different exposures. Do you think that having the time and film to bracket a lot takes the creativity out of photography?

SPRING: Oh, no. That makes it much more enjoyable. And the difference between being a professional and an amateur is how many pictures you're willing to throw away. One of the problems with amateurs is they want to show everything; every shot has some meaning to them. But favorite pictures seldom make it for other people.

BACKPACKER: Do you do all your scenic shooting while backpacking in wild areas?

SPRING: Heavens, no. I shoot often from roads. Quite a few people talk about the wilderness—the opposition, that is. They talk about the minute minority who get to see some of the most spectacular scenery in the country because there's no road to it. Hogwash! You can drive to the most beautiful places in the United States. If we could get pictures for calendars while backpacking, we would. But no, it's things like Mount Shuksen and the Tetons that you invariably see in calendars, taken right from the road.

It's not that photographers are lazy. They return from trips in ecstasy over other views they got while backpacking, because they put themselves into it. Look at the Banff-Jasper Highway, where there's one gorgeous view after another. You whiz along there at 60 miles an hour, and you get jaded. Now, if there were no road and you were walking and if those views slowly appeared, grew on you and then disappeared behind you, you would have day after day excitement.

BACKPACKER: It sounds like you'd rather backpack than take pictures.

SPRING: I have to admit that backpacking's first and the pictures, really, just support a bad habit. But that's not everything. I need to have more to interest me than just covering the miles. Certainly, I get a lot more out of hiking because I have photography.

GALEN ROWELL

The art of ''grab'' shooting

BACKPACKER: You're known as both a photographer and a climber, and you've done some really exciting things.

You must have developed a lot of special techniques for taking pictures when you're climbing. For instance, I'm sure you use a wide-angle lens.

ROWELL: I certainly use that a lot, and a 24mm lens stays on my camera as a normal lens. I keep it there until I need to change it. I do take other lenses. On a typical rock climb or light mountain trip or ski tour, I'll also take my very compact 45mm lens and a 105mm lens.

BP: What do you use the 105 for?

ROWELL: Scenery that needs to be moved closer—mountains, clouds, wildlife. But for climbing, I find there's very rarely a situation when I can get a good picture with the 105. Usually there's some sort of foreground in the climbing pictures that becomes hopelessly blurred. Once in a while it's absolutely a straight shot from me to the leader, and then the telephoto works just fine, but those situations are few and far between.

BP: I imagine with the grade of climbing that you're doing, you don't really have much opportunity to make special arrangements to take pictures.

ROWELL: Most of the time I don't; I usually don't set up pictures, other than maybe hoping I'll be somewhere at the right time of day and get myself into the right position. I don't use any complex set-ups to get people in the right places. I wait for them to create the scene and then try to capture the moment. I don't try to achieve that moment.

BP: It must be kind of disconcerting to a guy who's leading a new route to have you say, "Now, wait a minute . . . hold it." How do you manage to get shots when you're belaying?

ROWELL: Well, I'm able to hold my Nikkormat in my thumb and first two fingers. When I'm using a wide-angle lens, focusing is unnecessary once the subject is six or seven feet away. The rope is in the palm of my camera hand, and the camera and my arm are tight across my chest. I can see the leader and obviously have a moment's forewarning for any fall. With the camera on a neck loop, I can let go of it and have the rope held across my chest in a micro-second.

BP: How do you keep your camera from smashing against the wall while you're climbing?

ROWELL: First of all, I very rarely climb with the camera out of the pack, and I would never try climbing a crack or a chimney carrying the camera unless I had it inside a pack. When it *is* out, I put it down my back. I keep it in a good hard case so even if it does bang against the wall, it doesn't get damaged.

One thing I could say about climbing photography is that I've done it for two reasons. For something like the *Geographic* assignment, they wanted every possible bit of information that I could get on film. But when I'm climbing for myself, usually I'll take pictures for aesthetic reasons. If it's a climb I've done before, it's possible that I could climb without taking a single frame if nothing impressed me. If I'm doing a first ascent, I'll be more like I was on the *Geographic* climb and take informational pictures to have a record. However, I've found that I've never taken a photo for purely informational reasons which later satisfied my aesthetic values.

BP: What about lenses?

ROWELL: The lenses I carry depend on what I think I might encounter in the place I'm going.

BP: But in your car, you always take the three—the 24, 45 and 105?

ROWELL: At a minimum, yes. And on any kind of long trip in my car, more than overnight, I usually have a long lens—200mm, 300 or 500. Sometimes I'll go three or four trips without using it, but every time I leave it out, I need it.

BP: I'd like to talk about your climbing background. How did you get started with that?

ROWELL: Okay. My mountaineering background began with my mother, who participated in Sierra first ascents in the 1920s, became a concert musician with a classical trio that had its own radio program on NBC for more than a decade, and even climbed the ledge trail to play at the Glacier Point Hotel. Today, at 73 she's a professor of music at three colleges. We lived in a Sierra Club hotbed. I had a paper route that went by the homes of Dave Brower, Charlotte Mauk, Cicely Cristy and Richard Leonard, who were all active in the administration of the club. Two blocks from home was Pinnacle Rock, one of the Berkeley practice rocks where technical skills were developed for the first Yosemite climbs using ropes and pitons. I went on several Sierra Club pack trips with my family and I learned the rudiments of climbing. I told myself, though, I would never have much use for all that ''rock engineering'' stuff. The mountains meant more to me than just a testing ground of strength and skill. My first climb in Yosemite, in 1957, was preceded by a 60-mile walk from the eastern side of the Sierra.

BP: Was that when you started climbing the big walls?

ROWELL: No, I began to climb extensively in Yosemite in 1962. Later in the year I worked in a gas station, got married and in 1963 started my own auto repair and parts business, a veritable Horatio Alger of the grease, with $500

Galen Rowell on top of 14,375-foot Mount Williamson in the Sierra.

and a box of wrenches. Twenty-three years old.

BP: How did you get from there into journalism?

ROWELL: Until 1968, I never wrote anything for publication. Then a couple of stories of climbs were published in *Summit,* and my life began to change. Clubs approached me as a speaker. Friends advised me to take a camera on climbs. Other friends asked me to draft letters about mutual causes. I wrote more articles, and they were rarely turned down. A few photos began to sell to other places besides mountain periodicals. I had contact with the media and learned how the press operated, mostly because of climbs with Warren Harding. For Warren, after the Wall of the Early Morning Light, it was almost impossible to keep his name out of the news. He was 50 miles away in a cabin when *Sports Illustrated* descended on Yosemite for an interview, but they found him. A couple of papers called on me as a "mountaineering expert." I did a color photo essay and story for the Sunday *San Francisco Chronicle/Examiner.* I was criticized recently in a mountain periodical for spreading the word about mountain climbing.

BP: But you *are* spreading the word, of course. How do you view the relationship between the public image of climbing and your place as a spokesman?

ROWELL: Climbing's image has a large effect on the way climbers behave and the future of the sport. Already, the tight clique of a decade ago has been replaced by an amorphous group of newcomers. I'm in no way saying that the old guys were superior, but the scene was defini-

tely better. Not because the individuals were better people, but because everyone knew each other and there was a common bond. You could actually camp in Yosemite's Camp 4, for instance, and not expect to be ripped off for ropes, tents and sleeping bags. You never had situations where guys went on multi-day climbs without knowing each other's last names—something that's happened more than once in recent years. With so many mountaineers, and so much diffuseness, there's a need for accurate information. I'm constantly accused of being part of the problem because my writings and photographs have been in the public eye. But I never write an article without weighing its positive effects versus negative ones. I always try to gear toward an ethic or a philosophy that will unite people toward a better approach to the wilderness.

BP: How does that square with your big-wall days, which are obviously not yet over, and the fact that credit lines for some of your articles trumpet your 100-plus first ascents? Didn't you say you began by not liking "rock engineering?"

ROWELL: You're right, but I had an image shift rather than an ideological one. In 1957 I reasoned that climbing with "all that hardware" made one responsive not to the wild environment but to one's man-made gear. That was what I was trying to escape in the mountains. I wanted to orient myself toward natural things, not toward some gadgets I'd introduced, or else I would have stayed in the city working on cars all my life. But soon I realized that rock climbing, to paraphrase Bonatti, is raw adventure accomplished with a few classic tools. It's a fragile concept—one whose results often are destructive to the essence of the sport. I still find climbing a new route very satisfying, but I've never thought of it as conquering a virgin wall. It's really like the ant contemplating the rear of an elephant. Just because some puny humans sneak through nature's defenses doesn't mean the mountain is changed. If anyone is subjugated, it's the climbers, who've become submissive to the whims and fancies of the mountain until they're out of reach of its dangers. If a mountain is ever "conquered," it will be by changing the mountain, not by men climbing it.

BP: Other climbers you know must envy your making a living from doing what you love—climbing and being in the wilderness.

ROWELL: I'm not sure that's true. I meet a lot of climbers who think that by selling your experiences instead of savoring them individually and personally, you lose them. So I try to climb with light equipment in order to have the strongest possible experiences, as well as recording them on film. In other words, I try to let the writing and photographing interfere as little as possible with my mountaineering.

BP: Do you agree that recording takes away from the mountain experience?

ROWELL: Some of it I can see as just jealousy. Because I've noticed that the same people who complain bitterly about commercial enterprises having to do with climbing will jump at the possibility of making money the second they hear about a big enterprise in the mountains. On the other hand, I've certainly heard some very legitimate complaints. One of them came from a climber who frankly hates to climb with a photographer. I always thought that he was just stubborn or backward. Talking to him, I learned that he had an interesting objection to what I call informational photographs. His climbing is sort of a philosophy and a way of life in which he finds his consciousness expanded through intense action. Your perception is at the very highest during a moment of crisis, and you find your life the most precious of all during that kind of moment. The scenes that occur during such action get stamped in this climber's memory very firmly. He wishes to remember his experiences in terms of those moments imprinted in his mind, not by what his partner might have captured on film. I see that as a very valid critique.

BP: Ed Cooper says that when he quit climbing and turned to photography exclusively ("from the vertical wall to the horizontal valley," as he puts it), he found very much the same kind of heightened experience in photography that he did in this intense perception you're talking about. What do you think about that?

ROWELL: I wouldn't deny that heightened experience, but I think it's quite different. The experience that comes from putting your whole life on the line is quite a different thing from what a photographer gets from knowing that he's going to take a great picture, or from seeing something unusual. In some ways, they're similar, but in more ways, they're very different.

BP: You're having both those experiences these days, I presume. Which is the most important to you, your climbing career or your photography career?

ROWELL: They're both important in different ways, but if I were to choose between the two, I think I would put wilderness activities first. If I had to give up one or the other, I would not want in any way to give up my wilderness trips. 🖎

ED COOPER
His Trips, His Climbs, His Photographs

Backpacker: When you go out to take pictures do you have an idea of getting any particular kind of photograph?

Cooper: Yes. When I go on a trip, usually I have some photographs in mind. Sunrise on a particular mountain, or maybe the long shadows and erosion patterns on a desert. Certain shots I'll spend a good deal of time looking for. I'll be driving around, sightseeing, and I'll see something and think to myself, that will make a good picture but not right now. About four in the afternoon will be the best lighting. Or 10 o'clock in the morning. Occasionally, I'll find something good right away. Then of course I'll shoot it.

BP: Sometimes you'll camp in a place just to be there because of the shots you want, right?

Cooper: Yes. Now take Sahale Peak in the North Cascades. I went up there partially just for the aesthetic experience, knowing that with good weather I would enjoy being there. I wouldn't be under any pressure and I'd be by myself and I could just sit there and look at the sunset and watch the sunrise and during the night watch the stars.

But in addition to that I knew that I would get good shots from up there. I'd climbed the peak before, so I knew what to expect. Once before when near Mount Erie I could see there was going to be a very spectacular sunset: it was going to be hazy. You can shoot straight into the sun under that condition and the sun will appear as a circle; and it won't be too bright and fog your lenses. Since I could see it was going

to be a good sunset this time, I went up and waited, and when the sun got into the position I liked, I took a series of shots.

BP: What kind of equipment did you take?

Cooper: I took my 4 x 5 view camera and my usual amount of photo gear — small tripod, about 15 film holders, extra film, three lenses, exposure meter, filters.

BP: Do you load film when you're out in the backcountry?

Cooper: Yes. I have a changing bag so that when I use up what's in the film holders, I can load them up again.

BP: What kind of lenses did you take?

Cooper: A wide angle, a normal and a two-times normal. It would be the equivalent to a 100mm, a 50mm and a 35mm for a 35mm camera.

BP: What kind of a view

camera do you use?

Cooper: An old beat up thing. Several times I've looked around to buy a new one but I can't find any that

PHOTO: ED COOPER

Lenticular cloud cap over Alaska's Mt. McKinley, the highest peak in North America.
PHOTO: ED COOPER

does what this one does for me. The Linhof is too heavy. I couldn't find a new one that's as light as mine. It was in terrible shape. Eventually, I just spent a whole day fixing it up myself. I'm still using it.

BP: How much film do you use?

Cooper: It varies. but on a good day I'll go through 100 sheets of 4 x 5 color film, which costs in the neighborhood of $120, including processing.

BP: So it's pretty expensive if you're on a two- or three-week trip?

Cooper: Right. When I

was out this spring for two months in California, Oregon and the Southwest, I went through about 3,500 sheets of film, plus 60 to 70 rolls of 2¼ film. Of course I didn't average nearly 100 a day. Some of that time was traveling: some was bad weather. Then too, when I go to a new area, I'm not really oriented and it takes me a while to figure out where the best views are.

BP: But on any one backpacking trip, how much film do you use?

Cooper: Well, let's see, on my trip to Mount Sahale I spent two nights out—one

night down lower and then the second night on the summit. I'd planned to spend only one night, but the weather was good. So, it was a three-day trip. And I shot somewhat over 100 sheets of 4 x 5. I always take reserve film along, and this particular time I used it.

I take more film now than I used to. I learned by experience that shooting more film is more economical because I'll get a greater number of usable pictures. If you only take one or two exposures. and they're off, you lose it. But I'll shoot 10 exposures or more so that I'm sure of get-

ting several different pictures. As my markets expand. I have use for all the good pictures I can shoot. It pays me to shoot more, even though it's more expensive initially.

BP: How heavy is the film?

Cooper: I buy 4 x 5 film in 50-sheet boxes which weigh much less than five 10-sheet boxes. On an overnight trip I take two 50-sheet boxes. plus what's loaded in the film holders. which is usually an additional 30. If it's a three- or four-day trip, I'll take correspondingly more. It depends on the trip. I plan each one. I figure out how hard it's going to be. how good shape

I'm in. how much I can carry. how much vertical gain there is. how much photo gear I want to take. I also consider things like. will I be taking pictures of people up there. will I be taking pictures of animals or is it just going to be scenery? I'll take only a 4 x 5. or maybe just a 2¼ and a 35. or any combination of them. depending on what I think I'm going to run into.

BP: Do you take your 35mm for people?

Cooper: Yes. 35mm or 2¼.

BP: How about animals?

Cooper: I usually prefer the 35. I've got a zoom lens for it. It's the lightest equipment and that's the most convenient for animals. I take along the standard lens plus an 85-210 zoom. With the 35 I'll also shoot scenery. I use it for a lot of closeups. or just details – grass. mushrooms. Things that are hard to get with a larger camera.

BP: What's the longest you might stay out on a trip with a pack?

Cooper: My longest trip this past summer was three nights. I bivouacked. I didn't have a tent or a sleeping bag. I just lay down in my parka and an elephant foot. Also. I had a nylon shell that I could put over me to keep the wind off.

BP: Is it also waterproof?

Cooper: No. I'm what you might say out of luck if it rains.

BP: What about your camera equipment?

Cooper: I carry one poncho. If I do get caught by rain. I'll cover my equipment with the poncho. Everything else gets wet but not the equipment. But I've been caught out in bad weather only twice in the last four years. I'm very careful about the weather.

BP: For you. is backpacking a means to an end?

Cooper: Partly. I've got to come away with good pictures. Sure. I enjoy the aesthetic experience of backpacking and being out there. But I've also got to pay attention to the best times for photos. which generally are sunrises and sunsets. It's then I have to be active.

There is no time for campfires. In the morning. I'm busy shooting right through sunrise and there's no time for cooking. When I'm through shooting. I'm too tired and it's dark and I have to change film to get ready for the morning. So there's just no time for the usual sort of camping thing. It's a lot more convenient for me to take along food I can eat cold. I'd rather have a hot meal. But then, I'm glad that I am able to be out there. Other people are stuck working in offices.

BP: What kind of food do you take along?

Cooper: A bacon bar. nuts. candy bars. rye-krisp-type crackers. maybe a can of tuna fish or sardines. cheese. sometimes beef jerky.

BP: You don't take a stove?

Cooper: No. I take only a spoon and a knife. And a can opener.

BP: What kind of thing do you enjoy shooting the most?

Cooper: There's no one particular thing I enjoy more than anything else. I like variety: I like being outdoors. I like looking for the best shot and then taking it. I also like shooting buildings. such as the old Victorian ones in Fort Townsend and the ones in Olympia. the Washington State capital. I've taken a lot of telephoto shots of Mount Rainier from Seattle. showing the space needle and First National Bank Building. and pictures of Seattle at night. They are a little more touristy or a little more commercial. But I enjoy that. too. as long as I'm outdoors.

Of course. when I'm taking a picture. it's an aesthetic satisfaction. I like the stimulation of looking around for the best shot and then being there for about half an hour. I set up the camera and maybe I'll wait for the sun to get in a certain position. Finally I'll take a series of pictures and then when I am finished shooting I like to just stand there a bit more and look at the view before packing up.

BP: So would you say that the actual process of getting ready and taking a picture is as enjoyable for you as the end result – the picture itself?

Cooper: Oh yes. I enjoy the discovery. With my small cameras I frame the view in the viewfinder. or in the large format on the ground glass. With closeups I'll go around until I get it just the way I want it. I think photographers who take the kind of pictures I do have to enjoy it in order to get the right shots. It takes time.

A lot of people get to a real scenic spot and take pictures and if they don't turn out well. they don't understand why. The reason their pictures don't turn out. often. is that the eye sees differently from the camera. The camera lens sees exactly what's there. If the light is hazy or too blue. which you can get with overcast skies. that's what the camera lens sees and that's what will be in the picture. The amateur seldom understands this. The first thing you have to realize is that it's one thing for a scene to be spectacular but it's another thing to capture that feeling.

BP: How does one learn to do that?

Cooper: You take a lot of pictures and make a lot of mistakes. Trial and error. But even more than that. I think it's partly that some people have a natural ability and an enthusiasm. My first discovery of nature was the mountains. I really had enthusiasm for them. If you have a passionate feeling for something. you're more likely to get better pictures of it. Then your talent develops gradually. as you spend more time at it.

BP: So. it takes a lot of time, and you have to love what you're doing enough to put in that time?

Cooper: Sure. The average person tends to take pictures in the middle of the day. But early in the morning and late in the evening are the best times. The average tourist shot. say. of Mount Rainier or Mount Baker. if taken in the middle of the day is very bluish and tends to be flat. You've got to get up early in the morning if you want to get good photos. And who'd do that if he weren't really in love with what he was doing?

Of course. there are some shots that are good in the middle of the day. like water. You can shoot water. especially still water. almost any time. Some tree pictures will come out nicely in the middle of the day. Then too. any hour is good on cloudy days and rainy days. They're perfect for forests. Overcast weather tends to kill almost everything but gives you beautiful. the best. forest shots. And who. if he weren't passionate about it. would go out on rainy days to take photos?

BP: You say that your average day of shooting in the summertime is about 17 hours?

Cooper: Just about. What I like to do. especially on long days like that. is to arrange it so that I'll sleep right at the spot. I kind of roll out of the sack. and I may even have the tripod set up. so all I have to do is stick the camera on and get the pictures.

BP: Do you get up before dawn?

Cooper: No. I set my mental alarm clock. and when it gets light I wake up. Once in a while I'll oversleep.

BP: Do you shoot for a couple of hours after sunlight and then pack up your camera and that's that?

Cooper: I'll shoot from sunrise on until I get too tired. Then I'll take a nap if I'm really tired. But when I'm backpacking. I tend to shoot all day long. A lot of times it's difficult to stop and sleep. I'm moving around and the flies bother me and my sleeping gear will be in the bottom of my pack and I have to get everything else out to get at it. So I'll keep moving. I'll stop and take a few pictures, but I won't stop for any naps.

BP: How many miles do you cover in a day of shooting?

Cooper: This depends on the picture possibilities of the area I'm backpacking in. Last summer, when I went up to Cascade Pass, I covered about five miles the first day, the second day two miles or less. But there was a tremendous variety of picture possibilities in these seven miles. Some times I'll get to a place and spend the whole day there.

BP: In other words you just can't cover many miles and take pictures too?

Cooper: Right. But one day near the end of last summer I did 18 miles.

BP: Did you do much shooting that day?

Cooper: About the only shooting was early in the morning. I shot maybe for a couple of hours, and then I was out of film and finished for that trip. So I just packed all the way back out in one day.

BP: I hear you used to carry an 8 x 10 view camera into the mountains. Did you take that on backpacking trips?

Cooper: Well, the only place I've really backpacked the thing is up to Berg Lake at Mount Robson in the Canadian Rockies. That's a long way, about 14 miles.

BP: How much did your pack weigh then?

Cooper: The camera itself weighs about 10 pounds and the film holders are pretty heavy. I'd say I was carrying about 70 pounds and that's half of my weight. I usually weigh about 135 to 140 pounds.

BP: So much for the physical side of your trips. I understand that you're into meditation. Has that had an influence on your photography?

Cooper: I would say yoga and meditation have changed my photography and my life.

BP: Do you have a particular type of meditation? Like Transcendental Meditation?

Cooper: No, I use a free-lance kind. When you are trying to really know your inner self, and you set about it seriously, any method will work. There are many different ways of attaining self-realization.

BP: How much time do you spend on it?

Cooper: I like to spend about half an hour a day. Yesterday I spent half an hour, but lately I've been missing days here and there because there's been so much to do. Things will soon settle

down a bit though, and I'll get back to it.

BP: Do you meditate in the mountains?

Cooper: Sometimes. I'll take a period, generally in the afternoon when lighting is bad, and sit down and meditate. Since I started, all sorts of things have happened. It's as if I've opened a new source of energy. My life has improved dramatically, materially as well as spiritually.

BP: How did you get started meditating?

Cooper: First I became interested in yoga. Yoga can be purely physical or spiritual or both. I got into the physical end of it and then gradually into the spiritual end.

BP: So your self-realization half-hour includes yoga?

Cooper: No, the yoga is extra. A good yoga workout takes an hour.

BP: Do you do that every day?

Cooper: When I first started practicing yoga, I did. Then last spring I was very lax about it because of all the traveling. When I am out taking pictures, I can't do it. However, photographing partially takes the place of yoga.

BP: What is the relationship?

Cooper: I find I tend to have more spiritual experiences when I'm in the mountains. I've had a lot of strange things happen—for instance, with my wife, Debby. Lately I've picked up on a lot of things that apparently she's been thinking. Perhaps I'm becoming more attuned to the raw energy of the spirit, of the universe. The yogis of course are able to do this. They're close to what you might call a cosmic consciousness, where they're able to pick up on anything that's happening, anywhere.

BP: Could you describe one of these spiritual experiences that you've had in the mountains?

Cooper: Well, I had one experience where I left my body. I was lying down and this very strange feeling came upon me. I don't know how to describe it. It may be similar to a drug experience in that it's subjective. There's no way you can describe it well to someone who has not experienced something like it. I felt something very strange was happening. I was sliding right out of my body while I was fully conscious. I just let it happen; it was like falling down. I was lying on level ground, but I felt myself falling. The next thing I knew I was outside my body and went up above and looked down at myself and couldn't believe it. Then I went over and talked with Debby, who was sleeping near me, and I tried to wake her but didn't. Then

I tried going through solid objects such as rocks, and I just went through them. I was conscious throughout the whole thing from before it started till after I came back. Other weird things have happened to me. Occasionally, up in the mountains too, I've been meditating on God and the creation of the universe and suddenly felt a *presence*. It acts upon my consciousness like an explosion or something very strange—an outside force. What some people might call the Holy Spirit.

BP: In the days when you were climbing walls, you must have done a lot of work with your mind, too.

Cooper: Oh, sure. There was a lot of mind control involved there because there was a lot of raw terror to overcome. Basically, people who climb big walls, climb because they either need to or want to. Probably more climb because they *need* to. The reasons are complex.

Climbing can be an ego builder. I think most who climb the big walls are trying to do something that no one else has ever done, trying to set a record. You get involved in the climbing *game* and the climbing *group* and you are concerned about your status, so you try to climb more and more to improve your status. I believe the majority of climbers doing difficult climbs get into this ego trip to some extent. But, I remember climbing sometimes when I was consciously enjoying the aesthetic experience. And those are the times I enjoyed climbing the most.

BP: How old were you when you started climbing?

Cooper: I actually began back in 1955. But my brief interest in difficult technical climbing lasted five years, from 1957 to 1962.

BP: Your name appears quite frequently in the *American Alpine Journal* for that period. You had a number of first ascents, didn't you?

Cooper: Yes. Mostly in the Cascades and in the Bugaboos.

BP: I understand you were pretty much of a loner.

Cooper: That's right, although I did enjoy climbing with a number of northwestern climbers.

BP: At the time you started solo climbing, were there any other climbers soloing?

Cooper: Not in the northwestern part of the country. I don't think anyone had soloed Bugaboo or Snowpatch Spire, for instance.

BP: What was your most difficult climb?

Cooper: When I soloed the three peaks of Mount Index. That was quite a thing at the time. It was more hairy than anything I did in the Bugaboos.

BP: When was that?

Cooper: In 1960. Yes: I was about 23. They were very complicated peaks. And it was a lot different from the Bugaboos, when there were a lot of people around in case I got into serious trouble. And the rock was good in the Bugaboos, too. I felt secure when I was soloing there.

But when I climbed Mount Index, I was strictly on my own, and the rock was not very good. I did the South to North Traverse. No one had ever done that before. The first difficulty I had was coming down the South Peak, which is a complicated network of ridges and gullies. You have to understand. I was going down a route I had never been up. Once I rappelled down the first pitch I did not know whether I would be able to climb back up. And I had no idea what was ahead of me. The further I went, the more the commitment. And I ran out of water half-way through my second day. which was serious because the temperature was up around 80 degrees.

The most difficult climbing was going up the North Peak. On the crux pitch, there was an overhang where I had to chin myself. Then, finally, I went down a 2,500-foot rock face on the North Peak that required everything I knew about route finding. Twice, after rappelling down pitches, I discovered I had erred and had to reascend 300 feet to regain the route.

BP: How long did the climb take you?

Cooper: I believe it was two days and one night: I bivouacked one night on the mountain. It was the greatest challenge I ever faced. The only traverse of these peaks before had been from the opposite direction and that was just once, 10 years earlier. This climb was the one that I committed myself to totally—considering my capabilities at the time and my knowledge of climbing.

BP: Why did you do it?

Cooper: It's hard to say. I wouldn't do it now. If I had my life to live over again, I wouldn't do it either. It made me feel cocky whenever I "subdued" a new route. For some reason, in the rock climbing and mountaineering phase of my life, I felt it necessary to subdue

nature. Fortunately, this phase passed, and now reaching the summit is only incidental to the overall experience of the trip.

You know, I'm into my thing now. My thing is photography. It's my life's work and I am happy with it and it is stimulating. But at that period of my life I was still searching. I hadn't quite found what my thing was. I had some sort of vague idea that maybe I would find it in climbing. Of course, I didn't.

BP: And you just quit climbing one day, right?

Cooper: Well, yes I did. although I had been building up to it for some time. Right after I put in the Dihedral Wall on El Capitan, that was my last wall. Oh, I fooled around on some rock a little after that, but no more big walls.

BP: Why did you stop?

Cooper: I had decided I didn't want to be in the climbing game any more. I didn't want to have to keep doing more and more difficult climbs. And there was something else more positive. I had found that I really got enthusiastic about the aesthetic experience in the mountains. I came to like that more than the ego trip.

BP: Did you start right in taking photos?

Cooper: Actually. I was taking pictures before I started climbing, back in 1955. I always carried a 2¼ folding camera, sometimes even two (one with color and one with black-and-white), on backpacking and climbing trips. Of course, photography in this period of my life. up to 1962, was only an adjunct to my climbing and hiking. I did have a good feeling for light and composition. though. But technically most, if not all, of my photos were out of focus or a little too light or a little too dark.

BP: Then when you quit climbing you concentrated more on photography?

Cooper: I guess you could say that. In 1962 I obtained my first large-format camera, an old 4 x 5 Speed Graphic. My mountain rambles turned from vertical walls to more gentle alpine wandering. Sometimes, when I wasn't distracted photographically by interesting subjects at lower elevations, I climbed an occasional summit.

BP: What kind of shots were you most interested in?

Cooper: I was interested strictly in black-and-white photography and was greatly influenced by the masters, especially Edward Weston and Ansel Adams. I spent about three years exper-

imenting in the darkroom. Eventually, I felt I was able to turn out a print that almost matched the emotional impact of the scene at the time I photographed it.

BP: Why did you turn to color photography?

Cooper: There are snobs who shoot only black-and-white, feeling it allows more creativity than color. I, too, was very close to holding this viewpoint for a number of years. But how many photographers can make a living on high quality black-and-whites of wilderness subjects? Offhand, I can think of only one person, Ansel Adams. Frankly, I was anxious to make a living at photography. For a period of three years I did a stint on Wall Street as a salesman in a brokerage firm. But my spirit was not to be confined. One day when I was totally fed up with it, I broke out for good.

I began to realize that color has its creativity. One must rely on perfect exposure and composition while taking the picture, instead of correcting it later in the darkroom, since my final product is color transparencies, not color prints. I also was getting tired of darkroom work. I didn't like spending all those long hours with chemicals. I much preferred to be outdoors somewhere, shooting. With color, you send it to a processor after you manage to find one who does a decent job for you. This is an important consideration if you work in a larger film format, and I work today mostly in 4 x 5 Ektachrome.

BP: Then you are saying it requires more effort to take a color photo than a black-and-white while you are taking it – but more effort in the processing for black-and-white than for color?

Cooper: Yes. Unless you're shooting color negative film and intend to make color prints, which is even more work than black-and-white, once you have snapped the shutter, that is just about all you can do creatively with it. That is what I like most about color transparency photography—the amount of patience and time needed to get the shot in the first place. I would rather do my creative work outdoors than in a darkroom.

BP: When did you get into color, then?

Cooper: I mark my color period from 1971. This is not to imply that I didn't shoot color previously. But what color I did shoot was an afterthought to the black-and-white.

I discovered that the financial return from color was much higher than from black-and-white, with much less total effort. Even after you have the black-and-white negative, you have to print it. And turning out a very high quality black-and-white print is a painstaking process which requires a great deal of time.

Now, as my volume of color has gone up, so has my income. I finally am able to support myself, and support a family and even buy a home. I am able to do what I most like doing. And I feel very fortunate for that. ▶

ANSEL ADAMS
The Foremost Conservation Photographer
Interview conducted by PHILIP HYDE

In recent times, the one person who has used photography to the greatest extent on behalf of conservation is no doubt Ansel Adams. Furthermore, Adams has had a ripple effect in that he has inspired many other nature photographers to turn their efforts to the aid of conservation.

W.K.

BACKPACKER: You started out as an accomplished pianist. What made you switch to photography?

ADAMS: It's hard to say. I was spending all the time I could in the summers hiking around the Sierra, and I made hundreds of photographs, records of what I'd seen. Pretty soon I began to like the photographs, and I realized they were more than mere records. The camera simply took over.

BACKPACKER: When did you start hiking in the Sierra?

ADAMS: I first went to Yosemite with my family in 1916. Then in 1917 I made my first trip up to the High Sierra with Francis Holman and Bessie Pond, daughter of Admiral Pond, of Berkeley. The Ponds were an important family in the conservation world at that time. It rained all the way up to Merced Lake, and I spent my first night out with simply a piece of canvas and one blanket over me. I was exceedingly uncomfortable, but it cleared later, and the stars came out—I'd never seen so many stars in my life. At dawn I climbed up on a granite slope and looked at the crags under Mount Clark—beautiful, cathedral-like shapes—and they were all lit up in sunrise. That was my first real experience in the mountains. I've been coming back to the Sierra every year since!

After that, I acquired a sleeping bag, a ghastly piece of heavy, stiff canvas dyed a maroon color and waxed. I don't know what it weighed, but I had two blankets with the bag. At night I would go into it headfirst to load film. Then I'd creep out and somehow get the blankets back. By that time I was in such a condition I could have slept on bare rock.

BACKPACKER: What cameras were you carrying then?

ADAMS: The first cameras I backpacked with were a 3¼ × 4¼ Zeiss Mirrorflex, a Speed Kodak and a 4 × 5 Korona View. Then I had a 6½ × 8½ glass-plate camera. I backpacked that but not on overnight trips. That's the one I made *Monolith, the Face of Half Dome* with.

BACKPACKER: I've always wanted to hear how you made that. You had quite a scramble to get up there, didn't you?

ADAMS: Yes. I had the camera and those 6½ × 8½ glass plates to carry. The Le Conte Gully by Grizzly Peak was too steep for a heavy pack, so I went around Liberty Cap to Grizzly Peak and up the ridge to the north. There was snow on the ridge, and it was tough climbing. When I got up to the Diving Board, I had a wonderful view of the Dome, but for some reason, I photographed other things first. Then I made a conventional photograph of Half Dome on a Wratten panchromatic plate with a K-2 filter using a Zeiss Tessar lens. The lens didn't cover the plate completely so I didn't dare use any camera adjustments. I knew so little about photography then, it was a miracle I got anything. But that was the first time I realized how the print was going to look—what I now call visualization—and was actually thinking about the emotional effect of the image. I knew that with that K-2 filter

308

and panchromatic plate I was going to have gray skies with gray shadows, but most of the cliff was in shade, and little of the great monumentality of the rock would come through. I began to visualize the black rock and deep sky. I really wanted to give it a monumental, dark quality. So I used the last plate I had with a #29-F filter, dark red, and got this exciting picture. That was in 1926. The negative has lasted all these years (went through a fire in 1936) and I'm still printing from it.

On another trip I went up the old Tioga Road to Tenaya Lake and hiked down Tenaya Canyon to where you've got the wonderful shapes of Quarter Domes and Half Domes above you. I made a gorgeous 6½ × 8½ plate of the scene. Later in the year I had the plates at the Le Conte Memorial in Yosemite. I'd selected the plates I really liked and stood them on the chairs, against the backs. The one near the desk was the exceptional one. Later, I intended to sit down on that chair and write. I must have jarred the chair, for the plate fell over, and I sat down on the plate. I'll never forget the crumbling, shattering sensation of sitting on a glass plate—especially a fine one.

BACKPACKER: What makes you decide to take a photograph?

ADAMS: It's really the *impact* of recognition. I can see a wonderful bit of conventional scenery, but it may leave me utterly cold. Photographing "scenery" is the very thing I don't believe in, because that's often a two-dimensional affair. So the element of immediate, emotional impact is very important. Of all the pictures I've made, I can't think of one that has a contrived, carefully planned, waited-for image. When I took my Moonrise picture, the one with the church and the graveyard at Hernandez, New Mexico, I was driving back to Santa Fe from the Chama Valley and I saw this wonderful scene out the window. The reaction was so strong I practically drove off the road. I got out the tripod and camera, took the front part of the lens off, screwed it on the back of the shutter and began composing and focusing. All the time I was trying to think of what I'd have to do to make the picture. I couldn't find my exposure meter, but I knew the moon's luminance was 250 candles per square foot and that was placed

on Zone VII of the exposure scale. That gave me a shutter speed of a sixtieth of a second at f/8 with a film speed of ASA 64. The filter factor was 3×, so that made the basic exposure a twentieth of a second. I exposed for a long second at f/32, made one picture, and while I was turning the

---

The Zone System Simplified

Since light meters only give an "average" reading for the scene you want to photograph, you often have to add or subtract f/stops to the exposure indicated by your meter to determine the correct exposure. But how do you know when you should do this? And how many f/stops should you add or subtract?

Ansel Adams developed a great skill for determining the answers to such questions. Hence his great black and white photos. To teach his skill to other people he worked out a method in 1941 he called the Zone System.

The Zone System is based upon 10 shades of gray ranging from black to white, with the universally accepted photo industry "standard gray" in the middle.

The range of tones is as follows:

Zone 0—Deep black black.
Zone 1—Black that is lighter than Zone 0 but black enough so little detail is visible.
Zone 2—Light black. Some detail and texture visible.
Zone 3—Dark gray. Apparent detail and texture.
Zone 4—Gray. Good detail in shadows.
Zone 5—Medium gray, the same gray value as the standard gray card.
Zone 6—Light gray. The gray value related to the color of caucasian skin in a black and white photo.
Zone 7—Gray–white. Some detail visible.
Zone 8—White. Little detail. Almost pure white.
Zone 9—Paper white. No detail.

To use the Zone System, first study the scene and decide how you want to reproduce it on film. Let's say the subject is a whitewashed barn in Vermont. Depending upon the exposure you choose, you can make the sunlit side of the building appear white or one of several shades of gray.

You first work with the shadows. Do you want to picture the wheelbarrow that can be seen inside the barn? Or are you satisfied with holding texture and detail on the shadowed wall of the barn?

Suppose you want to photograph the shadowed side of the barn so as to show ample texture and "value." You would measure this side with your meter and perhaps find that it reads 32 candles-per-square-foot (c/ft²). If you are using a film of ASA speed 125 and you place this value on Zone IV of the Exposure-scale, you will see that 64 c/ft² would fall on Zone V (the "pivot" value). The desired exposure would be 1/64th of a second at f/11.

Now, if the sunlit side of the barn is 500 c/ft², this value would fall on Zone VIII. With normal processing, you would see just a trace of detail in the sunlit side. You are using the old golden rule of photography—"Expose for the shadows and let the high values take care of themselves."

The Zone System allows you to visualize the image you want in your mind's eye. An average reading of the sunlit and shadowed sides of the barn together probably would fail to give the desired image values. If you want to include the wheelbarrow, you would have to measure it; it would probably require at least two stops, or zones, more exposure. The sunlit side of the barn would then have two stops (zones) more exposure, and much less development of the negative would be indicated.

The Zone System can resolve such problems. It can tell a lot about many aspects of photography.

The above is an oversimplification. To get a working understanding of the Zone System, you should read *The Negative* and *Natural-Light Photography* by Ansel Adams and other books related to the subject.

holder around and pulling out the slide to make a duplicate, the sunlight went off the crosses. I got the picture by about 15 seconds!

If I had spent more time in the Chama Valley, I would have missed the entire thing. If I had come home earlier, I would have missed it. So there's always an element of chance in photography. If you have practiced and practiced, the process is intuitive. You suddenly recognize something, and you react.

BACKPACKER: Were most of your early photographs taken while you were backpacking?

ADAMS: Because I used the cameras so much, I didn't do much backpacking of camp equipment, so most trips were with one or two donkeys. But on the hikes I did make with other people, we divided up the load. Everyone would help carry the cameras and some of my films. Each of us would have about 50 pounds apiece.

BACKPACKER: Where were some of those trips?

ADAMS: I went all over the Yosemite Sierra with Francis Holman and climbed everything that was relatively easy by today's standards. We climbed all the Merced group, then Mount Starr King. That was mean; there was snow on it and we had to use a World War I trench pick to cut steps. Then we'd go toward Mount Clark, get as high as we could with the donkeys, find some grass for them and walk up as far as we could to camp. We would stay there a couple of days and climb Mount Clark and Gray Peak. Then we'd move to Red Creek and camp there, go up Red Peak, then on to Merced Peak. It's beautiful country, and we really explored it. Then we'd go to the Lyell Fork of the Merced, over Isberg Pass and down to the North Fork of the San Joaquin. One trip, from the lakes below Isberg Pass over by Mount Davis and across the Ritter Range and back, was quite hazardous. I always wonder what would have happened if one of us had sprained an ankle—or worse.

BACKPACKER: Did you ever get in trouble in the mountains?

ADAMS: Oh, yes. My most harrowing experience was in 1924. We had a lean-to camp at Merced Lake. I packed a bedroll and a Speed Kodak, and went up there the first of April.

I told my aunt in Yosemite I'd be gone three days. But I was so full of pep by the time I got up the Nevada Falls zigzags and met the High Sierra Camp crew coming back, I said, "Will you tell my aunt I'm going to stay out two more days?" I figured I had enough food—grapenuts and condensed milk. So I went to Merced Lake, then on to Triple Peak Fork. The ground was covered with snow, but I found a bare rock and slept on that. I nearly froze, but it was a beautiful night. Then I climbed to the top of Isberg Peak. I was alone, which was terribly dangerous because of the snow conditions, but I got to the top, and it was so wonderful I decided to stay all night. It was windy and cold, but there were protected places between the rocks, and I built a small shelter. The next afternoon I went down to Merced Lake. The snow was so soft that at times I literally disappeared. I'd go over a rock, fall through the snow and come up from beneath. By the time I got to Merced Lake I was very tired. I lit a fire and went down to the river flowing into the lake to get a drink. I had a terrible pain in my abdomen, so bad I couldn't eat. I knew something was really wrong. I was very weak. So I thought of hiking back to Yosemite Valley. There was a log, partly under water, and I tried to cross the river on that, but after crawling out about four feet I turned back. By instinct I filled a bucket with water and went back to the lean-to. That night I drank the whole bucket of water. The next morning the pain was gone, but I was weak as a cat, so I fussed around all day, and the next day I came home. It was appendicitis. If I had known it before, I would have died of fright. And if I'd had any kind of pill it would have killed me, but I just drank water.

BACKPACKER: I'd like to hear about your celebrated trip in the Minarets, the one with the Sierra Club, when you had a Minaret named after you.

ADAMS: That was in the early thirties when Robert L. M. Underhill was invited on the Sierra Club trip by the president of the club, Francis P. Farquhar. Underhill introduced modern rock climbing to America. On that trip he gave the first training in our part of the country in the use of the rope and belaying technique—what we now call Fourth-Class climbing.

Before that, Francis Holman and I would "scramble." We used window sash cord, an eighth of an inch thick and very strong. Of course, if one of us fell, it would have cut us in two. Several times we had some spills. In a sense it's a miracle I'm alive because we did have some hazardous experiences and didn't know anything about climbing technique. On that Sierra Club trip, we started at Red's Meadows, then went down Izaak Walton Creek. When Walter Starr, Jr., was killed, we went back to the Minarets to look for him. He had been climbing Michael Minaret alone and fell. Rondal Partridge was with me, and we climbed all the Minarets that were within our scale of climbing. For some reason they named one after me. It's not an important Minaret—more like a loose rock on a ridge. Later, we climbed all over Volcanic Ridge, to the east, which gives a spectacular view of the Minarets.

I went there in 1936 with Edward and Charis Weston. We rented some pack animals at Red's Meadows to carry our cameras and went up to Lake Ediza for a week.

BACKPACKER: That was the time you were eaten up by mosquitoes?

ADAMS: Yes, that was *one* time! I was changing Edward's film for him. God, it was awful. Charis was behind me killing mosquitoes—right ear, left ear, etc. There I was, partway in a sweaty bag, with 8 × 10 films. Edward would use 24 holders a day, 48 films. Changing film in a bag is an arduous technique, and it took hours! Edward had never used a changing bag and didn't dare use one the first time there. But he did get some beautiful pictures.

Those hikes around Yosemite were very important for me. Then I had two very fine summers with Joseph N. Le Conte and his family in the southern Sierra. That was in 1924 and 1925. We explored the Middle Fork and South Fork of the Kings, and the Kern River headwaters. They had two mules. If we were near Sequoia National Park, we used only one. Later, I had a mule that was just for my cameras.

BACKPACKER: People who backpack with modern camping equipment and Nikons don't realize that when you work with a view camera, it's backpacking just to carry the camera.

ADAMS: Of course, things are lighter

now. I don't know how a Nikon works with landscape, except for color. I think you could do beautiful details. But if I were going to climb again, I'd be happy with my little Zeiss Jewell 3½ × 4½. It was heavy, but all the accessories were light. I had three lenses for it, including a double Protar. And the lenses were all on bayonet mounts, so you didn't have separate lens boards. If the camera had been as light as a Deardorff, it would have been marvelous.

Food is different now, too, from when I was active in the mountains. We would have some bacon, and flour for flapjacks and biscuits. The Le Contes always made biscuits at least twice a day in a reflector oven. We'd have canned butter, and we'd fish and consume lots of canned beans. Most of it was pretty heavy. Now you have the marvelous compact packets of dehydrated food. It's amazing what's happened with the expansion of outdoor sports—especially in mountaineering. It's a different experience now.

BACKPACKER: What are some of the changes you find in the Sierra when you go back 40 years later?

ADAMS: The change in the forest in Yosemite is tremendous. One of my earliest photographs, of the forest in the Lyell Fork, was done in 1923. I went back there again in 1950. I could barely find the location. Most of the old trees were gone, and a lot of new ones had grown up. It was still beautiful, but the character has changed severely. This has happened all over Yosemite.

BACKPACKER: Do you think awareness about the quality of the environment has changed?

ADAMS: The awareness of the misuse of the environment has increased, but the idea of parks and preservation is no greater than it was. In fact there may be less in a proportionate sense because it is so easy for everyone to get places. The wilderness mystique is based on a special kind of experience, not just driving a car through a place. There are umptold thousands of people who come to a park just to camp, and all they've done is change the view outside their camper window. They still have their radios and tapes and dogs and poker games.

Some good legislation has been passed, and many people have become "aware," but there are still millions who don't care what happens to the environment.

Right now there's a bad situation in the national parks. The budget isn't sufficient to maintain them properly. But more important, there isn't a policy to preserve the original intent of the parks. The word "park" is a bad term, semantically, because the average person thinks of a park as a pleasuring ground, a merry-go-round, scenic railway, duck-boat on a lake,

Ansel Adams's Role in Conservation

Ansel Adams first became associated with the conservation movement in 1919. That summer he took on the job of custodian of the Sierra Club's Yosemite Valley headquarters. He worked there for four summers. His friendship with David Brower, who was to become a major force in the environmental movement, began on a mountain trail in 1933.

In 1934 Adams was elected to the Sierra Club's board of directors. He was continuously reelected to the board until his retirement in 1971. He was responsible for many of the philosophical concepts that led to the club's transformation from a local hiking group to an internationally known environmental organization.

In 1936 Adams was chosen to represent the Sierra Club at a conference to propose establishment of a national park in Kings Canyon in the southern Sierra. The club believed a portfolio of Adams's photographs would be a more persuasive argument for the park than several volumes of words. Adams showed his photographs to and discussed the park proposal with the secretaries of agriculture and the interior, the director of the National Park Service and key congressmen. Two years later his first photographic book, *Sierra Nevada: The John Muir Trail*, was published, containing his best photographs of the Kings Canyon region. When Congress established Kings Canyon National Park in 1940, Park Service Director Arno B. Cammerer wrote to Adams: "A silent but most effective voice in the campaign was your own book, *Sierra Nevada: The John Muir Trail.*"

Following Adams's lobbying success, Secretary of the Interior Harold Ickes invited him to undertake a photo-mural project for the Department of the Interior.

In 1946 Adams was given a Guggenheim Fellowship to photograph national parks and monuments. His work culminated in the publication of four books and portfolios displaying the beauty of the park system's wildlands.

In 1954 Adams, with Nancy Newhall, organized the Sierra Club conservation exhibit called "This Is the American Earth," consisting of photographs by Adams and 30 other photographers. It circulated widely in the United States and abroad. In 1960 the exhibit was published as a book. Supreme Court Justice William O. Douglas hailed it as "one of the great statements in the history of conservation." *This Is the American Earth* was the first in the Sierra Club Exhibit Format book series.

In addition to taking photographs, Adams wrote many articles and participated in such conservation battles as opposition to widening Yosemite's Tioga Road and construction of an oil refinery at Moss Landing on the California Coast. He also provided leadership in several campaigns to prevent overdevelopment of parks' commercial facilities.

Last year when Adams presented President Ford with one of his photographic prints, he took advantage of the meeting to urge the president to intervene against budget reductions in the national parks, to create seven new parks, to make additions to six existing parks and to establish a presidential commission on national parks. Later, Ford initiated a study of Adams's proposals.

Adams photos have been freely used by many conservation organizations—The Save the Redwoods League, Sierra Club, National Parks and Conservation Association—for a wide variety of fund-raising efforts. For his substantial contributions to conservation, Adams received the John Muir Award from the Sierra Club in 1963 and the Conservation Award from the Department of the Interior in 1968.

that kind of thing. People come to Yosemite and say, gee, it's nice here, but where's the park? What is there to do? So, it should be Yosemite National *Reserve*. We have a state park near Carmel, Point Lobos State Reserve, in which the term "reserve" helps keep it the way it is. If it were a state park, there would be more clamor for camping and tourist services. But it is a reserve. You can't camp, and you can't build fires. You go there to experience its inherent qualities. But as long as you have the word "park" in "national park," you're going to have a hard time keeping the place natural.

BACKPACKER: I'd like to discuss teaching versus making photographs. For some photographers teaching seems to take them away from working at photography. Then there is that old saw: those who can, do; those who can't, teach. It is not always true.

ADAMS: You should never get out of creative photography. I've been away from making pictures too long because of book projects. But teaching is a professional obligation.

BACKPACKER: To pass-on the torch?

ADAMS: Yes, but you should never become a pedant. Some have, and their teaching is reduced to quasi-cultism. A lot of it bothers me very much. It isn't directed to developing the student's qualities. It's imposing qualities and styles and cults and concepts on him. When I studied music, none of my teachers ever played anything for me. I was trained in a dialectic system. It was a questioning: Do you think you shaped that phrase? Did you realize it was weak? Did you want it that way? You had to do some thinking and feeling.

They'd guide you with the musical qualities, but they never would play so you could imitate them.

When I went to the Art Center School in Los Angeles to teach, I found I had nothing to teach about photography except the way I did it. That went against my grain. That's why the Zone System was developed. It gave the student technical controls so he could visualize what he wanted and could capture the image he saw with his eyes and mind. If he knew the basic mechanics, he could manage all kinds of problems. The Zone System caught on very quickly, and it has liberated people's vision.

BACKPACKER: Do you think the proliferation of workshops is in response to a great demand?

ADAMS: Yes, tremendous demand. There are a lot of colleges. Many are good, but the really good ones are filled. I advise everybody who is thinking seriously of photography and shows some talent to first take the workshop circuit. Not only do you learn the mechanics, but you get direction. You can go to a workshop and you might think, "This is my way of feeling." Or you might say, "It isn't for me," and go to another workshop where there's a person or group more in line with your thought and feeling. Often these kids in desperation go to some God-awful school. There are some good places, but they may teach only art appreciation or, I should say, photo appreciation.

People come to me, and I ask, what do you want to do? And they say, I'd like to make prints like you and sell them. Well, thanks for the flattery, but it was a long time before I sold prints! That comes after 50

years of work. When these people find they can't get into photography easily, they say they'll teach. So they go to a college and they get a degree. Then they get a job teaching photography in a high school. It's like a squirrel-cage — self-perpetuating mediocracy, which I think is tragic.

The teachers' group, the Society for Photographic Education, had a meeting at Asilomar recently. To me it was very discouraging—everybody related to schools and workshops, and damned few of them any good. A lot of them started out professionally and went bust. Workshops are increasing, and there are some very good ones, too: The Friends of Photography in Carmel, California, is initiating a lecture and workshop programs. My annual workshop is held in June in Yosemite Valley. Minor White's groups have always had an impressive success. Paul Caponegro has done well; Free-messer, up in Oregon, has done well, too, and Fred Picker in Vermont. The Arizona Center for Creative Photography in Tucson is going to be an important study source as well as an archives. Its emphasis will be on the student and photo–historian who wants to focus on the esthetic evaluation of photography. It will be wonderful for people who want a cultural appreciation of the visual arts. Thousands of people take art history and study art, not to be an El Greco, but to know and respond to various forms of expression and communication. If they have any means at all, they are in a good position to do that. But to earn your living from it, that's another world. ➤

CONSERVATION PHOTOGRAPHER PHILIP HYDE

Interview conducted by GARY BRAASCH

One of the most obvious protégés of Ansel Adams to use photography to help conservation is Philip Hyde. He's a master in his own right. And whereas Adams is known for his mastery of black-and-white photography, Hyde works mainly in color in large-format photography. When he backpacks his 4 X 5

view camera, with tripod, accessories, and film, he is totaling 30 pounds before he adds food, tent, and sleeping bag to his pack. The smallest format that Hyde works in is with a 2¼ X 2¼ Hasselblad. He prefers the larger camera, though, because of the amount of detail he can get into his photos.

W.K.

BACKPACKER: The world is so full of beautiful places. How do you, with a drive to photograph them all, decide when and where to travel?

HYDE: My trip planning evolves out of a combination of wanting to go back to places I really liked where I find a lot of subject matter, and the need to see new territory. Sometimes when I go to a new place I get certain images that I will never again get just because of the newness and the excitement of being in a place that's different.

BACKPACKER: What kind of kit do you take backpacking?

HYDE: This is always a great debate. Should I take the Hasselblad and have a lot of 2¼ x 2¼ inch exposures, or should I take the view camera and make a few good 4 x 5s? It depends on the situation and the place and how vigorous I feel. If I backpack the view camera for three or four days, I can carry three or four film magazines—36 or 48 sheets—and two or three lenses. My tripod weighs about five pounds. By the time I have it all thrown in I've got 30 pounds. The Hasselblad, with a lot of rolls, will add up to about half that.

BACKPACKER: But what kind of sacri-

fices do you make in the rest of your dunnage to survive the weight when you're going into the wilderness for any length of time?

HYDE: Everything else is minimal. We backpack with just a piece of plastic for tent, tarp and groundsheet combined. A down bag. We survive on stuff like muesli, and the cooking is pretty simple. I find that if I carry too much, I just don't have the energy or inclination to take pictures.

BACKPACKER: One answer, of course, is to go to a smaller camera. Why do you continue to use a 4 x 5 primarily rather than a 35mm, which is so much lighter?

HYDE: For one thing, I'm stubborn. But the basic reason is that I can't get the detail I want on 35mm. A 35mm original boosted up to 20 x 24 inches or even 8 x 10 doesn't have the sharpness I'm looking for. I'm always trying to compromise with the Hasselblad because with it I can go farther, faster and lighter. But then I get something I really like on the 2¼ x 2¼ inch film and wish I had taken my view camera along and done a little more struggling to get the picture on 4 x 5. Maybe that's pure stubbornness, but I still think there's a

difference, and the difference, as far as I'm concerned, is crucial.

There's something else, too: The view camera is a terrific discipline. I don't have nearly the discipline with the Hasselblad because I know the film's cheap and there's a lot of it. Expense-wise, I can shoot only about two exposures of 4 x 5 for a roll of 120 film or about 20 exposures of 35mm film. If I get one or two really good 4 x 5 pictures, I'm way ahead of the game because I often don't get that many on a roll of Hasselblad film.

BACKPACKER: The discipline you talk about—is it mostly a discipline of time? Waiting, walking around, getting the right angles and the right light?

HYDE: What I do is form a scene with my eyes and mind *before* exposure, rather than inside the camera. As an art-school-trained photographer, I have an axe to grind about getting people to look harder. I don't think the small camera does much for that because it's too easy. As for waiting, I don't wait. In fact it's almost always the other way around. A fellow who was here the other day looked at a photo of a meadow with a cloud up above it. He remarked; "Gee, you must have waited a long time until that cloud got just the way you wanted it." I had to laugh because that wasn't what happened at all. The cloud was already there when I saw it, and I had a hell of a time getting the view camera set up before it was gone. There are photographers who claim they work the other way. They know there's going to be a picture at a certain place and certain time of day, so they go there. But I can't imagine doing that, because the world is too full of pictures to wait a long time for any one of them. Also, it's very difficult for me to visualize a picture if it's not already there. It becomes something that's kind of put together—constructed. And if I were going to do that, it would be much more efficient to be a hand artist and paint the scene. Photography is the art of getting what's *there,* not creating something.

BACKPACKER: Are you saying that photography isn't creative—isn't a fine art?

HYDE: What I want to say about creativity in photography is that it is analyzing what is there, rather than constructing something out of one's imagination. Analysis consists of seeing strongly. If you define creativity as the expression of individuality, then the kind of photography you're talking about is "creative" when it communicates the maker's viewpoint and individual vision. This may be more subtle than in other mediums, and our audience, despite Marshall McLuhan, still isn't very educated

PHOTO: DAVID GUNN

The Minarets from lakelet above Lake Ediza, Sierra Nevada, California.
PHOTO: PHILIP HYDE

about appreciating photographs, which explains why there are still people around asking "But is it art?" But it's safe to say that photography can be art, and I see more and more evidences of individual expression by a growing number of photographers.

BACKPACKER: You have not only made your creativity into a successful way of life but taken photographs that have been instrumental in battles for very important wilderness areas. How can other photographers—skilled amateurs—use their creativity for conservation?

HYDE: Off the top of my head, they'd do a lot better by going to law school because it looks to me as if the fight is now in lawyers' hands. But on a local level, an individual can do a lot by becoming familiar with a place that needs protection and by studying the issues. The camera can be an important tool to him. The person can make himself an ad hoc committee on a project and carry it along until something gets done. The weekend photographer may have an even more important role in such cases than the professional, who is always hung up on having to make a living from photography. There are thousands of causes I could donate my photographs to if I were only privately endowed.

BACKPACKER: How did your career evolve?

HYDE: I got started in photography through nature, rather than vice versa, because of an early interest in mountains. Like everyone else, I carried a little camera around to take pictures of my favorite mountains, and one thing led to another. That was before World War II. Then just before I got out of the service I wrote to Ansel Adams. He said he was starting a school of photography; that's where I spent the next three years. Ansel knew I was interested in conservation and nature, and helped me get acquainted with people in the Sierra Club. My first major published photos were in the *Sierra Club Bulletin* of May, 1951. Getting photographs of Dinosaur National Monument was the first conservation project I did for the club. Even with that beginning my wife, Ardis, taught school for 12 years to support us.

BACKPACKER: There's a lot of Ansel's influence showing in your earlier work.

HYDE: Yes, some people have always said that. But I don't think I ever imitated him. That picture of Yosemite is a good example of my evolution. Twenty years ago, I had great difficulty making photographs in Yosemite because all I could see was Ansel Adams, and I was sure I didn't want to duplicate his pictures. Now I can go to Yosemite and see it through my own eyes. I have a tremendous debt to Ansel—not just for having taught me technique but for having inspired me, introduced me to the Sierra Club and helped me get on my way. I want to acknowledge that debt, but I don't agree that my pictures have ever been more than superficially like his pictures.

BACKPACKER: Let's discuss taking photos for straight illustration to show other people what a place is like, versus an artistic, creative image done to please yourself. The difference seems apparent in comparing many of your shots in *The Wild Cascades* with those in *Slickrock*. For instance, the photographs in the first book have much less emphasis on small detail.

HYDE: Several things happened between books. One was my own development. I think I started out with the idea of showing people what an area was like. When I went there I was very conscious of it as a place. Through the years as I visted more and more places, I began to realize that the PLACE, in capitals, is not really what we're looking for after all; PLACE has become a commercial object more than anything else. To illustrate: There is no difference between Capitol Reef National Monument and Capitol Reef National Park. The place is the same, but the name change was sponsored by Utah's industrial tourism because the term "national park" puts the place on the map. If the current wilderness proposal goes through the way it should, a very large percentage of the park will be preserved as wilderness, and the place will remain pretty much the same. Practically every book project I've ever worked on has had a very strong conservation aspect for saving a place.

Another difference between the two books you mentioned is not the photographer's approach but the editing. For *The Wild Cascades* and *The Last Redwoods* I produced many of the photographs, and I certainly edited them. I didn't just dump the takes on somebody's desk. But working with Dave Brower, he pretty much decided what ended up in a book. Practically all the exhibit format books were crash projects; that was Dave's way of working. When he got an idea, he wanted to see it in a book as fast as possible. I was sympathetic to that wish because some of the places were threatened, but it often meant that the people involved didn't really have time to do their best work. I think that shows up in the photographs as well as the texts.

Slickrock is a more finished book because I took all the photographs and I worked on the project a lot longer. I worked on it for several years before I ever talked to anyone about a book. I helped with the photo selection; the design and sequence of photographs were worked out by the book's editor and a designer.

BACKPACKER: It seems more and more nature photographers and editors are using images that suggest an area or give an impression of it without being specific about the exact location or subject, such as your exquisite photos of small details in *Slickrock* and here in BACKPACKER. Do you see this as a major trend in outdoor photography?

HYDE: I think that aspect is coming out more and more. You know, there are common elements to any scene. During the gasoline shortage I thought; "What can I do? I've got to go where the wild places are and make pictures of them." But if the subject were the little common things of nature, I wouldn't have to travel very far. Maybe, conservation-wise, that's what we all must do. Instead of flying off to another part of the world and burning up all that fuel getting there, maybe we should just look down at our feet. I'm fond of quoting what John Ruskin said: "There was always more in the world than a man could see, walked he ever so slowly. He will see no more if he goes fast." ▲

DAVE SUMNER
Photographing for the Land

"I care about the Wilderness. I'd like my photography to express that care and inspire it in others."

David Sumner, a contributing editor of BACKPACKER, moved to Colorado in 1966 from New Hampshire. He taught English literature for three years at the University of Denver and then turned to environmental writing and photography. His work has appeared in Time-Life books, the Sierra Club's Bulletin and calendars, The Living Wilderness, Colorado Magazine, which he edited for four years, National Wildlife, BACKPACKER, and other publications. David is co-author of The Regnery Guide to Sky Touring and author of Rocky Mountains, published by Graphic Arts Center Publishing Company with photographs by David Muench.

A nature photographer whose work is largely unappreciated and little known yet is Dave Sumner. He has a rare combination of talents both as a writer and photographer. And he has a burning need inside himself to help protect the Rocky Mountain roadless areas from the further encroachments of urban development.

The following interview with Dave develops some of his passionate concerns. I believe that in the years ahead we'll hear a good deal more about Dave's work.

W.K.

BACKPACKER: Many of your photos are taken on backpacking trips. Do you go backpacking mostly to photograph?
SUMNER: I backpack for several reasons and photography is an important one of them.

Photography has sharpened my vision. As I hike, I'm constantly looking for the play of light on rocks, for the patterns in reflections on a pond, for the textures of a leaf, for the colors of Indian paintbrush. Photography has quickened my whole awareness of the natural world.

Also, the more I photograph the wilderness, the more I want to learn about it. I can't photograph a ptarmigan or lichen without wanting to know more about them.

But I go into the wilderness for other reasons, too: to live by natural rhythms, to exercise, to be in a place I don't want to control, to satisfy and stimulate my curiosity.

No matter what, though. I always carry my cameras, and I'm disappointed if I don't come back with some good photos.
BACKPACKER: Do you consider your photography then to be primarily a personal record of what you see?
SUMNER: Yes, but I'm also using my photography as a conservation tool. I believe very strongly that wilderness needs attention—that people have to find out what's there before it gets messed up. So I'm trying to take photographs that attract attention. That makes me both a popularizer and a propagandist.

It also runs the danger of inviting more people into an area—people who are capable of loving the wilderness to death—but that seems a better alternative than logging or building roads and subdi-

Photo: Verna Huser

visions. I'm convinced that the wild open space we end up with in the United States is going to exist only through deliberate efforts to preserve it.

BACKPACKER: Do you look for anything in particular when you go out to photograph?

SUMNER: Yes. I try to get into country that's unfamiliar to most people. I'm proud of the shots I've made of places I've "discovered." Take the waterfalls on the unnamed tributary to Little Squaw Creek in the Weminuche Wilderness in southwestern Colorado. I was out bushwhacking on an elk hunt when I heard the sound of rushing water, so I made my way over to see what was there. I discovered not one fall but seven, one after another. It was only a mile back to camp, so I went back, left my bow and arrows, picked up my cameras and spent two hours scrambling around the waterfalls.

BACKPACKER: Do you often hike back to camp to pick up your cameras when you see something to photograph?

SUMNER: I found the waterfalls when I was hunting. I haven't hunted for four years. Now I carry my cameras with me all the time.

BACKPACKER: What made you want to go back and get your cameras on your hunting trip?

SUMNER: I was excited.

BACKPACKER: Do you usually get excited about photographs?

SUMNER: Yes, I do. A lot. Landscapes do that to me. They really move me. There are some photographs I take for commercial use, the kind that pay the freight. They're not really an intense thing. I may take a photograph of Yosemite Valley from Inspiration Point and simply put it in the stock file. It causes no excitement; it's a postcard. But with other photographs, where I'm concentrating on form and color arrangement, I can really get involved.

BACKPACKER: What makes you want to take a photograph? Are there particular qualities that attract you to one subject and not to another?

SUMNER: It can be different things. Take the photograph of the arctic willow. I tried to hike up Uncompahgre Peak in the Colorado Rockies that day and got chased down by some lightning. It was gray and overcast, and I was just trudging back to camp. Then I saw the willow. That patch of color leapt out at me. I stopped, squatted down and started to look. On one hand I was fascinated by the plant because it is a full-grown shrub—a very honest, bona fide member of the willow family, and it's only two inches tall when full grown! At the same time, it was a nice pattern, a comfortable arrangement for me. And the color, that's what caught me first. The oranges in the leaves are peculiar and exciting to me, too.

I like arrangements of forms. I'm better at perceiving forms and spatial relationships than I am at colors. That's why I like landscapes.

BACKPACKER: Do you have any favorite kinds of landscapes?

SUMNER: I like them stark and simple. For instance, there's a marvelously desolate side canyon winding off Grand Gulch in southeastern Utah called Cow Tanks Canyon. There you can feel the basic pulse of life. It's tough and gritty—barely holding its own under the heat of the sun. Lichens grow on sand, trees out of rock and in many places nothing lives, there's only caked dust. There are some good places in the mountains, too, above timberline— desolate, desperate landscapes with piles of bare rock, spatters of lichen and that's all, except for the intense sun. It's places like that that attract me most. But actually wilderness can be any type of country, even a few square yards which have been left substantially alone.

My photograph of the snow-covered aspen, for example, was taken at the edge of a subdivision in the foothills west of Denver.

BACKPACKER: What is your normal photographing routine?

SUMNER: Ideally, I like to set up a base camp, say five miles in, and from there I like to take day hikes, usually in circle routes so I'm always covering new ground.

I carry my cameras in a day pack.

BACKPACKER: How long do you stay out?

SUMNER: As long as I'm in a place long enough to get the feel of it, I'm satisfied. That usually means a few days of sinking in so I can get relaxed and attuned to the pulse of the place. Trips also are cumulative. I've done most of my hiking in the Colorado mountains, and I'm familiar with their ecosystems, weather patterns and geology. So when I go to the high country it doesn't take long for me to sink in— sometimes no more than 20 minutes. It is like going home.

But when I go someplace new, I need more time. The first few days I scatter-gun a bit—shooting away at this and that— before I'm able to zero in on the distinctive qualities of the place. The scatter-gunning is necessary to explore possibilities, and sometimes I get some very good shots in the process. However, if I don't have a modest feel for a place and its pulse, I don't think I photograph it well. I photograph *at* it instead.

BACKPACKER: Do you usually go into the wilderness alone?

SUMNER: It's about fifty-fifty. When I want to photograph intensely, I usually go alone because I'm more free to set my own pace and get utterly involved. Otherwise I like to go with a good friend or two. No more than three, though; a big group clutters things. I prefer to share the wilderness intimately.

BACKPACKER: What cameras do you carry?

SUMNER: A Nikon with three or four lenses: a 24mm, a 55mm macro, a 105mm and a 300mm. I also carry a beat-up old Linhof III 4 x 5 with a wide angle, standard and 2x lens. I carry as much film as I think I need, film holders, tripod and changing bag. The old Linhof is a good backpack camera for a 4 x 5. It's compact and weighs only about five pounds. They stopped making that model in the 1950s, so there are only a few of them around. I found mine through a classified ad in the *Denver Post*.

I didn't know how to work it at first and was actually scared of the thing. I carted it all over Wyoming when I was up there doing research in 1971 before I dared use it. Finally, I broke the ice in Grand Teton National Park. There was a soft copper sunset, so I did two shots of the mountains across Jackson Lake. One shot was washed out, but the other was beautiful. I've sold it four or five times.

BACKPACKER: Do you take different types of photos with each camera?

SUMNER: I use them together. I almost always have the Nikon in my hand or around my neck, and I am constantly viewing things. I reject a lot of scenes, or at least a lot of angles, but I still use plenty of film. When I hit upon something really interesting, I'll pull out the 4 x 5 and set up.

The two cameras complement each other. The Nikon gives me fluidity and freedom; sometimes with the Linhof I get too stiff. But the big camera gives me precision and tends to curb the scatter-gun sloppiness which creeps into my 35mm work.

BACKPACKER: How much does all this gear weigh?

SUMNER: I don't worry about that. I carry what I need and live with the weight. I weighed all the cameras and lenses once, and they came out to 22½ pounds.

BACKPACKER: When did you start backpacking?

SUMNER: When I moved to Colorado in 1966. I got into it through hunting—backpacking into the Weminuche Wilderness to bow hunt for elk.

BACKPACKER: Did you get into photography after you started backpacking?

SUMNER: No, I had a succession of Brownies, and Dad had an amateur darkroom where I learned how to develop film and make contact prints.

Then, in high school, Dad gave me an old Vöigtlander, and I got into sports photography.

In college I also shot a few athletic events, but it wasn't until 1963, when I made my first trip west, that I picked up a good camera, an old Zeiss-Ikon Contax.

BACKPACKER: Was that when you became serious about photography?

SUMNER: Not really. In late 1969 I became executive editor of *Colorado Magazine.* We used a lot of scenic color, and I was screening maybe 7,500 shots a year. I used to go straight up the wall because David Muench was the only Rocky Mountain photographer we used who consistently submitted fresh, top-quality work.

So about that time I became more serious with cameras. I tried a Hasselblad, but it didn't work out very well for me because my eye was conditioned to the needs of a magazine page. Pages are either vertical or horizontal but never square. So I went back to a 35mm camera, and then added the 4 x 5.

BACKPACKER: Then you're basically a self-taught photographer?

SUMNER: Mostly, yes. I couldn't be into photography the way I am without the experience I had of screening all the shots at *Colorado Magazine* and learning what makes a good photograph for publication. And I've tried to study the kind of photos that are being used in other magazines and books, which means I go through a lot of books and magazines.

I think Ernst Haas's *The Creation* is the most stimulating volume of nature photography I've seen. More recently I've been trying to sense what people like Edward Weston and Imogen Cunningham have done.

BACKPACKER: Do you try to apply this studying directly to your own photography?

SUMNER: I try to see the compositional possibilities that other people have used and then apply them in my own scenes. David Muench, for instance, made me realize a lot about foregrounds. In some of his stuff, you look at the scene, and it appears as if your feet were right there at the edge of the photo—as if you were there yourself.

David was the one who started me seeing the possibilities of wide-angle lenses for wilderness photography—the 90mm on the Linhof, the 24mm on the Nikon. I really like the inclusiveness they give to a picture; they pull more life into the frame—a tree or rock off to the left, some lichen or flowers at your feet. With a wide-angle lens I get pictures that surround me; it's an almost enveloping effect. And I think that's a real part of the wilderness experience for many people.

This is the kind of thing you can pick up from another person's work. Then you go out and try to extend it without being a mimic.

BACKPACKER: You say "mimic." Do you have any concerns that your photography might simply be a copy of someone else's?

SUMNER: Sure. Anyone who's into a creative pursuit worries about being original.

I used to duck the subject by refusing to take shots from locations that have been heavily photographed. At the least, I'd truck my cameras 100 yards off the beaten path before going to work. For this reason I've never photographed Old Faithful or the Maroon Bells, which are the most photographed peaks in Colorado.

But you can carry that only so far before you have to face the fact of other photographers. Last September I made my first trip to Yosemite. For the first two days I had a terrible time. I was confronted by a mixture of postcard scenery and Ansel Adams's images. I couldn't photograph Yosemite Falls or Half Dome or El Capitan at all. I felt they'd already been done to death.

With subjects that have been worked like that, I had to fight to be original. I visited El Cap one day, checking around for a good spot to set up my cameras. But it was cloudy, so I went back a day later to see how the light was then. Three days later, the elements fell together the way I'd hoped. The late afternoon sun was streaming up the Merced River. I could see the rays of light in the sky, a thin line on the granite face, part of its reflection in an eddy of the river, flickers of light in the trees on the opposite bank.

BACKPACKER: What do you think best expresses you in your work?

SUMNER: I care about wilderness. I'd like my photography to express that care and inspire it in others.

Although I am obviously manipulating and selecting when I photograph, I try to take the wilderness as it is instead of overcomposing, and hence, imposing myself on the scene. If I aspire toward a style, it's one that draws more attention to the subject I'm photographing than to my photographic skills. When a person looks at my work, I want him to think, "I want to be there."

Chapter Eleven

THE MAGIC OF MOUNTAINS

Of various types of terrain where one can backpack, the mountains have a special allure. It hasn't always been so. Until the last two hundred years of human history, people rarely felt compelled to venture into their heights. The two exceptions to this were the spiritual attraction of mountains, revealed in the Bible and other early religious writing, and military operations or explorations in search of mountain treasures—land, game, gold, and minerals, for example.

I'm sure that when we backpackers trek into the mountains today we seek a little bit of both—the spiritual as well as the adventure of exploration that our ancestors experienced.

Mountains were the least commercially attractive geographical terrain to our forebears. They were unsuitable for building cities, for farming, for industrial plants, and for cutting timber. There were even good commercial reasons for keeping ranges near urban centers free from development; for one, to pro-

tect their watershed values—a source of good water being essential to urban growth.

Hence, we backpackers are lucky that one of our most alluring types of geographical terrains has been preserved in its wildest state. Experiencing the call of mountains, we can identify easily with the American mountain men who confronted the vast wilderness in the nineteenth century. One of the most romantic tales is that of John Colter, who was a member first of the Lewis and Clark expedition, and then with a group of fur traders who discovered the Yellowstone country. John Muir sought in the mountains the solutions to the mysteries of the universe.

There are others, too, as you will see in this chapter, who have their own personal reasons for climbing—backpackers who have challenged the mountain ranges in this country and abroad for the sheer fascination of the terrain. Their accounts are exhilarating.

JOHN COLTER (1775–1813)

by WINIFRED BLEVINS

A biography with some legendary embellishments

On a hot August afternoon in 1806, on the dusty plains of what is now North Dakota, John Colter announced a decision that marked him as an adventurer without parallel, a badly misguided entrepreneur, a waywardly romantic adolescent or a dangerously antisocial man. Various contemporaries judged him to be all four, but on the whole their hostility outweighed their admiration.

Colter had traveled to the Pacific Ocean and back with Lewis and Clark, had learned something of the northwestern country and the Indians and had served the expedition ably. Now, as he sat in the village of the Mandan Indians beside the Missouri River, he described that country to two beaver trappers, Dixon and Hancock, who had an idea: they planned to open the Shining (or Stony, or Rocky) Mountains for beaver.

Colter told the trappers about the land, Indians and beaver, and Dixon and Hancock got the message: Colter knew what was out there and would be valuable. They put it to him: Would he go along with them as a partner? Colter asked permission from Lewis and Clark to muster out and return to the mountains, telling them that the venture looked like a good business proposition. They decided that Colter had served well and had earned the chance to go.

It was a surprising decision. Nicholas Biddle, the official chronicler of the Lewis and Clark expedition, saw in Colter's return to the mountains a lack of human feeling: "This hunter has now been absent for many years from the frontier, and might naturally be presumed to have some anxiety, or some curiosity at least, to return to his friends and his country; yet, just at the moment when he is approaching the frontiers, he is tempted by a hunting scheme to give up those delightful prospects, and go back without the least reluctance to the solitude of the woods."

What were Colter's real reasons for wanting to turn around? Perhaps his own explanation was sufficient. But profit was available back in civilization, as well. There is some evidence that he had a romantic wanderlust and a lifelong love of the wilds. He had seen small mountain creeks roiling in the spring; had breathed in the strong, sweet smell of buffalo chips on an open fire; had seen the mountain sky at night, with ten times as many stars as the prairie's, some of them as big as thistle balls; had felt the scorch of dust in his nostrils; had tasted hump ribs and beaver tail; had looked at the hugeness of high country.

In any case, Colter turned back to the Rocky Mountains with Dixon and Hancock. Then, after a year, he joined a trapping party headed by Manuel Lisa. Lisa erected a picket fort in the heart of Crow country, where the Big Horn River flows into the Yellowstone. Colter soon set out alone to spread the news of the trading post among the Crows. And so began his historic 1807-08 ramble through the Rockies.

Colter must have left in the autumn. He wore buckskins and moccasins and carried a skin bag filled with about 30 pounds of survival gear. He started south up the Big Horn, meeting Crows along the way, improving his crude Crow vocabulary, making friends, urging the Indians (and maybe huckstering them) to go to trade. They received him hospitably and told him about the country ahead, and other Crows he would find there. He followed the Big Horn to the place where it makes a right-angle turn along the Wind River Range, and then followed the Wind River (also called the Big Horn) north. At a favorite Crow wintering spot, he was befriended again by Crows and decided to sit out the winter. Probably, given typical Crow friendship, he passed the time exchanging stories, gambling at the hand game, borrowing wives and daughters of his new friends and learning about this tribe.

Early in 1808, before the thaw had occurred, Colter moved on. He was becoming a mountain man, simply rambling and exploring.

John Colter tells of the boiling springs, geysers, and other sights he'd seen as the first white man in the Yellowstone Rockies—stories that later earned him a reputation as a confirmed liar.

COLTER'S HELL, COURTESY OF THE PERMANENT COLLECTION OF THE NATIONAL PARK SERVICE, DEPARTMENT OF THE INTERIOR, WASHINGTON, D.C.

Probably it was in the valley of Pierre's Hole, at the base of the western slope of the Tetons, that Colter and his Crow and Flathead traveling companions fell into a pitched battle with the Blackfeet. Colter was shot in the leg and was noticed by the Blackfeet. No sense in trying to open trade with them now; he had become an enemy. To make matters worse, he discovered the next morning that his friends had slipped away and left him.

Alone now and walking north through Jackson Hole, Colter saw the lovely lakes and the Teton Range jutting up behind them.

How close Colter got to Yellowstone Lake or the famous geysers and boiling springs is a matter of speculation. (Later, he told stories about the boiling springs he had seen and was taken as a liar; but he may have seen springs other than the ones in today's national park.) Still traveling north, he came upon the Yellowstone River, which Clark had traveled in 1806, and followed it back to the fort at

the mouth of the Big Horn. He had hobbled for 300 miles. When he got there, in the summer of 1808, his companions had given him up for dead. They wondered why anyone would wander alone through the Rockies for nearly a year.

It had been a remarkable trip for a lone man. Colter had traveled more than a thousand miles through unexplored territory, much of it in high mountains, had crossed and recrossed the Continental Divide, had stayed mostly out of trouble with the Indians and had found enough water, wood and meat to live on. He was the first white man to see most of the sights he described—the upper Big Horn River, the Wind River and the mountains alongside it, Union Pass, the sources of the Green River, Jackson Hole and Yellowstone country.

Lisa, impressed with Colter's mountain sense, gave Colter a companion, a trapper named Potts, and sent them to the Blackfeet territory, near the Three

Forks of the Missouri, where Colter had been with Lewis and Clark. Waiting to make contact, they hid in the daytime and did some trapping at daylight and dusk. Colter wanted to choose his spot for the encounter with the Blackfeet. But one morning in their canoe on a creek six miles from Jefferson Fork, they were running late. Colter could see that the morning sun would angle onto the water surface and dissolve the covering mist in a few minutes.

Then the men heard noises. Quickly, Colter slid the canoe under an overhanging branch. Potts thought it was buffalo and wanted to continue on. But Colter said "Indians. Let's cache."

"Indians, hell," Potts replied. "Buffler trompin' around."

But then they saw them, Indians sprouting up on both banks. Several hundred Blackfeet, including women and children. They didn't look like a war party, though. A brave motioned Colter and Potts to bring the canoe to shore. Colter took a long, deep

It was a desperate run. A tribe of riled Blackfeet brandished tomahawks and spears behind Colter, the river and safety still three miles off. A numbing tide of pain swept over him, bringing on slow waves of nausea and dizziness.

PAINTING BY ROY KERSWILL

breath. His body was becoming a set of nerve endings to get hold of the situation, to feel its medicine, to figure out what to say, what to do. Maybe he and Potts would just be robbed.

Putting in at the riverbank, Colter stepped out and made the sign that he came in peace. Potts got halfway out of the bow, holding his rifle uncertainly, and a husky Indian snatched it from him. Instantly Colter grabbed the rifle and handed it back to Potts, who still had one foot in the canoe. Potts abruptly pushed off from shore and sat in the canoe in midstream.

"Put in," Colter said firmly, "right now. There's nowhere you can go. Put in, show them you ain't afraid of them."

"You crazy?" Potts came back. "Look at 'em. They're gonna kill us. Torture us, first. Don't make no difference what we do." An arrow cut off his last word with a *thock.* He doubled over, with the arrow sticking out of his hip. Before Colter realized what was happening, Potts came up from his clutched-over position and shot the Indian who had seized

his rifle. The Indian fell. The answering sounds were as soft as Potts's rifle had been loud, a nasty whir of arrows and little slapping sounds when they hit. Potts's body had been riddled.

Immediately, the Indians began to whoop and wail. Some braves charged into the water to get Potts's body and drag it ashore. Others began strange cries of vengeance. The squaws sent up ululations of grief. Colter knew that the Blackfeet were fully riled—in a mood to get even for the death of their tribesman with a slow, ritual revenge.

Colter felt hands on him, but did not flinch or protest. Women and children ripped all his clothing away. Yet he stood straight and looked directly at them, making no move to stop them. Out of the corner of his eye, he could see braves and squaws cutting at Potts and beating the body with clubs.

A squaw appeared in front of Colter and stared into his eyes. The noise died down a little as the other Blackfeet watched. She held something bloody in front of Colter's face: Potts's genitals. Then

she threw the bloody mess into his face and let out a fierce scream. The whoops soared again. Colter didn't need to look to know what was happening. He forced himself to keep his eyes open as more organs and chunks of flesh were thrown against his face and chest.

Then several braves pushed toward him, tomahawks in hand. But others held them back. They're going to make a ceremony of it, he thought. Maybe Potts was right. Colter remained still as a pine. He'd wait for whatever chance he had.

A dozen braves, important-looking ones, sat down and began to talk. Colter understood enough of what they said to realize that some of them were proposing to set him up as a shooting target. Others were arguing for a more lingering death by tomahawk. Colter waited.

Finally, an old chief came over to him and asked whether he was a fast runner. Colter guessed that they were considering letting him run for his life. Some chance, with 500 angry braves on his tail, and him running naked and barefoot through the cactus—but a chance.

Colter answered ambiguously, in his limited Blackfeet. "The long knife is a poor runner, and not swift. He is considered by the other long knives to be very swift, but he is not." A half-challenge. The chief returned to council.

When he came back, he signaled Colter to follow him onto the plain. After they had walked 20 or 30 yards, the chief said, "Walk farther, past the large boulder, and then you must run to try to save yourself." Then he went back to the party. Colter could see the young men were getting rid of their blankets and leggings, preparing for the race. He walked on slowly and calmly, passed the boulder and kept walking. He hoped to walk as far as possible, because they would come as soon as he started running. Finally he heard a series of whoops, glanced back to see the braves were starting out and began to run himself.

His legs turned toward the Jefferson Fork. From where he was, the creek arched down to the Jefferson like a bow. He would run as the bowstring would go. It was five or six miles to the Jefferson that way. He didn't know how far he would get. But he ran toward the river because that was his only chance. His hope was to get into the river, to destroy his trail, and then hide.

Plains and hills, plains and hills, as far as Colter could see. He noticed pain in his right foot first. He was not missing all the low, gnarly cactus. He made his eyes stay focused on the ground, cooperating with his legs and converting his body into one long motion of running.

He felt his breath coming full and deep, sucking in the thin air, bellowing it out, regular as the pendulum of a clock. He felt his feet hitting the sandy earth automatically as he loped along. He didn't feel the steps individually, but as a kind of glide. He was surprised at how fast he was going. But he thought that if he needed a little more speed, he would have it for a while.

He deliberately did not look back. He wondered how far he had run—a couple of miles, at the most. He put his pursuers out of his mind and forced himself again to concentrate on running.

Colter's mind floated. Images of packs of running horses came into his head, spread across a plain. Buffalo passed through, huge in foreshortening. He saw the water-wheel of a mill turning steadily with the flow of a wide, slow creek. A stick slid along

Colter set out from Fort Lisa in the fall of 1807. He entered unexplored territory, traveling along the Big Horn and Wind rivers, through Jackson Hole and Yellowstone. By the time he returned in the summer of 1808 he had walked more than 1,000 miles, mostly alone and in high mountains.

in a frictionless skim on ice covered by a thin layer of water. And Colter felt the evenness of his own slide. He would run until he died.

How close were they? He had to look back, just a quick glance. The Blackfeet were scattered all over the plain, most of them straggling far behind. But one of them was close, no more than a hundred yards behind. He was carrying a spear, and he was gaining.

Colter decided that now was the time for that extra speed he thought he had. He forced his legs to pick up the pace, and then let them settle into their own faster rhythm. It must still be two or three miles to the river.

He felt his breath coming faster now, maybe twice as fast, and rasping in his throat. He ignored it, and the pain that was growing in his chest. The rest of his body was getting logy, as though only his legs were alive.

When Colter snapped to, he realized that he had been dizzy for a moment. Dizzy! He fixed his eyes on the ground and made a point of holding them open. The dizziness came back in slow waves, and with it, nausea. For a couple of minutes he let the waves pass, observing himself dispassionately. Once he had the feeling that his bowels would let go, but ignored it. He snatched huge chunks of air into his lungs and forced himself on.

He decided he would look back quickly. Maybe he had left the Indian behind. He knew that his body would not stand much more of this punishment. He looked. The Indian was only about 20 yards back with his spear high, waiting for the moment when he would be close enough to throw it. Colter forced his legs a little harder.

Then Colter became aware of something on his knees. He looked down. Blood. The entire front of his body was covered with blood. He felt it on his lips, sticky and salty. Blood was gushing out of his nose.

Colter realized then that he would not be able to outrun the Indian. Abruptly he stopped, turned around, spread his arms and called to the Indian in the Crow language to spare his life. Startled, the Indian tried to stop and throw the spear at the same time. But he stumbled, just at the moment his arm started forward, and

pitched downward. The spear stuck in the ground and broke off in his hand. Colter pounced. He grabbed the head of the spear, pulled it out and, as the Indian pleaded for mercy, drove it into his stomach.

Suddenly Colter felt as though he had enough energy left to run to St. Louis. His legs tingled with new blood, and there were no Indians in sight. Yet. He started again toward the river with the loping motion he liked. Before long he heard one whoop, and then a series of whoops, as the Blackfeet found their dead comrade. No more than a mile from the river, he thought. He was going to make it. His legs took over once again.

Colter did make it, and only one step shorter than the others broke his rhythm as he shifted from run to dive. The water was a blast of ice. His head reeled as he came up. He began to swim toward a pile of driftwood near the head of an island. Reaching it, he slipped, beaverlike, beneath the surface, to grope for some kind of air space between the logs. He couldn't see anything, and his breath was running out. He found a hole big enough to accommodate his head and shoulders. He was under five or six feet of wood. He could see sideways out of small chinks, and straight up, through crevices, he saw blue sky and a cottonwood branch moving lazily in the wind. The hideout would do.

The Blackfeet soon began to splash in the water and prance along the bank, yelling and screeching. Several swam across to the island and trampled all over it, and even on top of the driftwood. Colter slipped back under the water, temporarily.

He wondered what they were thinking, now that they had lost his track. By now they must have learned that his trail didn't come out of the river for quite a distance, upstream or down. He had a sudden thought, and it chilled him. What if they decided to set fire to the driftwood? He stopped himself. They wouldn't; they had no reason to.

He waited. He was still up to his chest in the icy water, snow melted down from the Continental Divide. He managed to prop himself up and mostly out of the water. It was tiring, but he could do it.

It had been dark for two or three hours when Colter decided to risk

leaving his hideout. There had been no sound of Indians for quite a while. Noiselessly, he swam under the debris and surfaced alongside the island. Then, keeping his hands in the water so he wouldn't make any noise, he paddled slowly a long way downstream. (The Indians might look again for his track leaving the river.) Then he left the river and walked for the rest of the night.

At dawn he clambered onto some rock, walked trackless a ways, and finally lay down to sleep at the bottom of a rock chimney. His feet were bleeding from the beating they had taken. And because his body was white as the underside of a fish, he knew he wouldn't be able to expose it to much sun.

Well, he had done it before—traveled alone back to Fort Lisa after a scrap with the Blackfeet. That time he had had a wounded leg. But this time he was naked, so his feet would go raw, and he had no knife or gun. Bare-handed, he could survive, though, on roots and bark. Nearly 300 miles—a long walk.

Seven days later, Colter approached Fort Lisa, and the man at the gate did not recognize him. His face was gaunt, his body was emaciated and he was half-covered by scratches and dried blood. Only his beard identified him as a white man.

When Colter told his story, some people believed it, but others scoffed. A veteran mountain man decided not to travel with him anymore; Colter was obviously bad luck. A newcomer had little sympathy because Colter seemed such a queer fellow—he talked as though he were seeing faraway places and didn't care whether anyone listened.

Early in 1810 after the ice broke up on the river Colter surprised Manuel Lisa by announcing that he would return to civilization. He said he was fed up with fighting Blackfeet.

In St. Louis, Colter gave William Clark information for a forthcoming map and talked around town about his adventures. These stories earned him a reputation as a confirmed liar, and he was not vindicated for several years. Soon he acquired a piece of land on the Charrette Creek in Missouri and got married. Two years later, having left the mountains as hazardous to his health, he died in the settlements of jaundice.

Colter was the first mountain man, the precursor of such legendary trappers as Jim Bridger, Tom Fitzpatrick, Kit Carson and Jedediah Smith. It is enough to say that, as an explorer, trapper, woodsman and master of mountaincraft, he was legendary among those men. In the lone odyssey through unknown territory, he is without peer in American history.⬥

KEEP CLIMBING

by HARVEY MANNING

Too many mountains . . . not enough years. Don Woods climbed eight peaks in Wyoming's Tetons in the summer of 1946. Among the more than 365 peaks he has climbed around the world, he recalls his climb up the Exum Route on the Grand Teton as being one of the most enjoyable. In fact, he liked the mountain so much he climbed it twice.

WHAT IS AN APPROPRIATE way to spend your seventy-second summer? If you were Don Woods, it would be to set out with a 50-pound pack along the crest of Washington's North Cascades, and spend two weeks climbing four peaks and traversing half a dozen glaciers.

Unusual? Don Woods doesn't think so. "I've been climbing mountains since 1925. Maybe *you* know of a reason to quit. *I* don't."

It is exaggerating to say no mountaineer can match Woods' pace today. But few beginners can hope to match his half-century record. In a sport where 10 years are an average career and 30 an eye-opener, his 50 years are a jaw-dropper.

The statistics boggle: 41 extended climbing trips in the Cascades and Olympics; 44 in the High Sierra; 51 in Canada; travels in 34 mountain ranges on five continents; 365 peaks climbed (excluding walk-ups), many of them twice or more and a number of them first ascents.

No, for a young beginner it would be folly to think of catching up with Woods. Perhaps after 25 or 35 alpine years the possibility might be entertained. Until then, best simply to stand in awe, properly humbled—yet inspired, too.

Although Don Woods had lived near the Cascade volcanoes in Oregon's Willamette Valley since his birth in 1903 and often had gone family camping on the wilderness fringe, it was not until Labor Day of 1925, on a Boy Scout outing, that he climbed above the forest into bleak moraine, brilliant snow and wide horizons.

Atop 10,053-foot Middle Sister, he instantly thought, "This is where I belong!" Looking at the row of volcanoes from Mount Shasta in California to Mount Adams in Washington, he vowed, "I'm going to climb them all!"

He wasted no time getting started. Next year, joining the Mazamas, he scaled Middle Sister again, the neighboring South and North Sisters, and two other Oregon volcanoes, mounts Jefferson and Hood. In 1927 he crossed the Columbia River to Washington and climbed four more volcanoes—mounts St. Helens, Adams, Baker and Glacier Peak—and the equally impressive if nonvolcanic Mount Shuksan. At the end of his second season he was known throughout the climbing region as a young tiger, agile on rock and snow, with good sense and a cool head—the sort of lad meant by a club outing leader when, at the foot of a glacier or cliff, he shouted the order "Scouts forward!"

TODAY, THE MOTIVATION of 1920s mountaineers is perfectly familiar; it hasn't changed. But the equipment and techniques of the twenties are another matter. We groan or even go into eco-shock at the spectacle of 150 folk assaulting the wilderness, supported by a packtrain of half that many horses. But we forget two things.

First, the typical recreational mountaineer was poorly prepared for

There were few backpackers in the 1920s. Instead, most wilderness travelers relied upon packtrains to carry their heavy tents and clothing. Don Woods was an exception. He often backpacked for days at a time in the Cascades, a reason his packtrain-bound friends considered him a titan—if not a downright lunatic. He is shown here on Mount Rainier in 1927.

PHOTO: COURTESY OF DON WOODS

a Cascades trail trek. Existing instruction manuals were of little help. Written by Appalachian veterans, they were superb for keeping Boy Scouts busy with hatchets but totally irrelevant to trail life in the mountains of the West. Northwestern neophytes had to learn everything on their own. This was done most safely and comfortably in large outing groups.

Second, the weight of tents and clothing made the packtrain indispensable if the vacation were not to be an exercise in survival. Backpacking was customary only when a peak was too distant from the horse trail for a day's hike; and it was limited to ascending from an elaborate valley-bottom camp to an overnight "fly camp" or "bivouac."

Still, a few intrepid souls habitually risked damage to spine and

spirit by carrying homes on their backs for days at a time. Young Don Woods was among them.

To understand why Woods was looked upon by packtrain-bound friends as a titan, if not a downright lunatic, we must examine the backpacking outfit of the Northwest in the 1920s.

The hiking–climbing boot covered the calf nearly to the knee, and its sole was studded with hobnails or logger's caulks. More favored than trousers or knickers were cavalryman-style riding britches, flared at the thighs and narrow at the calves, with laces at the bottom to ensure a tight fit inside the high boots. For storm wear the local preference was a hiplength Filson jacket of tightly woven wool with a turn-up collar and snap-closed pockets. Of the various packboards, the choice of most experts was the wood-and-canvas Trapper Nelson, a recent adaptation from a sourdough design hailed as a boon to the aching back.

At night most hikers rolled up in wool blankets and snuggled next to the campfire. Shivering could be lessened by sewing the blankets together and adding a cotton-duck cover, thus constructing a "sleeping bag." Of course, Robert Peary, Vilhjalmur Stefansson and other travelers to the Far North had used down-filled bags. Their price, however, was excruciatingly high. Nevertheless, in 1927 Woods decided a down bag was the only rational alternative for a chap of his ambitions and steeled himself to face bankruptcy. The rectangular Woods (no relation) Arctic bag he bought from an Ogdensburg, New York, manufacturer was light and cozy, but it cost a staggering $47.50—half a month's salary.

Grudgingly, Woods lugged along a poplin Beebe tent weighing too much and protecting too little. Rigged as a tarp, it kept out drizzles but not downpours. Set up as a two-man A-tent, it was inferior in a bad blow to a clump of trees.

ON HIS FIRST BACKPACK in 1926, Woods tottered under 50 pounds of canned vegetables, fruits and soup. That blunder was not repeated; he gradually learned which foods could be carried without excessive pain and consumed with something resembling pleasure. The

standby suppers were based on pasta (not the modern speedy cooking variety): macaroni and cheese, noodles and canned tuna, spaghetti and corned beef. Dehydrated potatoes gave variety; the bland, lumpy sludge at least made one appreciate the pasta meals. Every breakfast was built around rolled oats, which with luck could be cooked in a half-hour and with constant stirring would burn only a little on the bottom. The accompanying powdered milk was not treated for quick mixing; to minimize lumps, shaker can and several minutes' exercise were required. Bacon and eggs were a frequent treat. Woods protected his eggs from breakage by carrying them in the rolled oats.

As for climbing gear and techniques, photos of mountain excursions in the twenties always are good for a chuckle—or a gasp of consternation. A helping hand or a shirt dangled from above was standard procedure on rock, supplemented on long pitches by a fixed rope for handholds. When Woods first tied into a rope in 1926, it was five-eighths- inch Manila hemp and much too weak (we moderns realize) to withstand a hard fall. But Woods' main complaint was that the hemp fibers worked into his skin and caused an itch.

Looking at a photo of a hundred men and women marching unroped up a crevassed glacier, each climber maintaining balance with an alpenstock (a walking stick five to eight feet long with a metal spike on one end and a leather wristloop on the other), we marvel that every mass ascent was not a mass slaughter. Woods, the young upstart, instinctively realized the "alpie" was inadequate and, despite the expostulations of his elders, switched in 1927 to an ice axe, which everybody who was anybody knew was strictly for Swiss guides and very dangerous in the hands of an amateur. He also dismayed friends by purchasing crampons. The prevailing philosophy was that lashing iron spikes to one's boots was unsporting.

Today's climbers may think Woods was too rapidly respected as a tiger. After all, in his second big season he scaled only five major peaks, for a career total of 10. And what is "major?" Nothing bragworthy about 10,541-foot Glacier Peak, says the modern hero, who leaves Seattle

Saturday noon, drives in two hours to the end of Whitechuck River road, and in four leisurely trail hours beds down in a moraine, from which on Sunday he dashes to the summit, then hikes and drives home in time for supper.

CLIMBING PEAKS WAS more complicated in 1927. To climb Glacier Peak, a party boarded the early morning train from Seattle and rode via Everett to Darrington, arriving around noon. To avoid walking 11 miles to the recently built Whitechuck River Trail, transport was negotiated on a logging-railroad "speeder," an open-air taxi fitted with flanged wheels to run on tracks. The first day concluded with a four-mile hike up the Whitechuck River to Stujack Creek. The second day covered 12 miles to Kennedy Hot Springs, and the third, seven miles to Whitechuck Meadows, from where Glacier Peak was climbed via the Whitechuck, Suiattle and Cool Glaciers. The two-day, 26-mile exit was made by hiking over Red Pass and White Pass and down the Sauk River to Barlow Pass, where one caught the Monte Cristo Railroad for the return to Everett. Allowing for at least a 50-percent proportion of stormy days, as one must in the Cascades, Glacier Peak was then a venture for an entire week—and might be an impossibility if the stormy weather failed to abate.

Climbing five major peaks was a triumph in 1927, and Woods returned home from Glacier Peak full of satisfaction—as well as another emotion.

Among the 28 members of the Mountaineers party was a Spokane girl, Lynda Mueller. An avid peakgrabber, she had climbed three of

---

When Woods first tied into a rope in 1926, it was five-eighths-inch Manila hemp and much too weak to withstand a fall. But Woods' only complaint was that the hemp fibers were itchy.

Washington's "Six Majors"— Rainier, Baker and Olympus—as well as Stuart and a score of lesser peaks.

The first evening, at Stujack Creek, Lynda had camped with the Dean of Women. (Females were

shielded from males by separation of camp into Men's Quarters and Women's Quarters and by a hawk-eyed Dean.) Seeking a quiet sleep, Lynda and the Dean had pitched their army pup tent at the edge of Women's Quarters.

IN THE MIDDLE OF THE NIGHT, Lynda awoke to heavy thudding, let out a scream and leapt up to do combat. Instead of the expected bear, her flashlight dazzled a young man under an enormous pack, trembling with relief that he had not, as he thought, disturbed a cougar.

Don contritely explained that his departure from Seattle had been delayed. Stumbling by starlight up the trail, he had seen a towel on a line and hoped he had found Men's Quarters.

The night encounter stirred camp gossip for the rest of the trip, especially after discussions revealed that Lynda and Don, two weeks earlier, had missed each other by a single day on the summit of Mount Baker. Commemorating their meeting at a campfire gathering, Lynda recited a composition she had written, "The Ballad of Don Woods." Its chorus:
"Oh-oh-oh, OH-OH dear lady,
Cease your howl!
I didn't come here to hurt you,
I merely saw your towel!"

Correspondence commenced between Spokane and Newberg, Oregon, where Woods, having in 1926 received a bachelor's degree in chemistry from the University of Oregon, was a science teacher. The letters led to his acceptance in February, 1928, of a position at North Central High School in Spokane where, by no coincidence, the school's biology teacher was Miss Lynda Mueller.

Although tender passion was growing in Don's heart, it had to coexist with an older, wilder passion. That summer the Sierra Club journeyed to the Canadian Rockies, and he was a guest member of the party. Compelled by circumstances to remain in Spokane, Lynda spent the summer reading letters that narrated conquests of mounts Geike, Edith Cavell, Resplendent and Lynx. Don reserved the supreme story for telling in person on his return.

Mount Robson, the 12,972-foot "roof of the Rockies," had repelled numerous assaults before yielding in

1913. By 1928 the summit, despite topping the American–Canadian "most wanted" list, had been attained fewer than 10 times. Most of these successes were in the "easy" year of 1924 when a crack in the key ice wall simplified passage. Since 1924 the mountain had frustrated every attempt, and North American mountaineers were wondering when, if ever, it would be climbed again.

An elite 12 of the large Sierra Club party were selected to join three of Canada's top Swiss guides in an attack; that Woods was among them indicates how quickly he'd proven himself to his new California friends. Only five of the 15 surmounted the ice wall: two guides, Hans and Heinrich Fuhrer; the Sierra Club's finest climber of the time, Norman Clyde; a doughty Illinois girl, Rusty Montgomery; and Don Woods. Next to the Swiss, Woods proved to be the best of the 15 on ice, although Clyde surpassed him on rock. The Robson victory gave Woods continent-wide fame and instant acceptance in any climbing group as a trusty man for tight spots.

THE CLIMBING SEASONS from 1929 to World War II placed Woods securely in the upper ranks of American mountaineers. His alpine skills, initially derived from innate agility and "being an eager beaver and fig-

Don Woods (left) on the summit of Canada's Mount Hungabee in 1929 with Norman Clyde, then the Sierra Club's finest climber. The boots are typical of the period's climbing garb, with Swiss edge nails crimped onto the overhang of the sole.
PHOTO: COURTESY OF DON WOODS

uring out how to do things as I went along," improved in 1929 on an Alpine Club of Canada outing to the Selkirk Mountains. For the first time he used a rope for belaying and rappelling. He also wore sneakers on rock for the first time, and found their traction and comfort far superior to that of the Swiss edge nails (chunks of soft iron crimped onto the overhang of the boot sole) with which he had supplemented his hobnails.

Woods further refined his skills while climbing 14 peaks on a 1930 Alpine Club of Canada outing to Maligne Lake. That trip was memorable for another reason: he and Lynda had been married in June. She later wrote, "By climbing a dozen summits on my honeymoon, I may have set some sort of record for women."

The newlyweds spent a year at the University of Oregon while Don obtained a master's degree in chemistry. They then moved in 1931 to their permanent home in San Jose, California, where Don became a science teacher at San Jose high school. In 1932 they became a family of three with the birth of their son, David.

In the thirties Woods began the string of 44 backpacking and climbing trips in the High Sierra during which he scaled more than a hundred peaks, including seven first ascents in the Sawtooth Range and Kearsarge Pinnacles. As a member of the new Sierra Club Rock Climbing Section, he became familiar with pitons, carabiners and slings. Using anchors, both for protection and direct aid, he accomplished such then notable climbs in Yosemite Valley as Lower Cathedral Spire, Split Pinnacle, Washington Column, Leaning Tower and Arrowhead Spire.

Woods also settled old scores in the Northwest. In 1934 he completed Washington's "Six Majors" when, after many weather-defeated attempts over the years, he at last climbed Mount Rainier via Emmons Glacier. He liked 14,410-foot Rainier so well that in 1938 he returned to lead the first ascent of Rainier's Sunset Ridge, at the time one of the three toughest routes ever done on the mountain. The same year he hiked with the Mazamas through the North Cascades, from the Trinity Mines to Stehekin on Lake Chelan. Among his ascents was Glacier Peak via the Chocolate Glacier.

Yet it was Canada where he climbed most often. His total ascents there ultimately exceeded 100 peaks. In the Canadian Rockies he made the first ascent of Rosita and of a route on the west face of Warren, and the first traverse of Castle (now Mount Eisenhower). Other climbs included mounts Brazeau and Louis, Victoria Peak, Lefroy and Hungabee. In the Selkirk Mountains he scaled Mount Sir Donald, Uto, Tupper, Selwyn, and Hasler. On a genuine if small-scale 1935 expedition, he slogged up the glaciers of the British Columbia Coast Range for the third ascent of the 13,-000-foot northwest summit of Mount Waddington. Nowadays airplane transport has eliminated Waddington from the expedition class, but in 1935 it was so well defended by wilderness that a dozen years earlier its very existence had been a mere rumor—thus its original name, Mystery Mountain.

D ON WOODS MIGHT WELL have let World War II, with its restrictions on travel, provide a graceful exit from high mountaineering, his place in history assured. But instead of relaxing at an age when most climbers are hanging up the rope and axe, he commenced a second alpine career as stunning as the first.

He returned to Canada and made first ascents in the Rockies of Hooge, Monehy, Pangman Two, Whiteaves and Helmar. In the Purcell Mountains he climbed a row of Bugaboos, and in the Selkirks he led the classic northwest ridge of Mount Sir Donald. He returned to the Olympics and the North Cascades for long wilderness traverses and ascents of new summits. He visited the Tetons and Wind River ranges of Wyoming, the northern Rockies of Glacier National Park, the central Rockies of Colorado, the southern Rockies of Arizona and the Wallowa Mountains of Oregon. Between far wanders he explored the High Sierra, not always solely to climb; with David now a long-legged lad, the Woodses took up family backpacking.

During drives to and from Canada, the Woods family attended to unfinished business in the Cascades. They ran up Mount St. Helens; thus Lynda finally completed the "Six Majors." They hiked through clouds to the top of Mount Shasta; thus Don finally kept his 1925 vow to "climb them all."

The special distinction of the Woodses' postwar climbing career, however, was their reaching out to peaks around the world. In 1951 they made a pilgrimage to the Alps. That taste aroused a voracious appetite. Don obtained a leave of absence from teaching and, from June 1959, to November, 1961, they roamed Europe in a Volkswagen camper. Don scaled 35 summits, including the Matterhorn and Mont Blanc, and traversed the Eiger. They also climbed Etna and Vesuvius in Italy, Mont Perdu in the Pyrenees, the slabs and cracks of Snowdon in Wales, and peaks leaping from Norwegian fjords.

Additional peaks on additional continents were not neglected:
• *1955, 1963 and 1966:* Mexico—Popocatepetl, Nevado de Toluca, Ixtacihuatl, La Malinche and Ajusco.
• *1963:* Peru—Chaco.
• *1966 and 1968-69:* New Zealand—Ngauruhoe, Ruapehu, Sebastopol and Egmont.
• *1967:* Africa—Alexandra in the Ruwenzori Mountains, Point Lenana in Kenya and up to 16,000 feet on Kilimanjaro.
• *1969:* Japan—Hokado (Nose).
• *1969:* Hawaii—traversed Haleakala Crater solo in one day; climbed Mauna Loa solo in 25 elapsed hours.

So you cry, "Hold, enough!" Not Don Woods. Retiring from teaching in 1968, he exulted that the entire year could now be devoted to exploring the world's mountains.

F EW CLIMBERS HAVE KNOWN SO many mountain ranges. And few climbers have known so many other mountaineers. Woods was a member of the Mazamas for 38 years and often climbed with the Seattle Mountaineers. In 1930 he was a charter member of the Obsidians of Eugene, and in 1933 a charter member of the Loma Prieta Chapter of the Sierra Club. Since 1929 he has belonged to the Alpine Club of Canada, and since 1930 to the American Alpine Club. He has attended outings of the Cascadians of Yakima, the Colorado Mountain Club, the Iowa Mountaineers, and the French and Austrian Alpine Clubs. Indeed, the roster of his friends and climbing companions amounts to a large proportion of world mountaineering's hall of fame during the past half-century.

But Woods' most cherished friend has been lost. On March 18, 1975, Lynda passed away. Yet the loss cannot mar his memories of 48 blithe high-country years with the girl from Spokane.

When asked to list the high points of his half-century on the peaks, Don Woods despairs; there are too many high points. Nevertheless, he recalls a dozen climbs that for one reason or another rank among his best:
• Mount Robson, Canada, 1928
• Sunset Ridge, Mount Rainier, Washington (first ascent), 1938
• Lower Cathedral Spire, Yosemite, 1937
• The Three Sisters in one day (the first time ever done), Oregon, 1931
• The Matterhorn, Switzerland, 1951
• Grande Charmoz-Grepon traverse, France, 1959
• Mont Blanc, traverse up Dome du Fouté, down Grande Mulets, France, 1951
• Mount Geike, Canada, 1928
• Northwest summit of Mount Waddington, Canada, 1935
• Three Teeth traverse, Sierra Nevada, 1936 .
• North Tower of Howser Spire, Bugaboos (new route on northeast ridge), Canada, 1946
• Bugaboo Spire, Canada, 1946

How did Don Woods spend his seventy-second summer and fifty-first climbing year? He shouldered pack, grasped axe and spent two weeks doing the Ptarmigan Traverse through the North Cascades in the company of four grandnephews and a grandniece, the five aged from 17 to 23.

Generation gap? What's that?

THE GRAND TETONS

by BOYD NORTON

The Tetons, leaping so startlingly from the surrounding plains, comprise one of America's most beautiful mountain ranges. Backpacking Congressman Goodloe E. Byron claimed Grand Teton National Park is our prettiest—and he had backpacked in all of the best-known national parks, including those in Alaska.

The Tetons have a rich and romantic history as Boyd Norton relates it here.

W.K.

Although the Lewis and Clark expedition passed well north of the Teton Range, the first white man to see it was a member of that expedition. John Colter joined Lewis and Clark in 1803 and traversed the rugged northern Rockies to the Pacific shore, returning over nearly the same route in 1806. Before the party returned to civilization, Colter left the group to join two trappers bound for the upper reaches of the Yellowstone River. Unfortunately, there is no record of this trio's wanderings. Colter mysteriously appeared alone in the spring of 1807 in time to join an expedition led by the celebrated trader Manuel Lisa near the confluence of the Platte and the Missouri rivers. Then, once again, he set out for the upper Yellowstone.

There is ample evidence concerning the 1807 journey. Sent ahead by Lisa to notify Indians of his arrival, Colter passed east of present-day Yellowstone National Park, traveled south to the Wind River and followed it northwest to its source. From there he crossed Union Pass and entered Jackson Hole from the southeast. He spent the winter of 1807-1808 in Pierre's Hole at the base of the western slope of the Tetons.

The next journey into the region was also a commercial venture. John Jacob Astor, seeking to control the fur trade, funded an expedition to follow the Lewis and Clark route from the Missouri River to the mouth of the Columbia River, there to establish a fort to serve as a center of commerce and exploitation of the Northwest. Wilson Price Hunt was the leader of this party.

In 1811 Hunt began his trip, but he soon departed from Lewis and Clark's route because of hostile Indians. He proceeded overland, ascending the Wind River as Colter had done four years earlier. In the vicinity of Union Pass, according to the account in Washington Irving's *Astoria:* "They came to a height that commanded an almost boundless prospect. Here one of the guides paused, and, after considering the vast landscape attentively, pointed to three mountain peaks glistening with snow, which rose, he said, above a fork of the Columbia River." The peaks were, of course, the Tetons. Hunt gave them the name "Pilot Knobs." The fort later established by the party on the Pacific Coast was named Astoria, after John Jacob Astor.

In the early summer of 1812 another party, headed by Robert Stuart,

The Grand Teton Mountains and the Snake River, Wyoming.
PHOTO: ED COOPER

left Astoria and, traveling eastward, traced Hunt's route in reverse. In 1818 or 1819 a party headed by Donald McKenzie explored the Teton and Yellowstone country, also approaching from the west. Their first glimpse was of three pointed peaks, which prompted some French-Canadian trappers in the group to name them *Les Trois Tetons* (the three breasts).

FASHION influenced the fate of the Teton country for the next 20 years. Fortunes were made from beaver pelts as tall beaver hats became the rage of society in the East and in Europe.

The "mountain men" came by the hundreds, working for such companies as the Rocky Mountain Fur Company, Hudson's Bay Company and John Jacob Astor's American Fur Company. Some of the men became legends in the history of the West: James Bridger, Jedediah S. Smith, Joseph Meek, David Jackson, Nathaniel

J. Wyeth, Captain Benjamin L.E. de Bonneville.

The fur trade provided quick fortunes for some. But as Bernard De-Voto pointed out, it was not solely profit that spurred on the mountain men. There was new country to be explored, lands never before seen by white men.

The trappers ranged over much of the northern and central Rockies—farther than they really needed to go for beaver alone. The spectacular valley east of the Tetons held a special attraction for David Jackson, and eventually it was given his name: Jackson Hole.

Unlike the gold seekers to come in a few decades, the mountain men had relatively little impact on the land. Rather than attempting to change it, they adapted. They seemed to share a profound feeling for beauty, wildness and adventure.

Their success as trappers, though, was depleting the resource. And more

significantly, the whims of fashion changed, and the market for beaver pelts declined. By the early 1840s the fur trade was a dying industry, and the trappers, with reluctance, were moving on. The Teton country was left in relative solitude.

THE DISCOVERY of gold farther west had little impact on the Tetons. The trails that carried hundreds of thousands of prospectors to California were situated well south of the range. Fortunately, the Tetons held no mineral wealth. While the insane pursuit of gold swept over much of the West, the valleys of the Tetons remained quiet and untouched by civilization for almost 20 years.

Around 1860 a period of rediscovery began. The government began to fund expeditions to explore the upper Yellowstone country. Even though much of the West had been roamed and combed, this particular

330

area was still a land of mystery. The tales of Bridger and his colleagues about smoking mountains and boiling springs continued to trickle out of the region.

First came the Captain W.F. Raynolds expedition of 1860, with Jim Bridger as guide. It traveled through Jackson Hole and Pierre's Hole on the way to Yellowstone, under the auspices of the U.S. Topographical Engineers. Ten years later the Washburn-Langford-Doane expedition was significant not for its exploration of the Tetons but for the idea it spawned of creating a national park. In 1872 the new concept was realized—Congress established Yellowstone National Park. Curiously, the Teton Range was not included in the park even though it had long been considered a part of Yellowstone country.

In 1871 Dr. Ferdinand V. Hayden, director of the U.S. Geological Survey, led the first of several expeditions under his direction to Yellowstone. The Hayden surveys were important not only for their thoroughness but for the pictorial records made by the noted photographer William Henry Jackson and the equally renowned artist Thomas Moran. Jackson and Moran captured on film and canvas the beauty of the Yellowstone and Teton country. Jackson roamed over a significant part of the Teton Range, in particular the western slope, where he made the first photographs of the Grand Teton.

In 1872 two members of the Hayden expedition, Nathaniel P. Langford and James Stevenson, made the first recorded ascent of the Grand Teton. Their route took them up its difficult west flank. After what Langford described as "ten hours of the severest labor of my life," they reached the 13,766-foot summit.

THE PHOTOGRAPHS of Jackson, the paintings of Moran and the words of Hayden, Langford and others unveiled the magnificence of the Tetons to the nation. Soon tourists visited Yellowstone Park, and settlers moved into the lovely valleys surrounding the Tetons. The most obvious characteristic of civilization—the political boundary—divided and subdivided the region. The land itself, which Indians believed belonged to no one and offered sustenance to everyone, was claimed and settled and bartered and sold. Preserving the Tetons was not easy.

To halt destruction by reckless timber barons, President Theodore Roosevelt established a system of forest preserves, the forerunner of the national forests. The Tetons became a part of the Teton Forest Preserve in 1897, but federal protection was minimal. Mining was allowed, and there was no guarantee against commercial development.

Most of Jackson Hole was carved into ranches. Some residents became concerned about callous development and the threat of irrigation schemes that would incorporate the lovely lakes at the base of the range. A small group of Jackson Hole residents met in 1923 with Horace M. Albright, then superintendent of Yellowstone National Park, to discuss means of preserving a portion of the region. There was no immediate action, but the seeds were sown.

John D. Rockefeller, Jr., who owned the JY Ranch near Phelps Lake, began to take an interest. In 1926 he established the Snake River Land Company, which would begin quietly purchasing private lands in Jackson Hole, planning to turn over these lands to the federal government for preservation. In the meantime, support for a park began to grow, and in 1929 President Calvin Coolidge signed into law the bill establishing Grand Teton National Park. The new park consisted of the rugged Teton Range plus a small fringe of valley lands immediately adjacent to the mountains, a total of 96,000 acres— less than a third of today's park area. It was Rockefeller's plan to continue to acquire many of the valley ranchlands to add to the park. But during the next two decades bitterness developed over the park's expansion.

Cattlemen feared that further encroachment would limit or perhaps curtail grazing rights. Citizens believed that removal of private lands from the tax rolls would bankrupt the county. Several bills were introduced in Congress to expand the park. All these measures failed to pass. Finally, in 1943, President Franklin D. Roosevelt felt compelled to take action lest the opportunity of acquiring the Rockefeller lands be lost. Under the Antiquities Act of 1906, he issued a presidential proclamation establishing Jackson Hole National Monument. It comprised the Rockefeller purchases plus federal lands in the northern and eastern portion of the valley.

This move seemed to confirm local suspicions of government takeover and precipitated swift action on the part of Wyoming lawmakers. Bills to abolish Jackson Hole National Monument were introduced almost immediately, and some came perilously close to passage. On one occasion, only President Roosevelt's threat of a veto prevented congressional action. Even as late as 1947, Congress held public hearings on a bill to abolish the monument.

Throughout this era, a small but solid core of citizens continued to support the preservation of the Tetons and Jackson Hole. Their devotion was rewarded. In 1950 a bill was signed authorizing a boundary change for Grand Teton National Park. The expansion took in nearly all of Jackson Hole National Monument, plus donations from Jackson Hole Preserve, Inc., for a new grand total of 310,442 acres. Permanent protection for the region was finally assured.

Yet backpackers and climbers are discovering that even the wilderness is becoming crowded. For years the detractors of the preservation-of-parks-and-wilderness philosophy have argued that only a "wealthy few" ever venture into wilderness country. But, as one park ranger points out, "There must be a hell of a lot of wealthy people in this country." There are: 939 people successfully climbed the Grand last summer. On an average climbing day, 16 people reach the summit, which measures only about 1,600 square feet. That's equivalent to a population density of 280,000 people per square mile, or 40 times the population density of Los Angeles.

Recently, there has been much publicity about overcrowding in the national parks. The problems of Grand Teton and nearby Yellowstone seem typical. While a great diversity of pressures plague the parks, most congestion stems from the internal combustion engine. The very dependence of our culture on the automobile, coupled with increased leisure time, has brought increasing numbers of park visitors.

IN ATTEMPTING to find a solution, it is probably best to begin by defining the national park concept, or, more specifically, to ask, What is Grand Teton National Park? What is the purpose of the boundary drawn around 310,442 acres?

In recent years the National Park Service has taken serious steps toward solving some of the problems, and one of the most powerful tools was provided by the Wilderness Act of 1964. As stipulated by that act, the National Park Service has conducted a ten-year review of the entire Park System and will recommend some parks or portions of them as candidates for protection in the National Wilderness Preservation System. In Grand Teton, 116,000 acres, or about 37 percent of the park, have been proposed for wilderness protection. If given this coverage, at least that much of the park will remain free of developments.

Wilderness designation solves only a part of the problem, however. Urgently needed are ways to regulate the increasing numbers who visit the park. The motorist and the backpacker usually have conflicting viewpoints. A widespread assumption has developed that virtually every place in the nation ought to be accessible by car. The auto's impact is even more dramatic when we realize that the nation has paved a greater amount of land than it has preserved in the entire National Park System. An estimated 35 million acres are now paved over by roads, streets, highways and parking lots; there are only 30 million acres in the National Park System.

To cope with the growing problem of the automobile, several national parks have initiated the use of mass transit systems, with some degree of success. Plans are now being developed for a bus system in Grand Teton National Park. A reservation system for the campgrounds there has already been moderately successful.

BUT WHAT OF the wilderness users? Should dispersal of backpackers from the high-use portions of the park to the undeveloped sections be encouraged? Certainly the wilderness has much less carrying capacity than valley lands and thus requires more stringent regulation of use. In Grand Teton National Park, it is now necessary to reserve a backcountry campsite. If particular areas are at carrying capacity, visitors are encouraged to change their backpacking itinerary and choose other campsites or destinations. Some backpackers feel that these restrictions are illogical because the National Park Service still allows continued use of horses in these areas, and horses obviously have more impact than hikers and backpackers. Therefore it seems imperative that the Park Service phase out the use of horses in park wilderness.

Another problem is that commercial interests in the region are pushing for expansion of the Jackson Hole Airport, the only airport located within a national park, to accommodate large jets. Conservationists argue that the high noise levels would further degrade the park experience.

It is easy to be misled in seeking solutions to the Teton jetport controversy. For example, an alternative jetport location has been suggested for Driggs, Idaho, on the western side of the Teton Range. This would remove the airport from the park, but it would destroy another, relatively unspoiled part of the Teton country. The noise would affect the western slope, which has been proposed for reservation as wilderness or as an addition to Grand Teton National Park. Besides, no matter where it were located, the jetport would not contribute to solving transportation problems in the park itself.

Economic pressure on the park takes many forms. The old Ashton-Flagg Ranch road, a primitive but passable route, traverses the Teton Corridor, the narrow strip of land separating the rugged Teton Range and the plateau area of Yellowstone Park. Ecologists feel that this is a biologically important area. It lies in the path of part of the seasonal elk migration and contains the headwaters of numerous lovely streams and rivers. For years motel and tourist interests have pushed hard to have the delightful, winding Ashton-Flagg Ranch road turned into a modern high-speed highway with massive recreation developments along the route. Conservationists have fought this proposal, but it seems clear that the battle may be won only by adding the Teton Corridor to either of the parks.

IT IS POSSIBLE that today's spark of environmental concern may be fanned into a blaze of environmental conscience. By altering our consumption patterns and by wiser use of our present resources, there is hope for our parks and wilderness areas. One would like to imagine that in the year 2029, the one-hundredth anniversary of the establishment of Grand Teton National Park, a visitor there will find it still a lovely and wild place; that through stabilized population and a tripling in size of the National Park System, the parks will be less crowded than they are today.

LONGS PEAK

by DAVID SUMNER

Landmark of the Rockies, Longs Peak.
Arapaho Indians caught eagles on its
rocky summit. White men said it couldn't
be climbed.

Why do some mountains have more of a history and more allure than others that are much higher? Sometimes it is their mere shape. Consider the Matterhorn. Everyone knows what the Matterhorn looks like. But few Americans know of Mont Blanc, which is a full 1,081 feet higher.

Likewise in the Rockies, far more people have heard about Pikes Peak and Longs Peak than have heard of Mt. Elbert, the highest peak

in Colorado. Longs Peak attracts far more viewers and climbers each year than any other mountain in Colorado. Yet it is only the 15th highest in the state.

No matter which side you view it from, Longs is a beauty. You see it, and you want to climb it. It's that kind of mountain. Dave Sumner tells about that allure in the fascinating piece that follows.

W.K.

At 8 A.M. on a bright, Colorado morning, a weary band of 22 explorers first spied what official expedition recorder J.H. Bell described as "a blue stripe, close in with the horizon on the West." Some thought it was merely a band of clouds; others maintained it was really the Rockies; none were sure. Led by Major Stephen H. Long, the party marched all day in doubt, until finally, toward late afternoon, the haze lifted.

"We had a distant view of the summit of a range of mountains," Bell wrote in his log for June 30, 1820. "To our great satisfaction and heartfelt joy, the commanding officer declared this to be the Rocky Mountains. A high peak was plainly to be distinguished—towering above all the others as far as the sight extended."

A high peak. Three weeks they had trudged across the sun-blistered plains at the footsteps of the Rockies, and now they had reached a landmark; everyone believed that the square-topped pinnacle bulking above the Front Range had to be Pikes Peak. They took their

bearings accordingly and soon were thoroughly, if temporarily, lost.

Of course, they were mistaken. It was not until some five years later—well after the party had completed its mission and scattered—that cartographers first began to pen "Longs Peak" on the rough maps of the early West. Yet today, according to Hugh Kingery, president of the Colorado Mountain Club, Major Long's "error" is the most climbed of all the state's 53 "fourteeners" (peaks rising above 14,000 feet). By the end of 1972 close to 85,000 people had stood on that rocky, windswept, four-acre summit. Among them were a five-year-old boy, an 85-year-old man, several cripples on crutches and members of the 1963 American expedition which conquered Mt. Everest. And that doesn't count repeaters like Shep Husted, a veteran mountain guide at the turn of the century, who was up top some 350 times.

Why is this one mountain so popular? At 14,255 feet, it ranks only fifteenth in height among the summits

of Colorado. Its massive form hardly matches the finer grace of the classic, angular volcanic peaks so prominent in the southwestern part of the state. The answer is simple: what Longs does have more than makes up for these minor deficiencies. Longs Peak is the scenic and symbolic center of Rocky Mountain National Park, now visited by some 2.5 million travelers annually. The peak's imposing bulk and squared-off summit dominate the view from almost any point east of the Continental Divide—from Horseshoe Park, along Deer Ridge, from Forest Canyon Overlook and along Trail Ridge Road, that breathtaking, overcrowded automobile route which bends and winds across the roof of the park. In addition, Longs has a seemingly limitless variety of climbing routes sufficient to satisfy novice and expert alike.

The unusually colorful fact and fiction surrounding the history of the peak is one of its principal attractions. August 1864 marks the first recorded (and unsuccessful) attempt on the summit. Only a year later, in his tale *From the*

333

Enos Mills, an irrepressible outdoorsman and naturalist who guided innumerable climbers to the summit in the early 1900s. As an author and lecturer, Mills worked tirelessly to publicize the mountain.
PHOTO: COURTESY OF THE DENVER PUBLIC LIBRARY, WESTERN HISTORY DEPARTMENT

Earth to the Moon, the French novelist Jules Verne described the installation on the summit of a 280-foot reflector telescope to observe the world's first lunar flight. The supposed date: September 1866. The actual conquest of Longs Peak had to wait about 23 months, until one-armed Major John Wesley Powell led the first successful ascent on August 23, 1868. (Within a year, Powell would make his historic exploration of the Grand Canyon.) After that, the typical firsts came thick and fast: first solo climb (Donald Brown, August, 1870); first woman to reach the summit (Addie Alexander of St. Louis, 1873); first fatality (Carrie J. Walton, 1884); first moonlight climb (H.C. Rogers, 1896); first winter climb (Enos Mills, 1903); first ascent of the mighty East Face (Professor J.W. Alexander of Princeton, 1922); first marriage service on the summit (in a spring snowstorm, 1927). But none of these firsts is as remarkable as the tales heard by white summiteers about the first conquerors of Longs Peak—the Arapaho Indians. Before the white man set foot on that mountain, Arapahos had built a small eagle trap on the summit. In the concealed, covered trap

baited with carrion a man had once crouched in hope of obtaining ceremonial feathers.

Considering the popularity of the peak during this century, another first is surprisingly recent. Until 1960 the Diamond—a smooth, perpendicular, 950-foot-high expanse on the

East Face—was thought unclimbable, but that year a pair of persistent Californians broke the spell. David Rearick and Robert Kamps spent 52 consecutive hours dangling from ropes and pitons, edging by tiny quarter-inch ledges along the forbidding wall. The pioneer winter ascent, by a new route, was put in by Wayne Goss and Layton Kor in 1967; William Forrest made the first solo climb of the Diamond in 1970.

In the rich history of Longs Peak, two figures stand out like giants: the Reverend Elkanah Lamb and the pioneer naturalist Enos Mills. Lamb arrived on the scene in 1871 and seven years later put up a 12-by-14-foot log homestead and lodge for climbers in Tahosa Valley at the eastern foot of the great peak. From this, the tenth cabin he'd built with his hands, Lamb and his son Carlyle began one of the first mountain-guiding enterprises in the West, taking visitors to the summit for $5 a trip.

But it was the irrepressible Mills—outdoorsman, author, lecturer and raconteur extraordinary—who once and for all established the great peak on the map and in the memories of thousands of Americans. In 1902, Mills bought out the old Lamb homestead, but only after some 40 meticulous trips up Longs did he feel himself qualified to guide climbers to the summit.

Soon others began flocking to the area to take part in Mills' excursions. He not only knew the peak like the

Instrumental in persuading Congress to establish Rocky Mountain Natural Park, Enos Mills also built Longs Peak Inn to lure city dwellers into the area.
PHOTO: COURTESY OF THE DENVER PUBLIC LIBRARY, WESTERN HISTORY DEPARTMENT

back of his hand, but also developed and refined the art of nature guiding, regaling his parties with carefully gleaned knowledge of the area's flora, fauna, geology and folklore. Many a contemporary park ranger still strives to emulate this old master.

For years, Mills worked tirelessly to establish Longs Peak, and the 358-odd square miles surrounding it, as a national park; he toured the nation making speeches, and he lobbied ardently in Washington. When the old Lamb cabin burned in 1906, Mills built the rustic Longs Peak Inn to lure city folk into the mountains; then he rigorously indoctrinated them. On September 4, 1915, the formal dedication of Rocky Mountain National Park finally ensured Mills' victory.

Then the tourist rush started, and it hasn't stopped since. Tourists drive through the park by the millions, "seeing" the Rockies with awe-struck eyes. But to really know a mountain demands much more than simply gazing at it from the distant comfort of a car. Thus, many thousands of people have determined to tackle Longs Peak on its own terms, with nothing between themselves and the mountain save the soles of their boots.

Today, the standard climb begins at the Longs Peak Campground on the eastern fringe of the park. From there, it's an eight-mile hike to the summit, with the usual trip running about 11 hours. During the regular climbing season (late June to early September) most people are on the trail by 5 or 6 A.M. This makes it a one-day hike and allows ample time to be off the summit and on the downhill leg before the usual midafternoon thunderstorms roll in. Altitude gain is a respectable 5,000 feet.

The first few hours are a steady uphill walk among rich mountain woods: aspen and lodgepole pine near the campground, Engelmann spruce, alpine fir, limber pine and willow higher up, with ample wildflowers scattered beneath both types of forest. The entire hike traverses three distinct life zones—montane, subalpine and alpine—creating an illusion of passage through vast spans of space and time, as if the northern coniferous forest had yielded, after thousands of miles, to the arctic barrens and the warmth of summer had given way, in only a few hours, to the chill of autumn or even the snows of winter.

At 11,500 feet only a few dwindling, twisted, scattered clumps of trees remain. From here to the summit is all alpine tundra, where the greatest growth may sprout only two or three inches from the ground and most of the plants hunch close to the soil like mossy cushions. Seen up close, on hands and knees, the vegetation is a miniature landscape specially designed to withstand the ravages of the harsh mountain climate: tiny blue forget-me-nots, pink fairy primrose, dwarf alpine sunflowers, varied small grasses and sedges, even a diminutive willow.

Down below it's possible to spook a mule deer or, less likely, an elk along the forest trail. But up on the tundra the smaller species take over. The ptarmigan, a mottled brown member of the grouse family (toward winter, he will molt to white to maintain his camouflage). The marmot, a mountain relative of the eastern woodchuck (his shrill call has earned him the name whistler). The pika—or cony, or rock rabbit—a chunky, short-eared, squeaking rodent with a preference for rock piles and slopes of broken talus.

Above timberline it's hard to keep the eye from lifting off into the distance, toward the spreading panorama of summits, ridges, gorges, canyons, lakes, rivers and plains. From the blocky Longs Peak massif alone, no less than six major summits jut against the sky: Mt. Meeker (13,911), Chief's Head (13,579), Pagoda Peak (13,491), Storm Peak (13,335), Mt. Lady Washington (13,269) and, of course, Longs itself.

Just above timberline a short spur trail forks to the left toward Chasm Lake, locked at the base of a huge catchment basin beneath the peak's vertical East Face and just below Mills Glacier (actually just a loose pack of perennial ice and snow). The stream flowing from Chasm Lake is the Roaring Fork; immediately beyond, it plummets over Columbine Falls and through Peacock Lake before dropping toward the Tahosa Valley to the east.

Above the Chasm Lake turnoff, the main trail angles up the sloping shoulder of Mt. Lady Washington before ending abruptly amid a chaotic jumble of rock aptly known as Boulder Field. From here on, it's a hands-and-knees scramble up the North Face to the summit. Part way up, the route skirts the brink of a sheer cliff and awesome vista known as Chasm View. Now the

two lakes and Mills Glacier are almost straight below, the East Face directly to the side. Vertical drop here is about 800 feet.

Minutes later comes the summit and a vast mountaintop panorama, rolling, buckling and breaking toward the horizon in all directions. Veteran Longs Peak hiker Paul Nesbit once figured that, on a clear day, the total vista takes in an area larger than the entire state of Ohio.

Eastward, the plains stretch for 120 miles—two-thirds of the way to Kansas—before finally curving out of sight. As the crow flies, Pikes Peak is 103 miles south. Closer in the same direction are five readily discernible fourteeners, several active glaciers and the newly proposed Indian Peaks Wilderness. Both Wyoming and Nebraska are visible toward the west and north, and more mountain ranges bulk against the skyline: the Gore, Never Summer, Park, Medicine Bow and Laramie. Closer by, within the confines of the national park itself, some 18 turquoise, jewellike lakes glisten in the sunshine.

This joyful panorama is open to anyone in reasonably good condition with a yen for hiking. The perpendicular, 1,675-foot East Face is not. Both Lamb and Mills made perilous descents down this wall in the early years, but it was not until the late 1950s and the advent of modern mountaineering technology that the full assault on the East Face—particularly the Diamond—began. Since then, with the relaxation of the climbing restrictions, one new route after another has been pioneered here, until today over 60 of them have been recognized. Zummies Chimney, Stepladder, Bongalong, Nexus Corner, Flying Buttress and Shining Slab are only a few of the routes, and more names join the official list with every passing season. 1966 was the summer of the Diamond. Thirteen parties assaulted this challenging route, but only three successful ascents were made. No ascents of the Diamond were made in 1972, but a total of 424 people essayed the vertical stage that is the East Face. Only 139 people reached the summit.

Once thought unclimbable, Longs Peak remains awesome when seen from afar. But this is only a promise of the delight awaiting the hardy climber who records his conquest in the brass cylinder among the rocks of the highest cairn.

MT. RAINIER

The Mountain That is God

by DEE MOLENAAR

When speaking of the beauty of mountains it is easy to mention Mt. Rainier. There is hardly anything more magnificent than watching, from a dining table in the Space Needle Restaurant in Seattle, the alpenglow turn Mt. Rainier into the appearance of great mounds of ice cream as the sun sinks into the ocean in the west. Unless it is watching the same sight from your tent high on the slopes of another Cascade Mountain peak.

Mt. Rainier continues to have a rich allure for hikers and climbers. While any route to its summit requires the use of technical climbing equipment, some are technically easy, though physically taxing, as any other 14,000-foot ascent would be.

In recent years it has become de rigueur

among the Seattle outdoorsy set to have climbed Rainier at least once. And today as many as 200 climb to the summit on a single day. Compare that to the day I climbed it with my friends Will Merritt and Dick Krenko in 1959. We met no one on the entire route. We were the first ones to use the stone shelter at Camp Muir at 12,000 feet that season, and had to dig our way down to the door through snow that covered the roof. Climbing Rainier was still so rare a feat at the time that a number of tourists lined the porch of Paradise Inn to watch our progress through the telescope there.

Dee Molenaar is one of the people who has climbed Rainier many times over numerous years and various weather conditions. Here is his history of Mt. Rainier.

W.K.

The earliest English record of Mount Rainier occurred on May 26, 1792, when Captain George Vancouver first observed the peak from his longboat while exploring Puget Sound and named it in honor of his friend, Rear Admiral Peter Rainier of the British Admiralty. But the Indians who had dwelled for several centuries at the base of the 14,410-foot volcano called it *Tah-ko-ba, Tahkoma* or *Tahoma*—"The Mountain that is God."

The real story of Mount Rainier began sometime during the Pleistocene ice age; along with the numerous other volcanoes rising along the Cascade Range, the massive peak has had a compositely violent and frigid history. It was constructed over thousands of years by alternating extrusions of lavas, ash, pumice, breccia and related mud flows. Moreover, geologic changes are still taking place. As recently as 1963, 14 million

cubic yards of rock avalanched away from the face of Little Tahoma Peak, Rainier's 11,117-foot satellite. Two or three times during each decade, mud flows flush down valleys below glacier snouts. Such occurrences, along with periodic recordings of new "hot spots," and a recent earthquake whose epicenter was seven miles directly beneath the mountain raise the question: Will Rainier erupt again soon? The answer from geologists and seismologists: Yes, maybe next year, maybe in 10,000 years.

Mount Rainier has the largest single-peak glacier system in the 48 contiguous states. Of its 26 named glaciers, six originate at the summit and extend four to six miles down to below treeline. During the late 1800s the ice on the peak covered about 55 square miles, but by 1950 it had shrunk to about 35 square miles. Since then several glaciers have

shown minor advances and thickenings.

The mountain owes its ice cover to its lofty position in the path of moisture-laden air masses flowing from the Pacific Ocean. From late October to early May it receives a heavy blanket of snow. During the winter of 1971-72 an accumulated total of 98 feet fell at Paradise Valley at 5,500 feet on the southwest flank—an all-time world record for a snow-gauging station. Most of the snow becomes compacted, so the maximum winter snow depth at Paradise normally ranges between 15 and 20 feet. By July 4 in many years a snow tunnel forms the entrance to Paradise Inn.

The snow usually remains on the ground near treeline until mid-July. Yet by late June colorful meadows of heather, lupine, Indian paintbrush, and avalanche and glacier lilies usually dominate the scene. Most al-

View of Mount Rainier from Tatoosh Range, above Paradise Valley.
PHOTO: DEE MOLENAAR

Radiating from the flanks of the mountain are deep, glacier-cut valleys separated by high, broad ridges which are characterized by jagged peaks and meadows. Below 4,500 feet the valleys are in the heavily forested Transition and Canadian zones, where Douglas fir, western hemlock, red cedar, yellow cedar and spruce provide picturesque frames for dramatic views of the gleaming peak. In midsummer, as one climbs from these valleys into the Hudsonian Zone of mountain hemlock, white-barked pine, Alaska cedar, and subalpine fir, open grassland and small lakes begin to appear. Finally there is a dazzling display of floral beauty in colorful meadows sprawled between clumps of stately firs in the Arctic-Alpine zone. Above is the mountain, sometimes seemingly suspended in the sky above a thin veil of fog or haze, with the browns and lavenders of its rocky ribs constantly changing and contrasting with the blues and greens of its ice cascades.

The variety of topographic features and the vegetation and wildlife of the four major life zones represented in Mount Rainier National Park have made it the number-one tourist and mountaineering attraction of the Pacific Northwest. More than 1.5 million people visited the park during 1973. While the majority were drive-through motorists making the loop trip around the mountain, many others lingered for recreational purposes. There were countless fishermen and day hikers, 90,000 camp-truck and trailer campers, 68,000 tent campers, 70,000 backpackers and 4,471 climbers who attempted the summit (2,619 made it). During the winter 4,100 skiers used the rope tows at Paradise, 7,300 headed out cross-country and 700 roared snowmobiles up snowed-in side roads.

The Wonderland Trail encircles the mountain in the Transition through Arctic-Alpine zones. It is about 90 miles long and is one of the most scenic footpaths in the entire National Park System. Bridging countless streams and passing from the rain forests of deep valleys upward to numerous high mountain lakes, fir-sprinkled meadows and summer snowfields, the trail ranges in altitude from 2,300 feet at Ipsut Creek campground in the Carbon River valley to about 6,800 feet at rocky, windswept

pine trails are open to foot travel by late July. From then through September cool, clear weather generally prevails, interrupted only occasionally by storms lasting two or three days. High winds are rare in summer.

Periods of settled weather are frequently accompanied by morning fog which fills the lower valleys up to 5,000 or 6,000 feet. It normally burns off through the morning and returns in the evening. Thus, summit climbers often are in bright sunshine high above a surrounding "cloud-sea" which other hikers are walking through on meadow and forest trails.

A meteorological phenomenon common to all Northwest volcanoes but which attains its greatest development on Rainier is the cloud cap, a lenticular mushroom cloud that settles on the summit. It is formed by an intimate rendezvous of moist warm air from the Pacific and cold air

over the peak. The mass of fog, snow or small ice particles that makes up the cap appears static, but in reality it is dissipating to the leeward as rapidly as it forms on the windward. It may be flowing across the summit at speeds of more than 60 miles per hour.

Although climbing into a cloud cap often is only an inconvenience to a well clothed, experienced party, the caps should not be taken lightly by the weather-wise. They have been factors in many tragedies. Sometimes climbers have doggedly continued their ascents into the whiteout of driving snow and sleet, hoping to gain protection inside the crater rim, only to find the wind there swirling from all directions. Parties forced to retreat often find the sleet descending with them and changing into a driving rain before they reach shelter below treeline.

Panhandle Gap. It can be traveled in segments of a day or two or completed at a semitrot in 4 or 5 days, but it is more enjoyably done in 9 or 10 days. Campsites situated at four- to six-hour hiking intervals allow a comfortable pace.

Unfortunately, the increasing popularity of hiking and backpacking has resulted in excessive soil compaction and trampling of flowers in the fragile meadows. Some segments of the trail at Paradise have been asphalted. Then there is thoughtless littering, despite trailhead signs pleading, "PACK IT OUT."

In 1973 the National Park Service began limiting the number and sizes of parties utilizing the designated backcountry campsites. Advance reservations and registration tags—"license plates" tied to packs—are now required for overnight stays in designated backcountry zones. Though the system has been well received by many local hikers, it has not been an unqualified success. People arriving on the scene unaware of the regulations—usually first-time visitors from out of state—face the frustrations of having to eliminate certain segments of the trail or cancel their plans entirely.

Mount Rainier may have been climbed by Indians long before the Caucasian invasion, although white men tend to categorize native accounts of ancestral adventures as dreams rather than reality. When whites first explored approaches to the peak, local Indians dreaded venturing much beyond treeline because of tales of a "lake of fire" at the summit. Recent explorations of steaming caverns beneath the snow-filled craters have disclosed that a small lake does exist beneath the west crater, so the Indians may well have seen a steaming lake on the summit within the past few hundred years.

Accounts of the earliest attempts by white men to ascend Mount Rainier are vague. In 1852 a party of three or four reportedly climbed part way up the south side via an approach from the Nisqually River Valley, but it is doubtful that they reached the crater. In 1855 two members of a group surveying the boundaries of the Yakima Indian Reservation were led by a young member of the tribe to the area of Mystic Lake on the mountain's northwest flank. From there, according to a story told years later by an old Indian named Saluskin, the whites made a one-day round trip to the top, presumably by the Winthrop Glacier. They described to their guide the crater and steam vents inside the rim.

In 1857 Lieutenant August Valentine Kautz made the first officially recorded attempt to climb Rainier and reached about 14,000 feet on the upper part of the glacier now bearing his name. Kautz was accompanied nearly to this point by two other soldiers and the Indian guide Wapowety.

The first widely recognized ascent of Mount Rainier to its highest point at Columbia Crest took place on August 17, 1870, by General Hazard Stevens, son of Isaac Stevens, the first governor of Washington Territory, and Philemon Beecher Van Trump. The story is well known in the state of Washington. There was the long journey by foot and horseback from Olympia to the mountain's base; the guided tour up the many peaks of the Tatoosh Range led by Sluiskin, the Indian; their farewell to him at treeline where they provided him with a written note exonerating him of all blame if they failed to return; their all-day climb to the summit by way of a ledge alongside the massive rib later named Gibraltar Rock; the night spent huddled in steam caves of the west summit crater; and the following day's discovery of the larger east crater and their return to a surprised Sluiskin, who thought they were ghosts returned from the dead.

After that the summit became the goal of many adventurers. Most of the climbs were made from Paradise Valley by way of the original route along Gibraltar Rock, which became known as the "Gib route." In 1888 the inveterate John Muir made the ascent in the company of several other distinguished scientists. He suggested that the pumice-covered ridge at 10,000 feet would make an ideal campsite for summit ascents. Muir later played a key role in establishing Rainier as a national park, and a spot on the ridge was named Camp Muir in his honor.

Fay Fuller was the first woman to scale the peak, in 1890. Her costume of bloomers and boy's hiking shoes raised eyebrows, but soon afterward other similarly attired women followed her up the peak.

In 1899 Mount Rainier was established as a national park. By then Paradise Valley had become a hub of climbing activity. Local woodsmen set themselves up as guides, operating out of tents in John Reese's Camp of the Clouds. In 1915 a road was completed to Paradise, providing auto access. The following year, with establishment of Rainier National Park Company, came construction of Paradise Inn, the impressive cedar-beamed structure that still accommodates tourists from all over the world. In 1920 the steep-roofed Guide House was built; other structures were added later. Paradise became a mecca for mountain lovers in the days of See America First tourism. Even European climbers were attracted to the park "Where Flowers and Glaciers Meet."

In 1966 Paradise Valley's long-cherished rustic atmosphere was destroyed by construction of a multipurpose visitor center which combines a restaurant, souvenir shop, lounge, museum, auditorium and ranger station within a large circular concrete structure resembling a stranded spaceship. People with memories of better days now prefer to visit Sunrise, on the opposite side of the mountain, where facilities constructed in the 1930s retain their mountain flavor.

At Camp Muir, during the twenties and thirties, two stone shelters built in 1916 and 1921 provided a sleeping point for hundreds of tourist-climbers led to the top via the Gib route. Many oldtimers still recall ascents to the crater, with 20 or 30 people grasping a single 100- to 150-foot rope held at each end by a guide as they passed along the ledge and up the ice chute to the summit dome, where a 20-foot wooden ladder facilitated the ascent of a large bergschrund.

Popular use of the Gib route ended in September, 1936, when a gigantic rock slide carried away the ledge trail. The guide route was shifted to the considerably longer climb from Paradise via the Kautz Glacier. This route was never as popular as the routes above Muir because it involved descending to and crossing the Nisqually Glacier, and climbing for six or eight hours to reach 11,300-foot Camp Hazard. Hazard's accommodations were merely a few rock-ringed windbreaks on the ridge crest below the intimidating 200-foot Kautz ice cliff. The cliff required either a direct ascent or a traverse westward into a steep ice chute leading to the upper snowfields.

After several reconnaissances, in 1948 a new ledge system was discovered across Gibraltar, and climbers returned to the relative comforts of Camp Muir for their approach. But Gib continued to harass climbers with its rockfall. Eventually the present-day route above Muir was developed, via the Ingraham Glacier and Disappointment Cleaver to the upper snow dome. In 1973 nearly 80 percent of the climbs were made by this route. The elevation and accessibility of Camp Muir and its adjacent glaciers resulted in its selection by Norman Dyhrenfurth as the training camp and equipment-testing site for the 1963 American Mount Everest Expedition.

Today Camp Muir is a complex of huts of various sizes and shapes. The two stone shelters and outhouses have been supplemented by a box-like plywood prefab dorm which accommodates about 40 guided guests, a small A-frame ranger patrol cabin and two one-holer outhouses. The water supply for the guide concession comes from a drum oil burner situated on the adjacent Cowlitz Glacier via a gravity hose to the smaller stone hut, the cook shack. Independent parties usually have to tent on the glacier, for unless they arrive in midweek the 18-bunk public shelter is filled and the rock-ringed windbreaks on the ridge are already occupied.

The problems of garbage and sewage disposal at Camp Muir have become very ugly. On busy weekends more than 200 climbers and 100 day hikers jam the facilities far beyond intended capacity. Many inconsiderate people throw picnic and camp refuse down toilets. The Park Service has taken drastic measures. Since 1974, a maximum of 35 guided climbers and 65 independent climbers are permitted to stay overnight at Camp Muir. If there are fewer than 35 guided climbers, more independents can be accommodated, for an overall total of 100 climbers. The limitation has somewhat relieved the situation where in predawn hours climbers used to line up 10-deep shuffling for their turn in the outhouses, Climbers who find Camp Muir filled to its limited capacity can continue onward and camp on the Ingraham Glacier, where a rela-

Insert: Joe Stampfler and party at Indian Henry Hunting Ground. Below: Camp Muir, circa 1927, showing large public shelter. Gibraltar Rock and trail on upper Cowlitz Glacier are beyond.
PHOTO: NATIONAL PARK SERVICE

tively broad area is available for numerous tents at about 11,000 feet.

The only high-camp facility on the mountain besides Camp Muir is Camp Schurman at 9,700-foot Steamboat Prow, on the divide between the Emmons and Winthrop glaciers on the east side. The stone-lined metal (Quonset-type) hut was constructed by volunteer labor during several summers from 1958 to 1963 and was named in memory of Clark Schurman, chief guide at Paradise from 1939 to 1942 and long-time advocate of an emergency shelter on the east slope.

On the Camp Schurman approach, 36 people can camp between Glacier Basin (near timberline en route to Schurman) and Camp Schurman, and 12 can camp between Camp Schurman and the summit (on upper Emmons-Winthrop Glaciers). On all other summit routes there are no restrictions on the number of climbers at one time or overnight. Advance reservations are not required for summit ascents or for use of backcountry campsites; however, advance reservations are recommended for use of Camps Muir and Schurman because of the above-noted numbers limitations. There is a restriction of no more than 12 persons per overnight party in backcountry areas.

Along with advance reservations for some routes, climbing Rainier requires registration by a data card which is filed in the Park Service's records. The card includes the usual information: name, age, address, next of kin, route planned, party size and a check list of equipment, clothing and food carried. In addition to keeping tabs on who's on the mountain and where, the cards permit rapid retrieval of information for the yearly summary of climbing statistics.

The ascent of Rainier by the guide route normally requires four to six hours from Paradise to Camp Muir, which is preferably reached in mid-afternoon to allow time for sufficient rest before the predawn (1:00 to 3:00 A.M.) start for the summit. Parties usually reach the crater about 8:00 to 9:00 A.M.; the crossing to Columbia Crest and the register box takes another half-hour. They start the descent by 10:00 or 11:00 A.M., before the sun has softened the snow and snow bridges, and reach Paradise by late afternoon.

The view from 14,410-foot Columbia Crest is more expansive than spectacular. The broad, undulating summit plateau, with 14,150-foot Point Success three-quarters of a mile to the southwest and 14,112-foot Liberty Cap a mile to the northwest, cuts off views of the rugged, lower peaks around Rainier's immediate base.

The two summit craters joined at Columbia Crest have been extensively explored in recent years with headlamps, compasses, measuring tapes and temperature-recording devices. Scientists have mapped an intricate system of sub-ice caverns and connecting tunnels which can be followed across the crater and down more than 300 feet below the surface. Formed by heat rising from countless fissures in the rocks, these caverns have sheltered many people from storms; early-day climbers customarily spent the night in them, being "parboiled on one side and frozen on the other. A small lake deep beneath the snow of the west crater has provided more rugged souls with the highest bath on the continent.

Before the 1930s, climbs on the west and north flanks of the mountain were limited to a few ascents of the Tahoma Glacier in the 1890s—by Van Trump who ran a small guide business from a tent camp in Indian Henry's Hunting Ground—and an ascent of Success Cleaver in 1905 by two eager young members of a joint Sierra Club-Mazamas outing. Completion of the West Side and Mowich Lake roads during the depression sparked interest among a few climbers in tackling the hitherto poorly accessible slopes. From 1935 to 1939 a dozen tough new routes were pioneered up Ptarmigan and Liberty ridges on the north flank and Sunset Ridge and Sunset Amphitheater on the west.

America's entry into World War II caused travel restrictions which stopped further exploration of new routes. The only notable activity in the park during the war years was in 1942 when the wintry slopes of Paradise were utilized by a small detachment, mostly well-known skiers, from Fort Lewis. Their objective was to lay the groundwork for formation of an army ski-troop unit which evolved into the 85th, 86th, and 87th Mountain Infantry Regiments of the Tenth Mountain Division.

Since the war, about 25 routes have been pioneered. Today, essentially all glaciers, ridges, and cirque headwalls on the peak have been climbed. Among the more stimulating efforts were a variety of climbs on the Mowich Face and Willis Wall.

Efforts to scale Willis Wall, a 4,-500-foot incline of black ice and rotten rock, began in 1960. The first attempts were failures, owing both to the psychological problems of facing the unknown and to hazards of the face, which is fringed along most of its upper rim by a 200- to 300-foot ice cliff. Finally, in late June, 1961, an easterner named Charlie Bell, after a reconnaissance to the wall's base with several local climbers, stayed on at high camp while the others returned to town.

A few days later Bell showed up in Seattle, claiming a solo ascent of Willis Wall. He described his route as up the westernmost of three ribs on the wall to the base of the upper ice cliff, a traverse westward to upper Liberty Ridge, from there to Liberty Cap and across to Columbia Crest, and after being unable to locate the register box buried in the snow, down the mountain via a first descent of Liberty Ridge. His climb had been unauthorized, and his story was treated as a fabrication. To prove his point, Bell returned the following June—again alone and illegally on the peak—and repeated much the same route and descent, but this time he carried a camera and returned with ample photographic evidence to substantiate at least his second climb.

In 1963 the first completed ascent of Willis Wall through the summit ice cap was made via the East Rib by Dave Mahre, Jim Wickwire, Fred Dunham and Don Anderson. In 1965 Dean Caldwell and Paul Dix made the first ascent of the Central Rib, joining the 1963 route through the ice cap. Then, Wickwire and Alex Bertulis made a February climb of Bell's West Rib. Wickwire, who has scaled about 20 of almost 40 routes on Rainier, is the only person to have climbed all three routes on Willis Wall and up the major ridges flanking the Wall—

340

Curtis, Liberty and Ptarmigan.

The restrictions against winter climbing (defined by the Park Service as climbs made between the weekend after Labor Day and the weekend before Memorial Day) were lifted in 1964 in the wake of improvements in cold-weather clothing and equipment and of appeals by local mountaineers for better opportunities to prepare for expeditions to Alaska, the Yukon, Antarctica and the Himalayas. Although the mountain had been climbed in winter "legally" (the much-publicized ascent by the Gib route in February, 1922) and illegally (a solo ascent by Delmar Fadden in January, 1936, which ended tragically on the upper Emmons Glacier), year-round climbing did not become fashionable until recently. Today, numerous winter climbs are made by various routes. So far the only problems have been the anticipated ones of new, unpacked snow, short periods of daylight and cold temperatures.

Mountaineers have enjoyed encircling Rainier above the 7,000-foot level. The 25-mile circuit offers continually changing and unrestricted views and involves crossing 16 to 18 major glaciers and ridges and gaining (and losing) about 11,000 feet of elevation. The trip can be done at a normal pace in about four days during early summer when the snowpack covers the major crevasses.

During the past 100 years more than 25,000 people have visited Rainier's summit. For the most part they traveled the well-established guide routes from Paradise, and the Emmons Glacier route from the White River Valley on the northeast. Fewer than 10 percent venture on some 35 other routes. Only 28 lives have been lost during climbs or descents. The first recorded tragedy took place in 1897 when Professor Edgar McClure of Oregon State University fell to his death from a rock now bearing his name. He was en route down the mountain from Camp Muir after dark.

Other deaths have resulted from a variety of causes. Falls into crevasses have claimed lives. Five people have died from exposure during storms. Three people have died as a result of rockfalls, two by falling from rocks and two from high-altitude pulmonary edema.

Probably the most widely publicized tragedy in Mount Rainier's climbing history was the Greathouse Accident of early July, 1929—five days of unbelievable suffering and heroism. Following a long slide down the upper part of the mountain in high winds and a blinding cloud cap, apprentice guide Forrest Greathouse and client Edwin Wetzel were killed and others in the six-man party were badly injured when the entire group fell into a deep crevasse. Before this, no official action recognizing Rainier's climbing hazards had been taken. But after the accident all guides and clients were required to wear caulked or nailed boots or crampons during summit ascents. Climbers were permitted to carry alpenstocks until after World War II.

Ever since the mountain was first ascended, certain impulsive climbers have added extra dimensions to their trips. Park Service records reveal an interesting assortment of trivia.

The youngest person to climb Rainier to date is 7-year-old Laura Ann Johnson; the oldest, 76-year-old Burr Singleton. Among the more ambitious have been George Smith of Denver, and his four sons. In 1969 the Smiths' ascent of Rainier marked their successful climbing of all 67 of the 14,000-foot peaks in the 48 states; 10-year old Tyle Smith probably is the youngest person to have accomplished this feat.

The fastest round-trip climb of the mountain was made in July, 1959, by guides Gil Blinn and Dick McGowan. They left the Paradise ranger station at midnight and were back in time for breakfast at 6:40 A.M., having ascended the mountain via Camp Muir, Cadaver Gap and the Ingraham Glacier. The slowest round-trip climb was that of Barry Prather and Dave Potter who spent 53 days in a tent camp at the summit during a summer of scientific observations.

The first wedding at the summit was that of Lenora Allain and Edward L. Hamilton on September 7, 1921, in a party of 16 led by Hans Fuhrer, a famous Swiss guide.

Rainier has been climbed in tennis shoes and Hush-Puppies. It has been climbed with a garden hoe, and in the nude. Summit activities have included a football game, golf-ball driving and a watermelon feast. A kite was temporarily lofted by a jogging climber during a rare windless days.

A black bear, a porcupine, a golden-mantled ground squirrel, a white-footed mouse, hummingbirds, a number of ravens and a squadron of bumblebees have all been seen at the summit.

How does the Park Service intend to preserve the natural environment in the face of the increasing hordes of visitors who drive on Rainier's roads, hike its trails and climb its peaks?

In 1974 the National Park Service presented to the public a draft master plan and wilderness proposal which incorporated recommendations for establishment of various wilderness areas, nonwilderness corridors and buffer zones, and limitations on public use and development. Among proposals considered before public hearings:

● Moving park headquarters outside the park.

● Mass transit—bus, minibus or cable tramways—to reduce private vehicle use to some areas.

● Rehabilitation and relocation of trails—even asphalting trails in heavy-use areas.

● Expansion of the reservation and permit system.

● Removal of shelters and closing of some campgrounds.

● Banning campfires.

● Expanding park boundaries.

During the public hearings there were nearly as many viewpoints as there were participants. Old-timers recalled happy days of carefree, unrestricted wandering, often in club groups of more than 50 and accompanied by sod-stomping, meadow-munching, trail-muddying pack animals carrying tentage, food and kitchen gear. These old-timers didn't like the idea that they might not be able to reach remote areas of the park in the future. There were ecology-oriented, long-maned collegians, apparently quite willing to hike into areas now accessible by auto. There was a delegation from the Good Samaritans, the pickup-camper and trailer-camping club with a record of helping other travelers in need. The Good Sams proclaimed their right to view the scenic features of the mountain from their motorized perches. And there were snowmobilers, whose use of snow-closed roads in the winter bothers snowshoers and cross-country skiers who desire their wilderness experience without the razz of revving engines.

As of 1978, the response to the master-plan proposals has resulted in the park headquarters' being moved about eight miles outside the park, at "Tahoma Woods" between the towns of Ashford and Elbe; rehabilitation of some well-traveled trails; expansion, then reduction, of a permit and reservation system; removal of some, and addition of some backcountry campsites; and recommendation for expansion of the park boundary along the Tatoosh Range. Campfires are still permitted in the backcountry, but only at certain designated sites where ample firewood is still available; no fires are permitted in trailless cross-country zones.

WE CLIMBED ZION'S GUARDIAN ANGELS

by KEN HORWITZ

There was no trail to follow across Zion's backcountry—merely paths used by deer and narrow canyons blocked by deep swirling pools and sandstone cliffs where the only way around was up.

When hard-rock men are not inching their way up vertical rock faces, what are they likely to be doing? Here is a trip taken by a trio of rock climbers, one the publisher of Off Belay, on a holiday in soft rock territory. Zion National Park has an abundance of vertical rock cliffs. But they are not suitable for rock climbing since the cliffs are of soft, crumbly sandstone.

The trio of hard-rock men, then, were there to see the sights, to loaf along in the backcountry. They were on a backpacking trip. Well, naturally, they couldn't just leave their ropes and hardware at home. Just in case, they brought along an armory of bongs, and rurps and nuts, chocks, slings and webs. They did some climbing, soft-rock climbing, and some rappelling. And they saw the sights—nature that is only seen by those who get off the highways and pathways and backpack in cross-country.

W.K.

One hundred short years ago, travelers scorned the same landscapes that today are searched out and relished by wilderness travelers eager to escape the confines of the civilized world. Such a region exists in the backcountry of Zion National Park, in southwestern Utah. Zion's backcountry is known only to a few. Wading its creeks and traversing its cliffs and pools of quicksand provide an unmatchable wilderness experience.

Three of us are going into Zion's backcountry. Our ambition is to reach and climb the North and South Guardian Angels, two white sandstone peaks at the entrance to the left fork of North Creek. The creek is a subsidiary of the Virgin River, the giant drainage that carved the gorges of the national park.

All that most people see of Zion is the scenery from a small highway that winds past a visitor's center and down into Zion Canyon, which is dominated by the towering Great White Throne and Zion Lodge. It comes as no surprise, then, that the majority of visitors here are vehicle oriented, whether it be to trailers, pickup campers or car campers. Rarely does anyone enter the park's vast wilderness areas. In 1973 only 3,000 man-nights were recorded for the backcountry, excluding campers along the rim trail at Zion Canyon. By

342

comparison, a very new national park, North Cascades, had 27,000 man-nights in the same year.

Rather than approach the peaks from a dirt road only two miles away from the North Guardian Angel, we choose to enter Wildcat Canyon far to the northeast and follow the watercourse until it abruptly turns into the Left Fork Canyon. This cross-country trek will have us exploring seldom-visited, rugged areas.

We travel as light as possible. Bulky frame packs give way to compact rucksacks, for we anticipate working in very close quarters in thick mesquite and manzanita. Two ropes and an odd assortment of climbing gear are included in case we have to scale a wall or rappel down into a canyon. We do not know what to expect on the peaks themselves. The park rangers think that the South Guardian Angel is perhaps unclimbed and that the North Guardian Angel might have been climbed by a fire aid working in the park the previous year. Nobody seems to know whether the Angels will be technical climbs or walkups.

We forgo the white-gas camp stove and take simply two pots and a lid for use over wood fires. The utensils are carefully wrapped in plastic bags because they will quickly turn black from burning wood, and the last thing we want is to spread carbon around on the inside of the packs. I take no extra clothes except a pair of socks, a down parka and a rain cagoule. Light sleeping bags, insulation pads and a very closely calculated supply of food complete our gear; we carry only about 25 pounds apiece.

As we wind our way down to the bottom of Wildcat Canyon, we see entire panoramas of cross-bedded walls. We are on a trail made by animals. They must be no more than a foot high, judging from the amount of foliage that reaches into the path and scratches our arms and legs.

The several layers of sandstone in Zion can be identified by color. The upper layer appears chalky white. This is the Carmel Formation; it makes up the higher peaks in the backcountry and most of Wildcat Canyon. Below it is the Navajo Sandstone, the flaming red rock that visitors to Zion describe later to friends. Below that is another white layer, the

Kayenta Formation. This formation is visible in the southern part of the park where it forms the bases of the huge red Navajo Sandstone monuments. All the formations were created during the Jurassic period about 150 million years ago, the time of dinosaurs. All have interesting textures of cross bedding; fine lines sweep and curve into one another, representing different times and varying amounts of deposition.

Following deer trails along Wildcat Creek, we know we are in wilderness because we see no footprints or cigarette butts. Only once do we cross some torn-down barbed wire, signifying a slow but promising expansion of Zion through the annexation of adjoining land. But Wildcat Canyon's easy terrain is very misleading.

Suddenly, as we approach the head of Left Fork Canyon, the canyon narrows. To continue, we would have to wade through deep potholes and spillways. We choose instead to traverse the top of the canyon. The change in terrain is remarkable. All around, the land drops suddenly, and we discover that we cannot reach the bottom of the Left Fork. We backtrack

and contour around the steep walls of the new formation to which we have descended, the red Navajo Sandstone. It is the cause of our difficulty: it tends to break away as cliffs, whereas the white sandstone above it had merely crumbled, allowing us to scramble up and down. We find a narrow tributary to the Left Fork and clamber down, keeping a good grip on roots and boughs of scrub bush. Then we follow the tributary until it narrows so tightly that we must squeeze between the walls sideways. At last we reach the creek in the Left Fork Canyon, only to be blockaded once again by innumerable impasses where the gorge narrows and plunges into many deep, black, swirling potholes. This exhausts our physical resources, so we decide to make camp. But camping on the creek floor is dangerous, even though the soft white sand looks inviting. When there is a storm miles away, flash floods can inundate the canyons in seconds, raising the water level in the narrow passages many tens of feet and leading to instant disaster. So we climb a hundred feet above the creek to make camp. The air will be as

Climbing South Guardian Angel, up sandstone steps formed by sediments of prehistoric seas and lakes, proved easier than reaching the peak in Zion's trailless backcountry.
PHOTO: KEN HORWITZ

much as 10 degrees warmer there during the night; even in this arid climate, the nights are quite cold.

Building a campfire leads to feelings of guilt. One of us feels badly that we are turning the rocks black. Although we can destroy all other evidence of our fire, the blackened rocks will remain. We rationalize by saying that they are sandstone, rather than granite, and that a season's rainfall will wash away the blackness. Besides, it may be five or 10 years before anyone else wanders through here.

The morning sun illuminates a white sandstone peak of 7100 feet to the south. Thinking that the view from the summit might be worth the effort, we decide to climb it. It is no more than a scramble by means of a steep gully on one shoulder, but there is a major difficulty in exiting the main canyon floor. One of our group, a little more daring than the others, climbs a section of wall and secures a rope around a tree, enabling us to climb the rope hand over hand to the lip of the canyon. The view from the summit is everything we had hoped for, and more. To the west, the Angels shine over the canyonlands between them. Gazing down the canyons, we see narrow spots that will certainly be impassable, and we wonder how we will ever get through. Nevertheless, we rappel into the canyon floor and resume our journey.

It is only two miles to the spot where we will make camp for our attempt on the 7164-foot South Guardian Angel, but those two miles will take more than six hours to travel. We are following the watercourse in the creek bottom. The canyon walls narrow so that we must walk through the water, which is several feet deep. Then we come to quicksand. By running, we are able to stay above the surface until we reach dry ground. Henceforth, we encounter quicksand continually, but only a few patches are treacherous, and we learn to test the solidity of the footing before transferring all our weight to one leg. Then we are blocked by potholes that are much too deep to wade through, so we again climb up the canyon, unaware that from now on traversing canyon walls will not be the walkup it was before.

Mountain lion tracks are preva-lent everywhere as we descend into the main canyon. We pass close to water-carved indentations in the upper cliffs that are now half-filled with smooth white sand; they obviously are frequented by the great cats. To our dismay, we cannot locate the route up the opposite wall that looked so promising on the topographic map. After considerable searching we climb a long chimney by wedging ourselves against the opposing walls and edging upward. Hauling the packs up after us, we do not stop to relish the climb because darkness is approaching and we have failed to locate a place to camp that has water. When we finally discover a very inviting dry stream bed, we find that the only water supply is a semistagnant pool with a natural oil film on top. Still, it is water, and it appears to support insect life, so it must be potable. And we are in position to climb the South Guardian Angel.

Next morning, winding our way up dry intermittent stream beds toward the Angel, we stumble upon the bedding grounds of what must be scores and scores of mule deer. Antlers lie everywhere. It is a tremendous contrast to see them lying about on hoof-trampled grass, bleached bright white by the sun, rather than strapped to the car-top carriers of greedy tourists.

The ridge leading up the South Guardian Angel appears promising. We clamber up the red sandstone, only occasionally having to use fingers to retain our balanced friction grip on the sharply sloped rock. The rock never steepens severely, and we attain the summit very quickly—so quickly that we are not at all surprised to find a summit register saying that no fewer than seven parties have previously made it to the summit. But the view is splendid. The sky is completely filled with strato cirrus wisps that accent the red canyon-rimmed horizon. Far to the north, near the well-known Cedar Breaks high country, there are traces of snow. To the south we spot the monuments and temples of Zion that are usually seen by motorized visitors. Dominating the scene, however, is the North Guardian Angel. Judging by the steepness of its ridges, it will be more of a challenge than the South Guard-ian Angel. Additionally, a gorge separates the two peaks. We had only climbed out of it yesterday; now we must descend into it and scale the opposite wall.

A terrible thirst brought on by the oil-contaminated water we have been drinking hastens our final descent into the canyon, by a series of hundred-foot rappels. At the bottom we enjoy huge gulps of what seems to be the finest water anywhere in Utah. After establishing our camp in a sandy nook somewhat higher than the riverbed, we stroll back upriver and observe the spring line, the permeable sandstone layer where groundwater is released as surface runoff. A community of algae and lichens lives among the moist red cracks in the sandstone. There are no other communities like it anywhere above the spring line in the maze of canyons.

On our final morning, we ascend for the last time the red walls of our now beloved but also hated, respected and rewarding canyon. We pass lion dens and manzanita handholds and emerge several canyons to the east of the North Guardian Angel. Careful map and compass reading enables us to reach the North Guardian, where we immediately reconnoiter and start up the east ridge. As we expected, it is more of a challenge than the peak to the south. We need ropes and anchors as we search out handholds. We put a sling around a bush rather than pound a pin into the fragile and chalky-white sandstone that constitutes most of the mountain. When we reach the summit, we know we have earned it. The North Guardian has been climbed only once before by a novice climber eight months earlier. The view of the South Guardian Angel complements yesterday's view of the peak on which we stand. Now we can admire the canyon much more, realizing that we do not have to descend it and match wits against its cracks and vegetation . . .

Our trio is silent as we trek cross-country toward the north to our van. We find it standing like a complacent cow in a meadow.

The Zion backcountry is such that I say to myself, "I'm going to come back someday." But there is always another area to visit, and I know that no matter how hard I try, I may never return.

EL CAPITAN

by TORY STEMPF

Where the backpacking is vertical

One of the most impressive scenes in Yosemite Park is the towering El Capitan granite wall. It is a mountain comprising the highest, most vertical cliff in North America. It is no wonder that its human history involves mainly technical rock climbing.

Tory Stempf's fine account of the history of climbing El Capitan leaves you wondering if there could be anything left for technical rock climbers to accomplish.

W.K.

Preeminent among the mammoth walls of Yosemite Valley stands El Capitan, the most famous piece of exposed white granite on earth. The mountain represents a unique saga of human exploration, as heroic and visionary as any historical drama. The saga began in 1864 when men of the first geological survey visited Yosemite and climbed most of the peaks rimming the valley, El Cap among them, presumably by easy routes. But other spectacular valley summits such as Half Dome and Lost Arrow Spire moved men to utter that they would "never be trodden by human foot."

Climbing progressed slowly in the ensuing decades. Only with the importation of piton techniques from Europe in the 1930s were climbs of increasing difficulty produced. The hitherto unclimbed summits were scaled, and the emphasis turned to more challenging routes rather than to bagging new peaks. But it was not until 1952 that exploration of El Capitan's elegant walls and buttresses commenced. That year Allen Steck, Will Siri, Bill Dunmire and Bob Swift attacked a weakness of the southeast face and beat out a line leading to a lone ponderosa pine 400 feet up. Even then the 1,600 feet to the top of the face remained untouched. Next, in 1953 Steck, Siri, Willi Unsoeld and Bill Long climbed the less intimidating East Buttress in three days.

The climb remains today one of the valley classics.

In the late fifties and early sixties many short routes, often ending nowhere, were established along the base of El Capitan. Here it seems most vulnerable, displaying a multitude of steep chimneys, cracks and exfoliation slabs which offer wonderful free routes of generally high difficulty. "Free' climbing is ascending a rock using only the natural hand- and footholds which the rock provides. This is in contrast to "aid" climbing in which the rock is so steep or smooth that artificial means—pitons, bolts, or artificial chockstones—must be inserted to provide the missing holds.

In 1957 a breakthrough came in the valley. Following the example of John Salathé's epic multiday ascents of Lost Arrow Chimney with Anton Nelson in 1947 and of Sentinel Rock with Allen Steck, in 1950, Royal Robbins, who was later to become *the* El Cap wall climber, pioneered the first Grade VI climb in America, a five-day effort on the northwest face of Half Dome. Man's potential for living in the vertical environment was then realized conclusively. We need not, like some mythic Antaean being, return to earth nightly for sustenance but can adapt to the exigencies of a world of up and down—sky, rock and space. Climbers now looked afresh at the behemothlike El Cap.

El Capitan juts into the valley with a prow like a titanic vessel. This 3,000-foot South Buttress, which cleaves the Capitan into two mighty facets, the southeast and southwest faces, is the finest line on the mountain . . . perhaps in Yosemite . . . perhaps anywhere. Warren Harding wanted this buttress for his own. With an assortment of partners, climbing during 47 days from the summer of 1957 to November of 1958, he slowly shrouded El Cap's Nose with fixed ropes. These allowed the men quick access to the upper reaches of the route and a means of expedient retreat if the weather turned nasty. The ever-present ropes offset the fear of becoming marooned on the face, and this technique became known as "siege" climbing.

The final assault on the Nose took 13 continuous days. Harding, Wayne Merry and George Whitmore pushed inexorably up into the last 1,000 feet of overhanging dihedrals and settled down for the final night beneath the final defense, the corbeled plating of the summit overhangs. In the twilight a lone figure drilled bolt holes in El Cap's summit armor. Harding, holding a flashlight in his mouth, created a final ladder to the top. The Nose yielded ultimately to one man's indefatigable will.

This route ushered in the Big Wall Age of American climbing. The concept of not merely climbing a rock

El Capitan from the Merced River.
PHOTO: ED COOPER

face but of living on it as well was to become the lasting contribution of the Yosemite method of mountaineering. El Cap became the age's ultimate challenge.

Now that everyone knew that El Capitan could be climbed mountaineering style, the rules of the game changed. The siege tactics of leaving fixed ropes to the ground gave way to the cleaner alpine-style ascent, the climb with no umbilicus—eating, sleeping and working autonomous of the world beneath. The odds would now swing more in El Cap's favor, for with no tangible line of communication with civilization a climber had to bring all his skill and courage with him: there could be no running down for psychological replenishment. Beside the technical difficulties (which always eventually yielded) there developed a race with time: the streak for the top before physical and emotional "burn out."

The second ascent of the Nose was done in 1960 in a single seven-day push. But the climbs that followed still saw assorted use of the fixed-rope principle: climb for a couple of days, fix ropes to the ground, do a reconnaissance of the intended route, come down for a rest and then re-ascend the ropes for a continuous climb to the summit.

This use of semi-siege techniques must not, in retrospect, diminish the climbers' achievements. Rather, it reflected the new age's visionary endeavors upon rock faces so huge as to defy intelligent comprehension. Sieging was the logical way to keep one's feet partially in sane reality. These matchless routes of the early sixties personify the grandeur of the mountaineers' dreams: the Salathé Wall in 1961, ("the greatest rock climb in the world"); the Dihedral Wall in 1962 ("no place to stand for the first 2,000 feet"), which was the first Grade VI by a non-Californian, Ed Cooper.

In 1964 attention turned from the southwest flank, the location of the aforementioned routes, to the North America (NA) Wall on the southeast face. Here was achieved what probably could be called the magnum opus of the Age of Wall Climbing in Yosemite. So-called for the resemblance of its geologic features to our continent, the NA Wall epitomized classic mountaineering: personal commit-

Dirty and Clean Climbing Hardware
Above: Bolts (dirty) are short rods hammered into holes drilled into solid rock and used as hand- and footholds, or anchors to which short rope ladders (etriers) can be attached to gain height.
PHOTO: GALEN ROWELL

Yvon Chouinard, epitome of a clean climber with nuts, wedges, chocks, stoppers, and hexentrics.
PHOTO: TOM FROST

Below: Unlike the piton, nuts (clean) are placed by hand into cracks and wedged there, and likewise retrieved by hand—all without damaging the rock.

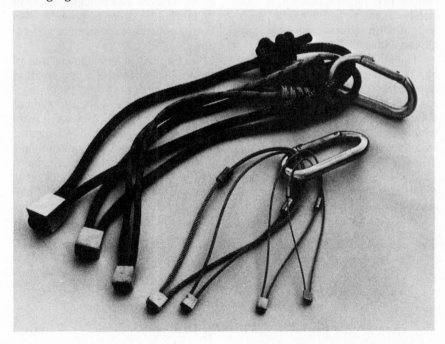

ment coupled with team solidarity on a long route of 2,500 feet up continuously steep, rotten, and above all, largely unknown rock. The nine-day climb marked the first time that no fixed ropes had been used on a first ascent of El Capitan. It gained the reputation of a "horror climb" and was not repeated until 1968. Its portentous pseudonyms have since disappeared with time and subsequent ascents. The NA Wall became so famous that a British expedition attempted it—a remarkable tribute to the El Cap pioneers, Robbins, Chuck Pratt, Yvon Chouinard and Tom Frost.

The next six years saw 10 more routes put up on El Capitan. They are all multiday climbs and among the longest in the world. Yet probably the Golden Age of Yosemite wall climbing ended with the tortuous eight-day ascent of El Capitan's Muir Wall in 1965 by Chouinard and T M Her-

bert. The new routes have tended not to be glorious, pioneering or classic of line—merely hard.

The noteworthy events do not end here, however. In 1968 Robbins did the first solo ascent of an El Cap route,

on the Muir Wall. This climb is long, very difficult and was inadequately described by the first ascensionists. Robbins's nine-day second ascent of a climb of such magnitude is surely one of the brilliant achievements of

*Warren Harding's 47–day siege of
El Cap's Nose ushered in the
Big Wall Age of American climbing.*

our time.

More recently, women have been demonstrating their prowess in big wall mountaineering. The Nose, the Integral Route and the NA Wall have been climbed either by all-woman teams or mixed teams in which the female did her share of the leading.

An event familiar to most readers was Harding's and Dean Caldwell's 27-day epic on the Wall of the Early Morning Light in 1970. It was the first time that rock climbing attracted widespread public notice from the U.S. press. This climb roused the indignation of much of the climbing world concerning the seeming overuse of bolts.

The controversy over the legitimacy of the climb, and its ominous implications for climbing in general, continues today. It is a poignant reminder that mountaineering is ultimately a social activity and is as fraught with ethical issues as any human endeavor.

The ethical conflagration sparked by the Harding/Caldwell odyssey demonstrates that climbing—even on the infinite acreage of El Cap—involves a relationship with nature which can be life-enhancing or destructive. We can no longer climb the hills alone as John Muir did before us. Those who follow our trails and routes also deserve the experience of an untrammeled wilderness.

When I first climbed El Cap's Nose, any preconceived notions of romantic solitude to which I clung were soon dashed by the punctured water bottles, rusting sardine cans (climbers always eat sardines, it seems) and liberal sprinkling of garbage on the bivouac ledges. In order to sleep one had to become a sanitation engineer. But my most startling encounter was with the long-accepted practice of using El Cap's cracks and chimneys as convenient latrines. As we neared Camp IV at 2,000 feet, the similarity to an overused state park privy was unavoidable.

The gist of these unpleasantries is that "freedom is not license." Climbers of today and tomorrow, in their quest for personal fulfillment, need to be aware that mountains are not indestructible; that even a colossus such as El Capitan needs the ongoing concern and thoughtfulness of its fanciers in order to provide everlasting adventure for ensuing generations.

El Cap has played a major role in the movement toward a conservation ethic in climbing practices and equipment. Pitons, once the symbol of modern extreme rockcraft, were designed to be hammered into natural cracks in the rock; but now we find that rock disintegrates beneath hammer blows and continual placement and removal of the devices. They have become anathema to the conservation-minded climber. El Cap's Nose is riddled with fist-sized holes caused by the pitons of our predecessors.

Alternatives do exist. The British have invented a climbing tool which is at once protective of the environment and exciting in its implications for the sport of mountaineering. The device began as ordinary pebbles found on the way up the Snowdon Cog Railway and carried in pockets on a climb. In a suitable crack the climber wedged a pebble and attached a rope to it, just as a piton would be used. In our culture all good things are eventually marketed, and so in Wales, I believe, the first artificial chockstones, called nuts, were manufactured—odd-shaped aluminum blocks of many sizes which could fit varying-sized cracks. The nuts are carried on short rope slings worn over the head and are made today to fit cracks from less than a quarter of an inch to six inches in width. This climbing nut replaces the piton as a device for aiding the climber.

Utilizing chockstones and the natural configurations of a cliff, or clean climbing, means developing an intimate knowledge of the nuances of the rock being scaled. Bristly knobs that were once grabbed for dear life now also become convenient projections to wrap a sling around; instead of uprooting the thistle bush occupying the only handhold, one ties a rope to it; each crack assumes a unique personality as it is inspected for the right spot for a nut. The climber has entered a relationship with the rock in which technical repertoire loses much meaning. *How* to get up supersedes in value simply *getting* up.

Clean climbing represents an awakened consciousness in mountaineering which philosophically assumes an enhanced awareness of the mountain environment. In the practical sense this new awareness prompts the individual to use his full range of skills in climbing, route finding, geological knowledge and self-awareness. The piton subdued the mountains. The key to personal fulfillment in our new age is not conquest but collaboration. ๐

*El Cap has played a major role
in the movement toward a conservation
ethic in Climbing practices.*

McKINLEY: THE GREAT ONE

by WILLIAM KUTIK

Approaching middle age, its explorations provoke continued controversy.

Not only is Mount McKinley the most imposing mountain in North America, but it is the highest mountain in the world, measured from its base to its summit. Climbing it is a mountaineering feat, though the first people to climb it were Alaskan sourdoughs out of a Fairbanks bar on a bet.

In its hugeness and massive snow cover, McKinley is symbolic to me of all of Alaska. Bill Kutik's interesting article tells mainly of McKinley's climbing history, which only reinforces the symbolism for me.

W.K.

Alaska's Mount McKinley tops the North American continent with its 20,320-foot peak surrounded by paradox and mystery. Shrouded in clouds four days out of five, its summit has provoked some of the fiercest exploration controversies of this century. Mount McKinley is at the same time one of the hardest and easiest mountains of its size to climb; at least 11 expeditions failed before its summit was touched. Dozens now tread on it every year, but seven died there just five years ago. Combining the hardships of the tropics and the arctic, its temperatures reach across a 237-degree span. First seen by a white man less than a hundred years ago, it now faces the twentieth-century problem of pollution. But it remains Denali, ''The Great One.''

The mountain is as remote as it is huge. More than a hundred miles inland from the headwaters of Cook's Inlet on Alaska's south coast, McKinley was no more than a blank space on the map used to ratify the purchase of Alaska from Russia in 1867. Once accessible from ''the lower 48'' only by weeks of overland and steamer travel, 29 miles still separate it from the National Park's Denali Highway—the nearest road—which opened in 1937. From the highway, the shortest route to the summit requires 36 miles of walking, one way, not including the vertical climb—a formidable backpack. Rising out of lowlands no more than 2,000 feet high, Denali's twin peaks form one of the world's great isolated uplifts. Part of the Alaskan Range, the McKinley massif extends 150 miles from the Anchorage-Fairbanks highway. In 1913, the first successful climber wrote: ''What a glorious, broad, massive uplift that mountain is! it is not a peak, it is a region.''

❝ Rising out of the lowlands, Denali's twin peaks form one of the world's greatest isolated uplifts. ❞

And a wilderness region besides, totally unexplored until 1889. The modern backpacker starting south from Denali Highway passes through primeval forest with 50-foot high spruce trees and moss underfoot. The mountain's first obstacle is the McKinley River – a fast waist-deep, glacially fed stream – that has to be forded. Several miles of tropical marshes follow, swarming with savage mosquitoes large enough to have visible body stripes and capable of biting through the thickest denim. Hardly a welcome mat from ''The Great One.''

Eight miles of barren rocky valley leave the treeline far below and lead to the pass to the lower Muldrow Glacier. Snow falls here and everywhere else on the mountain down to an elevation of 4,000 feet every month of the year. McKinley's 16,000 feet of vertical snow-cover is one of the world's largest. The Muldrow is easy walking until 7,000 feet, where crevasses described as ''big enough to engulf a freight train'' begin. Above the crevasses, Karsten's Ridge presents the only 500 feet of technically difficult climbing on the Muldrow route. Above 14,000 feet the terrain is almost unimportant (albeit snow-covered and passable) because McKinley lays down its trump card: the weather.

Mount McKinley (20,320 feet) reflected in tundra pond.
PHOTO: ED COOPER

A subarctic mountain more than 2,400 miles farther north than Everest, McKinley's climate has been proposed by expert Bradford Washburn as being on a yearly average the most severe of any non-polar spot on the face of the earth. A research expedition in the late '60s found McKinley's mean *summer* temperature to be nine degrees below zero including effective windchill factor. In June 1947, the area above Karsten's Ridge had an effective low of -101°, with a mean for the day of -38° Above 15,000 feet on the north slope, frostbite "danger" (exposed flesh freezing in one minute) prevails 60 percent of the time. Temperatures of -20° are common at night. On the other hand, hot summer days will reach 80° in the swampy northern approaches. And four years ago along the southern approach on the Kahiltna Glacier a high of 136° in the sun was recorded.

Despite these temperature extremes,

McKinley's summer storms pose the real danger. Some part of the mountain is experiencing inclement weather more than half the time. The air around McKinley is warmer than the mountain itself and usually moist. (Summer is the Alaskan interior's rainy season.) As it hits the peak, any brisk wind will form it into a double-convex cloud cap (as in the photograph seen above), bringing short, fierce blizzards. On a cloudless day these storms can gather, rage, and disappear in 20 minutes. Just such a storm killed seven young climbers in July 1967.

With all these weapons in McKinley's arsenal, how incredible that the first group to reach its lower North Peak in 1910 walked up from Fairbanks with neither a rope nor previous climbing experience. The Sourdough Expedition consisted of native Alaskans anxious to disprove the disputed claims of Brooklynite Dr. Frederick Cook. They hauled

a 16-foot spruce flagpole up the mountain and then planted it on the wrong peak. McKinley had fooled them. From town, the harder-to-climb North Peak looked higher than the true summit on the South Peak. Afterward, they claimed a second ascent—this time of the South Peak—but no one knows for sure whether or not they actually reached the top.

A modern version of this story involves climber Ed Cooper, who took the accompanying photographs. Alone in a blinding white-out, Cooper reached what he thought was McKinley's summit. However, he couldn't be certain, and returned to camp unsure of his success. The next day he had to climb it again—for a "second" time.

But the most incredible McKinley story involves the aforementioned Dr. Cook. A respected Arctic explorer, Cook and a horse-packer named Barrill left from a town 130 miles from McKinley and returned less than two weeks later claiming a successful ascent, complete with a photo of Barrill on the "summit." Before he could be challenged back at the New York Explorers' Club, Cook sailed off in search of the North Pole. His book, *To the Top of the Continent,* came out with the "summit" photograph showing an unexplained peak in the background. Cook came home in 1909 announcing he had reached the Pole, and all Europe believed him. Despite Admiral Peary's cable claiming that honor for himself, Cook received a conquering hero's welcome in New York and the keys to the city. Just as an investigation of his McKinley claim was initiated at the Club, Cook disappeared. Gentlemen to the last, the Club decided the only fair thing to do was mount an expedition that would check his story and maps.

Cook's friends Herschel Parker and Belmore Browne, now his severest critics, led that expedition and took a photograph showing his "summit" to be a 5,300-foot outcrop more than 19 miles away from McKinley. Barrill admitted the deception. Following a Congressional investigation, Cook's Pole claim was denied.

Two years later, Parker and Browne tried for the summit themselves by the Sourdoughs' route along the Muldrow Glacier. McKinley turned them back 200 yards and 150 vertical feet from the top with one of its summit storms. They would have succeeded the next week but for an axiom of modern mountaineering that was little known then: the body cannot digest fats at high altitude. Ten days of their rations were fatty meat pemmican, and they simply could not eat it. Parker and Browne left the mountain just in time to miss the famous Alaska earthquake of 1912. Had their food been adequate, they certainly would have been the first on the summit and would just as certainly have been killed by avalanches during the earthquake.

By then a total anticlimax, the first ascent came a year later. The first man on the top — Walter Harper, 21 — was the son of the first white man recorded to have seen McKinley.

Nineteen years passed before a second party attempted or gained the summit. Later in the '30s, the opening of the Denali Highway and the use of ski-equipped planes for airlifts opened McKinley to a post-war stream of climbers. When landings were banned in the Park, climbers shifted their attack to the south, landing outside the Park on the Kahiltna Glacier and climbing via the West Buttress, now the most popular route. The numbers tell the story: two successful parties up to 1940, six to 1950, 15 to 1960, and a total of 89 through 1970. The first all-woman expedition reached the summit on July 6, 1970.

The increase in climbers has given McKinley a pollution problem. Dumping garbage and excess baggage has always been an integral part of mountaineering and moon exploration. Last year, a group from the University of Oregon brought down 380 lbs. of cans, bottles, unused food, and new and broken equipment from a dump area at 17,200 feet. They say there is plenty more.

So McKinley enters its middle age — climbed by a dozen different routes, in the winter, and on skis — facing the prospect of becoming our continent's most elevated garbage dump. Only the backpackers and climbers who go to "The Great One" in the future can decide its fate for certain. 👢

HAWAII'S MAUNA LOA

by WILLIAM FINK

If the lava that formed Mauna Loa were poured over the earth, it would cover the entire surface to a depth of four inches.

Of all the mountains I've read about recently, Bill Fink's tale of Mauna Loa has given me the greatest desire for climbing it.

There is something very appealing in the idea of starting a mountain climb at the edge of the sea in the tropics, and ending on the top in a freezing snowstorm. And the idea that it is an active volcano adds more than a little spice to that.

W.K.

"Five-fourteen, headquarters."

"Five-fourteen."

"Bill, the volcano observatory reports heavy tremors near Kokoolau. Let's close Chain of Craters Road and get everyone out."

Kokoolau, a pit crater up the road. It had never erupted in historic times. Pauahi hadn't either, until 1973. And then the geologists had given us only four hours' warning. How MUCH THIS TIME?

The radio pops as I sign off. My job now is to get tourists to leave safely and speedily without becoming panicky.

I approach the first group, wondering whether my concern shows through the calm, confident smile I'm forcing on my face. "Folks, some unusual things are happening up the rift. Just to be on the safe side we're closing the road. Please leave the area right away without stopping."

The last two people I meet are at the end of the trail, more than a mile from the parking lot—two Japanese girls who speak no English. When I point back down the trail, they readily understand.

Back at the parking lot, the remaining people move slowly. Finally all the cars are heading up the road. I know it's been at least an hour now. How MUCH TIME?

The car I'm following is only going 25; the speed limit is 35. I turn on the public-address system: "Sir, please move out with

351

all due care. Ignore the speed limit." He gets the message.

I come to a sharp stop at Puhimau. There's a jeep I sent up the road five minutes ago; everyone is idly looking in the crater. The jeep's driver is coming around to his door; my window is down.

"Man—get the hell out of here. This is where it's at." He also gets the message. . .

The last car was out of danger 20 minutes ago. I wait; my car rocks with earthquakes. As I prepare to examine a new crack in the road, the radio sputters to life: "We have an eruption east of Keanakakoi—fountains to 200 feet!"

Keanakakoi! I'm right there, but where's the eruption? The 1971 vents are only 40 yards away; it must be here. I look around but see nothing.

I decide to just pay attention to the road ahead and leave the area, with all due care. Safely. Like a bat out of hell.

I'm a park ranger at Hawaii Volcanoes National Park, on the island of Hawaii. Fortunately, eruptions are not an everyday occurrence. But neither are they unusual.

Most of my time is spent helping visitors understand and appreciate the park, *their* park. People and parks combine to create a unique chemistry. A balance must be reached between protecting the park from the people and protecting the people from the park. It is a dynamic, challenging task.

MORE THAN A MILLION and a quarter visitors come here each year, mostly to witness the handiwork of Pele, the Hawaiian goddess of the volcano. And for good reason. A volcanic eruption is one of the most incredible experiences in nature. It assaults and overpowers the senses, ultimately making you humble at your mere humanity.

Yet very few visitors realize the park also offers a unique backcountry experience: in no other national park can you hike from the edge of the sea to an elevation above 13,000 feet—from a palm-bordered lagoon, up steep fault scarps, across a veritable desert, through "islands" of deep

The Shield Volcano

Geologists recognize several kinds of volcanoes. The shield vocano is one of them.

Volcanoes in Hawaii represent the classic shield form in its most imposing extreme. There, mountains rise more than 30,000 feet from their bases, built by repeated overlapping, interlocking flows from linear vent systems called rift zones. The most classic of these is Mauna Loa. Its gently sloping profile rises unbroken from the edge of the ocean to a height of more than 13,000 feet.

Hawaiian eruptions are characterized by their relative gentleness. Gases are released readily in the fluid lavas, so explosive eruptions are uncommon. Continental volcanoes, such as the Cascade peaks, are formed from thicker lavas interbedded with layers of cinder and ash. Their eruptions tend to be less hospitable to close observers than Hawaiian ones.

Rather than causing flight, Hawaiian eruptions have attracted viewers from throughout the world for the last 150 years. Visitors flock to intermittent eruptions of Mauna Loa and Kilauea, which now are protected in Hawaii Volcanoes National Park. The sight is extraordinary. Nowhere else in America can you look into the golden heart of the earth.

forest interspersed with savanna, then above tree line to the alpine summit of the world's most massive mountain, Mauna Loa, the long mountain.

Now and then people need a change of pace from whatever it is they do to keep beer in the refrigerator, an escape from the routine. I too feel the same need. On an evening patrol when the clouds lift and the broad shield of Mauna Loa reveals itself, I often look to its summit and wonder, "What's it like up there right now?"

Mountains have always been an important part of my life. I've done no major expeditions; I've made no major first ascents. But from the Blue Ridge to the Colorado Rockies, I have since childhood been drawn to any piece of vertically elevated real estate.

My first impression of Mauna Loa was typical of many visitors': "It's not very imposing, is it?" A broad, symmetrical shield volcano, it stands distantly aloof to the west of park headquarters. There is nothing on its slope revealing any size or distance.

From repeated eruptions and lava flows averaging only a few feet thick, Mauna Loa has grown from 18,000 feet beneath the sea to 13,680 feet above it. Mauna Kea, a sister peak nearby, a little more than 100 feet higher, often is touted as the tallest mountain in the world. Yet it is still small enough so its immensity can be comprehended by eye and mind. Mauna Loa's size, however, is almost

impossible to comprehend. Geologists estimate that 10,000 cubic miles of lava formed Mauna Loa, 100 times the volume of Fuji or Shasta.

Even a figure of 10,000 cubic miles had little meaning to me. So I decided to magically slice each cubic mile into a layer one foot thick and spread them out in a mosaic. I was so startled with the result that I had to check my calculation three times. The lavas that have made Mauna Loa could cover 91 percent of the earth's land surface with a layer of lava one foot thick.

I began to have a sense of the magnitude of this mountain. I knew then that I was being entranced by and somehow attracted to it. A familiar old feeling had returned. I know the symptoms. I don't know the cause, but I sure know the cure.

THE MORE I TRIED to comprehend the size of Mauna Loa, the more I realized I would have to walk from the edge of the sea to its summit. I would have to do it on my own time; that way no work projects would distract from my attempt to reach communion with the mountain.

I argued with myself. Must it be a continuous hike to preserve the integrity and pureness of the journey? At first I thought yes. Later I realized I had no desire to achieve any physical feat that would be cataloged and held in awe by people concerned with such matters. Continuity, a sense of wholeness; that I needed. I knew I could hold it in my head and heart as I alternated work with weekend segments of the trip.

Strictly speaking, the first 4000 feet of the hike is up the slope of Kilauea, the lower and more recently active neighbor of Mauna Loa. The national park includes the summit area of both volcanoes and the trail system links them conveniently.

My hike to the top began by hiking down. From the edge of Hilina Pali, part of a steeply sloping fault zone on the southern flank of Kilauea, the trail abruptly drops more than 1000 feet in little more than a mile. The trail surface is mostly aa, a jagged, clinkery kind of lava. Pahoehoe, a smoother, billowy kind, is usually a more pleasant hiking surface.

Trying to cover ground rapidly, I survived several episodes of none-too-graceful stepping maneuvers before gravity, momentum and the ball-bearing-like surface finally won. As I went down I thought, what a way to end the trip, a half-mile after the start. Fortunately, I received only a slightly jammed thumb and a few scrapes. The mountain was saying in its own way: don't worry, don't hurry. Good advice, I decided.

From the base of the Pali the trail strikes out across gently rolling land for several miles, then leads to the edge of Pu'u Kapukapu. Overlooking the coastline 1000 feet below, it is one of the most inspiring places in the park to eat lunch, which is just what I did. I could see the coconut grove

lape tank during the summer.

After arriving at the cabin and putting water on to boil, I went to the little sandy stretch of the lagoon. Lazily soaking and floating with the gentle swells, I watched big waves toss spray 40 feet into the air as they crashed along the open coast. I realized that for the present, at least, Mauna Loa and Kilauea have been able to stand fast and even make headway in their long struggle against the sea. I had the feeling that it was special to be there, at the interface of mountain, air and sea, and simply be a part of the interaction.

Soon I moved up on the beach, just out of the water, and idly fashioned a crescent-shaped breakwater in the sand. Suddenly, I stopped, shocked: Did I have to create a structure and try to outwit the forces of the sea to come to some understanding of it? Could I appreciate the waves only by trying to fight them? No, I decided, I merely get a kick out of playing in the sand. I returned to the water to wash off sand. As I walked back up the bank, I noticed only a faint trace of my breakwater.

After supper I read the cabin register by candlelight. Any register at a location like this is a curious blend of facts, banality and eloquence. Halape evokes differing reactions from visitors. Several months before, someone had written a passage he recalled reading someplace, saying it expressed his feelings very well: "You never really leave a place you love; part of it you take with you,

out to get some sunrise pictures. The overnight low had been 76 degrees.

THIS WAS THE DAY I would begin my ascent. Halape had been a beautiful place to sort out my thoughts, and the spectacular sunrise seemed a good omen. The weather was cloudy and threatened rain, but that would help mitigate the discomfort of the sea-level warmth, which was quite pronounced compared to the coolness of my home in a rain forest at 4000 feet. Another good omen.

I made surprising time to my water cache. Cool and fresh, all my insides seemed to cheer in unison as I took several healthy swallows.

Hiking along, my mind and body both slipped into low gear. Thoughts wandered as my legs chugged onward and upward. The trail finally topped out near 2700 feet, then traveled for a couple of miles to the Kipuka Nene campground.

A kipuka is an area of land that has been surrounded by younger lavas. If it survives long enough, the deep, rich soil can support a majestic grove of trees.

Kipuka Nene was once a beautiful forest area, but a fire from careless campers burned 3000 acres. Now the trees are towering white skeletons. Along the section of trail before the campground, the undergrowth has returned, and I always have mixed feelings when I'm there. One part of me cries at the destruction caused by a runaway campfire; yet another part is reassured. The bare trees and cool, brisk wind remind me of a warm, late-winter day back in the Blue Ridge.

At Kipuka Nene my weekend was over. It was back home and back to work.

I had been confident at first that I could keep a sense of continuity while I interspersed segments of my hike with my job. After returning from Halape, that ideal was put to its supreme test.

I was really tired after the first leg of my hike. My wife had to go to Hilo that night, and I had to babysit. My daughters seemed to have set up a conspiracy against me. After convincing both of them it was time for bed, I too succumbed shortly, stirring only briefly when my wife came home.

"The car rocks with earthquakes. In the distance, liquid rock fountains into the night sky from a mile-long line of fissures. A few minutes later, lava pours over the upper Ka'u Desert, covering the trail I hiked two months ago."

---

and lagoon where the Halape cabin sits beside the sea, my destination for the night.

Resisting the temptation to take a shortcut down the face of Kapukapu, I walked on around and down the back way—longer but safer. I stashed some water at the junction with the Kipuka Nene trail. I knew I would value it highly after a night of the brackish water we pump into the Ha-

leaving a part of yourself behind." It expressed my feelings, also.

Shortly after eight o'clock, two other hikers came in, having walked the last few miles by moonlight. As we settled in for the night, the sound of the surf ever present, I remarked, "Do you realize we are lying here listening to the surf break at the 18,000 foot level of a mountain?"

I awoke just before dawn and went

The phone rang at 2 A.M. It was the chief ranger. He said an automobile accident had been reported to the Kilauea Military Camp desk. The people said it looked bad.

I dressed and went to the park ambulance, mentally psyching myself for what I might have to face. The accident was a little farther down the road than originally reported. Finally I found the car, turned up on its side,

after I collected everything of value I could find. I forced myself to remain as detached and objective as I could.

Back at my office, I recorded in official-sounding language the results of my investigation. At last I realized I was being of no further use and went home.

My wife fixed supper. We sat down to eat. Finally I could no longer be objective. Finally, I cried.

The slow but steady work of wind, rain, ice and gravity inexorably changes the height of all mountains. In the Hawaiian volcanoes, change is much faster. It can happen overnight, or even in a terrifying moment's time.

---

slightly off the road, the body separated from the chassis, the windshield crushed against a tree. It looked vaguely familiar, but I couldn't place it.

No one was in the wreckage and my first thought was, "My God, someone climbed out of this?" But as I went around to the other side, my flashlight caught a figure in the ditch. I called out; no answer. I went down to him. His arms were crossed over his head; his jacket obscured his face. I freed one arm from the jacket and found a massive wound on his head. No signs of life.

I had prepared myself for the worst, and the worst had happened, or so I thought. When the ambulance arrived from Kilauea Military Camp, the medics confirmed my initial findings and began looking for some identification as I radioed my first report. Then one of the medics handed me an envelope he'd found in the car. It was addressed "Tom _____."

My heart sank. Now I knew the car, now I knew the battered profile of the face. The hardest, ugliest, dirtiest part of my job was happening. A co-worker, an acquaintance who had taken me, an outsider, into his confidence. Now I had to reconstruct as best I could his last moments of life in the land where he was born, the land he loved and knew so well.

I took the body to the morgue, returned and continued my investigation. I helped the towing company prepare the wreck to be hauled away

All during the following week, I wondered whether I could get back into the rhythm of my hike. Could I let the past be past and forget myself in the present?

The next leg was the Ka'u Desert.

As I walked west from the Hilina Pali road, the vegetation became more stunted and sparse. Sunny skies and a brisk cool wind helped me forget the immediate past and recall more distant memories.

The surroundings made it seem as if I were back in the upper Arizona desert—sand dunes, barren rock, scrubby trees clinging to life. The only difference was there were ferns growing in the shady areas instead of cactus. The Ka'u Desert receives 30 to 40 inches of rain a year, but the area lies to the southwest of Kilauea's summit. Influenced by a high water loss and sulfurous fumes, vegetation must struggle to survive.

WHATEVER THE REASONS for its existence, the desert added to my hike's striking variety. Only a few miles away, on the windward summit of Kilauea, 100 inches of rain a year supports a forest of tree ferns. Yet at the desert gray sand dunes pile up 20 feet or higher, and you have to keep reminding yourself that you are in tropical Hawaii. An added bonus is the vividly colored erosion patterns in the ash layers exposed along the trail.

The trail continued across gently rolling terrain. Ahead I saw two white

crater birds, the koa'e, seemingly hovering in the trade winds only 15 feet above the ground. Having walked the trail before, I knew their secret: they were actually 300 feet above the floor of the twin pit craters, which hide alongside the trail with nothing to belie their presence until you are almost upon them. I spent some time walking around the craters, trying to find a good vantage point for a picture. At each place I stopped I peered over the edge. I soon developed a queasy sense of vertigo and had to move carefully away.

From the pit craters I took off cross-country, aiming at the bluff called Uwekahuna, the high point of Kilauea and site of the Hawaiian Volcano Observatory.

Following an eruption a few weeks earlier, the observatory's instruments indicated the mountain had rapidly inflated, or recharged itself with magma. The level of inflation was extremely high and concentrated near the upper portion of the Southwest Rift, exactly where I was heading.

I walked parallel to the rift for several miles, finally cutting across at a right angle. After hopping over a crack, I decided it would be wise to use my "portable seismometer" before committing myself any deeper into the rift zone. I sat down and firmly extended my legs against the ground while I snacked and wrote some notes. My "seismometer" indicated nothing unusual, so I got up and continued on across.

The last mile to Uwekahuna trended back into the scrubby forest and rain, the 63-degree temperature heightened by moderate trade winds.

Then, it was back home and back to work.

The Mauna Loa strip road was the trip for the following weekend. In planning the hike I had decided that walking the 10 miles of road was an evil necessary for linking the ascent of Mauna Loa with Kilauea. I drive the road on routine patrol several times a week, but I felt I had to walk it to maintain a sense of continuity.

All week I had hoped for a sunny day, and the mountain proved most generous, with deep blue skies and a fresh breeze.

The first few miles of road led through Kipuka Ki, where a tall, rich forest obscured the sky. The wind in

Approaching the Pohaku Hanalei, at 12,400 feet, Mauna Loa's summit trail winds around cinder and spatter cone, evidence of the repeated eruptions that have built Mauna Loa from a rift 18,000 feet below the sea into a peak a hundred times the size of Fuji or Mount Shasta. Part of the trail was covered by an eruption in 1974.

PHOTO: NATIONAL PARK SERVICE: HAWAII VOLCANO NATIONAL PARK

the stately old koa trees forced them to reveal their age, bringing the forest alive with the sounds of creaking trunks and swaying limbs.

Soon I was using all my senses to experience the kipuka in ways denied me when I drove through in a patrol car. I heard small birds hiding in the treetops. I stopped and pondered a mound of moss eating away a rock, and young shoots growing from the decaying trunk of a fallen tree. An io, or Hawaiian hawk, not used to humans outside their machines, finally took to flight when I walked by his perch.

Emerging from Kipuka Ki, I saw the summit of Mauna Loa in the distance. I was now on the mountain itself. As I walked I wondered: fair weather after a week of rain and clouds; was I just lucky or was the mountain willing to indulge me?

Only a few cars passed; the feelings of intrusion they caused vanished as soon as they were out of sight. One couple stopped and offered a ride. Attempting to decline politely, I finally had to confess why I was walking up the road. They left me, perhaps not understanding fully but accepting the fact I did indeed want to walk.

As I moved higher, changes in vegetation indicated the ever increasing altitude. For several miles the road climbs through savanna with rich grasses and scattered groves of trees. Then, around 6000 feet, the grand koas become bent and contorted into grotesquely beautiful forms. They are victims of wind storms, perhaps of ice, periodic attempts by the mountain to force them down. Yet they struggle back with a tenacity for life I had to admire.

All too soon I passed above the koas and arrived at the shelter at the end of the road. I realized that what I had dreaded had become a beautiful, integral part of the hike.

There were 6662 feet down and 7015 vertical feet to go. Back home, back to work.

FOR THE LAST LEG of the hike I was joined by "fellow" ranger Margaret Thompson. We set aside five days for the trip, hoping to spend a full day at the summit.

It was raining when we left, and we were afraid the hike to Red Hill would be sodden. But as we drove up the strip road the clouds dropped away, leaving us in brilliant early morning light. Again I wondered, luck or something else?

We had seven trail miles to go and a 3300-foot climb to the Red Hill cabin with all day to get there. The first few miles was badly eroded; the footing was tricky and fatiguing.

The vegetation grew more stunted and sparse. At a little above 8000 feet, we took a fond look at the last tree, knowing there was more than 30 miles of hiking ahead of us before we would see it again.

Our pace was casual with frequent stops to admire the view or take pictures. Don't worry, don't hurry; good advice from the mountain. We were both enjoying the invigoration of the first day on the trail.

Eventually Margaret confessed she was experiencing a bit of discomfort from a developing blister and sore tendons. When she took off her sock to tend to the blister, I cringed in empathy. A *bit* of discomfort!

At 9000 feet Red Hill could be seen a few miles away, appearing de-

ceptively close. I could look back to Kilauea and trace my route down the desert, across to the Kipuka Nene area and see the ocean shimmering off the coast near the Halape cabin.

Soon after we reached the Red Hill cabin, at 10,000 feet, we were joined by two solo hikers, Kip from the Kona side of the island and Jeff from the mainland.

Originally built for patrols, the Red Hill and Summit cabins are now available for hikers year-round and are equipped with beds, cooking utensils, gas stoves and lanterns. The rain collected from the cabins' roofs provides the only dependable water supplies on most of the mountain.

During and after supper a plentiful supply of tales was swapped; then we all turned in. Shortly after dark the wind came up, and a moderate rain began.

Peering out the window in the predawn light, Margaret said, "Hey, there's snow on Mauna Kea!" Instantly everyone was rustling about to get dressed. The overnight low had been 34 degrees; it was somehow reassuring to step out into the brisk air of a rising mountain dawn and feel the cold air against my face. We climbed the few yards to the top of the Red Hill cinder cone and were confronted with a sublime spectacle. The cloud layer was at 5000 or 6000 feet, the sun not yet above it. Alternately I watched for the sun to peek above the clouds and the colors changing on Mauna Kea's fresh snow. The sun abruptly cleared the clouds, and we were bathed in a red glow that was accentuated by the red of the cinder cone on which we stood.

Soon we went down to have breakfast and pack up. Jeff and Kip left first. The early morning scrambling had given Margaret a chance to test her tendons. She said they were quite sore but we might as well hike.

We took a long time to go a short distance before we realized there was no possibility of continuing. We debated our options. Margaret said she knew it was important for me to reach the true summit, several miles from the summit cabin; that was the reason we had set aside a full day for up top. I countered that I placed safety above goals and that it would not be wise to split up and have her attempt to return to the car alone. I assured her I could go to the summit cabin the next day and feel I had attained my goal. Since we had a cushion day, we decided to stay at Red Hill to see whether things improved.

They did. We got up shortly after five o'clock, fixed breakfast, cleaned the dishes and packed. By six, we were on the trail, just as the sun rose. The morning low had again been 34 degrees, and we found scattered pockets of frost. Margaret was feeling much better. In 10 minutes we covered what had taken us 35 to cover the day before.

The early light was brilliant, illuminating all the features along the trail ahead of us. The path now led up the Northeast Rift, passing cinder cones, spatter ramparts and flow channels from both historic and prehistoric eruptions.

We met Kip and Jeff as they came down, exchanged pertinent information and said goodbye to them.

Climbing higher, Margaret and I constantly called each other's attention to one thing after another. The weather stayed clear and cool. Our pace was adequate; we knew we would make it. The only worry now was what toll the higher altitude would take.

AFTER LUNCH AT 12,000 feet, things began falling into place. The extra day at 10,000 feet had helped us acclimate. Margaret caught her second wind at about 12,800 feet and started chugging along; I had not quite fully adjusted and finally had to ask her to slow down.

We reached the junction of the summit cabin trail and the trail to the true summit, on the opposite side of Mokuaweoweo caldera. It was 2.1 miles to the cabin and 2.6 miles to the summit. We would be coming back this way the next day.

Margaret was studying the signs. She turned to me and asked, "How about making it 16 miles tomorrow instead of 11? Let's leave early and go to the summit." By then I too had acclimated, and I replied, "You're on!"

The summit cabin, whenever I look at it in pictures, is bleak and austere. But when we arrived, we had to agree with what many people had written in the register—this was the most beautiful building on Earth.

At sunset I walked a short distance to where I could reach my wife by citizens band radio. The same point provided a good place to watch the shadow of Mauna Loa as it was cast hundreds of miles to sea. Bundled against the wind and a 30-degree temperature, in clothes I'd not used since coming to Hawaii, I was content to simply witness the moment, to just stand there and be a silent spectator in the ageless transition from light to darkness.

Another day started at five o'clock—24 degrees outside, 27 degrees inside. Ice in the suntan lotion! Breakfast, cleanup, packing, interrupted by a beautiful sunrise.

We carried our packs as far as the junction with the North Pit trail and left them behind while we hiked the remaining two miles to the summit. Perhaps it was the buoyancy that came from walking without packs, but our spirits lifted, our steps were steady and we walked lightly. There were scattered patches of hard snow. Unable to resist temptation any longer, I picked up a piece and bit into it. Hawaiian snow tasted just like mainland snow!

As we climbed upward we discovered we could now look down to the ocean on the other side of the island, miles away and 13,000 feet below us. We knew we would soon stand at the top of the biggest mountain in the world.

We made the summit about 10 A.M. The temperature was 33 degrees with a 20- to 30-miles-per-hour wind. Cold. We snacked, took a few pictures and read and signed the register. We didn't talk much; for each of us this was a personal, special part of the trip, a time for reflection.

We had not achieved a conquest that would stun the world. Yet we both knew we had been granted a priceless treasure—a moment in time we would long cherish—a moment unique to all existence. We stood at the tip of almost six vertical miles of rock, satisfaction glowing within us.

We hiked down to Red Hill for the night, then out the next morning. The 18-mile hike provided time to sort out my thoughts about the mountain.

I realized that in addition to all the usual elements encountered on a big mountain, the element of fire, active or frozen, is dominant on Mauna Loa. The jaggedness of the lava formations, so beautiful to behold, also shreds boots mercilessly. Knowing that the mountain is far from dead, I wondered—just suppose—where would we run?

I had no answer until nearly eight months later. Then, after 25 quiet years, the world's biggest mountain started growing again. Lava broke forth in the floor of the summit caldera in the middle of a July night. Brilliant fumes rose above the mountain, and lava flows covered several miles of trail, obliterating part of the route I had followed.

That night I was at the Red Hill cabin on a routine patrol. No one suspected the mountain was finally poised, yet it went that night. After 25 years, nine others and I had a front row seat. The mountain seemed to have accommodated me again.

The next morning the hikers went down; I was instructed to wait and observe. Even though the eruption was waning, heavy tremors continued, apparently from magma moving down the rift beneath me. By evening the cabin was shaking and creaking every few minutes as the mountain adjusted to its change. At 11 P.M. I had a radio conference with the observatory, the jist of which was, "Run uphill, even if you have to run toward the vents."

The night passed safely, however, and I was soon off the mountain. I realized I had tempered my fear by reflecting on the tolerance the mountain seems to show me. Yet my imagination had conceived a weird scenario: I was running across the side of Mauna Loa and yelling into my radio, "Headquarters, five-fourteen." 🖐

NEW HAMPSHIRE'S MOUNT WASHINGTON

by GUY GOSSELIN

It is gentle and low and seemingly mild.
But for the unwary, deadly.

No doubt Mount Washington is the best-known mountain in the northeastern U.S. This has got to be because of its size, not because of its beauty. As northeast mountains go, I'd rank Mount Washington below such beauties as Maine's Mount Katahdin, the Adirondack mountains, Marcy, Pitchoff, Algonquin and Haystack, and New Hampshire's own Mount Franconia Ridge and Mount Chocorua, and Vermont's Mount Mansfield.

But Mount Washington has a reputation as a bad actor among mountains—killing more people than Mount Rainier or any other mountain in the lower 48 for that matter. And having some of the severest weather in the U.S.

Guy Gosselin knows the mountain well. He has lived through 16 winters on its summit, in his job as director of the Mount Washington Observatory there. He is the author of the following piece on Mount Washington.

W.K.

Although Mount Washington is only a minor mountain, its peak projects up into a major storm track and has some of the most severe weather conditions outside polar regions. Because of the mountain's harsh climate, the plant life of its alpine zone is similar to that of Labrador, 600 miles north. In minute cracks of scattered boulders and in broad grassy lawns grow heaths and highland rush, Bigelow sedge and mountain sandwort.

The mountain also supports unique plant life. One species of bluejoint grass has been recorded only once—in 1862 near Washington's summit—and may never be found again. Another plant, the dwarf cinquefoil, grows along the mountain's Crawford Path and on Franconia Ridge, the only places it is found in the entire world.

Mount Washington is unique in its history, too. No other mountain can boast of having had a carriage road, railway, daily newspaper, four hotels, two weather observatories, radio station and television station, or of being the birthplace of American mountaineering.

For nearly two centuries scientists have visited the peak to study geology, botany and weather. While explorers were seeking routes across the Rockies, hundreds of tourists were walking and riding on horseback to the summit of Mount Washington. This would have been impossible had Mount Washington been situated in a remote area, but travelers have been able to reach it with relative ease for more than 150 years. Innkeepers were quick to see the profits to be gained from travelers; by the 1870s the mountain's summit had become one of the major summer tourist attractions in northern New England.

No one can say for sure what relationship the Indians had with Mount Washington during their long occupancy near its base. They called it *Agiochook,* or *Waumbeket Methna,* meaning Mountain of the Snowy Forehead or Home of the Great Spirit, but rarely, if ever, climbed it.

The first European to take an interest in the mountain was the Florentine, Giovanni da Verrazano. As he sailed the Gulf of Maine in 1524 off what is now Portsmouth, New Hampshire, Verrazano reported seeing "high mountains within the land."

A scant 22 years after the landing of the Pilgrims, Darby Field of Exeter, New Hampshire, trekked through a hundred miles of wilderness and, with the help of two Indians, reached the summit of what was then known as "Christall Hill." Field was attracted to the mountain by the hope of riches. The diamonds he hauled back, however, proved to be quartz. The lure of easy money attracted sev-

On the peak, temperatures have plunged to 47 degrees below zero, 49 inches of snow have fallen in a single day and wind velocities exceed 75 mph an average of 104 days a year.

eral other groups that year, but they, too, found only quartz, and the diamond legend soon perished.

FOR THE NEXT 175 years the mountain drew the attention of only a few scientists and lettered travelers. In 1784 the first scientific expedition arrived, led by Dr. Jeremy Belknap of Dover, New Hampshire, author of the state's first history, and Manasseh Cutler of Ipswich, Massachusetts. Belknap was unable to reach the summit, but others in the party did and became the first people to spend a night on top. Cutler was the first to describe in detail the mountain's alpine plants. He and Belknap are credited with naming the mountain in honor of George Washington.

Later, other scientists followed, such men as Edward Tuckerman, a lichenologist, William Oakes, a biologist and author of *Scenery of the White Mountains,* Dr. Jacob Bigelow and Francis Boott, all of whom today have geographical features bearing their names.

By 1800 settlers had moved northward up the Connecticut, Saco and Androscoggin rivers, and roads followed them into the retreating wilderness. Years of intermittent warfare had ended with the Indians either shot or smallpoxed out of New England, and only a few place names remained on the maps to evoke a memory of their race. A new time was at hand, one of industry and expansion. Most significant for the future of Mount Washington was the growth of a leisure class in northeastern population centers.

Abel and Ethan Allen Crawford, father and son, were the first to open up the western side of the mountain in what is now Crawford Notch. They were innkeepers and guides. In 1819 Ethan, with the help of his father, built the first trail to the summit of Mount Washington: the Crawford Path. Today it is the oldest continuously used mountain trail in America.

Ethan is best remembered for his trail, but also for feats of strength he performed on a seemingly daily basis. He carried huge loads and claimed to have served as a "pack mule" for New Hampshire Secretary of State Philip Carrigan and his party in 1820 when they climbed the range to name the other peaks of the Presidentials. He even carried men and women along the trails.

IN 1821 ETHAN BUILT a bridle path to the present cog railway base station and a foot trail from there to the summit. In 1840 the foot trail was expanded into a bridle path by Ethan's brother Thomas. Abel Crawford, then 75 years old, was the first to ride up it to the summit.

By this time there were several inns at the base of Mount Washington competing for the tourist business. More were opened in the next few years. One of the most sumptuous was The Glen House, which was built at the upper end of Pinkham Notch in 1851. It had 700-foot piazzas and its own bridle path to the top of the mountain.

In 1852 a stone house measuring 64 by 24 feet was built on the summit. It offered meals and overnight accommodations. Another stone building, Tip-Top House, was erected the following year. Horses and men dragged up the mountain all the wood and fixtures for these mountaintop hostels, and the completed buildings were dependent upon daily pony trains for provisions.

As the railroads reached northern New Hampshire, the pace of development quickened. On August 8, 1861, after nearly eight years of labor, The Glen House completed a twisting eight-mile carriage road to the summit of Mount Washington. Tourists could then journey by train to Gorham, drive in coaches to The Glen House and there board 12-passenger wagons for the trip to the summit.

The novelty of the summit road helped make The Glen House the most popular resort in the White Mountains. By the 1870s it was housing as many as 500 guests who paid $4.50 per day for board, room and transportation to and from the trains at Gorham.

The next step in the development of Mount Washington was construction of the cog railway on the west side of the mountain. The idea had been proposed originally by Herrick and Walter Aiken of Franklin, New Hampshire, but railroad officials had turned them down.

Then, in 1858, Sylvester Marsh revived the idea. He had become lost in a storm while hiking on the mountain six years earlier and was convinced there had to be an easier and safer way to reach the summit. On his own, he sought permission to build a railroad to the top of the peak, and the New Hampshire legislators, although skeptical, granted it. An innovator and promoter, Marsh already had made and lost one fortune and recouped part of his losses in the Chicago meat-packing business. Many people thought he was crazy, but he persisted with his railroad plans.

With $20,000 backing from other railroad visionaries, Marsh began to construct a base station at the foot of the mountain in 1865. The laying of the track and the building of the first engine proceeded simultaneously. Four years later, the engine, named Peppersass, pushed its first carload of passengers to the summit.

THE SUMMIT BEGAN to take on the aspects of a community. A scientific expedition headed by state geologist Charles H. Hitchcock spent the entire winter of 1871-72 there in the newly built train depot. The scientists became the first people to operate a mountain weather station anywhere during winter. Their observations and experiences led to the establishment by the U.S. Signal Corps of a permanent weather station in 1874. It took regular readings until the 1890s.

In 1873 a new summit house was constructed. The project required 250 trainloads of material and cost $60,000. The building could accommodate 150 guests plus employees and boasted wall-to-wall carpeting in the lobby and a formal dining room complete with an orchestra.

In 1854, Mount Washington's Summit House (right) and Tip-Top House provided meals and overnight accommodations. Visitors who thought Washington's 6,288-foot summit was not high enough could climb 27-foot-high Estus Tower. In 1877 Tip-Top House was turned into an office for the newspaper Among the Clouds. The paper was published daily on the summit until 1908, when the complex of buildings burned in a fire.

PHOTO: MOUNT WASHINGTON OBSERVATORY

MOUNT WASHINGTON'S WEATHER: A HURRICANE EVERY THIRD DAY

Mount Washington's climate is comparable to that of Labrador. Its temperature, in the period that man has kept track of it, has never exceeded 71 degrees Fahrenheit. Major snowfields commonly last well into July and in isolated locations may last from one winter to the next. As much as 49 inches of snow has fallen in a single day, and as much as 566 inches in a year. Normal melted precipitation is computed at 76 inches yearly, and some snow usually falls even during the summer. Scientists believe that relatively minor climatic changes could even result in the reactivation of glaciation on the mountain.

But wind is the element that gives Mount Washington its claim to the world's worst weather. Velocities in excess of 75 mph—hurricane force—are achieved an average of 104 days a year; winds of 100 mph are common in winter and not unknown in summer. The average wind velocity is 35.3 mph. And the mountain holds the record for observed surface winds: 231 mph in April, 1934. While there are places in the world that are nearly as windy and many that have temperatures much lower than the minus 47 degrees F. recorded by the observatory in January, 1934, there are few, if any, that experience high winds in combination with below-zero temperatures. On many winter days the chill factor is so extreme the human body can no longer distinguish a drop in temperature.

The severity of Mount Washington's weather is caused largely by its location at the junction of major storm tracks. But topography also plays an important role, at least for wind speeds. They are caused by a phenomenon called the Bernoulli effect, whereby large volumes of air moving toward the peak become compressed and accelerate as they flow up its slopes.

Fog is present 60 percent of the time. Occasionally it is merely inconvenient, limiting visibility to a few feet or to the next trail cairn. At other times a dangerous whiteout condition can occur in which it becomes impossible to see your own feet.

Fog is significant for another reason. The freezing of supercooled fog droplets transforms the mountain and the summit's hodgepodge of buildings and antennae into a wonderland of frosted shapes, all dazzlingly white. And when the wind blows, it sculpts the rime ice into frost feathers that cover everything on the summit.

Rime ice typically covers the Mount Washington Observatory during winter months. It is formed by supercooled fog droplets and sculpted into feathery shapes by the mountain's high winds.
PHOTO: MOUNT WASHINGTON OBSERVATORY

Shortly after the hotel was finished, the summit community acquired a newspaper of its own, *Among the Clouds.* It was founded by Henry M. Burt in 1877.

By the turn of the century, Mount Washington's development reached a peak. Most of the summit was covered by buildings, platforms and walkways. Train sheds, barns and even a 27-foot-high observation tower combined to form a veritable town, the only one of its kind on a mountain peak. Then, on July 18, 1908, most of the complex burned down. Attempts to control the blaze were futile because of lack of manpower and equipment.

Nevertheless, recovery was rapid. Another more modest hotel was built on the ashes of its predecessor in 1915, and the ensuing years saw the emergence of a new summit community which eventually included a scientific observatory, a commercial FM station, a television station and a museum.

IN 1964 THE STATE of New Hampshire purchased most of the private land on top of the mountain. It now administers the summit as a state park. Under the auspices of the state-appointed Mount Washington Commission, plans are being promoted for the construction of a new summit building which will replace two existing structures and have a lower profile than the summit.

Despite the intensity of human activity that has taken place on its slopes, Mount Washington continues to lure backpackers in increasing numbers.

The peak rises more than 4000 feet from both the east and west to its maximum elevation of 6288 feet. From the west, along the ridge of Ammonoosuc which the cog railroad follows, the rise is fairly gradual. From the east it is sharper—up the glacial cirques of Tuckerman and Huntington ravines to the relatively level area surrounding the cone. Some geologists believe this level area is a remnant of an ancient peneplain that eroded away. It is the site of Bigelow Lawn and the Alpine Gardens, which fill with tiny alpine flowers in spring and early summer. Here the margin of the tree line is characterized by the presence of Krummholz—scrubby waist-high fir and spruce trees.

The cone of the mountain is bare and round. Its shape bespeaks its age, and the jumble of large mica-schist blocks that cover it disclose the effects of frost action over many centuries. The summit still is crowded with buildings and antennae, and the hiker who approaches the top on a clear, quiet day is likely to hear the cog train coming up the mountain and the low hum of diesel-powered machinery.

Looking north, a hiker sees the rugged northern Presidentials and the Great Gulf, which once held a tongue of ice six miles long fed by several subsidiary glaciers. Looking south, he sees that the rise to the summit is gentle. It starts at Bartlett, 12 miles away at the lower entrance of Crawford Notch at only 700 feet of elevation. The scene on all sides is dominated by great boulders that extend down into the forests and to the valley floor.

The mountain is crisscrossed by more than 40 trails and affords nearly every kind of climbing from long, lenient backpacking excursions to difficult rock- and ice-climbing routes.

MOST TRAILS IN the area were cut in the early part of the twentieth century by members of the Appalachian Mountain Club. Notable among the trail builders was J. Rayner Edmands, who built five trails at his own expense. Although his trails are more than 75 years old, they are so well built—graded and occasionally paved with flat stones—that they show less wear from erosion and hiker use than many newer trails. Additionally, the hut system for which the AMC is famous was begun in 1888 with the construction of Madison Hut, six miles north of Washington's summit.

North American mountaineering got its start on Mount Washington at about the time Mont Blanc was climbed in 1786. Although the climbs do not compare, the White Mountains were the center of American mountaineering activity until after the opening of the West.

Nowadays shelters and trails on Mount Washington are maintained by the Appalachian Mountain Club, the U.S. Forest Service and the Randolph Mountain Club. Most land in the White Mountains is national forest land, and some of it, principally the Great Gulf, has been designated as national wilderness.

What sets Mount Washington distinctly apart from other mountains is its weather. The Presidentials have recorded more than 80 fatalities. Several deaths were attributable to railroad and aircraft accidents, but most have been caused by exposure, falls and avalanches. And there have been countless narrow escapes.

The first fatality occurred in October, 1849, when an Englishman named Frederick Strickland became lost on Mount Washington in a sudden storm. In September, 1855, Lizzie G. Bourne of Kennebunk, Maine, died just below the summit after she and her uncle ignored the warnings of workmen at the Half-Way House to turn back because of a strong wind on the peak. The hikers were caught in a storm and forced to spend the night in the open.

A month later, Dr. B. L. Ball lost the trail in a storm and spent three days on the mountain huddled between rocks without food or water and with only an umbrella for protection. Rescuers finally heard his calls for help and hauled him off the mountain. Despite severe frostbite on hands and feet, Ball recovered.

ANOTHER NARROW ESCAPE occurred in October, 1925, when Max Englehardt, the caretaker of the summit stage office, ran out of firewood during a heavy snowstorm. He de-

cided to leave his post and make his way down the mountain. He, too, lost his way and spent three days on the mountain before being rescued. He lost part of one heel and all his toes because of frostbite.

On such a mountain, you are confronted with the extremes of nature and of yourself. As many as 50,000 hikers climb Mount Washington an-

nually. Yet, when you are alone and surrounded by fog with only the wind in your ears, you are truly alone; and the mountain is as full of wonder and mystery as it was in the time of the Indians. Only the rocks beneath your feet tie you to reality and to the present. And then, sometimes, only tenuously. ◢

TREKKING THROUGH THE TUCKAMOOR

by GUY and LAURA WATERMAN

Wet-weather wandering from
Moosechuckle Ridge to Celebration Cove
in Newfoundland's Gros Morne National
Park

WHAT DO YOU DO when you're a long day's bushwhack from the road, night is approaching, a Newfoundland southeaster—which has ripped your tent fly to tatters—has been slamming rain through the flapping tent fabric all day, and you face the night with water already soaking up through tent floor, foam pads and sleeping bags?

WELL, YOU GRIN AND bear it, remembering that the human mind is capable of serenity in the most trying circumstances. That's hardly enough, of course.

So you're thankful you knew this Newfoundland weather by reputation and did some careful planning: leaving down bags at home and taking fiberfill ones, instead; bringing sturdy raingear; carrying wool (not down) garments for warmth and wrapping them in plastic bags to keep them dry; and keeping meals simple and easy to prepare.

Still, these preparations were not enough to deal with the force of a Newfoundland storm in our particular situation.

And what a situation—a precarious tent site perched on a narrow strip of pebble beach next to a thicket of stunted fir. The site had been well protected against

the strong prevailing west wind when we set up camp, but when serious weather moved in, the wind shifted, roaring down eight miles of lake and slamming broadside into the tents.

So there we were, two New England trail walkers and BACKPACKER's Bill Kemsley, getting one more exercise on how to deal with wilderness. The storm-tossed night was the climax of a week in which we had learned many new lessons.

We spent that week fighting our way through the densest thickets imaginable in Newfoundland's newest national park, Gros Morne. Our legs and arms were scratched and scored from branches, our clothing ripped and soaked. The tangle of stunted fir and birch, two to six feet high, is known locally as "tuckamoor," though we often were tempted to call it other names.

Yet the adventure of exploring a route

where none existed and eventually finding our way to a remote alpine meadow was worth every minute, even of that wet, stormy day and night.

WE DO MOST OF our hiking in one of the country's most heavily trafficked backcountries, New England's White Mountains. Although we've bushwhacked some, especially in winter, we're usually zipping along well-tended trails and enjoying deep-green woods, not fighting them.

The prospect of a totally different backpacking environment had led to an enjoyable period of trip planning. We pored over the Canadian Surveys and Mapping Office's excellent maps of the region. We debated where to thread our way through the contours, how to deal with the fearsome tuckamoor, how long it might take to get from point to point, and where we might find water.

We corresponded with the then acting superintendent of the park, helpful young Eric Hiscock, whose concept of park planning demonstrates a greater respect for wilderness values than many of his stateside counterparts. (We visited the park headquarters when we arrived in Newfoundland, and Hiscock reviewed our

361

Ma and Pa Point drops precipitously 2,000 feet to the shore to Western Brook Pond and provides a spectacular view.
PHOTO: WILLIAM KEMSLEY, JR.

proposed itinerary and loaned us several aerial photos.)

Our planning extended to meticulous packing arrangements. Dinners were a compromise of volume and budget, achieved by alternating freeze-dried dinners with grains (bulghur, millet or semolina), legumes (chick peas or yellow split peas) and a cup of dehydrated mixed vegetables or a can of tuna fish or sardines. To these we always added a soup (usually Lipton Cup-a-Soup packets), a hot drink and, about half the time, a dessert (pudding, fruit or something else easy to mix). Breakfasts were a cereal with dried milk, wheat germ and raisins already added, plus a hot drink. For each day of the trip we packed one of these dinners, the next morning's breakfast, 12 squares of paper towels, candles and matches in one compact plastic bag bearing a number indicating the date for which it was intended.

For lunches we packed home-made bread that Laura has developed for camping and a tin of peanut butter. Every night we would slice half a loaf of bread and make two sandwiches apiece for the next day. Supplementing these, each person would carry a bag of gorp, chocolate bars and hard candies, which had to be spaced out over the eight days of the trip.

O N SOME POINTS our planning misfired. Laura took an umbrella—Eric Shipton had one on the damp trek into Everest. The high winds of Newfoundland promptly blew it inside out.

Bill purchased a machete, envisioning vigorous whacking through tuckamoor. The instrument provided great sport in practice, and we perfected a magnificent "Gros Morne stroke," which we longed to demonstrate in the aisles of the airplane going from Montreal to Deer Lake, New-

foundland, but didn't for fear the airline might misunderstand. If it had, and we'd ended up hijacking the plane to Cuba, we might at least have found use for the machete in sugar fields. It was ineffectual on Newfoundland tuckamoor, as the stunted fir, although small, was mean—often several inches thick.

But most of our preparations proved on target—and they certainly were a lot of fun.

We were blessed on one point: on many of the two- and three-day hikes we made in the summer before this trip (we went to Newfoundland in late September, to avoid black flies), we encountered frequent, hard rains. It was as if our New England hills were cooperating in training us for the damp and hostile Newfoundland environment.

When we finally reached the small fishing village of Deer Lake, we had scheduled not only the visit to park headquarters but a day's trial hike on the one mountain to which a trail already had been cut—the park's highest point, 2644-foot Gros Morne.

Once again, the weather cooperated—and showed us what Newfoundland hiking is so often like. A rain cloud sat over Gros Morne as we approached. When we ascended a long scree gully at the end of the three-mile approach trail, we entered that cloud, it began to rain and visibility dwindled to no more than 50 feet. At the top of the gully on the featureless plateau, we struck out across the flat summit. To ensure finding our way back to the gully, we constructed small cairns of four or five rocks, then knocked them over on our return so as not to confuse another party. The wind picked up stiffly, and the rain intensified. We spent an exciting hour wandering on that near-level plateau, in what seemed most like an uphill course, looking for an elusive summit cairn which we never found. We descended well chilled by dampness and wind. That night a retreat to the driers of Deer Lake's laundromat seemed prudent.

The next day our education began in earnest. We put on full packs, loaded for eight days' survival and grunted off. After following a two-mile approach trail through flat, boggy coastal wetlands, we arrived on the shore of Western Brook Pond, a ten-mile-long lake where the topography abruptly changed. The thicket-covered land jumped up in 2000-foot cliffs, giving the lake the appearance of a fjord spliced into a ring of hills that are actually the northernmost extension of the Appalachian Mountains.

A TRUE WILDERNESS stretched before us. Two miles down the lake, where the cliffs met the shore, the water narrowed to a canyonlike vista. But at our end of the lake there were gently rolling hillsides covered with low-growing fir, spruce and birch forest. The high table-land atop the distant cliffs looked like meadows which would be easy walking.

Our plans were simple: follow the shore and go through the woods until we reached those pleasant-looking meadows. We might even hike all the way around the lake. In the White Mountains, the total distance would take no more than two to three days. We had food and fuel for eight days. Simple, right?

Wrong! The first obstacle was the lake's outlet, a swift, ice-cold, 160-foot-wide, waist-deep stream. We know it's 160 feet because the first person to cross tied into a 150-foot rope and ran out of rope just before reaching the other side. We know it's waist-deep because we had to shed everything except our shirts to make it. Getting across took over an hour—and we had gone only 160 feet.

But now came two miles of shoreline. Simple waltzing along the stony beach for an hour or so, right?

Wrong again! For seven hours we alternated traversing steeply sloping cliffs with struggling through cliff-top tuckamoor. There were only occasional stretches of walkable beach. After all that time and effort, we still were near the lake, but we had made good progress toward the cliffs, where we could get up onto the high tableland.

Once or twice along the shore we found evidences of man: rough clearings evidently hewn by moose hunters, and the collapsed remains of a simple shack. (On our return we mentioned these camps to Acting Superintendent Hiscock, who looked surprised and commented that there was not supposed to be any hunting in the park.)

OUR FIRST NIGHT we stayed at a small cove about a quarter-mile wide, well sheltered from the strong west wind and with a beautiful sand and pebble beach.

We were so delighted with the natural beauty of the beach, and our legs and arms were so scratched by tuckamoor, that we steeled ourselves for a cooling but soothing swim in the September chill of the lake. But just as we started dinner, the well-known Newfoundland rain settled in.

We were slightly behind schedule—still down on the shore at the end of the first day—but the next day we'd move up to the high tableland and really start to move. Right?

Wrong! Although the rain did stop the next day, after taking a closer look at the woods we faced we elected to devote a day to reconnaissance without heavy packs.

After struggling, scratching, clawing, kicking, biting and fighting through unrelentingly dense tuckamoor—mostly balsam fir, with some spruce, birch and Canadian yew—we still were well below the

GREAT PLANS FOR GROS MORNE

Gros Morne National Park—one of Canada's newest parks, established in 1973—covers 716 square miles of highly varied, subarctic terrain. The park management is sensitive to modern environmental concerns and anxious to avoid the irreversible follies of overdevelopment. Therefore the area will be geared to the quieter forms of recreation—hiking, backpacking and boating in the lakes and fjords. Off-road vehicles, except for snowmobiles, are already prohibited.

At present there are just 10 miles of hiking trails, but 225 miles have been mapped out and are slowly being cut through tuckamoor and woods. Much of the high tableland can be traveled without trail. A first-rate climb of the highest point in the park (Gros Morne, 2644 feet) is already accessible. A strikingly barren uplands, The Serpentine Tableland, is almost devoid of vegetation and hauntingly like the surface of the moon.

The park management envisions a graduated scheme of well-manicured trails to potentially popular tourist spots; less-developed longer trails connecting outstanding natural areas, with primitive campsites at least four miles from the road; and no trails at all in wilder rugged places such as the high cliffs area described in the accompanying story.

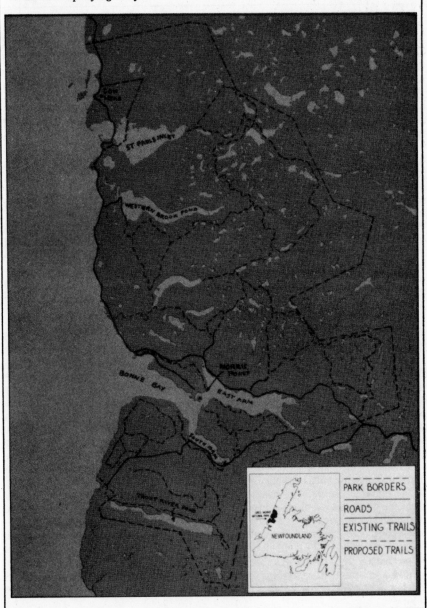

PARK BORDERS
ROADS
EXISTING TRAILS
PROPOSED TRAILS

THE RAUCOUS RAVEN OF THE TUCKAMOOR

(with apologies to Edgar Allan Poe)

Under a bleak and barren hill
Where cold north winds are never still
And driving rain hath power to chill,
We struggled 'round a ten-mile pond
In company of which I'm fond,
Mustachioed gent and pretty blond.
At end of day we stopped to dine,
Set up our tent on site so fine,
Secured it well with every line,
Wondering what the next day brings;
When above the wind that sings,
We thought we heard great flapping
    wings.
I opened up the door a crack,

Then suddenly I started back.
In flew this bird with feathers black,
A giant awful-looking raven,
With his enormous wings a-wavin'
And a look that made us craven;
Settled just above our door,
Which the north wind rudely tore;
Made our threesome into four.
A sight! We'd never seen one rarer
Inside our Gerry Himalayer
As the steely skies grew grayer.
The sight made Bill and Laura quake,
But I could conquer fear and spake:
"Tell us, bird, if words you fake,
If human language you can borrow,
Of what will we three find tomorrow,
And will it end in joy or sorrow?
What lies out there beyond the shore?
Speak to us above our door!"
    Quoth the raven: "Tuckamoor . . ."

This made us laugh and feel quite
    cheery
And we thought it oh so merry
To see this bird perched on our Gerry,
In mountain setting so spectacular
Chirping portents so oracular,
Frowning bleakly, like Count Dracula,
Looking darkly as could be,
Grimly warning just us three.
So we again addressed our plea:
"Lonesome bird, that hath no mate,
Read to us from destiny's slate!
Tell us what's to be our fate!
Will we make it back to shore?
Tell us, raven, what's in store?"
    Quoth the raven: "Tuckamoor . . ."

Three days we walked and did all right;
At further cove we camped that night
In the dim declining light;

---

ridge and ready to acknowledge we could never move our full packs up that route. We retreated to the beach for a second night.

We did not share the cove with people, but plenty of other creatures were there. Chickadees and a downy woodpecker flitted along the edge of the woods. Kingfishers patrolled the water. Three loons floated past the mouth of the cove. A snowshoe hare hopped along the beach, passing within ten feet of us. A weasel scurried close to the tent as we were inside eating dinner. And there were moose tracks and droppings all around. We had seen a gigantic bull moose far below us in a clearing on the second day and had been thankful that sighting was so distant.

The next day we pushed farther down the shoreline. We found several moose trails leading to the lake, and twice we used them to cut across impassable, rocky places. They made traveling through the tuckamoor easier, but they also made us nervous. What would you do if you were laboring along a three-foot-wide track under a 50-pound pack with an impenetrable wall of tuckamoor on either side, and you suddenly discovered you were going the wrong way on a 900-pound moose's one-way street? Fortunately, *we* never had to find out.

Eventually we arrived at a spot directly under the towering cliffs marking the start of the fjordlike canyon. We made camp there and spent the rest of the day exploring possible climbing routes. We hoped to avoid both the dense brush and the steep cliffs by sticking just to one side of the cliffs.

LATE IN THE DAY we enjoyed the unparalleled vistas of our new campsite and indulged in the prerogative of the explorer, naming the outstanding features that struck our view. A magnificent headland cliff which looked like the nose of Yosemite's El Capitan we called El Tuck, for the dreaded tuckamoor so effectively guarding its approaches. A particularly castlelike series of ramparts we dubbed Kenilworth, after the Sir Walter Scott novel we had just read. For reasons which now seem obscure, we named the first two dramatic points on the cliff above us Ma Point and Pa Point. The long approach ridge flanking the cliffs had received its name the day before when we had bogged down in frustration and fancied we heard a bull moose enjoying a hearty laugh at our predicament: Moosechuckle Ridge.

The next morning we started at daylight with just a rope and day packs. As we worked our way up a steepening stream bed, we could hear several waterfalls we had spotted from the shoreline the day before. The route alongside the falls proved steep and brushy, but we made progress. We stopped for a bit of lunch on a levelish spot beside the cascading falls. The wind blew the spray about, and we could see purple gentians blooming in the wet moss. Regaining strength, we tackled the brush again.

The route grew steeper and eventually butted into a wall which required intricate route selection. At one point we negotiated an overhang on vegetation alone, grasping roots and branches instead of rock handholds.

Toward the end of the morning we emerged on the crest of Moosechuckle

Ridge, at first into low-growing fir and birch but then, ever so gradually, into easier walking. Finally, on the fourth day of trying, we were up there, racing on wide open meadows of blueberries, alpine azalea, moss heather and lichens—a springy autumn carpet of purple, red and orange mosaic.

We skirted the edges of Ma and Pa points, stupendous rock promontories dropping 2000 feet to Western Brook Pond. We peered down steep scree gullies between the rock points and ran from one rocky promontory to the next. We realized we were at last covering ground at a great rate, bouncing over the promontories we had scanned so longingly for three days from below. Soon Ma and Pa points lay small below us as we lunched on the lofty battlements of Kenilworth. Then we turned inland to reach the true summit on that side of the lake, a bald, gently rounded eminence we called Blueberry Mountain. On it we found caribou scat, an antler and tracks.

But even on the high tableland there was occasional tuckamoor—dense impenetrable stands of stunted fir and birch, only two feet high in that harsh environment. Our plan to run around the lake in a day or two had clearly been overambitious. We realized that even if we had been able to get our gear up to the plateau, we would have had to make many wide detours around the tuckamoor growing in sheltered hollows between the rocky points.

At length we returned to our shoreline camp, skirting the cliffs even though it meant struggling with the tuckamoor. Once again we struck our claim on this wilderness: the camp became Celebration Cove.

En route our constant boon companion
Along the rim of that dread canyon—
Three musketeers had their D'Artagnan,
We had ours, though more absurd—
Just a black, infernal bird,
Who only seemed to know one word,
Repeated ever, evermore,
As if transfixed from ancient lore—
    Quoth the raven: "Tuckamoor . . ."

The next day we bogged down in
    thicket,
Really was a sticky wicket,
And we felt we couldn't lick it—
Dense-grown birch and stunted fir,
Through which no human foot could stir.
It would have stripped a bear of fur!
You would have cringed to hear our
    shrieks
Below those stark unconquered peaks:

"Why, we'll be stuck here for three
    weeks!"
"We'll never reach the hoped-for shore!
What is this stuff which we deplore?"
    Quoth the raven: "Tuckamoor . . ."

That night the rains came back again;
Our chance, we feared, went down the
    drain
With that damn thicket and all that rain.
The wind grew wild, the thunder shook,
And threatened our cold lonesome nook.
But still there sat that brooding rook,
That bird whose look seemed to deplore
Our very being there—and more—
Like some vengeful ancient Thor,
Brooding there above our door;
Caused us to cry out, implore:
"Dratted raven, just once more,
Will it ever cease to pour?

When can we get out of door?
Will we see our homes once more?"
    Quoth the raven: "Tuckamoor . . ."

So if you journey to Cow's Head*
To find if we're alive or dead,
And whether truth's in what I've said,
Go stand upon a lonesome shore
And listen to that north wind roar,
So shrill you've never heard before.
And drifting down to that chill shore,
Above the storm's eternal roar,
You'll hear these words just as before
Come haunting downward:
    "Tuckamoor . . ."

—Guy Waterman

*Nearest town to the trailhead.

W E HAD SET UP the tents head-on into the prevailing westerly winds and sheltered by a large rock outcrop. We knew the good weather would break soon, and we wanted to be in the best position to take the winds. Still, we hoped for clear skies. Although we had abandoned the idea of traversing the uplands, we wanted to continue our exploration by walking farther around the shoreline the next day. Right?

Wrong! We awoke to a hard rain. By mid-morning the wind was high, but worse, it had shifted. Now it was coming across the lake from the southeast, funneling down the canyon, picking up speed as it smashed into Celebration Cove, striking the tents broadside. We feared for Laura and Guy's tent fly on the windward side, and sure enough, when Laura stuck her head out into the driving rain after a particularly heavy late-morning gust, she saw the fly had ripped full-length down a seam. The shredded pieces slapped noisily near her face.

The wind was spraying tiny droplets through the tent walls. During a lull we all got out to make repairs. We turned the fly around and piled stones along the tent walls to keep the wind from whipping under the floor and pulling out the stakes.

No sooner had we settled back in the tent than the storm resumed, and a wild burst of wind ripped the other side of the fly.

We debated whether to move the tent. We could not turn it into the wind because the beach was too narrow. We could not move into the woods because of the tuckamoor and bog. We did, however, remove a section of wands so the tent would give somewhat with the wind.

All three of us waited out the lengthy afternoon in the flyless tent, reading, chatting and trying to keep the place mopped as dry as possible. Every now and then Bill stuck his arm out the door to take a temperature reading (low 40s), and whenever we heard a particularly heavy gust roaring down the canyon, he would hold out his wind gauge (gusts between 40 and 50 mph). It was exciting to watch the wind pick up the lake surface and drive the spray down the lake.

A T LAST IT WAS DINNER TIME. Wrestling with the stove, Guy had succeeded in getting the soup water nearly boiling when a particularly vicious gust hit the tent, shoving the poles inward and upsetting stove and pots. Bill and Guy struggled out into the storm, reset the poles and piled more rocks on the pullouts. We resumed dinner. Guy manned the stove, and Bill and Laura held the poles against the most furious blasts. Finally we managed to have a hot, satisfying dinner. It braced our spirits as the day slowly faded.

Bill moved over to his tent, which was weathering the storm nicely. We knew this would have to be our last night in this beautiful country, for with tent half-gone and equipment soaked, it would be foolish to expose ourselves to more wet weather.

It was a long, wet night. But the tent held, and we managed to drift in and out of sleep. Just before daylight we packed quickly and stepped into the wind and rain to dismantle what was left of the tent.

The wind fairly blew us along the rocky shore as we began the long walk back. Would we be able to get out in a day? It had taken us a hard day and a half

to reach the cove, but we hoped our early start and familiarity with the route would work in our favor. The thought of fording the river again was in all our minds. How much higher and swifter would the water be?

The rain finally stopped. Our excursions into the tuckamoor to avoid the lakeside cliffs were easier. Perhaps we were finally learning how to move in the wretched stuff?

By the time we reached the river crossing, Bill was reshuffling his pack and clothes. We contemplated the water. It was flowing much fuller and faster. We moved

The tuckamoor takes its toll. A mixture of stunted balsam, spruce, birch, Canadian yew, and a few other miscellaneous tormentors, tuckamoor proved to be a formidable adversary that could not be avoided. How does one negotiate such terrain? By kicking, scratching, clawing, and scrambling over, under, and through it.
PHOTO: WILLIAM KEMSLEY, JR.

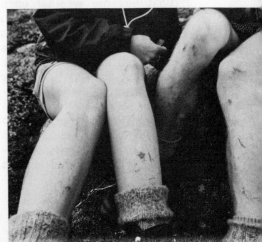

downstream from where we had crossed before, but found no better place.

BILL SHOULDERED HIS PACK, picked up a stout stick for balance and plunged in. We watched him with fascination. He made good progress to the middle of the river, and then he floundered as he tried to push his legs through the current eddying up over his thighs. Slowly and unsteadily he shuttled to the shallow water.

"That was rough," he shouted from the other side. "You might want to use the rope."

Laura tied on the rope and started out. About halfway across, at the place where Bill had had difficulty, she paused a moment, calmed herself, and then proceeded, fighting the current and using a staff to keep from slipping. Finally, just as the 150-foot rope was played out, she reached the shallow water. Soon Guy was across, too, and emptying the water from his boots.

Bill looked at his watch. It was five o'clock; we had made it. Just a two-mile jaunt down the easy access trail, and we'd be out before dark.

As we plodded along we looked at the tuckamoor, thick as ever, on either side. The trail was a relief. It was difficult to believe we had battered against such impenetrable tangles.

We stopped to look back at the canyon and cliffs now faint in the distance. They took on a remote and indifferent look, as though we had never been there—nor anyone else before. ◢

BACKPACKING ABOUT THE MATTERHORN

by HOWARD FRIEDMAN

Zermatt, Switzerland, is surrounded by more major peaks than any other region in the Alps. There are over 42 marked trails, 15 major glaciers, and—the guidebook says—Zermatt boasts the sunniest alpine climate north of Italy. We thought of all this when, having traveled 4,000 miles, we stepped off the cog railway into a very wet cloud.

The sign pointed to "Täsch, 1½ hours," and five minutes later a second sign read "Täsch, 2¼ hours." Someone had scrawled "Campground, 5 minutes." Beset with directions, we sloshed down the valley road and found the campground nestling between the railway embankment and the heliport.

"What has the weather been like?"—we had traveled through the worst drought in recent times and were apprehensive about its effects. "Well, in the mountains, you know, it changes." Studying the campground owner's utterance, we listened to the changes on the tent roof from light to heavy rain, from east rain to south rain, from billowing to flapping, and with thoughts of high

adventure among the peaks, we fell asleep.

The next morning the town was a sea of umbrellas. They were even mounted above the prize horses of the Hotel Sailer's guest carriage. Between droplets we sampled the delights of dark crusty rye bread (röggenbrot) and dairy-fresh butter. There were all varieties of splendid jams, a tangy milk-based drink, Rivella, and kiosks full of chocolate bars, which (my wife assured us) were well worth the entire trip. We also looked around for equipment, but with devalued dollars in our pocket we ended up buying less than we had planned. Still, the merchandise was of consistently good quality and would last many a season.

In the afternoon you could see over the dripping roofs to above timberline. Then the summer skiers, with faces tanned copper, came down from the brilliant sun-drenched ski area on the Plateau Rosa at 3,500 meters (11,550 feet). My barometer had risen slightly, the birds were flying higher, and if you were armed with a good imagination you could see

through the mists to the outline of the peaks behind them. Conditions could not be better! With more hope than conviction, we prepared to backpack into the high country. If the weather seemed to be clearing, we would leave in the morning.

Given the uncertain weather and our own untried condition, we decided to spend the first night camping by one of the mountain tarns at timberline, in the broad hanging valley above and to the east of town, below the Findeln glacier.

As ever, we—my 14-year-old son Peter and I—left later than planned and were behind other walkers. Our pack frames created some stir, for the trail is close to town and frequented mostly by strollers, or by those who take the chair lift to walk down from the terminal with a light pack and a sandwich.

When we told people—conversation was a convenient excuse for stopping—that we would spend the night at a given lake and the next night upon the glacier, the usual answer was, "You are mistaken. There's no

366

hotel there!" As in "The Three Little Pigs," life cannot be conceived of without a solid roof over one's head—and perhaps with some justice, for passing a night out in a severe alpine storm above timberline is an experience to be relished in retrospect, not when the wind gusts with enough force to rip up an unweighted tent and not when there is the smell of lightning on the rocks.

Anyway, we proceeded up through a deep forest of mixed hardwoods and passed the glade where two years earlier Peter and his sister had practiced the technique of using sliding friction knots to prusik up a rope over an overhanging boulder, so that they would not be totally hopeless if either had fallen into a crevasse. By the time we reached the upper forests of larch and spruce, veils of sky broke through the clouds. We might reasonably hope for a dry night.

Hours later, with the last strollers far behind, we reached a series of small alpine lakes. We pitched our tent above one of them at 2,300 meters (7,250 feet) in a meadow of flowering alpine mosses.

There were a few trees about and we even found a cache of dry wood below an overhanging boulder. A stream came down from a waterfall, and since I knew there were no major sources of contamination above, we figured, rightly, the water would be safe. If only the weather would cooperate, this would be an ideal campsite. If it did not, well, we would have to learn sometime whether my misgivings about the strength of a super-lightweight tent were justified. For the present we could enjoy the immense quiet spaces: The last clouds lifted for a while and the Matterhorn's twisted pyramid, just across the valley from us now, turned rose and purple in the evening light.

The tent held. The next night we planned to camp on one of the medial moraines of the Gorner glacier which drained three of the major Zermatt peaks: Monte Rosa, second highest in the Alps, Lyskamm, whose north wall held one of the major snow and ice

faces in Europe, and the serrated Breithorn. Although the glacier was only 1,000 feet higher than our camp at Grindjisee, the approach would be complex. First we would have to drop down to cross the outlet of the Findeln glacier, hike up to the Gornergrat, the high ridge opposite us, traverse this, and only then would we be in line for the descent to the glacier at its flank. All of this up and down would be at an altitude at which we would feel the lack of air, perhaps considerably. As it was, we had taken considerably more than guidebook time to reach the lake, but we had been jogging regularly all spring, and so, with a pulse rate lower than average, our systems had more latitude with which to adjust to the diminished oxygen.

Middle-ground hiking in most mountain areas is generally less interesting, for one is forever crossing the nondescript remains of retired glaciers. Fortunately the recent rain following the drought had brought out the alpine flowers. There were flowering mosses, asters, forget-me-nots, gentians, trolls in abundance. Also, we had chosen a trail indicated by faint dashes on the map and had the pleasant sense of hiking through an unfrequented area—until the trail steepened and both the dashes and the signs of trail became fewer and fewer. Whatever advantages a pack frame offers, increasing your stability on the loose rock of washed-out hillsides is not one of them. The old-time guides would take their clients walking on cow tracks the first days and then spend the rest of the week going up the steeper goat trails. Well, we must have taken the goat trail, I was thinking, when all of a sudden Peter, who was ahead, stopped and made a sign to be quiet.

There right in front of us, apparently using the same track, was a herd of steinbok, alpine cousins of our own mountain goats. We followed them at a distance and, I admit, slower. When the herd did stop, the animals were so totally engrossed, licking minerals from the rock, we were

able to approach them so closely we could see the reflections of an image in their eyes. Here certainly was a group of absolutely protected wild animals which had never had reason to learn fear of man.

We were so engrossed we had not even noticed that we had reached the ridge line and the Gorner glacier stretched below us at last. We did feel this, however, when we had to climb up the last stretch again, this time with our packs on. The steinbok now were gone, but in their place, rising beyond the ridge, was the great wall of ice-clad 4,000-meter peaks. We dropped down the trail to the glacier, surrounded by their presence, to follow the red blazes and flagged points onto the ice. In less than half an hour we came to a large moraine formed by the junction of tributary glaciers. The walking was easy and we left the trail to head upstream in search of a campsite.

Tenting that night was not a bed of roses. Peter had found a reasonably flat spot of rocks, close to a pool of clear water that had formed in the ice. We spent an hour leveling off the site: fresh glacial debris tends to be sharp.

Setting up camp on the rocky Gorner glacier.
PHOTO: HOWARD FRIEDMAN

We had taken, specially, a piece of lightweight plastic to protect the tent bottom—and as for ourselves, bottoms and all, we had ¼-inch cell pads, the airplane baggage labels still in place, and would be comfortable enough, all things considered.

A glacier is always in motion. All through the night we could hear the crack of opening crevasses, the shattering of seracs (upthrust ice masses), and the muffled explosion of some structure below, collapsing under internal pressures. Meanwhile, as after all storms, rock and snow avalanched down off the peaks. So we passed a sort of multimedia night in our tent, with sound and movement both above and below.

We awoke to splendid weather. Perhaps the guidebook had been right after all, for it looked like *le grand beau*, a condition of dry stable air associated with high barometric pressure. There would be no imminent threat of major storm. It was the time for difficult ascents and for easy photographs. Hardly in shape for the one, we chose the other.

It had been arranged for my wife and other son to come and join us for the day on the glacier. I met them at the trail's edge and led them across the slightly crevassed region to our camp. For Michaël, my younger son, who still had memories of being stuck in a snow cleft above Amphitheatre Lake in the Tetons, the crevasses seemed large enough, and I led him across with some tapes I had taken in the pack for the purpose.

We had planned to continue on to the Monte Rosa hut, an hour's walk across the glacier, so Michaël would have been in a hut, but time and fatigue were adding up and our recent arrivals were puffing. We had had three fine days in the mountains for this our first trip, and it would be nice to get down to the valley, unhurried, before night. So we climbed back up to the ridge and without too many qualms I deposited wife, younger son, and both packs in the cog railway car.

Free then as birds, Peter and I waltzed down the shortest route to the valley. Although we had the crazy temptation to race the train down part of the way, the secret of a successful alpine season is to conserve energy when one can—and by the end of the summer I would have hiked and climbed up the equivalent of three Mount Everests—so we allowed the cog railway to go down before us unchallenged.

The good weather was just the eye of the storm, and by the time we had sorted our gear in town and made the necessary modifications, the campground was again a large green sponge. But I enjoyed the varied company there from four continents and shared tea, soup, and reminiscences with them. In particular I remember a group from beyond the Iron Curtain. We spent long hours together talking in their weak English and my poor German and exchanged small gifts before leaving. It was painful, though, to realize what a gap separated our ways of life, for when I suggested that we take each other's addresses to write later, they smiled weakly but said it would be better not to. Suddenly there was fear in their eyes—the same expression I had seen in captured prisoners of war being herded to the rear lines—at the thought of the consequences of their stepping out of line. They left to drive back without stopping, without sightseeing,

Howard Friedman helps his son Michaël cross a crevasse in the Gorner glacier.
PHOTO: DIANE FRIEDMAN

without purchases, along the only route that had been permitted them.

When the weather is bad you hope for the moon to change and for the snow to descend to the valley. Days later the fresh snow was just a few hundred feet above the church steeple and we wondered whether the storm sequence had finally emptied itself. Rhetorical question, for, with more guts than brains, we were eager to get up again.

This time we took the long western side valley of the Zmutt glacier. Above us, when visible through the clouds, the entire north face of the Matterhorn was now as white as in midwinter. Hardly a rock could be seen. There was just this white triangle rising above us, so enormous we felt we had to bend backward to view it all. Here was alpine history compacted into one image. To the left was the stepped ridge up which Whymper led the first successful ascent in 1865. There in front was the 65-degree ice field and great central couloir up which the Schmid brothers had found a route for the first ascent of the great north face in 1931. And there, unthinkable even now, was the line of the audacious Diretissima route through the overhangs, which Bonatti first climbed alone in winter in temperatures of 40 below—to honor Whymper's ascent.

Our plans were more modest. We would go up and camp on the grassy moraine in the area of the Schönbiel Cabin. (In this unsettled weather we thought it unwise at that altitude to be too far from a fixed shelter.) The next morning, depending upon conditions, we would go up from our camp to or toward the relatively easy summit of the Point of Zinal, from which there is said to be a spectacular view.

Before evening a large herd of chamois romped over, wary but undisturbed, to browse on the small ridge opposite us. Shiest of the alpine fauna, they scattered with the click of my camera shutter, moving easily across the black, wet rock faces, only to take a stand again on a second ridge. I approached them quietly; this scene should not be disturbed. But my camera shutter, even when the camera was muffled inside my sweater, again disturbed them enough for them to continue loping on to a third ridge. We played this game until night and the altitude prevailed.

We were up early the next morning and the clouds were down again. We followed a steep line of cairns to a crest at 3,200 meters (7,200 feet) and then onto the Hohwäng glacier. Although this is a regular route from Zermatt to the adjacent valley of Zinal—in normal conditions—there was not a vestige of a track upon the gray, wrinkled surface of the ice. There must have been 10 to 15 feet less snow cover than in earlier years, and so there were few snow bridges linking the crevasses that, like black leeches, stretched across our line of ascent. To make matters worse, the recent snow had covered some crevasses with a thin, unstable cover.

We had taken a rope along for the glacial portion; still, I led up with some hesitation, for although I was relatively confident that I could take care of Peter were he to fall in, I was not certain what might happen if the roles were reversed. At other times in circumstances like this, I had watched amazed while local guides, the pattern of crevasses fixed in their minds, would thread their way effortlessly across dangerous areas. We instead proceeded slowly, for I was forced to probe with my ice ax with nearly every step: at least the clouds were thinner overhead, we might get a view after all, and preferably not from the bottom of a crevasse.

But just before the col at 3,455 we could see bad weather boiling over from the southwest, and it was heading our way fast. If that storm got worse, if there were a whiteout on these immense slopes, we would be unable to see the pattern of the crevasses and would be forced to thread our way back by map and compass. Already we could only see 50 feet in some directions, already the fresh snow swirled about our feet and rapidly covered our tracks. We turned around, knowing that it would be snow and storm all the long way down to the moraine below the tent. Except that for a few moments the cloud cover lifted and we could see the Matterhorn projected in the mist steeper and higher than I had ever remembered it. The low sun, breaking through other mists, rayed bright silver across the apex of the peak and streamed onto the clouds. For a brief moment this was the magnificence we had come to find.

It was the last week of Peter's alpine vacation, and as we walked up the gorge to the west of town, I thought this might very well be our last trip together that summer. Thinking about other matters, for it was hot in the gorge, the task of gaining altitude came easier. I remembered the afternoon all four of us had cooked together at our first mountain campsite above the tarn, and then of how well my younger son, despite his wee years, fitted into the life of an alpine camp when he and I spent the night there. . . . Or of Peter bivouacking with me on a ridge of the 4,165-meter (13,750 feet) Breithorn, when a quick change in weather forced us to turn back beneath avalanche-prone slopes, too late to reach the summit, too high to regain the tent. We had down jackets then and a nylon bivouac sack for protection, but the night was cold, starry, and long. Still, it is an ill bivouac that bears no good, for it is often only in these moments and from these otherwise awkward perches that the mountains can be seen to their best advantage. Afterward this is the compensation for a chill night on a ledge above some abyss, but at the moment it takes an act of will to clear your mind to go through the simple motions of taking a photograph.

But the weather had been glorious that day on the Breithorn and the sun had set in a row of clouds, back-lighting each peak between us and the French Alps. We were high enough: we could

Peter Friedman tucked into a protective nylon bivouac sack on a ridge of the 4,165-meter (13,750 feet) Breithorn.
PHOTO: HOWARD FRIEDMAN

see into four countries. . . .

The trail steepened and brought me back to the present. Would we ever find a place flat enough for a tent? In time we did, but there was a small stream flowing through the center and when the tent was up, it looked as if the tent weren't housebroken. Peter dammed—and damned—the stream. Tomorrow would be a two-o'clock start: I had promised to lead him up one of the major peaks, the Zinal Rothorn, by a route which is normally not particularly difficult, and we would have to get to sleep early.

It was two in the afternoon when we neared the summit. Conditions had not been normal. In contrast to an easy ascent of the Rothorn years ago by this route, there was considerable ice underfoot and on the rocks. Where we were resting on the summit ridge, the east face dropped in a series of vertical and overhanging walls the height of three Empire State Buildings down. On the Zinal side a 70-degree slope led into the sky. A slip in either direction would be repugnant.

We were on the subordinate summit at about 4,200 meters when again the weather gave unmistakable signs of worsening. Peter had never been this high in his life and we would have to get down quickly. I looked around with regret, too, for in no place in the Alps is one more surrounded by a sea of peaks.

Below the rock ridge, below the couloir, below the snow ridge, the snowfall caught up with us just above the long, snow-covered slope we had traversed shortly after dawn. But the snow had melted and an ice sheet was exposed below, green and uninviting. There are few ways of giving absolutely reliable protection on ice, and I belayed Peter with one of the best—an ice ax jammed in a fissure. Peter slipped, pendulumed below me, and I brought him to a stop. I was shaking, for there were hundreds of feet to descend across this ice sheet and I could not be sure of stopping him each time.

A Swiss mountaineering instructor came along at that time, climbing with his cousin. I proposed tying our ropes together for greater safety and I thought they agreed—I was talking in my college German and they in their Swiss dialect. Instead, they retied and the instructor led Peter down, separate from me and his cousin. The inevitable occurred: after slipping once (his crampons were not adequate), Peter slipped a second time and this time dislodged his companion. Slowly they slipped down 600 or so feet, unable to stop themselves, for their ice axes, which could have been used for braking, had been ripped from their hands. Below was a thin rock band and a ravine twice the size of Tuckerman, which funneled into an ice fall of several thousand feet.

It was the most dismal sight of my life to see the two of them fly over the rocks—one of them was hurt—and to continue being dragged down below. One stopped for a while but the other in sliding past drew him down. Nearing the funnel, one of them rolled out of the snow chute and slowly, slowly both of them stopped. The lower speck, say 1,000 feet below us, rose wobbling to his feet and waved. An avalanche of snow they had loosened rumbled down. The other sat in a crumpled heap.

I had gotten down by another route and the cousin went on to the hut for help. Peter was bloody but only scratched; the Swiss instructor, who had stopped them both, had been seriously contused where he had struck against the rocks, and could not move. I prepared them for the night. Snow was falling, debris rolling down the slope, the wind was up, and it was getting dark.

Two hours later, the sound of the storm seemed to worsen, but then we recognized the noise of a helicopter. We could see its lights the other side of the mountain. I shouted futilely, and then signaled with my flashlight. The sound and lights disappeared, only to reappear below the ice wall. I signaled again, and then, like an insect poised in the black, the lights turned and flashed toward us. The helicopter flew away. Peter thought they must be looking for someone else.

Later there were lights again, and suddenly a man came down out of the sky, swirling at the end of a cable. "How many hurt?" he asked. I told him. "We need a doctor," he called into his walkie-talkie. "Get down," he shouted, and a second rescuer came down with a stretcher. The 'copter disappeared.

A doctor, medical kit in his knapsack, was brought in the same way. "Hurry, there is lightning danger! If the wind is worse there will be avalanches and the heli can't stay!" In a short time the wounded man was fitted into a stretcher, tied to the cable, and (steadied by a guide) lifted away. The 'copter started back while he was being winched up.

After a long time, with the wind stronger, the 'copter again hovered above us. Attached by a ring at his chest, Peter was hauled up and I soon afterward. The 'copter was hardly holding its position in the storm. Through the open bay I could see its lights picking out the ice wall of a glacier *above us*. But we continued circling and reached the hut.

The Swiss climber had already been flown down to Zermatt and then to the hospital. It had taken less than four hours to get the news down, alert the rescuers, and rescue three people from a 14,000-foot alpine peak in a storm. René Arnold, who had come out of the sky to help us, like a pillar of vigor, was himself injured, seriously, several weeks later.

On the hike down the next day, Peter was pensive. "I never got to the summit after all," he said. I answered, as the chief of the guides had said earlier, "No hurry. The mountains are always there." I thought of a line of Goethe I had seen carved on the walls of a building in town, something to the effect that the mountains are the teachers of great thoughts and the masters of saying little.

IF YOU GO TO ZERMATT

Nearest airport: Geneva; also Zurich, Basel, Milan.

Train or bus to Brig, in the Rhone Valley. Then cog railway, via Visp, to Zermatt. Cog railway is expensive. Reduced tickets for most transport in Switzerland, including some cable cars, available through travel agents.

Alternatively drive to Täsch, south of Zermatt, and leave car in parking lot. Moderate overnight fee. Take cog railway from Täsch or hike 1½ hours on road or trail. Pleasant route but hot when sun is high.

Campground, unless relocated, at south end of Zermatt, just before helicopter landing station. Toilets. Hot showers. Alternatively, Hotel Bahnhof, opposite railroad station, traditionally friendly to hikers and climbers, has inexpensive dormitories, rooms, and cooking facilities for guests. Hot showers are free to guests.

Use General Delivery *(Poste Restante)*, Zermatt, Kanton Wallis, Switzerland, for mailing address. All-night telephone service at post office.

Several supermarkets and specialty food shops stock regular food. Migros will have some items such as dried milk, soup, and potatoes. Dehydrated meals probably not available. Migros cafeteria is a best buy. Also try Walliser Fleisch (dried meat) tasty, practical, expensive.

Replacement cylinders available for continental camping gas stoves. For gasoline stoves, regular gasoline may have to be used. Take spare parts if necessary.

Boutiques carry excellent lines of outdoor clothing and some camping gear. Generally expensive. La Cabane, owned by an alpine guide, has wide choice, fair prices. Skis, ski boots, hiking boots, and ice axes available on rental basis. Few lightweight tents and fewer adequate pack frames available for either rental or purchase.

Excellent topo maps, indispensable if leaving marked trails, on sale in bookshops and *papeterie*. Also splendid poster-sized mountain photographs.

For summer skiing Zermatt has probably the greatest number of lifts and cable cars, in fact too many. These, although expensive, provide a soft way uphill for hikers.

For further information contact Swiss National Tourist Bureau, offices in most major cities. In Zermatt contact Kurverein (Visitors' Bureau), Compagnie des Télépheriques (cable cars), and Guide's Office. This latter organizes relatively inexpensive glacial tours, as well as traditional climbs up the Matterhorn and other peaks.

Miscellaneous. For weather forecasts, you may telephone Wetter Bericht; up-to-date, detailed forecasts in German and French.

For doctor: Dr. Julen, clinic in center of town.

For drinking water in mountains: check first if it is safe and/or available. Traditional sources, e.g., troughs and fountains, are suspect. Courtesy above all: Remember American-style backpacking is in its infancy in the Alps. Respect the people, sites, and trails you employ, for nearly all land is either privately or communally owned and the freedom to camp nearly anywhere in the mountains can be revoked. Lastly, mountain accidents are serious, very costly, and speed of evacuation may be critical. Do not go on ice without proper equipment and training. Try to leave a detailed itinerary and timetable with a responsible person in the town. Consider moderate cost of helicopter rescue insurance. Expect a temperature range in town, for July and August, of 25-85 degrees, and 10 (or zero) to 80 in mountains, together with considerable wind chill at high altitudes.

Overnight accommodations and food are available at huts and mountain hotels located at the base of the peaks. Hut wardens in the former will generally also cook simple meals you bring them. If huts are to be used extensively, it is advisable to become a member, first, of a Swiss, French, Austrian, German, Belgian, or Italian mountain club, for which reduced hut taxes are in force.

ACROSS THE PATAGONIAN ICECAP

by LEO DICKINSON

Winds sweep across the ice at 100 miles an hour, and sulfurous clouds of steam billow out of volcanoes. Nothing lives on the icecap, and few people have ever been there.

A FAINT WIND GHOSTING across the Patagonian icecap filled the parachute, fattening it to the shape of a large nose cone. The two sleds to which it was attached moved smoothly forward, creaking under the weight of 700 pounds of climbing and expedition equipment. Mick was perched precariously on top, bread knife in hand, ready to cut free the parachute if a crevasse suddenly yawned in front of us. Eric and I hung on behind.

It was the final stage of a 300-mile journey across Patagonia's Heilo del Sur icecap, one of the most barren and inhospitable regions in the world. Located at the southern tip of Chile, the icecap is a sheet of ice 250 miles long and 20 miles wide. It is punctuated by active volcanoes and swept by fierce, freezing winds. Nothing lives on the icecap, and few people have ever been there.

With a desire to see the area, but wondering whether we could survive the inhospitable winds, British climbers Eric Jones and Mick Coffey, an Argentine—Ernesto O. Reilly—and I had set out to make a double crossing of the icecap in January, 1973. Our first objective was to climb Cerro Lautaro, an active volcano 90 miles northwest of Argentina's Fitzroy National Park.

Originally we had planned to parachute onto the icecap with our equipment and sleds. In preparation,

each of us had made four practice parachute jumps with the exception of Ernesto, to whom Eric had given a few minutes' instruction off the roof of a hen house with an umbrella.

But that plan was thwarted when Allende's government decided the idea was too risky and that bad publicity would accrue to the Chilean government in the event of accidents.

Undaunted, we adopted the more conventional approach of walking. This presented a problem, however: how to get 700 pounds of gear and two sleds up to the icecap. Also, the ship bringing our equipment from Liverpool had steamed off to Buenos Aires via Australia. By the time it arrived in Buenos Aires and customs had made double-sure we weren't trying to sneak anything past them, our departure had been delayed by six weeks. Ernesto had only three weeks left before taking his university exams. He volunteered to help haul the gear to the icecap, but once there he would have to leave us and return to Buenos Aires.

TO REACH THE PATAGONIAN icecap we flew to Río Gallegos in southern Argentina, near the Chilean border. There we transferred the equipment to a truck and bounced 200 miles through the interior to Fitzroy National Park, where the border police met us with a team of mules.

Once our gear was loaded onto the mules, we started off on foot through the park, a magnificent wedge of wild countryside separating the icecap from the vast grassy plains of the pampas. Gauchos live in the park, wandering vagabonds who tame horses from the plains and hire themselves out as ranch hands for $15 a week. Wildlife abounds, too: huge condors with 12-foot wing spans; the torrent duck, a rare comedian with webbed feet so large and strong it can paddle at high speeds up waterfalls; and hairy armadillos which demonstrated their formidable digging power by penetrating the ground sheet of our reserve tent. One night they left eight untidy holes in the tent floor through which some of the food stores disappeared.

For the final 15 miles of the approach to the icecap, we had to leave the mules behind and thread a delicate path up the Marconia glacier through gaping crevasses which pleated the ice. With each of us carrying 60-pound packs, it took us four trips and 18 days to ferry all the gear from the park to the icecap. The two sleds were especially tricky to transport. Though they weighed only 30 pounds each, they were 10 feet long. Even with one person on each end they were awkward to carry, especially when trying to maneuver around the crevasses. We finally succeeded with the help of a small winch and a deadman anchor, but not before almost losing a sled down a crevasse.

When we finally reached the icecap, our troubles began in earnest. To protect the gear from the elements while we were ferrying the final load, we had stored it in 9 x 14 inch biscuit tins and left them stacked on the ice. What we hadn't counted on was the wind. When we arrived with the sleds, we found the biscuit tins scattered across the ice. Nothing was missing, but it took us several hours to collect all the tins. Then the tent broke. Minutes after we erected it, the poles of the lightweight pyramid shelter bent and snapped beneath the force of 100-mile-an-hour winds. We

struggled to pin down what was left of it with large rocks, crawled into the wreckage and fell asleep, exhausted. Then Mick had a nightmare and woke the rest of us by thrashing around like an enraged chrysalis. He was dreaming about being in a tent in a violent storm on the Patagonian icecap, and he awoke to find he was.

THE NEXT DAY, in an effort to solve our shelter problem, we returned to Pier del Friely, a camp we had passed on the way through the park. There we were lucky enough to purchase a box tent from a group of South Africans who were attempting to

climb 11,073-foot Mount Fitzroy. The box is the brainchild of British mountaineer Don Whillans. It consists of a square frame of poles screwed together which one stakes into the ground. The tent solved the problem of accommodation, but there were additional problems as we embarked across the bleak expanse of ice. The prevailing winds always blow from west to east, and we were traveling northwest, so we could not use the parachute for pulling the sleds as we had planned. Instead, we were forced to pull them ourselves, trudging slowly across the white plateau like snails trailing overgrown shells behind them.

With their gear loaded on a sled, Eric Jones and Mick Coffey start off across the ice toward one of Patagonia's active volcanoes, 11,089-foot Cerro Lautaro. During the trek they were buffeted by winds and ice storms.
PHOTO: LEO DICKINSON

At first we were not optimistic about being able to move everything at once across the ice. Ernesto had left us, and we had made barely a dent in our 300-pound supply of biscuits, dehydrated meats and vegetables, tinned margarine, chocolate, tea, sugar and lemon powder. Then we loaded the sleds, and I found I could pull the lighter one by myself, while Eric and Mick sweated along with the bulk of the gear.

Often we traveled through whiteouts in which the sky and snow froze into a uniform grayness, erasing the horizon. Sanitation was a major problem. The region is struck frequently by vicious ice storms which come without warning, leaving their mark on any visible areas of exposed flesh. The answer seemed to be to dig a hole for protection. This turned out to be a mistake, for the winds immediately rushed into the hole at full force, leaving poor Mick—the first to try the method—with a trouserful of freezing ice. From then on it was a matter of trusting to luck. Miraculously, we all managed to escape frostbite.

For four days we trekked slowly toward our first goal, the volcano of Cerro Lautaro, which was discovered by explorer Eric Shipton in 1962. At first it was little more than a gray speck on the horizon that we glimpsed occasionally through mist, but each day it grew larger until it loomed 6,000 feet above us. The entire volcano was covered with hideously deformed ice sculptures created by the wind. With sulfurous clouds of steam billowing into the atmosphere, the volcano was an evil-smelling fortress. It had been climbed only once before, by two Argentines in 1964, and they had nearly been defeated by the overpowering sulfur fumes when only 500 feet from the summit.

We set up base camp at the foot of the volcano. Just in time, too. We were struck immediately by a storm and spent the next two weeks in the tent, playing cards and sleeping, while the wind howled around us. Despite the storm, the temperatures were not very cold. Even at night the thermometer never dropped far below zero. But the wind and chill factor were problems. To add warmth to our down sleeping bags, we put them inside heavy ventile outer bags. With this combination we managed to stay warm.

When the storm finally cleared, we began climbing Cerro Lautaro. We succeeded only at the third attempt. The first time we had to turn back when we were only 1500 feet up because of early morning mists. The second time we were defeated by a blanket of yellow ice crystals coming down the mountain. On the third attempt we left camp at 11 P.M. and climbed by torchlight for five hours through an intricate jungle of crevasses to a col just below the summit. At 11,089 feet above sea level, we could smell sulfur fumes seeping through the mountainside. Then the ice disappeared, and Cerro Lautaro became an intimidating cone of warm mud. Finally we were on top, standing on an ice raft surrounded by five vents discharging a haze of foul sulfur. Fortunately, the wind was in our favor and blew most of it away from us.

In the early morning light we could see the Pacific Ocean beyond the claw-shaped coastline of fjords 60 miles to the west. To the south fjords merged with higher mountains and a network of glaciers flowing from the icecap. I wanted to stay and film, but Eric and Mick said they preferred to make a hasty retreat. They were nervous about the volcano's antics and didn't want to be around if it erupted.

And, in fact, when we reached the col on the way down, the volcano gave a loud, evil-smelling belch and sent yellow fumes billowing from its vent holes. The mountain clearly had disliked our intrusion and now was angry and wanted us gone from its privacy of ice and fire.

After a two-day rest, we left base camp and set out with backpacks on downhill skis equipped with cross-country bindings toward our second mountain, an active volcano to the north. The 11,000-foot peak apparently had escaped the surveyor's attention, as it did not appear on our map.

A 10-mile ski run brought us to a small green lake at the foot of the volcano. We roped ourselves together, attached skins to our skis and, to the sound of howling wind and creaking ice, set off among the scars left by recently fallen cliffs of ice. Immediately we encountered the largest crevasse any of us had ever seen. Spanned by a fragile snow bridge, it seemed to extend right to the center of the earth in increasingly deep shades of blue. We gingerly scooted across the snow bridge, trying to keep ourselves from looking down into the yawning chasm.

It took three hours of climbing to reach the summit and the final obstacle—a vast, frozen mushroom of snow built up by the winds. From the top we again looked to the Pacific and, in deference to Eric, a Welshman, decided to name the peak Cerro Mimosa after the ship which carried the first Welsh settlers to Patagonia in 1867.

By now we were running low on food, so we returned to Cerro Lautaro, broke camp and set off on our return journey, 100 miles south across the icecap to Lago Viedma. We were able to use parachute power to propel us across the ice, an original idea devised by Eric and me. Neither of us had tried it before so we were a little apprehensive about how it would work. But after pulling the sleds for nearly 100 miles, we were ready to try anything. We attached the parachute to the sleds with 50 feet of climbing rope and thin nylon cord, which could be cut quickly if the sleds got out of control. Then the three of us climbed onto the sleds and hung on as the parachute billowed out in front. There was a jerk as it picked up the wind. Then suddenly we were sailing effortlessly across the ice at 15 knots.

On the second day of the return trip, owing to a miscalculation, we nearly ran out of rations. Our diet had not been a gourmet's delight, as it consisted of dehydrated dishes, tea, coffee and endless bars of chocolate; but from then on we had only a few bars of chocolate a day. Spurred by hunger, we finished the journey in four days, for a total of 52 days from the time we left Fitzroy National Park. All feelings of achievement were dulled by our monumental appetites. When we finally arrived at a ranch, the three of us devoured an entire sheep.

TRANS TASMANIA

by LLOYD SUMNER

Knifing through clouds wisping about its base, Federation Peak, first climbed in 1949, is regarded by many as Australia's most noble summit; yet the mountain is rarely climbed because of its remoteness and the severe weather that brews up in the Roaring Forties and continually buffets the area.

THE WESTERN AND EASTERN Arthur ranges in southwest Tasmania, the island–state off the southern coast of Australia, are set in the middle of one of the most inaccessible wilderness areas in the world. The mountains are not high by world standards, but they are craggy, rugged, covered with impenetrable scrub and cursed with bad weather. Storms brewed in the Roaring Forties, that tortuous piece of ocean on the 40th parallel between the Tasman Sea and the Indian Ocean, continually buffet the Arthurs with fierce rain and winds.

I had joined four bushwalkers (backpackers) from the Melbourne area for the traverse of the Arthurs and an ascent of Federation Peak, first climbed in 1949 and regarded by bushwalkers as Australia's most noble mountain. Peter Hay, a young lawyer whom I had met while climbing in New Zealand a year earlier, organized the trip and arranged the airdrop of additional supplies by a local charter service. Geoffrey Grantham and Bob Clemente, also Melbourne lawyers, and Richard Molesworth, a sheep and cattle rancher and classmate of the other Aussies, completed our party for this two-week "holiday."

We planned to traverse the Western Arthurs during the first week, pick up our airdrop at Pass Creek, traverse the Eastern Arthurs and climb Federation Peak. The area is rarely visited (we saw two other people the entire trip), and although members of the Hobart Walking Club made a similar trip several years ago and we acquired a copy of their notes for our "guidebook" plus a topographic map, sorrowfully lacking in detail, most of the time we would have to find our way on our own.

FROM OUR ACCESS POINT near Lake Peddor, we headed south along a mushy, barely distinguishable route lined with wet and scratchy bushes—no place for shorts—and dotted with knee-deep mudholes. My Aussie mates looked almost scornfully at my American style frame pack. They preferred their Mountain Mule packs, soft and close fitting, which they claimed were easier to maneuver in dense vegetation.

Every ridge crossed brought a closer view of the Arthurs and new awe of what we were about to attempt.

Our first camp was still in the flatlands. Bob quickly volunteered to do all the cooking for the group. We supplemented our dehydrated foods with rice, for which Bob had a variety of recipes. Geoff opted to wash the dishes.

During our first meal we were joined by what was to be the first of many unin-

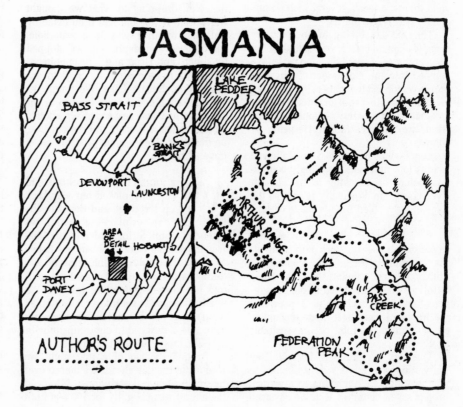

Weather varied: some days the mountains were engulfed in mist while other days the skies were clear and sunburn was a problem, although no one had time to worry about it while negotiating the tricky footing along the ridge leading up Federation Peak.
PHOTO: LLOYD SUMNER

vited diners: a leech, several inches long, quietly feasted on my leg.

The next day, hiking on land probably never walked on before, we made slow but steady progress toward the high peaks. We climbed into the clouds and finally into rain as we topped the main ridge. Donning oilskins (waterproof raincoats that breathe) and throwing a shoulder to the wind, we climbed Mount Hesperus by compass.

Engulfed in heavy mist, we followed a ridge to a precipice, seemingly bottomless, before backtracking to the summit and trying again. We finally descended the ridge and stumbled upon a sheltered lake to camp for the night.

We hiked the ridges on subsequent days, sometimes on rock but often on the horizontal trunks of scoparia, a prickly, densely growing scrub. We tried to follow the routes noted in our "guidebook," but the directions were poor and we frequently got lost and encountered unclimbable cliffs or impenetrable scrub.

One day we dropped down a deep gully, traversed onto a saddle, climbed to another ridge and encountered a vertical drop of several hundred feet. We traversed

that cliff, dropping to what we thought was a trail. It was but had been made by wallabies on their way to a waterhole. Discouraged and depressed, we stopped for lunch, and Geoff and I reconnoitered a possible route over rocky crags to one destination, Square Lake. We found the way impassable, but from the top of the ridge we had just descended we spotted an alternative: a descent to Crescent Lake on the other side—a route probably never traveled before.

WE JOINED OUR COMPANIONS and carefully picked our way back up the ridge and down to the lake. After an exhilarating swim, we ascended Mount Sirius, which left us 1000 feet above Lake Oberon, where we hoped to camp. The only possible descent was through a steep gully that offered not solid rock but knee-deep mud for traction. We finally managed to get into a rock chimney which was tight but not as slippery, and were able to descend to our campsite with only the loss of the seat of my pants.

Around the campfire that night we read about the day ahead. We mused over the understated descriptions: "Descend the almost vertical gully for 100 feet until

you can traverse to the northeast and drop down an even steeper fern-covered slope for another 150 feet. From here the going becomes incredibly steep."

The next morning we discovered that the least embellished directions often led us across the most difficult terrain. The Hobart Walking Club diary read simply, "Climb Mount Pegasus." To do so meant squeezing through small holes in the rock and sliding across a vertical slope on the tiny horizontal branches of twigs, with hundreds of feet of exposure below.

The days got rougher, but we got tougher. Crawling over, under, around and through the scrub became second nature. Dropping down steep, loose-rocked gullies became familiar. A lover's leap was encountered and jumped in alpine fashion, and we continued on to Haven Lake after climbing the Beggary Bumps and the West Horn of Mount Taurus.

Some days were beautiful, sunny all day, and we stopped at every lake we passed for a swim in the icy cold waters. The lakes didn't appear to support any fish but did have large numbers of tadpoles and mountain shrimp.

The mountain shrimp *(Anaspides tasmaniae)* has been extinct in the rest of the world for 200 million years, but it still thrives in the mountain lakes of Tasmania. We saw thousands of them, and we also kept a sharp eye out for the Tasmanian devil and the thylacine, or Tasmanian tiger—marsupial carnivores that exist no place else on earth. The thylacine, which has a pouch that opens backward, was once common throughout Tasmania, but may be extinct. Some experts believe it may yet have a foothold somewhere in these rugged mountains. We found possible tracks and dens, but no animals.

OUR LAST DAY in the Western Arthurs was the hardest. We covered 15 miles of trackless mountain country and headed off the range and into Pass Creek via Lucifer Ridge, an appropriately named, hellish piece of terrain covered with dense scoparia and clusters of button grass, which grows on tight hummocks up to three feet high. One can either walk on the tops of these mounds and risk a bad fall, or walk on the ground, stumbling and somersaulting over and around them.

After the long, tortuous climb down Lucifer Ridge we were thrilled to reach Pass Creek and find our airdrop. Only two oranges had been damaged in the drop. We quickly ate the undamaged ones and prepared ham, asparagus and bean salad for our evening meal and topped it off with canned peaches. Some backpackers before us had packed their airdrops in large tin cans which they left at the pass, the only litter problem we ran into the whole trip. We had packed our supplies in wooden boxes wrapped in burlap so that all packing material could be burned.

With 20 extra pounds in our packs we began the long tiring slog up Luckman's Lead to gain access to the Eastern Arthurs. In questionable safety we climbed the Boiler Plates and descended through deep scoparia to Stuart's Saddle. There we stopped to take a side trip to visit the grave of John Stuart, who died there of pneumonia when his party got caught in a storm. There was a crucifix on a rock but no apparent grave. A quick inspection soon revealed a pile of bones under the rock.

Next came a tree-hopping journey through junglelike growth of pandanus forest. I slipped on the moss-covered logs and hurt one leg. The pain was a most unwelcome nuisance while I led up a vertical mud and scree gully, climbing mostly on tree branches. Remembering John Stuart and the improbability of any kind of rescue, we tried to be extra careful.

Pandanus gave way to the ridge of the Needles, and we encountered severe conditions again. Our directions read, "Route finding on the Needles should be approached with extreme caution in mist." We had mist—and a strong headwind. But

the wind filled us with exhilaration and strength, and we galumphed over the craggy spires and felt our way into Goon Moor for the night.

FOR OUR FINAL TREK to Hanging Lake we had a beautiful day from the beginning—looking down on clouds, looking up at the peaks, looking out at the vast meadows.

When we arrived at the lake, I set up my small one-man tent on a flat spot on the shore and looked forward to a good night's sleep.

During the night fierce winds and hard rain battered the tents. I awoke, smiled to myself (my little tent had been through worse than this) and went back to sleep.

Soon a ripping noise jarred me awake. The rear end tie had pulled out, and the collapsed walls channeled rain straight into my sleeping bag. I pretended it was a nightmare and turned over, but there was to be no more sleep.

Finally I got up, and without getting dressed, tried to fix the damage. I ripped the tent a bit, stuffed in a pebble and tied the guyline around it. It held for a moment, but as I pulled it tight, the cord broke and the tent dropped again. With cold now jarring my bones, I groped frantically in the dark, found the broken cord and tent peg, and made another splice, which held.

I was almost comfortable back inside the wet sleeping bag when the cord broke again. I waited until I was lying in a pool of water before abandoning my tent and joining Peter and Richard.

Snuggled between the two of them was most uncomfortable, but I stayed dry. Peter and Rich, now forced against the sides of their tent, got soaked.

We arose tired, wet and cramped but excited over the prospect of climbing Federation Peak. After hopping along a rocky ridge, slithering down, across, then up a steep slope covered with pineapple grass, we finally reached the summit block, a 700-foot vertical peak standing sentry over all the lesser peaks. We had carried a rope along in case the climb was technical, but it turned out the ultimate scramble climb.

We ascended steadily but carefully, trying not to look at Lake Geeves, 2000 feet below. Our recent experiences in the Arthurs helped make the challenge easier and more enjoyable. We proudly signed the summit register. Because of its remoteness, difficult access and bad weather, Federation is rarely climbed. Then we carefully descended the southern face.

FEDERATION PEAK WAS supposed to be the climax of the trip. We intended to take the fastest route back to the

road, but the greatest excitement lay ahead of us.

After a day's descent down Moss Ridge and through dense rain forest entwined with creepers and vines and carpeted with moss two inches thick, we picked up a wallaby track by a river, which we crossed on a thin, nervous log, and followed a compass bearing across a vast button-grass plain. A hint of a trail, marked only by an occasional bent stalk of grass, took us through dense myrtle forests and finally to the top of Strike Ridge. From there, nothing; no one could be sure which way to go.

We elected to fall (literally) straight down the ridge. The vegetation was so dense that we fell over, stood up on the bent branches and fell again. After some distance we knew we were trapped. Horizontal scrub lay all around us.

Horizontal scrub grows vertically to about 40 feet, then breaks some 10 feet from the ground because the trunk cannot support the weight of the branches. New shoots grow out of the broken limbs until they too fall over. The eventual result is a tangled mass that defies imagination. The horizontal branches may form a dense mat which can fool a hiker into believing he is on the ground when he is actually ten feet up in the air. Multistoried forest floors are not uncommon.

Bob was leading at this point. He struggled for five minutes and made ten feet, then called out that it was impossible to get through. He was stuck. Being next in line, I launched my body hard to the left. Brute force got me a few feet, and I saw the possibility of dropping to a lower level. Suddenly my arms and pack were caught and my feet dangled 15 feet above what I thought to be the ground.

Worming and squirming, I finally dropped. It was midday but in the scrub darker than a full-moon night. I found a spring and proceeded to follow it downstream. The going was slow—more tree climbing and crawling than walking, much branch breaking and route finding.

We were genuinely lost and certainly the first humans ever to be there. We rotated the lead often and kept pushing hard until we finally broke out into the plains. The last quarter-mile had taken two and a half hours to cover.

A long hard slog brought us back to Pass Creek—12 hours on the move for that day.

As we tramped across the open Arthur Plains for the last day and a half, we looked back at the Arthurs with as much awe as before we had climbed them. We were amazed we had successfully completed our planned trip and thankful we had the chance to experience this magnificent, virgin wilderness. ☙

SANDY'S ROUTE

A Traverse of the Scottish Highlands

by SANDY COUSINS

Sandy Cousins, a marine engineer is in his mid-40s and has been climbing for over 20 years, mainly in Scotland. He is an ex-president of the Junior Mountaineering Club of Scotland, was a member of the Mountain Rescue Committee of Scotland for some years and is presently a member of the Scottish Mountain Leadership Training Board and Honorary Secretary of the Mountaineering Council of Scotland, which he was instrumental in forming in 1970. The MCS is run by the Scottish climbing clubs and it deals with a wide range of mountaineering matters, partnering the British Mountaineering Council. The equipment selected for the Highland traverse won a special prize in <u>Mountain Life</u> magazine's Backpacker Competition.

While camping on the West Coast of Scotland with my family during the July "monsoon," our holiday was brought to an abrupt end when one morning during the third gale we had survived the ridgepole, with a groan of despair, split and the tent collapsed. As my wife and I searched for the children in a confusion of canvas, clothes, and cornflakes I muttered,

"Let's go home."

"That's the first sensible thing you've said this holiday," she said.

The following year she took the children to seek the sun, so I was free to choose my own mountain holiday. Now if you like reading accounts of climbers moving slowly up a vertical wall on minute rugosities, swinging over the void on etriers secured by thumbnail pitons or traversing unbroken ice walls on daggers and front points, turn to another article—this will bore you. This is no account of a climb that was interesting until it leaned back to the vertical and became straightforward. But if you like to wander over the hills and corries of beautiful country, then fill your pipe, pour yourself a glass of malt whiskey, and come with me on a traverse of Scotland. This hill walk turned out to be the first traverse of the Scottish Highlands from Cape Wrath to Glasgow.

For some time I have wanted to spend a holiday climbing and staying in bothies, and I decided to combine this into a long trip across Scotland. I suggested the idea to two or three friends but there was little enthusiasm, so I resolved to go on my own. In the middle of winter I started to plan the trip. For many evenings our front-room floor was carpeted by Ordnance Survey (1″ = 1 mile) maps as I chose the summits, ridges, glens, and corries of my route. I had to expect bad weather, so to ease the navigation I marked my intended route on the maps, marking changes of direction with the bearing and distance to the next turning point. In this way I hoped to be able to maintain the route "blind." Alternative routes on lower ground were noted in case the high tops became too unpleasant. I wrote to various people on my route asking if some simple shelter was available, if they would keep a box of provisions I would send in advance, and if due to estate work or game management there was any area on their ground I should avoid. All were most helpful, some offering shelter and many offering to provide provisions if I advised my requirements in advance. Seventeen supply boxes were sent to various keepers, hotels, houses, and huts en route.

My route included some spots where there was no bothy or shelter and I intended to bivouac in an emergency polybag or whatever shelter I could make if required. However, just before I started, Vango provided a tent which proved excellent. This gave me freedom to have comfortable, secure nights out wherever I wanted. The tent could be satisfactorily set up with only four pegs in a few moments. I even practiced setting it up from a sitting position in case I should seriously injure my leg and require shelter. The Super Ariel sack with its inflatable tube pad provided by Brown Best gave a comfortable carry with about 30 pounds load. Hamish McInnes (well-known Scottish climber and Honorary Secretary of the Mountain Rescue Committee of Scotland) kindly agreed to be my emergency contact, and my wife had a schedule of about six dates when she could expect a telephoned progress report from me. If my call was a day overdue she would advise Hamish, who had a copy of my route. From the date and place of my last call he could estimate where I might be. If he heard nothing the next day he could assume something was wrong and set up some search. In this way, according to my schedule, the longest I could expect to wait if I became immobilized was about six days! Mountaineering is a risk

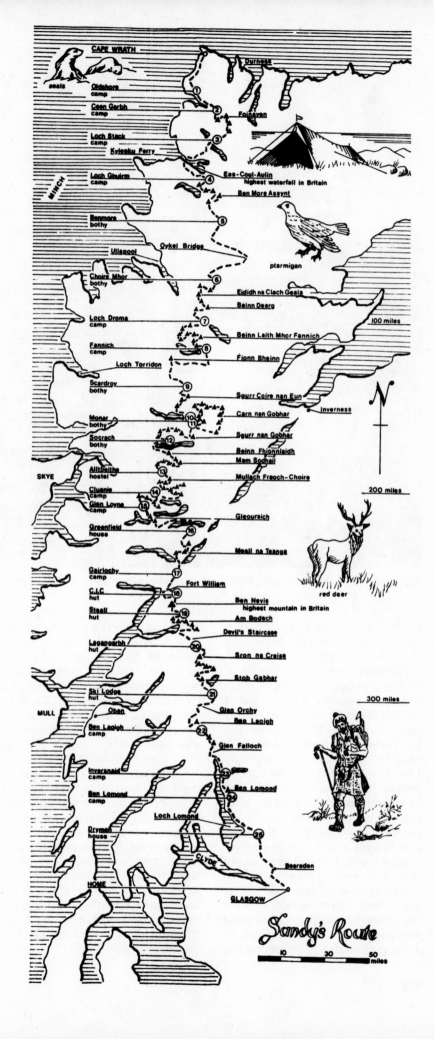

Sandy's Route

The author, on his first solo highland traverse, Cape Wrath to Glasgow, 1971.

sport; one shouldn't expect rescue "as of right." If one doesn't accept the risk—don't go!

Palatable food is essential if such a trip is to be enjoyed. I selected my provisions from a list of what I liked, modified to tinned and packet varieties, since the food would be packed about two months before use. For simplicity I made up a week's menu and repeated it four times in my food boxes. Although I was never hungry, I lost 15 pounds during the journey. Practically all the food was bought in one visit to a supermarket, and the bill was about five feet long! There would be boxes at most of my night stops, and these boxes would contain my dinner, breakfast for the next morning, and some lunch to carry. I always had one day's emergency

food, and with the spacing of the food boxes I only had to carry two days' food a couple of times. In some boxes I had clothes, paraffin, maps, film, batteries, etc. I could leave unwanted items in some boxes, to be posted home by my hosts. Thus the weight carried was minimized. Yes, I did cut short my toothbrush!

I arrived at the gear I was to carry by eliminating from a list of desirable items until I had a much smaller list of necessary items. Weight reduction was achieved by discarding containers and using polythene bags and using some homemade lightweight gear as listed. One sees very few Scots wearing the kilt these days, but I find it very good for hill walking. It is much more comfortable than breeches for wet summer

weather, and is cooler in hot weather. Even though I hiked through snow and gales I used my overtrousers only twice on the trip. My cromach was no ornament: it served as a bog-tester, fishing rod, spare tent pole, camera tripod, support for crossing rivers, and as a crutch if required.

The only preparation I felt I needed was to get used to carrying about 30 pounds, so for about three weeks I walked to my office, about three miles each way, carrying a load, and I had pleasant though tiring walks across the Stockiemuir out to Loch Lomond or across the Campsies (local hills) at the weekends. About three weeks before I was due to start, all my food had been sent off, all arrangements were completed, and I could relax and contemplate the exciting prospect ahead. Just about this time, through a neighbour in the BBC, a couple of chaps came along to film me walking to work, all rather comic, I thought.

On the first of June I arrived, with a co-driver, by car at Durness (280 miles from Glasgow by road) in glorious hot sunshine. I had stashed my first food box in the heather where I would cross the main road in a couple of days' time. We were ferried across the Kyle of Durness, then joined the tourist minibus for the run out to the lighthouse. Much of the area is used as a bombing and shelling range, and I heard that a hurried phone call had recently saved the bar being blown off the Keodale Hotel when someone got his bearings wrong!

At the Cape Wrath light I was given a warm send-off by the keeper and his wife and set off homeward across the short, dry grass of the undulating coast. I was on my first mile when, stepping into a hole, I almost twisted my ankle. It was a warning to keep alert all day, every day. I had been warned that some character inhabiting one of the bothies was rather undesirable, so I crossed the moor with dirk and cromach at the ready! Topping a rise I had my first view of the beautiful mile of sand at Sandwood Bay. Oyster catchers greeted me as I crossed the wide beach, which was empty though crisscrossed by footprints. The track from Sandwood took me to the road where my "chauffeur" met me, and we camped at Oldshore Beg.

We had breakfast in the sunshine early next morning; then he left for Glasgow by car and I set off on foot. This was a day of hot sunshine, and the views from the twisting road by Kinlochbervie were a delight. Sitting in a hayfield I shared my midmorning snack with a tramp and learned something about life on the road, while a corncrake's grating cry rose in the shimmering heat. By lunchtime I reached the Durness Road, and a kestrel flew suddenly from its concealed nest just a foot or so from my food box as I re-

trieved it from the heather. I lunched with some peat cutters, then crossed the rising moor toward Foinaven. By late afternoon I was in a corrie below the hill where I intended to bivouac. I felt fit, so I carried on up the steep, dry, mossy grass in warm sunshine and arrived at the top at about 5 P.M., to be greeted by gentlemen from the Yorkshire Ramblers Climbing Club (YRCC) who were just completing the ridge.

I camped beside the summit of Ganu Mor, 2,980 feet, and made a most comfortable bed of dry moss. The evening was calm, with a slow temperature inversion gradually drawing low mist across the moor below as the lights began to twinkle in the villages along the coast and on ships in the Minch. With my dinner over it was a delight to sit with glass in hand and watch my cigar smoke drifting slowly from the tent door. Just before turning in I had a walk around the summit and felt quite excited, looking south over the mass of peaks dimly lit by the gloaming light, at the prospect of the great journey ahead, yet relaxed in the knowledge that all my planning was done and my supplies were in position.

I woke early when the brilliant sun topped the cairn above me and shone hot in the open tent door. Banks of white clouds floated in low over the coast and evaporated over the land below me. By 9 A.M. I was packed and on my way along the ridge to Foinaven. I had a cool drink of Cremola Foam made from snow and continued along the ridge and down to Bealach Loch an Easain Uaine for a lunch stop as twelve fine stags in velvet ambled past me quite unaware of my presence. En route throughout the trip I left wax-chalk messages such as "Sandy 1200 3.6.71" at cairns, bothies, etc., so that if anything went wrong they could help anyone following my route. At Lone Both I picked up the food box left for me by the keeper at Loch Stack. I visited the YRCC, who entertained me to afternoon tea at their camp. This was in true safari

style—mess tent, tables, chairs, and an ample wine cellar—they do not believe in roughing it in hotels.

That evening I phoned the BBC's "Today in Scotland" program. They were going to do progress reports. As they were not ready to record and I could not arrange to phone at specific times, let alone specific days, I decided to scrap the idea. After a pleasant evening with the keeper, I returned to my tent and slept very comfortably on a fine bed of rushes.

A cool east wind which was to continue for a couple of weeks gave ideal hill-walking conditions next day. I crossed to Kylestrome on an old pony track with the ruins of the old pony shelter at the top of the pass. I noticed "Beware of the Bull" notices on the track (surely a right of way), which seemed contrary to the Countryside Act. Kylestrome must be among the most picturesque ferry crossings in Scotland, and as usual the seals were bobbing around in the tidal swirls.

A tourist took my sack up to the top of the road, so I enjoyed an unloaded stroll up to Loch na Gainmhich, then took to the path up toward the high lochan under Glas Bheinn. The path, a good one, goes over a pass to the top of the Glencoul waterfall (about 600 feet), the highest in Britain and well worth a visit. There is also an easy walk to the waterfall along the steep shore of the sea loch. An eagle passed low above me on the way and plovers with their beautiful plaintive alarm cry kept flying ahead of me, unfortunately warning deer of my coming, as shown by the continual scatter-away ahead of me.

With my tent at the edge of the lochan, I was able to sit in my sleeping bag and try a few casts as wisps of mist drifted into the corrie. My fishing rod was made by screwing a couple of rings into my cromach and fixing my reel to the handle. I enjoy camping in these isolated corners, and the wee tent gave a feeling of comfort and security should the weather change, as it was really watertight. My pocket radio was good company, and reception was usually very good on the high ground.

Thick mist surrounded me next morning, and my set line bore no trout, though I've had good fish from the lochan before. This was a gray day, on the gray quartzite tops of Glas Bheinn, 2,541 feet, Ben Uidhe, 2,824 feet, Conival, 3,234 feet, and Ben More Assynt, 3,278 feet. I was taking Dextrosol a couple of times a day, and though it was difficult to assess the effect, I felt I was going well.

I stopped for lunch, making a little boulder howff, and entertained myself singing—hoping there was no one around in the mist. I considered going along Breabag, but the glen below me was too tempting and soon I was down in sunshine again washing my undies in a burn and enjoying a smoke on the long trudge to Benmore Lodge. There the keeper put me in the bothy and I fed well from my food box. That evening in the keeper's house with fine old hunting engravings we sat cracking about game and salmon until about midnight. His friendly deerhound could stand easily resting its paws over my shoulder.

The walk from the lodge to Choire-mhor bothy was on road and track all day. A tourist took my sack along to Oykell Bridge, where I collected my food box and enjoyed a delicious lunch in the hotel. I found I had a yen for fresh meat and vegetables. For a while I walked with an elderly shepherd moving his lambs and ewes away from the road. I met the keeper, and he took my sack up to Corriemulzie, so I enjoyed the long walk up the glen without a load. From the lodge I followed the track to the bothy under Seana Braigh. This is a grand bothy in a fine situation.

After such a good lunch I had little appetite for dinner. I was tired after some 20 miles of road bashing, but enjoyed the evening sitting at the door of the bothy sipping Drambuie, listening to an opera, and watching deer playing like children in the shallow lochan in front of me. My pipe smoke drifted out on the calm air, and waiting for me across the

loch towered the sharp peak of Creag an Duine, 2,900 feet, as I turned in on a warm straw bed.

I was awake by 8:30 A.M.. It was calm and gray, and I climbed slowly and steadily to the narrow ridge leading to the Seana Braigh plateau, 3,040 feet. Having my route and bearings previously marked on my maps was useful as I was in mist until midday. I came on some ptarmigan chicks near the summit, and the hen flapped around trying to distract me as I photographed the chicks at my feet. By lunchtime the sky cleared and I lunched on the big open flat before Eididh nan Clach Geala, 3,039 feet, in bright sunshine. The high ground around me was ringed with deer watching me like Red Indians in a Western.

At the summit I found the boulder howff I had made three years ago. I crossed Meall nan Ceapraichean, 3,192 feet, and rather wearily climbed across snow patches to Beinn Dearg, 3,547 feet, then started the long descent and good path to Loch Droma via Lorguill, 2,862 feet. This had been a fine day's hill walking with a great feeling of being alone in a huge group of mountains and high plateaus with sunlit peaks all around as far as one could see. I was, however, looking forward to the arrival of a friend I had arranged to meet. I had just finished an enjoyable dinner when he arrived and camped beside me.

The second week began with the welcome sound of sizzling bacon for breakfast and—luxury—fresh bread. We climbed in cold mist and sleet showers to Meall a Crasgaigh, 3,062 feet, Am Baichdaich, Sgurr nan Clash Geala, 3,581 feet, and on to Sgurr nan Each, 3,026 feet—what beautiful names—as the weather cleared to sunshine. I had planned to go down to Nest bothy but Bill, a Munro-bagger, lured me eastward along the Fannichs with a promise of steak his wife had for us at camp at Fannich dam.

We crossed Sgurr nan Clach Geala again, Carn na Criche, 3,000 feet, Sgurr Mor, 3,637 feet, Beinn

Liath Mhor Fannaich, 3,000 feet, Creachan Rairgidh, Meal Gorm, 3,109 feet, and An Coileachan, 3,015 feet. There were several stone howffs along the tops. We could see across Scotland from the Beauly Firth on one side to Loch Torridon on the other. This was one of the big days of the journey, involving 19 miles, 6,400 feet of ascent and 10 summits.

Next morning we drove back west to Achnasheen so that I could rejoin my route, and Bill vanished into the wilds of the Loch Carron hills. I climbed Fionn Bheinn, 3,059 feet, in sunshine and snow showers, an easy ascent made interesting by the antics of ptarmigan distracting me from their chicks, and the views of the Fisherfield hills. As often happened on the journey, familiar hills reminded me of climbs I had enjoyed and friends I had been with there.

Back on my route again, I passed Loch Gowan and crossed the pass on a good path to Scardroy. This is a lovely spot. Rugged hillsides plunge down to the wooded loch and the bright green fields beside the river are dotted with a few tidy houses. The friendly atmosphere was confirmed when the keeper put me in his bothy complete with kitchen, hot bath, and room with fire. My dinner (all from my box) that night was typical: chicken soup, beef stew, potatoes, carrots, peas, rice, and fruit, Drambuie, cigar, tea, and lemonade. Breakfast next day was fruit juice, cereal, kipper fillets, oatcakes, etc., and lunch as usual was shortbread, biscuits, tea, jam, and sweets.

From Scardroy I went up Coire Mhoraigein and on to Sgurr Coire nan Eun, 2,581 feet, and An Sidhean, 2,661 feet. The tops were misty, and I found that with my radio on in my pocket the volume altered as I altered course; thus I navigated for about a mile on a steady course which landed me right at a col I wanted. I went down the Allt na Chois to Loch Morar, and along the path to the Lodge where Bill joined me in the evening. The keeper gave us the use of an excellent bothy with stove, cooker, and beds.

Our round of the Strathfarrar hills—Beinn na Muice, 2,272 feet, Carn na Daimh Bhan, 2,043 feet, Sgurr na Muice, 2,915 feet, Sgurr na Fearstaig, 3,326 feet, Sgurr Fhuar-Thuill, 3,439 feet, Creag Chorm a' Bhealaich, 3,378 feet, Sgurr a' Choire Ghlas, 3,554 feet, Carn nan Gobhar, 3,255 feet, Sgurr na Ruidh, 3,254 feet, and Garbh-Charr, 2,801 feet—was done in a mist driven by a strong northerly wind with occasional blasts of sleet, a wild day indeed. I found polythene bags made good gloves. We were both weary as we trudged back along the road to the bothy and I found my boot was holed at the toe.

The low cloud continued next day when we crossed the dam, waded the Uisge Misgeach and climbed Carn nan Gobhar, 3,251 feet, Sgurr na Lapaich, 3,775 feet, with its interesting rock ridge to the summit, and the An Riabhachan tops, flanked by slopes of deep old snow. From Coire Mhain we went down to Socrach bothy (private and locked), where the landowner had delivered my food box. This bothy, the Seldom Inn, was most comfortable.

The anticyclone had steadied up again next day, and we set off in shirt sleeves along to the west end of Loch Mullardoch, where we separated, Bill going to Sgurr nan Conbhairean and I to Mam Sodhail, 3,862 feet, via Beinn Fhionnlaidh, 3,294 feet. It seemed a long hot grind, and then, as I topped the ridge to Carn Eige, 3,880 feet, the cloud came in and I had cold sleet showers and dark mist again. I was not usually conscious of my load on the hills, but often felt it at the end of the day, especially if I had to finish along a road. I had map and compass work all afternoon as the ridge twisted around deep corries and passed looming shapes on the ridges. "This," I found myself thinking, "is what hill walking is all about." One has to be confident to navigate and to read the ground.

I crossed Ciste Dubh, 3,600 feet, Carn Conlavie, 3,508 feet, and emerged from the mist at Bealach Coire Ghaidheil, where I waited for Bill. He arrived and we found that we had passed within a few feet of each other minutes earlier in the mist. We spent the night in the deserted Alltbeithe youth hostel. By mistake, my map for next day's route was in my box awaiting me at Cluanie Inn, so I made a rough sketch from a map in the hostel.

A sprinkling of new snow on the summits glittered in the early sun next morning as Bill left for Mam Sodhail and home, and I headed south over Mullach Fraoch-Choire, 3,614 feet, with its interesting wee pinnacle ridge and A 'Chralaig, 3,673 feet, reaching Bealach Coir-a-Chait for a lunch stop. That day I had a glimpse of Ben Nevis, 4,406 feet, four days' journey away. It was like seeing an old friend, and I felt quite pleased that I was going well. All I had to do was relax mentally, keep going steadily, and enjoy this beautiful hill walking. I was averaging about 14 miles and 3,500 feet per day.

The hills were very dry and I had to seek about for tea-water for lunch. From Sgurr nan Conbhairean, 3,634 feet, I skirted the north corrie to another top. I had intended to stop the night down in Prince Charlie's cave. He and his companions rested in a howff in the corrie during the escape after the battle of Culloden. I could see the boulders of the howff a long way below me, but I decided to head for Cluanie as it was still early in the day. A golden eagle drifted along the edge of the ridge beside me for a few yards with its beady eye looking at me from under its wing. I went down the Allt Coire Lair to the road, trudged wearily along to the inn, and camped. I dined (poorly) in the inn, and the staff kindly gave me luxuries like milk, eggs, bacon, and bread— very tasty! Two weeks and two hundred miles lay behind me.

Ascot Day was one of mixed showers and sunshine on the south Cluanie hills. I went up Druim Shionnach along the ridge to Creag a 'Mhaim, 3,102 feet, then back along to Aonach air Chrith, 3,342 feet, and Maol Chinn Dearg, 3,214 feet, all interesting narrow-ridge walking, then steeply down to camp in Glen Loyne at a ruined bothy. I found that one boot was deteriorating a bit and did some sewing repairs as best I could, but began to wonder if this could be the end of the trip. With rain squalls lashing the tent I felt depressed. However, I was dry and snug, and things which seem problems at night are often minimal next morning, so I pushed despair aside, lit a fresh cigar, sipped more Drambuie, and settled into my bag.

Up into the mist again in the morning I walked rather carefully, avoiding straining my boot, and from the Bealach I followed the ridge to Gleouraich, 3,395 feet, then back over the Bealach to Spidean Mialach, 3,268 feet, and the weather cleared to sunshine by the time I reached the Quoich dam. It was a joy to walk down beautiful Glen Garry in warm sunshine with the birds singing and the dark cattle flicking their tails in birch-tree shades. At Greenfield the farmer insisted I avoid the midges, though I had felt none on the trip, by giving me a room in his house. I attacked my boots with glue and nails, and soon they were as good as new again. We talked late, and here as throughout the trip I found the folk I met most interesting and hospitable.

Fedden, a ruined house, was my lunch stop next day. I surprised some young ducks into their first splashing attempts at flight along a burn, and photographed a dappled newborn red deer calf, crouching in the heather as the hind barked nervously from a distance up the hillside. On the way to Cam Bealach I came on a small (6 inches) adder, and I was surprised at the needless cold shiver I felt. I climbed Sron a' Choire Ghairbh, 3,066 feet, in cold sunshine and crossed to Meall nan Teanga, 3,050 feet. This top seemed a kind of milestone, and I sat down for a time looking around. Northward I looked back over the glens, lochs, peaks, and ridges forming the distant horizon and realized I had crossed that seemingly enormous distance. I thought of the RAF party, led by a friend, John Hinde, who made a similar journey in 1968; of Hugh Munro's love of the hills; of past members of my club, the Scottish Mountaineering Club, who had explored these hills; and I felt in a small way part of that great company.

To the east and west lay country I did not know well, rough Knoydart and the Grey Corries of Lochaber. The southward view was dominated by the great dark hump of Ben Nevis still streaked white by snow in the gullies, high over the glittering waters of Loch Linnhe, and islands that seemed to float in shimmering sunlight. I was leaving the new country and crossing into familiar country. Even though I had been climbing around the country for some 20 years, over 60 of the tops I had just been on were new to me. Lord, what a beautiful country! The noises of civilization floated up from the Great Glen as I crossed to Meall Coire Lochain, Meall Odhar, and trotted down to Ruigh-na-Beinne into the forest and down to the narrow pass to Mile Drocha (the Dark Mile). I kept my mind off my seemingly heavy load and tired legs until I flopped down in my tent at Gairlochy. On the way I saw a wren, and earlier I had seen an eagle—our smallest and largest birds in the same day. Some tourists invited me into their caravan for supper and a cheery evening. The midges were fierce.

Before breakfast I telephoned a report to "Today in Scotland" and was amused to listen to it later during breakfast in the early sunshine. Walking along the canal to Inverlochy I thought how useful a canoe might have been. I had a desire for some fresh meat, so I had a good steak lunch in the cafe outside Fort William, went up the familiar path to the Charles Inglis Clark Hut (a Scottish Mountaineering Council hut). The hut is much improved due to the efforts of the custodian and his work squads. There I met the first people I had seen on the hill (excluding Bill) since Ceann Garbh 16 days earlier. The longest I had gone without seeing anyone, even in the distance, was about 30 hours.

In the small hours I woke with toothache. I had had some twinges since Scardroy, but this was different. The hut telephone is connected to the local police, so I called to ask if there was a dentist in Fort William. They told me to report there and a dentist would be standing by. After a quick breakfast I was in the Fort in a couple of hours, and I was directed to a dentist. Other pale-faced casuals arrived as I waited my turn. A man from Mallaig, some 30 miles away, awaited a verdict on his last few choppers. "Next please," and the pain vanished as I found it was my turn.

"Are you the fellow on the long walk?"

My ready story was cut short by "Open wide." Tap, tap. "Oops! there it is." Zip, zip, the bits flew and the hole was sealed. I was just entering Glen Nevis again when a car passed, and with a happy wave the man from Mallaig with toothless smile roared past. Early in the afternoon I was back at the hut, and I climbed the arete and soon reached the summit of Ben Nevis. I could just see my last top, Ben Lomond, and almost felt regret that the end was in sight. I dropped quickly down to the car park at the head of Glen Nevis and noticed there that the chaffinches hopping about the car park kept the humans in mobile cages! The path through the gorge had been thoughtfully repaired and improved so it still looked "natural." Steall Hut was a welcome sight. I was a day ahead of schedule and unfortunately missed some friends who came up next evening expecting to meet me.

Glen Nevis to Glencoe was a walk I had not done before, and I recommend it for its variety of ridges, wild scenery, and good walking tracks. The morning was wet as I made my way up through a jungle of dripping birches onto the misty slopes of Sgurr a' Mhaim, 3,601 feet, along the narrow south ridge with the impressive though easy gap, and on to Am Bodach, 3,382 feet, where the weather improved and the sun came out. The Loch Leven hills looked wonderfully rough and the sea lochs were like water-filled trenches. I followed the ridge past An Garbhanach and on to the double top of Na Gruagaichean, 3,442 feet. Because I still had to go a long way, I was reluctant to go out to Binnein Mor, so I headed down to Kinlochleven, where I had a good high tea before following the Devil's Staircase path to reach Glencoe in the lovely soft evening light. There was a halo round the sun foretelling wild weather to come in a few hours.

As I cleared the last rise, Bauchaille Etive Mhor rose majestically before me, with Lagangarbh (an SMC hut) nestling below. I remembered my first visit to the hut on a snowy February day years ago when I was a new boy all eyes and ears to catch the pearls of wisdom and technique from the old hands. I may be a bit sentimental, but I think the SMC (formed in 1898) is more than a club, it's a living tradition. The hut was empty of people but full of memories as I turned in.

It was raining heavily from low clouds scudding in from the west next morning, when I crossed the Coupal just above the waterfall and went up Sron na Creise, 2,952 feet. On the ridge the cold-front weather really hit me with a full gale so that I could hardly move, and squalls of hail and rain came across like wire. I wandered a bit, and, sure that the top of Clach Leathad, 3,602 feet, lay in one direction, I had to force myself to trust my compass, which told me it was in another direction. The compass as usual was right. For the second time on the trip I had put my day's map in the box ahead of me, but I had again made a sketch map and had been over this ground a few times before.

On the Bealach before Stob Gabhar, 3,565 feet, I was briefly below the mist so I stopped to fill up with some chocolate and Dextrosol to heat me up, and to wring out my socks. The roar of the wind on the ridge was awe-inspiring, and I had to keep just the right distance from the edge to seek the slightly calmer area one gets due to the uplift of the wind. At the summit I could just get shelter enough to eat more. As the rain had forced through my clothes, I was a bit chilled, so I set off down the familiar fence posts and soon emerged below the mist. The forecast had been for clearing skies in the late afternoon. I sat down for a rest just below the mist, and quite suddenly the rain stopped, the clouds shredded, and the warm sun shone from high patches of blue. It was 4 P.M. How's that for timing? I took off my wet clothes and hung them around me to dry off as I walked to Bridge of Orchy. Looking back at the sunlit hills there was no hint of the wild conditions I had just come through. The proprietor at Bridge of Orchy added fresh food to my food box, and I dried off my gear as I slept in Glencoe Ski Club Lodge.

After wading across the Orchy I strolled down sunny Glen Orchy and across Am Mam to the Dalmally road where I collected my box at a house, lunched, and set off up Ben Laoigh, 3,708 feet. New tree-planting may soon affect access to the west side. At over 3,000 feet on the south ridge I found a trickle of water and a flat site for my tent. During dinner I watched a lovely sunset over Cruachan as the evening shadows crept across the Arrochar hills.

The burbling of sheep in thick mist around me woke me at about 6 A.M. and I visited the summit a few feet above me. Early mist cleared as I crossed Ben Oss, 3,374 feet, and Ben Dubhcraig, 3,204 feet, on my way to Glen Falloch. On the road, some tourists leapt out to take my photograph and one was nearly run over in the process! From Ben Glass farm I headed through the tangled woods on the east side of the loch to Ardleish, where I dined from my box. A short way down the loch I climbed over the Maol an Fhithich ridge with unfamiliar views of the loch and the Arrochar hills, and went down the rough Garrison Glen to Inversnaid. From the former fort there the government troops tried to keep Rob Roy Macgregor under control. As usual, the midges at Inversnaid were vicious.

Real Loch Lomond weather (low mist and drizzle) greeted me in the morning, and I was soon soaked on my way through the dripping woods to Rowchoish bothy. I hope this side of Loch Lomond is left unspoiled for those who enjoy rough walking away from the rumble and peeps of the traffic on the west side. Climbing through the wood I emerged on the high moor below Ben Lomond, 3,192 feet, and watched a troop of some 40 wild goats with kids. One sees so much more wildlife when one is quiet and alone on the hills. At 4:30 P.M. I arrived at the familiar triangulation pillar on the summit and camped in mist and strong wind in a calm spot where the uprising wind lifts over the summit. After dinner, feeling a little disappointed that expected friends had not turned up, I listened to an orchestral concert from Glasgow, then slept soundly.

The walk to Drymen and to Glasgow is marred by the danger from traffic. Even where corners are being realigned there is no footpath. In Drymen I stayed with a friend. The last day's walking was one of enjoyable reflection. The view back northward to the hills, the trembling cry of the curlew on the Stockiemuir Road, the sweet scent of bog myrtle—these reminded me of the sights and sounds of the trip. The crisp early-morning light with mist drifting in the corries, sunlit ridge walking, wild days scrambling past dark shapes in the mist, the soft colors of the highland evenings in the hills—I can close my eyes and see them all.

Approaching Bearsden on the outskirts I had a panoramic view of the Clyde Valley and Glasgow. I was home from a superb mountain holiday.

Chapter Twelve

BACKPACKING, CONSERVATION, AND HOW YOU CAN MAKE A DIFFERENCE

Setting aside natural scenic lands has not been an easy job. It has come only with struggle against considerable odds. And by persistence. Nonetheless, much progress has been made over the years.

To me it is always surprising, in reading about the history of the conservation movement, to find how few people have had such far-ranging results. I've heard it said that these folks who devote themselves with such dedication to conservation serve as "a conscience for us all." I suspect that the reason they have accomplished so much with so few is because they are right, and those who oppose them know that they are right and that there is a power in righteousness which is difficult to fight against.

To realize this is encouraging to those of us who are involved in the struggle today. And it is inspiring to read the stories of the people who won some of the early battles. The tales of the people who waged the struggle in the past is not one of super-heroes. Many of the conservationists were ordinary people who were willing to patiently commit their time to the cause of conservation. The next 16 pieces should be an inspiration to us all in getting involved with preserving our natural resources.

WHERE DID ALL THESE DAMN HIKERS COME FROM?

by HARVEY MANNING

Anyone who has backpacked more than a couple of years can sometimes be heard to complain, "There are just too damned many backpackers in the wilderness today. It just isn't like it used to be." They are right, of course. There has been a big boom in backpacking lately. Just as much of a boom as there has been in all outdoor sports.

And there has been some speculation as to what caused this growing interest in strapping a whopping pack on one's back and hiking off into the woods. Harvey Manning, who is the author of the book Backpacking: One Step at a Time, has a theory about it. And he backs it up with some pretty solid research.

W.K.

IT'S HARD LINES when a guy can't encounter erstwhile friends in the wilderness without being snarled at and spat upon, but that's been my lot since 1965 when those of us running the book-publishing division of The Mountaineers began adding trail guides to our list. Mind you, I've never apologized for my role and won't start now. And I never put any stock in the mumblings about fixing me so I'd never type again. It was purely coincidental that in 1971, when irate club members instigated an official study of guidebook impact on the backcountry, I resigned as chairman of the publishing program and grew a beard.

Well, hell, I'm sick of defending guidebooks and won't go into my song and dance here. Anyway, books aren't my present subject. Boots are. Boots attached to people. Many many boots, many many people, and every passing year another thousand regiments taking the field in full battle gear. My God! Where did they all come from? While denying suppressed guilt feelings as my motive, I confess to having pondered this question more than most. And I believe I've found some answers.

Perhaps I can best expound my theory by going back to the beginning of the world—my world, that is—the Olden Days of the 1920s, when there were half as many Americans as now and we'd had eight fewer presidents and three fewer wars.

SHARPLY ETCHED in farthermost mists of my childhood are tall trees and roaring rivers, spooky nights and blazing campfires. Big slobbering bears and ingenious little periwinkles. Trout darting through pools of limeade and frying in the pan.

All unaware, being carted around by my folks, I was a pioneer of a new American recreation, car camping, which was then—in the West at least—opening wide to ordinary city dwellers scenic wonders of the nation formerly the exclusive domain of backwoodsmen on the one hand and monied sahibs on the other. Detroit, later to evolve into a mean master, was the Great Liberator of the day, its production lines enabling any but the destitute to probe wildlands via proliferating highways and forest roads.

Fondly I recall our favorite camp under huge and ancient firs, hemlocks and cedars, beside a glacier-fed torrent, and a mere two hours from Seattle. Solitude was nearly absolute. The scattered others who drove past on the single-lane dirt track invariably kept going, seeking their own private spots.

The 1920s and early 1930s were the Golden Age of car camping. Autos and roads had become dependable enough that on weekends city people could explore mountain vastnesses formerly too remote except for extended vacations. Still, no more than three or four places in the Cascades, such as the alpine meadows of Paradise on Mount Rainier, ever were short of elbow room—and they were not in the least so by today's standards. Though one sad day we arrived at our cherished camp to discover the Civilian Conservation Corps busy building fireplaces, picnic tables and privies, we'd no trouble gaining the isolation we wanted just down the road a piece.

Came the Depression. Strained to the limits providing food, clothing and shelter, our family finances could rarely be stretched to allow a camping trip. To make up for that lack, in the late 1930s I joined the Boy Scouts—and on mountain trails was dazzled by a new order of splendors beyond the reach of machines. The Olympics

and Cascades, however, though tantalizingly close on skylines west and east, remained far, far away across the dollar gap, and it was an ecstatic year when I managed as many as a dozen wilderness days. World War II replaced the money shortage with the gas shortage. The rule continued to be, look to the high horizons and dream, occasionally blowing a couple of gas stamps from the ration book to tramp green-colony forests and roam tundra ridges.

In the first gas-gushing postwar summer I busted loose and rambled 30-odd days through valley jungles

and alpine gardens. That season in Eden stimulated the next step. A decade of car camping had prepared me for trails; now a decade of trails had aroused a craving for glaciers and crags, for the final thrust into the ultimate wilderness, the sky. Thus I joined The Mountaineers, enrolled in the legendary Climbing Course, and became a fanatic peakbagger.

The disgruntlement of today's trail veterans was felt to a lesser degree by old-timers of that period. At war's end, with GIs home and defense workers released from the six-day week, tanks loaded with gas and pockets with coin, roads smoother and cars faster, the empty lands began filling. Car campgrounds were jammed and because of another exceedingly popular postwar sport teemed with infants building castles on sandbars, throwing pebbles in streams and chasing frogs—a new generation being initiated, even as mine had been. Trails grew loud with thudding boots; cirques previously entered once in several years now had campfires every summer.

Though startled by the trail crowds (a deluge of new hikers measured by prewar standards), I wasn't much bothered; when tenderfeet invaded my old lairs I had abundant lonesome retreats in reserve. But in the course of time my wife and I contributed our bit to the Baby Boom, and the logistical complexities resulting from two daughters born nearly as close together as nature allows forced us to briefly take a step down to car camping. Dear Lord! This wasn't what I remembered! Amid the din of portable radios and the glare of Coleman lanterns, I realized my affection for humans varies in inverse proportion to the square of their assembled numbers. As soon as it was practical, we converted the kids into donkeys and made our escape—and with no great difficulty. Well into the 1960s, a few miles of trail guaranteed peace. To be sure, there was a creeping loss of solitude, as there was of every other environmental amenity during that decade, and on weekends we no longer expected to have a meadow entirely to ourselves, but on weeklong hikes we generally met more bears than people.

Then, the mid-1960s. Just like that the whole bloody world came apart at the seams. I was horrified to find 300 strangers camped at Cascade Pass, a decade earlier the private realm of my friends and me. I was dumbfounded to climb a peak, thinking our ascent was the fifth or sixth and in the summit register discover the record of 30 parties.

One July day I went to Recreational Equipment Inc. to buy food for a trip, and the shelves were bare. I buttonholed Jim Whittaker, the general manager, and whined, "How the hell can I go hiking without dehydrated spinach?" Jim, glazed eyes roving the milling throng of frustrated customers, wailed, "I don't even have

any spinach for myself! Who could predict *this*? We doubled last year's order and it was all gone by June and they can't dehydrate spinach fast enough to keep us in stock."

Recalling the later years of that hectic era, Jim recently wrote, "REI's 1971 *increase* in sales over the previous year was more than its *total* sales in 1967, which could be interpreted to mean that more *new* people got out on the trails and into the mountains in 1971 than *all* the people who were there in 1967."

FRIGHTENING. Appalling. How did it happen? Where did all these damn hikers come from? The obvious answer (from their mothers' wombs) is insufficient. There are now about 212 million Americans compared to 130 million in 1940, an increase of 63 percent. But since 1940 the Cascades trail population has swelled some 1,000 percent.

Among us heavy-breathing bird-watchers striving to enlarge the National Wilderness Preservation System, a common explanation is that the quality of life in cities and slurbs has so deteriorated that more and more battered psyches require more and more wildland re-creation. I believe that the crudding of America is a contributing factor but not the triggering mechanism. After all, the urban–suburban–freeway madhouse doesn't necessarily impel a flight to the bosom of nature. Many choose instead such frenetic catharses as booze, drugs, rock festivals, drag races, bowling alleys, Disneyland, roller derbies, razzing around on motorcycles or watching football on TV.

Various villain theories have been propounded. The staggering multiplication of Cascades hikers occurred during the same years we were putting out trail guides for the range; thus many a distraught veteran thought he saw a causal relationship and attacked us as traitors revealing secrets to the enemy. Aside from objecting to the implicit fascism, I never grasped that reasoning. Certainly, publicizing a beauty spot attracts boots—indeed, we published guidebooks specifically because we felt a thousand boots are preferable to one bulldozer and that to save wildlands we must make them famous. For the life of me, though, I can't believe very

many hikers are recruited by words. First a person buys the boots. *Then* the book. The book influences *where* he goes but does not make him *go*.

If guides generated new hikers, a correlation should be found in any given area between the introduction of books and the amount of trail travel. But there ain't none. It seemed so in the Cascades, but that was simple coincidence; other areas thoroughly guidebooked for years suffered the same crush in the same period. To cite one case, the number of hikers in Grand Teton National Park doubled between 1967 and 1971. And areas completely blanked by the literature were also mobbed overnight. Whatever crimes may justly be charged to trail guides, creating new pedestrians isn't among them.

Should we blame Americans' unparalleled wealth and mobility? Sure. But money and leisure are as likely to stimulate a flight to Europe, a spree in Las Vegas, purchase of a sports car or membership in a country club. A rich hiker may hike more, but money doesn't set his boots in motion.

How about nailing Dick Kelty and his ilk to the wall? That wouldn't be nice. Agreed, the postwar hiking market became sizable enough to support innovative manufacturers for the first time, with the result that in the mid-1960s gear and foods were available that eliminated many former agonies of backpacking, easing the transition from car camps to trails. Yet one must avoid confusing cause and effect. Kelty and company pampered the crowds but didn't spawn them. Nor did Colin Fletcher, whose *Complete Walker,* published in 1968, popularized the notion that it's noble and romantic to act like an ass.

I suspect Backpacking Chic has begun to have a substantial impact, leading people to do what once was extremely rare: walk directly from sidewalks onto trails. About the time boys began to wear beards and girls no bras, rucksacks and Vibram soles attained "in" status on campus. Apparently a lot of fad-followers (who if born earlier would have thronged drive-ins, munching cheeseburgers and listening to Elvis Presley) decided to try backpacking, along with pot, Zen, casual sex and the other good things going around.

In my quest for answers I've paid

close attention to work done during the past decade by the Wildland Recreation Research Unit of the U.S. Forest Service. A paper by John C. Hendee, leader of the Northwest Research Unit, and Frederick L. Campbell describes a study showing how land managers unintentionally have contributed to trail crowds.

"The traditional small, primitive [roadside] camp once provided visitors with insulation from the social complexities of urban life, but it is the social characteristics of the modern developed campground which attract many recreationists . . . [who view] camping primarily as an opportunity to meet new people and to have an enjoyable social experience. . . . [They tend] to simply transfer their urban activity patterns to the campground. . . . Bicycles, toys, televisions, and all the things used for entertainment at home were brought to the campground. . . . Few displayed any concern for the flora, fauna, ecology, or natural history of the area. . . .

"Modern campgrounds have typically evolved from small, primitive camps that were enlarged and upgraded because they were popular, and responsive managers sought to protect the sites and make them available to greater numbers of people. Ironically, in their reflex action . . . recreation managers often created campgrounds attractive to those users with social rather than environmental orientations. The appearance of such users often forced the original clientele to seek solitude and close contact in other locations. This succession and displacement of different types of users resembles the models of human and plant ecology . . ."*

While Hendee, no fascist, insists that both socially and environmentally oriented car campers must be accommodated—in different places—he believes land managers must give more thought to the consequences of their actions, which may be quite different from what they in-

---

*"Social Aspects of Outdoor Recreation—The Developed Campground." *Trends in Parks and Recreation.* October, 1969. Reprint of journal article available from Pacific Northwest Forest and Range Experiment Station, U.S.D.A., Portland, Oregon.

tend. As he wrote in a recent letter, "I think we are beginning to realize now that putting in additional development, though generally motivated by a manager's desire to upgrade the *quality* of the experience opportunity, may not do that at all, but instead often merely changes the *nature* of the experience. In any case I think many people have been displaced into wilderness."

THE ABOVE FACTORS all doubtless have had a share in populating trails. But even in sum they are not enough; they do not explain the central, baffling mystery. Why did it happen so suddenly? Why, after decades of steady but reasonable growth in numbers of backcountry visitors, did every line on every graph for every national park and wilderness area of the West simultaneously and abruptly shoot straight up?

The crucial clue, I think, lies in another Wildland Recreation Research paper, written by William R. Burch, Jr. and Wiley D. Winger, Jr. The authors report the results of a study of three types of campers in the Oregon Cascades: easy access (car camping), remote (backpacking) and combination (those doing both). A few excerpts tell the story:

"About 90 percent of the sample of campers had experienced enjoyment of nature by the time they were 12 years old. . ."

(To interject further confirmation that enjoyment of nature is learned behavior normally beginning in childhood, a 1965 study by Hendee found that 70 percent of the wilderness users interviewed had taken their first wilderness trip before they were 15.)

"Persons . . . with childhood hiking experience are more likely now to be remote or combination campers rather than easy-access campers. Persons . . . with childhood auto camping experience . . . [also] tend to be combination or remote campers. The easy-access campers are most likely to be persons without either hiking or auto-camping experience as children with their parents.

"Therefore, it appears that remote campers tend to continue in the patterns learned in childhood. Combination campers are most likely persons who are continuing childhood pat-

terns or who have shifted from a childhood auto-camping pattern to a more primitive camping style. . .

"In summary, it appears . . . activities pleasantly familiar to a person in his childhood tend to attract his leisure-time attention as an adult. Furthermore, an adult with previous familiarity with the out-of-doors apparently prefers more challenging camping experiences, at least part of the time, than does the person new to the out-of-doors. . .

"Perhaps the present camping styles reflect attempts to retain the qualities of experience remembered from childhood years. If so, the present children of easy-access campers may very likely adopt a combination or remote camping style when they reach adulthood. The new experience for their parents now would be an old one for the children when they reach adulthood. Further, the old spots shared with their parents may be filling with new and inexperienced recruits whose presence tends to diminish the quality of experience as remembered.

"The pattern suggested by these data is the flow of new and less experienced campers into the easy-access areas with the 'old hands' feeling crowded and moving on . . ."**

THERE YOU HAVE IT, if you'll carefully digest those pregnant paragraphs—the firing device that triggered the bomb. Who caused the mass migration into wilderness? None other than Henry Ford. Little did I suspect, riding the family Model A to car camps in 1928, hiking with the scouts in 1938, climbing with The Mountaineers in 1948 and finally car camping and then hiking with kids, that my life would turn out to be so darn typical.

In the twenties and thirties, the Automobile Boom, I was among the first surge of car campers.

In the forties and fifties, we pioneers—partly seeking greater challenges and partly seeking escape from the second and even larger surge of
Continued on page 83

** "The Social Characteristics of Participants in Three Styles of Family Camping." Forest Service Research Paper PNW-48. Pacific Northwest Forest and Range Experiment Station, U.S.D.A., Portland, Oregon. 1967.

car campers—began giving the trails an unprecedented pounding. At the same time pioneers and newcomers began breeding up the storm of the Baby Boom and hauling swarms of infants to car camps and trails.

In the sixties and seventies, offspring of both the first and second surges of car campers were moving into adulthood. Together they hoisted packs and 300 people were camped at Cascade Pass and REI couldn't keep dehydrated spinach on the shelf and the Backpacking Boom was under way as abruptly as the Automobile Boom and the Baby Boom before it.

WHAT OF 1984? By then U.S. population is predicted to increase by 21 million, 89 percent of the growth in the 20–49 age category that does the most backpacking. Observe today's armies of car-camping children and imagine them as adults marching outward from the roads.

I gaze flinchingly into the probably horrid future and see quiet lands (and there are still plenty even in the High Sierra and Cascades if you know where to look) growing loud. I see a further displacement: old hands fleeing trails of their youth for off-trail scrambling and climbing, for journeys to Canada and Alaska. And I see winter lonesomeness diminishing as more and more people try to avoid mobs by snowshoeing and cross-country skiing.

I see no hike allowed anywhere without a permit and reservation obtained long in advance, and a hurricane of bitching. I see platoons of wilderness rangers deployed to enforce camping bans in fragile ecosystems, and incessant griping by violators issued citations.

I hope I see the bitchers and gripers realizing that they must support a biocentric rather than an anthropocentric approach to wildland management and must help educate ignorant novices. I also hope I see them taking a vigorous part in the movement to enlarge the National Wilderness Preservation System.

I hope I see land managers and land users realizing that they are all hooked up in the same grand ecosystem (the one we call Earth) and must do a better job of coordinated long-range planning. I hope I see the managers abandoning their accustomed stimulus-response pattern, particularly by recognizing that facilities for the "social" camper are best sited at a distance from the wilderness edge and that trail-building funds should be spent mainly on wilderness fringes and near urban centers rather than in the hearts of remote wildlands. I hope I see users consulting more closely with managers on the publication of guidebooks and other information that points boots in certain directions, thus constituting a form of land planning. I hope I see equipment manufacturers accepting responsibility for the impact of their products, rather than cranking them out simply because a market exists among the innocent or ignorant or vicious.

Enough! My crystal ball is going berserk with quick-flashing images, is suffering stress fatigue and getting murky. Do I see more and more people taking their weekends on Tuesday-Wednesday? Do I see wilderness hordes so nauseating that veterans give up in disgust and retreat to hermetically sealed city apartments to smoke dope and listen to Mozart quartets? Do I see the end of cheap energy gradually killing off the private automobile, with myriad implications?

Throw a blanket over my crystal ball. I don't want to see the future until I have to.

I can't help wondering, though, about children raised in the Kampgrounds of Amerika. Will the Winnebago and Air Stream kids who've never confronted night or storm and never slept on the ground, who value camping mainly for the freedom from noise-control ordinances, graduate from campground-razzing minibikes to tough and ugly trailbikes? Or will they one day accidentally hear birdsongs, try their feet, learn to pity energy-drunk parents and compound the wilderness crisis?

Danged if I know. ✍

OUTING IMPACT

by JACK HOPE

Six million backpackers could be saving the wilderness. Meanwhile, we're destroying it. Outing impact isn't misuse—it's just overuse. And it's caused by backpackers.

The backpacker, relative to other recreational users of the wilderness — the snowmobiler, the trailbiker, the motorboater, the downhill skier, the rock climber, the horseback camper — does little aesthetic and ecological damage to his natural surroundings. He does not roar across the landscape astride a noisy motor-powered vehicle. He does not damage the rock cliffs by driving pitons into the cracks. Unlike the pack animals favored by some campers, the backpacker does not graze on alpine vegetation, does not pulverize the earth with his hooves and does not deposit piles of manure on hiking trails.

Equally important, the backpacker's basic equipment—a pair of leather boots, a lightweight aluminum pack, a nylon tent—is relatively modest, requiring a small consumption of natural resources. The basic gear of the motor-powered outdoorsman, on the other hand, requires that 300 to 2,000 lbs of metal ore be mined from the earth and that an engine be created and fueled to propel his jeep, dune buggy, or snowmobile from spot to spot. Similarly, the sport of the downhill skier demands that mountain environments be cleared of trees, developed with lifts and lodges, and be supplied with the power to run these facilities.

The backpacker comes off very well in a comparison of this sort.

Nevertheless, he does cause wilderness impact. A lot of it. He erodes trails. (This erosion, incidentally, has increased with the introduction of Vibram soles.) He makes noise (especially in groups). He tramples natural vegetation, destroys delicate alpine meadows and the shorelines of lakes and streams. He consumes vast quantities of firewood. He litters. He pollutes backcountry watersheds with detergents and with human wastes. He creates (or causes others to create) man-made shelters, fireplaces, and a number of other physical structures in the backcountry that, despite their convenience, detract from the wilderness atmosphere.

Today, there are an estimated six million backpackers in the United States. More significantly, the ranks of the backpacking fraternity are swelling rapidly Based upon sales of boots and other backpacking gear, Seattle's Recreational Equipment, Inc. estimates that the number of people who took up backpacking in 1971 exceeded the total number of practicing backpackers just four years earlier. The National Park Service, which keeps accurate visitor records, estimates that while park use in general is rising at 7 percent annually, the number of wilderness backpacking trips is increasing at roughly 35 percent per year. A recent survey on the popular Appalachian Trail found that during daylight hours hikers passed the survey point on the average of once every 20 seconds, which is more frequently than people pass the door of my apartment building at the corner of 96th Street and West End Avenue in New York City.

With numbers of this magnitude, the individual hiker's opportunity for "wilderness solitude" is virtually nonexistent, at least during summer months, and the occurrence of backpacker-caused environmental damage is inevitable. In Rocky Mountain and Great Smokies National Parks, several sections of popular hiking trails have become worn down and eroded as much as five feet below adjacent ground level. In the backcountry of Sequoia-Kings Canyon National Park, pollution from detergents and human wastes has been detected in remote alpine lakes, and wilderness campers are now advised to boil all drinking water. In most national and state parks and forests, firewood cannot be found within a half-mile radius of popular campsites and fishing lakes. In some backcountry regions of the White Mountains, the Great Smokies, the Rockies and Sierra Nevadas, the use of wood fires is prohibited. Campers are now required to make a "cold camp" or to carry stoves. In the wilderness of Rocky Mountain National Park, the Park Service has been forced to install a battery of privy toilets and to run toilet-emptying missions by helicopter as frequently as twice a week. Due to campsite crowding, the destruction of vegetation and the accumulation of litter, limits have been placed on wilderness use within several national parks and along portions of the Appalachian Trail.

Planning for future wilderness use is as much a problem of psychology as it is of numbers.

In part, these problems can be remedied by education. As a group, backpackers have displayed a sincere concern for their natural surroundings and for the future of their recreation. In re-

cent years, organizations such as the Sierra Club, the Appalachian Mountain Club and the Boy Scouts have made efforts to educate their members in proper backcountry conduct and have contributed several thousand man-hours to wilderness clean-up projects.

However, it is unrealistic to rely solely upon education as a solution to the problems of wilderness impact. Even the best educational efforts do not reach all backpackers. And not all backpackers reached are willing to adhere to the standards required to minimize wilderness impact. It takes a great deal of self discipline, after all, to refrain from building a wood fire, to consistently erect a tent at least 100 feet from water or to resist the temptation to wash supper dishes in a stream.

Educational efforts are further complicated by the fact that we simply do not know what "ideal" wilderness behavior should consist of. Aside from one lengthy examination by the Sierra Club and several guides by such groups as the Appalachian Mountain Club, very few studies have been conducted to assess the pros and cons of various types of waste disposal and other backcountry activity. We do not know, for example, whether organic camp wastes are best buried in the earth or spread out over the surface of the ground. We cannot be certain as to the advisability of building latrines, either for groups of varying sizes or in soils of different porosity. We do not know if the consumption of firewood damages soil by depriving it of organic nutrients, or whether it actually benefits the environment by reducing the frequency and severity of naturally occurring forest fires.

Educational efforts cannot solve all the problems of impact because most of this impact is not a function of wilderness misuse, but of simple overuse—the inadvertent damage caused by millions of backpackers. While it may be theoretically possible to educate all hikers to carry stoves and to refrain from carving obscenities in tree trunks, it is highly unlikely that a hiker can be taught to lighten his footsteps on the trail, to pick up bread wrappers or scraps of tinfoil that he drops unknowingly, or to hold his bowels for the duration of a four-day hike. Given the estimated 35 percent annual increase in wilderness use, just to maintain the environment in its *current* condition

requires that every backpacker reduce his *personal* impact by 35 percent each year. An impossible goal.

Deterioration of the wilderness is self-reinforcing, to a certain extent. One tends to define "wilderness" in terms of one's early encounters with that environment. And if those early encounters are with a wilderness that is pawed over, littered and crowded, the human tendency is to accept this situation as the normal one.

It is significant, then, that most of the nation's six million backpackers have come to the wilderness only within the last few years. It seems logical to expect that the ideal toward which most wilderness users will strive in their interaction with their surroundings will not be that wilderness defined by the 1964 Wilderness Act—"an area with outstanding opportunities for solitude…untrammeled…where man is a visitor who does not remain"—but a wilderness more akin to New York's Central Park.

A first-time backcountry traveler, raised among the shopping centers and oil refineries of Los Angeles or Jersey City, may view the White Mountains—as crowded as they are—not only as a wilderness but as a veritable Garden of Eden. "Look at all those trees!"

What to do? Today, two basic wilderness-management systems are being considered to limit outing impact and to improve the individual's wilderness experience. The most sophisticated of these—which might be called the "rationing-dispersion" technique—is now being used on a trial basis in Rocky Mountain, Sequoia-Kings Canyon and Great Smokies National Parks. At present, the rationing program affects overnight wilderness campers only (as opposed to day hikers). It is designed to reduce overcrowding at traditionally popular (and therefore heavily damaged) backcountry campsites and to disperse overnight campers throughout the backcountry.

In Rocky Mountain National Park, for instance, the park superintendent has designated 198 backcountry campsites (each accommodating seven persons or less) and seven group campsites (accommodating up to 25 people). On a first-come, first-served basis, wilderness campers are issued free permits to camp at the site of their choice—until the limit is reached. Rangers may also issue overnight permits to 413 additional campers who are permitted to set up camp (but who are not permitted to build wood fires) at random locations throughout the backcountry, provided these sites are at least a half-mile from trails, roads and other campers. If the backcountry is filled (2,000 people), no additional permits are issued. To prevent local residents from obtaining all available permits early in the season, permits are only issued within 24 hours of the camper's expected wilderness trip. The issuance of permits is controlled through a central dispatching board.

This system disperses campers to prevent their interfering with one another and to ensure that their physical

---

In a recent survey on the Appalachian Trail, hikers passed the survey point on an average of once every 20 seconds throughout the day.

---

impact on a given site (the grass they trample, the wood they may burn, the human waste they leave) will be "absorbed" by the environment (grass straightens itself, new wood falls from trees, human and other organic wastes decay). If, after a period of time, specific sites show signs of marked deterioration, these sites are closed to camping until natural processes have restored (or partially restored) the site to its natural condition.

There is a highly arbitrary element to the rationing-dispersion technique at present, since there is little evidence of how many persons a wilderness can accommodate without becoming damaged (or without becoming a "non-wilderness" in terms of crowding or noise). However, experience with the pilot program should provide some of the needed evidence.

To date, visitor reaction to the program has been overwhelmingly positive. However, public land-managing agencies typically feel that they must please their customers—even at the expense of environment. Thus, the danger remains, should campers voice a dislike of the rationing procedure in the future,

that park superintendents will set wilderness camping capacities (or day-use capacities) that are too liberal to prevent heavy aesthetic and ecological damage.

Another weakness—not of the dispersion-rationing system, but of the Park Service's capacity to make it work—is the fact that land-managing agencies are notoriously understaffed. At Rocky Mountain, for example, the Park Service estimates that it needs roughly 1,400 employees to issue and process permits, to patrol sites and to issue fines to flagrant violators of the regulations. But due to a variety of factors, ranging from the cost of the Vietnam war to the indifference of most legislators to the problems of wilderness management, adequate funds have not been granted to hire the needed employees. At present the park has only 500 staff members.

Despite its weaknesses, however, the rationing-dispersion system is far superior to other schemes for relieving wilderness impact. It recognizes that the wilderness has a limited capacity to absorb human use, and, in time, may be improved and expanded to include day-use of the wilderness as well as overnight. Through its rationing device, it also holds symbolic value in reminding the public that our environment is not limitless.

A second plan for managing wilderness is the "concentration" technique, which involves the construction of permanent structures—overnight shelters, permanent toilets and septic tanks, lodges with bunks and meal services—within wilderness areas. The rationale for this technique is that the installation of permanent structures serves to concentrate wilderness impact in specific locations, thus sparing surrounding regions from these pressures. Yosemite, Glacier and Sequoia-Kings Canyon National Parks all have privately operated wilderness lodges that offer food and shelter to backcountry hikers. Along the 2,000-mile length of the Appalachian Trail, the Appalachian Trail Conference maintains a series of 238 lean-tos and a few more elaborate shelters that offer food and lodging. Similarly, various European alpine clubs operate "huts" which are in fact small mountain hotels.

This concentration technique has obvious shortcomings. First, it requires the construction of fixed structures which, in addition to destroying small wilderness enclaves, contradicts the essential

Permanent structures do not reduce hiker pressures. More trail shelters means more visitors means more shelters.

purpose of a wilderness experience—encountering nature on nature's terms, without the conveniences of man-made shelters, hot meals, and take-out lunches.

Secondly, once these new permanent wilderness structures are created, there is very little opportunity to remove them (they have cost time and money, after all) once that particular area becomes overused. The prime example of this is the Appalachian Trail, with its string of shelters. Around many of these shelters, use has become so heavy that the areas are littered, eroded and stripped of firewood and green vegetation. In recent years, as many as 138 people camped each night in and around a single shelter. During 1972, land-managing agencies were forced to restrict the use of some of these shelters with a permit system. Even if the Appalachian Trail were closed tomorrow, it would take decades for the environment to recover its natural condition in the areas around the shelters.

Finally, permanent structures in a wilderness area do not succeed in reducing hiker pressures in adjacent regions. Rather, the convenience of the shelters tends to attract people to the wilderness who would not visit these regions if they were required to bring their own tent, set up their own camp and prepare their own meals. In light of the current pressures on our backcountry environments, the attraction of new visitors by offering "convenience" can hardly be viewed as a responsible goal of wilderness management. (The Appalachian Mountain Club, by the way, has recently begun to tear down shelters and to erect tent platforms in some areas which receive unusually heavy use.)

Unfortunately, once the original structures become overtaxed, persuasive arguments will be heard for the construction of even more shelters to accommodate newcomers. One recent suggestion for "solving" the current overcrowding of existing Appalachian Trail shelters was the construction of more shelters. Similarly, one of the suggestions for relieving pressures on the battered trail itself was to create new, supplementary trail systems that would funnel off some of the trail's current users.

This type of thinking, it seems, is borrowed from the philosophy of highway engineers who have traditionally argued that the way to reduce auto traffic congestion is through the construction of new highways. But, as we know from experience, it simply doesn't work: new highways breed new cars breed new highways. And new wilderness accommodations breed new visitors breed new wilderness accommodations.

Essentially, the attempt to concentrate wilderness impact constitutes an admission that the impact in a region is already more than the environment can take. Unlike the rationing-dispersion technique, the concentration concept fails to recognize that natural environments have limited capacities for absorbing users.

Curiously, despite its drawbacks, the concentration technique has acquired considerable support in recent years. The National Parks Service, for instance, has sought approval of a plan that would create new wilderness lodges as well as permanent aerial gondolas to make wilderness areas more readily accessible.

In one sense, even a popular and well-advertised wilderness trail can be considered to be a sort of "permanent fixture" or "drawing card." To a very real extent, a trip on any of these trails may serve the hiker as an ego-balm, as an "accomplished" goal rather than a means of experiencing wilderness. This problem could be appropriately rectified by hiking clubs, many of which currently foster a sense of competition and goal orientation among their members. (Wit-

ness the "end-to-end" trail-travel badges, "peak-bagging" pins and other regalia now being dispensed in the manner of Olympic laurels.)

Admittedly, no one has ever spelled out what the appropriate purpose of a wilderness backpack trek should be. But in a society such as ours—busy, competitive, crowded, increasingly alienated from the natural world—the quality of a wilderness outing can probably be most appropriately defined in terms of the *contrast* it provides with our day-to-day lives. However, to the extent that our wilderness is damaged and developed, to the extent that it becomes overpopulated, to the extent that it is viewed as something to conquer, this contrast is destroyed, along with whatever perspective a wilderness experience might offer our nine-to-five existence. Planning for future wilderness use is as much a problem of psychology as it is of numbers.

And, speaking of numbers, there is no good reason to expect the level of wilderness backpackers to decline or even level off in the foreseeable future. "Getting back to nature" seems to be very much "in" today, and there is no sign that it will be "out" in years to come. More important, we should keep in mind that for economic reasons a large segment of our population currently has zero access to wilderness. A proper consideration of our wilderness resources and our future wilderness needs should make provisions for wilderness use by these people. In this sense society is justified in providing some encouragement (economic encouragement, not the encouragement offered by wilderness conveniences and by simplified physical access) to potential wilderness users.

Also, we should keep in mind and act upon the fact that increases in wilderness areas hold a considerable potential for improving the current problems of backcountry overuse. We cannot expect magically to expand the nation's total

wilderness area. However, it would behoove backpackers to exert political pressure upon land-managing agencies and upon elected representatives in Congress to officially designate more wilderness areas. Of the roughly 60 million acres of American wilderness in government hands, only 12 million have so far been given legal protection under the Wilderness Act of 1964.

In this case, of course, backpackers will come into head-on conflict with other recreational lobbies—snowmobilers, downhill skiers and horseback concessioners. But with any sort of organization and commitment, backpackers should easily overwhelm the opposition. If six million backpackers' letters were to land on the desks of Congressmen, they would hardly go unnoticed.

Yet, to a certain extent, this is simply an exercise in selfishness, an attempt to accommodate one's own pastime. It just happens, however, that backpacking, along with canoeing and cross-country skiing, is among the least destructive of land uses. Backpackers thus hold all the environmental cards. They can make a very honest and very convincing case for their activity, not only as a benefit to themselves, but as a benefit to society. Despite its quirks and quacks, its oddities and imperfections, backpacking holds more potential to foster a responsible and less consumptive attitude toward the environment than any other form of wilderness recreation. Which, after all, is precisely the point. ✒

FRANCIS OF ASSISI (1182–1226)

by GEORGE WILLIAMS

Can a 13th-century radical Christian mystic tell us anything about today's ecology problems?

I would rather call him Mister Francis than Saint Francis. My concept of him is sanitized. I have de-mythologized, de-romanticized and de-deified him for myself. For me Francis is now quite human. I often have tried to imagine what kind of person he would be if I should actually meet him coming along the trail. I have tried also to imagine what it would be like if I were he myself.

As I hike along alone, it is easy for me to do this. I am endowed with a fruitful imagination. When I walk in the forest where the path is wide and on a somewhat level grade, I imagine how it might have been 800 years ago when such paths were the highways by which everyone traveled from one town to the next. There were, of course, carts on the wide paths, and pack animals, too. By and large, though, most people traveled by foot. And whatever luggage they carried was on their backs. Sometimes there were great processions. That was a big thing in those days — hundreds of people walking along together, like parades from town to town and back again.

I think this is why backpacking today is so engaging to so many: It satisfies some primordial urges within us. I think it is another form of the back-to-fundamental-experiences we seek in today's push-button, painless, homogenized, sanitary world of plastic and chrome and flip-top cans. It is for this type of experience that some people go back to organic gardening or turn to health foods. Others wish to experience dramatic natural childbirth. There is an inordinate interest in survival skills at a time when wilderness survival has become the least likely danger that any of us may risk in our lifetime. Many others seek satisfaction in such pri-

CANTICLE OF BROTHER SUN

Most high almighty good lord,
Praises, glory, honor, and all blessings.

Praise be to you, my lord, through all your creatures,
Especially our brother sun
By whom you give us the light of day.
He is so beautiful and radiant and splendid.

Praise be to you, my lord, for sister moon and the stars
You formed them in the sky bright and precious and fair.

Praise be to you, my lord, for brother wind
And for the air and for cloudy and clear and every other
   kind of weather.
By which you nourish your creatures.

Praise be to you, my lord, for sister water.
Who is so useful and humble and precious and chaste.

Praise be to you, my lord, for brother fire
By whom you give us light at night.
He is so handsome and merry and mighty and strong.

Praise be to you, my lord, for our sister, mother earth.
Who sustains and governs us.
And brings forth various fruits with colorful flowers and leaves.

Praise and bless you, my lord, and thank you.
May we serve you in all humility.

– Saint Francis of Assisi

stars, moon, even wolves.

It is to experience these things with our senses wide open — if only for a few days and only modestly — that we go backpacking. To me, whoever would go backpacking with a hundred pounds of lightweight equipment is missing some of these things and consequently missing a good deal of the primordial experience. And the difference between backpackers and car campers is that the latter take along fully equipped, modernly convenient homes to the backcountry, while backpackers attempt to remove as many layers of their civilized paraphernalia as they can. Nevertheless, even they are closer to the primordial experience than city dwellers who spend their lives almost entirely in a man-made world.

My affections for Saint Francis go back to the late 1950s and early 1960s to the heyday of the beatniks. It was with considerable warmth that I first read historian Dr. Lynn White, Jr.'s proposal that Francis be made the patron saint of the ecologists, in his article entitled "The Historical Roots of Our Ecologic Crisis" in *Science* Magazine, March, 1967.

White said in his article that he doubted we would ever solve our ecologic problems by merely applying more science and technology. Our present environmental crisis, he pointed

out, was caused by already using too much science and technology. What is needed is a change in the fundamental attitude which we all seem to hold that man is the ruler over nature and that nature is there for us to subdue or conquer. This attitude is so deeply ingrained that most of us do not realize we hold it.

The reason this attitude is so deeply imbedded in our subconsciousness is that it is a fundamental tenet of our Judeo-Christian tradition. In the Book of Genesis God gives man dominion over all the other creatures of this earth. That idea is basic to Christian dogma as well as modern science, and is the father of modern technology. White

meval activities as fishing and hunting.

In backpacking it is not simply the visit to nature that entices us. There is a far more primeval lure for the backpacker which makes me believe that carrying all our necessities kindles deep within us reminiscences of an ancestral itinerancy.

Backpacking is as primordial for me as the experience my wife gets from digging her hands into the soil of her garden.

Mister Francis is for me the embodiment of the self-contained itinerant experience of mankind. He carried all of his earthly possessions, such as they were, with him. He regarded everything in nature as friendly and worthy of his undivided attention. He did not want to see the forest for the trees. He wanted to see each tree as a separate and sacred thing. Likewise, each bird, animal and blade of grass.

Mister Francis is a very appropriate hero for our time. He is a fine antidote for so much of what life is in today's hurried technological urban setting.

Thoughts of him serve the same function for me that a fine hike in solitude does.

Francis, first of all, was born rich, rejected his father's wealth and chose instead a life of poverty. He got away from the clutter of material possessions to gain possession of his own mind and soul. He rejected the commercial urban life of his home town, Assisi, and took to the backcountry. He walked extensively, making his home beside the path wherever he was. He traveled light, with little more than a bowl, the sandals on his feet and the sackcloth robe on his back. He depended upon berries and other fruits he picked along the roadside for his food, and augmented that by whatever he could beg from passersby. He refused title and position: He would not become a priest or even the titular head of the order he founded because he believed that would corrupt his spirit. He nurtured a deep perceptual relationship with his immediate surroundings, which were mostly nature — birds, trees, fire, sun,

reminded us that the roots of science and technology are firmly planted in medieval Christianity. These disciplines were actually spawned and nurtured by the Church. Thus, this attitude that man should subdue nature is an unquestioned assumption on several levels in our culture. It is an attitude held almost universally today regardless of one's religion. It is even a basic tenet for those who consider themselves entirely enlightened, scientific and completely nonreligious — such as the Individuals for a Rational Society, the followers of Ayn Rand.

If I read White correctly, what the attitude boils down to is an ego trip: We do not believe deep in our hearts, despite Charles Darwin, that we really are a part of the natural order of things. We consider ourselves on a higher plane, aloof from nature, superior to it. After all, we have superior intelligence; we have language; we have cybernetic goal-directed capabilities. Therefore, we are willing to use nature to satisfy our most capricious whims. Why not? Isn't nature there to serve us?

White warned that whatever we do about ecology in the future will depend largely upon whether we are able to alter this attitude of ours. We must rethink and refeel what the real nature of man is, and what our relationship to the natural world ought to be, and where we hope the planet should be headed with us on it. Since White saw the roots of the problem stretching so deeply back into the religious part of our heritage, he believed the remedy ought to be basically religious, also.

He thought that Zen might have possibilities for turning us in the right direction. But he distrusted Zen because its roots were so alien to our own Western culture that it would be difficult to assess the unintended social consequences if Zen were ever practiced widely. White thought that Francis of Assisi might be more help in pointing the way for us.

He settled upon Francis as a patron saint for ecologists because of two tactical considerations. First, he said that Saint Francis was the greatest Christian radical and that our ecological crisis calls for radical solutions. Second, he believed it important for us to understand very tangibly our own personalities to nature. Saint Francis, in the way he lived his life, taught humility toward nature; he tried "to depose man from his monarchy over nature." He asked us to see all of God's creatures as equal, with man but one of the creatures. Francis taught that we are sisters and brothers to the stars, sun, moon, flowers, birds, trees, fire and water — and that the only ruler over all was God.

White's idea had an immediate appeal for me. Although I never had considered Francis as the end-all, he certainly could be the begin-all of the ecology movement. I was completely for it. I suspect that White's idea has seeped silently and puissantly into our consciousness and already is doing its good work for us.

Then along came my latest ecology hero, Dr. Rene Dubos. I became captivated by his message in his book *A God Within*. But wait — he offhandedly dismisses White's suggestion of making Francis the patron saint of ecology as being "romantic and unworldly." That took me by surprise. I had to study his arguments. There are so few of us in the environmental movement that I believed we could not afford to have this sort of rift between two of our most important mentors. As I restudied the texts of both men, my eyes opened wide — Dubos did not really understand White. Thank God for that. There was a possibility for a reconciliation.

Dubos argues that man has never been purely a passive worshiper of nature. But Dubos is off on the wrong premise. White never said that man was or should be purely a passive worshiper of nature.

Man, as Dubos points out, from the Paleolithic hunters and Neolithic farmers down to Henry David Thoreau has always changed and reshaped nature. He points out that even Thoreau cleared the land to build his cabin and to plant his beans. Dubos concludes "human life inevitably implies changes in nature."

Additionally, he finds the idea of equality in nature uncongenial to his own spirit because he enjoys imposing his dominance over nature in the form of gardening and landscaping.

Therefore, Dubos proposes a different Christian — Saint Benedict of Nursia — as the patron of true conservation and as being more relevant to the modern world. His reasoning is that while Saint Benedict sticks to the Book of Genesis, he puts emphasis upon the second chapter with its idea of *benevolent* domination over nature, or more euphemistically, "stewardship."

Through the centuries, the Benedictines were good examples of the prudence of this benevolent domination. They developed windmills and water mills for their own power and produced leather, fabrics, paper and liqueurs. They exhibited a great wisdom "in adapting rituals and work to the cosmic rhythms."

Dubos argues that we won't find a solution to our environmental mess by retreating from the Judeo-Christian tra-

dition or from science and technology. But White didn't think so, either. White said we could not count on *merely* science and technology for a solution We must change our fundamental attitudes — not retreat from them.

Dubos argues further that reverence for nature is not enough. He says man "must read the book of external nature and the book of his own nature to discern the common patterns and harmonies."

Isn't that what White said in slightly different language? "What we do about ecology depends on our ideas of the man-nature relationship ... We must rethink and refeel our nature and destiny."

I cannot see why Dubos disagrees so with White. They don't differ in any material way — merely that Dubos seems to want to say things in his own words and use a different saint. That's okay with me.

I personally have a fond love for Saint Benedict and the Benedictines as well. A few years ago I spent considerable time in two Benedictine monasteries. I became imbued with the "adaptation of rituals to the cosmic rhythms." I can well see the value of Saint Benedict for conservation.

Nonetheless, Francis seems the more direct and the more capable of getting us back in touch with our relationship to the rest of nature. He can do it through our most fundamental feelings as well as through our open-minded perception, much more so than Benedict.

Look around you, wherever you are. See how many man-made objects there are compared to the number of simple, unadorned trees, plants, bugs, grasses, sun, wind, ants, leaves. If you go to Benedict for an understanding of yourself and your relationship to nature, you will do so in a man-made or man-cultivated world. I do not believe that gives you the same humility that raw nature does. This is an important difference. It is a real mind-bending starting point for getting right with the world.

I do not believe that backpacking *per se* makes one a better ecologist. But I do believe that the more closely and intimately we experience nature, the clearer and more benign our attitude toward it becomes. While Dubos makes good arguments for Benedict as the patron saint of conservation, I would like to propose that Mister Francis is the embodiment of the ideal most appropriate for backpacking.

I believe that with Mister Francis, a camera and a backpack we can save the world. 🍂

GENE STRATTON-PORTER (1863–1924)

by DEBORAH DAHLKE-SCOTT and MICHAEL PREWITT

While riding in the country, she
sometimes would clamber down from her
buggy to straighten a wild flower broken
by some careless foot, pat dirt around it,
prop it up with a stick, and give it a drink
from her Thermos bottle.

Gene Stratton-Porter was a wife and home-maker at the turn of the century, who was determined that this was not all there was going to be to her life. She raised her children, became a leading novelist, photographer, naturalist, outdoorswoman, and conservationist. Her achievements were impressive. She set an example worthy of emulating.

W.K.

DURING THE FIRST quarter of this century, Gene Stratton-Porter, now nearly forgotten by succeeding generations of readers, was one of America's most successful, most influential novelists. She drew her inspiration from the wilderness which was, even then, fast being plowed up, paved over and otherwise exploited. She became one of the first to speak publicly for the natural world and its wild creatures, and quickly became a leader in the emerging conservation movement.

The tools for her crusade were her novels. Her first passion had been her nature studies, books which documented her work with birds, moths and wild plants. But she realized early that these studies could never reach the wide audience she hoped to influence. So she wrote fiction.

The formula for a Gene Stratton-Porter novel—a plot woven skillfully through rich, descriptive nature lore—was at first doubted by her publishers. When she submitted her book *Freckles* to Doubleday and Page, her editors told her to "cut the nature stuff" or *Freckles* would never sell. For a while the editors were right. Then, three years after publication, the book caught on. Twenty years later, *Freckles*, the story of a crippled, orphaned young man who finds a home with the people and animals of the Limberlost, had sold nearly two million copies.

Gene Stratton-Porter published 22 books and wrote countless articles for magazines like *Century, Ladies' Home Journal* and *Saturday Evening Post*. Her books were translated into seven languages. *A Girl of the Limberlost*, published in 1909, told the story of a young girl's coming of age in the Limberlost Swamp. It gained such international acclaim that it was the first American book to be translated into Arabic. During the last 17 years of her life, Mrs. Stratton-Porter's books sold at the rate of 1,700 copies per day.

Her characters were often people deeply involved in the natural world. They perceived the woods and the swamps—the usual settings for the novels—just as the novelist herself did. This description of Elnora, the girl of the Limberlost, might easily characterize Gene Stratton-Porter herself:

The vast store of learning she had gathered from field and forest was a wealth of attraction no other girl possessed. Her frank, matter-of-fact manner was an inheritance from her mother, but there was something more. Once, as they talked, he thought "sympathy" was the word to describe it and again "comprehension." She seemed to possess a large sense of brotherhood for all human and animate creatures. She spoke to him as if she had known him all her life. She talked to the grosbeak in exactly the same manner, as she laid strawberries and potato bugs on the fence for his family. She did not swerve an inch from her way when a snake slid past her, while the squirrels came down

Gene Stratton-Porter was a naturalist, wildlife photographer, novelist, and one of the first people to speak out for the preservation of wildlife.

PHOTO: INDIANA DEPARTMENT OF NATURAL RESOURCES, DIVISION OF MUSEUMS AND MEMORIALS

from the trees and took corn from her fingers . . .

THIS SAME DEEP respect for the continuum of the natural world is the core of Gene Stratton-Porter's photography. Working in the days before there were high-speed films, miniature cameras and telephoto lenses, Mrs. Stratton-Porter lugged her 40 pounds of camera equipment through snake-infested swamps, up trees and around quicksand to record at close range the life processes of her subjects. Somehow, through a trust nurtured with birds and other wildlife, she got her camera within a few feet of some of the most intimate moments in the lives of wild creatures. This achievement is certainly one of the early high points in the history of nature photography.

She had gained her heightened awareness and delicately sensitive appreciation of nature from her parents on their Hopewell Farm near Wabash, Indiana. From her father, an ordained minister, she learned to love the beauty of the woods and fields which enmeshed the Stratton family's lives. She realized that birds were precious not only for their song and presence; they were also an integral part of the life chain of the farm, as protectors of fruit and crops from insect pests. Mark Stratton named his daughter protectress of all the birds on the farm and took Gene with him on his daily circuits inspecting and caring for the land. One of Mrs. Stratton-Porter's early memories was of her father tying a handkerchief around her mouth to quiet her. He then lifted her up to look into the nest of a hummingbird containing two tiny iridescent eggs.

At 23 Gene married Charles Darwin Porter, a druggist, who brought his bride to the natural setting which was later to make her famous: the Limberlost Swamp near Geneva in northeastern Indiana. The Limberlost was still uncharted backcountry when the Porters moved there in 1893 and built a 14-room log home on the swamp's edge. Mrs. Stratton-Porter adopted the Limberlost as her sanctuary.

Beyond her household obligations as a wife in small-town Indiana, Mrs. Stratton-Porter retained the independence that she carried throughout her life. Even her name speaks of this individualism. She characteristically insisted on using her maiden name, joining it to her husband's surname with a hyphen.

At the Limberlost cabin Gene Stratton-Porter first received a 4 × 5 view camera from her husband and daughter for Christmas in 1895. In her little black buggy, loaded with cameras, ropes, ladders and botanical specimens, she became a familiar sight to the country people who lived near the Limberlost.

As a child Mrs. Stratton-Porter had learned how to approach wildlife—especially birds. It was a long and tedious task to make friends with the builders of each of the nests. Approaching with extreme caution, she would imitate the bird's call as best she could. When she had gone so near that the brooding mother began to plaster her feathers against her body in fear, she would pause and allow the mother bird to settle. At first Mrs. Stratton-Porter would content herself with leaving a little of the food that the bird under study liked best. Going

Mrs. Stratton-Porter worked without a telephoto lens, sometimes spending weeks gaining the trust of animals so she could get close enough with her camera. These young field rabbits seem unaware that the photographer is only a few feet away.

PHOTO: INDIANA DEPARTMENT OF NATURAL RESOURCES, DIVISION OF MUSEUMS AND MEMORIALS

back daily to the same spot, she would advance farther, working cautiously toward the nest. In this manner she gradually won the confidence of the mother so completely that the bird would allow her to touch the babies as they brooded.

Gene Stratton-Porter commented about these remarkable encounters: "Few mothers were so careful about the food they feed their children. I gave those nestlings only a bite at a time and never a bite of anything until I watched what it was that the old birds were giving them."

All of this careful watching and waiting required even more patience when she began to record her encounters with a camera. She would locate the nest and set up her camera, covering the intruding equipment with a green cloth or a camouflage of twigs. Often this placement of the camera required hoisting the equipment up ladders or trees to find the closest spot to shoot from. Mrs. Stratton-Porter normally performed this painstaking work alone. But during the busiest season of her field-work, she had help in accustoming her subjects to people and photographic equipment. Bob Black, an oilman operating leases beside the Wabash River, spent his spare time locating nests for her. Black would set up a soapbox on stakes to simulate a camera and use his jacket for a lens cover. The birds became so used to his presence that they virtually "sat" for their portraits when the real photographs were taken.

Getting the birds accustomed to the photographer was by no means the only difficulty that Gene Stratton-Porter overcame. The Limberlost was

a dense and treacherous swamp, its bogs and swales filled with quicksand, mire and massasauga rattlesnakes (she sometimes carried a revolver as protection against the snakes). To Mrs. Stratton-Porter these obstacles were all part of her communion with the life of the swamp.

The studies made of a black vulture nest show her dedication to portraying the wildlife of the swamp. An oilman working within the swamp came to Mrs. Stratton-Porter and told her of the vulture's nest. Realizing the rarity of such a nest and the possibility of photographing a vulture chick, the Porters set off by carriage into the swamp after their prize. Gene Stratton-Porter describes the scene:

I shielded my camera in my arms, and before we reached the well I thought the conveyance would be torn to pieces. Starting out on foot, through the steaming fetid pools, through swarms of gnats, flies and mosquitoes and poisonous insects, keeping a watch for rattlesnakes, we sank ankle-deep at every step, and logs we thought solid broke beneath us. Our progress was a steady succession of prodding and pulling each other to the surface. Our clothing was wringing wet and exposed parts of our bodies lumpy with bites and stings. My husband found the tree, cleared an opening into the great prostrate log, traversed its unspeakable odors for nearly 40 feet to its farthest recess and brought the baby and egg to the light in his leaflike hat. We could endure the location only by dipping napkins into deodorant and binding them to our mouths and nostrils. Every third day for almost three months we made this trip . . .

IN HER PHOTOGRAPHIC work the surroundings were usually left undisturbed with the exception of tying back a branch here and there to allow sufficient light for exposure. For a photograph of an oriole's nest, two long painter's ladders were lashed to a telegraph pole. The camera was then fastened to the pole above the ladders, enabling the photographer to focus on the nest hanging in an adjacent tree. For each exposure in the series Mrs. Stratton-Porter had to climb down the ladders to change plates and reset the shutter.

The photographer's work with moths required an equal, if not greater, degree of patience. For more than 12 years she gathered material for her book, *Moths of the Limberlost.* Mrs. Stratton-Porter added greatly to the knowledge of her time about these silently beautiful creatures of the night.

The time and care that Gene Stratton-Porter demanded of herself in her photographic work is evident in her prints. Their quality and crispness was so exceptional that the Eastman Kodak Company sent an executive to the Limberlost cabin to observe her methods of development. Mrs. Stratton-Porter was too embarrassed to let him know that she used the family bathroom for a darkroom, stuffing rags around the doors and windows to make the room totally dark. For developing trays she appropriated the family turkey platters. Instead of confessing these "techniques" to Kodak, the photographer gave credit to her husband, a competent druggist, for his accurate mixing of the finest photographic chemicals money could buy—and to certain special qualities of the local water.

In 1913 the draining of the Limberlost began. Pressure to make the rich swampland productive—and the lure of oil—finally put an end to Mrs. Stratton-Porter's wild laboratory. While searching for a fitting place to continue her work in the wild, Mrs. Stratton-Porter remembered visits to Sylvan Lake, near Rome City, Indiana. In 1914 the Porters moved permanently to the new cabin which they built on 150 acres of woodland along the lake shore. They named their new home "Wildflower Woods" and set about turning the property into a preserve for birds and wild things.

This new cabin contained a bona fide darkroom where Mrs. Stratton-Porter continued her photographic work. There she sensed the rhythms and pace of the natural world. Calmly and with extreme care, she communicated to her subjects that they had nothing to fear from her. Then, as she wrote, she would take "sufficient time and patience until they became so accustomed to me that they would live out their lives before my lenses."

During her first two years at "Wildflower Woods," Gene Stratton-Porter brought in and set the roots of more than 3,000 trees, shrubs and wildflowers. Many of these plants were rare species, gathered in the last days of Limberlost and transplanted to help save them from extinction. She gathered the delicate fringed gentians, lady's-slipper orchids, wood lilies and other fine wildflowers to accompany cultivated flowers in their formal gardens. Other wildflowers were placed in the woods to be appreciated in their natural settings. An unusually large specimen of a jack-in-the-pulpit, transplanted by Mrs. Stratton-Porter 50 years ago, still emerges every spring near the grape arbor. The state of Indiana today maintains both the Limberlost cabin and the "Wildflower Woods" property at Sylvan Lake as state memorials.

Perhaps some words of her daughter Jeannette best capture the spirit of Gene Stratton-Porter: "In the old days, when we did field work together, I have seen her stop the horse, clamber down from the buggy, and straighten a wildflower, broken by some careless foot, pat the dirt around it, prop it up with a stick or stone, straighten the petals and leaves carefully, and give it a drink from her thermos bottle."

In 1919 Mrs. Stratton-Porter entered on a new career in Hollywood. With her usual energy and independence, she organized and financed her own movie company, then adapted and supervised the production of her story of an orphaned newsboy, *Michael O'Halloran.* She continued to write about and to photograph wildlife, often hiking in the canyons surrounding Los Angeles.

In 1924, still filled with her passion for the wild and the desire to show this world to others, she died, at the age of 61, following an automobile accident. ❧

THE LAST INTERVIEW WITH BENTON MAC KAYE (1879–1975)

by CONSTANCE L. STALLINGS

He started the Appalachian Trail, helped found The Wilderness Society, was an early advocate of garden cities, and devised a plan for the "Townless Highway."

IN THE BRILLIANT spring sun, the fine old clapboard house looked promising, but the question that had bothered me all the way to Shirley Center, Massachusetts, last May was still large in my mind. What could I expect from a man who was 96?

Benton MacKaye was born on March 6, 1879, only 14 years after the end of the Civil War. He had a fascinating, almost unbelievable career in conservation. He helped found The Wilderness Society. He worked as a forester under Gifford Pinchot, the man responsible for much of President Theodore Roosevelt's conservation program. He was an early advocate of garden cities. And he started

MacKaye in 1946, while attending a meeting of The Wilderness Society's Governing Council in Shenandoah National Park, Virginia. He was president of The Wilderness Society from 1945 to 1950.

PHOTO: COURTESY OF THE WILDERNESS SOCIETY

the Appalachian Trail. It was Mac-Kaye's association with the Appalachian Trail that had brought me to Shirley Center.

As I look back now on the visit, it has become tremendously important—an honor, really—for MacKaye was in the final year of his long life.

How much would MacKaye remember? My concern had grown along with my series of transfers from taxi to plane to taxi to bus. Would he be interested in answering my questions? Would he be able to hear them?

I crossed the lawn, soon to need its first mowing of the season, and stepped into the low-ceilinged, center-hall colonial with its wide-plank floor. There was scarcely time to admire the architecture, though, for MacKaye was standing just to the right, in the doorway to the dining room. Tall and erect, he wore a Scottish tartan robe. His white hair was neatly combed. Hand outstretched, he gave me a courtly welcome. Then he led me into the dining room.

A collection of antique lustre dishes caught my eye, several black stenciled tole trays stood against the walls and African violets bloomed in the center of the dining room table. MacKaye seated me in the corner nearest the front door, opposite an upholstered armchair where he sat

down himself. Index cards and other desk items were arranged close at hand on a window sill. Obviously, I thought, this man likes visitors and has many of them.

Unfortunately, the subject I had come to hear about, MacKaye's founding of the Appalachian Trail in 1921, was not what he wanted to discuss. Instead, he wanted to talk about the Pacific Northwest Trail, 1975. He knew that this trail, as proposed, will connect the Montana Rockies with the Pacific Ocean, but he wanted details, and he expected me to supply them. My questions had to wait while *he* questioned *me.*

"Will the trail begin at the point in Glacier National Park where the waters divide and drain three ways? What towns will the trail pass on its way across Washington State? What is the route for getting around Puget Sound to the Olympic Peninsula?" . . . Feeling hopelessly ignorant, I promised to have someone send him the answers. At least I knew that a bill for the creation of the trail had recently been introduced in the Senate. "By *which* senators?" he wanted to know. "Henry Jackson and Warren Magnuson of Washington? Good!"

HAVING EXTRACTED everything I knew about the Pacific Northwest Trail, MacKaye was willing to reminisce about his life. Although he wore no hearing aid, he had trouble seeing, and his eyes squinted under his bushy eyebrows as he talked. He spoke slowly and clearly, repeating sometimes like a professor making sure the students in the back row won't miss anything.

"I came to live in the house next-door in 1888," he said. It is still there, a smaller version of the house where he lived now. Shirley Center was then essentially a farming community. (Today it is a picturebook New England village—shade trees, winding roads, unnumbered houses and no sidewalks.) MacKaye attended the proverbial little red schoolhouse. But at age 12 while visiting in Washington, D.C., he was exposed to two important influences: Robert E. Peary talking about a forthcoming voyage to the Arctic, and John Wesley Powell lecturing on his explorations of the Grand Canyon.

Inspired by their spirit of adventure and the collections he'd seen in

the Smithsonian Institution, MacKaye decided to investigate the status of nature in his own surroundings in northern Massachusetts. When he was 14, he covered the countryside in a score of "expeditions," each of which he mapped and wrote up, with emphasis on the geography and plant and animal life. These trips marked the beginning of his concern for the land and of his appreciation of wilderness recreation.

Then he attended Harvard University, acquiring an A.B. degree and a master's degree in forestry. The year he received the master's was 1905.

Today we take national parks and forests, and many other areas protected by assorted public and private administrations, for granted. But in 1905 there were no national forests in the eastern United States. (There were few forests of any kind in the East because of the thorough clearcutting that had taken place during the nineteenth century.) There was no National Park Service; the U.S. Army cared for a handful of national parks, all in the West. Railroads were still new in many places, automobiles an absolute novelty. "Planning" was a meaningless word. Who needed it?— the growth of cities was viewed as A Good Thing. Audubon warden Guy Bradley was murdered with impunity by a plume hunter in 1905. Hardly anyone cared about the conservation of natural resources, and environmental awareness was at rock bottom.

But 1905 was also a time of change; the U.S. Forest Service was organized that year under Gifford Pinchot, who was interested in the conservation not only of trees but of all resources.

"I was in the Forest Service when it was started," MacKaye told me. "I knew Gifford Pinchot well. Those Pinchot–Roosevelt days were grand!"

Pinchot dispatched MacKaye to the White Mountains, which he had first visited in the summer of 1897 and considered his "home" mountains. ("I started on my bike with two other men. It took several days to get there. We all wore knapsacks of canvas.") MacKaye spent three months making a survey of forest cover. His conclusion, that the forests had an effect on the flow of the streams, helped lead to the establishment of national forests in New Hampshire and elsewhere in the East, from Maine to Florida, under the Weeks Act of 1911. This act and the National Park Service Act of 1916 are considered the two most important early conservation measures of the century. MacKaye has said, "I took more satisfaction from that job than any other I've done."

DURING THE TEENS, MacKaye began to realize that there was more to forestry than the scientific management of forests and that the use or nonuse of the country's riches had social consequences. So in 1918 he transferred to the Department of Labor, where they were trying to create jobs by using natural resources. He was put to work preparing a report on how to do it. In the course of this study and others that followed, he developed advanced views on conservation, the elimination of land speculation by public ownership, and the colonization of land into community units as a means of solving labor problems. In other words, he turned from a forester into a planner.

It was in connection with his Labor Department planning that MacKaye developed the idea for the Appalachian Trail. His original notion called for several features long since forgotten: shelter camps where city workers might spend vacations, farm communities and even industrial centers. MacKaye broached the trail idea in 1921 to Charles H. Whitaker, editor of the *Journal of the American Institute of Architects,* and Clarence S. Stein, chairman of the AIA's Committee on Community Planning. They liked it, and he wrote an article entitled "An Appalachian Trail, A Project in Regional Planning," which was published in the October 1921 issue of the AIA *Journal.* Many hiking clubs, government organizations and individual citizens were immediately interested, and the idea took root. The longest marked footpath in the world was on its way.

The first section of trail was completed the following year in New York State. "Some of us made a trail across Bear Mountain Park," Mac-Kaye told me. The field work there was done mainly by the Palisades Interstate Park Trail Conference, which had been formed several years earlier to develop trails in the Palisades preserve. When the group later expanded its efforts to build additional sections

of the Appalachian Trail east to the border of Connecticut and west to the Delaware River, it changed its name to the New York–New Jersey Trail Conference. It is still a going concern.

Then, in 1925, the Appalachian Trail Conference was organized in Washington, D.C., to further construction of the trail. It divvied up the trail and allotted each section to a committee whose members worked with local hiking organizations. Except for the linking of four existing trail systems (in the White and Green mountains, and the Connecticut River and Palisades Interstate Park areas), the job was a matter of pioneering.

"A lot of groups worked very hard on the trail," MacKaye recalled. "If I started to name names, I'd leave someone out who shouldn't be left out. But Clarence Stein was as much a founder as I was. He died just last February [1975] at the age of 92. And Major Welch was also very influential, a very important man." Major W.A. Welch had been in the army ("It might have been the Spanish War"), was general manager of the Palisades Interstate Park, served as the first chairman of the Appalachian Trail Conference and designed the AT trail markers. Originally made of embossed copper, they became so popular as souvenirs that they were later replaced by less expensive diamond-shaped markers of sheet iron. These are the markers seen today.

TRAIL WORK IN THE twenties and thirties had its ups and downs, what with innumerable problems of trail location and fluctuating enthusiasm. But newly formed Appalachian Trail clubs as well as individuals working on their own persevered, routing and clearing each section of trail bit by bit. Finally, in 1937, with the completion of a two-mile section on Mount Sugarloaf in Maine, and a one-mile section in the Great Smoky Mountains, the trail was finished, 15 years after the initial effort. It is 2,031 miles long and passes through 14 states. Although many changes have since been made in the route, they do not detract from the achievement.

MacKaye, nevertheless, was not content to stop there.

Two years after revealing his inspired trail idea, he and some friends founded the Regional Planning Association of America. A small

body, with never more than 20 members, the group had as its leaders Clarence Stein and writer Lewis Mumford. The association wanted to deter the haphazard growth of cities by planning entire regions so as to preserve natural resources and provide recreation areas and gardens for everybody's use. One result of its pioneering planning was Sunnyside Gardens in Long Island City, New York, a housing project for mixed-income families. From that grew an even more successful experiment, the "new town" of Radburn, New Jersey. These two projects were America's first garden cities.

Working together, MacKaye and Mumford edited a magazine that predicted an approaching strangulation of city life because of overcrowding. In 1928 MacKaye wrote a book called *The New Exploration* that outlined a practical regional approach to metropolitan problems. It became a classic and is still in print.

THEN IN 1931 in an article in *Harper's,* MacKaye described a plan he'd devised for a "Townless Highway." The townless highway of 1931 can be recognized as the expressway of today. Although we now may not appreciate having the countryside thoroughly laced by super-highways, MacKaye's brilliance in inventing a way to make cities more pleasant places should be recognized. As Mumford put it in *The Urban Prospect*: "In the Appalachian Trail and the Townless Highway this spiritual descendant of Thoreau effectually visualized the backbone of a better environment."

Incredibly, MacKaye wasn't through yet. "I was one of the eight founders of The Wilderness Society," he told me matter of factly, with only the slightest touch of well-deserved pride. "I was in Knoxville with the T.V.A. [Tennessee Valley Authority] and knew Harvey Broome. He was a lawyer but spent most of his time outdoors. Robert Marshall came down in July of 1934 to fight plans for roads along the top of the Appalachians. They were very controversial. . . Horace Albright? Yes, he had been director of the National Park Service during the battle over a sky-line road down the Smokies. I knew him slightly. A fine man, always very nice to me. . . Four years earlier Marshall had written a magazine article for the American Association for the Advancement of Science magazine, suggesting there should be an organization for the wilderness. I'd met him the year before in Washington. Harvey and I told Marshall it was time to start his society.

"In January of '35," he continued, "we formally organized The Wilderness Society. Eight of us were founders: Marshall, Ernest Oberholtzer, Robert Sterling Yard, Aldo Leopold, Harold Anderson, Broome, Bernard Frank and myself. Marshall was a rich young man. He put up the money. He paid Yard a salary to run it. Yard was executive director for 10 years, and then he died. I was made vice-president right from the start. When Yard died I was made acting president, and then president from '45 to '50.

"Marshall died on the Pullman going to meet his brother in New York City. I'd seen him just a few nights before. Howard Zahniser took over Yard's job and built the membership way up. He was there for 19 years and was the father of the Wilderness Bill. President Johnson signed it in September of '64. Zahniser didn't live long enough to see it signed, but he knew it would be. He died suddenly. It's very strange—Marshall, Zahniser and Broome all did."

MACKAYE REMAINED with the federal government during the thirties and forties. "I was in the Indian Service for a while in Arizona. And in St. Louis for a couple of years with the Rural Electrification Administration." That program brought electricity to 27 million farm people in the relatively short period of 15 years.

"In 1945 I retired," he concluded. "I considered Shirley Center home because I moved to the house next-door in 1888. Since then I've lived in these two houses off and on. My work has taken me to all the states except Alaska and Hawaii, but I've always come back here. When I was a boy, the Stone family lived in *this* house."

"This" house actually belongs to Lucy (Mrs. Harold P.) Johnson, a lively lady who bakes a mean brownie. Her husband was the nephew of the Stone boy whom MacKaye played with when he was growing up. To MacKaye's amusement, I had made arrangements for my interview believing that Mrs. Johnson was related to MacKaye, who, it turned out, had always been a bachelor. "I believe you thought Lucy was my daughter," he laughed. "It's just the other way around. She's my mother!"

The year MacKaye retired, a bill was introduced in Congress to create a national system of foot trails, of which the Appalachian Trail would have been one. The bill was pigeon-holed. A second try was made a few years later, but that bill was never reported out of committee. Finally, in 1968, with the passage of the National Trails System Act (P.L. 90-543), the Appalachian and Pacific Crest trails became the country's first national scenic trails.

Despite the federal protection, MacKaye said he was concerned about the Appalachian Trail, fearing that a complete permit system might be inevitable. "I don't see how they can do otherwise. There are so very many people at once." He declared emphatically: "What I hope is that it won't turn into a racetrack. I for one would give the prize to the person who took the longest time."

HE DESCRIBED A proposal to ease the crush by building a trail connection between the Appalachian Trail and the Bruce Trail in Ontario. "It would use some of the existing Finger Lakes trails and cross into Canada at Niagara Falls." The idea is three or four years old and is under consideration by the Appalachian Trail Conference.

MacKaye listened attentively as I described an idea I'd read about in Charlton Ogburn's recent book, *The Southern Appalachians*. It would extend the Appalachian Trail in two branches: from the Blue Ridge Mountains north through the Alleghenies, Poconos and Catskills to the Adirondacks, and from the Blue Ridge Mountains south through the Black Mountains to the vicinity of Tallulah Falls, Georgia. MacKaye focused inwardly with great concentration on maps he'd learned long ago and summoned up the names of several towns he thought the double-pronged extension might skirt.

It would be a mistake, however, to say that MacKaye loved only long trails. A favorite path of his is short and closer to home—the Wapack Trail, running 21 miles from Mount Watatic in Massachusetts north to the Pack Mountains in New Hampshire. It was built many years ago and there used to be a lodge on it. "Only the other day I got a notice saying it's being kept up," he said with pleasure.

Furthermore, he maintained an open mind about additional trail possibilities. He was intrigued by two trails I mentioned—the Illinois Prairie Path and Wisconsin's Elroy–Sparta Trail—which occupy abandoned railroad rights-of-way. "Still," he sighed, "it's a shame about the railroads."

As for his other major interest, The Wilderness Society, MacKaye volunteered that Stewart M. Brandborg, who replaced Howard Zahniser as executive director, was "doing a fine job." He liked "that thing that came from Brandy"—a hard-hitting poster about wildlife ranges that the society had mailed to its members. He did *not* mention that he and Ernest Oberholtzer, at the time the only surviving founders of the organization, were honorary president and vice-president. But he commented with a chuckle that the organization's current president, Thurman Trosper, "must have as much trouble with his name as I've had with mine." The second syllable of "MacKaye" does not rhyme with "hay," as most people assume, but with "high."

By then several hours had passed, and it was time for me to catch the last bus back to Boston. I stood up, and MacKaye did, too. Shaking my hand with formality, he thanked me for coming and said, "Don't forget that I want to know about the Pacific Northwest Trail."

John R. Ross, a former assistant professor of history at Virginia Polytechnic Institute and State University, is now writing a biography of Benton MacKaye. As I stepped out into the late-afternoon sunlight, I thought to myself that when the book appears, many thousands of walkers, hikers and backpackers would become aware of what this grand old man of conservation did for them. And then he would no longer have trouble with his name.

But the recognition, sadly, is already belated. Benton MacKaye died on December 11, 1975. ▰

BOB MARSHALL (1901–1939)

by ORVILLE E. BACH, JR.

Bob Marshall became a backpacking, canoeing, and conservationist legend in his brief 38 years.

"As a boy," recalled Robert Marshall, "I spent many hours in the heart of New York City, dreaming of Lewis and Clark and their glorious exploration into an unbroken wilderness. Occasionally," he added, "my reveries ended in a terrible depression, and I would imagine that I had been born a century too late for genuine excitement."

In part, of course, he was quite right. Most of the vast wilderness of the Lewis and Clark era had long since vanished by the turn of the century when Marshall was born. Nevertheless, in subsequent years, Marshall's love for the wilderness resulted in his making extensive hikes in the most remote corners of America's remaining wild areas.

By the time he was 36, Marshall had taken in the wilderness more than 200 day-hikes of 30 miles, 51 day-hikes of 40 miles; and several of up to 70 miles. With his brother George, and Herbert Clark, an Adirondack guide and close friend, he was the first to climb all 46 of the peaks above 4,000 feet in the Adirondacks.

Although Bob Marshall's physical accomplishments and explorations deserve legendary status, it was his contributions as a forester, administrator, author, lecturer and humanist which established him as one of America's true champions of the wilderness.

Bob Marshall was born January 2, 1901, to Louis and Florence Lowenstein Marshall in the brownstone house in New York City which his family occupied for more than 30 years. His father was a prominent and wealthy constitutional lawyer, and also a leader in Jewish affairs, a philanthropist, a fighter for minority rights and a conservationist.

Bob had two brothers, James and George, and a sister, Ruth, all of whom eventually obtained advanced degrees and entered a variety of professions. During most of the year, Bob's activities centered on the Marshall house, and from the third grade through high school, on the Ethical Culture School in New York City, from which he graduated in 1919.

The most favored part of the year for Bob was unquestionably summer. He spent his first 21 summers at the Marshalls' family camp, Knollwood, on Lower Saranac Lake in the heart of the Adirondacks in northern New York. He jumped at the chance to explore the Adirondack backcountry with his brother George and Herb Clark, and it wasn't long before his passion for wilderness was ignited. He climbed his first mountain, Ampersand, on August 15, 1916, and in 1918 his first high Adirondack peaks—Whiteface, Marcy, Algonquin and Iroquois. His first book, *High Peaks of the Adirondacks,* printed in 1922, was an account of the ascent of Adirondack peaks more than 4,000 feet high.

The issue of wilderness preservation came into prominence during Marshall's boyhood. When he was 13, his father successfully fought to retain the "forever wild" clause in the state constitution to protect New York's Adirondack State Forest Preserve. In later years Louis Marshall hardly needed to persuade his son to continue the wilderness "missionary work."

When he was only a high school junior, Marshall realized: "I love the woods and solitude . . . I should hate to spend the greater part of my lifetime in a stuffy office or in a crowded city." At the age of 15, while among his beloved Adirondacks, he made the decision to become a forester.

After attending Columbia College for a year, in 1920 he entered the New York State College of Forestry in Syracuse and was awarded a bachelor of science degree in 1924. That summer he entered the U.S. Forest Service and was assigned to the Wind River Forest Experiment Station in Washington. In 1925 he earned a master of forestry degree at Harvard University. From 1925-28 Marshall served as a junior forester, and later, as assistant silviculturist at the Forest Service's Northern Rocky Mountain Forest and Range Experiment Station in Missoula, Montana. During those years he spent as much time as possible exploring the great Montana outdoors, especially the Flathead South Fork wilderness region which now bears his name.

With growing qualifications, Marshall saw his career with the U.S. Forest Service blossom rapidly, and soon he began to extend his talents as a lecturer and writer. He was deeply concerned about the plight of our nation's forests and freely expressed his thoughts and opinions.

He was soon recognized as a powerful voice in Washington. Even the strongest of skeptics found themselves occasionally pondering what this articulate man had to say about wilderness values.

In the 1930s Marshall's fight to preserve wild areas was complicated by the fact that so few people visited the wilderness—far from the situation nowadays. He consequently had to present a convincing argument for preservation to the nonwilderness users while concurrently campaigning for more use.

In 1937 he presented to the public in *Nature* Magazine a classic entitled "The Universe of the Wilderness Is Vanishing," which offered a heartfelt plea for saving what wilderness remained. "The universe of the wilderness, all over the United States," wrote Marshall, "is vanishing with appalling rapidity. It is melting away like the last snowbank on some south-facing mountainside during a hot afternoon in June. It is disappearing while most of those who care more for it than anything else in the world are trying desperately to rally and save it."

Anticipating such negative responses as "What's the difference; where's the loss?" he added that the wilderness "is the last stand for that glorious adventure into the physically unknown that was commonplace in the lives of our ancestors . . . It is also the perfect esthetic experience because it appeals to all of the senses. It is vast panoramas, full of height and depth and glowing color, on a scale so overwhelming as to wipe out the ordinary meaning of dimensions. It is the song of the hermit thrush at twilight and the lapping of waves against the shoreline and the melody of the wind in the trees. It is the unique odor of balsams and of freshly turned humus and of mist rising from mountain meadows. It is the feel of spruce needles under foot and sunshine on your face and wind blowing through your hair. It is all of these at the same time, blended into a unity that can only be appreciated with leisure and which is ruined by artificiality." Surely, it was a rare individual who could read such an eloquent passage without being stirred by Marshall's love of the outdoors.

Marshall considered the wilderness skeptics' standard argument that rec-

reational land should always be managed for maximum use utterly ridiculous. He believed that any evaluation regarding recreation should take into consideration quality as well as quantity. When confronted with the typical "Why should we set aside a vast area for the enjoyment of a few hundred people when roads would make that area available for half a million?" he countered with:

"The doctrine of the greatest good to the greatest number does not mean that this laudable relationship has to take place on every acre. If it did, we would be forced to change our metropolitan art galleries into metropolitan bowling alleys. Our state universities, which are used by a minor fraction of the population, would be converted into state circuses where hundreds could be exhilarated for every one person who may be either exhilarated or depressed now. The Library of Congress would become a national hot dog stand, and the new Supreme Court building would be converted into a gigantic garage where it could house a thousand people's autos instead of Nine Gentlemen of the Law." To Marshall, his analogy was no more preposterous than the notions of his skeptics who adhered to the land management policy of maximum use.

While assigned to Missoula with the Forest Service, Marshall began championing the wilderness as early as 1928 when he wrote an article in the *Forest Service Bulletin* enlisting support to preserve portions of the national forests in their natural state. The following year he enthusiastically endorsed the Service's adoption of the "L" regulation which provided for the establishment of primitive areas. Though this new movement was encouraging, it was only a beginning to Marshall, who desired a more comprehensive and restrictive policy for protecting the wilderness.

In an attempt to achieve this goal he prepared a complete inventory of remaining American forest lands, proposing a zoning system for recreational use. "Superlative" areas denoted regions of splendid natural beauty, such as Yellowstone and Yosemite; "Wilderness" and "Primeval" areas both included uninhabited forest; and rounding out his survey were categories of "Roadside,"

"Camp-Site," "Outing" and "Residence" areas. He proposed that a total of 45 million acres of forest be set aside in all categories, or approximately 9 percent of the nation's commercial timberland. In 1932 his recommendations appeared in the Forest Service's report, "A National Plan for American Forests."

Marshall soon felt the need for a greater understanding of nature's forces at work and in 1929 he left for Johns Hopkins University, where in the spring of 1930 he was awarded a doctorate degree in plant physiology. In the summer of 1929, research for the degree provided him with an excuse to journey to the basin of the Koyukuk River within the Arctic Circle in Alaska. There he found land wild enough to meet the requirements of his boyhood dreams. His enthusiasm for the country and its scattered denizens was so intense that after graduation he departed for a 13-months' sojourn in the tiny Eskimo village of Wiseman in the Koyukuk watershed.

Marshall spent 21 summers exploring the Adirondacks, often with his good friend Herb Clark.
PHOTO: GEORGE MARSHALL, COURTESY OF THE LIVING WILDERNESS.

Despite his great love for the outdoors, Marshall rated the human values of the fascinating community of Eskimos first and gave of himself freely. He delved deeply into the lives of inhabitants of Wiseman and neighboring communities. He observed, interpreted and recorded every phase of life. The result was the first accurate map of the region, compiled after many first ascents of unnamed peaks, and *Arctic Village* (1933), a best seller, Literary Guild selection and probably his most important book. It was based on his observations and analysis of life in the Koyukuk region. *Arctic Village* inspired many fine reviews, such as one from *Forum* which called it "an unusually interesting and valuable sociological document, fit to join the works of Malinowsky and Margaret Mead, but more humanly appealing than either."

"It is obvious by the very wealth and detail of his information," *Forum* continued, "that these men and women loved, trusted, and respected Mr. Marshall. They told him things they never would have revealed to a purely scientific researcher, and we are the gainers thereby. *Arctic Village* will be a source book for sociologists, but most of us will remember it chiefly as the personal biography of a wilderness settlement. It has humor, and it also has dignity and nobility."

According to *Arctic Village*, "The inhabitants of the Koyukuk would rather eat beans with liberty, burn candles with independence, and mush dogs with adventure, than to have the luxury and restrictions of the outside world." Marshall revealed later that his 13 months in Wiseman were the most glorious of his life.

Following completion of *Arctic Village*, Marshall continued to exercise his considerable writing talents by beginning a book dealing with the American forests. As a forester, he was as concerned with proper forest management as he was with wilderness preservation. His chief contribution to forest policy occurred with the publication in 1933 of *The People's Forest*. In this book he traced the evolution of America's forests from the time the Pilgrims set foot on the New England shore to the devastating cut-and-run years which had extended into his own lifetime.

Although he felt satisfied with the record of public forest management,

Marshall expressed particular concern for private forests: "Under their present management, the American forests are drifting into constantly expanding ruin. Year by year the area of devastated lands keeps mounting, until today it has reached the appalling total of 83 million acres, to which nearly a million acres are being added annually ... The major cause of this sorry plight is the mismanagement of privately owned forests ... When this miserable failure is contrasted with the splendid record of public forest management, the moral seems inescapable."

Marshall suggested that the government purchase private forests so that effective management could be realized—a socialistic proposal that raised quite a few eyebrows, even though at the time the depression had prompted many loyal Americans to seriously question the capitalistic, free-enterprise system. Additionally, since little evidence of wise management in private forestry existed, Marshall probably underestimated the ability of private foresters to apply conservation principles.

I wonder what Marshall's opinion would be of public vs. private forest management today. During the last 40 years the Forest Service has changed and recently has drawn sharp criticism. I wonder what the Forest Service would be like today if Robert Marshall had only lived a normal life span. Private forest companies and many conservationists have observed that with present Forest Service timber-cutting practices, some areas will eventually have no more timber to be harvested.

I have personally examined the steep, cleanly shaven mountainsides of Montana's Bitterroots where clearcutting practices seem to violate the most basic principles of forest management. I witnessed attempts by the Forest Service, without having sought public opinion, to build a "recreation road" through the heart of what is now the Lincoln-Scapegoat Wilderness. If it had not been for one man— Cecil Garland of Lincoln, Montana— they might have succeeded. The Wilderness Society said in its 1973 annual report that its conflict with the Service regarding clearcutting and an apparent "desire to wipe out than to find wilderness potential" was one of its 10 major issues of concern.

With completion of *The People's Forest,* Marshall had to make a decision. Should he return to his beloved Arctic for further exploration and study? Should he go back to the U.S. Forest Service? Or should he devote himself to the intensely acute social problems boiling across the country? The year was 1933. Commissioner John Collier of the Bureau of Indian Affairs induced Marshall to take up the problems of the Indians and their forests.

Marshall became director of forestry for the Bureau of Indian Affairs. From his office he besieged government officials with phone calls, letters and personal visits on behalf of wilderness preservation. It was not uncommon for him to gather together a cross-section of people—congressmen, professional government officials, prima donna "brain trusters," various and sundry promoters—to hand them a dubious drink, and then insist that they seriously consider and debate a particular topic relating to the management of environmental resources. His acute observation, fearlessness and uncompromising integrity, together with his capacity for hard work and intense devotion to his cause, made him one of the most valued of government officials.

Through his unwearied zeal, a new "wilderness awareness" began to pervade Washington. In a 1934 memorandum to Secretary of the Interior Harold Ickes, Marshall issued a plea to keep roads out of undeveloped areas within his jurisdiction to preserve a "certain value of the timeless, the mysterious ... in a world overrun by split-second schedules, physical certainty, and man-made superficiality." Conceding that the nation faced other serious problems in 1934, he nevertheless felt that for a vast number of Americans "the most important passion of life is the overpowering desire to escape periodically from the clutches of a mechanistic civilization. To us the enjoyment of solitude, complete independence, and the beauty of undefiled panoramas is absolutely essential to happiness."

Marshall hoped that Secretary Ickes, as an advocate of national planning, would coordinate and help lead a program of preservation to be carried out by the Forest Service, National Park Service, Public Land Of-

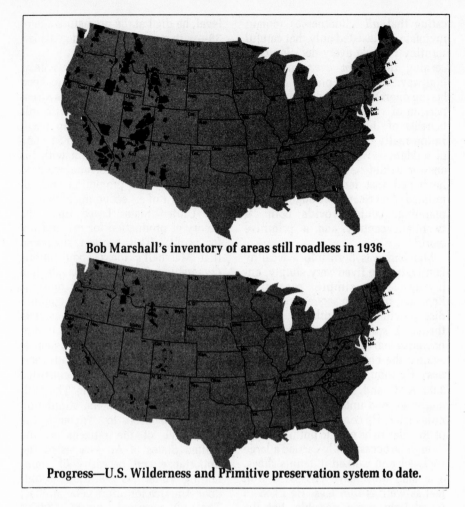

Bob Marshall's inventory of areas still roadless in 1936.

Progress—U.S. Wilderness and Primitive preservation system to date.

fice, Office of Indian Affairs, and state and private forest owners. He followed up his initial thrust with a lengthy paper to Secretary Ickes proposing which wilderness areas might be preserved. He recommended that a "Wilderness Planning Board," free of "stuffed shirts," be created to select areas to be preserved by act of Congress "just as National Parks are today set aside." Such unprecedented legal preservation differed sharply from existing government policy and marked Marshall as a radical, especially among some foresters. Nevertheless, his proposal anticipated in amazing detail the congressional action of 1964 establishing the National Wilderness Preservation System.

During the heyday of the New Deal, Marshall expressed concern about threats posed to wild country by public works projects. "What makes wilderness areas most susceptible to annihilation," he declared, "is that the arguments in favor of roads are direct and concrete, while those against them are subtle and difficult to express." But if anyone could express

them, Marshall could, and he cornered anyone who would listen. John Collier, Marshall's immediate supervisor, soon found himself caught up in the enthusiasm of his director of forestry. On October 25, 1937, Collier approved a Marshall plan creating 16 wilderness reserves on Indian reservations.

Yet Marshall realized that the bulk of remaining wilderness areas was located in the national forests and took care to maintain his earlier contacts with the Forest Service. Numerous Marshall memoranda on national forest wilderness areas were delivered directly to Chief Forester F. A. Silcox, who was impressed enough to invite him to express his ideas before a conference of western foresters in 1935.

The following year Marshall continued to apply pressure by preparing, along with Althea Dobbins, an inventory-map at his own expense of all remaining roadless areas larger than 300,000 acres in the United States. Of the 46 areas, 32 were in western national forests. Marshall

submitted the inventory and his recommendations to the appropriate regional foresters. There was no immediate action on his proposals, but in May, 1937, Chief Forester Silcox appointed Marshall to head the Service's Division of Recreation and Lands.

Immediately after attaining this position, Marshall made plans for enlarging the number of wilderness areas under Forest Service jurisdiction. During the summers of 1937-39 he seized the opportunity to return to his beloved backcountry to make inspection trips. Such work assignments became play for him because they deeply penetrated some of the nation's great wildernesses. They were followed by recommendations for placing nearly every roadless area of more than 100,000 acres into "Primitive" classification.

Marshall was eventually responsible for adding 5,437,000 acres to the Forest Service wilderness system. His most prized achievement occurred in September, 1939, with the adoption of the "U" regulations, which absolutely prohibited logging and road building in all areas designated "Wilderness" (100,000 acres or more) and "Wild" (5,000-10,000 acres). Although the process of reclassification would take time, and the new regulations did not automatically apply, they did extend wilderness status to more than 14 million acres in the West. Several of our greatest forest wildernesses, such as the Pasayten and the Three Sisters in the Cascades, and the mighty Selway-Bitterroot in the Rockies, were established under Marshall's powerful influence.

While Marshall was doing what he could in government circles to preserve wilderness, he also provided leadership for private citizens. In 1930 he had warned that the only hope for staving off an all-conquering civilization was an "organization of spirited people who will fight for the freedom of the wilderness."

After considerable organizational work designed to mobilize all friends of the American wilderness, not just a single region, Marshall and his colleagues declared on January 21, 1935: "For the purpose of fighting off invasion of the wilderness and of stimulating ... appreciation of its multiform emotional, intellectual, and scientific values, we are forming an organization to be known as The Wilderness Society." Headquarters were established in Washington, D.C., and the society proposed to defend wild country wherever it was in jeopardy. For the first few years Marshall was almost entirely responsible for the group's financial support. Gradually, membership increased. Today, The Wilderness Society continues to uphold Marshall's ideals and is recognized as one of the most politically influential conservation organizations in America.

Although Marshall's successful campaigns for wilderness preservation were his greatest achievements, he made other worthy contributions during his brief 38-year life span. He loved mankind and often expressed deep concern for human rights and civil liberties. To this cause he gave unstintingly of his time, means and great energy.

Though he never published anything in the field of social reform, he frequently expressed his position on general issues and defended his right and that of other government workers to do so. His long-range hopes for a better social order with more civil liberties paralleled his long-range views regarding proper use and management of the forests. One year before his death, Marshall wrote to a friend who had just been defeated in an election:

"We're all young enough that we'll probably meet many defeats in the next fifty years in the struggle for civil liberties and a decent economic system for this country and for democracy in the world at large. It's even conceivable that when we die we still will not have won the fight. That's happened before to many generations of people who have been working for goals which would make human beings happier. But win or lose, it will be grand fun fighting and knowing that whatever we do in the right direction will help eventual victory."

Marshall was aware that only a minority of the nation's population could visit his beloved wild areas, so he did everything in his capacity to create low cost recreational opportunities while he was in charge of the Forest Service's Division of Recreation and Lands.

Marshall was never considered a wilderness extremist; he was really quite reasonable. Rather than advocating that *all* wildernesses remain inviolate, he insisted only that careful scrutiny precede every decision concerning them. For every proposed highway, irrigation project or lumbering operation, he called for a comparison of values: "Do the increased benefits of this extension of civilization really compensate for the loss of wilderness values?" He knew the answer would never be simple. Yet, he hoped that far-sighted and fair-minded Americans, through careful planning, could provide both "a twentieth century and a primitive world."

Marshall was born into a wealthy family, but he lived very simply, enjoying life's simple pleasures. Repeated trips into sequestered paradise provided him with his greatest thrills. A spiritually and physically powerful man, he often tested himself against the challenges of the wilderness. He thought nothing of rising at 3:00 A.M. and starting a hike that might not end until 19 hours and 50 miles later. He considered a day hike of 20 miles to be next to nothing, even though he occasionally carried a large rucksack and walked in tennis shoes. The man must have possessed iron feet as well as iron legs. He liked to travel light when possible, but the mileages he covered in a single day are doubly incredible when you consider that today's ultra-light gear was not available.

Marshall's wilderness exploration occasionally produced unplanned, hair-raising adventures that ranged from the close call of bumping into an irate grizzly sow in the Selway-Bitterroot (his immediate thoughts at the moment of charge: "Theirs not to wonder why, theirs but to climb or die") to surviving electrical storms atop mountain summits, but he always managed to emerge unscathed. Once, when the boat in which he was traveling shattered against arctic ice, plummeting him into dark, freezing waters, he felt his time had surely come. His thoughts, as he later recorded them, were: "Gosh, I wish I had time to think over all the swell experiences of my 37 years before dying—to have the fun of recalling them just once more before I go." He survived the ordeal, but he was to live for only one more year.

Just as Marshall's influence in Washington was reaching its highest level, he died at the premature age of 38—with many projects and goals left in the balance.

Marshall was aware that his heart was weak, yet was reluctant to heed medical advice to abandon his strenuous tempo of life. Perhaps with this in mind he carefully made up a will which distributed more than $1,500,-000 in a manner consistent with his ideals. Half of the fortune went to trustees for "the promotion and advancement of an economic system in the United States based upon the theory of production for use and not for profit." This bequest suggested that Marshall's ideas about public ownership of American forests had been no casual whim but rather a reflection of a deep-rooted commitment to socialism. Individual freedom had always ranked high on Marshall's scale of values, so one-quarter of his estate went for the advancement of civil liberties. He entrusted $400,000 to his friends in The Wilderness Society with the stipulation that it be used to "increase the knowledge of the citizens of the United States of America as to the importance and necessity of maintaining wilderness conditions in outdoor America for future generations." The only personal bequest ($3,000) went to ease the declining years of Herb Clark, the old Adirondack guide who had played a large role in igniting Marshall's passion for the wilderness.

Robert Marshall died on November 11, 1939, on a train en route from Washington, D.C., to New York City. He was unmarried. A punishing trip two months earlier through Washington's northern Cascades—his last into the wilderness—probably contributed to the heart failure which ended his life.

Somebody once asked Marshall, "How many wilderness areas do we need?" His answer was unhesitatingly: "How many Brahms symphonies do we need?" Perhaps the greatest honor ever given him was the posthumous establishment in 1940 of the Bob Marshall Wilderness Area—nearly one million acres in Montana, scenic, spectacular and wild. It is truly appropriate that his name is immortalized in such a worthy manner.

I think it is safe to say that Bob Marshall represented the most powerful voice ever sounded in Washington for the cause of wilderness preservation. To me, he ranks right up there with John Muir as one of our nation's greatest crusaders for the wilderness. How tragic that he lived only half as long as Muir and was thus denied the chance of offering solutions to the nation's growing environmental crisis. Surely, *we* were

denied several classic books on the natural environment, for he was an outstanding writer. If Bob Marshall were alive today he would be only 73. One can only ponder what differences his contributions might have made.

Marshall believed the wilderness was an institution through which the human body, mind, soul and spirit

could be revivified. A century ago, Ralph Waldo Emerson defined an institution as "the lengthened shadow of one man." For many, people that man is Robert Marshall. May his lengthened shadow continue to lengthen. ♣

HOWARD ZAHNISER (1906–1964)

by ED ZAHNISER

Zahniser's language in writing the Wilderness Bill put government agencies in the ambiguous position of being unable to oppose the bill's objectives, though they hotly fought the legislation.

SHORTLY AFTER MY FATHER died in 1964 I dreamed he was sitting beside a trail wearing his red and black flannel shirt, blue windbreaker and old stained felt hat. That dream reconciled me to his death, which had occurred just four months before the passage of the Wilderness Act. To that far-reaching piece of legislation he had given 10 years of single-minded effort, if not his very life. The dream underlined a basic motivating idea he had tried to exemplify—the continuity of human experience. The wilderness setting of the dream also put his life's work in context, for my father greatly valued the wilderness as a testimony of permanence, continuity and interconnectedness. Going to the mountains, as John Muir had written in his description of the wilderness condition, was like going home.

In his youth, it would have struck Howard Zahniser as laughable that he would become the chief architect for the legislation creating the National Wilderness Preservation System. He did not believe in the "Great Man" theory of history. Even toward the end of the eight-year leg-

islative battle to pass a wilderness bill, when success was in sight, he saw himself as a mere cog in an inexorably turning wheel. He would joke that whoever had designed the wheel—*Zahniser* means "gear maker" in German — might have made a better choice of materials.

Yet he wrote toward the end of the ordeal, "If some of us may indeed become wearied physically, and profoundly . . . we should never lose heart. We are engaged in an effort that may well be expected to continue until its right consummation, by our successors if need be. Working to preserve [wilderness] in perpetuity is a great inspiration. We are not fighting a rearguard action, we are facing a frontier . . . We are not fighting progress. We are making it . . . We are not dealing with a vanishing wilderness. We are working for a wilderness forever."

ZAHNIE WAS AN UNLIKELY student of wilderness. He grew up in western Pennsylvania, the son of an evangelical Christian minister. Although he enjoyed the placid beauty of the Allegheny

River Valley, it provided no image of what we popularly visualize as wilderness. He lived in a stern household where religious dogma frowned on all expressions of exuberance except evangelical zeal.

He was, in fact, to become an evangelist for wilderness, traveling across the country articulating the need for it, expressing his compulsion that we save a viable remnant of it and, finally, drawing up a plan to do just that. Shunning dogma, he channeled his zeal into an untiring effort to save America's wilderness *forever.*

A schoolteacher in the sleepy Pennsylvania town of Tionesta first drew young Zahnie's attention to the appreciation of wildlife by helping him identify birdsongs. But his vision was so poor he could hardly see the birds. Money was scarce in the unsalaried minister's family, so Zahnie did not get glasses until he was a teenager. Putting them on for the first time, he jumped fences and ran through fields, marveling at how much there was to see and how distinctly beautiful it was. The response was characteristic.

411

When Zahnie was 17 a bout with osteomyelitis, an inflammatory disease of the bones, made it questionable whether he would ever walk again. "I crammed four years of college into five," he always joked, but when he arrived at Greenville College in Greenville, Illinois, he still did not know whether he was out of difficulty with the osteomyelitis. He spent four years taking the courses he was most interested in, only to discover then that he was still alive but lacked the credits necessary to graduate.

The college years, however, were more than a lark. He worked hard, editing the school paper, working on the local newspaper and later on the *Pittsburgh Press*. He immersed himself in literature, his most far-reaching interest. Following graduation he taught English for a year in the local high school. Although his college years in the midwestern farm town were still far from the wilderness, his interest in journalism and writing flourished there. And it was as a writer and publicist of wilderness that he later made his greatest contribution to America's wilderness movement.

In 1957 Greenville College conferred on him the honorary degree of Doctor of Letters. When he accepted it, he noted that he was so miserably far behind in his correspondence that the degree should be renamed a "Doctor of Postcards."

In 1930 Zahnie took an editorial position with the U.S. Department of Commerce in Washington, D.C. The following year he transferred to the Department of Agriculture and became assistant editor to the Bureau of Biological Survey. There he met and came under the tutelage of naturalist Edward Alexander Preble. Preble's friendship and influence, more than anyone else's, directed Zahnie toward a career as a conservationist.

ZAHNIE STAYED WITH THE Biological Survey for 10 years. During that time it became the Bureau of Sport Fisheries and Wildlife of the Department of the Interior. When its headquarters were transferred to Chicago, he transferred to the Bureau of Plant Industry as research writer and head of information. He remained with that bureau until the end of World War II.

Meanwhile, his conservation horizons were expanding. He had visited some of the nation's wildlife refuges. (Several are now part of the National Wilderness Preservation System.) More importantly, through Preble he had come in contact with The Wilderness Society and *Nature Magazine*. He became *Nature Magazine*'s book editor in 1935 (and held the position until 1954). Following the death of Robert Sterling Yard, the executive secretary of The Wilderness Society, Zahnie was asked to edit one issue of the society's *Living*

Wilderness magazine. The association grew into an offer to take on Yard's full responsibilities.

Zahnie's wife, Alice, was then pregnant with their fourth child, and the society could offer only half the salary he had received from the government. The society's membership numbered in the hundreds, a far cry from today's 75,000 members. Its funds came largely from the bequest of Robert Marshall. But Zahnie stood in awe of the accomplishments of people like Marshall and the society's other founders. With some hesitation he accepted the job.

Today the term "environmentalist" conjures up visions of wheeler-dealer lobbyists, pressure groups and flamboyant public interest lawyers. It implies large organizations with influential mailing lists of more than a quarter-million names and with annual budgets in the millions of dollars. In 1945, by contrast, Zahnie was the entire paid staff of The Wilderness Society. He had to preface every conversation about his work with a definition of the term "conservationist." There was no way to pretend he was influential. The whole thing was impractical, really, but he had succumbed to the allure of Marshall's vision. Marshall had pointed out the social need for wilderness and had foreseen the necessity of an organization of people to defend it.

ALTHOUGH ZAHNIE REPLACED YARD, he was heir to Bob Marshall's philosophy and began to slowly push Marshall's vision toward reality. The society was young, but it had the characteristic vigor of youthful organizations and what seems today a heavy intellectual endowment. Benton MacKaye, one of the other founders, also was the founder of the Appalachian Trail, a regional planner of great reputation and a prophet of the "townless highway," although he spent much of his life pointing out the automobile's negative effects on habitation patterns. Aldo Leopold, another founder, was instrumental in the establishment of the first official wilderness area, the Gila, on national forest land in New Mexico. He wrote the eloquent and timeless *Sand County Almanac* and other pieces which may be read in the anthology *Round River*. His incisive chapters on the land ethic, a term he coined, are persuasive plans for environmental consciousness. Today he is regarded as the patron saint of environmentalists.

My father never viewed himself as more than a publicist and popularizer of other people's ideas. The bulk of his essays, speeches and letters (apart from the material in *Nature Magazine*) constructed a program from the thoughts of such people as Marshall, MacKaye and Leopold.

Leopold gave America the notion of setting aside wilderness as an ecological phenomenon to be valued for itself. MacKaye was responsible for the idea that wild space had a role in healthy human culture. Zahnie picked up these ideas, along with Marshall's belief that the influence of the primitive must never be beyond our grasp, and began to build a national constituency for wilderness preservation. He molded the various abstractions into a concrete legislative program for protecting wilderness in perpetuity.

Zahnie, like Bob Marshall, cut his wilderness teeth on New York's Adirondack Mountain region. He did his first backpacking there in 1946 in the company of Paul Schaefer and Adirondack guide Ed Richards.

Zahnie's journal records a trip full of beauty, new realizations about wilderness and typical backcountry frustrations. Ed and Paul were in good shape, but my father suffered excruciating pains in one leg and, worse, his camera wouldn't work. He interpreted that as "more trouble to make the scene seem all the more lovely."

To Zahnie the experience emphasized the need for national legal protection for wilderness. The Adirondacks were protected on the state level by a "forever wild" clause—Article XIV, Section 1—in the state constitution. Since its enactment in 1894, the clause had successfully rebuffed the forces of exploitation. At the time, nevertheless, a portion of the park was being threatened by proposals for a hydroelectric power project.

AS HE BACKPACKED, Zahnie realized for the first time the significance of the forest preserve and the constitutional amendment which protects it: "The lands of the state, now owned or hereafter acquired, constituting the forest preserve as now fixed by law shall be forever kept as wild forest lands."

Forever—the word was to assume mystical significance in Zahnie's writings. It spearheaded a "transcendental" vocabulary of wilderness advocacy imbued with the sense of a future as unlimited as the past. His papers later abounded with such expressions as perpetuate, perpetuity, the eternity of the future, eternal and enduring.

The three men sat near the foot of Mount Marcy, on whose summit Bob Marshall had once exclaimed to Schaefer, "We simply must band together—all of us who love the wilderness. We must fight together—wherever and whenever wilderness is attacked. We must mobilize all our resources, all of our energies, all of our devotion to the wilderness." Zahnie suggested a strategy to protect the region from the well-financed threats of Higley Mountain and Panther Mountain dams. He promised to solicit the support of other national groups. Schaefer wrote of that strategy session, "A whole new battle to preserve the south branch of the Moose River began that night. No longer would a handful of New Yorkers be pitted alone against the most powerful commercial interests of their state." And the battle eventually was won by the concerted efforts of New York conservationists, The Wilderness Society, Sierra Club, National Parks Association and Wildlife Management Institute.

Backpacking up to Hanging Spear Falls on the Opalescent River inspired renewed commitment in Zahnie to try to preserve wilderness throughout the nation for future generations. His discussions with Schaefer gave new impetus to his growing belief that only a national program for protecting wilderness by law could provide such permanence. Schaefer recorded an observation Zahnie made in the Adirondacks which he found significant in light of the subsequent Wilderness Act: "In addition to such protection as national parks and monuments are now given, we need some strong legislation which will be similar in effect on a national scale to what Article XIV, Section 1, is to the New York State Forest Preserve. We need to reclaim for the people, perhaps through their representatives in the Congress, control over the wilderness regions of America."

THE YEAR 1946 WAS important for all wilderness proponents. Even before his death in 1939, Bob Marshall, from within the U.S. Forest Service, had begun to sense the inadequacy of federal agencies like the Forest Service and National Park Service having the last say about the future of wilderness areas. His death, in fact, marked the end of conservationists' confidence in federal agencies. (That confidence has not been renewed to any extent.) In 1946 the Forest Service was busy dismantling what it today likes to take credit for having established—wilderness areas championed from within its ranks by mavericks like Marshall and Leopold, with whom the bureaucracy of the 1930s had been decidedly uncomfortable. By the end of World War II most of the areas which Marshall had seen designated for protection had been declassified and committed to the chainsaw and bulldozer. And a new threat, that of the automobile-in-every-garage, promised to carve up more and more pristine areas.

The year 1946 also saw the drafting of legislation to promote a land planning proposal originated by Benton MacKaye which concerned wilderness "belts." Although the legislation never was introduced, it gave Zahnie and his fellow conservationists their first taste of the legislative process and of lobbying.

From then until the introduction of the Wilderness Bill in 1956, Zahnie and the other wilderness proponents spent their time fighting rear-guard actions and building a national constituency for conservation programs and policies. The Wil-

REMEMBERING ZAHNIE: NATURE WAS HIS GOD

BY PAUL H. OEHSER

On the evening of May 4, 1964, Benton MacKaye, Jack Durham and I had dinner with Howard Zahniser at the Cosmos Club in Washington, D.C. Zahnie looked tired but was cheerful as usual. In those days he was driving a blue Lincoln convertible, and that evening he was joking about the trouble he was having with it—he couldn't get it in reverse. As we left him that evening he was still joking and wondering how he would get out of the parking lot and home to Hyattsville, Maryland.

But off he went, and he made it home. That was the last time I saw him, for he died the following morning. It was so typical that no matter how burdened he was—and he was then unconscionably burdened with the weight of Wilderness Bill frustrations—he was always ready to relax with his friends, laugh and, as best he could, forget.

I knew Zahnie for more than 40 years, from the time we were in college together at Greenville, Illinois, back in the twenties. When, in 1931, I left my job as assistant editor of the U.S. Biological Survey, he took my place there, and from then on we saw each other often, and our friendship never ceased. We had a great deal in common—interest in journalism, poetry, nature, literature in general. We took many trips together, sometimes with our families, often to the Adirondacks, where we both eventually had "camps." He was a better backpacker than I, with a more acute nose for knowing where he was and where he was going.

Zahnie was famous for getting along with people. He had a way with him. Even his adversaries in the wilderness cause (I don't think he had any enemies) grew to respect and love him. He was persuasive but never caustic or vindictive, either in speech or in print. And this was the backbone of his integrity and effectiveness. He was articulate, and his talk, both on and off the platform, was always entertaining. His speeches were masterpieces of conviction and logic mixed with humor. He was a great companion, for he not only enjoyed good conversation along the trail but knew that silences in the great outdoors are often more eloquent than words.

His sense of humor was an inseparable part of him. It ranged from clownishness to wit of the first order. I remember Harvey Broome describing one of Zahnie's trips to the Great Smokies, where he had gone to talk with Harvey on important Wilderness Society matters. They hiked in the mountains all day, but Zahnie never had a serious word or moment the whole time, and the "important" discussion went by the board.

Zahnie was a great reader and loved to read aloud from his favorite authors, and my wife and I spent many a literary evening at the Zahniser home. He would pass around several copies of *Walden,* or the *Divine Comedy,* or the Book of Job or Blake's poems, and we would take turns. His knowledge of poetry was wide, and he had a large collection of it, as well as a sizable library of nature writers, on whom he was an authority. He loved music and playing records and was a devotee of symphony concerts. On Sundays he often took his children to Washington art galleries, hoping, I suppose, that they would learn to get as much thrill out of paintings as he did. He was a good father. He raised his sons and daughters in a manner that today might seem on the stern side—perhaps a relic of his evangelical upbringing. On a family trip through the West he made all four of them keep diaries, and if at the end of a day any one of them had failed his literary duty, he was denied his allowance. But I know them—all now are married—and they all are great people, perhaps living examples of the virtues of antipermissiveness.

It was one of the greatest experiences of my lifetime to have known Howard Zahniser. Nature was his God. He had an innate reverence for all life. As the *Washington Post* said in an editorial on his death, "He was in love with the open spaces, the rivers and mountains, the wild life, the music of nature, and the lure of the unspoiled world." He delighted in being a part of the physical universe.

derness Society enjoyed a slow, steady growth in membership and financial support, but it still was a beans and bacon organization in comparison with today's large environmental groups. Beginning in the 1950s Zahnie traveled a lot, speaking at wilderness conferences. While in any area for any reason, he visited newspaper editors and television and radio stations, and talked with anyone who would listen about the values of wilderness and the need for preserving it. He even had big pockets sewn inside his suit coats to accommodate large quantities of reprints, pamphlets and Wilderness Society membership applications, which he distributed at every opportunity.

The final event leading to the introduction of the Wilderness Bill was the so-called Echo Park dam controversy, the fight to protect Dinosaur National Monument from two dams planned by the Bureau of Reclamation, one to be called Echo Park. Building a dam in any unit of the National Park System seemed wrong. Dinosaur was small, little known and seldom visited, but a great principle was at stake. Zahnie, David Brower, Joseph Penfold and other conservationists decided to draw the line and fight to the end. The question was simply, "What is the use of designating parks, wild lands, wilderness or primitive areas if dam builders can move in and do their thing, protective status be damned?"

Zahnie and the others organized themselves into a group called the Council of Conservationists. Zahnie was chosen Washington representative. The council began to build important alliances with such future proponents of the Wilderness Bill as Congressman John P. Saylor and Hubert H. Humphrey and Senator Richard Neuberger. Against all odds, by rallying people in defense of the national park idea, they eventually won the battle. No dams were authorized, and dams were explicitly prohibited from the public works bill which had provided for their construction. It was a mammoth public works

bill—one of the largest ever—and a handful of men had brought it to a halt. To appreciate the significance of a conservation victory against a well-heeled pork barrel project in the early 1950s is hardly possible nowadays. It helps to remember that Zahniser, Brower and the other leaders often were the sole staff members of their organizations.

Echo Park publicized a growing momentum for a national wilderness preservation system, rallied conservationists in protection of the national park principle and, more important, received great national attention. It carried the word "conservation" into most newspapers, magazines and people's homes for the first time.

The conservationists were euphoric, yet they realized the moment they were waiting for had arrived. The week after Zahnie wrote Congressman Wayne Aspinall a final letter confirming the Echo Park settlement, he began drafting the Wilderness Bill.

He did not feel that he was the ideal person for the job. Nevertheless, as Sierra Club representative Douglas Scott recently said, "He was the ideal draftsman—certainly not a technician coldly turning living concepts into sterile jargon. He was an artist stating a noble policy and all its details in language that soared, carrying the reader's imagination, inspiring a recognition of its innate rightness of purpose." Indeed, the language of the bill was effectively used to argue for its own passage. It contended that preserving wilderness was for the good of the American people. The wording put government agencies in the position of being unable to argue against the objectives of the bill even though they hotly opposed the legislation.

There were, of course, frustrations with the bill's wording, and at one point Zahnie wrote to George Marshall, brother of Bob and a member of the boards of the Sierra Club and Wilderness Society, that he would "much prefer to state all this in iambic rhyming couplets

or even in the sequence of sonnets than attempt to do this in bill language."

The language often was remarkable. Zahnie looked for months for the word "untrammeled" as a definition of wilderness. That search, during which he discarded other words like "undeveloped" and "undisturbed," was made worthwhile in the recent protracted battle for an eastern wilderness bill. This entire battle focused on the definition and "purity" of wilderness. The language Zahnie contrived in the Wilderness Bill finally won passage of the Eastern National Forest Wilderness Areas Act in late 1974. It was signed into law by President Ford over the dead body of the U.S. Forest Service.

The fight for the Wilderness Bill was long and trying. Despite a serious heart attack in 1952 which cramped Zahnie's style from then on, and despite the loss of a lung in the early 1960s, his resolve did not weaken. He had enormous patience and steadfastness of purpose. Dave Brower called him in tribute "the constant advocate." In many ways the language of the bill and its underlying philosophy were an extension of his character. Olaus Murie reported to Wilderness Society leaders in 1955, "That fellow has grown in stature, if that is possible. His work is characterized by a moral flavor, an honesty that, however the present struggle turns out, will have an eventual effect."

Zahnie died quietly in his sleep on May 5, 1964, just two days after he had testified at the final hearing on the Wilderness Bill. The bill was signed into law in September, and the White House called his widow down from the Adirondacks to attend the ceremony.

I think Doug Scott best summarized my father's contribution when he said, "His proper memorial is simply this: that wherever there is wilderness today, in a world in which the only wilderness we shall save is that which we deliberately secure, it *can* be secured. And it will endure because of the basic tool he gave us, and the inspiration he gave us to use it well." ♠

THE NEW ETHIC

What the wilderness needs now is minimum-impact backpackers.

by DARA SUE ANDERSON

Some backpackers practice wilderness ethics and leave little trace of their passing. Others do not, thereby damaging the backcountry.

How often do you see backcountry trails littered with candy wrappers, beer cans, cigarette butts, and other rubbish? Or blackened fire rings filled with charred wood, bottles, cans, and foil? Or trees scarred by a camper who chopped off boughs to make a shelter or bed? Or human waste and soiled toilet paper left exposed? Or a section of a mountainside washed away because hikers took shortcuts between switchbacks, destroying the vegetation which protects the slope against erosion?

Do you ever see someone spitting toothpaste into a mountain stream, which just happens to be your source of drinking water? Or macaroni resting on the bottom of a lake where someone washed their dishes? Or someone's initials carved in the bark of an aspen tree? Or the sod of a lakeshore worn to bare soil by the wear and tear of campers? Or all of the branches within arm's reach broken off standing trees, leaving ugly stubs? Or have you ever returned to your campsite to find your solitude destroyed by a group of 20 camped a stone's throw away from you?

More people than ever before are backpacking in the wilderness. Rocky Mountain National Park, for instance, experienced a 700 percent increase in overnight backcountry use from 1965 to 1975. The increase in use resulted in damage to some of the more popular backcountry camping spots. For this reason a backcountry permit system, limiting the number of backpackers, is in effect to protect the fragile resources of the park.

The quality of your wilderness experience is being threatened by misuse and overuse. What can you do? You can minimize your impact on the environment to help protect the beauty of the backcountry. Here's how.

"I LOVE TO GO A-WANDERING ALONG THE MOUNTAIN TRACK"

Refrain from shortcutting between switchbacks. When shortcutters destroy plant life, the land loses its protection against erosion. While shortcutting may save a little time, it takes more energy than hiking the switchbacks and scars the environment—perhaps permanently. Also, shortcutting could be hazardous to people below you, if you happen to kick rocks loose.

When above timberline, stay off the delicate alpine tundra. " 'Walk only on the rocks' has become the watchword in Vermont and New Hampshire above treeline," says Laurence R. Van Meter, executive director of the Green Mountain Club. "Where bedrock outcrops are not extensive enough to permit walking only on the rocks, hikers should stay on the designated trails and not wander off through the alpine tundra. Impact from footsteps alone has severely damaged many acres of rare arctic-alpine flora in New England."

Due to the severe weather conditions, short growing season, and shallow, sandy soil at high altitudes, alpine tundra plants are so fragile they cannot survive your trampling feet. They grow slowly in the adverse conditions of their environment, and research shows it may take a plant five years to grow to ¼-inch in diameter. It has taken many of the plants that you see at high elevations several hundred years to achieve their growth! Let's take care to protect these delicate areas by staying on established trails. (Imagine having survived blizzards, droughts, hailstorms, and torrential cloudbursts for a hundred years only to be pulverized by a 220-pound waffle iron, the Vibram-soled step of a 180-pound mountain man carrying a 40-pound pack.)

ALL TRAILS LEAD TO "MECCA"

Leaving unsightly and unsanitary evidence of your presence is an annoying wilderness problem for those who follow you. Here's

*"Leave nothing but footprints;
take nothing but photos."*

how to dispose of your body's waste properly. Pick a spot for your "mecca" at least 100 feet from any open water, trail, or campsite. With a lightweight backpacker's trowel ("mecca" shovel), carefully remove the sod, keeping it intact if possible, and set aside. Dig about a 6-inch-deep cathole. Soil has various organisms at this depth that decompose organic material. Cover your cathole after use and replace the sod. Nature will do the rest.

Disposing of toilet paper is a problem. Burying it is not an ideal solution because frost or animal action may expose it later; and in dry climates it is especially slow to decompose. Put your used paper in a dark-colored plastic bag and burn it in your campsite fire, if campfires are permitted, or carry it out.

If you are not already accustomed to packing out your used TP, you are probably thinking that I'm some kind of a nut. (Here's a typical reaction: "You've

got to be kidding. That is gross! ") I, too, was skeptical when I was first introduced to the idea. I scoffed at the suggestion but agreed to try it. After I packed out my used TP for a while, I decided that it certainly didn't hurt me to carry it out; whereas, it could hurt the beauty of the backcountry to leave it. (Picture a forest littered with dirty TP blowing in the breezes. Now, *that* is gross!) Some suggest burning it in your cathole before covering as an alternative to packing it out, *unless burning creates a fire hazard.*

The National Outdoor Leadership School in Wyoming recommends that natural substitutes for toilet paper be used when practical. In Minnesota I have used leaves of a plant appropriately named lumberjack's toilet paper (*Aster macrophyllus*). In the wintertime I have used snow when I can compact it into a ball. Brrrr ... but it's more hygienic than TP and eliminates having to carry it out. One last suggestion—when

primitive toilet facilities are provided in the backcountry, use them rather than digging cat holes.

WHERE HAVE ALL THE FLOWERS GONE?

The fragile sod of meadows, lakeshores and streamsides is easily damaged by the wear and tear of campers. Once sod is destroyed, it may not grow back. Who enjoys seeing a lakeshore that bears the scars of an abandoned campsite?

Most backpackers come to the wilderness in search of peace and quiet, so camp well away from people who have arrived before you. You should select an isolated campsite where you won't be seen or heard by others. (Leave your radios and chain saws at home and keep your boisterous conduct below a magnitude of 2.5 on the Richter scale.)

If at all possible, camp on bare mineral soil or on an unvegetated forest floor so you won't destroy any plant life. Moist areas are particularly susceptible to soil deformation. (Be kind to your friends in the swamp—don't camp on top of them.) Broad-leaved herbaceous plants and tree seedlings are more easily destroyed than grasses. If you can't find a spot free of vegetation to pitch your tent, choose a dry meadow that has some resistance to your trampling feet. Then if you plan to stay in the same area more than one night, move your campsite at least several hundred yards every day to lessen your impact on one spot.

Some people are concerned about the destructive impact of Vibram-soled boots off the trail. Ed Menning, resource management specialist for Rocky Mountain National Park, is one. He likens Vibram soles to meat grinders which chew up the vegetation and suggests that once you arrive at your campsite you change into moccasins, tennis shoes, or other smooth-soled shoes. Because of the severe impact that occurs around your kitchen area, he stresses putting it in a rocky location.

WHERE DID YOU SLEEP LAST NIGHT?

Bough beds and shelters are no longer acceptable, because stripping the limbs off trees leaves unsightly scars. Use a foam or Ensolite pad or air mattress. They're lightweight, easy to carry, and comfortable for sleeping. Take a tent or tarp where a shelter is needed. Do not build tables, chairs, or other structures. (We were born too late to be pioneers!)

By all means refrain from digging a trench around your tent. Let's buy tents with waterproof floors and pitch them in well-drained locations so trenching won't be necessary. It mars the land and often results in erosion.

THIS IS THE WAY WE WASH OUR FACE

To protect the quality of our drinking water in the backcountry, soaps and detergents should not be used. You can adequately clean yourself and your clothes by thoroughly rinsing with plain water. Soap need not be used to wash your dishes either, particularly if you avoid cooking greasy foods. Immersing your dishes in boiling water after cleaning them with sand or pine needles is sufficient.

Wash yourself, your clothes, and your dishes well away (at least 100 feet) from the shores of lakes and streams. Bring a lightweight collapsible bucket or basin to carry water for washing away from its source; or to save carrying the extra weight in your backpack, a cooking pot will serve the purpose. (Please, no skinny-dipping until you have washed away the bacteria that grow on your skin.)

GOOD FOOD, GOOD MEAT, GOOD GOD, LET'S EAT!

Ideally, the modern backcountry traveler builds a fire *only* in emergencies. A portable cooking stove protects the wilderness from being denuded of wood and scarred by fireplaces. A stove leaves no trace, cooks efficiently, and is more convenient than cooking on a fire. It eliminates the chore of gathering wood, smoke blowing in your eyes, the difficulty of regulating the temperature of a fire, and soot-covered pots. "But the stove and fuel are extra weight in my pack," you say. True, but carrying a few extra pounds is a small price to pay for protecting our forests. (Besides, it will build your character.)

We may as well get into the habit of using a stove, since more and more fragile or heavily used areas are being restricted to stoves only. Wood was being burned faster than it could regenerate itself. Fires for cooking, warming, or social purposes are especially inappropriate where wood is scarce. A stove, then, is essential in subalpine areas, above timberline, and in desert country. (For warming and social purposes, try zip-together sleeping bags instead of building a fire.)

Ponder these words written by Colin Fletcher in *The Man Who Walked Through Time:*

> It was many nights now since I had needed a fire for warmth, or for cheer, so I rarely built one. This was not pure laziness. A campfire, for all its pulsating, dream-inducing fascination, cuts you off from the reality of the night, and as the days passed I found myself becoming less and less tolerant of any barrier that came between me and the reality of the Canyon.

If you must build a fire, use an existing fireplace. (For goodness' sake, don't build a new one!) A 1972 survey revealed 300 (!) fire rings at Upper and Lower Cathedral lakes in Yosemite National Park. Such blackened fire rings filled with burned wood and ashes detract from the beauty of the wilderness. Why make another ugly fireplace if there is already one where you are camping?

Let's leave axes and saws at home. They're heavy to carry, unnecessary when gathering small branches by hand, and campers too often deface the countryside with them. Gather firewood primarily from branches and sticks on the ground. Then gather from downed trees. Avoid breaking branches from standing trees—alive or dead. (A picturesque snag shouldn't be ruined.) Keep your fire small, using only as much wood as you absolutely need. Sitting close to a small fire is much cozier than backing off into the distance from the hot flames of a bonfire. Excessively large fires waste wood and are more apt to get out of control.

Always attend your fire to keep it under control. When the fire is burned to ashes, douse it with water and stir thoroughly. To make sure your ashes are cold, check them with your bare hands. Small hot embers cause many major fires.

If fires are permitted where you are camping and there is no existing fireplace, here's how to build a fire so you will leave no trace. According to National Outdoor Leadership School (NOLS), "to make camouflaging possible, one of the following two methods should be used to prepare a fireplace."

1. Flat Rock Method: Spread several inches of discreetly gathered mineral soil on a rock over a slightly larger area than the fire will occupy. After the fire is out, crush the coals to powder and scatter. Next remove the soil and rinse the rock.

2. Firepit Method: First, select a site with sod that is not too lush. Carefully remove the sod and set aside where it won't be trampled. Dig a pit several inches deep, setting the dirt aside in a neat pile. After the pit is dug, pat mineral soil around the perimeter to avoid drying out the surrounding grasses. The pit needs to be deep enough to hold the crushed coals and all the sod and large enough to avoid drying the surrounding grasses.

NOLS says the sod, both around the pit and removed from the pit, should be kept moist. "On breaking camp, after dousing the fire, the dirt and sod should be carefully replaced. The coals which can be crushed to a powder or paste should be scattered discreetly. That which can't be crushed should be buried in the pit. An effort should be made to burn wood as completely as possible to avoid having to deal with large, half-burned chunks of wood. You shouldn't put wood, especially large-diameter pieces, on your fire shortly before dousing it. Under winter conditions, it is virtually impossible to build a disguisable fireplace or to gather wood by acceptable means. Therefore, except in a real emergency, fires should not be used."

When selecting a site for your fire, NOLS suggests the following:

1. Fires should be built far from trees, branches, and root systems.

2. Fires should never be built in litter or duff. If there is a ground cover of duff, be sure to dig through it, well into the mineral soil when constructing a firepit. Be sure the pit is large enough to prevent the possibility of a coal smoldering in the duff.

3. Beware of coals falling off a flat-rock fire into the duff.

4. Especially when the woods are dry, be wary of using fires on windy days where sparks might be dangerous.

5. Fires should neither be ringed with rocks nor built against reflecting rocks to avoid permanent blackening and unnatural exfoliation.
(When you find an unnecessary fireplace in the backcountry, cast away the blackened rocks, scatter the ashes, and camouflage the unsightly scar.)

It was once considered a thoughtful gesture to stockpile wood for the next camper, but now the object is to leave no trace. After you erase all signs of your firepit, scatter your unused wood. Many backpackers believe finding a pile of wood destroys the solitude and independence they seek.

Keep in mind that many areas discourage and/or prohibit building fires. Cooking on a lightweight, compact stove is the modern way to go. Before you build a fire ask yourself: Are fires allowed? Is there a plentiful wood supply? Do I really need a fire? Consider going on a night hike or learning the constellations or watching beavers at work instead of letting a campfire come between you and the reality of the night.

IF WE CAN PACK IT IN, WE CAN PACK IT OUT

We can avoid canned and bottled foods in our backpacking menus by choosing dry foods from our supermarket and/or freeze-dried foods from a backpacking equipment store. Canned and bottled foods have several disadvantages. They are heavy to carry and leave you with empty cans and bottles to pack out. Some national parks prohibit the possession of food or beverage in discardable glass containers in the wilderness.

Burying cans, bottles, trash, and garbage was once considered acceptable. We now know that is not a satisfactory method of disposal. Animals and frost action often expose such rubbish after it's buried. Heavy-duty plastic bags work well for bringing out your trash and garbage. Carry everything out (or take a donkey or hire a sherpa to do it) that you carried in—plastic bags, aluminum foil, tampons, disposable diapers, orange peelings, cigarette butts, unused foodstuffs, and leftover food. Plan your food quantities carefully so you won't have leftovers to carry out. (Or invite a friend to come who will eat everything and anything that is left over.)

If fires are allowed and if there's a plentiful wood supply, destroy your "burnables" in your campfire. Watch for food packages lined with foil. Since foil won't burn, put them in your litter bag. (You can burn off the outer paper wrapping *if* you are sure to pick the foil from the ashes before you leave.) Where there are many scavenger animals

and birds, you can dispose of fish entrails in the brush for biological recycling rather than carrying them out in a plastic bag. Finally, we can all help by picking up litter thoughtlessly left by others.

LEAVE SOME OF YOUR FRIENDS AT HOME

Large groups have a destructive impact on the wilderness. Many areas in national parks and forests have been destroyed by overuse. Lassen Volcanic National Park has closed such areas to camping, so revegetation may occur. As a preventive measure, the park also has shut off areas that are too fragile to withstand the impact of campers. The Green Mountain Club suggests limiting the size of your group to 10 people.

Remember to obtain backcountry-use regulations for the area you plan to visit. Many areas require fire and/or camping permits.

TRESPASSERS WILL BE SHOT

To gain access to some trails it is sometimes necessary to cross private property. Secure the permission of the landowner before crossing or camping on his property. Respect his land just as you would want yours respected. Damage it in no way and close all gates behind you.

A TIME FOR FLUORESCENT ORANGE

To keep visual pollution to a minimum, buy backcountry equipment and clothing in subtle, earthy colors—browns, blues, greens—which blend with nature's colors. Bright reds, oranges, and yellows psychologically shrink the wilderness and may interfere with others' feelings of solitude. Says Peter Marsh of Rocky Mountain Ski Tours and Backpack Adventures in Estes Park, Colorado, "Even at 300 yards an orange tent is obvious. It tends to intrude on my privacy."

Backpacking during hunting season is an exception, of course.

To protect yourself, shout your presence with bright colors. In case of an emergency, you may want to have a piece of brightly colored equipment (a ground cloth) or clothing (a poncho or other rain gear) with which to make a ground-to-air signal for help. (Or carry a signal mirror.) Parents may wish to dress young children in bright clothing in case they get lost.

IN CLOSING . . .

It really takes just a little effort to minimize your impact on the wilderness. Practicing wilderness camping ethics insures a clean and attractive backcountry for others to enjoy—and for you to enjoy when you return.

As Jim Watters of the Sierra Club points out, it's impossible to get 100 percent agreement on minimum-impact camping techniques. "It's difficult to combine the ideal with the practical. Also, regional conditions often prescribe different techniques, obviously."

Leave-no-trace techniques are continually being developed and revised. I offer these guidelines as minimum standards to be adapted to your situation. They are not hard-and-fast rules by any means, but they can serve as a model for your own code of wilderness ethics. I agree with NOLS when they say that "to a large extent, practical conservation is an attitude that is tempered by judgment and experience rather than a rigid policy."

"Natural beauty and wonder are priceless heirlooms. How shall we escape the contempt of the coming generations if we suffer this irreplaceable heritage to be wasted?"
—Henry Van Dyke (1852-1933)

THE NEGLECTED HIKER

by ROBERT C. LUCAS and ROBERT P. RINEHART

Unless we begin to protect existing hiking trails and provide new ones to cope with projected demands, the hiker faces a grim future.

AMERICA'S 10 MILLION HIKERS are being neglected. Fifteen years ago, Congress set up the Outdoor Recreation Resources Review Commission to evaluate the needs of U.S. outdoorsmen. After what remains to this day the most exhaustive study of its kind, the commission reported, "It is something of a tribute to Americans that they do as much cycling and walking as they do, for very little has been done to encourage these activities, and a good bit, if inadvertently, to discourage them."

As far as the hiker is concerned, the situation reported by the commission has gone from bad to worse since the issuance of the report. While hikers have rapidly increased in numbers, trails have deteriorated or disappeared.

The United States has only about 100,000 miles of trails—less than one yard of trail per citizen. Give thanks that not everyone hikes and that all hikers do not hit the trail at the same time. If they did, they could all hold hands. There are approximately 50 yards of trail per square mile in our country, not including Alaska. (If Alaska were included, the average would be even lower.) England and Wales together have more miles of rural footpaths and bridlepaths than does the entire United States.

Most of the trails are in the West, the relics of past programs (mainly fire protection) rather than the product of recreation planning. This situation, recognized as early as 1952 in the annual report of the Chief of the U.S. Forest Service, has not changed. The 1968 National Trails System Act (P.L. 90-543) was passed to meet the need for recreational trails, but eight years later there are only a few active programs to build trails for recreation.

Trends are not encouraging. Total trail mileage in the United States is probably declining—we say "probably" because comparable annual fig-

ures for all parts of the trail system (federal, state and local) are not available. Most of America's trail mileage is in the national forests, but trail mileage in national forests has dropped almost one-third from a peak in 1945. Roads have replaced many trails, and aerial fire-fighting techniques have led to abandonment of other trails. Pack strings of mules supplying fire fighters and manned lookouts, which used to depend on trail access, are now rarities. Airplanes, helicopters and trucks have almost relegated pack animals to the realm of nostalgia.

Urban sprawl, limited-access highways and large airports have eliminated many other hiking opportunities, especially on unofficial, unmaintained paths around cities and towns. This loss of trails has occurred at the same time the number of hikers and other trail users has been increasing rapidly.

HIKING IS EASY TO NEGLECT. There are no long, conspicuous lines of people waiting their turn at the trailheads as there are at ski lifts. And hikers rarely buy admission tickets as campers and skiers do. Dispersal and lack of on-site payments hurt hiking in the competition for attention and public monies. Furthermore, hikers have not been as well represented by voluntary organizations as have many other types of recreationists. Although this situation may be starting to improve, hikers either tend to be absorbed in national wilderness-oriented groups or involved in hiking clubs that promote a particular trail or region, such as the Appalachian Trail. In either case, there has been practically no national pressure for hiking opportunities outside official wilderness areas.

The neglect applies to research, also. There are only a handful of studies of trail users or trails, and almost all of them concern visitors to designated wilderness areas, rather than hikers, horsemen or ski-tourers in general. Of course, there is overlap; some wilderness visitors are also hikers, but only a portion of the country's hikers visit designated wilderness areas.

Approximately 10 million Americans who are 12 years of age or older are hikers, the criterion being that they walk with packs on their backs. That is about 7 percent of the population in the age group. Based on rough calculations from U.S. Forest Service and National Park Service use reports, we estimate that 10 to 15 percent of all hiking takes place in established wilderness within national forests or in national parks. Another 10 to 15 percent of all hiking takes place on national forest trails outside wilderness areas. This means that about two-thirds of all hiking is done on state, county and private lands.

About 50 percent of Americans walk for pleasure, which is defined by the Bureau of Outdoor Recreation (BOR) as walking without a pack. National surveys show that "nature walks" have twice as many participants as hiking. All told, a lot of people are out using their legs.

Hiking is not as grueling as some think. In recent studies conducted by our U.S. Forest Service wilderness research unit in eight areas in Montana and Idaho, more than half of all hikers questioned spent only one day on the trail, and fewer than one-tenth stayed more than two nights. In our studies, and in others, the typical hiker is on a one-day outing and has traveled no more than a few hours from home.

The same studies show that most wilderness hikes are less than 10 miles in length, round trip, and are concentrated on a few favorite trails. For example, we found that about half of all trail use in the Spanish Peaks Primitive Area near Bozeman, Montana, occurs on only one-tenth of the area's trail system. Use is even more concentrated in the Selway-Bitterroot and Bob Marshall wildernesses in Idaho and Montana. Concentrated use has been typical of every area studied in the United States and Canada. One likely reason is that most trails were not designed for recreation; it is only a lucky accident that a few of them are attractive to hike. Another and probably more important reason could be lack of information about available trails. But to be honest, the reasons trail use varies so sharply are really not understood—hardly surprising, since it has been studied so little.

WHAT KINDS OF PEOPLE HIKE? Bureau of Outdoor Recreation surveys have shown that hikers are about evenly divided between males and females, and that women and girls outnumber men and boys in walking for pleasure, nature walks and bicycling (at least they did a few years ago). We have found, in the wildernesses we have studied, that men still outnumber women about three to one, although the proportion of women has risen in recent years.

Young people are most common in physically demanding activities. Participation gradually drops off as age increases. We found that 50 percent of all backpackers are under 30 years of age. This is not necessarily a reflection of ability declining with age. Part of the drop probably results from changing interests and desires. Furthermore, older people grew up in a society with fewer opportunities to develop interests in many types of outdoor recreation. (There are excep-

tions—more people used to live in rural areas where places to hunt and fish were easier to find.) Workweeks were longer; travel was less easy; efficient light packs and tents were not as common; and, most important, attitudes about leisure and its use were more restrictive. Perhaps the almost traditional neglect of hikers is understandable: most politicians and land managers old enough to be in positions of authority in public agencies grew up in this same society. If they

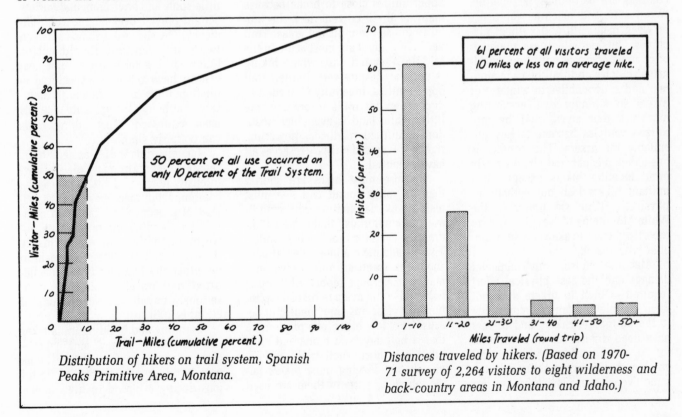

Distribution of hikers on trail system, Spanish Peaks Primitive Area, Montana.

Distances traveled by hikers. (Based on 1970-71 survey of 2,264 visitors to eight wilderness and back-country areas in Montana and Idaho.)

421

hiked and rode horses, it was usually work, not recreation.

What are future trends? Although only a few trails are presently being built and existing trails are not always being maintained, trail use is growing and seems sure to grow a lot more. Projections to 1980 by the BOR indicated that hiking will grow 78 percent over 1965 levels and that "walking for pleasure" will grow 49 percent. Based on past predictions, these estimates are probably too low. We just do not know enough about hikers to make reliable predictions, but we can support general predictions by citing recent growth of hiking and related activities. During a recent five-year period (1965 to 1970), when the population 12 years old and older grew eight percent, hiking increased 26 percent and walking for pleasure 57 percent—becoming the leading type of outdoor recreation in terms of numbers of occasions. (During the same period, horseback riding climbed 44 percent, and bicycling soared 92 percent.)

MORE AND MORE PEOPLE using fewer trails, and in new and different ways, have aggravated problems of overuse, of misuse and of conflicts between uses in wilderness areas and on backcountry trails. Use conflicts are particularly serious between man and machine—or really between men with and without machines. Outside wilderness, the hiker often must compete with four-wheel-drive vehicles and trail bikes in summer and snowmobiles in winter. But hikers so strongly dislike meeting machines that areas used by motorized vehicles become largely unsuitable for hikers. The conflict is one-sided; mechanized visitors rarely mind meeting hikers except when militant hikers lash out verbally or physically. (One ski tourer in the White Mountains of New Hampshire reportedly tried to skewer a snowmobiler with his ski pole.)

Machine noise, environmental damage and the less physical effort required—which to hikers does not seem like playing fair—all contribute to the antipathy. Hikers and drivers have deep differences in motivation for trail use, different desires and goals and different reactions to the same experiences. The hiker, in our

studies and in others, is generally less activity-oriented (not as interested in fishing, for example), less concerned with reaching a specific destination, less desirous of developed facilities, more motivated by an interest in scenic beauty and more often seeking solitude than the mechanized visitor. This means that the sort of area the trail-bike rider really wants and would enjoy most is often different from that desired by the hiker. On the other hand, the skier and snowshoer may prefer pretty much the same sort of country as the snowmobiler, which leads to conflict.

The conflict is intensified by a lack of clear trail-planning objectives and by a scarcity of active trail programs. More separation of mechanized and nonmechanized trail uses is essential. Each type needs areas suited to it. Land managers must now recognize and plan for diversity and variety in trail systems—long and short, hard and easy, close and far—and for different kinds of users.

The greatest need at this time is for trails for one-day hikes, most of which must be close to major population centers. Here is where the demand is the greatest, and where opportunities are most limited. The present recreation needs of inner-city people can best be met by providing opportunities close to home because many of these citizens lack the mobility to use more distant areas. Trail needs in general are most acute in the Middle West and East, where hiking is popular despite very limited trail opportunities. Ingenuity is needed to find places for trails in areas where little public land is available. Abandoned railroad roadbeds, powerline rights-of-way and military reserves all have potential.

Because most hikes are shorter than 10 miles round trip, we must resist an overfascination with grandiose "national trails" that run for hundreds or even for thousands of miles. These trails have a monumental aura about them and are impressive on a map, and perhaps reports of "trophy treks" give the average hiker inspiration and vicarious enjoyment. But because very few hikes take place more than a half-day from home and most hikes are short, such trails are obviously not serving most hikers (although some parts of them are used

for short hikes). The long trails are a part of the picture but are not top priority now.

TRAIL SYSTEMS NEED and deserve more attention outside established wilderness. Wilderness has its own special role to play, as a natural ecosystem with opportunities for solitude and challenge, but it cannot and should not become almost the only place to hike. Nonwilderness "trail recreation areas" could fill a real void and provide a great deal of enjoyment for many people, at lower cost. At the same time, nonwilderness trails could divert some kinds of use and help free wilderness to serve the purpose for which it was established. They also could give people a chance to experience a wide variety of landscapes —low elevation, big-tree forests; river bottoms; prairies; hardwood forests— in addition to the alpine, high-elevation areas that characterize so much of the present wilderness system. Because of mountainous settings, most of the wilderness system has only a short, summer-use season. Trails in other types of locations could provide for more spring and fall hiking.

Hiking trails should be designed primarily for scenic enjoyment, as an opportunity for esthetic experiences. Seeking out views, vistas, enchanting little spots and environmental variety should prevail over engineering efficiency. The shortest distance between two points generally should not be followed. A good trail does not necessarily have to lead to a specific destination; trails can be an end in themselves, although the opposite idea has been expressed. Most hiking trails can be fairly simple.

Incompatible trail uses need to be separated more. In many places, low-intensity horse- and hiker-use can be combined, but machines must be isolated if possible. This isolation complicates planning and raises costs, yet we think the benefits would justify the expense. The alternatives seem to be either the banning of all mechanized trail travel or allowing it to seriously impair the satisfactions of all other trail users.

Planning and building trails takes lots of time, money and labor—always scarce commodities. Some trail building might provide useful jobs during a period of high unem-

ployment. Much of the present trail system was built in the depression of the 1930s. Although an economic slump should not be required to get trails built, a slump could be an opportunity for trail building.

Meanwhile, better information about trails could help hikers to make better use of existing trails, quickly and at modest cost. Would-be hikers are often frustrated by ignorance about where to go. Published trail guides have greatly changed use patterns, without really intending to and not to everybody's satisfaction. The information shortage is especially acute in large cities where there is little public land for hiking nearby. Much more could be done to help people find that which is available.

FINALLY, MORE RESEARCH is needed. The management programs for all trail users need increased emphasis; but, even if funds and other resources were provided, the uncertainties discussed here would inevitably produce major mistakes and inefficiencies. Research could better identify fragile settings that trails should avoid and durable places where trails belong. This would produce more attractive trails and get more hiking opportunities from limited tax dollars. Much could be learned about what different trail users want in terms of design, length, level of difficulty and locations. Con-

Census regions	Percent hiking[1] (rank)	Miles of trail[2] (rank)	Miles of trail of 100 square miles (rank)	Miles of trail per 100,000 people[3] (rank)
Northeast	8 (3)	1,957 (6)	2.9 (3)	17 (3)
Middle Atlantic	5 (5)	1,663 (7)	1.6 (4)	5 (8)
East North Central	8 (3)	2,306 (4)	.9 (6)	6 (7)
West North Central	6 (5)	785 (9)	.2 (9	5 (8)
South Atlantic	3 (9)	4,263 (3)	1.5 (5)	14 (4)
East South Central	6 (5)	1,093 (8)	.6 (7)	9 (6)
West South Central	6 (5)	1,988 (5)	.5 (8)	11 (5)
Mountain	14 (1)	52,355 (1)	6.1 (1)	471 (1)
Pacific	10 (2)	32,027 (2)	3.5 (2)	117 (2)
Average, U.S.	7	98,437 (total)	2.7	48

Percent of population 12 years old or over that participated in hiking, and miles of public trail relative to area and population, by U.S. Census regions

[1]From Survey of Outdoor Recreation, BOR 1965.
[2]From *Trails for America*, BOR 1966.
[3]Based on 1970 census population reports.

flicts between different users need to be better understood to give everybody a fair shake. Unfortunately, the research effort to date has been too small and too scattered. The returns for the American people from good research, which could be implemented in better planning and management, would exceed the costs many fold.

To the hiker, places to hike are as vital as wilderness to the grizzly bear or free-flowing streams to the Atlantic salmon. Yet, unless we begin to protect existing hiking trails and provide new ones to cope with projected demands, the hiker faces a grim future—more and more hikers with fewer and fewer places to hike. If the current neglect continues, perhaps one day a manikin complete with waffle stompers and pack will stand in our museums alongside the passenger pigeon, great auk and other extinct species. The American hiker will have passed into history. ➨

JOE BOLAND
Fighting a Guerrilla Action
by DAVID SUMNER

He single-handedly blew the whistle on Yosemite Park development when others were lying back or afraid, kept the issue alive when others grew conciliatory or bored, and over the long haul gave it a precision and force it otherwise would have lacked.

Historians sometimes point out that the course of history often turns upon small pivotal incidences.

"For want of a nail the shoe was lost
For want of a shoe the horse was lost
For want of a horse the rider was lost
For want of a rider the battle was lost.
For want of a victory the kingdom was lost."

Joe Boland's story is of how a young, long-haired backpacker got curious about the power and the influence in the Yosemite master-planning process—and whose curiosity persisted until he'd provoked a congressional investigation which got a park director fired and the brakes applied to the concessionnaires' extraordinary influence in all of our nation's national parks.

One person can make a hell of a lot of difference. Read about what a difference Joe Boland made.

W.K.

On the evening of May 7, 1974, the National Park Service held an open meeting in Yosemite Valley. The purpose was to gather "public input" on a proposal to replace 150 tent cabins, the historic accommodation in the park, with a like number of modular motel units. The sponsor of the plan was the Yosemite Park and Curry Company, chief concessioner in the park and under government contract to run Yosemite's hotel, motels, restaurants, shops and other commercial facilities. The Curry Company, as it's commonly called, has been a subsidiary of the Music Corporation of America (MCA), the entertainment conglomerate, since August, 1973.

By chance Joe Boland dropped in on that meeting, the first of its kind he'd ever attended, and the proceedings made him furious. "It was a bloody kangaroo court," he recalls. "They'd already decided to build. It was just window dressing on a *fait accompli.*"

Boland left with a copy of the Curry Company's proposal, and at four o'clock the next morning he was still going over it — underlining, noting questions and writing rebuttals. "And then," he says, "I decided to look into what was behind it."

For the next 16 months Boland continued to look. During that time the proposal to "upgrade" the 150 tent cabins died, and a ten-year Yosemite Master Plan was killed because, in the words of then Interior Department Assistant Secretary Nathaniel P. Reed, "it appeared to have been written by the concessioner." A federal General Account-ing Office team visited the park to investigate charges of undue Curry Company influence. In Washington, Park Service Director Ronald Walker resigned under fire, and two congressional hearings were held on both Yosemite and park concessions policy nationwide.

All this did not happen just because of Joe Boland, but it's hard to imagine it happening without him. He raised an issue when others were lying back or afraid, kept it alive when others grew conciliatory or bored, and over the long haul gave it a precision and force it otherwise would have lacked. At the time he was 29, jobless and "just flippin' through life."

In college Boland had debated and for another two years he'd acted with the American Conservatory Theatre

424

The Agitator: Joe Boland
Simply because he loved the place, he spent 16 months digging up facts about MCA's plans for Yosemite and trying to get the attention of the press.
PHOTO: DAVE SUMNER

in San Francisco. But he much prefers quiet country living to city life and isn't the limelight type. For nine summers Boland worked in Yosemite on garbage and maintenance jobs. On days off he climbed — not for the intensity of the big walls but rather for the subtle play on the rounded domes east of Tuolumne Meadows off the Sierra Crest. During those years his love for the place deepened to the point that he now, almost reverently, calls Yosemite "home."

The morning after the May 7 meeting, Boland went to park headquarters in the valley. "I'd never done anything like this before," he says. "I asked to see all the preliminary drafts of the Curry Company proposal and all the correspondence that went with them." The information was "unavailable" there, and when he

hitchhiked over to the National Park Service's regional office in San Francisco the answer was, at first, the same.

Nevertheless, Boland could see that his requests made people edgy, so in a level way he persisted until he was referred to a sympathetic employee, who led him to a second employee and the documents he wanted. "I don't know if I should give you these papers," he was told, "but if I turn around and you take them, then I don't know where they went." Boland took the material to a corner desk and began reading. But soon a third staff member, a supervisor, moved to stop him.

This time Boland pleaded quietly and steadily for two hours. "I could see the man had a knot in his gut," he says. "He hated what was going on in

Yosemite, but he was locked in the bureaucracy and afraid to be open." Finally the legal department cleared the documents and only then did Boland learn of the Freedom of Information Act and the access that was his right as a citizen.

So Boland returned to Yosemite with his backpack full of Xeroxes and was soon able to figure out what was happening — "who wanted what, how they were getting it, who was browbeating whom and whom I could trust." This was the breakthrough. It showed (as reported in detail in BP-15) that MCA was forcing successively more favorable revisions in the Yosemite Master Plan through ties with the Nixon administration. And it made it clear that the tent cabin proposal was but part of a larger MCA design to intensively commercialize the park.

Now Boland formulated two simple goals: 1) to continue researching, and 2) to reach the public with what he found. For two more months he concentrated first on trench work: digging for more facts. Hitches to the Park Service regional office in San Francisco were regular, and doors opened in Yosemite. "I had good sources inside the Curry Company who were leaking me information," he recalls. "A lot of documentation came from wastebaskets." Boland was careful to protect his sources — by now the word on him was out — and often met with them at night up in the rocks by Yosemite Falls. He double- and triple-checked everything to offset the Yosemite rumor mill.

During this period Boland also worked to crack the media. This was tough. His first contact, a newsman in Oregon, buried a report on his desk for six months. The Sierra Club hierarchy in San Francisco was a blank wall and bounced him off to a local chapter because his story lacked "national significance." Most of his letters to Washington brought form letters in response. Jack Anderson dragged his feet until long after Boland's story had become safe. "Two months and nothing," he remembers. "Everyone was saying, 'Give up. You know you can't stop them.'"

By early July, 1974, Boland was temporarily burned out and decided to take a break in Colorado. Before leaving, however, he covered himself, working out assignments for three Yosemite friends to keep up while he was away. There was no telling when something might happen, and it did.

The press wouldn't buy Boland's story when it came from just a guy doing some digging. But as soon as Friends of Yosemite was invented, things were different.

Boland views his efforts as a guerrilla action "like the American Revolution," except he fears it will have only short-term effect.

While filming an episode for the MCA-Universal Studios TV series "Sierra," a production crew painted some rocks near the edge of the park so colors would match on the tube. The actual impact was trivial (lichen may have been killed), but the timing was superb. Watergate was the national agony of the day; doings in Yosemite had the same unseemly smell. "They're Painting Yosemite," read the classic headline of the hub-bub.

Boland's man-in-charge, Sky Lininger, seized the moment precisely. As the press flooded the park, he made sure it came away with more than a one-shot story about a painted rock. To accomplish this, he went public. From the Park Service he obtained a permit to place an information table on the Yosemite Village Mall, where thousands of summer visitors mill daily. He turned loose pickets with signs reading "Save Yosemite" and "Get MCA Out." He handed out a mimeographed newsletter detailing Boland's research. He talked to people, answered questions by the score, explained, and gathered signatures on a petition.

The Curry Company pressed the Park Service to stop the activity, but the move failed. When Boland returned, the three major networks had TV crews in the valley. They had not only an event to film but hard copy to go with it. The trench work was paying off.

Lininger did one more important thing: he began using the name Friends of Yosemite. All along the media had been asking Boland,

"Whom do you represent? Where are you from?" They wouldn't buy his story when it came from just a guy doing some digging. But as soon as Friends of Yosemite was invented, things were different. "All they wanted was a name," says Boland. "Any name to hang a story on."

Now so many doors were open that the situation became very different. Both the media and Washington, especially Representative John D. Dingell (D-Mich.), wanted all the information they could get. From July on, the detail work continued: more research, more double-checking, feeding the press and Washington, talking with park visitors on the mall and answering the mail, which was mounting. No form letters were sent; everyone who wrote Friends of Yosemite got an individual answer.

The rest — the GAO investigation, the congressional hearings — is public history. Boland plugged away in Yosemite until September, 1975. By then both he and Ann Baker, his steady co-worker through 16 months, had long since exhausted their $3,000 personal savings. "We were absolutely worn out, too," he adds. "We spread the word as far as we thought we could. It was time to leave, and we did."

Looking back, Boland views his effort as a guerrilla action "like the American Revolution," except he fears it will have only short-term effect. Friends of Yosemite never numbered more than five people, refusing to grow big and seek contributions. The Park Service correctly labeled Friends "a temporary group of uncertain membership" and never knew exactly who they were, let alone the identity of many of the group's sources.

As for results: "We accomplished a holding action," says Boland. "MCA came into Yosemite like corporate gangbusters, and it didn't work." He does not believe his campaign caused "any lasting change in basic awareness," but rather a chastisement. He thinks new designs to increase commercialization in the

park will surface soon and that Yosemite will continue to need its friends.

Why then did Boland bother? What kept him going?

During his months in Yosemite he thought about this, and since leaving he has continued to do so — not analytically but almost loosely, which may be the better way to fathom matters of passion. He talks of his love for Yosemite, of his experiences there, of special places at certain times of the day or year: an amphitheater at dusk, a dome in the fall, a meadow after rain.

If pressed beyond that for motives, Boland turns to an account from John Muir's book, *The Yosemite*, of the "relocation" of the native band of Miwok Indians from Yosemite Valley to a reservation on the plains near Fresno. The action occurred in the early 1850s, and the most striking thing about it was the Indians' deep reluctance to leave. After his favorite son had been shot and as the small band was about to be removed, the chief, Tenaya, gave this speech, addressing Captain John Boling of the Mariposa Battalion.

"Kill me, Sir Captain, yes, kill me as you have killed my son . . . You may kill me, Sir Captain, but you shall not live in peace. I will follow in your footsteps. I will not leave my home, but will be with the spirits among the rocks, the waterfalls, in the rivers and in the winds. Wherever you go I will be with you. You will not see me but you will fear the spirit of the old chief and grow cold."

"We're the Indians," says Boland, unable to explain further. ◣

FIRST WOMAN TO HIKE DEATH VALLEY

by BETTY J. TUCKER

For Betty Tucker, becoming an active
conservationist started with the second
hike of her life—a trek alone across the
entire length of Death Valley. She learned
a lot from that experience, about herself
and about the desert, as you will read in
the first of Betty's two pieces that follow.
Then continue to read about how she put
her love of the desert to action.

*Going hiking and backpacking is one thing for
a woman to do; going by herself is quite another experience. The experience of solo backpacking is a dramatic experience for anyone
who does it for the first time. For women it
presents different types of psychological problems.*

*Betty Tucker, at the age of 40, takes on the
full length of Death Valley alone. Some people
called it gutsy, some called it nutsy. No matter
what, it was an unusual experience worth
reading about.*

W.K.

I**F YOU WANT TO BE** considered a
crazy, just tell people you're going
to hike Death Valley. Mountaineers
can assault Annapurna, freeze off
their toes, get buried in an avalanche,
and still be considered sane. And
brave.

But *hike Death Valley?*

Think of the snakes, coyotes,
scorpions, tarantulas, the heat. Then
tell them you are a grandmother
planning to walk 140 miles down the
center of the valley alone, and they're
likely to bring a strait jacket for you
right then.

I was 45 years old and had long
since waded through the quicksands
of P.T.A., Brownies, girl and boy
scouts, and Y.M.C.A. Our son was a
high school senior. Our two daughters were grown and gone.

Still, with luck I was only half-

way through life. Surely there was
something I could do, not as
"mother" or "honey," but on my own,
as Betty.

One day my husband suggested
that I go backpacking in the mountains. I loved desert camping. So
much so, I often had gone car camping alone to sleep under the stars. But
backpacking in the mountains? "Oh
no!" I said. "Too much climbing; too
many bears."

"Well," Harry said, "how about
hiking in the desert?" I had just returned from Death Valley.

"I suppose I could do something
dramatic, like hike the length of
Death Valley," I replied.

He said, "Fantastic idea."

I took him seriously. I checked
backpacking catalogs. I tried on hiking boots. I planned menus. I bought

maps and figured the mileage for
water and food pickups.

Word got around. Soon it was either lose face or do the hike.

For a while, Harry had second
thoughts. But I persisted. At
Christmas he finally added his all-out
support by giving me a backpack.
Then he arranged to take two weeks
off from his job to help me make the
water and food drops.

A **MONTH BEFORE MY** departure, I
started to get in shape. I walked
every day until I got up to five miles
a day with a full pack. Finally, the
time arrived to head for the northern
end of Death Valley. For the entire
five-hour drive I worried about the
heat, blisters, breaking a leg, sprain-
ing an ankle. When Harry suggested
no one would blame me if I called off

Desert hikers must carry all their water, at least a gallon a day. To keep weight to a minimum during her hike through Death Valley, author Betty Tucker had her husband meet her every second day with a fresh supply.
PHOTO: HARRY TUCKER

the trip, I recovered. And so, on March 27, 1972, our twenty-fifth wedding anniversary, my husband kissed me goodbye and I began my hike.

Clad in long johns, mittens, wool socks, a sweater, jeans and down sweater, I circled Ubehebe Crater and shivered my way into what was supposed to be blistering heat. The sky was overcast. The wind caught my pack, turning me sideways. I started crying. I wanted to go home. It was cold, windy and ugly.

As I turned down Death Valley wash, thunder rolled ominously. I looked for an exit from the wash in case the clouds sent a flash flood my way. But there was none.

The wash, in its downward drop, had carved deep into the alluvium. I walked down between its eight-foot-high sides, passing islands where rushing waters had deposited a litter of twisted limbs. A bluejay whizzed past and landed on a branch of honey mesquite. I walked on looking for other signs of life.

Suddenly I rounded a bend and saw a bearded stranger less than 30 feet away. I stopped in my tracks.

The stranger grinned. In a disarming English accent he called out, "Hello there. Where are you off to?"

"Oh, just down to Saratoga Spring." I made it sound as if it were merely around the bend.

"You alone?"

Hesitantly, I nodded.

He stepped closer. Then he pulled four bananas from his jacket and handed them to me. Dumbfounded, I accepted.

"My wife made me take them along, but you're going farther than I. The wash gets a bit tacky around the bend after the campground." With that he waved and strode off.

I watched him go, then forged ahead and broke into song. The wash narrowed and cut through high gray hills. The mesquite, sparse until now, became tall and prolific. Yellow catkins lined the wash, giving off an aroma of orange blossoms.

At Mesquite Spring, Harry welcomed me with a steak and cold beer for our anniversary celebration. It had cleared, and the weather prediction was for sunny skies. The tent and rain gear were removed from my pack. In their place I put a gallon of water.

I was up before dawn the next day. My legs ached, and I had difficulty moving. After a quick breakfast, I shouldered my 30-pound pack and again headed down the wash. I wore all my warm clothes plus a brimmed hat.

AS THE SUN ROSE, its warmth eased my aches. Soon the walking became easier. High sedimentary cliffs, carved by eons of rushing waters, lined the wash. Here mastodons and prehistoric camels had once trod. I passed Bighorn Gorge, then Dry Bone Canyon. At noon I put on shorts and took out my stove to warm water for soup and tea.

Bees buzzed by to investigate this new water supply, along with a large wasp called a tarantula hawk. Its blue metallic body and reddish-orange wings flashed in the heat, then disappeared. The gentle hum of silence lulled me into security. I fell asleep.

Half an hour later I awoke hot and stiff. I repacked and staggered on. Now the wash was strewn with boulders. I moved ahead slowly. Though the footing was difficult, I was afraid I was behind schedule, which was important because of both the water pickup and the worry I would create if I were late. I began to hurry.

Soon I was stumbling over the rocks. Then my feet became tangled and I fell down in a sandy spot. I lay there for several minutes. The sand was warm, the sun penetrating, the breeze gentle. Slowly, I relaxed. I sat up and removed my pack. I poured water on a cloth and washed my face and hands. A feeling of contentment went through me. For the first time I did not feel threatened by the desert or that it was something I had to overcome.

At peace with myself, I picked my way on. As the sun began to drop I found a level spot and made camp. The sky darkened and filled with stars. But sleep did not come easily. Still enamored with my closeness to the desert, I wanted to see all and feel all. Later, awakening as the moon rose, I heard the distant yapping of coyotes. Then I slept soundly until the heat of day drove me from the sleeping bag.

And so day followed day. Inch-long horseflies became a nagging problem, and tiny midges flew into my eyes and nose. Rocks loomed larger and closer together. Finally, there was no way to step around and I was forced to go up and over. Mile upon mile I trudged through leg-straining sand and over rock-strewn terrain while lizards scooted out from underfoot at lightning speed.

As prearranged, Harry met me every two days with more water and supplies.

At LAST I WAS ON Westside Valley Road where I hoped walking would be a cinch. But as the rangers say, "There's one thing you can be sure of in Death Valley, and that's the wind." Which way it will blow, you never know. But blow it did, right into my face for the rest of the hike.

Finally I staggered into the ruins of the Eagle Borax works and found a shady grotto. It was infiltrated with buzzing insects and land and water birds. Moss covered the water where a killdeer and two green herons floated. An aristocratic phainopepla perched on a branch as I lay back on a mattress of duff under huge tamarisk trees.

As the sun set behind Telescope Peak, I started dinner. By the time I had finished eating, the insistent mosquitoes drove me onward for four more miles in the dark.

The next morning I climbed past the hills at the base of the Black Mountains. Telescope Peak in the Panamint Range was soon a memory; Confidence Hill beckoned, then faded into another memory. It was my longest day, 22 miles. By dusk I was too tired to eat and dropped into a dead sleep. I remember the day only as a wavy blur.

As I approached the end of the trail, I wanted to hurry. I put a thermometer under my hat, and it registered 106 degrees.

The trip had become a drag. I was too hot to care about the unchanging scenery. I no longer admired the speeding lizards. I just willed my feet on. It was like the final week of pregnancy—clumsy, ugly-feeling and lonely. But soon I would be able to rejoice.

At last I turned toward the Ibex Mountains, walked three miles across soft crusted dirt, through tall salt grass and across marshy ground. Then, finally, I stood gazing down into Saratoga Spring.

My husband, who had been waiting by the van, came up and kissed my dusty forehead. "One hundred-forty miles in ten days. Not bad, honey."

A tear slid down my cheek. I stood quietly, thinking back on the miles, knowing I had just become the first woman to hike Death Valley alone. But most of all, I thought of the deepened love I had developed for the desert, which would one day lead me to establish the Death Valley Hikers Association and to join those working on building the Desert Trail. ◣

BUILDING THE DESERT TRAIL

by BETTY J. TUCKER

It will stretch more than 2,500 miles from Canada to Mexico through the western deserts. And it will be an ideal place to hike in winter.

A LONE HIKER TRUDGED out of a sandy wash, stopped to look about, then built a small cairn. He marked the spot on his wrinkled topo map, dodged a spiny ocotillo and walked toward the thin shade of a smoke tree. At the tree he was met by a second hiker who had arrived from the opposite direction. The first hiker took out his canteen. "To the trail," he said. The hikers then took off their packs and began to compare and discuss their topo maps.

It was a scene that had taken place before and will take place many more times, by many other hikers, before the Desert Trail is fully established. When completed, the trail will stretch more than 2,500 miles from the Canadian border to Mexico. The proposed route passes through Idaho, Oregon, Nevada and California. To date, only 150 miles of the trail can be hiked, in Oregon. In other states much of the route has yet to be laid out and marked.

Putting together a trail takes time, as Russell Pengelly has discovered. A Burns, Oregon, high school biology teacher, he started planning the Desert Trail 13 years ago. He patterned the concept after the Pacific Crest Trail. Its success, and that of the

Appalachian Trail, had led him to speculate on the possibility of building a hiking and horseback trail that would traverse the western desert areas. He had two reasons for wanting to establish the trail: It would open up relatively unspoiled countryside to hikers, and he believed the existence of a trail would provide an incentive to preserve the desert's geological, biological, historical and scenic uniqueness. There would be additional advantages. The trail would take pressure off heavily used hiking areas and, since it was located in the desert, could be hiked when mountain trails were covered with snow.

Pengelly began studying maps in 1963 to determine possible routes. He found that more than 95 percent of the trail could be located on federal and state land. Where it would traverse private land, there was little development. Also, much of the terrain the trail would cross is relatively flat. This meant little construction—or expense—would be required to establish trail. Instead, in many places it could be marked simply with cairns and hiked as a point-to-point route.

Pengelly began writing letters to congressmen, public officials in the U.S. Forest Service and the Department of the Interior, recreation and wildlife groups, conservation organizations and hiking clubs to enlist support for the trail idea.

Slowly enthusiasm built. In 1968 the American Nature Study Society passed a resolution to support the Desert Trail concept. In 1970 The Izaak Walton League of America added its support. The same year the Bureau of Land Management in Oregon quietly endorsed the idea and began laying out possible routes. Unofficial support and help in trail routing came also from U.S. Forest Service officials in Oregon.

Later that year Ed Dolan and 25 other members of the Mazamas—a 75-year-old hiking and mountain-climbing club of Portland, Oregon—made the first official hike over a portion of the Desert Trail, from the Page Spring campground at the southern edge of the Malheur National Wildlife Refuge to Steens Mountain in southeastern Oregon. At a rest stop on the upper Blitzen River on Steens Mountain, a beaver swam up to Dolan's feet.

It was apparent the Desert Trail did not pass only through sagebrush flats and sandy washes.

In the fall of 1972, in Burns, Pengelly formed the Desert Trail Association to plot the route through Oregon and to enlist trail-building assistance from other states.

The section of trail that passes east of Burns was selected for the first step in the trail's development. The association decided the trail should go through Diamond Craters, where the most recent lava flows are believed to be only 400 years old. There the hiker could look through lava tubes created by molten magma flowing through tunnels of lava that had cooled more rapidly. At first the Desert Trail Association wanted to route the trail also through Malheur National Wildlife Refuge, the largest bird refuge in the United States and among the oldest. But after discussing the proposal with Refuge Manager Joseph Mazzoni, it was decided merely to skirt the reserve so as not to disrupt the habitat of the long-legged sandhill cranes and golden eagles. Provisions for future spur trails to areas of scenic or historic interest also were taken into account.

Slowly, a proposed route began to stretch across Oregon. In the spring of 1973 the Oregon State Recreational Trails Advisory Council proposed adding the Desert Trail to the state's trail system. That summer the Desert ing hike along the trail, to lay out the route from Diamond Craters to Steens Mountain. Accompanying the hikers were John Scharff, former manager of Malheur National Wildlife Refuge, Chris Vosler, manager of the Burns District of the Bureau of Land Management, Dick Gritman, public use specialist of the Malheur refuge, and Jack Remington, state trails coordinator for the State Parks and Recreation Section of the Oregon State Highway Division. All were along to study the trail concept.

By the end of the five-day hike the group had established a 30-mile route which was to become the first section of the new trail. At a celebration dinner on Steens Mountain, the section was designated the John Scharff Trail in recognition of Scharff's 36 years of service to the area.

It was a historic moment for Pen-

gelly. After 10 years of letter writing and discussions with state and federal officials, there was trail to walk on that could truly be called a desert trail.

In October, 1973, and again in January, 1975, Oregon Congressman Al Ullman introduced legislation in Washington to study the possibility of adding the Desert Trail to the National Scenic Trails System. If the measure is adopted, it will provide federal funds to establish campsites, water facilities and markers along the trail.

So far, only the Appalachian Trail and Pacific Crest Trail have been designated as national scenic trails. An additional 14 trails are under study for designation, but the Desert Trail is the only one which would take hikers through a variety of desert areas.

The proposed trail will lead the hiker through high desert peaks graced with mountain mahogany and trickling waterfalls. It will cross brush-carpeted basins and alkaline flats. It will skirt shallow lakes teeming with waterfowl, circle volcanic craters and pass by caves, near old mining camps and through areas rich in fossils and petrified wood.

Hikers will see towering joshua trees, cacti and tiny bellflowers and buttercups, as well as a diversity of wildlife: lizards, squirrels, coyotes, antelope, deer, fox, bighorn sheep and even, perhaps, the endangered pupfish, some of which live in Death Valley.

The oregon section of the trail now has been mapped. Last year, Pengelly's son David, then a junior at Oregon State University, completed a 35-day, 452-mile hike through the deserts and mountains of eastern Oregon. The Desert Trail in Oregon, at least, is becoming a reality.

Still, much of the trail is only in the planning stage. Pengelly has proposed a tentative route through Idaho and, in Nevada, the Bureau of Land Management has provided maps with suggested routes. But little has been done in either state to implement the trail.

In California the Desert Trail Association has fewer than two dozen members. Interest in the trail, however, is high. Three years ago The

Desert Protective Council voted to support the trail idea, and a committee was formed to plan a tentative route in California.

As proposed, the Desert Trail starts at the Canadian border in northwestern Idaho, swerves eastward near Priest River and follows the Montana border to Lolo Pass, where it turns southwest to follow the Snake River and enter Oregon at the southern end of Hells Canyon. From there it crosses the Wallowa Mountains and dips south of Baker to climb into the mountains near Sumpter. It then heads through the Wallowa-Whitman and Malheur national forests, along the Malheur River and past Malheur Cave, Diamond Craters and the Malheur National Wildlife Refuge. After climbing Steens Mountain, it drops down to the barren Alvord desert and enters Nevada near Denio.

From Denio, the trail crosses the Black Rock Desert, continues south toward Winnemucca, and then runs southwest to join the California section.

The California section goes through the Last Chance Range, circles the great Ubehebe Crater and

The proposed Desert Trail winds through four states from Canada to Mexico. Its route through Idaho and Nevada is only tentative.

> *Trail construction will be minimal. Instead, the path can be marked in many areas simply with cairns, and it can be hiked as a point-to-point route.*

enters Death Valley National Monument, where the Death Valley Hikers Association is planning both a winter and summer route the length of the valley. Then on to the great Mojave Desert—land of joshua trees, yucca, pinyon pines, coyotes and even mountain lions. There the hiker crosses salt flats, climbs desert peaks, peers into caverns and camps near ancient Indian petroglyphs. The trail passes through Joshua Tree National Monument, Painted Canyon and Mecca, then heads through the Anza-Borrego Desert State Park to the Mexican border.

PLOTTING A TRAIL on the map and having an actual usable trail, however, are two different things, as the California group discovered.

The biggest problem is water. While Oregon has enough water to keep a backpacker going, finding or developing water holes at 20-mile intervals over the entire route may be the ultimate challenge. In California what few seeps and springs exist along the state's proposed 1,450-mile route are necessary to wildlife. As a result, the California Chapter of the Desert Trail Association decided each hiker will have to be responsible for his own water supply and planned the route with access for caching in mind.

Areas of scenic and historic interest were taken into account, and the trail was planned to pass, if not through, at least near them. Private land was avoided wherever possible, as were areas set aside for motorcycle races. Wildlife habitats were considered, too, and the trail was routed where the disruption to desert life would be minimal.

Once the tentative route had been formulated, the California group decided to try the hike to be sure it was feasible. Last spring they began to put out the 30 food and water caches required for the trip. Almost at once they ran into problems. Some areas were described as "hotter than the

hinges of hell," and the route was modified accordingly. Then, midway along the route, their caching process ground to a halt. Private land and impassable back roads were going to force a massive review of part of the route.

A decision was made to forgo the center section of the trail and hike only the northern and southern sections, transferring from one section to the other by car.

Finally, on April 2, the hike began. But insect bites, heavy rains and heat soon proved too much. After only 55 miles, the hike was called off.

Nevertheless, it was not a total loss. The trail association found where they had gone wrong on their mapping. Also, they now know what 55 miles of the trail is like and how to assist those who want to hike other sections.

If you wish to, you can, of course, hike almost any part of the proposed Desert Trail right now simply because it is on public land. But you do so strictly on your own because no water has been provided and few trail markers of any kind have been placed. While parts of the trail have been officially recognized on maps, this is largely a form of advance planning by the Forest Service and Bureau of Land Management.

Still, the work begun by Russ Pengelly 13 years ago goes on. In June U.S. Senator Mark O. Hatfield (Oregon) introduced a Desert Trail Bill which, like Ullman's bill in the House, seeks to authorize a study of the Desert Trail for its designation as a national scenic trail. On August 24 the bill was approved by the Senate. Meanwhile, work continues on the trail in California and Oregon. Soon work will start on the trail in Nevada and Idaho.

But trails are built by individuals. Each person who even hikes a section and reports his findings to the Desert Trail Association will be helping to add another rock to the cairns along the trail. ◆

BUILDING THE FLORIDA TRAIL

by JAMES A. KERN

The success of the state's first footpath depends on self-motivated, self-reliant people who care about the land above all else. It may be the only warm-weather winter trail in the continental United States.

THE SIGHT WAS a little incongruous: Dr. David Wells, a staff physician at Plantation General Hospital in Hollywood, Florida, astride his swamp buggy, seven feet off the ground, handing down sections of pipe, a pitcher pump, bags of readi-mix cement, pipe wrenches, sledge hammers, and other paraphernalia to those below. It had taken three hours of strong-arm driving to get the buggy through the Big Cypress Swamp to this point on the Florida Trail, a spot about 50 miles west of Miami and seven miles north of U.S. Highway 41. The temperature was 85 degrees in mid-April, and the Big Cypress Swamp was bone-dry.

We were about to drive a well through the limestone cap rock and down into the sand, and we were sweating like mules in the dry heat.

Sinking the well turned out to be a hard two-day job, but now hikers can find water at two established campsites on the 31-mile stretch of trail between U.S. 41 and Alligator Alley.

David Wells has the responsibility of routing and maintaining one of 30 proposed sections that will eventually make up the Florida Trail. His contribution is part of a coordinated effort by hiking Floridians to build the first footpath in the state. Of a proposed 1,000-mile trail, 325 miles are already built, the result of the first

seven years' work. The Florida Trail Association is doing this job—Fred and Margaret and Tom and Al and Inez and Dorothy and dozens of other people who have a lot in common with David Wells, most of all their unwillingness to wait for the government to build their hiking trails for them.

Ten or 15 years ago hiking devotees knew that using trails also meant maintaining trails. But I wonder how many of those who have recently discovered the sport have asked: "Who built these trails? How can I contribute to their upkeep?" My concern for this problem has prompted me to describe something of what we are doing to build a footpath through Florida.

The Florida Trail begins at the Oasis Airport on Highway 41 not far from Everglades National Park. It presently runs northward through the Big Cypress Swamp and Ocala National Forest, turns westerly in Osceola National Forest, runs the bank of the Suwannee River for 75 miles, passes south of Tallahassee, and will extend through Apalachicola National Forest to Blackwater River State Forest. It is a flatland trail, hikeable when the heat and the rain of summer have disappeared. It is a winter trail, perhaps the only winter trail in the country; January, February, and March are the best months.

It is a private trail. People who want to hike it must sign a pledge agreeing to respect the rights of property owners, uphold trail ethics, and pay a modest fee before they can purchase maps.

"Hike in Florida?" asked personnel from the Florida Division of Recreation and Parks years ago. "It's hot, buggy, and swampy." Well, so it is in summer, but not in winter. From January to March, temperatures at night typically range from the 30s to the 60s, days from the 50s to the 80s. The dry season begins about November, so many marshy places are walkable by the first of the year. Since the entire state has a sandy soil, the walking is easy even when the ground is wet. Mosquitoes and other insects are scarce in winter. In fact, conditions for hiking then are ideal.

WHILE WINTER HIKING conditions in Florida are similar to summer hiking weather along ridge trails elsewhere in the country, the views are altogether different. For mile after mile in Big Cypress Swamp, the elevation doesn't vary more than two or three feet. Open pine "islands" occupy the higher land, some dotted with 90- and 100-foot slash-pine giants. The ground cover is usually saw palmetto, two to four feet high. These pine islands are ringed with grassy prairies,

Fronds of cabbage palms and waist-high palmettos grow faster than most other plants and add heavily to the maintenance problem along the Florida Trail.

PHOTO: JAMES A. KERN

usually dotted with dwarf cypress. The prairies run off into shallow depressions where summer and fall rains remain longest and where the cypress grow dense, straight, and tall.

Throughout the summer, several feet of water stand in the cypress depressions, or heads. The water is up to a foot deep on the prairies, and the ground on the pine islands is soggy. But when the rains stop in October the land begins to dry out, and by January most of the trail is dry. There are no rivers or lakes through this country, but at almost any point on the trail, hikers can doff their boots and wade into the cypress heads for water, carrying canteens and hala-zone tablets. By April the situation has reversed. Frequently no water at all can be found, even in the deepest heads. Hence the reason for installing wells.

But while the Florida Trail through the Big Cypress Swamp may be unlike any other trail in the country, it is also uniquely varied elsewhere in the state. Section 1 is entirely different from Section 12 through the sand pine country of Ocala National Forest, and Section 12 is very different from Section 18 along the banks of the Suwannee River. In the Ocala, pine islands are made up of stately long-leaf pines that spike a grassy floor devoid of an understory, while the "sea" around these islands

is dense stands of thin-barked sand pine that emerge from an understory of scrub oak, rosemary, and palmetto. Frequently only deer moss and pine needles carpet the white sand floor. Along the Suwannee live oaks draped with Spanish moss provide towering shade. Cypress and tupelo cling to the rocky ledges of the river. Not typical backpacking scenery, to be sure, but the miles of wildness are typical of what we Florida backpackers long to see again each year.

I N THE WINTER OF 1967 I made a 160-mile, 12-day hike through typical Florida backcountry to dramatize the idea of building a trail through Florida. The *Miami Herald* did a series of articles on the hike, culminating in a color cover article in a Sunday issue. Interested people were invited to write the Florida Trail Association, and in a few days we were 70-members strong.

We didn't need a highly structured organization—meetings, agendas, reports, committees for this and that. We needed self-reliant people who would grab the ball and run with it. A trail gets built because there are people to whom one can say, "We want to get the trail from Clearwater Campground on State Road 44 to Juniper Springs. Will you lay it out?" And someone says yes.

The volunteer must study aerial

photographs and contour maps, perhaps make an aerial inspection, talk to property owners if the land is privately owned and get their permission to cross the land, and then mark the trail. He must bushwack his way through woods, making dozens of decisions every thousand feet as the trail is affected by terrain, water, obstacles, natural beauty, and unsightly developments. Even the availability of suitable trees on which to place blazes and aligning the trail so that hikers will tend to stay on it when not watching for blazes are important considerations. Dozens of volunteers are needed to build just a few hundred miles of trail.

Fred Mulholland is an office supervisor at the General Telephone Company in Tampa. He loves to backpack. He has walked across the White Mountains on snowshoes in January at 10 degrees below zero, and he has crossed the Ocala National Forest in 90-degree heat in the middle of a mosquito and horsefly summer. A group of us, including Fred, went to the U.S. Forest Service in 1967 (before backpacking was the "in" thing it is today) and asked whether they had any interest in building a hiking trail through the Ocala. They weren't interested, so we asked if we could build one, and got the go-ahead.

Armed with a pair of loppers, machete, gloves, compass, canteens of water, mosquito repellent, and rain gear, Fred Mulholland took on the south half of Ocala National Forest. It was a 24-mile stretch. He had a lot of help from others in the Tampa area, including a scout troop, his wife, Ruth, and his children. In less than a year most of the work was done. Even before a suitable map had been made, hikers heard about the trail and started using it. They also began pumping U.S. Forest Service personnel with questions about the new trail. It was legitimate, it was growing, it was compatible, and it dawned on the Forest Service that they had better get in on it. So they announced plans to rebuild and maintain this hiking trail themselves.

Fortunately, the Forest Service employee assigned to build the trail through their land was a no-nonsense, hard-working guy named Bill Craig. Bill aligned the route of the Ocala Trail over much of the route

Pine woods along the trail provide good campsites. They are airy and open and let backpackers make good use of the day's last light.
PHOTO: JAMES A. KERN

THE
FLORIDA
TRAIL

DOTTED LINE REPRESENTS
THE PROPOSED TRAIL.
SUBSTANTIAL PORTIONS
OF WHICH HAVE BEEN
COMPLETED.

wasn't overseeing trail construction in the national forests, he could be found in the pine flatwoods south of his home in Tallahassee, blazing his own section of trail through Saint Joe Paper Company land.

Bill has been helped enormously by Dr. Inez Frink, a gray-haired lady who might just out-walk Colin Fletcher if the two were put on the trail together. Inez was a professor of business education and office management at Florida State University before retiring to wield a machete for the Florida Trail Association. But her greatest asset for us has been her desire to assist others in discovering the beauties and adventure of an on-foot encounter with nature. She leads several of the association's scheduled activities each year and introduces newcomers to what wilderness Florida has to offer.

THE ASSOCIATION'S patriarch is Al Stone, a retired Du Pont executive who used to make maps for Appalachian Trail hikers in Pennsylvania. He was able to meet with owners of large tracts of land on an equal basis and persuade them to let us go through their land. His biggest selling job was with Hudson Pulp & Paper Company, whose forward-thinking management not only agreed to allow hikers but provided Al with priceless (for us) aerial photographs for routing the trail. And when Al wanted to run the trail across some ancient earthen levees built during the British occupation of Florida in the 1790s for the purpose of raising rice, Hudson decided to contribute further by building the necessary foot bridges to connect the levee system at their expense. Al's map-making skills were equally helpful. After volunteering to make our maps, he began receiving rough data from section leaders around the state as their sections approached completion. Al turned out a simple, inexpensive map with detailed information on the reverse side for section leaders who did not have the background for this kind of work.

Much of our enterprise is carried on simply through the mail, two meetings a year, an occasional parley on the trail, and talks on the tele-

Fred had selected and made sure it emerged from the forest at points that were satisfactory to us. To show us his enthusiasm for the trail, he joined the Board of Directors; and when he

phone. Of considerable help for building enthusiasm and skills are a summer conference and an annual meeting when refresher courses on trail policies are held.

WHILE THE SUCCESS of a trail club depends on self-motivated, self-reliant people, finding them is easier than might be expected. Professional people make up a high percentage of those who enjoy walking in the woods, and they find that the diversion of trail building is a rewarding contrast to their office routine.

Dorothy Laker is a classic example. A librarian with double-A feet and gray-streaked hair, she has hiked the length of the John Muir Trail and probably more miles on the Florida Trail than anyone else. Her value to the association is that she is willing to lend a hand with anything that needs to be done.

Sometimes a man who works outdoors will take a busman's holiday and blaze trail on weekends. Tom Montoya is one of these. Tom is a lineman for the Tampa Electric Company and is now the Florida Trail Association's president. For years Tom routed, blazed, and maintained almost 50 miles of trail along the banks of the Suwannee with the help of an enthusiastic wife and four energetic daughters. His great talent is in making people happy in their work. Whenever Tom schedules a work weekend, people seem to come from all over north Florida to take part.

Margaret Scruggs has been an active member of the association from the first. The spirit of the outdoors rushes through her veins. Although canoeing and hiking are her primary interests, she has an extraordinary ability to manage details and see that myriad little jobs get done properly and on time. Today she is our executive secretary.

While these brief biographies give some idea of the kind of people needed to make a hiking association hum, no one should get the impression that the leadership remains in the hands of the old-timers. We try to prevent hardening of the arteries and have a relatively simple way to do it. We sponsored a few pleasure hikes from the beginning; now, with long sections of trail complete, we sponsor hundreds of them. Their primary purpose is to encourage newcomers to see and feel the beauty of a walk in the woods. We schedule work activities where the help of many hands in clearing trail and renewing paint blazes gets such routine work done fast. (These activities are fun, in part because people have the satisfaction of knowing they are helping to make the trail a reality.) After each of the hundred-odd hikes and canoe trips we sponsor each year, the leader turns in a short report. In it he mentions individuals who he thinks have leadership ability. Four times a year, before the quarterly newsletter goes to press, some of these people are telephoned and asked whether they would like to lead an activity. We build the activities around their preferences. As the association grows, leadership needs continue to grow, and this search for leaders is never-ending. A time limit for service on the board also forces the existing leadership to continually enroll new board members. Thus our trail group grows . . . at a healthy 50 percent per year, 6,000 people to date.

CONTEMPLATION OF what we are doing has made me wonder whether hikers in other parts of the country are as concerned about extending trails in their areas to accommodate the enormous number of new hikers. How many miles of new trail are being built each year? Even more important, I believe that the idea that only the government should build trails has got to go. The U.S. Forest Service spent $60,000 building 64 miles of the Florida Trail through the Ocala National Forest. Those 64 miles are beautiful, graded in places and in other places elevated by boardwalks through laurel, oak and cabbage palm sloughs. We are grateful. But with volunteer labor, we individuals spend less than a tenth of $60,000 in constructing an equal length of trail. (Trail maintenance costs are a bargain for the government, too, because most hikers adopt strict trail ethics.)

When we really do need help from the government, unfortunately we have a difficult time getting it—for instance, in the matter of continuity. A long trail involving private land simply cannot remain continuous without the power of eminent domain, the right of a government to appropriate private property for public use (frequently called condemnation). The power to condemn land in Florida can be used for vehicular traffic but not foot traffic. It applies to economic considerations such as building gas lines and power lines but not to recreational needs such as footpaths.

We made one effort to obtain eminent domain for footpaths from the state legislature and were put down promptly. The cattle interests were afraid bulls would gore us; the tourist industry was afraid we would tempt people away from the bright lights of the city; the orange-grove owners were afraid we would pick their fruit off trees as we hiked by, although the trail doesn't go through a single grove; the timber companies were afraid we would set the woods on fire. In fact, almost all the large lobbies in the state lined up against us.

ALL OF FLORIDA is flat and open to development. We have no long stretches of trail traversing high ridges that are government property and therefore safe from developers. Until regional zoning is instituted to protect portions of the state, every corner of it is vulnerable to dramatic changes in land use.

The Florida Trail Association has shown the need for and the value of hiking trails. We have shown that the cost-benefit ratio of hiking trails is very favorable, and our soaring membership is a good indication that hiking is not merely a fad that may soon disappear. The one thing state officials could provide is eminent domain. In the meantime, everyone who writes to Florida's Division of Recreation and Parks asking for information about the Florida Trail is referred to us, The Florida Trail Association.

For further information, write for the flyer entitled "Memo to Activity Leaders" and "Trail Policies for Section Leaders." Please enclose self-addressed, stamped envelope.
Florida Trail Association
4410 N.W. 18th Place
Gainesville. Florida 32605

TO SAVE A TRAIL

by CHARLES FERGUS

Ninety-two miles of the Appalachian Trail in Pennsylvania were threatened by development. Conservation groups and federal agencies had pushed for protective legislation since 1972, but their efforts were bogged down. Bills sat in committees. Then along came five concerned people, naive enough to think they could do something in eight weeks. And they did.

MILTON J. SCHAPP, GOVERNOR of Pennsylvania, stood in the crowded rotunda. Over him towered the dome of the capitol, blue, gold and white. Noise: flashguns popped, voices, footsteps on the worn red tile. State employees formed lines to get swine flu inoculations. The governor rubbed his arm where he had just received his shot; flanked by bodyguards, big men with quick eyes, Shapp started up the white marble stairs.

At the same time, a brown-haired woman carrying a wicker basket filled with sheaves of paper started down the stairs. She saw the governor and quickened her pace. "Governor Shapp," she said, pausing on the step above him. "We have some petitions here."

Shapp rubbed his arm through the fabric of his suit. Reporters edged closer. The woman stepped down and stood on the same step, eye to eye with the governor. "The Appalachian Trail is endangered in Pennsylvania. We need passage of a strong law to protect the trail and to qualify for matching federal funds."

"I've supported trail legislation for a long time," Shapp said with a smile. Microphones in front of his face tilted toward the woman as she lifted the basket.

"Governor, the petitions in this basket are signed by over 35,000 Pennsylvanians. And they represent the sentiments of many other Pennsylvanians, I'm sure."

"That's nice," the governor said, still smiling. "Go out and get me three or four more baskets." The discussion went on. Other Save the Trail people crowded in,

firing questions. Finally the governor held up his hand. "I will sign a bill," he said, "but without an appropriation. We have no money. We're broke."

The brown-haired woman answered quickly. "We've been told there *is* money available, that revenues have been running in excess."

"I will veto all appropriations."

Sue Daugherty's face lights up when she tells that story about her chance meeting with Governor Shapp. "He was really very kind," she says. "He talked with us for 15 or 20 minutes. When he left, one of his PR men gave us a card and told us to contact the governor's financial advisor."

Sue is the unofficial leader of Save the Trail, a citizens' committee which recently prodded the Pennsylvania government into passing a bill to protect the Appalachian Trail. She is 39 years old, poised and has piercing green eyes. A housewife? "I don't want that as my epitaph," she jokes. "I'm primarily interested in environmental education."

And in saving the Appalachian Trail. Her life and the lives of the four other committee members revolved around this task for eight hectic weeks—from October 1, 1976, when Save the Trail was born, to November 26, when Governor Shapp signed a bill allocating $250,000 for protection of the trail on private land in Pennsylvania.

ANOTHER STT MEMBER is Audrey McGahen, an environmental educator who has taught in Harrisburg-area schools. With short dark hair,

glasses and a measured tone of voice, she reminds you of a teacher you had, perhaps in fifth grade, a teacher who made you want to learn. Audrey is 50 and has three children. One of them, 23-year-old Carolyn, also belongs to Save the Trail. Like her mother, Carolyn is at home in the outdoors. Red-haired and ebullient, she has worked for the National Wildlife Federation as a counselor in environmental education.

At 55, Mary DeVincent is the oldest STT member. Although not a hiker, she's conservation chairman of the local Penn–Cumberland Garden Club. Indeed, the first trail action came from a petition campaign started by that club's Environmental Action Committee, which Sue chairs and to which Audrey is a special advisor. "We needed a project to work on for the year," Mary says, almost sheepishly in the face of Save the Trail's unimagined evolution. STT's fifth, final, and only male member is Gary Smith. Soft-spoken, he seems older than his 25 years. He works for the state's Department of Environmental Resources and is president of the Appalachian Audubon Society, a chapter of the National Audubon Society.

The need to protect the trail was evident back in 1969, when Audrey led a troop of girl scouts on a section of the AT near Boiling Springs. "When we started hiking, we found that part of the trail had been paved over for the main street of a housing development," she says. "In the woods, where the trail went, they had bulldozed the trees and brush into a big gulley." Plastic ribbon tacked to posts

Andy Coone of Belvedere, South Carolina, was on his second traverse of the AT when he met Save the Trail-ers, who explained the threat to the trail imposed by private landowners. Hiking north to south, Coone had left Katahdin in Maine on September 2, 1976, and expected to finish in Georgia in February.
PHOTO: CHARLES FERGUS

showed where houses would go; all along the ridge, the trail was marked off.

THE APPALACHIAN TRAIL cuts 224 miles through Pennsylvania, 92 miles on private holdings and the rest on state game and forestry lands. Audrey McGahen learned that the private land was subject to development—legally. And of those 92 miles, at least half were hemmed in by other development, which made rerouting impossible. She also discovered that Pennsylvania was one of the only places where such a situation existed. All of the other Appalachian Trail states except Vermont had responded to federal urging and passed laws providing a "green" corridor—a buffer zone bordering both sides of the trail where development was forbidden.

The women discussed the situation at a garden club meeting. They began to ask questions and make telephone calls to state offices. They learned that two bills—one in the Senate and the other in the House—had been proposed to protect the trail. The bills gave the state the power to buy, through eminent domain, if necessary, as much as 25 acres per mile of trail—thus preserving a green, undeveloped corridor up to 100 feet wide on each side of the trail.

"The bills were just sitting there, hung up in committees," says Carolyn. "In order to get money from the federal government, one of the bills had to pass in November." What were the chances of that happening? "No good, they told us. The reasons were lack of public interest and personal conflict between politicians. We decided to do something about it."

It would have to be fast. The committee discovered that if neither bill became law, Pennsylvania would probably lose $235,-000 in federal funds. This money was available under the National Scenic Trails Act only through early 1977. Another, more alarming note: bulldozers were ready to tear into at least three trail segments. Near Smith and Fox gaps and at Wolf Rocks in the Pocono Mountains, developers planned more than a thousand vacation homes. In addition, at White Rock Acres where Audrey's girl scouts had noticed damage seven years earlier, the builder's pamphlet boasted how close the development is to the Appalachian Trail.

SAVE THE TRAIL began a letter-writing campaign. They wrote to legislators; they cajoled friends into writing to their representatives; they telephoned the press (especially hometown newspapers of key lawmakers), outdoor columnists and even organizations that might care only slightly about the trail.

Later, when they visited the offices of individual lawmakers, they saw stacks of letters and mailgrams sent by concerned citizens.

"Some of the legislators grumbled at the volume of mail," Carolyn recalls. "But the movement began to gain momentum. At first we didn't know who held the power. Then, whenever we found a new point of sensitivity, that's where we hit."

Save the Trail members made timid visits to politicians' offices. "I went in to see a lot of people with my hat in my hand," Sue says. "I'd start by saying, 'We're trying to save the trail . . .' and they'd say, 'No way, baby.' Well, I never was one to take 'no' for an answer.

"I wish I had a nickel for every time someone told us we had about as much chance as a snowball in hell." Sue's eyes narrow slightly, and creases appear at their corners. "I remember talking to a man in the office of the Joint Conservation Committee. I asked him if he thought a petition might help. He said, 'Sue, can you get 10,000 names?' I picked myself up off the floor, thought about all the people we know who really care, and said, 'Yes. We *can* get 10,000 names.'"

So they printed petitions, cover letters and news releases. Help came from various organizations: the Keystone Trails Association, the Appalachian Trail Conference, National Audubon Society and other groups ranging from the boy scouts

A developer's proposal for Wolf Rocks. Note how the AT passes through the midst of the houses.
PHOTO: COURTESY OF THE APPALACHIAN TRAIL CONFERENCE

PROPOSAL FOR DEVELOPMENT OF THE AT AT FOX GAP, PENNA.

WOLF ROCKS

500   0   1000

DEVELOPER'S PLAN
FOX GAP, PENNA.

to the DAR. Save the Trail contacted BACKPACKER, and Executive Editor–Publisher William Kemsley, Jr. provided address labels of all Pennsylvania subscribers, as well as a letter explaining Save the Trail's goals.

Success mounted daily, and so did frustration. A friend of Audrey's called and offered support from the Pennsylvania State Education Association, which represents one of the most powerful voting blocks in the state. And there were other such groups: the Pennsylvania Federation of Sportsmen's Clubs, Sierra Club, Pennsylvania Environmental Council, League of Women Voters, Pennsylvania Forestry Association, Keystone Trails Association, Pennsylvania Chapter of the American Society of Landscape Architects—the list grew. Such lobbyists are part of the political world, and they began to apply their own special pressures.

AT FIRST, TRAIL CLUBS gave the committee a surprisingly cold shoulder. "You couldn't blame them," comments Audrey. "They'd worked for trail legislation for a long time, and they were bitter. 'What are you in it for?' they asked. We tried to explain that we were 'in it' only for the good of the trail." When confidence finally replaced suspicion, the trail groups joined forces with the newcomers.

Although Save the Trail members were political amateurs, there were two important things working in their favor: first, they lived only five miles from Harrisburg, the seat of government in Pennsylvania; and second, their mission had taken possession of them.

"We practically lived in the capitol for three weeks, and the rest of the time we were on the telephone," Sue says. "Our phone bills were humongous." Persistence began paying off as signatures, letters and petitions poured in from all over the state, and the rest of the nation, too. The Save the Trailers began to realize just how many politically knowledgeable contacts they had made in a few short weeks.

Carolyn got her fair share of frustration at a John Denver concert in Philadelphia. The evening's purpose had been two-fold: to enjoy the music and, if possible, contact the environmentally concerned entertainer and ask him to say a few words about Save the Trail. She talked to stage managers, concert police, even a member of Denver's band, but she couldn't get in to see Denver himself. Finally she arranged for him to be given a package of information. A sympathetic ticket seller had wangled her a seat only 11 rows from the stage, but Carolyn was too tense to really enjoy the concert.

"He was singing, 'the backcountry, that's where I belong.' And here was a chance for him to say to all those Philadelphians—'Look, here's a backcountry you can *save*.' And I couldn't get through to him. I still don't know if he even saw the information."

Later, Save the Trail received help from an unexpected source. Three backpackers—Dave Buttle, Tim Luria, and John Strange, all in their late twenties and from the Philadelphia–N.J. area—had arrived at the Pocono Mountain section of the Appalachian Trail. They'd started south from Maine in September and would trek into West Virginia before stopping for winter, but now they took a break. Complete with backpacks, trail dirt and beards, the hikers got a ride to Harrisburg and lobbied for the AT legislation.

BY THE END of October, the petitions had brought in 35,000 signatures; by mid-November, with time running out, the number stood at 48,000—a few more than the 10,000 names they'd been advised to get. But Save the Trail kept pushing. "A couple of times we were told to back off and take it easy," says Sue. "We did, because at that point we didn't want to antagonize anybody."

Carolyn adds: "We always made sure we were supporting the legislators, not chastising or berating them." Others, especially the press, were less diplomatic. One writer called the proposed $250,000 "a flyspeck sum in today's world of millions (spent for far less meaningful projects)"; another cited recent pay hikes that the legislators had okayed for themselves; many more sensed a certain irony in the public's having to complete a job for which their representatives were paid.

One problem Save the Trail faced from its inception was that the legislature would be in session only a few days following the November election. Rumor had it the lawmakers would vote on matters they judged more important and pressing than a bill to save a footpath.

Then on November 15, 1976, House Bill 2359—a catchall for appropriations—made its way into the Joint Conference Committee. The House majority leader began to outline and explain various provisions. When he reached the section, "For establishing, maintaining and preserving the Appalachian Trail," he paused. "You all know about that," he said, skipping ahead to a Health Department grant. In the gallery, the people of Save the Trail exchanged glances, nods and smiles.

Less than two weeks later Governor Shapp signed the bill. "That's when we knew we were in the clear," Sue says. "And that's when we celebrated!"

The bill sets aside a quarter-million dollars which will be matched by the federal government and used to maintain the all-important undeveloped zone bordering the trail. This will be done by acquiring rights-of-way and easements from private landowners—or, if necessary, by condemning and purchasing the corridor.

The complete package of laws needed to set the program in motion will come later. As of this writing, the Save the Trail committee has met with representatives of the Pennsylvania Department of Environmental Resources (the agency handling the money), the Appalachian Trail Conference, the Keystone Trails Association and the federal government. Together, they will hash out an overall plan to be made law during the next session of the legislature. ◆

NINE STEPS TO POLITICAL ACTION

Besides being inspiring, the story of Save the Trail is a fine primer in political action. No one said working through the political system is easy, but it can be done effectively. Perhaps one of the biggest stumbling blocks is being heard. Here are some thoughts on communicating with your representatives:

1. Write a personal letter. Form letters are much less effective.
2. If you have a personal letterhead, use it. And sign your name clearly and be sure your return address is on both letter and envelope.
3. Identify your subject clearly. Supply the number of the bill with which you are concerned, if possible.
4. Give your reason for writing and your personal experience in the matter. Explain how the issues affect you, your family, business and community.
5. Use your own language. Don't try to sound like a lawyer or regurgitate prepared statements supplied by a lobby group.
6. Be polite and reasonable. Don't threaten with the loss of your vote.
7. Ask for a statement of your representative's position on the issue. You're entitled to it.
8. Remember that things do not happen overnight in politics. Consider the timing and write your letter when the bill is in committee rather than the day before it comes up for a vote.
9. Politicians are people and appreciate a thank-you note. They will remember such a courtesy the next time you write with a request or comment.

VOLUNTEERS

Salvation for the Nation's Forests

by DOROTHY ALDRIDGE

"There's more work to be done on national forests than can ever be accomplished by all the Forest Service employees in all of its history," says Bill Ruskin, organizer of the VCC. He's right, and he may have the solution.

THE HIGHLY SUCCESSFUL Volunteer Conservation Corps, organized in 1974 near Colorado Springs, Colorado, is proof that there are thousands of Americans willing to work in U.S. national forests if given the opportunity.

A project of the National Hiking and Ski Touring Association (NAHSTA), the volunteer concept proved its worth in a cooperative effort by citizens, free enterprise and the U.S. Forest Service.

NAHSTA inaugurated the first nationwide recruitment of a volunteer crew to work on trails in a U.S. national forest. Hundreds of volunteers from across the United States saw in the invitation the opportunity for personal contribution—the chance to sweat a little and sacrifice the questionable reward of cash in doing work for the common good.

The Volunteer Conservation Corps (VCC) was the brainchild of William R. Ruskin, founder and president of the Colorado Springs-based NAHSTA. Ruskin recognized the problems caused by a shortage of Forest Service funds for building, maintaining and repairing trails, and the willingness of individual citizens to personally do something about them.

In September, 1973, Ruskin asked Region 2 Forester William Lucas of Denver what he thought of bringing 50 people together at Monument Environment Center in Pike National Forest to participate in a pilot program to be called the Volunteer Conservation Corps. The program would be centered around trail building but would involve other forest work, including recreation, training and environmental education. Volunteers would have a unique vacation experience while mak-

ing a valuable contribution to the National Forest System. The objective would be to ignite enough interest and provide sufficient training so corps members would return to their communities and start similar projects at the grassroots level.

Lucas not only agreed that the volunteer idea had merit but explained that little-known Public Law 92-300 of 1972 would support exactly what Ruskin had in mind. The law authorizes the secretary of agriculture to establish a program of volunteers in the national forests, working under supervision and protected by federal law if injured on the job.

Consequently, in January, 1974, a single NAHSTA advertisement in a magazine with limited circulation called for volunteer trail builders. The ad emphasized that all ages would be welcome to spend two weeks in Colorado building trails, that no previous experience was necessary and that volunteers would receive no monetary remuneration. But there would be benefits of other kinds: camping in a beautiful area while learning physical, intellectual and organizational skills, and helping to reverse a 30-year trend by adding eight miles to America's declining mileage of hiking trails.

"The response was overwhelming," Ruskin recalls. "By April, more than 1,300 persons from just about every state had volunteered to spend their vacations building trails in Colorado."

FROM THE LANDSLIDE of applicants, only 60 persons from 14 states could be chosen to constitute the first VCC because facilities were limited. One hundred other volunteers were recruited by the

Forest Service's Region 2, eager to have help building the Colorado Trail—the state's most ambitious recreational project. When completed, this nonvehicular trail will extend more than 300 miles through six national forests, from Denver to Durango.

Among those chosen were the president of a daily newspaper, his son and two nephews; a Utah electronics worker, his two daughters and two sons; a part-time waitress–student from New Jersey; and an Iowa grain merchant and his family in search of a healthful, educational, high-country experience. Similar thoughts were expressed by a school custodian, probation officer, registered nurse, cable machine operator, radiological technologist, clothing corporation president and a teacher of industrial arts.

"Many volunteers had spent a lifetime developing skills in particular trades and professions," Ruskin says. "That they were willing to share their knowledge as service on public lands was impressive."

The volunteers agreed to provide their own transportation and personal items and pay for meals. Then, private enterprise got behind the project and donated $2,000 in food, money and such equipment as family-size tents and backpacks.

Walter H. Schrader, Jr., was selected as project director. From 1912 to 1931 he had lived in Pike National Forest at the project site, which was then the Forest Service's Monument Nursery. (His father had been in charge of the facility.) For 25 years he had been a wildlife biologist and plant-material specialist with the U.S. Soil Conservation Service in Rock Hill, South Carolina. And for the previous 15 sum-

GRANNY ON THE TRAIL
BY DOROTHY STANLEY MOORE

THE RAIN POURED DOWN the night I arrived in Crestone, Colorado, a two- by three-block hamlet at the base of the west slope of the Sangre de Cristo Mountains. I left my car—and the amenities of civilization—and huddled in miserable silence with other VCC workers in the back of a Forest Service pickup for a three-mile, cold, wet ride to our base camp. "I was ready to pack up and go home," Marlene, a mother with three children, later told me, and others agreed.

There was more rain the next day, and our spirits were as damp as our clothes as we attended lectures and demonstrations on trail maintenance, and learned how to use shovels, pruning saws, axes and pulaskis—wicked-looking double-bladed picks. Toward the end of the day, Linda Cooper, a volunteer leader in charge of 19 workers, approached me and asked, "Will you be in charge of a trail crew?" Surprised, yet no less flattered that she would choose a 48-year-old grandmother, I accepted the job and was assigned a crew: Marlene and her children, 18-year-old Rich, and Lynn, a girl of 19. We were not by any stretch of the imagination a stereotype trail maintenance crew.

The next morning the sun rose behind a backdrop of drying clothes, and Lynn, Rich and I backpacked two steep miles to our assigned campsite, an aspen-ringed spot at 9000 feet next to a plunging stream. Marlene and her youngsters, Kim (14), Clay (11) and Scott (10), followed later.

Work began the following day. We tackled the open slopes in the morning when the sun was least intense, yet sweat ran into our eyes anyway and rest breaks were frequent. Scott, small for his age, carried messages and water and sometimes worked with a shovel, while the rest of us toiled with heavy pulaskis or shovels, trading tools occasionally to even out the workload. We were self-sufficient, highly dependent on each other (although Linda visited us daily, carrying a heavy radio and backpack) and, within a few days, were functioning like a team.

At the end of the first week, we were rewarded with the weekend off. After hot showers, we all took a busman's holiday—hiking in the Great Sand Dunes National Monument and on the strenuous trail to North Crestone Lake. Both evenings we attended local bicentennial celebrations.

The second week we traded campsites with the base camp crew so they could enjoy the high country. In return for our

thoughtfulness, we were introduced to the joys of building water bars, diversionary "dams" for channeling water across trails. We often started a bar by wrenching out grapefruit-sized rocks that grew into watermelons the moment we touched them. After five hours a day of such labor, our tools weighed twice as much as when we started. Yet we got good at our job, and we stopped counting water bars after we reached 100.

For a change of pace, we spent a day filling and leveling two abandoned garbage pits—hardly a glamorous task, but one which we tackled with an ever-increasing dedication and sense of purpose. We all worked hard, and only once was there a note of complaint—from 10-year-old Scott.

"I know you're tired. I understand," I said. "I just don't want to hear about it." And I didn't.

At the end of the week, after a "real meal" of grilled hamburgers served up in style by the Forest Service, we exchanged addresses, posed for pictures, made promises to visit and said goodbyes. Meeting as strangers, we had lived and worked with each other for two weeks and were now close friends.

"I'm glad I didn't go home," Rich said as we parted. So was I.

Trail chief (and grandmother) Moore works on a water bar, a barrier for channeling water runoff across a trail.

PHOTO: DOROTHY STANLEY MOORE

mers he had directed the coeducational South Carolina Conservation Corps—200 high school volunteers who spent the summer doing conservation projects.

"One important thing we determined," Ruskin declares, "is that it's highly feasible to bring inexperienced families with children into a forest and involve them in rigorous work." The youngest member of the corps was five years old. "In such a situation, it's important to have adequate training before work starts and experienced supervision from field personnel during the project."

Because most of the volunteers were inexperienced, four days of training in forest skills were conducted by personnel from the U.S. Forest Service and the Colorado State Forest Service. Sessions included environmental training, operation of the U.S. Forest Service, use of hand tools, living in the backcountry, weather conditions, hypothermia and mountain medicine.

Harold Wadley, overall director of volunteer programs in Region 2, gave instruction in safety and trail construction; state Forest Service representatives provided lessons in controlling the pine bark beetle and mistletoe. Ruskin taught orienteering and the use of map and compass. Additionally, special speakers gave presentations during the evening. They talked about wilderness, the natural history of the Pikes Peak region and land-use planning.

"We believed that trail building in the wilderness and land-use planning in urban areas should be regarded together," Ruskin explains. "The VCC would not be working on just a trail in a forest but one related to urban Colorado Springs, miles away."

After project leaders had been selected from among the volunteers and trained by Schrader to lead group projects, the first nationally recruited trail crew went to work.

In evaluating the pilot program, Ruskin says, "I think we scheduled too many activities and didn't permit enough leisure time to take care of personal matters like laundry and sightseeing. However, the volunteers were partly responsible. We couldn't slow them down! They were very enthusiastic and actually accomplished more work than we had scheduled."

DURING THE TWO-WEEK PERIOD, the group constructed 11,100 feet of a nature trail around Monument Environmental Center. The center is designed for school teachers, who then bring their students from Colorado Springs, Denver and Pueblo to follow the nature trail. Along it live examples of all the plants, insects and wildlife in the Front Range of the Rocky Mountains, with the possible exception of big game.

The corps assisted the state Forest Service in locating and eradicating infestations of pine bark beetle and mistletoe in trees at the center. They made a biological inventory of the center and policed the grounds, as well as leveling and raking a newly installed leach field.

Additionally, the volunteers maintained four miles of the Mount Herman Trail and one mile of North Beaver Trail. They flagged approximately five miles of new trail, a connecting link in the Front Range Trail between Colorado Springs and Pueblo, and cleaned up and maintained 12 miles of historic Barr Trail and 10 miles of other trails on the slopes of 14,110-foot Pikes Peak.

They also worked on constructing approximately 2,000 feet of trail around the new Rampart Reservoir, a cooperative project of the city of Colorado Springs and the U.S. Forest Service. Their efforts were partially responsible for the reservoir being opened to the public on Labor Day that year instead of the following spring.

The total income for the first season was $2,264.75; the estimated cost of the program was $2,827. Some of the expenses, according to Ruskin, were one-time expenses that will not occur in other projects. And the U.S. Forest Service found the VCC work valuable. Based on current Forest Service rates for similar activities, it was worth approximately $7,000.

"However impressive the figures are, the social significance of the project should not be overlooked," says Ruskin. "The group, a diverse cross-section, became one family for two weeks. Working on projects of common interest, members were patient with the fact that it was a pilot project. There was some criticism, but for the most part they offered good suggestions on how to improve the program. And no one quit or even left early."

During the following winter NAHSTA was deluged with letters from across the country from individuals and agencies interested in starting similar programs in their areas, as well as from people volunteering for the summer 1975 program. The association also received offers of assistance in dealing with public agencies and the private sector to get VCC projects under way in areas other than Colorado.

As a result, the conservation corps was expanded in 1975 to 100 volunteers working at eight sites in four national forests: the Pike–San Isabel National Forest in Colorado, the Shoshone and Big Horn national forests in Wyoming, the Black Hills National Forest in South Dakota and the Gallatin National Forest in Montana. After a specific training period, volunteers spent from one week to two weeks in the backcountry performing a variety of trail work and related activities, including maintenance and construction.

"We found that members of the first VCC wanted to get away from base camp and spend more time in the backcountry," Ruskin recalls. "The first year we had a base camp operation where the corps went out on a day-to-day basis to do their work. There was a central kitchen facility, and the logistics of that got pretty rough. To solve the problem of serving food in 1975 we went into a self-sustaining, backpacking arrangement where everyone took care of his own meals. It proved to be very workable."

In the second VCC program, the volunteers were involved in a wider variety of conservation work. In one instance national forest personnel laid out a trail for the VCC to build.

"Crew members had to decide how they'd organize to build it," says Ruskin. "After looking over the situation they determined that for ecological reasons the trail should not be built in that particular area, and they recommended it be relocated. The Forest Service did so because of the sound reasons behind the recommendation."

Forest fire control also was part of the VCC work in 1975. And there was at least one surprise: a crew working on a Wyoming trail discovered significant archeological sites, which led to an investigation by a team from the University of Wyoming.

THE VOLUNTEER PROGRAM for 1976 mushroomed to more than 200 volunteers with 18 sponsors from private enterprise. Crew members were involved in a number of conservation-related projects, but the main focus was on trail maintenance and construction. There were 12 projects—in Pike –San Isabel and Rio Grande national forests in Colorado, Carson National Forest in New Mexico, Shoshone, Big Horn and Medicine Bow national forests and Yellowstone and Grand Teton national parks in Wyoming, and Lake of the Ozarks State Park in Missouri.

NAHSTA, is interested in establishing contacts with outdoor groups, private forest landowners and others interested in the program, as well as from manufacturers that might like to sponsor a VCC camp in 1977. Each two-week camp of 20 to 25 volunteers requires $500 for food and miscellaneous costs. No salaries are paid to volunteers. Further information about the program can be obtained by writing to NAHSTA, American Hiking Society, 317 Pennsylvania Avenue, S.E., Washington, D.C. 20003.

441

And, in Michigan, the volunteers worked on the High Country Pathway Trail, part of the transcontinental North Country Trail.

BACKPACKER sponsored a VCC project in 1976 in Grand Teton National Park. Other sponsors and their projects were Hine/Snowbridge, Sierra Designs and Woolrich, Shoshone National Forest; Silva Company, Gerry and Eastern Mountain Sports, Lake of the Ozarks State Park; Class 5, Carson National Forest; L. L. Bean, Medicine Bow National Forest; North Face, Big Horn National Forest; Holubar Mountaineering, Yellowstone National Park; Snow Lion, Rio Grande National Forest; Fabiano, Rogue River National Forest, Oregon; Eddie Bauer, Shoshone National Forest; Colorado Mountain Trails Foundation and Barge Transports, Pike — San Isabel National Forest. Both the Johnson's Wax company and J.C. Penney Company have supported the VCC program since its inception.

Ruskin says that the success of the VCC projects has proven the worth of Public Law 92-300 and the potential of the vol-unteer program. "However," he continues, "until NAHSTA can find sufficient friends to adequately staff the Volunteer Conservation Corps, the program out of administrative necessity will be limited to ten projects and 200 to 225 volunteers which the association is actively seeking for the 1977 summer season." All of the projects will be in the Rocky Mountain region— Colorado, Wyoming and New Mexico.

Three years ago Ruskin was invited to Washington, D.C., where he described the VCC at a U.S. Forest Service meeting, which included deputy chief foresters, nine regional foresters from across the country and top Forest Service researchers.

"There's more work to be done in national forests than can ever be accomplished by all the Forest Service employees in all its history," he told the group. "There aren't enough of you, there isn't enough time and there isn't enough money." But, he continued, there are untapped citizen resources that can help reforest millions of idle acres, prune and thin slow-growing timber stands, combat insects and forest diseases, and build and maintain trails.

Ruskin believes the Forest Service should take more advantage of Public Law 92-300 and the pioneer spirit which still exists in America to help get the job done in the nation's forests. The response to that single ad for the first volunteer trail crew, he says, proves the manpower is out there.

An alternative to the VCC for high school and college students is offered by the Student Conservation Program (see BP-5). Student volunteers have the opportunity to maintain trails, patrol backcountry areas, lead nature walks and assist in research programs in 40 parks and forests across the nation. For further information and an application form, write to: Student Conservation Association, P.O. Box 550, Charlestown, New Hampshire 03603. ▰